Fundamentals of
Financial Accounting

The Robert N. Anthony/Willard J. Graham Series in Accounting

FUNDAMENTALS OF FINANCIAL ACCOUNTING

Glenn A. Welsch
Daniel G. Short
both of the
College of Business Administration
The University of Texas at Austin

Fifth Edition
1987

Homewood, Illinois 60430

To
Irma, Maryrose,
Jenni, and Heather

© RICHARD D. IRWIN, INC. 1974, 1977, 1981, 1984, and 1987

ISBN 0-256-03613-6

Library of Congress Catalog Card No. 86–82802

Printed in the United States of America

2 3 4 5 6 7 8 9 0 DO(C) 4 3 2 1 0 9 8

PREFACE

The fifth edition of this textbook retains all of the features that the numerous faculty who have used the prior editions have regarded favorably. It has been substantially updated to reflect changes in business practice, accounting rules, and the economy. Most chapters have been revised to make them more understandable and interesting to read. This revision reflects both continuity and change.

TO STUDENTS:

Fundamentals of Financial Accounting, 5th edition, is an introduction to the communication of relevant financial information to investors, creditors, analysts, and other individuals. This book is designed to meet the needs of students who plan to major in accounting as well as those who do not. If you understand the material in *Fundamentals of Financial Accounting*, it will be much easier for you to be successful in subsequent courses. Nonaccounting majors will benefit from their study of this book because they must understand the language of business as well as the uses and limitations of accounting information. Senior business executives often state that they need a better understanding of accounting. Careful study of this text will prepare you for the future. This book is able to meet the needs of both accounting and nonaccounting majors because of its emphasis on concepts. An understanding of the technical aspects of accounting is important for subsequent accounting courses and for the analysis of financial information. The text gives a sound introduction to accounting practice. And with a continuing emphasis on concepts, it clarifies the "why" of each practice. Our discussion of this conceptual framework ties together topics that might otherwise seem unrelated. Also, you will be able to generalize your knowledge and, for example, see similarities between accounting for inventory and property, plant and equipment. Your understanding of these concepts will (1) aid in your study of accounting, (2) permit you to adapt to changes in accounting practice, and (3) help you to appreciate the uses and limitations of accounting information.

This text contains many special features designed to help both the student and the instructor.

SPECIAL FEATURES FOR STUDENTS

There is a complete package of study aids to help you. Each study aid was prepared by the authors of the text to ensure consistency in terminology, approach, and quality. These aids are:

1. A Study Guide that includes chapter outlines, additional illustrations, and sample exam questions with detailed solutions.
2. Working Papers that include all forms needed for solving homework assignments. The forms contain captions and information that you would otherwise have to copy from the text.
3. A Practice Set that covers the complete information processing cycle. It can be used anytime after Chapter 5 and concluded anytime after Chapter 11.

Each chapter begins with a special introduction that gives you a complete overview of the topics to be covered. The introduction includes a brief statement of purpose and explains how the chapter relates to prior discussions. The introduction also includes broad learning objectives to provide a "road map" for your study of the chapter. Each introduction provides a financial reporting perspective that relates the topics in the chapter to actual financial statements.

Accounting has its own technical language and jargon. The book will help you learn these new words by providing both a comprehensive index and, at the end of each chapter, a list of "important terms used in this chapter". This list includes the key words, the definition of the word, and the page reference that tells you where the word was first introduced.

A unique format is used in many of the exhibits. To facilitate your study, these exhibits give the illustrative data, analysis, and accounting entries and reporting on a single page.

Each exercise, problem, and case begins with a brief statement of the purpose of the assignment. You will get much more out of homework assignments when you understand your role more clearly.

An actual set of financial statements is included in Special Supplement B (immediately preceding the Index) to help you learn how various accounting issues are handled by a typical company.

The discussions in each chapter have been carefully integrated with other chapters. When we refer to a topic from a prior chapter, a reference is provided to help you locate and review the prior discussion.

TO INSTRUCTORS:

This textbook is designed to give you maximum flexibility in selecting topics and scheduling. Discussions with a large number of accounting educators have convinced us that there is no single "best" way to teach accounting. We selected topics for this text and organized them in a sound and logical way but we have given you the flexibility to easily include or exclude topics and to rearrange the organization. Adopters have told us that this text permits them to custom design their courses based on the preferences and needs of their students.

SPECIAL FEATURES FOR INSTRUCTORS

Several teaching aids are available for instructors:

1. A Comprehensive Teachers Manual that includes answers (with detailed computations) to all questions, exercises, problems, and cases. It also includes suggested course plans, assignment schedules, and instructional ideas.
2. A list of Check Figures for exercises, problems, and cases. This aid is available in quantity for free distribution to students.
3. An extensive Bank of Examination Questions coordinated by chapter and coded by topic, type of question, and level of difficulty. Computest, a computerized test-generating system, is also available.
4. Teaching Transparencies to assist in the preparation and delivery of lectures.
5. A Practice Set that is a complete integrated problem covering the entire information processing cycle. The Practice Set can be introduced after Chapter 5 and concluded anytime after Chapter 11. The section on the Statement of Changes in Financial Position can be completed after Chapter 15.

Most chapters are divided into two parts, an arrangement that permits the instructor to give balanced reading assignments. Also, it provides complete flexibility in selecting topic coverage. With this arrangement each instructor can easily emphasize or eliminate selected topics.

This book includes 17 supplements that discuss either procedural or advanced topics. It is unlikely that any instructor would assign all 17 chapters and 17 supplements. Instead, one objective of the textbook is to provide maximum flexibility in topic selection and to have sufficient additional material available to permit changes based on the objectives of the course.

A brief statement of objectives is given at the start of each exercise, problem, and case. These statements are designed to assist the student, but they can also help the instructor select appropriate assignment material.

This book has an unusually large number of homework assignments. Instructors are able to vary assignments from semester to semester. In addition each chapter contains assignments that have different levels of difficulty. Exercises tend to be applications of a single concept discussed in the chapter; problems are more difficult and may require an understanding of several concepts; cases typically require analysis and judgment. All end-of-chapter material is keyed either to a chapter part or supplement.

Each chapter gives a case based on the Chesebrough-Pond's financial statements included in the book. These cases provide an excellent overview of current accounting practice.

The book places an important emphasis on understanding accounting terminology. Each chapter has at least one exercise on terminology that can be assigned to assess student understanding.

Many faculty members and students have commented that this book is unusually easy to read and understand. We have achieved that objective through careful writing and selection of illustrations. Clarity has not been attained by ignoring or "sliding over" difficult topics. The book discusses a number of advanced topics that are ignored in many other fundamentals textbooks. For example, we include discussions of purchases versus pooling, comprehensive inflation adjustments, and both present and future value concepts. These special topics are organized to facilitate inclusion or exclusion based on the objectives of the instructor.

The list of students and faculty members to whom the authors feel a sense of gratitude for ideas and suggestions is too long to enumerate here. For the 5th edition, we are particularly grateful to the following individuals who devoted considerable time in discussions, reviewing parts of the manuscript, and testing materials:

The following students at The University of Texas at Austin: Vicky Conway, Annick Barton, Jody Daughtler, Melissa Gan, Erica Peters, and Lynette Broders. We recognize the valuable editorial suggestions provided by Petria Sandlin and Kathy Springer. We are especially grateful to Professors Janet Daniels, University of Hartford, Harry Dickinson, University of Virginia, Ralph Drtina, Lehigh University, Sandra and David Byrd, Southwest Missouri State University, Stuart Webster, Lehigh, and LaVern Krueger, University of Missouri, for their valuable suggestions.

Consultation with Kathy Springer was especially valuable in preparing the special supplement on income taxes.

Finally, we express our thanks to numerous users of the prior editions for their valuable suggestions.

Our thanks to the American Institute of Certified Public Accountants, American Accounting Association, Financial Accounting Standards Board, and the authors identified by citations for permission to quote from their publications. To Chesebrough-Pond's, our special thanks for permission to use its annual reports.

Suggestions and comments on the text and the related materials are invited.

Glenn A. Welsch
Daniel G. Short

CONTENTS

Depreciation—Concepts. *Depreciation and Income Tax. Which Depreciation Method Should Be Used?* Depreciation Effects on the Income Statement and Balance Sheet: *Effects of Depreciation on Cash Flow.* Depreciation for Interim Periods. Change in Depreciation Estimates.

PART B—REPAIRS AND MAINTENANCE, NATURAL RESOURCES, AND INTANGIBLE ASSETS

Repairs, Maintenance, and Additions: *Ordinary Repairs and Maintenance. Extraordinary Repairs.* Natural Resources. Intangible Operational Assets: *Amortization of Intangible Operational Assets.* Deferred Charges. Disposal of Operational Assets. Demonstration Case. Supplement 9A—Capitalization of Interest as a Cost of Operational Assets. Supplement 9B—Trading in Assets.

PART A—MEASURING, RECORDING, AND REPORTING LIABILITIES

Liabilities Defined and Classified. Measuring Liabilities. Current Liabilities: *Accounts Payable. Accrued Expenses. Payroll Liabilities. Deferred Revenues.* Long-Term Liabilities: *Notes Payable. Deferred Income Tax.* Contingent Liabilities. Controlling Expenditures with a Voucher System.

PART B—FUTURE VALUE AND PRESENT VALUE CONCEPTS

Concepts. Future and Present Values of a Single Amount: *Future Value of a Single Amount(f). Present Value of a Single Amount (p).* Future and Present Values of an Annuity: *Future Value of an Annuity (F). Present Value of an Annuity (P).* Demonstration Cases—Accounting Applications of Future and Present Values. Summary of Chapter. Supplement 10A—Payroll Accounting. *Required Deductions. Optional Deductions. Accounting for Employee Deductions. Accounting for Employer Payroll Taxes.* Supplement 10B—The Voucher System. Supplement 10C—Lease Liabilities.

PART A—FUNDAMENTALS OF MEASURING, RECORDING, AND REPORTING BONDS PAYABLE

Characteristics of Bonds Payable: *Special Characteristics of Bonds.* Measuring Bonds Payable and Interest Expense: *Interest Rates on Bonds.* Accounting for Bonds Illustrated: *Bonds Sold at Par. Bonds Sold at a Discount. Bonds Sold at a Premium.* Advantages of Issuing Bonds: *Financial Leverage Illustrated.* Disadvantages of Issuing Bonds.

PART B—ADDITIONAL PROBLEMS IN ACCOUNTING FOR BONDS PAYABLE

Accounting for Bonds Sold between Interest Dates. Adjusting Entry for Accrued Bond Interest. Bond Sinking Funds. Effective-Interest Amortization of Bond Discount and Premium. Demonstration Case.

12 MEASURING AND REPORTING OWNERS' EQUITY   605

PART A—STOCKHOLDERS' EQUITY

Nature of a Corporation. Structure of a Corporation. Authorized, Issued, and Outstanding Capital Stock. Types of Capital Stock: *Common Stock. Preferred Stock.* Accounting for, and Reporting of, Capital Stock: *Sale and Issuance of Par Value Capital Stock. Capital Stock Sold and Issued for Noncash Assets and/or Services. Reporting Stockholders' Equity. Sales and Issuance of Nopar Capital Stock.* Treasury Stock.

PART B—ACCOUNTING FOR DIVIDENDS AND RETAINED EARNINGS AND UNINCORPORATED BUSINESSES

Dividends Defined. Dividends from the Perspectives of the Investor and the Issuer. Dividends on Preferred Stock: *Current Dividend Preference on Preferred Stock. Cumulative Dividend Preference on Preferred Stock.* Stock Dividends: *Reasons for Stock Dividends.* Stock Splits. Dividend Dates. Stockholder Records. Reporting Retained Earnings: *Prior Period Adjustments. Restrictions on Retained Earnings.* Accounting and Reporting for Unincorporated Businesses. Demonstration Case. Supplement 12A—Participating Dividend Preference on Preferred Stock. Supplement 12B—Accounting for Owners' Equity for Sole Proprietorships and Partnerships: *Owners' Equity for a Partnership.*

13 MEASURING AND REPORTING LONG-TERM INVESTMENTS   663

PART A—LONG-TERM INVESTMENTS IN EQUITY SECURITIES (STOCKS)

Measuring Long-Term Investments in Voting Common Stock. Cost Method. Equity Method.

PART B—LONG-TERM INVESTMENTS IN DEBT SECURITIES (BONDS)

Measuring and Reporting Bond Investments. Accounting for Bonds Illustrated. Bonds Purchased at Par. Bonds Purchased at a Discount.

Bonds Purchased at a Premium. Bonds Purchased between Interest Dates. Sale of a Bond Investment. Effective-Interest Amortization on Bond Investments. Demonstration Case.

14 CONSOLIDATED STATEMENTS—MEASURING AND REPORTING 705

PART A—ACQUIRING A CONTROLLING INTEREST

Criteria for Consolidated Financial Statements. Methods of Acquiring a Controlling Interest. Pooling of Interests Method. Purchase Method. Comparison of the Effects on the Balance Sheet of Pooling versus Purchase Methods.

PART B—REPORTING CONSOLIDATED OPERATIONS AFTER ACQUISITION

The Impact of the Pooling and Purchase Methods One Year after Acquisition. Demonstration Case. Supplement 14A—Consolidation Procedures—100% Ownership: *Developing Consolidated Statements for Periods Subsequent to Acquisition.* Supplement 14B—Consolidation Procedures—Less than 100% Ownership.

15 STATEMENT OF CHANGES IN FINANCIAL POSITION 757

PART A—STATEMENT OF CHANGES IN FINANCIAL POSITION, CASH BASIS

Concepts of the Statement of Changes in Financial Position. How the SCFP, Cash Basis, Helps Decision Makers. Format of the SCFP, Cash Basis: *Sources of Cash. Uses of Cash. Net Increase (Decrease) in Cash during the Accounting Period.* All-Resources Concept of the SCFP. Preparing the SCFP, Cash Basis: *Direct Analysis to Prepare the SCFP, Cash Basis. Relationships among the Income Statement, Balance Sheet, and the SCFP.* Worksheet Analysis to Prepare SCFP, Cash Basis: *Analysis of Disposal of an Asset.*

PART B—STATEMENT OF CHANGES IN FINANCIAL POSITION, WORKING CAPITAL BASIS

Concept of Working Capital: *Sources of Working Capital. Uses of Working Capital.* Format for the SCFP, Working Capital Basis. Worksheet to Prepare the SCFP, Working Capital Basis: *Steps to Prepare the SCFP, Working Capital Basis.* Working Capital versus Cash Basis for the SCFP. Demon-

Fundamentals of
Financial Accounting

This chapter introduces financial statements as the means a business uses to communicate economic information to others. Below are selected summary financial data communicated by one large company on its final report. The magnitude of the numbers is interesting.

Report of Management

    The accompanying financial statements, which consolidate the accounts of American Telephone and Telegraph Company and its subsidiaries, have been prepared in conformity with generally accepted accounting principles.

Summary Data from the 1985 Financial Statements (in millions):

Income Statement (Statement of Operations):
Revenues (during 1985)	$34,909.5
Expenses (during 1985)	33,352.7
Income (during 1985)	$ 1,556.8

Balance Sheet (Statement of Financial Position):
Assets (at end of 1985)	$40,462.5
Liabilities (at end of 1985)	24,372.1
Owners' equity (at end of 1985)	$16,090.4

Statement of Changes in Financial Position (Cash):
Beginning cash balance (January 1, 1985)	$2,139.9
Sources of cash during 1985	6,756.4
Uses of cash during 1985	(6,682.6)
Ending cash balance (December 31, 1985)	$2,213.7

*Note: The primary purposes of these "Perspectives" are: (a) to emphasize an important issue discussed in the chapter and (b) to show you how a company resolves that issue.

PERSPECTIVES— ACCOUNTING OBJECTIVES AND COMMUNICATION

PURPOSE:

In our environment, people need information to make rational economic decisions. Most consumers use product and price information prior to purchasing a specific item. Investors and creditors need financial information before they provide funds to a business entity. A primary source of financial information is the periodic financial statements provided by a business entity. The primary purpose of this chapter is to define accounting, review the environment in which accounting is done, and describe how accounting serves our society.

ORGANIZATION:

Part A—The Objectives and Environment of Accounting

1. Accounting defined.
2. Use of accounting information by decision makers.
3. Historical accounting perspectives.
4. Groups involved in accounting innovation.

LEARNING OBJECTIVES—TO BE ABLE TO:

1. Write and explain the objectives of accounting.
2. Explain how accounting reports help decision makers.
3. Tell how the business environment influences accounting.
4. Give an overview of the financial statements used to communicate information.
5. Expand your business vocabulary by learning the "important terms defined in this chapter" (page 31).
6. Apply the knowledge learned from this chapter by completing the homework assigned by your instructor.

Part B—Communication of Accounting Information

1. Communication concepts.
2. Overview of external financial reports.

PART A—THE OBJECTIVES AND ENVIRONMENT OF ACCOUNTING

ACCOUNTING DEFINED

Accounting can be defined as the collection of financial data about an organization and the analysis, measurement, recording, and reporting of that information to decision makers. An accounting system processes the *(a)* flows of resources into (inflows) and out (outflows) of an organization, *(b)* resources controlled (i.e., assets) by the organization, and *(c)* claims against those resources (i.e., debts). Accounting requires judgment and interpretation in analyzing, reporting, and using the reported financial results. The flow of accounting information of an entity can be summarized as in Exhibit 1–1, which shows that the end products of an accounting system are **financial statements** that are prepared for decision makers.

Economics has a special relationship with accounting. Economics has been defined as the study of how people and society choose to employ scarce productive resources that could have alternative uses to produce various commodities and distribute them for consumption, now or in the future, among various persons and groups in society.[1] Like economics, accounting has a conceptual foundation that provides guidelines for the collection, measurement, and communication of financial information about an organization. In general, accounting reports how an entity has allocated its scarce resources. Thus, accounting collects, measures, interprets, and reports financial information on the same

---

EXHIBIT 1–1

Flow of economic information in an accounting system

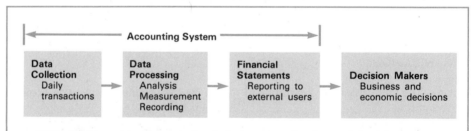

* Financial statements are prepared primarily for investors and creditors and those that advise investors and creditors. Financial statements are prepared under the assumption of reasonably sophisticated and diligent users (FASB, *Statement of Financial Accounting Concepts No. 1*).

---

[1] Paul A. Samuelson, *Economics*, 9th ed. (New York: McGraw-Hill).

activities that are the focus of economics. Economics explains economic relationships on a conceptual level, whereas accounting reports the economic relationships primarily on a practical level. However, accounting measurements are as consistent with economic concepts as is possible. Accounting must cope with the complex and practical problems of measuring in monetary terms the economic effects of **exchange transactions** (i.e., resource inflows and outflows). These effects relate to the resources held and the claims against the resources of an entity. Throughout this textbook, the theoretical and practical issues that arise in the measurement process are discussed from the accounting viewpoint.

ACCOUNTING OPERATES IN A COMPLEX ENVIRONMENT

The environment in which accounting operates is affected by such forces as the type of (a) government (e.g., democracy versus communism), (b) economic system (e.g., free enterprise versus socialism), (c) industry (e.g., technological versus agrarian), (d) organizations within that society (e.g., labor unions), and (e) regulatory controls (i.e., private sector versus governmental). Accounting is influenced significantly by the educational level and economic development of the society.

Each of us is associated with social, political, and economic organizations such as businesses, churches, fraternal organizations, political parties, states, environmental groups, and professional associations. These organizations face important resource allocation decisions. Organizations are essential to the workings of a society; in fact, they constitute much of society.

Fundamental to a dynamic and successful society is the ability of each organization to measure and report its accomplishments, to undergo critical self-analysis, and, through sound decisions, to renew itself and grow. In this way, individual and societal objectives are served best. Essentially, society, and the various organizations that comprise it, thrive in direct proportion to the efficiency with which scarce resources of human talent, materials, services, and capital are allocated. To achieve this goal, organizations need information about how the resources are obtained and used. Accounting information is designed to meet this need.

Accounting is a management information system that is continuously changed to meet the evolving needs of society. The environmental characteristics of a society are diverse and complex; therefore, accounting is always facing new challenges. For example, an inflationary spiral necessitates the development of accounting concepts and procedures that will report "real" effects separately from purely inflationary effects (discussed in Chapter 17).

Throughout this textbook you will study how accounting responds to the unique environment of the United States. In the next few paragraphs we will discuss two environmental characteristics—types of business entities and measurement in dollars. These characteristics have pervasive effects on accounting concepts and procedures.

TYPES OF BUSINESS ENTITIES

This textbook emphasizes **accounting for profit-making entities.** In our environment there are three main types of business entities—sole proprietorship, partnership, and corporation. Their primary characteristics are given in the paragraphs that follow.

A **sole proprietorship** is an unincorporated business owned by one person. This type of business entity is common in the services, retailing, and farming industries. Usually, the owner is the manager. Legally, the business and the owner are not separate entities—they are the same. However, accounting views the business as a separate entity to be accounted for separate from its owner.

A **partnership** is an unincorporated business that is owned by two or more persons known as partners. The agreements between the owners are specified in a partnership contract. This contract deals with such matters as division of income each reporting period and distribution of resources of the business upon termination of its operations. A partnership is not legally separate from its owners. Legally, each partner in a general partnership is responsible for the debts of the business. This means that each general partner has **unlimited liability.** However, accounting views the partnership as a separate business entity to be accounted for separately from its several owners.

A **corporation** is a business that is incorporated under the laws of a particular state. The owners are stockholders or shareholders. Ownership is represented by shares of capital stock that usually can be bought and sold freely. When an approved application is filed by the organizers, the state issues a charter. This charter gives the corporation the right to operate as a separate legal entity, separate and apart from its owners. The owners enjoy **limited liability.** That is, the owners are liable for the debts of the corporation only to the extent of their investments. The charter specifies the types and amounts of capital stock that can be issued. Most states require a minimum of two or three stockholders and a minimum amount of resources to be contributed at the time of organization. The stockholders elect a governing board of directors, which in turn employs managers and exercises general supervision of the corporation.[2] Accounting for the business entity focuses on the corporation, not on the directors and managers as individuals.

In terms of economic importance, the corporation is the dominant form of business organization in the United States. The advantages of the corporate form include *(a)* limited liability for the stockholders, *(b)* continuity of life, *(c)* ease in transferring ownership (stock), and *(d)* opportunities to raise large amounts of money by selling shares to a large number of people. The primary disadvantages of a corporation are that *(a)* they tend to be impersonal and *(b)* their income is subject to double taxation. First, corporate income is taxed when

---

[2] There are a number of specialized types of entities that we do not discuss, such as joint ventures, mutual funds, cooperatives, investment trusts, and syndicates. Consideration of these entities is appropriate for advanced accounting courses.

earned and then again when stockholders receive dividends. Because of several advantages, most large and medium-sized businesses (and many small ones) are organized as corporations. Therefore, we shall emphasize this form of business. Nevertheless, the accounting concepts, standards, and measurement procedures that we will discuss also apply to the other types of businesses.

MEASUREMENT IN DOLLARS

A monetary system provides the primary way to measure and communicate economic information about the flow of resources in and out of an organization. In a monetary system, the unit of exchange (dollars in our case) is the common denominator used to measure value. Thus, the monetary unit provides a means for expressing the available resources and the resource flows of an entity.

Accounting uses the monetary system of each country within which it operates. One of the critical problems in accounting is the conversion of financial amounts from one monetary system to another monetary system in measuring resources and resource flows for multinational activities.

Measurement fundamentals

Essential in any measurement process is a precise definition of what is to be measured. Examples of specific items often measured are the population of California, the rainfall in Michigan, the voter registrations in New York, and the bank deposits in Texas (each for a stipulated time). Similarly, in the measurement of resources and debts of a business, accounting requires precise definition of the specific entity for which financial data are to be collected, measured, and reported. When a specific entity is defined for financial reporting purposes, it often is referred to as an **accounting entity.** In any measurement scheme, the definition of what should be measured often involves problems. For example, in measuring the population of California, should the total include military personnel? college students? jail inmates? long-term visitors? hotel guests? Similarly, in defining an accounting entity, important problems must be resolved. First, we must define a separate and specific accounting entity. An accounting entity has a specialized definition that is known as the separate-entity assumption.[3] The separate-entity assumption requires that for accounting measurement purposes, the particular entity being accounted for be distinguished carefully from all similar and related entities and persons. Under this assumption, an accounting entity is separate and distinct from its owner(s). Such an entity is viewed as owning the resources (i.e., assets) used by it and as owing the claims (i.e., debts) against those resources. For measurement purposes, the assets, debts, and activities of the entity are kept separate from those of the owners and other entities.

---

[3] A list of the fundamental assumptions and principles underlying accounting is summarized in Exhibit 4–5.

THE USE OF ACCOUNTING INFORMATION BY DECISION MAKERS

Your role as a decision maker is significant, whether you are a manager, investor, professional person, owner of a business, or an interested citizen. Decision makers use various approaches to select one solution to a given problem from among a set of several alternative solutions. Selection of the best alternative is the basic decision. In making decisions, a decision maker is concerned about the future because a decision cannot change the past. However, an effective decision maker should not neglect to consider past events and their outcomes. Knowledge and interpretation of what has happened in the past can aid in making decisions because history may shed considerable light on what the future is likely to hold. Thus, one of the fundamental inputs to decision making is dependable and relevant historical data. A large portion of historical data that are relevant to business decisions are expressed in monetary terms. They include costs (i.e., resources expended), revenues (i.e., resources earned), assets (i.e., things owned), liabilities (i.e., amounts owed), and owners' equity (i.e., total assets less total liabilities of the entity). Thus, accounting provides important information for decision making. The information provided by financial reports must be understandable and relevant to the decision. This is a primary reason why measurements in accounting must adhere to acceptable standards and concepts.

Accounting reports (i.e., financial statements) serve those who use the reported information in three related ways:

1. Accounting provides information that is helpful in making decisions. Most important decisions, regardless of the type of endeavor involved, are based, in part, upon complex financial considerations. Accounting provides an important information base and a particular analytical orientation that help the decision maker assess the future financial implications and potential outcomes of various alternatives that are considered.

2. Accounting reports the economic effects of past decisions on the entity. Once a decision is made and implementation starts, significant and often subtle financial economic effects on the entity occur. These economic effects often are critical to the success of the endeavor. The evolving effects of past decisions must be measured continuously and periodically reported so that the decision maker can be informed of continuing and newly developing problems, and of successes, over time. Accounting provides a continuing feedback of the economic effects of a series of decisions already made, the results of which are communicated to the decision maker by means of periodic financial statements.

3. Accounting keeps track of a wide range of items to meet the financial scorekeeping and safeguarding responsibilities that must be assumed by all organizations. These include how much cash is available for use; how much customers owe the company; what debts are owed by the organization; what

items are owned by the company, such as machinery and office equipment; and inventory levels on hand.

Accounting Information in Decision Making

Most organizations engage in activities for an extended period of time. During this time resources are committed and used with the expectation that there will be desirable results in the future. During the period of continuing activities, those involved in the organization need information about the continuing amounts of resources committed, resources used, resources on hand, and outputs (goods and services). This information should be reported, interpreted, and evaluated periodically. The accounting process is designed to provide a continuing flow of such information to all interested parties. A typical flow of accounting information in an entity is diagrammed in Exhibit 1–2. The financial statements constitute the primary source of relevant information on a continuing basis. This information is important feedback concerning the outcome of particular decisions.

Now we will examine two different entities—a local business and a municipal hospital.

EXHIBIT 1–2

Accounting information flows in a decision and implementation cycle

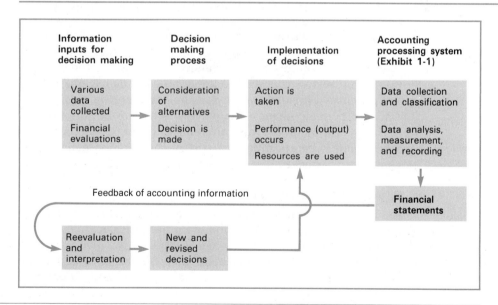

A local business

The objectives of a business are determined by the organizers. Initially, the owners provide the funds, which often are supplemented by funds provided by creditors. These funds are used by the managers of the business to acquire equipment, inventory, services, and other assets. Assume you are the manager of the entity and that you develop a **business plan** for operating the business. As the business operates, additional resources flow in from the sale of goods and services and flow out for expenses. As the manager of the business, you need information, on a continuing basis, about sources and amounts of funds, revenues (products and services sold), expenses, the amounts invested in equipment and inventory, the cash situation, the amount spent for research and development, and the amount of money used in the sales efforts.

As the manager, you need such information for two reasons. First, accounting information will help you to make sound decisions about the entity that can improve its effectiveness and efficiency. Second, accounting information reports what the score was during the immediate past periods. This scorekeeping is important to the evaluation and control of performance. Exhibit 1–2 shows financial evaluations and interpretations as important information inputs to the decision-making process.

Now, assume instead that you are a stockholder (an owner) of the business. You have a substantial amount of money invested in the business. As a stockholder, you must continuously select from among three alternatives: (1) retain your ownership interest, (2) expand or contract it, or (3) dispose of it completely. As a stockholder, you also are interested in management decisions that will expand the business and make it more profitable. Therefore, you, and the other stockholders, need financial information about the trend of sales, the level of expenses, the amount of earnings, the amount invested by the entity in various assets (such as inventory and machinery), the debts of the business, and cash flow. As an investor, you need to know how the management is allocating the scarce resources provided by the stockholders and the creditors. The primary objective of periodic financial statements is to provide, on a continuing basis, information bearing on the three alternatives listed. The accounting information provided should be an important part of the decision-making process of the stockholders in ways similar to those depicted in Exhibit 1–2.

A municipal hospital

Assume you are on the board of governors of a municipal-owned hospital. Therefore, you share the responsibility for the basic decisions and guidelines for its continued operation at an efficient level. Like the owner of a business, you have a wide variety of questions about its revenues, expenses, funds tied up in buildings and equipment, cost of charity services, and so on, that are in the scorekeeping category. Also, you are concerned with whether enough resources are being allocated to such activities as emergency care, sanitation, and nursing services. To make sound decisions in these areas, you need information about prior allocation of resources and about the quality and quantity of resulting output or benefits. Thus, as a member of the board, you have many information needs that are important to your decisions.

Consider the manager of the hospital. The manager needs accounting information about the operations of the hospital similar to that discussed above for the manager of a business, and for the same reasons. Typically, the manager will need more detailed accounting information than the sponsor. However, whether one is a sponsor or manager of the hospital, financial measurement and the reported results should be continuing inputs to the decision-making process. This situation suggests the importance of accounting information which was emphasized in an interesting way in *Forbes* magazine as follows:

> In all of mainland China there are about 30 CPAs. Some might call this a sign of how advanced the Chinese civilization really is, but for the Chinese—who are making an effort to bring their economy into the 20th century—it's a major obstacle. Now the leaders in the Chinese government want modern accounting systems—translation: Western accounting systems—and they want them fast. After all, this is a nation with some 400,000 manufacturing concerns and one accounting firm.

HISTORICAL PERSPECTIVES

Accounting is as old as the exchange processes (whether barter or monetary) that gradually developed with civilization. The earliest written records, including the Scriptures, contain references to what now is called accounting.

Accounting evolved in response to the economic needs of society. Prior to the 15th century, accounting had no well-defined pattern except that it developed in answer to governing and trading needs of the era. The first known treatment of the subject of accounting was written in 1494, two years after the discovery of America. An Italian monk and mathematician, Fr. Luca Paciolo, described an approach developed by Italian merchants to account for their activities as owner-managers of business ventures. Paciolo laid the foundations of the basic "accounting model" that is used to this day. As economic activity progressed from the feudal system to agriculture and then to the Industrial Revolution, accounting continued to adapt to the needs of society. As business units became more complex and broader in scope, accounting evolved in response to the increased planning and control responsibilities of management. As governments grew in size and became more centralized, accounting was developed to meet the increased accountabilities.

In the 17th and 18th centuries, the Industrial Revolution in England provided the impetus for developing new approaches in accounting. That impetus was on the accumulation of data about the cost of manufacturing each product. In the latter half of the 19th century, English accountants, small in numbers but large in competence, appeared on the American scene. By 1900, the lead in accounting developments, provided earlier by the English, began to shift to Americans.

Since the turn of this century, spearheaded by the accounting profession in the United States, accounting has experienced dynamic growth.

THE ACCOUNTING PROFESSION TODAY

Since 1900, accounting has attained the stature of such professions as law, medicine, engineering, and architecture. As with all recognized professions, accounting is subject to licensing, observes a code of professional ethics, requires a high level of professional competence, is dedicated to service to the public, requires a high level of academic study, and rests on a "common body of knowledge." In addition to meeting specified academic requirements, the accountant may be licensed to be a **Certified Public Accountant, or CPA.** This designation was first established in 1896. It is granted only upon completion of requirements specified by resident state statutes. Although the CPA requirements vary among states, they include a college degree with a major in accounting, good character, one to five years experience, and successful completion of a three-day examination. The CPA examination, scheduled in each state simultaneously on a semiannual basis, is prepared by the American Institute of Certified Public Accountants. This examination covers accounting theory, auditing, business law, and accounting practice.

As with physicians, engineers, lawyers, and architects, accountants (including CPAs) commonly are engaged in professional practice or are employed by businesses, government entities, nonprofit organizations, and so on. Accountants employed in these activities often take and pass a professional examination to become a **Certified Management Accountant, or CMA.**

Practice of Public Accounting

A CPA can offer professional services to the public for a fee, as does the lawyer and physician. In this role, the accountant is known as an **Independent CPA** because certain responsibilities also extend to the general public (third parties) rather than being limited to the specific business or other entity that pays for the services. Independent CPAs, although paid by their clients, are not employees of their clients. This independence from the client is a unique characteristic of the accounting profession. The consequences of this uniqueness are not widely understood. For example, in case of malpractice or incompetence, lawyers and physicians generally are subject to potential lawsuits that may extend only to the client or patient involved (and the family). In contrast, in case of malpractice or negligence in the audit function, the independent CPA is subject to potential liability that may extend to all parties (whether known to the CPA or not) who have suffered loss because of reliance on financial statements "approved" by the CPA.

While an individual may practice public accounting, usually two or more individuals organize an accounting firm in the form of a partnership (in some states incorporation is permitted). Firms vary in size from a one-person office to regional firms and the "big-eight" firms, which have hundreds of offices located worldwide. Accounting firms usually render three types of services: auditing, management advisory services, and tax services.

Auditing

The most important function performed by the CPA in public practice is the **audit or attest function.** Its purpose is to lend reliability to the financial reports; that is, to assure that they are believable (i.e., relevant, accurate, and not biased). Primarily, this function involves an examination of the financial reports prepared by the management of the entity in order to assure that they conform with **generally accepted accounting principles (GAAP),** which are discussed later. In performing this function, the independent CPA examines the underlying transactions, including the collection, classification, and assembly of the financial data incorporated in the financial reports. In performing these tasks, established professional standards must be maintained. To appreciate the magnitude of these reponsibilities, the number of transactions involved in a major enterprise such as General Motors involves billions of dollars each year. However, the CPA does not examine each of these transactions; rather, professional approaches are used to ascertain beyond reasonable doubt that they were measured and reported properly.

Occasionally, the auditor may encounter attempts to manipulate accounting reports, for example, to increase reported profit by omitting certain expenses or to overstate financial position by omitting certain debts. There are many intentional and unintentional opportunities to prepare misleading financial reports. The audit function performed by an independent CPA is the best protection available to the public. Many investors have learned the pitfalls of making investments in enterprises that do not have their financial reports examined by an independent CPA.

At the conclusion of an audit, the independent CPA must provide an auditor's opinion that indicates whether the financial statements are appropriate and not misleading. For example, a recent auditor's report was as follows:

> Because of the materiality of the matters discussed in paragraphs 2, 3, and 4, we are unable to, and do not express an opinion on the financial statements referred to above of Consolidated Packaging Corporation and Subsidiaries (Debtor-in-Possession) as of December 31, 1984, and for the year then ended.
>
> In our opinion, subject to the effects on the financial statements of such adjustments, if any, as might have been required had the outcome of the uncertainty referred to in paragraph 4 been known, the financial statements referred to above present fairly the financial position of Consolidated Packaging Corporation and Subsidiaries as of December 31, 1983 and 1982, and the results of their operations and the changes in their financial position for each of the two years in the period ended December 31, 1983, in conformity with generally accepted accounting principles applied on a consistent basis." (Source: AICPA, *1985 Accounting Trends & Techniques*, page 402.)

Management advisory services

Many independent CPA firms also offer advisory or consulting services. These services usually are accounting based and encompass such activities as the design and installation of accounting, data processing, profit-planning and control (i.e., budget) systems; financial advice; forecasting; inventory controls; cost-effectiveness studies; and operational analyses. This facet of public practice is growing rapidly.

Tax services

CPAs in public practice usually provide income tax services to their clients. These services include both tax planning as a part of the decision-making process, tax compliance, and also determination of the income tax liability (reported on the annual income tax return). Because of the increasing complexity of state and federal tax laws, particularly income tax laws, a high level of competence is required. CPAs specializing in taxation can provide this competence. The CPA's involvement in tax planning often is quite significant. Most major business decisions have significant tax impacts; so much so that tax-planning considerations often govern the decision.

Employment by Organizations

Many accountants, including CPAs and CMAs, are employed by profit-making and nonprofit organizations. An organization, depending upon its size and complexity, may employ from a few to hundreds of accountants. In a business enterprise, the chief financial officer (usually a vice president or controller) is a member of the management team. This responsibility usually entails a wide range of management, financial, and accounting duties. Exhibit 1–3 shows a typical organizational arrangement of the financial function in a business.

In a business entity, accountants typically are engaged in a wide variety of activities, such as general management, general accounting, cost accounting, profit planning and control (i.e., budgeting), internal auditing, and electronic data processing. A common pattern in recent years has been the selection of a "financial expert" as the chief executive or president of the company. One primary function of the accountants in organizations is **management accounting,** that is, to provide data that are useful for internal managerial decision making and for controlling operations. Also, the functions of external reporting, tax planning, control of assets, and a host of related responsibilities normally are performed by accountants in industry.

Employment in the Public Sector

The vast and complex operations of governmental units, from the local to the international level, create a need for accountants. Accountants employed in the

EXHIBIT 1–3

Typical organization of the financial function

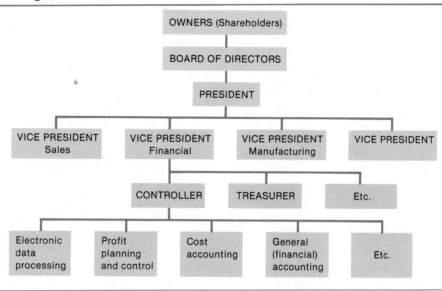

public sector perform functions similar to those performed by their counterparts in private organizations. Also, the General Accounting Office (GAO) and the regulatory agencies, such as the Securities and Exchange Commission (SEC), Interstate Commerce Commission (ICC), Federal Power Commission (FPC), and Federal Communications Commission (FCC), use the services of accountants in carrying out their regulatory duties.

Finally, accountants are involved in varying capacities in the evolving programs of pollution control, health care, minority enterprises, and other socially oriented programs, whether sponsored by private industry or by government.

GROUPS INVOLVED IN ACCOUNTING INNOVATION

In the United States, five groups predominate in the development of financial accounting concepts and practice. A general knowledge of their respective historical and continuing roles is important to your understanding of accounting. The groups are the Financial Accounting Standards Board (FASB), American Institute of Certified Public Accountants (AICPA), U.S. Securities and Exchange Commission (SEC), American Accounting Association (AAA), and Financial Executives Institute (FEI). The past and present roles of each group are briefly reviewed below.

Financial Accounting Standards Board (FASB)

The FASB began operating June 1, 1973. It was established to develop accounting standards to enhance the usefulness and reliability of financial reports. The development of accounting standards is important because accounting standards tend to prevent the reporting of unreliable and misleading financial information. The intensity of the controversies in recent years is indicated by the wide range of interested individuals and special interest groups who have given significant amounts of resources and time to influence the development of accounting concepts and standards. On occasion, the controversy has been an issue in the U.S. Congress. The Congress generally is viewed as an inappropriate forum in which to establish sound accounting concepts and standards. Increasingly, accounting issues have been important in litigation in the courts.

As you study accounting you will realize that the economic results reported in the financial statements, such as asset valuations, earnings, and earnings per share, may have impacts on the economy, on the capital markets (including the stock market), and on many major decisions of individuals, groups, and entities. You also may appreciate how the selection of a particular financial accounting approach often has a significant effect on the financial results reported through the accounting process (such as earnings and earnings per share).

The FASB has seven members who are appointed by an independent board of trustees and serve on a full-time basis. It was organized to be independent. Its sole function is the **establishment and improvement of accounting concepts and standards.** Through the FASB, the accounting profession intends to keep the standards-setting function in the private sector rather than to have the standards imposed by laws and governmental agencies.

American Institute of Certified Public Accountants (AICPA)

The AICPA was organized a few years before the turn of the century by a group of accountants engaged in public and industrial accounting. Membership currently is limited to certified public accountants (see page 12). In terms of direct impact on financial accounting practice, the AICPA has been the strongest force in accounting in recent decades. It carries on a wide-ranging program including professional development, publications (including the magazine *Journal of Accountancy*), and the development and communication of accounting standards and procedures. During the period from 1930 to 1950, the AICPA's Committee on Accounting Procedure issued a number of *Accounting Research Bulletins (ARBs)* that enunciated certain recommended financial accounting principles and procedures. These recommendations were followed by much of the accounting profession. Realizing the need for a more concentrated effort to develop accounting standards and more adherence to prescribed accounting guidelines, in 1959 the AICPA organized the **Accounting Principles Board (APB)** to replace the former committee. The FASB (discussed above) was established to replace the APB. The APB issued 31 numbered *Opinions* during its existence from 1959 through mid-1973. The *Opinions* dealt with many of the difficult issues of financial accounting; therefore, many of them were controversial. Throughout this textbook you will notice a few references to the *ARBs* and numerous references to *APB Opinions* because some of them are still recognized by the FASB.

Securities and Exchange Commission (SEC)

The SEC, a government regulatory agency, operates under authority granted by the Securities Acts of 1933 and 1934. These acts were enacted in response to the manipulations, irrational speculation, and lack of credible financial information that existed when the stock market crashed in 1929–30. The acts gave the SEC authority to **prescribe accounting guidelines for the financial reports required to be submitted by corporations that sell their securities in interstate commerce** (i.e., registered companies, which are primarily those listed on the stock exchanges). This list includes most of the large, and some medium-sized, corporations. The SEC requires these corporations to submit periodic financial reports, which are maintained in the files of the Commission as a matter of public record. Also, a **prospectus,** which is a preliminary statement presented to prospective buyers or investors, is required before the sale of securities. As a matter of policy, the SEC usually has followed the accounting concepts, standards, and procedures established by the accounting profession. The SEC publishes *Regulation S-X* and issues *Financial Reporting Releases (FRR)*, which prescribe the guidelines to be followed by registered companies in preparing the financial reports submitted in conformance with the Securities Acts. Throughout its existence, the SEC has had a significant impact on accounting. Its staff has worked closely with the accounting profession on the evolution and improvement of accounting standards.

American Accounting Association (AAA)

The AAA was organized during the World War I period by a group of college accounting professors. The Association sponsors and encourages the improvement of accounting teaching and accounting research and publishes *The Accounting Review.* Its committees issue reports that, along with the research activities of individual academicians, exert a pervasive influence on the development of accounting theory and standards.

Financial Executives Institute (FEI)

The membership in the FEI is primarily CPAs and CMAs employed in industry. They are financial vice presidents, controllers, and other accounting executives. This group provides important and responsible inputs to the FASB.

Summary of Part A

The prior discussions of the environment in which accounting operates suggest the importance of competitive and successful businesses (from the smallest to the largest) to a free enterprise economy. Economic success in a competitive business economy means earning reasonable profits and providing funds (cash) to meet broad reinvestment needs. Adequate reinvestment in businesses means more jobs, better wages, continuing technological advances, expansion of efficient productive capacity, adequate dividends for investors, and more tax revenue to the government (to support socially desirable programs and other governmental activities). The economic dimensions of this success by individual businesses are communicated in accounting reports.

PART B—COMMUNICATION OF ACCOUNTING INFORMATION

This part of the chapter presents an overview of the end product of the accounting processing system—the **periodic financial statements** of a business. These statements are viewed as the primary way to communicate financial information about an entity. Chapter 2 will continue this overview of the basic financial statements.

The remaining chapters will discuss and illustrate how the financial statements are derived. Therefore, those chapters will focus on the economic analyses, measurements, and recording of transactions that precede the preparation of financial statements.

COMMUNICATION CONCEPTS AND APPROACHES

Communication is a flow of information from one party to one or more other parties. **Effective communication** means that the recipient understands what the sender intends to convey. Communication involves problems in understanding the words, symbols, and sounds used by the parties involved. Accounting uses words and symbols to communicate financial information that is relevant to the decisions made by investors, creditors, and other interested parties. As decisions are made, reliance is placed upon certain information that often is unique to the issue involved. Often, decisions are made without adequate information. Either the needed information is not available in time or the cost of developing it is too high when compared to its potential usefulness.[4] The form in which information is "packaged" and the avenues used to communicate it sometimes affect the decision. For example, some individuals are more influenced by graphic than by quantitative presentations. However, others find

---

[4] This sentence suggests the concept of cost-benefit analysis; that is, a comparison of the cost of pursuing a particular course of action compared with the economic benefits or advantages derived from that course of action.

narrative preferable to tabular expression, while some prefer summaries rather than details. Still others are not interested in technical presentations.

Financial information and the means used to communicate it often have strong and pervasive behavioral impacts on decision makers.[5] The behavioral impacts of accounting extend to both positive and negative motivations of people. The frequency, form, and quality of one's communications with others are often important to the recipients.

The terminology of accounting was developed to communicate financial information effectively. As is common with other professions, such as law and medicine, the terminology of accounting is technical because precision is essential. Accounting has developed in direct response to the needs of its environment. Therefore, accounting is continuously evolving new concepts, terminology, procedures, and means of communication. In the chapters to follow, you should learn the basic terminology of accounting. That terminology is referred to as the "language of business."

OVERVIEW OF EXTERNAL FINANCIAL STATEMENTS

Financial statements often are classified as (1) internal (i.e., management accounting) statements and (2) external (i.e., financial accounting) statements. **Internal financial statements** are not given to parties outside the entity. They are used exclusively by, and are prepared under the direction of, the managers of the entity; therefore, they are prepared to meet specific internal policies and guidelines established by those managers.

External financial statements are the end product of an accounting system. They are given to parties (i.e., external decision makers) outside the entity (which include stockholders and creditors). External parties are unable to specify guidelines for preparation of the statements. The information presented on external financial statements helps investors and others make better economic decisions about the entity. Thus, financial statements must present information that is relevant to economic decisions. That is, they must be useful for predicting the future successes (and failures) of the business. **Relevance** is an important qualitative characteristic of financial statements.

To ensure that external parties can rely on the information reported in financial statements, the entity is required to conform to specific and well-known **generally accepted accounting principles (GAAP)** that are developed by the accounting profession. GAAP will be discussed in the remaining chapters.

---

[5] A behavioral impact is an individual's response to external forces. An individual may be motivated toward or away from certain courses of action by information or observations that come to his or her attention. For example, one may be motivated to purchase a large automobile rather than a small one because of prestige. However, a financial report showing the relative costs of operating the two automobiles may motivate the individual to purchase the small automobile. Thus, the financial report exerted a significant behavioral impact on the decision maker.

This textbook discusses the **preparation and interpretation** of external financial reports only. The next several pages present an overview of the external financial statements required by GAAP.

A general understanding of financial statements at the outset helps you to understand the accounting process when it is discussed in later chapters. The three required financial statements for a profit-making entity for **external reporting** to owners, potential investors, creditors, and other decision makers are the—

1. **Income statement** (also called the statement of revenues, expenses, and income).
2. **Balance sheet** (also called the statement of assets, liabilities, and owners' equity and statement of financial position).
3. **Statement of changes in financial position** (also called the statement of cash inflows and outflows; abbreviated SCFP).

These three required statements summarize the financial activities of the business entity for each specific period of time. They can be prepared at any time (such as end of the year, quarter, or month) and can apply to any time span (such as 10 years, 1 year, 1 quarter, or 1 month). The heading of each statement has a specific statement of the **time dimension** of the report. Although these three statements directly relate to each other, for instructional convenience, they are considered separately. First, we will illustrate these statements for a simple business case. The next chapter discusses and illustrates them in a more complex case.

The Income Statement

The income statement reports the **profit performance** of a business entity. The term profit is used widely in our language, but accountants prefer to use the technical term income. The **accounting model** for the income statement is:

REVENUES − EXPENSES = INCOME

An income statement reports the revenues and expenses for a specified period. Revenues cause inflows of resources into a business, and expenses cause outflows of resources. Income statements present the results of operations for a specific period of time, which is called the **time-period assumption** (e.g., "For the Year Ended December 31, 19A"). Results of operations include **revenues, expenses,** and the resulting **income.**

Illustration.   The income statement of Business Aids, Inc., is presented in Exhibit 1–4. Business Aids is a company that provides professional secretarial, reproduction, and mailing services for a fee. Business Aids was organized by three individuals as a **corporation.** Each owner (called a stockholder) received 1,000 shares of capital stock as proof of ownership. The **heading** of the statement specifically identifies the name of the entity, the title of the report, and the **time period** over which the net income was earned (one year). Notice that there are

Exhibit 1–4

Income statement (simplified)

BUSINESS AIDS, INC.	←Name of entity	
Income Statement	←Title of report	HEADING
For the Year Ended December 31, 19A	←Time period	

Revenues:
Stenographic revenue	$30,000	
Printing revenue	20,000	
Mailing revenue	13,000	
Total revenues		$63,000

Expenses:
Salary expense	30,750	
Payroll tax expense	1,100	
Rent expense for office space	2,400	
Rental payments for copiers	6,600	
Utilities expense	400	
Advertising expense	960	
Supplies expense	90	
Interest expense	100	
Depreciation expense on office equipment	600	
Total expenses (excluding income tax)		43,000
Pretax income		20,000
Income tax expense ($20,000 × 17%)		3,400
Net income		$16,600
Earnings per share (EPS) ($16,600 ÷ 3,000 shares)		$5.53

three major captions: **revenues, expenses,** and **net income.** The detail given under each caption meets the needs of decision makers interested in Business Aids, Inc. This latter point is significant because the composition and the detail of a financial statement vary, depending on the characteristics of the business entity and the needs of the decision makers.

Next we will discuss the four primary elements on an income statement—revenues, expenses, net income, and earnings per share.

Revenues

Revenues are earned from the sale of goods or services rendered by the entity to others for which the entity will receive (or has received) cash or something else of value. When a business sells goods or renders services, it usually receives cash immediately. If goods or services are sold on credit, the business receives an **account receivable,** which is collected in cash later. In either case, the business recognizes revenue for the period as the sum of sales of goods and services for cash and on credit. Revenue is measured in dollars as the bargained

cash-equivalent price agreed on by the two parties to the transaction.[6] Various terms are used in financial statements to describe revenue, such as sales revenue, service revenue, rental revenue, and interest revenue. Revenues are discussed in more detail in Chapter 4.

Expenses

Expenses represent the dollar amount of resources expended or used up by the entity during a period of time to earn revenues. Expenses may require the immediate payment of cash and/or some other resource such as services or inventory items. The payment may be on credit so that cash or some other resource is paid after the expense is incurred. For accounting purposes, the **period in which an expense is incurred**[7] **is the period in which the goods are used or the services are received.** The expense may be incurred in one period, and the payment made in another period.

An expense may represent the cost of **using** equipment or buildings that were purchased earlier for continuing use in operating the business rather than for sale. Such items often have a high acquisition cost. Through use, each one is worn out (or becomes obsolete) over an extended period of time known as useful life. As such items are used in operating the business, a portion of their cost becomes an expense. This kind of expense is called **depreciation expense.** For example, on January 1, 19A, Business Aids purchased office equipment for its own use at a cash cost of $6,000. It was estimated that the office equipment would have a useful life of 10 years. Therefore, the depreciation expense each year for using the equipment is measured as $6,000 ÷ 10 years = $600. The income statement for 19A (Exhibit 1–4) reports this amount as a noncash expense.[8]

Business Aids also reported **interest expense** for one year on the $1,000, 10% note payable (i.e., $1,000 × 10% = $100) because this debt was outstanding for all of 19A.

As a corporation, Business Aids has a 17% income tax rate on income. Therefore, Business Aids incurred **income tax expense** of $3,400 (i.e., $20,000 × 17% = $3,400).

Net income

Net income (often called profit by nonaccountants) is the excess of total revenues over total expenses. If the total expenses exceed the total revenues, a **net loss** is reported. When revenues and expenses are equal for the period, the business has operated at **break even.**

---

[6] Revenue sometimes is called income, such as rent income, interest income, and royalty income, but this practice causes confusion. Ideally, **income should be used to refer only to the difference between revenues and expenses.**

[7] Incurred, as used in this context, means that the amount involved should be accounted for (i.e., recorded in the accounting system) during the specific period.

[8] Accounting for depreciation is discussed in detail in Chapter 9.

Notice that Business Aids reported *(a)* pretax income, *(b)* income tax expense, and *(c)* net income, which is an **aftertax** amount.[9]

Earnings per share (EPS)

The amount of earnings per share (EPS) is reported immediately below net income on the income statement of corporations. EPS is computed by dividing net income by the number of shares of **common** stock outstanding. Because Business Aids had 3,000 shares of common stock outstanding (i.e., 1,000 shares were owned by each of the three stockholders) and a net income of $16,600, EPS was computed as $16,600 ÷ 3,000 shares = $5.53 per share for the year. EPS is given extensive attention by security analysts and investors.

Some people view the income statement as the most important of the three required financial statements because it is designed to report the amount of **net income** and the details of how that amount was earned.

The Balance Sheet

The purpose of the balance sheet is to report the financial position of a business at a particular point in time. Financial position is the amount of resources (i.e., assets) and the liabilities (i.e., debts) of a business. Therefore, the balance sheet is frequently called the statement of financial position. The **accounting model** for the balance sheet is:[10]

ASSETS = LIABILITIES + OWNERS' EQUITY

Assets represent resources owned by the entity, liabilities are the debts (obligations) of the entity, and owners' equity represents the interests of the owners.[11]

Illustration.   The balance sheet of Business Aids, Inc., is presented in Exhibit 1–5. Notice that the **heading** specifically identifies the name of the entity, the title of the report, and the specific date of the statement. Note that the specific point in time—in this case, December 31, 19A—is stated clearly on the balance sheet. This contrasts with the dating on the income statement, which indicates a period of time (such as one year). After the statement heading, the **assets** are listed on the left and the **liabilities** and **owners' equity** (called stockholders' equity for a corporation) on the right. The result is that the two sides "balance" in conformity with the accounting model given above. In the

---

[9] Corporations, except those that qualify under Subchapter S of the Internal Revenue Code, are required to pay federal income taxes as follows. The income tax rates are determined by Congress and are changed periodically. Sole proprietorships and partnerships, as business entities, and Subchapter S corporations, are not subject to income taxes. In each of these cases, the owner, or owners, must report the income of the entity on their own individual income tax returns. For illustrative purposes, an average tax rate is used herein to ease the arithmetic.

[10] The accounting model is an algebraic equation that can be rearranged. For example, it frequently is expressed as: Assets − Liabilities = Owners' Equity.

[11] Owners' equity for a corporation usually is called stockholders' equity.

EXHIBIT 1–5

Balance sheet (simplified)

BUSINESS AIDS, INC.
Balance Sheet
At December 31, 19A

Assets			Liabilities		
Cash		$13,600	Accounts payable.............	$ 900	
Accounts receivable..........		13,000	Income taxes payable	500	
Land		20,000	Note payable,		
Office equipment	$6,000		short term, 10%	1,000	
Less: Accumulated			Total liabilities..........		$ 2,400
depreciation..............	600	5,400*			
			Stockholders' Equity		
			Contributed capital:		
			Capital stock (3,000 shares,		
			par value $10		
			per share)................	$30,000	
			Contributed capital in excess		
			of par value	3,000	
			Retained earnings.............	16,600	
			Total stockholders'		
			equity		49,600
			Total liabilities and		
Total assets		$52,000	stockholders' equity.........		$52,000

* This is the **undepreciated** cost; it is usually called the "book value" of the asset.

following chapters we will learn that the accounting model for the balance sheet is the basic building block for the entire accounting process.

Next we will discuss the three elements reported on a balance sheet—assets, liabilities, and owners' equity.

Assets

Assets are the resources owned by the entity. Assets may be tangible (physical in character) such as land, buildings, and machinery. Or they may be intangible (characterized by legal claims or rights) such as amounts due from customers (legal claims called accounts receivable) and patents (protected rights).

Notice in the balance sheet given in Exhibit 1–5 that each **asset** listed has an assigned dollar amount. An asset should be measured on the basis of the total cost incurred to acquire it. For example, the balance sheet for Business Aids reports "Land, $20,000"; this is the amount of resources paid for the land when it was acquired. It may be that because of market changes, the market value of the land at December 31, 19A (date of the balance sheet), actually was more or less than $20,000. Nevertheless, the balance sheet reports the land at its **original acquisition cost.** It follows that the balance sheet does not purport to show the **current market value** of the assets listed.

Notice that the balance sheet reports **Office equipment,** $6,000, which was its **acquisition cost. Accumulated depreciation** of $600 is subtracted from the original cost. This $600 is the same as the amount of depreciation expense on the income statement (Exhibit 1–4). This amount is deducted because it represents the portion of the original cost that is "worn out or used up" to earn the revenues. This is a cumulative amount; therefore, at the end of the next year (19B) the deduction for accumulated depreciation will be $1,200 (i.e. $600 × 2 years).

You may ask why accountants do not change the measurement of each asset for each subsequent balance sheet to reflect the new market values. This revaluation is not done because the acquisition cost is factually objective (i.e. not an estimate), whereas the current market value of the assets owned by the entity would have to be estimated at the end of each year. The estimate would be subjective because the assets are not sold each year-end. Such subjectivity could reduce the reliability of the financial statements.

Liabilities

Liabilities are the debts or obligations of the entity. They arise primarily because of the purchase of goods or services from others on credit and through cash borrowings to finance the business.

If a business does not pay its creditors, the law may give the creditors the right to force the sale of assets sufficient to meet their claims.

Business entities often borrow money by entering into a formal note contract. In this case, a liability called **notes payable** is created. A note payable, which may be short term or long term, specifies a definite maturity or payment date and the rate or amount of interest charged by the lender. Also, many businesses purchase goods and services on credit that do not involve notes. This transaction creates a liability known as **accounts payable.** Another type of liability arises because income taxes often are paid, at least in part, several months after the end of the year. Therefore, a liability to the government, **income taxes payable,** must be reported until the taxes are fully paid. Notice in Exhibit 1–5 that Business Aids listed three liabilities and the amount of each.

Owners' Equity

The accounting model (page 23) shows that owners' equity is equal to total assets minus total liabilities of the business. Because creditors' claims legally come first, owners' equity represents a **residual interest** or claim of the owners to the assets. Owners' equity sometimes is called net worth or capital. However, the preferable designations are (a) "owner's equity" for a sole proprietorship; (b) "partners' equity" for a partnership; and (c) "stockholders' equity" for a corporation. Owners' equity in a business comes from two sources: (1) **contributed capital,** which is the investment of cash and other assets in the business by the owners; and (2) **retained earnings,** which is the amount of accumulated earnings kept in the business.[12]

In Exhibit 1–5, the stockholders' equity section reports the following:

1. **Contributed capital**—The three stockholders invested a total of $33,000 in the business. Each stockholder received 1,000 shares of capital stock having a par value of $10 per share (par value will be discussed in Chapter 12). They invested an average price of $11 per share, or $1 per share above par value. The 3,000 shares issued are reported at their par value (3,000 × $10) as "Capital stock" and the remainder, often called a premium on capital stock (3,000 shares × $1 = $3,000), is reported as "Contributed capital in excess of par value."

2. **Retained earnings**—The accumulated amount of earnings less all losses and dividends paid to the stockholders since formation of the corporation is reported as "Retained earnings." During the first year, Business Aids earned $16,600, as shown on the income statement (Exhibit 1–4). This amount is reported as retained earnings on the balance sheet for Business Aids at this date because no dividends were declared or paid to the stockholders during the first year (since organization).

3. **Total stockholders' equity**—The sum of the owners' investment ($33,000) plus the retained earnings ($16,600) equals $49,600. This amount may be verified in terms of the basic accounting model: Assets ($52,000) − Liabilities ($2,400) = Stockholders' Equity ($49,600).

A cash dividend is the payment by a corporation of an equal amount to each share of capital stock outstanding. For example, if a cash dividend of $6,000 had been declared and paid by Business Aids to the three stockholders during the year, the balance sheet would have reflected cash of $7,600 (i.e., $13,600 − $6,000) and retained earnings of $10,600 (i.e., $16,600 − $6,000).

Statement of Changes in Financial Position (SCFP)

A business requires substantial cash for operations and expansion. Cash comes primarily from four sources: (1) owner investments, (2) borrowings, (3) earnings, and (4) selling noncash assets. Users of financial statements need information about the sources and uses of cash because such information helps them project their own future cash flows. Therefore, a **statement of changes in financial position (SCFP)** is required.

The objective of the SCFP is to communicate to decision makers information about the sources (inflows) and uses (outflows) of cash. The **accounting model** for the SCFP is:

---

[12] The term **retained earnings** usually is used by businesses organized as corporations. In contrast, sole proprietorships and partnerships usually do not use this term because it is included in the owners' capital account(s). These distinctions are discussed later.

$$\begin{array}{ccc} \text{CASH SOURCES} & - \text{ CASH USES } & = \text{ NET CHANGE IN CASH} \\ \text{(inflows)} & \text{(outflows)} & \text{(increase or decrease)} \end{array}$$

Illustration. The SCFP of Business Aids, Inc., is presented in Exhibit 1–6. Notice that the heading is dated the same as the income statement because it covers a period of time (i.e., "For the Year Ended December 31, 19A"). At this point you do not need to be concerned about the derivation of the amounts illustrated. Rather, you should notice the detailed information about the cash inflows and cash outflows for the year. This information is relevant to investors and creditors in projecting the future cash flows of the business.[13]

The SCFP is derived from an analysis of the balance sheet and the income statement. For example, total revenue reported on Exhibit 1–4 (the income statement) of $63,000, less $13,000 of the revenue (mailing) extended on credit, equals $50,000. This amount represents the cash inflow from revenue in Exhibit 1–6. Total expenses of $46,400 (including income tax expense), shown on Exhibit 1–4 (income statement), less the **noncash expenses** of $600 for depreciation, $900 for accounts payable, and $500 for income taxes payable, equals the $44,400 reported in Exhibit 1–6 as the cash used for expenses. Thus, the earned net

EXHIBIT 1–6

Statement of changes in financial position (SCFP) (simplified)

BUSINESS AIDS, INC.
Statement of Changes in Financial Position, Cash Basis
For the Year Ended December 31, 19A

Sources of cash (inflows):		
From operations:		
From cash revenues	$50,000	
Less: Cash used for expenses	44,400	
Cash inflow from operations		$ 5,600
From other sources:		
Investment by owners (stock issued for cash)	33,000	
Loan—note payable	1,000	
Cash inflow from other sources		34,000
Total cash inflow during the year		39,600
Uses of cash (outflows):		
To purchase office equipment	6,000	
To purchase land	20,000	
Total cash used during the year (outflows)		26,000
Change—increase in cash during the year		$13,600

---

[13] Some companies prepare the SCFP using "funds" defined as working capital, rather than as cash (discussed in Chapter 15).

income of $16,600 caused a cash inflow of $5,600. Shares of capital stock were sold and caused a cash inflow of $33,000. Also, a loan was obtained to secure another $1,000, giving a total cash inflow during the year of $39,600. During the year, $26,000 cash was expended for office equipment and land. Therefore, the statement reports that $13,600 more cash was received than was spent during the year.

A detailed discussion of the SCFP is deferred to Chapter 15 because its preparation requires special procedures that are best understood after your knowledge of accounting is substantial.

DEMONSTRATION CASE

At the end of most chapters, one or more demonstration cases are presented. These cases provide an overview of the primary issues discussed in the chapter. Each demonstration case is followed by a recommended solution. The case should be read carefully; then you should prepare your own solution before you study the recommended solution. This self-evaluation is highly recommended.

The introductory case presented below will start you thinking in monetary terms of some of the resource inflows and outflows of a business. (Note: The case will test your comprehension of Part B of the chapter and also your analytical skills.)

ABC Service Corporation was organized by Able, Baker, and Cain on January 1, 19A. On that date each investor bought 1,000 shares of capital stock (par value $10 per share) at $12 cash per share. On the same day, the corporation borrowed $10,000 from a local bank and signed a three-year, 15%, note payable. The interest is payable each December 31. On January 1, 19A, the corporation purchased two service trucks for $20,000 cash. Operations started immediately.

At the end of 19A, the corporation had completed the following additional business transactions (summarized):

a. Performed services and billed customers for $100,500, of which $94,500 was collected in cash by year-end.
b. Paid $55,500 cash for expenses (including the annual interest on the note payable).
c. Paid $7,000 cash to the Internal Revenue Service (IRS) for income taxes. At the end of the year, ABC still owed the IRS $1,000 (the average income tax rate was 20%).
d. Depreciated the cost of the two service trucks on the basis of a four-year useful life (disregard any residual value at the end of the four-year life).

Required:

Complete the two 19A financial statements shown in Exhibit 1–7 by entering the correct amounts. The suggested solution is given in Exhibit 1–8.

EXHIBIT 1–7

Format of financial statements—demonstration case

ABC SERVICE CORPORATION
Income Statement

Date _____

Revenues: Computations
  Service revenues......... $ _____ _____
Expenses:
  Various expenses........ $ _____
  Interest expense......... _____ _____
  Depreciation expense.... _____ _____
    Total expenses........ _____
Pretax income............. _____
  Income tax expense...... _____
Net income............... $ _____ _____
Earnings per share........ $ _____ _____

ABC SERVICE CORPORATION
Balance Sheet

Date _____

Assets:
  Cash.................. $ _____ _____
  Accounts receivable...... _____ _____
  Service trucks.......... $ _____ _____
  Less: Accumulated
    depreciation........... _____ _____ _____
Total assets.............. $ _____
Liabilities:
  Note payable........... $ _____ _____
  Income taxes payable.... _____
    Total liabilities....... $ _____ _____
Stockholders' equity:
  Capital stock, par $ _____
    shares _____ .... _____ _____
  Contributed capital in
    excess of par value..... _____ _____
  Retained earnings....... _____ _____
    Total stockholders'
      equity.............. _____
Total liabilities and
  stockholders' equity...... $ _____

EXHIBIT 1–8

Suggested solution—demonstration case

ABC SERVICE CORPORATION
Income Statement

Date _____ *For the Year ended December 31, 19A* _____

		Computations
Revenues:		
Service revenues.........	$100,500	*Given*
Expenses:		
Various expenses........	$54,000	*Given (minus interest)*
Interest expense.........	1,500	*$10,000 × 15%*
Depreciation expense	5,000	*$20,000 ÷ 4 years*
Total expenses	$ 60,500	
Pretax income.............	40,000	
Income tax expense......	8,000	*$40,000 × 20%*
Net income	$ 32,000	
Earnings per share.........	$ 10.67	*$32,000 ÷ 3,000 shares*

ABC SERVICE CORPORATION
Balance Sheet

Date _____ *At December 31, 19A* _____

Assets:				*$36,000 + $10,000 + $94,500*
Cash			$ 58,000	*− $55,500 − $7,000 − $20,000*
Accounts receivable......			6,000	*$100,500 − $94,500*
Service trucks		$20,000		*Given, cost of trucks*
Less: Accumulated				
depreciation...........		5,000	15,000	*$20,000 ÷ 4 years = $5,000*
Total assets			$ 79,000	
Liabilities:				
Note payable...........		$10,000		*Given, bank loan*
Income taxes payable		1,000		*Given, amount unpaid*
Total liabilities.......			$ 11,000	
Stockholders' equity:				
Capital stock, par $ _10_				
shares _3,000_		30,000		*3,000 × $10*
Contributed capital in				
excess of par value.....		6,000		*3,000 × ($12–$10)*
Retained earnings		32,000		*From income statement**
Total stockholders'				
equity			68,000	
Total liabilities and				
stockholders' equity......			$ 79,000	

* Beginning RE ($-0-) + Net Income ($32,000) − Dividends ($-0-) = Ending RE ($32,000).

SUMMARY OF CHAPTER

Accounting interacts with almost all aspects of the environment: social, economic, and political. Any open society is complex and is characterized by a large number of organizations. Each organization, whether local, national, or international, can be an **accounting entity**. The essence of accounting is the measurement and reporting of financial information for an accounting entity. **Measurement** and **reporting** of the financial effects of transactions on accounting entities are relevant to interested decision makers. Your decision-making potential is enhanced if you understand the financial impacts of alternative solutions to particular problems.

Part B of the chapter explained and illustrated the basic features of the three required external financial reports—the income statement, the balance sheet, and the statement of changes in financial position (SCFP).

The income statement is a statement of operations that reports revenues, expenses, and net income for a stated period of time. Earnings per share (EPS), which gives the relationship between net income and the number of shares of common stock outstanding, was illustrated.

The balance sheet is a statement of **financial position** that reports dollar amounts for the assets, liabilities, and owners' equity at a specific point in time.

The statement of changes in financial position (SCFP) is a statement of the inflows and outflows of cash that reports those flows for a specific period of time.

The accounting model for the balance sheet, **Assets = Liabilities + Owners' Equity,** is the **foundation for the entire accounting process.**

The financial statements for a small company were illustrated. In the next chapters, you will move one step forward by learning more about the basic accounting model and the analysis of business transactions.

IMPORTANT TERMS DEFINED IN THIS CHAPTER

Terms (alphabetically)	Key words in definitions of important terms used in chapter	Page reference
AAA	American Accounting Association.	17
Accounting entity	A business or other organization; separate and distinct from its owners.	7
AICPA	American Institute of Certified Public Accountants.	16
Assets	Items owned; have value.	24
Auditing	Attest function; reliability; auditor's opinion.	13
Balance sheet	Position statement; Assets = Liabilities + Owners' Equity.	23
Cash inflows	Cash received; increase Cash.	26
Cash outflows	Cash paid; decrease Cash.	26
Contributed capital	Total amount invested by stockholders.	26
Corporation	A separate legal entity; shares of stock represent ownership.	6
CMA	Certified Management Accountant.	12
CPA	Certified Public Accountant.	12
Depreciation	Allocation of the cost of operational assets; based on use.	22

Dividend (cash)	A cash payment from a corporation to its stockholders based on the number of shares held.	26
EPS	Earnings per share; common stock.	23
Expenses	Outflow of resources; for goods and services used.	22
FASB	Financial Accounting Standards Board.	16
FEI	Financial Executives Institute	17
GAAP	Generally accepted accounting principles.	13
Income statement	Required report; operations; income; EPS.	20
Liabilities	Obligations; debts; promises to pay.	25
Management advisory services	Service rendered by CPA firms; consulting; complements audit and tax services (MAS).	14
Net income	Revenues − Expenses = Income.	22
Owners' equity	Assets − Liabilities = Owners' Equity.	25
Partnership	Nonstock; two or more owners.	6
Retained earnings	Accumulated earnings; reduced by dividends.	26
Revenues	Inflow of resources; from sale of goods and services.	21
SCFP	Statement of changes in financial position.	26
SEC	Securities and Exchange Commission; government.	17
Separate entity assumption	An entity must be accounted for separately and apart from its owners.	7
Sole proprietorship	Nonstock; one owner.	6
Stockholders' equity	Assets − Liabilities = Stockholders' Equity.	25

QUESTIONS

PART A

1. Define accounting.

2. Explain the use of the monetary unit in accounting.

3. Briefly distinguish among a sole proprietorship, partnership, and corporation.

4. What is an accounting entity? Why is a business treated as a separate entity for accounting purposes?

5. Briefly explain the three ways that financial statements serve statement users.

6. List and briefly explain the three primary services provided by CPAs in public practice.

7. Briefly explain the role of the:
   a. FASB.
   b. SEC.
   c. AAA.

PART B

8. Financial statements are the end products of the accounting process. Explain.

9. Define communication.

10. The accounting process generates financial reports for both "internal" and "external" users. Identify some of the groups of users.

11. Complete the following:

Name of statement		*A more descriptive name*
a. Income statement	a.	_____
b. Balance sheet	b.	_____
c. Statement of changes in financial position (SCFP)	c.	_____

12. What information should be included in the heading of each of the three required financial statements?

13. Explain why the income statement and the SCFP are dated "For the Year Ended December 31, 19X," whereas the balance sheet is dated "At December 31, 19X."

14. Define revenue.

15. Define expense.

16. Briefly define the following: net income, net loss, and break even.

17. What are the purposes of (a) the income statement, (b) the balance sheet, and (c) the SCFP?

18. Explain the accounting model for the income statement. What are the three major items reported on the income statement?

19. Explain the accounting model for the balance sheet. Define the three major components reported on the balance sheet.

20. Explain the accounting model for the SCFP. Explain the three major components reported on the statement.

21. Why is owners' equity referred to frequently as a residual interest?

22. What are the two primary sources of owners' equity in a business?

23. What are the appropriate titles for owners' equity for (a) sole proprietorship, (b) partnership, and (c) corporation?

EXERCISES

(Note: The booklet of working papers that accompanies this textbook provides forms with the problem data already entered.)

PART A

E1–1   (Identifying Important Accounting Organizations)

Below is a list of important abbreviations used in Part A of the chapter. These abbreviations also are used widely in business. For each abbreviation give the full designation. The first one is an example.

	Abbreviation	Full designation
	(1) CPA	Certified Public Accountant
	(2) APB	
	(3) GAO	
	(4) AAA	
	(5) CMA	
	(6) AICPA	
	(7) SEC	
	(8) FASB	
	(9) ICC	
	(10) FEI	

E1–2   (Characteristics of the Environment of Accounting)

Match each description with its related term or abbreviation by entering the appropriate letter in the blanks provided.

Related term or abbreviation

_____ (1) SEC
_____ (2) Auditing
_____ (3) Sole proprietorship
_____ (4) Corporation
_____ (5) Accounting
_____ (6) Separate entity
_____ (7) Auditor's report
_____ (8) CMA
_____ (9) Partnership
_____ (10) AICPA
_____ (11) FASB
_____ (12) CPA
_____ (13) Unit of measure
_____ (14) FEI
_____ (15) American Accounting Association

Description

A. The collection, analysis, measurement, recording, and reporting information about an entity to decision makers.
B. Measurement of information about an entity in the monetary unit—dollars.
C. An unincorporated business owned by two or more persons.
D. An entity defined for accounting purposes, separate from its owners.
E. An incorporated entity that issues shares of stock as evidence of ownership.
F. A Certified Management Accountant.
G. Attest function by an independent CPA.
H. Certified Public Accountant.
I. An unincorporated business owned by one person.
J. Independent CPA's statement that indicates whether the financial statements are appropriate and not misleading.
K. Securities and Exchange Commission.
L. Financial Accounting Standards Board.
M. American Accounting Association.
N. Financial Executives Institute.
O. Encourages improvement of accounting teaching and accounting research.
P. American Institute of Certified Public Accountants.

PART B

E1–3   (Using the Income Statement and Balance Sheet Models)

Review the chapter explanations of the income statement and the balance sheet models. Apply these models in each independent case below to compute the two missing amounts for each case. Assume it is the end of 19A, the first full year of operations for the company.

Independent Cases	Total Revenues	Total Assets	Total Expenses	Total Liabilities	Net Income (Loss)	Stockholders' Equity
A	$95,000	$150,000	$88,000	$92,000	$	$
B		112,000	61,000		10,000	70,000
C	80,000	92,000	86,000	26,000		
D	65,000			40,000	9,000	77,000
E			81,000	73,000	(6,000)	88,000

E1–4   **(Analyzing an Income Statement)**

Rose Corporation was organized by three individuals on January 1, 19A, to provide electronic repair services. At the end of 19A, the following income statement was prepared:

ROSE CORPORATION
INCOME STATEMENT
FOR THE YEAR ENDED DECEMBER 31, 19A

Revenues:
  Service sales (cash) $178,000
  Service sales (credit)   12,000
    Total revenues $190,000

Expenses:
  Salaries   71,000
  Rent   12,000
  Utilities   10,000
  Advertising   11,000
  Supplies   18,000
  Interest   3,000
  Depreciation   5,000
    Total expenses   130,000
Pretax income   60,000
  Income tax expense   13,200
Net income .... $ 46,800
EPS $2.34

Required:

a. What was the average monthly revenue amount?
b. What was the monthly rent amount?
c. Explain why "Supplies, $18,000" is an expense.
d. Explain why "Interest, $3,000" is reported as an expense.
e. Explain what is meant by "Depreciation, $5,000."
f. What was the average income tax rate for Rose Corporation?
g. How many shares of capital stock were outstanding?
h. Can you determine how much cash the company had on December 31, 19A? Explain.

E1–5 **(Preparing a Simple Income Statement)**

Assume you are the owner of "The Drop-In Shop," which specializes in items that interest college students. At the end of January 19A you find that (for January only):

a. Sales, per the cash register tapes, totaled $80,000, plus one sale on credit (a special situation) of $1,000.

b. With the help of a friend (who majored in accounting), you determined that all of the goods sold during January had cost you $30,000 when they were purchased.

c. During the month, according to the checkbook, you paid $35,000 for salaries, utilities, supplies, advertising, and other expenses; however, you have not yet paid the $600 monthly rent for January on the store and fixtures.

On the basis of the data given, what was the amount of income for January (disregard income taxes)? Show computations. (Hint: A convenient form to use would have the following major side captions: revenue from sales, expenses, and the difference—income.)

E1–6 **(Analysis of Cash Inflow from Operations)**

SuperServ Company, a service organization, prepared the following special report for the month of January 19A:

Service Revenues, Expenses, and Income

Service revenues:		
Cash services (per cash register tape)	$95,000	
Credit services (per charge bills; not yet collected by end of January)	30,000	$125,000
Expenses:		
Salaries and wages (paid by check)	50,000	
Salary for January not yet paid	2,000	
Supplies used (taken from stock, purchased for cash during December)	1,000	
Estimated cost of wear and tear on used delivery truck for the month (depreciation)	500	
Other expenses (paid by check)	21,500	75,000
Pretax income		50,000
Income tax expense (not yet paid)		10,000
Income for January		$ 40,000

Required:

a. The owner (who knows very little about the financial part of the business) asked you to compute the "amount that cash increased in January 19A from the operations of the company." You decided to prepare a detailed report for the owner with the following major side captions: cash inflows (collections), cash outflows (payments), and the difference—net increase (or decrease) in cash.

b. What was the average income tax rate?

c. See if you can reconcile the "difference—net increase (or decrease) in cash" you computed in (a) with the income for January 19A.

E1–7 **(Preparing a Simple Income Statement and Balance Sheet)**

Dusty Corporation was organized by five individuals on January 1, 19A. At the end of January 19A, the following monthly financial data are available:

Total revenues $110,000
Total expenses (excluding income taxes) 80,000
Cash balance, January 31, 19A 18,000
Receivables from customers (all considered collectible) 12,000
Merchandise inventory (by inventory count at cost) 35,000
Payables to suppliers for merchandise purchased
     from them (will be paid during February 19A) 9,000
Capital stock, par $10, 2,600 shares 26,000
No dividends were declared or paid during 19A.

Assume a 20% tax rate on the income of this corporation; the income taxes will be paid during the first quarter of 19B.

Required:

Complete the following two statements:

DUSTY CORPORATION
Income Statement
For the Month of January 19A

Total revenues .... $ _____
     Less: Total expenses (excluding income tax) .... _____
Pretax income .... _____
     Less: Income tax expense .... _____
Net income .... $ _____

DUSTY CORPORATION
Balance Sheet
At January 31, 19A

Assets:
     Cash .... $ _____
     Receivables from customers .... _____
     Merchandise inventory .... _____
Total assets .... $ _____

Liabilities:
     Payables to suppliers .... $ _____
     Income taxes payable .... _____
          Total liabilities .... _____

Stockholders' equity:
     Capital stock .... $ _____
     Retained earnings .... _____
Total liabilities and stockholders' equity .... $ _____

E1–8   (Completing a Simple Balance Sheet)

Cutrate Bookstore was organized as a corporation by Mary Newell and Joe Owens; each contributed $40,000 cash to start the business. Each received 3,000 shares of common stock, par $10 per share. The store completed its first year of operations on December 31, 19A. On that date, the following financial items for the year were determined: December 31, 19A, cash on hand and in the bank, $41,100; December 31, 19A, amounts due from customers from sales of books, $19,000; store and office equipment, purchased January 1, 19A, for $50,000 (estimated useful life 10 years; depreciate an equal amount each year); December 31, 19A, amounts owed to publishers for books purchased,

$7,000; and a note payable, 10%, one year, dated July 1, 19A, to a local bank for $2,000. No dividends were declared or paid to the stockholders during the year.

Required:

a. Complete the balance sheet at the end of 19A shown below.
b. What was the amount of net income for the year?
c. Show how the $100 liability for interest payable was computed. Why is it shown as a liability on this date?

Assets			**Liabilities**			
Cash	$ _____		Accounts payable	$ _____		
Accounts receivable	_____		Notes payable	_____		
Store and office equipment ... $ _____			Interest payable	100		
Less: Accumulated			Total liabilities		$ _____	
depreciation to date	_____	_____				
			Stockholders' Equity			
			Common stock	_____		
			Contributed capital in excess			
			of par	16,000		
			Retained earnings			
			Total stockholders' equity		_____	
			Total liabilities and			
Total assets	$ _____		stockholders' equity		$ _____	

E1–9   (Preparing a Simple SCFP, Cash Basis)

Blue Manufacturing Corporation is preparing the annual financial statements for the stockholders. A SCFP, cash basis, must be prepared. The following data on cash flows were developed for the entire year ended December 31, 19D; cash inflow from operating revenues, $250,000; cash expended for operating expenses, $190,000; sale of unissued Blue stock for cash, $20,000; cash dividends declared and paid to stockholders during the year, $15,000; and payments on long-term notes payable, $50,000. During the year, a tract of land was sold for $10,000 cash (which was the same price that Blue had paid for the land in 19C), and $33,000 cash was expended for two new machines. The machines were used in the factory.

Required:

Prepare a SCFP, cash basis, for 19D. Follow the format illustrated in the chapter.

E1–10   (Completing a Simple Income Statement)

Quality Reality Corporation has been operating for five years and is owned by three investors. J. Doe owns 60% of the total outstanding stock of 9,000 shares and is the managing executive in charge. On December 31, 19C, the following financial items for the entire year were determined: commissions earned and collected in cash, $140,000, plus $14,000 uncollected; rental service fees earned and collected, $16,000; salaries expense paid, $56,700; commissions expense paid, $40,000; payroll taxes paid, $3,000; rent paid, $2,200 (not including December rent yet to be paid); utilities expense paid, $900; promotion and advertising paid, $6,000; and miscellaneous expenses paid, $400. There were no other unpaid expenses at December 31. Quality Realty rents its office space but owns the furniture therein. The furniture cost $6,000 when acquired and has an estimated life of 10 years (depreciate an equal amount each year). The average income tax rate for this corporation is 30%. Also during the year, the company paid the owners "out of profit" cash dividends amounting to $10,000. Complete the following income statement:

Revenues:		
Commissions earned	$ _____	
Rental service fees	_____	
Total revenues		$ _____
Expenses:		
Salaries expense	_____	
Commission expense	_____	
Payroll tax expense	_____	
Rent expense	_____	
Utilities expense	_____	
Promotion and advertising	_____	
Miscellaneous expenses	_____	
Depreciation expense	_____	
Total expenses (excluding income taxes)		_____
Pretax income		_____
Income tax expense		_____
Net income		$ ____42,000____
Earnings per share (EPS)		$ _____

E1–11 (Applying the Balance Sheet Model)

On June 1, 19F, Rand Corporation prepared a balance sheet just prior to going out of business. The balance sheet totals showed the following:

Assets (no cash) $100,000
Liabilities 60,000
Stockholders' equity 40,000

Shortly thereafter, all of the assets were sold for cash.

Required:

a. How would the balance sheet appear immediately after the sale of the assets for cash for each of the following cases? Use the format given below.

	Cash received for the assets	Balances immediately after sale		
		Assets	− Liabilities =	Stockholders' Equity
Case A	$110,000	$_____	$_____	$_____
Case B	100,000	_____	_____	_____
Case C	90,000	_____	_____	_____

b. How should the cash be distributed in each separate case? (Hint: Creditors have a priority claim over owners upon dissolution.) Use the format given below.

	To creditors	To stockholders	Total
Case A	$_____	$_____	$_____
Case B	_____	_____	_____
Case C	_____	_____	_____

PROBLEMS

(Note: The booklet of forms that accompanies this textbook provides forms with the problem data already entered.)

PART A

P1–1   (Analyzing Transactions)
Below are listed five transactions completed by VT Company during the year 19A:

a. Sold services for cash, $40,000.
b. Purchased a microcomputer for use in performing the accounting function of the company: cost, $6,000; paid cash.
c. Paid salaries, $20,000 cash.
d. Borrowed cash, $15,000 on a 12% interest-bearing note.
e. The owner of VT Company purchased a special pickup for his personal use: cost, $16,000; paid cash from his personal funds.

Required:
Complete the tabulation given below. Indicate the effects (in dollars) of each of the above transactions on the balance sheet, income statement, and SCFP of VT Company. Consider only the effects on the date the transactions were completed. Provide explanatory comments to support your response for each transaction. Use "+" for increase and "−" for decrease on the income statement and balance sheet.

Financial statements	Transaction				
	(a)	(b)	(c)	(d)	(e)
Income statement:					
Revenues	$	$	$	$	$
Expenses					
Balance sheet:					
Assets					
Liabilities					
Owners' equity					
SCFP:					
Cash inflow					
Cash outflow					

Explanations:

P1–2   (Analysis of Data to Support a Loan Application)

On January 1, 19A, three individuals organized Quick Service Company. Each individual invested $10,000 cash in the business. On December 31, 19A, they prepared a list of resources (assets) owned and a list of the debts (liabilities) to support a company loan request of $50,000 submitted to a local bank. None of the three investors had studied accounting. The two lists prepared were as follows:

Company resources:
Cash	$ 8,000
Service supplies inventory (on hand)	5,000
Service trucks (four practically new)	64,000
Personal residences of organizers (three houses)	190,000
Service equipment used in the business (practically new)	24,000
Bills due from customers (for services already completed)	13,000
Total	$304,000

Obligations of the company:
Unpaid wages to employees	$ 18,000
Unpaid taxes	6,000
Owed to suppliers	8,000
Owed on service trucks and equipment (to a finance company)	40,000
Loan from organizer	15,000
Total	$ 87,000

Required:

a. If you were advising the local bank about the two lists, what issues would you raise? Explain the basis for each question and include any recommendations that you have (consider the separate-entity assumption).

b. In view of your response to (a), what do you think the amount of **net resources** (i.e., assets minus liabilities) of the company would be? Show your computations.

P1–3   **(Comparison of Income with Cash Flow)**

Rush Service Company was organized on January 1, 19A. At the end of the first quarter (three months) of operations, the owner prepared a summary of its operations as shown in the first column of the following tabulation:

Summary of Transactions	Computation of	
	Income	Cash
1. Services performed for customers, $66,000, of which one sixth remained uncollected at the end of the quarter.	$ + 66,000	$ + 55,000
2. Cash borrowed from the local bank, $20,000 (one-year note).	_____	_____
3. Purchased a small service truck for use in the business; cost, $8,000; paid 20% down, balance on credit.	_____	_____
4. Expenses, $42,000, of which one fifth remained unpaid at the end of the quarter.	_____	_____
5. Purchased service supplies for use in the business, $2,000, of which one fourth remained unpaid (on credit) at the end of the quarter. Also, one fifth of these supplies were unused (still on hand) at the end of the quarter.	_____	_____
6. Wages earned by employees, $18,000, of which one sixth remained unpaid at the end of the quarter.	_____	_____
7. Purchased land for future use for $20,000 cash.	_____	_____

Based only on the above transactions, compute the following for the quarter:
    Income (or loss)
 	
    Cash inflow (or outflow)
	$ _____	
		
		$ _____

Required:

a. For each of the seven transactions given in the tabulation above, enter what you consider the correct amounts. Enter a zero when appropriate. The first transaction is illustrated.

b. For each transaction, explain the basis for your dollar responses. (Hint: Income and cash flow totals are not the same.)

PART B

P1–4   **(Completing a Simple Balance Sheet)**

DC Corporation was organized by Donald Dunn and Cynthia Cummings; they had previously operated the company as a partnership. Each owner has 10,000 shares of capital stock of DC Corporation. At the end of the accounting year, 19H, the company bookkeeper prepared the following incomplete balance sheet (amounts simplified for problem purposes):

DC CORPORATION
Balance Sheet

(1) Assets:			
(2) Cash			$28,000
(3) Accounts receivable			15,000
(4) Equipment*	$		
(5) Less: Accumulated depreciation		10,000	40,000
(6) Total _____			$83,000
(7) _____			
(8) Accounts payable		8,000	
(9) Income tax payable		1,000	
(10) Note payable, short term, 15%†		4,000	
(11) _____			
(12) _____			_____
(13) Capital stock, $_____ par value		20,000	
(14) Contributed capital in excess of par		10,000	
(15) Retained earnings		40,000	
(16) _____			70,000
(17) Total liabilities and stockholders' equity			$_____

* Equipment has a 10-year estimated life; equal amounts expensed each year.
† Note dated July 1, 19H, time to maturity, 12 months.

Required (the lines are numbered above for problem reference purposes):

1. Define the term *assets* as used on the balance sheet.
2. What would be DC's cash balance in the bank assuming the company has $500 cash on hand on December 31, 19H?
3. Explain why "Accounts receivable" represents an asset.
4. Compute the amount that the equipment cost when it was acquired by DC Corporation.
5. Explain "Accumulated depreciation." What does the $10,000 indicate?
6. Enter the correct caption.
7. Enter the correct caption.
8. Explain why "Accounts payable" is a liability.
9. Explain what this liability represents.
10. What amount of interest expense applies to the year 19H? Note that the amount computed will be shown on the income statement as "Interest expense."
11. Enter the appropriate caption and amount.
12. Enter the appropriate caption.
13. Enter the amount of the par value per share of capital stock.
14. What was the total issue price per share of capital stock?
15. Explain what the $40,000 amount means.
16. Enter appropriate caption.
17. Enter correct amount.
18. Do you have any suggestions about the heading of the statement?

P1–5   (Redraft an Incorrect Income Statement)

Surfir Realty Company was organized early in 19A as a corporation by four investors, each of whom invested $6,000 cash. The company has been moderately successful, even though internal financial controls are inadequate. Although financial reports have been prepared each year (primarily in response to income tax requirements), sound accounting procedures have not been followed. Therefore, the financial performance of the company is known only vaguely by the four stockholders. Recently, one of the stockholders, with the agreement of the others, sold his shares to a local accountant. The new stockholder was amazed when handed the report below. This report was prepared by an employee for the last meeting of the board of directors. The accountant could tell immediately that the reported profit was wrong. She quickly observed that no interest expense was shown on a $10,000, 12%, note payable that had been outstanding throughout the year. Also, no recognition had been given to depreciation expense of office equipment that was purchased on January 1, 19D, at a cost of $12,000 with an estimated six-year useful life.

SURFIR REALTY
Profit Statement
December 31, 19D

Commissions earned (all collected)	$155,400
Property management revenue (exclusive of $1,200 not collected)	9,000
Total	164,400
Salaries paid	35,000
Commissions paid	36,000
Payroll taxes paid	3,200
Office supplies expense	150
Rent paid	3,000
Utilities paid	600
Advertising (excluding the December bill for advertising of $4,000 not yet paid)	26,000
Miscellaneous expenses	450
Total	104,400
Profit for the year (pretax)	$ 60,000

EPS: $60,000 ÷ 10,000 shares = $6.

Required:

You were asked to redraft the income statement, including corrections. Assume an average income tax rate of 30%. (Hint: The correct EPS is $3.78)

P1–6   (Prepare a Simple Income Statement and Balance Sheet)

Assume you are president of Salt Lake Company. At the end of the first year (December 31, 19A) of operations, the following financial data are available for the company:

Cash	$ 35,000
Receivables from customers (all considered collectible)	15,000
Inventory of merchandise (based on physical count and priced at cost)	80,000
Equipment owned, at cost	25,000
Depreciation expense (equipment)	2,500
Note payable, one year, 12% annual interest, owed to the bank (dated July 1, 19A)	30,000
Interest on the note through December 31, 19A (due to be paid to the bank on June 30, 19B; $30,000 × 12% × 6/12)	1,800
Salary payable for 19A (on December 31, 19A, this was owed to an employee who was away because of an emergency; will return around January 10, 19B, at which time the payment will be made)	1,000
Total sales revenue	120,000
Expenses paid, including the cost of the merchandise sold (excluding income taxes at a 30% rate; the taxes will be paid during the first quarter of 19B)	75,000
Capital stock, 10,000 shares outstanding	80,000

No dividends were declared or paid during 19A.

Required (show computations):

a. Prepare a summarized income statement for the year 19A. (Hint: EPS is $2.78, rounded.)

b. Prepare a balance sheet at December 31, 19A.

P1–7 (**Analyze a Student's Business and Prepare a Simple Income Statement**)

During the summer between her junior and senior years, Jeri Brown needed to earn sufficient money for the coming academic year. Unable to obtain a job with a reasonable salary, she decided to try the lawn-care business for three months. After a survey of the market potential, Jeri bought a used pickup truck on June 1 for $1,200. On each door she painted "Jeri's Lawn Service, Ph. XX." Also, she spent $600 for mowers, trimmers, and tools. To acquire these items she borrowed $2,000 cash on a note (endorsed by a friend) at 15% interest per annum, payable at the end of the three months (ending August 31).

At the end of the summer, Jeri realized that she had "done a lot of work, and her bank account looked good." This fact prompted her to become concerned about how much profit the business had earned.

A review of the check stubs showed the following: Deposits in the bank of collections from customers totaled $11,400. The following checks were written: gas, oil, and lubrication, $830; pickup repairs, $175; repair of mowers, $80; miscellaneous supplies used, $100; helpers, $4,400; payroll taxes, $175; payment for assistance in preparing payroll tax forms, $25; insurance, $150; telephone, $90; and $2,075 to pay off the note including interest (on August 31). A notebook kept in the pickup, plus some unpaid bills, reflected that customers still owed her $600 for lawn services rendered and that she owed $100 for gas and oil (credit card charges). She estimated that the "wear and tear" for use of the truck and the other equipment for three months amounted to $300.

Required:

a. Prepare a quarterly income statement for Jeri's Lawn Service for the months June, July, and August 19A. Use the following main captions: revenues from services, expenses, and net income. Because this is a sole proprietorship, the company will not be subject to income tax. (Hint: Total revenues amounted to $12,000.)

b. Do you see a need for one or more additional financial reports for this company for 19A and thereafter? Explain.

P1–8 (**Analyze a Student's Business and Prepare a Simple Income Statement**)

Upon graduation from high school, Jack Kane immediately accepted a job as a plumber's helper for a large local plumbing company. After three years of hard work, Jack received a plumber's license and decided to start his own business. He had saved $5,000 which he invested in the business. First, he transferred this amount from his savings account to a business bank account for "Kane Plumbing Company, Incorporated." His lawyer had advised him to start as a corporation. He then purchased a used panel truck for $3,000 cash and secondhand tools for $800; rented space in a small building; inserted an ad in the local paper; and opened the doors on October 1, 19A. Immediately, Jack was very busy, and after one month, he employed a helper. Although Jack knew practically nothing about the financial side of the business, he realized that a number of reports were required and that costs and collections had to be controlled carefully. At the end of the year, prompted in part by concern about his income tax situation (previously he only had to report salary), he recognized the need for financial statements. His wife, Jane, "developed some financial statements for the business." On

December 31, 19A, with the help of a friend, she gathered the following data for the three months just ended: Deposits in the bank account of collections for plumbing services totaled $30,000. The following checks were written: plumber's helper, $7,550; payroll taxes paid, $150; supplies purchased and used on jobs, $9,000; oil, gas, and maintenance on truck, $1,100; insurance, $300; rent, $500; utilities and telephone, $650; and miscellaneous expenses, $400 (including advertising). Also, there were uncollected bills to customers for plumbing services amounting to $2,000. The rent for December amounting to $100 had not been paid. The average income tax rate is 20%. The "wear and tear on the truck and tools due to use during the three months" was estimated by Jack to be $250.

Required:

a. Prepare a quarterly income statement for Kane Plumbing for the three months October–December 19A. Use the following main captions: revenue from services, expenses, pretax income, and net income. (Hint: Expenses, excluding income taxes, totaled $20,000.)
b. Do you think that Jack may have a need for one or more additional financial reports for 19A and thereafter? Explain.

CASES

PART A

C 1–1   (Analysis of the Assets and Liabilities of a Business)

D. X. Jones owns and operates the DXJ Sporting Goods Company (a sole proprietorship). An employee prepares a financial report for the business at each year-end. This report lists all of the resources (assets) owned by Jones (including such personal items as the home owned and occupied by Jones). It also lists all of the debts of the business (but not the "personal" debts of Jones).

Required:

a. From the accounting point of view, in what ways do you disagree with what is being included in and excluded from the report of business assets and liabilities?
b. Upon questioning, Jones responded, "Don't worry about it, we use it only to support a loan from the bank." How would you respond to this comment?

C 1–2   (A Decision about a Proposed Audit)

You are one of three partners who own and operate the Triple X Refreshments Company. The company has been operating for seven years. One of the other partners has always prepared the company's annual financial statements. Recently you proposed that "the statements should be audited each year because it would benefit the partners and preclude possible disagreements about the division of profits." The partner that prepares the statements proposed that his "Uncle Ray, who has a lot of financial experience can do the job and at little cost." Your other partner remained silent.

Required:

a. What position would you take on the proposal? Justify your response.
b. What would you strongly recommend? Give the basis for your recommendation.

PART B

C 1-3   (Identifying Deficiencies in an Income Statement and Balance Sheet)

Slack Corporation was organized on January 1, 19A. At the end of 19A, the company had not yet employed an accountant. However, an employee who was "good with numbers" prepared the following statements at that date:

SLACK CORPORATION
December 31, 19A

Income from sales of merchandise	$180,000
Total amount paid for goods sold during 19A	(95,000)
Selling costs	(30,000)
Depreciation (on service vehicles used)	(15,000)
Income from services rendered	50,000
Salaries and wages paid	(60,000)
Income taxes (at tax rate of 20%)	(6,000)
Profit for the year 19A	$ 24,000

SLACK CORPORATION
December 31, 19A

Resources:		
Cash		$ 31,000
Merchandise inventory (held for resale)		44,000
Service vehicles		45,000
Retained earnings (profit earned in 19A)		24,000
Grand total		$144,000
Debts:		
Payables to suppliers		$ 15,000
Note owed to bank		20,000
Due from customers		12,000
Total		47,000
Supplies on hand (to be used in rendering services)	$12,000	
Accumulated depreciation (on service vehicles)	15,000	
Capital stock, 10,000 shares	70,000	
Total		97,000
Grand total		$144,000

The above amounts, except for some totals, are correct.

Required:

a. List all of the deficiencies in the above statements that you can identify. Give a brief explanation on each one.

b. Prepare a proper income statement (correct net income is $24,000) and balance sheet (correct balance sheet total is $129,000).

C 1-4   (Introduction to an Actual Set of Financial Statements)

A complete set of financial statements is given in the Special Supplement B immediately preceding the Index. Throughout this course you may be asked to examine those statements to become familiar with actual financial statements that you will encounter in other courses and after you graduate.

Required:

a. What is the full name of this company?

b. What is the ending date of the current reporting year?

c. Give the exact title and date that the company uses for the income statement, balance sheet, and statement of changes in financial position.

d. What is the amount of net income reported by the company for the current year?

e. What is the amount of total assets reported by the company for the current year?

f. There is a section in the financial statements titled "Notes to Consolidated Financial Statements." How many numbered notes are given?

g. What is the name of the independent Certified Public Accountants (the audit firm)?

This chapter introduces the fundamental accounting model and shows how transactions are recorded in that model. Below is a diagram that shows how all companies apply the fundamental model.

Balance Sheet (fundamental model)

Assets	=	Liabilities	+	Owners' Equity
Cash $29,300		Notes payable $5,000		Capital stock $20,000
Accounts receivable 3,000		Accounts payable . . . 1,500		Retained
Delivery truck . . . 8,000				earnings 12,200
Less: Accumulated				
depreciation . . . (1,600)				
Totals $38,700		$6,500		$32,200

- Typical transaction that affects **only** the balance sheet:
    - (a) Sold (issued) capital stock:
        - Debit: Cash 20,000
            - Credit: Capital stock 20,000

- Typical transaction that affects **both** the balance sheet and income statement:
    - (b) Incurred operating expenses on credit:
        - Debit: Operating expenses 2,000
            - Credit: Accounts payable 2,000

Income Statement

Revenue	$44,000
Operating expenses	(29,400)
Interest expense	(600)
Net income	$14,000

- Note: When you complete this chapter you will know how all companies record transactions in journal entries such as these.

THE FUNDAMENTAL ACCOUNTING MODEL AND TRANSACTION ANALYSIS

PURPOSE:

Chapter 1 emphasized the importance of the communication of accounting information to certain decision makers. It also presented an overview of external financial statements. The purpose of Chapter 2 is to begin our discussions of how the accounting function collects data about business transactions and how those data are processed to provide the periodic financial statements. To accomplish this purpose, this chapter discusses the fundamental accounting model, transaction analysis, and how the results of transaction analysis are recorded in an accounting system.

ORGANIZATION:

1. The fundamental accounting model.
2. Nature of business transactions.
3. Debits = Credits.
4. Transaction analysis.
5. Journal entries and T-accounts.

LEARNING OBJECTIVES—TO BE ABLE TO:

1. Explain what constitutes a business transaction.
2. Analyze some simple business transactions in terms of the fundamental accounting model: Assets = Liabilities + Owners' Equity, and Debits = Credits.
3. Record the results of transaction analysis in two basic ways: (a) journal entries and (b) T-accounts.
4. Use the T-account balances to prepare a simple income statement and balance sheet.
5. Expand your business vocabulary by learning about the "Important Terms Defined in this Chapter" (pages 76 and 77).
6. Apply the knowledge learned from this chapter by completing the homework assigned by your instructor.

THE FUNDAMENTAL ACCOUNTING MODEL

Chapter 1 presented the accounting model:

ASSETS = LIABILITIES + OWNERS' EQUITY

It is both an algebraic model and an economic model. As an **algebraic model,** it can be rearranged in various ways, such as Assets − Liabilities = Owners' Equity. As an **economic model,** it expresses an economic truism: "What I own less what I owe equals my net worth." For example, if on December 31 you own assets of $100,000 and owe debts of $30,000, your net worth (i.e., "owners' equity") is $70,000. All of us measure our **net** resources in this way.

Let's carry our personal example one step further to see how you stand at the end of the next month. To do this you must **record each and every transaction** that you complete. The amounts for assets, liabilities, and owners' equity will change as follows:

Recording transactions in terms of the fundamental accounting model (personal), month of January:

Transactions	Assets	=	Liabilities	+	Owners' Equity
Your beginning financial situation	$100,000		$30,000		$70,000
a. Received $3,000 salary	+3,000		–0–		+3,000
Revised situation	103,000		30,000		73,000
b. Paid monthly bills, $2,000	−2,000		–0–		−2,000
Revised situation	101,000		30,000		71,000
c. Paid a debt, $10,000 (no interest now)	−10,000		−10,000		–0–
Revised situation	91,000		20,000		71,000
d. Paid cash for IBM stock as an investment, $5,000	−5,000				
	+5,000				
Your ending financial situation	$91,000		$20,000		$71,000

Notice two important points in the above schedule: (1) Each transaction had a **dual** effect in the model; and (2) after each transaction is recorded, the model is in balance (i.e., A = L + OE).

Now, let's apply the fundamental accounting model to a business. The model is used to **analyze and record** each and every transaction completed by the business entity. Assume that B. Bass and three friends organized a corporation called Bass Cleaners, Inc.

The **separate-entity assumption** (Chapter 1) requires that this business be accounted for as an entity separate and apart from its owners (i.e., stock-holders). From the previous personal illustration, we see that (*a*) revenues **increase** stockholders' equity, (*b*) expenses **decrease** stockholders' equity, and (*c*) dividends (i.e., withdrawals) paid by the corporation to stockholders **decrease** stockholders' equity in the company. Therefore, for a business, we can elaborate on the fundamental accounting model as follows:

ASSETS = LIABILITIES + OWNERS' EQUITY

Decreased by:	Increased by:
• Owner withdrawals	• Investments
• Expenses	• Revenues

The fundamental accounting model applied to a business is a broad economic description of an accounting entity that accommodates the recording of each transaction that directly affects the entity. The **dual economic effect** of each transaction is recorded in terms of this expanded accounting model. The dual effect is recorded in terms of this model regardless of whether the accounting system is handwritten, mechanized, or computerized. Before illustrating our hypothetical business situation, we will examine the nature of business transactions.

NATURE OF TRANSACTIONS

Accounting focuses on certain events that have an economic impact on the entity. Those events are recorded as a part of the accounting process and generally are referred to as **transactions.** A broad definition of transactions includes (1) exchanges of resources (assets) and/or obligations (liabilities) between the business (i.e., the accounting entity) and one or more parties other than the entity; and (2) certain events (or economic occurrences) that are not between the entity and one or more parties but have a direct and measurable effect on the accounting entity. Examples of the first category of transactions include the purchase of a machine, the sale of merchandise, the borrowing of cash, and the investment in the business by the owners. Examples of the second category of transactions include: (1) **economic events,** such as a drop in the replacement cost of an item held in inventory and a flood loss; and (2) **time adjustments,** such as depreciation of an operational asset (as a result of use) and the "using up" of prepaid insurance. Throughout this textbook, the word **transaction** will be used in the broad sense to include both types of events.[1]

Most transactions are evidenced by a **business document.** In the case of a sale on credit, a charge ticket is prepared, and in the case of a purchase of goods for resale, an invoice is received. In other transactions, such as a cash sale, the only document may be the cash register tape. The documents that underlie, or support, transactions usually are called **source documents.** From the accounting

---

[1] A narrow definition of a transaction limits it to the first category, that is, events between the entity and one or more parties other than the entity. This definition is useful in certain circumstances and is conceptually correct. However, accounting recognizes a number of events that are not transactions in the strict sense. Therefore, we have defined the term in the broader sense to generalize our terminology.

point of view, the important requirement is that procedures be established to capture the data on each transaction as it occurs. Once this is done, the accounting system transfers and summarizes the economic impact of each transaction on the entity from its initial recording to the end product—the **periodic financial statements.**

The fundamental feature of most transactions with external parties is an exchange where the business entity both gives up something and receives something in return. In the case of a sale of merchandise for cash, the entity gives up resources (the goods sold) and receives in return another resource (cash). In the case of a credit sale of merchandise, the resource received at the time of sale is an account receivable (an asset). Later, another transaction occurs when the account receivable is collected; here, the resource relinquished is the receivable, and the resource received is cash. In the purchase of an asset (either merchandise for resale or a truck purchased for use in the business), the entity acquires the noncash asset and gives up cash, or in the case of a credit purchase, the entity incurs a liability. Another transaction occurs later when the debt is paid. At that time, the entity gives up a resource (cash) and "receives" satisfaction of the debt. The sale or purchase of services can be analyzed in the same way.

THE FUNDAMENTAL ACCOUNTING MODEL ILLUSTRATED

B. Bass and three others organized Bass Cleaners, Inc., on January 1, 19A. Each of the four organizers invested $5,000 cash, and each received 200 shares of capital stock. The company immediately started operations. Therefore, each transaction completed by the business must be recorded in the company's accounting system in terms of the fundamental accounting model:

$$\text{Assets} = \text{Liabilities} + \text{Stockholders' Equity}$$

Exhibit 2–1 lists a series of transactions completed during the year 19A. The exhibit shows how each transaction is recorded in terms of the fundamental accounting model for Bass Cleaners. You should study it carefully and notice that (1) each transaction is recorded separately; (2) in recording each transaction, the equality of the fundamental accounting model is maintained (that is, assets will always equal liabilities plus owners' equity); and (3) the dual effect, as discussed in the preceding section, is recorded for each transaction.

Each transaction is **analyzed,** then entered in terms of the accounting model. The last line of Exhibit 2–1 shows the financial position of the business at December 31, 19A (end of Year 1):

$$\text{Assets, } \$38,700 = \text{Liabilities, } \$6,500 + \text{Stockholders' Equity, } \$32,200$$

Exhibit 2–1 shows what is done in an accounting system. However, it does not show how the 19A **periodic financial statements** are prepared. Exhibit 2–2 shows the 19A **income statement** and **balance sheet** for Bass Cleaners. These statements were explained in Chapter 1, Part B.

The three required financial statements for external parties are the income statement, balance sheet, and statement of changes in financial position. The primary categories of items reported on the financial statements are called elements. These elements are:[2]

Income statement—revenues, expenses, gains, and losses.
Balance sheet—assets, liabilities, and owners' equity.

These statements and the elements are discussed throughout this textbook.

The 19A income statement and balance sheet for Bass Cleaners were prepared by selecting data from Exhibit 2–1 for each element reported. The financial statement elements for Bass Cleaners are:

Income statement:
- Revenues
- Expenses

Balance sheet:
- Assets
  Accounts:
    Cash
    Accounts receivable
    Delivery truck
      Accumulated depreciation
- Liabilities
  Accounts:
    Notes payable
    Accounts payable
- Owners' equity
  Accounts:
    Capital stock
    Retained earnings

The method used in Exhibits 2–1 and 2–2 to (a) record each transaction and (b) prepare the financial statements would be inefficient for a business that had numerous transactions. This data collection and reporting process can be facilitated in an accounting system by establishing a separate record, called an **account,** for each item included in the financial statement elements (see the five elements and the related accounts listed above for Bass Cleaners). Let's see how an account is used.

THE ACCOUNT

An account is a standardized format used to accumulate data about each element in order to (a) facilitate **preparation** of the periodic financial statements and (b) to provide a continuous check on the **accuracy** of the recording of transactions.

---

[2] FASB *Statement of Financial Accounting Concepts No. 3,* "Elements of Financial Statements of Business Enterprises" (Stamford, Conn., December 1980). The elements of financial statements are discussed in detail in Chapter 4 of this textbook.

EXHIBIT 2–1

Transaction analysis illustrated

BASS CLEANERS, INC.
Transaction Analysis—19A

	Dual effect of each transaction on the entity			
Transactions	Assets	= Liabilities	+	Stockholders' Equity
a. Bass Cleaners received $20,000 cash invested by owners; 800 shares ($25 par value) of stock issued to the four owners.......... Cash	+ $20,000			Capital stock (800 shares) + $20,000
b. Borrowed $5,000 cash on 12% note payable .... Cash	+ 5,000	Note payable + $5,000		
c. Purchased delivery truck for cash at cost of $8,000 .... Cash Delivery truck	− 8,000 + 8,000			
d. Cleaning revenue collected in cash, $40,000.......... Cash	+ 40,000			Cleaning revenue + 40,000
e. Cleaning revenue earned in 19A, but the bill is not collected, $4,000 .... Accounts receivable +	4,000			Cleaning revenue + 4,000
f. Operating expenses paid in cash, $25,800.......... Cash	− 25,800			Operating expenses − 25,800

g. Operating expenses incurred in 19A but
   not paid, $2,000 .... Accounts payable + 2,000 Operating expenses – 2,000

h. Paid 12% interest on the $5,000
   note payable, (b) above, with cash
   ($5,000 × 12% = $600) .... Cash – 600 Interest expense – 600

i. Depreciation expense for one year on
   truck ($8,000 ÷ 5 years = $1,600) ...... Truck – 1,600 Operating ex-
                                                            penses,
                                                            depreciation – 1,600

j. Cash dividend of $1,800 declared and
   paid to stockholders* .... Cash – 1,800 Retained earnings
                                                          (or dividends
                                                          paid) – 1,800

k. Collected $1,000 cash on accounts
   receivable in (e) .... Cash + 1,000
              Accounts receivable – 1,000

l. Paid $500 cash on accounts payable
   in (g) .... Cash – 500 Accounts payable – 500

   Totals (end of accounting period) ..... Total assets $38,700 = Total liabilities $6,500 + Total stockholders' equity $32,200

Observe how these items and their respective ending balances flow into the financial
statements, Exhibit 2–2.

* A cash dividend is not an expense; it is a withdrawal of resources from the business and is paid to the owners.

EXHIBIT 2–2

Income statement and balance sheet illustrated

Observe that these items and their respective amounts were developed in the transaction analysis illustrated in Exhibit 2–1.

BASS CLEANERS, INC.
Income Statement
For the Year Ended December 31, 19A

Cleaning revenue ($40,000 + $4,000)		$44,000
Operating expenses ($25,800 + $2,000 + $1,600)	$29,400	
Interest expense	600	30,000
Net income		$14,000

Note: To simplify the illustration, income taxes are disregarded.

BASS CLEANERS, INC.
Balance Sheet
At December 31, 19A

Assets

Cash ($20,000 + $5,000 − $8,000 + $40,000 − $25,800 − $600 − $1,800 + $1,000 − $500)		$29,300
Accounts receivable ($4,000 − $1,000)		3,000
Delivery truck	$ 8,000	
Less: Accumulated depreciation	1,600	6,400
Total assets		$38,700

Liabilities

Notes payable	$ 5,000	
Accounts payable ($2,000 − $500)	1,500	
Total liabilities		$ 6,500

Stockholders' Equity

Contributed capital:		
Capital stock (800 shares)	20,000	
Retained earnings (beginning retained earnings, $–0–, plus net income, $14,000, minus dividends declared and paid, $1,800)	12,200	
Total stockholders' equity		32,200
Total liabilities and stockholders' equity		$38,700

EXHIBIT 2–3

Account (T-account format) illustrated

Cash*

Left or Debit Side		Right or Credit Side	Acct. No. 101
(Increases)		(Decreases)	
Investment by owners	20,000	To purchase truck	8,000
Loan from bank	5,000	Operating expenses	25,800
Cleaning revenue	40,000	Interest expense	600
Collections on accounts		Dividends declared and paid	1,800
receivable	1,000	Payment on accounts payable	500
	66,000		36,700

* The data shown in this account were taken from Exhibit 2–1.

A separate account is set up for each individual asset, liability, and owners' equity[3] (including separate accounts for each kind of revenue and expense). In most accounting systems, you will find separate accounts, individually labeled, for each **asset** (such as cash, inventory, accounts receivable, equipment, land); for each **liability** (such as accounts payable, notes payable, taxes payable); and for each element of **owners' equity** (such as capital stock, sales revenue, service revenue, and various kinds of expenses). The **Cash account** for Bass Cleaners may appear as shown in Exhibit 2–3.

Now we will discuss how accounts are used to (a) facilitate preparation of the financial statements and (b) attain accuracy in the accounting system.

a. **Keeping track of the amounts for each element**—To do this, a separate account is set up for each element that will be reported on the financial statements. Each account is designed so that all **increases** are entered on one side (e.g., on the left side of the Cash account in Exhibit 2–3) and all **decreases** are entered on the other side (e.g., on the right side of the Cash account in Exhibit 2–3). To illustrate the increased efficiency possible, compare the list of plus and minus amounts on the cash lines of Exhibit 2–1 with the location arrangement in Exhibit 2–3. Also, imagine thousands or millions of such increases and decreases during the year in a typical business. The Cash account shown in Exhibit 2–3 reflects a left side total of $66,000 and a right side total of $36,700; the difference, $29,300, is the ending cash balance (as

---

[3] Owners' equity usually is designated to indicate the kind of ownership arrangement used as follows:

Corporation .... Stockholders' equity
Sole proprietorship .... Owner's capital
Partnership .... Partners' capital

reported on the balance sheet in Exhibit 2–2). When the total amount on the decrease side of the Cash account is larger than the total amount on the increase side, a cash deficit (bank overdraft) is indicated. The account system is very flexible; for example, instead of being set up in the "T-account" format shown in Exhibit 2–3, it can be set up in other formats such as the columnar form shown in Exhibit 3–4. The account system can be used with either (or a combination of) handwritten, mechanical, or computerized approaches.

b. **Providing a systematic method of checking for accuracy during the recording process**—To resolve this problem, the account was designed to provide two **equalities or balances** that may be summarized as follows:

Equalities	Basis
1. Assets = Liabilities + Owners' Equity	Algebraic relationship in the fundamental accounting model
2. Debits = Credits	Algebraic relationship between account increases and decreases

These two basic equalities may be explained as follows:

First equality—Assets = Liabilities + Owners' Equity. This model is an algebraic representation of the economic position of an entity at any point in time. By definition, it always balances and can be rearranged mathematically (e.g., Assets − Liabilities = Owners' Equity). Observe in Exhibit 2–1 that the analysis of each transaction and the cumulative effects of all transactions were always in balance in terms of this algebraic model (also shown in the balance sheet in Exhibit 2–2). Thus, the first check for accuracy listed above is applied continuously throughout the accounting process as each transaction is recorded.

Second equality—Debits = Credits. In this context, it is useful to think of an account as having two sides (i.e., parts): the **left side,** which is always called the **debit** side, and the **right side,** which is always called the **credit** side. These designations were used in Exhibit 2–3.[4]

The Debits = Credits feature in accounting has an interesting history. In 1494, Paciolo (a mathematician) first described the fundamental accounting model used today. Knowing the importance of accuracy, and after designing the T-account (similar to that illustrated in Exhibit 2–3), Paciolo applied an algebraic concept that has proven to be of great significance in minimizing errors in the accounting process. The fundamental accounting model, **Assets = Liabilities + Owners' Equity,** is an algebraic model that has mathematical equality. Paciolo added another algebraic balance feature to the basic model to minimize errors in recording increases and decreases in each account. Let's see how it was done.

---

[4] Handwritten or manually maintained accounts in the formats shown here are used in small businesses. Highly mechanized and computerized systems retain the concept of the account but not this format. T-accounts are useful primarily for instructional purposes.

Paciolo perceived that having designed the T-account with two sides to reflect increases and decreases, he could add another algebraic **balancing feature** by simply **reversing** the position in the account of the "increases" and "decreases" on the **opposite sides** of the basic accounting model. This second algebraic balance feature is still used today; it has the "+" and "−" **in reverse order** on the opposite sides of the accounting model in this way:

Assets		=	Liabilities		+	Owners' Equity	
Debit	*Credit*		*Debit*	*Credit*		*Debit*	*Credit*
+	−		−	+		−	+

Notice that **debit** always refers to the left side of an account and **credit** always refers to the right side of an account. Thus, debit and credit positions do not change; only the plus and minus signs change positions. The addition of this algebraic concept resulted in the second "balancing" feature, that is, **debits always should equal credits.** Thus, the system used for recording increases and decreases in the accounts may be tabulated as follows:[5]

	Increases	Decreases
Assets	Debit	Credit
Liabilities	Credit	Debit
Owners' equity	Credit	Debit

Debits and credits for revenues and expenses

After some practice you will become comfortable using the words **debit** and **credit** to signify changes in assets, liabilities, and owners' equity accounts. However, some persons are confused about the proper terms to reflect changes in revenue and expense accounts. Remember that owners' equity is increased by credits and decreased by debits. Revenues increase owners' equity; therefore, **revenues are recorded as credits.**

Expenses decrease owners' equity; therefore, **expenses are recorded as debits.** In other words, the debit-credit relationship for owners' equity accounts is applied to revenues and expenses.[6]

In summary, the balance features of the fundamental accounting model are:

1. **Assets = Liabilities + Owners' Equity.**
2. **Debits = Credits.**

---

[5] Historically, and today, accountants refer to the left side as the debit side and to the right side as the credit side. For accounting purposes, the terms **debit** and **credit** have no other meanings. The words **to debit** and **to credit** should not be confused with "increase" or "decrease" as will become clear in the next few paragraphs. Contrary to what some people think, there is no implication of "goodness" attached to credits or "badness" attached to debits (or vice versa).

[6] To "charge an account" is a frequently used expression meaning to **debit** an account. Thus, the word *debit* is used as both a verb and a noun.

The next section of this chapter illustrates the use of accounts and emphasizes application of the fundamental accounting model and its dual-balancing feature.

TRANSACTION ANALYSIS

Transaction analysis is a term frequently used to describe the process of studying a transaction to determine its dual effect on the entity in terms of the accounting model. Transaction analysis starts when a business document is available that indicates a completed transaction. Based upon the (*a*) nature of the transaction and (*b*) proper application of the fundamental accounting model, the effects of the transaction are recorded in the accounting system.

Application of the fundamental accounting model and accounting principles require that **accrual basis accounting** be used. This means that assets, liabilities, revenues, expenses, and the other elements should be recognized (i.e., recorded) when the transaction that caused them was completed. The related cash collected or paid at a later date is recorded as a separate transaction. For example, a sale made on the last day of Year 1, with 30-day credit terms must be recorded in Year 1, and the cash collection must be recorded in Year 2. In contrast, **cash basis accounting,** which is not appropriate, would record the sale only in Year 2 when the cash is collected. In contrast, the concept of accrual accounting requires that revenues and expenses be measured and reported in the accounting period in which the transactions occur rather than when the related cash is received or paid.

Now, let's see how **each transaction** is subjected to transaction analysis to determine (1) its dual economic effect on the entity and (2) how that dual effect is recorded in the accounts (i.e., in terms of the fundamental accounting model).

Recall that for each transaction recorded, **two separate balances** must be maintained: (1) Assets = Liabilities + Owners' Equity, and (2) Debits = Credits.

Transaction Analysis and Recording

Bass Cleaners, Inc., will be used again to demonstrate transaction analysis and the basic recording process. We analyze each transaction (given in Exhibit 2–1) and trace the manner in which the dual effect is recorded in the accounting model by using T-accounts (rather than using the simple plus and minus signs shown in Exhibit 2–1). The transactions (repeated for convenience) are identified with letters for ready reference.

For each transaction, Exhibit 2–4 gives its (*a*) nature, (*b*) analysis, (*c*) journal entry, and (*d*) T-account effect. The **journal entry** is an accounting method of expressing the results of transaction analysis in a Debits = Credits format. Notice that for each transaction (*a*) the debits are written first, (*b*) the credits are written below all of the debits, and (*c*) the credits are indented (both words and amounts).

You should study Exhibit 2–4 carefully (including the explanations of transac-

EXHIBIT 2–4

Transaction analysis, journal entries, and T-accounts illustrated, Bass Cleaners, Inc.

BASS CLEANERS, INC.

a. **Received $20,000 cash invested by the four owners and in turn issued 800 shares of capital stock (par value $25 per share).**

Transaction analysis—This transaction increased the company's cash by $20,000, which is recorded in the **Cash** account as a debit (increase); liabilities were unaffected; and owners' equity was increased by $20,000, which is recorded in the **Capital Stock** account as a credit (increase). The journal entry (recording) in the accounting system may be summarized conveniently in what often is called a **journal entry.** This format lists the **debit** first—account name and amount—then lists the credit—account name and amount (which is indented for clarity).

Journal Entry		
	Debit	*Credit*
(*a*) Cash (asset) 20,000		
Capital stock (owners' equity)		20,000

The two T-accounts would appear as follows:

Cash (asset)		**Capital Stock (owners' equity)**	
Debit	*Credit*	*Debit*	*Credit*
(*a*) 20,000			(*a*) 20,000

Dual check for accuracy—The entry meets both tests: Assets (+$20,000) = Liabilities (–0–) + Owners' Equity (+$20,000), and Debits ($20,000) = Credits ($20,000).

b. **Borrowed $5,000 cash from the bank on a 12% interest-bearing note payable.**

Transaction analysis—This transaction increased cash by $5,000, which is recorded in the **Cash** account as a debit (increase); liabilites were increased by $5,000, which is recorded in the **Notes Payable** account as a credit (increase); and owners' equity was not changed. The journal entry may be summarized as follows:

(*b*) Cash (asset) 5,000		
Notes payable (liability)		5,000

The accounts affected would appear as follows (new items are boxed):

Cash (asset)		**Notes Payable (liability)**	
Debit	*Credit*	*Debit*	*Credit*
(*a*) 20,000			(*b*) 5,000
(*b*) 5,000			

Dual check for accuracy—The entry meets both tests: Assets (+$5,000) = Liabilities (+$5,000) + Owners' Equity(–0–), and Debits ($5,000) = Credits ($5,000).

EXHIBIT 2–4 *(continued)*

Transaction analysis, journal entries, and T-accounts illustrated, Bass Cleaners, Inc.

c. **Purchased a delivery truck for cash at a cost of $8,000.**

Transaction analysis—This transaction increased the asset, **Delivery Truck,** by $8,000, which is recorded in that asset account as a debit (increase); and the cash was decreased by $8,000, which is recorded in the asset account **Cash** as a credit (decrease). Liabilities and owners' equity were not affected. The journal entry may be summarized conveniently as follows:

(c) Delivery truck (asset)	8,000	
Cash (asset)		8,000

The two accounts affected would appear as follows:

	Delivery Truck (asset)				**Cash (asset)**		
	Debit	*Credit*			*Debit*	*Credit*	
(c)	8,000			(a)	20,000	(c)	8,000
				(b)	5,000		

Dual check for accuracy—The entry meets both tests: Assets (delivery truck, +$8,000 and cash, −$8,000) = Liabilities (–0–) + Owners' Equity (–0–), and Debits ($8,000) = Credits ($8,000).

d. **Cleaning revenue earned and collected in cash, $40,000.**

Transaction analysis—This transaction increased cash by $40,000, which is recorded in the asset account **Cash** as a debit (increase); liabilities were not affected; and owners' equity was increased by $40,000 as a result of earning revenue. Owners' equity is credited (increased) for $40,000. A separate owners' equity account, **Cleaning Revenue,** is used to keep track of this particular revenue. The journal entry may be summarized as follows:

(d) Cash (asset)	40,000	
Cleaning revenue (owners' equity)		40,000

The two accounts affected would appear as follows:

	Cash (asset)				**Cleaning Revenue (owners' equity)**		
	Debit	*Credit*			*Debit*	*Credit*	
(a)	20,000	(c)	8,000			(d)	40,000
(b)	5,000						
(d)	40,000						

Dual check for accuracy—The entry meets both tests: Assets (+$40,000) = Liabilities (–0–) + Owners' Equity (+$40,000), and Debits ($40,000) = Credits ($40,000).

EXHIBIT 2–4 *(continued)*

Transaction analysis, journal entries, and T-accounts illustrated, Bass Cleaners, Inc.

e. Cleaning revenue earned, but the cash was not yet collected, $4,000.

Transaction analysis—This transaction increased the company's asset, **Accounts Receivable,** by $4,000, which is recorded as a debit (increase) to that account; liabilities were not affected; and owners' equity was increased by $4,000. Owners' equity is credited (increased) by $4,000 using a separate account, **Cleaning Revenue,** which is used to keep track of this particular revenue. The journal entry may be summarized as follows:

(e) Accounts receivable (asset) 4,000	
Cleaning revenue (owners' equity)	4,000

The effect on the two accounts would appear as follows:

Accounts Receivable (asset)			**Cleaning Revenue (owners' equity)**	
Debit	*Credit*		*Debit*	*Credit*
(e) 4,000			(d)	40,000
			(e)	4,000

Dual check for accuracy—The entry meets both tests: Assets (+ $4,000) = Liabilities (–0–) + Owners' Equity (+$4,000), and Debits ($4,000) = Credits ($4,000).

f. Expenses incurred and paid in cash, $25,800.

Transaction analysis—This transaction decreased cash by $25,800, which is recorded in the **Cash** account as a credit (decrease); liabilities were not affected; and owners' equity was decreased by $25,800 as a result of paying expenses. Owners' equity is decreased by debiting a separate account **Operating Expenses,** which is used to keep track of this particular expense. The journal entry may be summarized as follows:

(f) Operating expenses (owners' equity) 25,800	
Cash (asset)	25,800

The effect on the two accounts would appear as follows:

Operating Expenses (owners' equity)			**Cash (asset)**		
Debit	*Credit*		*Debit*		*Credit*
(f) 25,800		(a)	20,000	(c)	8,000
		(b)	5,000	(f)	25,800
		(d)	40,000		

Dual check for accuracy—The entry meets both tests.

EXHIBIT 2–4 *(continued)*

Transaction analysis, journal entries, and T-accounts illustrated, Bass Cleaners, Inc.

g. **Expenses incurred, but the cash not yet paid, $2,000.**

Transaction analysis—This transaction did not affect the company's assets; liabilities were increased by $2,000, which is recorded as a credit (increase) to **Accounts Payable;** and owners' equity was decreased $2,000 by debiting a separate account, **Operating Expenses,** which is used to keep track of this particular type of expense. The journal entry summarized is:

(g) Operating expenses (owners' equity)	2,000	
Accounts payable (liability)		2,000

The two accounts affected would appear as follows:

Operating Expenses (owners' equity)		**Accounts Payable (liability)**	
Debit	*Credit*	*Debit*	*Credit*
(f) 25,800		*(g)*	2,000
(g) 2,000			

Dual check for accuracy—The entry meets both tests.

h. **Paid cash interest incurred on note payable in (*b*) ($5,000 × 12% = $600).**

Transaction analysis—This transaction decreased cash by $600, which is recorded as a credit (decrease) in the **Cash** account; the principal amount of the related liability ($5,000) was not changed; however, owners' equity was decreased by the amount of the interest ($600) because the payment of interest (but not the principal of the note) represents an expense. Owners' equity is decreased by debiting a separate account, **Interest Expense,** which is used to keep track of this particular type of expense. The journal entry summarized is:

(h) Interest expense (owners' equity)	600	
Cash (asset)		600

The two accounts affected would appear as follows:

Interest Expense (owners' equity)		**Cash (asset)**	
Debit	*Credit*	*Debit*	*Credit*
(h) 600		*(a)* 20,000 *(c)*	8,000
		(b) 5,000 *(f)*	25,800
		(d) 40,000 *(h)*	600

Dual check for accuracy—The entry meets both tests.

EXHIBIT 2–4 *(continued)*

Transaction analysis, journal entries, and T-accounts illustrated, Bass Cleaners, Inc.

i. **Depreciation expense on the truck for one year ($8,000 ÷ 5 years = $1,600).**

Transaction analysis—This transaction is caused by the **internal** use (wear and tear) of an asset owned for operating purposes (rather than for resale). This use is measured in dollars and recorded as depreciation expense. Owners' equity was decreased by this expense, which is recorded as a debit to a separate account for this type of expense, **Operating Expenses** (alternatively, a separate expense account, called depreciation expense, could have been used). Assets (i.e., the delivery truck) were decreased because a part of the cost of the asset was "used up" in operations. Instead of directly crediting (decreasing) the asset account, Delivery Truck, a related **contra account, Accumulated Depreciation, Delivery Truck,** is credited so that the total amount of depreciation can be kept separate from the cost of the asset. This procedure will be explained and illustrated in detail in Chapter 9. The journal entry summarized is:

> (i) Operating expenses (owners' equity)   1,600
>   Accumulated depreciation, delivery truck
>   (contra account)   1,600

The two accounts affected would appear as follows:

Operating Expenses (owners' equity)		**Accumulated Depreciation, Delivery Truck (contra account)**	
Debit	*Credit*	*Debit*	*Credit*
(f) 25,800		(i)	1,600
(g) 2,000			
(i) 1,600			

Dual check for accuracy—The entry meets both tests: Assets (−$1,600) = Liabilities (−0−) + Owners' Equity (−$1,600), and Debits ($1,600) = Credits ($1,600).

j. **Declared and paid cash dividends to stockholders, $1,800.**

Transaction analysis—This transaction decreased the company's cash by $1,800, which is recorded in the **Cash** account as a credit (decrease); liabilities were unaffected; owners' equity was decreased by $1,800 as a result of the resources (cash) paid out of the business to the stockholders. Owners' equity is debited (decreased) by using a separate account, **Retained Earnings,** which is used to keep track of this kind of decrease in owners' equity (and certain increases explained later). Dividends declared and paid decrease owners' equity but do not represent an expense (which also decreases owners' equity), rather dividends represent a cash distribution of "earnings" to the owners. The journal entry summarized is:

> (j) Retained earnings (or dividends paid)   1,800
>   Cash (asset)   1,800

EXHIBIT 2–4 *(continued)*

Transaction analysis, journal entries, and T-accounts illustrated, Bass Cleaners, Inc.

The two accounts would appear as follows:

Retained Earnings (owners' equity)		Cash (asset)	
Debit	*Credit*	*Debit*	*Credit*
(j) 1,800		*(a)* 20,000	*(c)* 8,000
		(b) 5,000	*(f)* 25,800
		(d) 40,000	*(h)* 600
			(j) 1,800

Dual check for accuracy—The entry meets both tests.

k. Collected $1,000 cash on accounts receivable in *(e)*.

Transaction analysis—This transaction increased the asset cash by $1,000, which is recorded as a debit (increase) in the **Cash** account; another asset, **Accounts Receivable,** was decreased, which is recorded as a credit (decrease) of $1,000. Liabilities and owners' equity were not affected because there was a change in two assets with no change in total assets. The journal entry summarized is:

(k) Cash (asset) 1,000
     Accounts receivable (asset)   1,000

The two accounts would appear as follows:

Cash (asset)		Accounts Receivable (asset)	
Debit	*Credit*	*Debit*	*Credit*
(a) 20,000	*(c)* 8,000	*(e)* 4,000	*(k)* 1,000
(b) 5,000	*(f)* 25,800		
(d) 40,000	*(h)* 600		
(k) 1,000	*(j)* 1,800		

Dual check for accuracy—The entry meets both tests.

l. Paid $500 cash on accounts payable in *(g)*.

Transaction analysis—This transaction decreased cash by $500, which is recorded as a credit (decrease) in the **Cash** account; the $500 decrease in liabilities is recorded as a debit (decrease) to the **Accounts Payable** account. Owners' equity was not affected because there was no revenue or expense involved in this transaction. The journal entry summarized is:

(l) Accounts payable (liability) 500
     Cash (asset)   500

EXHIBIT 2–4 *(concluded)*

Transaction analysis, journal entries, and T-accounts illustrated, Bass Cleaners, Inc.

The two accounts would appear as follows:

	Accounts Payable (liability)				Cash (asset)		
	Debit		*Credit*		*Debit*		*Credit*
(l)	500	*(g)*	2,000	*(a)*	20,000	*(c)*	8,000
				(b)	5,000	*(f)*	25,800
				(d)	40,000	*(h)*	600
				(k)	1,000	*(j)*	1,800
						(l)	500

Dual check for accuracy—The entry meets both tests.

For further illustration purposes, all of the above accounts are repeated in Exhibit 3–3 with their respective balances (i.e., the total increases minus the total decreases in each account) shown in Exhibit 3–5.

tion analysis). Careful study is essential to understand (*a*) application of the fundamental accounting model, (*b*) transaction analysis, (*c*) recording the dual effects of each transaction, and (*d*) the dual-balancing system. Exhibit 2–4 emphasizes these important aspects of the accounting processing system. Notice that the amounts for each additional entry illustrated are shown in boxes to facilitate your study of this exhibit.

In summary, Exhibit 2–4 presented the following features of an accounting system:

1. **Collecting information about each completed transaction** that is necessary for accounting purposes.
2. **Analyzing each transaction** to determine how it affected the fundamental accounting model—Assets = Liabilities + Owners' Equity.
3. **Recording the effects of transactions is accomplished in the "journal entry format"** commonly used in accounting as follows:

Account name (debit) . . . . $xx
    Account name (credit) . . . . $xx

4. **Showing the effects in T-accounts** which provide for increases and decreases in each account as follows:

Assets		=	Liabilities		+	Owners' Equity	
(Debit)	(Credit)		(Debit)	(Credit)		(Debit)	(Credit)
+	−		−	+		−	+

5. **Preparing periodic financial statements** from the data accumulated in the accounts (discussed in Chapter 3).

DEMONSTRATION CASE

On January 1, 19A, an ambitious college student started the ABC Service Company. The primary purpose was to earn money to complete a college education. Completed transactions (summarized) through December 31, 19A, for ABC Service Company (a sole proprietorship) were:

a. Invested $5,000 cash in the business.
b. Purchased service supplies, $600; paid cash. These supplies were placed in a storeroom to be used as needed.
c. Revenues earned, $32,000, collected in cash, except for $2,000 on credit.
d. Operating expenses incurred, $17,000; paid cash except for $1,000 on credit.
e. Used $500 of the service supplies from the storeroom for operating purposes.
f. Owner withdrew $3,000 cash from the business.
g. At year-end purchased a tract of land for a future building site. Paid cash, $2,000, and gave a $5,000, 10%, interest-bearing note payable for the balance.

Requirement 1:

Set up T-accounts for Cash, Accounts Receivable (for services on credit); Service Supplies (for supplies on hand in the storeroom); Land; Accounts Payable (for operating expenses on credit); Note Payable; Owner's Equity; Service Revenues; and Operating Expenses. Next, analyze each transaction, prepare journal entries, and then enter the effects on the fundamental accounting model in the appropriate T-accounts. Identify each amount with its letter given above.

Requirement 2:

Refer to the three financial statements illustrated in Chapter 1: income statement (Exhibit 1–4); balance sheet (Exhibit 1–5); and the statement of changes in financial position (Exhibit 1–6). Use the **amounts in the T-accounts,** prepared in Requirement 1, to prepare these three 19A statements for ABC Service Company. The solutions to these two requirements are shown in Exhibit 2–5.

EXHIBIT 2–5

Transaction analysis, journal entries, T-accounts, and financial statements—a demonstration case

Requirement 1—Transaction analysis and journal entries:

a. Increase cash, $5,000; increase owner's equity account, $5,000.

Journal entry:

Cash	5,000	
Owner's equity		5,000

b. Increase asset, service supplies, $600; decrease cash, $600 (supplies are not an expense until used).

Journal entry:

Service supplies	600	
Cash		600

c. Increase assets, cash, $30,000, and accounts receivable, $2,000; increase service revenues (an owner's equity account), $32,000.

Journal entry:

Cash	30,000	
Accounts receivable	2,000	
Service revenues		32,000

d. Decrease asset, cash, $16,000; increase liability, accounts payable, $1,000; increase operating expenses, $17,000 (which decreases owner's equity).

Journal entry:

Operating expenses	17,000	
Cash		16,000
Accounts payable		1,000

e. Decrease asset, service supplies, $500; increase operating expenses, $500 (which decreases owner's equity).

Journal entry:

Operating expenses	500	
Service supplies		500

f. Decrease asset, cash, $3,000; decrease owner's equity account, $3,000.

Journal entry:

Owner's equity	3,000	
Cash		3,000

EXHIBIT 2–5 *(continued)*

Transaction analysis, journal entries, T-accounts, and financial statements—a demonstration case

Requirement 1 (continued)

g. Increase assets, land, $7,000; decrease asset, cash, $2,000; increase liability, note payable, $5,000.

Journal entry:

Land 7,000
    Cash   2,000
    Note payable   5,000

T-accounts:

Cash				
(a)	5,000	*(b)*	600	
(c)	30,000	*(d)*	16,000	
		(f)	3,000	
		(g)	2,000	

Accounts Payable	
(d)	1,000

Note Payable	
(g)	5,000

Accounts Receivable	
(c)	2,000

Owner's Equity Account			
(f)	3,000	*(a)*	5,000

Service Supplies			
(b)	600	*(e)*	500

Service Revenues	
(c)	32,000

Land	
(g)	7,000

Operating Expenses	
(d)	17,000
(e)	500

Requirement 2—Periodic financial statements:

ABC Service Company
Income Statement
For the Year Ended December 31, 19A

Revenues:
    Service revenues $32,000
Expenses:
    Operating expenses   17,500
Net income $14,500

EXHIBIT 2–5 *(concluded)*

Transaction analysis, journal entries, T-accounts, and financial statements—a demonstration case

Requirement 2 (continued)

ABC Service Company
Balance Sheet
At December 31, 19A

Assets		Liabilities	
Cash	$13,400	Accounts payable	$ 1,000
Accounts receivable	2,000	Note payable	5,000
Service supplies	100	Total liabilities	6,000
Land	7,000		
		Owner's Equity	
		Owner's equity account .... $ 2,000	
		Net income (Req. 2) 14,500	
		Total owner's equity	16,500
		Total liabilities and owner's	
Total assets	$22,500	equity	$22,500

ABC Service Company
Statement of Changes in Financial Position, Cash Basis
For the Year Ended December 31, 19A

Sources of cash (inflows):
From operations:
   Revenues $30,000
   Less: Cash used for expenses ($16,000 + $600)   16,600
     Cash inflow from operations   13,400
From other sources:
   Investment by owner (cash)   5,000
    Total cash sources during the year (inflows)   18,400
Uses of cash (outflows):
   To pay cash to owner (withdrawals) $3,000
   To pay on land purchased 2,000
    Total cash used during the year (outflows)   5,000
    Change: Increase in cash during the year $13,400*

* Agrees with the increase in cash from a beginning zero balance to $13,400 on the balance sheet above.

Preparation of the 19A **income statement** involved selection of the **account balances** for all revenues and expenses. The **income statement model** (page 20) is applied—Revenues − Expenses = Net Income.

The 19A **balance sheet** required use of the **account balances** for **all** assets and liabilities. The **balance sheet model** (page 23) is applied—Assets = Liabilities + Owners' Equity. Notice that owner's equity includes the net income amount ($14,500) reported on the income statement because it increased owner's equity.

The 19A statement of changes in financial position requires an analysis of the Cash account. The model for this statement (page 27)—Cash sources (inflows) − Cash uses (outflows) = Net change in cash (increase or decrease). Notice two aspects of this statement:

a. **Net cash** inflow from continuing operations must be reported as the difference between cash received from revenues $30,000 (which excludes revenues on credit) and cash paid for expenses ($16,000 plus the $600 cash paid for the supplies, even though some of them have not yet been used).

b. **Uses of cash** include the $2,000 cash paid on the $7,000 cost of the land because the remaining $5,000 was on credit, and the $3,000 withdrawn by the owner for personal use.

SOME MISCONCEPTIONS

Some people confuse a bookkeeper with an accountant and bookkeeping with accounting. In effect, they confuse one of the parts with the whole of accounting. Bookkeeping involves the routine and clerical part of accounting and requires only minimal knowledge of the accounting model and its application. A bookkeeper may record the repetitive and uncomplicated transactions in most businesses and may maintain the simple records of a small business. In contrast, the accountant is a highly trained professional competent in the design of information systems, analysis of complex transactions and economic events, interpretation and analysis of financial data, financial reporting, financial advising, auditing, taxation, and management consulting.

Another prevalent misconception is that all of the financial affairs of an entity are subject to precise and objective measurement each period and that the accounting results reported in the financial statements are exactly what happened that period. In contrast, accounting numbers are influenced by estimates as illustrated in subsequent chapters. Many people believe that accounting should measure and report the market value of the entity (including its assets), but accounting does not attempt to do this. To understand financial statements and to interpret them wisely for use in decision making, the user must be aware of their limitations as well as their usefulness. One should understand what the financial statements do and do not try to accomplish.

Finally, financial statements are often thought to be inflexible because of their quantitative nature. As you study accounting, you will learn that it requires considerable **professional judgment in application** on the part of the accountant to capture the economic essense of complex transactions. Thus, accounting is stimulating intellectually; it is not a cut-and-dried subject. Rather, it calls upon your intelligence, analytical ability, creativity, and judgment. Accounting is a communication process involving an audience (users) with a wide diversity of knowledge, interest, and capabilities; therefore, it will call upon your ability as a communicator. The language of accounting uses concisely written phrases and symbols to convey information about the resource flows measured for specific organizations.

As you study accounting and later as a decision maker, you must be wary of these misconceptions. To understand financial statements and to be able to interpret the "figures" wisely, you must have a certain level of knowledge of the concepts and the measurement procedures used in the accounting process. You should learn what accounting "is really like" and appreciate the reasons for using certain procedures. This level of knowledge cannot be gained by reading a list of the "concepts" and a list of the misconceptions. Neither can a generalized discussion of the subject matter suffice. A certain amount of involvement, primarily problem solving (similar to the requirement in mathematics courses), is essential in the study of accounting focused on the needs of the user. Therefore, we provide problems aimed at the desirable knowledge level for the user (as well as the preparer) of financial statements.

SUMMARY OF CHAPTER

This chapter discussed the **fundamental accounting model** and illustrated its application in the accounting system for a business. For accounting purposes, transactions were defined as (a) exchanges between the business and other individuals and organizations, and (b) certain events that exert a direct effect on the entity (such as a fire loss), and events caused by the passage of time (such as depreciation of a building).

Application of the model—Assets = Liabilities + Owners' Equity—was illustrated for a small business. The application involved: (a) transaction analysis, (b) journal entries, and (c) the accounts (T-account format).

An extended illustration, Exhibit 2–4, was presented. This exhibit demonstrated that each transaction caused at least two different accounts to be affected because the economic position of the entity in terms of the fundamental accounting model—Assets = Liabilities + Owners' Equity—always has a dual effect. This characteristic of the model is the reason its application often is referred to as a **double-entry** system.

The fundamental accounting model and the mechanics of the debit-credit concept in T-account format can be summarized as follows, where + means increase and − means decrease:

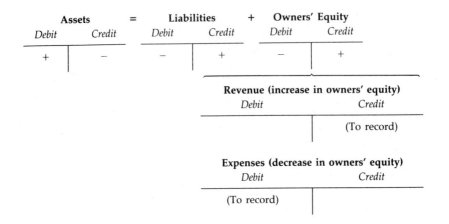

An increase in **revenue** (a credit) represents an **increase** in owners' equity. When a revenue is earned, the resources (i.e., assets) of the business are increased (or liabilities may be decreased), and because of the dual effect, owners' equity is increased by the same amount. In contrast, when an **expense** is incurred, the net resources of the business are decreased (i.e., assets are decreased and/or liabilities increased), and because of the dual effect, owners' equity is decreased by the same amount.

IMPORTANT TERMS DEFINED IN THIS CHAPTER

Terms (alphabetically)	Key word in definitions of important terms used in this chapter	Page reference
Account	A standardized format used to accumulate data about each financial statement element. It provides for recording increases and decreases in these elements caused by transactions.	55
Accrual basis accounting	All financial statement elements—assets, liabilities, revenues, expenses, etc.—are recognized (recorded) when the related transaction occurs. In contrast, cash basis accounting is not appropriate because it recognizes **only** cash transactions.	62
Business (source) document	A document that evidences (supports) a business transaction.	53
Cash basis accounting	See accrual basis accounting.	62
Debits and credits	Debit is the name for the left side of a T-account. Debits represent increases in assets and decreases in liabilities and owners' equity. Credit is the name for the right side of a T-account. Credits represent decreases in assets and increases in liabilities and owners' equity.	60

Elements of financial statements	Items that are reported on financial statements, such as revenues, expenses, assets, liabilities, and owners' equity.	55
Journal entry	An accounting method of expressing the results of transaction analysis in a Debits = Credits format.	62
Periodic financial statements	The financial statements that must be prepared each reporting period for external parties—balance sheet, income statement, and statement of changes in financial position.	55
Transaction	An exchange between a business and one or more external parties and certain other events, such as a fire loss.	53
Transaction analysis	The process of studying a completed transaction to determine its economic effect on a business in terms of the fundamental accounting model: Assets = Liabilities + Owners' Equity.	62

QUESTIONS

1. Give (a) the fundamental accounting model and (b) define each of its elements.

2. Assume your personal financial condition is assets, $30,000; and debts, $20,000. You pay a $10,000 debt plus 12% interest for the year. Show how your personal financial condition will change in terms of the fundamental accounting model.

3. Define a business transaction in the broad sense and give an example of the two different kinds of transactions.

4. Explain why owners' equity is increased by revenues and decreased by expenses.

5. Demonstrate the dual effect on the fundamental accounting model of (a) a cash sale of services for $1,000 and (b) a cash payment of $300 for office rent for the business.

6. Explain what the "separate-entity assumption" means in accounting.

7. What are the owners of a business organized as a corporation called? What is the basis for this name?

8. Explain why a "business document" is important in accounting for a business entity.

9. At December 31, 19A (end of year 1), the fundamental accounting model for YOUR Company showed the following: owners' equity, $70,000; and liabilities, $20,000.
   a. Show how YOUR Company stands in terms of the fundamental accounting model.
   b. Show the summarized balance sheet.

10. For accounting purposes, what is an "account"? Explain why accounts are used in an accounting system.

11. Explain what debit and credit mean.

12. Explain why revenues are recorded as credits and expenses as debits.

13. What is meant by the "two equalities" in accounting.

14. Complete the following matrix by entering either debit or credit in each cell.

Item	Increases	Decreases
Assets		
Liabilities		
Owners' equity		
Revenues		
Expenses		

15. Complete the following matrix by entering either increases or decreases in each cell.

Item	Debit	Credit
Assets		
Liabilities		
Owners' equity		
Revenues		
Expenses		

16. Briefly explain what is meant by transaction analysis.

17. Define accrual accounting. Contrast it with cash basis accounting.

18. What is a T-account? What is its purpose?

19. What is a "journal entry"?

20. Assume you and a friend started a new business called Y and M Corporation. Each of you invested $10,000. Give the effect of this transaction on the company in terms of:
    a. The fundamental accounting model.
    b. A journal entry.
    c. How it is shown in the T-accounts.

21. Complete the following tabulation:

Transaction	Assets	Liabilities	Owners' Equity
a. Investment of cash by organizers, $15,000			
b. Borrowed cash, $4,000			
c. Sold goods for cash, $8,000			
d. Paid expenses, $6,000, cash			
e. Purchased equipment, $9,000, cash			
Ending balances			

22. XR Company paid a $10,000, 12%, one-year note on the due date. Show how this transaction would affect the fundamental accounting model.

EXERCISES

E2–1   **(Learning Terminology)**

Match the items listed under Terminology with the descriptions by entering letters in the spaces provided.

Terminology	Description
__C__ (1) (Example) Separate-entity assumption	A. Liabilities + Owners' Equity.
____ (2) Business document	B. Reports assets, liabilities, and owners' equity.
____ (3) Credits	C. Accounts for a business separate from its owners.
____ (4) Assets	D. Increase assets; decrease liabilities and owners' equity.
____ (5) Elements of financial statements	E. An exchange between an entity and other parties.
____ (6) Transaction	F. Evidence of a completed transaction.
____ (7) Income statement	G. Decrease assets; increase liabilities and owners' equity.
____ (8) T-account	H. Reports revenues, expenses, and net income.
____ (9) Balance sheet	I. Items reported on the financial statements.
____ (10) Debits	J. A standardized format used to accumulate data about each element reported on financial statements.

E2–2   **(Fundamental Accounting Model—Personal)**

You have just finished college and have been working for CC Business for one month. At the start of the month your financial situation was shown in the following schedule. You are to complete the schedule by "recording" your transactions summarized in the first column and indicating your ending financial position on the last line.

Transactions	Assets	Liabilities	Owners' Equity
a. Beginning (personal items, including your rather "used" auto).	$2,000	$800	$1,200
b. Borrowed $1,000 to "get through" the first month.			
c. Paid rent on apartment, $500.			
d. Paid utility deposits, $200.			
e. Personal expenses; food, cleaning, etc., $700.			
f. Auto payment, $400 (including $10 interest).			
g. Trip to visit a "special" person, $300.			
h. Received a "gift" from your family, $150 cash.			
i. You gave your date a special present, $50.			
j. You received your first pay check (net of deductions), $1,400.			
k. Your ending financial position.			

E2–3   (Use of T-accounts; Summarize the Results)

Small Company has been operating one year (19A). At the start of 19B, its T-accounts were:

Assets:

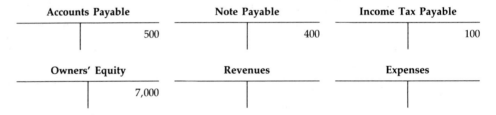

Liabilities:

Owners' Equity:

Required:

1. Enter the following 19B transactions in the T-accounts:
   a. Paid the income tax.
   b. Collected the accounts receivable.
   c. Paid the accounts payable.
   d. Revenue earned, $30,000; including 10% on credit.*
   e. Expenses incurred, $18,000; including $2,000 on credit.*
      * Hint, each of these transactions will affect three accounts.

2. Respond to the following by using data from the T-accounts:

   a. On January 1, 19B, amounts for the following were:

      Assets, $_____ = Liabilities, $_____ + Owners' Equity, $_____.

   b. Net income for 19B was $_____.

c. On December 31, 19B, amounts for the following were:

Assets, $_____ = Liabilities, $_____ + Owners' Equity $_____.

3. Complete the following schedule at December 31, 19B:

Accounts	Assets	Liabilities	Owners' Equity
Cash	$	$	$
Accounts receivable			
Land			
Accounts payable			
Note payable			
Income tax payable			
Owners' equity			
Total assets	$		
Total liabilities		$	
Total owners' equity			$

E2–4   (Learning Terminology)

Match each item listed under Terminology with its appropriate description by entering letters in the space provided.

Terminology

_D__ (1) (Example) Journal entry
_____ (2) Note payable
_____ (3) Assets = Liabilities + Owners' Equity
_____ (4) Expenses
_____ (5) Accounts payable
_____ (6) A = L + OE, and Debits = Credits
_____ (7) Balance sheet, income statement, statement of changes in financial position
_____ (8) Revenues
_____ (9) Accounts receivable
_____ (10) Double-entry system

Description

A. Fundamental accounting model.
B. The three required periodic financial statements.
C. The two equalities in accounting that aid in providing accuracy.
D. An accounting method of expressing the results of transaction analysis.
E. The account that is credited when money is borrowed from a bank.
F. The account that is credited when a sale is made.
G. The account that is debited when an expense is incurred.
H. The account that is debited when a credit sale is made.
I. The account that is credited when an expense is incurred on credit.
J. Application of the fundamental accounting model— Assets = Liabilities + Owners' Equity.

E2–5   (Preparing Simple Journal Entries)

Use the space provided to express the results of your transaction analysis for each of the following six transactions. Use only the journal entry format.

a. Example: Three investors organized XT Corporation, and each one invested $20,000 cash.

Cash ($20,000 × 3)	60,000	
Stockholders' equity		60,000

b. Borrowed $5,000 cash and signed a 10% note.
c. Earned revenues, $40,000, of which $4,000 was on credit.
d. Incurred expenses, $25,000, of which $3,000 was on credit.
e. Paid a debt, accounts payable, $1,000.
f. Collected an amount due, accounts receivable, $2,000.
g. Paid cash interest on note payable, $500.

E2–6   **(Balance Sheet, Income Statement, and Cash Flow Relationships)**
Small Corporation has been operating for one year, 19A. At the end of 19A, the
financial statements have been prepared. Below are a series of independent cases based
on the 19A financial statements. For each independent case and the financial relationship
it relates to, you are to supply the missing item and its amount.

Case	Data	Missing Item	Amount
Example	Assets, $70,000; owners' equity, $20,000	Liabilities	$50,000
A	Revenues, $100,000; expenses, $60,000		
B	Liabilities, $30,000; owners' equity, $52,000		
C	Cash inflows, $80,000; increase in cash, $50,000		
D	Liabilities, $40,000; assets, $80,000		
E	Net income, $35,000; expenses, $60,000		
F	Net income, $20,000; revenues, $95,000		
G	Expenses, $80,000; revenues, $80,000		
H	Revenues, $80,000; expenses, $95,000		
I	Increase in cash, $20,000; cash outflows, $60,000		
J	Cash outflows, $60,000; cash inflows, $50,000		

E2-7 **(Transaction Analysis—Nonquantitative)**

For each transaction given below indicate the effect upon assets, liabilities, and owners' equity by entering a plus for increase and a minus for decrease.

Transaction	Effect on		
	Assets	Liabilities	Owners' Equity
a. Issued stock to organizers for cash (example).	+		+
b. Borrowed cash from local bank.			
c. Purchased equipment on credit.			
d. Earned revenue, collected cash.			
e. Incurred expenses, on credit.			
f. Earned revenue, on credit.			
g. Paid cash for (e).			
h. Incurred expenses, paid cash.			
i. Earned revenue, collected three-fourths cash, balance on credit.			
j. Theft of $100 cash.			
k. Declared and paid cash dividends.			
l. Collected cash for (f).			
m. Depreciated equipment for the period.			
n. Incurred expenses, paid four-fifths cash, balance on credit.			
o. Paid income tax expense for the period.			

E2-8 **(Understanding Transactions; Effects on Balance Sheet and Income Statement)**

During its first week of operations, January 1–7, Tiny Retail Company completed ₋ight transactions, the dollar effects of which are indicated in the following schedule:

Account	Dollar Effect of Each of the Eight Transactions								Ending Balance
	1	2	3	4	5	6	7	8	
Cash	$10,000	$15,000	$(4,000)	$80,000	$(9,000)	$(50,000)	$(11,000)	$7,000	$38,000
Accounts receivable				10,000				(7,000)	3,000
Store fixtures					9,000				9,000
Land			12,000						12,000
Accounts payable						20,000	(11,000)		9,000
Notes payable, 10%		15,000	8,000						23,000
Capital stock	10,000								10,000
Revenues				90,000					90,000
Expenses						70,000			70,000

Required:

1. Write a brief explanation of each transaction. Explain any assumptions that you make.
2. Complete the following tabulation after the eight transactions:

Balance sheet:
    Total assets .... $_____
    Total liabilities .... $_____
    Total owners' equity .... $_____

Income statement:
    Total revenues .... $_____
    Total expenses .... $_____
    Net income .... $_____

E2–9   (Applying the Fundamental Accounting Model)

Sampson Service Company, Inc., was organized by five investors. The following transactions were completed:

a. The investors paid in $50,000 cash to start the business. Each one was issued 1,000 shares of capital stock, par value $10 per share.
b. Equipment for use in the business was purchased at a cost of $10,000, one half was paid in cash, and the balance is due in six months.
c. Service fees were earned amounting to $54,000, of which $6,000 was on credit.
d. Operating expenses incurred amounted to $33,000, of which $3,000 was on credit.
e. Cash was collected for $4,000 of the service fees performed on credit in (c) above.
f. Paid cash, $1,000, on the operating expenses that were on credit in (d) above.
g. Investor A borrowed $10,000 from a local bank and signed a one-year, 10% note for that amount.

Required:

Set up a schedule similar to the following and enter thereon each of the above transactions that should be recorded by Sampson. Transaction (a) is used as an example.

Transactions	Assets	= Liabilities + Owners' Equity
a. Investment of cash in the business	Cash + $50,000	Capital stock + $50,000

After the last transaction (on the last line of the schedule), total each dollar column to prove the correctness of your solution.

E2–10   (Application of Debits and Credits; Nonquantitative)

The 12 transactions given below were completed by Duster Service Company during the year 19X:

1. The organizers paid in cash and in turn received 10,000 shares of capital stock.
2. Duster borrowed cash from the local bank.
3. Duster purchased a delivery truck, paid three fourths cash, and the balance is due in six months.
4. Revenues earned, collected cash in full.
5. Expenses incurred, paid cash in full.
6. Revenues earned, on credit (cash will be collected later).
7. Expenses incurred, on credit (cash will be paid later).

8. Declared and paid a cash dividend to stockholders.
9. Collected half of the amount on credit in 6.
10. Paid all of the credit amount in 7.
11. A spare tire was stolen from the delivery truck (not insured).
12. At the end of 19X, the delivery truck is depreciated by a dollar amount (an expense).

Required:

For each transaction given above enter in the tabulation given below, a D for debit and a C for credit to reflect the increases and decreases of the assets, liabilities, and owners' equity (separate accounts are given for owners' equity). Transaction 1 is used as an example.

Fundamental Fundamental Accounting Model	Twelve Transactions											
	1	2	3	4	5	6	7	8	9	10	11	12
a. Assets	D											
b. Liabilities												
Owners' equity: c. Investments by owners	C											
d. Revenues												
e. Withdrawals (dividends)												
f. Expenses												

(Note: In some cases there may be both a D and C in the same box.)

E2–11   (Using T-accounts; Summarizing the Results)
Snappy Service Company, Inc., was organized and issued 10,000 shares of its capital stock for $30,000 cash. The following transactions occurred during the current accounting period:

a. Received the cash from the organizers, $30,000.
b. Service fees earned amounted to $35,000, of which $25,000 was collected in cash.
c. Operating expenses incurred amounted to $23,000, of which $17,000 was paid in cash.
d. Bought two machines for operating purposes at the start of the year at a cost of $9,000 each; paid cash.
e. One of the machines was destroyed by fire one week after purchase; it was uninsured. The event to be considered is the fire. (Hint: Set up a fire loss expense account.)
f. The other machine has an estimated useful life to Snappy of 10 years (and no residual value). The event to be considered is the depreciation of the equipment because it was used for one year in rendering services.
g. Stockholder Able bought a vacant lot (land) for $5,000 cash.

Required:

1. Set up appropriate T-accounts and record in them the dual effects on the fundamental accounting model of each of the above transactions that should be recorded by

Snappy. Key the amounts to the letters starting with (*a*). Number the following required accounts consecutively starting with 101 for cash: Cash, Accounts Receivable, Machines, Accumulated Depreciation, Accounts Payable, Service Fees Earned, Operating Expenses, Fire Loss Expense, Depreciation Expense, and Capital Stock.

2. Use the data in the completed T-accounts (Requirement 1) to complete the following:

Debits = Credits:
   Total debits .... $_____
   Total credits .... $_____

Income statement:
   Total revenues .... $_____
   Total expenses .... $_____
   Net income .... $_____

Balance sheet:
   Total assets .... $_____
   Total liabilities .... $_____
   Total owners' equity .... $_____

PROBLEMS

P2–1   (Transaction Analysis, Recording, and Reporting)

Toni Company was organized on January 1, 19A, by J. B. Tory, S. T. Olen, R. R. Neans, and B. T. Irwin. Each organizer invested $8,000 in the company, and, in turn, each was issued 8,000 shares of capital stock. To date they are the only stockholders.

During the first quarter (January–March 19A), the company completed the following six transactions (summarized and simplified for instructional purposes):

1. Collected a total of $32,000 from the organizers and, in turn, issued the shares of capital stock.
2. Purchased equipment for use in the business; paid $8,000 cash in full.
3. Purchased land for use in the business; paid $4,000 cash and gave a $6,000, one-year, 12% interest-bearing note for the balance; total cost, $10,000.
4. Earned service revenues of $40,000 of which $36,000 was collected in cash, the balance was on credit. (Hint: Two asset accounts are increased.)
5. Incurred $28,000 operating expenses of which $25,000 was paid in cash, the balance was on credit. (Hint: Three different accounts will be affected.)
6. In addition, stockholder Tory reported to the company that 500 shares of his Toni stock had been sold and transferred to stockholder Irwin for a cash consideration of $6,000.

Required:

a. Was Toni Company organized as a sole proprietorship, a partnership, or a corporation? Explain the basis for your answer.
b. What was the issue price per share of the capital stock?
c. During the first quarter, the records of the company were inadequate. You were asked to prepare the summary of transactions given above. To develop a quick assessment of their economic effects on Toni Company, you have decided to complete the tabulation that follows and to use plus (+) for increases and minus (−) for decreases for each account. The first transaction is used as an example.

Accounts	Six Transactions—Effects						Ending Amounts (total)
	1	2	3	4	5	6	
Cash	$+32,000	$	$	$	$	$	$
Accounts receivable							
Land							
Equipment							
Accounts payable							
Notes payable							
Capital stock	+32,000						
Service revenues							
Operating expenses							

d. Did you include the Tory-Irwin transaction in the above tabulation? Why?

e. Based only upon the completed tabulation above, provide the following amounts (show computations):

(1) Income for the quarter.

(2) Total assets at the end of the quarter.

(3) Total liabilities at the end of the quarter.

(4) Total owners' equity at the end of the quarter.

(5) Cash balance at the end of the quarter.

(6) Net amount of cash inflow from operations, that is, from revenues and expenses combined.

(7) How much interest must be paid on the note at its maturity date?

P2–2 (Identifying Accounts for Assets, Liabilities, and Owners' Equity; Also, Usual Balance— Debit versus Credit)

Listed below are the accounts of the AAA Rental Corporation:

a. Cash.

b. Accounts receivable.

c. Capital stock (issued to stockholders).

d. Bonds payable.

e. Rent revenue.

f. Insurance premium paid in advance of use.

g. Interest revenue.

h. Investments, long term.

i. Interest expense.

j. Machinery and equipment.

k. Patents.

l. Income tax expense.

m. Property taxes payable.

n. Loss on sale of machinery.

o. Land, plant site (in use).

p. Accounts payable.

q. Supplies inventory (held for use as needed).

r. Notes payable, short term.

s. Retained earnings.

t. Investments, short term.

u. Certificates of deposit (CDs) held.

v. Operating expenses.

w. Income taxes payable.

x. Gain on sale of equipment.

y. Land held for future plant site.

z. Revenue from investments.

aa. Wages payable.

bb. Accumulated depreciation.

cc. Merchandise inventory (held for resale).

Complete a tabulation similar to the following (enter two check marks for each account listed above). Account a. is used as an example.

Type of account

Account	Asset	Liability	Owner's equity (including revenues and expenses)	Usual balance Debit	Credit
a.	✓			✓	

Etc.

P2–3 **(Transaction Analysis, Recording; Debits = Credits; Financial Statements)**

Bayside Service Company has been operating for three years. At the end of 19C, the accounting records reflected assets of $320,000 and liabilities of $120,000. During the year 19D, the following summarized transactions were completed:

a. Revenues of $160,000, of which $10,000 was on credit.
b. Issued an additional 1,000 shares of capital stock, par $10 per share, for $10,000 cash.
c. Purchased equipment that cost $25,000, paid cash $10,000, and the balance is due next year.
d. Expenses incurred were $110,000, of which $15,000 was on credit.
e. Collected $8,000 of the credit amount in (a).
f. Declared and paid cash dividends to stockholders of $12,000.
g. Paid $10,000 of the credit amount in (d).
h. Borrowed $20,000 cash, on a 12% interest-bearing note, from a local bank (on December 31, 19D), payable June 30, 19E.
i. Cash amounting to $400 was stolen (not covered by insurance).
j. Depreciation on equipment was $600 for 19D (because of use).

Required:

1. Enter each of the above transactions in the following schedule. The first transaction is used as an example.

Transactions	Assets Debit	Credit	Liabilities Debit	Credit	Owners' Equity Debit	Credit
Balances, January 1, 19D	$320,000			$120,000		$200,000
a. Revenues	150,000					160,000
	10,000					
b.						
Etc.						

2. Respond to the following:
    a. Why were two debits entered in the above schedule for transaction (a)?
    b. Complete the following at the end of 19D:

    Income statement:
    Revenues .... $_____
    Expenses .... $_____
    Net income .... $_____

    Balance sheet:
    Assets .... $_____
    Liabilities .... $_____
    Owners' equity .... $_____

    c. Explain why the dividend declared and paid is not an expense.

P2–4   **(Transaction Analysis; Recording Debits and Credits)**
        Listed below is a series of accounts for Service Corporation, which has been operating for three years. These accounts are listed and **numbered** for identification. Below the accounts is a series of transactions. For each transaction indicate the account(s) that should be debited and credited by entering the appropriate account number(s) to the right of each transaction. The first transaction is used as an example.

Account No.	Account title	Account No.	Account title
1.	Cash.	10.	Wages payable.
2.	Accounts receivable.	11.	Income tax payable.
3.	Supplies inventory (on hand, pending use).	12.	Capital stock, par $10.
4.	Prepaid expense.	13.	Retained earnings.
5.	Equipment (used in the business).	14.	Service revenues.
6.	Accumulated depreciation, equipment.	15.	Operating expenses.
7.	Patents.	16.	Income tax expense.
8.	Accounts payable.	17.	Interest expense.
9.	Notes payable.	18.	None of the above (explain).

Transactions	Debit	Credit
a. Example—Purchased equipment for use in the business; paid one-third cash and gave a note payable for the balance.	5	1, 9
b. Investment of cash in the business; capital stock was issued (at par).	___	___
c. Paid cash for salaries and wages.	___	___
d. Collected cash for services performed this period.	___	___
e. Collected cash for services performed last period.	___	___
f. Performed services this period on credit.	___	___
g. Paid operating expenses incurred this period.	___	___
h. Paid cash for operating expenses incurred last period.	___	___
i. Incurred operating expenses this period, to be paid next period.	___	___
j. Purchased supplies for inventory (to be used later); paid cash.	___	___
k. Used some of the supplies from inventory for operations.	___	___
l. Purchased a patent; paid cash.	___	___

m. Made a payment on the equipment note (*a*) above; the payment was part principal and part interest expense.   ____ ____

n. Collected cash on accounts receivable for services previously performed.   ____ ____

o. Paid cash on accounts payable for expenses previously incurred.   ____ ____

p. Paid three fourths of the income tax expense for the year; the balance to be paid next period.   ____ ____

q. On last day of current period, paid in cash for an insurance policy covering the next two years.   ____ ____

P2–5   (Transaction Analysis; Recording in the Accounts)

Listed below is a series of accounts (with identification numbers) for Silver Service Corporation.

Account No.	Account titles	Account No.	Account titles
1.	Cash.	20.	Capital stock, par $10 per share.
2.	Accounts receivable.	21.	Contributed capital in excess of par.
3.	Service supplies inventory.	25.	Service revenues.
4.	Trucks and equipment.	26.	Operating expenses.
5.	Accumulated depreciation.	27.	Depreciation expense.
10.	Accounts payable.	28.	Interest expense.
11.	Notes payable.	29.	Income tax expense.
12.	Income tax payable.	30.	None of the above (explain).

During 19X, the company completed the selected transactions given in the tabulation that follows.

Required:

To the right indicate the accounts (by identification number) that should be debited and credited and the respective amounts. The first transaction is used as an example.

Transaction	Debit		Credit	
	Acct. No.	Amount	Acct. No.	Amount
a. Example: Purchased panel truck for use in the business for $18,000; paid $10,000 cash and signed a 10% interest-bearing note for the balance, $8,000.	4	18,000	1 11	10,000 8,000
b. Service revenues earned, $150,000, of which $10,000 was on credit.				
c. Operating expenses incurred, $100,000, of which $20,000 was on credit.				
d. Purchased service supplies, $500, paid cash (placed in supplies inventory, for use as needed).				
e. Collected $8,000 of the credit amount in (b).				
f. Paid $15,000 of the credit amount in (c).				
g. Used $400 of the service supplies (taken from inventory) for service operations.				
h. Depreciation on the truck for the year, $3,000.				
i. Paid six months' interest on the note in (a).				
j. Income tax expense for the year, $4,000, paid three-fourths cash, balance payable by April 1 of next year.				

CASES

C2–1   (Inspection of a Balance Sheet to Evaluate Its Reliability)

J. Doe asked a local bank for a $50,000 loan to expand his small company. The bank asked Doe to submit a financial statement of the business to supplement the loan application. Doe prepared the balance sheet shown below.

Balance Sheet
June 30, 19X6

Assets:
Cash and CDs	$ 9,000
Inventory	30,000
Equipment	46,000
Residence (monthly payments, $18,000)	300,000
Remaining assets	20,000
Total assets	$405,000

Liabilities:
Short-term debt to suppliers	$ 62,000
Long-term debt on equipment	38,000
Total debt	100,000
Owners' equity, J. Doe	305,000
Total liabilities and owners' equity	$405,000

Required:

The balance sheet has several flaws; however, there is at least one major deficiency. Identify it and explain its significance.

C2-2   (Analyzing and Restating an Income Statement that Has Major Deficiencies; a Challenging Case)

Allen Jenkins started and operated a small service company during 19A. At the end of the year, he prepared the following statement based on information stored in a large filing cabinet.

Jenkins Company
Profit for 19A

Service fees income collected during 19A		$80,000
Cash dividends received		12,000
Total		92,000
Expense for operations paid during 19A	$58,000	
Cash stolen	300	
Supplies purchased for use on service jobs (cash paid)	1,700	
Total		60,000
Profit		$32,000

A summary of completed transactions was:

a. Service fees earned during 19A, $87,000.
b. The cash dividends received were on some Dow Jones common stock purchased six years earlier.
c. Expenses incurred during 19A, $62,000.
d. Supplies on hand (unused) at the end of 19A, $200.

Required:

1. Did Jenkins prepare the above statement on a cash basis or an accrual basis? Explain how you can tell. Which basis should be used? Explain why.
2. Revise the above statement to make it consistent with proper accounting and reporting. Explain (using footnotes) the reason for each change that you make.

C2-3   (A Challenging Analytical Case Related to Application of the Fundamental Accounting Model)

SEC Company was organized during January 19A by T. E. Scott, W. D. Evans, and R. L. Cates. On January 20, 19A, the company issued 5,000 shares to each of its organizers. Below is a schedule of the **cumulative** account balances immediately after each of the first 10 transactions.

Accounts	Ten Transactions—Cumulative Balances									
	1	2	3	4	5	6	7	8	9	10
Cash	$75,000	$70,000	$87,000	$77,000	$66,000	$66,000	$70,000	$58,000	$55,000	$54,000
Accounts receivable			8,000	8,000	8,000	11,000	11,000	11,000	11,000	11,000
Office fixtures		20,000	20,000	20,000	20,000	20,000	20,000	20,000	20,000	20,000
Land				14,000	14,000	14,000	14,000	14,000	14,000	14,000
Accounts payable					2,000	2,000	2,000	7,000	4,000	4,000
Notes payable		15,000	15,000	19,000	19,000	19,000	19,000	19,000	19,000	19,000
Capital stock*	75,000	75,000	75,000	75,000	75,000	75,000	79,000	79,000	79,000	79,000
Revenues			25,000	25,000	25,000	28,000	28,000	28,000	28,000	28,000
Expenses					13,000	13,000	13,000	30,000	30,000	31,000

* Owners' equity.

Required:

1. Analyze the changes in the above schedule for each transaction; then explain the transaction. Transactions 1 and 2 are used as examples:
   a. Cash increased $75,000, and capital stock (owners' equity) increased $75,000. Therefore, the transaction was an issuance of the capital stock of the corporation for $75,000 cash.
   b. Cash decreased $5,000, office fixtures (an asset) increased $20,000, and notes payable (a liability) increased $15,000. Therefore, the transaction was a purchase of office fixtures that cost $20,000. Payment was made as follows: cash, $5,000; note payable, $15,000.

2. Based only upon the above schedule (disregarding your response to Requirement 1) respond to the following after transaction 10:
   a. Income statement:
      Revenues .... $_____
      Expenses .... _____
      Net income .... $_____
   b. Balance sheet:
      Total assets .... $_____
      Total liabilities .... _____
      Total owners' equity .... _____

C2–4   **(Overview of an Actual Set of Financial Statements)**

Refer to the financial statements of Chesebrough–Pond's Inc. given in Special Supplement B immediately preceding the Index. Answer the following questions for the 1985 annual accounting period:

1. What is the name of the company?
2. What is the beginning date and the ending date for the current reporting year?
3. What is the name of the independent CPA firm (i.e., auditor)?
4. What current-year amounts are reported for the following?

Total assets .... $_____.
Total liabilities .... $_____.
Total owners' equity .... $_____.

5. What current-year amounts are reported for the following?

Total cash sources (inflows) .... $_____.
Total cash uses (outflows) .... $_____.
Change in cash (increase or decrease) .... $_____.

6. What years are included in the Ten-Year Financial Summary?
7. What is the name of the auditors' report?
8. What are the position titles of the two managers who signed the report "Management's Responsibility for Financial Reporting"?

This chapter expands your knowledge of financial statements. Some users may not be able to understand these statements because of the technical accounting language. Notice below how a familiar company used an innovative approach to make its annual report more understandable.

Southwestern Bell Corporation

Selected Financial Data*

Dollars in Millions — Except Per Share Amounts

At December 31 Or For The Year Ended:	1985	1984
A **Operating revenues**		
Local telephone service	$3,036	$2,838
B Network access	2,656	2,238
Long distance service	891	912
Directory advertising	948	744
Other	394	459
Total operating revenues	7,925	7,191
Expenses		
C Operating	5,802	5,254
Interest	541	520
Other	(69)	(45)
D Income taxes	655	579
Total expenses	6,929	6,308
E **Net Income**	$ 996	$ 883

Financial Terms Made Simple
The specialized language used in financial reports can sometimes be difficult to comprehend. We hope these simplified definitions of financial terminology help make your review of our financial report easier. Each phrase explained in this section is marked by a letter in red to indicate where that term appears within the selected financial data on the opposite page.

A   Operating Revenues
Southwestern Bell Corporation in 1985 recorded $7.9 billion in revenues from the products and services sold or provided by all its subsidiaries. The 1985 revenues represent a 10 percent increase from 1984.

B   Network Access Charges
These are the fees Southwestern Bell Telephone assesses long distance companies and end users to help pay for "fixed" costs of the telephone network. Access charges became a new revenue source after divestiture.

C   Operating Expenses
The majority of operating revenues paid for operating expenses. This category basically shows our cost of doing business. Employee salaries and benefits, along with costs to purchase and maintain facilities, are the largest expense categories. In 1985 operating expenses and costs increased 10 percent compared to the previous year.

D   Income Taxes
The Corporation's provision for income taxes for 1985 was $655 million. These taxes include federal, state and local income taxes.

E   Net Income
Our net income—also called profit or earnings—was $996 million during 1985. With this income, we pay dividends to shareowners and reinvest in the business. Our 1985 net income is a 13 percent increase from 1984. However, it's important to note that our 1985 earnings included non-recurring net income of $57 million from Yellow Pages operations.

THE ACCOUNTING INFORMATION PROCESSING CYCLE

PURPOSE:

Chapter 2 emphasized the fundamental accounting model and transaction analysis. It also discussed the use of journal entries and T-accounts to record the results of transaction analysis for each business transaction. The purpose of Chapter 3 is to discuss the **accounting information cycle,** which processes financial data from the transaction to the end result—the periodic income statement, balance sheet, and statement of changes in financial position. This chapter will expand your knowledge of journal entries, accounts, and financial statements.

ORGANIZATION:

1. Characteristics of an accounting system.
2. Application of the accounting information processing cycle—six sequential phases.
3. Subclassifications on the:
   a. Income statement.
   b. Balance sheet.
   c. Statement of change in financial position (SCFP).
4. Demonstration case—the accounting information processing cycle.

LEARNING OBJECTIVES—TO BE ABLE TO:

1. Identify and explain the characteristics of an accounting system.
2. List and explain the six sequential phases of the accounting system.
3. Apply the six phases of the accounting information processing cycle using simple situations.
4. Prepare simple financial statements—income statement, balance sheet, and SCFP.
5. Expand your vocabulary by learning about the "Important Terms Defined in This Chapter" (page 124).
6. Apply the knowledge gained from this chapter by completing the homework assigned by your instructor.

CHARACTERISTICS OF AN ACCOUNTING SYSTEM

An accounting system, regardless of the size of a business, is designed to collect, process, and report periodic financial information about the entity. **Financial reports** are prepared at the end of each **reporting period,** often called the **accounting period.** For external reporting, the reporting period is one year, which may, or may not, be the calendar year (January 1 to December 31). Therefore, during each reporting period, the accounting system must systematically collect and process economic data about all of the transactions completed by the entity. This collecting and processing activity is called the **accounting information processing cycle.** It is called a cycle because it must be repeated each accounting period for the new economic data. This processing cycle involves a series of sequential phases (steps), starting with the transactions and extending, in the accounting system, through the accounting period and finally to the preparation of the required financial statements—income statement, balance sheet, and statement of changes in financial position. We will discuss the primary sequential phases in the information processing cycle in the order in which they usually are accomplished. The phases are outlined in Exhibit 3–1.

APPLICATION OF THE ACCOUNTING INFORMATION PROCESSING CYCLE

This section discusses the first six phases of a typical accounting information processing cycle. Each phase is discussed in order and illustrated by using Bass Cleaners, Inc. (see Exhibit 2–4). At the end of this chapter, a comprehensive

_____ **EXHIBIT 3–1** _____

Phases of the accounting information processing cycle

SEQUENTIAL ACTIVITIES COMPLETED DURING THE ACCOUNTING PERIOD

Phases

1   **COLLECT INFORMATION** about each transaction as it occurs.
2   **ANALYZE EACH TRANSACTION** in terms of (*a*) Assets = Liabilities + Owners' Equity, and (*b*) Debits = Credits.
3   **RECORD THE ECONOMIC EFFECTS** of each transaction in the journal.
4   **TRANSFER THESE ECONOMIC** effects from the journal to the ledger.

COMPLETED AT THE END OF THE ACCOUNTING PERIOD.

5   **PREPARE A TRIAL BALANCE** from the ledger.
6   **PREPARE FINANCIAL STATEMENTS.**
7–11   Other phases at end of the accounting period—discussed in Chapter 5.

demonstration case, with its solution, is given to tie all of these six phases together.

Phase 1—Collect Original Data

The initial phase in the accounting information processing cycle is the collection of original economic data about each transaction affecting the entity. Such economic data are collected continuously throughout the accounting period as transactions occur. Each transaction that involves **external** parties usually generates one or more source documents that provide essential data about that transaction. Examples are sales invoices, cash register tapes, purchase invoices, and signed receipts. Documentation must be generated **internally** for certain economic effects such as depreciation and the using up of office supplies already on hand.[1] Importantly, the original economic data (from the supporting source documents) entered into an accounting system are not generated by the accounting function but through the various **operating** functions of a business. The quality of the **outputs** of an information processing system is determined primarily by the quality (and timeliness) of the inputs of original data based on transactions. Therefore, a carefully designed and controlled data collection system is essential throughout a business. The initial data collection procedure constitutes an integral and important subsystem of an accounting information processing system.

To illustrate the collection of original data, return to Bass Cleaners, Inc. (Exhibit 2–4). The first transaction was the issuance of 800 shares of capital stock for $20,000 cash. The business documents to support this transaction would be a copy of the cash receipt given to each stockholder and an internal memorandum that identifies the number of shares issued to each of the four organizers.

Phase 2—Analyze Each Transaction

This phase in the accounting information processing cycle was explained and illustrated in Exhibit 2–4 of Chapter 2. Recall from Chapter 2 that the objective of this analytical activity is to determine the **economic effects** on the entity of each transaction in terms of the basic accounting model, Assets = Liabilities + Owners' Equity, and the equality, Debits = Credits. When this analysis of a business transaction is completed, the economic effects are then formally entered into the accounting system in the Debits = Credits format.

Transaction analysis requires an understanding of the nature of business transactions, the operations of the business, and a sound knowledge of the concepts and procedures of accounting.

To illustrate, analysis of the first transaction of Bass Cleaners, Inc. (Exhibit

---

[1] Recall from Chapter 2 that transactions include (*a*) events that involve an exchange between two or more separate entities (or persons) and (*b*) events that are not between entities but nevertheless have a particular economic impact on the entity being accounted for.

2–4)—the issuance of 800 shares of capital stock to the organizers for $20,000 cash—would be:

ASSETS		LIABILITIES		STOCKHOLDERS' EQUITY
Cash debit, $20,000	=	No effect	+	Capital stock credit, $20,000

Phase 3—Record Transactions in the Journal

After transaction analysis, the economic effect of each transaction is formally entered into the accounting system in a record known as the **journal.** The journal is a simple form used to record the economic effects of each transaction using the Debits = Credits format.

In a simple situation, after the analysis of a business transaction, it could be recorded directly in the separate accounts for each asset, liability, and owners' equity. However, in more complex situations, it is essential that the economic effects of each transaction on the accounting model be recorded in one place in **chronological order** (i.e., in order of date of occurrence). The accounting record designed for this purpose is the journal. Typically, the effects of transaction analysis are recorded first in the journal and later transferred to the appropriate accounts (refer to the various journal entries and T-accounts used for Bass Cleaners in Exhibit 2–4).

The journal contains a chronological listing of each entry for all of the transactions. The **format** of the entry in the journal for each transaction is designed to facilitate posting so that the economic effects on the accounting model and the debit and credit features are physically linked. For example, in Exhibit 2–4, the first transaction by Bass Cleaners would appear in the journal in the following format:

JOURNAL	Debit	Credit
(Date) Cash	20,000	
Capital stock		20,000
To record investment of cash by owners.		

Notice that the **debit always is listed first** and the **credit is listed last and indented** to avoid incorrect identification.

The physical linking of the dual effects of each transaction in the journal contrasts with the separate accounts, where the debits and credits associated with each transaction must be separated physically between two or more accounts. For example, recall that the economic effects of the above entry for Bass Cleaners appear in separate accounts as follows:

Cash		Capital Stock	
(Date) 20,000		(Date) 20,000	

The **journal** is the place of initial (or first) entry of the economic effects of each transaction. Therefore, it has been referred to as the **book of original entry.** The journal serves three useful purposes:

1. It provides for the initial and orderly listing (by date) of each transaction immediately after its transaction analysis is completed.
2. It provides a single place to record the economic effects of each transaction without further subclassifications of the data.
3. It facilitates later **tracing;** checking for possible errors; and reconstruction of each transaction, its analysis, and its recording.

Knowledge of the approximate date of a transaction often is used in tracing activities. In this regard, the journal is the only place in the accounting system where the economic effects of each transaction are linked physically and recorded chronologically.

Let's see how the journal is used in a manually maintained system. The first three transactions for Bass Cleaners have been entered in a typical journal shown in Exhibit 3–2. Recording transactions in the journal in this manner is called **journalizing,** and the entries made are called **journal entries.**

To summarize the discussion about journal entries: (1) each transaction and event is first recorded in the journal as a separate entry; (2) each entry in the journal is dated, and entries are recorded in chronological order; (3) for each transaction, the debits (accounts and amounts) are entered first, the credits follow and are indented; and (4) for each transaction, the economic effects on the accounting model and the debits and credits are linked in one entry. These features provide an "audit or tracing trail" that facilitates subsequent examination of past transactions and assists in locating errors. Also the journal is designed to simplify subsequent accounting (as will be shown later).

Phase 4—Transfer to the Ledger

As shown in Exhibit 2–4, for Bass Cleaners, a separate account was set up for each asset, liability, and owners' equity. An accounting system typically contains a large number of such accounts. Collectively, these individual accounts are contained in a record known as the **ledger.** The ledger may be organized in many ways. Handwritten accounting systems may use a loose-leaf ledger—one page for each account. In the case of a "machine" accounting system, a separate machine card is kept for each account. With a computerized accounting system, the ledger is kept on electronic storage devices, but there are still individual accounts under each system. Each account is identified by a descriptive **name**

EXHIBIT 3–2

Journal illustrated

	Journal			Page ___1___
Date	Account Titles and Explanation	Folio	Debit	Credit
Jan. 1	Cash	101	20,000	
	Capital stock	301		20,000
	Investment of cash by owners			
Jan. 3	Cash	101	5,000	
	Note payable	202		5,000
	Borrowed cash on 12% note			
Jan. 6	Delivery truck	111	8,000	
	Cash	101		8,000
	Purchased delivery truck for use in the business			

and an **assigned number** (e.g., Cash, 101; Accounts Payable, 201; and Capital Stock, 301).

Exhibit 3–3 shows the ledger for Bass Cleaners in handwritten T-account format. The ledger (i.e., all of the accounts) contains information that initially was recorded in the journal and then **posted** (i.e., transferred) to the appropriate accounts in the ledger. The transfer of information from the journal to the ledger is called posting. This transfer from the chronological arrangement in the journal to the account format in the ledger is a very important **reclassification** of the data because the ledger reflects the data classified as assets, liabilities, owners' equity, revenues and expenses (i.e., by individual accounts) rather than chronologically.

EXHIBIT 3–3

Ledger illustrated (T-accounts)

BASS CLEANERS, INC.
LEDGER at December 31, 19A

ASSETS	=	LIABILITIES	+	OWNERS' EQUITY

Cash   101

(a)	20,000	(c)	8,000
(b)	5,000	(f)	25,800
(d)	40,000	(h)	600
(k)	1,000	(j)	1,800
		(l)	500

(Net debit balance, $29,300)

Accounts Receivable 102

(e)	4,000	(k)	1,000

(Net debit balance, $3,000)

Delivery Truck   120

(c)	8,000

Accumulated Depreciation, Delivery Truck†   121

		(i)	1,600

Accounts Payable   201

(l)	500	(g)	2,000

(Net credit balance, $1,500)

Notes Payable   205

		(b)	5,000

Capital Stock   301

		(a)	20,000

Retained Earnings* 310

(j)	1,800	

Cleaning Revenue   312

		(d)	40,000
		(e)	4,000

(Net credit balance, $44,000)

Operating Expenses 320

(f)	25,800
(g)	2,000
(i)	1,600

(Net debit balance, $29,400)

Interest Expense   325

(h)	600

Totals	$38,700	=	$6,500	+	$32,200

Note: The accounting model, Assets = Liabilities + Owners' Equity, given at the top of this exhibit and the totals at the bottom are shown for your convenience in study; they would not appear in an actual ledger.

* Retained Earnings is an owners' equity account that reports accumulated earnings minus dividends paid to date. Dividends paid reduce cash and owners' equity (see Chapter 12). Dividends paid is a distribution to owners—not an expense because it does not contribute to earning revenue.

† The delivery truck is depreciated over a five-year period because that is its estimated useful life to Bass Cleaners. Depreciation refers to the "wearing out" of the truck due to use. The truck is assumed to wear out at a steady rate each year throughout its life; therefore, the annual depreciation is $8,000 ÷ 5 years = $1,600. This amount is recorded in an account called Accumulated depreciation; it is a negative, or contra, account to the Delivery Truck account. The $1,600 also is an expense for the year. For further explanation of depreciation, see Chapter 9.

A business using a handwritten system will record the transactions in the journal each day and **post** to the ledger less frequently, say, every few days. Of course, the timing of these **information processing activities** varies with the data processing system used and the complexity of the entity.

The T-account format shown in Exhibit 3–3 is useful for instructional purposes. However, the typical account used is the columnar format shown in Exhibit 3–4. It retains the debit-credit concept, but it is arranged to provide columns for date, explanation, folio (F), and a running balance.

To post to the ledger, the debits and credits shown in the journal entries are transferred directly, as debits and credits, to the appropriate accounts in the ledger. In both the journal (Exhibit 3–2) and the ledger (Exhibit 3–3) there is a **Folio** column for **cross-reference** between these two records. In the journal, shown in Exhibit 3–2, the numbers in the Folio column indicate the account **to which** the dollar amounts were posted (i.e., transferred). In the ledger account for Cash, the numbers in the Folio column indicate the journal page **from which** the dollar amounts were posted. Folio numbers are used in the posting phase to (a) indicate that posting has been done and (b) provide an "audit trail."

___ **EXHIBIT 3–4** ___

Ledger account in columnar format illustrated

Account Title __Cash__   Account Number __101__

Date	Explanation	Folio	Debit	Credit	Balance
Jan. 1	Investments	1	20,000		20,000
3	Borrowing	3	5,000		25,000
6	Truck purchased	3		8,000	17,000
7	Cleaning revenue	4	40,000		57,000
8	Operating expenses	4		25,800	31,200
10	Interest expense	5		600	30,600
15	Payments to owners	7		1,800	28,800
16	Collections on receivables	8	1,000		29,800
17	Payments on accounts payable	8		500	29,300

The economic data ends up in the ledger; therefore, it has been called the **book of final entry.**

Phase 5—Develop a Trial Balance

At the end of the **accounting period** (also called the reporting period), to verify recording accuracy, and for subsequent processing uses, a **trial balance** is prepared directly from the ledger. A trial balance is a listing, in ledger account order, of the individual ledger **accounts** and their respective **net ending** debit and credit balances. The ending balance shown for each individual account is the difference between the total of its debits and the total of its credits. Exhibit 3–5 shows the trial balance of Bass Cleaners at December 31, 19A. It was prepared directly from the ledger accounts given in Exhibit 3–3.

A trial balance has two purposes in the accounting information processing cycle:

1. It provides a check on the equality of the debits and credits as shown in the ledger accounts at the end of the period.
2. It provides financial data in a convenient form to help in preparing the financial statements.

Phase 6—Prepare Financial Statements

At the end of the reporting period, the first four phases of the accounting information processing cycle will have been completed—data collection, analysis, journal entries, and posting to the ledger.[2] Phase 5, illustrated above, starts the end-of-period phases.

The next phase (i.e., Phase 6) is preparation of the three required financial statements—income statement, balance sheet, and statement of changes in financial position. The trial balance provides basic data that are needed to prepare the financial statements at the end of the reporting period. The 19A income statement and balance sheet for Bass Cleaners are shown in Exhibit 3–6. Notice that the amounts on these statements were taken directly from the trial balance, except for retained earnings. Retained earnings is computed as: Beginning balance, $–0– (this is Year 1 for Bass Cleaners), + Net income (from the income statement), $14,000, − Dividends paid to stockholders, $1,800, = Ending balance, $12,200.[3]

---

[2] Chapter 5 will expand the accounting information cycle to include some additional activities to develop the financial statements in complex situations.

[3] Notice how much easier it is to prepare these statements from a trial balance than when the accounts are used directly (as was done in Chapter 2, Exhibit 2–2). Retained earnings, an element of stockholders' equity, will be discussed in detail later.

EXHIBIT 3–5

Trial balance illustrated

BASS CLEANERS, INC.
Trial Balance
December 31, 19A

Account No.	Account titles	Net balance Debit	Net balance Credit
101	Cash	$29,300	
102	Accounts receivable	3,000	
120	Delivery truck	8,000	
121	Accumulated depreciation, delivery truck		$ 1,600
201	Accounts payable		1,500
205	Notes payable		5,000
301	Capital stock (800 shares)		20,000
310	Retained earnings (explained later)	1,800	
312	Cleaning revenues		44,000
320	Operating expenses	29,400	
325	Interest expense	600	
	Totals	$72,100	$72,100

CLASSIFICATION OF ELEMENTS REPORTED ON THE FINANCIAL STATEMENTS

External decision makers who use financial statements have varied backgrounds, education, experience, financial interests, and problems. These decision makers include investors, creditors, employees, governmental agencies, unions, customers, and other interested parties. Often financial statements are referred to as **general-purpose financial statements** because they are prepared to serve the diverse needs of these groups.

To make financial statements clearer and more useful to the wide range of decision makers, **subclassifications** of the economic information presented are included on the financial statements. Standard subclassifications have evolved; however, they have some acceptable variations, and changes are sometimes made (especially by the FASB). Throughout this textbook the subclassifications given in the next few paragraphs will usually be used.

For continuing reference as you study the remaining chapters, the typical subclassifications on each of the three required financial statements are outlined on the next few pages. Following each outline some of the major distinctions are briefly discussed. Future chapters will discuss these subclassifications in more detail.

EXHIBIT 3–6

Income statement and balance sheet, Bass Cleaners, Inc.

BASS CLEANERS, INC.
Income Statement
For the Year Ended December 31, 19A

Cleaning revenues		$44,000
Expenses:		
Operating expenses	$29,400	
Interest expense	600	
Total expenses		30,000
Net income		$14,000

Earnings per share (EPS), $14,000 ÷ 800 shares = $17.50

BASS CLEANERS, INC.
Balance Sheet
At December 31, 19A

Assets

Cash		$29,300
Accounts receivable		3,000
Delivery truck	$ 8,000	
Less: Accumulated depreciation	1,600	6,400
Total assets		$38,700

Liabilities

Accounts payable		$ 1,500
Notes payable		5,000
Total liabilities		$ 6,500

Stockholders' Equity

Contributed capital:		
Capital stock, par, $25 (800 shares)	$20,000	
Retained earnings ($14,000 − $1,800)	12,200	
Total stockholders' equity		32,200
Total liabilities and stockholders' equity		$38,700

Subclassifications on the Income Statement

An income (or earnings) statement is subclassified as follows:

A. **Revenues**
   By type:
     Sales
     Services

B. **Expenses**
>   By kind:
>>   Cost of goods sold (an expense)
>>   Operating expenses
>>   Administrative expenses
>>   Financial expenses
>>   Income tax expense

C. **Income before extraordinary items (A − B)**

D. **Extraordinary items (unusual and nonrecurring)**
>   Gains and losses

E. **Net income (C − D)**

F. **Earnings per share (EPS)**

Cost of goods sold is an expense incurred when goods or merchandise is sold. The goods or merchandise had to be purchased before they were sold. The amount paid to the supplier for the items sold is called cost of goods sold. Assume goods purchased for resale cost $40,000. If three fourths of these goods are sold for $50,000, the effect can be shown on an income statement as:

Sales revenue	$50,000
Less: Cost of goods sold ($40,000 × 3/4)	30,000
Gross margin on sales	20,000
Operating expenses:	
Etc.	

Extraordinary items are gains and losses that are (*a*) unusual in nature and (*b*) infrequent in occurrence. These items must be separately reported on the income statement. Since they seldom occur, separate reporting informs decision makers that they are not likely to recur.

Income tax expense is incurred by a corporation but not by a sole proprietorship or partnership.[4] Income taxes are payable each year (partially in advance on quarterly estimates). A corporation must report income tax expense on its income statement separately for operations and extraordinary items. Assume XT Corporation computed **pretax** amounts as follows: income from operations, $80,000; and an extraordinary gain, $10,000. If the income tax rate is 30%, the income statement would show the following:

Pretax income from operations		$80,000
Less: Income tax ($80,000 × 30%)		24,000
Income before extraordinary items		56,000
Extraordinary gain	$10,000	
Less: Income tax ($10,000 × 30%)	3,000	7,000
Net income		$63,000

---

[4] The earnings of a sole proprietorship and a partnership must be reported on the **personal** income tax returns of the owners. Under specified conditions a closely held corporation can avoid corporate income tax as a "Subchapter S corporation."

Earnings per share relates only to the common stock of a corporation. It is computed by dividing income by the average number of common shares outstanding during the reporting period. If an extraordinary gain or loss is reported, these earnings per share amounts must be reported. Assume ART Corporation reported the following **aftertax** amounts on its income statement:

Income before extraordinary items	$100,000
Less: Extraordinary loss	20,000
Net income	$ 80,000

If 40,000 shares of common stock are outstanding, EPS would be reported as follows:

Income before extraordinary items	($100,000 ÷ 40,000 shares) =	$2.50
Extraordinary loss	($20,000 ÷ 40,000 shares) =	(0.50)
Net income	($80,000 ÷ 40,000 shares) =	$2.00

Subclassifications on the Balance Sheet

Typically a balance sheet (or statement of financial position) is subclassified as follows:

A. **Assets (by order of liquidity):***
   (1) Current assets (short term)
   (2) Long-term investments and funds
   (3) Operational assets (property, plant, and equipment)
   (4) Intangible assets
   (5) Deferred charges
   (6) Other (miscellaneous) assets
      Total assets

B. **Liabilities (by order of time to maturity):**
   (1) Current liabilities (short term)
   (2) Long-term liabilities
      Total liabilities

C. **Owners' equity (by source):**
   (1) Contributed capital (by owners)
   (2) Retained earnings (accumulated earnings minus accumulated dividends declared)
   (3) Unrealized capital

Current assets are resources owned by the entity that are reasonably expected to be realized in cash or used up within one year from the balance sheet date or during the normal operating cycle of the business, whichever is longer. The **normal operating cycle** for a merchandising company may be shown graphically as in Exhibit 3–7.

---

* Liquidity refers to the average period of time required to convert a noncash asset to cash.

EXHIBIT 3–7

Typical operating cycle of a business

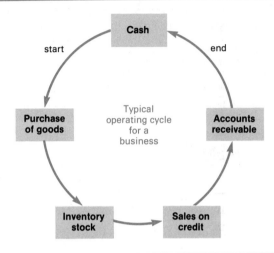

The usual current assets are cash, short-term investments, accounts receivable and other short-term receivables, inventory, and prepaid expenses (i.e., expenses paid in advance of usage).

Current liabilities are those short-term debts at the balance sheet date that are expected to be paid out of the current assets listed on the same balance sheet. Short-term liabilities are expected to be paid during the coming year or the normal operating cycle of the business, whichever is longer. Current liabilities include accounts payable, short-term notes payable, wages payable, income tax payable, and other expenses incurred (used) but not yet paid.

The difference between total current assets and total current liabilities is called **working capital.** It is a widely used measure of a company's liquidity.

Operational assets are often called property, plant, and equipment or fixed assets. This group includes those assets that have physical substance (i.e., they are tangible) and were acquired for use in **operating the business** rather than for resale as inventory items or held as investments. The assets included are buildings owned; land on which the buildings reside; and equipment, tools, furniture, and fixtures used in operating the business. Operational assets, with the exception of land, are depreciated as they are used (i.e., worn out). Because their usefulness decreases as they are used, their initial cost is apportioned to expense over their estimated useful lives. This apportionment of cost over useful life is called **depreciation.** Land is not depreciated because it does not wear out like machinery, buildings, and equipment. The amount of depreciation computed for **each period** is reported on the income statement as depreciation **expense.** The **accumulated** amount of depreciation expense for all past periods from acquisition date is **deducted** (as a contra amount) on the balance sheet from the initial cost of the asset to derive **"book or carrying value"** at the balance sheet date. To illustrate, Bass Cleaners purchased a delivery truck for $8,000. It had an estimated useful life of five years. Therefore, depreciation expense was computed as $8,000 ÷ 5 years = $1,600 depreciation expense per year. The five balance sheets developed during the five-year period would report the following:

	19A	19B	19C	19D	19E
Delivery truck	$8,000	$8,000	$8,000	$8,000	$8,000
Less: Accumulated depreciation	1,600	3,200	4,800	6,400	8,000
Book or carrying value	$6,400	$4,800	$3,200	$1,600	$ –0–

Intangible assets have no **physical existence** and have a long life. Their value is derived from the **rights and privileges** that accompany ownership. Examples are patents, trademarks, copyrights, franchises, and goodwill. Intangible assets usually are not acquired for resale but rather are directly related to the operations of the business.

Owners' equity, called stockholders' equity for a corporation, represents the residual claim of the owners (i.e., A − L = OE). This claim results from the initial contributions of the stockholders (contributed capital) plus retained earnings, which is the accumulated earnings of the company less the accumulated dividends declared. Thus, retained earnings represents the amount of earnings that have been left in the company for growth. Typically long-time successful companies have grown more from retained earnings than from additional contributions by investors for capital stock.

Capital stock usually has a par value which is a legal amount per share. It has little or no relationship to the **market price** of the shares. When a corporation issues capital stock above the par value, the excess must be recorded in a separate account. Assume a corporation issued 6,000 shares of its capital stock, par $10 per share, for $80,000 cash. The required journal entry would be:

Cash	80,000	
Capital stock (6,000 shares × par $10)		60,000
Contributed capital in excess of par ($80,000 − $60,000)		20,000

This topic will be discussed in detail in Chapter 12.

Subclassifications on the Statement of Changes in Financial Position (SCFP)

A SCFP, cash basis, is subclassified as follows:

A. **Sources of cash:**
   (1) From continuing (or primary) operations
   (2) From extraordinary items
   (3) From other sources
        Total cash sources (inflows)

B. **Uses of cash:**
   (1) To purchase long-term assets
   (2) To pay liabilities
   (3) To pay dividends
   (4) Other (miscellaneous) payments
        Total cash uses (outflows)

C. **Net change in cash during the period (increase or decrease)**
D. **Direct exchanges (noncash trades)**

The SCFP will be discussed in Chapter 15. The preceding summaries of each financial statement were given to (*a*) provide an overview of financial statements and (*b*) use as a reference when you study the subsequent chapters.

DEMONSTRATION CASE—THE ACCOUNTING INFORMATION PROCESSING CYCLE

We chose the case of a small business to show an actual **accounting information processing cycle** from the capture of the raw economic data during the reporting period to the financial statements prepared at the end of the accounting year. Only representative and summary transactions are used to simplify the illustration. You should study each step in the solution carefully because it reviews the discussion in Chapters 1, 2, and 3.

On January 3, 19A, M. Hall and P. Garza organized a corporation, La Paloma Apartments, to build and operate apartment complexes. At the start, each one invested $40,000 cash and in turn received 3,000 shares of $10 par value capital stock. On that date the following entry was recorded in the journal:

January 3, 19A:

Cash 80,000		
Capital stock, par $10 (6,000 shares)	60,000	
Contributed capital in excess of par	20,000	

Then land was acquired for $30,000 cash, and a construction contract was signed with a builder. The first apartments were rented on July 1, 19B. The owners decided to use an **accounting year** of July 1 through June 30 for business purposes (instead of a period that agrees with the calendar year).

It is now July 1, 19C, the beginning of the second year of rental operations; therefore, certain **accounts in the ledger** have balances carried over from the

---

EXHIBIT 3–8

Trial balance and transactions for demonstration case

LA PALOMA APARTMENTS
Ledger Balances
July 1, 19C (start of Year 2 of rental operations)

Account No.	Account titles	Balance Debit	Balance Credit
101	Cash	$ 18,000	
103	Accounts receivable (or rent receivable)		
105	Supplies inventory	2,000	
112	Prepaid insurance		
121	Land (apartment site)	30,000	
122	La Paloma apartment building	200,000	
123	Accumulated depreciation, apartment building		$ 10,000
125	Furniture and fixtures	60,000	
126	Accumulated depreciation, furniture and fixtures		12,000
131	Land for future apartment site		
201	Accounts payable		6,000
202	Property taxes payable		
203	Income taxes payable		
204	Mortgage payable, 10% (apartment building)		180,000
205	Note payable, long term, 12%		
301	Capital stock (par $10, 6,000 shares)		60,000
302	Contributed capital in excess of par		20,000
303	Retained earnings (accumulated earnings to June 30, 19C)		22,000
401	Rent revenue		
521	Utilities and telephone expense		
522	Apartment maintenance expense		
523	Salary and wage expense		
524	Insurance expense		
525	Property tax expense		
526	Depreciation expense		
527	Miscellaneous expenses		
531	Interest expense		
532	Income tax expense		
	Totals	$310,000	$310,000

(Assets, $288,000 = Liabilities, $186,000 + Stockholders' Equity, $102,000)

prior accounting year ended June 30, 19C. A complete list of the accounts in the ledger that will be needed for this case, their folio numbers, and the balances carried over from the previous year is given in Exhibit 3–8. **Typical transactions** (summarized) for the 12-month accounting year—July 1, 19C, through June 30, 19D—are also given in Exhibit 3–8. Instead of using dates, we will use the letter notation to the left of each transaction.

EXHIBIT 3–8 *(concluded)*

Trial balance and transactions for demonstration case

Transactions, July 1, 19C, through June 30, 19D:

Date   *Description*

a. On November 1, 19C, paid $3,000 cash for a two-year casualty insurance policy covering the building, its contents, and liability coverage.

b. Rental revenue earned: collected in cash, $105,500; and uncollected by June 30, 19D, $2,000.

c. Paid accounts payable (amount owed from the prior year for expenses), $6,000.

d. Bought a tract of land, at $35,000, as a planned site for another apartment complex to be built in "about three years." Cash of $5,000 was paid, and a long-term note payable (12% interest per annum, interest payable each six months) was signed for the balance of $30,000.

e. Operating expenses incurred and paid in cash were:

Utilities and telephone expense	$23,360
Apartment maintenance expense	1,200
Salary and wage expense	6,000

f. At the end of the accounting year (June 30, 19D), the following bills for expenses incurred had not been recorded or paid: June telephone bill, $40; and miscellaneous expense, $100.

g. Paid interest for six months on the long-term note at 12% per annum. (Refer to item [d].) (Hint: Interest = Principal × Rate × Time.)

h. An inventory count at the end of the accounting period, June 30, 19D, showed remaining supplies on hand amounting to $400. Supplies used are considered a miscellaneous expense.

i. By the end of the accounting period, June 30, 19D, one third (8 months out of 24 months) of the prepaid insurance premium of $3,000 paid in transaction (a) had expired because of passage of time.

j. Depreciation expense for the year was based on an estimated useful life of 20 years for the apartment and 5 years for the furniture and fixtures (assume no residual or salvage value).

k. The property taxes for the year ending June 30, 19D, in the amount of $2,700 have not been recorded or paid.

l. Cash payment at year-end on the mortgage on the apartment was:

On principal	$20,000
Interest ($180,000 × 10%)	18,000
Total paid	$38,000

m. Income tax expense for the year ending June 30, 19D, was $5,940 (i.e., a 20% average rate). This obligation will be paid in the next period.

Required:

Complete the accounting information processing cycle by doing each of the following:

1. **Set up a ledger** with T-accounts that has all of the accounts listed on the trial balance given in Exhibit 3–8; include the account numbers as given. Enter the July 1, 19C, balances in each account in this manner:

	Cash	101
Balance	18,000	

2. **Analyze,** then **journalize** (i.e., enter in the journal), each transaction listed above for the accounting period July 1, 19C, through June 30, 19D. Number the journal pages consecutively starting with 1.
3. **Post all entries** from the journal to the ledger; use the folio columns for account numbers.
4. **Prepare a trial balance** at June 30, 19D.
5. **Prepare an income statement** for the reporting year ending June 30, 19D. Use the following subclassifications:

> Revenue
> Operating expenses:
>   Total operating expenses
> Income from apartment operations
> Financial expense
> Pretax income
>   Income tax expense
> Net income
> EPS

6. **Prepare a balance sheet** at June 30, 19D. Use the following subclassifications:

> **Assets**
> Current assets
> Operational assets
> Other assets
>
> **Liabilities**
> Current liabilities
> Long-term liabilities
>
> **Stockholders' Equity**
> Contributed capital
> Retained earnings

Suggested Solution:

Requirement 1—Ledger (see pages 118 and 119):

Requirement 2—Journal (Note: Be sure you understand all of these entries):

JOURNAL   Page <u>1</u>

Date	Account Titles and Explanation	Folio	Debit	Credit
a.	Prepaid insurance	112	3,000	
	Cash	101		3,000
	Paid insurance premium for two years in advance.			
	(Explanatory note: An asset account, Prepaid Insurance, is debited because a future service, insurance coverage, is being paid for in advance.)			
b.	Cash	101	105,500	
	Accounts receivable (or rent receivable)	103	2,000	
	Rent revenue	401		107,500
	To record rent revenues earned for the year, of which $2,000 has not yet been collected.			
c.	Accounts payable	201	6,000	
	Cash	101		6,000
	Paid a debt carried over from previous year.			
d.	Land for future apartment site	131	35,000	
	Cash	101		5,000
	Note payable, long term (12%)	205		30,000
	Bought land as a site for future apartment complex. (This is a second tract of land acquired; the present apartment building was built on the first tract.)			
e.	Utilities and telephone expense	521	23,360	
	Apartment maintenance expense	522	1,200	
	Salary and wage expense	523	6,000	
	Cash	101		30,560
	Paid current expenses.			
f.	Utilities and telephone expense	521	40	
	Miscellaneous expenses	527	100	
	Accounts payable	201		140
	Expenses incurred, not yet paid.			
g.	Interest expense	531	1,800	
	Cash	101		1,800
	Paid six months' interest on a long-term note ($30,000 × 12% × 6/12 = $1,800).			

Requirement 2 (continued)

JOURNAL   Page 2

Date	Account Titles and Explanation	Folio	Debit	Credit
h.	Miscellaneous expenses Supplies inventory	527 105	1,600	1,600
	To record as expense supplies used from inventory during the year.			
	(Explanatory note: Supplies are bought in advance of use. Therefore, at that time they are recorded as an asset, Supplies Inventory. As the supplies are used from inventory, the asset thus used becomes an expense. Refer to Supplies Inventory account [$2,000 − $400 = $1,600].)			
i.	Insurance expense Prepaid insurance	524 112	1,000	1,000
	To record as an expense the cost of the insurance that expired ($3,000 × 8/24 = $1,000).			

j.	Depreciation expense
	    Accumulated depreciation, apartment building
	    Accumulated depreciation, furniture and fixtures
		526
		
		123
		
		126
			22,000	
				
				10,000
				
				12,000

	Depreciation expense for one year. Computation: Apartment: $200,000 ÷ 20 years = $10,000. Furniture and fixtures: $60,000 ÷ 5 years = $12,000.			
k.	Property tax expense Property taxes payable	525 202	2,700	2,700
	Property taxes for the current year, not yet paid.			
l.	Mortgage payable Interest expense Cash	204 531 101	20,000 18,000	38,000
	Payments on principal of mortgage payable plus interest expense ($180,000 × 10%).			
m.	Income tax expense Income tax payable	532 203	5,940	5,940
	Income tax for the year; payable later.			

Requirements 1 and 3—ledger:

LEDGER

Cash — 101

Date	F	Amount	Date	F	Amount
Balance		18,000	(a)	1	3,000
(b)	1	105,500	(c)	1	6,000
			(d)	1	5,000
			(e)	1	30,560
			(g)	1	1,800
			(l)	2	38,000

(Net debit balance, $39,140)

Accounts Receivable — 103

Date	F	Amount	Date	F	Amount
(b)	1	2,000			

Supplies Inventory — 105

Date	F	Amount	Date	F	Amount
Balance		2,000	(h)	2	1,600

Prepaid Insurance — 112

Date	F	Amount	Date	F	Amount
(a)	1	3,000	(i)	2	1,000

Land (Apartment Site) — 121

Date	F	Amount	Date	F	Amount
Balance		30,000			

La Paloma Apartment Building — 122

Date	F	Amount	Date	F	Amount
Balance		200,000			

Accumulated Depreciation, Apartment Building — 123

Date	F	Amount	Date	F	Amount
			Balance		10,000
			(j)	2	10,000

Furniture and Fixtures — 125

Date	F	Amount	Date	F	Amount
Balance		60,000			

Accumulated Depreciation, Furniture and Fixtures — 126

Date	F	Amount	Date	F	Amount
			Balance		12,000
			(j)	2	12,000

Land for Future Apartment Site — 131

Date	F	Amount	Date	F	Amount
(d)	1	35,000			

Accounts Payable — 201

Date	F	Amount	Date	F	Amount
(c)	1	6,000	Balance		6,000
			(f)	1	140

Property Taxes Payable — 202

Date	F	Amount	Date	F	Amount
			(k)	2	2,700

Income Taxes Payable — 203

Date	F	Amount	Date	F	Amount
			(m)	2	5,940

Mortgage Payable (10%) (apartment building) — 204

Date	F	Amount	Date	F	Amount
(l)	2	20,000	Balance		180,000

Requirements 1 and 3 (continued)

Notes Payable, Long Term (12%)						205
Date	F	Amount	Date	F	Amount	
			(d)	1	30,000	

Capital Stock				301
		Balance	60,000	

Contributed Capital in Excess of Par				302
		Balance	20,000	

Retained Earnings				303
		Balance	22,000	

Rent Revenue				401
		(b)	1	107,500

Utilities and Telephone Expense			521
(e)	1	23,360	
(f)	1	40	

Apartment Maintenance Expense			522
(e)	1	1,200	

Salary and Wage Expense			523
(e)	1	6,000	

Insurance Expense						524
Date	F	Amount	Date	F	Amount	
(i)	2	1,000				

Property Tax Expense			525
(k)	2	2,700	

Depreciation Expense			526
(j)	2	22,000	

Miscellaneous Expenses			527
(f)	1	100	
(h)	2	1,600	

Interest Expense			531
(g)	1	1,800	
(l)	2	18,000	

Income Tax Expense			532
(m)	2	5,940	

Requirement 4:

LA PALOMA APARTMENTS
Trial Balance
June 30, 19D

Account No.	Account titles	Balance Debit	Balance Credit
101	Cash	$ 39,140	
103	Accounts receivable (or Rent receivable)	2,000	
105	Supplies inventory	400	
112	Prepaid insurance (16 months)	2,000	
121	Land (apartment site)	30,000	
122	La Paloma apartment building	200,000	
123	Accumulated depreciation, apartment building		$ 20,000
125	Furniture and fixtures	60,000	
126	Accumulated depreciation, furniture and fixtures		24,000
131	Land for future apartment site	35,000	
201	Accounts payable		140
202	Property taxes payable		2,700
203	Income taxes payable		5,940
204	Mortgage payable (10%) (apartment building)		160,000
205	Note payable, long term (12%)		30,000
301	Capital stock (par $10, 6,000 shares)		60,000
302	Contributed capital in excess of par		20,000
303	Retained earnings (accumulated earnings to June 30, 19C)		22,000
401	Rent revenue		107,500
521	Utilities and telephone expense	23,400	
522	Apartment maintenance expense	1,200	
523	Salary and wage expense	6,000	
524	Insurance expense	1,000	
525	Property tax expense	2,700	
526	Depreciation expense	22,000	
527	Miscellaneous expenses	1,700	
531	Interest expense	19,800	
532	Income tax expense	5,940	
	Totals	$452,280	$452,280

Requirement 5:

LA PALOMA APARTMENTS
Income Statement
For the Year Ended June 30, 19D

Revenue:		
Rent revenue		$107,500*
Operating expenses:		
Utilities and telephone expense	$23,400	
Apartment maintenance expense	1,200	
Salary and wage expense	6,000	
Insurance expense	1,000	
Property tax expense	2,700	
Depreciation expense	22,000	
Miscellaneous expenses	1,700	
Total operating expenses		58,000
Income from apartment operations		49,500
Finance expense:		
Interest expense		19,800
Pretax income		29,700
Income tax expense		5,940
Net income		$ 23,760
EPS ($23,760 ÷ 6,000 shares)		$3.96

* Notes:
a. These amounts were taken directly from Requirement 4, the trial balance.
b. No products are sold by this business; therefore, gross margin cannot be reported.

Requirement 6:

LA PALOMA APARTMENTS
Balance Sheet
At June 30, 19D

Assets

Current assets:			
Cash		$ 39,140*	
Accounts receivable		2,000	
Supplies inventory		400	
Prepaid insurance		2,000	
Total current assets			$ 43,540
Operational assets:			
Land (apartment site)		30,000	
La Paloma apartment building	$200,000		
Less: Accumulated depreciation, building	20,000	180,000	
Furniture and fixtures	60,000		
Less: Accumulated depreciation, furniture and fixtures	24,000	36,000	
Total operational assets			246,000
Other assets:			
Land acquired for future apartment site†			35,000
Total assets			$324,540

* These amounts were taken directly from Requirement 4, the trial balance.
† Classified as "other" rather than "operational" because this land is not being used currently for operating purposes.

Liabilities

Current liabilities:		
Accounts payable	$ 140	
Property taxes payable	2,700	
Income taxes payable	5,940	
Total current liabilities		$ 8,780
Long-term liabilities:		
Mortgage payable	160,000	
Note payable, long term	30,000	
Total long-term liabilities		190,000
Total liabilities		198,780

Stockholders' Equity

Contributed capital:		
Capital stock, par $10 (6,000) shares	60,000	
Contributed capital in excess of par	20,000	
Total contributed capital		80,000
Retained earnings (beginning balance, $22,000 +		
net income, $23,760)		45,760
Total stockholders' equity		125,760
Total liabilities and stockholders' equity		$324,540

SUMMARY OF CHAPTER

An accounting system is designed to collect, process, and report financial information about an entity. During each period, an **accounting information processing cycle** starts with data collection and ends with the periodic financial statements. The phases of this sequential cycle are summarized in Exhibit 3–9. Let's briefly review the essence of this accounting cycle.

The fundamental accounting model—Assets = Liabilities + Owners' Equity —gives the basic framework for transaction analysis and recording the dual effect of each transaction. The accounting model has two balancing features that must be met for each transaction and event recorded: (1) assets must equal liabilities plus owners' equity and (2) debits must equal credits. After transaction analysis, the dual effects of each transaction are recorded first in the journal and then are posted to the ledger. The journal provides a chronological record of the transactions, and the ledger reflects a **separate account** for each kind of asset, liability, and owners' equity. Normally, asset accounts will have debit balances, whereas liability accounts will have credit balances. Owners' equity accounts normally will show credits for the capital stock and retained earnings accounts— expenses will show debit balances, and revenues will show credit balances. The accounting information processing cycle accumulates the financial data needed to develop the periodic financial statements: the income statement, balance sheet, and statement of changes in financial position (SCFP).

The chapter also gave an outline of the subclassifications on the required financial statements—income statement, balance sheet, and statement of changes in financial position.

EXHIBIT 3–9

Sequential phases of an accounting information processing cycle summarized*

ACTIVITY	FLOW OF DATA

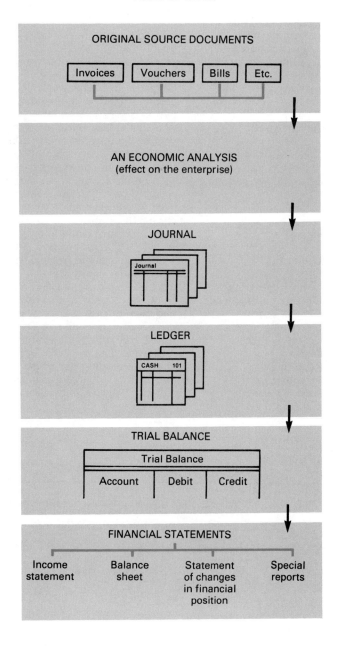

(1) COLLECT RAW DATA

(capture the economic data about each **transaction**)

ORIGINAL SOURCE DOCUMENTS

Invoices | Vouchers | Bills | Etc.

(2) ANALYZE EACH TRANSACTION

(determine economic effects of each transaction on the entity)

AN ECONOMIC ANALYSIS
(effect on the enterprise)

(3) JOURNALIZE

(record the economic effects of each transaction on the accounting model in chronological order)

JOURNAL

Journal

(4) POST TO THE LEDGER

(accumulate each asset, liability, and owners' equity in separate accounts)

LEDGER

CASH 101

(5) DEVELOP A TRIAL BALANCE

(list of account balances to facilitate preparation of financial reports)

TRIAL BALANCE

Trial Balance

Account | Debit | Credit

(6) PREPARE FINANCIAL STATEMENTS

(To help decision makers make better decisions.)

FINANCIAL STATEMENTS

Income statement | Balance sheet | Statement of changes in financial position | Special reports

* This cycle will be expanded in Chapter 5.

IMPORTANT TERMS DEFINED IN THIS CHAPTER

Terms (alphabetically)	Key words in definitions of important terms used in chapter	Page reference
Accounting information processing cycle	Sequential accounting phases used to process data from initial transaction to financial statements	98
Accounting (or reporting) period	Time period; usually one year; the period covered by the financial statements	98
Accounting system	Designed to collect, process, and report financial information about an entity	98
Cost of goods sold	An expense that represents the cost of purchasing goods and merchandise that were sold during the accounting period	108
Current assets	Assets that are expected to be converted to cash within one year or the operating cycle if longer	109
Current liabilities	Liabilities that will be paid by using current assets within one year or the operating cycle if longer	110
Extraordinary gain or loss	A gain or loss that is unusual and infrequent; separately reported on the income statement	108
Journalizing	Recording transactions in the journal; original entry; chronological order	101
Journal entry	An original entry made in the journal in terms of: $A = L + OE$, and Debits = Credits	101
Ledger	Contains all of the individual accounts for assets, liabilities, and owners' equity	101
Normal operating cycle of a business	Used to define current assets and current liabilities; the time from cash to purchase of inventories; to sale on credit, and back to cash.	109
Operational assets	Assets used to operate a business; not for resale; often called property, plant, and equipment	110
Posting	Transferring data from the journal to the ledger	102
Reporting period	Same as accounting period (see above)	98
Trial balance	A list of all of the accounts in the ledger and their balances	105
Working capital	Difference between total current assets and total current liabilities	110

QUESTIONS

1. What is the function of an accounting system?

2. Explain the accounting information processing cycle.

3. How does a company collect the data needed for accounting purposes?

4. What is meant by transaction analysis?

5. Explain the meaning of "to debit" and "to credit."

6. Define the following terms: (a) accounting period and (b) reporting period.

7. What is the (a) book of original entry and (b) book of final entry?

8. Define the journal. What is its purpose?

9. Define the ledger. What is its purpose?

10. Explain the difference between journalizing and posting.

11. What is the purpose of the folio notations in the journal and in the ledger accounts?

12. What is a trial balance? What is its purpose?

13. What is an audit trail?

14. What is the primary purpose of subclassification of the information presented on financial statements?

15. What are the six major classifications on the income statement?

16. Define extraordinary items. Why should they be reported separately on the income statement?

17. List the six subclassifications of assets reported on a balance sheet.

18. Briefly define (a) current assets, (b) current liabilities, and (c) working capital.

19. What is a prepaid expense?

20. For operational assets, as reported on the balance sheet, explain (a) cost, (b) accumulated depreciation, (c) book value, and (d) carrying value.

21. What are the subclassifications of liabilities on a balance sheet?

22. Briefly explain the major subclassifications of owners' equity for a corporation.

23. What are the three major subclassifications on a SCFP, cash basis?

EXERCISES

E3–1   (Phases in the Accounting Information Processing Cycle)
Match the following phases with the descriptions of the accounting processing cycle by writing the correct letters in the blanks to the left.

Phases of the accounting information processing cycle (sequential order)	Description of phases
_____ Data collection	A. Income statement, balance sheet, SCFP.
_____ Transaction analysis	B. Transfer of amount for each account affected by the transaction; results in a reclassification of the data.
_____ Journalizing	C. A listing of each account and its debit or credit ending balance; checks Debits = Credits.
_____ Posting	D. Source documents that underlie each transaction.
_____ Trial balance	E. A chronological record is prepared that reflects the economic effects of each transaction.
_____ Financial statements	F. A careful study of each transaction and determination of its economic effects on the entity.

E3–2 **(Overview of the Accounting Information Processing Cycle)**

On January 1, 19A, Joe Hotstrike started the Hotstrike Electric Company (a single-owner business). During 19A, the company completed the following summarized transactions:

a. Cash invested by the owner, $20,000.
b. Service revenues earned, $80,000 (all cash).
c. Operating expenses incurred, $30,000 (all cash).
d. Cash withdrawn from the business by the owner, $4,000 per month for twelve months.

Required:

You are to process these four transactions through the accounting information processing cycle by phases as given below. (Hint: Refer to Exhibit 3–1 and the related discussions.)

Phase 1—Collect information—already done above.

Phase 2—Analysis. Write your analysis of each transaction in terms of Assets = Liabilities + Owner's Equity, and Debits = Credits.

Phase 3—Journalize each transaction.

Phase 4—Post the journal entries to the ledger. Use only the following T-accounts: Cash, Owner's Equity, Hotstrike, Service Revenues, and Operating Expenses.

Phase 5—Prepare a trial balance.

Phase 6—Prepare the following financial statements:
a. Income statement.
b. Balance sheet.

E3–3 **(Write Journal Entries from T-accounts)**

The following T-accounts for Ringer Service Company, Inc., show five different transactions (entries). Prepare a journal entry for each transaction and write a complete description of each one. (Hint: Notice that some transactions have two debits or two credits.)

Cash				Accounts Payable				Capital Stock, Par $10			
(a)	70,000	(c)	9,000	(e)	1,500	(c)	2,000			(a)	70,000
(b)	20,000	(e)	1,500								
(d)	2,000	(f)	5,000								

Accounts Receivable				Note Payable				Service Revenue			
(b)	4,000	(d)	2,000			(f)	15,000			(b)	24,000

Equipment								Operating Expenses			
(f)	20,000							(c)	11,000		

E3–4   (Journalize and Compute Account Balances)

On January 1, 19A, Wilson and Young organized the WY Service Company, Inc. The completed transactions from January 1, 19A, through February 3, 19A, can be summarized as follows:

Jan.   1   Cash invested by the organizers was: Wilson, $30,000 (for 3,000 shares); and Young, $20,000 (for 2,000 shares).

   3   Paid monthly rent, $1,500.

   15   Purchased equipment for use in the business that cost $24,000; paid one third down and signed a 12% note payable for the balance. Monthly payments (24) made up of part principal and part interest are to be paid on the note.

   30   Paid cash for operating expenses amounting to $20,000; in addition, operating expenses of $4,000 were incurred on credit.

   30   Service fees earned amounted to $50,000, of which $40,000 was collected and the balance was on credit.

Feb.   1   Collected $6,000 on account for services performed in January and originally recorded as an account receivable and service revenue.

   2   Paid $3,000 on the operating expenses incurred in January and originally recorded as an account payable and operating expenses.

   15   Paid the first installment of $753 on the equipment note, including $160 interest expense.

Required:

1. Analyze and journalize each of the above transactions (refer to Exhibit 3–2 and the Demonstration Case, Requirement 2).
2. Based on your journal entries only, compute the following:
   a. Cash balance at February 3, 19A.
   b. Pretax income for the period January 1, 19A, through February 3, 19A.

E3–5   (Terminology Related to the Income Statement)

Below are terms related to the income statement. Match the terms with the definitions by writing the correct letter to the left for each term.

Terms	*Brief definition*
__E__ (Example): Cost of goods sold	A. Sales revenue minus cost of goods sold.
____ Interest expense	B. Items that are both unusual and infrequent.
____ Extraordinary items	C. Sales of services for cash or on credit.
____ Service revenue	D. Revenues + Gains − Expenses − Losses (including EO items).
____ Income tax expense on operations	E. Amount of resources used to purchase the goods that were sold during the reporting period.
____ Income before extraordinary items	F. Income tax on revenues minus operating expenses.
____ Net income	G. Time cost of money (borrowing).
____ Gross margin on sales	H. Income divided by shares outstanding.
____ EPS	I. Income before extraordinary items and the related income tax.
____ Operating expenses	J. Total expenses directly related to operations.
____ Pretax income from operations	K. Income before all income tax and before extraordinary items.

E3–6   (Complete a Partial Income Statement with Income Tax and an Extraordinary Loss)
Cotten Corporation (common stock, 10,000 shares outstanding) is preparing the income statement for the year ended December 31, 19D. The pretax operating income was $100,000, and there was a $30,000 pretax loss on earthquake damages to one of the plants properly classified as an extraordinary item. Total tax expense is $28,000 on the basis of a 40% tax rate on operations and on the earthquake loss.

Required:

1. Complete the following income statement:

> (Already completed to here)
> Pretax operating income
> Less: Income tax
> Income before EO items:
>   Extraordinary loss
>   Less: Income tax
> Net income
> Earnings per share

2. Why is the income tax of $28,000 separated into two parts?

E3–7   (Ordering the Classifications on a Typical Balance Sheet)
Following is a list of major classifications and subclassifications on the balance sheet. Number them in the order in which they normally appear on a balance sheet. (Hint: Start with Assets as No. 1.)

No.	Title
_____	Current liabilities
_____	Liabilities
_____	Owners' equity
_____	Long-term liabilities
_____	Long-term investments and funds
_____	Intangible assets
_____	Operational assets (property, plant, and equipment)
_____	Current assets
_____	Retained earnings
_____	Contributed capital
_____	Assets
_____	Other assets
_____	Deferred charges
_____	Unrealized capital

E3–8   (Terminology Related to the Balance Sheet)
Below are terms related to the balance sheet. Match the terms with the definitions by writing the correct letter to the left for each term.

Terms	Definitions
__G__ (Example) Retained earnings	A. A miscellaneous category of assets.
_____ Current liabilities	B. Current assets minus current liabilities.
_____ Liquidity	C. Total assets minus total liabilities.
_____ Contra asset account	D. Nearness of assets to cash (in time).
_____ Accumulated depreciation	E. Assets expected to be realized within one year or operating cycle, if longer.
_____ Intangible assets	F. Same as carrying value; cost less accumulated depreciation to date.
_____ Other assets	
_____ Shares outstanding	

——— Normal operating cycle
——— Book value
——— Working capital
——— Liabilities
——— Operational assets
——— Owners' equity
——— Current assets
——— Assets
——— Long-term liabilities

G. Accumulated earnings minus accumulated dividends.
H. Asset offset account (subtracted from asset).
I. Balance of the capital stock account divided by the par value per share.
J. Assets that do not have physical substance.
K. Items owned by the business that have future economic values.
L. Liabilities expected to be paid out of current assets within the next year or operating cycle, if longer.
M. The average cash-to-cash time involved in the operations of the business.
N. Sum of the annual depreciation expense on an asset from its acquisition to the current date.
O. All liabilities not classified as current liabilities.
P. Property, plant, and equipment.
Q. Obligations to give up (pay) economic benefits in the future.

E3–9   **(Classification of Investments in Common Stock on the Investor's Balance Sheet)**
Tucker Manufacturing Corporation is preparing its annual financial statements at December 31, 19B. The company has two investments in shares of other corporations:

a. Common stock of X Corporation: 1,000 shares purchased for $80,000 during 19A. X Corporation is a supplier of parts to Tucker Corporation; therefore, the latter "intends to hold the stock indefinitely." The shares acquired represented 2% of the shares outstanding. X stock was selling at $95 at the end of 19B.

b. Common stock of Y Corporation: purchased 500 shares at a cost of $60 per share on August 15, 19B. Tucker made this investment to "temporarily use some idle cash that probably will be needed next year." Y stock was selling at $70 at the end of 19B.

Required:

Illustrate and explain the basis for the classification and amount that should be reported for each investment on the 19B balance sheet of Tucker Corporation.

E3–10   **(Prepare a Simple SCFP, Cash Basis)**
At the end of the annual reporting period, December 31, 19B, the records of BT Company showed the following:

a. Cash account: beginning balance, $36,000; ending balance, $22,000.
b. From the income statement:
   (1) Cash revenues $180,000
   (2) Cash expenses   135,000
c. From the balance sheet:
   (1) Additional capital stock sold: common stock, par $10; sold 2,000 shares at $15 per share.
   (2) Borrowed cash on a long-term note, $25,000.
   (3) Purchased equipment for use in the business, $110,000; paid cash, $75,000; balance on credit.
   (4) Paid a long-term note, $25,000.
   (5) Declared and paid a cash dividend, $14,000.

Required:

1. Prepare the 19B statement of changes in financial position for BT Company. Use the following captions: Sources of cash, Uses of cash, Net increase (decrease) in cash during 19B.
2. Prove your answer.

PROBLEMS

P3–1   **(Journalize, Post, and Compute Account Balances)**

Kool Air Conditioning Service Company, Incorporated, has been operating for three years. I. M. Kool, the majority stockholder, built it from a one-person organization to an operation requiring 10 employees. In the past, few records were kept; however, Kool now realizes the need for a complete accounting system. The size and complexity of the business is partially indicated by the following selected transactions completed during January 19E:

Jan.   1   Purchased three new service trucks at $12,000 each; paid a third down and signed a 12% one-year, interest-bearing note for the balance. Twelve monthly payments, each including principal and interest, are to be made on the note.

31   Service revenue earned in January amounted to $85,000, which included $5,000 on credit (due in 90 days).

31   Operating expenses incurred in January amounted to $60,000, which included $4,000 on credit (payable in 60 days).

31   Dividends declared and paid of $2,000; in cash to the stockholders.

31   Paid $2,132 on the truck note, which included $240 interest.

31   Paid 19D taxes on business property, $150; this amount was recorded in 19D as a liability (property taxes payable) and as an expense.

31   Collected $4,400 on the services extended on credit in January.

Required:

1. Analyze and journalize each of the above transactions. Number the first journal page, 51; etc. (Hint: Refer to the Demonstration Case, Requirement 2.)
2. Post the journal entries to the following T-accounts. Use folio numbers.

Account No.	Account titles	Balance, January 1, 19E
101	Cash	$40,000 (debit)
102	Accounts receivable	20,000 (debit)
103	Trucks	None
104	Accounts payable	9,000 (credit)
105	Notes payable	None
106	Property taxes payable	150 (credit)
107	Retained earnings	80,000 (credit)
108	Service revenues	None
109	Operating expenses	None
110	Interest expense	None

Remaining accounts—not needed.

3. Compute the following amounts based on the above data only:
   a. Cash balance at the end of January 19E.
   b. Pretax income for the month of January 19E.

P3–2   **(Complete Phase 2, Transaction Analysis, and Phase 3, Journalize)**

Fast Stenographic and Mailing Service, Incorporated, was organized by three persons during January 19A. Each investor paid $11,000 cash, and each received 1,000 shares of

$10 par value stock. During 19A, the transactions listed below occurred (Phase 1). The letters at the left of each item will serve as the date notation.

a. Received the $33,000 investment of cash by the organizers and issued the shares.
b. Purchased office equipment which cost $6,000; paid cash.
c. Paid $400 cash for a two-year insurance policy on the office equipment for 19A and 19B (debit the asset account, Prepaid Insurance, because the premium is paid in advance on this date).
d. Purchased a delivery truck at a cost of $12,000; paid $7,000 down and signed a $5,000, 90-day, 12%, interest-bearing note payable for the balance.
e. Purchased office supplies for cash to be used in the stenographic and mailing operations, $2,000. The supplies are for future use (therefore, debit the asset account, Office Supplies Inventory—an asset account because they have not yet been used).
f. Revenues earned during the year were:

	Cash	On credit
Stenographic fees	$55,000	$6,000
Mailing fees	8,000	2,000

g. Operating expenses incurred during the year were (excluding transactions [h] through [l]):

Cash	$26,000
On credit	14,000

h. Paid the $5,000 note on the panel truck. Cash paid out was for the $5,000 principal plus the interest for three months.
i. Purchased land for a future building site at a cost of $20,000; paid cash.
j. Depreciation on the truck for 19A was computed on the basis of a 5-year useful life; on the office equipment, a useful life of 10 years was assumed (compute full-year depreciation on each and assume no residual value).
k. By December 31, 19A, insurance for one year had expired. Prepaid Insurance should be decreased and an expense recorded because half of the insurance was "used" during 19A.
l. An inventory of the office supplies reflected $300 on hand at December 31, 19A. Supplies Inventory should be reduced and an expense recognized because some, but not all, of the supplies were used in 19A.
m. Income tax expense, based on a 20% rate, was $5,190 (to be paid in 19B).

Required:

1. Analyze and journalize each of the above transactions. Use journal format illustrated in Exhibit 3–2. Write a brief explanation after each journal entry.
2. What was the balance in the cash account at the end of 19A?

P3–3   **(Complete an Income Statement with Income Tax, Extraordinary Loss, and EPS)**
Bill and Marcie Day organized the Day Hardware Company, Inc., on January 1, 19A. On that date, 20,000 shares of common stock were issued to three owners (Bill, Marcie, and a relative) for $100,000 cash.
At the end of the first year, December 31, 19A, the records kept by Marcie showed the following:

a. Merchandise sold: for cash, $200,000; on credit, $20,000.
b. Interest on debt; paid in cash, $2,000.
c. Salaries and wages paid in cash, $53,000.
d. Other operating expenses, $5,000, incurred (used) but not yet paid.
e. Cost of the merchandise sold, $100,000.
f. Services sold (all for cash), $10,000.
g. Extraordinary (EO) loss, $5,000 (subject to income tax).
h. Average corporate income tax rate on all items, 20%.

Required:

a. Complete the following income statement for the year, 19A:

Revenues
Expenses:
   Cost of goods sold
   Operating expenses
   Interest expense
Pretax income from operations
   Income tax expense
Income before EO item
   EO loss
   Less: Income tax saving
Net income
EPS

b. What was the total amount of income tax for 19A? Explain.
c. Explain why the $100,000 cash paid by the organizers is not considered to be revenue.

P3–4   **(Prepare a Balance Sheet and Analyze Some of Its Parts)**
Ace Jewelers is developing the annual financial statements for 19C. The following amounts were correct at December 31, 19C: cash, $41,200; accounts receivable, $49,000; merchandise inventory, $110,000; prepaid insurance, $600; investment in stock of Z corporation (long term), $31,000; store equipment, $50,000; used store equipment held for disposal, $9,000; allowance for doubtful accounts, $800; accumulated depreciation, store equipment, $10,000; accounts payable, $43,000; long-term notes payable, $40,000; income taxes payable, $7,000; retained earnings, $80,000; and common stock, 100,000 shares outstanding, par $1 per share (originally sold and issued at $1.10 per share).

Required:

1. Based on the above data, prepare a 19C balance sheet. Use the following major captions (list the individual items under these captions):

   Assets: Current assets; long-term investments and funds; operational assets; and other assets.

   Liabilities: Current liabilities; and long-term liabilities.

   Stockholders' equity: Contributed capital; and retained earnings.

   (Hint: The balance sheet total is $280,000.)
2. What is the book or carrying value of the:
   (1) Inventory?
   (2) Accounts receivable?

(3) Store equipment?

(4) Notes payable (long term)?

Explain what these values mean.

3. What is the amount of working capital?

P3–5   (Prepare the Stockholders' Equity Section of a Balance Sheet)

At the end of the 19A annual reporting period, the balance sheet of Avon Corporation showed the following:

AVON CORPORATION
Balance Sheet
At December 31, 19A

Stockholders' Equity

Contributed capital:

Common stock, par $10; 5,000 shares outstanding .... $ 50,000

Contributed capital in excess of par 10,000

    Total contributed capital 60,000

Retained earnings:

Ending balance 40,000

    Total stockholders' equity $100,000

During 19B, the following selected transactions (summarized) were completed:

a. Sold and issued 1,000 shares of the common stock at $16 cash per share (at year-end).

b. Net income, $30,000.

c. Declared and paid a cash dividend on the beginning shares outstanding of $3 per share.

Required:

1. Prepare the stockholders' equity section of the balance sheet at December 31, 19B.

2. Give the journal entry to record the sale and issuance of the 1,000 shares of common stock.

P3–6   (Complete Phase 6, Income Statement and Balance Sheet, from a Trial Balance)

Mission Real Estate Company (organized as a corporation on April 1, 19A) has completed Phase 1 (data collection) Phase 2 (analyses), Phase 3 (journal entries), and Phase 4 (posting) for the second year, ended March 31, 19C. Mission also has completed a correct trial balance (Phase 5) as follows:

MISSION REAL ESTATE COMPANY
Trial Balance
At March 31, 19C

Account titles	Debit	Credit
Cash	$ 41,000	
Accounts receivable	53,800	
Office supplies inventory	200	
Automobiles (company cars)	26,000	
Accumulated depreciation, automobiles		$ 12,000
Office equipment	2,000	
Accumulated depreciation, office equipment		1,000
Accounts payable		12,150
Income tax payable		
Salaries and commissions payable		1,000
Notes payable, long term		20,000
Capital stock (par $1; 30,000 shares)		30,000
Contributed capital in excess of par		5,000
Retained earnings (on April 1, 19B)		7,350
Dividends declared and paid during the current year	10,000	
Sales commissions earned		90,000
Management fees earned		8,000
Operating expenses (detail omitted to conserve your time)	46,000	
Depreciation expense (on autos and including $333 on office equipment)	6,000	
Interest expense	1,500	
Income tax expense (not yet computed)		
Totals	$186,500	$186,500

Required:

1. Complete the financial statements, as follows:
   a. Income statement for the reporting year ended March 31, 19C. Include income tax expense, assuming a 30% tax rate. (Hint: EPS is $1.04.) Use the following major captions: Revenues; Expenses; Pretax income; Income tax; Net income; and EPS (list each item under these captions).
   b. Balance sheet at the end of the reporting year, March 31, 19C. Include (1) income taxes for the current year in income tax payable, and (2) dividends in retained earnings. Use the captions that follow (list each item under these captions). (Hint: Total assets is $110,000.)

   Assets
   Current assets
   Operational assets

   Liabilities
   Current liabilities
   Long-term liabilities

   Stockholders' Equity
   Contributed capital
   Retained earnings

2. Give the journal entry to record income taxes for the year (not yet paid).

P3–7   **(Reporting Building, Land, and Depreciation Expense)**

Tabor Company is preparing the balance sheet at December 31, 19X. The following assets are to be reported:

1. Building, purchased 15 years ago (counting 19X); original cost, $330,000; estimated useful life, 20 years from date of purchase; and no residual value.
2. Land, purchased 15 years ago (counting 19X); original cost, $25,000.

Required:

a. Show how the two assets should be reported on the balance sheet. What is the total book value of these operational assets?
b. What amount of depreciation expense should be reported on the 19X income statement? Show computations.

P3–8   **(Prepare a Simple Statement of Changes in Financial Position, Cash Basis)**

Sweet Bakery is preparing its annual financial statements at December 31, 19X. The income statement and balance sheet are finished. The statement of changes in financial position must be prepared. Therefore, the following cash flow data have been determined to be correct for 19X:

a. Sales and service revenues, $300,000, including $15,000 on credit and not yet collected.
b. Expenses, $256,000, including $6,000 noncash items.
c. Sold Sweet's used delivery truck for $3,000 cash (the gain on the sale was $1,000).
d. Borrowed cash, $20,000 on a three-year note payable (10% interest payable each year-end). The note was dated December 31, 19X.
e. Purchased a new delivery truck for $14,000 cash.
f. Paid a $40,000 long-term note payable.
g. Paid cash dividend of $12,000.
h. Purchased a tract of land for a future building site that cost $24,000. Paid one-third cash and signed a note payable for the balance.
i. Cash account: balance January 1, 19X, $36,000; balance December 31, 19X, $20,000.

Required:

1. Prepare the 19X statement of changes in financial position, cash basis, for Sweet Bakery. Use the following format, with appropriate details under each caption:

Heading
Sources of cash:
   From continuing operations
   From other sources
      Total sources of cash
Uses of cash:
Net increase (decrease) in cash

2. Prove your answer.
3. What was the major *(a)* source of cash and *(b)* use of cash?

P3-9   **(Short Problem; Completion of the First Six Phases of the Accounting Information Process-ing Cycle)**

Super Service Company, Inc., was started on Janury 1, 19A. During the first year ended December 31, 19A (end of the accounting period), the following summarized entries were completed:

Date	Transaction
a.	Issued 20,000 shares of its common stock (par $1 per share) for $60,000 cash.
b.	Purchased equipment for use in operations that cost $40,000 cash. Estimated life, 10 years.
c.	Borrowed $50,000 cash on a long-term note payable (10% interest).
d.	Revenues earned, $100,000, of which $8,000 was on credit (not yet collected at year-end).
e.	Expenses incurred (including interest on the note payable), $60,000, of which $5,000 was on credit (not yet paid at year-end).
f.	Paid cash dividend, $10,000. (Hint: Debit retained earnings.)
g.	Recorded depreciation expense. Assume no income tax.

Required:

Process the above transactions through the accounting information processing cycle by phases as follows:

Phase 1—Collect information about each transaction; already done above.

Phase 2—Analysis; write your analysis of each transaction in terms of: Assets = Liabilities + Stockholders' Equity, and Debits = Credits.

Phase 3—Journalize each transaction. Start your journal with page 1. Use the date letters for identification of transactions.

Phase 4—Post the journal entries to the ledger accounts (as you complete each journal entry or after the last journal entry). Set up the following ledger accounts and account numbers: Cash, 101; Accounts Receivable, 102; Equipment, 105; Accumulated Depreciation, 106; Accounts Payable, 201; Note Payable, Long Term, 205; Common Stock, 301; Contributed Capital in Excess of Par, 302; Retained Earnings, 303; Revenues, 310; and Expenses, 315.

Phase 5—Prepare a trial balance. (Hint: Debit total is $219,000.)

Phase 6—Prepare the following 19A financial statements:

  a. Income statement. (Hint: EPS is $1.80.)
  b. Balance sheet. (Hint: Total assets is $141,000.)

P3-10   **(Comprehensive Problem: Completion of the First Six Phases of the Accounting Informa-tion Cycle)**

Able, Baker, and Cain organized ABC Realty as a corporation to conduct a real estate and rental management business. Each one contributed $20,000 cash and received 1,500 shares of stock (par value $10 per share). They began business on January 1, 19A. The transactions listed below, representative of those during the first year (19A), were selected from the actual transactions.

Assume that these transactions comprise all of the transactions for 19A. All of the accounts needed in the ledger are given below (Phase 1). Use the letters given at the left as the date notation.

  a. Received $60,000 cash invested by stockholders and issued 4,500 shares of stock.
  b. On January 1, 19A, purchased office equipment that cost $6,000; paid one-third cash and charged the balance (one third due in 6 months, and the remaining third is due in 12 months). Credit Accounts Payable for the amount not paid in cash.

c. Purchased land for future office site: cost, $20,000; paid cash.

d. Paid office rent in cash, 12 months at $200 per month (debit Rent Expense).

e. Sold nine properties and collected sales commissions of $56,000.

f. Paid salaries and commissions expense to salespersons amounting to $52,000 and miscellaneous expenses amounting to $1,000.

g. Collected rental management fees, $20,000.

h. Paid utilities, $1,400.

i. Paid auto rental fees (auto rented for use in business), $3,600.

j. Paid for advertising, $7,500.

k. The estimated life of the office equipment was 10 years; assume use for the full year in 19A and no residual value.

l. Additional commissions earned during 19A on sale of real estate amounted to $64,000 of which $14,000 was uncollected at year-end.

m. Paid the installment of $2,000 on the office equipment (see [b] above). Assume no interest.

n. Assume an average income tax rate of 30%; 19A tax expense of $21,450 will be paid in 19B.

Required:

1. Set up T-accounts as follows (no beginning balances because this is the first year):

Account No.	Account titles	Account No.	Account titles
101	Cash	402	Rental management revenue
102	Accounts receivable	501	Rent expense
103	Office equipment	502	Salary and commission expense
104	Accumulated depreciation, office equipment	503	Miscellaneous expense
105	Land for future office site	504	Utilities expense
201	Accounts payable	505	Auto rental expense
203	Income tax payable	506	Advertising expense
301	Capital stock, par $10	507	Depreciation expense
302	Contributed capital in excess of par	508	Income tax expense
401	Realty commission revenue		

2. Complete Phase 2 (analyze) and Phase 3 (journalize) each of the above transactions. Use the journal format shown in Exhibit 3–2. Use the letters for dates. Number the journal pages starting with 1. Write a brief explanation of each entry.

3. Complete Phase 4—Post each transaction from the journal to the ledger. Use folio cross-references when posting. You may post each entry as it is made, or wait until all of the journal entries are made.

4. Complete Phase 5—Prepare a trial balance. (Hint: The trial balance total is $224,050, including cash, $94,100.)

5. Complete Phase 6—Prepare the following 19A financial statements:

a. Income statement—major captions:
   Revenues; Expenses; Pretax income; Income tax expense; Net income; and EPS (enter individual items under each). (Hint: EPS is $11.12.)

b. Balance sheet—major captions:
   Assets: Current assets; Operational assets; and Other assets.
   Liabilities: Current liabilities.
   Stockholders' equity: Contributed capital; and Retained earnings.
   (Enter individual items under each.)

P3–11   (A Challenging Analysis of the Amounts on an Income Statement)
Below is a partially completed income statement of WRY Corporation for the year ended December 31, 19B.

Item	Other Data		Amounts
Net sales revenue			$200,000
Cost of goods sold			
Gross margin on sales	Average markup on sales, 40%		
Expenses: Selling expenses			
General and administrative expenses		$23,000	
Interest expense		2,000	
Total expenses			
Pretax income			
Income tax on operations			
Income before EO items:			
EO gain		10,000	
Income tax effect			
Net EO gain			
Net income			
EPS (on common stock): Income before EO gain			1.00
EO gain			
Net income			
* EO = Extraordinary.			

Required:

Based upon the data given above, and assuming (1) a 20% income tax rate on all items and (2) 20,000 common shares outstanding, complete the above income statement. Show all computations.

CASES

C3–1   **(Analysis of Financial Statements)**

The amounts listed below were selected from the annual financial statements for Small Corporation at December 31, 19C (end of the third year of operations):

From the 19C income statement:

Sales revenue	$300,000
Cost of goods sold	(180,000)
All other expenses (including income tax)	(90,000)
Net income	$ 30,000

From the December 31, 19C, balance sheet:

Current assets	$100,000
All other assets	265,000
Total assets	$365,000
Current liabilities	$ 60,000
Long-term liabilities	79,000
Capital stock, par $10	150,000
Contributed capital in excess of par	15,000
Retained earnings	61,000
Total liabilities and stockholders' equity	$365,000

Required:

Analyze the data on the 19C financial statements of Small by answering the questions that follow. Show computations.

a. What was the gross margin on sales?
b. What was the amount of EPS?
c. What was the amount of working capital?
d. If the income tax rate were 25%, what was the amount of pretax income?
e. What was the average sales price per share of the capital stock?
f. Assuming no dividends were declared or paid during 19C, what was the beginning balance (January 1, 19C) of retained earnings?

C3–2   **(Identification and Correction of Several Accounting Errors)**

The bookkeeper of Careless Company prepared the following trial balance at December 31, 19B:

Account titles	Debit	Credit
Notes receivable	$ 4,000	
Supplies inventory		$ 200
Accounts payable	800	
Land	16,000	
Capital stock		20,000
Cash	7,045	
Interest revenue	200	
Notes payable		5,000
Operating expenses	19,000	
Interest expense		800
Other assets	9,583	
Service revenues		30,583
Totals	$56,583	$56,583

An independent CPA (auditor) casually inspected the trial balance and saw that it had several errors. Draft a correct trial balance and explain any errors that you discover. All of the amounts are correct except "Other Assets."

C3-3   **(A Complex Situation that Requires Technical Analysis of an Income Statement; Challenging)**

Simon Lavoie, a local attorney, decided to sell his practice and retire. He has had discussions with an attorney from another state who wants to relocate. The discussions are at the complex stage of agreeing on a price. Among the important factors have been the financial statements on Lavoie's practice. Lavoie's secretary, under his direction, maintained the records. Each year they developed a "Statement of Profits" on a cash basis from the incomplete records maintained, and no balance sheet was prepared. Upon request, Lavoie provided the other attorney with the following statements for 1986 prepared by his secretary:

S. LAVOIE
Statement of Profits
1986

Legal fees collected		$92,000
Expenses paid:		
Rent for office space	$10,400	
Utilities	360	
Telephone	2,900	
Office salaries	19,000	
Office supplies	900	
Miscellaneous expenses	1,600	
Total expenses		35,160
Profit for the year		$56,840

Upon agreement of the parties, you have been asked to "examine the financial figures for 1986." The other attorney said: "I question the figures because, among other things, they appear to be on a 100% cash basis." Your investigations revealed the following additional data at December 31, 1986:

a. Of the $92,000 legal fees collected in 1986, $28,000 was for services performed prior to 1986.

b. At the end of 1986, legal fees of $7,000 for services performed during the year were uncollected.

c. Office equipment owned and used by Lavoie cost $3,000 and had an estimated remaining useful life of 10 years.

d. An inventory of office supplies at December 31, 1986, reflected $200 worth of items purchased during the year that were still on hand. Also, the records for 1985 indicate that the supplies on hand at the end of that year were about $125.

e. At the end of 1986 a secretary, whose salary is $12,000 per year, had not been paid for December because of a long trip that extended to Janaury 15, 1987.

f. The phone bill for December 1986, amounting to $1,500, was not paid until January 11, 1987.

g. The office rent paid of $10,400 was for 13 months (it included the rent for January 1987).

Required:

a. On the basis of the above information, prepare a correct income statement for 1986. Show your computations for any amounts changed from those in the statement prepared by Lavoie's secretary. (Suggested solution format with four column headings: Items; Cash Basis per Lavoie Statement, $; Explanation of Changes; and Corrected Basis, $.)

b. Write a comment to support your schedule prepared in (a). The purpose should be to explain the reasons for your changes and to suggest some other important items that should be considered in the pricing decision.

C3–4 **(Analysis of the Income Statement and Balance Sheet Included in an Actual Set of Financial Statements)**

Refer to the financial statements of Chesebrough-Ponds given in Special Supplement B immediately preceding the Index. Answer the following questions for the 1985 annual accounting period:

1. On what date did the 1985 accounting period end? How were the dollar amounts rounded?

2. Complete the following fundamental accounting model by providing the 1985 amounts for:

    Assets, $ _____ = Liabilities, $ _____ + Owners' Equity, $ _____.

3. How much was the 1985 net sales revenue? _____.

4. What was the dual economic effect on the company of the total revenues?

    a. _____ $ _____

    b. _____ $ _____

5. What was the dual economic effect on the company of the cost of the products sold?

    a. _____ $ _____

    b. _____ $ _____

6. What was the dual economic effect on the company of the cash dividends paid?

    a. _____ $ _____

    b. _____ $ _____

7. Interest income was _____ debited; _____ credited for $ _____, and interest expense was _____ debited; _____ credited for $ _____.

8. Prepare a journal entry to record miscellaneous expenses assuming they were all paid in cash.

9. What amounts were reported for (a) long-term debt and (b) goodwill and trademarks?

10. What was the amount of depreciation expense? Prepare a journal entry to record this amount.

11. List the subclassifications that the company emphasized on the income statement.

12. List the subclassifications that the company emphasized in the balance sheet.

Accounting (including financial reporting) is based on a conceptual framework. The FASB issues (a) statements of accounting concepts and (b) standards. This chapter discusses the conceptual framework of accounting. Below is the cover and introductory paragraph of the latest statement of concepts.

No. 017 | December 1985

Financial
Accounting Series

Statement of
Financial Accounting
Concepts No. 6

Elements of Financial Statements

a replacement of FASB Concepts Statement No. 3
(incorporating an amendment of
FASB Concepts Statement No. 2)

This Statement of Financial Accounting Concepts is one of a series of publications in the Board's conceptual framework for financial accounting and reporting. Statements in the series are intended to set forth objectives and fundamentals that will be the basis for development of financial accounting and reporting standards. The objectives identify the goals and purposes of financial reporting. The fundamentals are the underlying concepts of financial accounting — concepts that guide the selection of transactions, events, and circumstances to be accounted for; their recognition and measurement; and the means of summarizing and communicating them to interested parties. Concepts of that type are fundamental in the sense that other concepts flow from them and repeated reference to them will be necessary in establishing, interpreting, and applying accounting and reporting standards.

CONCEPTUAL FRAMEWORK OF ACCOUNTING AND ADJUSTING ENTRIES

PURPOSE:

Chapter 3 discussed the accounting information processing cycle. That cycle rests upon a foundation of accounting concepts called the **conceptual framework of accounting.** A primary purpose of Chapter 4 is to present that framework and to explain how it is used in transaction analysis, recording, and reporting accounting information.

The other primary purpose of this chapter is to discuss the implications of accrual basis accounting related to the time-period assumption. This topic leads to discussion of a group of entries called **adjusting** entries. These entries are made at the end of each reporting period so that the revenue and matching principles can be properly applied.

LEARNING OBJECTIVES—TO BE ABLE TO:

1. Identify and explain the essential characteristics of accounting information.
2. Give an overview of the conceptual framework of accounting.
3. Use the conceptual framework as a qualitative supplement while studying the other chapters.
4. Expand your accounting vocabulary by learning about the "Important Terms Defined in this Chapter" (page 174).
5. Apply the knowledge learned from this chapter by completing the homework assigned by your instructor.

ORGANIZATION:

Part A—Conceptual Framework of Accounting

1. Essential characteristics of accounting information.
2. Fundamental concepts of accounting: assumptions, principles, elements of financial statements, and constraints.
3. Types of adjusting entries.

Part B—Adjusting Entries Illustrated

1. Revenues.
2. Expenses.

143

PART A—CONCEPTUAL FRAMEWORK OF ACCOUNTING

IMPORTANCE OF THE CONCEPTUAL FRAMEWORK

The prior chapters discussed the fundamental accounting model (A = L + OE), financial statements, and the accounting information processing cycle. Those discussions emphasized **applications**—the how of accounting. Part A of this chapter discusses the **conceptual framework of accounting.** The concepts are important because they (a) help explain the "why" of accounting, (b) provide guidance when new accounting situations are encountered, and (c) significantly reduce the need to memorize accounting procedures when learning about accounting.

Discussion of the conceptual framework of accounting is included in this early chapter for two important reasons. First, it will help you understand the reasons for particular accounting methods and approaches. Second, the conceptual framework will provide a qualitative, rather than a mechanical, understanding of accounting. Your analytical and interpretive skills will be enhanced significantly.

Finally, a word of caution. The learning objective of Part A of this chapter is to help you develop a general understanding of the concepts. You should not expect to memorize them, nor be able to realize their full effect and importance. Throughout all of the chapters the concepts will be used to support the discussions. In that way you will learn more about what the concepts mean and how they are applied in recording and reporting accounting information.

OVERVIEW OF THE CONCEPTUAL FRAMEWORK

The conceptual framework of accounting is like a basic law of science. It is continually modified to meet certain changing needs of society and has evolved through experience and consensus. The Financial Accounting Standards Board (FASB; see Chapter 1, Part A) has published five *Statements of Financial Accounting Concepts* that state its view of a conceptual framework. The discussions that follow are based on the FASB *Statements of Financial Accounting Concepts.*

The FASB conceptual framework of accounting can be viewed from the perspective of (a) the essential **characteristics** of accounting information and (b) the **concepts** that make up the overall framework.

ESSENTIAL CHARACTERISTICS OF ACCOUNTING INFORMATION

The conceptual framework of accounting starts with definitions of the **essential characteristics** that accounting information must possess. These essential characteristics are outlined in Exhibit 4–1. First, the **users** of accounting information are defined as **decision makers.** Users of financial statements are primarily

---

EXHIBIT 4–1

Essential characteristics of accounting information

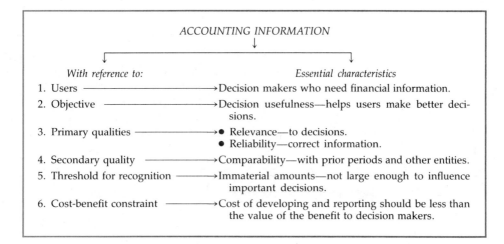

ACCOUNTING INFORMATION

With reference to:	*Essential characteristics*
1. Users	Decision makers who need financial information.
2. Objective	Decision usefulness—helps users make better decisions.
3. Primary qualities	• Relevance—to decisions. • Reliability—correct information.
4. Secondary quality	Comparability—with prior periods and other entities.
5. Threshold for recognition	Immaterial amounts—not large enough to influence important decisions.
6. Cost-benefit constraint	Cost of developing and reporting should be less than the value of the benefit to decision makers.

---

decision makers defined as average, prudent investors, creditors, and experts who provide financial advice. Users are expected to have a reasonable understanding of accounting concepts and procedures (which may be one of the reasons you are studying accounting).

The second essential characteristic of accounting concerns the necessary **qualities of accounting information.** Accounting information must help the users make better decisions. To satisfy this objective, it must have the primary **qualitative characteristics** of relevance and reliability. **Relevance** means that accounting information must be capable of influencing decisions. **Reliability** means that accounting information must be accurate, unbiased, and verifiable.

Also, accounting information must have a secondary qualitative characteristic called **comparability.** This means that accounting information must help users compare the information of a business entity with information about other businesses and prior time periods. Comparability is designated as a secondary characteristic because it is not as important as relevance and reliability.

The two remaining qualitative characteristics of accounting information given in Exhibit 4–1 focus on the cost of preparing accounting information. The **threshold for recognition** (often called materiality) means that accounting for a specific item (i.e., transaction) need not conform precisely to specified accounting guidelines if the amount of the item is not large enough to affect important decisions. Second, the **cost-benefit** (also called utility) **constraint** recognizes that it usually is costly to produce and report accounting information. Under this constraint, accounting should not use more resources to develop and report a specific item than its value to decision makers—to do so would clearly be uneconomic. Measurement of the cost-benefit relationship is very subjective—especially the value of the benefits.

FUNDAMENTAL CONCEPTS OF ACCOUNTING

The fundamental concepts build upon the characteristics of accounting shown in Exhibit 4–1. The fundamental concepts of accounting provide the conceptual guidelines for application of the accounting information cycle. This cycle was introduced in Chapter 3 and is expanded in Chapter 5.

Exhibit 4–2 gives an overview of the **fundamental concepts of accounting.** Notice the five categories—assumptions, principles, constraints, elements of

EXHIBIT 4–2

Fundamental concepts of accounting

A. Assumptions of Accounting
1. Separate-entity assumption.
2. Continuity assumption.
3. Unit-of-measure assumption.
4. Time-period assumption.

B. Principles of Accounting
1. Cost principle.
2. Revenue principle.
3. Matching principle.
4. Full-disclosure principle.

C. Constraints of Accounting*
1. Materiality threshold constraint.
2. Cost-benefit constraint.
3. Conservatism constraint.

D. Elements of Financial Statements
↓

Income statement	*Balance sheet*	*Statement of changes in financial position*
1. Revenues	1. Assets	1. Sources of funds.
2. Expenses	2. Liabilities	2. Uses of funds.
3. Gains	3. Owners' equity	3. Net increase (decrease) in funds.
4. Losses		

↓   ↓   ↓

E. Detailed Practices and Procedures of Accounting
(Used to apply the assumptions, principles, and constraints)

* The FASB used the same terminology here as in the characteristics of accounting information (see Exhibit 4–1) because it is descriptive and it emphasizes these concepts.

financial statements, and detailed practices and procedures. Because of the significance of these fundamental concepts, each category is discussed below.

Assumptions of Accounting

The four assumptions are primarily based on the business environment in which accounting operates. They reflect the scope of accounting and the expectations that set certain limits on the way accounting information is reported.

Separate-entity assumption

Each business must be accounted for as an individual organization, separate and apart from its owners, all other persons, and other entities. The personal transactions of the owners are not considered as transactions of the business. A business entity usually is a sole proprietorship, partnership, or corporation.

Continuity assumption

For accounting purposes a business is assumed to have an indefinite life. This assumption is sometimes called the "going-concern assumption" because accounting assumes that a business will continue to follow its objectives indefinitely.

Unit-of-measure assumption

Each entity will account for, and report, its financial results primarily in terms of the national monetary unit. Therefore, the financial statements of companies in the USA must use the dollar. This assumption implies that the monetary unit is a stable measuring unit, without a changing value (due to inflation and deflation).

Time-period assumption

The time-period assumption recognizes that decision makers require **periodic information** about the financial condition of a business. The periodic **reporting period** does not have to conform to the calendar year. However, the accounting information processing cycle and the primary financial statements cover one full reporting year.

All of the chapters discuss the effects of these four assumptions on accounting and financial reporting.

Principles of Accounting

The four principles of accounting are important because they provide the conceptual guidelines for application of the basic accounting model (A = L + OE). Also, they give the measurement, recording, and reporting phases of the accounting information processing cycle. They can be characterized as "how to apply" concepts.

Cost principle

This principle defines the conceptual basis for measuring the assets, liabilities, and owners' equity (including revenues and expenses) of a business. The cost principle states that the **cash-equivalent** cost should be used for recognizing (i.e., recording) all financial statement elements (discussed later). Under the cost principle, cost is **measured** as the cash paid plus the current value of all noncash considerations.

Revenue principle

The revenue principle relates to the income statement model (Revenues − Expenses = Income). This principle specifies when revenue should be **recognized** (i.e., recorded) and how it should be measured. Revenue should be recognized when there is an inflow of net assets from the sale of goods or services. Revenue is **measured** as the cash received plus the current dollar value of all noncash considerations received.

Matching principle

This principle relates directly to the income statement (Revenues − Expenses = Income). Resources that are used to earn revenues are called **expenses.** The matching principle holds that when the period's revenues are properly recognized in conformity with the revenue principle, all of the expenses incurred in earning those revenues must be **matched** with the revenues of that period. For example, if the revenue from selling a television set is recognized in 19X, the purchase cost of the set must be recognized as an expense in 19X only.

Full-disclosure principle

The periodic financial statements of a business must clearly report (i.e., disclose) all of the relevant information about the economic affairs of a business. This principle requires (a) complete financial statements and (b) notes to the financial statements to elaborate on the "numbers."

Constraints of Accounting

The constraints of accounting are practical guidelines to reduce the **volume** and **cost** of reporting accounting information without reducing its value to decision makers. The constraints are materiality, cost benefit, and conservatism.

Materiality threshold constraint

Although items and amounts that are of low significance must be accounted for, they **do not have to be separately reported if they would not influence reasonable decisions.** Accountants usually designate such items and amounts as **immaterial.**

Cost-benefit constraint

The **benefits of accounting information to decision makers should be higher than the cost of providing that information.** This concept is economically sound; however, measurement of benefits is difficult.

Conservatism constraint

Special care should be taken to **avoid (a) overstating assets and revenues and (b) understating liabilities and expenses.** This constraint produces conservative income statement and balance sheet amounts.

ELEMENTS OF FINANCIAL STATEMENTS

The **elements** of financial statements are the broad classifications (e.g., assets, revenues) of information that should be reported on the required financial statements. These elements were discussed briefly in Chapter 3, which presented practical definitions of the elements. Exhibit 4–3 gives the conceptual definitions of all of the elements for each required financial statement.

_____ **EXHIBIT 4–3** _____

Elements of financial statements defined*

Income statement:
1. **Revenues**—Inflows of net assets or settlements of liabilities from sale of goods and services that constitute the entity's **ongoing or major operations.**
2. **Expenses**—Outflows or using up of assets or incurrence of liabilities for delivery of goods or services, and other activities that constitute the entity's **ongoing or major operations.**
3. **Gains**—Increases in net assets from **peripheral or incidental transactions,** and all other activities except those from revenues or investments by owners.
4. **Losses**—Decreases in net assets from **peripheral or incidental transactions** and other events except those from expenses or distributions to owners.

Balance sheet:
1. **Assets**—Probable future economic benefits owned by the entity as a result of past transactions.
2. **Liabilities**—Probable future sacrifices of economic benefits as a result of past transactions; involves transfer of assets or services.
3. **Owners' equity**—Residual interest of the owners after all debts are paid (i.e., Assets − Liabilities = Owners' Equity).

Statement of changes in financial position:
1. **Sources of funds**—Cash (or cash plus short-term investments) actually received during the period.
2. **Uses of funds**—Cash (or cash plus short-term investments) actually paid during the period.

* Adapted from: FASB, _Statement of Financial Accounting Concepts No. 3,_ "Elements of Financial Statements of Business Enterprises" (Stamford, Conn., December 1980), pp. xi and xii.

PRACTICES AND PROCEDURES OF ACCOUNTING

The "practices and procedures of accounting" were listed last in Exhibit 4–2 because they primarily involve implementation of the fundamental concepts. Practices and procedures are practical and detailed guidelines. They have been developed to attain a reasonable degree of uniformity in applying the fundamental concepts. The practices and procedures of accounting are discussed in all of the chapters of this textbook. A major portion of the illustrations given in Chapter 3 involved accounting practices and procedures—journal, ledger, trial balance, subclassifications on the financial statements, depreciation, etc.

CONCEPTUAL FRAMEWORK RELATED TO THE FINANCIAL STATEMENTS

The conceptual framework of accounting determines how each phase of the accounting information cycle—transaction analysis, recording, and reporting—is done. **The end product—the periodic financial report—must be in conformity with the conceptual framework.** The three required financial statements—the balance sheet, income statement, and statement of changes in financial position—were discussed in the preceding chapters. This section emphasizes the **relationships** among these financial statements. These three financial statements and their accompanying notes, supporting schedules, and the auditors' opinion (see page 13) should be viewed as the entire financial report for the selected time period. This entire reporting package is necessary to meet the varied needs of a diverse population of financial statement users. Exhibit 4–4 gives the basic relationships among the three required financial statements for a reporting period, such as January 1, 1987 through December 31, 1987. The exhibit shows that the beginning balance sheet was changed to the ending balance sheet by the items reported on the income statement and statement of changes in financial position. You can see changes in the financial position of a business by comparing its balance sheets at the beginning and the end of the year.

The income statement and statement of changes in financial position are often referred to as **change** statements because they help users understand what caused the period's change in financial position. Exhibit 4–4 shows that the **income statement** explains one change in financial position—retained earnings. The income statement gives detailed information that "explains" net income. The **statement of changes in financial position** explains all of the changes in financial position (i.e., assets, liabilities, and owners' equity) in terms of cash inflows and cash outflows.

Thus, the three financial statements are linked in important ways. This linking often is called **articulation;** that is, an amount in one statement (e.g., net income on the income statement) is carried to another statement (e.g., the statement of retained earnings). Similarly, net income is tied to the balance sheet

EXHIBIT 4-4

Relationships among the three required financial statements

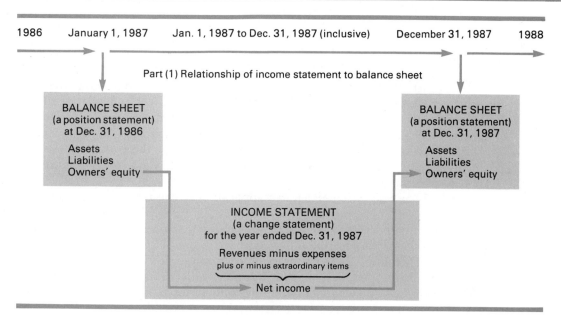

| 1986 | January 1, 1987 | Jan. 1, 1987 to Dec. 31, 1987 (inclusive) | December 31, 1987 | 1988 |

Part (1) Relationship of income statement to balance sheet

BALANCE SHEET
(a position statement)
at Dec. 31, 1986

Assets
Liabilities
Owners' equity

BALANCE SHEET
(a position statement)
at Dec. 31, 1987

Assets
Liabilities
Owners' equity

INCOME STATEMENT
(a change statement)
for the year ended Dec. 31, 1987

Revenues minus expenses
plus or minus extraordinary items

Net income

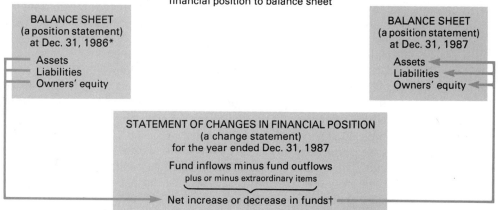

Part (2) Relationship of statement of changes in
financial position to balance sheet

BALANCE SHEET
(a position statement)
at Dec. 31, 1986*

Assets
Liabilities
Owners' equity

BALANCE SHEET
(a position statement)
at Dec. 31, 1987

Assets
Liabilities
Owners' equity

STATEMENT OF CHANGES IN FINANCIAL POSITION
(a change statement)
for the year ended Dec. 31, 1987

Fund inflows minus fund outflows
plus or minus extraordinary items

Net increase or decrease in funds†

* The balance sheet of December 31, 1986 also is the balance sheet at the beginning of 1987.
† Funds are measured as either cash or working capital in the SCFP (discussed later).

(through retained earnings)—and to the SCFP (discussed later). Decision makers can better interpret the financial statements when they clearly understand these relationships. Understanding these relationships will be helpful as you study the remaining chapters.

ACCRUAL BASIS ACCOUNTING

The conceptual framework of accounting (Exhibits 4–1 and 4–2) requires that **accrual basis accounting** be used for the income statement and balance sheet.

Accrual basis accounting means that all **completed transactions** are recorded when they occur, regardless of when any related cash receipts or payments occur. In contrast, **cash basis accounting** means that these transactions are recorded only when the related cash is received or paid. Cash basis accounting is not in conformity with GAAP.

Accrual basis accounting requires application of the revenue and matching principles.

The revenue principle specifies that revenues are **earned** (i.e., recognized) in the period when the revenue transaction occurs, rather than when the cash is collected. Therefore, the total amount of revenues reported on the income statement for the period should include sales and services of that period collected in cash. Also included are all sales and services of the period on credit, even though the cash may be collected in the next period. Similarly, when rent (for example) is collected in advance, rent revenue should be reported on the income statement for the period in which occupancy occurred, rather than in the period of cash collection. Assume rent revenue of $1,200 is collected on December 1, 19A, for 12 months' future occupancy ending November 30, 19B. Rent revenue **earned** in 19A would be $100 and in 19B, $1,100.

To apply the **revenue principle,** the general guideline is that revenue is considered earned (realized) when the **earning process** is substantially completed. In the case of the sale of goods, the earning process is substantially completed when ownership of the goods passes from the seller to the buyer. In the case of the sale of services, the earning process is substantially completed as the services are performed (rather than when the services finally are completed in all respects). This general guideline is applied to most revenue transactions; however, there are a few exceptions that will be discussed in later chapters.

Expenses are **incurred** in the period when the goods or services are **used or consumed.** Therefore, the total amount of expense incurred should be reported on the income statement of the period. In some cases, the expense-incurring services and goods are obtained on credit whereby the cash is paid in a later period; and in other cases, the cash is paid in advance of use of the goods or services (as in the case of prepayment of a three-year insurance premium on a building). In each of these cases, the date of the cash flow is not used to determine the period in which the expense should be reported on the income statement. In contrast, individuals and very small businesses sometimes use the

cash basis for their records. That is, all revenues are considered earned only when the cash is collected. All expenses are considered incurred only when the cash is paid. This method does not conform to GAAP because it incorrectly measures revenues and expenses when their transaction dates precede or lag the related cash flow dates.

Accrual Basis Accounting and the Time-Period Assumption

The above discussion of the relationships among the three required financial statements emphasized the dating of financial statements. Each financial statement should specifically identify its **time dimension** (see Chapter 1, pages 20, 23, and 27). Exhibit 4–4 reemphasizes that the time dimension of the balance sheet is at a specific date (such as "At December 31, 19X"). In contrast, the two "change" statements cover a **specified period of time** (such as, "For the Year Ended December 31, 19X").

The life span of most business entities is indefinite. However, decision makers need **current** information about the entity. Therefore, the life span of an entity is divided into a series of short time periods, such as one year, for many financial reporting purposes. This division of the activities of a business into a series of equal time periods is known as the **time-period assumption.**

Because annual periods tend to be dominant in our society, the accounting period usually is 12 consecutive months. Consequently, accounting emphasizes annual financial statements. Many companies use a year that corresponds to the natural cycle of their business, such as July 1 through June 30, rather than to the calendar year.

In addition to the annual financial statements, many businesses prepare and publish quarterly financial reports for external distribution. These statements usually are called **interim reports.** In addition to annual reports, monthly financial statements often are prepared exclusively for **internal management** purposes. The monthly reports are not distributed to outsiders.

Dividing the life span of a business into short time periods, such as a year, for measurement purposes often causes complex accounting problems because **some transactions start in one accounting period and are, in effect, concluded in a subsequent period.** This continuity of the effects of a transaction may occur for all classifications. For example:

a. **Assets**—A machine that is purchased in year 19A will be depreciated over its estimated useful life, for example, 10 years.
b. **Liabilities**—A note payable is signed that requires interest payments in each of three years and payment of the principal at the end of the third year.
c. **Owners' equity**—Shares of stock are sold in one year with a cash down payment plus two equal annual installment payments and issuance of the shares at the date of the last installment.
d. **Revenues**—Rent is collected in one year for six months in advance, and two of the occupancy periods (months) extend into the next year.

e. **Expenses**—An insurance premium on property is paid in advance for two years of future coverage.

When the effects of a transaction, such as those listed above, overlap two or more accounting periods, accrual basis accounting necessitates a **cutoff** point at each year-end. At this cutoff point the effects of the transaction must be separated between the two accounting periods. To explain—the "bottom line" on an income statement is called **net income.** Accrual basis accounting requires that both revenues and expenses be correctly measured each accounting period. The revenues of the period are determined in conformity with the revenue principle, then the expenses must be matched with the revenues that they earned. This measurement process is complicated because some revenue and expense transactions start in one period and extend over one or more future periods. Therefore, a careful cutoff of all revenues and expenses between accounting periods must be made. This cutoff is done by applying the revenue and matching principles.

The **matching principle** focuses on the measurement of expenses and the matching of them with the periodic revenues **earned** during the period. The matching principle states that all of the **expenses incurred in earning revenues** should be identified, or matched, with only those revenues.

To apply the matching principle, it is necessary to consider the **purposes** for which the expenses were incurred. If the expenses are associated with a specific revenue, as is the usual case, the expenses should be identified with the period in which that revenue was earned. Resources used in one period to earn revenues in other periods should be assigned to those other periods. Some expenses, such as general company overhead and institutional advertising, do not have a direct relationship to the revenues of a specific accounting period. Therefore, such expenses, are recognized on the income statement of the period in which they were incurred.

Accrual basis accounting involves a cutoff at the end of each accounting period to satisfy the revenue and matching principles. That is, at the end of each accounting period, accounting entries must be made for those transactions whose effects extend beyond the year in which the initial transaction occurred. These entries are called **adjusting entries.**

Adjusting Entries

Adjusting entries are made to change certain account balances at the end of the accounting period. For example, assume a company purchased a machine for use in the business on January 1, 19A. The machine cost $50,000 and had an estimated useful life of five years (no residual value). On January 1, 19A (the date the transaction was completed), an asset account—Machinery—was debited (increased) for $50,000. However, by December 31, 19A (end of the first accounting period), the machine had depreciated to $40,000. Therefore, due to an internal economic event (use of the machine), an **adjusting entry** must be made to (a) decrease the book value of the asset by $10,000 and (b) record depreciation expense of $10,000.

Adjusting entries have four basic characteristics as follows:

1. An **income statement** account balance (revenue or expense) is changed.
2. A **balance sheet** account balance (asset or liability) is changed.
3. They usually are recorded at the end of the accounting period.
4. They never directly affect the Cash account.

The four different types of adjusting entries are as follows:

Revenues (revenue principle applied):

1. **Revenue collected in advance but not yet earned**—Revenue collected in advance of being **earned** must be deferred to the future period or periods in which it will be earned. In this case, cash collection **leads** (precedes) revenue recognition.

    Example: On December 1, 19A, Alpha Company collected $1,000 cash for December 19A and January 19B rent (i.e., $500 per month). On the transaction date, the company debited Cash and credited Rent Revenue for $1,000.

    Analysis on December 31, 19A: Rent revenue was earned in 19A for only one month, December; the other monthly rent will be earned in 19B; however, cash was collected in 19A for both months. Therefore, on December 31, 19A, an **adjusting entry** for $500 must be made to (a) decrease (debit) Rent Revenue and (b) increase (credit) Rent Revenue Collected in Advance. The $500 credit balance in this account must be reported on the 19A balance sheet as a **liability** because the company owes the renter occupancy for one month (January 19B).
2. **Revenue earned but not yet recorded or collected**—Revenue not collected or recorded but earned in the current accounting period should be recorded as **earned** in the current period, even though the related cash will be collected in a subsequent period. In this case, cash collection lags revenue recognition.

    Example: On December 31, 19A, Alpha Company finished two phases of a service job for a customer; the third phase will be done in January 19B. The total contract price was $1,200 (i.e., $400 per phase) cash, payable upon completion of all phases.

    Analysis on December 31, 19A: Service revenue of $800 (i.e., $1,200 × 2/3) was earned in 19A, although not yet recorded or collected. Therefore, an **adjusting entry** for $800 must be made on December 31, 19A. This entry will (a) increase (debit) Accounts Receivable and (b) increase (credit) Service Revenue because revenue for the first two phases has been earned in 19A. A receivable must be recorded because the collection of cash will be made in 19B.

Expenses (matching principle applied):

3. **Expense paid in advance but not yet incurred**—Expense paid in advance of use of the services or goods must be deferred to the future period, or periods, in which such services or goods will be used. In this case, cash payment **leads** expense recognition.

    Example: On January 1, 19A, Alpha Company paid a two-year premium of $800 for property insurance; the coverage is for 19A and 19B (i.e., $400 per year). The company recorded this transaction on January 1, 19A, as a debit (increase) of $800 to Prepaid Insurance (an asset), and a decrease (credit) to Cash.

    Analysis on December 31, 19A: On this date half of the benefit of the insurance coverage has been used. Half of the related insurance premium has expired (i.e., $800 ÷ 2 = $400); the other half remains prepaid. Therefore, on December 31, 19A, an **adjusting entry** for $400 must be made to (a) increase (debit) Insurance Expense and (b) decrease (credit) Prepaid Insurance. This entry records the $400 expense for 19A and leaves $400 in the asset account, Prepaid Insurance. Prepaid insurance is an asset because Alpha Company has an obligation from the insurance company to provide insurance coverage for 19B (the premium already has been paid).

4. **Expense incurred but not yet recorded or paid**—Expense incurred (the services or goods have been used) in the current accounting period but not yet recorded or paid (the related cash payment will be in a subsequent period) should be recorded as expense in the current period. In this case, cash payment **lags** expense recognition.

    Example: On December 31, 19A, Alpha Company employees have earned $1,000 in wages that will be paid in cash on the next payroll date January 6, 19B.

    Analysis on December 31, 19A: The company has incurred wage expense in 19A of $1,000 (the employees were helping to earn 19A revenues). Because the employees have not been paid, the company has a $1,000 liability on December 31, 19A. Therefore, an **adjusting entry** for $1,000 must be made on December 31, 19A. This entry will (a) debit (increase) Wage Expense and (b) credit (increase) Wages Payable. This liability will be reported on the 19A balance sheet and will be paid on the next payroll date, January 6, 19B.

In summary, adjusting entries usually are made at the end of each accounting period, after the regular entries are completed. At this time, the accountant must make a careful check of the records and supporting documents to determine whether there are any cases such as those listed above that need **adjusting entries.** In most cases, one or more such entries will be required. If any required adjusting entries are not made, revenue for the period may be measured incorrectly, and/or expenses may not be matched with the revenues earned during the period. In either case, the result would be an incorrect measurement of amounts on both the income statement and the balance sheet for both the current and subsequent period or periods. Adjusting entries are not unusual. They require only a knowledge and analysis of the actual facts about each item.

Terminology—accrue and defer

Accountants often use two technical terms in respect to adjusting entries and in a more general sense. Throughout this textbook and in many of your other courses (and in the outside environment), you will encounter the terms **accrued** (or to accrue) and **deferred** (or to defer). Definitions for accounting purposes are: Accrued, in the case of expenses, means not yet paid; in the case of revenues, not yet collected. Deferred, in the case of revenues, means collected in advance; in the case of expenses, paid in advance. To summarize:

Term	Definition	Example
1. Accrued expense.	An expense incurred; not yet paid or recorded.	Wages earned by employees but not yet paid.
2. Accrued revenue.	A revenue earned; not yet collected or recorded.	Services performed in advance of collection.
3. Deferred revenue.	A revenue not yet earned; collected in advance.	Rent collected in advance of occupancy.
4. Deferred expense.	An expense not yet incurred; paid in advance.	Insurance premium paid in advance.

PART B—ADJUSTING ENTRIES ILLUSTRATED (A CASE STUDY)

This part of the chapter continues the discussion of adjusting entries. It provides detailed illustrations and explanations of numerous adjusting entries. Our emphasis will be on the **analysis** of specific examples to determine the appropriate adjusting entry and the related entries that are made in subsequent periods. These illustrations will increase your understanding of the application of the accounting model, measurement of periodic revenues and expenses, and determination of income. Throughout the examples we will refer to High-Rise Apartments (organized as a corporation on January 1, 19A) and will assume that the current annual accounting period ends December 31, 19B. This case is continued in Chapter 5 to illustrate the complete accounting information processing cycle. Adjusting entries are entered in the journal and posted to the ledger accounts. All adjusting entries are recorded and dated at the end of the accounting period.

REVENUE COLLECTED IN ADVANCE (DEFERRED REVENUE)

Businesses may collect cash and record it in advance of earning the related revenue from the sale of services or goods. The amount collected in advance is called unearned or deferred revenue. Unearned revenue must be apportioned to the period in which the services are performed or the sale is completed in conformity with the **revenue principle.** When unearned revenue has been received, an **adjusting entry** usually is required at the end of the period. This entry will recognize (1) the correct amount of revenue **earned** during the current period and (2) the remaining obligation in the future to provide the related goods or services. We will analyze one such case for High-Rise Apartments that occurs because some tenants pay their rent in the middle of each month. Each adjusting entry is letter coded for reference.

Example: On December 11, 19B, two tenants paid rent for one month from December 11, 19B, through January 10, 19C, in the amount of $1,500. The sequence of entries recorded by High-Rise would be:

December 11, 19B—date of the transaction:

Cash	1,500	
Rent revenue		1,500
To record one month's rent for the period December 11, 19B, through January 10, 19C.		

December 31, 19B—end of the accounting period:

Analysis: The $1,500 cash collected included rent revenue for December 19B of $1,500 $\times$ 20/30 = $1,000, and rent revenue collected in advance for January 19C of $1,500 $\times$ 10/30 = $500. Therefore, an **adjusting entry** is required on December 31, 19B, to (a) reduce the balance in Rent Revenue by $500 and (b) record the obligation to furnish occupancy in 19C for one third of a month which was paid in advance of that year. This $500 is a current liability that will be paid in January 19C by providing occupancy rights.

a. December 31, 19B (end of the accounting period) **adjusting entry:**[1]

Rent revenue	500	
Rent revenue collected in advance		500
To adjust the accounts for revenue collected in advance as of the end of the current period.		

---

[1] The entry at collection date, December 11, 19B, could have been recorded so that it would preclude the need for an adjusting entry later:

Cash	1,500	
Rent revenue		1,000
Rent revenue collected in advance		500

(*footnote continued on next page*)

The $1,000 (i.e., $1,500 − $500) rent revenue is reported on the 19B income statement. The rent revenue collected in advance of $500 is reported on the 19B balance sheet as a current liability.

January 19C:

Rent revenue collected in advance	500	
Rent revenue		500
To transfer the rent revenue from the liability account to the 19C revenue account because it now has been earned.		

REVENUE EARNED PRIOR TO COLLECTION (ACCRUED REVENUE)

At the end of the current accounting period, analysis may reveal that some revenue has been **earned** (in conformity with the revenue principle) but has **not yet been recorded or collected.** Such unrecorded revenue usually is called accrued revenue.

The revenue principle states that if revenue was earned in the current accounting period, it must be recorded and reported in that period along with the asset that has been created (an account receivable). This is accomplished by making an **adjusting entry** to recognize (a) a receivable for the amount earned but not yet collected and (b) the amount of revenue earned. We will analyze a typical situation for High-Rise Apartments and give the sequence of entries.

Example: On December 31, 19B, the manager of High-Rise Apartments analyzed the rental records and found that one tenant had not paid the December rent amounting to $600. The sequence of entries recorded by High-Rise would be:

Also, it could be accounted for as follows with the same end result:

December 11, 19B:

Cash	1,500	
Rent revenue collected in advance		1,500

December 31, 19B—adjusting entry:

Rent revenue collected in advance	1,000	
Rent revenue		1,000

b. December 31, 19B (end of the accounting period)—adjusting entry:

```
Rent revenue receivable  ........................................    600
    Rent revenue  ...............................................            600
    To record rent revenue earned in 19B but not collected by year-end.
```

January 19C—date of collection:

```
Cash  ...............................................................    600
    Rent revenue receivable  ..................................            600
    To record collection of receivable for 19B rent revenue.
```

The adjusting entry at the end of 19B has two measurement purposes: (1) to record rent revenue earned in 19B of $600 and (2) to record a receivable (an asset) for occupancy provided in 19B for which $600 cash will be collected in January 19C. Rent revenue receivable is reported on the December 31, 19B, balance sheet as a current asset.

EXPENSES PAID IN ADVANCE (DEFERRED OR PREPAID EXPENSE)

Often a company either pays cash or incurs a liability in one accounting period for assets purchased or services obtained that will be used in one or more future accounting periods to help earn revenues during those future periods. Such transactions create an asset because of the future benefits. The asset usually is called a **prepaid expense** (or a deferred expense). As the future periods pass, the related revenues are earned in conformity with the revenue principle. Then, as the revenues are earned, period by period, the prepaid expense amount must be apportioned to the appropriate periods in conformity with the **matching principle.**

For example, if the related revenues are earned over three accounting periods, the prepaid expense must be apportioned to each of those three periods in order to measure net income for each period.

For High-Rise Apartments we will analyze three such transactions that occurred in 19B.

Prepaid Insurance

On January 1, 19B, High-Rise paid cash of $2,400 in advance for a two-year insurance policy on the apartment building. The entries by High-Rise for this prepaid expense would be:

January 1, 19B—date of the transaction:

Prepaid insurance (an asset account) 2,400
    Cash   2,400
    To record prepayment of a two-year premium on building.

December 31, 19B—end of the accounting period:

Analysis: The $2,400 cash paid on January 1, 19B, was for insurance coverage for two full years; therefore, insurance expense for each of the two years will be $1,200. At the end of 19B, an adjusting entry must be made to (a) reduce prepaid insurance by $1,200 and (b) record insurance expense of $1,200 for 19B.

c. December 31, 19B (end of the accounting period)—adjusting entry:

Insurance expense 1,200
    Prepaid insurance   1,200
    To record 19B insurance expense for 12 months ($2,400 × 12/24
    = $1,200).

The adjusting entry has two measurement purposes: (1) it apportions insurance expense to the current period for **matching** purposes and (2) it adjusts (reduces) the Prepaid Insurance account to the correct asset amount ($1,200) for the unexpired insurance remaining at the end of 19B. That is, at the end of 19B, the company was entitled to one more year of insurance protection (with a cost of $1,200), which is a current asset.

December 31, 19C (end of next accounting period)—adjusting entry:

Insurance expense 1,200
    Prepaid insurance   1,200
    To record 19C insurance expense.

This entry apportions insurance expense to 19C and reduces the prepaid insurance balance to zero because the policy term ends on December 31, 19C.

Depreciation

On January 1, 19A, a contractor finished an apartment building for High-Rise. The contract price of $360,000 was paid in cash. The building has an **estimated useful life** of 30 years and an estimated $60,000 **residual value** at the end of the 30 years. This transaction involved the acquisition of an asset (building) that may affect the financial statements for the next 30 years (including 19A). At this point, we will consider one continuing effect—depreciation. The entries by High-Rise are discussed below.

January 1, 19A—date of acquisition of the building:

Apartment building 360,000	
Cash	360,000
To record full payment for construction cost of the building.	

d. December 31, 19B (end of the accounting period)—adjusting entry:

Depreciation expense 10,000	
Accumulated depreciation, building	10,000
To record straight-line depreciation expense for one year ($360,000 − $60,000) ÷ 30 years = $10,000.	

The adjusting entry for depreciation expense will be repeated at the end of each year over the 30-year life of the building. The estimated amount expected to be recovered when the asset is sold or disposed of is known as the **residual value** (sometimes it is called scrap or salvage value). For computing depreciation, the cost of the asset must be **reduced** by the residual value. The difference ($360,000 − $60,000 = $300,000) is the net amount of cost to be depreciated over the estimated useful life. Thus, the annual depreciation expense on the apartment building is ($360,000 − $60,000) ÷ 30 years = $10,000.[2] The residual value of $60,000 is deducted because it is the amount of cost that is expected to be recovered at the end of the useful life (of the building) to the company.

The adjusting entry has two measurement purposes: (1) it allocates a part of the cost of the building to expense for the current period for **matching** purposes and (2) it adjusts (reduces) the amount of the asset to its undepreciated cost. The credit to Accumulated Depreciation, Building could have been made directly to the building account with the same effect. However, it is desirable, for reporting

---

[2] This example assumes straight-line depreciation, that is, an equal amount of depreciation expense is apportioned to each period. Other methods of depreciation will be discussed in Chapter 9.

purposes, to keep the balance of the asset account Apartment Building at original cost. This is accomplished by an asset **contra,** or **offset,** account titled Accumulated Depreciation, Building. The difference between the acquisition cost and accumulated depreciation is called **book** or **carrying value.** The book or carrying value does not represent the current **market** value of the asset because accounting for depreciation is a cost allocation process rather than a market valuation process.

Supplies Inventory and Expense

High-Rise purchases maintenance supplies not for resale but for use as needed. They are kept in a small storeroom from which supplies are withdrawn as needed. On January 1, 19B, the inventory of maintenance supplies was $100; these were **unused** supplies on hand carried over from the previous year. On March 18, 19B, additional supplies were purchased for $500 and placed in the storeroom. No accounting entry is made when the supplies are withdrawn for use. To determine the amount of supplies **used** during the period, an inventory of the supplies remaining is taken at the end of the period. At December 31, 19B, the inventory of the supplies in the storeroom showed $200. The entries by High-Rise would be:

March 18, 19B—date of purchase of supplies:

Inventory of maintenance supplies (an asset)	500	
Cash		500
To record purchase of maintenance supplies for addition to inventory.		
Note: This entry increases the inventory account balance from $100 to $600.		

e. December 31, 19B (end of the accounting period)—adjusting entry:

Maintenance expense	400	
Inventory of maintenance supplies		400
To record the amount of supplies used from inventory: Beginning inventory, $100 + Purchases, $500 − Ending inventory, $200 = Supplies used, $400.		

Analysis: Before the adjusting entry is made, the balance in the Inventory of Maintenance Supplies account is $600 (i.e., beginning inventory, $100, plus the purchase, $500); however, the actual inventory count at this date showed $200, which means that usage of supplies was $400 (i.e., $100 + $500 − $200 = $400). The above adjusting entry is required to (*a*) reduce the inventory account by $400 (so that the asset, inventory, will be shown as $200 per the inventory count) and *(b)* to record an expense for the amount of supplies used, $400. Therefore, the 19B income statement will report supplies expense of $400. The 19B balance sheet will report a current asset—inventory of maintenance supplies—of $200.

EXPENSES INCURRED PRIOR TO PAYMENT (ACCRUED EXPENSES)

Most expenses are incurred and paid for during the same period; however, at the end of the accounting period there usually are some expenses that have been **incurred** (i.e., the goods and/or services that already have been used) but are **not yet recorded.** Such unpaid expenses are called **accrued expenses.** These expenses must be recorded in the current period because they must be **matched** with the revenues of the current period in conformity with the matching principle. Also, the liability for those unpaid expenses must be recorded and reported on the balance sheet of the current period. These effects are recorded by using an adjusting entry. We will analyze and illustrate three such transactions, each of which required an adjusting entry by High-Rise Apartments.

Salary and Wage Expense

On December 31, 19B, the manager of High-Rise was on vacation and would return January 10, 19C. Therefore, the manager's December salary of $900 was not paid or recorded by December 31, 19B. The sequence of entries by High-Rise for the accrued salary expense (disregard payroll taxes at this time) would be:

f. December 31, 19B (end of the accounting period)—adjusting entry:

```
Salary expense ...................................................    900
    Salaries payable (or accrued salaries payable) .................        900
    To record salary expense and the liability for December salary not yet
    paid.
```

January 10, 19C—date of payment of the December 19B salary:

```
Salaries payable ..................................................    900
    Cash ..........................................................        900
    To record payment of a December 19B salary.
```

The adjusting entry had two measurement purposes: (1) to record an expense incurred in 19B for matching with revenues and (2) to record the liability for the salary owed at the end of 19B for balance sheet purposes. The entry in 19C recorded the payment of the liability.

Property Taxes

On December 28, 19B, a tax bill for $5,700 was received from the city for 19B property taxes. The taxes are due on February 15, 19C; therefore, they were unpaid and unrecorded at the end of 19B. The entries for High-Rise would be:

g. December 31, 19B (end of the accounting period)—adjusting entry:[3]

```
Property tax expense ............................................. 5,700
    Property tax payable ........................................          5,700
    To record 19B property taxes incurred and the related liability.
```

This adjusting entry records the incurred, but unpaid, tax expense for 19B, and also the tax liability that must be reported on the 19B balance sheet.

February 15, 19C—payment of the 19B liability for property tax:

```
Property tax payable ............................................. 5,700
    Cash ......................................................          5,700
    To record payment of property tax liability.
```

Interest Expense

On November 1, 19B, High-Rise borrowed $30,000 cash from a local bank on a 90-day note with an annual interest rate of 12%. The principal plus interest is due in three months. The entries by High-Rise are:

November 1, 19B—date of transaction:

```
Cash ...................................................... 30,000
    Note payable, short term ...............................          30,000
    To record a loan from a bank.
```

---

[3] This is an example of a case where there may or may not be an adjusting entry. For example, assume the tax bill was received on December 5, 19B. At that date, a **current entry** probably would be made identical to the adjusting entry given above. Under these circumstances, an adjusting entry at December 31, 19B, would not be needed.

Analysis: At December 31, 19B, the end of the accounting period, two months have passed since the note was signed. Therefore, interest expense for two months has accrued on the note because interest legally accrues with the passage of time. At year-end, there is a **liability** for interest for the two months. This expense and the related liability have not yet been recorded. Therefore, an **adjusting entry** is necessary to (*a*) debit interest expense for $600 (i.e., $30,000 × 12% × 2/12 = $600) and (*b*) credit interest payable for the same amount. The adjusting and payment entries would be:

h. December 31, 19B (end of the accounting period)—adjusting entry:

Interest expense	600	
Interest payable (or accrued interest payable)		600
To record accrued interest expense for two months on note payable ($30,000 × 12% × 2/12 = $600).		

January 31, 19C—maturity date; payment of the principal of the note and interest:

Note payable, short term	30,000	
Interest payable (per adjusting entry)	600	
Interest expense (19C—$30,000 × 12% × 1/12)	300	
Cash		30,900
To record payment of principal plus interest on note payable at maturity date.		

RECORDING ADJUSTING ENTRIES

The preceding examples showed the application of the revenue and matching principles at the end of the accounting period by using adjusting entries. In cases when certain economic effects have not been recorded, appropriate adjusting entries are necessary to ensure that both the income statement and balance sheet will be correct. Adjusting entries are made to allocate revenue and expense among the current and one or more future periods so that expenses are properly matched with revenues each accounting period.

Adjusting entries relate to transactions that start in one period and, in effect, continue into one or more subsequent periods. Therefore, an analysis to determine whether an adjusting entry is needed, and if so, how it should be made, must be based on the sequence of related events covering the periods affected. The demonstration case at the end of this chapter illustrates how adjusting entries are influenced by particular situations.

Adjusting entries are entered first in the journal (dated the last day of the accounting period) immediately after all of the regular transactions are recorded. Then the adjusting entries are posted from the journal to the ledger accounts. Recording in the journal and posting to the ledger are necessary because adjusting entries reflect economic events, and their effects must be processed through the accounting information system and into the financial statements in the same manner as the regular transactions. These procedures are illustrated in the next chapter within the context of a complete information processing cycle.

In some instances, it is difficult to draw a clear line between regular and adjusting entries. Also, there are no reasons to make the distinction, other than the fact that adjusting entries (*a*) usually must be made at the **end** of the accounting period and (*b*) **update** certain income statement and balance sheet accounts. The important point is that adjusting entries (as well as many other entries) are necessary to appropriately measure periodic revenues and to match expenses with those revenues that were earned during the period.

DEMONSTRATION CASE

(Try to resolve the requirements before proceeding to the suggested solution that follows.)

New Service Corporation is owned by three stockholders and has been in operation for one year, 19A. Cash flow and expenses are critical control problems. Minimal recordkeeping has been performed to save money. One secretary performs both the secretarial and recordkeeping functions. Because of a loan application made by the corporation, the bank has requested an income statement and balance sheet. The secretary prepared the following (summarized for case purposes):

NEW SERVICE CORPORATION
Profit Statement
Annual—December 31, 19A

Revenues:	
Service	$78,500
Expenses:	
Salaries and wages	(43,200)
Utilities	(1,800)
Miscellaneous	(4,000)
Net profit	$29,500

NEW SERVICE CORPORATION
Balance Sheet
December 31, 19A

Assets

Cash	$ 4,000
Accounts receivable	35,500
Supplies on hand	8,000
Equipment	40,000
Other assets	16,000
Total assets	$103,500

Liabilities

Accounts payable	$ 9,000
Income taxes payable	
Note payable, one year, 12%	10,000

Net Worth

Capital stock, par $10	50,000
Premium	5,000
Retained profits	29,500
Total liabilities and net worth	$103,500

After reading the two statements, the bank requested that an independent CPA examine them. The CPA found that the secretary used some obsolete captions and terminology and did not include the effects of the following data (i.e., the adjusting entries):

a. Supplies inventory on hand at December 31, $3,000.
b. Depreciation for 19A. The equipment was acquired during January 19A; estimated useful life, 10 years, and no residual value.
c. The note payable was dated August 1, 19A. The principal plus interest are payable at the end of one year.
d. Rent expense of $3,600 was included in miscellaneous expense.
e. Income taxes; assume an average tax rate of 17%.

Required:

1. Recast the above statements to incorporate the additional data, appropriate captions, preferred terminology, and improved format. Show computations.
2. Prepare the adjusting entries (in journal form) for the additional data at December 31, 19A.
3. Comment on any part of this situation that the bank loan officer should note if it appears to be unusual.

Suggested Solution

Requirement 1:

NEW SERVICE CORPORATION
Income Statement
For the Year Ended December 31, 19A

	Amounts reported	Effects of adjusting entries*	Corrected amounts
Revenue:			
Service revenue	$ 78,500		$78,500
Expenses:			
Salaries and wages	43,200		43,200
Utilities	1,800		1,800
Supplies expense		(a) + 5,000	5,000
Depreciation expense		(b) + 4,000	4,000
Interest expense		(c) + 500	500
Rent expense		(d) + 3,600	3,600
Miscellaneous expense	4,000	(d) − 3,600	400
Total expenses	49,000		58,500
Pretax income	$ 29,500		20,000
Income tax expense ($20,000 × 17%)		(e) + 3,400	3,400
Net income			$16,600
EPS ($16,600 ÷ 5,000 shares)			$3.32

NEW SERVICE CORPORATION
Balance Sheet
At December 31, 19A

Assets

Cash	$ 4,000		$ 4,000
Accounts receivable	35,500		35,500
Supplies inventory	8,000	(a) − 5,000	3,000
Equipment	40,000		40,000
Accumulated depreciation		(b) − 4,000	(4,000)
Other assets	16,000		16,000
Total assets	$103,500		$94,500

Liabilities

Accounts payable	$ 9,000		$ 9,000
Income taxes payable		(e) + 3,400	3,400
Interest payable		(c) + 500	500
Note payable, one year, 12%	10,000		10,000
Total liabilities	19,000		22,900

Stockholders' Equity

Capital stock, par $10 (5,000 shares)	50,000		50,000
Contributed capital in excess of par	5,000		5,000
Retained earnings	29,500	−29,500 + 16,600	16,600
Total liabilities and stockholders' equity	$103,500		$94,500

Note: Observe changes in captions, terminology, and format.
* The letters identify the adjustments shown under Requirement 2.

Requirement 2:

Adjusting entries at December 31, 19A:

a. Supplies expense 5,000
      Supplies inventory   5,000
      To reduce supplies inventory to the amount on hand December 31,
      19A, $3,000, and to record supplies expense, $8,000 − $3,000 =
      $5,000.

b. Depreciation expense 4,000
      Accumulated depreciation   4,000
      Depreciation for one year, $40,000 ÷ 10 years = $4,000.

c. Interest expense 500
      Interest payable   500
      To record interest expense and the interest accrued (a liability) from
      August 1 to December 31, 19A ($10,000 × 12% × 5/12 = $500).

d. Rent expense 3,600
      Miscellaneous expense   3,600
      To record rent expense in the proper account.

e. Income tax expense 3,400
      Income taxes payable   3,400
      To record income tax expense and the liability for unpaid tax as
      computed on the income statement.

Requirement 3:

The loan officer should note particularly the following:

a. The overstatement of net income by 78%; [i.e., ($29,500 − $16,600) ÷ $16,600] and total assets by 10% [i.e., ($103,500 − $94,500) ÷ $94,500]. This suggests either (1) an attempt to mislead or (2) a need for better accounting.
b. The very high amount in accounts receivable compared to cash and total assets. This fact suggests inadequate evaluation of credit and/or inefficiency in collections.
c. The small amount of cash compared with accounts payable (a current liability).
d. Inclusion of rent expense in miscellaneous expense.
e. Inappropriate captions, terminology, and format shown in the financial statements.

SUMMARY OF CHAPTER

Part A of the chapter discussed the conceptual framework of accounting. Those discussions are summarized in Exhibit 4–5. This exhibit will be particularly useful as you study the other chapters.

EXHIBIT 4–5

Summary of the conceptual framework of accounting (based on *FASB Statements of Financial Accounting Concepts Nos. 1, 2, 3;* and 5)

Fundamentals	Brief explanation	Example
USERS of financial statements (persons to whom they are directed—the audience)	Primarily decision makers who are "average prudent investors" and are willing to study the information with diligence.	Investors, creditors, including those who advise or represent investors and creditors.
OBJECTIVES of financial statements (decision usefulness)	To provide economic information about a business that is useful in projecting the future cash flows of that business.	The operations of a business are summarized in net income which is the primary long-term source of cash generated by a business.
QUALITATIVE characteristics of financial statements (necessary to make the reported information useful to decision makers)	Characteristics that make financial statements useful, viz: 1. Relevance—affects decisions; timely presentation; has predictive and feedback value. 2. Reliability (believable)—unbiased, accurate, and verifiable. 3. Comparability—comparable with other periods and entities	1. The financial statements are available soon after their data have been audited and present complete information. 2. Audited financial statements. 3. Use FIFO for merchandise inventory from period to period
IMPLEMENTATION ASSUMPTIONS of financial statements (imposed by the business environment)	1. Separate-entity assumption—each business is accounted for separately from its owners and other entities. 2. Continuity (going-concern) assumption—assumes the entity will not liquidate, will continue to pursue its objectives. 3. Unit-of-measure assumption—accounting measurements will be in the monetary unit. 4. Time-period assumption—accounting reports are for short time periods.	1. XYZ Company is a separate entity; its owners and creditors are other entities. 2. Accounting for XYZ Company will assume it will carry on its normal operations. 3. Assets, liabilities, owners' equity, revenues, expenses, etc., are measured in dollars in the United States. 4. Financial statements of XYZ Company are prepared each year.

EXHIBIT 4–5 *(continued)*

Summary of the conceptual framework of accounting (based on *FASB Statements of Financial Accounting Concepts Nos. 1, 2, 3;* **and 5)**

Fundamentals	*Brief explanation*	*Example*
IMPLEMENTATION PRINCIPLES of accounting	1. Cost principle—Cost (cash equivalent cost given up) is the appropriate basis for initial recording of assets, liabilities, owners' equity, revenues, expenses, gains, and losses.	1. XYZ Company purchased a machine; record the cash equivalent given up, $10,000 as the cost of the machine.
	2. Revenue principle—The cash equivalent amount received for the sale of goods or services is recognized as earned revenue when ownership transfers or as the services are rendered.	2. Sale of merchandise for $2,000, half cash and half on credit—record sales revenue of $2,000 on date of sale.
	3. Matching principle—Revenues are recognized in conformity with the revenue principle; then all expenses incurred in earning that revenue must be identified and recorded in the period in which those revenues are recognized.	3. Sales of merchandise during the period of $100,000 are recorded as earned; the cost of those goods, $60,000, is recorded as expense of that period.
	4. Full-disclosure principle—The financial statements of an entity should disclose (present) all of the relevant economic information about that entity.	4. Report inventory on the balance sheet and explain in a note the inventory accounting policies.
CONSTRAINTS OF ACCOUNTING (based on practical reasons)	1. Materiality—Amounts of relatively small significance must be recorded; however, they need not be accorded strict theoretical treatment (for cost-benefit reasons).	1. Purchase of a pencil sharpener for $4.98 (an asset) may be recorded as expense when purchased.
	2. Cost-benefit—The value of a financial item reported should be higher for the decision makers than the cost of reporting it.	2. An expense report costs $3,000; its potential cost saving is $1,000.
	3. Conservatism—Exercise care not to overstate assets and revenues and not to understate liabilities and expenses.	3. A loss and a gain are probable, but not for sure. Report the loss but not the gain.

_____ **EXHIBIT 4–5** *(concluded)* _____

Summary of the conceptual framework of accounting (based on *FASB Statements of Financial Accounting Concepts Nos. 1, 2, 3; and 5*)

Fundamentals	Brief explanation	Example
ELEMENTS of financial statements (basic items reported on the financial statements)	Income statement: 1. Revenues—Inflows of net assets, or settlements of liabilities from sale of goods and services that constitute the entity's ongoing or major operations.	1. Sale of merchandise for cash or on credit.
	2. Expenses—Outflows or using up of assets, or incurrence of liabilities for delivery of goods or services, and other activities that constitute the entity's ongoing or major operations.	2. Wages earned by employees paid in cash or owed.
	3. Gains—Increases in net assets from peripheral or incidental transactions, and all other activities except those from revenues or investments by owners.	3. Sale of a tract of land for a price more than its cost when acquired.
	4. Losses—Decreases in net assets from peripheral or incidental transactions and other events except those from expenses or distributions to owners.	4. Sale of a tract of land for a price less than its cost when acquired.
	Balance sheet: 5. Assets—Probable future economic benefits, owned by the entity as a result of past transactions.	5. Land, buildings, equipment, patent.
	6. Liabilities—Probable future sacrifices of economic benefits as a result of past transactions; involves transfer of assets or services.	6. Note owed to the bank, taxes owed but not yet paid, unpaid wages.
	7. Owners' equity—Residual interest of owners after all debts are paid (i.e., Assets − Liabilities = Owners' Equity).	7. Capital stock outstanding plus retained earnings.
DETAILED accounting practices and procedures (detailed measurement and recording guidelines)	1. Those related to asset and income measurement. 2. Those related to reporting accounting information. 3. Other accounting procedures.	1. Straight-line versus accelerated depreciation. 2. Separate reporting of extraordinary items (net of income tax); terminology. 3. Control and subsidiary ledgers; special journals; bank reconciliations, worksheets.

Part B of the chapter discussed **adjusting entries** that are necessary to apply those principles. Matching expenses with revenue for the period is critical because the life span of an enterprise, although indefinite in length, must be divided into a series of short time periods (usually one year each) for the periodic financial statements.

To measure net income, the **revenue principle** states that revenues earned during the period from the sale of goods or services must be identified, measured, and reported for that period. The **matching principle** states that the expenses incurred in earning those revenues must be identified, measured, and matched with the revenues earned in the period to determine periodic net income. To implement the revenue and matching principles, certain transactions and events whose economic effects extend from the current period to one or more future accounting periods, must be analyzed at the end of the accounting period. This analysis is the basis for allocating their effects to the current and future periods. The allocation of some revenues and expenses to two or more accounting periods requires the use of **adjusting entries.** Adjusting entries follow the same concepts and procedures as entries for the usual transactions except that they are made at the end of the accounting period.

IMPORTANT TERMS DEFINED IN THIS CHAPTER

Terms (alphabetically)	Key words in definitions of important terms used in chapter	Page reference
Accrue (accrued)	An expense incurred but not yet paid; a revenue earned but not yet collected.	157
Accrual basis accounting	Record completed transactions when they occur, regardless of when the related cash is received or paid.	152
Adjusting entries	End-of-period entries required by the revenue and matching principles to attain a cutoff between periods.	154
Cash basis accounting	Record only cash basis transactions; not in conformity with GAAP.	152
Conceptual framework of accounting	See Exhibit 4–5.	171
Conservatism constraint	Do not overstate assets and revenues; do not understate liabilities and expenses.	149
Contra account	An account, related to a primary account, that is an offset (or reduction) to the primary account.	163
Cost principle	All assets, liabilities, and owners' equity items are recorded initially at cost.	148
Cost-benefit constraint	Accounting information should have a higher use value than the cost of reporting it.	149
Defer (deferred)	An expense paid in advance of use; a revenue collected in advance of being earned.	157
Depreciation	Expense of using (wearing out) a building, machinery, fixtures, etc., each period of useful life.	162
Elements of financial statements	Major classifications on the financial statements.	149

Terms (alphabetically)	Key words in definitions of important terms used in chapter	Page reference
Expenses paid in advance	Cash paid for goods, or services, before those goods or services are used; prepaid expenses.	156
Expenses incurred but not recorded	Expenses actually incurred but not yet paid or recorded.	156
FASB, *Statements of Financial Accounting Concepts*	Gives the conceptual framework of accounting; summarized in Exhibit 4–5.	171
Full-disclosure principle	Financial statements must report all relevant information about the economic affairs of a business.	148
Interest expense	Time value of money; the cost of borrowing money (or other assets acquired).	164
Interim reports	Financial reports for periods of less than one year; quarterly or monthly reports.	153
Matching principle	All costs incurred to earn the revenues of the period must be identified then matched with revenue by recording as expense.	148
Materiality constraint	Items of low significance need not be separately reported.	148
Residual value	Value (estimated) of an operational asset at the end of its useful life to the business (scrap or salvage value).	162
Revenue collected in advance	Revenue collected in cash before that revenue is earned. Precollected revenue.	154
Revenue earned but not yet collected or recorded	Revenue not yet collected, or recorded, but already earned. Accrued revenue.	155
Revenue principle	Recognize revenue in the period earned rather when the cash is received; earning process completed.	148
Separate-entity assumption	A business is accounted for separate and apart from its owners and all others.	147
Supplies inventory	Supplies purchased and still on hand; unused supplies at the end of period.	163
Time-period assumption	Division of the operating activities of a business into a series of equal time periods (usually one year) for accounting purposes.	147
Unit-of-measure assumption	Financial statements measured in terms of the monetary unit—U.S. dollars.	147

QUESTIONS

PART A

1. Briefly explain why a conceptual framework of accounting is important.

2. Explain the purpose of defining the six essential characteristics of accounting information.

3. Briefly explain the cost-benefit characteristic of accounting information.

4. An essential characteristic of accounting information that is considered to be a secondary characteristic involves what two comparisons?

5. What are the two primary characteristics of accounting information? Briefly explain each.

6. List the five categories that comprise the fundamental concepts of accounting. Briefly explain each.

7. List and briefly explain the three accounting constraints.

8. List the four elements reported on the income statement. Explain the primary difference between revenues and gains and expenses and losses.

9. Explain why the balance sheet is dated differently than the income statement and the statement of changes in financial position.

10. Explain the basic difference between accrual basis accounting and cash basis accounting.

11. What basis of accounting is required by GAAP on the *(a)* income statement, *(b)* balance sheet, and *(c)* statement of changes in financial position?

12. Briefly explain why the time-period assumption and the accrual basis of accounting require a precise "cutoff" at the end of each accounting period.

13. Briefly explain adjusting entries. List the four types of adjusting entries.

PART B

14. AB Company collected $600 rent for the period December 15, 19A, to January 15, 19B. The $600 was credited to Rent Revenue Collected in Advance on December 15, 19A. Give the adjusting entry required on December 31, 19A (end of the accounting period).

15. On December 31, 19B, Company T recorded the following adjusting entry:

Rent revenue receivable	500	
Rent revenue		500

Explain the situation that caused this entry and give the subsequent related entry.

16. On July 1, 19A, M Company paid a two-year insurance premium of $400 and debited Prepaid Insurance for that amount. Assuming the accounting period ends in December, give the adjusting entries that should be made at the end of 19A, 19B, and 19C.

17. Explain "estimated residual value." Why is it important in measuring depreciation expense?

18. Explain why adjusting entries are entered in the journal on the last day of the accounting period and then are posted to the ledger.

EXERCISES

PART A

E4–1   (Pair the Essential Characteristics of Accounting Information with Conceptual Designations)

Match the essential characteristics of accounting information with the related designations by entering appropriate letters in the blanks provided.

Designations	*Essential characteristics*
_____ (1) Users	A. Comparability with prior periods and other entities.
_____ (2) Utility constraint	B. Decision usefulness—helps users make better decisions.
_____ (3) Secondary quality	C. Decision makers who need financial information.
_____ (4) Purpose	D. Relevance to decisions and reliability.
_____ (5) Threshold for recognition	E. Immaterial amounts—not large enough to influence important decisions.
_____ (6) Primary qualities	F. Cost of developing and reporting is less than the use-value to decision makers.

E4–2 **(Pair Financial Statements with the Elements of Financial Statements)**

Match the financial statements with the financial statement elements by entering appropriate letters in the spaces provided.

Elements of financial statements	*Financial statements*
_____ (1) Liabilities	A. Income statement.
_____ (2) Uses of funds	B. Balance sheet.
_____ (3) Losses	C. Statement of changes in financial position.
_____ (4) Assets	D. None of the above.
_____ (5) Revenues	
_____ (6) Sources of funds	
_____ (7) Gains	
_____ (8) Owners' equity	
_____ (9) Expenses	
_____ (10) Assets owned by proprietor	

E4–3 **(Pair Descriptive Statements with Conceptual Terms)**

Match the following brief descriptions with the terms by entering an appropriate letter in each space provided.

Term	*Brief description*
_____ (1) Primary users of financial statements	A. To prepare the income tax return of the business.
_____ (2) Broad objective of financial reporting	B. Separate entity, going concern, time periods, and unit of measure.
_____ (3) Qualitative characteristics of financial statements	C. Guidelines to apply the assumptions and principles.
_____ (4) Implementation assumptions	D. To provide financial information that is useful in projecting future cash flows.
_____ (5) Elements of financial statements	E. Relevance and reliability.
_____ (6) Implementation principles	F. Investors, creditors, and those who advise and represent them (decision makers).
_____ (7) Exceptions to implementation principles	G. Materiality, cost benefit, conservatism.
_____ (8) Detailed accounting practices and procedures	H. Assets, liabilities, owners' equity, revenues, expenses, gains and losses, source of funds, use of funds.
_____ (9) None of the above	I. Revenue, cost, matching, full disclosure.

E4–4 **(Terminology Related to Adjusting Entries)**

Match the following terms with the statements by entering appropriate letters in the spaces provided. There will be two answers for each term.

	Term		Statements
_____ _____	(1) Accrued expense	A.	A revenue not yet earned; collected in advance.
_____ _____	(2) Deferred expense	B.	Office supplies on hand; will be used next accounting period.
_____ _____	(3) Accrued revenue	C.	Interest revenue collected; not yet earned.
_____ _____	(4) Deferred revenue	D.	Rent not yet collected; already earned.

Term

Statements

A. A revenue not yet earned; collected in advance.
B. Office supplies on hand; will be used next accounting period.
C. Interest revenue collected; not yet earned.
D. Rent not yet collected; already earned.
E. An expense incurred; not yet paid or recorded.
F. A revenue earned; not yet collected or recorded.
G. An expense not yet incurred; paid in advance.
H. Property taxes incurred; not yet paid.

E4–5   **(Two Simple Adjusting Entries)**

Simplex Company has completed its first year of operations on December 31, 19A. All of the 19A entries have been recorded, except for the following:

a. At year-end, employees have earned wages of $6,000. These wages will be paid on the next payroll date, January 6, 19B.

b. At year-end, interest revenue of $2,000 has been earned by the company. The cash will be collected March 31, 19B.

Required:

1. What is the annual reporting period for this company under the time-period assumption?

2. Give the required adjusting entry for transactions (a) and (b) above. Give appropriate dates and write a brief explanation of each entry.

E4–6   **(Pairing Transactions with Types of Adjusting Entries)**

Match the following transactions with the terms by entering the appropriate letter in each blank space.

Term

_____ (1) Deferred revenue
_____ (2) Accrued revenue
_____ (3) Deferred expense
_____ (4) Accrued expense

Transaction

A. At the end of the year wages payable of $2,500 had not been recorded or paid.
B. Supplies for office use were purchased during the year for $600 and $100 of the office supplies remained on hand (unused) at year-end.
C. Interest of $300 on a note receivable was earned at year-end, although collection of the interest is not due until the following year.
D. At the end of the year, service revenue of $1,000 was collected in cash but was not yet earned.

PART B

E4–7   **(Effects of Three Adjusting Entries on the Income Statement and Balance Sheet)**

XT Company started operations on January 1, 19A. It is now December 31, 19A (end of the annual accounting period). The part-time bookkeeper needs your help to analyze the following three transactions:

a. On January 1, 19A, the company purchased a special machine for a cash cost of $15,000 (debited to the machine account). The machine has an estimated useful life of five years and no residual value.

b. During 19A, the company purchased office supplies that cost $400. At the end of 19A, office supplies of $100 remained on hand.

c. On July 1, 19A, the company paid cash of $300 for two years premium on an insurance policy on the machine.

Required:

Complete the following schedule of the amounts that should be reported for 19A:

**Selected Balance Sheet Amounts at
December 31, 19A:**

*Amount to be
reported*

Assets:
Machine .... $_____
Accumulated depreciation .... _____
Carrying value .... _____
Office supplies inventory .... _____
Prepaid insurance .... _____

**Selected Income Statement Amounts for
the Year Ended December 31, 19A:**

Depreciation expense .... $_____
Office supplies expense .... _____
Insurance expense .... _____

E4–8 (Journalize Seven Typical Adjusting Entries)

Rich Department Store is completing the accounting process for the year just ended, December 31, 19B. The transactions during 19B have been journalized and posted. The following data in respect to adjusting entries are available:

a. Office supplies inventory at January 1, 19B, was $120. Office supplies purchased and debited to Office Supplies Inventory during the year amounted to $360. The year-end inventory showed $80 of supplies on hand.

b. Wages earned during December 19B, unpaid and unrecorded at December 31, 19B, amounted to $1,400. The last payroll was December 28; the next payroll will be January 6, 19C.

c. Three fourths of the basement of the store is rented for $800 per month to another merchant, J. B. Smith. Smith sells compatible, but not competitive, merchandise. On November 1, 19B, the store collected six months' rent in advance from Smith for $4,800, which was credited in full to Rent Revenue when collected.

d. The remaining basement space is rented to Spears Specialty; for $360 per month, payable monthly. On December 31, 19B, the rent for November and December 19B was not collected nor recorded. Collection is expected January 10, 19C.

e. Delivery equipment that cost $21,000 was being used by the store. Estimates for the equipment were (1) useful life five years and (2) residual value at the end of five years' use, $1,000. Assume depreciation for a full year for 19B. The asset will be depreciated evenly over its useful life.

f. On July 1, 19B, a two-year insurance premium amounting to $1,000 was paid in cash and debited in full to Prepaid Insurance.

g. Rich operates an alteration shop to meet its own needs. Also, the shop does alterations for J. B. Smith. At the end of December 31, 19B, J. B. Smith had not paid for alterations completed amounting to $450. This amount has not been recorded as Alteration Shop Revenue. Collection is expected during January 19C.

Required:

Give the adjusting entry for each situation that should be recorded in the journal of Rich Department Store at December 31, 19B.

E4–9   (Adjusting Entries for Interest on Two Notes Receivable)

On April 1, 19B, Davis Corporation received a $4,000, 15% note from a customer in settlement of a $4,000 open account receivable. According to the terms, the principal of the note, plus the $600 interest, is payable at the end of 12 months. The annual accounting period for Davis ends on December 31, 19B.

Required:

a. Give the journal entry for Davis for receipt of the note on April 1, 19B.
b. Give the adjusting entry required on December 31, 19B.
c. Give the journal entry on date of collection, March 31, 19C, for the principal and interest.

On August 1, 19B, to meet a cash shortage, Davis Corporation obtained a $20,000, 12% loan from a local bank. The principal of the note, plus interest expense is payable at the end of 12 months.

Required:

d. Give the journal entry for Davis on the date of the loan, August 1, 19B.
e. Give the adjusting entry required on December 31, 19B.
f. Give the journal entry on date of payment, July 31, 19C.

E4–10   (Adjusting Entries for Prepaid Insurance—Two Cases)

Kay Company is making adjusting entries for the year ended December 31, 19B. In developing information for the adjusting entries, the accountant learned that on September 1, 19B, a two-year insurance premium of $2,400 was paid.

Required:

a. What amount should be reported on the 19B income statement for insurance expense?
b. What amount should be reported on the December 31, 19B, balance sheet for prepaid insurance?
c. Give the adjusting entry at December 31, 19B, under each of two cases:

Case 1—Assume that when the premium was paid on September 1, 19B, the bookkeeper debited the full amount to Prepaid Insurance.

Case 2—Assume that when the premium was paid September 1, 19B, the bookkeeper debited Insurance Expense for the full amount.

(Hint: In Case 2 be sure that after the adjusting entry, you end with the same amount in the Prepaid Insurance account as in Case 1.)

E4–11   (Adjusting Entry for Supplies Inventory)

Wise Manufacturing Company uses a large amount of shipping supplies that are purchased in large volume, stored, and used as needed. At December 31, 19B, the following data relating to shipping supplies were obtained from the records and supporting documents:

Shipping supplies on hand, January 1, 19B .... $ 2,000
Purchases of shipping supplies during 19B 13,000
Shipping supplies on hand, per inventory December 31, 19B 4,000

Required:

a. What amount should be reported on the 19B income statement for shipping supplies expense?

b. What amount should be reported on the December 31, 19B, balance sheet for shipping supplies inventory?

c. Give the adjusting entry at December 31, 19B, assuming the purchases of shipping supplies were debited in full to Shipping Supplies Inventory ($13,000).

d. What adjusting entry would you make assuming the bookkeeper debited Shipping Supplies Expense for the $13,000? (Hint: In solving (c) and (d), be sure that each solution ends up with the same amount remaining in the Shipping Supplies Inventory account.)

E4–12   **(Correct Income Statement and Balance Sheet Amounts for the Effects of Three Adjusting Entries)**

On December 31, 19B, Wag Company prepared an income statement and balance sheet and failed to take into account three adjusting entries. The income statement, prepared on this incorrect basis, reflected a pretax income of $20,000. The balance sheet reflected total assets, $90,000; total liabilities, $30,000; and owners' equity, $60,000. Wag is not a corporation; therefore, it does not pay income tax. The data for the three adjusting entries were:

a. Depreciation was not recorded for the year on equipment that cost $55,000; estimated useful life, 10 years, and residual value, $5,000.

b. Wages amounting to $8,000 for the last three days of December 19B not paid and not recorded (the next payroll will be on January 10, 19C).

c. Rent revenue of $3,000 was collected on December 1, 19B, for office space for the period December 1, 19B, to February 28, 19C. The $3,000 was credited in full to Rent Revenue when collected.

Required:

Complete the following tabulation to correct the financial statement amounts shown (indicate deductions with parentheses):

Item	Net Income	Total assets	Total liabilities	Owners' equity
Balances reported	$20,000	$90,000	$30,000	$60,000
Effects of depreciation				
Effects of wages				
Effects of rent revenue				
Correct balances				

E4–13   **(Prepare Correct Income Statement to Include Effects of Seven Adjusting Entries; Give Adjusting Entries)**

Supreme Auto Rentals, Inc., completed its first year of operations on December 31, 19A. Because this is the end of the annual accounting period, the company bookkeeper prepared the following tentative income statement:

Income Statement, 19A

Rental revenue		$102,000
Expenses:		
Salaries and wages	$26,400	
Maintenance expense	10,000	
Rent expense (on location)	8,000	
Utilities expense	3,000	
Gas and oil expense	2,000	
Miscellaneous expense (items not listed above)	400	
Total expenses		49,800
Income		$ 52,200

An independent CPA reviewed the income statement and developed additional data as follows:

1. Wages for the last three days of December amounting to $600 were not recorded or paid (disregard payroll taxes).
2. The telephone bill for December 19A amounting to $200 has not been recorded or paid.
3. Depreciation on rental autos, amounting to $20,000 for 19A, was not recorded.
4. Interest on a $20,000, one-year, 12% note payable dated November 1, 19A, was not recorded. The 12% interest is payable on the maturity date of the note.
5. Rental revenue includes $2,000 rental revenue for the month of January 19B.
6. Maintenance expense includes $1,000, which is the cost of maintenance supplies still on hand (per inventory) at December 31, 19A. These supplies will be used in 19B.
7. The income tax rate is 20%. Payment of income tax will be made in 19B.

Required:

a. Prepare a correct income statement for 19A, assuming 10,000 shares of stock are outstanding. Show computations.
b. Give the adjusting entry at December 31, 19A, for each of the additional data items. If none is required, explain why.

E4–14 **(Prepare Three Adjusting Entries and Recast the Income Statement and Balance Sheet)**
On December 15, 19C, the bookkeeper for Seattle Company prepared the income statement and balance sheet summarized below but neglected to consider three of the adjusting entries.

	As prepared	Effects of adjusting entries	Corrected amounts
Income statement:			
Revenues	$95,000		
Expenses	(83,000)		
Income tax expense			
Income	$12,000		
Balance sheet:			
Assets			
Cash	$18,000		
Accounts receivable	26,000		
Rent receivable			
Equipment*	40,000		
Accumulated depreciation	(8,000)		
	$76,000		
Liabilities			
Accounts payable	$10,000		
Income tax payable			
Owners' Equity			
Capital stock	50,000		
Retained earnings	16,000		
	$76,000		

* Acquired January 1, 19A, 10-year life, no residual value; straight-line depreciation.

Data on the three adjusting entries:

1. Depreciation on the equipment was not recorded for 19C.
2. Rent revenue earned of $1,000 for December 19C was neither collected or recorded.
3. Income tax for 19C, was not paid or recorded. The average rate was 20%.

Required:

a. Complete the two columns to the right in the above tabulation to show the correct amounts on the income statement and balance sheet.
b. Prepare the three adjusting entries (in journal form) that were omitted. Use the account titles given above.

PROBLEMS

PART A

P4–1 **(Pair Definitional Statements with Concepts)**
Match the following descriptive statements with the fundamental concepts of accounting by entering appropriate letters in the spaces provided.

Fundamental concepts	*Descriptive statements*

Fundamental concepts

_____ (1) Separate-entity assumption

_____ (2) Continuity assumption

_____ (3) Unit-of-measure assumption

_____ (4) Time-period assumption

_____ (5) Cost principle

_____ (6) Revenue principle

_____ (7) Matching principle

_____ (8) Full-disclosure principle

_____ (9) Materiality threshold

_____ (10) Cost-benefit constraint

_____ (11) Conservatism constraint

Elements of financial statements:

_____ (12) Income statement

_____ (13) Balance sheet

_____ (14) Statement of changes in financial position

_____ (15) Practices and procedures of accounting

Descriptive statements

A. Used to apply the assumptions, principles, and constraints.

B. The reporting period usually is one year.

C. Expenses are matched with revenues period by period.

D. Items of low significance do not need to be reported separately.

E. Account for the business separate from owners.

F. Report in terms of the monetary unit.

G. Inflow of net assets from the sale of goods and services that is measurable in dollars.

H. All relevant information about the financial activities must be reported.

I. The entity is a going concern.

J. Financial statement elements are initially recorded at cash equivalent cost.

K. Reports revenues, expenses, gains, and losses.

L. Value of user benefits must exceed cost of providing the item of financial information.

M. Reports cash inflows, outflows, and net change.

N. Reports Assets = Liabilities + Owners' Equity.

O. Do not overstate assets and revenues and do not understate liabilities and expenses.

P4–2 **(Pair Definitional Statements with Elements of Financial Statements)**

Match the following definitions with the elements of financial statements by entering the appropriate letters in the spaces provided.

Elements

Income statement:

_____ (1) Revenues

_____ (2) Expenses

_____ (3) Gains

_____ (4) Losses

Balance sheet:

_____ (5) Assets

_____ (6) Liabilities

_____ (7) Owners' equity

Statement of changes in financial position:

_____ (8) Sources of funds

_____ (9) Uses of funds

Brief definitions

A. Cash received during the accounting period.

B. Probable future sacrifices of economic resources.

C. Increase in net assets from peripheral transactions.

D. Outflow of assets for delivery of goods or services.

E. Residual interest of owners.

F. Inflow of net assets from major ongoing operations.

G. Cash paid out during the period.

H. Probable future economic benefits; owned by the entity.

I. Decreases in net assets from incidental transactions.

P4–3   **(Pair Transactions and Events with Concepts)**

Below are listed the concepts of accounting. Match each brief description of a transaction or event with a concept by entering the appropriate letter in the spaces provided. Use one letter for each blank.

Concept applied

_____ (1) Users of financial statements
_____ (2) Objective of financial statements

Qualitative characteristics:

_____ (3) Relevance
_____ (4) Reliability

Implementation assumptions:

_____ (5) Separate entity
_____ (6) Continuity
_____ (7) Unit of measure
_____ (8) Time period

Elements of financial statements:

_____ (9) Revenues
_____ (10) Expenses
_____ (11) Gains
_____ (12) Losses
_____ (13) Assets
_____ (14) Liabilities
_____ (15) Owners' equity

Implementation principles:

_____ (16) Cost
_____ (17) Revenue
_____ (18) Matching
_____ (19) Full disclosure

Constraints of accounting:

_____ (20) Materiality threshold
_____ (21) Cost-benefit constraint
_____ (22) Conservatism constraint

Brief description of transaction or event

A. Recorded a $1,000 sale of merchandise on credit.
B. Counted (inventoried) the unsold items at the end of the period and valued them in dollars.
C. Acquired a vehicle for use in operating the business.
D. Reported the amount of depreciation expense because it likely will affect important decisions of statement users.
E. Identified as the investors, creditors, and others interested in the business.
F. Used special accounting approaches because of the uniqueness of the industry.
G. Sold and issued bonds payable of $1 million.
H. Paid a contractor for an addition to the building with $10,000 cash and $20,000 market value of the stock of the company ($30,000 was deemed to be the cash equivalent price).
I. Engaged an outside independent CPA to audit the financial statements.
J. Sold merchandise and services for cash and on credit during the year then determined the cost of those goods sold and the cost of rendering those services.
K. Established an accounting policy that sales revenue shall be recognized only when ownership to the goods sold passes to the customer.
L. To design and prepare the financial statements to assist the users to project the future cash flows of the business.
M. Established a policy not to include in the financial statements the personal financial affairs of the owners of the business.
N. Sold an asset at a loss that was a peripheral or incidental transaction.
O. The user value of a special financial report exceeds the cost of preparing it.
P. Valued an asset, such as inventory, at less than its purchase cost because the replacement cost is less.
Q. Dated the income statement "For the Year Ended December 31, 19B."
R. Used services from outsiders—paid cash for some and the remainder on credit.
S. Acquired an asset (a pencil sharpener that will have a useful life of five years) and recorded as an expense when purchased for $1.99.
T. Disclosed in the financial statements all relevant financial information about the business; necessitated the use of notes to the financial statements.
U. Sold an asset at a gain that was a peripheral or incidental transaction.
V. Assets, $500,000 − Liabilities, $300,000 = Owners' Equity $200,000.
W. The accounting and reporting assumes a "going concern."

P4–4   (Convert from Cash to Accrual Basis)

At the end of 19A, the accounting records of Sly Service Company showed the following data:

	For the year		
	19A	19B	19C
Service revenue:			
Cash	$40,000	$50,000	
On credit	15,000	11,000	
19C revenue collected in advance of 19C (not included in the $50,000)		3,000	
Additional cash collections for:			
19A service revenue	6,000	5,000	
19B service revenue	2,000	7,000	$3,000
Expenses:			
Paid in cash	25,000	30,000	
On credit	5,000	7,000	
19C expenses paid in advance of 19C (not included in the $30,000)		1,000	
Additional cash payments for:			
19A expenses	3,000	2,000	
19B expenses	1,000	3,000	3,000

Required:

Complete the following tabulation (show computations):

	For the Year	
	19A	19B
a. Service revenue that would be reported:		
Accrual basis	$_____	$_____
Cash basis	$_____	$_____
b. Expenses that would be reported:		
Accrual basis	$_____	$_____
Cash basis	$_____	$_____

P4–5   (Restate Income Statement from Cash Basis to Accrual Basis)

Art Little Company (not a corporation) prepared the income statement given below including the two footnotes:

ART LITTLE COMPANY
Income Statement, Cash Basis
For the Year Ended December 31, 19B

Sales revenue (does not include $20,000 sales on credit because collection will be in 19C)	$100,000
Expenses (does not include $10,000 expenses on credit because payment will be made in 19C)	75,200
Profit	$ 24,800

Additional data:

a. Depreciation on operational assets (a company truck) for the year amounted to $15,000. Not included in expenses above.

b. On January 1, 19B, paid a two-year insurance premium on the truck amounting to $400. This amount is included in the expenses above.

Required:

a. Recast the above income statement on the accrual basis in conformity with GAAP. Show computations and explain each change.

b. Explain why the cash basis does not measure income as well as the accrual basis.

P4–6   **(Challenging; Convert Income Statement and Balance Sheet from Cash to Accrual Basis)**
At the end of 19A, Foster Corporation prepared the following annual income statement and balance sheet:

FOSTER CORPORATION
Income Statement
For the Year Ended December 31, 19A

Revenues	$280,000
Expenses	248,000
Income before taxes	32,000
Income taxes (average rate, 30%)	9,600
Net income	$ 22,400

FOSTER CORPORATION
Balance Sheet
At December 31, 19A

Assets			**Liabilities**		
Cash		$ 18,000	Accounts payable		$ 8,000
Accounts receivable		22,000	Income taxes payable (This is the		
Inventory (by count)		76,800	one half unpaid)		4,800
Fixtures	$25,000		Notes payable, 12%		
Less: Accumulated			(due June 20, 19B)		20,000
depreciation	7,000	18,000	Total liabilities		32,800
Total assets		$134,800			
			Stockholders' Equity		
			Common stock, par $10		
			5,000 shares	$50,000	
			Contributed capital in		
			excess of par	10,000	
			Retained earnings	42,000	
			Total stockholders'		
			equity		102,000
			Total liabilities and		
			stockholders' equity		$134,800

An independent audit of the above statements and underlying records showed the following:

1. Depreciation expense included in total expense was $2,000 for 19A; it should have been $2,500.
2. A tentative order was received from a customer on December 31, 19A, for goods having a sales price of $10,000 and was included in sales revenue and accounts receivable. The goods were on hand (and included in the ending inventory). It is quite likely that a sale may not materialize; the customer will decide by January 20, 19B. This tentative order should not have been recognized as a sale in 19A.

Required:

Other than these two items, the amounts on the financial statements were correct. Recast the two statements to take into account the depreciation error and the incorrect recognition of the tentative order. Show computations and assume an average income tax rate of 30%. (Hint: Revised EPS is $3.01.)

P4-7   **(Prepare Four Simple Adjusting Entries)**

The annual accounting year used by Jones Service Company ends on December 31. It is December 31, 19X, and all of the 19X entries have been made except the following adjusting entries:

a. On September 1, 19X, Jones collected six months rent of $1,200 on some storage space. At that date Jones debited Cash and credited Rent Revenue for $1,200.

b. The company earned service revenue of $1,000 on a special job which was completed December 29, 19Y. Collection will be made during January 19Y, and no entry has been recorded.

c. On November 1, 19X, Jones paid a one-year premium for property insurance, $600. Cash was credited and Insurance Expense was debited for this amount.

d. At December 31, 19X, wages earned by employees not yet paid, $400. The employees will be paid on the next payroll date, January 15, 19Y.

Required:

Give the adjusting entry required for each transaction. Provide a brief explanation for each entry.

P4-8   **(Prepare Four Types of Adjusting Entries)**

Vitro Service Company started operations on September 1, 19A. It is now August 31, 19C, end of its second year of operations. All entries for the annual accounting period have been journalized and posted to the ledger accounts. The following end-of-year entries are to be recorded:

a. Service revenue collected in advance, $1,500. On August 15, 19C, the company debited Cash and credited Service Revenues for this amount. The services will be performed during September 19C.

b. Revenue earned but not yet collected or recorded, $5,000. The company completed a large service job, which passed inspection on August 31, 19C. Collection is expected on September 6, 19C.

c. Expense paid in advance, $3,000. The company purchased service supplies on August 1, 19C, at which time Expense was debited and Cash credited for this amount. At August 31, 19C, one third of these supplies were on hand (will be used later on other jobs).

d. Expense incurred but not yet paid or recorded. The company used the consulting services of an engineer during the last two weeks of August, 19C. The services have been performed, and Vitro expects to pay the $500 billing on September 15, 19C.

Required:

1. What is the accounting (i.e., reporting) year for this company? What accounting assumption supports your answer?

2. Prepare the required adjusting entry for each situation, including a brief explanation of each entry.

3. Explain the effect on net income if these entries are not made on August 31, 19C (disregard income tax).

PART B

P4–9 **(Give Six Adjusting Entries and Related Balance Sheet Classifications)**

Jackson Service Company is preparing the adjusting entries for the year ended December 31, 19B. On that date, the bookkeeper for the company assembled the following data:

1. On December 31, 19B, salaries earned by employees but not yet paid or recorded, $6,000.

2. Depreciation must be recognized on a service truck that cost $9,000 on July 1, 19B (estimated useful life is six years with no residual value).

3. Cash of $1,000 was collected on December 28, 19B, for services to be rendered during 19C (Service Revenue was credited).

4. On December 27, 19B, Jackson received a tax bill of $200 from the city for 19B property taxes (on service equipment) that is payable (and will be paid) during January 19C.

5. On July 1, 19B, the company paid $840 cash for a two-year insurance policy on the service truck (2 above).

6. On October 1, 19B, the company borrowed $10,000 from a local bank and signed a 12% note for that amount. The principal and interest are payable on maturity date, September 30, 19C.

Required:

a. The bookkeeper has asked you to assist in preparing the adjusting entries at December 31, 19B. For each situation above, give the adjusting entry and a brief explanation. If none is required, explain why.

b. Based on your entries given in Requirement *(a)*, complete the following schedule to reflect the amounts and balance sheet classifications:

Item No.	Accounts	19B amount	Balance sheet classification (one check on each line)		
			Assets	Liabilities	Owners' Equity
1	Salaries payable	$_____	_____	_____	_____
2	Accumulated depreciation	_____	_____	_____	_____
3	Revenue collected in advance	_____	_____	_____	_____
4	Property tax payable	_____	_____	_____	_____
5	Prepaid insurance	_____	_____	_____	_____
6	Interest payable	_____	_____	_____	_____

P4–10 **(Prepare Seven Adjusting Entries and Recompute Income to Include Their Effects)**

Slow Transportation Company is at the end of its accounting year December 31, 19B. Slow is not a corporation; therefore, it does not pay income tax. The following data that must be considered were developed from the company's records and related documents:

1. On July 1, 19B, a three-year insurance premium on equipment was paid amounting to $900 that was debited in full to Prepaid Insurance on that date.

2. During 19B, office supplies amounting to $1,000 were purchased for cash and debited in full to Supplies Inventory. At the end of 19A, the inventory count of supplies remaining on hand (unused) showed $200. The inventory of supplies on hand (unused) at December 31, 19B, showed $300.

3. On December 31, 19B, B&R Garage completed repairs on one of Slow's trucks at a cost of $650; the amount is not yet recorded and, by agreement, will be paid during January 19C.

4. In December 19B, a tax bill, on trucks owned during 19B, amounting to $1,400 was received from the city. The taxes, which have not been recorded, are due and will be paid on February 15, 19C.

5. On December 31, 19B, Slow completed a hauling contract for an out-of-state company. The bill was for $7,500 payable within 30 days. No cash has been collected, and no journal entry has been made for this transaction.

6. On July 1, 19B, Slow purchased a new hauling van at a cash cost of $21,600. The estimated useful life of the van was 10 years, with an estimated residual value of $1,600. No depreciation has been recorded for 19B (compute depreciation for six months in 19B).

7. On October 1, 19B, Slow borrowed $6,000 from the local bank on a one-year, 15% note payable. The principal plus interest is payable at the end of 12 months.

Required:

a. Give the adjusting entry required on December 31, 19B, related to each of the above transactions. Give a brief explanation with each entry.

b. Assume Slow Transportation Company had prepared a tentative income statement for 19B that did not include the effect of any of the above items and that the tentative net income computed was $30,000. Considering the above items, compute the corrected net income for 19B. Show computations.

P4–11   (Compute Income Statement Amounts for Three Items and Identify Any Adjusting Entries)
The following information was provided by the records and related documents of Greene Garden Apartments (a corporation) at the end of the annual fiscal period, December 31, 19B:

Revenue:

a. Rent revenue collected in cash during 19B for occupancy in 19B (credited to Rent Revenue) $497,000

b. Rent revenue earned for occupancy in December 19B; will not be collected until 19C 8,000

c. In December 19B, collected rent revenue in advance for January 19C (credited to Rent Revenue) 6,000

Salary expense:

d. Cash payment made in January 19B for salaries incurred (earned) in December 19A 3,000

e. Salaries incurred and paid during 19B (debited to Salary Expenses) 58,000

f. Salaries earned by employees during December 19B; will not be paid until January 19C 2,000

g. Cash advance to employees in December 19B for salaries that will be earned in January 19C (debited to Receivable from employees) 4,000

Supplies used:

h. Maintenance supplies inventory on January 1, 19B (balance on hand) 2,000

i. Maintenance supplies purchased for cash during 19B (debited to Maintenance Supplies Inventory when purchased) 8,000

j. Maintenance supplies inventory on December 31, 19B 1,500

Required:

1. In conformity with the revenue and matching principles, what amounts should be reported on Greene's 19B income statement for:
   a. Rent revenue .... $_____
   b. Salary expense .... _____
   c. Maintenance supplies expense ...... _____
   Show computations.
2. Check the items that would need an adjusting entry at the end of 19B:
   a. ____; *b.* ____; *c.* ____; *d.* ____; *e.* ____; *f.* ____; *g.* ____; *h.* ____; *i.* ____; *j.* ____.

P4–12   (Determine the Effect of Five Adjusting Entries on the Income Statement)

Rapid Service Company has completed its annual financial statements for the year ended December 31, 19C. The income statement (summarized) reflected the following:

Revenues:	
Service	$95,600
Rental (office space)	2,400
Total revenues	98,000
Expenses:	
Salaries and wages	44,000
Service supplies used	2,600
Depreciation expense	2,000
Maintenance of equipment	2,000
Rent expense (service building)	8,400
Oil and gas for equipment	1,800
Insurance expense	200
Utilities expense	800
Other expenses	6,200
Total expenses	68,000
Net income	$30,000

Rapid is a partnership; therefore, it does not pay income taxes. An audit of the records and financial statements by a CPA revealed that the following items were not considered:

1. Service revenue of $700 earned but not collected on December 31, 19C, was not included in the $95,600 on the income statement.
2. The $2,600 of service supplies used included $600 of service supplies still on hand in the supplies storeroom on December 31, 19C.
3. Rent revenue of $100 that was collected in advance and not yet earned by December 31, 19C, was included in the $2,400 on the income statement.
4. Property tax for 19C of $400 was billed during December 19C, but will be due and paid during January 19D (not included in the above amounts on the income statement).
5. A two-year insurance premium of $400 was paid on July 1, 19B; no premiums were paid in 19C.

Required:

a. Recast the above income statement to include, exclude, or omit each of the items identified by the CPA. Use a format similar to the following:

Items	Amounts as reported	Corrections	Amounts that should be reported

    b. The owner of the company asked you to explain the following:

        (1) The insurance premium was paid in 19B; therefore, why was insurance expense reported in 19C?

        (2) Although the company paid no cash for depreciation expense, $2,000 was included in 19C as expense. Why was this so?

P4–13   **(Determine the Effects of Six Entries on the Income Statement and Balance Sheet)**

It is December 31, 19B, end of the annual accounting period for TT Service Company. Below are listed six independent transactions (summarized) that affected the company during 19B. The transactions are to be analyzed as to their effects on the balance sheet and income statement for 19B.

    a. On January 1, 19A, the company purchased a machine that cost $10,000 cash (estimated useful life five years and no residual value).

        (1) Show how the machine should be reported on the 19B balance sheet.

        (2) Show how the 19B income statement should report the effects of the machine usage.

    b. On September 1, 19B, the company signed a $10,000, 12%, one-year note payable. The principal plus interest is payable on maturity date.

        (1) Show how the liability should be reported on the 19B balance sheet.

        (2) Show how the effects of the note should be reported on the 19B income statement.

    c. During 19B, service revenues of $90,000 were collected of which $10,000 was collected in advance.

        (1) Show how the $10,000 should be reported on the 19B balance sheet.

        (2) Show how the 19B income statement should report the effects of the transaction.

    d. In 19B, expenses paid in cash amounted to $60,000 of which $5,000 was paid for expenses yet to be incurred (prepaid).

        (1) Show how the 19B balance sheet should report the $5,000.

        (2) Show how the income statement should report this situation.

    e. In 19B, $85,000 cash revenues were collected, and in addition revenues of $5,000 were on credit.

        (1) Show how the $5,000 should be reported on the 19B balance sheet.

        (2) Show how the 19B income statement should report the revenues.

    f. In 19B, expenses amounting to $56,000 were paid in cash, and in addition expenses of $3,000 were on credit.

        (1) Show how the $3,000 should be reported on the 19B balance sheet.

        (2) Show how the expenses should be reported on the 19B income statement.

P4–14   **(Analytical—Compare Two Sets of Account Balances to Determine What Adjusting Entries Were Made)**

Modern Service Company is completing the information processing cycle at the end of its fiscal year, December 31, 19B. Below is listed the correct balance for each account at December 31, 19B *(a)* before the adjusting entries for 19B and *(b)* after the adjusting entries for 19B.

	Account balance, December 31, 19B			
	Before adjusting entries		After adjusting entries	
Item	Debit	Credit	Debit	Credit
a. Cash	$ 8,000		$ 8,000	
b. Service revenue receivable			400	
c. Prepaid insurance	300		200	
d. Operational assets	120,200		120,200	
e. Accumulated depreciation, equipment		$ 21,500		$ 25,000
f. Income taxes payable				5,500
g. Capital stock		70,000		70,000
h. Retained earnings, January 1, 19B		14,000		14,000
i. Service revenue		60,000		60,400
j. Salary expense	37,000		37,000	
k. Depreciation expense			3,500	
l. Insurance expense			100	
m. Income tax expense			5,500	
	$165,500	$165,500	$174,900	$174,900

Required:

a. Compare the amounts in the columns before and after the adjusting entries in order to reconstruct the four adjusting entries that were made in 19B. Provide an explanation of each.

b. Compute the amount of income assuming (1) it is based on the amounts, "before adjusting entries" and (2) it is based on the amounts, "after adjusting entries." Which income amount is correct? Explain why.

P4–15 **(Compute Effects of Adjusting Entries on the Balance Sheet and Income Statement; Two Consecutive Years)**

On January 1, 19A, four persons organized WAS Company. The company has been operating for two years, 19A and 19B. Given below are data relating to six selected transactions that affect both years. The annual accounting period ends December 31.

a. On January 1, 19A, the company purchased a computer for use in the business at a cash cost of $14,000. The computer has an estimated useful life of seven years and no residual value. It will be depreciated on a straight-line basis.

b. On September 1, 19A, the company borrowed $10,000 cash from City Bank and signed a one-year, 12%, interest-bearing note. The interest and principal are payable on August 31, 19B.

c. The company owns its office building. On October 1, 19A, the company leased some of its office space to A. B. Smith for $6,000 per year. Smith paid this amount in full on October 1, 19A, and expects to use the space for one year only. The company increased (debited) Cash for $6,000 and increased (credited) Rent Revenue for $6,000 on October 1, 19A.

d. Office supplies were purchased for use in the business. Cash was decreased (credited), and Office Supplies Inventory was increased (debited). The unused supplies at each year-end are determined by inventory count. The amounts were:

Year	Purchased	Inventory
19A	$700	$200
19B	500	300

e. Wages are paid by the company at the end of each two weeks. The last payroll date in December usually is four days before December 31. Therefore, at each year-end, unpaid wages exist that are paid in cash on the first payroll date in the next year. The wages paid in cash and the wages incurred but not yet paid or recorded at each year-end were:

Year	Wages paid in cash during the year	Wages unpaid and unrecorded Dec. 31
19A	$30,000	$2,000
19B	36,000	3,000

f. On July 1, 19A, the company paid a two-year insurance premium (on the computer) of $240. At that date, the company increased (debited) an asset account—Prepaid Insurance—and decreased (credited) Cash, $240.

Required:

Complete the following schedule for 19A and 19B by entering the amounts that should be reported on the financial statements of WAS Company. Show computations.

Balance sheet:

	19A	19B
Assets		
Computer	$_____	$_____
Less: Accumulated depreciation	_____	_____
Carrying value	_____	_____
Office supplies inventory	_____	_____
Prepaid insurance	_____	_____
Liabilities		
Note payable, City Bank	_____	_____
Interest payable	_____	_____
Rent revenue collected in advance	_____	_____
Wages payable	_____	_____

Income statement:

	19A	19B
Rent revenue	$_____	$_____
Depreciation expense	_____	_____
Interest expense	_____	_____
Office supplies expense	_____	_____
Wage expense	_____	_____
Insurance expense	_____	_____

P4–16   (A Comprehensive Bonus Problem; Prepare Six Adjusting Entries and Recast the Income Statement and Balance Sheet)

Morris Transportation Corporation has been in operation since January 1, 19A. It is now December 31, 19A, the end of the annual accounting period. The company has not done well financially during the first year, although transportation revenue has been fairly good. The three stockholders manage the company, but they have not given much attention to recordkeeping. In view of a serious cash shortage, they asked a local bank for a $10,000 loan. The bank requested a complete set of financial statements. The 19A annual financial statements given below were prepared by a clerk and then were given to the bank.

MORRIS TRANSPORTATION CORPORATION
December 31, 19A

Income Statement

Transportation revenue $90,000

Expenses:
Salaries 20,000
Maintenance 15,000
Other expenses 25,000
Total expenses 60,000
Net income $30,000

Balance Sheet

Assets

Cash .... $ 1,000
Receivables 4,000
Inventory of maintenance supplies 5,000
Equipment 30,000
Remaining assets 37,000
Total assets $77,000

Liabilities

Accounts payable .... $ 7,000

Capital

Capital stock 40,000
Retained earnings 30,000
Total liabilities and capital $77,000

After briefly reviewing the statements and "looking into the situation," the bank requested that the statements be redone (with some expert help) to "incorporate depreciation, accruals, inventory counts, income taxes, and so on." As a result of a review of the records and supporting documents, the following additional information was developed:

1. The inventory of maintenance supplies of $5,000 shown on the balance sheet has not been adjusted for supplies used during 19A. An inventory count of the maintenance supplies on hand (unused) on December 31, 19A, showed $2,000. Supplies used are debited to Maintenance Expense.
2. The insurance premium paid in 19A was for years 19A and 19B; therefore, the prepaid insurance at December 31, 19A, amounted to $1,000. The total insurance premium was debited in full to Other Expenses when paid in 19A.
3. The equipment cost $30,000 when purchased January 1, 19A. It has an estimated useful life of five years (no residual value). No depreciation has been recorded for 19A.
4. Unpaid (and unrecorded) salaries at December 31, 19A, amounted to $1,500.
5. At December 31, 19A, hauling revenue collected in advance amounted to $3,000. This amount was credited in full to Transportation Revenue when the cash was collected earlier during 19A.
6. Assume an income tax rate of 20%.

Required:

a. Give the six adjusting entries (in journal form) required by the above additional information for December 31, 19A.

b. Recast the above statements after taking into account the adjusting entries. You do not need to use subclassifications on the statements. Suggested form for the solution:

		Changes		
	Amounts			*Correct*
Items	*reported*	*Plus*	*Minus*	*amounts*
(List here each item from the two statements)				

(Hint: The correct balance sheet total is $69,000.)

c. Omission of the adjusting entries caused:

(1) Net income to be incorrect by: $_____, ___ overstated, or ___ understated.

(2) Total assets on the balance sheet to be incorrect by: $_____, ___ overstated, or ___ understated.

Write a brief, nontechnical report to the bank explaining the causes of these differences.

CASES

PART A

C4–1   (A Question of Full Disclosure)

Forbes magazine (December 8, 1980, p. 57) reported the following: "One firm sold shares for a new coal mining company. The prospectus stated that the firm had acquired 15,000 acres of land with proven coal deposits. What the 'entrepreneurs' who raked in some $20 million didn't mention in the prospectus was that they had only leased surface rights to the land. So the only way they could possibly get any coal out of it was if the black stuff came popping out of its own volition."

Explanation:

A prospectus is defined in *Webster's Dictionary* (7th edition) as "A preliminary printed statement that describes an enterprise (as a business) and is distributed to prospective buyers, investors, or participants."

The company sold all of the shares in one state; therefore, it was not under the jurisdiction of the SEC (see Chapter 1 discussion of the Securities and Exchange Commission).

Required:

If the firm were to prepare a financial report for external decision makers should they disclose the facts cited above? Give the basis for your decision.

PART B

C4–2   (Analysis of Four Transactions of a Real Estate Company that Involve Adjusting Entries)

Fast Company, a closely held corporation, invests in commercial rental properties. Fast's annual accounting period ends on December 31. At the end of each year, numerous adjusting entries must be made because many transactions completed during current and prior years have economic effects on the financial statements of the current and future years. This case is concerned with four transactions that have been selected for your analysis. Assume the current year is 19D.

Transaction A:

On July 1, 19A, the company purchased office equipment for use in the business that cost $12,000. The company estimates that the equipment will have a useful life of 10 years and no residual value.

a. Over how many accounting periods will this transaction affect the financial statements of Fast? Explain.
b. Assuming straight-line depreciation, how much depreciation expense should be reported on the 19A and 19B income statements?
c. How should the office equipment be reported on the 19C balance sheet?
d. Would an adjusting entry be made by Fast at the end of each year during the life of the equipment? Prove your answer.

Transaction B:

On September 1, 19D, Fast collected $18,000 rent on some office space. This amount represented the monthly rent in advance for the six-month period, September 1, 19D, through February 28, 19E. Rent Revenue was increased (credited), and Cash was debited for $18,000.

a. Over how many accounting periods will this transaction affect the financial statements of Fast? Explain.
b. How much rent revenue on this office space should Fast report on the 19D income statement? Explain.
c. Did this transaction create a liability for Fast as of the end of 19D? Explain. How much?
d. Should an adjusting entry be made by Fast on December 31, 19D? Explain why. If your answer is yes, give the adjusting entry.

Transaction C:

On December 31, 19D, Fast owed employees unpaid and unrecorded wages of $5,000 because the payroll was paid on December 27, and between this day and year-end, employees worked three more days in December 19D. The next payroll date is January 5, 19E.

a. Over how many accounting periods would this transaction affect the financial statements of Fast? Explain.
b. How would this $5,000 affect the 19D income statement and balance sheet of Fast?
c. Should an adjusting entry be made by Fast on December 31, 19D? Explain why. If your answer is yes, give the adjusting entry.

Transaction D:

On January 1, 19D, Fast agreed to supervise the planning and subdivision of a large tract of land for a customer—J. Ray. This service job, to be performed by Fast, involved four separate phases. By December 31, 19D, three phases had been completed to the satisfaction of Ray. The remaining phase will be done during 19E. The total price for the four phases (agreed upon in advance by both parties) was $40,000. Each phase involves about the same amount of services. On December 31, 19D, no cash had been collected by Fast for the services already performed.

a. Should Fast record any service revenue on this job for 19D? Explain why. If yes, how much?
b. If your answer to (a) is yes, should Fast make an adjusting entry on December 31, 19D? If yes, give the entry. Explain.
c. What entry will be made by Fast when the last phase is completed, assuming the full contract price is collected on completion date, February 15, 19E?

C4–3   **(Analysis of How Alternative Ways of Recording a Transaction Affect Adjusting Entries)**
General situation: On December 1, 19A, Voss collected $4,000 cash for office space rented to an outsider. The rent collected was for the period December 1, 19A, through March 31, 19B. The annual accounting period ends on December 31.

Required:

a. How much of the $4,000 should Voss report as revenue on the 19A annual income statement? How much of it should be reported as revenue on the 19B income statement?
b. What is the amount of rent revenue collected in advance as of December 31, 19A? How should Voss report this amount on the 19A financial statements?
c. On December 1, 19A, Voss could have recorded the $4,000 collection in one of three different ways as follows:

Approach A:

Cash	4,000	
Rent revenue		4,000

Approach B:

Cash	4,000	
Rent revenue collected in advance		4,000

Approach C:

Cash	4,000	
Rent revenue		1,000
Rent revenue collected in advance		3,000

For each approach, give the appropriate adjusting entry (in journal form) at December 31, 19A. If no adjusting entry is required, explain why.
d. Do you believe one of the approaches shown above is better than the other two? Which one? Explain.

C4–4   **(An Overview of a Complete Set of Actual Financial Statements)**
Refer to the Chesebrough-Ponds financial statements given in Special Supplement B at the end of this textbook immediately preceding the Index. Answer the following questions for the 1985 annual accounting period.

1. On what date did the 1985 accounting year end? How were the dollar amounts rounded?

2. What was the name of the firm of independent CPAs? What was the title of their report?

3. What is the name of the schedule in which the company implements the full-disclosure principle in the long term? How many years does it cover? What is the number of (a) employees and (b) shareholders for 1981 through 1985?

4. What two lines on the income statement, that involve large amounts, directly reflect the matching principle? Compute the ratio between these two amounts (a cost ratio) for 1985 and 1984.

5. What two lines on the balance sheet specifically refer to the cost principle?

6. What item under "Notes to the Consolidated Financial Statements," note No. 1, specifically uses the term "is stated at cost"?

7. How many "Notes to the Consolidated Financial Statements" were included?

8. When are advertising costs and sales promotion costs expensed (refer to the notes)?

9. Give the titles that the company used for the three required financial statements.

10. What is the name of the discussion prepared by the management? List its major captions.

Companies have an information processing accounting system. All such systems must use an *annual* information processing cycle as shown below. All financial statements show when this cycle starts and when it ends.

End of Year	Last Day	First Day	During Year

THE ANNUAL ACCOUNTING INFORMATION PROCESSING CYCLE

Phase 10
Prepare post-closing trial balance

Phase 9
Journalize and post closing entries

Phase 8
Journalize and post adjusting entries

Phase 7
Prepare statements

Phase 6
Prepare the accounting worksheets

Phase 5
Prepare an unadjusted trial balance

Phase 1
Collect data about each transaction

Phase 2
Analyze each transaction in terms of A = L + OE

Phase 3
Enter (record) each transaction in a **journal**

Phase 4
Post data from the journals to the ledger

INFORMATION PROCESSING IN AN ACCOUNTING SYSTEM

PURPOSE:

Chapter 3 introduced the accounting information processing cycle, and Chapter 4 discussed an important phase of the cycle—adjusting entries. The purpose of Chapter 5 is to expand and complete the cycle. The expansion in this chapter involves additional phases that are performed at the end of the accounting (i.e., reporting) year. Accounting worksheets, adjusting entries, closing entries, and financial statements are emphasized. A clear understanding of this chapter will help you learn more applications of the (a) conceptual framework of accounting (Chapter 4, Part A) and (b) accounting information processing cycle.

ORGANIZATION:

1. Data processing approaches in an accounting system—manual, mechanical, electronic.
2. Phases of the accounting information processing cycle during the accounting year.
3. Phases of the accounting information processing cycle at the end of the accounting year.
4. Interim financial statements.

LEARNING OBJECTIVES—TO BE ABLE TO:

1. Define and explain the complete accounting information processing cycle.
2. Apply the four phases of the cycle that are performed during the accounting year.
3. Apply each of the seven phases of the cycle that are performed at the end of the accounting year.
4. Expand your accounting vocabulary by learning the "Important Terms Defined in This Chapter" (page 225).
5. Apply the knowledge learned from this chapter by completing the homework assigned by your instructor.

DATA PROCESSING APPROACHES IN AN ACCOUNTING SYSTEM

Data processing in an accounting system refers to the flow of data through the accounting information processing cycle during each accounting period. Although data processing can be time consuming and costly to the enterprise, a well-designed processing system provides an efficient flow of data from the daily transactions to the financial statements at the end of the accounting period. The processing of accounting data may be done in one of three ways, or, as is the usual case, by a combination of them. The three approaches are: manual data processing, mechanical data processing, and electronic data processing.

Manual data processing

With this approach, the accounting work is done by hand (i.e., manually). The manual approach is used in small entities. In large and medium-sized businesses, certain parts of the information process often are done manually. The manual approach also is used in accounting textbooks to illustrate data processing because you can see what is being done. You cannot see what is going on inside a computer.

Mechanical data processing

Mechanical data processing is used to record repetitive transactions that occur in large numbers. Mechanical processing of accounting data uses accounting machines that vary in type and application. These mechanical devices range from cash registers to posting machines. Although mechanical data processing is used today, it is being rapidly replaced by electronic data processing.

Electronic data processing

Electronic processing of accounting data uses electronic computers of varying size and sophistication. When electronic data processing is used, the use of manual and mechanical activities in an accounting system is minimal. Because of the large capability to store data and the speed with which such data can be manipulated and recalled, electronic data processing is widely used in accounting. Electronic data processing needs "hardware" and "software." The computer and equipment related to it (usually called peripheral equipment) make up the **hardware. Software** includes (a) the computer programs that are instructions to the computer and (b) other items related to the operation of the system. Electronic data processing is applied widely to such accounting problems as payrolls, billings for goods and services, accounts receivable, accounts payable, inventories, and to the preparation of detailed financial statements. Because of the rapid development of microcomputers and software "packages" for them, it is technically and economically feasible for even the smallest businesses (and individuals) to have an electronic accounting system.

EXPANDING THE ACCOUNTING INFORMATION PROCESSING CYCLE

This section expands, but does not change, the **accounting information processing cycle** introduced in Chapter 3. You should review those discussions (particularly Exhibit 3–8). The expansion has additional phases related to the end-of-period activities. Exhibit 5–1 shows the additional phases.

EXHIBIT 5–1

Phases of the accounting information processing cycle expanded

Phases Completed During the Accounting Period

1. **Collection of economic data** about each transaction of the entity; supported with business documents.
2. **Transaction analysis** of each current transaction (when completed) to determine the economic effects on the entity in terms of the accounting model.
3. **Journalizing** the results of the analysis of the current transactions. This phase encompasses recording the entries in chronological order in the **journal.**
4. **Posting** the current entries from the journal to the respective accounts in the **ledger.**

Phases Completed Only at the End of the Accounting Period

5. **Prepare an unadjusted trial balance** from the ledger.
*6. **Prepare an accounting worksheet:**
   a. Collection of data for adjusting entries and analysis of the data in the context of the accounting model. Enter the adjusting entries on the worksheet.
   b. Separation of the adjusted data among the income statement, balance sheet, and statement of retained earnings. Prepare SCFP worksheet (discussed in Chapter 15).
7. **Prepare financial statements:**
   a. Income statement.
   b. Balance sheet.
   c. Statement of changes in financial position (SCFP; discussed in Chapter 15).
*8. **Adjusting entries** (at the end of the period):
   a. Recorded in the journal.
   b. Posted to the ledger.
*9. **Closing** the revenue and expense accounts in the **ledger:**
   a. Recorded in the journal.
   b. Posted to the ledger.
*10. **Prepare a post-closing trial balance.**

Phase Completed Only at the Start of the Next Accounting Period

11. Optional **reversing entries** (see Supplement 5A).

* Phases added in this chapter to expand the cycle.

Phases Completed during the Accounting Period

The phases completed during the accounting period were discussed and illustrated in Chapter 3. For study convenience, these phases are summarized below.

Phase 1—Collection of economic data about each transaction

This phase is a continuing activity that collects **source documents** (such as sales invoices) from all of the transactions as they occur. The collection process involves all operations of the entity and a large number of employees (including nonaccountants). Source documents provide data to be analyzed and recorded in the accounting system. The source documents must be collected in a timely manner and must provide **complete and accurate data** about each transaction.

Phase 2—Transaction analysis

This phase is an analysis of source documents to identify and measure the economic impact of each transaction on the entity in terms of the basic accounting model: Assets = Liabilities + Owners' Equity, and Debits = Credits. It requires determination of the specific asset, liability, and owners' equity accounts that should be increased and/or decreased to properly reflect the economic consequences of each transaction.

Phase 3—Journalizing

This phase involves recording by date the analysis of each transaction in the **journal** in the Debits = Credits format. Thus, the economic impacts of each transaction on the entity are recorded first in the journal in chronological order.

Phase 4—Posting

This phase involves transferring the data in the journal to the **ledger.** The ledger has separate accounts; one for each kind of asset, liability, and owners' equity. Thus, posting to the ledger reorders the data from the chronological order in the journal to the classifications in the fundamental accounting model— Assets = Liabilities + Owners' Equity. The ledger is viewed as the basic accounting record because it provides appropriately classified economic data about the entity that will be used to **complete the remaining phases** of the accounting information processing cycle (including preparation of the periodic financial statements).

Phases of the Accounting Information Processing Cycle Completed at the End of the Accounting Period

The phases of the accounting information cycle discussed in Chapter 3 are expanded in this chapter to *(a)* handle large volumes of accounting data, *(b)* facilitate the end-of-period accounting activities, and *(c)* minimize accounting errors and omissions. The specific procedures associated with the remaining phases are discussed in detail in this section.

Phase 5—Unadjusted trial balance

At the end of the accounting period, after all current transactions have been recorded in the journal (journalized) and then posted to the ledger, a listing of all **ledger** accounts and their balances is prepared. This listing is called the **unadjusted trial balance.** This trial balance has two purposes: (a) it can be used to check the two accounting equalities—Assets = Liabilities + Owners' Equity, and Debits = Credits—and (b) it provides basic data needed to prepare the financial statements.

This trial balance is called **unadjusted** because it does not include the effects of the **adjusting** entries (discussed in Chapter 4). The expanded phases—6 through 10—show how the adjusting entries are included in the (a) financial statements and (b) the accounting records.

Phase 6—The accounting worksheet

The outline given in Exhibit 5–1 lists six different phases that are completed at the end of the accounting period, including an **accounting worksheet.** The worksheet is prepared before the financial statements are prepared and before the adjusting and closing entries are recorded. The **completed worksheet provides all of the data needed to complete the remaining end-of-period phases** by bringing together in one place, in an orderly way, the (1) unadjusted trial balance, (2) adjusting entries, (3) income statement, (4) statement of retained earnings, (5) balance sheet, and (6) the closing entries (explained later).[1]

Prepare an accounting worksheet.   The simplified case used in Chapter 4 (pages 157–66) for High-Rise Apartments will be used to illustrate preparation of a typical worksheet at the end of the accounting year, December 31, 19B. To make the illustration easier, two exhibits are given:

Exhibit 5–2—Worksheet format with the unadjusted trial balance and adjusting entries.

Exhibit 5–3—Worksheet completed; shows the **income statement, statement of retained earnings, and balance sheet.**

The sequential steps used to develop the worksheet are:

Step 1—Set up the worksheet format by entering the appropriate column headings. This step is shown in Exhibit 5–2. The left column shows the account titles (taken directly from the ledger). There are six separate pairs of debit-credit money columns. Notice that the last six debit-credit columns show the data for the financial statements.

---

[1] This entire section on the worksheet can be omitted without affecting the remaining chapters because it is only a facilitating procedure.

Step 2—Enter the **unadjusted** trial balance as of the end of the accounting period directly from the ledger into the first pair of debit-credit columns. When all of the current entries for the period, **excluding** the adjusting entries, have been recorded in the journal and posted to the ledger, the amounts for the **unadjusted** trial balance are the balances of the respective ledger accounts. Before going to the next step, the equality of the debits and credits in the unadjusted trial balance should be tested by totaling each column (totals $491,460). When a worksheet is used, there is no need to develop a **separate** unadjusted trial balance (Phase 5) because it can be developed on the worksheet.

Step 3—The second pair of debit-credit columns, headed "Adjusting Entries," is completed by developing and then entering the adjusting entries directly on the worksheet. The adjusting entries for High-Rise Apartments shown in Exhibit 5–2 were shown (with the same letter codes) and discussed in detail in Chapter 4, Part B. To facilitate examination (for potential errors), future reference, and study, the adjusting entries usually are coded on the worksheet as illustrated in Exhibit 5–2. Some of the adjusting entries may need one or more account titles in addition to those of the original trial balance listing (see last four account titles in Exhibit 5–2). After the adjusting entries are completed on the worksheet, the equality of debits and credits for those entries is checked (totals $19,900).

The remaining steps to complete the worksheet are shown by the shaded area in Exhibit 5–3; these steps are:

Step 4—The pair of debit-credit columns headed "Adjusted Trial Balance" is completed. Although not essential, this pair of columns helps to assure accuracy. The adjusted trial balance is the line-by-line combined amounts of the unadjusted trial balance, plus or minus the amounts entered as adjusting entries in the second pair of columns. For example, the Rent Revenue account shows a $128,463 credit balance under Unadjusted Trial Balance. To this amount is **added the credit** amount, $600, **minus the debit amount,** $500, for combined amount of $128,563, which is entered as a **credit** under Adjusted Trial Balance. For those accounts that were not affected by the adjusting entries, the unadjusted trial balance amount is carried directly across to the Adjusted Trial Balance column. After each line has been completed, the equality of the debits and credits under Adjusted Trial Balance is checked (total $509,260).

Step 5—The amount on each line, under Adjusted Trial Balance, is **extended horizontally** across the worksheet and entered (a) as a debit, if it is a debit under Adjusted Trial Balance, or as a credit, if it is a credit under Adjusted Trial Balance; and (b) under the financial statement heading (income statement, retained earnings[2], or balance sheet) on which it must be reported.

---

[2] The statement of Retained Earnings is discussed below under Phase 7.

EXHIBIT 5–2

Worksheet format with unadjusted trial balance and adjusting entries (already entered)

HIGH-RISE APARTMENTS, INC.
Worksheet for the Year Ended December 31, 19B

Account Titles	Unadjusted Trial Balance Debit	Unadjusted Trial Balance Credit	Adjusting Entries Debit	Adjusting Entries Credit	Adjusted Trial Balance Debit	Adjusted Trial Balance Credit	Income Statement Debit	Income Statement Credit	Retained Earnings Debit	Retained Earnings Credit	Balance Sheet Debit	Balance Sheet Credit
Cash	12,297											
Prepaid insurance	2,400			(c) 1,200								
Inventory of maintenance supplies	600			(e) 400								
Land	25,000											
Apartment building	360,000											
Accumulated depreciation, building		10,000		(d) 10,000								
Notes payable, long term		30,000										
Rent collected in advance				(a) 500								
Mortgage payable, long term		238,037										
Capital stock, par $10, 5,000 shares*		50,000										
Contributed capital in excess of par		5,000										
Retained earnings, Jan. 1, 19B		29,960										
Dividends declared and paid	12,000											
Rent revenue		128,463	(a) 500	(b) 600								
Advertising expense	500											
Maintenance expense	3,000		(e) 400									
Salary expense	17,400		(f) 900									
Interest expense	19,563		(h) 600									
Utilities expense	34,500											
Miscellaneous expenses	4,200											
Insurance expense			(c) 1,200									
Depreciation expense			(d) 10,000									
Salaries payable				(f) 900								
Property tax expense			(g) 5,700									
Property tax payable				(g) 5,700								
Interest payable				(h) 600								
Rent revenue receivable			(b) 600									
	491,460	491,460	19,900	19,900								

* Average issue price per share: ($50,000 + $5,000) ÷ 5,000 shares = $11. This topic is discussed in Chapter 12.

EXHIBIT 5–3

Accounting worksheet completed

HIGH-RISE APARTMENTS, INC.
Worksheet for the Year Ended December 31, 19B

Account Titles	Unadjusted Trial Balance Debit	Unadjusted Trial Balance Credit	Adjusting Entries* Debit	Adjusting Entries* Credit	Adjusted Trial Balance Debit	Adjusted Trial Balance Credit	Income Statement Debit	Income Statement Credit	Retained Earnings Debit	Retained Earnings Credit	Balance Sheet Debit	Balance Sheet Credit
Cash	12,297				12,297						12,297	
Prepaid insurance	2,400			(c) 1,200	1,200						1,200	
Inventory of maintenance supplies	600			(e) 400	200						200	
Land	25,000				25,000						25,000	
Apartment building	360,000				360,000						360,000	
Accumulated depreciation, building		10,000		(d) 10,000		20,000						20,000
Notes payable, long term		30,000				30,000						30,000
Rent collected in advance				(a) 500		500						500
Mortgage payable, long term		238,037				238,037						238,037
Capital stock, par $10, 5,000 shares		50,000				50,000						50,000
Contributed capital in excess of par		5,000				5,000						5,000
Retained earnings, Jan. 1, 19B		29,960				29,960				29,960		
Dividends declared and paid	12,000				12,000				12,000			
Rent revenue		128,463	(a) 500	(b) 600		128,563		128,563				
Advertising expense	500				500		500					
Maintenance expense	3,000		(e) 400		3,400		3,400					

Financial Statements

Account	Trial Balance Dr	Trial Balance Cr	Adjustments Dr	Adjustments Cr	Adjusted Trial Balance Dr	Adjusted Trial Balance Cr	Income Statement Dr	Income Statement Cr	Retained Earnings Dr	Retained Earnings Cr	Balance Sheet Dr	Balance Sheet Cr
Salary expense	17,400		(f) 900		18,300		18,300					
Interest expense	19,563		(h) 600		20,163		20,163					
Utilities expense	34,500				34,500		34,500					
Miscellaneous expenses	4,200				4,200		4,200					
Insurance expense			(c) 1,200		1,200		1,200					
Depreciation expense			(d) 10,000		10,000		10,000					
Salaries payable				(f) 900		900						900
Property tax expense			(g) 5,700		5,700		5,700					
Property tax payable				(g) 5,700		5,700						5,700
Interest payable				(h) 600		600						600
Rent revenue receivable			(b) 600		600						600	
	491,460	491,460	19,900	19,900	509,260	509,260	97,963	128,563				
Income tax expense†			(i) 6,120		6,120		6,120					
Income tax payable‡				(i) 6,120		6,120						6,120
Net income							24,480			24,480		
							128,563	128,563		54,440		
Retained earnings, Dec. 31, 19B§									12,000			42,440
									42,440			399,297
									54,440		399,297	

* Explanation of adjusting entries is provided in Exhibit 5-4.
† Revenues, $128,563 − Pretax expenses, $97,963 = $30,600; $30,600 × tax rate, 20% = $6,120.
‡ Pretax income, $30,600 − Income tax, $6,120 = $24,480.
§ $54,440 − $12,000 = $42,440.

You can see that (1) each amount extended across was entered under only one of the six remaining columns, and (2) debits remain debits and credits remain credits in the extending process.

Step 6—At this point, the two Income Statement columns are summed (subtotals). The difference between these two subtotals is the **pretax income (or loss).** Income tax expense then is computed by multiplying this difference by the tax rate. In Exhibit 5–3, the computation was (Pretax revenues, $128,563 − Pretax expenses, $97,963) × Tax rate, 20% = $6,120. The **adjusting entry** for income tax then was entered at the bottom of the worksheet (a "loopback"). Income tax expense and income tax payable now can be extended horizontally to the Income Statement and Balance Sheet columns. Net income is entered as a **balancing debit** amount in the Income Statement column and as a credit (i.e., increase) in the Retained Earnings column.

Step 7—The two Retained Earnings columns are summed. The difference is the ending balance of retained earnings. This balance amount is entered as a balancing debit amount (under Retained Earnings) and also as a balancing credit amount (i.e., an addition to owners' equity). At this point, the two Balance Sheet columns should sum to equal amounts. The continuous checking of the equality of debits and credits in each pair of debit-credit columns helps to assure the correctness of the worksheet. However, the balancing feature alone does not assure that the worksheet has no errors. For example, if an expense amount (a debit) were extended to either the Retained Earnings debit column or to the Balance Sheet debit column, the worksheet would balance in all respects; however, at least two money columns would have one or more errors. Therefore, special care must be used in selecting the appropriate debit-credit columns during the horizontal extension process.[3]

The completed worksheet, Exhibit 5–3, provides the data needed to complete the remaining phases of the accounting information processing cycle as follows (summarized from Exhibit 5–1):

Phase	Phase description	Source on worksheet
7	Prepare income statement	Income Statement columns
	Prepare balance sheet	Balance Sheet columns
	Prepare statement of retained earnings	Retained Earnings columns
8	Record adjusting entries in journal and post to ledger	Adjusting Entries columns
9	Record closing entries in journal and post to ledger	Income Statement and Retained Earnings columns
10	Post-closing trial balance	Prepare from ledger and check with Balance Sheet columns

---

[3] The number of paired columns on a worksheet can be reduced by omitting both, or either, the Adjusted Trial Balance columns and the Retained Earnings columns. Also, the number of columns can be reduced further by using only one money column for each set instead of separate debit and credit columns (for example, the credits can be indicated by parentheses).

Phase 7—Prepare financial statements from the worksheet

The completed worksheet provides the accounts and amounts needed to prepare the income statement, balance sheet, and statement of retained earnings.The statement of retained earnings, although not a required statement, usually is prepared by corporations. The **retained earnings statement** ties together the income statement and the stockholders' equity section of the balance sheet.

The financial statements for High-Rise Apartments, prepared directly from the worksheet, Exhibit 5–3, are shown below. Notice that all of the figures were provided by the last three pairs of columns headed "Income Statement," "Retained Earnings," and "Balance Sheet."

HIGH-RISE APARTMENTS, INC.
Income Statement
For the Year Ended December 31, 19B

Revenue:		
Rent revenue		$128,563
Operating expenses:		
Advertising expense	$ 500	
Maintenance expense	3,400	
Salary expense	18,300	
Interest expense	20,163	
Utilities expense	34,500	
Miscellaneous expenses	4,200	
Insurance expense	1,200	
Depreciation expense	10,000	
Property tax expense	5,700	
Total operating expenses		97,963
Pretax income		30,600
Income tax expense ($30,600 × 20%)		6,120
Net income		$ 24,480
EPS ($24,480 ÷ 5,000 shares)		$4.90

HIGH-RISE APARTMENTS, INC.
Statement of Retained Earnings
For the Year Ended December 31, 19B

Retained earnings balance, January 1, 19B	$29,960
Add net income of 19B	24,480
Total	54,440
Less dividends declared and paid in 19B	12,000
Retained earnings balance, December 31, 19B	$42,440

HIGH-RISE APARTMENTS, INC.
Balance Sheet
At December 31, 19B

Assets

Current assets:

Cash	$ 12,297	
Prepaid insurance	1,200	
Inventory, maintenance supplies	200	
Rent revenue receivable	600	
Total current assets		$ 14,297

Operational assets:

Land		25,000	
Apartment building	$360,000		
Less: Accumulated depreciation	20,000	340,000	365,000
Total assets			$379,297

Liabilities

Current liabilities:

Salaries payable	$ 900	
Property tax payable	5,700	
Interest payable	600	
Income tax payable	6,120	
Rent collected in advance	500	
Total current liabilities		$ 13,820

Long-term liabilities:

Note payable	30,000	
Mortgage payable	238,037	
Total long-term liabilities		268,037
Total liabilities		281,857

Stockholders' Equity

Contributed capital:

Capital stock, par $10; outstanding 5,000 shares	50,000	
Contributed capital in excess of par	5,000	
Total contributed capital	55,000	
Retained earnings (see statement of retained earnings)	42,440	
Total stockholders' equity		97,440
Total liabilities and stockholders' equity		$379,297

Phase 8—Journalize and post the adjusting entries

This phase is needed to enter the effects of the adjusting entries into the accounts. Immediately after finishing the worksheet, the financial statements are prepared and distributed to the users. By using a worksheet, preparation and distribution of the financial statements are not delayed by the remaining phases of the accounting cycle. After the financial statements have been prepared, the **adjusting entries shown on the completed worksheet are entered in the journal and then posted to the ledger.** These entries are "dated" as of the last day of the accounting period. This task is a clerical one because the entries merely are copied from the worksheet into the journal. The adjusting entries for High-Rise Apartments, with a **folio notation** to show that posting is completed, are shown in Exhibit 5–4. The ledger, with the adjusting entries posted (in color for identification), is shown in Exhibit 5–6. You should trace the posting from the journal to the ledger.

Phase 9—Closing entries for the income statement accounts

Chapters 2 and 3 emphasized that the revenue and expense accounts are subdivisions of retained earnings which is a part of owners' equity. The revenue, gain, expense, and loss accounts are **"income statement" accounts.** The remaining accounts are **"balance sheet" accounts.** The revenue, gain, expense, and loss accounts are often called **temporary** (or nominal) accounts because they are used to accumulate data for the **current accounting period only.** At the end

EXHIBIT 5–4

Adjusting entries recorded in the journal

	HIGH-RISE APARTMENTS, INC.				
	JOURNAL				Page 6
Date 19B	Account Titles and Explanation	Folio	Debit	Credit	
Dec. 31	*a.* Rent revenue	340	500		
	Rent collected in advance	204		500	
	To adjust the accounts for revenue collected in advance (see pages 157 and 158).				
31	*b.* Rent revenue receivable	102	600		
	Rent revenue	340		600	
	To adjust for rent revenue earned in 19B, but not yet collected (see pages 159–60).				
31	*c.* Insurance expense	356	1,200		
	Prepaid insurance	103		1,200	
	To adjust for insurance expired during 19B (see pages 160–61)				
31	*d.* Depreciation expense	360	10,000		
	Accumulated depreciation, building	113		10,000	
	To adjust for depreciation expense for 19B (see pages 162–63).				
31	*e.* Maintenance expense	351	400		
	Inventory of maintenance supplies	104		400	
	To adjust for supplies used from inventory during 19B (see page 163).				

EXHIBIT 5–4 *(concluded)*

Adjusting entries recorded in the journal

HIGH-RISE APARTMENTS, INC.

JOURNAL   Page 6

Date 19B	Account Titles and Explanation	Folio	Debit	Credit
31	*f.* Salary expense	352	900	
	Salaries payable	206		900
	To adjust for salaries earned but not yet recorded or paid (see page 164).			
31	*g.* Property tax expense	361	5,700	
	Property tax payable	207		5,700
	To adjust for 19B property tax incurred, but not yet recorded or paid (see page 165).			
31	*h.* Interest expense	353	600	
	Interest payable	209		600
	To adjust for accrued interest expense for two months on note payable ($30,000 × 12% × 2/12 = $600) (see pages 165–66).			
31	*i.* An adjusting entry for income tax expense is computed on the worksheet when the pretax income is computed thereon (see page 170 and 210). The entry is:			
	Income tax expense	370	6,120	
	Income tax payable	208		6,120

of each period, their balances are transferred, or **closed,** to the Retained Earnings account. This periodic closing (or clearing out) of the balances of the income statement accounts into Retained Earnings is done by using closing entries. The closing entries have two purposes: (1) to transfer net income (or loss) to retained earnings (i.e., owners' equity), and (2) to establish a **zero balance** in each of the temporary accounts to start the next accounting period. In this way, the **income statement accounts** again are ready for their **temporary** periodic collection function for the next period.

In contrast, the **balance sheet accounts** (assets, liabilities, and owners' equity) are not closed periodically; therefore, they are often called **permanent** (or real) accounts. To illustrate, the ending cash balance of one accounting period must be the beginning Cash balance of the next accounting period. The only time a permanent account has a zero balance is when the item represented (such as machinery or notes payable) is no longer owned (or is fully depreciated) or no longer owed. The balance at the end of the period in each balance sheet account is carried forward in the ledger as the **beginning** balance for the next period.

The **closing entries** made at the end of the accounting period to transfer the balances of all of the income statement accounts is only a clerical phase. To close an account means to transfer its balance to another designated account by means of an entry. For example, an account that has a credit balance (such as a revenue account) is closed by **debiting** that account for an amount equal to its balance and crediting the account to which the balance is transferred. In the closing process, a credit balance is always transferred to another account as a credit, and a debit balance is always transferred to another account as a debit. Closing entries are **dated** the last day of the accounting period, entered in the journal in the usual Debits = Credits format, and immediately posted to the ledger.

A special summary account, called Income Summary, sometimes is used in the closing process. All of the income statement accounts—revenues, gains, expenses, and losses—are closed to Income Summary. The summarized difference is net income or net loss, which is then closed to the Retained Earnings account. The following summarized data for High-Rise Apartments (from Exhibit 5–3) is used to illustrate the Income Summary account: total revenues, $128,563, total expenses, $104,083, and net income, $24,480. The three closing entries, as they would be shown in the ledger accounts, would be as follows:

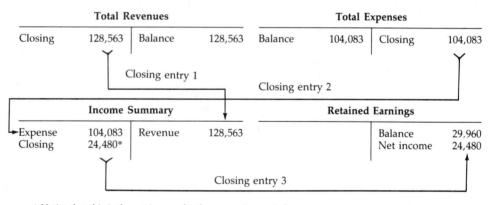

* Notice that this is the net income for the accounting period.

The detailed closing entries are shown in Exhibits 5–5 and 5–6. The data used in the detailed closing entries can be taken directly from the worksheet, Exhibit 5–3.

The last journal entry shown on Exhibit 5–5 closed Dividends Declared and Paid to Retained Earnings (not to Income Summary). High-Rise Apartments, Inc., declared and paid a $12,000 cash dividend to its stockholders. Dividends Declared and Paid was debited, and Cash was credited for this amount. Dividends are payments to the stockholders out of earnings. A dividend reduces retained earnings. Therefore, the dividend account is closed to Retained Earn-

EXHIBIT 5–5

Closing entries recorded in the journal (Source of data is Exhibit 5–3)

HIGH-RISE APARTMENTS, INC.

JOURNAL   Page 7

Date 19B	Account Titles and Explanation	Folio	Debit	Credit
Dec. 31	Rent revenue	340	128,563	
	Income summary	330		128,563
	To transfer revenues into Income Summary.			
31	Income summary ($97,963 + $6,120)	330	104,083	
	Advertising expense	350		500
	Maintenance expense	351		3,400
	Salary expense	352		18,300
	Interest expense	353		20,163
	Utilities expense	354		34,500
	Miscellaneous expenses	355		4,200
	Insurance expense	356		1,200
	Depreciation expense	360		10,000
	Property tax expense	361		5,700
	Income tax expense	370		6,120
	To transfer expense amounts into Income Summary.			
31	Income summary	330	24,480	
	Retained earnings	305		24,480
	To transfer Net Income into Retained Earnings.			
31	Retained earnings	305	12,000	
	Dividends declared and paid	306		12,000
	To transfer Dividends Declared and Paid into Retained Earnings.			

ings.[4] Notice that the **ending** balance in the ledger account for Retained Earnings is: $29,960 + $24,480 − $12,000 = $42,440. Net income and dividends paid are included in the statement of retained earnings (see page 211).

After the closing process is completed, all of the temporary (i.e., the income statement) accounts have been closed to a zero balance. These accounts then are ready for reuse during the next accounting period for accumulating the revenues and expenses of the new period. When T-accounts are used, as in Exhibit 5–6, a zero balance is indicated by a double ruling on each side of the account.

---

[4] When the dividend was declared and paid, the debit could have been made directly to Retained Earnings. In this case, the closing entry would not be made.

EXHIBIT 5–6

Ledger accounts illustrated with adjusting and closing entries

HIGH-RISE APARTMENTS, INC.
LEDGER—19B

Cash		101
12,297		

Property Tax Payable		207
	(g)	5,700

Maintenance Expense		351
3,000	(7)	3,400
(e) 400		

Rent Revenue Receivable		102
(b) 600		

Income Tax Payable		208
	(i)	6,120

Salary Expense		352
17,400	(7)	18,300
(f) 900		

Prepaid Insurance		103
2,400	(c)	1,200

Interest Payable		209
	(h)	600

Interest Expense		353
19,563	(7)	20,163
(h) 600		

Inventory of Maintenance Supplies		104
600	(e)	400

Mortgage Payable		251
		238,037

Utilities Expense		354
34,500	(7)	34,500

Land		110
25,000		

Capital Stock		301
		50,000

Miscellaneous Expenses		355
4,200	(7)	4,200

Contributed Capital in Excess of Par		302
		5,000

EXHIBIT 5–6 *(concluded)*

Ledger accounts illustrated with adjusting and closing entries

Apartment Building	111		Retained Earnings		305		Insurance Expense		356
360,000		(7) 12,000		29,960	(c)	1,200	(7)	1,200
				(7) 24,480		═══		═══

Accumulated Depreciation, Building	113		Dividends Declared and Paid		306		Depreciation Expense		360
	10,000	12,000	(7) 12,000	(d)	10,000	(7)	10,000
(d)	10,000		═══	═══		═══		═══

Notes Payable (long term) 201		Income Summary		330		Property Tax Expense		361
	30,000	(7) 104,083	(7) 128,563	(g)	5,700	(7)	5,700
		(7) 24,480	═══		═══		═══

Rent Collected in Advance	204		Rent Revenue		340		Income Tax Expense		370
	(a) 500	(a) 500	128,463	(i)	6,120	(7)	6,120
		(7) 128,563	(b) 600		═══		═══
		═══	═══				

Salaries Payable	206		Advertising Expense		350
	(f) 900	500	(7) 500
		═══	═══

For illustrative purposes:
- Unadjusted balances are in black.
- Adjusting entries are in color.
- Closing entries are enclosed in boxes.

The permanent (i.e., balance sheet) accounts will have an **ending** balance, which is carried forward as the beginning balance for the next period. The balance carried forward in a T-account can be shown as follows:[5]

Retained Earnings			305
Dividends (19B)	12,000	Jan. 1, 19B, balance	29,960
Balance carried forward to 19C	42,440	Net income (19B)	24,480
	54,440		54,440
		Jan. 1, 19C, balance	42,440

Phase 10—Post-closing trial balance

This phase is a clerical verification of the account balances after all closing entries have been posted. In computerized accounting systems this verification can be done automatically. In other systems it may be done with a printing calculator or an adding machine. Some accountants prefer to prepare another formal trial balance, called a **post-closing trial balance**, before starting a new period. All of the income statement accounts have been closed to Retained Earnings; therefore, the post-closing trial balance will show balances **only** for the permanent accounts classified as assets, liabilities, and owners' equity. These balances should be the same as those shown in the last two columns of the worksheet (Exhibit 5–3). The ending balances shown in the ledger accounts after the closing process will be the beginning balances for the next period.

Phase 11—Reversing entries

Some accountants add an **optional phase** to the accounting information processing cycle called **reversing entries.** This phase is dated as of the first day of the next accounting period. It is used for the sole purpose of **facilitating** certain subsequent entries in the accounts. Reversing entries are related specifically to certain adjusting entries that already have been journalized and posted to the accounts. When appropriate, such adjusting entries are reversed on the first day of the next period (i.e., the debits and credits simply are reversed by the reversing entry). Reversing entries involve bookkeeping skills rather than accounting concepts and principles. Supplement 5A at the end of this chapter discusses and illustrates reversing entries for those who want to learn about this optional facilitating technique.

---

[5] Exhibit 3–4 shows the columnar format for ledger accounts that is always used. The T-account format is used only for instructional convenience.

INTERIM FINANCIAL STATEMENTS

Financial statements for a reporting period of less than one year are called **interim financial statements.** Such statements usually are prepared quarterly or monthly. **Monthly** financial statements almost always are for internal management uses only. In contrast, many larger companies prepare quarterly financial statements for internal management use and also present summarized versions of them to their stockholders and other external parties.

When monthly or quarterly interim financial statements are prepared, the company usually does not go through the phases of interim adjusting and closing entries. The formal phases of journalizing and posting adjusting entries typically are performed only at the end of the annual accounting period. Instead, the company prepares a worksheet to facilitate preparation of the interim financial statements. Therefore, the worksheet has another very useful purpose when interim monthly or quarterly financial statements are prepared. At the end of each interim period, an unadjusted trial balance is taken from the ledger accounts and entered directly on an interim (say, monthly) worksheet. The interim worksheet then is completed by entering the interim adjusting entries on it and extending the adjusted amounts to the Retained Earnings, Income Statement, and Balance Sheet columns. The interim statements (say, monthly) are prepared on the basis of the worksheet. In such cases, the remaining phases of the accounting information processing cycle (adjusting entries recorded, closing entries recorded, and post-closing trial balance) are not completed at the end of each interim period.

SUMMARY OF CHAPTER

This chapter discussed the accounting information processing cycle that is completed in cases where periodic financial statements are developed for both external and internal users. The cycle captures economic data on transactions as they occur and then records and processes their economic effects on the entity and communicates these effects by means of the periodic financial statements. The accounting information system must be designed to measure net income, financial position, and funds flow accurately and effectively. Such an information system also must be designed to fit the specific characteristics of the entity.

The worksheet, the closing entries, and the post-closing trial balance phases are clerical data processing procedures and do not involve any new accounting principles. The 11 phases discussed in this chapter constitute the accounting information processing cycle that is repeated each accounting period in most accounting systems.

Many adaptations of the procedures used to implement the cycle are observed in actual situations because entities have different characteristics such as size, type of industry, complexity, accounting expertise, and sophistication of the management.

The information processing activities in a particular entity can be effective in terms of the outputs (the financial statements), but unfortunately, the opposite may be true. The effectiveness of the system depends on the competence of those performing the data processing tasks and the importance attached by the management and owners to the financial measurement of operating results and financial position. In this context, the information processing system of an entity is significant to all parties interested in the entity because the end results—the financial statements—are important in decision making.

SUPPLEMENT 5A—REVERSING ENTRIES ILLUSTRATED

After finishing Phase 10 of the accounting information processing cycle (i.e., the post-closing trial balance), an **optional facilitating phase** may be added as Phase 11 (see Exhibit 5–1). This optional phase involves reversing entries. **Reversing entries are dated at the beginning of the next period and relate only to certain adjusting entries made at the end of the prior period.** Certain adjusting entries may be reversed on the first day of the next period solely to facilitate recording subsequent related entries. Unlike most of the prior phases in the accounting information processing cycle, reversing entries are optional and involve only bookkeeping skills rather than accounting principles or concepts.

The reversing entry phase is presented because (1) it introduces a common data processing technique used in most companies, whether the system is manual, mechanical, or computerized; and (2) a knowledge of the circumstances under which this phase may be used gives some additional insight into certain relationships in the efficient processing of accounting information.[6]

Reversing entries are given this name because they reverse, at the start of the next accounting period, the effects of certain adjusting entries made at the end of the previous period. Reversing entries are always the opposite of the related adjusting entry. It may be desirable to "reverse" certain adjusting entries; the other adjusting entries should not be reversed.

To illustrate reversing entries and the type of situation where a reversing entry will simplify the subsequent accounting entry, assume that Day Company is in the process of completing the information processing cycle at the end of its accounting period, December 31, 19B. To place the reversing entry in context, Exhibit 5–7 presents a situation that shows (1) an adjusting entry on December 31, 19B; (2) the reversing entry that could be made on January 1, 19C; and (3) the subsequent entry on January 13, 19C, that was facilitated or simplified. To demonstrate the facilitating effect of a reversing entry, we also have presented entries in the exhibit reflecting the same situation assuming no reversing entry. You should study carefully the two sets of entries and the explanatory comments in Exhibit 5–7. The reversing entry is shown in color for emphasis.

---

[6] Knowledge of reversing entries is important primarily to students who plan to study advanced accounting. This knowledge is not significant for study of the remaining chapters in this book.

EXHIBIT 5–7

Purpose of reversing entries illustrated with wages

DAY COMPANY

Situation: The payroll was paid on December 28, 19B; the next payroll will be on January 13, 19C. At December 31, 19B, wages of $3,000 were earned for the last three days of the year that had not been paid or recorded.

With reversing entry ‖ Without reversing entry

a. **The preceding adjusting entry:**

December 31, 19B, adjusting entry to record the $3,000 accrued (unpaid) wages:

With reversing entry		‖	Without reversing entry	
Wage expense 3,000		‖	Wage expense 3,000	
Wages payable		‖	Wages payable	
(a liability)	3,000	‖	(a liability)	3,000

b. **The closing entry:** The revenue and expense accounts are closed to Income Summary after the adjusting entries are completed and posted to the ledger.

December 31, 19B, closing entry:

With reversing entry		‖	Without reversing entry	
Income summary 3,000		‖	Income summary 3,000	
Wage expense	3,000	‖	Wage expense	3,000

Exhibit 5–8 presents another illustration of the effects of reversing entries. It is presented to emphasize the facilitating feature of reversing entries as shown in both the journal and ledger. The reversing entry is shown in color to facilitate your study.

In the above discussion we explained that certain adjusting entries could be reversed to facilitate or simplify subsequent related entries and that certain adjusting entries would **not** be reversed. How does one decide which entries may be reversed to advantage? There is no inflexible rule that will answer this question. The accountant must analyze each case and make a rational choice. In general, short-term accruals and deferrals are candidates for reversal.

The adjusting entry to record depreciation and other entries of this type should never be reversed. In these cases, the adjusting entry is not followed by a subsequent "collection or payment" entry; therefore, it would be not only pointless to reverse the adjusting entry for depreciation but would introduce an

EXHIBIT 5–7 *(concluded)*

Purpose of reversing entries illustrated with wages

c. **The reversing entry:** The information processing cycle in 19B is complete. All closing entries have been posted, and the post-closing trial balance has been verified. At this point in time, January 1, 19C, the accountant should decide whether it is desirable to reverse any of the 19B adjusting entries (i.e., any reversing entries) to simplify the **subsequent related entries.** Question: Would a reversing entry on January 1, 19C, simplify the entry to be made on January 13, 19C, when the wages are paid?

January 1, 19C, reversing entry.

Wages payable			No reversing entry assumed.
(a liability)	3,000		
Wage expense		3,000	

d. **The subsequent entry that was facilitated:** The payroll of $25,000 was completed and paid on January 13, 19C. This subsequent payment entry is to be recorded. Question: Did the reversing entry facilitate or simplify this entry?

January 13, 19C, payroll entry:*

Wage expense	25,000		Wages payable	3,000	
Cash		25,000	Wage expense	22,000	
			Cash		25,000

* **Explanation:** Observe that when the reversing entry was used, this last entry required only one debit, contrasted with two debits when no reversing entry was made. This difference was due to the fact that the reversing entry served to (1) clear out the liability account, Wages Payable, and (2) set up a temporary **credit** in the Wage Expense account. After the last entry, to record the payment of the payroll, both accounts affected—Wage Expense and Wages Payable—are identical in balance under both approaches. If the reversing entry is not made, the company must go to the trouble of identifying how much of the $25,000 paid on January 13, 19C, was expense and how much of it was to pay the liability set up in the adjusting entry at the end of the prior period ([*a*] above).

error into the accounts because the accumulated depreciation account would reflect a zero balance for the first period. Thus, many adjusting entries are not candidates for reversal. Those that are candidates are easily identified if one considers the nature of the subsequent related entry (i.e., whether there is a subsequent collection or payment).

Perhaps the most compelling reason for reversing entries is to increase the likelihood that the effects of certain adjusting entries will not be overlooked when recording the next related transaction in the following period.

EXHIBIT 5-8

Reversing entries illustrated, journal and ledger (with interest revenue)

Situation: On September 1, 19A, Company X loaned $1,200 on a one-year, 10%, interest-bearing note receivable. On August 31, 19B, the company will collect the $1,200 principal plus $120 interest revenue. The annual accounting period ends December 31.

JOURNAL

a. September 1, 19A—To record the loan:

Note receivable   1,200
   Cash   1,200

b. December 31, 19A (end of the accounting period)—Adjusting entry for four months' interest revenue earned but not collected ($1,200 × 10% × 4/12 = $40):

Interest receivable   40
   Interest revenue   40

c. December 31, 19A—To close interest revenue:

Interest revenue   40
   Income summary   40

d. January 1, 19B—To reverse adjusting entry of December 31, 19A:

Interest revenue   40
   Interest receivable   40

Observe that after this entry, the Interest Receivable account reflects a zero balance and Interest Revenue reflects a **debit** balance of $40 (four months interest).

e. August 31, 19B—Subsequent entry; to record collection of note plus interest for one year:*

Cash   1,320
   Note receivable   1,200
   Interest revenue   120

LEDGER

Cash

	x,xxx	(a) 9/1/19A 1,200
(e) 8/31/19B 1,320		

Note Receivable

(a) 9/1/19A 1,200	(e) 8/31/19B 1,200

Interest Receivable

(b) 12/31/19A 40	(d) 1/1/19B 40

Interest Revenue

(c) 12/31/19A 40	(b) 12/31/19A 40
(d) 1/1/19B 40	(e) 8/31/19B 120

Income Summary

	(c) 12/31/19A 40

Note: To demonstrate the facilitating feature, assume the reversing entry (d) was not made. The August 31, 19B, entry would be more complex, viz:

Cash   1,320
   Note receivable   1,200
   Interest receivable   40
   Interest revenue   80

* Observe that after this entry the Note Receivable account has a zero balance and the Interest Revenue an $80 balance which represents eight months' interest revenue earned in 19B.

IMPORTANT TERMS DEFINED IN THIS CHAPTER

Terms (alphabetically)	Key words in definitions of terms used in chapter	Page reference
Accounting information processing cycle	Accounting phases (steps) from the time a transaction is completed to the financial statements.	203
Closing entries	End-of-period entries to close all revenue and expense accounts to Retained Earnings (through Income Summary).	213
Computer hardware	Computer and other equipment used with it.	202
Computer software	Computer programs and instructions for using an electronic computer.	202
Electronic data processing	Accounting process performed (in whole or in part) using electronic computers.	202
Manual data processing	Accounting process performed (in whole or in part) in handwriting; manually.	202
Mechanical data processing	Accounting process performed (in whole or in part) using machines.	202
Permanent (real) accounts	Permanent (or real) accounts are the balance sheet accounts; no closing entries.	214
Post-closing trial balance	Trial balance prepared after all of the closing entries have been posted.	219
Reversing entries	Recorded at beginning of next accounting period; backs out certain adjusting entries; facilitates subsequent entries.	219
Statement of retained earnings	Reports increases and decreases in retained earnings; ties together the income statement and balance sheet.	213
Temporary (nominal) accounts	Income statement accounts; closed at the end of the accounting period.	213
Unadjusted trial balance	A trial balance that does not include the effects of the adjusting entries.	205
Worksheet	A "spread sheet" designed to minimize errors and to provide data for the financial statements.	205

QUESTIONS

1. Distinguish among manual, mechanical, and electronic data processing. How does each relate to accounting information processing?

2. Identify, in sequence, the 11 phases of the accounting information processing cycle.

3. Contrast transaction analysis with journalizing.

4. Compare journalizing with posting.

5. How does posting reflect a change in the classification of the data?

6. Contrast an unadjusted trial balance with an adjusted trial balance. What is the purpose of each?

7. What is the basic purpose of the worksheet?

8. Why are adjusting entries entered on the accounting worksheet?

9. Why are adjusting entries recorded in the journal and posted to the ledger even though they are entered on the worksheet?

10. What is the purpose of closing entries? Why are they recorded in the journal and posted to the ledger?

11. Distinguish among (a) permanent, (b) temporary, (c) real, and (d) nominal accounts.

12. Why are the income statement accounts closed but the balance sheet accounts are not?

13. What is a post-closing trial balance? Is it a useful part of the accounting information processing cycle? Explain.

14. What are reversing entries? When are reversing entries useful? Give one example of an adjusting entry that (a) should be reversed and (b) another one that should not be reversed (based on Supplement 5A)?

EXERCISES

E5–1   **(Pairing Brief Descriptive Statements with the 11 Phases of the Accounting Information Processing Cycle)**
Match the descriptive statements with the phases by entering the appropriate letter in each blank provided.

Phase

_____ (1) Data collection
_____ (2) Transaction analysis
_____ (3) Journalizing
_____ (4) Posting
_____ (5) Unadjusted trial balance
_____ (6) Worksheet
_____ (7) Financial statements
_____ (8) Adjusting entries recorded
_____ (9) Closing entries recorded
_____ (10) Post-closing trial balance
_____ (11) Reversing entries

Descriptive statements

A. Reduces income statement accounts to zero.
B. Converts chronological data to A = L + OE basis.
C. Collection of source documents.
D. Backs out certain adjusting entries.
E. Income statement, balance sheet, and SCFP.
F. Recording the results of transaction analysis.
G. Checks equalities after the adjusting entries.
H. Determines effects of transactions on A = L + OE.
I. Records transactions and events at the end of the accounting period that are not yet recognized properly.
J. Checks equalities before the adjusting entries.
K. Facilitates, in an orderly way, completion of the remaining phases of the cycle.

E5–2   **(Pairing Brief Definitions with Important Terms Used in the Chapter)**
Match the following brief definitions with the terms by entering the appropriate letter in each space provided.

Term

_____ (1) Interim financial statements
_____ (2) Permanent accounts
_____ (3) Closing entries

Brief definition

A. A "spread sheet" used to facilitate completion of the financial statements.
B. Computer instructions and programs.
C. Reconciles the income statement with the balance

Term	Brief definition
_____ (4) Computer hardware	sheet at the end of each accounting period.
_____ (5) Statement of retained earnings	D. Recorded only on the first day of each accounting period to facilitate subsequent entries.
_____ (6) Temporary accounts	E. A computer and dot matrix printer.
_____ (7) Accounting worksheet	F. All of the income statement accounts.
	G. Cause all temporary accounts to have a zero balance.
_____ (8) Adjusting entries	H. Recorded to recognize items only at the end of the accounting period.
_____ (9) Computer software	
_____ (10) Folio notation	I. All of the balance sheet accounts.
_____ (11) Reversing entries	J. Prepared after adjusting entries and before closing entries to check equalities.
_____ (12) Adjusted trial balance	K. Used to indicate that posting has been done.
	L. Financial statements that cover less than one year.
_____ (13) Income summary account	M. A special clearing account used only during the closing process.
_____ (14) Nominal accounts	
_____ (15) Real accounts	

E5–3 **(Prepare a Simple Income Statement and Balance Sheet, Including Four Adjusting Entries, Without a Worksheet)**

Vista Company prepared the unadjusted trial balance given below at the end of the accounting year, December 31, 19B. To simplify the case, the amounts given are in thousands of dollars.

Account titles	Debit	Credit
Cash	$ 33	
Accounts receivable	27	
Prepaid insurance	4	
Machinery (10-year life, no residual value)	50	
Accumulated depreciation, machinery		$ 4
Accounts payable		6
Wages payable		
Income tax payable		
Capital stock, nopar (2,000 shares)		62
Retained earnings		10
Dividends declared and paid during 19B	3	
Revenues (not detailed)		60
Expenses (not detailed)	25	
Totals	$142	$142

Other data not yet recorded at December 31, 19B:

1. Insurance expired during 19B, $2.
2. Depreciation expense for 19B, $5.
3. Wages payable, $3.
4. Income tax rate, 20%.

Required:

(Note: A worksheet may be used but is not required.)

_a._ Complete the income statement and balance sheet given below for 19B.
_b._ Give the adjusting entries for 19B.

c. Give the closing entries for 19B.

Income Statement, For the Year Ended December 31, 19B

Revenues (not detailed)	$	_____
Expenses (not detailed)		_____
Pretax income		_____
Income tax expense		_____
Net income	$	_____
EPS	$	_____

Balance Sheet, December 31, 19B

Assets		Liabilities	
Cash .... $ _____		Accounts payable .... $ _____	
Accounts receivable .... _____		Wages payable .... _____	
Prepaid insurance .... _____		Income tax payable .... _____	
Machinery .... _____		**Stockholders' Equity**	
Accumulated			
depreciation .... _____		Capital stock .... _____	
		Retained earnings .... _____	
Total .... $ _____		Total .... $ _____	

E5–4   **(Determining How to Extend an Unadjusted Trial Balance to Complete a Worksheet; Uses Answer Codes)**

The worksheet at December 31, 19B, for Bustle Realty Corporation has been completed through the adjusted trial balance. You are ready to extend each amount to the several columns to the right. The columns that will be used are listed below with code letters:

Code	Columns
A	Income Statement, debit
B	Income Statement, credit
C	Retained Earnings, debit
D	Retained Earnings, credit
E	Balance Sheet, debit
F	Balance Sheet, credit

Below are listed representative accounts to be extended on the worksheet. You are to give, for each account, the code letter that indicates the proper worksheet column to the right of "Adjusted Trial Balance" to which the amount in each account should be extended. Assume normal debit and credit balances.

Account titles	Code
(1) Cash (example)	E
(2) Inventory of office supplies	
(3) Interest payable	
(4) Capital stock	
(5) Commission revenue earned	
(6) Rent revenue collected in advance	
(7) Salary expense	
(8) Prepaid insurance	
(9) Retained earnings, beginning balance (a credit)	
(10) Building	
(11) Mortgage payable	
(12) Income tax payable	
(13) Sales commissions receivable	
(14) Accumulated depreciation on building	
(15) Contributed capital in excess of par	
(16) Dividends declared and paid	

	Account titles	Code
(17)	Income tax expense	
(18)	Investment in bonds	
(19)	Net income amount (indicate both the debit and credit on the worksheet)	
(20)	Net loss amount (indicate both the debit and credit on the worksheet)	
(21)	Retained earnings, positive ending balance amount (indicate both the debit and credit on the worksheet)	

E5–5   (Completing a Worksheet Starting with an Unadjusted Trial Balance)

Miller Company is completing the annual accounting information processing cycle at December 31, 19B. The worksheet, as shown below, has been started (to simplify, amounts given are in thousands of dollars).

Account No.	Account titles	Unadjusted trial balance Debit	Credit
101	Cash	$20	$
102	Accounts receivable	38	
103	Inventory	22	
104	Prepaid insurance	3	
110	Equipment (10-year life, no residual value)	70	
111	Accumulated depreciation, equipment		7
119	Accounts payable		11
120	Wages payable		
121	Income tax payable		
122	Revenue collected in advance		
123	Note payable, long term (10% each December 31)		20
130	Capital stock, par $10		60
131	Contributed capital in excess of par		10
140	Retained earnings		15
141	Dividends declared and paid	8	
145	Revenues		99
146	Expenses	61	
147	Income tax expense		
	Totals	$222	$222

Data not yet recorded for 19B:

a. Insurance expense, $1.

b. Depreciation expense, $7.

c. Wages earned by employees; not yet paid, $2.

d. Revenue collected by Miller; not yet earned, $3.

e. Income tax rate, 20%.

(Note: No accrued interest is recorded because interest is paid on each December 31.)

Required:

Complete the worksheet in every respect (you may use account numbers instead of account titles). Set up additional column headings for Adjusting Entries, Adjusted Trial Balance, Income Statement, Retained Earnings, and Balance Sheet. Record all revenues and expenses (except income tax) in the two accounts given (145 and 146).

E5–6   **(Completing a Worksheet Starting with an Unadjusted Trial Balance)**

Scott Corporation, a small company, is completing the annual accounting information processing cycle at December 31, 19B. The worksheet, prior to the adjusting entries, has been started as shown below.

Account Titles	Unadjusted Trial Balance	
	Debit	Credit
Cash	$ 24,000	
Accounts receivable	14,000	
Equipment	30,000	
Accumulated depreciation		$ 9,000
Other assets	64,000	
Accounts payable		11,000
Long-term note payable		10,000
Capital stock, par $10		40,000
Contributed capital in excess of par		11,000
Retained earnings		14,000
Revenues		90,000
Expenses	53,000	
	$185,000	$185,000
Income tax expense		
Income tax payable		
Net income		

Data not yet recorded for 19B:

a. Depreciation expense, $3,000.

b. Income tax rate, 25%.

Required:

Complete the worksheet in all respects. Set up additional column headings for Adjusting Entries, Adjusted Trial Balance, Income Statement, Retained Earnings, and Balance Sheet.

E5–7   **(Identifying Adjusting Entries by Comparing Unadjusted and Adjusted Trial Balances)**
Moline Service Company is in the process of completing the information processing
cycle at the end of the accounting year, December 31, 19B. The worksheet and financial
statements have been prepared. The next step is to journalize the adjusting entries. The
two trial balances given below were taken directly from the completed worksheet.

| Account Titles | December 31, 19B | | | |
| | Unadjusted Trial Balance | | Adjusted Trial Balance | |
	Debit	Credit	Debit	Credit
a. Cash	$ 9,000		$ 9,000	
b. Accounts receivable			800	
c. Prepaid insurance	300		150	
d. Equipment	120,000		120,000	
e. Accumulated depreciation, equipment		$ 21,300		$ 26,300
f. Income tax payable				3,300
g. Capital stock, par $10		50,000		50,000
h. Retained earnings, January 1, 19B		15,000		15,000
i. Service revenues		61,000		61,800
j. Salary expense	18,000		18,000	
k. Depreciation expense			5,000	
l. Insurance expense			150	
m. Income tax expense			3,300	
	$147,300	$147,300	$156,400	$156,400

Required:

By examining the amounts in each trial balance, reconstruct the four adjusting entries
that were made between the unadjusted trial balance and the adjusted trial balance. Give
an explanation of each adjusting entry.

E5–8   **(Journalizing Adjusting and Closing Entries Based on a Completed Worksheet)**
The accountant for Rocky Corporation has just completed the following worksheet for
the year ended December 31, 19D (note the shortcuts used by the accountant to reduce
the number of vertical columns on the worksheet—credits in parens, and no column for
adjusted trial balance):

Account Titles	Unadjusted Trial Balance (credits)	Adjusting Entries Debit	Adjusting Entries Credit	Income Statement (credits)	Balance Sheet (credits)
a. Cash	15,000				15,000
b. Prepaid insurance	300		100		200
c. Accounts receivable	20,000				20,000
d. Machinery	80,000				80,000
e. Accumulated depreciation	(24,000)		8,000		(32,000)
f. Other assets	13,700				13,700
g. Accounts payable	(7,000)				(7,000)
h. Rent collected in advance			200		(200)
i. Interest payable			450		(450)
j. Income tax payable			3,375		(3,375)
k. Notes payable, long term	(10,000)				(10,000)
l. Capital stock, par $10	(50,000)				(50,000)
m. Retained earnings	(18,000)				(18,000)
n. Revenues	(80,000)	200		(79,800)	
o. Expenses (not detailed)	60,000	100		60,100	
p. Depreciation expense		8,000		8,000	
q. Interest expense		450		450	
r. Income tax expense		3,375		3,375	
s. Net income				7,875	(7,875)
Totals	–0–	12,125	12,125	–0–	–0–

Required:

a. Prepare the adjusting entries in journal form required on December 31, 19D. Write a brief explanation with each entry.

b. Prepare the closing entries at December 31, 19D.

E5–9   (Recording Adjusting Entries in Journal Format)

For each of the 10 independent situations, give the journal entry by entering the appropriate code(s) and amounts.

Code	Account	Code	Account
A	Cash	K	Interest revenue
B	Office supplies inventory	L	Wage expense
C	Revenue receivable	M	Depreciation expense
D	Office equipment	N	Interest expense
E	Accumulated depreciation	O	Supplies expense
F	Note payable	P	Capital stock
G	Wages payable	Q	Retained earnings
H	Interest payable	R	Dividends declared and paid
I	Rent revenue collected in advance	S	Income summary
J	Service revenues	X	None of the above

Independent Situations	Debit		Credit	
	Code	Amount	Code	Amount
a. Accrued wages, unrecorded and unpaid at year-end, $400 (example).	L	400	G	400
b. Service revenue collected and recorded as revenue, but not yet earned, $700.				
c. Dividends declared and paid during year and debited to Dividends account, $900. Give entry at year-end.				
d. Depreciation expense for year not yet recorded, $650.				
e. Balance at year-end in Service Revenue account, $59,000. Give the closing entry at year-end.				
f. Service revenue earned but not yet collected at year-end, $300.				
g. Balance at year-end in Interest Revenue account, $360. Give the closing entry at year-end.				
h. Office Supplies Inventory account at year-end, $550; inventory of supplies on hand at year-end, $100.				
i. At year-end interest on note payable not yet recorded or paid, $180.				
j. Balance at year-end in Income Summary account after all revenue and expense accounts have been closed, $9,900 (credit).				

E5–10   **(Based on the Supplement 5–A; Determining When to Use a Reversing Entry)**

Dover Company has completed the accounting information processing cycle for the year ended December 31, 19A. Reversing entries are under consideration (for January 1, 19B) for two different adjusting entries (of December 31, 19A). For case purposes, the relevant data are given in T-accounts:

Prepaid Insurance

1/1/19A Balance	600	(a) 12/31/19A Adj. entry	400

Insurance Expense

(a) 12/31/19A Adj. entry	400	(c) 12/31/19A Closing entry	400

Accrued Wages Payable

		(b) 12/31/19A Adj. entry	1,000

Wage Expense

Paid during 19A	18,000	(d) 12/31/19A Closing entry	19,000
(b) 12/31/19A Adj. entry	1,000		

Income Summary

12/31/19A Closing entries		12/31/19A	
(c)	400	Closed to Retained	
(d)	19,000	Earnings	19,400

Required:

Would a reversing entry on January 1, 19B, facilitate the next related entry for (a) Prepaid Insurance and (b) Accrued Wages Payable? Explain why.

PROBLEMS

P5–1 **(Prepare an Income Statement and Balance Sheet from an Unadjusted Trial Balance and Include the Effects of Five Adjusting Entries)**

AAA Services Company, Inc., a small service company, keeps its records without the help of an accountant. After much effort, an outside accountant prepared the following unadjusted trial balance as of the end of the annual accounting period, December 31, 19C:

Account titles	Debit	Credit
Cash	$ 30,000	
Accounts receivable	31,000	
Service supplies inventory	700	
Prepaid insurance	800	
Service trucks (5-year life, no residual value)	20,000	
Accumulated depreciation, service trucks		$ 8,000
Other assets	10,400	
Accounts payable		2,000
Wages payable		
Income tax payable		
Note payable (3 years, 10% each December 31)		10,000
Capital stock, par $1		30,000
Contributed capital in excess of par		3,000
Retained earnings		6,500
Dividends declared and paid	2,000	
Service revenues		75,000
Remaining expenses (not detailed)*	39,600	
Income tax expense		
Totals	$134,500	$134,500

* Excludes income tax expense.

Data not yet recorded at December 31, 19C:

1. The supplies inventory count on December 31, 19C, reflected $200 remaining on hand; to be used in 19D.
2. Insurance expired during 19C, $400.

3. Depreciation expense for 19C, $4,000.
4. Wages earned by employees not yet paid on December 31, 19C, $500.
5. Income tax rate, 20%.

Required:

Note: A worksheet may be used but is not required.

a. Complete the financial statements given below (show computations) for 19C to include the effects of the five transactions listed above.
b. Give the 19C adjusting entries. (Hint: Journalize the above five data items.)
c. Give the 19C closing entries. (Hint: Use the income statement column).

(Hint: The EPS amount is $0.80.)

Income Statement, for the Year Ended December 31, 19C

Service revenues		$_____
Remaining expenses (not detailed)	$_____	
Supplies expense	_____	
Insurance expense	_____	
Depreciation expense	_____	
Remaining wage expense	_____	
Total expenses		_____
Pretax income		_____
Income tax expense		_____
Net income		$_____
EPS		$_____

Balance Sheet, at December 31, 19C

Assets		Liabilities	
Cash	$_____	Accounts payable	$_____
Accounts receivable	_____	Wages payable	_____
Service supplies inventory	_____	Income tax payable	_____
Prepaid insurance	_____	Note payable, long term	_____
Service trucks	_____	Total liabilities	_____
Accumulated depreciation, trucks	_____	**Stockholders' Equity**	
Other assets (not detailed)	_____	Capital stock, par $1	_____
		Contributed capital in excess of par	_____
		Retained earnings	_____
		Total stockholders' equity	_____
		Total liabilities and	
Total assets	$_____	stockholders' equity	$_____

P5–2   (Use the Ledger Balances to Explain the Adjusting Entries Recorded and to Give the Closing Entries; Answer Three Analytical Questions)

The ledger accounts of Home Service Company at the end of the second year of operations, December 31, 19B (prior to the closing entries), were as shown below. The 19B adjusting entries are identified by letters, and account numbers are given to the right of the account name.

Cash		101		Note Payable, 10%		201		Capital Stock, Par $1		301
Bal.	20,000				Jan. 1, 19B	10,000			Bal.	50,000

Inventory, Maintenance Supplies		102		Wages Payable		202		Cont. Capital in Excess of Par		302
Bal.	500	(a)	400		(e)	600			Bal	6,000

Service Equipment		103		Interest Payable		203		Retained Earnings		303
Jan. 1, 19A	90,000				(b)	1,000			Bal.	9,000

Accumulated Depreciation, Service Equipment		104		Revenue Collected in Advance		204		Service Revenues		304
		Bal.	18,000		(c)	7,000	(c)	7,000	Bal.	220,000
		(d)	18,000							

Remaining Assets		105		Income Tax Payable		205		Expenses		305
Bal.	42,500				(f)	6,600	Bal.	160,000		
							(a)	400		
							(b)	1,000		
							(d)	18,000		
							(e)	600		
							(f)	6,600		

Required:

a. Develop three 19B trial balances of Home Service Company using the following format:

Account No.	Unadjusted Trial Balance		Adjusted Trial Balance		Post-Closing Trial Balance	
	Debit	Credit	Debit	Credit	Debit	Credit
101						

b. Write an explanation of each adjusting entry for 19B.
c. Give the closing journal entries (do not use Income Summary).
d. What was the apparent useful life of the service equipment? What assumptions must you make to answer this question?
e. What was the average income tax rate for 19B?
f. What was the average issue (sale) price per share of the capital stock?

P5–3   (Complete a Worksheet Starting with the Adjusted Trial Balance; Compute the Amounts for the Adjusting Entries; and Give the Closing Entries)

Avis Corporation has partially completed the following worksheet for the year ended December 31, 19E:

Account Titles	Unadjusted Trial Balance		Adjusting Entries	
	Debit	Credit	Debit	Credit
Cash	18,000			
Accounts receivable	26,000			
Supplies inventory	200			(a) 120
Interest receivable			(b) 200	
Long-term note receivable, 10%, dated				
Sept. 1, 19E	6,000			
Equipment (10-year life)	75,000			
Accumulated depreciation		30,000		(c) 7,500
Accounts payable		11,000		
Short-term note payable, 12% dated				
June 1, 19E		8,000		
Interest payable				(d) 560
Income tax payable				(e) 3,620
Capital stock, par $1		40,000		
Contributed capital in excess of par		2,000		
Retained earnings		7,000		
Service revenue		68,000		
Interest revenue				(b) 200
Expenses (not detailed)	40,800		(a) 120	
Depreciation expense			(c) 7,500	
Interest expense			(d) 560	
Income tax expense			(e) 3,620	
Totals	166,000	166,000	12,000	12,000

Required:

1. Use additional columns for Adjusted Trial Balance, Income Statement, Retained Earnings, and Balance Sheet; and complete the worksheet.
2. Show how the following amounts were computed in the adjusting entries:
   a. $120.
   b. $200.
   c. $7,500.
   d. $560.
3. Give the closing entries.
4. Why are the adjusting and closing entries journalized and posted?

P5–4   (Start with a Partially Completed Worksheet and Complete Phases 6–9 in Order)

Virginia Corporation is completing the accounting information processing cycle for the year ended December 31, 19C. The unadjusted trial balance, taken from the ledger, was as follows:

Account No.	Account title	Unadjusted trial balance Debit	Credit
101	Cash	$ 43,550	
103	Accounts receivable (net)	17,000	
105	Prepaid insurance	450	
107	Interest receivable		
120	Long-term note receivable, 12%	6,000	
150	Equipment (10-year life)	100,000	
151	Accumulated depreciation, equipment		$ 20,000
170	Other assets	30,000	
201	Accounts payable		14,000
203	Wages payable		
205	Interest payable		
210	Long-term note payable, 15%		10,000
300	Capital stock, par $10		80,000
301	Contributed capital in excess of par		12,000
310	Retained earnings		34,000
311	Dividends declared and paid during 19C	8,000	
320	Service revenue		150,000
322	Interest revenue		
350	Expenses (not detailed)*	115,000	
351	Depreciation expense		
360	Interest expense		
370	Income tax expense		
207	Income tax payable		
	Totals	$320,000	$320,000

* Includes wage expense and insurance expense.

Additional data for adjusting entries:

a. Expired insurance during 19C was $150.
b. Interest on the long-term note receivable (dated September 1, 19C) is collected annually each August 31.
c. The equipment was acquired on January 1, 19A (assume no estimated residual value).
d. At December 31, 19C, wages earned but not yet paid or recorded, amounted to $3,000.
e. Interest on the long-term note payable (dated May 1, 19C) is paid annually each April 30.
f. Assume a 20% average income tax rate.

Required:

a. Phase 6—Complete a worksheet for the year ended December 31, 19C. Key the adjusting entries with letters. (Hint: Net income is $16,872.)
b. Phase 7—Prepare an income statement (use two captions: Revenues and Expenses), a statement of retained earnings, and a balance sheet; use three captions only (Assets, Liabilities, Stockholders' Equity).
c. Phase 8—Write an explanation of each adjusting entry reflected on the worksheet.
d. Phase 9—Give the closing entries in journal form. Explain why they must be journalized and posted to the ledger.

P5–5   **(A Comprehensive Problem to Cover Chapters 2 through 5, Starting with an Unadjusted Trial Balance and Ending with the Closing Entries)**

W&P Moving and Storage Service, Inc., has been in operation for several years. Revenues have increased gradually from both the moving and storage services. The annual financial statements prepared in the past have not conformed to GAAP. The newly employed president decided that a balance sheet, income statement, and cash flow statement would be prepared in conformity with GAAP. The first step was to employ a full-time bookkeeper and engage a local CPA firm. It is now December 31, 1987, the end of the current accounting year. The bookkeeper has developed a trial balance from the ledger. A member of the staff of the CPA firm will advise and assist the bookkeeper in completing the accounting information processing cycle for the first time. The unadjusted trial balance at December 31, 1987, is shown below.

Unadjusted Trial Balance, December 31, 1987

Debits		*Credits*	
Cash	$ 25,880	Accumulated depreciation	$ 18,000
Accounts receivable	2,030	Accounts payable	6,000
Office supplies inventory	150	Wages payable	
Prepaid insurance	600	Interest payable	
Land for future building		Revenue collected advance	
site	6,000	Income tax payable	
Equipment	68,000	Note payable (12%)	30,000
Remaining assets		Capital stock, par $1	
(not detailed)	27,000	(20,000 shares)	20,000
Salary expense	74,000	Retained earnings,	
Advertising expense	1,000	January 1, 1987	21,600
Utilities expense	1,270	Hauling revenue	106,400
Maintenance expense	6,500	Storage revenue	14,000
Miscellaneous expenses	570		
Insurance expense			
Wage expense			
Depreciation expense			
Interest expense			
Income tax expense			
Dividends declared and paid	3,000		
	$216,000		$216,000

Examination of the records and related documents provided the following additional information that should be considered for adjusting entries:

a. A physical count of office supplies inventory at December 31, 1987, reflected $40 on hand. Office supplies used are a miscellaneous expense. Office supplies purchased during 1987 were debited to this inventory account.

b. On July 1, 1987, a two-year insurance premium was paid amounting to $600; it was debited to prepaid insurance.

c. The equipment cost $68,000 when acquired. Annual depreciation expense is $6,000.

d. Unpaid and unrecorded wages earned by employees at December 31, 1987, amounted to $1,200.

e. The $30,000 note payable was signed on October 1, 1987, for a 12% bank loan; principal and interest are due at the end of 12 months from that date.

f. Storage revenue collected and recorded as earned before December 31, 1987, included $400 collected in advance from one customer for storage time to be used in 1988. (Hint: Reduce storage revenue.)

g. Gasoline, oil, and fuel purchased for the vehicles and used during the last two weeks of December 1987 amounting to $300 have not been paid for nor recorded (this is considered maintenance expense).

h. The average income tax rate is 20% which produces income tax expense of $5,600.

Required:

a. Phase 6—Enter the unadjusted trial balance on a worksheet; then, based on the above data, enter the adjusting entries. Complete the worksheet. (Hint: The adjusted trial balance total is $230,000.)

b. Phase 7—Using the worksheet, prepare an income statement (use two captions: Revenues and Expenses), statement of retained earnings, and balance sheet. Use subclassifications as shown in Chapter 3, page 121. (Hint: The balance sheet total is $105,400.)

c. Phase 8—Using the worksheet, prepare the 1987 adjusting entries in journal form.

d. Phase 9—Using the worksheet, prepare 1987 closing entries in journal form.

P5–6   (An Alternate Comprehensive Problem to Cover Chapters 2 through 5, Starting with an Unadjusted Trial Balance and Ending with the Closing Entries)

Charter Air Service, Incorporated, was organized to operate a charter service in a city of approximately 350,000 population. The 10 organizers were issued 7,500 shares of $10 par value stock for a total of $75,000 cash. To obtain facilities to operate the charter services, the company rents from the city hangar and office space at the city airport for a flat monthly rental. The business has prospered because of the excellent service and the high level of maintenance on the planes. It is now December 31, 1987, end of the annual accounting period, and the accounting information processing cycle is in the final phases. Representative accounts and unadjusted amounts selected from the ledger at December 31, 1987, are as follows:

Unadjusted Trial Balance, December 31, 1987

Debits		*Credits*	
Cash	$ 24,600	Accumulated depreciation,	
Prepaid insurance	6,000	aircraft	$ 60,000
Maintenance parts inventory	18,000	Notes payable, 12%	100,000
Aircraft	260,000	Capital stock, par $10	75,000
Salary expense	90,000	Retained earnings,	
Maintenance expense	24,000	January 1, 1987	20,600
Fuel expense	63,000	Charter revenue	262,400
Advertising expense	2,000		
Utilities expense	1,400		
Rent expense	14,000		
Dividends declared and paid	15,000		
	$518,000		$518,000

For the 1987 adjusting entries, the following additional data were developed from the records and supporting documents:

a. On January 1, 1987, the company paid a three-year insurance premium amounting to $6,000.

b. The aircraft, when purchased on January 1,1984, cost $260,000; and the estimated useful life to the company is approximately 10 years. The equipment has an estimated residual value of $60,000. Annual depreciation expense is $20,000 (can you verify this amount?).

c. On July 1, 1987, the company borrowed $100,000 from the bank on a five-year, 12% loan. Interest is payable annually starting on June 30, 1988.

d. Charter revenue, on occasion, is collected in advance. On December 31, 1987, collections in advance amounted to $1,000; when collected, this amount was recorded as Charter Revenue.

e. Rent amounting to $14,000 on hangar and office space was paid during the year and recorded as Rent Expense. This included rent paid in advance amounting to $2,000 for January and February 1988. The total amount was recorded as Rent Expense in 1987.

f. The inventory of maintenance parts at December 31, 1987, showed $7,000. All parts purchased are debited to Maintenance Parts Inventory when purchased.

g. For case purposes, assume an average income tax rate of 20%, which results in income tax expense of $6,000.

Required:

a. Enter the above accounts and unadjusted balances from the ledger on a worksheet. (The following accounts should be added at the bottom of the worksheet because they will be needed for the adjusting entries: Insurance Expense, Depreciation Expense, Interest Expense, Interest Payable, Revenue Collected in Advance, Prepaid Rent Expense, Income Tax Expense, and Income Tax Payable.)

b. Based on the additional data given above, enter the 1987 adjusting entries on the worksheet.

c. Phase 6—Complete the worksheet. (Hint: The adjusted trial balance total is $550,000.)

d. Phase 7—Based on the worksheet, prepare the 1987 income statement (use two captions, Revenues and Expenses), statement of retained earnings, and the balance sheet (classified as shown in Chapter 3, page 121). (Hint: The total on the balance sheet is $217,600.)

e. Phase 8—Journalize the 1987 adjusting entries.

f. Phase 9—Journalize the 1987 closing entries.

P5–7 **(A Mini-Practice Set Starting with Transactions and Continuing Through a Complete Accounting Information Cycle; Simplified by Using Only 10 Basic Entries plus 5 Adjusting Entries)**

Little Service Company (a corporation) began operations on January 1, 19A. The annual reporting period ends December 31. The trial balance on January 1, 19B, was as follows (rounded to even thousands to simplify):

Account No.	Account titles	Debit	Credit
01	Cash	$ 2	$
02	Accounts receivable	6	
03	Service supplies inventory	15	
04	Land		
05	Equipment	80	
06	Accumulated depreciation, equipment		8
07	Remaining assets (not detailed to simplify)	5	
11	Accounts payable		7

Account *No.*	*Account titles*	*Debit*	*Credit*
12	Note payable		
13	Wages payable		
14	Interest payable		
15	Income tax payable		
21	Capital stock, par $1		83
31	Retained earnings		10
35	Service revenues		
40	Depreciation expense		
41	Income tax expense		
42	Interest expense		
43	Remaining expenses (not detailed to simplify)		
50	Income summary		
	Totals	$108	$108

Transactions during 19B, summarized in thousands of dollars (the letters indicate dates):

a. Borrowed $12,000 cash on a 10% note payable, dated March 1, 19B.
b. Purchased land for future building site, paid cash, $12.
c. Revenues for 19B, $140, including $20 on credit.
d. Sold 2,000 shares of capital stock for $1 cash per share.
e. Remaining expenses for 19B, $80, including $6 on credit.
f. Collected accounts receivable, $14.
g. Purchased "remaining" assets, $10 cash.
h. Accounts payable paid, $9.
i. Purchased service supplies for future use, $10 (debit to Account No. 3).
j. Signed a $15 service contract to start February 1, 19C.
k. Declared and paid cash dividend, $15. (The accountant decided to debit Account No. 31 rather than a special account.)

Data for adjusting entries:

1. Service supplies inventory counted on December 31, 19B, $10 (debit Remaining Expenses).
2. Equipment, useful life 10 years (no residual or scrap value).
3. Accrued interest on note payable (to be computed).
4. Wages earned since the December 24 payroll; not yet paid, $16.
5. Income tax rate, 20%; payable in 19C.

Required:

Phases 1, 2 and 3—Analyze and journalize each of the 11 transactions. Give a description below each entry. Start with journal page 1 and provide a column for "Folio."

Phase 4—Set up the 20 ledger accounts. Use the following format (see page 104) (enter the beginning balances):

Cash   **Account No. 01**

Date	Explanation	Folio	Debit	Credit	Balance
19B	Beginning balance	√			2
a	Borrowed cash	1	12		14

Note: Cash requires 10 lines; the remainder, 4 lines each.

Post the journal; use the folio columns.

Phase 5—Set up an accounting worksheet like Exhibit 5–2 and enter the unadjusted trial balance at December 31, 19B. (Hint: The total is $249.)

Phase 6—Complete the worksheet. (Hint: Net income is $16.)

Phase 7—Prepare the 19B income statement and balance sheet. To save time use only major captions.

Phase 8—Journalize and post the adjusting entries.

Phase 9—Journalize and post the closing entries.

Phase 10—Prepare a post-closing trial balance. (Use account numbers rather than titles to save time.)

Phase 11—Identify the two reversing entries that could be made.

P5–8   **(Based on the Supplement 5A; Selecting Adjusting Entries that Often Are Reversed)**

Alvin Corporation has completed all information processing including the annual financial statements at December 31, 19D. The adjusting entries recorded at that date were as follows:

a. Insurance expense	150	
Prepaid insurance		150
b. Interest receivable	200	
Interest revenue		200
c. Supplies expense	80	
Supplies inventory		80
d. Depreciation expense	2,000	
Accumulated depreciation		2,000
e. Wage expense	500	
Wage payable		500
f. Interest expense	300	
Interest payable		300
g. Income tax expense	4,000	
Income tax payable		4,000

Required:

For each of the above adjusting entries indicate whether it usually would be reversed. Give the reversing entry in each instance (if none, so state) and explain the basis for your response.

CASES

C5–1 **(Analyze Some Simple Errors to Determine the Effects of Each on Income, Assets, and Liabilities)**

Lax Company (not a corporation) was very careless about its financial records during its first year of operations, 19A. It is December 31, 19A, end of the annual accounting period. An outside CPA examined the records and discovered numerous errors. All of those errors are described below. Assume each error is independent of the others. Analyze each error and indicate its effect on 19A and 19B income, assets, and liabilities *if not corrected.* Do not assume any other errors. Use these codes to indicate the effect of each dollar amount: O = overstated; U = understated, and N = no effect. Write an explanation of your analysis of each transaction to support your response. The first error is used as an example.

Independent Errors	Effect on					
	Net Income		Assets		Liabilities	
	19A	19B	19A	19B	19A	19B
a. Depreciation expense for 19A, not recorded in 19A, $950.	O $950	N	O $950	O $950	N	N
b. Wages earned by employees during 19A, not recorded or paid in 19A, but will be paid in 19B, $200.						
c. Revenue earned during 19A, but not collected or recorded until 19B, $400.						
d. Amount paid in 19A and recorded as expense in 19A, but not an expense until 19B, $500.						
e. Revenue collected in 19A and recorded as revenue in 19A, but not earned until 19B, $600.						
f. Sale of services and cash collected in 19A. Recorded as a debit to Cash and as a credit to Accounts Receivable, $800.						
g. On December 31, 19A, bought land on credit for $9,000, not recorded until payment was made on February 1, 19B.						

Explanation of analysis of errors if not corrected:

a. Failure to record depreciation in 19A caused depreciation expense to be too low; therefore, income was overstated by $950. Also, accumulated depreciation is too low by $950, which causes assets to be overstated by $950 until the error is corrected.

C5-2   (Analytical—Prepare Adjusting and Closing Entries by Analyzing Unadjusted and Adjusted Trial Balances; Then Answer 10 Analytical Questions)

Delta Company was organized on January 1, 19A. At the end of the first year of operations, December 31, 19A, the bookkeeper prepared the following two trial balances (amounts in thousands of dollars):

Account No.	Account titles	Unadjusted trial balance Debit	Unadjusted trial balance Credit	Adjusted trial balance Debit	Adjusted trial balance Credit
11	Cash	$ 30	$	$ 30	$
12	Accounts receivable	25		25	
13	Prepaid insurance	3		2	
14	Rent receivable			1	
15	Operational assets	48		48	
16	Accumulated depreciation, operational assets				6
17	Other assets	4		4	
18	Accounts payable		11		11
19	Wages payable				2
20	Income tax payable				2
21	Rent revenue collected in advance				3
22	Note payable, 10% (dated January 1, 19A)		30		30
23	Capital stock, par $1 per share		50		50
24	Retained earnings				
25	Dividends declared and paid	2		2	
26	Revenues (total)		92		90
27	Expenses (total including interest)	71		80	
28	Income tax expense			2	
	Totals	$183	$183	$194	$194

Required:

a. Based upon inspection of the two trial balances, give the 19A adjusting entries developed by the bookkeeper (provide brief explanations).
b. Based upon the above data, give the 19A closing entries with brief explanations.
c. Answer the following questions (show computations):
  (1) How many shares of stock were outstanding at year-end?
  (2) What was the estimated useful life of the operational assets assuming no residual value?
  (3) What was the amount of interest expense that was included in the total expenses?
  (4) What was the balance of Retained Earnings on December 31, 19A?
  (5) What was the average income tax rate?
  (6) How would the two accounts (a) Rent Receivable and (b) Rent Revenue Collected in Advance be reported on the balance sheet?
  (7) Explain why cash increased by $30,000 during the year even though net income was very low comparatively.
  (8) What was the amount of EPS for 19A?
  (9) What was the average selling price of the shares?
  (10) When was the insurance premium paid and over what period of time did the coverage extend?

C5–3   **(Analysis of Adjusting and Closing Entries—Related to an Actual Set of Financial Statements)**

Refer to the financial statements of Chesebrough-Ponds given in Special Supplement B immediately preceding the Index. Respond to the following questions for the 1985 annual accounting period. Use an Income Summary account.

1. What dates should the company use for the *(a)* adjusting entries, *(b)* closing entries, and *(c)* reversing entries?
2. Give the 1985 adjusting entry that the company made for depreciation (on continuing operations).
3. Give the closing entry for cash dividends paid.
4. Give the closing entry for net sales.
5. Give the closing entry for cost of goods sold and selling, advertising, and administrative expenses.
6. Give the closing entry for net income.
7. List five accounts that would not appear on the post-closing trial balance.
8. List five accounts that would appear on the post-closing trial balance.
9. Give the entries, if any, to close *(a)* interest expense and *(b)* interest revenue (income).
10. Give the entry, if any, to close accumulated depreciation.

This chapter discusses accounting for sales revenue and cost of sales. Notice that cost of sales (also cost of goods sold) is usually a large percentage of sales revenue. Small changes in cost of sales can result in large changes in net income. Summary data from income statements:

You can be sure. . .
if it's Westinghouse

(millions of dollars)

Statement of Income

Year Ended December 31	1984	1983	1982
Sales and operating revenues	**$10,264.5**	$9,532.6	$9,745.4
Cost of sales	**7,579.8**	6,991.0	7,215.6
Marketing, administration and general expenses	**1,648.7**	1,680.8	1,684.0
Depreciation and amortization	**426.0**	383.0	322.0
Operating costs and expenses	**9,654.5**	9,054.8	9,221.6
Operating profit	**610.0**	477.8	523.8

(thousands of dollars except per share data)	Year Ended		
	Sept. 29, 1985	Sept. 30, 1984	Sept. 25, 1983
NET SALES	**$1,732,278**	$1,532,883	$1,167,752
Cost of products sold	**1,107,228**	953,841	742,986
	625,050	579,042	424,766
Selling, general and administrative expenses	**531,763**	428,614	332,985
OPERATING INCOME	**93,287**	150,428	91,781

ACCOUNTING FOR SALES REVENUE AND COST OF GOODS SOLD

PURPOSE:

The previous five chapters discussed the various phases of the information processing cycle and the conceptual framework of accounting. In this chapter, you will apply that knowledge by examining typical business transactions that involve the purchase and sale of merchandise. Net income reported on the income statement is a measure of the operating success of a business. As a result, proper recording of sales revenue and the related cost of goods sold is important to both managers and users of financial statements.

LEARNING OBJECTIVES—TO BE ABLE TO:

1. Apply the revenue principle and record sales revenue.
2. Account for credit sales and sales discounts.
3. Use the allowance method to record bad debts.
4. Apply the matching principle to record cost of goods sold.
5. Identify and explain two inventory systems.
6. Describe the cost of goods sold model.
7. Make closing entries with each of the inventory systems.
8. Expand your accounting vocabulary by learning about the "Important Terms Defined in this Chapter" (page 288).
9. Apply the knowledge gained from this chapter by completing the homework assigned by your instructor.

ORGANIZATION:

Part A—Accounting for Sales Revenue

1. Recording sales revenue.
2. Measuring bad debt expense.
3. Sales returns and allowances.

Part B—Accounting for Cost of Goods Sold

1. Nature of cost of goods sold.
2. Inventory systems.
3. Taking a physical inventory.

PART A—ACCOUNTING FOR SALES REVENUE

APPLYING THE REVENUE PRINCIPLE

Determination of the amount of sales revenue that should be recorded and the appropriate accounting period in which to record it sometimes presents complex problems. Sales may be for cash or on credit and may involve the trade-in of a noncash asset. Sales activities often begin in one accounting period and end in another. Problems associated with accounting for sales revenue are easier to resolve if you know the revenue principle (Exhibit 4–5). In conformity with the revenue principle, sales revenue is measured as the **market value** of the considerations received, or the market value of the item sold, whichever is more clearly determinable. Also, sales revenue should be recognized in the accounting period when ownership of the goods passes from the seller to the buyer. Problems in implementing this principle will be discussed in this part of the chapter.

Observe the income statement for Campus Corner in Exhibit 6–1. Cost of goods sold[1] (an expense) is set out separately from the remaining expenses,[2] which makes it possible to report a step difference called **gross margin on sales.**[3] The difference between net sales revenue and cost of goods sold reflects the total amount of **markup** on all goods sold during the period. It is expressed in dollars on the income statement ($40,000) and often is reported as the gross margin ratio (Gross margin on sales, $40,000 ÷ Net sales revenue, $100,000 = 0.40, or 40%). For Campus Corner, the average markup maintained on sales was 40% of sales.[4] This amount of markup is typical for a full service department store. The markup for a discount store typically is much less.

RECOGNIZING SALES REVENUE

In most cases, the seller records sales revenue when ownership of goods passes from the seller to the buyer. Under the revenue principle, the sales price (net of any discounts) is the measure of the amount of revenue that should be recorded. If the sale is for cash, the amount of revenue to be recorded simply is the amount of cash that was received. If the sale is on credit, the revenue is the

---

[1] Similar titles sometimes used are "cost of sales" and "cost of products sold." Regardless of title, it is an **expense.**

[2] In this chapter, to simplify the illustrations, we ordinarily shall not show the detailed operating expenses. In the single step format for the income statement, revenues would be reported as above under a major caption "Revenues." However, all expenses, including cost of goods sold, would be reported under a major caption "Expenses." Therefore, in the single-step format, gross margin on sales is not reported.

[3] This often is called gross profit on sales or simply gross margin or gross profit. In the *Accounting Terminology Bulletins* the AICPA recommended against use of the term **profit** in this context.

[4] This percent is based on sales revenue rather than cost. The markup percent on **cost** would be $40,000 ÷ $60,000 = 66⅔%.

EXHIBIT 6–1

Income statement

CAMPUS CORNER
Income Statement (multiple-step format)
For the Year Ended December 31, 19F

	Amount	Percentage analysis
Gross sales	$108,333	
Less: Sales returns and allowances	8,333	
Net sales revenue	100,000	100
Cost of goods sold	60,000	60
Gross margin on sales	40,000	40
Operating expenses:		
Selling expenses (detailed) $15,000		
Administrative expenses (detailed) 10,000	25,000	25
Pretax income	15,000	15
Income tax expense	3,000	3
Net income	$ 12,000	12
EPS ($12,000 ÷ 10,000 shares)	$1.20	

cash equivalent of the assets to be received excluding any financing charges (i.e., interest). If the sale involves the trade-in of a noncash asset (such as the trade-in of an old car for a new car), the amount of revenue to record is the cash equivalent of the goods received or given up, whichever is the more clearly determinable. Thus, under the revenue principle, Campus Corner would recognize a sale in 19F (i.e., when ownership passed) as follows:

a. Cash sales for the day per the cash register tapes:

Jan. 2	Cash	2,000	
	Sales revenue		2,000

b. Credit sales for the day per all charge tickets:

Jan. 2	Accounts receivable	1,000	
	Sales revenue		1,000

Alternatively, a **separate sales revenue** account could be kept in the ledger for the sales of each department. The two journal entries above would be as follows:

```
Jan. 2  Cash .................................................. 2,000
        Accounts receivable ...................................... 1,000
              Sales, Department 1 ...................................    1,000
              Sales, Department 2 ...................................    1,500
              Sales, Department 3 ...................................      500
```

Credit Sales and Sales Discounts

A large portion of the sales made by many businesses is on credit. When merchandise is sold on credit, the terms of payment should be definite so there will be no misunderstanding as to the amounts and due dates. Credit terms usually are printed on each credit document. Often, credit terms are abbreviated using symbols such as, "n/10, EOM," which means the net amount (i.e., the sales amount less any sales returns) is due not later than 10 days after the end of the month (EOM) in which the sale was made. In other cases, **sales discounts** (often called cash discounts) are granted to the purchaser to encourage early payment. For example, the credit terms may be "2/10, n/30," which means that if cash payment is made within 10 days from the date of sale, the customer may deduct 2% from the invoice price; however, if not paid within the 10-day discount period, the full sales price (less any returns) is due in 30 days from date of sale.

Usually customers will pay within the discount period because the savings are substantial. For example, with terms 2/10, n/30, 2% is saved by paying 20 days early, which is approximately 37% annual interest. Credit customers conceivably may borrow cash from a bank in order to take advantage of cash discounts. Normally the bank's interest rate is less than the high interest rate that would result from not taking cash discounts. Because the cash discount on sales almost always will be taken, the amount of sales revenue that is recorded should be based on the amount of cash that probably will be received rather than for the gross sales amount. To do otherwise would be inconsistent with the **revenue principle** which holds that sales revenue should be measured as the cash or cash equivalent received for the goods sold. Assume a sale by Campus Corner of $1,000 with terms 2/10, n/30. The sequence of journal entries is:

a. January 18, date of sale on credit:

> Accounts receivable 980
>   Sales revenue   980
>   Terms: 2/10, n/30 ($1,000 × 0.98 = $980).

b. January 27, date of collection if payment is made **within** the discount period (the usual case):

> Cash 980
>   Accounts receivable   980

c. January 31, date of collection if payment is made **after** the discount period (the unusual case):

> Cash 1,000
>   Sales discount revenue*   20
>   Accounts receivable   980
>   * Interest revenue sometimes is used because conceptually it is in the nature of
>   interest revenue earned.

The preferred method for recording sales revenues, illustrated above, is called the **net method.** As an alternative, some companies use the **gross method of recording sales revenue.** Under the gross method, sales revenue is recorded without deducting the amount of the cash discount. The following journal entries would be made for a $1,000 sale if the gross method were used instead of the net method:

a. January 18, date of sale on credit:

> Accounts receivable 1,000
>   Sales revenue   1,000

b. January 27, date of collection if payment is made **within** the discount period (the usual case):

```
Cash ................................................................. 980
Sales discounts ....................................................  20
      Accounts receivable ..........................................        1,000
   Terms 2/10, n/30 ($1,000 × 0.98 = $980).
```

c. January 31, date of collection if payment is made **after** the discount period (the unusual case):

```
Cash ................................................................. 1,000
      Accounts receivable ..........................................         1,000
```

The Sales Discounts account (used with the gross method) may be reported as *(a)* a contra revenue account, or *(b)* an addition to selling expense. The gross method overstates both accounts receivable and sales revenue. The net method is theoretically preferable, but most companies choose the method that they believe involves the least clerical effort. However, the bookkeeping differences between the two methods are not significant.

Cash discounts are not the same as **trade discounts.** A cash discount is a price concession given to encourage early payment of an account. A trade discount is sometimes used by vendors for quoting sales prices; the amount **after** the trade discount is the sales price. For example, an item may be quoted at $10 per unit subject to a 20% trade discount on orders of 100 units or more; thus, the price for the large order would be $8 per unit.

In recent years there has been a trend toward more credit sales, particularly at the retail level. However, the use of cash discounts appears to be declining. In some jurisdictions, they are not legal in certain situations because the effect is to charge the cash customers more than the credit customers who pay within the discount period. Also, the discount not taken by credit customers is a hidden financing charge that may be governed by legislation dealing with credit practices.

Extending credit usually involves an increase in the amount of bookkeeping required because detailed records must be kept for each credit customer. Some businesses have their credit sales handled by a credit card company (such as Mastercard or Visa), which charges a fee for this service. The fee paid to the credit card company is recorded as a collection expense (and not a sales discount). Supplement 6A discusses some aspects of the detailed records kept for credit customers.

MEASURING BAD DEBT EXPENSE

Despite careful credit investigations, a few credit customers will not pay their bills. If an account receivable is uncollectible, the business has incurred a **bad debt expense.** Businesses that extend credit know that there will be a certain amount of bad debt losses on credit sales. An extremely low rate of bad debt losses may indicate too tight a credit policy. If the credit policy is too restrictive, many good credit customers may be turned away causing a loss of sales volume. Bad debt losses can be thought of as a necessary expense associated with generating credit sales.

In conformity with the matching principle, bad debt expense must be matched with the sale revenues that caused those losses. This requirement is difficult to implement because it may be one or more years after the sale was made before the business will know that the customer will be unable to pay.

To satisfy the matching principle, the **bad debt allowance method** is used to measure bad debt expense. The allowance method recognizes that bad debt expenses must be recorded in the year in which the sales that caused those losses were made rather than in the year that the customer is unable to pay. There is no way of knowing in advance which individual customers will not pay. Therefore, the allowance method is based upon **estimates** of the probable amount of bad debt losses from uncollectible accounts. The estimate is made in each accounting period based on the total credit sales for the period.

Estimating the probable amount of expense due to uncollectible accounts is not difficult. A company that has been operating for some years has sufficient experience to project probable future bad debt losses. New companies often rely on the experience of similar companies that have been operating for a number of years, if such information is available. Assume an analysis of accounting data on total credit sales and total uncollectible accounts for the past five years by Campus Corner indicated on average bad debt loss of 0.9% of total credit sales as follows:

Year	Bad debt losses	Credit sales
19A	$ 440	$ 54,000
19B	480	57,000
19C	620	53,000
19D	500	66,000
19E	660	70,000
	$2,700	$300,000

Aggregate: $2,700 ÷ $300,000 = 0.9% average loss rate for the five-year period 19A–E

Usually a company will adjust the average loss rate of the past to reflect future expectations. Campus Corner expects a small increase in uncollectible accounts from 19F sales; therefore, it increased the expected loss rate to 1.0%.

Assuming net credit sales in 19F of $40,000, we would record bad debt expense of $40,000 × 1% = $400 in 19F. This estimate would require the following **adjusting entry** at the end of the accounting period, December 31, 19F:

Bad debt expense	400	
Allowance for doubtful accounts (or bad debts)		400

To adjust for the estimated bad debt loss based on credit sales with an average expected loss rate of 1% ($40,000 × 1% = $400).

Bad debt expense of $400 would be reported on the 19F income statement. It would be matched with the related sales revenue for 19F, the year in which the credit was granted. The Bad Debt Expense account is closed at the end of each accounting period along with the other expense accounts. The credit in the above journal entry was made to a **contra account** titled "Allowance for Doubtful Accounts."[5] Accounts Receivable cannot be credited because there is no way of knowing which account receivable is involved. The balance in Allowance for Doubtful Accounts **always** is a subtraction from the balance of Accounts Receivable. The two accounts would be reported in the current asset section of the balance sheet as follows:

CAMPUS CORNER
Balance Sheet (partial)
At December 31, 19F

Current assets:		
Cash		$34,000
Accounts receivable	$100,000	
Less: Allowance for doubtful accounts	2,400*	97,600

   * This amount assumes a balance of $2,000 carried forward prior to the above entry.

Allowance for Doubtful Accounts has a cumulative credit balance. It is not closed at the end of the accounting period because it is a balance sheet account. The balance of the allowance account is the total amount of the accounts receivable that is estimated to be uncollectible. The difference between the balances of Accounts Receivable and the allowance account measures the **estimated net realizable** value of accounts receivable. In the above example, the difference between the two accounts—$97,600—represents the **estimated net**

---

[5] Other acceptable titles for this account are "Allowance for Bad Debts" and "Allowance for Uncollectible Accounts."

realizable value of accounts receivable (also called the book value of accounts receivable).

The bad debt estimate should be based only on credit sales. Sometimes, a company bases the estimate on total sales (i.e., cash plus credit sales). This practice is illogical because (1) it is impossible to have a bad debt loss on a cash sale (except in the case of a "hot" check that is uncollectible), and (2) a shift in the relative proportion between cash and credit sales would affect the accuracy of the estimate. The total amount of credit sales for each period can be determined (because these transactions are recorded in Accounts Receivable as debits); therefore, there is no reason for not using credit sales as the base for the estimate. Another method of estimating bad debt expense (called aging accounts receivable) is explained in Supplement 6B.

Writing Off a Bad Debt

When a specific customer's account receivable is determined to be uncollectible, the amount should be removed from the Accounts Receivable account with an offsetting debit to the allowance account. This entry does not record a bad debt expense because the estimated expense was recorded with an adjusting entry in the period of sale, and the related allowance account was established. Assume Campus Corner sold J. Doe merchandise on credit in 19D amounting to $100 (which was properly credited to 19D Sales Revenue and debited to Accounts Receivable). At the end of 19F, Campus Corner decided that it would never collect the $100. The journal entry to record the write-off would be:

December 31, 19F:

Allowance for doubtful accounts	100	
Accounts receivable (J. Doe)		100
To write off a receivable from J. Doe determined to be uncollectible.		

Notice that the above journal entry did not affect any income statement accounts. The expense already had been recorded (when the adjusting entry was made at the end of 19D). Also, the entry did not change the **net realizable value** (i.e., the book value) of Accounts Receivable. The difference between Accounts Receivable and the allowance account is the same as before the entry:

	Before write-off	After write-off
Accounts receivable	$100,000	$99,900
Less: Allowance for doubtful accounts	2,400	2,300
Difference—estimated net realizable value	$ 97,600	$97,600

Actual write-offs compared with estimates

The amount of uncollectible accounts actually written off seldom will equal the estimated amounts previously recorded. If the accounts actually written off are less than the estimated amount, the Allowance for Doubtful Accounts will continue with a credit balance.[6] If an account is written off as bad and the customer subsequently pays it, the write-off entry should be reversed and the collection should be recorded in the usual way.

Terminology

The caption "Accounts Receivable" often appears on the balance sheet under current assets without additional descriptive terms; however, a more descriptive phrase such as "Receivables from trade customers" is preferable. Receivables from other than the regular trade customers, such as loans to officers or employees, should not be included in the accounts receivable category. Instead, such nontrade receivables should be reported as separate items.

SALES RETURNS AND ALLOWANCES

Many businesses let customers return unsatisfactory or damaged merchandise and receive a refund. In some cases, rather than taking back such merchandise, an adjustment may be given to the customer. To measure correctly sales revenue, returns and adjustments are recorded by reversing the original sales entry. Although the Sales account could be debited (i.e., reduced) to record these reductions in sales, a separate account "Sales Returns and Allowances" often is used. This account has an important purpose. It informs management of the volume of returns and allowances. If cash is refunded, the Cash account is credited. If a credit adjustment is given, accounts receivable of the customer must be credited. The Sales Returns and Allowances account is a contra revenue account; therefore, it is a deduction from gross sales revenue (as shown in Exhibit 6–1). Assume a customer, F. Fox, bought five new lamps from Campus Corner for $500. Fifteen days after payment, Fox returned one damaged lamp. The sequence of journal entries by Campus Corner would be:

Date of sale:

Accounts receivable (F. Fox)	500	
Sales revenue		500
To record sale.		

---

[6] On the other hand, if the amount written off is more than the allowance balance, there will be a temporary debit balance in the allowance account. This situation will be resolved when the next adjusting entry is made. It indicates that the estimated loss rate used may be too low.

Date of sale return:

Sales returns and allowances 100
　　Cash* 100
　To record sale return, 1 unit.
　　* If payment had not been made, this credit would be to Accounts Receivable.

PART B—ACCOUNTING FOR COST OF GOODS SOLD

NATURE OF COST OF GOODS SOLD

Cost of goods sold is a major expense item for most nonservice businesses. Cost of goods sold (CGS) is directly related to sales revenue. Sales revenue for a product during an accounting period is the number of units sold multiplied by the sales price. Cost of goods sold is the same number of units multiplied by the unit cost. Revenue and expense are matched on the income statement in conformity with the **matching principle** (see Exhibit 4–5). Cost of goods sold includes the cost of all merchandise sold during the period. However, it excludes the cost of all merchandise remaining on hand at the end of the accounting period (i.e., the ending merchandise inventory).

A business will start each accounting period with a stock of merchandise on hand for resale called the **beginning inventory (BI).** The merchandise on hand at the end of an accounting period is called the **ending inventory (EI).** The ending inventory for one accounting period automatically becomes the beginning inventory for the next period.

During the accounting period, the beginning inventory is increased by the purchase or manufacture of more merchandise. The sum of the beginning inventory and the **purchases (P)** during the period represents the **goods available for sale** during that period. If all of the goods available for sale were sold during the period, there would be no ending inventory. Typically, not all of the goods available for sale are sold, and there is an ending inventory for the period. From these relationships, we can compute cost of goods sold as follows:

$$BI + P - EI = CGS$$

To illustrate, Campus Corner reported cost of goods sold of $60,000 (Exhibit 6–1), which was computed as follows:

Beginning inventory (January 1, 19F) $40,000
Add purchases of merchandise during 19F 55,000
　Goods available for sale 95,000
Deduct ending inventory (December 31, 19F) 35,000
　Cost of goods sold $60,000

TWO DIFFERENT INVENTORY SYSTEMS

To compute cost of goods sold, three amounts must be known: (1) beginning inventory, (2) purchases of merchandise during the period, and (3) ending inventory. The beginning inventory of one accounting period is the ending inventory of the previous period. The amount of purchases for the period is accumulated in the accounting system. The amount of the ending inventory can be determined by using one of two different inventory systems:

1. **Periodic inventory system**—Under this system, no up-to-date record of inventory is maintained during the year. An actual physical count of the goods remaining on hand is required at the **end of each period.** The number of units of each type of merchandise on hand is multiplied by the purchase cost per unit to compute the dollar amount of the ending inventory. Thus, the amount of goods on hand is not known until the last day of the period when the inventory count is done. Also, the amount of cost of goods sold cannot be determined until the inventory count is done.
2. **Perpetual inventory system**—This system involves the maintenance of up-to-date inventory records in the accounting system during the period. For each type of merchandise stocked, a detailed record is maintained that shows *(a)* units and cost of the beginning inventory, *(b)* units and cost of each purchase, *(c)* units and cost of the goods for each sale, and *(d)* the units and cost of the goods on hand at any point in time. This up-to-date record is maintained on a transaction-by-transaction basis throughout the period. **Thus, the inventory record gives both the amount of ending inventory and the cost of goods sold amount at any point in time.**

Periodic Inventory System

The periodic inventory system requires an actual count of the goods on hand at the end of the period and valuation of the units at their purchase cost. The primary reasons for using the periodic inventory system are low cost and convenience. Consider the expense and difficulty associated with a grocery store attempting to keep track of the number of units sold and the cost of each purchase and sale for thousands of low-priced items that usually are stocked. In many stores, no record is made at the cash register of the cost and quantity of each item sold. Instead, the total sales price is entered into the cash register. The primary disadvantage of a periodic inventory system is the lack of inventory control (for purchasing purposes and detection of theft).[7]

---

[7] Because of this important disadvantage, large chain stores now have computerized perpetual inventory systems tied in directly to the cash registers.

A periodic inventory system applies the cost of goods sold computation as follows:

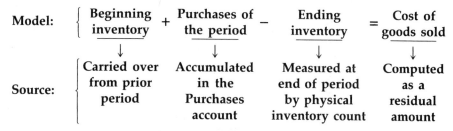

Model:	Beginning inventory	+	Purchases of the period	−	Ending inventory	=	Cost of goods sold
	↓		↓		↓		↓
Source:	Carried over from prior period		Accumulated in the Purchases account		Measured at end of period by physical inventory count		Computed as a residual amount

A periodic inventory system may be outlined sequentially as follows:

1. **Record all purchases**—During the period, the cost of all goods purchased is recorded in an account called Purchases (or Merchandise Purchases). A credit or cash purchase would be recorded as follows:

January 14, 19F:

```
Purchases ......................................................  9,000
     Accounts payable (or Cash) ...................................      9,000
```

2. **Record all sales**—During the period, the sales price received for all goods sold is recorded in a Sales Revenue account. A credit or cash sale would be recorded as follows:

January 30, 19F:

```
Accounts receivable (or Cash) ........................................ 8,000
     Sales revenue ................................................      8,000
```

3. **Count the number of units on hand**—At the end of each accounting period, the inventory account balance still shows the ending inventory amount carried over from the prior period because **no journal entries** are made to the inventory account during the period. To measure the ending inventory for the current period, a physical inventory count must be made. A physical count is needed because under the periodic inventory system, a transaction-by-transaction record is not maintained. Taking a physical inventory count is discussed later.

4. **Compute the dollar valuation of the ending inventory**—The dollar amount of the ending inventory quantities is computed by multiplying the number of units on hand by their unit purchase cost. The dollar amounts of all of the types of goods stocked are summed to determine the total ending inventory valuation for the company.
5. **Compute cost of goods sold**—After the ending inventory valuation is determined, cost of goods sold for the period is computed. The calculation of cost of goods sold for Campus Corner is shown below.

CAMPUS CORNER
Schedule of Cost of Goods Sold
For the Year Ended December 31, 19F

Beginning inventory (carried over from the last period in the inventory account)	$40,000
Add purchases for the period (accumulated balance in the Purchases account)	55,000
Goods available for sale	95,000
Less ending inventory (determined by physical count, per above)	35,000
Cost of goods sold (as shown in Exhibit 6–1)	$60,000

Perpetual Inventory System

A perpetual inventory system typically involves a large amount of clerical effort. However, the maintenance of a separate inventory record for each type of goods stocked on a transaction-by-transaction basis usually is desirable, particularly for control purposes. To minimize clerical difficulties, most perpetual inventory systems are computerized. Whether the accounting system is manual, mechanical, or computerized, the data that are recorded and reported are the same. Assume, for this illustration only, that Campus Corner stocks and sells only one item, called Super X. The following events apply to 19F:

Jan. 1   Beginning inventory—8 units, at unit cost of $5,000.
July 14   Purchased—11 additional units, at unit cost of $5,000.
Nov. 30   Sold—13 units, at unit sales price of $8,333.
Dec. 31   Return sale—1 unit (returned to stock and refunded sales price).

The perpetual inventory record for the Super X item is shown in Exhibit 6–2.[8]

When the perpetual inventory system is computerized, the computer does exactly what was done manually in Exhibit 6–2; however, a computerized system does it with tremendous speed and accuracy. Computers overcome many of the difficulties associated with the perpetual system. Computers permit large, medium, and small companies to use the perpetual system.

A perpetual inventory system may be outlined sequentially as follows:

---

[8] Measuring inventories and cost of goods sold when there are different unit purchase costs is deferred to Chapter 7.

Exhibit 6-2

Perpetual inventory record

PERPETUAL INVENTORY RECORD

Item ___Super X___   Code   No. 33___   Minimum stock 10___

Location Storage No. 4___   Valuation basis Cost___   Maximum stock 20___

Date	Explanation	Goods Purchased			Goods Sold			Balance on Hand		
		Units Rec'd	Unit Cost	Total Cost	Units Sold	Unit Cost	Total Cost	Units	Unit Cost	Total Cost
Jan. 1	Beginning inventory							8	5,000	40,000
July 14	Purchase	11	5,000	55,000				19	5,000	95,000
Nov. 30	Sale				13	5,000	65,000	6	5,000	30,000
Dec. 31	Return sale				(1)	5,000	(5,000)	7	5,000	35,000
Recap: Total purchases		11		55,000						
Total cost of goods sold					12		60,000			
Ending inventory								7		35,000

1. **Record all purchases**—During the period, the cost of all goods purchased is recorded in the **inventory** ledger account and is entered in a detailed perpetual inventory record (Exhibit 6–2). A cash or credit purchase of goods for resale would be recorded as follows:

July 14, 19F:

```
Inventory* (Super X, code 33) ...................................... 55,000
    Accounts payable (or Cash) ....................................        55,000
    * Also entered in the perpetual inventory record as shown in Exhibit 6–2.
```

2. **Record all sales**—During the period, each sale is recorded using **two companion journal entries.** One entry is to record the sales revenue, and the

other entry is to record the cost of goods sold. A credit or cash sale would be recorded as follows (refer to data presented in Exhibit 6–2):

a. To record the sales revenue at the sales price of $8,333 per unit:

```
Accounts receivable (or Cash) ...........................  108,329
     Sales revenue (13 units @ $8,333) ...................          108,329
```

b. To record the cost of goods sold (at cost per the perpetual inventory record—Exhibit 6–2):

```
Cost of goods sold* .....................................  65,000
     Inventory (13 units @ $5,000) ........................          65,000
     * Also entered in the perpetual inventory record as shown in Exhibit 6–2.
```

3. **Record all returns**—During the period, the costs of both **purchase returns and sales returns** are recorded in the Inventory account and on the perpetual inventory record. The return by a customer of one unit of Super X on December 31 requires companion journal entries to reverse the two entries made on the date of sale (but only for the number of units returned). The return is recorded as follows:

a. To record the sales return at sale price (one unit):

```
Sales returns and allowances (1 unit @ $8,333) .............  8,333
     Accounts receivable (or Cash) ........................          8,333
```

b. To record the return of the unit to inventory at cost:

```
Inventory (1 unit @ $5,000) ..............................  5,000*
     Cost of goods sold ...................................          5,000
     * This amount was provided by the perpetual inventory record; also it is restored to the
     perpetual inventory record as shown in Exhibit 6–2.
```

4. **Use cost of goods sold and inventory amounts**—At the end of the accounting period, the balance in the Cost of Goods Sold account is the amount of that expense reported on the income statement. It is not necessary to compute cost of goods sold because under the perpetual inventory system the Cost of Goods Sold account is up-to-date. Also, the Inventory account shows the ending inventory amount reported on the balance sheet. The sum of all the inventory balances in the various perpetual inventory records should equal the balance in the Inventory account in the ledger at any point in time.

When a perpetual inventory system is used, it is not necessary to take a physical inventory count in order to measure the inventory and cost of goods sold. However, because clerical errors, theft, and spoilage may occur, a physical inventory should be taken from time to time to check upon the accuracy of the perpetual inventory records. If an error is found, the perpetual inventory records and the Inventory account must be changed to agree with the physical count.

To summarize, there are two basic accounting differences between periodic and perpetual systems:

1. Inventory account:
   a. Periodic system—During the period, the balance in the Inventory account is not changed; thus, it reflects the beginning inventory amount. During the period, each purchase is recorded in the Purchases account. Therefore, the ending inventory for each accounting period must be measured by physical count, then valued (or "costed") at unit purchase cost.
   b. Perpetual system—During the period, the Inventory account is increased for each purchase and decreased (at cost) for each sale. At any point during the period, it measures the correct amount of inventory.
2. Cost of Goods Sold account:
   a. Periodic system—During the period, no entry is made for cost of goods sold. At the end of the period, after the physical inventory count, cost of goods sold is calculated as follows:

$$\text{Beginning inventory} + \text{Purchases} - \text{Ending inventory} = \text{Cost of goods sold}$$

   b. Perpetual system—During the period, cost of goods sold is recorded at the time of each sale and the Inventory account is reduced (at cost). This system directly measures the amount of cost of goods sold for the period.

The perpetual inventory system provides the following advantages over the periodic inventory system:

1. It gives up-to-date inventory amounts (units and dollar cost for each item).
2. It gives the cost of goods sold amount without having to take a periodic inventory count.

3. It gives continuing information needed to keep minimum and maximum inventory levels by appropriate timing of purchases.
4. It gives continuing information about the quantity of goods on hand at various locations.
5. It gives a basis for measuring the amount of theft.
6. It gives cost of goods sold information needed to record sales at both selling price and cost.
7. It is adaptable for use by computers that quickly process large quantities of inventory data.

For these reasons there has been an increase in the use of the perpetual inventory system and a decrease in use of the periodic inventory system.

ADDITIONAL ISSUES IN MEASURING PURCHASES

Goods purchased for resale are recorded as a purchase at the date that **ownership** passes from the seller to the buyer. Ownership usually passes when the goods are received and not when the purchase order is placed. Goods purchased should be recorded at their **cash equivalent cost** in conformity with the cost principle. Cost includes the cash equivalent price paid to the vendor (seller) plus other amounts paid for transportation and handling in order to get the goods into location and condition for intended use. Cost does not include interest paid on cash borrowed to make the purchase. Many of the problems associated with accounting for purchases are the same as those discussed in Part A of this chapter from the perspective of the seller.

Purchase Returns and Allowances

Goods purchased may be returned to the vendor if they do not meet specifications, arrive in unsatisfactory condition, or otherwise are unsatisfactory. When the goods are returned or when the vendor makes an allowance because of the circumstances, the effect on the cost of purchases must be measured. The purchaser will receive a cash refund or a reduction in the liability to the vendor for the purchase. Assume Campus Corner returned unsatisfactory goods that cost $1,000 to Company B. The return would be recorded by Campus Corner (which uses the periodic system) as follows:

Accounts payable (or cash)	1,000	
Purchase returns and allowances*		1,000
* Inventory is credited when the perpetual inventory system is used.		

Purchase returns and allowances are accounted for as a deduction from the cost of purchases.

Transportation-In

The **purchase cost** of goods acquired for resale should include all freight and other transportation-in costs incurred by the purchaser. When a perpetual inventory system is used, transportation costs paid on goods purchased should be apportioned to each inventory item and included in the inventory cost amount entered in the perpetual inventory. When a periodic inventory system is used, such costs should be recorded as a debit (i.e., increase) to the Purchases account. It is difficult to apportion a freight bill to the several items it may cover. It is more practical to enter the amount of the bill in a separate account "Transportation-In," or "Freight-In." Also, for control purposes it is often useful to classify separately this significant cost. The journal entry to record a payment for transportation charges upon delivery of merchandise acquired for resale is:

Jan. 17	Transportation-in	3,000	
	Cash		3,000

At the end of the accounting period, the balance in the Transportation-In account is reported as an addition to the cost of purchases.

Assuming freight-in and purchase returns, cost of goods sold may be shown as follows on the income statement when periodic inventory procedures are used:

Cost of goods sold:		
Beginning inventory		$40,000
Purchases	$53,000	
Add: Freight-in	3,000	
Deduct: Purchase returns and allowances	(1,000)	
Net purchases		55,000
Goods available for sale		95,000
Less: Ending inventory		35,000
Cost of goods sold		$60,000

Purchase Discounts

Cash discounts must be accounted for by both the seller and the buyer (accounting by the seller was discussed in Part A of this chapter). When merchandise is bought on credit, terms such as 2/10, n/30 sometimes are specified.

This means that if payment is made within 10 days from date of purchase, a 2% cash discount is granted. If payment is not made within the discount period, then the full invoice cost is due 30 days after purchase. Assume on January 17, Campus Corner bought goods that had a $1,000 invoice price with terms 2/10, n/30. The purchase should be recorded on the net basis by Campus Corner as follows:[9]

January 17—date of purchase:

Purchases*	980	
Accounts payable		980
* Inventory is debited when a perpetual inventory system is used.		

January 26—date of payment, within the discount period:

Accounts payable	980	
Cash		980

If for any reason Campus Corner did not pay within the 10-day discount period, the following entry would be needed:

Feb. 1 Accounts payable	980	
Purchase discounts lost (or Interest expense)	20	
Cash		1,000

Purchase discounts lost should be reported on the income statement as a **financial expense** along with interest expense.

---

[9] Some persons prefer to record the transaction at the date of purchase at the gross amount, that is, at $1,000. In this instance, payment within the discount period would result in credit to an account called Purchase Discounts, $20. The purchase discount credit would then be reported as a revenue, or as a deduction from purchases. This credit is not revenue and if deducted in full from purchases on the income statement would tend to misstate both inventory and purchases. In contrast, the net basis has the distinct advantage in that recording the **purchase discount lost** calls direct attention to inefficiency—failure to take the discount. The gross approach conceptually and practically is deficient for reasons similar to those cited with respect to sales discounts.

TAKING A PHYSICAL INVENTORY

A physical inventory count must be taken from time to time. When a **periodic** inventory system is used, the inventory must be counted (and costed) at the **end of each period** because the financial statements cannot be prepared without this key amount. When a perpetual inventory system is used, the inventory count may be scheduled at various times to verify the perpetual inventory records. The two steps in taking a **physical inventory** are:

1. **Quantity count**—The **count** of merchandise is made after the close of business on the inventory date. Normally, it would be difficult to count the goods accurately during business hours when sales activities are taking place. A physical count is made of all items of merchandise on hand and entered on an appropriate form. An inventory form, such as the one shown in Exhibit 6–3, may be used. Special care must be used so that all of the merchandise owned by the business is included, wherever located. Also, all items for which the

EXHIBIT 6–3

Physical inventory form

Campus Corner
PHYSICAL INVENTORY SHEET

Date of Inventory _12/31/87_ Department _4 (and last)_ Taken by _M. R._

Location	Identification of Merchandise	Quantity on Hand	Date Purchased	Unit Cost	Unit Market Price*	Unit Cost (LCM)	Inventory Amount
1	Headsets #8-16	20	12/2/87	$20	$21	$20	$400
2	Television sets #17-961	7	11/5/87	300	300	300	2,100
2	Radios #23-72	4	10/26/87	52	50	50	200

| Total Department Inventory | | | | | | | 6,000 |
| TOTAL INVENTORY VALUE—ALL DEPARTMENTS | | | 12/31/87 | | | | $35,000 |

* Replacement cost that would have to be paid if the item were being purchased on the inventory date (see lower of cost or market discussion in Chapter 7).

business does not have legal ownership should be excluded. Sometimes, a business will have possession of goods it does not own (see discussion of consignments in Chapter 7).

2. **Inventory costing**—After the physical count of goods on hand has been completed, each kind of merchandise must be assigned a **unit cost.** The quantity of each kind of merchandise is multiplied by the unit cost to derive the inventory amount (as shown in Exhibit 6–3). The sum of the inventory amounts for all merchandise on hand is the total ending inventory amount for the business. Exhibit 6–3 shows computation of the ending inventory shown on the income statement for Campus Corner. To determine the value of inventory, the cost principle must be applied. A problem arises if there are different unit costs for inventory items that are the same. When this situation occurs, there are several ways to identify unit cost for inventory purposes such as the first-in, first-out (FIFO), last-in, first-out (LIFO), or average cost approaches. These alternative approaches to costing inventories are discussed in Chapter 7.

Management must deal with complex problems associated with planning and control of inventories. An excessive amount of inventory may tie up resources (i.e., cash) that could be used more economically in other ways in the business. Insufficient inventory often results in lost sales. Decisions must be made concerning maximum and minimum levels of inventory that should be kept; when to reorder; how much to reorder; and the characteristics of the items to stock, such as size, color, style, and specifications. From the viewpoint of the investor, creditor, and other interested parties, information concerning the investment in inventory is important in decision making. Therefore, explanatory footnotes related to inventories are included in the financial reports.

DATA PROCESSING—CLOSING ENTRIES FOR SALES REVENUE, COST OF GOODS SOLD, AND MERCHANDISE INVENTORY

Closing the Sales Revenue and Bad Debt Expense Accounts

Revenue and expense accounts are **temporary** accounts that must be closed at the end of the accounting period. Sales Revenue is closed by recording a debit in that account and a credit in the Income Summary. Sales Discount Revenue is closed in the same way. Bad Debt Expense is closed by recording a credit in that account and a debit to the Income Summary. Sales Returns and Allowance (a contra revenue account) is closed by recording a credit to that account and a debit to the Income Summary. The closing entries for cost of goods sold (an expense) and the merchandise inventory amounts depend upon the inventory system (periodic versus perpetual) used.

Closing Entries When a Periodic Inventory System Is Used

When a periodic inventory system is used, there is no Cost of Goods Sold account in the ledger. The merchandise inventory account requires two directly related closing entries: (1) an entry to close the **beginning inventory** amount to the Income Summary account and (2) an entry to transfer the **ending inventory** amount from the Income Summary account to the Inventory account. A third entry is needed to close the Purchases account. Campus Corner would make closing entries for the merchandise inventories as follows:

December 31, 19F.

a. To close (transfer) the **beginning** merchandise inventory amount into Income Summary:

Income summary	40,000	
Merchandise inventory (beginning)		40,000

b. To transfer the **ending** merchandise inventory amount from the Income Summary account to the Merchandise Inventory account:

Merchandise inventory (ending)	35,000	
Income summary		35,000

The effects of these two journal entries are (a) to replace the beginning inventory amount in the Merchandise Inventory account with the ending inventory amount and (b) to enter the beginning inventory amount in the Income Summary account as an **expense** (a debit) and (c) to remove the ending inventory amount from the Income Summary account (a credit) as a cost transfer to the asset account Merchandise Inventory.

c. In addition, the Purchases account is closed to Income Summary as follows:

Income summary	55,000	
Purchases		55,000

The reason for the two closing entries for merchandise inventories under the **periodic inventory system** can be understood if you recall that the ending inventory of the one year automatically is the beginning inventory for the next year. Also, the Inventory account balance is not changed during the year because all purchases of merchandise are entered in the Purchases account rather than in the Inventory account. Therefore, at the end of the accounting period, the beginning inventory amount ($40,000 for Campus Corner) is still in the Inventory account. It must be transferred out as an expense and be replaced with the ending inventory amount ($35,000 for Campus Corner). Notice that when the ending inventory amount is transferred out of the Income Summary, the Income Summary is decreased by the amount of cost of goods sold (beginning inventory plus purchases minus ending inventory equals cost of goods sold). After completion of these closing entries, the Merchandise Inventory, Purchases, and Income Summary accounts for Campus Corner would appear as follows:

PERIODIC INVENTORY SYSTEM

Merchandise Inventory

12/31/19E (beginning)	40,000	(a) To close	40,000
(b) 12/31/19F (ending)	35,000		

Purchases

12/31/19F (balance)	55,000	(c) To close	55,000

Income Summary

Operating expenses (not shown)		Revenues (not shown)	
(a) 12/31/19E (beginning inventory)	40,000	(b) 12/31/19F (ending inventory)	35,000
(c) (purchases)	55,000		

(Note that these three amounts net to $60,000, the amount of cost of goods sold.)

These closing entries, along with all the other closing entries, are shown in the demonstration case (Rote Appliance Store) at the end of this chapter.[10] This demonstration case should be studied carefully because it ties together the discussion in this chapter.

Closing Entries When a Perpetual Inventory System Is Used

When a perpetual inventory system is used, the Merchandise Inventory account and Cost of Goods Sold account always show the correct up-to-date balance. Therefore, no adjusting or closing entries are needed for the Merchan-

---

[10] There are several mechanical variations in how the closing entries can be made; all of them give the same end results. For example, some persons prefer to record the two inventory entries as adjusting, rather than closing, entries. Also, some persons prefer to use a temporary Cost of Goods Sold account in the closing process under a periodic inventory system; in this approach the two inventory amounts and purchases are first transferred to the Cost of Goods Sold account, which is then closed to Income Summary.

dise Inventory account; it shows the ending inventory amount that will be reported on the balance sheet. Because the Cost of Goods Sold account is an expense account, it will be closed. For example, Campus Corner would record the following closing entry under the perpetual inventory system:

Income summary	60,000	
Cost of goods sold		60,000

Inventory Shrinkage

Inventory shrinkage occurs because of theft, breakage, spoilage, and incorrect measurements. The measurement of inventory shrinkage is important for internal control purposes and, if large, is a major concern for investors and creditors. The dollar amount of shrinkage is reported on **internal** financial statements, but seldom are such amounts significant enough to be reported **separately** on **external** financial statements. Accurate measurement of this loss is related directly to the inventory system used.

When a **periodic inventory** is used, measurement of inventory shrinkage often is difficult, and may be impossible. The inventory, as counted at the end of the period, does not give a basis for measurement of shrinkage. An implicit assumption underlying the calculation of cost of goods sold (i.e., Beginning inventory + Purchases − Ending inventory = Cost of goods sold) is that if an item is not in ending inventory, it must have been sold. Therefore, under the periodic inventory system, cost of goods sold includes inventory shrinkage.

In contrast, a perpetual inventory system gives data on shrinkage loss. The inventory record gives both cost of goods sold and the ending inventory. These data make it possible to measure shrinkage loss. Assume the perpetual inventory records showed cost of goods sold for the period, 12 units, $60,000, and ending inventory of 7 units, $35,000. An inventory count at the end of the period showed 6 units on hand. An inventory shrinkage would be reported as 1 unit, and the loss amount would be $5,000 (assuming no insurance recovery). The journal entry to record the shrinkage, using a perpetual inventory system, is:

Inventory shrinkage*	5,000	
Inventory		5,000
* Closed to Income Summary.		

DEMONSTRATION CASE

(Try to resolve the requirements before proceeding to the suggested solution that follows.)

Rote Appliance Store has been operating for a number of years. It is a relatively small but profitable retail outlet for major appliances, such as refrigerators and air conditioners. Approximately 40% of the sales are on short-term credit. This case has been simplified to demonstrate information processing when there are significant selling activities (the service activities have been deleted). The case shows the application of both perpetual and periodic inventory systems with the same data. The annual accounting period ends December 31, 19D. Two independent cases will be assumed:

Case A—Perpetual inventory system.
Case B—Periodic inventory system.

The trial balance at December 31, 19D, was:

| | Unadjusted trial balance | | | |
| | Case A—Perpetual inventory system used | | Case B—Periodic inventory system used | |
Account titles	Debit	Credit	Debit	Credit
Cash	$ 34,100		$ 34,100	
Accounts receivable	5,000		5,000	
Allowance for doubtful accounts		$ 1,000		$ 1,000
* Merchandise inventory:				
January 1, 19D			20,000	
December 31, 19D	16,000			
Store equipment	30,000		30,000	
Accumulated depreciation, equipment		9,000		9,000
Accounts payable		8,000		8,000
Income tax payable				
Capital stock, par $10		40,000		40,000
Retained earnings, January 1, 19D		9,000		9,000
Sales revenue		102,000		102,000
Sales returns and allowances	2,000		2,000	
* Cost of goods sold	60,000			
* Purchases			57,000	
* Purchase returns and allowances				1,000
Expenses (not detailed)	21,900		21,900	
Depreciation expense				
Income tax expense				
Totals	$169,000	$169,000	$170,000	$170,000

* These account balances are different between the two cases because of the effects of the two inventory systems used.

Data developed by Rote as a basis for the adjusting entries at December 31, 19D, were:

a. Credit sales in 19D were $40,000; the average loss rate for bad debts is estimated to be 0.25% of credit sales.

b. The store equipment is depreciated on the basis of an estimated 10-year useful life with no residual value.

c. On December 31, 19D, the periodic inventory count of goods remaining on hand was $16,000.

d. The average income tax rate is 20%.

e. The beginning inventory, January 1, 19D, was as shown on the trial balance (Case B).

Required:

a. Based upon the above data, complete a worksheet at December 31, 19D, similar to that shown in Exhibit 5–3. You may omit the columns for Adjusted Trial Balance. **Prepare a separate worksheet for each separate case.**

b. Based upon the completed worksheets, present an income statement for each case. Use a single-step format for Case A and a multiple-step format for Case B.

c. Based upon the two worksheets, present, in parallel columns, the adjusting entries for each case at December 31, 19D.

d. Based upon the two worksheets, present, in parallel columns, the closing entries for each situation at December 31, 19D.

In preparing the worksheet when a **perpetual inventory** system is used, no new complications are presented. The inventory amount is extended across the worksheet as an asset because the balance in the Inventory account reflects the ending inventory when a perpetual inventory system is used. The expense—cost of goods sold—is extended to the Income Summary debit column along with the other expenses. See Exhibit 6–4.

In preparing the worksheet with a **periodic inventory system,** both the beginning and ending inventory amounts must be used. First, the beginning inventory amount must be extended horizontally as a debit to the Income Statement column (because it now is an expense). A special line, "Merchandise inventory, ending" is added to the bottom of the worksheet, and the ending inventory amount is entered on this line under Income Statement credit. This amount also is listed on the same line under Balance Sheet, debit.[11]

---

[11] There are several mechanical ways of handling the inventories on the worksheet when a periodic inventory system is used. Some accountants view the inventory entries as closing rather than adjusting entries. The various approaches arrive at the same net result, and each has its particular mechanical advantages and disadvantages.

EXHIBIT 6-4

Worksheets compared for perpetual and periodic inventory systems

ROTE APPLIANCE STORE
Worksheet, December 31, 19D
Case A—Assuming Perpetual Inventory System Is Used

Account Titles	Trial Balance Debit	Trial Balance Credit	Adjusting Entries* Debit	Adjusting Entries* Credit	Income Statement Debit	Income Statement Credit	Retained Earnings Debit	Retained Earnings Credit	Balance Sheet Debit	Balance Sheet Credit
Cash	34,100								34,100	
Accounts receivable	5,000								5,000	
Allowance for doubtful accounts		1,000		(a) 100						1,100
Merchandise inventory Dec. 31, 19D	16,000								16,000	
Store equipment	30,000								30,000	
Accumulated depreciation, equipment		9,000		(b) 3,000						12,000
Accounts payable		8,000								8,000
Income tax payable				(c) 3,000						3,000
Capital stock, par $10		40,000								40,000
Retained earnings, Jan. 1, 19D		9,000						9,000		
Sales revenue		102,000				102,000				
Sales returns and allowances	2,000				2,000					
Cost of goods sold	60,000				60,000					
Expenses (not detailed)	21,900		(a) 100		22,000					
Depreciation expense			(b) 3,000		3,000					
	169,000	169,000			87,000	102,000				
Income tax expense†			(c) 3,000		3,000					
Net income					12,000				12,000	
			6,100	6,100	102,000	102,000	–0–	21,000		
Retained earnings, Dec. 31, 19D							21,000			21,000
							21,000	21,000	85,100	85,100

* Note that a **simplifying mechanical change** is used—the "Adjusting Entries" total is not entered until **after** the income tax is computed and entered.
† ($102,000 − $87,000) × 20% = $3,000 income tax expense.

Requirement a (concluded):

EXHIBIT 6–4 *(concluded)*

ROTE APPLIANCE STORE
Worksheet, December 31, 19D
Case B—Assuming Periodic Inventory System Is Used

Account Titles	Trial Balance		Adjusting Entries*		Income Statement		Retained Earnings		Balance Sheet	
	Debit	Credit	Debit	Credit	Debit	Credit	Debit	Credit	Debit	Credit
Cash	34,100								34,100	
Accounts receivable	5,000								5,000	
Allowance for doubtful accounts		1,000		(a) 100						1,100
Merchandise inventory, Jan. 1, 19D	20,000				20,000					
Store equipment	30,000								30,000	
Accumulated depreciation, equipment		9,000		(b) 3,000						12,000
Accounts payable		8,000								8,000
Income tax payable				(c) 3,000						3,000
Capital stock, par $10		40,000								40,000
Retained earnings, Jan. 1, 19D		9,000						9,000		
Sales revenue		102,000				102,000				
Sales returns and allowances	2,000				2,000					
Purchases	57,000				57,000					
Purchase returns and allowances		1,000				1,000				
Expenses (not detailed)	21,900		(a) 100		22,000					
Depreciation expense			(b) 3,000		3,000					
Merchandise inventory, Dec. 31, 19D						16,000			16,000	
	170,000	170,000			104,000	119,000				
Income tax expense†			(c) 3,000		3,000					
Net income					12,000			12,000		
			6,100	6,100	119,000	119,000	–0–	21,000		
							21,000			21,000
							21,000	21,000	85,100	85,100

* Note that a **simplifying mechanical change** is used—the "Adjusting Entries" total is not entered until after the income tax is computed and entered.
† ($119,000 − $104,000) × 20% = $3,000 income tax expense.

Requirement b:

ROTE APPLIANCE STORE
Income Statement
For the Year Ended December 31, 19D
Case A—Perpetual Inventory System and Single-Step Format

Revenues:

Gross sales revenue	$102,000	
Less: Sales returns and allowances	2,000	
Net sales revenue		$100,000

Expenses:

Cost of goods sold	60,000	
Expenses (not detailed for case purposes)	22,000	
Depreciation expense	3,000	85,000
Pretax income		15,000
Income tax expense ($15,000 × 20%)		3,000
Net income		$ 12,000
EPS ($12,000 ÷ 4,000 shares)		$3.00

ROTE APPLIANCE STORE
Income Statement
For the Year Ended December 31, 19D
Case B—Periodic Inventory System and Multiple-Step Format

Gross sales revenue		$102,000
Less: Sales returns and allowances		2,000
Net sales revenue		100,000

Cost of goods sold:

Inventory, January 1, 19D	$ 20,000	
Purchases	57,000	
Purchase returns and allowances	(1,000)	
Goods available for sale	76,000	
Less: Inventory, December 31, 19D	16,000	
Cost of goods sold		60,000
Gross margin on sales		40,000

Operating expenses:

Expenses (not detailed for case purposes)	22,000	
Depreciation expense	3,000	25,000
Pretax income		15,000
Income tax expense ($15,000 × 20%)		3,000
Net income		$ 12,000
EPS ($12,000 ÷ 4,000 shares)		$3.00

Requirement c:

Adjusting Entries
December 31, 19D

	Case A		Case B	
	Perpetual inventory		*Periodic inventory*	
a. Expenses (estimated bad debt loss)	100		100	
Allowance for doubtful accounts		100		100
Bad debt loss estimated, $40,000 × 0.25% = $100.				
b. Depreciation expense	3,000		3,000	
Accumulated depreciation, equipment		3,000		3,000
Depreciation for one year, $30,000 ÷ 10 years = $3,000.				
c. Income tax expense	3,000		3,000	
Income tax payable		3,000		3,000
Income tax for year, $15,000 × 20% = $3,000				

Requirement d:

Closing Entries
December 31, 19D

	Case A	Case B
	Perpetual inventory	*Periodic inventory*
1. Sales revenue 102,000		102,000
Sales returns and allowances	2,000	2,000
Income summary	100,000	100,000
To transfer the revenue amounts to Income Summary.		
2. Income summary .... (Not applicable)		56,000
Purchase returns and allowances		1,000
Purchases		57,000
To transfer purchase amounts to Income Summary.		
3. Income summary .... (Not applicable)		20,000
Merchandise inventory (beginning)		20,000
To transfer beginning inventory to Income Summary.		
4. Merchandise inventory (ending) .... (Not applicable)		16,000
Income summary		16,000
To transfer ending inventory from Income Summary.		
5. Income summary 60,000		(Not applicable)
Cost of goods sold	60,000	
6. Income summary 28,000		28,000
Expenses (not detailed)	22,000	22,000
Depreciation expense	3,000	3,000
Income tax expense	3,000	3,000
To transfer expense amounts to Income Summary.		
7. Income summary 12,000		12,000
Retained earnings	12,000	12,000
To transfer net income to Retained Earnings.		

SUMMARY OF CHAPTER

This chapter discussed the measuring, recording, and reporting of the effects on income of the selling and purchasing activities of various types of business.

In conformity with the matching principle, the total cost of the goods sold during the period must be matched with the sales revenue earned during the period. The Cost of Goods Sold account measures the **cost** of merchandise that was sold while the Sales Revenue account measures the **selling price** of the same merchandise. When cost of goods sold is deducted from sales revenue for the period, the difference is called gross margin on sales. From this amount, the remaining expense must be deducted to derive income.

This chapter also discussed the effect on cost of goods sold of the beginning and ending inventory amounts. We observed that the ending inventory of one period is the beginning inventory of the next period. Two inventory systems were discussed for measuring the merchandise remaining on hand at the end of the period (ending inventory) and cost of goods sold for the period: (1) the perpetual inventory system, which is based on the maintenance of detailed and continuous inventory records for each kind of merchandise stocked; and (2) the periodic inventory system, which is based upon a physical inventory count of ending inventory and the costing of those goods in order to determine the proper amounts for cost of goods sold and ending inventory.

SUPPLEMENT 6A—DATA PROCESSING; CONTROL ACCOUNTS AND SUBSIDIARY LEDGERS

Control accounts and subsidiary ledgers facilitate keeping records in situations where a large number of similar transactions occur. Their use does not involve accounting theory, principles, or standards but involves only the mechanics of data processing. The use of control accounts and subsidiary ledgers will be explained for accounts receivable; however, the procedure also is applicable in any situation that involves numerous transactions that are similar and require detailed records, such as accounts payable and operational assets.

Some businesses carry thousands of individual customers on a credit status. If a separate Accounts Receivable account was kept in the general ledger for each customer, there would be thousands of receivable accounts in the general ledger. Instead, in most large businesses, the Accounts Receivable account is an aggregation of all of the individual customer accounts. However, to maintain adequate control, and for billing purposes, a business also must keep detailed records about each customer's account.

GENERAL LEDGER

Date 19A		Folio	Debit	Credit	Balance
Cash #101					
Jan. 12		3	1 000		

		Accounts Receivable Control #102			
Jan. 5		1	2 400		2 400
7		2		140	2 260
12		3		1 000	1 260

		Sales #610			
Jan. 5		1		2 400	2 400

		Sales Returns #620			
Jan. 7		2	140		140

Most large businesses keep a **single control account** in the general ledger for Accounts Receivable and a **separate subsidiary ledger** that carries an individual account for each credit customer. Thus, in the above example, the **general ledger** would include Accounts Receivable as a **single control account,** and the **subsidiary ledger** may include several thousand **individual receivable accounts.** The **sum** of the individual account balances in the receivable subsidiary ledger always should equal the single balance in the Accounts Receivable control account in the general ledger. The individual customer accounts, as subdivisions of the control account, are subsidiary to the control account; thus they are called subsidiary ledgers.

SUBSIDIARY LEDGER

		Adams, J. K. 102.1						
Jan.	5			1	740			740
	7	Return		2		140		600
	12			3		400		200

		Baker, B. B. 102.2					
Jan.	5			1	120		120

		Ford, C. E. 102.3					
Jan.	5			1	340		340
	12			3		340	-0-

		Moore, W.E. 102.4					
Jan.	5			1	320		320
	12			3		220	100

		Price, V. T. 102.5					
Jan.	5			1	430		430
	12			3		40	390

		Ward, B. L. 102.6					
Jan.	5			1	450		450

To illustrate the use of a control account with a subsidiary ledger for Accounts Receivable, we will assume several transactions for the Mayo Department Store. Mayo uses a manual system, but control accounts and subsidiary ledgers also are used extensively with computerized systems. Credit sales could be recorded in the general journal as follows:

GENERAL JOURNAL   Page 1

Date	Account Titles and Explanation	Folio	Debit	Credit
Jan. 5	Accounts receivable	102	2,400	
	Sales revenue	610		2,400
	To record the following credit sales:			
	Adams, J. K. .... $ 740	102.1		
	Baker, B. B. 120	102.2		
	Ford, C. E. 340	102.3		
	Moore, W. E. 320	102.4		
	Price, V. T. 430	102.5		
	Ward, B. L. 450	102.6		
	Total $2,400			

Posting of the above journal entry to the control account in the general ledger is indicated by entering the Accounts Receivable and Sales Revenue **account numbers** in the folio column in the usual manner. Posting to the individual customer accounts in the subsidiary ledger is indicated by entering an individual customer's account number in the folio column of the journal. Thus, the total amount was posted to the control account, Accounts Receivable (a debit total of $2,400), and the several single amounts were posted to the subsidiary ledger. Note that the debit-credit-balance form is used in the Mayo subsidiary ledger rather than the T-account form that often is used for instructional purposes.

On January 7, one customer, J. K. Adams, returned some unsatisfactory merchandise purchased on January 5. Mayo accepted the goods and gave Adams credit on his account. The journal entry was:

GENERAL JOURNAL   Page 2

Date	Account Titles and Explanation	Folio	Debit	Credit
Jan. 7	Sales returns	620	140	
	Accounts receivable	102		140
	To record the return of goods:			
	Adams, J. K. $140	102.1		

The folio column shows that the above entry has been posted in total to the control account in the general ledger. Also, the single amount has been posted to the individual customer account in the subsidiary ledger.

Cash collections from customers are recorded in the journal entry given below. The folio column shows that the entry has been posted in total to the control account and each single amount to the individual customer accounts in the subsidiary ledger.

GENERAL JOURNAL | Page 3

Jan. 12	Cash	101	1,000	
	Accounts receivable	102		1,000
	To record collections on accounts as follows:			
	Adams, J. K. .... $ 400	102.1		
	Ford, C. E. 340	102.3		
	Moore, W. E. 220	102.4		
	Price, V. T. 40	102.5		
	Total $1,000			

The subsidiary ledger should be reconciled frequently with the control account in order to determine whether errors were made in posting. This reconciliation is accomplished by summing the balances in the subsidiary ledger to determine whether that total agrees with the total shown by the control account in the general ledger. A reconciliation schedule for Mayo follows:

MAYO DEPARTMENT STORE
Schedule of Accounts Receivable
January 28, 19A

No.	Account Customer	Amount (per subsidiary)
102.1	Adams, J. K.	$ 200
102.2	Baker, B. B.	120
102.4	Moore, W. E.	100
102.5	Price, V. T.	390
102.6	Ward, B. L.	450
102	Total accounts receivable (per control account)	$1,260

The subsidiary ledger total should agree with the balance in the control account. If there is disagreement, one or more errors are indicated; however, agreement does not necessarily mean there are no errors. A transaction could be posted to the wrong customer's account, and the two ledgers would still reconcile in total.

The **Sales Revenue** account also could be established as a control account. This account would be supported by a subsidiary ledger that would contain separate accounts for the sales of **each department** or for **each product.** Another common application of control accounts relates to **accounts payable** when there are numerous purchases on credit.

Control accounts are also useful when accounting for **operational assets.** For example, the Office Equipment account usually is included in the general ledger as a control account. This control account is supported by a subsidiary ledger of office equipment that has an account for each different kind of office equipment, such as copiers, typewriters, calculators, and furniture. These examples show that the control account/subsidiary ledger procedure is an important element of the accounting information processing system of most enterprises.

One advantage of the use of subsidiary ledgers in a manual system is that it facilitates the subdivision of work. A person can be trained in a short time to maintain a subsidiary ledger because a knowledge of the broad field of accounting is not needed for such routine bookkeeping tasks.

In the journal entries given above, the individual amounts relating to each individual customer account were listed in the Explanation column of the journal and then were posted to the subsidiary ledger. There are two approaches to simplifying this phase of the bookkeeping. Amounts could be transferred directly from the charge tickets to the subsidiary ledger accounts and thus avoid the detailed listing in the journal entry. This approach is used sometimes by small companies. Another simplifying approach involves the use of a related procedure known as **special journals.** This procedure is explained in Supplement 8B.

Although our illustration used a manual approach to show subsidiary ledgers, most companies apply the procedure using computers. The computer can be programmed to process credit sales, returns, collections on account, reconciliation of account balances, and a printout of monthly bills to be mailed to the customers.

SUPPLEMENT 6B—AGING ACCOUNTS RECEIVABLE

Usually as an account receivable gets older there is an increase in the probability that the account will be uncollectible. Therefore, an analysis of the age of accounts receivable provides management with valuable information about probable losses due to uncollectible accounts. This information is used by some companies to provide amounts needed to make the **adjusting entry** at the end of each period for estimated bad debt expense.

An aging analysis of the individual accounts receivable balances is done to **estimate** the amount of bad debts instead of estimating bad debt expense on the basis of credit sales for the period, as illustrated in this chapter. The amount estimated to be uncollectible under the aging method is the balance that should be in the account "Allowance for Doubtful Accounts" at the end of the period. The **difference** between the **actual balance** in that account and the **estimated balance** is the amount recorded as bad debt expense in the adjusting entry at the end of the period.

For example, the general ledger for Macon Appliance Store reflected the following account balances:

Accounts receivable .... $ 40,000 (debit balance)
Allowance for doubtful accounts ....   900 (credit balance)
Sales on credit for 19B 200,000

The company uses the aging method for determining the amount of the adjusting entry for bad debt **expense** that must be made at December 31, 19B. The following aging analysis of accounts receivable was completed:

Aging Analysis of Accounts Receivable, December 31, 19B						
Customer	Total	Not Yet Due	1–30 Days Past Due	31–60 Days Past Due	61–90 Days Past Due	Over 90 Days Past Due
Adams, A. K.	$ 600	$ 600				
Baker, B. B.	1,300	300	$ 900	$ 100		
Cox, R. E.	1,400			400	$ 900	$ 100
Day, W. T.	3,000	2,000	600	400		
Zoe, A. B.	900					900
Total	$40,000	$17,200	$12,000	$8,000	$1,200	$1,600
Percent	100%	43%	30%	20%	3%	4%

The management, on the basis of experience and knowledge of specific situations, can use the above analysis as a basis for realistically estimating the probable **rates of uncollectibility for each age group.** Assume the management **estimated** the following probable bad debt loss rates: not yet due, 1%; 1–30 days past due, 3%; 31–60 days, 6%; 61–90 days, 10%; over 90 days, 25%. The following estimating schedule can be prepared:

Estimate of Probable Uncollectible Accounts, December 31, 19B			
Age	Amount of Receivable	Percent Estimated to Be Uncollectible	Balance Needed in Allowance for Doubtful Accounts
Net yet due	$17,200	1	$ 172
1–30 days past due	12,000	3	360
31–60 days past due	8,000	6	480
61–90 days past due	1,200	10	120
Over 90 days past due	1,600	25	400
Total	$40,000		$1,532

The adjusting entry on December 31, 19B, is:

```
Dec. 31  Bad debt expense  ............................................  632
              Allowance for doubtful accounts  ...........................         632
         To adjust Allowance for Doubtful Accounts to the estimated balance
         needed.
         Computations
              Balance needed (per schedule above) ......................    $1,532
              Balance before adjustment (page 286) .......................       900
              Difference—adjustment needed (increase) ..................    $  632
```

Some persons argue that the aging method approach to estimate the amount of bad debt expense does not apply the **matching principle** as effectively as the percent-of-credit-sales method discussed in the chapter. When the estimate is based on the amount of credit sales from which uncollectible accounts ultimately will occur, bad debt expense is best matched with revenues.

The aging method is based on the ending balance in Accounts Receivable. It tends to match bad debt expense with credit sales for a number of periods. As a result, the matching principle may not be served well each period. However, the aging method produces a good measurement of the net realizable value of accounts receivable because it takes into account probable losses by actual age distribution of the amounts in each account.

In practice, the percent-of-credit-sales method appears to be used more widely.

IMPORTANT TERMS DEFINED IN THIS CHAPTER

Terms (alphabetically)	Key words in definitions of important terms used in chapter	Page reference
Aging accounts receivable	Method to estimate uncollectible accounts based on the age of each account receivable.	286
Bad debt allowance method	Method that bases bad debt expense on an estimate of uncollectible accounts.	255
Bad debt loss	Expense associated with estimated uncollectible accounts receivable.	255
Gross margin on sales	As a dollar amount, net sales minus cost of goods sold; as a ratio, gross margin divided by net sales revenue.	250
Gross method to record revenue	Sales revenue is recorded without deducting the authorized cash discount.	253

Terms (alphabetically)	Key words in definitions of important terms used in chapter	Page reference
Inventory shrinkage	Missing inventory caused by theft, breakage, spoilage, and incorrect measurements.	273
Markup	The difference between net sales revenue and cost of goods sold.	250
Net method to record revenue	Sales revenue is recorded after deducting the amount of any authorized cash discount.	253
Periodic inventory system	Ending inventory and cost of goods sold are determined at the end of the accounting period.	260
Perpetual inventory system	A detailed inventory record is maintained continuously during the accounting period.	260
Physical inventory count	Actual count of units in inventory.	269
Purchase discount	Cash discount received for prompt payment of an account payable.	267
Purchase returns and allowances	A deduction from the cost of purchases associated with unsatisfactory goods.	266
Sales discount	Cash discount offered to encourage prompt payment of an account receivable.	252
Sales returns and allowances	A contra revenue account which is associated with un-satisfactory goods.	258
Subsidiary ledgers	A group of sub-accounts that provides more detail than the general ledger control account.	282
Trade discount	A discount that is deducted from list price to derive the actual sales price.	254

QUESTIONS

PART A

1. In a company that has extensive selling and purchasing activities, the **quantity** of goods included in sales revenue also must be included in a particular **expense** amount. Explain the basis for this statement.

2. Explain the difference between gross sales and net sales.

3. What is gross margin on sales? How is the gross margin ratio computed (in your explanation, assume that net sales revenue was $100,000 and cost of goods sold was $60,000)?

4. What is a sales discount? Use 1/10, n/30 in your explanation.

5. When merchandise, invoiced at $1,000, is sold on terms 2/10, n/30, the vendor must make the following entry:

    Accounts receivable ....
       Sales revenue ....

    What amounts should be used in this entry under the net method of recording sales discounts? Why is the net method preferred over the gross method?

6. A sale is made for $500; terms are 2/10, n/30. At what amount should the sale be recorded under the net method of recording sales discounts? Give the required entry with an explanation. Also, give the collection entry assuming it is after the discount period.

7. Because the actual time of cash collection is not relevant in determining the date on which a sale should be given accounting recognition, what factor is relevant?

8. Why is an estimate, instead of the actual amount of bad debts, used as a measure of periodic bad debt expense?

9. What is a contra account? Give two examples.

10. Define the book value of accounts receivable.

11. Why should estimated bad debt losses be based on credit sales rather than on total sales for the period?

12. What is the distinction between sales allowances and sales discounts?

PART B

13. Define goods available for sale. How does it differ from cost of goods sold?

14. Define beginning inventory and ending inventory.

15. Briefly distinguish between the perpetual and periodic inventory systems. How does each measure (a) inventory and (b) cost of goods sold?

16. Describe the calculation of cost of goods sold under the periodic inventory system.

17. Why is it necessary to take an actual physical inventory count at the end of the period when the periodic inventory system is used?

18. Under the cost principle, at what amount should a purchase be recorded? Be specific.

19. What is the purpose of a perpetual inventory record for each item stocked?

20. What accounts are debited and credited for a purchase of goods for resale (a) when a perpetual inventory system is used and (b) when a periodic inventory system is used?

21. What accounts are debited and credited for a sale of goods on credit (a) when a perpetual inventory system is used and (b) when a periodic inventory system is used?

22. Why is there no purchases account when the perpetual inventory system is used?

23. Why is transportation-in considered to be a cost of purchasing merchandise?

EXERCISES

PART A

E6–1   (Pair definitions with terms)

Match the following brief definitions with the terms by entering the appropriate letter in each space provided.

Terms

_____ (1) Cost of goods sold
_____ (2) Trade discount
_____ (3) Bad debt loss
_____ (4) Sales returns and allowances
_____ (5) Gross margin on sales
_____ (6) Inventory shrinkage
_____ (7) Aging accounts receivable
_____ (8) Periodic inventory system
_____ (9) Physical inventory count
_____ (10) Markup
_____ (11) Purchase returns and allowances
_____ (12) Net method to record revenue
_____ (13) Perpetual inventory method
_____ (14) Bad debt allowance method
_____ (15) Gross method to record revenues
_____ (16) Sales discount
_____ (17) Subsidiary ledger
_____ (18) Purchase discount

Definitions

A. Analysis of the elements of individual accounts receivable according to the time elapsed after the dates of billing.

B. Use of this method establishes a contra account titled "Allowance for Doubtful Accounts" which is considered a subtraction from the balance of "Accounts Receivable."

C. Receivables determined to be uncollectible.

D. Synonym for gross profit.

E. Method of recording revenue which, without adjusting entries, may overstate both accounts receivable and sales revenue.

F. The difference between the value of inventory if there were no theft, breakage, or clerical errors, and the value of inventory when it is physically counted.

G. A percentage often reported as the gross margin ratio.

H. The preferred method for recording sales on credit.

I. Method where the cost of goods sold is computed periodically by relying solely on physical counts and not keeping any day-to-day records.

J. A system that keeps a continuous record that tracks inventories and cost of goods sold on a day-to-day basis.

K. A process which involves two steps: (1) a quantity count and (2) an inventory costing.

L. A cash discount received by a credit customer for prompt payment.

M. Products returned by the customer, or a reduction in the selling price resulting in a deduction from the cost of purchases.

N. A price concession offered by a seller to a customer for prompt payment.

O. A contra revenue account used to record goods returned by customers.

P. A supporting ledger that provides details for specific accounts in the general ledger.

Q. A price concession often offered on volume orders that applies a reduction to the list price resulting in a lower invoice price.

R. Beginning inventory + Purchases − Ending inventory.

E6–2   **(Analysis of Income Statement Relationships)**

Supply the missing dollar amounts for the 19B income statement of Better Retail Company for each of the following independent cases:

	Case A	Case B	Case C	Case D	Case E
Sales revenue	$900	$800	$800	$?	$?
Selling expenses	?	200	80	120	180
Cost of goods sold	?	480	?	500	610
Income tax expense	?	30	30	20	40
Gross margin	400	?	?	?	390
Pretax income	100	40	?	180	?
Administrative expenses	100	?	60	100	90
Net income	80	?	120	?	80

E6–3   **(Preparation of an Income Statement Using the Gross Margin)**

The following data were taken from the records of Strickland Appliances, Incorporated, at December 31, 19D:

Sales revenue	$150,000
Administrative expenses	15,000
Distribution (selling) expenses	20,000
Income tax rate	20%
Gross margin ratio	40%
Shares of stock outstanding	4,000

Required:

Prepare a complete income statement for Strickland. Show all computations. (Hint: Set up side captions starting with sales revenue and ending with earnings per share; rely on the percents given.)

E6–4   **(Preparation of a Multiple-Step Income Statement)**

The following data were taken from the records of Teen Center at December 31, 19B:

Gross margin (40% ratio)	$24,000
Selling (distribution) expenses	9,000
Administrative expenses	?
Pretax income	10,000
Income tax rate, 20%	
Shares of stock outstanding	4,000

Required:

Prepare a complete multiple-step income statement for Teen Center. Show all computations. (Hint: Set up the side captions starting with sales revenue and ending with earnings per share; rely on the percents given.)

E6–5   **(Preparation of a Multiple-Step Income Statement and Analysis of Gross Margin)**

The following data were taken from the records of Burton Corporation on December 31, 19B:

Sales of merchandise for cash	$145,000
Sales of merchandise for credit	257,000
Sales returns and allowances	2,000
Selling expenses	100,000
Cost of goods sold	242,000
Administrative expenses	40,500

Items not included in above amounts:
Estimated bad debt loss, 2% of net credit sales.
Average income tax rate, 20%.
Number of shares of common stock outstanding, 10,000.

Required:

a. Based on the above data, prepare a multiple-step income statement. There were no extraordinary items. Include a column for percentage analysis.

b. How much was the gross margin? What was the gross margin ratio? Explain what these two amounts mean.

E6–6   **(Using Percentage Analysis with an Income Statement)**

The following summarized data were provided by the records of Melody's Music Store, Incorporated, for the year ended December 31, 19B:

Sales of merchandise for cash	$124,000
Sales of merchandise on credit	80,000
Cost of goods sold	120,000
Distribution expenses	30,800
Administrative expenses	20,000
Sales returns and allowances	4,000

Items not included in above amounts:
Estimated bad debt loss, 1¼% of credit sales.
Average income tax rate, 20%.
Number of shares of common stock outstanding, 5,000.

Required:

a. Based upon the above data, prepare a multiple-step income statement. Include a Percentage Analysis column.

b. What was the amount of gross margin? What was the gross margin ratio? Explain.

E6–7   **(Recording Sales Revenue Using the Net Method)**

During the months of January and February, the WNH Corporation sold goods to three customers. The sequence of events was as follows:

Jan.   6   Sold goods for $800 to J. Doe and billed that amount subject to terms 3/10, n/30.
6   Sold goods to R. Roe for $600 and billed that amount subject to terms 2/10, n/30.
14   Collected cash due from J. Doe.
Feb.   2   Collected cash due from R. Roe.
28   Sold goods for $500 to B. Moe, and billed that amount subject to terms 2/10, n/45.

Required:

a. Give the appropriate journal entry for each date. Assume a periodic inventory system is used and that the net method is used to record sales revenue.

b. Explain how each account balance as of February 28 should be reported, assuming that this is the end of the accounting period.

E6–8 **(Using the Net Method to Record Sales Revenue)**

The following transactions were selected from among those completed by Martin Retailers:

Nov. 25 Sold 20 items of merchandise to Customer A at an invoice price of $2,000 (total); terms 3/10, n/30.

   28 Sold 10 items of merchandise to Customer B at an invoice price of $4,000 (total); terms 3/10, n/30.

   30 Customer B returned two of the items purchased on the 28th; the items were defective and credit was given to the customer.

Dec. 6 Customer B paid the account balance in full.

   30 Customer A paid in full for the invoice of November 25, 19B.

Required:

a. Give the appropriate journal entry for each of the above transactions assuming Martin Retailers uses the periodic inventory system and records sales revenue under the net method.

b. Assume it is December 31, 19B, end of the accounting period. Show how the various account balances would be reported on the balance sheet and the income statement.

E6–9 **(Accounting for Bad Debts Using the Allowance Method)**

Luther Company started business on January 1, 19A. During the year 19A, the company's records indicated the following:

Sales on cash basis	$200,000
Sales on credit basis	100,000
Collections on accounts receivable	75,000

The manager of Luther Company is concerned about accounting for the bad debts. At December 31, 19A, although no accounts were considered bad, several customers were considerably overdue in paying their accounts. A friend of the manager suggested a 1% bad debt rate on sales, which the manager decided to use at the start.

Required:

a. You have been employed, on a part-time basis, to assist with the recordkeeping for Luther Company. The manager told you to set up bad debt expense of $3,000. Give the required entry.

b. You are concerned about how the $3,000 was determined and the manager told you it was from another manager "who knew his business" and used 1% of sales. Do you agree with the $3,000? If you disagree, give the correct entry and explain the basis for your choice.

c. Show how the various accounts related to credit sales should be shown on the December 31, 19A, income statement and balance sheet.

E6–10 **(Analysis and Evaluation of a Bad Debt Estimate)**

During 19G, Joan's Ready-to-Wear Shop had sales revenue of $110,000, of which $40,000 was on credit. At the start of 19G, Accounts Receivable shows a debit balance of $8,000 and the Allowance for Doubtful Accounts, a $500 credit balance. Collections on accounts receivable during 19G amounted to $33,000.

Data during 19G:

1. December 31, 19G, an account receivable (J. Doe) of $700 from a prior year was determined to be uncollectible; therefore, it was written off immediately as a bad debt.
2. December 31, 19G, on the basis of experience, a decision was made to continue the accounting policy of basing estimated bad debt losses on 2% of credit sales for the year.

Required:

a. Give the required journal entries for the two items on December 31, 19G (end of the accounting period).
b. Show how the amounts related to accounts receivable and bad debt expense would be reported on the income statement and balance sheet for 19G. Disregard income tax considerations.
c. On the basis of the data available, does the 2% rate appear to be reasonable? Explain.

PART B

E6–11 **(Analysis of Income Statement Relationships)**

Supply the missing dollar amounts for the 19B income statement of Janice Retailers for each of the following independent cases:

Case	Sales Revenue	Beginning Inventory	Purchases	Total Available	Ending Inventory	Cost of Goods Sold	Gross Margin	Expenses	Pretax Income or (Loss)
A	900	100	700	?	200	?	?	200	?
B	900	180	750	?	?	?	?	100	0
C	?	140	?	?	300	650	350	100	?
D	900	?	600	?	210	?	?	150	50
E	900	?	650	900	?	?	100	?	(50)

E6–12   (Finding Missing Amounts Based on Income Statement Relationships)

Supply the missing dollar amounts for the 19D income statement of Albert Company for each of the following independent cases:

	Case A	Case B	Case C
Sales revenue	6,000	6,000	?
Sales returns and allowances	150	?	100
Net sales revenue	?	?	5,920
Beginning inventory	9,000	9,500	8,000
Purchases	5,000	?	5,300
Freight-in	?	120	120
Purchase returns	40	30	?
Goods available for sale	?	14,790	13,370
Ending inventory	10,000	9,000	?
Cost of goods sold	?	?	5,400
Gross margin	?	110	?
Expenses	690	?	520
Pretax income	1,000	(500)	–0–

E6–13   (Accounting for Sales and Purchases Using the Periodic Inventory System)

The following transactions involving University Book Store were selected from the records of January 19B:

1. Sales: cash, $150,000; and on credit, $40,000 (terms n/30).
2. Some of the merchandise sold on credit in 1 was subsequently returned for credit, $800.
3. Purchases: cash, $80,000; and on credit, $15,000 (terms n/60).
4. Some of the merchandise purchased was subsequently returned for credit, $700.
5. Shipping costs paid in cash on the merchandise purchased, $400 (debit Freight-In).
6. Bad debt losses, on the basis of experience, are estimated to be 2% of credit sales net of sales returns and allowances.
7. An account receivable amounting to $400 was written off as uncollectible. The sale was made two years earlier.

Required:

a. Give the journal entry that would be made for each transaction, assuming the company uses a periodic inventory system.
b. Prepare an income statement for January 19B, through the caption "Gross margin on sales" and show the details of cost of goods sold. The December 31, 19A, inventory of merchandise was $75,000; and the physical inventory count of merchandise taken on January 31, 19B, amounted to $90,000.

E6–14   (Recording Sales and Purchases Using the Net Method)

L&L Sport Shop sells merchandise on credit terms of 2/10, n/30. A sale invoiced at $800 was made to K. Williams on February 1, 19B. L&L uses the net method of recording sales discounts.

Required:

a. Give the journal entry to record the credit sale.

b. Give the journal entry assuming the account was collected in full on February 9, 19B.

c. Give the journal entry assuming, instead, the account was collected in full on March 2, 19B.

On March 4, 19B, L&L purchased sporting goods from a supplier on credit, invoiced at $6,000; the terms were 1/15, n/30. L&L uses the net method to record purchases.

Required:

d. Give the journal entry to record the purchase on credit. Assume periodic inventory system.

e. Give the journal entry assuming the account was paid in full on March 12, 19B.

f. Give the journal entry assuming, instead, the account was paid in full on March 28, 19B.

E6–15   **(Accounting for Inventory Using the Perpetual System)**

Hill Company uses a perpetual inventory system. Because it is a small business and sells only five different high-cost items, a perpetual inventory record is maintained for each item. The following selected data relate to Item A for the month of January:

1. Beginning inventory—quantity 5, cost $77 each.
2. Purchased—quantity 4, cost $72 each; paid $20 total freight.
3. Sold—quantity 6, sales price $150 each.
4. Returns—two sold in 3 were returned for full credit.

Required:

a. Give the journal entries for the above transactions assuming a perpetual inventory system and cash transactions.

b. Prepare the perpetual inventory record for Item A.

c. For January, give the following amounts for Item A:

 a. Sales revenue .... $ _____
 b. Cost of goods sold .... $ _____
 c. Gross margin on sales .... $ _____
 d. Ending inventory .... $ _____

d. Is it possible to determine if there was any inventory shrinkage? Explain.

E6–16   **(Accounting for Sales and Purchases under the Perpetual Inventory System)**

Flower Company uses a perpetual inventory system that provides amounts for the period for (a) cost of goods sold and (b) ending inventory. Physical inventory counts are made from time to time to verify the perpetual inventory records. On December 31, 19B, the end of the accounting year, the perpetual inventory record for Item No. 18 showed the following (summarized):

	Units	Unit cost	Total cost
Beginning inventory	500	$2	$1,000
Purchases during the period	900	2	1,800
Sales during the period (sales price $3.50)	800		

Required:

a. Give the journal entry to record the purchase of 900 units for cash during the period.

b. Give the journal entry to record the sales for cash during the period.

c. Assume a physical inventory count was made after the above transactions and it shows 595 units of Item No. 18 on hand. Give any journal entry required.

d. Give the following amounts for 19B related to Item No. 18:

1. Ending inventory .... units_____ $ _____
2. Cost of goods sold .... units_____ $ _____
3. Shrinkage loss .... units_____ $ _____

e. As a manager, would you investigate in this situation? How?

E6–17   (Comparison of the Periodic and Perpetual Inventory Systems)

During 19B, Iota Corporation's records reflected the following for one product stocked:

1. Beginning inventory .... 1,000 units, unit cost $2
2. Purchases .... 8,000 units, unit cost $2
3. Sales .... 7,000 units, unit sales price $3
4. Purchase returns .... 10 units, for $2 per unit refund from the supplier
5. Sales returns .... 5 units, for $3 per unit refund to the customer

Required:

a. All transactions were in cash; give the journal entries for the above transactions assuming:

Case A—A perpetual inventory system.

Case B—A periodic inventory system.

b. How would the amount of cost of goods sold be determined in each case?

c. Would you expect the cost of goods sold amount to be the same for Case A as for Case B? Why?

E6–18   (Use of a Worksheet; Periodic Inventory System)

The trial balance for Mountain Store, Incorporated, at December 31, 19B (the end of the accounting year), is given below. Only selected accounts are given to shorten the case. The company uses a periodic inventory system. With the exception of the ending inventory, all of the accounts (before adjusting and closing entries) that you will need are listed in the trial balance.

Data developed as a basis for the adjusting entries at December 31, 19B, were:

a. Estimated bad debt expense for 19B was 1% of net credit sales of $12,000.

b. An inventory of store supplies on hand taken at December 31, 19B, reflected $50.

c. Depreciation on the store equipment is based on an estimated useful life of 10 years and no residual value.

d. Wages earned through December 31, 19B, not yet paid or recorded, amounted to $500.

e. The beginning inventory is shown in the trial balance. A physical inventory count of merchandise on hand and unsold, at December 31, 19B, reflected $2,000.

f. Assume an average income tax rate of 20%.

Required:

Prepare a worksheet similar to the one in the demonstration case. If desired, you may omit columns for Adjusted Trial Balance and Retained Earnings. Enter the trial balance, adjusting entries, ending inventory, and complete the worksheet.

Debits		Credits	
Cash	$ 8,000	Allowance for doubtful	
Accounts receivable	3,000	accounts	$ 150
Merchandise inventory,		Accumulated depreciation	900
January 1, 19B	4,000	Accounts payable	5,000
Store supplies inventory	250	Wages payable	
Store equipment	3,000	Income tax payable	
Sales returns	150	Capital stock, par $10	6,000
Purchases	6,000	Retained earnings	1,870
Bad debt expense		Sales revenue	13,000
Depreciation expense		Purchase returns	480
Freight-in (on purchases)	100		
Income tax expense			
Other operating expenses	2,900		
	$27,400		$27,400

E6–19   (Use of a Worksheet; Perpetual Inventory System)

The trial balance for Modern Appliances, Incorporated, at December 31, 19B (end of the accounting year), is given below. Only selected items have been used in order to shorten the case. The company uses a perpetual inventory system. All of the accounts you will need are listed in the trial balance.

Trial Balance
December 31, 19B

Account titles	Debit	Credit
Cash	$ 6,800	
Accounts receivable	13,000	
Allowance for doubtful accounts		$ 700
Merchandise inventory, ending	64,000	
Operational assets	40,000	
Accumulated depreciation		13,000
Accounts payable		8,000
Income tax payable		
Capital stock, par $10		60,000
Retained earnings, January 1, 19B		14,300
Sales revenue		105,000
Sales returns and allowances	1,200	
Cost of goods sold	56,000	
Expenses (not detailed)	20,000	
Bad debt expense		
Depreciation expense		
Income tax expense		
	$201,000	$201,000

Additional data developed for the adjusting entries:

a. Estimated bad debt expense is 2% of net credit sales. Net credit sales for 19B amounted to $35,000.
b. The operational assets are being depreciated $4,000 each year.
c. The average income tax rate is 20%.

Required:

Prepare a worksheet similar to the one in the demonstration case. If desired, you may omit columns for Adjusted Trial Balance and Retained Earnings. Enter the trial balance, adjusting entries, and complete the worksheet.

PROBLEMS

PART A

P6–1   **(Understanding the Income Statement)**

The following data were taken from the year-end records of Erbs Company. You are to fill in all of the missing amounts. Show computations.

	Independent cases	
Income statement items	*Case A*	*Case B*
Gross sales revenue	$110,000	$212,000
Sales returns and allowances	?	12,000
Net sales revenue	?	?
Cost of goods sold .... (62%)	?	?
Gross margin on sales	? (40%)	?
Operating expenses	18,000	?
Pretax income	?	35,000
Income tax expense (20%)	?	?
Income before extraordinary items	?	?
Extraordinary items .... (gain)	5,000 (loss)	5,000
Less: Income tax (20%)	?	?
Net income	?	?
EPS (10,000 shares)	2.00	?

P6–2   **(Preparation of a Multiple Step Income Statement)**

Dryden Equipment Company, Inc., sells heavy construction equipment. There are 10,000 shares of capital stock outstanding. The annual fiscal period ends on December 31. The following condensed trial balance was taken from the general ledger on December 31, 19D:

Account titles	*Debit*	*Credit*
Cash	$ 15,000	
Accounts receivable	20,000	
Allowance for doubtful accounts		$ 1,000
Inventory (ending)	90,000	
Operational assets	40,000	
Accumulated depreciation		12,000
Liabilities		17,000
Capital stock		100,000
Retained earnings, January 1, 19D		20,000
Sales revenue		208,000
Sales returns and allowances	8,000	
Cost of goods sold	110,000	
Selling expenses	37,000	
Administrative expenses	20,000	
Interest expense	3,000	
Extraordinary loss, unusual and infrequent storm damage	5,000	
Income tax expense*	10,000	
Totals	$358,000	$358,000

* Assume a 40% average tax rate on both operations and the extraordinary loss.

Required:

a. Prepare a multiple-step income statement.
b. Prepare the following ratio analyses:
   (1) Gross margin on sales ratio.
   (2) Profit margin ratio (see Chapter 2).
   (3) Return on investment; use owners' equity (see Chapter 2).
c. To compute (*b*2) and (*b*3), what amount did you use as the numerator? Explain why.
d. Briefly explain the meaning of each of the three ratios computed in (*b*).

P6–3   (Preparation and Analysis of an Income Statement)

Stevenson Corporation is a local grocery store organized seven years ago as a corporation. At that time, a total of 10,000 shares of common stock was issued to the three organizers. The store is in an excellent location, and sales have increased each year. At the end of 19G, the bookkeeper prepared the following statement (assume all amounts are correct; also note the inappropriate terminology and format):

STEVENSON CORPORATION
Profit and Loss
December 31, 19G

	Debit	*Credit*
Sales		$305,000
Cost of goods sold	$169,500	
Sales returns and allowances	5,000	
Selling expenses	60,000	
Administrative and general expenses	30,000	
Interest expense	500	
Extraordinary loss	4,000	
Income tax expense (on operations, $12,000 less $1,200 saved on the extraordinary loss)	10,800	
Net profit	25,200	
Totals	$305,000	$305,000

Required:

a. Prepare a multiple-step income statement. Assume an average 30% income tax rate.
b. Prepare the following ratio analyses:
   (1) Profit margin on sales ratio (see Chapter 2).
   (2) Gross margin on sales ratio.
   (3) Return on investment; use owners' equity of $200,000 (see Chapter 2).
c. In computing ratios (*b*1) and (*b*3), what amount did you use for income? Explain why.
d. Generally, it is conceded that of the three ratios in (*b*), return on investment has the highest information content for the typical investor. Why?

P6–4   (Recording Sales, Returns and Bad Debts)

The data below were selected from the records of Baldwin Company for the year ended December 31, 19C.

Balances January 1, 19C:
Accounts receivable (various customers) $80,000
Allowance for doubtful accounts 6,000

Transactions during 19C:

1. Sold merchandise for cash, $300,000. Sold merchandise and made collections, on credit terms 2/10, n/30, in the order given below (assume a unit sales price of $1,000 in all transactions and use the net method to record sales revenue):
2. Sold merchandise to T. Smith; invoice price, $18,000.
3. Sold merchandise to K. Jones; invoice price, $30,000.
4. T. Smith returned one of the units purchased in 2 above, two days after purchase date and received account credit.
5. Sold merchandise to B. Sears; invoice price, $20,000.
6. T. Smith paid his account in full within the discount period.
7. Collected $72,000 cash from customer sales on credit in prior year, all within the discount periods.
8. K. Jones paid the invoice in 3 above within the discount period.
9. Sold merchandise to R. Roy; invoice price, $10,000.
10. Three days after paying the account in full, K. Jones returned one defective unit and received a cash refund.
11. Collected $5,000 cash on an account receivable on sales in a prior year, after the discount period.
12. Baldwin wrote off a 19A account of $2,500 after deciding that the amount would never be collected.
13. The estimated bad debt rate used by Baldwin is 1% of **net** credit sales.

Required:

a. Give the journal entries for the above transactions, including the write-off of the uncollectible account and the adjusting entry for estimated bad debts. Assume a periodic inventory system. Show computations for each entry. Hint: Set up T-accounts on scratch paper for Cash, Accounts Receivable by customer, Allowance for Doubtful Accounts, Sales Revenue, Sales Returns, Sales Discount Revenue, and Bad Debt Expense (this will provide the data needed for the next requirement).
b. Show how the accounts related to the above sale and collection activities should be reported on the 19C income statement and balance sheet.

P6–5   (Comparison of the Net and Gross Methods Using the Periodic Inventory System)
The following transactions were selected from the records of Electric Company:

July 15 Sold merchandise to Customer A at an invoice price of $4,000; terms 2/10, n/30.
     20 Sold merchandise to Customer B at an invoice price of $3,000; terms 2/10, n/30.
     21 Purchased inventory from Alpha Supply Company at an invoice price of $500; terms 3/10, n/45.
     22 Purchased inventory from Beta Supply Company at an invoice price of $1,000; terms 1/20, n/30.
     23 Received payment from Customer A, within the discount period.
     25 Paid invoice from Alpha Supply Company, within the discount period.
Aug. 25 Received payment from Customer B, after the discount period.
     26 Paid invoice from Beta Supply Company, after the discount period.

Required:

a. Give the appropriate journal entry for each of the above transactions. Assume that Electric Company uses the periodic inventory system and records sales and purchases using the net method.

b. Give the appropriate journal entry for each of the above transactions. Assume that Electric Company uses the periodic inventory system and records sales and purchases using the gross method.

P6–6   **(Based on Supplement 6B; Use Aging Analysis)**

Farley Equipment Company uses the aging approach to estimate bad debt expense at the end of each accounting year. Credit sales occur frequently on terms n/60. The balance of each account receivable is aged on the basis of three time periods as follows: *(a)* not yet due; *(b)* up to one year past due; and *(c)* more than one year past due. Experience has shown that for each age group the average loss rate on the amount of the receivable at year-end due to uncollectibility is *(a)* 1%, *(b)* 5%, and *(c)* 30%.

At December 31, 19F (end of the current accounting year), the Accounts Receivable balance was $50,500 and the Allowance for Doubtful Accounts balance was $1,500. To simplify, only five customer accounts are used; the details of each on December 31, 19F, follow:

A. Able—Account Receivable

Date	Explanation	Debit	Credit	Balance
3/11/19E	Sale	15,000		15,000
6/30/19E	Collection		5,000	10,000
1/31/19F	Collection		3,000	7,000

C. Carson—Account Receivable

2/28/19F	Sale	21,000		21,000
4/15/19F	Collection		10,000	11,000
11/30/19F	Collection		3,000	8,000

M. May—Account Receivable

11/30/19F	Sale	18,000		18,000
12/15/19F	Collection		8,000	10,000

T. Tyler—Account Receivable

3/2/19D	Sale	5,000		5,000
4/15/19D	Collection		5,000	–0–
9/1/19E	Sale	12,000		12,000
10/15/19E	Collection		10,000	2,000
2/1/19F	Sale	19,000		21,000
3/1/19F	Collection		1,000	20,000
12/31/19F	Sale	1,500		21,500

Z. Ziltch—Account Receivable

12/30/19F	Sale	4,000	4,000

Required:

a. Set up an aging analysis schedule and complete it; follow the illustration given in supplement 6B.
b. Compute the estimated uncollectible amount for each age category and in total.
c. Give the adjusting entry for bad debt expense at December 31, 19F.
d. Show how the amounts related to accounts receivable should be presented on the 19F income statement and balance sheet.

PART B

P6–7   (Accounting for Cash Discounts by the Seller and the Purchaser)

Assume the following summarized transactions between Company A, the vendor, and Company B, the purchaser. Use the letters to the left as the date notations. Assume each company uses a periodic inventory system and each uses the net method to record sales revenue and purchases.

1. Company A sold Company B merchandise for $10,000; terms 1/10, n/30.
2. Prior to payment, Company B returned $1,000 (one tenth) of the merchandise for credit because it did not meet B's specifications.

Required:

Give the following journal entries in parallel columns for each party:

a. The sale/purchase transaction.
b. The return transaction.
c. Payment in full assuming it was made within the discount period.
d. Payment in full assuming, instead, it was made after the discount period.

Use a form similar to the following:

		Co. A—Vendor		Co. B—Purchaser	
Date	Accounts	Debit	Credit	Debit	Credit

P6–8   (Recording Sales and Purchases Using the Net Method)

University Store, Incorporated, is a student co-op. On January 1, 19X, the beginning inventory was $200,000; the Accounts Receivable balance was $3,000; and the Allowance for Doubtful Accounts had a credit balance of $400. A periodic inventory system is used and purchases are recorded using the net method.

The following transactions (summarized) have been selected from 19X for case purposes:

1. Merchandise sales for cash $300,000
2. Merchandise returned by customers as unsatisfactory, for cash refund 1,400
   Merchandise purchased from vendors on credit; terms 2/10, n/30:
3. May Supply Company invoice price, before deduction of cash discount 4,000
4. Other vendors, invoice price, before deduction of cash discount 115,000
5. Purchased equiment for use in the store; paid cash 1,800

6. Purchased office supplies for future use in the store; paid cash 600
7. Freight on merchandise purchased; paid cash (set up a separate account for
    this item) 500
    Accounts payable paid in full during the period as follows:
8.   May Supply Company, paid after the discount period 4,000
9.   Other vendors, paid within the discount period 98,000

Required:

a. Prepare journal entries for each of the above transactions.
b. Give the closing entry required at December 31, 19X, for:
  (1) Beginning inventory.
  (2) Ending inventory (assume $130,000).
c. Prepare a partial income statement through gross margin on sales.
d. Explain why it was preferable to record purchases using the net method.

P6–9   **(Reporting Sales Transactions on the Financial Statements)**
The transactions listed below were selected from those occurring during the month of January 19D for Polo Department Store, Incorporated. A wide line of goods is offered for sale. Credit sales are extended to a few select customers; the usual credit terms are n/EOM.

1. Sales to customers:
    Cash $350,000
    On credit 30,000
2. Unsatisfactory merchandise returned by customers:
    Cash 4,000
    Credit 1,000
    Merchandise purchased from vendors on credit; terms 1/20, n/30:
3.   AB Supply Company, amount billed, before deduction of cash discount 1,000
4.   From other vendors, amount billed, before deduction of cash discount 120,000
6. Freight paid on merchandise purchased; paid cash (set up a separate account for this
    item) 2,000
6. Collections on accounts receivable 17,000
    The accounts payable were paid in full during the period as follows:
7.   AB Supply Company, paid after the discount period 1,000
8.   Other vendors, paid within the discount period 118,800
9. Purchased two new typewriters for the office; paid cash 900
10. An account receivable from a customer from a prior year amounting to $300 was
    determined to be uncollectible and was written off.
11. At the end of January the adjusting entry for estimated bad debts is to be made. The loss
    rate, based on experience, is 1% of net credit sales for the period (i.e., on credit
    sales less credit returns).

Relevant account balances on January 1, 19D, were Accounts Receivable, $3,200 (debit); and Allowance for Doubtful Accounts, $900 (credit). Total assets at the end of the period, $250,000.

Required:

a. Prepare journal entries for the above transactions assuming a periodic inventory system is in use and record purchases using the net method.
b. Show how the following amounts should be reported on the January 19D income statement and balance sheet. Show computations.
  (1) Bad debt expense.

(2) Balance in accounts receivable.

(3) Balance in allowance for doubtful accounts.

c. Explain why bad debt expense should not be debited for the $300 uncollectible account written off in January.

P6–10 **(Application of the Perpetual Inventory System)**

Air Express Distributing Company uses a perpetual inventory system for the items it sells. The following selected data relate to Item 10, a small but high-cost item stocked during the month of January 19B.

1. Beginning inventory—quantity, 70; cost, $50 each.
2. Purchases—quantity, 90; cost, $48 each plus $180 for transportation on the purchases.
3. Sales—quantity, 120; sale price, $95 each.
4. Returns—Air Express accepted a return of two of the items sold in 3 because they were not needed by the customer and they had not been used.
5. At the end of January 19B a physical inventory count showed 40 items remaining on hand.

Required (assume all transactions were cash):

a. Prepare the perpetual inventory record for Item 10.
b. Give journal entries for each of the above transactions.
c. Prepare the income statement for January 19B through gross margin on sales as it related to item 10. What was the gross margin ratio?
d. As the responsible manager, would you investigate the inventory shrinkage? How?
e. Assume that you observe quite often that the required items are out of stock. How can a perpetual inventory system be helpful in avoiding this problem?

P6–11 **(Use of the Perpetual Inventory System and Analysis of Shrinkage)**

Green Company uses a perpetual inventory system. During the month of January 19D, the perpetual inventory record for Item A, which is one of the 23 items stocked, is shown below (summarized):

PERPETUAL INVENTORY RECORD

Date	Explanation	Goods Purchased		Goods Sold		Balance	
		Units	Total Cost	Units	Total Cost	Units	Total Cost
1	Beginning inventory					40	3,200
2	Purchase (at $80 each)	20					
3	Sale (sales price $150 each)			31			
4	Purchase return (one unit)						
5	Purchase (at $80 each)	30					
6	Sales return (one unit)						
7	Sale (sales price $150 each)			29			
8	Inventory shortage (four units)						

Required:

a. Complete the perpetual inventory record.
b. Give the journal entry for each transaction reflected in the perpetual inventory record (assume transactions are cash).
c. Complete the following tabulation:

Income statement:
    Sales .... $ _____
    Cost of goods sold .... _____
    Gross margin on sales .... _____
    Gross margin ratio .... _____

Balance sheet:
    Inventory .... _____

d. Explain how the inventory shortage should be reported.
e. As the responsible manager, would you investigate this situation? How?
f. Assume "stockout" has been a problem. What would you recommend?

P6–12 **(Comparison of Periodic and Perpetual Inventory Systems)**
The following transactions, relating to one product sold by Jackson Company, were completed in the order given during January:

a. Purchased—quantity, 120; cost, $20 each.
b. Sold—quantity, 100; $35 each.
c. Purchase return—returned one of the units purchased in *(a)* because it was the wrong size.
d. Sales return—accepted two units from a customer that were sold in *(b)*. The customer did not need them, and they were not damaged.
e. Inventories:

    Beginning inventory, January 1—30 units at total cost of $600.

    Ending inventory, January 31—per periodic inventory count, 51 units @ $20 = $1,020.

f. Cost of goods sold for January—98 units @ $20 = $1,960.

Required:

Give the journal entries that would be made for the above transactions assuming: Case A—a perpetual inventory system is used; and Case B—a periodic inventory system is used. To do this, set up the following form (assume cash transactions):

		Amounts			
		Perpetual		Periodic	
Date	Explanation	Debit	Credit	Debit	Credit
a.	To record the purchase				
b.	To record the sale				
c.	To record the purchase return				
d.	To record the sales return				
e.	To record the closing entries for inventories				
f.	To record the closing entry for cost of goods sold				
g.	To close purchases and purchase returns				

P6–13   **(Completion of a Worksheet)**

   Quality Retailers Inc., is completing the accounting information processing cycle for the year ended December 31, 19D. The worksheet given below has been completed through the adjusting entries. (An optional column, "Adjusted Trial Balance," may be helpful in completing the requirements.)

Required:

a. Complete the following worksheet (periodic inventory system is used). Assume an average income tax rate of 20%.

b. Give the closing journal entries at December 31, 19D. Close all revenue and expense accounts to Income Summary.

QUALITY RETAILERS, INC.
Worksheet—December 31, 19D

Account Titles	Trial Balance		Adjusting Entries*		Income Statement		Retained Earnings		Balance Sheet	
	Debit	Credit	Debit	Credit	Debit	Credit	Debit	Credit	Debit	Credit
Cash	27,200									
Accounts receivable	12,000									
Allowance for doubtful accounts		300		(a) 400						
Merchandise inventory, Jan. 1, 19D	30,000									
Equipment	22,500									
Accumulated depreciation, equipment		9,000		(b) 1,500						
Other assets	20,000									
Accounts payable		8,000								
Interest payable				(c) 300						
Note payable, long term, 12%		10,000								
Capital stock, par $10		50,000								
Contributed capital in excess of par		7,500								
Retained earnings, Jan. 1, 19D		13,000								
Dividends declared and paid (19D)	6,000									
Sales revenue		95,000								
Sales returns and allowances	1,000									
Purchases	52,000									

QUALITY RETAILERS, INC.
Worksheet—December 31, 19D

Account Titles	Trial Balance		Adjusting Entries*		Income Statement		Retained Earnings		Balance Sheet	
	Debit	Credit	Debit	Credit	Debit	Credit	Debit	Credit	Debit	Credit
Freight-in	2,000									
Purchase returns and allowances		1,100								
Operating expenses (not detailed)	20,300									
Bad debt expense			(a) 400							
Depreciation expense			(b) 1,500							
Interest expense	900		(c) 300							
Merchandise inventory, Dec, 31, 19D ($32,000)										
	193,900	193,900								
Income tax expense										
Income tax payable										
Net income										
Retained earnings, Dec. 31, 19D										

P6–14   **(Related to Supplement 6A; Use of Subsidiary Ledgers)**

City Department Store, Incorporated, is a large department store located in a midwestern city with a population of approximately 200,000 persons. The store carries top brands and attempts to appeal to "quality customers." Approximately 80% of the sales are on credit. As a consequence, there is a significant amount of detailed recordkeeping related to credit sales, returns, collections, and billings. The accounts receivable records are maintained manually; however, the store is considering computerizing this phase of the accounting information system. Included in the general ledger is a control account for Accounts Receivable. Supporting the control account is an accounts receivable subsidiary ledger which has individual accounts for more than 20,000 customers. For case purposes, a few accounts and transactions with simplified amounts have been selected. The case requirement is intended to indicate the nature of the data processing work that City Store plans to computerize; however, here it will be completed manually.

On January 1, 19F, the Accounts Receivable control account (No. 52), in the general ledger, shows a debit balance of $4,000 and the subsidiary ledger shows the following balances:

52.1	Akins, A. K.	$400
52.2	Blue, V. R.	700
52.3	Daley, U. T.	900
52.4	Evans, T. V.	300
52.5	May, O. W.	800
52.6	Nash, G. A.	100
52.7	Roth, I. W.	600
52.8	Winn, W. W.	200

During the month of January, the following transactions and events relating to sales activities occurred (use the notation at the left for date):

a. Sales of merchandise on credit.

Akins, A. K.	$300
Blue, V. R.	250
Winn, W. W.	730
May, O. W.	140
Daley, U. T.	70
Roth, I. W.	370
Evans, T. V.	410

b. Unsatisfactory merchandise returned by customers:

Roth, I. W.	$30
Winn, W. W.	70
Akins, A. K.	20

c. Collections on accounts receivable:

Winn, W. W.	$800
May, O. W.	940
Akins, A. K.	200
Roth, I. W.	700
Blue, V. R.	750
Daley, U. T.	600

d. The account for G. A. Nash has been inactive for several years. After an investigation, the management decided that it was uncollectible; therefore, it is to be written off immediately.

e. The estimated loss rate is 2% of net credit sales (i.e., credit sales less returns for credit).

Required:

a. Set up the general ledger control account for Accounts Receivable. Also, set up the general ledger account for Allowance for Doubtful Accounts (No. 53) with a credit balance of $600. Indicate the beginning balance as "Bal." and for convenience use T-accounts for these two accounts.

b. Set up an accounts receivable subsidiary ledger; use three columns—Debit, Credit, and Balance. Enter the beginning balances with the notation "Bal."

c. Prepare journal entries for each of the above transactions.

d. Post the entries prepared in (c) to the Accounts Receivable control account, Allowance for Doubtful Accounts, and the subsidiary ledger. Use folio numbers.

e. Prepare a schedule of accounts receivable to show how much each customer owed at the end of January.

f. Show how accounts receivable and the related allowance amounts would be reported in the January balance sheet.

P6–15   **(A Review of Chapters 3, 4, 5, and 6.)**

Discount Furniture Store, Inc., has been in operation for a number of years and has been quite profitable. The losses on uncollectible accounts and on merchandise returns are about the same as for other furniture stores. The company uses a perpetual inventory system. The annual fiscal period ended December 31, 19B, and the end-of-period accounting information processing cycle has been started. The following trial balance was derived from the general ledger at December 31, 19B.

Account titles	Debit	Credit
Cash	$ 28,880	
Accounts receivable	36,000	
Allowance for doubtful accounts		$ 4,600
Merchandise inventory (ending)	110,000	
Store equipment	22,000	
Accumulated depreciation		10,000
Accounts payable		10,000
Income tax payable		
Interest payable		
Notes payable, long term (12%)		50,000
Capital stock, par $10		70,000
Retained earnings, January 1, 19B		11,400
Sales revenue		441,000
Sales returns and allowances	25,000	
Cost of goods sold	223,350	
Selling expenses	102,700	
Administrative expenses	49,070	
Bad debt expense		
Depreciation expense		
Interest expense		
Totals	$597,000	$597,000
Income tax expense		
Net income		

Data for adjusting entries:

a. The bad debt losses due to uncollectible accounts are estimated to be $6,000.

b. The store equipment is being depreciated over an estimated useful life of 11 years with no residual value.

c. The long-term note of $50,000 was for a two-year loan from a local bank. The interest rate is 12%, payable at the end of each 12-month period. The note was dated April 1, 19B. (Hint: Accrue interest for nine months.)

d. Assume an average 20% corporate income tax rate.

Required:

a. Based upon the above data, complete a worksheet similar to the one illustrated in the chapter for the demonstration case. If you prefer, you may omit columns for Adjusted Trial Balance and Retained Earnings. (Hint: Net income is $22,704.)

b. Based upon the completed worksheet, prepare a multiple-step income statement and classified balance sheet.

c. Based upon the completed worksheet, prepare the adjusting and closing journal entries for December 31, 19B. Close all revenue and expense accounts to Income Summary.

P6–16   **(A Review of Chapters 3, 4, 5, and 6)**

Northwest Appliances, Incorporated, is owned by six local investors. It has been operating for four years and is at the end of the 19D fiscal year. For case purposes, certain accounts have been selected to demonstrate the information processing activities at the end of the year for a corporation that sells merchandise rather than services. The following trial balance, assumed to be correct, was taken from the ledger on December 31, 19D. The company uses a periodic inventory system.

Debits		Credits	
Cash	$ 18,000	Allowance for doubtful	
Accounts receivable	28,000	accounts	$ 600
Merchandise inventory,		Accumulated depreciation	12,000
January 1, 19D	80,000	Accounts payable	15,000
Prepaid insurance	300	Notes payable,	
Store equipment	40,000	long term (12%)	30,000
Sales returns and		Capital stock, par $10	40,000
allowances	3,000	Retained earnings,	
Purchases	250,000	January 1, 19D	2,000
Freight-in	11,000	Sales revenue	400,000
Operating expenses	76,300	Purchase returns	7,000
	$506,600		$506,600

Additional data for adjusting entries:

a. Credit sales during the year were $100,000; based on experience, a 1% loss rate on credit sales has been established.

b. Insurance amounting to $100 expired during the year.

c. The store equipment is being depreciated over a 10-year estimated useful life with no residual value.

d. The long-term note payable for $30,000 was dated May 1, 19D, and carries a 12% interest rate per annum. The note is for three years, and interest is payable on April 30 each year.

e. Assume an average income tax rate of 30%.

f. Inventories:

Beginning inventory, January 1, 19D (per above trial balance) $80,000.

Ending inventory, December 31, 19D (per physical inventory count), $75,000.

Required:

a. Prepare a worksheet at December 31, 19D, similar to the one shown in the demonstration problem in the chapter. If you prefer, you may omit columns for Adjusted Trial Balance and Retained Earnings. To save time and space, all operating expenses have been summarized. However, you should set up additional expense accounts for depreciation, bad debts, interest, and income tax. Also, you will need additional liability accounts for interest payable and income tax payable. (Hint: Net income is $37,940.)

b. Based upon the completed worksheet, prepare a multiple-step income statement and classified balance sheet.

c. Based upon the completed worksheet, prepare the adjusting and closing journal entries at December 31, 19D. Close all revenue and expense accounts to Income Summary.

CASES

C6–1   **(Analysis of the Impact of Uncollectible Accounts)**

A recent annual report for Sears Roebuck & Company contained the following information at the end of their fiscal year:

	Year 1	Year 2
Accounts receivable	$7,022,075,000	$7,336,308,000
Allowance for doubtful accounts	(86,605,000)	(96,989,000)
	$6,935,470,000	$7,239,319,000

A footnote to the financial statements disclosed that uncollectible accounts amounting to $55,000,000 were written off as bad during Year 1 and $69,000,000 during Year 2. Assume that the tax rate for Sears was 40%.

Required:

a. Determine the bad debt expense for Year 2 based on the facts given above.

b. Working capital is defined as current assets minus current liabilities. How was Sears' working capital affected by the write-off of $69,000,000 in uncollectible accounts during Year 2? What impact did the recording of bad debt expense have on working capital in Year 2?

c. How was net income affected by the $69,000,000 write-off during Year 2? What impact did the recording of bad debt expense have on net income for Year 2?

C6–2   **(Analysis of Accounts Receivable and Sales Revenue Using an Actual Financial Statement)**

Refer to the financial statements of Chesebrough-Pond's given in Special Supplement B immediately preceding the Index.

Required:

a. What is the amount of the Allowance for Doubtful Accounts for 1985? Assume that Bad Debt Expense for 1985 was $15,000,000. Determine the amount of individual customer accounts that were written off during 1985.

b. Many businesses are seasonal, with high sales activity during certain months and low sales activity during others. Is Chesebrough-Pond's a seasonal business?

c. What was the amount of trade accounts receivable for 1985?

d. Can you approximate the amount of goods that were purchased during the year? If not, explain why.

Accounting for inventories affects both the balance sheet (current assets) and the income statement (cost of goods sold). Most financial statements contain detailed notes concerning inventories.

 **COLGATE-PALMOLIVE** COMPANY

5. Inventories

At December 31, inventories were as follows:

	1985	1984
Raw materials and supplies	$247,797	**$278,025**
Work-in-process	45,670	**45,663**
Finished goods	322,600	**353,053**
Total	$616,067	**$676,741**

Inventories valued under LIFO amounted to $300,652 at December 31, 1985, and $233,897 at December 31, 1984. The excess of current cost over LIFO cost at the end of each year was $75,613 and $89,611, respectively.

You can be sure . . . if it's Westinghouse

■ Note 5: Inventories and Progress Billings

The excess of production cost over the cost of inventories valued on the LIFO basis was approximately $440 million and $555 million at December 31, 1984 and 1983. Cost of sales was reduced by $92 million in 1984, $123 million in 1983 and $69 million in 1982 due to decreases in inventories valued on the LIFO method.

Raw materials, work in process and finished goods included costs related to short- and long-term contracts of approximately $718 million and $655 million at December 31, 1984 and 1983. All costs in long-term contracts in process, progress payments to subcontractors and recoverable engineering and development costs were contract-related.

Inventories
(in millions)

	1984	1983
Raw materials	$ 152.2	$ 134.2
Work in process	851.5	721.9
Finished goods	281.5	237.7

COSTING METHODS FOR MEASURING INVENTORY AND COST OF GOODS SOLD

PURPOSE:

Chapter 6 discussed accounting for sales revenue and cost of goods sold. You were introduced to the periodic and perpetual inventory systems. In Chapter 6, we assumed that the cost of items purchased for inventory did not change over time. In reality, however, the unit cost of inventory items often will change each time a new purchase order is placed. In this chapter, we will discuss accounting for inventory and cost of goods sold when unit costs are changing.

ORGANIZATION:

Part A—Measuring Ending Inventory and Cost of Goods Sold with a Periodic Inventory System

1. Inventory effects on the measurement of income.
2. Measuring inventory cost.
3. Application of the inventory costing methods with the periodic inventory system.

LEARNING OBJECTIVES—TO BE ABLE TO:

1. Analyze the effects of inventory errors.
2. Identify what items should be included in inventory.
3. Describe and use the four inventory costing methods with the periodic and perpetual inventory systems.
4. Explain the comparability principle.
5. Apply the lower of cost or market rule.
6. Estimate ending inventory and cost of goods sold.
7. Expand your accounting vocabulary by learning about the "Important Term Defined in this Chapter" (page 345).
8. Apply the knowledge gained from this chapter by completing the homework assigned by your instructor.

Part B—Application of a Perpetual Inventory System and Selected Inventory Costing Problems

1. Application of the inventory costing methods with a perpetual inventory system.
2. Lower of cost or market; damaged goods; estimating inventory and cost of goods sold.

PART A—MEASURING ENDING INVENTORY AND COST OF GOODS SOLD WITH A PERIODIC INVENTORY SYSTEM

INVENTORY EFFECTS ON THE MEASUREMENT OF INCOME

A direct relationship exists between ending inventory and cost of goods sold. When the periodic inventory system (Chapter 6) is used, items not in the ending inventory are assumed to have been sold. Thus, the measurement of ending inventory affects both the balance sheet (assets) and the income statement (cost of goods sold and net income). The measurement of ending inventory affects not only the net income for that period but also the net income for the **next accounting period.** This two-period effect occurs because the ending inventory for one period is the beginning inventory for the next accounting period. The 19A and 19B income statements for SAL Company are shown in panel A of Exhibit 7–1. The reported 19A ending inventory was $10,000. Notice that this amount is shown as the beginning inventory for 19B.

An error in measuring the 19A ending inventory would affect both 19A and 19B income. For example, if the 19A ending inventory for SAL Company should have been $11,000 (i.e., $1,000 more than reported), both 19A and 19B income would be incorrect by $1,000. The restated income statements for SAL Company are shown in panel B of Exhibit 7–1. The various accounts that are affected by the $1,000 error are identified in panel C. Two generalizations can be made concerning the impact of an inventory error:

1. **In the period of the change**—An increase in the amount of the ending inventory for a period decreases cost of goods sold by the same amount, which in turn increases pretax income for that period by the same amount. A decrease in the amount of ending inventory increases cost of goods sold, which in turn decreases pretax income for that period by the same amount.
2. **In the next period**—An increase in the amount of the ending inventory for a period increases the beginning inventory for the next period. The increase in beginning inventory increases cost of goods sold, which decreases the pretax income of the **next period** by the same amount. In contrast, a decrease in the amount of the ending inventory for a period decreases cost of goods sold of the next period, which increases pretax income of the **next period** by the same amount.

An error in measuring ending inventory is caused by either incorrectly counting the inventory or by using an incorrect unit cost to value the inventory. Accountants use great care in counting and valuing inventory, but errors do occur. For example, several years ago the financial statements of Lafayette Radio Electronics Corporation had the following note:

> Subsequent to the issuance of its financial statements the company discovered a computational error in the amount of $1,046,000 in the calculation of its year-end inventory which resulted in an overstatement of ending inventory.

EXHIBIT 7–1

Impact of error in measuring inventory

Panel A:

SAL COMPANY
Income Statement (as reported)

	19A		19B	
Sales revenue		$100,000		$110,000
Cost of goods sold*				
Beginning inventory	$ –0–		$10,000	
Purchases	70,000		58,000	
Goods available for sale	70,000		68,000	
Ending inventory	10,000		–0–	
Cost of goods sold		60,000		68,000
Gross margin		40,000		42,000
Expenses		35,000		35,500
Pretax income		$ 5,000		$ 6,500

    * See Chapter 6: BI + P – EI = CCS

Panel B:

SAL COMPANY
Income Statement (corrected)

	19A		19B	
Sales revenue		$100,000		$110,000
Cost of goods sold:				
Beginning inventory	$ –0–		$11,000	
Purchases	70,000		58,000	
Goods available for sale	70,000		69,000	
Ending inventory	11,000		–0–	
Cost of goods sold		59,000		69,000
Gross margin		41,000		41,000
Expenses		35,000		35,500
Pretax income		$ 6,000		$ 5,500

Panel C—Comparison:

		As reported	Corrected
19A	Ending inventory	$10,000	$11,000
19A	Cost of goods sold	60,000	59,000
19A	Gross margin	40,000	41,000
19A	Pretax income	5,000	6,000
19B	Beginning inventory	10,000	11,000
19B	Goods available for sale	68,000	69,000
19B	Gross margin	42,000	41,000
19B	Pretax income	6,500	5,500

ITEMS INCLUDED IN INVENTORY

Usually, inventory includes tangible property that (1) is held for sale in the normal course of business or (2) will be used in producing goods or services for sale. Inventory is reported on the balance sheet as a current asset because it usually will be used or converted into cash within one year or within the next operating cycle of the business, whichever is the longer. Because inventory is less liquid (i.e., less readily convertible to cash) than accounts receivable, it usually is listed below accounts receivable on the balance sheet.

The kinds of inventory normally held depend upon the characteristics of the business:[1]

Retail or wholesale business:

Merchandise inventory—goods (or merchandise) held for resale in the normal course of business. The goods usually are acquired in a finished condition and are ready for sale without further processing.

Manufacturing business:[2]

Finished goods inventory—goods manufactured by the business, completed and ready for sale.

Work in process inventory—goods in the process of being manufactured but not yet completed as finished goods. When completed, work in process inventory becomes finished goods inventory.

Raw materials inventory—items acquired by purchase, growth (such as food products), or extraction (natural resources) for processing into finished goods. Such items are accounted for as raw materials inventory until used. When used, their cost is included in the work in process inventory (along with other processing costs such as direct labor and factory overhead). The flow of inventory costs in a manufacturing environment can be diagrammed as follows:

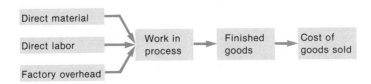

The work in process inventory includes (1) the cost of raw materials used, (2) the **direct** labor incurred in the manufacturing process, and (3) the factory

---

[1] Supplies on hand usually are reported as prepaid expenses.
[2] Subsequent accounting courses present a complete discussion of inventory measurement and accounting in a manufacturing environment.

overhead costs. Direct labor cost represents the earnings of employees who work directly on the products being manufactured. Factory overhead costs include all manufacturing costs that are not raw material or direct labor costs. For example, the salary of the plant supervisor is included in factory overhead.

When counting the **physical quantity** of goods in the inventory, a company should include all items to which it has **ownership,** regardless of their locations. In purchase and sale transactions, accounting focuses on the passage of ownership. Usually when ownership passes, one party records a sale and the other party records a purchase. At this point, goods should be included in the inventory of the purchaser and not in the inventory of the seller. In a sale transaction, the basic guideline is that ownership to the goods passes at the **time intended by the parties** to the transaction. Usually, ownership passes when the seller gives the goods to the buyer; however, there are situations in which this is not the case.

When the intentions of the parties concerning the passage of ownership are not clear, all of the circumstances must be assessed. Judgment must then be applied as to when the buyer and seller intended ownership to pass. For example, the buyer may ask the vendor (seller) to hold the goods pending shipping instructions. In this instance, ownership appears to have passed, regardless of the delivery date. A similar problem arises when a third party has physical possession of the goods for a period of time. For example, an independent transportation company may move the goods from the seller's location to the buyer's location. If the terms of the sale provide that the buyer must pay the transportation charges (known as FOB shipping point), then ownership usually is assumed to pass when the vendor delivers the goods to the transportation agent. However, if the terms of the sale are FOB destination (i.e., the seller must pay the freight), ownership is assumed to pass when the goods are delivered to the buyer at destination. FOB stands for "free on board" and is used in business to indicate who is responsible for paying transportation charges. FOB destination means that the seller pays the freight; FOB shipping point means that the buyer pays the freight.

The passage-of-ownership guideline is used to apply the revenue principle (Exhibit 4–5). Without the passage-of-ownership guideline, the financial statements could be manipulated to overstate revenue by entering **sales orders** received, regardless of whether ownership to the goods has passed to the buyer. Conversely, costs could be manipulated by not recording purchases even though ownership to the goods has passed.

When a company has possession of goods that it does not own, it should exclude those goods from the inventory. This situation often occurs when goods are on **consignment** for sale on a commission basis. The supplier (called the consignor) legally retains ownership to the goods on consignment, although the goods are in the physical possession of the party that will sell them (called the consignee). The consignor should include the goods in the ending inventory, while the consignee should exclude them from the ending inventory.

MEASURING INVENTORY COST

Goods in inventory are recorded in conformity with the **cost principle** as follows:

> The primary basis of accounting for inventory is cost, which is the price paid or consideration given to acquire an asset. As applied to inventories, cost means, in principle, the sum of the applicable expenditures and charges directly or indirectly incurred in bringing an article to its existing condition and location.[3]

In conformity with the cost principle, indirect expenditures related to the purchase of goods, such as freight, insurance, and storage, theoretically should be included in measuring the purchase cost of the goods acquired. However, because these incidental costs often are not **material in amount** (see the materiality constraint, Exhibit 4–5), they do not have to be assigned to the inventory cost. Thus, for practical reasons, some companies use the **net invoice price** to assign a unit cost to goods and record the indirect expenditures as a separate cost which is reported as an expense.

Chapter 6 discussed the assignment of **dollar cost** to (a) the ending inventory and (b) cost of goods sold in situations in which unit purchase (or manufacturing) cost remained constant. This chapter expands those discussions to the typical situation in which the cost per unit of the goods stocked changes during the annual accounting period.

Chapter 6 presented two alternative inventory systems used to accumulate data to facilitate determination of (a) the ending inventory and (b) cost of goods sold. The two alternative inventory systems are:[4]

1. **Periodic inventory system**—This system accumulates total merchandise acquisition cost (including the beginning inventory). At the **end of the accounting period,** the ending inventory is measured by means of a physical inventory count of all goods remaining on hand. The units counted on hand then are valued (costed) in dollars by using appropriate unit purchase costs. The periodic inventory system measures **cost of goods sold** as a residual amount; that is:

$$BI + P - EI = CGS$$

2. **Perpetual inventory system**—This system keeps a detailed daily inventory record throughout the period for each item stocked. This record includes (a) the beginning inventory, (b) each purchase, (c) each issue (i.e., sales), and (d) a continuous (perpetual or running) balance of the inventory. This system measures cost of goods sold and ending inventory without a physical inventory count at the end of each accounting period. Under this system, the **ending inventory** can be viewed as a residual amount; that is:

---

[3] AICPA, *Accounting Research Bulletin No. 43* (New York, 1961), chap, 4, statement 3.

[4] Often a company will use one of the systems for certain items stocked and the other system for the remaining items. The choice usually depends upon such factors as the nature of the item (size), unit cost, number of units stocked, and cost to implement the system.

$$BI + P - CGS = EI$$

In this part of the chapter, we discuss several alternative inventory costing methods using the **periodic inventory system**. Part B of this chapter discusses these methods with a perpetual inventory system.

PURPOSE OF INVENTORY COSTING METHODS

There are four generally accepted inventory costing methods:

1. Weighted average.
2. First-in, first-out (FIFO).
3. Last-in, first-out (LIFO).
4. Specific identification.

If unit costs of items purchased for inventory did not change, there would be no need for alternative inventory costing methods. When unit costs change, an accounting method is needed to assign the various costs to units in the ending inventory and to the units that have been sold. Consider Summer Retail Store (Exhibit 7–2). The total cost of goods available for sale is $3,630. There are four different unit costs ($6, $7, $8, and $9). The amounts of ending inventory and

---

EXHIBIT 7–2

Illustrative inventory data

SUMMER RETAIL STORE
19A Illustrative Data—Beginning Inventory, Purchases, and Sales

Transactions	Symbol	Number of units	Unit cost	Total cost	
Beginning inventory, January 1, 19A (carried over from last period)	BI	100	$6		$ 600
Purchases during 19A:					
January 3, first purchase	P	50	7	$ 350	
June 12, second purchase	P	200	8	1,600	
December 20, third purchase	P	120	9	1,080	
Total purchases during 19A		370			3,030
Goods available for sale during the year		470			3,630
Goods sold during 19A:					
January 6 (unit sales price, $10)	S	40			
June 18 (unit sales price, $12)	S	220			
December 24 (unit sales price, $14)	S	60			
Total sales during 19A		320			?
Ending inventory, December 31, 19A (units 470 − 320)	EI	150			?

cost of goods sold that are reported depend upon the costing method that is selected.

The four inventory costing methods are **alternative allocation methods** for assigning the total amount of goods available for sale (BI + P) between (a) ending inventory (reported as an asset at the end of the period) and (b) cost of goods sold (reported as an expense of the period). Refer to the data for Summer Retail Store given in Exhibit 7–2. The two allocated amounts were calculated using the weighted-average inventory costing method, as shown below. At this point you need not be concerned about how the two amounts were calculated.

	Units	Amount
Goods available for sale (total amount to be allocated)	470	$3,630
Cost allocation:		
Ending inventory (determined by inventory count and then costed at weighted-average unit cost)	150	1,158
Cost of goods sold (residual amount)	320	$2,472

The amount of **goods available for sale** ($3,630) was allocated between **ending inventory** ($1,158) and **cost of goods sold** ($2,472). The sum of these two

---

EXHIBIT 7–3

Illustration of cost allocation

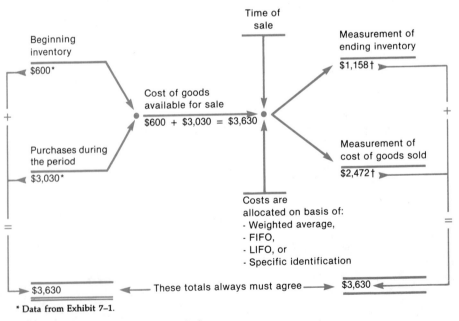

* Data from Exhibit 7–1.

† Based on the weighted-average cost method.

amounts (and the related units) must be the same as goods available for sale. This cost allocation procedure also is shown graphically in Exhibit 7–3.

INVENTORY COSTING METHODS ILLUSTRATED

The choice among the four inventory costing methods is not based on the physical flow of goods on and off the shelves. For most companies, the actual **physical flow** of goods is first-in, first-out (FIFO). Regardless of the physical flow of goods, a company can use any of the inventory costing methods. Generally accepted accounting principles only require that the inventory costing method used be rational and systematic.

A company is not required to use the same inventory costing method for all inventory items, and no particular justification is needed for the selection of one or more of the acceptable methods. However, a change in method is significant and needs special disclosures in the notes to the financial statements.

Weighted-Average Inventory Costing Method

The weighted-average method requires computation of the weighted-average unit cost of the goods available for sale. In a periodic inventory system, the computed unit cost is multiplied by the **number of units** in inventory to derive the total cost of ending inventory. Cost of goods sold is determined by subtracting the ending inventory amount from the amount of goods available for sale. For example, the weighted-average method would be applied by Summer Retail Store (Exhibit 7–2) as follows using a **periodic** inventory system.[5]

Step 1—Computation of the weighted-average unit cost for the period:

$$\frac{\text{Total goods available for sale—at cost}}{\text{Total goods available for sale—units}} = \frac{\$3,630}{470} = \$7.72 \quad \left\{ \begin{array}{l} \text{Weighted-} \\ \text{average} \\ \text{cost per} \\ \text{unit for} \\ \text{the period} \end{array} \right.$$

Step 2—Allocation of the cost of goods available for sale under the periodic inventory system:

	Units	Amount
Goods available for sale (Exhibit 7–2)	470	$3,630
Ending inventory (150 units × $7.72)	150	1,158*
Cost of goods sold (residual amount)	320	$2,472†

  * Reported on the balance sheet.
  † Reported as an expense on the income statement. This amount can be verified as 320 units × $7.72 = $2,470 (a $2 rounding error).

---

[5] When an average cost is used, uneven unit cost amounts usually are rounded to the nearest cent. The rounded unit cost amount is used to compute the ending inventory amount which allocates any rounding error to cost of goods sold. Under the perpetual inventory system, a moving average unit cost (rather than the weighted-average unit cost) usually is used (see Part B).

The weighted-average cost method is rational, systematic, easy to apply, and not subject to manipulation. It is representative of costs during the entire period including the beginning inventory rather than of the cost only at the beginning, end, or at one point during the period.[6] Representative costs are reported on both the balance sheet (ending inventory) and the income statement (cost of goods sold).

First-In, First-Out Inventory Costing Method

The first-in, first-out method, frequently called **FIFO,** assumes that the oldest units (i.e., the first costs in) are the first units sold (i.e., the first costs out). The units in the beginning inventory are treated as if they were sold first. Then the units from the first purchase are sold next, and so on until the units left in the ending inventory all come from the most recent purchases. FIFO allocates the oldest unit costs to cost of goods sold and the most recent unit costs to the ending inventory.

Often, FIFO is justified because it is consistent with the actual physical flow of the goods. In most businesses, the first goods placed in stock are the first goods sold. However, FIFO can be used regardless of the actual physical flow of goods because the objective of FIFO is to allocate costs to ending inventory and to cost of goods sold in a systematic and rational manner.

FIFO is applied by Summer Retail Store (Exhibit 7–2) as follows under a **periodic** inventory system:

	Units	Unit cost	Total cost
Goods available for sale (Exhibit 7–2)	470		$3,630
Valuation of ending inventory (FIFO):			
At latest unit costs, 150 units:			
From December 20 purchase (latest)	120	$9	$1,080
From June 12 purchase (next latest)	30	8	240
Valuation, FIFO basis	150		1,320*
Cost of goods sold (residual FIFO amount)	320		$2,310†

* Report on balance sheet.
† Report as an expense on income statement. This amount can be verified as follows: Units sold at oldest costs—100 units × $6 = $600, plus 50 units × $7 = $350, plus 170 units × $8 = $1,360, which sum to $2,310.

The FIFO method is rational, systematic, easy to apply, and not subject to manipulation. On the balance sheet, the FIFO ending inventory amount is valued on the basis of the most recent unit costs. It is likely to provide a realistic valuation prevailing at the balance sheet date. In contrast, on the income statement, cost of goods sold is at the oldest unit costs, which may not reflect the current cost of items that were sold. The significance of the impact of FIFO on the income statement (i.e., cost of goods sold and income) and the balance sheet

---

[6] A weighted-average unit cost rather than a simple average of the unit costs must be used. For example, ($6 + $7 + $8 + 9) ÷ 4 = $7.50 would be incorrect because it does not consider the number of units at each unit cost.

(i.e., the ending inventory amount) depends on how much the unit costs change during the period.

Last-In, First-Out Inventory Costing Method

The last-in, first-out method, often called **LIFO,** assumes that the most recently acquired goods are sold first. Regardless of the physical flow of goods, LIFO treats the costs of the most recent units purchased as cost of goods sold. Therefore the unit costs of the beginning inventory and the earlier purchases remain in the ending inventory. The LIFO flow assumption is the exact opposite of the FIFO flow assumption.

LIFO is applied by Summer Retail Store (Exhibit 7–2) as follows under a **periodic** inventory system:

	Units	Unit cost	Total cost
Goods available for sale (Exhibit 7–2)	470		$3,630
Valuation of ending inventory (LIFO):			
At older unit costs, 150 units:			
From beginning inventory (oldest)	100	$6	$600
From January 3 purchase (next oldest)	50	7	350
Valuation, LIFO basis	150		950*
Cost of goods sold (residual LIFO amount)	320		$2,680†

* Report on balance sheet.
† Report as an expense on income statement. This amount can be verified as follows: Units sold at latest costs— 120 units @ $9 = $1,080, plus 200 units @ $8 = $1,600, which sum to $2,680.

The LIFO method is rational and systematic. However, it can be manipulated by buying (or not buying) goods at the end of a period when unit costs have changed. By this action, it is possible to manipulate cost of goods sold and, hence, reported income. On the income statement, LIFO cost of goods sold is based on the latest unit costs, which is a realistic measurement of the current cost of items that were sold. In contrast, on the balance sheet, the ending inventory amount is based on the oldest unit costs, which may be an unrealistic valuation. The comparative impact of LIFO will be discussed later.[7]

Specific Identification Inventory Costing Method

When the specific identification method is used, the cost of each item sold is individually identified and recorded as cost of goods sold. This method requires keeping track of the purchase cost of each item. This is done either by (1) coding the purchase cost on each unit before placing it in stock, or (2) keeping a separate

---

[7] This discussion assumes an item-by-item application of LIFO and costing of goods sold currently throughout the period. For income tax purposes, LIFO costing must be done at the end of the taxable year. Although the concepts are the same, many companies use a method known as dollar-value LIFO, and the costing is at the end of the year. These complexities are beyond the scope of this course.

record of the unit and identifying it with a serial number. If the 40 units sold by Summer Retail (Exhibit 7–2) on January 6 were selected from the units that were purchased at $6 each, the cost of goods sold amount for that sale would be measured as 40 units × $6 = $240. Alternatively, if 20 of the units were selected from those that cost $6 each and the other 20 from those that cost $7 each, cost of goods sold would be measured as (20 units × $6) + (20 units × $7) = $260.

The specific identification method is tedious and impractical when unit costs change frequently or a large number of different items are stocked. On the other hand, when there are "big-ticket" items such as automobiles and expensive jewelry, this method is appropriate because each item tends to be different from the other items. In such situations, the selling price of an item usually is based on a markup over its cost. However, the method may be manipulated when the units are identical because one can affect the cost of goods sold and the ending inventory accounts by "picking and choosing" from among the several available unit costs, even though the goods are identical in other respects. In the previous example, cost of goods sold was either $240 or $260, depending on which items were chosen for sale.

COMPARISON OF THE INVENTORY COSTING METHODS

Each of the four alternative inventory costing methods is in conformity with generally accepted accounting principles. However, each method may produce significantly different income and asset (i.e., ending inventory) amounts. To illustrate this difference, the comparative results for Summer Retail Store are as follows:

	Sales revenue	Cost of goods sold	Gross margin	Balance sheet (inventory)
Weighted average	$3,880	$2,472	$1,408	$1,158
FIFO	3,880	2,310	1,570	1,320
LIFO (end of period)	3,880	2,680	1,200	950

From the above results, we see that when unit costs are changing, each method will give different income and different inventory amounts. Notice that the difference in **the gross margin** among each of the methods is the same as the difference in the inventory amounts. The method that gives the highest ending inventory amount also gives the highest income amount and vice versa. The weighted-average cost method will give income and inventory amounts that are between the FIFO and LIFO extremes.

We will focus now on a comparison of the FIFO and LIFO methods because they usually represent the extreme, opposite effects. Note in the comparison above that unit costs were **increasing. When unit costs are rising, LIFO produces lower income and a lower inventory valuation than FIFO. Conversely, when unit costs are declining, LIFO produces higher income and higher inventory valuation than FIFO.** These effects occur because LIFO will cause the new unit costs to be reflected on the income statement whereas FIFO will cause the older unit costs to be reflected on the income statement.

INCOME TAX EFFECTS RELATED TO INVENTORY METHODS

The selection of an inventory costing method often has a significant impact on income taxes that must be paid. The various inventory costing methods produce different amounts of pretax income among accounting periods. When prices are rising, **LIFO** often is preferred for income tax purposes because an immediate tax deduction is preferred to a later tax deduction. The shifting of tax liability to later years is important because the company can earn interest on money that otherwise would be paid as taxes.

In recent years, many businesses have adopted LIFO because it minimizes early income tax payments. Prices have been rising, and with rising prices, LIFO allocates higher costs to cost of goods sold. This in turn reduces pretax income so the income tax bill is lower. Of course, the inventory effect suggests that should prices decline at some future date, those businesses may want to change from LIFO to FIFO to minimize income taxes on the downward trend of prices. In many cases, it is difficult to get permission from the Internal Revenue Service to change the inventory costing method.

EXHIBIT 7–4

Income tax effects illustrated

A. Fact situation for 19B (when prices increased rapidly):

a. Sales revenue	$900,000
b. Cost of goods sold:	
FIFO basis	400,000
LIFO basis	600,000
c. Remaining expenses (excluding income taxes)	250,000
d. Average income tax rate	30%

B. Effect on income tax expense:

	Inventory costing method	
	FIFO	LIFO
Sales revenue	$900,000	$900,000
Cost of goods sold	400,000	600,000
Gross margin	500,000	300,000
Less: Remaining expenses (except income taxes)	250,000	250,000
Pretax income	250,000	50,000
Income tax expense (30% rate)	75,000	15,000
Net income	$175,000	$ 35,000
EPS (100,000 shares common stock outstanding)	$1.75	$0.35

Reduction in income tax expense ($75,000 − $15,000) = $60,000.
Cash saved ($75,000 − $15,000) = $60,000.

The income tax effects associated with LIFO and FIFO are shown in Exhibit 7–4.

In this situation, ending inventory, cost of goods sold, and pretax income were different by $200,000, which was caused by the differences between the FIFO and LIFO methods. Costs were rising, and there was a significant difference between the "old" and "new" unit costs. When multiplied by the 30% income tax rate, the $200,000 difference indicates a cash saving of $60,000 in 19B. The internal revenue code specifies a LIFO conformity rule: If LIFO is used on the income tax return, it also must be used on the financial reports. LIFO cannot provide permanent tax savings because (a) when inventory levels drop or (b) costs drop, the income effect reverses and the income taxes deferred will have to be paid. The only advantage of deferring income taxes in such situations is due to the fact that interest can be earned on the money that otherwise would be paid as taxes for the current year.

EVALUATION OF ALTERNATIVE INVENTORY COSTING METHODS

No single method of inventory costing can be considered the "best." Tax consequences are an important consideration in the choice of method. Many accountants believe that the best inventory costing method is the one that best reflects the sales pricing policy of the company. Many companies do price units for sale in each of the ways implied by these four costing methods. Other accountants believe that the choice of method should be based upon whether the measurement emphasis should be on the income statement or on the balance sheet. Those who believe that the income statement should be given primary emphasis tend to defend LIFO because it matches the most recent purchase cost with current sales revenue. Those who prefer to emphasize the balance sheet tend to prefer FIFO because it reports the ending inventory on the balance sheet at the most current cost price. Because of these considerations, it is easy to understand why the accounting profession and the income tax laws have accepted several alternative inventory costing methods.

COMPARABILITY

Different income statement and balance sheet amounts are caused by the use of different inventory costing methods. These differences in reported financial data cause problems for statement users in comparing companies that use different accounting methods. Problems also occur when an individual business changes accounting methods over time. The **comparability quality** (Exhibit 4–5) is applied to maximize comparability when accounting alternatives are permitted. The comparability quality holds that all accounting concepts, principles, and measurement approaches should be applied in a similar or consistent way from one period to the next. This characteristic is necessary to assure that the data reported in the financial statements are reasonably comparable over time. It prevents arbitrary changes from one accounting or measurement approach to another, but the comparability quality does not preclude change. Changes in accounting are permitted when they improve the measurement of financial results and financial position. Comparability is a difficult concept to define precisely and poses problems in application.

A business is not allowed to change from one inventory costing method to another from period to period. Changing from one inventory costing method to another is a major event. Such a change requires full disclosure about the reason for the change and the accounting effects.

PART B—APPLICATION OF A PERPETUAL INVENTORY SYSTEM AND SELECTED INVENTORY COSTING PROBLEMS

This part of the chapter discusses **application of each of the inventory costing methods with a perpetual inventory system.** Separate discussion of the two inventory systems is essential because:

a. The timing of the application of the inventory costing methods between the two systems causes some differences in the allocated amounts. The periodic inventory system costs inventory units at the end of the period; the perpetual inventory system costs units on a day-to-day basis.
b. The accounting entries vary between the two systems.
c. The inventory controls that are available with the two systems vary.

APPLICATION OF THE INVENTORY COSTING METHODS WITH A PERPETUAL INVENTORY SYSTEM

A perpetual inventory system requires the maintenance of a day-to-day **perpetual inventory record** for each kind of goods or merchandise. This record shows units, unit costs, and dollar amounts for (a) beginning inventory, (b) goods received (purchases), (c) goods sold (issues), and (d) balance of goods on hand (ending inventory). Each purchase and each sale transaction is entered in the perpetual inventory record when it occurs. The perpetual inventory record is designed so that cost of goods sold and the ending inventory are measured on a perpetual or continuous basis.

In the following discussions, a **perpetual inventory record** will be shown for each of the four inventory costing methods. We will use the data for Summer Retail Store given in Exhibit 7–2. The beginning inventory of 100 units at a unit cost of $6 would have been carried over in the records from the prior period.

Each purchase is recorded as follows and at the same time entered on the perpetual inventory record (see Exhibit 7–5):

Jan. 3   Inventory (50 units × $7) 350
              Cash (or accounts payable)   350

EXHIBIT 7–5

Moving weighted-average method—perpetual inventory system

PERPETUAL INVENTORY RECORD

Item   Item A   Cost Basis   Moving average

Location   320   Minimum
                                                    Level   100
Code   13
                                                    Maximum
                                                    Level   300

Date	Received (purchases)			Issued (sales)			Inventory Balance		
	Units	Unit Cost	Total Cost	Units	Unit Cost	Total Cost	Units	Unit Cost	Total Cost
1/1 bal.							100	6.00	600
1/3	50	7.00	350				150	6.33	950
1/6				40	6.33	253	110	6.33	697
6/12	200	8.00	1,600				310	7.41*	2,297
6/18				220	7.41	1,630	90	7.41	667
12/20	120	9.00	1,080				210	8.32*	1,747
12/24				60	8.32	499	150	8.32	1,248
Total cost of goods sold						2,382			
Total ending inventory									1,248

  * New moving weighted-average unit cost computed.

A sale generates two companion entries when a perpetual inventory system is used; one at sales price and one at cost:

```
Jan. 6  Cash ......................................................... 400
            Sales revenue (40 units × $10) .............................       400

        Cost of goods sold (FIFO basis) .................................. 240
            Inventory (40 units × $6) ....................................       240
```

Weighted-Average Inventory Costing Method

When the weighted-average cost method is applied with a perpetual inventory system, a **moving weighted-average** unit cost is used because the cost of goods sold amount is measured and recorded at the **time of each sale.** It is impossible to use an **annual** weighted average with the perpetual system because the recording of cost of goods sold would be delayed until year-end, which is the only time an annual average unit cost can be computed.

Under the perpetual inventory system, a **new** average unit cost is computed at the time of **each purchase.** Cost of goods sold and the remaining inventory are measured at the then current moving average unit cost. A perpetual inventory record on a moving weighted-average basis for the Summer Retail Store is shown in Exhibit 7–5. The moving weighted-average unit cost was recomputed three times during the period because there were three purchases. Units sold are removed from the inventory record at the current moving average unit cost. For example, the moving weighted-average unit cost was computed on the date of the first purchase as follows:

	Units	Cost
Beginning inventory	100	$600
Purchase, January 3	50	350
Totals	150	$950

Moving average unit cost:
$950 ÷ 150 units = $6.33 per unit.

The companion journal entries for the sale on January 6 would reflect sales revenue of $400 and cost of goods sold of $253 (from the perpetual inventory record) as follows:

```
Jan. 6  Cash ......................................................... 400
            Sales revenue (40 units × $10) ..........................       400

        Cost of goods sold (moving average basis) ..................... 253
            Inventory .................................................       253
            From Exhibit 7–5, 40 units × $6.33 = $253.
```

FIFO Inventory Costing Method

When the FIFO method is applied with a perpetual inventory system, after each issue the remaining units on hand must be "layered" by the different unit costs. These layers are called "inventory cost layers." The identification of inventory cost layers is necessary because goods are removed from the perpetual inventory record in FIFO order; that is, the oldest unit cost is taken off first. A perpetual inventory record on a FIFO basis is shown in Exhibit 7–6. Each purchase and each sale of goods is entered in the inventory record at the time of the transaction. At each transaction date, the balance column on the perpetual inventory record is restated to show the units and amount on hand for each different unit cost. At the same time, each transaction is recorded in the journal. The two companion journal entries to record the sales of June 18 are:

```
June 18  Cash  ..................................................  2,640
             Sales revenue (220 units × $12)  ......................       2,640

         Cost of goods sold (FIFO basis)  ..........................  1,590
             Inventory  ...........................................       1,590
             From Exhibit 7–6, $360 + $350 + $880 = $1,590.
```

LIFO Inventory Costing Method

When the LIFO method is used with a perpetual inventory system, the inventory cost layers must be identified separately on the perpetual inventory record, as was the case with FIFO. This identification is necessary so that the units (and their costs) can be removed at the time of sale from the inventory record in the opposite order that they came in. Unit costs are removed from the perpetual inventory record at the time of each issue, which means that the **timing of costing is during the period rather than at the end of the period.** A perpetual inventory record on a LIFO basis is shown in Exhibit 7–7.

Specific Identification Inventory Costing Method

When the specific identification method is applied with a perpetual inventory system, the item-by-item choice (for entry in the perpetual inventory record and in the accounts) should be made at the time of sale. Use of the specific identification costing method with a perpetual inventory system is done in a manner like that shown in the preceding illustrations.

_____ **EXHIBIT 7–6** _____

FIFO method—perpetual inventory system

	PERPETUAL INVENTORY RECORD								
	(heading—same as in Exhibit 7–5, except cost basis—FIFO)								
Date	Received (purchases)			Issued (sales)			Inventory Balance*		
	Units	Unit Cost	Total Cost	Units	Unit Cost	Total Cost	Units	Unit Cost	Total Cost
1/1 bal.							100	6	600
1/3	50	7	350				100	6	600
							50	7	350
1/6				40	6	240	60	6	360
							50	7	350
6/12	200	8	1,600				60	6	360
							50	7	350
							200	8	1,600
6/18				60	6	360			
				50	7	350			
				110	8	880	90	8	720
12/20	120	9	1,080				90	8	720
							120	9	1,080
1/24				60	8	480	30	8	240
							120	9	1,080
Total cost of goods sold						2,310			
Total ending inventory									1,320

  * Maintained by FIFO unit cost inventory layers.

EXHIBIT 7–7

LIFO method, costed currently—perpetual inventory system

	PERPETUAL INVENTORY RECORD								
	(heading—same as in Exhibit 7–5, except cost basis—LIFO)								
Date	Received (purchases)			Issued (sales)			Inventory Balance*		
	Units	Unit Cost	Total Cost	Units	Unit Cost	Total Cost	Units	Unit Cost	Total Cost
1/1 bal.							100	6	600
1/3	50	7	350				100	6	600
							50	7	350
1/6				40	7	280	100	6	600
							10	7	70
6/12	200	8	1,600				100	6	600
							10	7	70
							200	8	1,600
6/18				200	8	1,600			
				10	7	70			
				10	6	60	90	6	540
12/20	120	9	1,080				90	6	540
							120	9	1,080
12/21				60	9	540	90	6	540
							60	9	540
Total cost of goods sold						2,550			
Ending inventory									1,080

* Maintained by LIFO unit cost inventory layers.

COMPARISON OF PERIODIC AND PERPETUAL INVENTORY SYSTEMS

There are two important implementation differences between the periodic inventory system and the perpetual inventory system:

a. The perpetual system requires more clerical effort than the periodic system.
b. The periodic system requires a year-end physical inventory; the perpetual system does not.

In the past, most businesses used the periodic inventory system because of its relative low cost and convenience. However, recent advances in computer technology have produced a significant reduction in the cost of maintaining a perpetual inventory system. As a result, many businesses have adopted the perpetual system. The perpetual system offers the advantage of providing management with up-to-date inventory information.

The periodic and perpetual inventory systems often produce different valuations of cost of goods sold and ending inventory because of differences within the timing of the costing of cost of goods sold and inventory. The **periodic** inventory system costs ending inventory and cost of goods sold at the **end** of the accounting period. The **perpetual** inventory system costs inventory and cost of goods sold **throughout** the accounting period.

The FIFO inventory method gives identical valuations of ending inventory and cost of goods sold under both the periodic and perpetual inventory systems. The results are identical because of the basic FIFO assumption that the first goods into inventory are the first goods taken out of inventory, and that order is always maintained. Compare the following FIFO results for Summer Retail Store:

FIFO	Perpetual inventory system	Periodic inventory system
Source	Exhibit 7–6	Page 333
Ending inventory	$1,320	$1,320
Cost of goods sold	2,310	2,310
Total goods available	$3,630	$3,630

In contrast, results typically will be different under periodic and perpetual systems when either the LIFO or the average inventory costing method is used. The results will be different under the **average cost** method because the **periodic** inventory system applies an **annual** weighted average for cost allocation whereas the **perpetual** inventory system applies a series of **moving** averages throughout the accounting period.

Results will be different under the **LIFO** method because the **periodic** inventory system allocates the most recent purchase cost to cost of goods sold at the end of the accounting period. In contrast, the **perpetual** system allocates the most recent purchase costs to cost of goods sold **during** the accounting period on the date that each sales transaction occurs.

To show the differences that can occur between LIFO and weighted average, compare the following results for Summer Retail Store:

LIFO	Perpetual inventory system	Periodic inventory system
Source	Exhibit 7–7	Page 334
Ending inventory	$1,080	$ 950
Cost of goods sold	2,550	2,680
Total goods available	$3,630	$3,630

Weighted Average		
Source	Exhibit 7–5	Page 330
Ending inventory	$1,248	$1,158
Cost of goods sold	2,382	2,472
Total goods available	$3,630	$3,630

To summarize, the four **inventory costing methods** (weighted average, FIFO, LIFO, and specific identification) are alternative methods of measuring the valuation of ending inventory and cost of goods sold. Each method assumes a different flow of unit costs during the accounting period; therefore, each method produces different results. The **periodic** and **perpetual inventory systems** are two different accounting approaches for applying the inventory costing methods to measure cost of goods sold and ending inventory. The periodic inventory system allocates costs at the end of the accounting period (using one of the four inventory costing methods). The perpetual inventory system allocates costs currently during the accounting period (again, using one of the inventory costing methods). Because of these two different timing assumptions, the two systems give different valuations of ending inventory and cost of goods sold under the weighted average, LIFO, and specific identification costing methods. Valuations are always the same under FIFO.

SELECTED INVENTORY PROBLEMS

The remaining discussions in this chapter relate to three issues that may affect the valuation of the ending inventory reported on the balance sheet and the amount of income reported on the income statement. They are (a) lower of cost or market (LCM) valuation, (b) damaged items, and (c) estimating the ending inventory.

Inventories at Lower of Cost or Market (LCM)

Inventories should be measured at their unit purchase cost in conformity with the cost principle. However, when the goods remaining in the ending inventory can be replaced with identical goods at a lower cost, the lower unit cost should be used as the inventory valuation. This rule is known as measuring inventories on a **lower of cost or market (LCM) basis.** It is a departure from the cost principle because of the conservatism constraint (Exhibit 4–5). The LCM basis recognizes a "holding" loss in the period in which the replacement cost of an item dropped, rather than in the period in which the item actually is sold. The holding loss is the difference between purchase cost and the subsequent lower replacement cost. To illustrate, assume that an office equipment dealer has 10 new electronic calculators in the 19B ending inventory. The calculators were bought for $450 each and were marked to sell at $499.95. At the end of the year, the same new calculators can be purchased for $400 and will be marked to sell for $429.95. The 10 calculators should be costed in the ending inventory at the lower of cost ($450) or current market ($400). The LCM basis costs the ending inventory at $400 per unit. There are several effects caused by using a replacement cost of $400 instead of the original purchase cost of $450 for the 10 calculators included in the ending inventory. By costing them at $50 per unit below their purchase cost, 19B pretax income will be $500 less (i.e., 10 × $50) than it would have been had they been costed in the inventory at $450 per unit. This $500 loss in the value of the inventory (i.e., the holding loss) was due to a decline in the replacement cost. Because the loss is included in cost of goods sold, 19B pretax income will be reduced by $500 in the period in which the replacement cost dropped (19B) rather than in the later period when the goods actually are sold. The $500 loss also reduces the amount of inventory that is reported on the 19B balance sheet. These effects are shown in Exhibit 7–8. LCM usually is applied to

EXHIBIT 7–8

Effect of inventory measurement at LCM

	Inventory measured at—	
	Cost (FIFO)	LCM
Sales revenue	$41,500	$41,500
Cost of goods sold:		
Beginning inventory	$ 5,000	$ 5,000
Add purchases	20,000	20,000
Goods available for sale	25,000	25,000
Less ending inventory (10 calculators):		
At purchase cost of $450	4,500	
At LCM of $400		4,000
Cost of goods sold	20,500	21,000
Gross margin on sales	21,000	20,500
Expenses	15,000	15,000
Pretax income	$ 6,000	$ 5,500

all inventories on an item-by-item basis rather than on the aggregate inventory as a whole.[8]

Damaged and Deteriorated Goods

Merchandise on hand that is damaged, obsolete, or shopworn should not be measured and reported at original cost. Instead this merchandise should be reported at its present **net realizable value** when it is below cost. Net realizable value is the **estimated amount** that will be realized when the goods are sold in their deteriorated condition, less all repair and sale costs.

Assume a retail store has on hand two television sets that have been used as demonstrators and cannot be sold as new sets (i.e., they are shopworn). When purchased, the sets cost $300 each. Because of their present condition, realistic estimates are:

	Per set
Estimated sales price in present condition	$175
Estimated repair costs of $20 and sales costs of $15	35
Estimated net realizable value	$140

Based on these estimates, the two television sets would be included in the inventory at $140 each, rather than at the original cost of $300 each. Net realizable value is used, rather than cost, because it records the loss in the period in which it occurred rather than in the period of sale. This method also avoids overstatement of the asset on the balance sheet.

If a **periodic** inventory system is used, the item is included in the ending inventory of **damaged goods** at its estimated net realizable value. The loss is reflected in cost of goods sold. However, if a **perpetual** system is used, the following entry would be made:

Inventory of damaged goods (2 × $140)	280	
Loss on damaged goods (an expense) ($600 − $280)	320	
Inventory (2 × $300)		600

The perpetual inventory record also would be changed to show this entry.[9]

---

[8] In contrast, if the replacement cost had increased to $500 each, there would have been a **holding gain** of 10 units × $50 = $500. Generally accepted accounting principles do not permit recognition of holding gains because revenue is recognized only at date of sale of the goods. Because of the unfavorable connotations, holding gains are called windfall profits in the political arena.

[9] The subsequent entries may be as follows:

a. To record actual repair costs of $25:

Inventory of damaged goods	25	
Cash		25

Estimating Ending Inventory and Cost of Goods Sold

When a periodic **inventory system** is used, a physical inventory count must be taken to determine the amount of the ending inventory. Taking a physical inventory is a time-consuming task in many businesses. Therefore, physical inventories often are taken only once a year. Nevertheless, managers may want financial statements for internal use on a monthly or a quarterly basis. When a periodic inventory system is used, some businesses **estimate** the ending inventory for the monthly or quarterly financial statements rather than taking a physical inventory. The **gross margin method** is used for this purpose. The method uses an **estimated gross margin ratio** as the basis for the computation.

The gross margin ratio is computed by dividing the gross margin amount by net sales revenue. The gross margin method assumes that the **gross margin ratio** for the current period should be the same as it was in the recent past. Therefore, the average gross margin ratio from one or more prior periods is used as an estimate of the ratio for the current period. This estimated ratio then can be used to compute **estimated amounts** for (1) gross margin on sales, (2) cost of goods sold, and (3) ending inventory.

Patz Company uses the periodic inventory system and is preparing **monthly** financial statements at January 31, 19D. The accounting records give the following data:

PATZ COMPANY
Income Statement
For the Month Ended January 31, 19D

Sales revenue		$100,000*
Cost of goods sold:		
Beginning inventory	$15,000*	
Add purchases	65,000*	
Goods available for sale	80,000	
Less ending inventory	?	
Gross margin on sales		?
Expenses		30,000*
Pretax income		$?

    * Provided by the accounts.

The January ending inventory is to be **estimated** rather than determined by physical count. The yearly net sales for 19C amounted to $1,000,000, and gross margin was $400,000; therefore, the actual gross margin ratio for 19C was $400,000 ÷ $1,000,000 = 0.40. Management has decided that this ratio is a realistic estimate for use during 19D. Using the 0.40 as our estimate for 19D, we

---

b. To record sale of the two sets for $360 (less actual selling costs of $15):

Cash ($360 − $15)	345	
Selling expense	15	
Inventory ($280 + $25)		305
Gain on sale of damaged goods		55

can compute an **estimated** inventory valuation. The computational steps, in lettered sequence, are shown below:

PATZ COMPANY
Income Statement
For the Month Ended January 31, 19D (estimated)

			Computations (sequence a, b, c)
Sales revenue		$100,000	Per accounts
Cost of goods sold:			
Beginning inventory	$15,000		Per accounts
Add purchases	65,000		Per accounts
Goods available for sale	80,000		
Less ending inventory	20,000		*c.* $ 80,000 − $60,000 = $20,000
Cost of goods sold		60,000	*b.* $100,000 − $40,000 = $60,000*
Gross margin on sales		40,000	*a.* $100,000 × 0.40 = $40,000
Expenses		30,000	Per accounts
Pretax income		$ 10,000	

* Or alternatively, $100,000 × (1.00 − 0.40) = $60,000.

The balance sheet can be completed by reporting the $20,000 estimated ending inventory amount as a current asset.

The gross margin method has other uses. Auditors and accountants may use this method to test the reasonableness of the amount of the inventory determined by other means. If the current gross margin ratio has changed materially from the recent past, it may suggest an error in the ending inventory. The method also is used in the case of a casualty loss when an inventory of goods is destroyed or stolen and its valuation must be estimated for settlement purposes with an insurance company.[10]

DEMONSTRATION CASE A

(Try to resolve the requirements before proceeding to the suggested solution that follows.)

This case focuses on the effects of an error in the amount of the ending inventory. It does not introduce any new accounting concepts or procedures.

Metal Products, Incorporated, has been operating for eight years as a distributor of a line of metal products. It is now the end of 19C, and for the first time the company will undergo an audit by an independent CPA. The company uses

---

[10] Another method, known as the retail inventory method, is used widely to estimate the ending inventory by department stores. It is essentially the same as the gross margin method, but differs in detail. Discussion of it is deferred to more advanced courses.

a **periodic** inventory system. The annual income statements, prepared by the company, were:

| | For the year ended December 31 | |
	19B	19C
Sales revenue	$750,000	$800,000
Cost of goods sold:		
Beginning inventory	45,000	40,000
Add purchases	460,000	484,000
Goods available for sale	505,000	524,000
Less ending inventory	40,000	60,000
Cost of goods sold	465,000	464,000
Gross margin on sales	285,000	336,000
Operating expenses	275,000	306,000
Pretax income	10,000	30,000
Income tax expense (20%)	2,000	6,000
Net income	$ 8,000	$ 24,000

During the early stages of the audit, the independent CPA discovered that the ending inventory for 19B was understated by $15,000.

Required:

a. Based on the above income statement amounts, compute the gross margin ratio on sales for each year. Do the results suggest an inventory error? Explain.
b. Reconstruct the two income statements on a correct basis.
c. Answer the following questions.
   (1) What are the correct gross margin ratios?
   (2) What effect did the $15,000 understatement of the ending inventory have on 19B pretax income? Explain.
   (3) What effect did the inventory error have on 19C pretax income? Explain.
   (4) How did the inventory error affect income tax expense?

Suggested Solution

Requirement a—Gross margin ratios as reported:

$$19B: \$285,000 \div \$750,000 = 0.38$$
$$19C: \$336,000 \div \$800,000 = 0.42$$

The change in the gross margin ratio from 0.38 to 0.42 suggests the possibility of an inventory error in the absence of any other explanation.

Requirement b—Income statements corrected:

| | For the year ended December 31 | |
	19B	19C
Sales revenue	$750,000	$800,000
Cost of goods sold:		
Beginning inventory	45,000	55,000*
Add purchases	460,000	484,000
Goods available for sale	505,000	539,000
Less ending inventory	55,000*	60,000
Cost of goods sold	450,000	479,000
Gross margin on sales	300,000	321,000
Operating expenses	275,000	306,000
Pretax income	25,000	15,000
Income tax expense (20%)	5,000	3,000
Net income	$ 20,000	$ 12,000

* Increased by $15,000.

Requirement c:

1. Correct gross margin ratios:

$$19B: \$300,000 \div \$750,000 = 0.400$$
$$19C: \$321,000 \div \$800,000 = 0.401$$

The inventory error of $15,000 was responsible for the difference in the gross margin ratios reflected in Requirement *(a)*. The error in the 19B ending inventory affected gross margin for both 19B and 19C, in the opposite direction, but by the same amount ($15,000).

2. Effect on pretax income in 19B: **Ending inventory understatement** ($15,000) caused an **understatement of pretax income** by the **same amount.**
3. Effect on pretax income in 19C: Beginning inventory **understatement** (by the same $15,000 since the inventory amount is carried over from the prior period) caused an **overstatement** of pretax income by the same amount.
4. Total income tax expense for 19B and 19C combined was the same ($8,000) regardless of the error. However, there was a shift of $3,000 ($15,000 × 20%) income tax expense from 19B to 19C.

   Observation—An ending inventory error in one year affects pretax income by the amount of the error and in the next year affects pretax income again by the same amount but in the opposite direction.

DEMONSTRATION CASE B

(Try to resolve the requirements before proceeding to the suggested solution that follows.)

This case presents the effects on ending inventory, cost of goods sold, and the related accounting entries of a **periodic** inventory system compared with a **perpetual** inventory system assuming the LIFO inventory costing method is applied in each system.

Balent Appliances distributes a number of high-cost household appliances. One product, microwave ovens, has been selected for case purposes. Assume the following summarized transactions were completed during the accounting period in the order given below (assume all transactions are cash).

	Units	Unit cost
a. Beginning inventory	11	$200
b. Sales (selling, price $420)	8	?
c. Sales returns (can be resold as new)	1	200
d. Purchases	9	220
e. Purchase returns (damaged in shipment)	1	220

Required:

a. Compute the following amounts assuming application of the LIFO inventory costing method:

	Ending inventory		Cost of goods sold	
	Units	Dollars	Units	Dollars
(1) Periodic inventory system (costed at end of period)	___	___	___	___
(2) Perpetual inventory system (costed during period)	___	___	___	___

b. Give the indicated journal entries for transactions (b) through (e) assuming:
   (1) Periodic inventory system.
   (2) Perpetual inventory system.

Suggested Solution

Requirement a:

	Ending inventory		Cost of goods sold	
	Units	Dollars	Units	Dollars
1. Periodic inventory system (costed at end of the period)	12	$2,420	7	$1,540
2. Perpetual inventory system (costed during the period)	12	2,560	7	1,400

Computations:
   Goods available for sale: (11 units × $200 = $2,200) + (8 units × $220 = $1,760) = $3,960.
   1. Periodic LIFO inventory (costed at end):
      Ending inventory: (11 units × $200 = $2,200) + (1 unit × $220 = $220) = $2,420.
      Cost of goods sold: (Goods available, $3,960) − (Ending inventory, $2,420) = $1,540.
   2. Perpetual LIFO inventory (costed during period):
      Ending inventory: (8 units × $220 = $1,760) + (4 units × $200 = $800) = $2,560.
      Cost of goods sold: 7 units × $200 = $1,400.

Requirement b—Journal entries:

1. Periodic Inventory System		2. Perpetual Inventory System	

b. Sales:
    Cash (8 × $420) 3,360
        Sales revenue ....
	
	3,360
		Cash 3,360
		    Sales revenue ....
			
			3,360

		Cost of goods sold .... 1,600 Inventory (8 × $200)	 1,600

c. Sales returns:
    Sales returns 420
        Cash (1 × $420) ....
	
	420
		Sales returns 420
		    Cash ....
			
			420

		Inventory (1 × $200) .... 200 Cost of goods sold	 200

d. Purchases:
    Purchases 1,980
        Cash (9 × $220) ....
	
	1,980
		Inventory 1,980
		    Cash ....
			
			1,980

e. Purchase return:
    Cash 220
        Purchase returns ....
	
	220
		Cash 220
		    Inventory ....
			
			220

SUMMARY OF CHAPTER

This chapter focused on the problem of measuring cost of goods sold and ending inventory when unt costs change during the period. Inventory should include all the items for resale to which the entity has ownership. Costs flow into inventory when goods are purchased (or manufactured) and flow out (as expense) when the goods are sold or disposed of otherwise. When there are several unit cost amounts representing the inflow of goods for the period, a rational and systematic method must be used to allocate unit cost amounts to the units remaining in inventory and to the units sold (cost of goods sold). The chapter discussed four different inventory costing methods and their applications in both a perpetual and a periodic inventory system. The methods discussed were weighted-average cost, FIFO, LIFO, and specific identification. Each of the inventory costing methods is in conformity with generally accepted accounting principles. The selection of a method of inventory costing is important because it will affect reported income, income tax expense (and hence cash flow), and the inventory valuation reported on the balance sheet. In a period of rising prices, FIFO gives a higher income than does LIFO; in a period of falling prices, the opposite result occurs.

Damaged, obsolete, and deteriorated items in inventory should be assigned a unit cost that represents their current estimated net realizable value. Also, the ending inventory of new items (not damaged, deteriorated, or obsolete) should be measured on the basis of the lower of actual cost or replacement cost (i.e., LCM basis).

This chapter explained another fundamental accounting concept (Exhibit 4–5) known as the comparability quality, which means that all accounting concepts, principles, and measurement approaches should be applied in a consistent manner from period to period.

IMPORTANT TERMS DEFINED IN THIS CHAPTER

Terms (alphabetically)	Key words in definitions of important terms used in chapter	Page reference
Comparability quality	Accounting methods should be consistently applied from one period to the next.	328
Consignments	Goods in possession of a seller but legal title is retained by the supplier.	319
Finished goods inventory	Manufactured goods that are completed and ready for sale.	318
First-in, first-out	Inventory costing method that assumes the oldest units are the first units sold.	324
Gross margin method	Method to estimate ending inventory based on the gross margin ratio.	339
Last-in, first-out	Inventory costing method that assumes the newest units are the first units sold.	325
Lower of cost or market	Departure from cost principle that serves to recognize a "holding" loss when replacement cost drops below cost.	336
Merchandise inventory	Goods held for resale in the ordinary course of business.	318
Moving weighted average	Weighted-average inventory costing method applied in the perpetual inventory system.	331
Net realizable value	Estimated amount to be realized when goods are sold, less repair and disposal costs.	338
Periodic inventory system	Ending inventory and cost of goods sold are determined at the end of the accounting period; a physical inventory count must be taken.	320
Perpetual inventory system	A detailed daily inventory record is updated continuously during the accounting period; provides ending inventory and cost of goods sold.	320
Raw materials inventory	Items acquired for the purpose of processing into finished goods.	318
Specific identification	Inventory costing method that identifies the cost of the specific item that was sold.	325
Weighted average	Inventory costing method used with a periodic inventory system that averages all purchase costs to calculate a weighted-average unit cost on an annual basis.	323
Work in process inventory	Goods in the process of being manufactured that are not yet complete.	318

QUESTIONS

PART A

1. Assume the 19A ending inventory was understated by $100,000. Explain how this error would affect the 19A and 19B pretax income amounts. What would be the effects if the 19A ending inventory were overstated by $100,000 instead of understated?

2. Match the type of inventory with the type of business in the following matrix:

Type of Inventory	Type of Business	
	Trading	Manufacturing
Merchandise		
Finished goods		
Work in process		
Raw materials		

3. Why is inventory an important item to both internal management and external users of financial statements?

4. What are the general guidelines for deciding which items should be included in inventory?

5. In measuring cost of goods sold and inventory, why is passage of ownership an important issue? When does ownership to goods usually pass? Explain.

6. Identify the two parties to a consignment. Which party should include the goods on consignment in inventory? Explain.

7. Explain the application of the cost principle to an item in the ending inventory.

8. When a perpetual inventory system is used, unit costs of the items sold are known at the date of each sale. In contrast, when a periodic inventory system is used, unit costs are known only at the end of the accounting period. Why are these statements correct?

9. The periodic inventory calculation is BI + P − EI = CGS. The perpetual inventory calculation is BI + P − CGS = EI. Explain the significance of the difference between these two calculations.

10. The chapter discussed four inventory costing methods. List the four methods and briefly explain each.

11. The four inventory costing methods may be applied with either a periodic inventory system or a perpetual inventory system. Briefly explain how the methods are applied in each system.

12. Explain how income can be manipulated when the specific identification inventory costing method is used.

13. Contrast the effects of LIFO versus FIFO on reported assets (i.e., the ending inventory) when (a) prices are rising and (b) prices are falling.

14. Contrast the income statement effect of LIFO versus FIFO (i.e., on pretax income) when (a) prices are rising and (b) prices are falling.

15. Contrast the effects of LIFO versus FIFO on cash outflow and inflow.

PART B

16. What is the purpose of a perpetual inventory record? List the four main column headings and briefly explain the purpose of each.

17. When a perpetual inventory system is used, a moving weighted average is used. In contrast, when a periodic inventory system is used, an annual weighted average is used. Explain why the different averages are used.

18. The weighted-average inventory costing method usually produces different results when a perpetual inventory system is used rather than a periodic inventory system. Explain why.

19. Explain briefly application of the LCM concept to the ending inventory and its effect on the income statement and balance sheet when market is lower than cost.

20. When should net realizable value be used in costing an item in the ending inventory?

21. The chapter discussed the gross margin method to estimate inventories. Briefly explain this method and indicate why it is used.

22. Briefly explain the comparability quality. How might it relate to the inventory costing methods?

EXERCISES

PART A

E7–1   (Pair Definition with Terms)

Match the following definitions with the terms by entering the appropriate letter in each space provided.

Terms	*Definitions*
_____ (1) Specific identification	A. Prevents arbitrary changes from one accounting or measurement approach to another from one period to another.
_____ (2) Work in process inventory	
_____ (3) Merchandise inventory	B. Goods held on this basis should be excluded from inventory because legal title still resides with the consignor.
_____ (4) Periodic inventory system	
_____ (5) Last-in, first-out	C. An account reported on the balance sheet as a current asset; represents goods completed in the manufacturing process.
_____ (6) Weighted average	

Terms	*Definitions*

<table>
<tr><td>

_____ (7) Finished goods inventory

_____ (8) Comparability quality

_____ (9) Perpetual inventory system

_____ (10) Gross margin method

_____ (11) First-in, first-out

_____ (12) Net realizable value

_____ (13) Lower of cost or market

_____ (14) Raw materials inventory

_____ (15) Moving weighted average

_____ (16) Consignment

</td><td>

D. An inventory costing method that assumes that those items which have been in inventory the longest are sold first.

E. Uses a ratio derived by dividing the gross margin amount by the net sales revenue to compute estimates for CGS, gross margin on sales, and ending inventory.

F. An inventory method that assumes that the units acquired most recently are sold first.

G. Recognizes a holding loss when replacement cost drops below cost.

H. The inventory of a retailer or wholesaler.

I. An inventory costing method in which a new average unit cost is computed at the time of each new purchase.

J. Estimated selling price of a product in the ordinary course of business, less reasonably predictable costs of completion and disposal.

K. Requires computation of the ending inventory by means of a physical count of the goods remaining on hand; CGS is computed as a residual amount.

L. System that maintains a detailed daily inventory record throughout the period for each item stocked and therefore does not require a physical count at the end of each accounting period.

M. Those items acquired by purchase, growth, or extraction of natural resources for further processing into finished goods.

N. An inventory costing method that may be appropriate for "big ticket" items but may be impractical when unit costs are low and unit costs change frequently.

O. An inventory costing method that weights the number of units purchased and unit costs that prevailed during the period; used in conjunction with a periodic inventory system.

P. An asset that includes the cost of raw materials used, the direct labor incurred in the manufacturing process, and factory overhead costs.

</td></tr>
</table>

E7–2   (Analysis of the Impact of an Inventory Error)

Dallas Corporation prepared the two income statements that follow (simplified for illustrative purposes):

	First quarter 19B	Second quarter 19B
Sales revenue	$11,000	$13,000
Cost of goods sold:		
Beginning inventory	$ 2,000	$ 3,000
Purchases	9,000	10,000
Goods available for sale	11,000	13,000
Ending inventory	3,000	4,000
Cost of goods sold	8,000	9,000
Gross margin	3,000	4,000
Expenses	1,000	1,000
Pretax income	$ 2,000	$ 3,000

During the third quarter it was discovered that the ending inventory for the first quarter should have been $2,500.

Required:

a. What effect did this error have on the combined pretax income of the two quarters? Explain.
b. Did this error affect the EPS amounts for each quarter? Explain.
c. Prepare corrected income statements for each quarter.
d. Set up a schedule that reflects the comparative effects of the correct and incorrect amounts.

E7-3   (Use of a Periodic Inventory System)

Laura Fashions purchased 100 new shirts and recorded a total cost of $2,940 determined as follows:

Invoice cost	$2,000
Less: Cash discount 3%	
Shipping charges	530
Import taxes and duties	110
Interest paid in advance (15%) on $2,000	
borrowed to finance the purchase	300
	$2,940

Give the journal entry(s) to record this purchase assuming a periodic inventory system. Show computations.

E7-4   (Use of the Four Inventory Methods)

The records at the end of January 19B for Olds Company showed the following for a particular kind of merchandise:

Transactions	Units	Total cost
Inventory, December 31, 19A	30	$390
Purchase, January 9, 19B	60	900
Sale, January 11, 19B (at $35 per unit)	50	
Purchase, January 20, 19B	35	490
Sale, January 27, 19B (at $36 per unit)	41	

Required:

Assuming a periodic inventory system, compute the amount of (1) goods available for sale, (2) ending inventory, and (3) cost of goods sold at January 31, 19B, under each of the following inventory costing methods (show computations and round to the nearest dollar):

a. Weighted-average cost.
b. First-in, first-out.
c. Last-in, first-out.
d. Specific identification (assume the sale on January 11 was "identified" with the purchase of January 9, the sale of January 27 was "identified" with the purchase of January 20, and any excess identified with the beginning inventory).

E7-5   (Comparison of Alternative Inventory Methods)

Tower Company uses a periodic inventory system. At the end of the annual accounting period, December 31, 19B, the accounting records provided the following information for Product 2:

Transactions	Units	Unit cost
1. Inventory, December 31, 19A	2,000	$20
For the year 19B:		
2. Purchase, April 11	2,000	22
3. Sale, May 1 (@ $52 each)	3,000	
4. Purchase, June 1	6,000	24
5. Sale, July 3 (@ $53 each)	4,000	
6. Operating expenses (excluding income tax expense), $140,000.		

Required:

a. Prepare a separate income statement through pretax income that details cost of goods sold for:

    Case A—Annual weighted average.

    Case B—FIFO.

    Case C—LIFO.

    Case D—Specific identification assuming two thirds of the first sale was "selected" from the beginning inventory and one third was "selected" from the items purchased on April 11, 19B. The second sale was "selected" from the purchase of June 1, 19B.

    For each case, show the computation of the ending inventory. (Hint: Set up adjacent columns for each case.)

b. For each case, compare the pretax income and the ending inventory amounts. Explain the similarities and differences.

E7–6   **(Comparison of LIFO and FIFO)**

    Use the data given in Exercise 7–4 for this exercise (assume cash transactions and a periodic inventory system).

Required:

a. Compute (1) goods available for sale, (2) cost of goods sold, and (3) ending inventory for Case A—FIFO and Case B—LIFO.

b. In parallel columns, give the journal entries for each purchase and sale transaction, assuming a periodic inventory system is used for each case. Set up captions as follows:

	FIFO		LIFO	
Accounts	Debit	Credit	Debit	Credit

c. Prepare an income statement through gross margin and explain why the FIFO and LIFO ending inventory, cost of goods sold, and gross margin amounts are different.

d. Which inventory costing method may be preferred for income tax purposes? Explain.

E7–7   **(Comparison of Cash Flow and Income Effects of LIFO and FIFO)**

    During January 19B, Ford Company reported sales revenue of $425,000 for the one item stocked. The inventory for December 31, 19A, showed 7,500 units on hand with a cost of $165,000. During January 19B, two purchases of the item were made: the first was for 1,500 units at $24 per unit; and the second was for 7,600 units at $25 each. The periodic inventory count reflected 8,600 units remaining on hand on January 31, 19B. Total operating expense for the month was $84,900.

Required:

a. On the basis of the above information, complete the 19B summary income statements under FIFO and LIFO. Use a single list of side captions including computation of cost of goods sold. Set up three separate column headings as follows: Units, FIFO, and LIFO. Show your computations of the ending inventory.

b. Which method gives the higher pretax income? Why?

c. Which method gives the more favorable cash flow effects? By how much, assuming a 20% tax rate?

E7–8 **(Comparison of Alternative Inventory Methods Using the Periodic Inventory System)**
Luther Company uses a periodic inventory system. Data for 19B were: beginning merchandise inventory (December 31, 19A), 1,600 units @ $15; purchases, 6,000 units @ $18; expenses (excluding income taxes), $51,800; ending inventory per physical count at December 31, 19B, 1,500 units; sales price per unit, $35; and average income tax rate of 25%.

Required:

a. Prepare income statements under the FIFO, LIFO, and weighted-average costing methods. Use a format similar to the following:

| | | | Inventory costing method | |
| | | | | |
Income statement	Units	FIFO	LIFO	Weighted average
Sales revenue	_____	$ _____	$ _____	$ _____
Cost of goods sold:				
Beginning inventory	_____	_____	_____	_____
Purchases	_____	_____	_____	_____
Goods available for sale	_____	_____	_____	_____
Ending inventory	_____	_____	_____	_____
Cost of goods sold	_____	_____	_____	_____
Gross margin	_____	_____	_____	_____
Expenses	_____	_____	_____	_____
Pretax income		_____	_____	_____
Income tax expense		_____	_____	_____
Net income		_____	_____	_____

b. Comparing FIFO and LIFO, which method is preferable in terms of (1) net income and (2) cash flow? Explain.

c. What would be your answer to Requirement *(b)* assuming prices were falling? Explain.

E7–9 **(Analysis of Cash Flow Effects of Alternative Inventory Methods)**
Following is partial information for the income statement of Lime Company under three different inventory costing methods assuming a periodic inventory system:

	FIFO	LIFO	Weighted average
Unit sales price, $30.			
Cost of goods sold:			
Beginning inventory (480 units)	$ 9,600	$ 9,600	$ 9,600
Purchases (520 units)	13,000	13,000	13,000
Goods available for sale			
Ending inventory (530 units)			
Cost of goods sold			
Expenses, $1,200			

Required:

 a. Compute cost of goods sold under the FIFO, LIFO, and weighted-average inventory costing methods.
 b. Prepare an income statement through pretax income for each method.
 c. Rank the three methods in order of favorable cash flow and explain the basis for your ranking.

PART B

E7–10   (Use of FIFO with a Perpetual Inventory System)

United Company uses a perpetual inventory system and FIFO. The inventory records reflected the following for January 19B:

Transactions	Units	Unit cost
Beginning inventory, January 1	80	$1.00
Purchase, January 6	200	1.10
Sale, January 10 (at $2.40 per unit)	110	
Purchase, January 14	100	1.30
Sale, January 29 (at $2.50 per unit)	160	

Required:

 a. Prepare the perpetual inventory record for January.
 b. Give journal entries indicated by the above data for January (assume cash transactions).
 c. Prepare a summary income statement for January through gross margin.

E7–11   (Comparison of Periodic and Perpetual Inventory Systems Using LIFO)

At the end of the accounting period, the inventory records of Egger Company reflected the following:

Transactions (in order of date)	Units	Unit cost
Beginning inventory	500	$10
1. Purchase No. 1	600	12
2. Sale No. 1 (@ $23 per unit)	(700)	
3. Purchase No. 2	800	13
4. Sale No. 2 (@ $25 per unit)	(500)	
Ending inventory	(700)	

Required:

 a. Compute goods available for sale in units and dollars.
 b. Compute the (1) ending inventory valuation and (2) cost of goods sold assuming a periodic inventory system under the LIFO inventory costing method.
 c. For comparative purposes compute the (1) ending inventory valuation and (2) cost of goods sold assuming a perpetual inventory system under the LIFO inventory costing method. To do this prepare a perpetual inventory record and cost each sale when made. See Exhibit 7–4 for an example of a perpetual inventory record.
 d. Compare the results of *(b)* and *(c)* and explain why the valuations of ending inventory and cost of goods sold are different as between the periodic and perpetual inventory systems.

E7–12   (Analysis of the Moving Weighted Average Cost Inventory Method)
Use the data given in Exercise 7–4 for this exercise (assume cash transactions).

Required:

a. Prepare the perpetual inventory record for January on a moving weighted average basis. Round to the nearest cent on unit costs and the nearest dollar on total cost. See Exhibit 7–5 for an example of a perpetual inventory record.
b. Give the journal entry to record the purchase of January 9.
c. Give the journal entries to record the sale on January 11.
d. Prepare a summarized income statement through gross margin for January.
e. Explain why a moving weighted average rather than a weighted average for the period was used.
f. When the weighted average cost method is used, would the ending inventory and cost of goods sold amounts usually be different between periodic and perpetual inventory systems? Explain why.

E7–13   (Comparison of FIFO, Periodic and FIFO, Perpetual)
Fairfield Company uses a perpetual inventory system and applies FIFO inventory costing. The data below were provided by the accounting records for 19B:

Transactions (in order of date)	Units	Unit cost	Total cost
Beginning inventory	125	$10	$1,250
1. Purchase No. 1	300	12	3,600
2. Sale No. 1 (@ $21 each)	(275)		
3. Purchase No. 2	400	14	5,600
4. Sale No. 2 (@ $23 each)	(200)		
Ending inventory	350		

Required:

a. Compute the valuation of (1) cost of goods sold and (2) ending inventory assuming a perpetual inventory system and application of the FIFO inventory costing method.
b. Give the journal entries to record transactions 1 and 2 assuming FIFO:

   Case A—A perpetual inventory system.

   Case B—A periodic inventory system.

   Use adjacent amount columns for each system and assume cash transactions.
c. Explain why the journal entries are different between the perpetual and periodic inventory systems.

E7–14   (Accounting for Damaged Goods under a Perpetual Inventory System)
Contemporary Sound Company is preparing the annual financial statements at December 31, 19D. Two different types of tape recorders that were used as demonstrators remained on hand at year-end. These items will be sold as damaged (used) merchandise; therefore, they must be removed from the ending inventory of new merchandise. The company uses a perpetual inventory system. These items will be included in the inventory of damaged goods. Data on the tape recorder models are:

	Model 2—206	Model 112A
Quantity damaged	1	2
Actual unit cost	$400	$300
Regular sales price	700	500
Estimated unit market value in present condition	380	250
Estimated unit cost to sell	80	35

Required:

a. Compute the valuation of each item that should be used for 19D inventory purposes. Show computations.
b. Give the required journal entry(s) to reflect the appropriate inventory valuations in the accounts.

E7–15   (Alternative Applications of LCM)

Anderson Company is preparing the annual financial statements dated December 31, 19B. Ending inventory information about the five major items stocked for regular sale is:

Ending inventory, 19B

Item	Quantity on hand	Unit cost when acquired (FIFO)	Replacement cost (market) at year-end
A ...	50	$20	$18
B ...	100	45	45
C ...	20	60	62
D ...	40	40	40
E ...	500	10	8

Required:

a. Compute the valuation that should be used for the 19B ending inventory using the LCM rule applied on an item-by-item basis. (Hint: Set up columns for Item, Quantity, Total cost, Total market, and LCM valuation).
b. Compute the valuation of ending inventory using the LCM rule applied to total cost and total market value of the inventory.
c. Which method (a) or (b) is preferable? Why?

E7–16   (Estimating Ending Inventory)

Reston Retail Company prepares annual financial statements each December 31. The company uses a periodic inventory system. This system requires an annual detailed inventory count of all items on the store shelves and items stored in a separate warehouse. However, the management also desires quarterly financial statements but will not take a physical inventory count four times during the year. Accordingly, they use the gross margin method to estimate the ending inventory for the first three quarters.

At the end of the first quarter, March 31, 19D, the accounting records provided the following information:

1. Beginning inventory, January 1, 19D	$ 60,000

Data for the first quarter of 19D:

2. Sales revenue	405,000
3. Sales returns	5,000
4. Purchases	296,000
5. Freight-in	4,000
6. Operating expenses (excluding income tax expense)	50,000

7. Estimated average income tax rate, 20%.
8. Estimated gross margin ratio, 30%.

Required:

Based on the above information prepare a detailed income statement for the first quarter of 19D. Show all computations.

E7–17 (Estimating Inventory Based on Partial Records)

On November 2, 19C, a fire destroyed the inventory of College Book Store. The accounting records were not destroyed; therefore, they provided the following information:

	19A	19B	19C to date of fire
Sales revenue	$120,000	$142,000	$120,000
Cost of goods sold	73,200	85,200	?
Gross margin on sales	46,800	56,800	?
Expenses	34,800	42,800	35,000
Pretax income	$ 12,000	$ 14,000	?
Ending inventory	$ 20,000	$ 22,000	?
Purchases during year	70,000	87,200	75,000

Required:

a. Based on the data available, prepare an estimated income statement for 19C up to the date of the fire. Show details for the cost of goods sold. Disregard income taxes and show computations.

b. What amount of loss on the inventory should be submitted to the insurance company (a casualty loss insurance policy is in effect)? Write a brief statement in support of the amount of indemnity claimed.

PROBLEMS

PART A

P7–1 (Analysis and Correction of an Error in Ending Inventory)

The income statement for Pitts Company summarized for a four-year period shows the following:

	19A	19B	19C	19D
Sales revenue	$1,000,000	$1,200,000	$1,300,000	$1,100,000
Cost of goods sold	600,000	610,000	870,000	650,000
Gross margin	400,000	590,000	430,000	450,000
Expenses	300,000	328,000	362,000	317,000
Pretax income	100,000	262,000	68,000	133,000
Income tax expense (30%)	30,000	78,600	20,400	39,900
Net income	$ 70,000	$ 183,400	$ 47,600	$ 93,100

An audit revealed that in determining the above amounts, the ending inventory for 19B was overstated by $30,000. The company uses a periodic inventory system.

Required:

a. Recast the above income statements on a correct basis.
b. Did the error affect cumulative net income for the four-year period? Explain.
c. Did the error affect cash inflows or outflows? Explain.

P7–2   **(Analysis of Possible Inventory Errors)**

Monroe Company has just completed a physical inventory count at year-end, December 31, 19B. Only the items on the shelves, in storage, and in the receiving area were counted and costed on a FIFO basis. The inventory amounted to $90,000. During the audit, the independent CPA developed the following additional information:

a. Goods costing $400 were being used by a customer on a trial basis and were excluded from the inventory count at December 31, 19B.
b. Goods in transit on December 31, 19B, from a supplier, with terms FOB destination, cost, $700. Because these goods had not arrived, they were excluded from the physical inventory count.
c. On December 31, 19B, goods in transit to customers, with terms FOB shipping point, amounted to $900 (expected delivery date January 10, 19C). Because the goods had been shipped, they were excluded from the physical inventory count.
d. On December 28, 19B, a customer purchased goods for cash amounting to $1,500 and left them "for pickup on January 3, 19C." Monroe Company had paid $800 for the goods and, because they were on hand, included the latter amount in the physical inventory count.
e. Monroe Company, on the date of the inventory, received notice from a supplier that goods ordered earlier, at a cost of $2,400, had been delivered to the transportation company on December 27, 19B; the terms were FOB shipping point. Because the shipment had not arrived by December 31, 19B, it was excluded from the physical inventory.
f. On December 31, 19B, Monroe Company shipped $750 worth of goods to a customer, FOB destination. The goods are expected to arrive at their destination no earlier than January 8, 19C. Because the goods were not on hand, they were not included in the physical inventory count.
g. One of the items sold by Monroe Company has such a low volume that the management planned to drop it last year. In order to induce Monroe Company to continue carrying the item, the manufacturer-supplier provided the item on a consignment basis. At the end of each month, Monroe Company (the consignee) renders a report to the manufacturer on the number sold and remits cash for the cost. At the end of December 19B, Monroe Company had five of these items on hand; therefore, they were included in the physical inventory count at $2,000 each.

Required:

Begin with the $90,000 inventory amount and compute the correct amount for the ending inventory. Explain the basis for your treatment of each of the above items. (Hint: The correct amount is $82,750. Set up three columns: Item, Amount, and Explanation.)

P7–3   **(Use of Four Alternative Inventory Methods with the Periodic System)**

Ross Company uses a periodic inventory system. At the end of the annual accounting period, December 31, 19E, the accounting records for the most popular item in inventory showed:

Transactions	Units	Unit cost
Beginning inventory, January 1, 19E	300	$20
Transactions during 19E:		
1. Purchase, February 20	500	22
2. Sale, April 1 (@ $40 each)	(600)	
3. Purchase, June 30	400	24
4. Sale, August 1 (@ $40 each)	(200)	
5. Sales return, August 5, (related to transaction 4)	10	

Required:

Compute the amount of (1) goods available for sale, (2) ending inventory, and (3) cost of goods sold at Deceember 31, 19E, under each of the following inventory costing methods (show computations and round to the nearest dollar):

a. Weighted-average cost.

b. First-in, first-out.

c. Last-in, first-out.

d. Specific identification, assuming the April 1, 19E, sale was "selected" one third from the beginning inventory and two thirds from the purchase of February 20, 19E. Assume the sale of August 1, 19E, was "selected" from the purchase of June 30, 19E.

P7–4   (Analysis and Use of Alternative Inventory Methods)

At the end of January 19B, the records at Chicago Company showed the following for a particular item that sold at $20 per unit:

Transactions	Units	Amount
Inventory, January 1, 19B	700	$4,200
Sale, January 10	(600)	
Purchase, January 12	600	4,200
Sale, January 17	(550)	
Purchase, January 26	310	2,790
Purchase return, January 28	(10)	Out of Jan. 26 purchase

Required:

a. Assuming a periodic inventory system, prepare a summarized income statement through gross margin on sales under each method of inventory: (1) weighted-average cost, (2) FIFO, (3) LIFO, and (4) specific identification. For specific identification, assume the first sale was out of the beginning inventory and the second sale was out of the January 12 purchase. Show the inventory computations in detail.

b. Between FIFO and LIFO, which method will derive the higher pretax income? Which would derive the higher EPS?

c. Between FIFO and LIFO, which method will derive the lower income tax expense? Explain, assuming a 20% average tax rate.

d. Between FIFO and LIFO, which method will produce the more favorable cash flow? Explain.

P7–5   (Manipulation of Income Under the LIFO Inventory Method)

Import Company sells large computers that it acquires from a foreign source. During the year 19W, the inventory records reflected the following:

	Units	Unit cost	Total cost
Beginning inventory	20	$25,000	$500,000
Purchases	30	20,000	600,000
Sales (35 units @ $45,000)			

The company uses the LIFO inventory costing method. On December 28, 19W, the unit cost of the computer was decreased to $18,000. The cost will be decreased again during the first quarter of the next year.

Required:

a. Complete the following income statement summary using the LIFO method and the periodic inventory system (show computations):

Sales revenue .... $ _____
Cost of goods sold .... _____
Gross margin .... _____
Expenses 300,000
Pretax income .... $_____
Ending inventory .... $_____

b. The management, for various reasons, is considering buying 20 additional units before December 31, 19W, at $18,000 each. Restate the above income statement (and ending inventory) assuming this purchase is made on December 31, 19W.
c. How much did pretax income change because of the decision on December 31, 19W? Is there any evidence of income manipulation? Explain.

P7–6   (Change in Inventory Method from FIFO to LIFO)

Quick Stop Corporation reported the following summarized annual data at the end of 19X:

	(millions)
Sales revenue	$950
Cost of goods sold*	500
Gross margin	450
Expenses	200
Pretax income	$250

* Based on ending FIFO inventory of $150 million. On a LIFO basis this ending inventory would have been $80 million.

Before issuing the preceding statement the company decided to change from FIFO to LIFO for 19X because "it better reflects our operating results." The company has always used FIFO.

Required:

a. Restate the summary income statement on a LIFO basis.
b. How much did pretax income change due to the LIFO decision for 19X? What caused the change in pretax income?
c. If you were a stockholder, what would be your reaction to this change? Explain.

P7-7   **(Comparison of LIFO and FIFO when Costs Are Rising and Falling)**
Income to be evaluated under four different situations as follows:

Prices are rising:
    Situation A—FIFO is used.
    Situation B—LIFO is used.
Prices are falling:
    Situation C—FIFO is used.
    Situation D—LIFO is used.

The basic data common to all four situations are sales, 600 units for $5,600; beginning inventory, 500 units; purchases, 500 units; ending inventory, 400 units; and operating expenses, $3,000. The following tabulated income statements for each situation have been set up for analytical purposes:

	Prices rising		Prices falling	
	Situation A FIFO	Situation B LIFO	Situation C FIFO	Situation D LIFO
Sales revenue	$5,600	$5,600	$5,600	$5,600
Cost of goods sold:				
Beginning inventory	1,000	?	?	?
Purchases	1,500	?	?	?
Goods available for sale	2,500	?	?	?
Ending inventory	1,200	?	?	?
Cost of goods sold	1,300	?	?	?
Gross margin	4,300	?	?	?
Expenses	3,000	3,000	3,000	3,000
Pretax income	1,300	?	?	?
Income tax expense (30%)	390	?	?	?
Net income	$ 910			

Required:

a. Complete the above tabulation for each situation. In Situations A and B (prices rising), assume the following: beginning inventory, 500 units @ $2 = $1,000; and purchases, 500 units @ $3 = $1,500. In Situations C and D (prices falling), assume the opposite; that is, beginning inventory, 500 units @ $3 = $1,500; and purchases, 500 units @ $2 = $1,000. Use periodic inventory procedures.
b. Analyze the relative effects on pretax income and on net income as demonstrated by Requirement (a) when prices are rising and when prices are falling.
c. Analyze the relative effects on the cash position for each situation.
d. Would you recommend FIFO or LIFO? Explain.

PART B

P7-8   **(Analysis of Inventory Errors)**
The income statements for four consecutive years for Clark Company reflected the following summarized amounts:

	19A	19B	19C	19D
Sales revenue	$60,000	$60,000	$78,000	$65,000
Cost of goods sold	36,000	38,300	50,100	39,000
Gross margin	24,000	21,700	27,900	26,000
Expenses	15,000	16,700	17,200	15,800
Pretax income	$ 9,000	$ 5,000	$10,700	$10,200

Subsequent to development of the above amounts, it has been determined that the physical inventory taken on December 31, 19B, was understated by $4,000.

Required:

a. Recast the above income statements to reflect the correct amounts, taking into consideration the inventory error.

b. Compute the gross margin ratio for each year (1) before the correction and (2) after the correction. Do the results lend confidence to your corrected amounts? Explain.

c. What effect would the error have had on the income tax expense assuming a 20% average rate?

P7–9   (Analysis of the Effects of Damaged Goods in Inventory)

Washington Company has completed taking the periodic inventory count of merchandise remaining on hand at the end of the fiscal year, December 31, 19D. Questions have arisen concerning inventory costing for five different items. The inventory reflected the following:

	Units	Original unit cost
Item A—The two units on hand are damaged because they were used as demonstrators. The company estimated that they may be sold at 20% below cost and that disposal costs will amount to $60 each.	2	$260
Item B—Because of a drop in the market, this item can be replaced from the original supplier at 10% below the original cost. The sale price also was reduced.	20	70
Item C—Because of style change, it is highly doubtful that the four units can be sold; they have no scrap value.	4	20
Item D—This item no longer will be stocked; as a consequence it will be marked down from the regular sale price of $110 to $50. Cost of selling is estimated to be 20% of the original cost.	3	80
Item E—Because of high demand and quality, the cost of this item has been raised from $120 to $125; hence, all replacements for inventory in the foreseeable future will be at the latter price.	15	120

The remaining items in inventory pose no valuation problems: their costs sum to $50,000.

Required:

Compute the total amount of the ending inventory including the damaged goods. List each of the above items separately and explain the basis for your decision with respect to each item.

P7–10   (Comparison of LIFO and FIFO Using a Perpetual Inventory System)

Waco Hardware Store uses a perpetual inventory system. This problem will focus on one item stocked, designated at Item A. The beginning inventory was 2,000 units @ $4. During January, the following transactions occurred that affected Item A:

Jan 5. Sold 500 units at $10 per unit.
   10 Purchased 1,000 units at $5 per unit.
   16 Sold 1,800 units at $12 per unit.
   18 Purchased 2,300 units for $13,800.
   24 Sold 500 units at $12 per unit.

Required (assume cash transactions):

a. Prepare a perpetual inventory record for January on (1) a FIFO basis and (2) a LIFO basis.
b. Give the journal entry for each basis for the purchase on January 10.
c. Give the journal entries for each basis for the sale on January 16.
d. Complete the following financial statement amounts for each basis:

	January	
	FIFO	LIFO
Income statement:		
Sales revenue	$?	$?
Cost of goods sold	?	?
Gross margin	?	?
Expenses	12,000	12,000
Pretax income	?	?
Balance sheet:		
Current assets:		
Merchandise inventory	?	?

e. Which method gives the higher pretax income? Under what conditions would this comparative effect be the opposite?
f. Assuming a 20% average tax rate, which method would provide the more favorable cash position? By how much? Explain.
g. Which basis would you recommend for Waco? Why?

P7–11   **(Use of a Perpetual Inventory Record)**
Box Elder Company uses a perpetual inventory system. Below is a perpetual inventory record for the period for one product sold at $6 per unit.

PERPETUAL INVENTORY RECORD

Date								
a.						400		1,200
b.	800	3.30				1,200		
c.			500		1,600	700		2,240
d.	300		1,050					3,290
e.			200			800		2,632
f.			600		1,974	200		
g.	500	3.60						

Required:

1. Complete the column captions for the perpetual inventory record.
2. What inventory costing method is being used?
3. Enter all of the missing amounts on the perpetual inventory records.
4. Complete the following tabulation:

	Units	Per unit	Amount
a. Beginning inventory	_____	_____	_____
b. Ending inventory	_____	_____	_____
c. Total purchases	_____	_____	_____
d. Total cost of goods sold	_____	_____	_____

5. Give the journal entry(s) for date *(b)*.
6. Give the journal entry(s) for date *(c)*.
7. Assume a periodic inventory taken at the end of the period reflected 490 units on hand. Give any journal entry(s) required.
8. Disregard Requirement 7 and assume that on date *(h)*, 10 units of the beginning inventory were returned to the supplier and a cash refund of $2.90 per unit was recovered. Give the required entry.

P7–12   (Comparison of FIFO and LIFO Using a Perpetual Inventory System)
Super Company executives are considering their inventory policies. They have been using the moving weighted average method with a perpetual inventory system. They have requested an "analysis of the effects of using FIFO versus LIFO." Selected financial statement amounts (rounded) for the month of January 19B, based upon the moving weighted average method, are as follows:

	Units	Amounts
Income statement:		
Sales revenue	180	$10,600
Cost of goods sold	180	5,710
Gross margin on sales		4,890
Less: Expenses		2,000
Pretax income		$ 2,890
Balance sheet:		
Merchandise inventory		$ 2,620

Transactions during the month were:

Beginning inventory 50 units @ $30.

Jan. 6 Sold 40 units @ $55.
    9 Purchased 100 units @ $32.
  16 Sold 80 units @ $60.
  20 Purchased 110 units @ $33.
  28 Sold 60 units @ $60.

Required:

a. Copy the above statement data and extend each item to the right by adding columns for FIFO and LIFO using a perpetual inventory system. This statement will provide one basis for analyzing the different results among the three inventory costing methods.

b. Which inventory costing method produces the highest pretax income? Explain.

c. Between FIFO and LIFO, which inventory costing method provides the more favorable cash position for 19B? Explain.

P7-13   **(Use of LCM under the Periodic Inventory System)**

Durwin Company prepared their annual financial statements dated December 31, 19B. The company uses a periodic inventory system and applies the FIFO inventory costing method; however, the company neglected to apply LCM to the ending inventory. The preliminary 19B income statement is summarized below:

Sales revenue		$310,000
Cost of goods sold:		
Beginning inventory	$ 40,000	
Purchases	206,000	
Goods available for sale	246,000	
Ending inventory (FIFO cost)	50,000	
Cost of goods sold		196,000
Gross margin		114,000
Operating expenses		58,000
Pretax income		56,000
Income tax expense (30%)		16,800
Net income		$ 39,200

Assume you have been asked to restate the 19B financial statements to incorporate LCM. You have developed the following data relating to the 19B ending inventory:

Item	Quantity	Acquisition cost Unit	Acquisition cost Total	Current replacement unit cost (market)
A	2,000	$ 2	$ 4,000	$ 4
B	3,000	6	18,000	5
C	4,000	4	16,000	5
D	1,000	12	12,000	10
			$50,000	

Required:

a. Restate the above income statement to reflect LCM valuation of the 19B ending inventory. Apply LCM on an item-by-item basis and show computations.

b. Compare and explain the LCM effect on each amount that was changed in (a).

c. What is the conceptual basis for applying LCM to merchandise inventories?

d. Thought question: What effect did LCM have on the cash flow of 19B? What will be the long-term effect on cash flow?

P7-14   **(Estimating the Amount of Inventory Damaged in a Flood for Insurance Purposes)**

On April 15, 19B, North Sea Company suffered a major flood that damaged their entire merchandise inventory. Fortunately, North Sea carried a casualty insurance policy that covered floods. The company uses the periodic inventory system. The accounting records were not damaged; therefore, they provided the following information for the period January 1 through April 14, 19B:

Merchandise inventory,
December 31, 19A .... $ 21,000

Transactions through April 14, 19B:
Purchases   70,000
Purchase returns   2,000
Freight-in   1,000
Sales 103,000
Sales returns   3,000

Required:

For insurance indemnity purposes you have been asked to estimate the amount of the inventory loss. Your analysis to date indicates that *(a)* a 30% gross margin rate is reasonable and *(b)* the damaged merchandise can be sold to a local salvage company for approximately $4,000 cash.

What amount should be presented to the insurance company as a claim for insurance indemnity? Show computations.

P7–15   (Preparing an Interim Income Statement without Taking an Inventory Count)

The president of ET Company has been presented with the March 19B financial statements. They reflect data for three months as summarzied below:

	January	*February*	*March*	*Quarter*
Sales revenue	$100,000	$106,000	$90,000	$296,000
Cost of goods sold	61,000	59,360	?	?
Gross margin on sales	39,000	46,640	?	?
Expenses	32,000	33,500	32,000	97,500
Pretax income	$ 7,000	$ 13,140	$?	$?
Gross margin ratio	.39	.44	.42 (estimated)	
Ending inventory	$ 14,000	$ 16,000		

Income statements

The company uses a periodic inventory system. Although monthly statements are prepared, a monthly inventory count is not made. Instead, the company uses the gross margin method for monthly inventory purposes.

Required:

a. Complete computations in the following tabulation to estimate the results for March.

	Amounts	*Computations*
Cost of goods sold:		
Beginning inventory	$16,000	From records
Purchases	51,000	From records
Goods available for sale	?	?
Ending inventory	?	?
Cost of goods sold	?	

b. Complete the income statements given above (March and Quarter). Disregard income tax.

c. What level of confidence do you think can be attributed to the results for March? Explain.

d. Would you recommend continued use of the gross margin method for the company? Explain.

CASES

C7–1   **(Analysis of the Effects of a Reduction in the Amount of LIFO Inventory)**
An annual report of Standard Oil Company (Indiana) contained the following footnote:

> During both 1981 and 1980, the company reduced certain inventory quantities which were valued at lower LIFO costs prevailing in prior years. The effect of these reductions was to increase aftertax earnings by $71 million, or $.24 per share, and $74 million, or a $.25 per share, in 1981 and 1980 respectively.

Required:

a. Explain why the reduction in inventory quantity increased aftertax earnings (net income) for Standard Oil.
b. If Standard Oil had used FIFO, would the reductions in inventory quantity in 1980 and 1981 have increased aftertax earnings? Explain.

C7–2   **(Analysis of the Effect of an Inventory Error Disclosed in an Actual Note to a Financial Statement)**
Several years ago, the financial statements of Lafayette Radio Electronics Corporation contained the following footnote:

> Subsequent to the issuance of its financial statements, the company discovered a computational error in the amount of $1,046,000 in the calculation of its year-end inventory which resulted in an overstatement of ending inventory.

Assume that Lafayette reported an incorrect net income amount of $3,101,000 for the year in which the error occurred and that the income tax rate is 40%.

Required:

a. Compute the amount of net income that Lafayette should report after correcting the inventory error. Show computations.
b. Assume that the inventory error had not been discovered. Identify the financial statement accounts that would have been incorrect for the year the error occurred and for the subsequent year. State whether each account was understated or overstated.

C7–3   **(Analysis of LIFO and FIFO Based on an Actual Note to the Financial Statements)**
An annual report for General Motors Corporation included the following footnote:

> Inventories are stated generally at cost, which is not in excess of market. The cost of substantially all domestic inventories was determined by the last-in, first-out (LIFO) method. If the first-in, first-out (FIFO) method of inventory valuation had been used by the Corporation for U.S. inventories, it is estimated they would be $2,077.1 million higher at December 31, 1981, compared with $1,784.5 million higher at December 31, 1980.

In 1981, GM reported net income (after taxes) of $320.5 million. On December 31, 1981, the balance of the GM retained earnings account was $15,340 million.

Required:

a. Determine the amount of net income that GM would have reported in 1981 if the FIFO method had been used (assume a 48% tax rate).

b. Determine the amount of retained earnings that GM would have reported on December 31, 1981, if the FIFO method had always been used (assume a 48% tax rate).

c. Use of the LIFO method reduced the amount of taxes that GM had to pay for 1981 compared with the amount that would have been paid if FIFO had been used. Calculate the amount of this reduction (assume a 48% tax rate).

C7–4   (Analysis of Inventory and Cost of Goods Sold Using an Actual Financial Statement)
Refer to the financial statements of Chesebrough-Pond's given in Special Supplement B immediately preceding the Index.

Required:

a. What method does Chesebrough-Pond's use to determine the cost of its inventory?

b. Total inventory was $657,498,000 in 1985. What amount of inventory was finished goods (as opposed to raw materials and work in process)?

c. If the company had used FIFO for all of its inventory would net income have been higher or lower? If it cannot be determined, explain why.

d. What was the cost of goods sold for the first quarter of 1985?

This chapter discusses accounting for cash, marketable securities, and accounts receivable. These are the most liquid of the current assets.

GENERAL ELECTRIC

ASSETS

Cash (note 8)	$ 2,194	$ 2,219
Marketable securities (note 8)	393	252
Current receivables (note 9)	4,740	4,872
Inventories (note 10)	3,029	3,461
Current assets	10,356	10,804

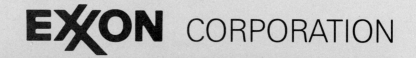

ASSETS

Current assets		
Cash, including time deposits of $1,922,987,000 and $1,474,938,000	$1,279,367,000	$2,216,262,000
Marketable securities	1,404,154,000	1,232,478,000
Notes and accounts receivable, less estimated doubtful amounts of $145,828,000 and $161,222,000	9,664,888,000	8,366,098,000
Inventories		
Crude oil, products and merchandise	5,573,689,000	3,798,532,000
Materials and supplies	1,611,438,000	1,737,689,000
Prepaid taxes and expenses	2,508,712,000	2,441,627,000
Total current assets	23,242,248,000	19,792,686,000

CASH, SHORT-TERM INVESTMENTS IN SECURITIES, AND RECEIVABLES

PURPOSE:

The discussions in the two preceding chapters have focused primarily on the income statement. In this chapter, the focus will shift to the balance sheet. Our discussion of balance sheet classifications will begin with the most liquid (or current) assets: cash, short-term investments, and receivables. In the previous chapter, we discussed accounting for another important current asset, inventories.

ORGANIZATION:

Part A—Safeguarding and Reporting Cash

1. Internal control of cash.
2. Bank reconciliation.

Part B—Measuring and Reporting Short-Term Investments

1. Definition of short-term investments.
2. Lower of cost or market rule.

Part C—Measuring and Reporting Receivables

1. Classification of receivables.
2. Interest on receivables.

LEARNING OBJECTIVES—TO BE ABLE TO:

1. Identify internal control procedures for cash.
2. Perform a bank reconciliation.
3. Apply the lower of cost or market rule to short-term investments.
4. Calculate interest on receivables.
5. Account for a discounted note receivable.
6. Apply the materiality concept.
7. Expand your accounting vocabulary by learning about the "Important Terms Defined in this Chapter" (page 408).
8. Apply the knowledge gained from this chapter by completing the homework assigned by your instructor.

PART A—SAFEGUARDING AND REPORTING CASH

CASH DEFINED

Cash is defined as money and any instrument that banks will accept for deposit and immediate credit to the depositor's account, such as a check, money order, or bank draft. Cash **excludes** such items as notes receivable, IOUs, and postage stamps (a prepaid expense). Cash usually is divided into three categories: cash on hand, cash deposited in banks, and other instruments that meet the definition of cash. All cash accounts are combined as one amount for financial reporting purposes, even though a company may have several bank accounts.

Many businesses receive a large amount of cash from their customers each day. Cash can be spent by anyone, so management must develop procedures to safeguard the cash that is used in the business. Effective cash management involves more than protecting cash from theft, fraud, or loss through carelessness. Other cash management responsibilities are:

1. Accurate accounting so that relevant reports of cash inflows, outflows, and balances may be prepared periodically.
2. Control to assure that enough cash is on hand to meet (a) current operating needs, (b) maturing liabilities, and (c) unexpected emergencies.
3. Planning to prevent excess amounts of idle cash from accumulating. Idle cash produces no revenue; therefore, it often is invested in securities to get a return (i.e., revenue) pending future need for the cash.

INTERNAL CONTROL OF CASH

Internal control refers to those policies and procedures of an entity designed to safeguard all of the **assets** of the enterprise. Internal control procedures should extend to all assets—cash, receivables, investments, operational assets, and so on.

Because cash is the asset most vulnerable to theft and fraud, a significant number of internal control procedures should focus on cash. You have already observed internal control procedures for cash, although you may not have known it at the time. At most movie theaters, one employee sells tickets and another employee collects the tickets. It would be less expensive to have one employee do both jobs, but it would be easier for an employee to steal cash.

Effective internal control of cash should include:

Separation of functions and routines:

1. Complete separation of the **functions** of receiving cash from disbursing cash.
2. Complete separation of the **procedures** for cash receipts from cash disbursements.

3. Complete separation of *(a)* the **physical** handling of cash from *(b)* all phases of the **accounting** function.
4. Require that all cash receipts be deposited in a bank daily. Keep any cash held on hand (for making change) under strict control.
5. Require that all cash payments be made by prenumbered checks with a separate approval of the expenditures and separate approval of the checks in payment.

Responsibilities assigned to individuals:

6. Assign the cash receiving and cash paying responsibilities to different individuals.
7. Assign the cash handling and cash recordkeeping responsibilities to different individuals.
8. Assign the cash payment approval and check signing responsibilities to different individuals.
9. Assign responsibilities for the cash function and the accounting function to different individuals.

The separation of individual responsibilities and the use of prescribed policies and procedures are important phases in the control of cash. Separation of duties and responsibilities deters theft because collusion would be needed among two or more persons to steal cash and then conceal the theft in the accounting records. Prescribed procedures are designed so that the work done by one individual is checked by the results reported by other individuals.

To show how easy it is to hide cash theft when internal control is lacking, two examples are provided:

Case 1—An employee handles both cash receipts and the recordkeeping. Cash amounting to $100 was collected from J. Doe in payment of an account receivable. An employee pocketed the cash and made an entry for $100 crediting Accounts Receivable (J. Doe) and debiting Allowance for Doubtful Accounts.

Case 2—Occasionally an employee with cash payment authority would send a fictitious purchase invoice through the system. The check, payable to a fictitious person, was not mailed but was cashed by the employee.

In each case, the accounting records did not reveal the theft. Also, the financial statements did not provide any evidence that theft had occurred. The thefts could have been prevented with simple internal control procedures.

All cash disbursements should be made with prenumbered checks. Cash payments should involve separate routines and responsibilities specified for (1) payment approvals, (2) check preparation, and (3) check signing. When procedures similar to these are followed, it is difficult to conceal a fraudulent cash disbursement without the collusion of two or more persons. The level of internal control, which is reviewed by the outside independent auditor, increases the reliability of the financial statements of the business.

BANK STATEMENTS TO DEPOSITORS

Proper use of the bank accounts of a business can be an important internal control procedure for cash. When a business opens a bank account, a **signature card** is completed. The card shows the names and signatures of the persons authorized to sign checks drawn against the account. By authorizing a minimum number of individuals to sign checks, a business gains important internal control over its bank accounts.

Each month, the bank provides the depositor with a **bank statement** that lists (1) each deposit recorded by the bank during the period, (2) each check cleared by the bank during the period, and (3) the balance of the depositor's account. The bank statement also will show the bank charges or deductions (such as service charges) made directly to the depositor's account by the bank. The bank statement includes copies of the deposit slips and all checks that cleared through the bank during the period covered by the statement. A typical bank statement (excluding the deposit slips and canceled checks) is shown in Exhibit 8–1.

Example of a Bank Statement

Exhibit 8–1 lists three items that need explanation. Notice that on June 20, listed under "Checks and Debits," is a deduction for $18 coded with "NC."[1] A check for $18 was received from a customer, R. Roe, which then was deposited by J. Doe Company with its bank, the Texas Commerce Bank. The bank processed the check through banking channels to Roe's bank. Roe's account did not have sufficient funds to cover it; therefore, Roe's bank returned it to the Texas Commerce Bank which then charged it back to J. Doe Company. This type of check often is called an **NSF check** (not sufficient funds). The NSF check is now a receivable; consequently, J. Doe Company must make an entry to debit Receivables (R. Roe) and credit Cash for the $18.

Notice the $6 listed on June 30 under "Checks and Debits" and coded "SC." This is the code for **bank service charges.** The bank statement included a memo by the bank explaining this service charge (which was not documented by a check). J. Doe Company must make an entry to reflect this $6 decrease in the bank balance as a debit to an appropriate expense account, such as Bank Service Expense, and a credit to Cash.

Notice the $100 listed on June 12 under "Deposits" and coded "CM" for "credit memo." The bank collected a note receivable owned by Doe and increased the depositor account of J. Doe Company. The bank service charge (SC) included the collection service cost. J. Doe Company must record the collection by making an entry to debit Cash and credit Note Receivable for the $100 (assume interest on the note had been recorded).

---

[1] These codes vary among banks.

___EXHIBIT 8–1___

Example of a bank statement

Texas
Commerce
Bank

Austin
NATIONAL ASSOCIATION

7TH & LAVACA
AUSTIN, TEXAS 78789
PHONE: 512/476-6611

ACCOUNT NUMBER	STATEMENT DATE	PAGE NO.
877–95861	6–30–87	1

J. Doe Company
1000 Blank Road
Austin, Texas 78703

STATEMENT OF ACCOUNT

Please examine statement and checks promptly. If no error is reported within ten days, the account will be considered correct. Please report change of address.
For questions or problems
call TCB-Austin's Hotline · 476-6100

ON THIS DATE	YOUR BALANCE WAS	DEPOSITS ADDED		CHECKS AND DEBITS SUBTRACTED		SERVICE COST	RESULTING BALANCE
		NO.	AMOUNT	NO.	AMOUNT		
6–1–87	7 562 40	5	4 050 00	23	3 490 20	6 00	122 20

CHECKS AND DEBITS			DEPOSITS	DATE	DAILY BALANCE
				6–1–87	7 562 40
			3 000 00	6–2–87	10 562 40
500 00				6–4–87	10 062 40
55 00	5 00	40 00		6–5–87	9 962 40
100 00			500 00	6–8–87	10 362 40
8 20	16 50	160 00		6–10–87	10 177 70
2 150 00	10 00		*100 00CM	6–12–87	8 117 70
7 50	15 30			6–16–87	8 094 90
35 00	1 50		150 00	6–17–87	8 208 40
40 20	15 00	6 00		6–18–87	8 147 20
*18 00NC				6–20–87	8 129 20
125 50	80 00	2 00		6–21–87	7 921 70
18 90			300 00	6–24–87	8 202 80
7 52	19 60			6–27–87	8 175 68
15 00	32 48			6–28–87	8 128 20
*6 00SC				6–30–87	8 122 20

Code:
   CM-Credit Memo-Customer note collected
   NC-Not sufficient funds
   SC-Service charge

MEMBER F.D.I.C.   IMPORTANT: SEE REVERSE SIDE OF STATEMENT.

CASH ACCOUNTS IN THE LEDGER

A balance sheet reports **cash** as the first current asset because it is the most liquid asset. The amount of cash reported on a balance sheet is the **total amount** of cash at the end of the last day of the accounting period. The total amount of cash reported on the balance sheet includes:

1. Cash on deposit in all checking accounts subject to current checking privileges (offset by any overdrafts).[2]
2. Cash on hand (not yet transmitted to a bank for deposit).
3. Cash held in all petty cash funds.

A company will have a separate account in the **ledger** for each bank account.[3] Often companies keep a small amount of **cash on hand.** Although such amounts are included in the balance of the **regular Cash account,** those amounts have not been deposited. They represent *(a)* amounts of cash received since the last deposit was made and/or *(b)* a stable amount of cash needed for making change to start the next day.

Often, a **petty cash system** is kept to make **small cash payments** (not to make change) in lieu of writing a separate check for each such item. This system necessitates the use of another separate cash account, usually called Petty Cash (discussed later).

BANK RECONCILIATION

A **bank reconciliation** is the process of comparing (reconciling) the **ending** cash balance shown in the **Cash ledger account** and the **ending** cash balance reported by the bank on the monthly **bank statement.** A bank reconciliation should be completed for each separate checking account (i.e., for each bank statement received from each bank) at the end of each month.

Usually, the ending cash balance as shown on the bank statement does not agree with the ending cash balance shown by the related Cash ledger account on the books of the depositor. For example, the Cash ledger account at the end of June of J. Doe Company showed the following (Doe has only one checking account):

Cash

June 1	Balance	7,010.00*	June	Checks written	3,800.00
June	Deposits	5,750.00			

(Ending balance, $8,960.00)

* Including $200 undeposited cash held for change.

The $8,122.20 **ending cash balance** shown on the **bank statement** (Exhibit 8–1) is different from the $8,960.00 **ending book balance** of cash shown on the books of the J. Doe Company. This difference exists because (1) some transactions affecting cash were recorded in the books of depositor Doe but were not shown on the bank statement, and (2) some transactions were shown on the

---

[2] Adjusted for deposits in transit and outstanding checks (discussed later).
[3] Larger companies often carry one Cash control account in the ledger, which is supplemented with a series of separate cash subsidiary accounts for the depository banks. Refer to Supplement 6A.

bank statement but had not been recorded in the books of the depositor, Doe. The most common causes of differences between the ending bank balance and the ending book balance of cash are:

1. **Outstanding checks**—checks written by the depositor and recorded in the depositor's ledger as credits to the Cash account. These checks have not cleared the bank (they are not shown on the bank statement as a deduction from the bank balance). The outstanding checks are identified by comparing the canceled checks returned with the bank statement and with the record of checks (such as the check stubs) maintained by the depositor.
2. **Deposits in transit**—deposits sent to the bank by the depositor and recorded in the depositor's ledger as debits to the Cash account. These deposits have not been recorded by the bank (they are not shown on the bank statement as an increase in the bank balance). Deposits in transit usually happen when deposits are made one or two days before the close of the period covered by the bank statement. Deposits in transit are determined by comparing the deposits listed on the bank statement with the copies of the deposit slips retained by the depositor.
3. **Bank service charges**—an expense for bank services; listed on the bank statement. This expense must be recorded in the depositor's ledger by making a debit to an appropriate expense account, such as Bank Service Expense, and a credit to Cash.
4. **NSF checks**—a "bad check" that was deposited and must be deducted from the depositor's account. The depositor must make a journal entry to debit a receivable and credit Cash.
5. **Credit memo**—a note receivable collected by the bank for the depositor. It is recorded by making a debit to Cash and credits to Notes Receivable and Interest Revenue.
6. **Errors**—both the bank and the depositor may make errors, especially when the volume of cash transactions is large.

In view of these factors, a **bank reconciliation** should be made by the depositor immediately after each bank statement is received. A bank reconciliation is an important element of internal control and is needed for accounting purposes. To encourage bank reconciliation by depositors, many banks provide a form on the back of the bank statement for this purpose. A typical form is shown in Exhibit 8–2.

Bank Reconciliation Illustrated

The bank reconciliation for the month of June prepared by J. Doe Company to reconcile the **ending bank balance** (Exhibit 8–1, $8,122.20) with the **ending book balance** ($8,960) is shown in Exhibit 8–3. On the completed reconciliation, Exhibit 8–3, the **correct** cash balance is $9,045. This balance is different from both the reported bank and book balances before the reconciliation.

EXHIBIT 8–2

Sample form and instructions for a bank reconciliation

	CHECKS OUTSTANDING	
	NO.	AMOUNT

THIS IS PROVIDED TO HELP YOU BALANCE
YOUR BANK STATEMENT

BANK BALANCE
SHOWN ON THIS STATEMENT $_____

ADD + (IF ANY)
DEPOSITS NOT SHOWN
ON THIS STATEMENT _____

TOTAL _____

SUBTRACT - (IF ANY)
CHECKS OUTSTANDING _____

THIS IS PROVIDED TO HELP YOU BALANCE
YOUR CHECKBOOK

CHECKBOOK BALANCE
$_____

SUBTRACT - (IF ANY)
ACTIVITY CHARGE _____

SUB-TOTAL _____

SUBTRACT - (IF ANY)
OTHER BANK CHARGES _____

TOTAL

BALANCE $_____
SHOULD AGREE WITH YOUR CHECKBOOK BALANCE

BALANCE $_____
SHOULD AGREE WITH YOUR STATEMENT BALANCE

IF YOUR ACCOUNT DOES NOT BALANCE
PLEASE CHECK THE FOLLOWING CAREFULLY

☐ HAVE YOU CORRECTLY ENTERED THE AMOUNT OF EACH CHECK ON YOUR CHECKBOOK STUB?

☐ ARE THE AMOUNTS OF YOUR DEPOSITS ENTERED ON CHECKBOOK STUBS THE SAME AS IN YOUR STATEMENT?

☐ HAVE ALL CHECKS BEEN DEDUCTED FROM YOUR STUBS?

☐ HAVE YOU DEDUCTED ALL BANK CHARGES FROM YOUR STUBS?

☐ HAVE YOU CARRIED THE CORRECT BALANCE FORWARD FROM ONE CHECKBOOK STUB TO THE NEXT?

☐ HAVE YOU CHECKED ALL ADDITIONS AND SUBTRACTIONS ON YOUR CHECKBOOK STUBS?

The format of a bank reconciliation can vary. A simple and flexible one uses a balancing format with the "Depositor's Books" and the "Bank Statement" identified separately. This format starts with two different amounts: (1) the **ending balance per books** and (2) the **ending balance per bank statement.** Space is provided for additions to, and subtractions from, each balance so that the last line shows the same correct cash balance (for the bank and the books). This correct balance is the amount that should be shown in the Cash account **after the reconciliation.** In this example it is also the correct amount of cash that should be reported on the balance sheet (J. Doe Company has only one checking account and no petty cash system). J. Doe Company followed these steps in preparing the bank reconciliation:

1. **Identify the outstanding checks**—A comparison of the canceled checks returned by the bank with the records of the company of all checks drawn showed the following checks still outstanding (not cleared) at the end of June:

EXHIBIT 8–3

Bank reconciliation illustrated

J. DOE COMPANY
Bank Reconciliation
For the Month Ending June 30, 1987

Depositor's Books		Bank Statement	
Ending cash balance per books $8,960.00		Ending cash balance per bank statement .... $ 8,122.20	
Additions:		Additions:	
Proceeds of customer note collected by bank 100.00		Deposit in transit 1,800.00	
Error in recording check No. 137 .... 9.00		Cash on hand 200.00	
	9,069.00		10,122.20
Deductions:		Deductions:	
NSF check of R. Roe $18.00		Outstanding checks 1,077.20	
Bank service charges 6.00 24.00			
Ending correct cash balance $9,045.00		Ending correct cash balance .... $ 9,045.00	

Check No.	Amount
101	$ 145.00
123	815.00
131	117.20
Total	$1,077.20

This total was entered on the reconciliation as a **deduction** from the bank account. These checks will be deducted by the bank when they clear the bank.

2. **Identify the deposits in transit**—A comparison of the deposit slips on hand with those listed on the bank statement revealed that a deposit made on June 30 for $1,800 was not listed on the bank statement. This amount was entered on the reconciliation as an **addition** to the bank account. It will be added by the bank when the deposit is recorded by the bank.

3. **Cash on hand**—On the date of the bank statement, cash on hand (i.e., undeposited cash held for making change) was $200. This amount is included in the company's Cash account but was not included in the bank statement balance (it was not deposited). Therefore, it must be entered on the reconciliation as an addition to the bank balance (as it would be, if deposited).

4. **Record bank charges and credits:**
   a. Proceeds of note collected, $100—entered on the bank reconciliation as an

addition to the book balance; it already has been included in the bank balance. A journal entry is needed to debit Cash and credit Note Receivable and Interest Revenue.

b. NSF check of R. Roe, $18—entered on the bank reconciliation as a **deduction** from the book balance; it has been deducted from the bank statement balance. A journal entry is needed to credit Cash to debit a receivable account.

c. Bank service charges, $6—entered on the bank reconciliation as a **deduction** from the book balance; it has been deducted from the bank balance. A journal entry is needed to credit Cash and to debit an expense account.

5. **Determine the impact of errors**—At this point J. Doe Company found that the reconciliation did not balance by $9. Because this amount is divisible by 9, they suspected a transposition. (A transposition, such as writing 27 for 72, always will cause an error that is exactly divisible by 9.) Upon checking the journal entries made during the month, they found that a check was written for $56 to pay an account payable. The check was recorded in the company's accounts as $65. The incorrect entry made was a debit to Accounts Payable and a credit to Cash for $65 (instead of $56). Therefore, $9 (i.e., $65 − $56) must be **added** to the book cash balance on the reconciliation; the bank cleared the check for the correct amount, $56. The following correcting entry must be made in the accounts: Cash, debit $9; and Accounts Payable, credit $9.

Note in Exhibit 8–3 that the "Depositor's Books" and the "Bank Statement" parts of the bank reconciliation now agree at a **correct cash balance** of $9,045. This amount will be reported as cash on a balance sheet prepared at the end of the period.

A bank reconciliation as shown in Exhibit 8–3 accomplishes two major objectives:

1. Checks the accuracy of the bank balance and the company cash records, which involves development of the **correct cash balance.** The correct cash balance is the amount of cash that must be in the Cash account for financial reporting purposes (i.e., the balance sheet) and the amount that would be in the bank if all cash items were recognized by the bank.

2. Identifies any previously unrecorded transactions or changes that are necessary to cause the company's Cash account(s) to show the **correct cash balance.** These transactions or changes need journal entries. The explanations given above of the development of the bank reconciliation of J. Doe Company cite such transactions and changes. Therefore, the entries shown in Exhibit 8–4, taken directly from the "Depositor's Books," part of the bank reconciliation (Exhibit 8–3), must be entered into the company's records.

Notice that all of the additions and deductions on the "Depositor's Books" side of the reconciliation need journal entries to update the Cash account. The

EXHIBIT 8–4

Entries from bank reconciliation (Exhibit 8–3)

Accounts of J. Doe Company:

a. Cash 100
    Note receivable   100
        To record note collected by bank.

b. Accounts receivable 18
        Cash   18
        To record NSF check.

c. Bank service expense 6
        Cash   6
        To record service fees charged by bank.

d. Cash 9
        Accounts payable (name)   9
        To correct error made in recording a check payable to a creditor.

Cash account of J. Doe Company:

The Cash account prior to reconciliation was given on page 374. After the above journal entries are posted, the Cash account is as follows:

Cash (after recording results of bank reconciliation)

June 1	Balance	7,010.00	June	Checks written	3,800.00
June	Deposits	5,750.00	June 30	NSF check*	18.00
June 30	Note collected*	100.00	June 30	Bank service charge*	6.00
June 30	Correcting entry*	9.00			

(Correct cash balance, $9,045.00)

* Based on the bank reconciliation.

---

additions and deductions on the "Bank Statement" side do **not** need journal entries because they will work out automatically when they clear the bank. The cash amount reported on the balance sheet and reflected in the Cash account will be the **correct cash balance** only if the proper journal entries are made after the bank reconciliation is completed.

CASH OVER AND SHORT

Errors in handling cash inevitably occur when a large number of cash transactions is involved. These errors cause cash shortages or cash overages at the end of the day when the cash is counted and compared with the cash records for the day. Cash overages and shortages must be recorded in the accounts. Assume that the count of cash from sales amounted to $1,347 but the cash register tapes for sales totaled $1,357—a **cash shortage** of $10 is indicated. The sales for the day should be recorded as follows:

Cash	1,347.00	
Cash over and short	10.00	
Sales		1,357.00
To record cash sales and cash shortage.		

In the case of a cash **overage,** the Cash Over and Short account is credited. Sales revenue should be recorded for the correct amount shown on the register tapes regardless of any cash overage or shortage. At the end of the period, a debit balance in the Cash Over and Short account usually is reported as miscellaneous expense. If a credit balance exists, it is reported as miscellaneous revenue.

PETTY CASH

Disbursements of cash should be made by **prenumbered checks.** However, many businesses find it inconvenient and expensive to write checks for small payments for items such as taxi fares, newspapers, and small amounts of supplies. To avoid this inconvenience and expense, businesses often set up a **petty cash fund** to handle small miscellaneous cash payments. To set up a petty cash fund, a check should be drawn "Pay to the order of Petty Cash" for the amount needed in the fund and cashed. Small cash payments, supported by written receipts, are made from this fund, and no journal entry is made at the time of payment. When the petty cash fund gets low and at the end of each accounting period, the expenditures from the fund are summarized and a journal entry is made to reflect the payments from the fund (debits to expenses) and to record the check written to reimburse the fund for the total amount spent (credit to Cash). For balance sheet reporting, the amount in the Petty Cash account must be added to the other cash balances. The details of accounting for a petty cash fund are discussed in Supplement 8A.

COMPENSATING BALANCES

A **compensating balance** exists when the bank requires a business to keep a minimum amount in its bank account. A compensating balance may be required by the bank explicitly (by a loan agreement) or implicitly (by informal understanding) as part of a credit-granting arrangement. Information on compensating balances is important to statement users because of two major effects on the business: (1) a compensating balance requirement imposes a restriction on the amount of cash readily available; and (2) if it arises in connection with a loan, the compensating balance increases the real rate of interest on the loan because not all of the cash borrowed can be used (i.e., the minimum must remain on deposit).

Information concerning a compensating balance must be reported in the notes to the financial statements because of its relevance to statement users.

DATA PROCESSING OF CASH

Small businesses usually process cash transactions manually. In contrast, large businesses write checks and process cash information using computers. However, recent developments with microcomputers and software have brought computer processing of cash information within the cost-benefit range of small and medium-sized businesses. Essentially, the basic data activities of accounting are the same whether manual, mechanical, or computerized approaches are used. For most instructional situations, the basic characteristics of accounting information processing are best illustrated with a manual system.

Supplement 8B presents an information processing procedure known as **special journals.** Two of these special journals relate to information processing of cash inflows (i.e., cash receipts journal) and cash outflows (i.e., cash payments journal).

PART B—MEASURING AND REPORTING SHORT-TERM INVESTMENTS

Most businesses hold extra cash in addition to the minimum required for normal daily transactions. This extra cash may be held to meet unexpected needs or may be the result of normal seasonal variations in the level of business operations. Cash that is deposited in most checking accounts does not earn interest. A company can earn revenue by investing such idle cash in short-term investments. These investments include savings accounts and certificates of deposit, commercial paper (short-term debt issued by corporations), bonds, and capital stock. Investments in commercial paper, bonds, and stock can be quickly converted into cash because they can be sold on stock exchanges such as the New York Stock Exchange.

When bonds of another company are acquired, the purchaser becomes a creditor of the issuing company because bonds represent debt owed by the other company similar to a long-term note payable. As the holder of a bond, the investor is entitled to receive interest on the principal of the bond and the principal if held to maturity. In contrast, when shares of capital stock are purchased as an investment, the purchaser becomes one of the owners of the company that issued the stock. As an owner, the stockholder receives dividends when they are paid by the other company. Most capital stock confers voting rights, which means a stockholder can exercise some **control** over the issuing company. The degree of control depends upon the number of voting shares owned by the stockholder in relation to the total number of such shares of stock outstanding.

Investments made by one company in the stocks or bonds of another company may be either (1) short-term investments (also called marketable securities) or (2) long-term investments. This chapter discusses the measurement and reporting of short-term investments; long-term investments are discussed in Chapter 13.

SHORT-TERM INVESTMENTS DEFINED

To be classified as a short-term investment, a security must meet a twofold test of (1) marketability and (2) an expected short-term holding period. **Marketability** means that the security must be readily converted into cash or it must be traded regularly on the market so that it easily can be converted to cash. Short-term investments usually must be listed on an established stock exchange. A short-term holding period means that it must be the **intention** of the management to convert the investment into cash in the near future for normal operating purposes.[4] Short term refers to the longer of the normal operating cycle of the business or one year as specified in the definition of current assets. The distinction between short-term and long-term investments is important because (1) accounting for the two types of investments is different; and (2) short-term investments are classified as a current asset, and long-term investments are classified as a noncurrent asset.

MEASUREMENT OF SHORT-TERM INVESTMENTS

In conformity with the **cost principle,** short-term investments are initially recorded at their acquisition cost. Cost includes the market price paid plus all additional costs incurred to buy the security. Assume that in December, Brown Corporation purchased 1,000 shares of American Telephone & Telegraph (AT&T) stock for $56,000, including all broker's fees, transfer costs, and taxes related to the purchase. This transaction is recorded in Exhibit 8–5.

Short-term investments are reported at the **lower of cost or market** (LCM) on the balance sheet (lower of cost or market is discussed in the next section). The **current market value** of the short-term investment should be shown parenthetically. For example, at the end of the accounting period, December 31, 19A,

---

[4] We shall see later that long-term investments also include marketable securities. Thus, the basic distinction between short-term and long-term investments hinges primarily on the intention of management in respect to their expected disposal date. As a result, the same kind of security may be a short-term investment in one company and a long-term investment in another company, depending upon the intentions of the respective managements.

EXHIBIT 8–5

Accounting for short-term investments illustrated

December 1, 19A—Purchase of 1,000 shares of AT&T common stock for $56,000 including all transfer costs:

Short-term investments (1,000 shares @ $56)	56,000	
Cash		56,000

December 31, 19A (end of the accounting period)—on this date the AT&T stock was selling at $57 (i.e., **above** acquisition cost)*

Balance sheet at December 31, 19A:

Current assets:

Cash (assumed amount)	$62,000
Short-term investments at cost (current market value, $57,000)	56,000

February 2, 19B—Received a quarterly cash dividend on the AT&T stock of $0.70 per share:

Cash (1,000 shares × $0.70 per share)	700	
Investment revenue		700

April 5, 19B—Sold 250 shares of the AT&T stock at $58 per share (cash):

Cash (250 shares @ $58)	14,500	
Short-term investments (250 shares @ $56)		14,000
Gain on sale of investments		500

   * See next section on LCM when the market price is **less** than the acquisition price.

Brown Corporation would report the short-term investment of AT&T stock, assuming a market value **above** cost of $57 per share, as shown in Exhibit 8–5.

When either a cash dividend or interest is received, Cash is debited for the amount received, and a revenue account, such as Investment Revenue, is credited for the same amount. Assume Brown Corporation received a cash dividend of $0.70 per share on the AT&T stock on February 2, 19B. This transaction would be recorded by Brown as shown in Exhibit 8–5.

When a short-term investment is sold, the difference between the sale price and the original cost of the security is recorded as a gain, or loss, as shown in Exhibit 8–5.

When a company owns short-term equity securities in several other companies, the securities held are referred to collectively as a **short-term portfolio of equity securities.** If debt securities also are held, they are considered to be a separate **portfolio** of **debt securities.** Each portfolio of short-term investments is managed (i.e., acquired, held, and sold) with the objective of maximizing the return while minimizing the risk. Thus, each **investment portfolio** is accounted for as a whole rather than as a number of separate investments.

Short-Term Investments Valued at Lower of Cost or Market (LCM)

Accounting for short-term investments is usually in conformity with the cost principle. There is an important exception related **only** to equity securities. The exception occurs when the **current** market value of the **short-term portfolio of equity securities** drops below the recorded acquisition cost.[5]

Chapter 7 discussed the lower of cost or market (LCM) basis for inventory. The same rule applies to the **short-term portfolio of equity securities.** When market value drops below cost, a short-term portfolio of equity securities loses a part of its value as a short-term source of **cash.** The drop in value is viewed as an **unrealized loss** that should be recognized in the period in which the price drop occurred. However, an unrealized holding gain is **not** recorded when the current market value is **above** the acquisition cost. The LCM basis is an exception to the cost principle because the **conservatism exception** (see Exhibit 4–5) overrides the cost principle. The LCM rule does not have to be applied to short-term investments in **debt** securities. They are accounted for at cost (with parenthetical disclosure of their current market value).

When the end-of-period market value of short-term investments in equity is lower than cost, an unrealized loss must be recorded. The loss is recorded as a debit to an **expense** account called Unrealized Loss on Short-Term Investments and a credit to an **asset contra** account called Allowance to Reduce Short-Term Investments to Market. This entry records the holding (market) loss as an expense in the period in which the market dropped and revalues the short-term investment on an LCM basis.

At the end of 19B, Brown Corporation (Exhibit 8–5) still owned 750 shares of the AT&T common stock acquired at $56 per share (i.e., total cost is, $42,000). At the end of 19B, the AT&T stock was selling on the stock exchange at $55 per share, which was $1 per share less than its cost. Therefore, the LCM rule must be applied. An **unrealized** loss of $750 must be recorded and reported as shown in Exhibit 8–6.

The illustration given in Exhibit 8–6 involved only one stock (AT&T) in the investment portfolio. Often the portfolio includes several different equity securities. In such cases, LCM is applied by comparing the **total portfolio cost and the total portfolio market** value rather than on an item-by-item basis. To illustrate, assume Cox Company has three separate stocks, A, B, and C, in its short-term **investment portfolio.** The measurement at the end of the accounting period would be derived as follows:

---

[5] FASB, *Statement of Accounting Standards No. 12*, "Accounting for Certain Marketable Securities" (Stamford, Conn., December 1975). The procedures and accounting entries in this section specifically follow the **requirements** of *FASB Statement 12*. This statement **does not apply LCM to investments in debt securities.**

EXHIBIT 8–6

Recording and reporting short-term equity investments at LCM

Entries:

December 31, 19B (end of accounting period)—AT&T common stock held as a short-term investment; 750 shares, cost $56, current market, $55 per share.

Unrealized loss on short-term investments 750*		
Allowance to reduce short-term investments to market	750	

Computation:
Cost (750 shares @ $56) $42,000
Market (750 shares @ $55) 41,250
Unrealized loss .... $ 750

Financial statements:

Balance sheet at December 31, 19B:

Current assets:
Short-term investments (at cost) $42,000
Less: Allowance to reduce short-term investments to market ...   750 $41,250

or alternatively:

Current assets:
Short-term investment, at LCM (cost $42,000) $41,250

Income statement for year ended December 31, 19B:

Expenses:
Unrealized loss on short-term investments $750

Security	Acquisition cost	Current market
A Company common stock	$10,000	$ 9,000
B Company preferred stock	23,000	22,000
C Company common stock	7,000	8,000
Total portfolio	$40,000	$39,000

Under the LCM basis, the Short-Term Investments account of Cox Company would be written down to $39,000 by recognizing a $1,000 unrealized loss as follows:

Unrealized loss on short-term investments 1,000		
Allowance to reduce short-term investments to market	1,000	

The LCM rule is applied to the total portfolio because the portfolio typically is managed as a single investment instead of as several individual investments with different objectives.[6]

When investments that were written down to a lower market (i.e., LCM) are **sold**, the realized gain or loss is the difference between the sale price and the original cost regardless of any balance in the allowance account. Any balance in the allowance account at the end of the accounting period is adjusted (up or down) to reflect any difference between total portfolio cost and a lower total portfolio market of the short-term investments held at the end of the accounting period.

Assume that Cox Company sold all of the portfolio on January 15, 19C, for $39,400 cash. This transaction would be recorded as follows:[7]

Cash	39,400	
Loss on sale of short-term investments	600	
Short-term investments (at cost)		40,000

Note: At the end of the period, the allowance to reduce short-term investments to market must be adjusted.

CERTIFICATES OF DEPOSIT

A commonly used short-term investment is called a **certificate of deposit** (CD). A "CD" is an investment contract (a certificate is received) that may be purchased from a bank for cash. The contract specifies (1) a limited period of time for the investment, such as 90 days, 6 months, 1 year, and so on; and (2) a guaranteed interest rate. Usually, a higher interest rate is available for large investments. The interest rate also tends to be higher for longer time periods to maturity. Certificates of deposit and similar commercial paper often are used for

---

[6] In contrast, when the LCM rule is applied to merchandise inventories, the item-by-item basis usually is used because merchandise is not viewed "as a single item" but as separate items.

[7] Assuming no short-term investments were held at the end of 19C, the following entry would be made:

December 31, 19C:

Allowance to reduce short-term investments to market	1,000	
Recovery of unrealized loss on short-term investments*		1,000

* Some accountants prefer the title: "Unrealized Gain on Short-Term Investments."

Note that the LCM effect is to record a holding loss in the period that the market dropped below cost and to record an offset (a holding gain) in the period of sale. This anomalous effect occurs because LCM is not consistent with either cost basis accounting or market value accounting for Investments.

the short-term investment of idle cash because of the relatively high interest return and the liquidity factor.

Certificates of deposit are accounted for on the cost basis (not LCM) because they are **debt** securities. At the end of the accounting period, an **adjusting entry** is made for any accrued interest earned but not yet collected. The interest earned is reported on the income statement as **investment revenue.** For external reporting purposes, certificates of deposit are reported on the balance sheet as a current asset.

ADJUSTING ENTRIES FOR INVESTMENT REVENUE

At the end of the accounting period, **no adjusting entry is made for dividend revenue** on capital stock held as an investment because dividends (1) do not accrue on the basis of time and (2) are not paid unless formally declared by the board of directors of the issuing corporation. In contrast, when CDs, bonds, or other **debt securities are held, an adjusting entry is needed** for accrued interest revenue because interest is a legal liability that increases in amount with the passage of time. Accrual of interest is illustrated in Chapter 4 and in Part C of this chapter.

PART C—MEASURING AND REPORTING RECEIVABLES

RECEIVABLES DEFINED

Receivables include all claims of the entity against other entities or persons for money, goods, or services. In most businesses there are two types of receivables: trade receivables and special (nontrade) receivables. Either type may include both short-term receivables and long-term receivables. For example, a balance sheet may report the following receivables:

Current assets:		
Trade accounts receivable	$40,000	
Less: Allowance for doubtful accounts	3,000	$37,000
Trade notes receivable, short term		5,000
Special receivables:		
Due from employees		400
Equipment note receivable, short term		600
Long-term investments:		
Note receivable, long term		10,000
Special receivable, long term		8,000
Other assets:		
Utility deposits		2,000
Due from company officers		1,000

TRADE RECEIVABLES

Trade receivables include **accounts receivable** and trade notes receivable. Either may be short term or long term, although the latter is rare. Trade receivables arise from the normal operating activities of the business, that is, from the sale of merchandise and/or services.

Trade accounts receivable and the contra account, Allowance for Doubtful Accounts, were discussed in Chapter 6.

Many businesses **sell** their accounts receivable instead of holding them until they are collected. Factoring is a term used for the **sale** of accounts receivable to a financial institution, which usually occurs on the date that the goods and/or services are sold. Factoring is used widely because the company immediately receives the cash for sales. The rate of interest for factoring arrangements is high. A discussion of the detailed accounting involved for factoring is included in advanced accounting courses.

SPECIAL RECEIVABLES

Special (or nontrade) receivables arise from transactions other than the normal sale of merchandise and/or services. Special receivables may be short term or long term and should be given descriptive titles. They should not be included in the caption "Accounts receivable." Other than for appropriate classification on the balance sheet, special receivables seldom involve unusual accounting problems.

NOTES RECEIVABLE

Notes receivable may be either **trade** notes receivable or **special** notes receivable, depending upon the source of the note. A note is an unconditional promise in writing (i.e., a formal document) to pay (1) a specified sum of money on demand or at a definite future date known as the maturity or due date and (2) specified interest at one or more future dates. The person who signs a note is called the **maker.** The person to whom payment is to be made is known as the **payee.** The maker views the note as a "note payable," whereas the payee views the note as a "note receivable." A note involves two distinctly different amounts: (1) **principal,** which is the amount that the interest rate is based upon; and (2) **interest,** which is the specified amount charged for use of the principal. The **face amount** of a note is the amount that is payable at maturity.

Interest Calculations on Notes

Interest represents the cost of using money over time. To the payee of a note, interest is **revenue;** while to the maker it is **expense.** The formula for computing interest is:

Principal × Annual rate of interest × Fraction of year = Interest amount

Interest rates are quoted on an **annual basis** and, therefore, must be restated for time periods of less than one year. Thus, the interest on a $10,000, 12%, 90-day note is calculated as follows:

$$\$10,000 \times 12\% \times 90/360 = \$300$$

When a note specifies a number of days, the exact days must be counted on the calendar to determine the due date and then related to the number of days in the year. For simplicity, sometimes it is assumed that the year has 360 days. Therefore, each day's interest is $\frac{1}{360}$ of a year rather than $\frac{1}{365}$. This simplification has the effect of making the actual interest cost for a short-term loan slightly higher than the stated amount of interest.[8]

All commercial notes have interest, either explicitly or implicitly, because money borrowed or loaned has a value that cannot be ignored.[9]

Accounting for Notes Receivable

Notes receivable usually arise as a result of a business selling merchandise or services. Although most businesses use open accounts (i.e., accounts receivable), those selling high-priced items on credit often require notes from their customers. To illustrate, assume Jackson Company received a $10,000, 12%, interest-bearing note from a customer as a result of the sale of goods; the payee would record it on the date of the sale as follows:

Notes receivable (trade)	10,000	
Sales revenue		10,000
To record 90-day, 12%, interest-bearing note received from customer.		

Note: Assuming the note was in settlement of an open account receivable, which frequently happens, the credit would have been to Accounts Receivable instead of to Sales Revenue.

When **collection** is made at **maturity date** 90 days later, the entry to record the principal amount and the interest would be:

---

[8] For simplicity throughout this book, interest dates are given in a manner that avoids the needless counting of exact days on a calendar. Most lending institutions use 365 days in the calculations.

[9] An **interest-bearing note** explicitly specifies a stated rate of interest (such as 12%) on the face of the note, and the interest is to be paid in addition to the **face amount** of the note. In contrast, a **noninterest-bearing note** does not explicitly state an interest rate on the note because the interest charge is included in the face amount of the note (i.e., the interest is implicit).

Cash 10,300		
Notes receivable (trade)		10,000
Interest revenue		300

To record collection of a 90-day, 12%, interest-bearing note receivable of $10,000 plus interest ($10,000 × 12% × 90/360 = $300).

Default of a Note Receivable

A note receivable that is not collected at maturity is **dishonored** or **defaulted** by the maker. Immediately after default, an entry should be made by the payee transferring the amount due from the Notes Receivable account to a special account such as Special Receivable—Defaulted Trade Notes. The maker is responsible for both the unpaid principal and the unpaid interest. The receivable account should reflect the full amount owed to the payee. If the above note receivable was defaulted by the maker, the entry made by the payee is:[10]

Special receivable—defaulted trade notes 10,300		
Notes receivable (trade)		10,000
Interest revenue		300

To record the principal and interest earned on defaulted note.

Special Receivable—Defaulted Trade Notes is reported as a current or noncurrent asset depending upon the probable collection date.

Discounting a Note Receivable

Many businesses prefer a note receivable rather than an open account receivable from customers involved in large purchases on credit. The primary reasons are (1) the note provides formal evidence of the receivable; and (2) notes, if negotiable, often can be sold to a financial institution, such as a bank, to get needed cash before the maturity date. Selling a note receivable to a financial institution frequently is called **discounting** a note receivable.

---

[10] From date of default, the amount due at that date (principal plus interest) continues to draw interest either at the stipulated rate or the legal rate as specified by the law of the state. There may be a question about the propriety of recognizing the interest revenue before collection is made when there is a reasonable probability that collection will not be made.

A negotiable instrument is one that can be transferred by the endorsement of the payee (there are other technical legal requisites for negotiability). The most common negotiable instrument is a check. Notes and a number of other instruments can be transferred by endorsement. An endorsement may be made by signature of the holder. The note may be negotiated **with recourse,** which means that the endorser is liable for repayment if the maker defaults. An endorsement may be made without recourse by writing this phrase on the instrument before the endorsement signature. **Without recourse** means that the endorser cannot be held contractually liable in the case of default by the maker. Most banks, businesses, and individuals will not accept endorsements without recourse. As a result, financial institutions can rely on both the maker and the endorser. An endorsement with recourse makes the endorser **contingently liable.** If the maker does not pay the note at maturity, the endorser pays. The **full-disclosure principle** (Exhibit 4–5) requires that such contingent liabilities be reported as a note to the financial statements.

The sale of a note receivable gives the payee immediate cash and causes the transfer of the asset (note receivable) to the lender. Often there will be a difference between the interest rate specified on the note and the interest rate charged by the purchaser of the note.

For example, assume that Jackson Company held a $10,000, 10%, 90-day interest-bearing note receivable for 30 days, then sold it to the Texas Commerce Bank at an interest rate of 12%. The bank's interest rate is applied to the **maturity value** of the note (that is, the principal amount of the note **plus** the amount of interest due at maturity). The bank's rate of interest is applied to the number of days the bank will hold the note (in this case, 60 days). Computation of the amount of cash the bank will pay for the note is:

Discounting a note receivable:

Note: Principal, $10,000; annual interest rate, 10%; term, 90 days.
Discounted: Thirty days after date; discount rate, 12% per year.

Principal amount	$10,000.00
Plus: Interest due at maturity ($10,000 × 10% × 90/360)	250.00
Maturity value—amount subject to discount rate	10,250.00
Less: Discount—interest charged by bank ($10,250 × 12% × 60/360)	205.00
Cash proceeds—amount the bank pays for the note	$10,045.00

The discounting or sale of the above note receivable is recorded by the payee (Jackson Company) as follows:[11]

---

[11] The credit of $45 to Interest Revenue may be explained as follows: Had the note been held to maturity, the payee would have earned $250 interest revenue; however, the bank charged interest amounting to $205. The difference is $45, which is the net interest earned by the payee for holding it 30 of the 90 days. The discount rate is applied to the maturity value of the note because that is the amount the bank will advance, less the interest required by the bank.

Cash 10,045.00		
Notes receivable (trade)		10,000.00
Interest revenue		45.00
To record discounting of note receivable.		

Even though the note was sold, the bank has recourse against the endorser in case of default by the maker. Therefore, Jackson Company must disclose a **contingent liability** in a note to the financial statements similar to the following:

Note: At December 31, 19B, the company was contingently liable for notes receivable discounted in the amount of $10,250.

CONSTRAINTS TO ACCOUNTING PRINCIPLES

The preceding chapters used the terms **materiality** and **conservatism**. The conservatism constraint was cited earlier as the reason for using the LCM rule in measuring inventory (Chapter 7) and short-term investments (Chapter 8). The terms **materiality** and **conservatism** modify the accounting principles listed in Exhibit 4–5. That exhibit lists three constraints to accounting principles: (1) materiality, (2) conservatism, and (3) cost benefit.

Although compliance with the fundamental accounting assumptions and principles is essential, the benefits of absolute compliance with concepts sometimes are offset by practical considerations. Under certain **limited conditions,** a constraint may be permitted to override one or more of the other principles. The accounting constraints are:

1. **Materiality**—The fundamental accounting principles must be followed without exception for each transaction when the amount involved in the transaction is **material** (i.e., significant) in relationship to its overall effect on the financial statements. All amounts must be accounted for, but **immaterial amounts need not be accorded theoretically correct treatment.** For example, a pencil sharpener that cost $8 and has a five-year estimated life need not be depreciated under the matching principle. The $8 may be expensed in the period of acquisition because the amount involved is not material. The clerical cost alone of recording depreciation over the five-year period would exceed the cost of the asset. Also, the $1.60 annual depreciation expense would not affect any important decisions by statement users.

2. **Conservatism**—If more than one accounting alternative is acceptable for a transaction, the one having the **least favorable immediate effect on income or owners' equity usually should be selected.** For example, the LCM basis is used in measuring the amount of short-term investments and merchandise inventory. In this case, conservatism overrides the cost principle so that an

unrealized loss (but not a gain) that occurs before the asset is sold is recorded and reported.

3. **Cost benefit**—This is a general utility constraint. It specifies that the cost of preparing and reporting accounting information should not exceed the value of the benefits of that information to the users of financial statements.

DEMONSTRATION CASE

(Try to resolve the requirements before proceeding to the suggested solution that follows.)

Dotter Equipment Company has been selling farm machinery for more than 30 years. The company has been quite successful in both sales and repair services. A wide range of farm equipment, including trucks, is sold. The company policy is to seek "high volume and quality service, at the right price." Credit terms with varying conditions are typical. Although most of the credit granted is carried by several financial institutions, Dotter will carry the credit in special circumstances. As a result, the company occasionally accepts a promissory note and keeps it to maturity. However, if a cash need arises, some of these notes may be sold (i.e., discounted) to the local bank with which Dotter has its checking account. This case focuses on two farm equipment notes that were received during 19D. By following these notes from date of sale of farm equipment to final collection, we can see the various measurement problems posed and the accounting for them. The accounting period ends December 31, 19D.

The series of transactions in respect to the two notes follows:

Equipment Note No. 1:

19D

Jan. 15 Sold a farm tractor to S. Scott for $20,000 and received a 25% cash down payment plus a $15,000 equipment note receivable for the balance. The note was due in nine months and was interest bearing at 12% per annum. A mortgage on the tractor was executed as a part of the agreement.

Apr. 15 The Scott equipment note was sold to the local bank at the 13% per annum discount rate. Dotter endorsed the note, with recourse, and the proceeds were deposited in Dotter's checking account.

Oct. 15 Scott paid the bank the face amount of the note plus the interest, $15,000 + ($15,000 × 0.12 × $\frac{9}{12}$) = $16,350.

Required:

a. Give appropriate journal entries for Dotter Equipment Company on each of the three dates. Show the interest computations and give an explanation for each entry.

b. Assume that instead of payment on October 15, 19D, S. Scott defaulted on the note. When notified by the bank, Dotter paid the note and interest in full. Give the appropriate entry for this assumption and one for the further assumption that Scott later paid Dotter in full on December 1, 19D.

Equipment Note No. 2:

19D

Oct. 1 Sold a farm truck to B. Day for $7,000; received a down payment of $1,000 and set up an account receivable for the balance; terms n/30.

Nov. 1 Day came in and wanted an extension on the account receivable "until he sold some equipment." After some discussion it was agreed to settle the account receivable with a six-month, 12%, interest-bearing note. Day signed the $6,000 note and a mortgage on this date.

Dec. 31 End of the accounting period. An adjusting entry is required.

19E

Jan. 1 Start of the new accounting period.

May 1 On this due date, Day paid the face amount of the note plus interest in full. The note was marked paid, and the mortgage was canceled by Dotter.

Required:

c. Give appropriate journal entries on each date, including any adjusting entries at year-end and the entry on maturity date. Omit closing entries at year-end. Explain what could be done on January 1, 19E, to simplify subsequent accounting. Provide a brief explanation with each entry.

Suggested Solution

The solutions for Requirements (a), (b), and (c) are given in Exhibit 8–7 and 8–8.

EXHIBIT 8–7

Accounting for discounted and defaulted notes receivable illustrated

Requirement *a*—Equipment Note No. 1:

January 15, 19D—Note executed:

Cash	5,000.00	
Equipment notes receivable	15,000.00	
Sales revenue		20,000.00

Sale of tractor to S. Scott for cash and equipment note; terms of note, nine months, 12% interest, including a mortgage.

April 15, 19D—Note discounted:

Cash	15,287.25	
Equipment notes receivable		15,000.00
Interest revenue		287.25

Discounted Scott equipment note receivable at bank discount rate of 13%.

Proceeds computed:

Principal amount	$15,000.00
Interest to maturity ($15,000 × 12% × 9/12)	1,350.00
Maturity value	16,350.00
Discount ($16,350 × 13% × 6/12)	(1,062.75)
Cash proceeds	$15,287.25

October 15, 19D—Maturity date of note:

No entry required; Scott paid the bank that owned the note. During the period from April 15, 19D, until the note was paid, Dotter was contingently liable for the note because of the possibility that Scott would default.

Requirement *b*—Note defaulted:

October 15, 19D—Under the assumption that Scott defaulted on the note on due date, Dotter would have to pay the principal plus interest in full.

Special receivable (defaulted note—S. Scott)	16,350.00	
Cash		16,350.00

Scott note defaulted; payment to bank of the $15,000 principal plus interest ($15,000 × 12% × 9/12 = $1,350).

December 1, 19D—Scott paid Dotter the full amount of the note plus interest.

Cash	16,350.00	
Special receivable (defaulted note, S. Scott)		16,350.00

Payment received in full on Scott note in default.

Note: In most states, Dotter could have assessed Scott interest at the **legal** rate on the $16,350 amount overdue; in this case, there would be a credit to Interest Revenue.

_____ **EXHIBIT 8–8** _____

Accounting for interest accrual on notes receivable illustrated

---

Requirement c—Equipment Note No. 2:

October 1, 19D—Sale:

Cash	1,000	
Accounts receivable	6,000	
Sales revenue		7,000

   Sold truck to B. Day; terms of the receivable, n/30.

November 1, 19D—Note executed:

Equipment notes receivable	6,000	
Accounts receivable		6,000

   Settled account receivable with a six-month, 12% interest bearing note.

December 31, 19D—Accrual (end of accounting period):

Interest receivable	120	
Interest revenue		120

   Adjusting entry for two months' interest accrued at 12% on Day equipment note ($6,000 × 12% × 2/12 = $120).

January 1, 19E—Start of next accounting period:

   No entry is required on this date; however, a **reversal** of the adjusting entry could be made to facilitate the subsequent entry when the interest is collected on April 30, 19E. The **optional reversing entry** would be (see Supplement 5A):

Interest revenue	120	
Interest receivable		120

   Reversing entry on Day note.

April 30, 19E—Maturity date (assuming **no** reversing entry was made on January 1, 19E):

Cash $6,000 + ($6,000 × 12% × 6/12)	6,360	
Note receivable (principal amount)		6,000
Interest revenue ($6,000 × 12% × 4/12)		240
Interest receivable		120

SUMMARY OF CHAPTER

This chapter discussed cash, short-term investments, and receivables. Cash is the most liquid of all assets, and it flows continually into and out of a business. As a result, cash presents some of the most critical control problems facing the managers. Also, cash may be of critical importance to decision makers who rely on financial statements for relevant information. The measurement and reporting of cash includes such problems as controlling and safeguarding cash, reconciling bank balances, accounting for petty cash, and recording the cash inflows and outflows.

The use of short-term investments to employ idle cash was discussed. Marketability and the length of the expected holding period are fundamental in the classification of an investment as short term as opposed to long term. Short-term investments are accounted for in conformity with the **cost principle;** however, in conformity with the conservatism constraint, the LCM rule is applied to the short-term investment portfolio of **equity securities** at the end of each accounting period. **Debt securities** held as short-term investments are accounted for at **cost** (not LCM). Long-term investments are discussed in Chapter 13.

Receivables include trade receivables (usually called accounts receivable), special receivables, and notes receivable. Each of these should be accounted for separately. Interest calculations and discounting of notes receivable were discussed.

The chapter emphasized the importance of careful measurement of these liquid assets and the importance of examining their characteristics before classifying them as current assets for reporting purposes. Financial statement users often are faced with decisions in which these liquid assets are critical; therefore, they should be measured properly and reported adequately.

SUPPLEMENT 8A—PETTY CASH

A petty cash fund is established to avoid the inconvenience and cost of writing checks for the many small payments that occur daily in some businesses. This supplement discusses the detailed accounting and recordkeeping for a petty cash fund (also called an imprest fund).

Establishing the petty cash fund

To establish a petty cash fund, a check should be written for the estimated amount needed to meet the expected payments, say, for an average month. The check, made payable to "Petty Cash," is cashed. The money is kept in a safe place under the direct control of a **designated individual** known as the **custodian.** The entry to set up a **separate Cash account** and to record the initial check would be:

Petty cash	100	
Cash		100
To record establishment of a petty cash fund.		

Disbursements from the petty cash fund

The custodian should keep a perpetual record of all disbursements and the amount of cash on hand. No entry is made in the regular ledger accounts at the time each payment is made from the petty cash fund. Instead, the custodian keeps a separate **petty cash record** in which each disbursement is recorded when made. This record is supported by documentation, such as a signed bill, voucher, or receipt for each payment made. As an internal control feature, occasional surprise audits of the fund, and the records of disbursements should be conducted. "Borrowing" from the fund by the custodian or others should not be allowed. Careless handling of petty cash often leads to theft.

Replenishment of the petty cash fund

When the amount of cash held by the custodian gets low, and at the end of each accounting period, the fund should be reimbursed (or replenished) with an amount of cash sufficient to restore it to the original amount (to $100 in the example). Reimbursement is made by having the custodian submit the petty cash record and the supporting documents to the accountants. On the basis of these records, a check to "Petty Cash" is written for the amount of cash needed for replenishment which is the same as the sum of the expenditures reported by the custodian. The check is cashed, and the money is given to the custodian, which increases the cash held by the custodian to the original amount ($100 in the example). A journal entry is made to credit Cash for the amount of the check and to debit expenses. The petty cash documents turned in by the custodian provide the underlying support for this journal entry.

To illustrate, assume that by the end of the month there was $8.50 petty cash on hand. This means that cash expenditures by the custodian were $91.50 for the month. Assuming no shortage or overage, the bills, vouchers, and receipts accumulated by the custodian should equal this amount. These documents provide support for the additional check to petty cash for $91.50.

The detailed data for recording the replenishment check in the following journal entry are based on the supporting documents:

Telephone expense	12.40	
Office supplies expense	6.32	
Postage expense	21.45	
Delivery expense	6.33	
Taxi fare expense	14.87	
Repair expense, office equipment	15.00	
Coffee expense	10.04	
Miscellaneous expense	5.09	
Cash		91.50

Notice that the Petty Cash account is debited **only** when the petty cash fund is first established and when the fund amount is increased on a permanent basis. The Petty Cash account shows a stable balance at all times ($100 in the above example). Expense accounts, not Petty Cash, are debited, and the **regular** Cash account is credited when the fund is replenished. Therefore, there will be no further entries in the petty cash account once it is established unless management increases or decreases the original amount on a permanent basis. The fund must be replenished (a) when the balance of cash in the fund is low, and (b) always at the end of the accounting period, whether low or not. Replenishment at the end of the accounting period is necessary to (a) record the expenses incurred by the fund up to the date of the financial statements and (b) have the amount of petty cash on hand that is shown in the Petty Cash account. The petty cash fund should be subject to rigid internal control procedures to remove all temptations to misuse it.

SUPPLEMENT 8B—SPECIAL JOURNALS

In the preceding chapters, the **general journal** was used to record all transactions in chronological order (i.e., by order of date). The general journal can be used to record any transaction. However, it is inefficient if used for recording transactions that occur frequently, such as credit sales, credit purchases, cash receipts, and cash payments. The **general journal** is inefficient in three ways: (1) the same journal entry must be recorded repeatedly (except for changed amounts), (2) a large number of journal entries must be posted to the ledger, and (3) division of labor is difficult with a single journal. Special journals are designed to reduce these inefficiencies.

No new accounting principles or concepts are involved with special journals. They involve only the mechanics of data processing. Special journals should be designed to meet a special need when a particular type of data processing problem arises. We will limit this discussion to the four special journals that often are used: credit sales, credit purchases, cash receipts, and cash payments.

Credit sales journal

This journal is designed to accommodate **only credit sales.** Cash sales are entered in the cash receipts journal as explained below. Recall that the journal entry to record a credit sale (assuming a periodic inventory system) is:[12]

Jan. 3 Accounts receivable (customer's name) 100	
Sales	100
To record credit sale; Invoice No. 324; terms n/30.	

The credit sales journal is designed to simplify (1) recording this kind of entry and (2) subsequent posting to the ledger. The design of a credit sales journal is

---

[12] For instructional purposes, we will utilize simplified amounts, a limited number of transactions and customers, T-accounts, and a manual system. In many companies these procedures are computerized.

shown in Exhibit 8–9. Notice the **saving** in space, time, and accounting expertise required to journalize a credit sale.

EXHIBIT 8–9

Credit sales journal and accounts receivable subsidiary ledger illustrated

	CREDIT SALES JOURNAL				Page 9

Date		Customer	Terms	Invoice Number	Folio	Amount
Jan.	3	Adams, K. L.	n/30	324	34.1	100
	4	Small, C. C.	n/30	325	34.6	60
	6	Baker, C. B.	n/30	326	34.2	110
	10	Roe, R. R.	n/30	327	34.5	20
	11	Mays, O. L.	n/30	328	34.3	200
	16	Roe, R. R.	n/30	329	34.5	90
	18	Null, O. E.	n/30	330	34.4	30
	20	Baker, C. B.	n/30	331	34.2	180
	21	Small, C. C.	n/30	332	34.6	150
	31	Null, O. E.	n/30	333	34.4	260
		Total				1,200
		Posting				(34) (81)

ACCOUNTS RECEIVABLE SUBSIDIARY LEDGER

Adams, K. L			34.1
Jan. 3		9	100

Baker, C. B.			34.2
Jan. 6		9	110
20		9	180	290

Mays, O. L.			34.3
Jan. 11		9	200

Null, O. E.			34.4
Jan. 18		9	30
31		9	260	290

Roe, R. R.			34.5
Jan. 10		9	20
16		9	90	110

Small, C. C.			34.6
Jan. 4		9	60
21		9	150	210

GENERAL LEDGER

Accounts Receivable (control)			34
Jan. 31	9	1,200	

Sales Revenue			81
	Jan. 31	9	1,200

Posting the credit sales journal

Posting the special credit sales journal involves two distinct phases. First, the **individual charges** (i.e., debits) must be posted daily to the customers' individual accounts in the accounts receivable subsidiary ledger. This task may be divided among several employees. Second, periodically (usually weekly or monthly), the **totals** are posted to the **general ledger** accounts—Accounts Receivable (debit) and Sales Revenue (credit). There is a significant saving in time compared with posting each transaction to the general ledger.

Posting on a daily basis to the **subsidiary ledger,** as shown in Exhibit 8–9, is indicated in the folio column by entering the account number for each individual customer. Daily posting to the subsidiary ledger is necessary because customers may, on any day, want to pay the current balance of their accounts.

The second phase in posting the sales journal is to transfer to the general ledger the total credit sales for the month. Thus, the $1,200 total will be posted to the general ledger as (1) a debit to the Accounts Receivable **control account** and (2) a credit to the Sales Revenue account. This posting is shown in Exhibit 8–9; note in the credit sales journal that two ledger account numbers were entered for the $1,200 total to indicate the posting procedure.

The credit sales journal can be adapted readily to fill special needs. For example, sales taxes could be recorded by adding a column headed "Sales Taxes Payable," and separate sales columns can be added to accumulate sales by department or product. You should observe the following efficiencies: (1) recording in the credit sales journal is much less time consuming than separately entering each credit sale in the general journal, (2) posting is reduced by transferring the **total** to the general ledger instead of posting separate debits and credits for each sales transaction, (3) the opportunity for division of labor, and (4) additional information (such as sales revenue by department) can be recorded easily.

Credit purchases journal

Following the same pattern as described above, a credit purchases journal may be designed to record the entry common to all purchases on credit:

Jan. 8	Purchases* 392	
	Accounts payable, C. B. Smith	392

To record purchase on credit from C. B. Smith, Purchase Order No. 139; invoice dated January 5, 19B; terms 2/10, n/30. Recorded net of discount, $400 × 0.98 = $392.

* This debit assumes a periodic inventory system; if a perpetual system is used this account would be Merchandise Inventory.

Only credit purchases are recorded in the credit purchases journal. Cash

EXHIBIT 8-10

Credit purchases journal illustrated

CREDIT PURCHASES JOURNAL						Page 4
Date	Creditor's Account	Purchase Order No.	Date of Invoice	Terms	Folio	Amount
Jan. 8	Smith, C. B. Etc.	139	Jan. 5	2/10, n/30	51.8	392
	Total					784
	Posting					(6) (51)

purchases are entered in the cash payments journal as illustrated later. The design of a purchases journal is as shown in Exhibit 8–10.

Notice that purchases are recorded net of the purchase discount (as explained in Chapter 6). The cash payments journal will be used to record the subsequent payment of cash for the purchase including situations where the purchase discount is lost.

Exhibit 8–10 was not completed in detail for illustrative purposes because it follows the same pattern already shown for the credit sales journal. Daily posting would involve transfer to the creditors' individual accounts in the **accounts payable subsidiary ledger.** Periodically, the total would be posted to the **general ledger** as (1) a debit to the Purchases account and (2) a credit to the Accounts Payable control account. The efficiencies cited for the sales journal also are realized by a purchases journal.

Cash receipts journal

All cash receipts can be recorded in the cash receipts journal, but no other transactions can be recorded in it. The design of a special journal to accommodate **cash receipts** is more complex because there are many different accounts that are **credited individually** when the Cash account is debited. To resolve this problem, more than one **credit** column is needed to record the various credits. The number and designation of the debit and credit columns depends upon the character of the repetitive cash receipts transactions in the particular business.

A typical cash receipts journal with some usual transactions recorded is shown in Exhibit 8–11. Notice that there are separate debit and credit sections. Each column is used as follows:

EXHIBIT 8–11

Cash receipts journal illustrated

Date		Explanation	DEBITS	CREDITS				
			Cash	Account Title	Folio	Accounts Receivable	Sundry Accounts	Cash Sales
Jan.	2	Cash sales	1,237					1,237
	3	Cash sales	1,482					1,482
	4	Sale of land	2,500	Land	43		2,000	
				Gain on sale of land	91		500	
	4	Cash sales	992					992
	6	Invoice #324	100	Adams, K.L.	34.1	100		
	6	Cash sales	1,570					1,570
	10	Bank loan, 12%	1,000	Notes payable	54		1,000	
	15	Invoice #328	200	Mays, O.L.	34.3	200		
	26	Cash sales	1,360					1,360
	31	Invoice #326	110	Baker, C.B.	34.2	110		
	31	Cash sales	1,810					1,810
		Totals	12,361			410	3,500	8,451
		Posting	(12)			(34)	(NP)	(81)

CASH RECEIPTS JOURNAL — Page 14

1. **Cash debit**—This column is used for **each** debit to cash. The column is totaled at the end of the month and posted as one debit amount to the Cash account in the general ledger. The posting number at the bottom indicates the total was posted to account number "12," which is the Cash account.[13]
2. **Accounts Receivable credit**—This column is used to enter the individual amounts collected on trade accounts which must be posted to the individual customer accounts in the **accounts receivable subsidiary ledger** (as indicated by the posting numbers in the folio columns). The **total** of this column is posted at the end of the month as a credit to the Accounts Receivable **control** account in the general ledger as indicated by the posting number "34."
3. **Sundry Accounts credit**—This column is used for recording credits to all accounts other than those for which special credit columns are provided (in this example Accounts Receivable and Sales Revenue). The titles of the accounts to be credited are entered under the column "Account Title."

---

[13] This design assumes that the company correctly records credit sales at net of discounts. If credit sales are recorded at "gross," then a Sales Discount debit column also would be needed in this special journal.

Because the Sundry Accounts column represents a number of **accounts,** the **total** is not posted; rather, each individual amount must be posted as a credit directly to the indicated general ledger account. Account numbers entered in the related folio column indicate the posting.

4. **Cash Sales credit**—This column is used to record **all cash sales.** The total at the end of the month is posted as a credit to the Sales Revenue account in the general ledger.

Posting the cash receipts journal involves the same two phases explained previously for the credit sales and credit purchases journals. The **daily posting** phase involves posting the individual credits to the accounts receivable subsidiary ledger. The **second phase** involves posting the totals periodically to the accounts in the general ledger, with the exception of the column total for "Sundry Accounts," as explained above.

The individual accounts shown in the "Sundry Accounts" column can be posted daily or at the end of the month. Posting through January is indicated by account code numbers in the illustrated cash receipts journal.

The representative entries shown in the illustrated cash receipts journal are summarized in Exhibit 8–12, in **general journal form,** for convenience in assessing the increased efficiencies of the cash receipts journal approach in journalizing and posting a large number of individual cash transactions.

Other debit and credit columns can be added to the cash receipts journal to accommodate repetitive transactions that also involve cash receipts.

Cash payments journal

The special cash payments journal (often called the check register) is designed to accommodate efficiently the recording of **all cash payments.** Only cash payments can be recorded in the cash payments journal. The basic credit column is for Cash; columns for debits are incorporated into the format to accommodate repetitive transactions that involve cash payments. The cash payments journal also must include a column for "Sundry Accounts, Debits" to accommodate the nonrecurring transactions involving cash payments for which a special debit column is not provided.

A typical cash payments journal with some usual transactions recorded is shown in Exhibit 8–13. Notice that there are separate debit and credit sections. Each column illustrated is used as follows:

1. **Cash credit**—This column is for **every credit** to the Cash account. The column is totaled at the end of the month and posted as a credit to the Cash account in the general ledger.

2. **Accounts Payable debit**—This column is used to enter the individual amounts paid on accounts payable. The individual amounts are posted as debits to the **accounts payable subsidiary ledger** (as indicated by the account numbers under folio), and the total at the end of the month is posted as a debit to the Accounts Payable control account in the general ledger.

_____ **Exhibit 8–12** _____

Journal entries for cash receipts

Jan. 2	Cash 1,237	
	Sales revenue	1,237
	To record total cash sales for the day.	
3	Cash 1,482	
	Sales revenue	1,482
	To record total cash sales for the day.	
4	Cash 2,500	
	Land	2,000
	Gain on sale of land	500
	To record sale of land for $2,500 that originally cost $2,000.	
4	Cash 992	
	Sales revenue	992
	To record total cash sales for the day.	
6	Cash 100	
	Accounts receivable	100
	To record total collection of K. L. Adams account for Invoice No. 324 (no discount).	
6	Cash 1,570	
	Sales revenue	1,570
	To record total cash sales for the day.	
10	Cash 1,000	
	Notes payable	1,000
	To record bank loan, 90-day, 12%.	
15	Cash 200	
	Accounts receivable	200
	To record collection of O. L. Mays account for Invoice No. 328 (no discount).	
26	Cash 1,360	
	Sales revenue	1,360
	To record total cash sales for the day.	
31	Cash 110	
	Accounts receivable	110
	To record total collection of C. B. Baker account for Invoice No. 326 (no discount).	
31	Cash 1,810	
	Sales revenue	1,810
	To record total cash sales for the day.	

EXHIBIT 8–13

Cash payments journal illustrated

Date	Check No.	Explanation	CREDITS	DEBITS				
			Cash	Account Title	Folio	Accounts Payable	Sundry Accounts	Cash Purchases
Jan 2	101	Purchased mdse.	1,880					1,880
4	102	Invoice #37	2,970	Ray Mfg. Co	51.3	2,970		
5	103	Jan. rent	1,200	Rent expense	71		1,200	
8	104	Purchased mdse.	250					250
10	105	Freight on mdse.	15	Freight in	63		15	
14	106	Invoice #42	980	Bows Supply Co	51.1	980		
15	107	Paid note, plus	2,200	Notes payable	54		2,000	
		interest		Interest expense	79		200	
20	108	Insurance premium	600	Prepaid insurance	19		600	
26	109	Purchased mdse.	2,160					2,160
29	110	Invoice #91 - after	500	Myar Corp	51.2	490		
		discount period		Discount lost	80		10	
31	111	Wages	1,000	Wage expense	76		1,000	
		Totals	13,755			4,440	5,025	4,290
		Posting	(12)			(51)	(NP)	(61)
Feb 1		Etc.						

CASH PAYMENTS JOURNAL   Page 16

3. **Sundry Accounts debit**—This column is used to record all accounts debited for which special columns are not provided (in this example Accounts Payable and Purchases are provided). The titles of the accounts to be debited are entered under the column "Account Titles." Because this column represents a number of accounts, the total cannot be posted; rather, each individual amount is posted as a debit directly to the indicated general ledger account.

4. **Cash Purchases debit**—All cash purchases are entered in this column. The total at the end of the month is posted as a debit to the Purchases account in the ledger.

Posting the cash payments journal involves two phases: (1) **daily posting** of the individual credit amounts to the **accounts payable subsidiary ledger;** and (2)

periodic posting of the totals to the **general ledger,** with the exception of the total of "Sundry Accounts." The posting of the individual amounts in the "Sundry Accounts" column can be done during the period, say, daily.

The illustrative transactions entered in the cash payments journal (Exhibit 8–13) were:

Jan. 2 Issued Check No. 101 for cash purchase of merchandise costing $1,880.
      4 Issued Check No. 102 to pay account payable owed to Ray Manufacturing Company within the discount period. Discount allowed, 1%; Invoice No. 37, $3,000.
      5 Issued Check No. 103 to pay January rent, $1,200.
      8 Issued Check No. 104 for cash purchase of merchandise costing $250.
   10 Issued Check No. 105 for freight-in on merchandise purchased, $15.
   14 Issued Check No. 106 to pay account payable owed to Bows Supply Company within the discount period. Discount allowed, 2%; Invoice No. 42, $1,000.
   15 Issued Check No. 107 to pay $2,000 note payable plus 10% interest for one year.
   20 Issued Check No. 108 to pay three-year insurance premium, $600.
   26 Issued Check No. 109 for cash purchase of merchandise costing $2,160.
   29 Issued Check No. 110 to pay account payable to Myar Corporation; terms 2/10, n/30; Invoice No. 91, $500. Therefore, accounts payable to Myar was credited for $490 at the purchase date (see Chapter 6). The payment was made after the discount period; hence, the full invoice price of $500 was paid and purchase discount lost of $10 was recorded.
   31 Issued Check No. 111 to pay wages amounting to $1,000.

Additional debit and credit columns can be added to the cash payments journal to accommodate other repetitive transactions involving cash disbursements.

Many companies control expenditures with a **voucher system** rather than using the credit purchases and the cash payments journals. A voucher system is adaptable to computerized accounting and gives tight control mechanisms on the sequence of events for each transaction from incurrence until final cash payment. The voucher system is explained and illustrated in Chapter 10.

In summary, special journals do not involve new accounting principles or concepts. Rather, they represent a mechanical technique designed to increase efficiency in the data processing cycle. Special journals are not standardized. They should be designed to fit each situation. Although a manual approach has been illustrated for instructional purposes, many companies have computerized the procedures represented by special journals. In computerized systems, essentially the same mechanics illustrated for the manual system are accomplished by the computer.

IMPORTANT TERMS DEFINED IN THIS CHAPTER

Terms (alphabetically)	Key words in definitions of terms used in chapter	Page reference
Bank reconciliation	Process of verifying the accuracy of both the bank statement and the cash accounts of the business.	374
Bank statement	Monthly report from a bank that shows deposits recorded, checks cleared, and a running bank balance.	372
Cash	Money and any instrument that banks will accept for immediate increase in depositor's checking account.	370
Cash over and short	Difference between the amount of cash held at a particular time and the amount the cash records call for.	379
Certificates of deposit	A CD; an investment contract that can be purchased from banks; specifies amount, time, and interest rate.	386
Compensating balances	Exists when a bank requires that a specified minimum cash balance must be maintained in the depositor's account.	380
Conservatism	When more than one alternative is acceptable in accounting, use the one that has the least short-term favorable effect on income and owners' equity.	392
Contingent liability	An endorser (on a negotiable instrument) is liable for its payment if the maker defaults; a contingent liability exists for the endorser.	391
Default of note receivable	Failure of the maker (payor) of a note to pay it by its maturity date.	390
Deposits in transit	Deposits made by a depositor that have not yet been reported on the bank statement.	375
Discounting a note receivable	Sale of a note receivable to another party prior to its maturity date.	390
Exceptions to accounting principles	Implementation principles may be modified in application for (a) immaterial amounts, (b) conservatism, and (c) cost benefit constraint.	392
Internal control	Policies and procedures of a business designed to safeguard the assets of the business.	370
Investment portfolio	A group of securities (stock or bonds) held as an investment; grouped to be accounted for as one unit.	383
Lower of cost or market	Valuation of an investment at either (a) original cost or (b) current market whichever is lower.	382
Materiality	Small amounts involved in transactions must be recorded; however, the theoretically correct way may, but need not, be followed; use a simple accounting approach.	392
Negotiable instrument	A formal (written) instrument that specifies the terms of a debt; it is **transferable by endorsement.**	391
Notes receivable	A written promise that requires another party to pay the business under specified conditions (amount, time, interest).	388
Outstanding checks	Checks written by a depositor that have not yet been cleared (cashed) by the depositor's bank.	375
Petty cash	A small amount of cash set aside for making small cash payments instead of writing checks.	374
Receivables, short-term	Short-term notes and accounts owed to the business by regular trade customers.	387

Terms (alphabetically)	Key words in definitions of terms used in chapter	Page reference
Short-term investment	An investment that *(a)* is marketable and *(b)* will have a short-term holding period.	381
Special receivables	Receivables that arise from transactions other than merchandise and services sold.	388
Trade receivables	Another name for accounts receivable; open accounts owed to the business by trade customers.	388
Unrealized loss	Difference between original purchase cost of an investment and its current market value, if market value is **lower,** there is an unrealized loss (if not sold).	384

QUESTIONS

PART A

1. Define cash in the context of accounting and indicate the types of items that should be included and excluded. Identify typical categories of cash.

2. Summarize the primary characteristics of an effective internal control system for cash.

3. Why should cash-handling and cash-recording activities be separated? How is this separation accomplished?

4. What are the purposes of a bank reconciliation? What balances are reconciled?

5. Briefly explain how the total amount of cash reported on the balance sheet is computed.

6. What is the purpose of petty cash? How is it related to the regular Cash account?

PART B

7. Define a short-term investment. What is the twofold test for classification of an investment as short term?

8. Is a marketable security always classified as a short-term investment? Explain.

9. How does the cost principle apply in accounting for short-term investments in *(a)* debt securities and *(b)* equity securities?

10. What is the rationale for application of the LCM rule to the short-term investment portfolio of equity securities?

11. Explain the purpose of the Allowance to Reduce Short-Term Investments to Market account.

PART C

12. Distinguish between accounts receivable and special receivables.

13. Define a promissory note indicating the designation of the parties and explain what is meant by principal, maturity date, face amount, and interest rate.

14. Distinguish between an interest-bearing and noninterest-bearing note.

15. What is a negotiable note?

16. What is a defaulted note? Who is responsible for its payment? Explain.

17. What is meant by discounting a note receivable?

18. What is a contingent liability? How does one arise in respect to a note receivable?

19. Identify and briefly explain the three accounting constraints related to the implementing accounting principles.

EXERCISES

E8–1 **(Pair Definition with Terms)**
Match the following brief definitions with the terms by entering the appropriate letter in each space provided.

Terms	*Definitions*
_____ (1) Bank statement	A. An analysis that explains any differences existing between the cash balance shown by the depositor and that shown by the bank.
_____ (2) Short-term investment	
_____ (3) Cash over and short	B. Provided by the bank to the depositor each month listing deposits, checks cleared, and running balance.
_____ (4) Petty cash	
_____ (5) Compensating balances	C. Examples of this, by definition, are currency, checks, money orders, or bank drafts.
_____ (6) Contingent liability	D. Account to record errors that occur inevitably when a large number of cash transactions is involved.
_____ (7) Bank reconciliation	
_____ (8) Special receivables	E. Required minimum cash balances on deposit.
_____ (9) Internal control	F. Selecting the accounting method that yields the most pessimistic immediate financial results.
_____ (10) Cash	
_____ (11) Conservatism in accounting	G. A potential liability that depends on a future event arising out of a past transaction.
_____ (12) Materiality	H. A note receivable not collected at maturity.
_____ (13) Deposits in transit	I. Deposits recorded in the depositor's ledger as debits to cash that have not been recorded by the bank.
_____ (14) Notes receivable	
_____ (15) Discounting a note receivable	J. Selling a negotiable note receivable before its maturity date to obtain cash.
_____ (16) Negotiable instrument	K. Methods and procedures concerned with the accuracy of financial records.
_____ (17) Outstanding checks	L. An exception to accounting principles that says that amounts not material must be accounted for but need not be accorded theoretically correct treatment.
_____ (18) Default of note receivable	

M. The most common example of this is a check.

N. Promissory notes that are evidence of a debt and state the terms of payment.

O. Checks not listed on the bank's statement.

P. Currency used for disbursements that are usually relatively minor and conveniently made from cash on hand.

Q. A temporary investment in marketable securities.

R. Receivables, short or long term, that arise from transactions other than the sale of goods and/or services.

E8–2 **(Reporting Cash When There Are Several Bank Accounts)**

Modern Furniture Corporation has manufacturing facilities in several cities and has cash on hand at several locations as well in several bank accounts. The general ledger at the end of 19A showed the following accounts: Petty Cash—Home Office, $500 City Bank—Home Office, $57,300; Cash Held for Making Change, $1,000 (included in the regular Cash Account balance); Petty Cash—Location A, $100; National Bank—Location A, $4,458; Petty Cash—Location B, $200; Southwest Bank—Location B; $864; Petty Cash—Location C, $100; State Bank—Location C, $965; and Metropolitan Bank—Savings account, $8,700; and postdated checks held that were received from two regular customers, $600.

The four bank balances given represent the current cash balances as reflected on the bank reconciliations.

Required:

What cash amount should be reported on Modern Furniture's 19A balance sheet? Explain the basis for your decisions on any questionable items.

E8–3 **(Analysis of Items to Determine Correct Cash Balance)**

Lakeview Company prepared a December 31, 19B, balance sheet that reported cash, $7,489. The following items were included in the reported cash balance:

Balance per bank statement at City Bank	$4,934*
a. A deposit made to the local electric utility	500
b. Postage stamps on hand	80
c. Check signed by a customer, returned NSF	30
d. Petty cash on hand	150
e. IOUs signed by employees	80
f. Check signed by the company president for an advance to him; to be held until he "gives the word to cash it."	1,500
g. Money orders on hand (received from customers)	45
h. A signed receipt from a freight company that involved a $10 overpayment to them. They have indicated "a check will be mailed shortly."	10
i. A money order obtained from the post office to be used to pay for a special purchase upon delivery; expected within the next five days	160
Total cash shown on the 19B balance sheet	$7,489

* Items not considered: deposit in transit, $500; checks outstanding, $175; and cash held for making change, $100 (all included in the regular Cash account).

Required:

a. The reported cash balance is not correct. Compute the correct cash amount that should be reported on the balance sheet. Give appropriate reporting for any items that you exclude. (Hint: Set up a form similar to the above.)

b. Assume the company carries two cash accounts in the general ledger—Cash and Petty Cash. What is the correct balance that should be reflected in each cash account at December 31, 19B (end of the accounting period)? Show computations.

E8–4 **(Bank Reconciliation, Entries, and Reporting)**

Howard Company has the June 30, 19B, bank statement and the June ledger accounts for cash, which are summarized below:

Bank Statement

	Checks	Deposits	Balance
Balance, June 1, 19B			$ 4,900
Deposits during June		$17,000	21,900
Checks cleared through June	$17,700		4,200
Bank service charges	75		4,125
Balance, June 30, 19B			·4,125

Cash

June	1	Balance	4,900	June	Checks written	18,100
June		Deposits	19,000			

Petty Cash

June 30	Balance	200	

Required:

a. Reconcile the bank account. A comparison of the checks written with the checks that have cleared the bank show outstanding checks of $900. Cash on hand (for making change) on June 30 is $500 (included in the Cash account). Some of the checks that cleared in June were written prior to June. There were no deposits in transit carried over from May, but there is a deposit in transit at the end of June.

b. Give any journal entries that should be made as a result of the bank reconciliation.

c. What is the balance in the cash account after the reconciliation entries?

d. What total amount of cash should be reported on the balance sheet at June 30?

E8–5   **(Bank Reconciliation, Entries, and Reporting)**

The September 30, 19D, bank statement for Witt Company and the September ledger accounts for cash are summarized below:

Bank Statement

	Checks	Deposits	Balance
Balance, September 1, 19D			$ 5,100
Deposits recorded during September		$27,000	32,100
Checks cleared during September	$27,300		4,800
NSF check—J. J. Jones	80		4,720
Bank service charges	100		4,620
Balance, September 30, 19D			4,620

Cash

Sept.	1	Balance	5,300	Sept.	Checks written	27,800
Sept.		Deposits	29,500			

Petty Cash

Sept. 30	Balance	450	

Cash on hand for making change (included in the Cash account) on September 1 and September 30 amounted to $200. There were no outstanding checks and no deposits in transit carried over from August; however, there are deposits in transit and checks outstanding at the end of September.

Required:

a. Reconcile the bank account.
b. Give any journal entries that should be made as a result of the bank reconciliation.
c. What should be the balance in the Cash account after the reconciliation entries?
d. What total amount of cash should Witt report on the September 30 balance sheet?

E8–6   **(Bank Reconciliation with an Overage or Shortage)**

The March 31, 19C, bank statement for Star Company and the March ledger accounts for cash are summarized below:

Bank Statement

	Checks	Deposits	Balance
Balance, March 1, 19C			$ 8,600
Deposits during March		$28,000	36,600
Note collected for depositor			
(including $100 interest)		1,060	37,660
Checks cleared during March	$32,200		5,460
Bank service charges	35		5,425
Balance, March 31, 19C			5,425

Cash

Mar.	1	Balance	8,320	Mar.	Checks written	32,500
Mar.		Deposits	31,000			

Petty Cash

Mar. 31	Balance	200	

A comparison of March deposits recorded with deposits on the bank statement showed deposits in transit of $3,000. Outstanding checks at the end of March were determined to be $900. Cash on hand (not petty cash) for making change (included in the Cash account) was $300 at March 31.

Required:

a. Prepare a bank reconciliation for March. The bank figures have been verified as correct.
b. Give any journal entries that should be made by Star based on the reconciliation.
c. What amount should be shown as the ending balance in the Cash account after the reconciliation entries? What total amount of cash should be reported on Star's balance sheet at the end of March?

PART B

E8–7   **(Recording and Reporting Short-Term Investments)**

In July 19B, White Company had accumulated excess cash that would not be needed for 10 to 15 months. To employ the idle cash profitably, the management decided to purchase some shares of stock as a short-term investment. The following related transactions occurred:

19B
July 30   Purchased 5,000 shares of the common stock of Sharp Corporation. The cash price, including fees and transfer costs, was $20,000.
Dec. 15   Received a cash dividend of $0.40 per share on the Sharp shares.
      30   Sold 1,000 of the Sharp shares at $5 per share.

Required:

a. Give the journal entries that White Company should make on each date for this short-term investment. The accounting period of White Company ends on December 31.
b. Show how this short-term investment should be reported on the balance sheet at December 31, 19B. Assume the market value of the Sharp stock was $5 per share on December 31, 19B.

E8–8   (Recording and Reporting a Single Equity Security)

Danbury Company purchased some common stock in Bay Corporation as a short-term investment. The following related transactions occurred:

19B
Feb. 1   Purchased 10,000 shares of Bay Corporation common stock for $60,000 cash.
Aug. 15   Received a cash dividend on the Bay stock of $0.30 per share.
Dec. 30   Sold 3,000 shares of the Bay stock at $5.80 per share.
      31   End of the accounting year. Bay stock was selling at $5.75 per share.

Required:

a. Give the journal entries for Danbury Company on each date (including December 31) for the investment in Bay stock. Danbury Company had no other short-term investments.
b. Show how the effects of this short-term investment should be reported on the financial statements at December 31, 19B.
c. Give the entry on January 15, 19C, assuming the remaining shares were sold at $5.50 per share.
d. Explain what Danbury Company should do about the allowance account on December 31, 19C, assuming no short-term investments are held on that date.

E8–9   (Recording and Reporting a Short-Term Investment in Several Securities)

During March 19B, Meigs Company acquired 200 shares of common stock in each of three corporations at the following costs: Corporation A, $8,000; Corporation B, $6,000; and Corporation C, $12,000. At the end of the annual accounting period, December 31, 19B, the quoted market prices per share were Corporation A, $40; Corporation B, $25; and Corporation C, $61.

Required:

a. Give the journal entry for Meigs to record the acquisition of these short-term investments.
b. Give the entry to record cash dividends of $1,800 received on the short-term investments in November 19B.
c. Give the entry to reflect the investments at LCM at December 31, 19B. Show computations.
d. Show how the investments would be reported on the financial statements at December 31, 19B.

e. Give the entry on January 5, 19C, assuming all of the shares were sold for $24,000 cash.

f. Give any entry required at December 31, 19C, assuming no short-term equity investments are held at that time (disregard any closing entries).

E8–10   **(Accounting for an Investment in a Debt Security)**

On October 1, 19B, Johnson Company purchased a debt security as a short-term investment for $25,000 cash. The security (due in 12 months) earns 8% annual interest on its principal amount of $25,000, payable on the date of maturity. At the end of the annual accounting period (December 31), the same security could be purchased for $24,200 cash.

Required:

a. Give all of the journal entries for Johnson Company on the following dates and provide an explanation for each date:
   (1) October 1, 19B.
   (2) December 31, 19B.
   (3) September 30, 19C.
b. Show how the security would be reported on the 19B financial statements.

PART C

E8–11   **(Accounting for a Credit Sale through Accounts Receivable, to Notes Receivable, to Final Collection)**

Approximately 40% of the merchandise sold by King Company is sold on credit. Accounts receivable that are overdue, if material in amount, are "converted" to notes receivable when possible. The related transactions during 19B were:

Jan. 10   Sold merchandise on account to B. A. Cable for $10,000; terms n/30.
Mar. 1   The account was unpaid. King Company asked Cable to sign a six-month, 10%, interest-bearing note for the account. Cable executed the note on this date.
Aug. 31   Cable paid the principal of the note plus interest.

Required:

a. Give the journal entry that King should make on each of the three dates.
b. Give the journal entry that should be made on September 1, 19B, assuming Cable defaulted.
c. Give the journal entry assuming the default in (b) and also that Cable paid the note in full on September 15, 19B (no additional interest was paid).

E8–12   **(Accounting for a Credit Sale with a Note Payable)**

Pyle Company sells a line of products that has a high unit sales price. Credit terms are traditional in the industry. Pyle frequently takes a promissory note for the sale price. The accounting year ends December 31. The transactions and events were:

19B
Dec. 1   Sold merchandise to B. T. Hamm on a three-month, 12%, interest-bearing note for $10,000.
   31   End of accounting year.

19C

Jan. 1   Start of new accounting period.

Mar. 1   Collected the note plus interest.

Required:

a. Give the journal entries for Pyle Company at each of the four dates; if none, so state.

b. With respect to the note, what item(s) and amount(s) should be reported on the 19B income statement?

c. With respect to the note, what item(s) and amount(s) should be reported on the balance sheet at December 31, 19B?

E8–13   (Accounting for a Defaulted Note)

Sidney Company frequently sells merchandise on a promissory note. These notes frequently are sold (i.e., discounted) to the local bank to obtain cash needed before maturity date. The following transactions relate to one note:

19B

Apr. 1   Sold merchandise for $9,000 to R. C. Day; took a six-month, 12%, interest-bearing note.

June 1   Discounted the note at the local bank at a 10% discount rate.

Oct. 1   Due date of the note plus interest.

Required:

a. Give the journal entries of the three dates, assuming Day paid the bank for the note on due date.

b. Give the journal entry on October 1, 19B, assuming Day defaulted on the note and Sidney Company had to make payment plus a $50 protest fee. This protest fee will be charged to Day.

c. Give the journal entry assuming Day paid in full on October 5, 19B (no additional interest was paid).

E8–14   (Based on Supplement 8A—Accounting and Reporting Petty Cash)

On January 1, 19B, Boston Company established a petty cash fund of $300 by writing a check to "Petty Cash." The fund was assigned to J. Wright, an employee, to administer as custodian. At the end of January, $60 cash remained in the fund. Signed receipts for expenditures during January were summarized as follows: postage, $63; office supplies, $28; transportation, $101; newspapers, $34; and miscellaneous (coffee for the office), $14.

Required:

a. Give the journal entry to establish the petty cash fund on January 1, 19B.

b. Give the journal entry to replenish the fund on January 31, 19B.

c. What balance would be shown in the Petty Cash account in the ledger at January 31? Explain.

d. How would petty cash be reported on the balance sheet at January 31, 19B?

e. Explain how the petty cash fund affected the January 19B income statement?

f. Assume it is January 5, 19C, and the management has decided to decrease the petty cash fund to $250. Give the required journal entry.

PROBLEMS

PART A

P8–1   **(Analysis of Internal Control)**

Pedernales Company has one trusted employee who, as the owner said, "handles all of the bookkeeping and paperwork for the company." This employee also is responsible for counting, verifying, and recording cash receipts and payments, such as making the weekly bank deposit, preparing checks for major expenditures (signed by the owner), making small expenditures from the cash register for daily expenses, and collecting accounts receivable. The owners asked the local bank for a $25,000 loan. The bank asked that an audit be performed covering the year just ended. The independent auditor (a local CPA), in a private conference with the owner, presented some evidence of the following activities of the trusted employee during the past year:

1. Cash sales sometimes were not entered in the cash register, and the trusted employee pocketed approximately $40 per month.
2. Cash taken from the cash register (and pocketed by the trusted employee) was replaced with expense memos with fictitious signatures (approximately $10 per day).
3. A $500 collection on an account receivable of a valued out-of-town customer was pocketed by the trusted employee and was covered by making a $500 entry as a debit to Sales Returns and a credit to Accounts Receivable.
4. A $700 collection on an account receivable from a local customer was pocketed by the trusted employee and was covered by making a $700 entry as a debit to Allowance for Doubtful Accounts and a credit to Accounts Receivable.

Required:

a. What was the approximate amount stolen during the past year?
b. What would be your recommendations to the owner?

P8–2   **(Prepare a Bank Reconciliation and Related Journal Entries)**

The bookkeeper at Rapid Growth Company has not reconciled the bank statement with the Cash account, saying, "I don't have time." You have been asked to prepare a reconciliation and review the procedures with the bookkeeper.

The April 30, 19D, bank statement and the April ledger accounts for cash showed the following (summarized):

Bank Statement

	Checks	Deposits	Balance
Balance, April 1, 19D			$23,550
Deposits during April		$38,000	61,550
Note collected for depositor			
(including $90 interest)		1,090	62,640
Checks cleared during April	$44,700		17,940
NSF check—A. B. Cage	140		17,800
Bank service charges	50		17,750
Balance, April 30, 19D			17,750

Cash

Apr.	1	Balance	23,050	Apr. Checks written	44,500
Apr.		Deposits	42,000		

Petty Cash

Apr. 30	Balance	200	

A comparison of checks written before and during April with the checks cleared through the bank showed outstanding checks at the end of April of $600. No deposits in transit were carried over from March, but there was a deposit in transit at the end of April. Cash on hand, held for change, at the end of April was $300 (included in the regular Cash account).

Required:

a. Prepare a detailed bank reconciliation for April.
b. Give any required journal entries as a result of the reconciliation. Why are they necessary?
c. What were the balances in the cash accounts in the ledger on May 1, 19D?
d. What total amount of cash should be reported on the balance sheet at the end of April?

P8–3   **(Compute Outstanding Checks and Deposits in Transit; Prepare a Bank Reconciliation and Journal Entries)**

The August 19B bank statement for Zork Company and the August 19B ledger accounts for cash are given below:

Bank Statement

		Checks	*Deposits*	*Balance*
Aug.	1			$16,000
	2	$ 300		15,700
	3		$7,000	22,700
	4	400		22,300
	5	200		22,100
	9	900		21,200
	10	300		20,900
	15		9,000	29,900
	21	700		29,200
	24	21,000		8,200
	25		8,000	16,200
	30	800		15,400
	30		2,180*	17,580
	31	75†		17,505

* $2,000 note collected plus interest.
† Bank service charge.

Cash

Aug. 1 Balance	15,250	Checks written:	
Deposits:		Aug. 2	300
Aug. 2	7,000	4	900
12	9,000	15	850
24	8,000	17	550
31	6,000	18	800
		18	700
		23	21,000

Petty Cash

Aug. 31 Balance	400

Cash on hand for making change at the end of August is $150 (included in the regular Cash account). Outstanding checks at the end of July were $200, $400, and $300. There were no deposits in transit at the end of July.

Required:

a. Compute the deposits in transit at the end of August.
b. Compute the outstanding checks at the end of August.
c. Prepare a bank reconciliation for August.
d. Give any journal entries that should be made as a result of the bank reconciliation by Zork Company. Why are they necessary?
e. After the reconciliation journal entries are posted, what balances would be reflected in the cash accounts in the ledger?
f. What total amount of cash should be reported on the August 31, 19B, balance sheet?

P8–4   **(Compute Outstanding Checks and Deposits in Transit; Prepare Bank Reconciliation)**
The December 31, 19B, bank statement for Myles Company and the December 19B ledger accounts for cash are given below.

Bank Statement

Date	Checks	Deposits	Balance
Dec. 1			$41,000
2	$400, 150	$16,000	56,450
4	7,000, 80		49,370
6	120, 180, 1,500		47,570
11	900, 1,200, 90	21,000	66,380
13	450, 700, 1,900		63,330
17	17,000, 2,000		44,330
23	40, 23,500	36,000	56,790
26	1,800, 2,650		52,340
28	2,200, 4,800		45,340
30	13,000, 1,890, 200*	19,000	49,250
31	1,650, 1,200, 28‡	6,360†	52,732

* NSF check, J. Doe, a customer.
† Note collected, principal, $6,000 plus interest.
‡ Bank service charge.

Cash

Dec. 1 Balance	56,000	Checks written during December:		
Deposits:		40	5,000	2,650
Dec. 11	21,000	13,000	4,800	1,650
23	36,000	700	1,890	2,200
30	19,000	4,400	1,500	7,000
31	18,000	1,200	120	150
		180	80	450
		17,000	23,500	2,000
		90	900	1,900
		1,800	1,200	

Petty Cash

Dec. 31 Balance	150	

The November 19B bank reconciliation showed the following: Correct cash balance at November 30, $55,700; deposits in transit on November 30, $16,000; and outstanding checks on November 30, $400 + $900 = $1,300. At the end of December 19B, cash held on hand for making change was $300 (included in the regular Cash account).

Required:

a. Compute the deposits in transit December 31, 19B.
b. Compute the outstanding checks at December 31, 19B.
c. Prepare a bank reconciliation at December 31, 19B.
d. Give any journal entries that should be made as a result of the bank reconciliation made by Myles Company. Why are they necessary?
e. After the reconciliation journal entries, what balances would be reflected in the cash accounts in the ledger?
f. What total amount of cash should be reported on the December 31, 19B, balance sheet?

PART B

P8–5   **(Accounting for a Portfolio of Short-Term Investments; Use of LCM)**
     Heather Company usually acquires common stocks as a short-term investment. This problem focuses on the purchase of three different common stocks during 19B. The annual accounting period ends December 31. The sequence of transactions was:

19B
  Apr. 2 Purchased (with cash) the following common stocks as a short-term invest-
       ment:

Corporation	Number of shares	Total price per share
X	300	$50
Y	400	70
Z	200	90

Sept. 8 Received a cash dividend of $4 per share on Corporation Z stock.

Dec. 30   Sold the stock of Corporation Y for $76 per share.

     31   Quoted market prices on this date were Corporation X stock, $53; Corporation Y stock, $75; and Corporation Z stock, $80.

Required:

a. Give the journal entry for Heather Company on each date.

b. How would the effects of these investments be shown on the 19B income statement and the balance sheet at December 31, 19B?

c. What was the amount of the 19B unrealized loss? Explain what this means.

d. Assume it is December 31, 19C, and that all of the X and Z shares still are held and that their market values per share are X, $51; and Z, $80. Give the required LCM entry. (Hint: Leave the correct balance in the Allowance account.)

P8–6   (Accounting for Short-Term Investments in Debt Securities)

On July 1, 19D, Dakota Corporation purchased, as a short-term investment, ten $1,000, 10% bonds of Lowe Corporation at par (i.e., at $1,000 each). The bonds mature on June 30, 19G. Annual interest is payable on June 30 each year. The accounting period for Dakota Corporation ends on December 31.

Required:

a. Give the journal entries required for Dakota Corporation on the following dates (if no entry is required, explain why): July 1, 19D, and December 31, 19D.

b. At the end of 19D, the bonds were quoted on the market at $975 each. Give any LCM basis journal entry required on December 31, 19D. If none is required, explain why.

c. Show how this investment should be reported on the 19D balance sheet and income statement.

d. Give the journal entry required on June 30, 19E.

P8–7   (Accounting for Short-Term Investments in Equity and Debt Securities; Use of LCM)

Superior Manufacturing Company produces and sells one main product. Demand is seasonal, and the unit sales price is high. Superior's accounting year ends December 31. Typically, in the busy months of the demand cycle, the company collects large amounts of cash, which is not needed during the slow months. The company often purchases short-term investments to earn a return on idle cash. Recently, the company purchased 1,000 shares of common stock in each of two other corporations—Corporations A and B. The prices per share, including fees and related costs, were A, $30; and B, $70. In addition, Superior purchased a $10,000 bond of James Corporation. The bond pays 9% annual interest on each March 31. The bond was purchased for $10,000 cash (i.e., at par).

The sequence of transactions was:

19B

Apr. 1   Purchased the common stock and the bond. (Hint: Account for the stock and bond portfolios separately.)

Oct. 3   Received a cash dividend of $1 per share on the stock of Corporation B.

Nov. 30   Sold 600 shares of the stock of Corporation A at $26 per share and 600 shares of the stock of Corporation B at $75 per share.

Dec. 31   End of the accounting period. The market prices on this date were A stock, $31; B stock, $68; and James bonds, 100 (i.e., at par). (Hint: Do not overlook accrued interest.)

Required:

a. Give the journal entries for Superior at each of the four dates given above. Omit any closing entries.
b. Show how the effects of the investment should be reported on the balance sheet at December 31, 19B.
c. What items and amounts should be reported on the 19B income statement?

PART C

P8–8   **(Accounting for Accounts Receivable and Notes Receivable)**

Watertown Company sells approximately 80% of its merchandise on credit; terms n/30. Occasionally, a note will be received as a part of the collection process of a delinquent account. The annual accounting period ends December 31. The sequence of transactions was:

Note No. 1:

19B
Feb. 15   Sold merchandise for $5,000 to A. B. Lee; received $3,000 cash, and the balance was debited to Accounts Receivable.
Apr.   1   Received a 12% interest-bearing note in settlement of the overdue account of Lee. The note is due in four months.
July 31   Due date for note; Lee defaulted.
Oct.   1   Lee paid the defaulted note plus interest, plus 8% interest on the defaulted amount for the period July 31–October 1. The 8% is the legal rate of interest on overdue obligations.

Note No. 2:

19B
Oct.   1   Sold merchandise for $3,000 to J. K. Pope on account.
Nov.   1   Received a 12% interest-bearing note in settlement of the overdue account from Pope. The note is due in three months.
Dec. 31   End of accounting period.

19C
Jan.   1   Start of new accounting period.
       30   Maturity date of the note. Pope paid the principal plus interest.

Required:

a. Note No. 1—Give the journal entries for Watertown Company on each date. Show interest calculations. Omit any closing entries.
b. Note No. 2—Give the journal entries for Watertown Company on each date. Show interest calculations. Omit any closing entries.
c. Note No. 2—How much interest revenue should be reported on the 19B income statement of Watertown Company?
d. Note No. 2—How will this note affect the 19B balance sheet of Watertown Company?

P8–9   **(Accounting for Notes Receivable, Including Discounting)**

Formex Company sells heavy machinery. Credit terms are customary and usually involve promissory notes and a mortgage on the machinery sold. The annual accounting period ends December 31. The transactions involving notes were:

Note No. 1:

19B

Feb. 1   Sold equipment to W. D. Fort for $40,000; received a $16,000 down payment and a four-month, 12%, interest-bearing note for the balance.

Mar. 1   Sold the note to the local bank at a 10% discount rate.

June 1   Due date of the note plus interest; Fort paid the note and interest in full.

Required:

a. Give the journal entry for Formex Company on each of the three dates. Show interest computations. Assume that Fort paid the bank the principal plus interest on the due date.

b. Give the journal entry on the due date, June 1, 19B, assuming instead that Fort defaulted on the note and Formex paid the local bank the face amount of the note plus interest, and a $25 protest fee.

c. How much interest revenue should be reported on the 19B income statement for Note No. 1?

Note No. 2:

19B

Dec. 1   Sold equipment to W. T. Owens for $30,000; received $5,000 cash down payment and a three-month, 12%, interest-bearing note for the balance.

      31   End of accounting period.

19C

Jan. 1   Start of new accounting period.

Mar. 1   Due date of the principal plus interest; Owens paid the note plus interest in full.

Required:

d. Give the journal entry for Formex Company on each of the four dates (omit any closing entries). State any assumptions you make.

e. How much interest revenue (Note No. 2) should be reported on the 19B income statement?

f. Show how Note No. 2 should be reported on the balance sheet at December 31, 19B.

P8–10   **(Based on Supplement 8B—Use of Control Accounts and Subsidiary Ledgers)**

New Company completes a variety of transactions each year. A number of them are repetitive in nature; therefore, the company maintains five different journals: general, credit sales, credit purchases, cash receipts, and cash payments. Selected transactions are listed below that are to be appropriately entered in these journals. To shorten this problem, amounts have been simplified and the number of transactions limited. All credit sales and credit purchases are recorded net of discount.

Selected transactions are listed below (use the letter to the left in lieu of the date and use the letter *v* for the last day of the period):

a. Sold merchandise to K. K. May at invoice cost of $250; terms 2/10, n/20; Invoice No. 38.

b. Received merchandise from Sable Company at invoice cost of $300; credit terms 1/10, n/20; Purchase Order No. 17.

c. Sold merchandise to B. B. Wise for $200 on credit; terms 2/10, n/20; Invoice No. 39.

d. Received merchandise from Rex Supply Company at an invoice cost of $200 on credit; terms 1/10, n/20; Purchase Order No. 18.

e. Sold merchandise to A. B. Cox for $750.

f. Received merchandise from Baker Manufacturing Company at a cost of $360; paid cash (number the checks consecutively starting with No. 81).

g. Purchased an operational asset (machinery) at a cost of $5,000; gave a 90-day, 12%, interest-bearing note payable for the purchase price.

h. Sold a tract of land for $9,000 that previously was used by the company as a parking lot and originally cost $4,000; collected cash.

i. Collected the account receivable from B. B. Wise within the discount period; Invoice No. 39.

j. Paid $600 for a three-year insurance policy on operational assets.

k. Obtained a $5,000 bank loan; signed a one-year, 12%, interest-bearing note payable.

l. Paid the account payable to Rex Supply Company within the discount period.

m. Paid monthly rent, $1,200.

n. Sold merchandise for cash, $1,400.

o. Purchased merchandise for cash, $980.

p. Sold merchandise on credit to C. C. Coe for $700; terms 2/10, n/20; Invoice No. 40.

q. Purchased merchandise on credit from Stubbs Company at an invoice cost of $400; terms 2/10/, n/30; Purchase Order No. 19.

r. Collected the account receivable from K. K. May after the discount period.

s. Paid the account payable to Sable Company after the discount period.

t. Paid monthly salaries, $2,400.

u. By year-end, six months of the prepaid insurance had expired.

Use the following general ledger account code numbers for posting: Cash, 11; Accounts Receivable, 14; Prepaid Insurance, 16; Machinery, 17; Land, 19; Accounts Payable, 21; Notes Payable, 22; Purchases, 31; Purchase Discounts Lost, 33; Sales Revenue, 41; Sales Discount Revenue, 43; Expenses, 51; and Gain on Sale of Operational Assets, 53. For journals, use the following page numbers: General, 15; Credit Sales, 18; Credit Purchases, 14; Cash Receipts, 21; and Cash Payments, 34.

Required:

1. Draft a format for each of the five journals, including a general journal, following the illustrations included in Supplement 8B. Include folio columns.

2. Set up separate T-accounts for each of the general ledger accounts listed above.

3. Set up separate T-accounts (with account numbers) for the subsidiary ledgers as follows:

Accounts receivable (14)	Accounts payable (21)
Coe—14.1	Stable—21.1
May—14.2	Stubbs—21.2
Wise—14.3	Rex—21.3

4. Enter each transaction in the appropriate journal.

5. Indicate all postings to the subsidiary ledgers by entering appropriate account numbers in the folio columns.

6. Total each money column in the special journals and indicate all postings to the general ledger accounts by entering the account code numbers in the folio columns and below total amounts posted. Use the account code numbers given above.

CASES

C8–1   (Analysis and Evaluation of Internal Controls)

Hall Manufacturing Company is a relatively small local business that specializes in the repair and renovation of antique jewelry, brass objects, and silverware. The owner is an expert craftsman. Although a number of skilled workers are employed, there is always a large backlog of work to be done. A long-time employee, who serves as clerk-book-keeper, handles cash receipts, keeps the records, and writes checks for disbursements. The checks are signed by the owner. Small amounts are paid in cash by the clerk-bookkeeper, subject to a month-end review by the owner. Approximately 100 regular customers regularly are extended credit that typically amounts to less than $500. Although credit losses are small, in recent years the bookkeeper had established an Allowance for Doubtful Accounts, and all write-offs were made at year-end. During January 19E (the current year), the owner decided to start construction as soon as possible of a building for the business that would provide many advantages over the presently rented space and would have space usable for expansion of facilities. As a part of the considerations in financing, the financing institution asked for "19D audited financial statements." The company statements never had been audited. Early in the audit, the independent CPA found numerous errors and one combination of amounts, in particular, that caused concern.

There was some evidence that a $1,500 job completed by Hall had been recorded as a receivable (from a new customer) on July 15, 19D. The receivable was credited for a $1,500 cash collection a few days later. The new account never was active again. The auditor also observed that shortly thereafter three write-offs of Accounts Receivable balances had been made to Allowance for Doubtful Accounts as follows: Jones, $250; Adams, $750; and Coster, $500; all of whom were known as regular customers. These write-offs drew the attention of the auditor.

Required:

a. What caused the CPA to be concerned? Explain. Should the CPA report the suspicions to the owner?

b. What recommendations would you make in respect to internal control procedures for this company?

C8–2   (Analysis of Cash, Short-Term Investments, and Receivables Using an Actual Financial Statement)

Refer to the financial statements of Chesebrough-Pond's in Special Supplement B immediately preceding the Index.

Required:

a. Is it possible to determine the causes of the decrease in cash and short-term investments during 1985?

b. How much cash was invested in additions to property, plant, and equipment?

c. Evaluate the adequacy of the reporting of short-term investments.

d. In 1985, the company sold $100,000,000 of trade receivables without right of recourse (see footnote 4). Explain the nature of this transaction.

e. Analyze the increase in the allowance for doubtful accounts from 1984 to 1985.

This chapter discusses operational assets owned and used by a company. Notice how a successful company reports these assets in its balance sheet and also provides related supplementary disclosure notes.

Consolidated Balance Sheets

March 31, 1985, and 1984 (rounded to nearest $1,000)	1985	1984
Total Current Assets	**$ 58,401,000**	$ 55,946,000
Property, Plant and Equipment	**41,692,000**	34,837,000
Less accumulated depreciation and amortization	**18,390,000**	15,579,000
Net Property, Plant and Equipment	**23,302,000**	19,258,000

Notes to Financial Statements

Note 1. Significant Accounting Policies
Depreciation and Amortization — Depreciation is provided generally on the straight-line method over the estimated useful lives of the property. Leasehold costs are amortized over the life of the related asset or the life of the lease, whichever is shorter.

Note 3. Property, Plant and Equipment
Property, plant and equipment and accumulated depreciation and amortization at March 31, 1985 and 1984 consisted of:

	1985	1984
Land	$ 1,457,000	$ 1,458,000
Buildings and ground improvements	8,132,000	7,447,000
Machinery and equipment	26,621,000	21,409,000
Leasehold improvements	3,116,000	2,340,000
Capital leases:		
Buildings	1,645,000	1,645,000
Machinery and equipment	721,000	538,000
Total	41,692,000	34,837,000
Less accumulated depreciation and amortization (including $1,260,000 in 1985 and $1,123,000 in 1984 related to capital leases)	18,390,000	15,579,000
Net Property	$23,302,000	$19,258,000

OPERATIONAL ASSETS— PROPERTY, PLANT, AND EQUIPMENT; NATURAL RESOURCES; AND INTANGIBLES

PURPOSE:

The operation of a business requires a combination of assets that are classified on a balance sheet as current, investments and funds, operational, and other. The purpose of this chapter is to discuss operational assets. These assets usually are called property, plant, and equipment and intangible assets (and sometimes fixed assets). **Operational assets are the noncurrent assets that a business retains more or less permanently (not for sale) to carry on its continuing and ongoing operations.** Operational assets include land, buildings, equipment, fixtures, natural resources, and certain intangible assets (such as a patent). Operational assets are important in carrying out the normal profit-making activities of a business.

LEARNING OBJECTIVES—TO BE ABLE TO:

1. Define, classify, and explain the nature of operational assets.
2. Apply the cost principle to measure and record operational assets.
3. Apply the matching principle to record and report depreciation and depletion.
4. Define, record, and amortize intangible operational assets.
5. Expand your accounting vocabulary by learning about the "Important Terms Defined in This Chapter" (page 466).
6. Apply the knowledge gained from this chapter by completing the homework assigned by your instructor.

ORGANIZATION:

Part A—Property, Plant, and Equipment, Including Depreciation

1. Measuring and recording acquisition cost.
2. Depreciation concepts and methods.
3. Effects of depreciation on the financial statements.
4. Depreciation and cash flow.

Part B—Repairs and Maintenance, Natural Resources, and Intangible Assets

1. Repairs and maintenance, and additions.
2. Natural resources and depletion.
3. Intangible operational assets and amortization.
4. Disposal of operational assets.

CLASSIFICATION OF OPERATIONAL ASSETS

The combination of assets held by a business is reported on the balance sheet. Operational assets have different characteristics depending on the nature of the business. Therefore, operational assets are classified as follows:

1. **Tangible operational assets**—the operational assets that have **physical substance;** that is, they are tangible. This classification usually is called property, plant, and equipment. There are three kinds of tangible operational assets:
   a. Land—held for use in operations; it is **not** subject to depreciation.
   b. Buildings, fixtures, equipment; subject to **depreciation.**
   c. Natural resources; subject to **depletion.**
2. **Intangible operational assets**—the operational assets that do not have physical substance that are held by the business because of the **use rights** they confer to the owner. Examples are patents, copyrights, franchises, licenses, and trademarks. Intangible assets are subject to periodic **amortization.**

ACCOUNTING CONCEPTS APPLIED TO ACCOUNTING FOR OPERATIONAL ASSETS

The life span of operational assets owned by a business varies from 2 years to 5, 10, 20, or more years. Therefore, the following accounting concepts usually must be applied (refer to Exhibit 4–5, page 171):

1. **Cost principle**—at purchase date, each operational asset is measured and recorded at its **cash-equivalent** cost.
2. **Matching principle**—during the period from acquisition date to disposal date, the expense of using each asset is measured and recorded in a way to match this expense with the revenues that the asset helped to earn.
3. **Recognition of gain or loss** (elements of financial statements)—at disposal date of operational assets.

Parts A and B will discuss these three application problems.

PART A—PROPERTY, PLANT, AND EQUIPMENT, INCLUDING DEPRECIATION

MEASURING AND RECORDING ACQUISITION COST

Under the **cost principle,** all reasonable and necessary costs incurred in **acquiring** an operational asset, **placing** it in its operational setting and **preparing** it for use, **less** any cash discounts, should be recorded in a designated asset account. Cost is measured as the **net cash equivalent** amount paid or to be paid.

Aquisition cost can be readily determined when an operational asset is purchased for cash. The acquisition cost of a machine on January 1, 19A, may be measured as follows:

Invoice price of the machine	$10,000
Less: Cash discount allowed ($10,000 × 2%)	200
Net cash invoice price	9,800
Add: Transportation charges paid by purchaser	150
Installation costs paid by purchaser	200
Sales tax paid ($10,000 × 2%)	200
Cost—amount debited to the Machinery account	$10,350

The seller agreed to give a 2% discount for immediate cash payment. Otherwise, the full invoice price ($10,000) must be paid. Even if the $200 discount is not taken, it still is deducted because the extra amount paid is a cost of credit; it is recorded as interest expense. Notice that the cost includes transportation, installation, and sales tax. The journal entry to record the purchase of this machine is:[1]

January 1, 19A:		
Machinery	10,350	
Cash		10,350

When an operational asset is purchased and a **noncash** consideration is included in part, or in full, payment for it, the cash equivalent cost is measured as any cash paid plus the **current market value** of the noncash consideration given. Alternatively, if the market value of the noncash consideration given cannot be determined, the current market value of the asset purchased is used for measurement purposes. Assume a tract of timber (a natural resource) was acquired by Fast Corporation. Payment in full was made as follows: $28,000 cash plus 2,000 shares of Fast Corporation capital stock (nopar).[2] At the date of the purchase, Fast stock was selling at $12 per share. The cost of the tract would be measured as follows:

Cash paid	$28,000
Market value, noncash consideration given (2,000 shares nopar stock × $12)	24,000
	52,000
Title fees, legal fees, and other costs paid in cash (incidental to the acquisition)	1,000
Cost—amount debited to the asset account	$53,000

---

[1] If the invoice is not paid immediately, this entry would be:

Machinery	10,350	
Interest expense	200	
Liability, equipment purchase		10,000
Cash ($150 + $200 + $200)		500

[2] See Chapter 12 for discussion of capital stock.

The journal entry to record the acquisition of this natural resource is:

January 1, 19A:

Timber tract (No. 12)	53,000	
Cash		29,000
Capital stock, nopar (2,000 shares × $12)		24,000

When land is purchased, all of the incidental costs paid by the purchaser, such as title fees, sales commissions, legal fees, title insurance, delinquent taxes, and surveying fees, should be included in the cost of the land. Because land is **not** subject to depreciation, it must be recorded and reported as a separate operational asset.

Sometimes, an **old** building or used machinery is purchased for operational use in the business. Renovation and repair costs incurred by the purchaser **prior to use** should be debited to the asset account as a part of the cost of the asset. Ordinary repair costs incurred **after** the asset is placed in use are normal operating expenses when incurred.

Basket Purchases of Assets

When two or more kinds of operational assets are acquired in a single transaction and for a single lump sum, the cost of each kind of asset acquired must be **measured and recorded separately.** When a building and the land on which it is located are purchased for a lump sum, at least two separate accounts must be established. One is for the building (which is subject to depreciation), and one is for the land (which is not subject to depreciation). Therefore, the single sum must be apportioned between the land and the building on a **rational** basis.

Relative market value of the several assets at the date of acquisition is the most logical basis on which to allocate the single lump sum. Appraisals or tax assessments often have to be used as indications of the market values. Assume Fox Company paid $300,000 cash to purchase a building suitable for an additional plant and the land on which the building is located. The separate, true market values of the building and land were not known; therefore, a professional appraisal was obtained that showed the following estimated market values; building, $189,000; and land, $126,000 (apparently the buyer got a good deal). The apportionment of the $300,000 purchase price and the journal entry to record the acquisition are shown in Exhibit 9–1.

Under limited conditions during the construction period of an operational asset, interest cost may be included in acquisition cost. This topic is discussed in Supplement 9A.

EXHIBIT 9–1

Recording a basket purchase of assets

Situation:

Fox Company purchased a building and the related land for $300,000 cash. Estimated current market values: building, $189,000; and land, $126,000.

Allocation of acquisition cost:

	Appraised value		Apportionment of lump-sum acquisition cost	
Asset	Amount	Ratio	Computation	Apportioned cost
Building	$189,000	0.60*	$300,000 × 0.60 =	$180,000
Land	126,000	0.40†	300,000 × 0.40 =	120,000
	$315,000	1.00		$300,000

* $189,000 ÷ $315,000 = 0.60.
† $126,000 ÷ $315,000 = 0.40.

Entry to record the acquisition:

Plant building	180,000	
Land—plant site	120,000	
Cash		300,000

MATCHING COSTS WITH REVENUES GENERATED FROM OPERATIONAL ASSETS

In conformity with the **matching principle,** the costs of using an operational asset must be matched with revenues earned each accounting period. These **use costs** are called (1) depreciation, depletion, and amortization (discussed in Part A of this chapter); and (2) repairs and maintenance (discussed in Part B).

Nature of Depreciation, Depletion, and Amortization

For **accounting purposes** (not income tax purposes), an operational asset that has a limited useful life represents the **prepaid cost** of a bundle of **future** services or benefits that will help earn future revenues.[3] The **matching principle** (Exhibit 4–5) requires that the acquisition cost of operational assets (other than land) be

---

[3] A careful distinction must be maintained between depreciation for accounting purposes (prescribed by GAAP) and for income tax (prescribed by tax laws and regulations). Usually income tax must be paid by corporations, not by sole proprietorships and partnerships.

allocated as expense to the periods in which revenue is earned as a result of using those assets. Thus, the acquisition cost of this kind of operational asset is matched in a systematic and rational manner in the future with the future revenues to which it contributes by way of services and benefits.

Three different terms are used to identify the allocation of the **use-costs** required by the matching principle. These terms are:

1. **Depreciation**—the systematic and rational allocation of the acquisition cost of **tangible** operational assets, other than natural resources, to future periods in which the assets contribute services or benefits to help earn revenue. Example—depreciation of the $10,350 cost of a machine over its estimated useful life of 10 years and no residual value (see page 429). The accounting year ends December 31, and it is the end of 19B (the second year after purchase):[4]

> December 31, 19B (adjusting entry):
>
> Depreciation expense ($10,350 ÷ 10 years) 1,035
>   Accumulated depreciation, machinery 1,035

2. **Depletion**—the systematic and rational allocation of the acquisition cost of **natural resources** to future periods in which the use of those natural resources contributes to revenue. Example—depletion of the $53,000 cost of timber tract over the estimated period of cutting based on "cutting" rate of approximately 20% per year (see page 429):

> December 31, 19B (adjusting entry):
>
> Depletion expense ($53,000 × 20%) 10,600
>   Timber tract (No. 12) 10,600
>   Note: A contra account could be used, such as Accumulated Depletion.

3. **Amortization**—the systematic and rational allocation of the acquisition cost of **intangible** operational assets to future periods in which the benefits

---

[4] Adjusting entries made at the end of 19A would be the same as the following three entries because the allocation shown uses a straight-line assumption.

contribute to revenue. Example—amortization of the $8,500 purchase cost of a patent over its estimated economic useful life to the entity of 17 years:

December 31, 19B (adjusting entry):

Patent expense ($8,500 ÷ 17 years) 500

Patents 500

Note: A contra account, such as Accumulated Patent Amortization, could be used for the credit.

The three terms—depreciation, depletion, and amortization—relate to the same basic objective; that is, the allocation of the acquisition cost of an operational asset to the future periods in which the benefits of its use contribute to earning revenue.

The amounts of depreciation, depletion, and amortization measured and recorded during each period are reported as expenses for the period. The amounts of depreciation, depletion, and amortization **accumulated since acquisition** date are reported on the balance sheet as deductions from the assets to which they pertain. An operational asset, such as the machine illustrated above, would be reported on the balance sheet (at the end of the second year in the example) as follows:

Balance Sheet
At December 31, 19B

Property, plant, and equipment:
  Machinery $10,350
  Less: Accumulated depreciation 2,070 $8,280*

or

Machinery (less accumulated depreciation, $2,070) $8,280*

  * Called book value or carrying value.

We stress that the amounts for operational assets reported on the balance sheet do not represent their market values at the balance sheet date. Rather, the amounts are called book, or carrying, values. The **book,** or **carrying value,** of an operational asset is its acquisition cost, less the accumulated allocation to expense of that cost from acquisition date to the date of the balance sheet. Recording and reporting depreciation is a process of **cost allocation.** It is not a process of determining the current market value of the asset. Under the **cost principle,** the cost of an operational asset is measured and recorded at acquisition date at its current market value. The cost is not remeasured on a market value basis at subsequent balance sheet dates. Instead, the acquisition cost is reduced by the accumulated expense allocation for depreciation, depletion, or amortization.

DEPRECIATION CONCEPTS

Tangible operational assets, except land, are subject to depreciation because they have limited economic lives. Usually, land is not subject to depreciation because it does not wear out and is not considered to be scrap.

Tangible operational assets (except land) decrease in economic utility to the user because of a number of **causative factors,** such as wear and tear, the passage of time, effects of the elements (such as the weather), obsolescence (i.e., becoming out-of-date), technological changes, and inadequacy. These causative factors always affect such assets during the periods in which the assets are being used to earn revenues. Thus, under the **matching principle,** at the end of each accounting period an **adjusting entry** is needed to record these expense-causing factors. In developing the adjusting entry, accounting principles require the use of a rational and systematic allocation to match the acquisition cost of tangible operational assets with the revenue earned each period.[5]

Because of the wide diversity of operational assets subject to depreciation and the varying effects of the causative factors listed above, a number of **depreciation methods** have been developed that provide rational and systematic allocations.

The depreciation methods require three amounts for each asset: (1) **actual acquisition cost,** (2) **estimated net residual value,** and (3) **estimated useful life.** Of these three amounts, two are **estimates** (residual value and useful or service life). Therefore, the periodic amount of depreciation expense that is recorded and reported is an **estimate.** Depreciation expense may be measured as follows:

Acquisition cost	$625
Less: Estimated residual value	25
Amount to be depreciated over useful life	$600
Estimated useful life	3 years
Annual depreciation expense: $600 ÷ 3 = ...	$200

Estimated residual value[6] must be deducted from acquisition cost to compute depreciation. It represents that part of the acquisition cost that is expected to be recovered by the user upon disposal of the asset at the end of its estimated useful life to the entity. **Residual value** is the total estimated amount to be recovered **less** any estimated costs of dismantling, disposal, and selling. Disposal costs may approximately equal the gross residual amount recovered. Therefore, many depreciable assets are assumed to have no residual value. It is important to realize that the estimated net residual value is not necessarily the value of the asset as salvage or scrap. Rather, it may be the value to another user

---

[5] AICPA, *Accounting Research Bulletin No. 43* (New York, 1961), chap. C, par. 5, defines depreciation accounting as "a system of accounting which aims to distribute the cost or other basic value of tangible capital assets, less salvage value (if any), over the estimated useful life of the unit (which may be a group of assets) in a systematic and rational manner. It is a process of allocation, not of valuation."

[6] Residual value also is called scrap value or salvage value; however, "residual value" is a more descriptive term because the asset may not be scrapped or sold as salvage upon disposition—a subsequent buyer may renovate it and reuse it for many years.

at the date on which the **current owner** intends to dispose of it. A company whose policy is to replace all trucks at the end of three years normally would use a higher estimated residual value than would a user of the same kind of truck whose policy is to replace the trucks at the end of five years.

Estimated useful or service life should be seen as the useful **economic** life to the **present owner** rather than as the total economic life to all potential users. In the example above, for accounting purposes, one owner would use a three-year estimated useful life, whereas the other owner would use a five-year estimated useful life.

Estimates are necessary to allocate a known cost amount (the acquisition cost of an operational asset) over a number of future periods during which the asset will contribute to the earning of revenues. The allocation must be made at the end of each accounting period. To defer all cost allocations until the date of disposal of an operational asset that is "used up" would not be very useful in the measurement of periodic income.

The determination of estimated useful life of an operational asset must conform to the **continuity assumption** (see Exhibit 4–5, page 171). This assumption holds that the business will continue as a going concern; that is, that the business will continue indefinitely to pursue its commercial objectives (it will not liquidate in the foreseeable future). This assumption prevents a business from estimating the life of an operational asset to be less than its potential life because of some conjecture that the business will liquidate in the near future.

DEPRECIATION METHODS

The depreciation methods commonly used for **accounting purposes** are discussed in this section. The different depreciation methods are the same in concept; each method allocates a portion of the cost of a depreciable asset to each of a number of future periods in a systematic and rational manner. Nevertheless, each method allocates to each accounting period a different portion of the net cost to be depreciated. The discussions that follow will define, illustrate, and evaluate the following depreciation methods:[7]

1. Straight-line (SL).
2. Productive-output (PO) (units of production).
3. Sum-of-the-years' digits (SYD).
4. Declining-balance (DB).

The common set of facts and notations shown in Exhibit 9–2 will be used to illustrate these methods.

---

[7] AICPA, *Accounting Trends and Techniques* (Annual Survey of Accounting Practices Followed in 600 Stockholders' Reports), 39th ed. (New York, 1985), p. 268, reports on the use of the various depreciation methods used by the 600 companies surveyed (some companies use more than one method) during 1984: straight line, 567; declining balance, 54; sum-of-the-years' digits, 15; accelerated method—not specified, 76; and the units of production, 60.

EXHIBIT 9-2

Illustrative data for depreciation

DEP CORPORATION

	Symbols	Illustrative amounts
Acquisition cost of a particular operational asset (a productive machine)	C	$625
Estimated net residual value at end of useful life	RV	$ 25
Estimated service life:		
Life in years	N*	3
Life in units of productive output	P*	10,000
Depreciation rate	R	
Dollar amount of depreciation expense per period	D	

* Lowercase letters will be used for the current period. The accounting period ends December 31.

Straight-Line (SL) Method

Under the straight-line (SL) method, an **equal portion** of the acquisition cost less the estimated residual value is allocated to each accounting period during the estimated useful life. Thus, the annual depreciation expense is measured as follows (refer to Exhibit 9-2):

$$D = \frac{C - RV}{N} \quad \text{or} \quad D = \frac{\$625 - \$25}{3 \text{ years}} = \$200 \text{ depreciation expense per year}$$

A depreciation schedule for the entire useful life of the machine is:

Depreciation Schedule—Straight-Line Method

		End of year	
Year	Periodic depreciation expense	Balance in accumulated depreciation	Book value
At acquisition			$625
1	$200	$200	425
2	200	400	225
3	200	600	25
	$600		

The adjusting entry for straight-line depreciation expense on this machine is the same for each of the three years of the useful life:

	Year 1	Year 2	Year 3
Adjusting entry			
Depreciation expense 200		200	200
Accumulated depreciation, machinery	200	200	200

Notice that *(a)* depreciation expense is a constant amount for each year (often called a fixed expense), *(b)* accumulated depreciation increases by an equal amount each year, and *(c)* book value decreases by the same amount each year. This is the reason for the designation, straight line.

Evaluation. The straight-line method is simple, rational, and systematic (i.e., logical, stable, consistent, and realistically predictable from period to period). It is appropriate when the asset is used at about the same rate each period. It implies an approximately equal decline in the economic usefulness of the asset each period. For these reasons, it is used more often than all of the other methods combined (see footnote 7).

Productive-Output Method

The productive-output method relates acquisition cost less estimated residual value to the estimated productive output. Therefore, a depreciation rate per **unit of output** is computed as follows (refer to Exhibit 9–2):

$$R = \frac{C - RV}{P} \quad \text{or} \quad R = \frac{\$625 - \$25}{10{,}000 \text{ units}} = \$0.06 \text{ depreciation rate per unit of output}$$

Assuming 3,000 units of actual output from the illustrative machine in Year 1, depreciation expense for Year 1 would be:

$$D = R \times p \quad \text{or} \quad D = \$0.06 \times 3{,}000 = \$180 \text{ depreciation expense}$$

Assuming actual output is 5,000 units in Year 2 and 2,000 units in Year 3, the depreciation schedule is:

Depreciation Schedule—Productive-Output Method

	Periodic depreciation expense			End of Year	
Year	Actual units	Rate	Amount	Balance in accumulated depreciation	Book value
At acquisition					$625
1	3,000 ×	$0.06	$180	$180	445
2	5,000 ×	0.06	300	480	145
3	2,000 ×	0.06	120	600	25
			$600		

The adjusting entry for productive output depreciation at the end of each year is:

	Year 1	Year 2	Year 3
Adjusting entry			
Depreciation expense	180	300	120
Accumulated depreciation, machinery	180	300	120

Notice that depreciation expense, accumulated depreciation, and book value vary from period to period directly with the periodic outputs. When the productive-output method is used, depreciation expense is said to be a **variable** expense.

Evaluation.   The productive-output method, sometimes called the units-of-production method, is based upon the assumption that the revenue-generating benefits derived each period from a depreciable asset are related directly to the periodic **output** of the asset. Many accountants believe that such equipment as a machine should be depreciated on the basis of units produced each period (i.e., based on a measure of output) rather than on the passage of time as is assumed by the straight-line method. These accountants believe that many productive assets contribute to the earning of revenues only when they are used productively, not because time has passed.

The productive-output method is simple, rational, and systematic. It is appropriate if **output** of the asset can be measured realistically. Also, it is appropriate when the economic utility of the asset to the entity decreases with productive use rather than with the passage of time. Also, when the productive use varies significantly from period to period, a more realistic **matching** of expense with revenue is attained. Despite these conceptual and practical advantages, it is not widely used, primarily because of the problems associated with measuring output (see footnote 7).

Accelerated Depreciation—Concepts

Accelerated depreciation means that in the early years of the useful life of an asset, depreciation expense amounts should be higher, and correspondingly lower in the later years. Accelerated depreciation is supported by the following arguments:

1. A depreciable asset is more efficient in the early years than in the later years.
2. Repair costs increase in later years; therefore, **total use-cost** per period should include decreasing depreciation expense to "offset" the increasing repair expense each period.

3. Accelerated depreciation expense decreases income tax in the case of a corporation (discussed later).

The relationship between accelerated depreciation expense, repair expense, and total use expense can be illustrated as follows for DEP Corporation:

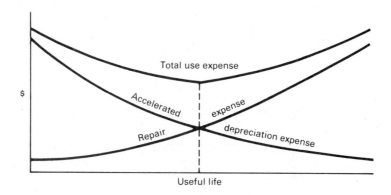

There are several variations of accelerated depreciation; however, the two accelerated methods used more often are the sum-of-the-years'-digits method and the declining balance method.

Sum-of-the-years'-digits (SYD) method

Under this method depreciation expense is computed for each accounting year by multiplying the acquisition cost, less estimated residual value, by a fraction that is successively **smaller** each year. Each of the decreasing fractions is determined by using the sum of the digits that make up the estimated useful life as the denominator. The numerator is the specific year of life in **inverse order.** Using the data given in Exhibit 9–2, the computations are:

1. Compute the annual depreciation fraction:

   Denominator—Sum of digits in useful life:[8] $1 + 2 + 3 = \underline{\underline{6}}$

   Numerators—Digits (specific year of life) in inverse order: $\underline{\underline{3}}, \underline{\underline{2}}, \underline{\underline{1}}$.

   Depreciation fractions—Year 1, ³⁄₆; Year 2, ²⁄₆; Year 3, ¹⁄₆ (total, ⁶⁄₆).

---

[8] The denominator (i.e., sum of the digits) can be computed by using the formula:

$$SYD = n\left(\frac{n + 1}{2}\right)$$

For example, a five-year life would be:

$$SYD = 5\left(\frac{5 + 1}{2}\right) = 15$$

2. Compute annual SYD depreciation and related balances based on the data given in Exhibit 9–2:

Depreciation Schedule—Sum-of-the-Years'-Digits Method

Year	Computations	Periodic depreciation expense	End of Year Balance in accumulated depreciation	Book value
At acquisition				$625
1	$600 × ⅜ =	$300	$300	325
2	600 × 2/6 =	200	500	125
3	600 × ⅙ =	100	600	25
Total		$600		

The adjusting entry for SYD depreciation expense by year is:

Adjusting entry	Year 1	Year 2	Year 3
Depreciation expense	300	200	100
Accumulated depreciation, machinery	300	200	100

Notice that, compared to straight-line results (page 437), depreciation expense under the SYD method is higher in the earlier years and lower in the later years. The total amount of depreciation expense over the entire life of the asset is the same under both methods.

Evaluation. The SYD method is used because it produces a significant accelerated effect, and it is simple to apply, rational, and systematic. However, the SYD method is criticized because it often does not relate depreciation expense to use or output. In such cases, its conformity to the **matching** principle is questionable. Footnote 7 states that it is not widely used.

Declining balance (DB) method

There are several variations of the declining balance method. One variation is based upon an acceleration rate applied to the straight-line rate. The **declining balance (DB) rate** is found by (1) computing the straight-line rate, ignoring residual value, then (2) multiplying that straight-line rate by a **selected acceleration rate.** Assuming a five-year estimated useful life, the SL rate, excluding residual value, is:

1 period of life ÷ 5 total periods = 20%

Computation of the DB rate for three different income tax acceleration rates (for illustrative purposes):

$$
\begin{array}{llll}
\textit{SL rate} & \textit{Selected} & \textit{DB} \\
\textit{(excluding RV)} \times \textit{acceleration rate} = \textit{depreciation rate}
\end{array}
$$

Case A 20% × 200% or 2.00 = 40% or 0.40
Case B 20% × 175% or 1.75 = 35% or 0.35
Case C 20% × 150% or 1.50 = 30% or 0.30

Computation of DB depreciation expense is illustrated below using the data given in Exhibit 9–2 and assuming a **selected acceleration rate** of 150%:

1. To compute the DB acceleration rate:

   SL rate (ignoring residual value) = 1 year ÷ 3 years = 33.3%, or 0.333.
   150% acceleration DB rate = 33.3% × 1.50 = <u>50%, or 0.50.</u>

2. Depreciation schedule—declining balance (DB) method:

			End of year	
Year	Computations	Periodic depreciation expense	Balance in accumulated depreciation	Book value
At acquisition				$625
1	0.50 × $625 =	$313	$313	312
2	0.50 × 312 =	156	469	156
3	0.50 × 156 =	78	547	78*

* This must be the computed amount, but it cannot be less than the estimated residual value (in this illustration, not less than $25).

The adjusting entry for DB depreciation at each year-end is:

	Year 1	Year 2	Year 3
Adjusting entry			
Depreciation expense	313	156	78
Accumulated depreciation, machinery	313	156	78

Evaluation. This method began because it was acceptable for income tax purposes. The method is criticized because the **selected acceleration rate** is subjectively determined for accounting purposes. Income tax provisions have been changed; therefore, this method is not widely used. However, notice in footnote 7 that acceleration methods collectively are often used.

Depreciation and Income Tax

Usually corporations must pay income tax the same as individuals (see Special Supplement A). Sole proprietorships and partnerships do not pay income tax; however, the individual owners must include the company's earnings on their **personal** income tax returns.

The last section discussed depreciation for **accounting** purposes in conformity with GAAP. This section discusses depreciation and income tax for corporations in conformity with the tax laws and regulations. Each year a corporation must file a corporate income tax return. A distinction must be made between the accounting records kept in conformity with GAAP and data used to conform to the income tax regulations. Some of the depreciation methods discussed in the last section are not allowed for income tax purposes. However, the accelerated methods evolved from prior income tax provisions.

The Economic Recovery Tax Act of 1981 established an accelerated tax method for depreciation (called ACRS). It set up classes of property: (1) **3-year** property (e.g., light trucks and special tools); (2) **5-year** property (e.g., machinery and equipment); (3) **10-year** property (e.g., public utility property); and (4) **15-year** property (e.g., real estate). This legislation set up depreciation percentages, by year, for each class of property. The percent for "3-year property" are: Year 1, 25%; Year 2, 38%; and Year 3, 37%. The tax reform act of 1986 reclassified certain assets according to their present class life and created class lives for 7-year, 20-year, 27.5-year, and a 31.5-year class. However, the legislation provides for an **optional straight-line method** for **all classes of property** and a "half-year convention", for property other than real estate. The half-year convention permits half of the annual depreciation in the first and last years of useful life. Residual value is ignored. An asset that cost $60,000 would be depreciated on the **income tax return** under the straight-line method as follows:

Year

19A	($60,000 ÷ 3) × ½ =	$10,000
19B	($60,000 ÷ 3) =	20,000
19C	($60,000 ÷ 3) =	20,000
19D	($60,000 ÷ 3) × ½ =	10,000
	Total depreciated	$60,000

Because of the short lives permitted by ACRS depreciation and most of the tax rates specified, this legislation gives a significant acceleration of depreciation amounts.

ACRS depreciation is not used for accounting purposes. However, for instructional purposes, we assume that depreciation expense (on the income statement and the tax return) are the same. This assumption permits illustration of depreciation and its income tax effects without involvement in the complexities of the corporate income tax return.

Which Depreciation Method Should Be Used?

To date, the accounting profession has not provided definitive guidelines for selection of a depreciation method that would be preferable for each type of depreciable asset. Therefore, each of the several methods can be characterized as an acceptable alternative for financial reporting purposes. That is, any of the above depreciation methods may be used regardless of the characteristics of the

EXHIBIT 9–3

Depreciation methods compared   (DEP Corporation)

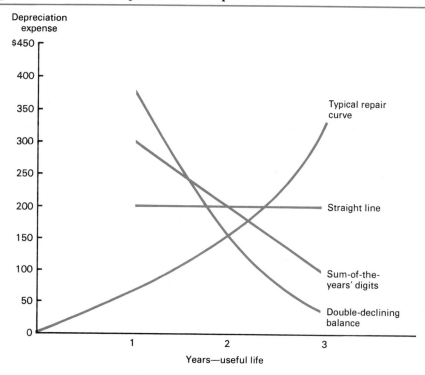

operational asset and the way it is used. Exhibit 9–3 further shows the differences among the three most commonly used depreciation methods.

GAAP requires that the depreciation method selected must be "rational and systematic." Also, it should reliably measure net income of the company considering the circumstances in which the asset is used. Thus, it is usual for a company to use more than one depreciation method. The selection of a method of depreciation is important. It has a significant impact on net income and amounts reported on the balance sheet for operational assets. Exhibit 9–3 compares depreciation amounts under each method discussed above.

DEPRECIATION EFFECTS ON THE INCOME STATEMENT AND BALANCE SHEET

Each depreciation method has different effects on the income statement and balance sheet because each method has a different pattern of allocation of depreciation expense. Exhibit 9–4 shows the different effects of SL versus SYD

_____ EXHIBIT 9–4 _____

Effects of depreciation methods on net income, cash flow, and operational assets

DEP Corporation

Panel A—Situation given in Exhibit 9–2:

- Straight-line depreciation, Year 1, $200,000; SYD depreciation, Year 1, $300,000 (as previously illustrated).
- Income tax rates, for Year 1, on pretax income: Over $350,000, 45%; below $350,000, 40%.
- Financial data given below (in thousands). Income tax expense is paid at year-end.

Panel B—SL and SYD depreciation effects compared:

Financial Statements	Year 1 ($000)	
	SL Depreciation	SYD Depreciation
Income statement:		
Revenues	$ 920	$ 920
Depreciation expenses	(200)	(300)
Remaining expenses	(320)	(320)
Pretax income	400	300
Income tax expense	($400 × 45%) (180)	($300 × 40%) (120)
Net income	$ 220	$ 180
Balance Sheet:		
Cash	$ 10	(+180 − $120) $ 70
Operational assets	625	625
Accumulated depreciation	(200)	(300)
Remaining assets	400	400
Total assets	$ 835	$ 795
Liabilities	$ 215	$ 215
Income tax payable	–0–	–0–
Common stock	400	400
Retained earnings	220	180
Total liabilities plus stockholders' equity	$ 835	$ 795

depreciation (Year 1) for DEP Corporation. The following differences are significant:

1. **Income statement**—Accelerated depreciation (SYD) caused *(a)* depreciation expense to be $100 **more,** *(b)* pretax income to be $100 **less,** *(c)* income tax expense to be $60 **less,** and *(d)* net income to be $40 **less.**
2. **Balance sheet**—Accelerated depreciation (SYD) caused *(a)* cash to be $60 **more** (because the corporation paid less income tax—a cash saving), *(b)* book

value of the operational assets to be $100 **less,** (c) total assets to be $40 **less,** (d) retained earnings to be $40 **less,** and (e) total liabilities plus owners' equity to be $40 **less.**

Effects of Depreciation on Cash Flow

When an operational asset is acquired, there is a cash outflow (i.e., payment) for its acquisition (and/or later cash outflows for any related debt). Subsequent journal entries for depreciation do not involve cash outflows because the expense lags the cash outflow already made. Therefore, depreciation expense does not represent a current cash outflow; it is a noncash expense on the income statement. However, depreciation expense does affect cash flow each period. It **reduces** the amount of income tax that otherwise would be paid by a corporation. In this way it reduces the amount of cash outflow for income tax (this reduction is often called a "tax saving"). Thus, if depreciation expense is increased for the period, the cash outflow for income tax is decreased. This cash flow effect is shown in Exhibit 9–4. In summary, as the amount of depreciation expense is increased, net income is decreased, and cash inflow is increased (i.e., by the tax saving).

Finally, let's discuss some misleading terminology that may be used. Analysts and others often say that "cash is provided by depreciation." Depreciation is not a source of cash. Also, the accumulated depreciation amount does not represent cash or a fund of cash available to replace the operational asset when it is disposed of. Accumulated depreciation is a contra asset account (not cash). Exhibit 9–4 shows that a significant effect of depreciation expense is a reduction of the cumulative balance of retained earnings. A lower balance in retained earnings could reduce cash dividends. If cash dividends are reduced because of the depreciation effect, cash outflows would be less than otherwise.[9]

DEPRECIATION FOR INTERIM PERIODS

The preceding illustrations assumed recognition of depreciation expense with an adjusting entry. Many businesses record depreciation for interim periods, such as monthly, quarterly, or semiannually. Also, a depreciable asset may be acquired or disposed of during the accounting year, which requires that depreciation expense be recognized for periods of less than one year. It is usual to compute depreciation proportionally to either the nearest month, quarter, or six-month period. Depreciation for a full month may be assumed to start or end at

---

[9] The discussion in this section assumes a corporation because other types of businesses do not pay income tax. The discussions also assume that the same depreciation method is used for financial reporting and income tax purposes. Chapter 10 discusses the reporting implications of the use of different depreciation methods for financial reporting and tax purposes.

the nearest first of the month. For all of the methods shown, except productive output, monthly depreciation usually is determined by computing the annual amount of depreciation as shown, then dividing by 12 to obtain the monthly amount.[10] In Exhibit 9–4, sum-of-the-years'-digits (SYD) depreciation for the first year was $300. Assume the asset was acquired on August 12, 19A, with a December 31 fiscal year end. The depreciation expense for 19A would be (nearest-month basis):

$$\frac{\$300}{12} \times 5 \text{ months} = \$125$$

Depreciation expense is an estimate; therefore, small depreciation amounts should not be recognized because this would suggest a higher degree of accuracy than is warranted. Also, for this reason, depreciation expense should be rounded to the nearest amount—one, ten, hundred, or even thousand dollars—depending on the cost of the depreciable asset compared with total depreciable assets. This is in conformity with the **materiality constraint** (see Exhibit 4–5).

CHANGES IN DEPRECIATION ESTIMATES

Depreciation is based on two estimates—useful life and residual value. These estimates are made at the time a depreciable asset is acquired. One, or both, of these initial estimates may have to be revised as experience with the asset accumulates. When it is clear that either estimate should be revised (to a material degree), the undepreciated asset balance, less any residual value, at that date should be apportioned, based on the new estimate, over the **remaining** estimated life. This is called a **change in estimate.**

Assume the following for a machine:

Cost of machine when acquired	$33,000
Estimated useful life	10 years
Estimated residual value	$ 3,000
Accumulated depreciation through Year 6 (assuming the straight-line method is used); ($33,000 − $3,000) × 6/10	$18,000

Shortly after the start of Year 7, the initial estimates were changed to the following:

Revised estimated total life	14 years
Revised estimated residual value	$ 1,000

No entry is needed when this decision is reached. However, the **adjusting entry at the end of Year 7** would be:

---

[10] Under the productive-output method, monthly depreciation is computed by multiplying the unit depreciation rate by the output for the particular month.

Depreciation expense 1,750
    Accumulated depreciation 1,750

Computation:
Acquisition cost $33,000
Accumulated depreciation, Years 1–6 18,000
Undepreciated balance 15,000
    Less: Revised residual value 1,000
Balance to be depreciated $14,000

Annual depreciation:
    $14,000 ÷ (14 years − 6 years) .... $ 1,750

Under GAAP, changes in accounting estimates and depreciation methods should be made only when the new estimate or accounting method "better measures" the periodic income of the business. The **characteristic of comparability** (Exhibit 4–5) requires that accounting information reported in the financial statements should be comparable across accounting periods and among similar entities. This principle has a significant constraint on changing depreciation estimates and methods unless the effect is to improve the measurement of depreciation expense and net income.

PART B—REPAIRS AND MAINTENANCE, NATURAL RESOURCES, AND INTANGIBLE OPERATIONAL ASSETS

REPAIRS, MAINTENANCE, AND ADDITIONS

Subsequent to the acquisition of a tangible operational asset, related cost outlays often must be made for such items as ordinary repairs and maintenance, major repairs, replacements, and additions. The main measurement problem is determination of which expenditures should be recorded as expenses of the period when incurred, and which should be recorded as assets (i.e., as a prepayment) to be matched with **future** revenues. In this context, the term **expenditure** means the payment of cash or the incurrence of a debt for an asset or service received. The purchase of a machine or a service, such as repairs on a truck, may be for cash or on credit. In either case, there is an expenditure.

Accounting for expenditures made after the acquisition date are called revenue expenditures and capital expenditures. **A revenue expenditure is recorded as expense when incurred. A capital expenditure is recorded as an asset when incurred.**[11]

---

[11] The term **revenue** expenditure is widely used. It suggests that the expenditure is to be deducted in the current period from revenue in deriving income. However, a term such as expense expenditure would be more descriptive.

Ordinary Repairs and Maintenance

Ordinary repairs and maintenance are expenditures for normal maintenance and upkeep of operational assets that are necessary to keep the assets in their usual condition. These expenditures are recurring in nature, involve small amounts at each occurrence, and do not directly lengthen the useful life of the asset. Ordinary repairs and maintenance are **revenue expenditures.** They are recorded as expense in the accounting period in which incurred.

Extraordinary Repairs

Extraordinary repairs are classified as **capital expenditures;** therefore, an extraordinary repair is debited to the related asset account and depreciated over the **remaining life** of that asset. **Extraordinary repairs** seldom occur, involve large amounts of money, and increase the economic usefulness of the asset in the future because of either greater efficiency or longer life, or both. They are represented by major overhauls, complete reconditioning, and major replacements and improvements. The complete replacement of a roof on the factory building would be an extraordinary repair. Patching the old roof would be an ordinary repair.

To illustrate the accounting for extraordinary repairs, assume a machine that originally cost $40,000 is being depreciated on a straight-line basis over 10 years with no estimated residual value. At the beginning of the seventh year, a major reconditioning was finished that cost $12,700. The estimated useful life changed from 10 years to 13 years (i.e., a change in estimate). A typical sequence of entries would be:

At acquisition date:

Machinery	40,000	
Cash		40,000
Purchase of machinery.		

End of each accounting period (depreciation):

Depreciation expense	4,000	
Accumulated depreciation, machinery		4,000
Adjusting entry to record annual depreciation ($40,000 ÷ 10 years).		

Extraordinary repair—at the start of Year 7:[12]

Machinery	12,700	
Cash		12,700
Capital expenditure.		

Revised annual depreciation, Years 7–13:

Depreciation expense	4,100	
Accumulated depreciation, machinery		4,100
Adjusting entry to record annual depreciation.		

Computation:

Original cost	$40,000	
Depreciation, Years 1–6	24,000	
Book value remaining		$16,000
Extraordinary repair		12,700
Balance to be depreciated over remaining life		$28,700

Annual depreciation: $28,700 ÷ (13 − 6 years) = $4,100.

Additions

Additions are extensions to, or enlargements of, existing assets, such as the addition of a wing to a building. These additions are **capital expenditures;** therefore, the cost of additions should be debited to the existing account for the asset and depreciated over the remaining life of the asset to which the cost is related. However, if the life of the addition is shorter than the life of the related asset, the addition should be depreciated over its remaining useful life (less its residual value).

NATURAL RESOURCES

Natural resources, such as a mineral deposit, oil well, or timber tract, are often called "wasting assets" because they are **depleted** (i.e., physically used). When acquired or developed, a natural resource is measured and recorded in the accounts in conformity with the **cost principle.** As a natural resource is used up, its acquisition cost, in conformity with the **matching principle,** must be apportioned among the various periods in which the resulting revenues are earned. The term **depletion** describes the process of periodic cost allocation over

---

[12] Alternatively, the debit could be made to the account for accumulated depreciation; the result would be the same.

the period of use of a natural resource. A **depletion rate** per unit of the resource produced is computed by dividing the total acquisition and development cost (less any estimated residual value, which is rare) by the **estimated units** that can be withdrawn economically from the resource. The depletion rate, thus computed, is multiplied each period by the **actual** number of units withdrawn during the accounting period. This procedure is the same as the productive-output method of calculating depreciation (see page 439).

To illustrate accounting for a natural resource, assume that a gravel pit was developed that cost $80,000. A reliable estimate was made that 100,000 cubic yards of gravel could be economically withdrawn from the pit. The **depletion rate per unit** is computed as follows (assuming no residual value):

$80,000 ÷ 100,000 cubic yards = $0.80 per cubic yard (depletion rate per unit)

Assuming 5,000 cubic yards of gravel were actually withdrawn and sold during the year, depletion expense for the first year would be recorded by making the following adjusting entry.[13]

Depletion expense	4,000	
Gravel pit		4,000
Depletion for the year, 5,000 cubic yards × $0.80 = $4,000.		

At the end of the first year, this **natural resource** should be reported as follows:

Balance Sheet

Operational assets:
  Gravel pit (cost, $80,000 − $4,000 accumulated depletion) $76,000

Since it is difficult to estimate the recoverable units from a natural resource, the depletion rate often must be revised. This is a **change in estimate;** therefore, the undepleted acquisition cost is spread over the estimated remaining recoverable units by computing a new depletion rate. Assume in Year 2 that the estimate of recoverable units remaining was changed from 95,000 to 150,000 cubic yards. The depletion rate to be applied to the cubic yards of gravel withdrawn in Year 2 would be:

($80,000 − $4,000) ÷ 150,000 cubic yards = $0.51 per cubic yard

---

[13] Consistent with the procedure for recording depreciation, an Accumulated Depletion account may be used. However, as a matter of precedent, the asset account itself usually is credited directly for the periodic depletion. Either procedure is acceptable. The same is true for intangible operational assets, discussed in the next section.

When buildings and similar improvements are built for the development and exploitation of a natural resource, they should be recorded in separate asset accounts and **depreciated**—not depleted. Their estimated useful lives cannot be longer than the time needed to exploit the natural resource unless they have a significant use-value after the resource is depleted.

INTANGIBLE OPERATIONAL ASSETS

An intangible operational asset, like any other asset, has value because of certain rights and privileges conferred by law upon the owner of the asset. However, an intangible asset has **no material or physical substance** as do tangible assets such as land and buildings.[14] Examples of intangible operational assets are patents, copyrights, franchises, licenses, trademarks, and goodwill. The acquisition of an intangible asset usually requires the expenditure of resources. For example, an entity may buy a patent from the inventor. An intangible asset should be measured and recorded in the accounts of the entity at its cash-equivalent cost in conformity with the **cost principle.** Subsequently, it is recorded at cost less accumulated amortization.

Each kind of intangible operational asset should be recorded in a separate asset account when acquired. Assume that on Janaury 1, 19A, Mason Company bought a patent from its developer, J. Doe, at a cash price of $17,000. The acquisition of this intangible asset is recorded as follows:

```
January 1, 19A:

   Patents ..................................................... 17,000
      Cash ....................................................          17,000
      Bought a patent from J. Doe.
```

Under the cost principle, although an intangible right or privilege may have value, it is not recorded unless there has been an identifiable expenditure of resources to acquire or develop it. The demise of a competitor's patent may cause the company's patent to be more valuable. This increase in value would not be recorded because there was no expenditure of resources that caused the increase in value.

Research and development (R&D) costs are recorded as expenses in. the period incurred, even though they sometimes result in the development of a patent that has future value.

---

[14] Intangible operational assets often are called intangible assets.

Amortization of Intangible Operational Assets

Intangible operational assets normally have limited lives; however, they seldom have a residual value. Intangible assets have a limited life because the **rights or privileges** that help earn revenues terminate or disappear. Therefore, in conformity with the **matching principle,** the acquisition cost of an intangible operational asset must be written off over its estimated economic life. This systematic write-off is called **amortization.** *APB Opinion 17* states that for accounting purposes, the estimated useful life of an intangible asset cannot exceed 40 years. The *Opinion* does not permit an arbitrary and immediate write-off of an intangible asset. These rules are intended to avoid income manipulation.

An intangible asset may be amortized by using any "systematic and rational" method that reflects the actual expiration of its economic usefulness. However, the **straight-line** method is used almost exclusively. The primary intangible assets are discussed below.

Patents

A patent is an exclusive right, recognized by law, that enables the owner to use, manufacture, and sell the subject of the patent, and the patent itself. A patent that is **purchased** is recorded at its cash-equivalent cost. An **internally developed** patent is recorded at only its registration and legal cost. **GAAP does not permit** the capitalization of research and development costs. In conformity with the **matching principle,** the capitalized cost of a patent must be amortized over the **shorter** of its economic life or its remaining legal life (of the 17 years from date of grant). Assume the patent acquired by Mason Company had an estimated 10-year remaining economic life. At the end of 19A, the **adjusting entry** to record amortization for one year would be (see footnote 13):

December 31, 19A:

Patent expense 1,700
    Patents   1,700
    Adjusting entry to record amortization of patent over the estimated
    economic life of 10 years ($17,000 ÷ 10 years = $1,700).

The amount of patent amortization expense recorded for 19A is reported on the income statement as an operating expense. The patent would be reported on the December 31,19A, balance sheet as follows:

        Intangible assets:
            Patents (cost, $17,000, less amortization) $15,300

Copyrights

A copyright is similar to a patent. A copyright gives the owner the exclusive right to publish, use, and sell a literary, musical, or artistic piece of work for a period not exceeding 50 years after the author's death. The same principles, guidelines, and procedures used in accounting for and reporting the cost of patents also are used for copyrights.

Franchises and licenses

Franchises and licenses frequently are granted by governmental and other units for a specified period and purpose. A city may grant one company a franchise to distribute gas to homes for heating purposes, or a company may sell franchises, such as the right for a local outlet to operate a Kentucky Fried Chicken restaurant. Franchises and licenses usually require an investment by the franchisee to acquire them; therefore, they represent intangible operational assets that should be accounted for as shown above for patents.

Leaseholds

Leasing is a common type of business contract. For a consideration called rent, the owner (or lessor) extends to another party (the lessee) certain rights to use specified property. Leases may vary from simple arrangements, such as the month-to-month lease of an office or the daily rental of an automobile, to long-term leases having complex contractual arrangements. The rights granted to a lessee frequently are called a **leasehold.**

Long-term leases sometimes require a lump-sum advance rental payment by the lessee. In such cases, the lessee should record the advance payment as a debit to an intangible asset account (usually called Rent Paid in Advance or Leaseholds). This cost should be amortized to expense over the contractual life of the lease. Total rent expense includes the amortization of the leasehold. Therefore, the annual amortization is debited to Rent Expense. Assume Favor Company leased a building for its own use on January 1, 19A, under a five-year contract that required in addition to the monthly rental payments of $2,000, a single payment in advance of $20,000. The advance payment is recorded as follows:

January 1, 19A:

Leasehold (or Rent paid in advance)	20,000	
Cash		20,000
Rent paid in advance.		

At the end of each year, 19A through 19E, the following **adjusting entry** is made to amortize the cost of this intangible asset:[15]

December 31, 19A:

Rent expense 4,000
    Leasehold 4,000
Adjusting entry to record amortization of leasehold over five years
($20,000 ÷ 5 years = $4,000).

The $2,000 monthly rental payments would be debited to Rent Expense when paid each month. Thus, the 19A income statement would report rent expense of $28,000 [i.e., ($2,000 × 12) + $4,000 = $28,000]. The December 31, 19A, balance sheet would report an asset, Leasehold, of $16,000 (i.e., Cost, $20,000 − Amortization, $4,000 = $16,000).

Leasehold improvements

In most cases, when buildings, improvements, or alterations are built by the **lessee** on leased property, such assets legally belong to the owner of the property at the end of the lease. The lessee has full use of such improvements during the term of the lease. Therefore, the cost should be recorded as an intangible operating asset, Leasehold Improvements. These expenditures should be amortized over the estimated useful life of the related improvement or the remaining life of the lease, whichever is shorter.

Goodwill

Often when a successful business is sold, the price will be higher than the market values of its recorded assets less its liabilities. A business may command a higher price because an intangible operational asset called goodwill is attached to a successful business.

Goodwill represents the potential of a business to earn above a normal rate of return on the recorded assets less the liabilities. Goodwill arises from such factors as customer confidence, reputation for dependability, efficiency and internal competencies, quality of goods and services, and financial standing. From the date of organization, a successful business continually builds goodwill. In this context, the goodwill is said to be "internally generated at no identifiable cost." On the other hand, when a business is purchased as an entity, the

---

[15] This discussion presumes an **operating** type of lease. In some cases a lease is in effect a sale/purchase agreement. Such leases, known as financing leases, involve complex accounting problems that are discussed in a subsequent chapter.

purchase price may include a payment for any goodwill that exists at that time. **In conformity with the cost principle, goodwill is recorded as an intangible operational asset only when it actually is purchased at a measurable cost.**

Assume Richard Roe purchased the College Men's Store on January 1, 19A, for $200,000 cash. At the date of purchase, the recorded assets had a total **market value** of $160,000, comprised of the market values of inventory, $110,000; fixtures, $35,000; prepaid rent, $1,000; and remaining assets, $14,000. Roe did not accept any of the store's liabilities. The purchase is recorded by Roe as follows:

January 1, 19A:

Inventory	110,000	
Furniture and fixtures	35,000	
Prepaid rent	1,000	
Remaining assets	14,000	
Goodwill	40,000	
Cash		200,000
Purchase of College Men's Store.		

The intangible asset—goodwill—must be amortized to expense over its estimated economic life not to exceed 40 years *(APB Opinion 17)*. Assuming a 40-year economic life, the amortization for 19A is recorded in an **adjusting entry** as follows:

December 31, 19A:

Goodwill amortization (expense)	1,000	
Goodwill		1,000
Adjusting entry to record goodwill amortization for one year based on 40-year economic life ($40,000 ÷ 40 years = $1,000).		

Many other kinds of intangible operational assets are reported in financial statements. Examples are formulas, processes, and film rights. These types are accounted for, and reported, in a manner similar to that shown above.

DEFERRED CHARGES

An asset category called **deferred charges** occasionally is reported on the balance sheet. A deferred charge, like a prepaid expense, is an **expense paid in advance.** That is, goods or services were acquired that will be used later to earn future revenues. A deferred charge is a **long-term** prepaid expense. Therefore, it cannot be classified as a current asset. A prepaid expense is a short-term prepayment, and for this reason, it is classified as a current asset. Thus, the only difference between the two is time. For example, a $1,000 insurance premium for five years' coverage paid in advance at the start of Year 1 would be reported as follows at the end of Year 1:

```
Income statement:
    Insurance expense ($1,000 ÷ 5 years)  ................... $200
Balance sheet:
    Current assets:
        Prepaid insurance ($1,000 ÷ 5 years) ...................  200
    Deferred charges:
        Insurance premium paid in advance ($1,000 × 3/5) ......  600
```

Common examples of deferred charges are bond issuance costs (Chapter 11), start-up costs, organization costs, and plant rearrangement costs. In conformity with the **matching principle,** deferred charges are amortized to expense each period over the future periods benefited.

DISPOSAL OF OPERATIONAL ASSETS

Operational assets may be disposed of in two ways: **voluntarily** by sale, trade-in, or retirement; or **involuntarily** as a result of a casualty, such as a storm, fire, or accident. Whatever the nature of the disposal, the cost of the asset and any accumulated depreciation, depletion, or amortization must be removed from the accounts at the date of disposal. The difference between any resources received upon disposal of an operational asset and the **book or carrying value** of the asset at the date of disposal is a **gain or loss on disposal of operational assets.** This gain (or loss) is reported on the income statement. However, it is not revenue (or expense) because it is from "peripheral or incidental" activities rather than from normal operations (see Exhibit 4–5). Assume a machine is sold for $3,500 cash when the account balances showed Machine, $10,000; and Accumulated Depreciation, Machine, $7,000 (i.e., a book value of $3,000). The entry to record this disposal is:

```
Cash ............................................................... 3,500
Accumulated depreciation, machine ................................. 7,000
    Machine .......................................................        10,000
    Gain on disposal of operational asset ..........................          500

Gain computed:
    Sale price ........................................................ $3,500
    Book value at date of sale ($10,000 − $7,000) ..................... 3,000
    Difference, gain .................................................. $ 500
```

EXHIBIT 9–5

Disposal of an operational asset

Panel A—Situation of Bye Company:

January 1, 19A—Purchased a heavy-duty truck for $38,000 cash; estimated useful life eight years and $6,000 residual value (straight-line depreciation).

December 31—End of accounting year.

June 30, 19D—The truck was wrecked, and the insurance company paid a claim of $21,000 (i.e., the replacement cost of the truck at the date of the wreck).

Panel B—Entries during the life of the truck:

January 1, 19A—To record purchase of the truck:

Truck	38,000		
Cash		38,000	

December 31—To record annual depreciation 19A–19C:

	19A	19B	19C
Depreciation expense	4,000	4,000	4,000
Accumulated depreciation	4,000	4,000	4,000

Computation: ($38,000 − $6,000) ÷ 8 years = $4,000.

Panel C—June 30, 19D—Entries on date of disposal (wreck):

1. To record depreciation for six months (to date of wreck):

Depreciation expense	2,000	
Accumulated depreciation		2,000

Computation: $4,000 × 6/12 = $2,000.

2. To record the involuntary disposal of the asset and the insurance indemnity:

Cash (insurance indemnity)	21,000	
Accumulated depreciation ($4,000 × 3) + $2,000	14,000	
Casualty loss on operational assets	3,000	
Truck		38,000

Panel D—Reporting (by year):

	19A	19B	19C	19D
Income statement (for the year):				
Depreciation expense	$ 4,000	$ 4,000	$ 4,000	$2,000
Loss on disposal				3,000
Balance sheet (at December 31):				
Truck	$38,000	$38,000	$38,000	$ –0–
Accumulated depreciation	(4,000)	(8,000)	(12,000)	–0–
Book value	$34,000	$30,000	$26,000	$ –0–

Disposals of operational assets seldom occur on the last day of the accounting period. That is, the depreciation, depletion, or amortization must be updated to the date of disposal. Therefore, the disposal of a depreciable operational asset usually requires two entries: (1) an adjusting entry to update the depreciation expense and accumulated depreciation accounts, and (2) a disposal entry to remove all related account balances and to record a disposal gain or loss. Exhibit 9–5 illustrates a typical disposal. Panel A gives the situation, Panels B and C show the journal entries, and Panel D presents the reporting of a disposal.

A gain or loss on disposal occurs because (1) depreciation expense is based on estimates that may differ from actual experience, and (2) depreciation is based on original cost, not current market values.

DEMONSTRATION CASE

(Resolve the requirements before proceeding to the suggested solution that follows.)

Diversified Industries has been operating for a number of years. It started as a residential construction company. In recent years it expanded into heavy construction, ready-mix concrete, sand and gravel, construction supplies, and earth-moving services.

The transactions below were selected from those completed during 19D. They focus on the primary issues discussed in this chapter. Amounts have been simplified for case purposes.

19D

Jan. 1   The management decided to buy a building that was about 10 years old. The location was excellent and there was adequate parking space. The company bought the building and the land on which it was situated for $305,000 cash. A reliable appraiser provided the following market values: land, $126,000; and building, $174,000.

12   Paid renovation costs on the building of $38,100.

June 19   Bought a third location for a gravel pit (designated No. 3) for $50,000 cash. The location had been carefully surveyed. It was estimated that 100,000 cubic yards of gravel could be removed from the deposit.

July 10   Paid $1,200 for ordinary repairs on the building.

Aug. 1   Paid $10,000 for costs of preparing the new gravel pit for exploitation.

December 31, 19D (end of the annual accounting period)—the following data were developed as a basis for the adjusting entries:

a. The building will be depreciated on a straight-line basis over an estimated useful life of 30 years. The estimated residual value is $35,000.

b. During 19D, 12,000 square yards of gravel were removed and sold from gravel pit No. 3. Use an Accumulated Depletion account.

c. The company owns a patent right that is used in operations. On January 1, 19D, the Patent account had a balance of $3,300. The patent has an estimated remaining useful life of six years (including 19D).

Required:

1. Give the journal entries for the five transactions completed during 19D.
2. Give the adjusting entries on December 31, 19D.
3. Show the December 31, 19D, balance sheet classification and amount for each of the following items: land, building, gravel pit, and patent.

Suggested Solution:

Requirement 1—Entries during 19D:

January 1, 19D:

Land (building site)	128,100	
Building	176,900	
Cash		305,000

Allocation of cost (based on appraisal):

Item	Appraisal value	Percent	Computation	Allocation
Land	$126,000	42 ×	$305,000 =	$128,100
Building	174,000	58 ×	305,000 =	176,900
Totals	$300,000	100		$305,000

January 12, 19D:

Building	38,100	
Cash		38,100
Renovation costs on building prior to use.		

June 19, 19D:

Gravel pit (No. 3)	50,000	
Cash		50,000
Purchased gravel pit; estimated production, 100,000 cubic yards.		

July 10, 19D:

    Repair expense 1,200
        Cash   1,200
    Ordinary repairs.

August 1, 19D:

    Gravel pit (No. 3) 10,000
        Cash   10,000
    Preparation costs.

Requirement 2—Adjusting entries:

December 31, 19D:

a. Depreciation expense, building 6,000
        Accumulated depreciation   6,000

    Computation:
      Cost ($176,900 + $38,100) $215,000
        Less: Residual value 35,000
      Cost to be depreciated $180,000
    Annual depreciation: $180,000 ÷ 30 years = $6,000.

b. Depletion expense 7,200
        Accumulated depletion, gravel pit (No. 3)   7,200

    Computation:
      Cost ($50,000 + $10,000) $60,000
    Depletion rate:
      $60,000 ÷ 100,000 cubic yards = $0.60
    Depletion expense: $0.60 × 12,000 cubic yards = $7,200

c. Patent expense 550
        Patent   550

    Computation:
      $3,300 ÷ 6 years = $550.

Requirement 3—Balance sheet, December 31, 19D:

Assets			
Operational assets:			
Land		$128,100	
Building	$215,000		
Less: Accumulated depreciation	6,000	209,000	
Gravel pit	60,000		
Less: Accumulated depletion	7,200	52,800	
Total operational assets			$389,900
Intangible assets:			
Patent ($3,300 − $550)			2,750

SUMMARY OF CHAPTER

This chapter discussed accounting for operational assets. These are the non-current assets that a business retains for long periods of time for use in the course of normal operations rather than for sale. They include tangible assets and intangible assets. At acquisition, an operational asset is measured and recorded in the accounts at cost. Cost includes the cash equivalent purchase price plus all reasonable and necessary expenditures made to acquire and prepare the asset for its intended use.

An operational asset represents a bundle of future services and benefits that have been paid for in advance. As an operational asset is used, this bundle of future services gradually is used to earn revenue. Therefore, in conformity with the **matching principle,** cost (less any estimated residual value) is allocated to periodic expense over the periods benefited. In this way, the expense associated with the use of operational assets is matched with the revenues earned. This allocation process is called **depreciation** in the case of property, plant, and equipment; **depletion** in the case of natural resources; and **amortization** in the case of intangibles.

Four methods of depreciation are used widely: straight-line, productive-output, sum-of-the-years' digits, and declining-balance.

Expenditures related to operational assets are classified as:

1. **Capital expenditures**—those expenditures that provide benefits for one or more accounting periods beyond the current period; therefore, they are debited to appropriate asset accounts and depreciated, depleted, or amortized over their useful lives; or
2. **Revenue expenditures**—those expenditures that provide benefits during the current accounting period only; therefore, they are debited to appropriate current expense accounts when incurred.

Ordinary repairs and maintenance costs are revenue expenditures. Extraordinary repairs and asset additions are capital expenditures.

Operational assets may be disposed of voluntarily by sale or retirement, or involuntarily through casualty, such as storm, fire, or accident. Upon disposal, such assets must be depreciated, depleted, or amortized up to the date of disposal. The disposal transaction is recorded by removing the cost of the old asset and the related accumulated depreciation, depletion, or amortization amount from the accounts. A gain or loss on disposal of an operational asset will result when the disposal price is different from the book value of an old asset. Special rules apply to the trade-in of an asset as all, or part, of the consideration given for another asset (trade-ins are discussed in Supplement 9B).

SUPPLEMENT 9A—CAPITALIZATION OF INTEREST AS A COST OF OPERATIONAL ASSETS

When an operational asset is purchased and a loan is incurred as all, or part, of the payment, periodic interest on the debt is recorded and reported as **interest expense** during the term of the loan. However, *FASB Statement 34* provides an exception to this principle. The exception is that interest cost **must be capitalized** as a part of the cost of acquiring assets that require a lengthy period of time to get them ready for their intended use. In such cases, interest on the average expenditures incurred during the construction or acquisition period is recorded as a part of the cost of the operational asset. Interest is included in the cost of the asset *(a)* **only** during the construction or acquisition period and *(b)* not in excess of total interest cost incurred by the entity during the period. It is not necessary that the debts of the company be related to the construction of the operational asset.[16]

To illustrate capitalization of interest during construction, assume that on January 1, 19A, Byers Corporation signed a contract that required Dow Construction Company to build a new plant building at a contract price of $1,000,000. The construction period started March 1, 19A, and the building was substantially complete and ready for its intended use on December 31, 19A (end of the 10-month construction period). Byers Corporation was required to make the following quarterly cash progress payments on the contract during 19A:

---

[16] FASB, *Statement of Financial Accounting Standards No. 34*, "Capitalization of Interest Cost (Stamford, Conn., October 1979). Under this *Statement*, interest cannot be capitalized for assets that are (1) in use or ready for their intended use, or (2) not used in the earnings activities of the entity. *Statement 34* specifies the qualifying assets as follows: "Assets that are constructed or otherwise produced for an enterprise's own use (including assets constructed or produced for the enterprise by others for which deposits or progress payments have been made)."

Date of payment	Amount
a. March 31, 19A	$ 120,000
b. June 30, 19A	220,000
c. September 30, 19A	480,000
d. December 31, 19A	180,000
Total	$1,000,000

To make the progress payments, Byers Corporation borrowed 60% of each payment from a financial institution at 10% annual interest; the remaining cash needed was from within Byers Corporation. Total interest cost incurred by Byers during the period was $70,000 (at an average rate of 10%).

Upon completion, December 31, 19A, Byers Corporation should reflect the following acquisition cost in the operational asset account, Plant Building:

Contract price (paid in full)		$1,000,000
Add interest during the construction period:		
a. $120,000 × 10% × 9/12	$ 9,000	
b. $220,000 × 10% × 6/12	11,000	
c. $480,000 × 10% × 3/12	12,000	
d. $180,000—no interest	–0–	32,000*
Total acquisition cost		$1,032,000

* Note that this amount was not based on the specific borrowings of 60% but on the expenditures. This amount cannot exceed the $70,000 total interest cost for the period (19A).

FASB Statement 34 provides the following guidelines that must be observed.

1. Interest is capitalized **only** during the construction or acquisition period.
2. Interest is computed on the average **expenditures** during the construction period.
3. The applicable **borrowing interest rate** for the company is used.
4. Interest is computed **regardless of the source** of the funds (which may be borrowed or obtained from normal operations of the entity).
5. Interest added to the cost of the operational assets **cannot exceed** the total amount of total interest cost incurred by the entity in that period (for all purposes).

SUPPLEMENT 9B—TRADING IN ASSETS

It is not unusual when acquiring an asset to trade in another asset. Although there may be a direct trade of two assets, the typical case involves the trading in of an old asset plus the payment of cash for the difference (often called boot). In such transactions, the asset acquired must be recorded in the accounts and the old asset is removed from the accounts.

Accounting for the exchange of one asset for another asset depends on two factors:[17]

1. Whether the two assets are similar or dissimilar.
2. Whether cash for the difference (boot) is paid or received.

The trading in of an old truck for a newer truck would involve similar assets. In contrast, the trading in of a plot of land for a new truck would involve dissimilar assets.

The basic principle for recording the exchange of assets can be stated as follows: If the assets exchanged are similar, the exchange should be recorded on a "book value" basis because there is no completed earning process.[18] If the assets exchanged are dissimilar, the exchange should be recorded on a "market value" basis because there is a completed earning process (for the old asset).

Exhibit 9–6 illustrates accounting for the acquisition of an asset when another asset is given as a trade-in. Four independent cases are illustrated:

Case	Situation
A	Similar assets are exchanged; no cash boot is paid.
B	Dissimilar assets are exchanged; no cash boot is paid.
C	Similar assets are exchanged; cash boot is paid.
D	Dissimilar assets are exchanged; cash boot is paid.

The four cases shown in Exhibit 9–6 explain the exchange of assets. Sometime the terms of the transaction involving a trade-in also include the **receipt** of cash boot, in which case the recording becomes more complex.

Under fundamental accounting principles *(APB Opinion 29)*, an asset, when acquired, never should be recorded at an amount greater than its market value (i.e., its cash equivalent price). In some cases, this constraint will reduce a gain (or increase a loss) on disposal.

In the illustration in Exhibit 9–6, the market value of old Asset O was $200 in excess of its book value [i.e., $2,200 − ($5,000 − $3,000)]. Therefore, in Cases B and D (relating to dissimilar assets), this amount was recorded as a gain. In contrast, if the market value of old Asset O had been $1,900 (i.e., $100 below book value), a loss of $100 would be reported in Cases B and D. A loss would be recorded for Cases A and C (similar assets) when the market value of either asset is below book value because it indicates an impairment of value.

---

[17] *APB Opinion 29*, "Accounting for Nonmonetary Transactions" (New York, May 1973), specifies the appropriate accounting for transactions that involve the exchange of assets when either or both of these factors are present.

[18] In the case of an exchange of similar productive assets, because the asset acquired performs essentially the same productive function as the asset given up, the exchange is only one step in the earning process. The earning process in these situations is completed when the goods or services are sold that the similar productive assets helped to produce. In contrast, in the case of an exchange of dissimilar productive assets, the earning process is completed because the productive function of the productive asset given up is terminated. The asset acquired serves a different economic purpose for the entity and begins a new earning process of its own.

EXHIBIT 9–6

Trading in used assets illustrated

Situation of Company T:

Transaction: Company T acquired Asset N and traded in Asset O. At the date of the transaction, the accounts of Company T reflected the following:

Asset O:

Cost when acquired	$5,000
Accumulated depreciation	3,000
Estimated market value	2,200

Asset N:

Market value	2,250

Case A—Similar assets are exchanged; **no** cash boot paid.

Principle applied: The asset acquired is recorded at the **book value** of the asset traded in.

Asset N	2,000	
Accumulated depreciation, Asset O	3,000	
Asset O		5,000

Case B—Dissimilar assets are exchanged; **no** cash boot paid.

Principle applied: The asset acquired is recorded at the **market value** of the asset traded in.

Asset N	2,200	
Accumulated depreciation, Asset O	3,000	
Asset O		5,000
Gain on disposal of operational asset		200

Case C—Similar assets are exchanged; $60 cash boot is **paid.**

Principle applied: The asset acquired is recorded at the **book value** of the asset traded in **plus the cash boot** paid.

Asset N ($2,000 + $60)	2,060*	
Accumulated depreciation, Asset O	3,000	
Asset O		5,000
Cash		60

* This amount cannot exceed the market value of the asset acquired, $2,250.

Case D—Dissimilar assets are exchanged; $60 cash boot is **paid.**

Principle applied: The asset acquired is recorded at the **market value** of the asset traded in **plus the cash boot** paid.

Asset N ($2,200 + $60)	2,250*	
Accumulated depreciation, Asset O	3,000	
Asset O		5,000
Cash		60
Gain on disposal of operational assets		190

* This amount cannot exceed the market value of the asset acquired, $2,250.

IMPORTANT TERMS DEFINED IN THIS CHAPTER

Terms (alphabetically)	*Key words in definitions of important terms used in chapter*	*Page reference*
Accelerated depreciation	Higher depreciation expense in early years, and lower in later years of an operational asset.	438
Acquisition cost	Net cash equivalent amount paid for an asset.	432
Amortization	Systematic and rational allocation of the cost of an intangible operational asset over its useful life.	432
Basket purchase	Acquisition of two or more assets in a single transaction for a single lump sum.	430
Book (or carrying) value	Acquisition cost of an operational asset less accumulated depreciation, depletion, or amortization.	433
Capital expenditures	Expenditures that are debited to an asset account; the acquisition of an asset.	447
Capitalization of interest	Interest expenditures included in the cost of an operational asset; interest capitalized during construction period.	462
Copyrights	Exclusive right to publish, use, and sell a literary, musical, or artistic work.	453
Deferred charges	An expense paid in advance of usage of the goods or services; long-term prepayment.	455
Depletion	Systematic and rational allocation of the cost of a natural resource over the period of exploitation.	432
Depreciation	Systematic and rational allocation of the cost of property, plant and equipment (but not land) over its useful life.	432
Declining depreciation	An accelerated depreciation method based upon a multiple of the straight-line rate; it disregards residual value.	440
Estimated useful life	Estimated service life of an operational asset to the present owner.	435
Extraordinary repairs	Major, high cost, and long-term repairs; debited to an asset account (or accumulated depreciation); a capital expenditure.	448
Goodwill	Acquisition cost of the purchase of a business that is in excess of the market value of the other assets of the business purchased.	454
Intangible operational assets	Assets used in the operations of a business that have special rights but not physical substance.	451
Leaseholds	Rights granted to a lessee under a lease contract that have been paid for.	453
Leasehold improvements	Expenditures by the lessee on leased property that have use value beyond the current accounting period.	454
Natural resources	Mineral deposits, timber tracts, oil, and gas.	449
Operational assets	Tangible and intangible assets owned by a business and used in its operations.	428
Productive-output depreciation	Cost of an operational asset is allocated over its useful life based upon the periodic output related to total estimated output.	437
Repairs and maintenance	Expenditures for normal operating upkeep of operational assets; debit expense for ordinary repairs.	447
Residual value	Estimated amount to be recovered, less disposal costs, at the end of the estimated useful life of an operational asset.	434

Terms (alphabetically)	Key words in definitions of important terms used in chapter	Page reference
Revenue expenditures	Expenditures that are debited to an expense account; the incurrence of an expense.	447
Straight-line depreciation	Cost of an operational asset is allocated over its useful life in equal periodic amounts.	436
Sum-of-the-years'-digits depreciation	Cost of an operational asset is allocated over its useful life based upon a fraction when the denominator is the total of all of the useful years and the numerator is the year of life in inverse order.	439
Tangible operational assets	Assets used in the operations of a business that have physical substance.	428

QUESTIONS

PART A

1. Define operational assets. Why are they considered a "bundle of future services?"

2. What are the classifications of operational assets? Explain each.

3. Relate the cost principle to accounting for operational assets.

4. Describe the relationship between the matching principle and accounting for operational assets.

5. Define and illustrate the book value of a three-year-old operational asset that cost $11,500, has an estimated residual value of $1,500, and an estimated useful life of five years. Relate book value to carrying value and market value.

6. Under the cost principle, what amounts usually should be included in the acquisition cost of an operational asset?

7. What is a "basket purchase"? What measurement problem does it pose?

8. Distinguish between depreciation, depletion, and amortization.

9. In computing depreciation, three values must be known or estimated; identify and explain the nature of each.

10. Estimated useful life and residual value of an operational asset relate to the current owner or user rather than to all potential users. Explain this statement.

11. What kind of a depreciation-expense pattern is provided under the straight-line method? When would its use be appropriate?

12. What kind of depreciation-expense pattern emerges under the productive-output method? When would its use be appropriate?

13. What are the arguments in favor of accelerated depreciation?

14. Explain how monthly depreciation should be computed when the sum-of-the-years'-digits method is used for an asset having a 10-year life.

PART B

15. Distinguish between capital expenditures and revenue expenditures.

16. Distinguish between ordinary and extraordinary repairs. How is each accounted for?

17. Over what period should an addition to an existing operational asset be depreciated? Explain.

18. Define an intangible operational asset.

19. What period should be used to amortize an intangible operational asset?

20. Define goodwill. When is it appropriate to record goodwill as an intangible operational asset?

21. Distinguish between a leasehold and a leasehold improvement.

22. Over what period should a leasehold improvement be amortized? Explain.

23. Compare the accounting for a prepaid expense with accounting for a deferred charge.

24. When an operational asset is disposed of during the accounting period, two separate entries usually must be made. Explain this statement.

EXERCISES

PART A

E9–1   **(Pair Allocation Terms with Assets)**

For each asset listed below, enter a code letter to the left to indicate the allocation terminology for each asset. Use the following letter codes:

Allocation Term

A—Amortization   P—Depletion
D—Depreciation   N—None of these

Assets

A (1) Patent (example)	_____ (11) Copyright
_____ (2) Land	_____ (12) Investment in common stock
_____ (3) Building	_____ (13) Mineral deposit
_____ (4) Cash	_____ (14) Machinery
_____ (5) Oil well	_____ (15) License right
_____ (6) Trademark	_____ (16) Deferred charge
_____ (7) Goodwill	_____ (17) Inventory of goods
_____ (8) Stamps	_____ (18) Timber tract
_____ (9) Franchise	_____ (19) Tools
_____ (10) Plant site in use	_____ (20) Gravel pit

E9-2 **(Pair Brief Definitions with Terms)**
Match the definitions given below with the terms by entering the code letters in the blanks provided.

Terms	*Definition*
___E___ (1) Acquisition cost (example)	A. Assets used in operations; have physical substance.
_____ (2) Depreciation	B. Declining expense; numerator year of life in inverse order.
_____ (3) Straight-line depreciation	C. Use cost is the same amount per year during useful life.
_____ (4) Productive-output depreciation	D. Estimated recovery less costs of disposal.
_____ (5) Tangible operational assets	E. Cash equivalent amount.
_____ (6) Natural resource	F. Periodic expense fluctuates with actual output.
_____ (7) Useful life	G. A timber tract.
_____ (8) Depletion	H. Estimated productive life to the current user.
_____ (9) Basket purchase	I. Systematic allocation of the cost of a natural resource.
_____ (10) Book value	J. Must allocate a single purchase cost to two or more assets.
_____ (11) SYD depreciation	K. Systematic allocation of the cost of a tangible operational asset.
_____ (12) Residual value	L. Acquisition cost minus accumulated allocation of original cost.

E9-3 **(Record Asset Acquisition and Straight-Line Depreciation; Basket Purchase)**
Tony Company bought a building and the land on which it is located for a total cash price of $197,000. Also, Tony paid transfer costs of $3,000. Renovation costs on the building were $16,000. An independent appraiser provided market values of building, $145,152; and land, $56,448.

Required:

a. Apportion the cost of the property on the basis of the appraised values. Show computations.

b. Give the journal entry to record the purchase of the property, including all expenditures. Assume that all transactions were for cash and that all purchases occurred at the start of Year 1.

c. Give the journal entry to record straight-line depreciation at the end of one year assuming an estimated 20-year useful life and a $24,000 estimated residual value.

d. What would be the book value of the property at the end of Year 2?

E9-4 **(Apply Cost Principle and Record Straight-Line Depreciation)**
A machine was purchased by Mason Company on March 1, 19A, at an invoice price of $15,000. On date of delivery, March 2, 19A, Ryan Company paid $10,000 on the machine, and the balance was on credit at 12% interest. On March 3, 19A, $150 was paid for freight on the machine. On March 5, installation costs relating to the machine were paid amounting to $750. On October 1, 19A, Ryan Company paid the balance due on the machine plus the interest.

Required (round all amounts to the nearest dollar):

a. Give the journal entries on each of the above dates through October 19A.

b. Give the adjusting entry for straight-line depreciation at the end of 19A, assuming an estimated useful life of 10 years and an estimated residual value of $1,900. Depreciate to the nearest month. The accounting period ends December 31, 19A.

c. What would be the book value of the machine at the end of 19B?

E9–5   (Compute Depreciation for Four Years Using Four Different Depreciation Methods)
Vista Corporation bought a machine at a cost of $2,700. The estimated useful life was four years, and the residual value, $300. Assume that the estimated productive life of the machine is 60,000 units and each year's production was Year 1, 24,000 units; Year 2, 20,000 units; Year 3, 10,000 units; and Year 4, 6,000 units.

Required:

a. Determine the amount for each cell in the following schedule. Show your computations, and round to the nearest dollar.

Year	Depreciation Expense			
	Straight Line	Productive Output	Sum-of-the-Years' Digits	150% Declining Balance
1				
2				
3				
4				
Total				

b. Assuming the machine was used directly in the production of one of the products manufactured and sold by the company, what factors might be considered in selecting a preferable depreciation method in conformity with the matching principle?

E9–6   (Compute Depreciation and Book Value for Two Years Using Four Depreciation Methods)
XIT Company bought a machine for $35,000. The estimated useful life was five years, and the estimated residual value, $5,000. Assume the estimated useful life in productive units is 60,000. Units actually produced were Year 1, 12,000; and Year 2, 11,000.

Required:

a. Determine the appropriate amounts to complete the schedule below. Show computations, and round to the nearest dollar.

| | Depreciation expense | | Book value at end of | |
Method of depreciation	Year 1	Year 2	Year 1	Year 2
Straight-line	——	——	——	——
Productive-output	——	——	——	——
Sum-of-the-years' digits	——	——	——	——
140% declining-balance	——	——	——	——

b. Which method would result in the lowest EPS for Year 1? For Year 2?

E9–7   **(Monthly Depreciation Using Two Depreciation Methods; Effect on Income Statement)**
Stoner Company acquired, and paid for, a machine that cost $5,300 on July 1, 19B. The estimated useful life is four years, and the estimated residual value is $500. The accounting period ends December 31.

Required:

a. Compute monthly depreciation expense for July 19B and July 19C assuming (a) the straight-line method and (b) the SYD method.

b. Assume cash revenues of $50,000 and cash expenses of $30,000 for the year 19B and an income tax rate of 30%. Complete the following tabulation for 19B:

	Straight Line	Sum-of-the-Years' Digits
Revenues		
Expenses		
Depreciation expense		
Pretax income		
Income tax expense		
Net income		

c. Which method produced the higher net income? By how much? Why do the net incomes differ (use amounts)?

E9–8   **(Record and Explain Change in Useful Life and Residual Value)**
Belt Company owns the office building occupied by its administrative office. The office building was reflected in the accounts on the December 31, 1985, balance sheet as follows:

Cost when acquired $250,000
Accumulated depreciation (based on straight-line
depreciation, an estimated life of 30 years,
and a $40,000 residual value) 105,000

During January 1986, on the basis of a careful study, the management decided that the total estimated useful life should be changed to 25 years (instead of 30) and the residual value reduced to $35,000 (from $40,000). The depreciation method will not be changed.

Required:

a. Give the adjusting entry (or entries) related to depreciation at the end of 1986. Show computations.

b. Explain the basis for the entry (or entries) that you gave in (a).

PART B

E9–9   **(Identify Capital and Revenue Expenditures)**

For each item listed below, enter the correct letter to the left to show the type of expenditure. Use the following:

Type of Expenditure
A—Capital expenditure
B—Revenue expenditure
C—Neither

Transaction

_____ (1) Paid $500 for ordinary repairs.
_____ (2) Paid $6,000 for extraordinary repairs.
_____ (3) Addition to old building; paid cash, $10,000.
_____ (4) Routine maintenance; cost, $300; on credit.
_____ (5) Purchased a machine, $6,000; gave long-term note.
_____ (6) Paid $2,000 for organization costs.
_____ (7) Paid three-year insurance premium, $600.
_____ (8) Purchased a patent, $3,400 cash.
_____ (9) Paid $10,000 for monthly salaries.
_____ (10) Paid cash dividends, $15,000.

E9–10   **(Pair Brief Definitions with Terms)**

Match the definitions given below with the terms by entering the code letters in the blanks provided.

Terms

H	(1) Patents (example)
_____	(2) Goodwill
_____	(3) Leaseholds
_____	(4) Amortization
_____	(5) Copyrights
_____	(6) Capitalization of interest
_____	(7) Intangible operational assets
_____	(8) Deferred charges
_____	(9) Ordinary repairs and maintenance
_____	(10) Additions (to assets)
_____	(11) Leasehold improvements
_____	(12) Franchise

Definition

A. Cash paid or received when operational assets are exchanged.
B. Ownership right to publish, use, or sell a literary, musical, or artistic work.
C. An expense paid in advance that represents a long-term payment.
D. Long-term, major, high-cost repairs.
E. Price paid for a business in excess of the market value of the net assets.
F. Assets used in the operations of a business because of their special rights.
G. Rights granted to a lessee that have been paid for.
H. An exclusive to use, manufacture, and sell a right that is protected by law.
I. Time cost of money allocated as a part of the cost of an operational asset.

Terms	Definition
——— (13) Gain (loss) on disposal of an operational asset	J. A right granted by a governmental or business entity to offer services or products under a contract.
——— (14) "Boot" involved in the exchange of operational assets	K. Costs expended by a lessee on leased property (e.g., a building on leased land).
——— (15) Extraordinary repairs	L. Difference between consideration received and book value of an operational asset disposed of.
	M. Systematic and rational allocation of the cost of an intangible asset.
	N. Normal low cost, regularly recurring expenditures for upkeep of operational assets.
	O. Extensions to, or enlargements of, an operational asset; a capital expenditure.

E9–11   **(Record Depreciation, Repairs, and Amortization)**

Florida Company operates a small manufacturing facility as a supplement to its regular service activities. At the beginning of 19L, an operational asset account for the company showed the following balances:

Manufacturing equipment $70,000
Accumulated depreciation through 19K 48,400

During 19L, the following expenditures were incurred for repairs and maintenance:

1. Routine maintenance and repairs on the equipment $1,000
2. Major overhaul of the equipment 6,400

The equipment is being depreciated on a straight-line basis over an estimated life of 15 years and a $4,000 estimated residual value. The annual accounting period ends on December 31.

Required:

a. Give the adjusting entry for depreciation on the manufacturing equipment that was made at the end of 19K. Starting with 19L, what is the remaining estimated life?
b. Give the journal entries to record the two expenditures for repairs and maintenance during 19L.
c. Give the adjusting entry that should be made at the end of 19L for depreciation of the manufacturing equipment assuming no change in the estimated life or residual value. Show computations.

E9–12   **(Record Depreciation; Extraordinary Repairs; Change in Estimated Useful Life and Residual Value)**

At the end of the annual accounting period, December 31, 19C, the records of Wang Company reflected the following:

Machine A:
Cost when acquired $34,000
Accumulated depreciation 12,000

During January 19D, the machine was renovated, including several major improvements at a cost of $8,000. As a result, the estimated life was increased from 8 years to 10 years, and the residual value was increased from $2,000 to $5,500.

Required:

a. Give the journal entry to record the renovation. How old was the machine at the end of 19C?

b. Give the adjusting journal entry at the end of 19D to record straight-line depreciation for the year.

c. Explain the rationale for your entries in *(a)* and *(b)*.

E9–13   (Record Acquisition and Depletion of a Natural Resource)

In February 19A, ACE Extractive Industries paid $500,000 for a mineral deposit. During March, $220,000 was spent in preparing the deposit for exploitation. It was estimated that 800,000 total cubic yards could be extracted economically. During 19A, 50,000 cubic yards were extracted. During January 19B, another $80,000 was spent for additional developmental work. After conclusion of the latest work, the estimated remaining recovery was increased to one million cubic yards over the remaining life. During 19B, 35,000 cubic yards were extracted.

Required:

Give the appropriate journal entry on each of the following dates:

a. February 19A, for acquisition of the deposit.

b. March 19A, for developmental costs.

c. Year 19A, for annual depletion assuming the company uses a contra account (show computations).

d. January 19B, for developmental costs.

e. Year 19B, for annual depletion (show computations).

E9–14   (Record Acquisition, Amortization, and Reporting of Three Different Intangible Assets)

Reo Manufacturing Company had three intangible operational assets at the end of 19F (end of the accounting year):

1. Patent—purchased from J. Ray on January 1, 19F, for a cash cost of $4,260. Ray had registered the patent with the U.S. Patent Office five years earlier on January 1, 19A. Amortize over the remaining legal life.

2. A franchise acquired from the local community to provide certain services for 10 years starting on January 1, 19F. The franchise cost $26,000 cash.

3. On January 1, 19F, the company leased some property for a five-year term. Reo immediately spent $4,800 cash for long-term improvements (estimated useful life, eight years, and no residual value). At the termination of the lease, there will be no recovery of these improvements.

Required:

a. Give the journal entry to record the acquisition of each intangible asset. Provide a brief explanation with the entries.

b. Give the adjusting journal entry at December 31, 19F, for amortization of each intangible. Show computations. The company does not use contra accounts.

c. Show how these assets, and any related expenses, should be reported on the financial statements for 19F.

E9–15   **(Record a Patent, Copyright, and Goodwill and Amortize Each)**

Bebie Company acquired three intangible operational assets during 19F. The relevant facts were:

1. On January 1, 19F, the company purchased a patent from J. Doe for $4,800 cash. Doe had developed the patent and registered it with the Patent Office on January 1, 19A. Amortize over the remaining legal life.
2. On January 1, 19F, the company purchased a copyright for a total cash cost of $12,000, and the remaining legal life was 25 years. The company executives estimated that the copyright would have no value by the end of 20 years.
3. Bebie Company purchased a small company in January 19F at a cash cost of $150,000. Included in the purchase price was $20,000 for goodwill; the balance was for plant, equipment, and fixtures (no liabilities were assumed). Amortize the goodwill over the maximum period permitted.

Required:

a. Give the journal entry to record the acquisition of each intangible.
b. Give the adjusting journal entry that would be required at the end of the annual accounting period, December 31, 19F, for each intangible. The company uses contra accounts. Include a brief explanation and show computations.
c. What would be the book (carrying) value of each intangible asset at the end of 19G?

E9–16   **(Record and Amortize Rent Paid in Advance, Leasehold Improvements, and Periodic Rent)**

WT Company conducts operations in several different sites. In order to expand into still another city, the company obtained a 10-year lease, starting January 1, 19D, on a downtown location. Although there was a serviceable building on the property, the company had to build an additional structure to be used for storage. The 10-year lease required a $10,000 cash advance rental payment, plus cash payments of $2,000 per month during occupancy. During January 19D, the company spent $60,000 cash building the structure. The new structure has an estimated life of 12 years with no residual value (straight-line depreciation).

Required:

a. Give the journal entries for WT Company to record the payment of the $10,000 advance on January 1, 19D, and the first monthly rental.
b. Give the journal entry to record the construction of the new structure.
c. Give any adjusting entries required at the end of the annual accounting period for WT Company on December 31, 19D, in respect to (1) the advance payment and (2) the new structure. Show computations.
d. What is the total amount of expense resulting from the lease for 19D?

E9–17   **(Reporting Intangible Assets on the Balance Sheet)**

Doe Company is in the process of preparing the balance sheet at December 31, 19B. The following are to be included:

Prepaid insurance .... $ 300
Long-term investment in common stock of
    X Corporation, at cost (market $10,600)   10,000

Patent (at cost)	3,400
Accumulated amortization, patent	1,000
Accounts receivable	24,000
Allowance for doubtful accounts	700
Franchise (at cost)	1,000
Accumulated amortization, franchise	600
Land—site of building	40,000
Building	400,000
Accumulated depreciation, building	160,000

Required:

Show how each of the above assets would be reflected on Doe Company's balance sheet at December 31, 19B. Use the following subcaptions: Current assets, Investments and funds, Tangible operational assets, and Intangible operational assets. The company uses the "accumulated" accounts as listed above.

E9–18   (Record the Disposal of an Asset at Three Different Assumed Sale Prices)

Daly Company sold a small truck that had been used in the business for three years. The records of the company reflected the following:

Delivery truck	$25,000
Accumulated depreciation	20,000

Required:

a. Give the journal entry for disposal of the truck assuming the sales price was $5,000.
b. Give the journal entry for the disposal of the truck assuming the sales price was $5,400.
c. Give the journal entry for the disposal of the truck assuming the sales price was $4,400.
d. Summarize the effects of the disposal of the asset under the three different situations above.

E9–19   (Record the Disposal of an Operational Asset; Compute Estimated Life)

The records of Phoenix Company on December 31, 19D, showed the following data about a particular machine:

Machine, original cost	$27,000
Accumulated depreciation	16,000*

* Based on a six-year estimated useful life, a $3,000 residual value, and straight-line depreciation.

On April 1, 19E, the machine was sold for $10,700 cash. The accounting period ends on December 31.

Required:

a. How old was the machine on January 1, 19E? Show computations.
b. Give the journal entry, or entries, related to the sale of the machine.

E9–20   (Record Accident and Insurance Indemnity on an Operational Asset)

On August 31, 19C, a delivery truck owned by Prince Corporation was a total loss as a result of an accident. On January 1, 19C, the records showed the following:

Truck (estimated residual value, 10% of cost)	$10,000
Accumulated depreciation (straight line, two years)	3,000

The truck was insured; therefore, Prince Corporation collected $6,300 cash from the insurance company on October 5, 19C.

Required:

a. Based on the data given, compute the estimated useful life and the estimated residual value of the truck.

b. Give all of the journal entries with respect to the truck from January 1 through October 5, 19C. Show computations.

PROBLEMS

PART A

P9–1 **(Apply the Cost Principle to Determine the Cost of an Operational Asset)**

On January 1, 19A, Flye Company bought a machine for use in operations. The machine has an estimated useful life of 10 years and an estimated residual value (given below). The expenditures given below were provided by the company:

a. Invoice price of the machine, $60,000.

b. Less: Cash discount of 3% on all cash paid by January 10.

c. Freight paid by the vendor per sales agreement, $1,000.

d. Flye incurred installation costs, $1,500.

e. Payment of the $60,000 was made by Flye on January 15, 19A, as follows:

Flye common stock, par $1; 3,000 shares (market value, $4 per share).

Note payable, $30,000, 10% due April 16, 19A (principal plus interest).

Balance of the invoice price settled with cash.

Required:

Compute the cost of the machine that Flye should record. Explain the basis you used for any questionable items.

P9–2 **(Basket Purchase Allocation; Record Cost and Depreciation—Three Methods)**

Bush Company bought three used machines from J. Doe for a cash price of $48,000. Transportation costs on the machines were $2,000. The machines immediately were overhauled, installed, and started operating. The machines were different; therefore, each had to be recorded separately in the accounts. An appraiser was employed to estimate their market values at date of purchase (prior to the overhaul and installation). The book values shown on Doe's books also are available. The book values, appraisal results, installation costs, and renovation expenditures were:

	Machine A	Machine B	Machine C
Book value—Doe	$6,000	$10,000	$7,000
Appraisal value	7,200	24,400	8,400
Installation costs	300	500	200
Renovation costs prior to use	1,000	600	400

Required:

a. Compute the cost of each machine by making a supportable allocation. Explain the rationale for the allocation basis used.

b. Give the journal entry to record the purchase of the three machines assuming all payments were cash. Set up a separate asset account for each machine.

c. Give the entry to record depreciation expense at the end of Year 1, assuming:

		Estimates	
Machine	*Life*	*Residual value*	*Depreciation method*
A	6	$1,300	Straight line
B	4	1,600	SYD
C	5	1,100	200% DB

P9–3 **(Compute and Record Depreciation Using Four Methods; Explain Effect of Depreciation on Cash Flow and EPS)**

Bye Company bought a machine that cost $34,375. The estimated useful life is 10 years, and the estimated residual value is 4% of cost. The machine has an estimated useful life in productive output of 110,000 units. Actual output was Year 1, 15,000; and Year 2, 12,000.

Required:

a. Determine the appropriate amounts for the table below. Show your computations.

	Depreciation expense		*Book value at end of*	
Depreciation method	*Year 1*	*Year 2*	*Year 1*	*Year 2*
Straight line	$_____	$_____	$_____	$_____
Productive output	_____	_____	_____	_____
Sum-of-the-years' digits	_____	_____	_____	_____
200% declining balance	_____	_____	_____	_____

b. Give the adjusting entries for Years 1 and 2 under each method.

c. In selecting a depreciation method, some companies assess the comparative effect on **cash flow** and **EPS.** Briefly comment on the depreciation methods in terms of effects on cash flow and EPS.

P9–4 **(Compute Depreciation Expense and Accumulated Depreciation for Four Depreciation Methods; Also a Change in Useful Life and Residual Value)**

On January 1, 19A, AA Company bought a special heavy-duty truck that cost $28,500. The truck has an estimated five-year life and a $6,000 residual value. Estimated total mileage by disposal date is 50,000. Actual mileage was: Year A, 12,000; Year B, 14,000; Year C, 16,000; Year D, 6,000; and Year E, 3,000.

Required:

a. Complete the following comparative depreciation schedule:

Depreciation Method	Year				
	A	B	C	D	E

1. Straight line (SL):
    Depreciation expense
    Accumulated depreciation
	$	$	$	$	$

2. Sum-of-the-years' digits (SYD):
    Depreciation expense
    Accumulated depreciation					

3. Productive output (PO):
    Depreciation expense
    Accumulated depreciation					

4. Declining balance, 150% (DB):
    Depreciation expense
    Accumulated depreciation					

b. The interim depreciation expense for January 19A would be: SL, $_____; SYD, $_____; PO, $_____; DB, $_____.

c. Assume that at the start of 19D, the estimates were changed; total life, seven years; residual value, $4,000. Give all related entries for 19D, for the SL method.

P9–5   (Compute and Analyze Net Cash Flow)

Stable Corporation bought an operational asset on January 1, 19A, at a cash cost of $34,000. The estimated useful life is five years, and the estimated residual value is $4,000. Assume a constant 30% income tax rate; all paid in cash.

The company is deciding whether to use either straight-line (SL) depreciation or declining balance (DB) depreciation for both accounting and income tax purposes. The five-year projected all-cash incomes (before depreciation and income tax) are shown in the second column below.

Schedule to Compare Projected SL and DB Results

Year	Income (all-cash) before Depreciation and Income Tax	Depreciation Expense (dollars)		Income Tax Expense (dollars)		Net Income (dollars)		Net Cash Inflow (dollars)	
		SL	200% DB	SL	200% DB	SL	200% DB	SL	200% DB
1	$ 40,000	6,000	13,600	10,200	7,920	23,800	18,480	29,800	32,080
2	40,000								
3	40,000								
4	40,000								
5	40,000								
Total	200,000	30,000		51,000		119,000		149,000	

Required:

a. Complete the above schedule. Round to the nearest dollar. (Hint: Use the total line to prove your computations.)

b. Respond to each of the following items, based on your answer in *(a)*:
   (1) Total depreciation under each method.
   (2) Explain the periodic depreciation amounts of SL versus DB.
   (3) Total income tax under each method.
   (4) Explain the periodic income tax amounts of SL versus DB.
   (5) Total net income under each method.
   (6) Explain the periodic net income under each method.
   (7) Total cash flow under each method.
   (8) Explain the periodic cash flow amounts in terms of DB and SL.

P9–6   **(Analyze and Give Entries Related to a Change in Estimated Life and Residual Value)**

Tirpo Company owns an existing building that was built at an original cost of $500,000. It is being depreciated on a straight-line basis over a 20-year estimated useful life and has a $60,000 estimated residual value. At the end of 19H, the building had been depreciated for a full eight years. In January 19I, a decision was made, on the basis of new information, that a total estimated useful life of 30 years, and a residual value of $82,000 would be more realistic. The accounting period ends December 31.

Required:

a. Compute (1) the amount of depreciation expense recorded in 19H and (2) the book value of the building at the end of 19H.

b. Compute the amount of depreciation that should be recorded in 19I. Show computations.

c. Give the adjusting entry for depreciation at December 31, 19I.

P9–7   **(This Problem Relates to Supplement 9A; It Requires Computation of Interest that Must be Capitalized on an Operational Asset).**

On January 1, 19A, Stonewall Corporation bought land at a cost of $120,000 and paid transfer fees of $6,000. Clearing the land and planning for the building construction was started immediately. Construction of an office building for company use was started on April 1, 19A. The company borrowed about 80% of the funds to purchase the land and construct the office building at a 12% interest rate. The remaining cash needed was paid from company funds. Total interest cost for 19A was $36,000. The company made the following cash expenditures at the dates indicated:

January 1, 19A, down payment on the land (20%) .... $ 24,000
January 1, 19A, transfer costs on the land 6,000
March 1, 19A, fees for preliminary surveys and work prior to start of construction 12,000

Progress payments to contractor for construction costs:
May 31, 19A, No. 1 200,000
August 31, 19A, No. 2 300,000
November 30, 19A, No. 3 (end of the construction period) 200,000

Required:

a. Compute the cost of the tangible operational asset with separate amounts for the land and building. Assume the construction period started on April 1, 19A. Show computations.

b. How much interest expense should be reported on the 19A income statement?

PART B

P9–8 **(Recording Repairs and an Addition)**

Case Company made extensive repairs on its existing building and added a new wing. The existing building originally cost $360,000; and by the end of 19J (10 years), it was half depreciated on the basis of a 20-year estimated useful life and no residual value. During 19K, the following expenditures were made that were related to the building:

1. Ordinary repairs and maintenance expenditures for the year, $7,500 cash.
2. Extensive and major repairs to the roof of the building, $21,000 cash. These repairs were completed on June 30, 19K.
3. The new wing was completed on June 30, 19K, at a cash cost of $150,000. The wing had an estimated useful life of 10 years and no residual value.

Required:

a. Give the journal entry to record each of the 19K transactions.
b. Give the adjusting entry that would be required at the end of the annual accounting period, December 31, 19K, for the building after taking into account your entries in (a) above. Assume straight-line depreciation. The company computes depreciation based on the nearest month.
c. Show how the assets would be reported on the December 31, 19K, balance sheet. (Hint: Depreciation expense for 19K is $27,000.)

P9–9 **(Analyze, Record, Give Adjusting Entries, and Compute Book Value Related to Five Different Intangible Operational Assets)**

Dakota Company has five different intangible operational assets to be accounted for and reported on the financial statements. The management is concerned about the amortization of the cost of each of these intangibles. Facts about each intangible are:

1. **Patent**—The company purchased a patent at a cash cost of $26,000 on January 1, 19E. The patent had a legal life of 17 years from date of registration with the U.S. Patent Office, which was January 1, 19A. Amortize over the remaining legal life.
2. **Copyright**—On January 1, 19E, the company purchased a copyright for $15,000 cash. The legal life remaining from that date is 30 years. It is estimated that the copyrighted item will have no value by the end of 25 years.
3. **Franchise**—The company obtained a franchise from X Company to make and distribute a special item. The franchise was obtained on January 1, 19E, at a cash cost of $10,000 and covered a 10-year period.
4. **License**—On January 1, 19D, the company secured a license from the city to operate a special service for a period of five years. Total cash expended to obtain the license was $8,000.
5. **Goodwill**—The company started business in January 19C by purchasing another business for a cash lump sum of $400,000. Included in the purchase price was "Goodwill, $80,000." Dakota executives stated that "the goodwill is an important long-term asset to us." Amortize over the maximum period permitted.

Required:

a. Analyze each intangible asset and give the journal entry to record each of the five acquisitions.
b. Give the adjusting entry for each intangible asset that would be necessary at the end of the annual accounting period, December 31, 19E. Provide a brief explanation and

show computations. If no entry is required for a particular item, explain the basis for
your conclusion.
  c. Give the book value of each intangible on January 1, 19G. (Hint: The total book value
     for the five intangibles is $119,000.)

P9-10   **(Record the Purchase of a Business Including Goodwill; Depreciation of Assets, Acquired
and Amortization of Goodwill)**
  On January 1, 19A, Investor Corporation was organized by five individuals to purchase and operate a successful business known as Kampus Korner. The name was
retained, and all of the assets, except cash, were purchased for $300,000 cash. The
liabilities were not assumed by Investor Corporation. The transaction was closed on
January 5, 19A, at which time the balance sheet of Kampus Korner reflected the book
values shown below:

KAMPUS KORNER
January 5, 19A

	Book value	Market value*
Accounts receivable (net)	$ 30,000	$ 30,000
Inventory	180,000	175,000
Operational assets (net)	19,000	50,000
Other assets	1,000	5,000
Total assets	$230,000	
Liabilities	$ 80,000	
Owners' equity	150,000	
Total liabilities and owners' equity	$230,000	

   * These values for the assets purchased were provided to Investor
Corporation by an independent appraiser.

As a part of the negotiations, the former owners of Kampus Korner agreed not to engage
in the same or similar line of business in the same general region.

Required:

  a. Give the journal entry by Investor Corporation to record the purchase of the assets of
     Kampus Korner. Include goodwill. (Hint: Record the assets at market value in confor-
     mity with the cost principle.)
  b. Give the adjusting journal entries that would be made by Investor Corporation at the
     end of the annual accounting period, December 31, 19A, for:
     (1) Depreciation of the operational assets (straight line) assuming an estimated re-
         maining useful life of 20 years and no residual value.
     (2) Amortization of goodwill assuming the maximum amortization period is used.

P9-11   **(Record the Disposal of Three Operational Assets)**
  During 19K, Hammer Company disposed of three different assets. On January 1, 19K,
prior to their disposal, the accounts reflected the following:

Assets	Original cost	Residual value	Estimated life	Accumulated depreciation (straight line)
Machine A	$20,000	$2,000	10 years	$12,600 (7 years)
Machine B	35,400	3,000	9 years	21,600 (6 years)
Machine C	65,200	6,400	14 years	46,200 (11 years)

The machines were disposed of in the following ways:

Machine A—Sold on January 1, 19K, for $6,400 cash.

Machine B—Sold on May 1, 19K, for $13,200; received cash, $3,200, and a $10,000 interest-bearing (12%) note receivable due at the end of 12 months.

Machine C—On July 2, 19K, this machine suffered irreparable damage from an accident. On July 10, 19K, it was given to a salvage company at no cost. The salvage company agreed to remove the machine immediately at no cost. The machine was insured, and $18,000 cash was collected from the insurance company.

Required:

Give all journal entries related to the disposal of each machine. Explain the accounting rationale for the way that you recorded each disposal.

P9–12 **(Analyze Five Transactions to Give Original Entry and Any Related Depreciation and Amortization Adjusting Entries)**

During the 19X5 annual accounting period, Baker Company completed the following transactions:

1. On January 10, 19X5, paid $6,000 for a complete reconditioning of each of the following machines acquired on January 1, 19X1(Total Cost $12,000):

   Machine A—Original cost, $23,000, accumulated depreciation to December 31, 19X4, $16,000 (straight line, $3,000 residual value).

   Machine B—Original cost, $28,000, accumulated depreciation, $12,000 straight line, ($4,000 residual value).

2. On July 1, 19X5, purchased a patent for $14,000 cash (estimated useful life, seven years).
3. On January 1, 19X5, purchased another business for cash $50,000 including $12,000 for goodwill. No liabilities were assumed by Baker.
4. On September 1, 19X5, constructed a storage shed on some land leased from J. Doe. The cost was $14,400; the estimated useful life was 10 years with no residual value. Baker Company uses straight-line depreciation. The lease will expire at the end of 19X8.
5. Total expenditures during 19X5 for ordinary repairs and maintenance was $4,500.
6. On July 1, 19X5, sold Machine A for $7,000 cash.

Required (compute depreciation to the nearest month):

a. For each of the above transactions, give the entry (or entries) that should be made during 19X5.

b. For each of the above transactions, give any adjusting entry that should be made at December 31, 19X5.

P9–13 **(A Challenging Analytical Problem; Five Different Situations Are Analyzed—Two Involve Accounting Errors, One Involves a Basket Purchase, and One Involves Some Noncash Payments; Related Entries Are Required)**

It is the end of the annual accounting period, December 31, 19F, for Modern Company. The following items must be resolved before the financial statements can be prepared:

1. On January 1, 19F, a used machine was bought for $5,000 cash. This amount was properly debited to an operational asset account, Machinery. Prior to use, cash was expended for (a) major overhauling the machine, $600, and (b) for installation, $150; both of these amounts were debited to Expense. The machine has an estimated remaining useful life of five years and a 10% residual value. Straight-line depreciation will be used.

2. A small warehouse (and the land on which it is located) was purchased on January 1, 19F, at a cash cost of $40,000 which was debited in full to an operational asset account, Warehouse. The property was appraised for tax purposes near the end of 19E as follows: warehouse, $21,250; and land, $8,250. The warehouse has an estimated remaining useful life of 10 years and a 10% residual value; 200% declining balance depreciation will be used.

3. During the year 19F, usual recurring repair costs of $1,200 were paid. During January 19F, major repairs (on the warehouse purchased in 2 above) of $1,000 were paid. Repair expense was debited $2,200, and Cash was credited.

4. On June 30, 19F, the company purchased a patent for use in the business at a cash cost of $2,040. The patent was dated July 1, 19A. The Patent account was debited for the full amount.

5. On December 31, 19F, the company acquired a new truck that had a list price of $15,000 (estimated life, five years; residual value, $2,000). The company paid for the truck with cash, $7,000, and issued to the seller 600 shares of its own capital stock, par $10. The market value of the stock was $12 per share. This purchase has not been recorded.

Required:

a. Give the journal entry or entries that should be made to correct the accounts at December 31, 19F, before the adjusting entries are made. If none is required, so state.

b. Give the adjusting journal entries at December 31, 19F, after the corrections in Requirement (a) have been made.

P9–14   **(A Challenging Problem; Focuses on the Cash Flow Effects of Income Tax for Straight-Line Depreciation versus Accelerated Depreciation)**

On January 1, 19A, Brown Corporation bought a special machine for use in the business for $33,000. The machine has a three-year useful life and a residual value of $3,000. The company is considering using either the straight-line (SL) method or the 200% declining balance (DB) method of depreciation. Assume an average income tax rate of 30% (for both accounting and income tax purposes) and that it is paid in full in cash.

Requirement a:

Prepare an analysis of the effects of SL versus 200% DB depreciation on the projected financial statements and cash flows over the life of the machine (19A–19C). You have decided to complete the following schedules—one set based on straight-line depreciation and another set based on 200% declining balance depreciation:

	Year 1	Year 2	Year 3
Income statements:			
Revenues (all cash)	$90,000	$95,000	$99,000
Expenses (all cash)	(60,000)	(62,000)	(63,000)
Depreciation expense	_____	_____	_____
Pretax income	_____	_____	_____
Income tax expense	_____	_____	_____
Net income	_____	_____	_____
EPS (5,000 shares)	_____	_____	_____
Balance sheets:			
Operational assets:			
Machine	_____	_____	_____
Accumulated depreciation	_____	_____	_____
Book value	_____	_____	_____
Cash flows:			
Revenues	_____	_____	_____
Expenses	_____	_____	_____
Depreciation expense	_____	_____	_____
Income tax	_____	_____	_____
Net cash inflow	_____	_____	_____

Requirement b:

Complete the following summary of **relevant comparisons** based upon your answer to Requirement *(a)*:

Items Compared	Year 1		Year 2		Year 3		Total (each method)
	SL	200% DB	SL	200% DB	SL	200% DB	
1. Net income							
2. Machine, book value							
3. Net cash inflow							

Requirement c:

List, and explain, any generalizations that you can make about the three items summarized in Requirement *(b)*: (1) net income, (2) book value, and (3) net cash inflow.

Requirement d:

Which method would you recommend? Explain the basis for your recommendation.

Instructional note: This problem assumes a constant income tax rate in order to focus on the different effects of SL versus DB depreciation. Also, the time period is limited to a three-year useful life only to reduce the computational burden.

P9–15 **(This Problem Relates to Supplement 9B; Record the Sale of an Operational Asset under Two Assumptions: All Cash and Exchange)**

Quick Manufacturing Company operates a number of machines. One particular group of machines has five identical machines acquired on the same date. At the beginning of 19G, the operational asset account for the five machines showed the following:

Machinery (Type A, five machines) $200,000
Accumulated depreciation (Type A machines) 108,000*

  * Based on 10-year estimated useful life and $4,000 residual value per machine and straight-line depreciation.

One of the machines (Type A) was disposed of on September 1, 19G.

Required:

a. How old were the Type A machines at January 1, 19G? Show computations.
b. What was the book value of the machine sold (at date of disposal)? Show computations. The company computes depreciation to the nearest full month.
c. Give all journal entries to record the disposal of the machine under two independent assumptions:
 (1) It was sold outright for $14,000 cash.
 (2) It was exchanged for a new similar machine having a "quoted" price of $47,000; however, it was determined that it could be purchased for $44,000 cash. The old machine was traded in, and $30,000 was paid in cash. Assume the machines were similar. No reasonable market value was determinable for the old machine.

P9–16 **(This Problem Relates to Supplement 9B; Record Exchanges of Similar and Dissimilar Machine, with and without a Cash Difference)**

Mason company owned a particular machine (designated Machine O for case purposes) which no longer met the needs of the company. On December 31, 19F, the records reflected the following:

Machine O:
 Original cost $30,000
 Accumulated depreciation 17,000

On January 3, 19G, the company acquired another machine (Machine N) and traded in Machine O. On this date, a reliable estimate of the market value of Machine O was $15,000.

Required:

a. Give the journal entry by Mason to record the transaction completed on January 3, 19G, for each of the following independent cases:

 Case A—The machines were similar, and no cash difference was paid or received by Mason.

 Case B—The machines were dissimilar, and no cash difference was paid or received by Mason.

 For each case, explain the underlying reasons for the amount that you recorded as the cost of Machine N.

b. Use the facts and requirements given above, except that for each case assume Mason paid a $1,000 cash difference and that the market value of Machine N was $16,100.

CASES

C9–1 **(Comprehensive Case; Involves Computation and Evaluation of Cash Flow Effects for 10 Years for Three Different Depreciation Methods)**
    Slick Corporation acquired a large machine for use in its productive activities at a cash cost of $189,000. The machine was acquired on January 1, 19A, at which time its estimated useful life was 500,000 units of output over a period of 10 years. The estimated residual value was $24,000. Assume a 40% income tax rate for Slick for both accounting and income tax purposes.
    The management of Slick is considering using either straight-line (SL), productive-output (PO), or sum-of-the-years' digits (SYD) depreciation. The management also is developing a 10-year profit plan. The 10-year projected all-cash incomes (before depreciation and income tax) are shown in the first column below.

Required:

a. Complete the following tabulation (round to nearest $1):

Year	Income (all-cash) before Depreciation and Income Tax		Depreciation Expense (dollars)			Income Tax Expense (dollars)			Net Income (loss) (dollars)		
	Units	Dollars	SL	PO	SYD	SL	PO	SYD	SL	PO	SYD
1	70,000	96,500	16,500	23,100	30,000	32,000	29,360	26,600	48,000	44,040	39,900
2	75,000	103,400									
3	80,000	102,300									
4	75,000	103,400									
5	60,000	82,700	16,500	19,800	18,000	26,480	25,160	25,880	39,720	37,740	38,820
6	60,000	82,700									
7	50,000	69,000									
8	20,000	27,600	16,500	6,600	9,000	4,440	8,400	7,440	6,660	12,600	11,160
9	8,000	11,000									
10	2,000	2,400	16,500	660	3,000	(5,640)	696	(240)	(8,460)	1,044	(360)
Σ	500,000	681,000	165,000	165,000	165,000	206,400	206,400	206,400	309,600	309,600	309,600

b. List and explain any generalizations that you can make from the columns for (1) depreciation expense, (2) income tax expense, and (3) net income.

c. Which method would you recommend in this situation? Explain the basis for your recommendation.

C9–2   **(Analysis of Some Amounts Related to Property, Plant, and Equipment Reported on Actual Set of Financial Statements)**

Refer to the financial statements of Chesebrough-Pond's given in Special Supplement B immediately preceding the Index. Respond to the following questions for 1985.

1. What amount was reported in 1985 for "accumulated depreciation and amortization"?
2. What methods of depreciation were used?
3. What total amount of "depreciation and amortization" expense was reported for 1985?
4. Give your explanation of why depreciation and amortization expense was added to net income in the computation of "Total funds provided from operations" on the SCFP.
5. Were any deferred charges reported on the balance sheet? If deferred charges are not reported separately, what amount on the balance sheet would include them?
6. How much interest did the company capitalize?
7. What were the amounts of (a) total interest and (b) interest expense reflected on the income statement?
8. What segment (line of business) of the company had the highest amount of identifiable assets at year-end 1985?
9. What segment (line of business) of the company had the highest amount of income before income taxes?
10. Which quarter of 1985 reported the highest net income?
11. How much did the company spend for property, plant, and equipment during 1985?
12. How much of property, plant, and equipment is represented by construction in progress?
13. What percent of property, plant, and equipment has been depreciated?
14. Does the company own any intangible operational assets?

This chapter discusses liabilities. Notice below how one prominent company reports its debts and provides a supplementary disclosure note.

LIQUID AIR CORPORATION

CONSOLIDATED BALANCE SHEET

(Thousands of dollars)

December	1985	1984
Current Liabilities		
Bank indebtedness	$ 17,941	$ 4,764
Accounts payable	61,917	50,529
Accrued interest	2,160	2,065
Accrued taxes, other than income taxes	3,434	3,742
Due to parent and other affiliates	5,346	4,024
Income taxes	11,736	3,724
Current maturities of long-term debt	8,264	5,946
Total current liabilities	110,798	74,794
Long-term Debt, exclusive of current maturities	141,179	170,969

NOTES TO CONSOLIDATED FINANCIAL STATEMENTS:

E—Long-Term Debt

	1985	1984
Industrial Revenue Bonds at rates from 6.5% to 8%, payable in varying maturities through 2004	$ 14,370	$ 15,800
8.75% note payable to an insurance company, due February 1, 1996, payable in annual installments of $2,000	22,000	24,000
9% note payable to an insurance company, due April 1, 1993, payable in annual installments of $1,000	8,000	9,000
Prime rate or less, revolving loans to a maximum of $175,000 due in 1990	61,500	65,321
Prime rate or less, revolving loans to a maximum of $15,000 due in 1992	5,000	11,000
11.875% note payable to an insurance company due April 1, 1990	20,000	20,000
11.91% note payable to a bank due 1990, payable in varying annual installments	7,000	9,000
Notes payable to affiliates at rates from 7.9% to 12%, payable through 1987	6,186	17,081
Various long-term indebtedness at rates from 6% to 13% payable in varying maturities through 1994	5,387	5,713
Total long-term debt	149,443	176,915
Less current maturities	8,264	5,946
Long-term debt, exclusive of current maturities	$141,179	$170,969

Long-term debt includes the U.S. dollar equivalent (approximately $3,192 and $3,861 at December 31, 1985 and 1984) of loans repayable in foreign currencies.

The principal payments required on long-term debt at December 31, 1985, during the succeeding five years, are as follows:

1986	1987	1988	1989	1990
$8,264	$8,451	$5,642	$4,641	$86,163

MEASURING AND REPORTING LIABILITIES

PURPOSE:

A business generates or receives resources from three sources: *(a)* capital contributed by owners, *(b)* income from operations, and *(c)* borrowing from creditors. **Creditors** provide resources by making cash loans and by selling property, goods, and services on credit. For users of financial statements, the liabilities reported on the balance sheet and the related interest expense reported on the income statement are important factors in evaluating the financial performance of a business. The purpose of this chapter is to discuss the measurement, recording, and reporting of liabilities and the related interest expense.

LEARNING OBJECTIVES—TO BE ABLE TO:

1. Define and classify liabilities.
2. Record and report current liabilities.
3. Apply deferred income tax allocation.
4. Record and report contingent liabilities.
5. Apply the concepts of the future and present values of a single amount.
6. Apply annuity concepts to liabilities.
7. Expand your accounting vocabulary by learning the "Important Terms Defined in This Chapter" (page 536).
8. Apply the knowledge gained from this chapter by completing the homework assigned by your instructor.

ORGANIZATION:

Part A—Measuring, Accounting, and Reporting Liabilities

1. Liabilities defined and classified.
2. Measuring liabilities.
3. Short-term liabilities.
4. Long-term liabilities.

Part B—Future Value and Present Value Concepts

1. Concepts.
2. Future and present values of a single amount.
3. Future and present values of annuities.
4. Ordinary annuities and annuities due compared.

PART A—MEASURING, RECORDING, AND REPORTING LIABILITIES

LIABILITIES DEFINED AND CLASSIFIED

Liabilities are **defined** as probable future sacrifices of economic benefits.[1] Liabilities **arise** from present obligations of an entity to transfer assets or provide services to other entities in the future as a result of past transactions or events. Liabilities often are called debts or obligations.

Usually a business has several kinds of liabilities and a wide range of creditors. Therefore, the users of financial statements must rely on those statements for relevant information about the kinds and amounts of liabilities owed by the entity. The accounting model, along with an audit by an independent CPA, gives the user reliable evidence that all liabilities are identified, properly measured, and fully reported in conformity with the **full-disclosure principle.** To meet these requirements, liabilities usually are classified as follows:

1. Current liabilities:
   a. Accounts payable.
   b. Short-term notes payable.
   c. Other short-term obligations.
2. Long-term liabilities:
   a. Long-term notes payable and mortgages.
   b. Bonds payable.
   c. Other long-term obligations.

Bonds payable will be discussed in Chapter 11. The other classifications will be discussed and illustrated in this chapter.

MEASURING LIABILITIES

Usually a liability involves the payment of two different amounts: (a) the **principal** of the debt and (b) the **interest** on the principal. Assume that you borrowed $1,000 cash on January 1, 19A, and signed a $1,000 note payable that specified 10% interest and a time to maturity (repayment) of one year. You would receive $1,000 cash and repay $1,100 ($1,000 principal plus $100 interest). This liability would be measured and recorded on January 1, 19A, at its principal amount. The transaction would be recorded as follows:

---

[1] FASB, *Statement of Financial Accounting Concepts No. 3,* "Elements of Financial Statements of Business Enterprises" (Stamford, Conn., December 1980).

```
January 1, 19A:
    Cash .................................................................. 1,000
        Note payable ................................................        1,000
```

Liabilities are measured in conformity with the **cost principle.** When initially incurred, the amount of a liability is equivalent to the current market value of the resources received when the transaction occurred. In most cases, liabilities are measured, recorded, and reported at their **principal** amounts. This amount usually is the same as the face amount or maturity value.[2] However, there are two important exceptions to the general case:

1. **Noninterest-bearing notes**—Some notes do not specify a rate of interest, but there is **implicit** interest in the transaction. Assume you borrow $1,000 cash on January 1, 19A, and agree to repay $1,100 in one year. You sign a $1,100 note that does not specify an interest rate (called a noninterest-bearing note). The difference between the cash you repay and the cash you borrow ($1,100 − $1,000 = $100) is implicit interest expense.
2. **Liabilities with an unrealistic interest rate**—In some cases, the **stated** interest rate is higher or lower than the **market** interest rate for the transaction.[3] For example, the stated rate on the above note may have been 6%, although its market rate was 10%. Measuring liabilities with a market interest rate that is different than the stated interest rate requires application of present value concepts (discussed in Part B of this chapter).

In most cases, the stated and effective interest rates for liabilities will be the same; in these cases, the liabilities are measured at their **principal** amounts. Notes payable usually specify a stated rate of interest on the principle. This kind of note is called an **interest-bearing note.**

CURRENT LIABILITIES

Current liabilities are defined as **short-term obligations that will be paid within the current operating cycle of the business or within one year of the balance sheet date, whichever is longer.** This definition presumes that current

---

[2] The principal amount of a debt does not include interest because interest is an expense that is incurred only after a debt is incurred.

[3] The market rate of interest also is called the **going** or **effective** rate of interest. As discussed later, interest expense is based on the market rate, rather than the stated rate, when the two rates are different.

liabilities will be paid with assets that are classified as current assets on the same balance sheet.[4]

An important financial relationship is the dollar difference between total current assets and total current liabilities. This difference is called **working capital.** The relationship between current assets and current liabilities also is measured as a ratio called the **current ratio** (or the working capital ratio). The current ratio is computed by dividing total current assets by total current liabilities. Assume the balance sheet for State Company on December 31, 19B, reported total current assets of $900,000 and total current liabilities of $300,000. The amount of working capital would be $900,000 − $300,000 = $600,000. The current ratio would be $900,000 ÷ $300,000 = 3.00, or 3 to 1. A current ratio of 3 to 1 means that at the balance sheet date there were $3 of current assets for each $1 of current liabilities. These relationships often help creditors and others in assessing the ability of a company to meet its short-term obligations.[5]

Current liabilities include trade accounts payable, short-term notes payable, accrued expenses (such as wages payable, taxes payable, and interest payable), cash dividends payable, the current portion of long-term debt, and revenues collected in advance (also called deferred or unearned revenues).

Accounts Payable

Trade accounts payable are created by purchases of goods for resale and services received in the normal course of business. The term **accounts payable** is used in accounting to mean trade accounts payable. Typical journal entries for an account payable are:

March 6, 19B (purchase on credit; terms 2/10, n/30; periodic inventory system):		
Purchases	980	
Accounts payable		980
Purchase of merchandise on credit; terms 2/10, n/30. (Invoice price, $1,000 × 0.98 = $980.)		

---

[4] Current assets and current liabilities were defined and discussed in Chapter 2. Current assets are defined as cash and other resources reasonably expected to be realized in cash or sold or consumed within one year from the date of the balance sheet or during the **normal operating cycle,** whichever is longer.

The AICPA Committee on Accounting Procedure defined current liabilities as follows: The term **current liabilities** is used principally to designate obligations whose liquidation is reasonably expected to require the use of existing resources properly classifiable as current assets, or the creation of other current liabilities.

[5] Interpretation of financial ratios is discussed in Chapter 16.

March 11, 19B (payment of liability):[6]

Accounts payable	980	
Cash		980

Payment of account payable within the discount period.

Accrued Expenses

Accrued expenses (also called accrued liabilities) arise when expenses have been incurred but have not yet been paid or recorded at the end of the accounting period. These liabilities are recorded as **adjusting entries.** To illustrate a typical accrued expense, assume that on December 31, 19B, the annual amount of property taxes for 19B was $1,600, which had not been paid or recorded. At the end of the accounting period, December 31, 19B, the expense and related liability must be recorded and reported. However, the amount will not be paid until January 15, 19C.[7] Therefore, the following **adjusting entry** must be made:

December 31, 19B (adjusting entry):

Property tax expense	1,600	
Property taxes payable		1,600

Adjusting entry to record property taxes incurred in 19B not yet recorded or paid.

The entry in 19C for payment of the above liability would be:

January 15, 19C:

Property taxes payable	1,600	
Cash		1,600

Payment of liability for property taxes accrued in 19B.

---

[6] In case of payment **after** the discount period, the entry would be (see Chapter 6):

Accounts payable	980	
Purchase discounts lost (or Interest expense)	20	
Cash		1,000

[7] If these taxes already had **been paid** (i.e., Expense debited and Cash credited), there would be no accrued liability to record at year-end. If these taxes **already had been recorded but not paid** (i.e., Expense debited and Taxes Payable credited), there would be no need to make an adjusting entry at year-end.

Payroll Liabilities

When employees perform services, the employer incurs an obligation that is not settled until the employees are paid on a weekly or monthly payroll basis. In previous chapters, accounting for wage and salary expense was simplified by ignoring payroll taxes and payroll deductions; we will now discuss these complications.

Besides the obligation to the employee for salary or wages, the employer incurs other liabilities that are related directly to the payment of salaries and wages. These liabilities usually arise as a result of federal and state laws (e.g., social security taxes), and contractual obligations (such as pension plans and union dues). Some of these liabilities are paid by the **employees** through the employer (as payroll deductions); others must be paid by the **employer** and thus are additional expenses to the business.

The take-home pay of most employees is considerably less than the gross salary or wages. This difference is caused by **payroll deductions** for employee income taxes withheld, social security taxes (known as FICA taxes) that must be paid by the employee, and other employee deductions such as insurance and union dues. The employer must pay the amounts deducted from the wages to the designated governmental agencies and other organizations such as the union. From the date of the payroll deduction until the date of payment to the agencies or organizations, the employer must record and report the **current liabilities** that are owed to the designated taxing agencies and other parties. A typical journal entry for a $100,000 payroll would be as follows:

January 31, 19B:

Salary and wage expense	100,000	
Liability for income taxes withheld—employees		21,000
Liability for union dues withheld—employees		400
FICA taxes payable—employees		7,150
Cash (take-home pay)		71,450

To record the payroll including employee deductions (see Supplement 10A).

Besides the payroll taxes that the **employees** must pay through the employer, the **employer** is required by law to pay additional specified payroll taxes. These taxes include the employer's share of social security taxes (FICA) and Federal Unemployment Compensation (FUTA). These taxes cause an operating expense for the business. Therefore, a second entry related to the payroll is needed to record the payroll taxes to be paid by the **employer**. A typical entry related to the above payroll would be as follows:

January 31, 19B:

Payroll tax expense 10,550*
    FICA taxes payable—employer (matching) 7,150
    FUTA taxes payable—employer 700
    State unemployment taxes payable—employer 2,700
  Employer payroll taxes for January payroll.
  * Total payroll expense: $100,000 + $10,550 = $110,550.

The six current liabilities recorded in the two entries immediately above will be paid in the near future. At that time the company remits the requisite amounts of cash to the appropriate taxing agencies and other parties. Payroll accounting does not entail any new accounting concepts or principles; however, much clerical detail is involved. Details involved in payroll accounting are discussed and illustrated in Supplement 10A.

Deferred Revenues

Deferred revenues (often called unearned revenues or revenues collected in advance) arise when revenues are collected during the current period that will not be earned until a **later** accounting period (see Chapter 4).

Deferred revenues create a liability because cash has been collected but the related revenue has not been earned by the end of the accounting period. Therefore, there is a **current obligation** to render the services or to provide the goods in the future. For example, on November 15, 19B, rent revenue of $6,000 was collected. This amount was recorded as a debit to Cash and a credit to Rent Revenue. At the end of 19B, $2,000 of this amount was for January 19C rent. Thus, there is a current liability of $2,000 for deferred rent revenue that must be recognized. The sequence of entries for this case would be as follows:

November 15, 19B (collection of rent revenue):

Cash 6,000
    Rent revenue 6,000
  Collection of rent revenue.[8]

---

[8] On November 15, 19B, the $6,000 credit could have been made to Rent Revenue Collected in Advance. In that case the adjusting entry to give the same results on December 31, 19B, would be:

               Rent revenue collected in advance 4,000
                  Rent revenue 4,000

December 31, 19B (adjusting entry for unearned rent revenue):

Rent revenue 2,000
    Rent revenue collected in advance (deferred revenue)   2,000
    Adjusting entry to record unearned rent revenue at the end of the
    accounting period.

LONG-TERM LIABILITIES

Long-term liabilities include all obligations of the entity not classified as current liabilities. Long-term liabilities often are incurred when purchasing operational assets or borrowing large amounts of cash for asset replacements and major expansions of the business. Long-term liabilities usually are represented by long-term **notes payable** or **bonds payable.** A long-term liability often is supported by a mortgage on specified assets of the borrower **pledged** as security for the liability. A mortgage has a separate document that is appended to the note payable. A liability supported by a mortgage is a "**secured** debt." An **unsecured** debt is one for which the creditor relies primarily on the integrity and general earning power of the borrower.

Long-term liabilities are reported on the balance sheet (immediately following current assets) under a separate caption "Long-term liabilities." As a long-term debt approaches the maturity date, the part of it that is to be paid from current assets is reclassified as a current liability. For example, a five-year note payable of $50,000 was signed on January 1, 19A. Repayment is in two installments as follows: December 31, 19D, $25,000; and December 31, 19E, $25,000. The December 31, 19B, 19C, and 19D balance sheets would report the following:

December 31, 19B:
  Long-term liabilities:
    Note payable $50,000
December 31, 19C:
  Current liabilities:
    Maturing portion of long-term note 25,000
  Long-term liabilities:
    Long-term note 25,000
December 31, 19D:
  Current liabilities:
    Maturing portion of long-term note 25,000

Notes payable may be either short term or long term. A short-term note payable usually has a maturity date within one year from the balance sheet date. Short-term notes often arise as a result of borrowing cash or from purchasing merchandise or services on credit. Bonds payable (discussed in Chapter 11) always are long-term liabilities, except for any currently maturing portion as shown above for the long-term note payable.

Notes Payable

A note payable (short term or long term) is a written promise to pay a stated sum at one or more specified future dates. A note payable may require a single-sum repayment at the due or maturity date or it may call for installment payments (called an annuity). Consider the purchase of a sailboat for $3,000, with a $1,000 cash down payment and a note payable for the balance. The note specifies 12 equal monthly payments that include principal and interest.

Notes payable require the payment of interest and the recording of interest expense. Interest expense is incurred on liabilities because of the **time value of money.** The word **time** is significant because the longer borrowed money is held, the larger is the total dollar amount of interest expense. Thus, one must pay more interest for a two-year loan of a given amount, at a given **interest rate,** than for a one-year loan. To the **borrower, interest is an expense;** whereas to the **lender (creditor), interest is a revenue.** Interest rates usually are quoted on an **annual** basis.

To calculate interest, three variables must be considered: (1) the principal, (2) the interest rate, and (3) the duration of time. Therefore, the interest formula is:

$$\textbf{Interest} = \textbf{Principal} \times \textbf{Rate} \times \textbf{Time}$$

Accounting for an interest-bearing note

On November 1, 19A, Baker Company borrowed $10,000 cash on a six-month, 12%, interest-bearing note payable. The interest is payable at the maturity date of the note. The computation of interest expense would be: $10,000 \times 12\% \times \frac{6}{12} = \$600$. Ths note would be recorded in the accounts as follows:

```
November 1, 19A:

  Cash ...................................................... 10,000
      Note payable, short term ....................................       10,000
      Borrowed on short-term note; terms, six months at 12% per annum;
      interest is payable at maturity.
```

Interest is an expense of the period when the money is used (unpaid); therefore it is measured, recorded, and reported on a **time basis** rather than when the cash actually is paid or borrowed. This concept is based on legal as well as on economic considerations. For example, if the $10,000 loan cited above was paid off in two months instead of in six months, interest amounting to $10,000 \times 12\% \times \frac{2}{12} = \$200$ would have to be paid.

The **adjusting entry** for accrued interest payable would be made at the end of the accounting period on the basis of time expired from the last interest date or from the date of the note. Assume the accounting period for Baker Company ends December 31, 19A. Although the $600 interest for the six months will not be paid until April 30, 19B, two months' unpaid interest (i.e., November and December 19A) must be **accrued** by means of the following adjusting entry by Baker Company:

December 31, 19A:

Interest expense 200
    Interest payable 200
    Adjusting entry to accrue two months' interest ($10,000 × 12% × $\frac{2}{12}$
    = $200).

At maturity date the payment of principal plus interest for six months would be recorded as follows:[9]

April 30, 19B:

Notes payable, short term 10,000
Interest payable (per prior entry) 200
Interest expense ($10,000 × 12% × $\frac{4}{12}$) 400
    Cash ($10,000 + $600 interest) 10,600
    To record payment of note payable including interest.

Accounting for a note payable is the same whether it is classified as a current or as a long-term liability. Accounting for a note payable also is the same regardless of the purpose for which the note was executed.

Accounting for a noninterest-bearing note

A noninterest-bearing note includes the interest amount in the face amount of the note. This causes a difference in the accounting entries. For example, if the Baker note above was noninterest bearing, its face amount would be $10,600 (i.e., the principal amount plus interest). The journal entries would be:

---

[9] This journal entry assumes no reversing entry was made on January 1, 19C. (See Supplement 5A.) If a reversing entry of the accrual had been made on January 1, 19C, the payment entry would have been:

Notes payable, short term 10,000
Interest expense 600
    Cash 10,600

November 1, 19A (date of note):

Cash 10,000
Discount on note payable 600
   Note payable (noninterest-bearing) 10,600

December 31, 19A (adjusting entry):

Interest expense ($10,000 × 12% × 2/12) 200
   Discount on note payable 200

April 30, 19B (maturity date):

Note payable (noninterest-bearing) 10,600
Interest expense ($10,000 × 12% × 4/12) 400
   Discount on note payable ($600 − $200) 400
   Cash 10,600

The 19A balance sheet will report the note at $10,200 (i.e., Face amount, $10,600 − Unamortized discount, $400).

Deferred Income Tax

The preceding chapters discussed income taxes paid by corporations. Income tax expense is reported on the income statement, and income tax payable is reported as a liability on the balance sheet. In addition to income tax payable, most corporate balance sheets report another tax item called **deferred income tax.**

The concept of deferred income tax is that **income tax expense** should be based on the **taxable income** reported on the income statement. However, **income tax payable** necessarily must be based on the taxable income shown on the **tax return** (i.e., as specified in the tax laws). Often there is a difference between the time when certain revenues or expenses (which affect income taxes) appear on the income statement and when they appear on the tax return. Thus, a deferred income tax amount will occur whenever there is a **timing difference** between when a taxable revenue or tax-deductible expense appears on the income statement and when it appears on the tax return. Deferred taxes are created only by a timing difference. Deferred taxes always will "reverse" or "turnaround" because the taxable items will appear on both the income statement and tax return but in different periods. Consider a $10,000 taxable revenue that is reported on the 19A income statement but not on the 19A tax return. This timing difference will cause the recording of a deferred tax liability in 19A. In 19B, when the $10,000 taxable revenue is reported on the tax return (but not on the income statement), the deferred tax amount is reduced to zero (i.e., it "reverses"). Likewise, when a tax-deductible expense is on the income statement and the tax return in different periods, a timing difference must be accounted for. Accounting for deferred income taxes is illustrated in Exhibit 10–1.

Notice in Exhibit 10–1 that income tax expense for Web Corporation (on the income statement) does not agree with income tax payable on the balance sheet in years 19A and 19C. However, the total income tax for the three years agree: Income statement, $9,000 × 3 = $27,000; tax return, $8,400 + $9,000 + $9,600 = $27,000.

The yearly differences between "Income tax expense" on the income statement and "Income tax payable" on the balance sheet in Exhibit 10–1 were due to a single expense—depreciation. Web Corporation bought a depreciable asset at the beginning of 19A that cost $12,000. It had a useful life of three years with no residual value. The company used straight-line depreciation in its accounts (and on its income statement) and accelerated depreciation on its tax return.

Deferred income tax is recorded when a difference exists between income tax expense and income tax payable. Web Corporation would record deferred tax each year as shown in Exhibit 10–1.

The $600 deferred income tax amount would be reported as a liability on the balance sheet of Web Corporation in 19A and 19B. No deferred income tax liability would be reported in 19C because the deferred tax amount "reversed" during 19C. This effect occurred because the advantage of the increased depreciation deduction in early years using accelerated depreciation for tax purposes was offset in 19C. Recall that regardless of the method of depreciation used, only the cost of the asset (less any residual value) can be depreciated for both accounting and tax return purposes ($12,000 in the example above). Also, this illustration shows what has been noted before—the economic advantage of accelerated depreciation over straight line is only the time value of money. That is, the tax savings resulting from use of accelerated depreciation in early years can be invested to earn a certain return during 19B and 19C.

Deferred income tax amounts are reported by most corporations. For example, *Accounting Trends & Techniques* (AICPA, 1985) reported the following for the 600 companies surveyed:

Deferred income taxes:
As noncurrent liabilities 504 (84%)
As noncurrent assets 126 (21%)
As current assets 13 (2%)

It is possible to have a **debit** balance in deferred income taxes. However, this situation is not typical because the tax law usually does not require "early" tax payments. If the deferred income tax account has a debit balance, it would be reported under assets on the balance sheet as a prepaid expense (if short term) or deferred charge (if long term).

APB Opinion 11, "Accounting for Income Taxes" (December 1967), states that deferred income tax shall be recorded **only** when there is a timing difference between the income statement and the tax return. A timing difference occurs only when an item of revenue or expense will be included on **both** the income

EXHIBIT 10–1

Deferred income tax illustrated

Situation—Web Corporation:

a. Depreciation—Straight-line depreciation on income statement and accelerated depreciation on income tax return:

	19A	19B	19C
Income statement:			
Income before depreciation expense and before income tax expense	$34,000	$34,000	$34,000
Depreciation expense (see computation [a] below)	4,000	4,000	4,000
Pretax income	30,000	30,000	30,000
Income tax expense (30%)	9,000	9,000	9,000
Net income	$21,000	$21,000	$21,000
Balance sheet (December 31):			
Liabilities:			
Income tax payable (see computation [c] below)	$ 8,400	$ 9,000	$ 9,600
Deferred income tax (see entries below)	600	600*	

* Cumulative balance.

Computation of income tax and income tax payable as reported above:

a. Depreciation expense computed:

Year	Straight-line depreciation (for income statement)	Accelerated depreciation (for tax purposes)
19A	$4,000	$6,000
19B	4,000	4,000
19C	4,000	2,000

b. Computation of tax **expense** as reported on the income statement:

	19A	19B	19C
Income before depreciation expense and before income tax expense	$34,000	$34,000	$34,000
Less: Depreciation expense (straight-line)	4,000	4,000	4,000
Amount subject to tax	30,000	30,000	30,000
Income tax **expense** (30%)	$ 9,000	$ 9,000	$ 9,000 ←

c. Computation of income tax **payable** as reported on the tax return:

	19A	19B	19C
Income before depreciation expense and before income taxes	$34,000	$34,000	$34,000
Less: Depreciation expense (accelerated)	6,000	4,000	2,000
Amount subject to tax	28,000	30,000	32,000
Income tax **payable** (30%)	$ 8,400	$ 9,000	$ 9,600 ←

Compare these amounts

Entries to record income tax:

	19A	19B	19C
Income tax expense (from income statement)	9,000	9,000	9,000
Income tax payable (from tax return)	8,400	9,000	9,600
Deferred income tax (the difference)	600		600

statement and the tax return in different years. Therefore, the deferred tax effect automatically will reverse (as illustrated in Exhibit 10–1). Another type of difference between the income statement and tax return amounts is called a **permanent difference.** A permanent difference does not create deferred income tax because the revenue or expense appears on either the income statement or the tax return but not both. For example, interest revenue on tax-free municipal bonds is included on the income statement of the recipient. It is not reported on the recipient's income tax return. A permanent difference never will "reverse or turn around."

On the balance sheet, the total amount of deferred income tax must be reported in part as a current liability (or asset), and in part as a long-term liability (or asset). The classification depends on the specific asset that gave rise to the deferred tax amount. Thus, the deferred income tax amount for Web Corporation would be classified as noncurrent because it was related to a noncurrent asset.

This discussion of deferred income taxes will help you understand the nature of a deferred income tax reported on the balance sheets of most medium and large corporations. Income tax payable (a liability) is easy to understand; however, many statement users have difficulty understanding the other tax item—deferred income tax.[10]

CONTINGENT LIABILITIES

A contingent liability is defined as a potential liability that has arisen because of an event or transaction that **already has occurred.** However, its conversion to an effective liability depends on the occurrence of one or more **future events** or transactions (i.e., a future contingency). A contingent liability also causes a **contingency loss.** For accounting purposes, contingencies are classified as follows:[11]

a. **Probable**—the future event or events are likely to occur.
b. **Reasonably possible**—the chance of the occurrence of the future event or events is more than remote but less than likely.
c. **Remote**—the chance of occurrence of the future event or events is slight.

At the end of the accounting period, the company must determine whether the **amount** of any contingent liability can be **"reasonably estimated."** The

---

[10] It is unfortunate that the accounting profession adopted the term **deferred income taxes** because it is not descriptive of an item that may be reported as either a liability or an asset. More descriptive (but less succinct) titles are:

Liabilities:
  Estimated future income taxes payable due to tax timing differences

Assets:
  Estimated future income tax savings due to tax timing differences

[11] Financial Accounting Standards Board (FASB), Statement 5, "Accounting for Contingencies."

general accounting guidelines are: (1) a contingent liability that is both **probable** and can be **reasonably estimated** must be **recorded** and reported in the financial statements, (2) a contingent liability that is **reasonably possible** (whether reasonably estimated or not) must be **disclosed** in a note in the financial statements, and (3) remote contingencies are not disclosed. For example, during 19B, Baker Company was sued for $200,000 damages based on an accident involving one of the trucks owned by the company. The suit is scheduled to start during March 19C. Whether there is an effective (i.e., enforceable) liability at the end of 19B (end of the accounting period) depends upon a future event—the decision of the court at the end of the trial.

Case A.   Baker Company and its legal counsel determines that (1) it is probable that damages will be assessed, and (2) a reasonable estimate is $150,000. Therefore, Baker must make the following entry:

December 31, 19B:

Loss due to accident 150,000
    Estimated liability due to accident   150,000

The loss is reported on the 19B income statement, and the liability is reported on the 19B balance sheet.

Case B.   Baker Company determines that (1) it is reasonably possible that damages will be assessed, and (2) a reasonable estimate cannot be made. Therefore, Baker must disclose the contingency by a note in the 19B balance sheet similar to the following:

> The company was sued for $200,000 based on an accident involving a company vehicle. Legal counsel believes that the suit lacks merit; however, it is reasonably possible that some damages will be assessed. The amount cannot be reasonably estimated at this date. The trial is scheduled for March 19C.

CONTROLLING EXPENDITURES WITH A VOUCHER SYSTEM

The purchase of merchandise, services, and operational assets often requires that either a short-term or long-term liability be recorded. Therefore, a large number of cash payments on liabilities are made in a business. In most companies, control over cash expenditures prevent the misapplication of cash in the cash-disbursement process. In a very small business, it is possible for the owner to give personal attention to each transaction and to make each cash payment. This personal attention may assure that the business is getting what it pays for, that cash is not being disbursed carelessly, and that there is no theft or fraud involving cash.

As a business grows and becomes more complex, the owner or top executive cannot devote personal attention to each transaction involving the processing of cash disbursements. In such cases, these activities must be assigned to various employees. The assignment of these responsibilities to others creates a need for systematic and effective procedures for the control of cash expenditures. This facet is important in the internal control of a well-designed accounting system.

Chapter 8 discussed the essential features of effective **internal control.** The emphasis was on the control of cash receipts. Similar internal control procedures were discussed for cash disbursements: the separation of duties, disbursement of cash by check, petty cash, and two special journals—the purchases journal and the cash disbursements journal. In larger companies and in computerized accounting systems, the method usually used for maintaining control over cash expenditures is the **voucher system.** This system replaces the cash disbursements journal that was explained in Supplement 8B.

A voucher system establishes strict control over those transactions that create a legal obligation for an **expenditure of cash.** The system requires that a **written authorization,** called a **voucher,** be approved by one or more designated managers at the time each such transaction occurs. An approved voucher is required regardless of whether the transaction involves the purchase of merchandise or services, the acquisition of operational assets, the payment of a liability, or an investment. The system permits checks to be issued only in payment of properly prepared and approved vouchers. Check writing is kept separate from the voucher-approval, check-approval, and check-distribution procedures.

The voucher system requires that every obligation be supported by a previously approved voucher and that each transaction be recorded when incurred. The incurrence of each obligation is treated as an independent transaction. Also, each payment of cash is treated as another independent transaction. This sequence of voucher approval, followed by payment by check, is required even in strictly cash-disbursement transactions. A **cash** purchase of merchandise for resale would be recorded under the voucher system as follows:

1. To record the incurrence of an obligation (with a periodic inventory system):

Purchases	1,000	
Vouchers payable		1,000

2. To record payment of the obligation by check (immediately thereafter):

Vouchers payable	1,000	
Cash		1,000

In a voucher system, the account designated **Vouchers Payable** replaces the account entitled Accounts Payable; but the designation on the balance sheet continues to be "Accounts Payable." The incurrence entries (1 above) are entered in a **voucher register,** and the payment entries (2 above) are entered in a **check register.**

The primary objective of the voucher system is to have continuous control over each step in an expenditure from the incurrence of an obligation to the final disbursement of cash to satisfy the obligation. Thus, each transaction that leads to a cash payment, and the cash payment itself, are reviewed systematically. Then it is subjected to an approval system based on separately designated responsibilities. Supplement 10B discusses and illustrates the **mechanics** of the voucher system.

PART B—FUTURE VALUE AND PRESENT VALUE CONCEPTS

CONCEPTS

The measuring and reporting of liabilities, when they are first recorded in the accounts and during the periods they are outstanding, often involve application of the concepts of present value and future value. These concepts also are used in measuring the effects of long-term investments in bonds, leases, pension plans, and sinking funds. In accounting, most of these applications involve either measurement of a liability or a receivable, or the establishment of a fund of cash to be used in the future for some special purpose (such as for the retirement of debt).

The concepts of future value (FV) and present value (PV) focus on the time value of money, which is another name for interest. The **time value of money** refers to the fact that a dollar received today is worth more than a dollar received one year from today (or at any other future date). If a dollar received today can be invested at 10%, it will increase to $1.10 in one year. In contrast, if the dollar is to be received one year from today, the opportunity to earn the $0.10 interest revenue for the year is lost. The difference between the $1 and $1.10 is interest that can be earned during the year. Interest is the cost of the use of money for a specific period of time, just as rent represents the cost for use of a tangible asset for a period of time. Interest may be specified (i.e., stated explicitly), as in the case of an interest-bearing note. Also, it may be unspecified, as in a noninterest-bearing note (but interest is still paid; i.e., it is implicitly incurred).

For many years, the time value of money was overlooked in accounting for some transactions. In recent years, several *Opinions* issued by the APB have required the application of present value determinations. Of particular significance was *Opinion 21* entitled "Interest on Receivables and Payables." This *Opinion* requires the application of present value determinations to a number of transactions. For example, the *Opinion* states: "In the absence of established exchange prices for the related property, goods, or service or evidence of the market value of the note, the present value of a note that stipulates either no interest or a rate of interest that is clearly unreasonable should be determined by **discounting** all future payments on the notes using an imputed rate of interest." For example, company A bought a machine for $20,000. Company A will pay the $20,000 at the end of two years. There is an implied interest rate of 12% (which is the market rate of interest). The $20,000 to be paid represents the current cash equivalent amount of the debt **plus** the interest that will be paid during the two years. In conformity with the **cost principle,** the machine account should be debited for the present value (current cash equivalent cost, excluding interest) of the debt, or $15,944 (see page 519).

There are four different types of problems related to the time value of money; they are identified in Exhibit 10–2. Each type of problem is based on the interest formula that was discussed in Part A of this chapter.

$$\text{Interest} = \text{Principal} \times \text{Rate} \times \text{Time}$$

In **future value** problems, you will be given the amount of cash (principal) to be invested at the current date and you will be asked to use the basic interest formula to calculate the amount of principal plus interest that will be available at some **future date.** In contrast, **present value** problems involve a rearrangement of the basic interest formula. In present value problems, you will be given the amount that will be available at some **future date** (principal plus interest) and you will be asked to calculate the **current** cash equivalent of that amount.

Tables are used to avoid the detailed arithmetic calculations that are required in future value and present value computations. These tables (pages 512–15) give values for each of the four types of problems for different periods of time (*n*) and at different rates of interest (*i*). The values given in the tables are based on payments of $1. If a problem involves payments other than $1, it is

EXHIBIT 10–2

Four types of future and present value problems

	Symbol	
Payment or Receipt	Future Value	Present Value
Single amount	f	p
Annuity (equal payments or receipts for a series of equal time periods)	F	P

necessary to multiply the value from the table by the amount of the payment.[12] We will examine each of the four types of present value and future value problems.

FUTURE AND PRESENT VALUES OF A SINGLE AMOUNT

Future Value of a Single Amount (f)

The future value of a single amount (i.e., the principal) is the sum to which that amount will increase at i interest rate for n periods. The future sum will be the **principal plus compound interest.** The future value concept is based on compound interest. Therefore, the amount of interest for each period is calculated by multiplying the interest rate by the principal plus any interest that accrued in prior interest periods but was not paid out.

To illustrate, on January 1, 19A, $1,000 was deposited in a savings account at 10% annual interest, compounded annually. At the end of three years, that is, on December 31, 19C, the $1,000 originally deposited would increase to $1,331 as follows:

Year	Amount at start of year	+	Interest during the year	=	Amount at end of year
1	$1,000	+	$1,000 × 10% = $100* =		$1,100
2	1,100	+	1,100 × 10% =	110 =	1,210
3	1,210	+	1,210 × 10% =	121 =	1,331

     * Rounded.

However, we can avoid the detailed arithmetic by referring to Table 10–1, **Future value of $1** (f). For $i = 10\%$; $n = 3$, we find the value 1.331. Therefore, we can compute the balance at the end of Year 3 as $1,000 × 1.331 = $1,331. The increase of $331 was due to the time value of money. It would be interest revenue to you and interest expense to the savings institution. A convenient format to display the computations for this problem is: $1,000 × $f_{i=10\%;\ n=3}$ (Table 10-1; 1.3310) = $1,331. The table value for the future value of $1 always will be greater than $1. Exhibit 10–3 gives a summary of this future value concept.

Present Value of a Single Amount (p)

Present value of a single amount is the value now (i.e., at the present time) of an amount to be received at some date in the future. It is the **inverse** of the future value concept. To compute the present value of a sum to be received in the

---

[12] Present value and future value problems assume cash flows. The basic concepts are the same for cash inflows (receipts) and cash outflows (payments). Thus, there are no fundamental differences between present value and future value calculations for cash payments versus cash receipts.

EXHIBIT 10–3

Overview of future and present value determinations

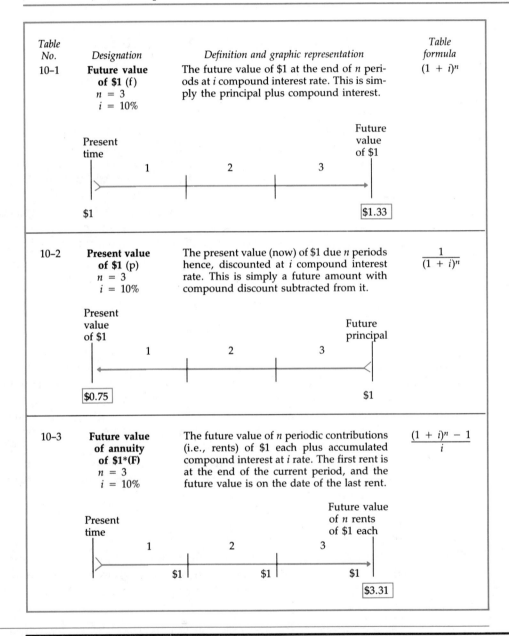

Table No.	Designation	Definition and graphic representation	Table formula
10–1	**Future value of $1 (f)** $n = 3$ $i = 10\%$	The future value of $1 at the end of n periods at i compound interest rate. This is simply the principal plus compound interest.	$(1 + i)^n$
10–2	**Present value of $1 (p)** $n = 3$ $i = 10\%$	The present value (now) of $1 due n periods hence, discounted at i compound interest rate. This is simply a future amount with compound discount subtracted from it.	$\dfrac{1}{(1 + i)^n}$
10–3	**Future value of annuity of $1*(F)** $n = 3$ $i = 10\%$	The future value of n periodic contributions (i.e., rents) of $1 each plus accumulated compound interest at i rate. The first rent is at the end of the current period, and the future value is on the date of the last rent.	$\dfrac{(1 + i)^n - 1}{i}$

EXHIBIT 10–3 (*concluded*)

Overview of future and present value determinations

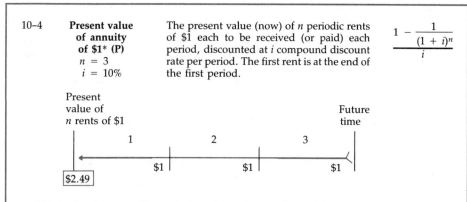

| 10–4 | **Present value of annuity of $1* (P)** $n = 3$ $i = 10\%$ | The present value (now) of n periodic rents of $1 each to be received (or paid) each period, discounted at i compound discount rate per period. The first rent is at the end of the first period. | $\dfrac{1 - \dfrac{1}{(1 + i)^n}}{i}$ |

* Notice that these are ordinary annuities; that is, they are often called end-of-period annuities. Thus, the **table values** for **F**, the future amount, is on the date of the last rent; and for **P**, the present value, is at the beginning of the period of the first rent. Annuities due assume the opposite; that is, they are "beginning-of-period" annuities. Ordinary annuity values can be converted to annuities due simply by multiplication of $(1 + i)$.

future, the sum is subjected to compound **discounting** at i interest rate for n periods. In compound discounting, the interest is subtracted rather than added (as in compounding). To illustrate, today is January 1, 19A, and you will receive $1,000 cash on December 31, 19C; that is, three years from now. With an interest rate of 10% per year, how much would the $1,000 be worth today; that is, what is its present value (today, on January 1, 19A)? We could set up a discounting computation, year by year, that would be the **inverse** to the tabulation shown above for the future value.[13] However, to facilitate the computation, we can refer to the **Present value of $1 table** (p), Table 10–2. For $i = 10\%$; $n = 3$, we find the present value of $1 is 0.7513. The $1,000, to be received at the end of three

---

[13] The detailed discounting would be as follows:

Periods	Discounting, inverse with reciprocal	Present value*
1	$1,000 − ($1,000 × 1/1.10 = $90.90) =	$909.10
2	$909.10 − ($909.10 × 1/1.10 = $82.60) =	826.40
3	$826.40 − ($826.40 × 1/1.10 = $75.10) =	751.30

* Verifiable in Table 10–2.

TABLE 10–1

Future value of $1, f = (1 + i)^n$

Periods	2%	3%	3.75%	4%	4.25%	5%	6%	7%	8%
0	1.	1.	1.	1.	1.	1.	1.	1.	1.
1	1.02	1.03	1.0375	1.04	1.0425	1.05	1.06	1.07	1.08
2	1.0404	1.0609	1.0764	1.0816	1.0868	1.1025	1.1236	1.1449	1.1664
3	1.0612	1.0927	1.1168	1.1249	1.1330	1.1576	1.1910	1.2250	1.2597
4	1.0824	1.1255	1.1587	1.1699	1.1811	1.2155	1.2625	1.3108	1.3605
5	1.1041	1.1593	1.2021	1.2167	1.2313	1.2763	1.3382	1.4026	1.4693
6	1.1262	1.1941	1.2472	1.2653	1.2837	1.3401	1.4185	1.5007	1.5869
7	1.1487	1.2299	1.2939	1.3159	1.3382	1.4071	1.5036	1.6058	1.7138
8	1.1717	1.2668	1.3425	1.3686	1.3951	1.4775	1.5938	1.7182	1.8509
9	1.1951	1.3048	1.3928	1.4233	1.4544	1.5513	1.6895	1.8385	1.9990
10	1.2190	1.3439	1.4450	1.4802	1.5162	1.6289	1.7908	1.9672	2.1589
20	1.4859	1.8061	2.0882	2.1911	2.2989	2.6533	3.2071	3.8697	4.6610

Periods	9%	10%	11%	12%	13%	14%	15%	20%	25%
0	1.	1.	1.	1.	1.	1.	1.	1.	1.
1	1.09	1.10	1.11	1.12	1.13	1.14	1.15	1.20	1.25
2	1.1881	1.2100	1.2321	1.2544	1.2769	1.2996	1.3225	1.4400	1.5625
3	1.2950	1.3310	1.3676	1.4049	1.4429	1.4815	1.5209	1.7280	1.9531
4	1.4116	1.4641	1.5181	1.5735	1.6305	1.6890	1.7490	2.0736	2.4414
5	1.5386	1.6105	1.6851	1.7623	1.8424	1.9254	2.0114	2.4883	3.0518
6	1.6771	1.7716	1.8704	1.9738	2.0820	2.1950	2.3131	2.9860	3.8147
7	1.8280	1.9487	2.0762	2.2107	2.3526	2.5023	2.6600	3.5832	4.7684
8	1.9926	2.1436	2.3045	2.4760	2.6584	2.8526	3.0590	4.2998	5.9605
9	2.1719	2.3579	2.5580	2.7731	3.0040	3.2519	3.5179	5.1598	7.4506
10	2.3674	2.5937	2.8394	3.1058	3.3946	3.7072	4.0456	6.1917	9.3132
20	5.6044	6.7275	8.0623	9.6463	11.5231	13.7435	16.3665	38.3376	86.7362

years, has a **present value** (today) of $1,000 × 0.7513 = $751.30. The difference (i.e., the discount) of $248.70 is the time value of money; it is the interest. A convenient format to display the computations for this problem is: $1,000 × $P_{i=10\%;\ n=3}$ (Table 10-2; 0.7513) = $751.30. The table value for the present values of $1 will always be less than $1. The concept of the present value of $1 is summarized in Exhibit 10–3.

FUTURE AND PRESENT VALUES OF AN ANNUITY

An annuity means that instead of a single amount, there is a **series of consecutive payments** (often called rents) characterized by:

1. An equal amount each interest period.
2. Interest periods of equal length (year, semiannual, or month).
3. An equal interest rate each interest period.

_____ TABLE 10–2 _____

Present value of $1, $p = \dfrac{1}{(1 + i)^n}$

Periods	2%	3%	3.75%	4%	4.25%	5%	6%	7%	8%
1	0.9804	0.9709	0.9639	0.9615	0.9592	0.9524	0.9434	0.9346	0.9259
2	0.9612	0.9426	0.9290	0.9246	0.9201	0.9070	0.8900	0.8734	0.8573
3	0.9423	0.9151	0.8954	0.8890	0.8826	0.8638	0.8396	0.8163	0.7938
4	0.9238	0.8885	0.8631	0.8548	0.8466	0.8227	0.7921	0.7629	0.7350
5	0.9057	0.8626	0.8319	0.8219	0.8121	0.7835	0.7473	0.7130	0.6806
6	0.8880	0.8375	0.8018	0.7903	0.7790	0.7462	0.7050	0.6663	0.6302
7	0.8706	0.8131	0.7728	0.7599	0.7473	0.7107	0.6651	0.6227	0.5835
8	0.8535	0.7894	0.7449	0.7307	0.7168	0.6768	0.6274	0.5820	0.5403
9	0.8368	0.7664	0.7180	0.7026	0.6876	0.6446	0.5919	0.5439	0.5002
10	0.8203	0.7441	0.6920	0.6756	0.6595	0.6139	0.5584	0.5083	0.4632
20	0.6730	0.5534	0.4789	0.4564	0.4350	0.3769	0.3118	0.2584	0.2145

Periods	9%	10%	11%	12%	13%	14%	15%	20%	25%
1	0.9174	0.9091	0.9009	0.8929	0.8850	0.8772	0.8696	0.8333	0.8000
2	0.8417	0.8264	0.8116	0.7972	0.7831	0.7695	0.7561	0.6944	0.6400
3	0.7722	0.7513	0.7312	0.7118	0.6931	0.6750	0.6575	0.5787	0.5120
4	0.7084	0.6830	0.6587	0.6355	0.6133	0.5921	0.5718	0.4823	0.4096
5	0.6499	0.6209	0.5935	0.5674	0.5428	0.5194	0.4972	0.4019	0.3277
6	0.5963	0.5645	0.5346	0.5066	0.4803	0.4556	0.4323	0.3349	0.2621
7	0.5470	0.5132	0.4817	0.4523	0.4251	0.3996	0.3759	0.2791	0.2097
8	0.5019	0.4665	0.4339	0.4039	0.3762	0.3506	0.3269	0.2326	0.1678
9	0.4604	0.4241	0.3909	0.3606	0.3329	0.3075	0.2843	0.1938	0.1342
10	0.4224	0.3855	0.3522	0.3220	0.2946	0.2697	0.2472	0.1615	0.1074
20	0.1784	0.1486	0.1240	0.1037	0.0868	0.0728	0.0611	0.0261	0.0115

Examples of annuities include: equal monthly payments on an automobile or a home, equal yearly contributions to a savings account, and equal monthly retirement benefits received from a pension fund.

Future Value of an Annuity (F)

The future value of an annuity includes **compound interest** on each payment (i.e., rent) from its payment date to the end of the term of the annuity. Therefore, each payment will accumulate less interest than the prior payments only because the number of periods (n) that it accumulates interest will be less. To illustrate, you decide to deposit $1,000 cash in a savings account each year for three years at 10% interest per year (i.e., a total principal of $3,000). The first $1,000 deposit is made on December 31, 19A; the second one on December 31, 19B; and the third and last one on December 31, 19C. How much would you have in the savings account at the end of Year 3, that is, immediately after the third deposit on December 31, 19C? In this case, the first $1,000 deposit would

TABLE 10-3

Future value of annuity of $1 (ordinary), $F = \dfrac{(1 + i)^n - 1}{i}$

Period rents*	2%	3%	3.75%	4%	4.25%	5%	6%	7%	8%
1	1.	1.	1.	1.	1.	1.	1.	1.	1.
2	2.02	2.03	2.0375	2.04	2.0425	2.05	2.06	2.07	2.08
3	3.0604	3.0909	3.1139	3.1216	3.1293	3.1525	3.1836	3.2149	3.2464
4	4.1216	4.1836	4.2307	4.2465	4.2623	4.3101	4.3746	4.4399	4.5061
5	5.2040	5.3091	5.3893	5.4163	5.4434	5.5256	5.6371	5.7507	5.8666
6	6.3081	6.4684	6.5914	6.6330	6.6748	6.8019	6.9753	7.1533	7.3359
7	7.4343	7.6625	7.8386	7.8983	7.9585	8.1420	8.3938	8.6540	8.9228
8	8.5830	8.8923	9.1326	9.2142	9.2967	9.5491	9.8975	10.2598	10.6366
9	9.7546	10.1591	10.4750	10.5828	10.6918	11.0266	11.4913	11.9780	12.4876
10	10.9497	11.4639	11.8678	12.0061	12.1462	12.5779	13.1808	13.8164	14.4866
20	24.2974	26.8704	29.0174	29.7781	30.5625	33.0660	36.7856	40.9955	45.7620

Period rents*	9%	10%	11%	12%	13%	14%	15%	20%	25%
1	1.	1.	1.	1.	1.	1.	1.	1.	1.
2	2.09	2.10	2.11	2.12	2.13	2.14	2.15	2.20	2.25
3	3.2781	3.3100	3.3421	3.3744	3.4069	3.4396	3.4725	3.6400	3.8125
4	4.5731	4.6410	4.7097	4.7793	4.8498	4.9211	4.9934	5.3680	5.7656
5	5.9847	6.1051	6.2278	6.3528	6.4803	6.6101	6.7424	7.4416	8.2070
6	7.5233	7.7156	7.9129	8.1152	8.3227	8.5355	8.7537	9.9299	11.2588
7	9.2004	9.4872	9.7833	10.0890	10.4047	10.7305	11.0668	12.9159	15.0735
8	11.0285	11.4359	11.8594	12.2997	12.7573	13.2328	13.7268	16.4991	19.8419
9	13.0210	13.5795	14.1640	14.7757	15.4157	16.0853	16.7858	20.7989	25.8023
10	15.1929	15.9374	16.7220	17.5487	18.4197	19.3373	20.3037	25.9587	33.2529
20	51.1601	57.2750	64.2028	72.0524	80.9468	91.0249	102.4436	186.6880	342.9447

* There is one rent each period.

draw compound interest for two years (for a total principal and interest of $1,210); the second deposit would draw interest for one year (for a total principal and interest of $1,100); and the third deposit would draw no interest because it was made on the day that the balance is computed. Thus, the total amount in the savings account at the end of three years would be $3,310 ($1,210 + $1,100 + $1,000). We could use Table 10–1 values to compute the interest on each deposit to derive the future value of this annuity. However, we can refer to Table 10–3, **Future value of annuity of $1 (F)** for $i = 10\%$; $n = 3$, we find the value 3.3100. Therefore, the total of your three deposits (of $1,000 each) would have increased to $1,000 × 3.31 = $3,310 by December 31, 19C. The increase of $310 was due to the time value of money; it is interest revenue to you on the $3,000 principal. A convenient format for this problem is: $1,000 × $F_{i=10\%;\ n=3}$ (Table 10-3; 3.3100)

_____ TABLE 10–4 _____

Present value of annuity of $1 (ordinary), $P = \dfrac{1 - \dfrac{1}{(1 + i)^n}}{i}$

Period rents*	2%	3%	3.75%	4%	4.25%	5%	6%	7%	8%
1	0.9804	0.9709	0.9639	0.9615	0.9592	0.9524	0.9434	0.9346	0.9259
2	1.9416	1.9135	1.8929	1.8861	1.8794	1.8594	1.8334	1.8080	1.7833
3	2.8839	2.8286	2.7883	2.7751	2.7620	2.7232	2.6730	2.6243	2.5771
4	3.8077	3.7171	3.6514	3.6299	3.6086	3.5460	3.4651	3.3872	3.3121
5	4.7135	4.5797	4.4833	4.4518	4.4207	4.3295	4.2124	4.1002	3.9927
6	5.6014	5.4172	5.2851	5.2421	5.1997	5.0757	4.9173	4.7665	4.6229
7	6.4720	6.2303	6.0579	6.0021	5.9470	5.7864	5.5824	5.3893	5.2064
8	7.3255	7.0197	6.8028	6.7327	6.6638	6.4632	6.2098	5.9713	5.7466
9	8.1622	7.7861	7.5208	7.4353	7.3513	7.1078	6.8017	6.5152	6.2469
10	8.9826	8.5302	8.2128	8.1109	8.0109	7.7217	7.3601	7.0236	6.7101
20	16.3514	14.8775	13.8962	13.5903	13.2944	12.4622	11.4699	10.5940	9.8181

Period rents*	9%	10%	11%	12%	13%	14%	15%	20%	25%
1	0.9174	0.9091	0.9009	0.8929	0.8850	0.8772	0.8696	0.8333	0.8000
2	1.7591	1.7355	1.7125	1.6901	1.6681	1.6467	1.6257	1.5278	1.4400
3	2.5313	2.4869	2.4437	2.4018	2.3612	2.3216	2.2832	2.1065	1.9520
4	3.2397	3.1699	3.1024	3.0373	2.9745	2.9137	2.8550	2.5887	2.3616
5	3.8897	3.7908	3.6959	3.6048	3.5172	3.4331	3.3522	2.9906	2.6893
6	4.4859	4.3553	4.2305	4.1114	3.9975	3.8887	3.7845	3.3255	2.9514
7	5.0330	4.8684	4.7122	4.5638	4.4226	4.2883	4.1604	3.6046	3.1611
8	5.5348	5.3349	5.1461	4.9676	4.7988	4.6389	4.4873	3.8372	3.3289
9	5.9952	5.7590	5.5370	5.3282	5.1317	4.9464	4.7716	4.0310	3.4631
10	6.4177	6.1446	5.8892	5.6502	5.4262	5.2161	5.0188	4.1925	3.5705
20	9.1285	8.5136	7.9633	7.4694	7.0248	6.6231	6.2593	4.8696	3.9539

* There is one rent each period.

= $3,310. The table value for the future value of an annuity of $1 will always be greater than the sum of its rents. This concept is summarized in Exhibit 10–3.

Present Value of an Annuity (P)

The present value of an annuity is the value now (i.e., the present time) of a series of equal amounts (i.e., rents) to be received each period for some specified number of periods in the future. It is the **inverse** of the future value of an annuity explained above. It involves compound **discounting** of each of the equal periodic amounts.

To illustrate, it now is January 1, 19A, and you are to receive $1,000 cash on each December 31, 19A, 19B, and 19C. How much would the sum of these three $1,000 future amounts be worth now, on January 1, 19A (i.e., the present value), assuming an interest rate of 10% per year? We could use Table 10–2 values to calculate the discounting of each rent as follows:

Year	Amount	Value from Table 10–2 $i = 10\%$	Present Value
1	$1,000	× 0.9091 ($n = 1$) =	$ 909.10
2	1,000	× 0.8264 ($n = 2$) =	826.40
3	1,000	× 0.7513 ($n = 3$) =	751.30
		Total present value	$2,486.80

However, the present value of this annuity can be more easily computed by using one PV amount from Table 10–4 as follows:

$$\$1{,}000 \times P_{i=10\%;\; n=3} \text{ (Table 10–4; 2.4869)} = \$2{,}487 \text{ (rounded).}$$

The difference of $513 (i.e., $3,000 − $2,487) is interest. The present value of an annuity of $1 will always be less than the sum of its rents. This concept is summarized in Exhibit 10–3.

Interest rates and interest periods

Notice that the preceding illustrations assumed annual interest rates and annual periods for compounding and discounting. While interest rates almost always are quoted on an annual basis, interest compounding periods often are less than one year (such as semiannually or quarterly). When interest periods are less than a year, the values of n and i must be restated to be consistent with the length of the interest period. To illustrate, 12% interest compounded annually for five years requires use of $n = 5$ and $i = 12\%$. If compounding is quarterly, the interest period is one quarter of a year (i.e., four periods per year), and the quarterly interest rate would be one quarter of the annual rate (i.e., 3% per quarter); therefore, 12% interest compounded quarterly for five years requires use of $n = 20$ and $i = 3\%$.

There are two kinds of annuities, called ordinary annuities and annuities due. The only difference between them is the timing of the periodic rents. **Ordinary annuities** assume that the periodic rents are made at the **end of each interest period.** This chapter illustrates ordinary annuities only. **Annuities due** assume that the periodic rents are made at the **beginning of each interest period.** Therefore, an annuity due involves one more interest period (but the same number of rents) as an ordinary annuity. Therefore, the **table value** for an annuity due can be readily computed as: Ordinary annuity value (Table 10–3 or 10–4) × (1 + i) = Annuity due value. Ordinary annuities (often called end-of-period annuities) and annuities due (often called beginning-of-period annuities) may be compared as shown in Exhibit 10–4. The homework for this chapter uses only ordinary annuities. Therefore, this discussion may be conveniently omitted.

_____ **EXHIBIT 10–4** _____

Ordinary annuities and annuities due compared

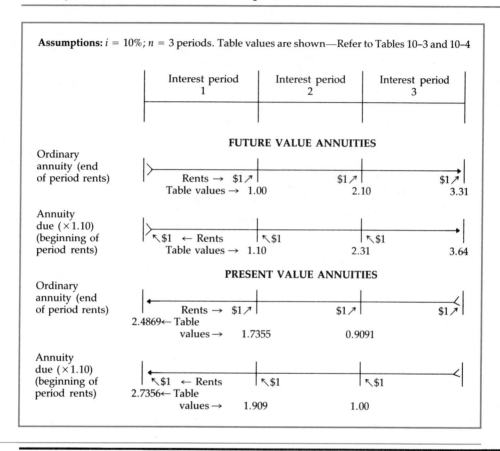

Assumptions: $i = 10\%$; $n = 3$ periods. Table values are shown—Refer to Tables 10–3 and 10–4

	Interest period 1	Interest period 2	Interest period 3

FUTURE VALUE ANNUITIES

Ordinary annuity (end of period rents)
Rents → $1
Table values → 1.00   2.10   3.31

Annuity due (×1.10) (beginning of period rents)
$1 ← Rents $1 $1
Table values → 1.10   2.31   3.64

PRESENT VALUE ANNUITIES

Ordinary annuity (end of period rents)
2.4869 ← Table   Rents → $1 $1 $1
values → 1.7355   0.9091

Annuity due (×1.10) (beginning of period rents)
2.7356 ← Table $1 ← Rents $1 $1
values → 1.909   1.00

DEMONSTRATION CASES—ACCOUNTING APPLICATIONS OF FUTURE AND PRESENT VALUES

There are many transactions when the concepts of future and present value must be used for accounting measurements. Four such cases are presented below.

Case A:

On January 1, 19A, Company A set aside $200,000 cash in a special building fund (an asset) to be used at the end of five years to construct a new building.

The fund is expected to earn 10% interest per year, which will be added to the fund balance each year end. On the date of deposit the company made the following entry:

> January 1, 19A:
>
> Special building fund 200,000
>   Cash   200,000

Required:

1. What will the balance of the fund be at the end of the fifth year?

   Answer: This case requires application of the future value of a single amount as follows:

   $$\$200,000 \times f_{i=10\%;\ n=5};\ (\text{Table 10-1; 1.6105}) = \underline{\underline{\$322,100}}$$

2. How much interest revenue was earned on the fund during the five years?

   Answer:

   $$\$322,100 - \$200,000 = \underline{\underline{\$122,100}}$$

3. What entry would be made on December 31, 19A, to record the interest revenue for the first year?

   Answer: Interest for one year on the fund balance is added to the fund and recorded
   as follows:

> December 31, 19A:
>
> Special building fund 20,000
>   Interest revenue ($200,000 × 10%)   20,000

4. What entry would be made on December 31, 19B, to record interest revenue for the second year?

Answer:

December 31, 19B:

Special building fund 22,000
    Interest revenue   22,000
    ($200,000 + $20,000) × 10% = $22,000.

Case B:

On January 1, 19A, Company B bought a new machine that had a list price of $20,000. A $20,000, two-year noninterest-bearing note payable was signed by Company B. The $20,000 is to be paid on December 31, 19B. The market interest rate for this note was 12%.

Required:

1. The company accountant is preparing the following journal entry:

January 1, 19A:

Machinery ....   ?
    Note payable (noninterest-bearing) ....   ?

What amount should be recorded in this entry?

Answer: This case requires application of the present value of a single amount. In conformity with the **cost principle,** the cost of the machine is its current cash equivalent price, which is the present value of the future payment. The present value of the $20,000 is computed as follows:

$$\$20,000 \times p_{i=12\%:\ n=2} \text{ (Table 10-2; 0.7972)} = \underline{\$15,944}$$

Therefore, the journal entry is as follows:

January 1, 19A:

Machinery 15,944
    Note payable (noninterest-bearing)   15,944

2. What journal entry would be made at the end of the first and second years for interest expense?

   Answer: Interest expense for each year on the amount in the Note Payable account would be recorded in an adjusting entry, as follows:

December 31, 19A:

    Interest expense 1,913
        Note payable (noninterest-bearing)   1,913

    $15,944 × 12% = $1,913
      Note: The note payable would be reported on the 19A balance sheet at $15,944 + $1,913 = $17,857.

December 31, 19B:

    Interest expense 2,143
        Note payable (noninterest-bearing)   2,143

    ($15,944 + $1,913) × 12% = $2,143.

---

3. What journal entry should be made on December 31, 19B, to record payment of the debt?

   Answer: At this date the amount to be paid is the balance of Note Payable, which is the same as the maturity amount on the due date, that is, $15,944 + $1,913 + $2,143 = $20,000.[14]

---

[14] The following entries also could be made with the same results:

January 1, 19A:

    Machinery 15,944
    Discount on note payable 4,056
        Note payable   20,000

December 31, 19A:

    Interest expense ($15,944 × 12%) 1,913
        Discount on note payable   1,913

At the end of 19A, the liability would be reported at net as $20,000 − $2,143 = $17,857.

December 31, 19B:

    Interest expense ($17,857 × 12%) 2,143
    Note payable (special) 20,000
        Cash   20,000
        Discount on note payable   2,143

The journal entry to record full payment of the debt would be:

```
December 31, 19B:
    Note payable ............................................. 20,000
        Cash ...............................................          20,000
```

Case C:

Company C will make five equal annual payments of $30,000 each with a financial institution to accumulate a debt retirement fund. The payments will be made each December 31, starting December 31, 19A. The fifth and last payment will be made December 31, 19E. The financial institution will pay 8% annual compound interest, which will be added to the fund at the end of each year.

1. What entry should be made to record the first payment?
   Answer:

```
December 31, 19A:
    Debt retirement fund ...................................... 30,000
        Cash ...............................................          30,000
```

2. What will be the balance in the fund immediately after the fifth and last payment (i.e., on December 31, 19E)?
   Answer: This case requires application of future value of an annuity as follows:

$$\$30,000 \times F_{i=8\%;\ n=5} \text{ (Table 10-3; 5.8666)} = \underline{\$175,998}$$

3. What entries would be made at the end of 19B?
   Answer:
   a. Interest for one year on the fund balance is added to the fund and recorded as follows:

```
December 31, 19B:
    Debt retirement fund ...................................... 2,400
        Interest revenue ($30,000 × 8%) ......................          2,400
```

b. The second payment would be recorded as follows:

December 31, 19B:

Debt retirement fund 30,000

    Cash   30,000

4. What is the amount of interest revenue that should be recorded at the end of the 19C?

Answer: Interest would be computed on the increased fund balance as follows:

$$(\$30,000 + \$2,400 + \$30,000) \times 8\% = \underline{\$4,992}$$

December 31, 19C:

Debt retirement fund 4,992

    Interest revenue   4,992

5. Prepare a **fund accumulation** schedule that shows the entry for each deposit and the increasing balance in the fund.

Fund Accumulation Schedule

Date	Cash payment (cr)	Interest revenue (prior balance × 8%) (cr)	Fund increase (dr)	Fund balance
12/31/19A	$ 30,000		$ 30,000	$ 30,000
12/31/19B	30,000	$ 30,000 × 8% = $ 2,400	32,400 [a]	62,400 [b]
12/31/19C	30,000	62,400 × 8% = 4,992	34,992	97,392
12/31/19D	30,000	97,392 × 8% = 7,791	37,791	135,183
12/31/19E	30,000	135,183 × 8% = 10,815	40,815	175,998
Total	$150,000	$25,998	$175,998	

Computations:
(a) $30,000 + $2,400 = $32,400, etc.
(b) $30,000 + $32,400 = $62,400, etc.

Case D:

On January 1, 19A, Company D bought a new machine that cost $40,000. The company was short of cash so it executed a $40,000 note payable, to be paid off in three equal annual installments. Each installment includes principal plus interest on the unpaid balance at 11% per year. The equal annual installments are due on December 31, 19A, 19B, and 19C. The acquisition was recorded as follows:

January 1, 19A:

Machinery	40,000	
Note payable		40,000

Required:

1. What is the amount of each equal annual installment?

   Answer: The $40,000 is the amount of the debt today. Therefore, $40,000 is the present value of the debt, $i = 11\%$ and $n = 3$. This is an **annuity** because payment is made in three equal installments. The amount of each equal annual payment is computed by **dividing** the amount of the debt by the present value of an annuity of $1 as follows:

   $$\$40,000 \div P_{i=11\%; \ n=3} \text{ (Table 10-4; 2.4437)} = \underline{\$16,369}$$

2. What was the total amount of interest expense in dollars?
   Answer:

   $$\$16,369 \times 3 = \$49,107 - \$40,000 = \underline{\$9,107}$$

3. What journal entry should be made at the end of each year to record the payment on this $40,000 note payable?
   Answer:
   a. To record the first installment payment on the note:

December 31, 19A:

Note payable	11,969	
Interest expense ($40,000 × 11%)	4,400	
Cash (computed above)		16,369

b. To record the second installment payment on the note:

```
December 31, 19B:
    Note payable ............................................  13,285
    Interest expense [($40,000 − $11,969) × 11%] ...........   3,084
        Cash (computed above) .............................          16,369
```

c. To record final installment payment on the note:

```
December 31, 19C:
    Note payable .........................................  14,746
    Interest expense .....................................   1,623
        Cash (computed above) ............................          16,369
    Interest: ($40,000 − $11,969 − $13,285) × 11% = $1,623
    (rounded to accommodate rounding errors).
```

4. Prepare a **debt payment schedule** that shows the entry for each payment and the effect on interest expense and the unpaid amount of principal each period.

Debt Payment Schedule

Date	Cash payment (cr)	Interest expense (prior balance × 11%) (dr)	Principal decrease (dr)	Unpaid principal
1/1/A				$40,000
12/31/A	$16,369	$40,000 × 11% = $4,400	$11,969[a]	28,031[b]
12/31/B	16,369	28,031 × 11% = 3,084	13,285	14,746
12/31/C	16,369	14,746 × 11% = 1,623*	14,746	–0–
Total	$49,107	$9,107	$40,000	

* To accommodate rounding error.
  Computations:
    (a) $16,369 − $4,400 = $11,969, etc.
    (b) $40,000 − $11,969 = $28,031, etc.

Notice in the debt payment schedule that of each successive payment an increasing amount is payment on principal and a decreasing amount is interest expense. This effect occurs because the interest each period is based on a lower amount of unpaid principal. When an annuity is involved, schedules such as this one often are essential.

SUMMARY OF CHAPTER

Liabilities are obligations of either a known or estimated amount. Detailed information about the liabilities of an entity is important to many decision makers, whether internal or external to the enterprise, because liabilities represent claims against the resources of an entity. Decision makers often may not be able to identify the kinds and amounts of liabilities without reliable financial statements. The existence and amount of liabilities sometimes are easy to conceal from outsiders. The accounting model and the verification by an independent CPA are the best assurances that all liabilities are disclosed.

Current liabilities are obligations that will be paid from the resources reported on the same balance sheet as current assets. They are short-term obligations that will be paid within the coming year or within the normal operating cycle of the business, whichever is longer. All other liabilities (except contingent liabilities) are reported as **long-term liabilities.** A **contingent liability** is a potential claim due to some event or transaction that has happened, but whether it will materialize as an effective liability is not certain because that depends upon some future event or transaction. At the end of the accounting period, a contingent liability must be recorded (as a debit to a loss account and a credit to a liability account) if (a) it is **probable** that a loss will occur, and (b) if the amount of the loss can be estimated reasonably. Contingent liabilities that are **reasonably possible** must be disclosed in the notes to the financial statements.

Future and present value concepts often must be applied in accounting for liabilities. These concepts focus on the time value of money (i.e., interest). Future value is the amount that a principal amount will increase in the future due to compound interest. Present value is the amount that a future principal amount will decrease due to compound discounting. Future and present values are related to (a) a single amount (of principal) or (b) a series of equal periodic amounts of principal (called annuities). Typical applications of future and present values are to: create a fund, determine the cost of an asset, account for notes payable, and account for installment debts and receivables.

SUPPLEMENT 10A—PAYROLL ACCOUNTING

Payroll accounting does not involve any new accounting concepts or principles. However, payroll accounting needs additional discussion because it is necessary to pay employees for their services promptly and correctly. Also, detailed payroll accounting is necessary to fulfill legal requirements under federal and state laws concerning withholding taxes, social security taxes, and unemployment taxes. Further, the management of an enterprise, for planning and control purposes, needs detailed and accurate cost figures for wages and salaries. Often, salaries and wages constitute the largest category of expense in an enterprise. Because a large amount of detailed recordkeeping is required, payroll accounting often is computerized, including the production of individual checks for the employees.

A detailed payroll record must be kept for each employee. The payroll record varies with the circumstances in each company; however, it must include for each individual such data as social security number, number of dependents (for income tax withholding), rate of pay, a time record (for hourly paid employees), and deductions from gross pay.

In payroll accounting, a distinction must be made between (1) payroll deductions and taxes that must be paid by the **employee** (i.e., deducted from the employee's gross earnings); and (2) payroll taxes that must be paid by the **employer.** Both types of payroll amounts must be remitted to the governmental unit or other party to whom the amounts are owed. Payroll taxes and deductions apply only in cases where there is an employer-employee relationship. Independent contractors that are not under the direct supervision of the client, such as outside lawyers, independent accountants, consultants, and building contractors, are not employees; hence, amounts paid to them are not subject to payroll taxes and related deductions.

An employee usually receives take-home pay that is much less than the gross earnings for the period. This is due to two types of payroll deductions:

1. Required deductions for taxes that must be paid by the employee as specified by state and federal laws.
2. Optional deductions authorized by the employee for special purposes.

Required Deductions

There are two categories of taxes that the employee must pay and thus must be deducted from the employee's gross earnings. They are income taxes and social security taxes. The employer must remit the total amount deducted to the appropriate government agency.

Employee income taxes

Most employees must prepare an annual federal income tax return. Wages and salaries earned during the year must be reported on the income tax return as income. Federal laws require the employer to deduct an appropriate amount of income tax each period from the gross earnings of each employee. The amount of the deduction for income tax is obtained from a tax table (provided by the Internal Revenue Service) based upon the earnings and number of exemptions (for self and dependents) of the employee. The amount of income tax withheld from the employee's wages is recorded by the employer as a current liability between the date of deduction and the date the amount withheld is remitted to the government. The total amount withheld must be paid to the Internal Revenue Service within a specified short period of time. A form that accompanies each remittance is provided by the Internal Revenue Service. The form identifies the employees and the amounts withheld. Some states also require withholding for state income tax.

Employee FICA taxes

The social security taxes paid by the employee are called FICA taxes because they are required by the Federal Insurance Contributions Act. This act provides that persons who are **qualified** under the provisions of the act, upon reaching age 62, may retire and receive the minimum monthly benefits for life, plus certain medical benefits after age 65.[15] Retirement at age 65 provides maximum pension benefits. It also provides benefits for the family of a deceased person who was qualified.

The funds required by the government to provide the benefits under the Social Security Act are obtained by payroll taxes, which are imposed in equal amounts on **both the employee and the employer.** Effective January 1, 1986, the FICA rate was 7.15% on the first $42,000 paid to each employee during the year.

At the end of each year, the employer is required to give each employee a **Withholding Statement, Form W-2,** which reports to the employee (1) gross earnings for the year, (2) earnings subject to FICA taxes, (3) income taxes withheld, and (4) FICA taxes withheld. A copy of this form also is sent to the Internal Revenue Service.

Optional Deductions

Many companies encourage programs of voluntary deductions from earnings by employees. These voluntary deductions include savings funds, insurance premiums, charitable contributions, supplementary retirement programs, repayment of loans, stock purchase plans, and the purchase of U.S. savings bonds. The employer agrees to make these deductions, subject to employee authorization, as a convenience to the employees. The amounts deducted are remitted in a short time to the organization or agency in whose behalf the deduction was authorized. Another type of deduction is for union dues as specified in the union contract. In some states, this deduction may not be voluntary. The employer is required to remit the deductions, along with the employee list, to the union each month.

---

[15] To qualify under the act for retirement and medical benefits, the employee must be in "covered" employment for a specified period of time. Covered employment requires payroll deductions for these taxes. The amount of benefits and the FICA tax deductions are frequently changed by the U.S. Congress.

Accounting for Employee Deductions

The employer must keep detailed and accurate records of all deductions from the earnings of each employee. From the employer's viewpoint, the employee deductions are **current liabilities** from the date of the payroll deduction to the date of remittance to the government or other entity.

To illustrate the basic accounting entry for the payment of a payroll and the accrual of liabilities for the **employee deductions,** assume that Real Company accumulated the following data in the detailed payroll records for the month of January 19B:

```
Gross earnings:
    Salaries ...............................................  $60,000
    Wages (hourly paid employees) .........................   40,000
    Income taxes withheld .................................   21,000
    Union dues withheld ...................................      400
    FICA taxes (assume no maximums were exceeded
        in January, $100,000 × 7.15%) .....................    7,150
```

The entry to record the payroll and employee deductions would be:

```
January 31, 19A:

    Salary and wage expense ....................................  100,000
        Liability for income taxes withheld—employees ..............         21,000
        Liability for union dues withheld—employees ................            400
        FICA taxes payable—employees ($100,000 × 7.15%) ...........          7,150
        Cash (take-home pay) ......................................         71,450
    Payroll for January, including employee payroll deductions.
```

Accounting for Employer Payroll Taxes

Remember that the payroll taxes illustrated above are those levied on the **employees.** The employer simply acts as a tax collector. Also, specific payroll taxes are levied on the employer. These taxes represent **operating expenses** of the business. The liability for these taxes is settled when the taxes are paid to the designated agencies of the state and federal governments. Usually, three different payroll taxes must be paid by the employer—FICA taxes, FUTA taxes, and state unemployment compensation taxes.

Employer FICA taxes

The employer must pay an additional FICA tax equal to the amount withheld from the employee's wages. Thus, the FICA tax paid by the employer is at the same rate as the FICA employee tax and on the same amount of wages (i.e., for 1986, 7.15% on the first $42,000 of gross earnings of each employee).

Employer FUTA taxes

The Social Security Act provides for another program known as unemployment compensation. This program derives its monetary support under the provisions of the Federal Unemployment Tax Act. The FUTA, or unemployment tax, is paid **only by the employer.** Currently, the federal tax amounts to 3.4% of the first $6,000 in wages paid to each employee during the year.

State unemployment compensation taxes

The unemployment program specified in the Federal Unemployment Tax Act is a joint federal-state program. Therefore, each state participates in the program by sharing both in providing benefits and in funding the program through payroll taxes. Although state laws vary in some respects, 2.7% is payable to the state (of employment). The remaining 0.7% is payable to the Federal Treasury (i.e., the total of 3.4% on the first $6,000 wages paid). Most states have a merit-rating plan that provides for a reduction in the tax rate for employers that establish a record of stable employment over a period of time.

Payroll taxes paid by the employer are debited to an expense account and credited to a current liability when the payroll is paid each period. The January entry for the employer's payroll taxes for Real Company (data shown on page 000), assuming a 2.7% state unemployment tax rate, would be as follows:[16]

Payroll tax expense	10,550*	
FICA taxes payable—employer		
($100,000 × 7.15% matching)		7,150
FUTA taxes payable—employer ($100,000 × 0.7%)		700
State unemployment taxes payable—		
employer ($100,000 × 2.7%)		2,700
To record employer payroll taxes.		
* Total payroll expenses, $100,000 + $10,550 = $110,550.		

When the taxes are remitted to the government, the liability accounts are debited, and Cash is credited.

SUPPLEMENT 10B—THE VOUCHER SYSTEM

The voucher system is designed to attain strict control over cash expenditures from the point an obligation is incurred (by means of purchase of merchandise for resale, services, operational assets, investments, etc.) through the payment

---

[16] In this and the preceding entries, it was assumed that none of the employees received remuneration above the $42,000 and $6,000 maximums for the year.

of cash. The incurrence of an obligation and the payment of cash to satisfy it are viewed as separate and independent transactions. When a voucher system is used, an account called **Vouchers Payable** replaces the account called **Accounts Payable** in the ledger. Similarly, a **voucher register** and a **check register** replace the purchases journal and the cash disbursements journal, respectively (see Supplement 8B).

The basic document in the voucher system is the **voucher.** A voucher is a form, prepared and used within the business, on which a transaction is (1) summarized and supported, (2) approved, (3) analyzed for recording, and (4) approved for payment. Thus, it is a comprehensive document that follows a transaction from the transaction date to the final cash payment. A voucher is prepared for **each** transaction involving the payment of cash, such as the purchase of assets, the use of services, the incurrence of expenses, and the payment of debt. The form of a voucher varies between companies because it is designed to meet the specific internal requirements of the individual company. For control purposes, all voucher forms and checks should be numbered consecutively when printed.

After approval, each voucher is entered in the voucher register numerically. The voucher register is designed to record the basic data from the voucher, including the accounts to be debited and credited.

To illustrate the mechanics of a voucher system, we will follow a purchase of merchandise for resale through the system from the **order date** to the final cash payment date. Each step in the sequence may be illustrated and explained as follows:

19A

Jan. 10   Merchandise ordered from Box Supply Company, cost $1,000; terms n/15. A purchase order is prepared and approved.

12   Merchandise ordered from Box Supply Company on January 10 is received; invoice is received. Voucher No. 47 is drawn, and the purchase order is attached (see Exhibit 10–5). Goods are checked for quantity and condition; a receiving report is prepared.

12   Receiving report and invoice sent to accounting department; they are attached to the voucher. Voucher is approved, and then recorded in the voucher register (see Exhibit 10–6).

26   Voucher is approved by designated manager for payment on January 27 and sent to disbursements department; Check No. 90 is prepared.

27   Check No. 90 is signed by treasurer and mailed.

28   The accounting department enters Check No. 90 in the check register (see Exhibit 10–7); enters payment notation in the voucher register (see Exhibit 10–6); and files the voucher in the **Vouchers Paid File.**

For illustrative purposes, two more transactions are recorded in the voucher register, one of which is unpaid.

At the end of the month the voucher register and the check register are totaled, and the equality of the debits and credits is verified. Posting to the

EXHIBIT 10–5

Voucher format

Voucher No.   47

MAY DEPARTMENT STORE
Boston, Mass.

Date of Voucher   *Jan. 12, 19A*   Date Paid   *Jan. 27, 19A*

Pay to: *Box Supply Company*   Check No.   *90*

           1119 Brown Street

           Philadelphia, Pa.

For the following goods or services: (attach all supporting documents)

Date Incurred	Terms	Explanation of Details	Amount
Jan. 12	*n/15*	*Merchandise, Dept. 8*	*1,000.00*
		Invoice No. 17-8132	
		Receiving Report No. 123	
		Net payable	*1,000.00*

Approvals:

Voucher Approval: Date   *1/12/A*   Signature   *R. C. Roe*

Payment Approval: Date   *1/26/A*   Signature   *A. B. Doe*

Accounting Analysis:

Account Debited:	Acct. No.	Amount
Purchases	*91*	*1,000.00*
Office Supplies		
Sales Salaries		
Operational Assets		
Etc.		
Total, Voucher Payable Credit *41*		*1,000.00*

EXHIBIT 10–6

Voucher register

Date	Vou. No.	Payee	Payment Date	Payment Check No.	Vouchers Payable (Credit)	Purchases (Debit)	Selling Expense Control Account Code	Selling Expense Control Folio	Selling Expense Control Amount (Debit)	Adm. Expense Control Account Code	Adm. Expense Control Folio	Adm. Expense Control Amount (Debit)	Other Accounts to Be Debited Account Name	Folio No.	P	Amount (Debited)
Jan 12	47	Box Supply Co	1/27	90	1,000.00	1,000.00										
Jan. 14	48	John Day-salary	1/15	89	600.00		64	√	600.00							
Jan. 31	98	Capital Nat'l Bank - note			2,160.00								Notes payable Interest expense	44 82	√ √	2,000.00 160.00
		Totals			27,605.00	14,875.00			7,410.00			3,160.00				2,160.00
		Posting notations			(41)	(91)			(60)			(70)				(√)

EXHIBIT 10–7

Check register

Date	Payee	Voucher No. Paid	Check No.	Vouchers Payable (Debit)*	Cash (Credit)*
Jan. 15	John Day	48	89	600.00	600.00
27	Box Supply Co.	47	90	1,000.00	1,000.00
31	Totals			18,751.00	18,751.00
	Posting notation			(41)	(11)

* These two columns could be combined.

ledger from these two special journals follows the same pattern as for the special journals explained in Supplement 8B. Posting involves two separate phases:

1. **Current posting**—During the period, and even daily, the details in the Voucher Register columns are posted to (a) the selling expense subsidiary ledger (under the selling expense control); (b) the administrative expense subsidiary ledger (under the administrative expense control); and (c) other accounts to be debited. No current posting is required from the check register as illustrated.
2. **Monthly posting**—The totals from the voucher register, except for the "Other Accounts to Be Debited" are posted at the end of each month. The account number to which each total is posted is entered below the amount. The column for "Other Accounts to Be Debited" was posted individually; hence, the total should not be posted. The totals from the check register are posted to the accounts at the end of each month as shown by the account numbers entered below the total.

The balance in the ledger account Vouchers Payable is reported on the balance sheet as a liability and is designated as Accounts Payable. The amount should be allocated and classified between current and long-term liabilities, depending on due dates.

The Vouchers Payable account is a control account. Its balance represents all of the **unpaid** vouchers for any given time. The total of all vouchers in the **Unpaid Voucher File** must agree with the balance of the Vouchers Payable account; therefore, the Vouchers Payable account replaces the Accounts Payable control account in the ledger (see Supplement 6A).

In studying the mechanics of the voucher system, you should not overlook its most important aspect—the high degree of **internal control** attained through formalization of the sequence of acquiring operational assets, services, and merchandise, and in making the cash payments. The internal control feature rests on (1) clear-cut separation and designation of specific approval responsibilities, (2) a prescribed routine for carrying out these responsibilities, and (3) accounting for the results.

Although a manual approach was illustrated, these routines can be adapted easily for the computer. A computer program can be designed to accomplish the same steps and procedures illustrated above. Most companies have a computerized voucher system to attain a high degree of control over expenditures and to accelerate the processing of a large volume of transactions, including cash disbursements.

SUPPLEMENT 10C—LEASE LIABILITIES

For accounting purposes, leases are classified as operating leases and capital leases.

1. **Operating lease**—a short-term lease in which the owner (called the lessor), for a stated rental, grants the user (called the lessee) the right to use property under specified conditions. The **lessor** is responsible for the costs of ownership (such as taxes, insurance, and major maintenance). The **lessee** pays a monthly rental (and usually the utilities). The lease of an automobile on a daily basis and office space on a monthly basis are typical operating leases. When the monthly rent is paid, the lessor records rent revenue and the lessee records rent expense. Any unpaid rent is a current liability for the lessee and a current asset for the lessor.

2. **Capital lease**—a long-term, noncancelable lease contract in which the lessor transfers most of the **ownership rights** to the **lessee** during the lease term. Thus, the **lessee** must pay most of the costs of ownership (such as taxes, insurance, and maintenance). In addition, the lessee pays a periodic rental. For accounting purposes, this type of lease is a **sale of the leased property by the lessor and a purchase of it by the lessee.** Therefore, when a capital lease is signed, the lessee records a sale of the property (on the installment basis) and the lessor records a purchase of it that involves recognition of a long-term liability. Accounting for capital lease requires the use of present value concepts (discussed in Part B of this chapter).

A typical operating and a typical capital lease are shown in Exhibit 10–8. On January 1, 19A, Daly Construction Company must acquire a heavy-duty machine ready to operate. The machine has a cash price of $100,000, and it has a five-year estimated useful life and no residual value. In the face of a serious cash problem, Daly's top management is considering three alternative ways of acquiring the machine: (a) purchase by signing a note for the full purchase price, (b) lease the machine on an **operating** lease, and (c) lease the machine on a **capital** lease. The basic entries for each alternative are given in Exhibit 10–8. Let's examine each alternative.

Alternative a. Purchase the machine and sign a two-year interest-bearing note; 15% interest and principal payable each month-end (i.e., 24 equal payments). On January 1, 19A, Daly would record the purchase at cost and a liability as illustrated in Exhibit 10–8. Equal monthly payments of principal plus interest ($4,849) are to be made; the journal entry to record the first payment is illustrated in Exhibit 10–8. Under this alternative Daly would own the machine. Therefore, Daly would record depreciation expense, and all other expenses incurred, such as maintenance, insurance, and taxes.

Alternative b. Lease the machine on a month-to-month **operating lease** at a monthly rental of $6,000 (as determined by the lessor), payable at each month-end. Under this alternative Daly would not own the machine. Therefore, the only journal entries to be recorded by Daly would be for the monthly rental payments as illustrated in Exhibit 10–8. Under this alternative Daly would have to continue lease payments as long as the machine is used and would never own the machine.

_____ EXHIBIT 10–8 _____

Operating lease and capital lease compared

Situation:

Daly Construction Company intends to acquire a heavy-duty machine that will cost $100,000 cash equivalent price. Estimated useful life of the machine is five years and no residual value. Daly is considering three alternatives: (a) purchase by signing note, (b) rent on an operating lease, and (c) rent on a capital lease.

Alternative a:

On January 1, 19A, purchased the machine for $100,000 and signed a two-year 15% note that requires equal month-end payments (24) of $4,849.

Journal entries:

Purchase, January 1, 19A:

Machinery	100,000	
Note payable, long term		100,000

Payment on note, January 31, 19A:

Interest expense ($100,000 × 1¼%)	1,250	
Note payable ($4,849 − $1,250)	3,599	
Cash (per note)		4,849

Alternative b:

Lease on a month-to-month **operating lease;** month-end rental payments of $6,000, as required by lessor.

Journal entries:

January 31, 19A:

Machinery rental expense	6,000	
Cash (per lease agreement)		6,000

Alternative c:

Lease on a **capital lease** that requires month-end payments of $3,321 for 36 months (the implied interest rate is 12%). Daly is required by the lease to pay all ownership costs.

Journal entries:

January 1, 19A—Inception date of the lease (record as a purchase):

Machinery (under capital lease)	100,000	
Liability, capital lease		100,000

Computation:

$$\text{Present value} = \text{Payments} \times \text{Table 10–4 } (i = 1\%; n = 36)$$
$$= \$3,321 \times 30.0175^*$$
$$= \$100,000 \text{ (rounded)}$$

January 31, 19A, first monthly rental payment:

Interest expense ($100,000 × 1%)	1,000	
Liability, capital lease ($3,321 − $1,000)	2,321	
Cash (per lease contract)		3,321

* This value is given for illustrative purposes. Table 10–4 does not contain values for 36 periods.

Alternative *c.* Lease the machine on a three-year **capital lease.** The contract requires Daly to pay 36 month-end rentals of $3,321, computed by the **lessor** to earn 12% on the $100,000 cash equivalent price. Also, Daly must pay most of the "ownership" costs, such as maintenance, insurance, and taxes. The lessee learned that the rental of $3,321 was based on 12% interest; therefore, the **lessee** computed the **present value** of the future lease rentals as follows:

Present value = **Rents (payments)** × **(Table 10–4,** *i* = **1%;** *n* = **36)**
= **$3,321 × 30.1075 (given; Table 10–4 does not contain values for 36 periods)**
= **$100,000 (rounded)**

In accounting, a **capital lease** is a sale of the asset by the lessor to the lessee. Daly (the lessee) would record a purchase of the machine on the date of the lease contract for $100,000 (its present value).

On January 1, 19A, Daly would debit machinery and credit a lease liability for $100,000 as shown in Exhibit 10–8. Each of the 36 month-end lease payments would be recorded, in part as payment of principal and in part as payment of interest expense. Exhibit 10–8 shows entries at the inception of the lease (i.e., a "purchase" of the machine is recorded) and the first interest payment on January 31, 19A.

Because Daly is assumed to "own" the machine during the lease term, Daly will record depreciation expense and all other "ownership" expenses incurred, such as maintenance, insurance, and taxes. Under this alternative, Daly will own the machine after the last rental payment with no further obligations to the lessor.

The above example does not suggest which alternative is the "best" for Daly. Such a determination would need more information than given. Rather, it is intended to differentiate between the required accounting approaches for an operating lease versus a financial lease. The basic difference requires the application of **present value** determination for **capital lease.**

IMPORTANT TERMS DEFINED IN THIS CHAPTER

Terms (alphabetically)	Key words in definitions of important terms used in chapter	Page reference
Accrued expenses	Expenses that have been incurred but have not yet been paid or recorded at the end of the accounting period; a liability.	495
Annuities due	Beginning-of-period annuities; payments are assumed to be on the first day of each interest period.	516
Annuity	A series of periodic cash receipts or payments that are equal in amount each interest period.	512
Capital lease	A lease that is viewed as a purchase/sale, for accounting purposes.	534

Terms (alphabetically)	Key words in definitions of important terms used in chapter	Page reference
Contingent liability	Potential liability that has arisen as the result of a past event; not an effective liability until some future event occurs.	504
Current liabilities	Short-term obligations that will be paid within the current operating cycle or one year, whichever is longer.	493
Deferred income tax	Difference between income tax expense and income tax liability; caused by timing differences; may be a liability or an asset.	501
Deferred revenues	Revenues that have been collected but not earned; a liability until the goods or services are provided.	497
Future value	The sum to which an amount will increase as the result of compound interest.	509
Interest-bearing note	A note that explicitly gives a stated rate of interest.	505
Liabilities	Probable future sacrifices of economic benefits that arise from past transactions.	492
Long-term liabilities	All obligations that are not properly classified as current liabilities.	498
Noninterest-bearing note	A note that does not explicitly state a rate of interest but has implicit interest; interest is included in the face amount of the note.	493 & 500
Operating lease	A rental agreement between a lessor and lessee that is not viewed as a purchase/sale in accounting.	534
Ordinary annuities	End-of-period annuities; payments are assumed to be on the last day of each interest period.	516
Permanent difference	An income tax difference that does not cause deferred taxes.	501
Present value	The current value of an amount to be received in the future; a future amount discounted for compound interest.	509
Time value of money	Interest that is associated with the use of money over time.	507
Timing difference	An income tax difference that causes deferred taxes; will reverse or turn around in the future.	501
Working capital	The dollar difference between total current assets and total current liabilities.	494
Working capital ratio	The ratio of total current assets divided by total current liabilities; also known as the current ratio.	494

QUESTIONS

PART A

1. Define a liability. Distinguish between a current liability and a long-term liability.

2. How can external parties be informed about the liabilities of a business?

3. Liabilities are measured and reported at their current cash equivalent amount. Explain.

4. A liability is a known obligation of either a definite or estimated amount. Explain.

5. Define working capital. How is it computed?

6. What is the current ratio? What is another name for the current ratio? How is the current ratio related to the classification of liabilities?

7. Define an accrued liability. What kind of an entry usually reflects an accrued liability?

8. Define a deferred revenue. Why is it a liability?

9. Define a note payable. Distinguish between a secured and an unsecured note.

10. Distinguish between an interest-bearing note and a noninterest-bearing note.

11. Define deferred income tax. Explain why deferred income tax "reverses, or turns around," in subsequent periods.

12. What is a contingent liability? How is a contingent liability reported?

13. Explain the primary purpose of a voucher system.

14. Compute 19A interest expense for the following note: face, $6,000; 10% interest; date of note, April 1, 19A.

PART B

15. Explain the time value of money.

16. Explain the basic difference between future value and present value.

17. If you deposited $10,000 in a savings account that would earn 10%, how much would you have at the end of 10 years? Use a convenient format to display your computations.

18. If you hold a valid contract that will pay you $10,000 cash 10 years hence and the going rate of interest is 10%, what is its present value? Use a convenient format to display your computations.

19. What is an annuity?

20. Complete the following schedule:

Concept	Symbol	Table Values		
		$n = 4; i = 5\%$	$n = 7; i = 10\%$	$n = 9; i = 15\%$
FV of $1 PV of $1 FV of annuity of $1 PV of annuity of $1				

21. If you deposit $1,000 for each of 10 interest periods (ordinary annuity) that would earn 10% interest, how much would you have at the end of period 10? Use a convenient format to display your computations.

22. You purchased an XIT auto for $20,000 by making a $5,000 cash payment and six semiannual installment payments for the balance at 10% interest. Use a convenient format to display computation of the amount of each payment.

EXERCISES

PART A

E10–1   (Pair Definitions with Terms)

Match the brief definitions given below with the terms by entering the code letters in the blanks provided.

Term	*Brief definition (or statement)*
_B_ (1) Liabilities (example)	A. Provides resources to a business by selling its goods and services on credit.
____ (2) Interest expense	
____ (3) Current ratio	B. Probable future sacrifices of economic benefits.
____ (4) Full-disclosure principle	C. The two major classifications of liabilities on a balance sheet.
____ (5) Interest-bearing note	D. All liabilities must be reported in conformity with this principle.
____ (6) Secured debt	
____ (7) Short term and long term	E. A liability requires the payment of these two different amounts.
____ (8) Deferred revenues	F. Interest payable on a noninterest-bearing note.
____ (9) Principal and interest	G. Current assets divided by current liabilities.
____ (10) Working capital	H. A liability that represents trade accounts payable only.
____ (11) Noninterest-bearing note	I. A liability that is supported by a mortgage on specified assets.
____ (12) Accounts payable	J. A note that does not specify a stated rate of interest but interest nevertheless is paid.
____ (13) Accrued expenses	
____ (14) Creditors	K. Unearned revenues or revenues collected in advance.
____ (15) Implicit interest	L. Principle × Rate × Time, related to a liability.
	M. Expenses incurred by the end of the period but not yet recorded or paid.
	N. Current assets minus current liabilities.
	O. A note that specifies a stated rate of interest on the principal amount.

E10–2   (Pair Definitions or Statements with Terms)

Match the brief definitions given below with the terms by entering the code letters in the blanks provided.

Term	*Brief definition (or statement)*
_E_ (1) A timing difference (example)	A. Amount of the difference between income tax expense and income tax payable.
____ (2) A permanent tax difference	B. A potential liability from an event that has already happened but depends on a future event.
____ (3) A contingent liability that must be recorded as a loss and a liability	C. A contingent liability that is reasonably possible.
	D. A system used to attain control over cash expenditures.
____ (4) Voucher system	E. A deferred income tax item that will "reverse or turn around."
____ (5) Contingent liability	
____ (6) Deferred income tax	F. A liability that is not supported by a mortgage on specific assets.
____ (7) Working capital ratio	
____ (8) A contingent liability that must be reported only in a footnote	G. All liabilities are measured in conformity with this principle.
	H. A contingent liability that is probable and can be reasonably estimated.
	I. Current assets divided by current liabilities.
____ (9) An unsecured debt	J. An income tax difference that will never "reverse or turn around."
____ (10) Cost principle	

E10–3   **(Compute Owners' Equity, Working Capital, and Interest Expense; Provide an Adjusting Entry)**

Rath Corporation is preparing its 19B balance sheet. The company records show the following related amounts at the end of the accountng period, December 31, 19B.

Total current assets	$160,100
Total all remaining assets	665,000
Liabilities:	
Note payable (10%, due in 5 years)	24,000
Accounts payable	50,000
Income tax payable	15,000
Liability for withholding taxes	2,000
Rent revenue collected in advance	3,000
Bonds payable (due in 15 years)	200,000
Wages payable	5,000
Property taxes payable	1,000
Note payable, 12% (due in 6 months)	8,000
Interest payable	100

Required:

a. Compute total owners' equity.
b. Compute (1) working capital and (2) the current ratio (show computations).
c. Compute the amount of interest expense for 19B on the 10% note. Assume it was dated October 1, 19B.
d. Give any adjusting entry required for the 10% note payable on December 31, 19B.

E10–4   **(Accounting for, and Reporting, Accrued Expenses and Deferred Revenue)**

During 19B, the two transactions given below were completed by RV Company. The annual accounting period ends December 31.

1. Wages paid and recorded during 19B were $120,000; however, at the end of December 19B, there were three days' wages unpaid and unrecorded because the weekly payroll will not be paid until January 6, 19C. Wages for the three days were $4,000.
2. On December 10, 19B, the company collected rent revenue of $1,500 on office space that it rented to another party. The rent collected was for 30 days from December 10, 19B, to January 10, 19C, and was credited in full to Rent Revenue.

Required:

a. Give (1) the adjusting entry required on December 31, 19B, and (2) the January 6, 19C, journal entry for payment of any unpaid wages from December 19B.
b. Give (1) the journal entry for the collection of rent on December 10, 19B, and (2) the adjusting entry on December 31, 19B (compute rent to the nearest 10 days).
c. Show how any liabilities related to the above transactions should be reported on RV's balance sheet at December 31,19B.

E10–5   **(Accounting for an Interest-Bearing Note Payable through Its Time to Maturity)**

On November 1, 19A, Modesto Company borrowed $60,000 cash from the City Bank for working capital purposes and gave an interest-bearing note with a face amount of $60,000. The note was due in six months. The interest rate was 10% per annum payable at maturity. The accounting period ends December 31.

Required:

a. Give the journal entry to record the note on November 1.

b. Give any adjusting entry that would be required at the end of the annual accounting period.

c. Give the journal entry to record payment of the note and interest on the maturity date, April 30, 19B.

E10–6   **(Record a Payroll, Including Deductions)**

Simplex Manufacturing Company has completed the payroll for January 19B, reflecting the following data:

Salaries and wages earned	$80,000
Employee income taxes withheld	9,000
Union dues withheld	1,000
FICA payroll taxes*	5,720
FUTA payroll taxes	560
State unemployment taxes	2,160

   * Assessed on both employer and employee (i.e., $5,720 each).

Required:

a. Give the journal entry to record payment of the payroll and employee deductions.

b. Give the journal entry to record employer payroll taxes.

c. What was the amount of additional labor expense to the company due to tax laws? What was the amount of the employees' take-home pay?

d. List the liabilities, and their amounts, that are reported on Simplex's January 31, 19B, balance sheet.

E10–7   **(Accounting for Accounts Payable and an Interest-Bearing Note Payable)**

Victor Company sells a wide range of goods through two retail stores that are operated in adjoining cities. Most purchases of goods for resale are on invoices with credit terms of 2/10, n/30. Occasionally, a short-term note payable is used to obtain cash for current use. The following transactions were selected from those occurring during 19B:

1. On January 10, 19B, purchased merchandise on credit, $20,000; terms 2/10, n/30. Record at net (see Chapter 6); the company uses a periodic inventory system.
2. On March 1, 19B, borrowed $60,000 cash from Town Bank and gave an interest-bearing note payable: face amount, $60,000; due at the end of six months, with an annual interest rate of 12% payable at maturity.

Required:

a. Give the journal entry for each of the above transactions. Record purchases and accounts payable at net.

b. Give the journal entry if the account payable of January 10, 19B, was paid within the discount period.

c. Give the journal entry if the account payable of January 10, 19B, was paid after the discount period.

d. Give the journal entry for the payment of the note payable plus interest on its maturity date.

E10–8   **(Accounting for a Noninterest-Bearing Note Payable)**

On September 1, 19A, Foxy Company borrowed $20,000 and signed a one-year note payable for $22,400. The accounting period ends December 31.

Required:

a. What kind of note was involved? Explain.

b. How much interest was paid? What was the implicit interest rate?

c. Give the required entries (if any) on the following dates: September 1, 19A, December 31, 19A, and October 31, 19B. Assume that reversing entries are not used.

E10–9   (Accounting for a Deferred Income Tax Credit)

The comparative income statements of Rowan Corporation at December 31, 19B, showed the following data (summarized and excluding income taxes):

	Annual income statement for	
	19A	19B
Sales revenue	$50,000	$61,000
Expenses	40,000	48,000
Pretax income	$10,000	$13,000

Included on the 19B income statement given above was an expense of $7,000 that was deductible on the income tax return in 19A rather than in 19B. Assume an average tax rate of 20%.

Required:

a. For each year compute (1) income tax expense, (2) income tax payable, and (3) any deferred tax.

b. Give the journal entry for each year to record income tax, including any deferred tax.

c. Show how the income tax liabilities should be reported on the balance sheet for each year assuming the tax is paid the following April.

E10–10   (Accounting for a Deferred Income Tax Debit)

The comparative income statement for Nader Corporation for the years ended December 31, 19A, and 19B, provided the following data (summarized and excluding income taxes):

	Annual income statement for	
	19A	19B
Revenues	$90,000	$94,000
Expenses	75,000	78,000
Pretax income	$15,000	$16,000

Included on the 19B income statement given above was a revenue item of $7,000 that was included on the income tax return for 19A rather than in 19B. Assume an average income tax rate of 20%.

Required:

a. For each year, compute (1) income tax expense, (2) income tax payable, and (3) deferred income tax. (Hint: Deferred income tax will have a debit balance for 19A.)

b. Give the journal entry for each year to record income tax, including any deferred tax.

c. Show how income tax would be reported on the balance sheet each year if the tax is paid the following April.

E10–11 **(Accounting for Deferred Income Tax and Analysis of the Related Cash Flows)**
Green Corporation reported the following income statement data (summarized):

	Income statement for year ended December 31		
	19A	19B	19C
Revenues	$150,000	$150,000	$150,000
Expenses (including depreciation)	110,000	110,000	110,000
Pretax income	$ 40,000	$ 40,000	$ 40,000

Depreciation expense included on the income statement was computed as follows:

Machinery cost (acquired on January 1, 19A), $60,000; estimated useful life, three years, no residual value; annual depreciation (straight-line) $60,000 ÷ 3 years = $20,000.

The company uses sum-of-the-years'-digits depreciation on the income tax return and has an average income tax rate of 30%.

Required:

a. For each year, compute (1) income tax expense for the income statement and (2) income tax payable for the tax return (show computations).
b. Give the journal entry for each year to record income tax including any deferred income tax.
c. What kind of "tax difference" was involved? Explain.
d. What advantage was gained by using SYD depreciation on the tax return?

PART B

E10–12 **(Pair Definitions with Terms)**
Match the brief definitions given below with the terms by entering the code letters in the blanks provided.

Terms	Brief definition (or statement)
<u> C </u> (1) Interest (example)	A. Future value of a single amount at 10% interest for five interest periods.
_____ (2) Principal × Rate × Time	B. A series of consecutive equal rents each interest period.
_____ (3) $f_{i=10;\ n=5}$ = 1.6105	C. Time cost of using money.
_____ (4) Balance in a fund for $i = 8\%$; n = 4	D. Present value of a series of equal rents at 10% interest for five periods.
_____ (5) $P_{i=10\%;\ n=5}$ = 3.7908	E. Formula for computing interest.
_____ (6) Ordinary annuity	F. A beginning-of-period annuity.
_____ (7) $F_{i=10\%;\ n=5}$ = 6.1051	G. Value today of a single future amount.
_____ (8) Annuity	H. $30,000 × $f_{i=8\%;\ n=4}$ (1.3605) = $40,815.
_____ (9) Future value of 1	I. An end-of-period annuity.
_____ (10) Table value for an annuity due	J. Future value of a series of equal rents at 10% interest for five periods.
_____ (11) Annuity due	K. Value in the future of a single present amount.
_____ (12) $p_{i=10\%;\ n=5}$ = 0.6209	L. Present value of a single amount at 10% interest for five interest periods.
_____ (13) Balance in a fund with equal rents for $i = 8\%$; n = 4	M. $20,000 ÷ $P_{i=12\%;\ n=3}$ (2.4018) = $8,327.
_____ (14) Present value of 1	N. Table value of an ordinary annuity × (1 + i).
_____ (15) Periodic payments on a debt, $i = 12\%$; n = 3	O. $5,000 × $P_{i=8\%;\ n=4}$ (4.5061) = $22,531.

E10–13   **(Application of the Four Kinds of Present and Future Values)**

On January 1, 19A, Hyper Company completed the following transactions (assume a 12% annual interest rate):

1. Deposited $20,000 in a fund (designated Fund A).
2. Established a fund (designated Fund B) by making six equal annual deposits of $3,000 each.
3. Established a fund (designated Fund C) by depositing a single amount that will increase to $60,000 by the end of Year 7.
4. Decided to deposit a single sum in a fund (designated Fund D) that will provide 10 equal annual year-end payments of $10,000 to a retired employee (payments starting December 31, 19A).

Required (show computations and round to the nearest dollar):

a. What will be the balance of Fund A at the end of Year 9?
b. What will be the balance of Fund B at the end of Year 6?
c. What single amount must be deposited in Fund C on January 1,19A?
d. What single sum must be deposited in Fund D on January 1, 19A?

E10–14   **(Accounting for a Savings Account; a Single Amount)**

On January 1, 19A, you deposited $12,000 in a savings account. The account will earn 8% annual compound interest, which will be added to the fund balance at the end of each year. You recorded the deposit as follows:

Savings account	 5,000	
Cash	....	5,000

Required (round to the nearest dollar):

a. What will be the balance in the savings account at the end of 10 years?
b. What is the time value of the money in dollars for the 10 years?
c. How much interest revenue did the fund earn in 19A? 19B?
d. Give the journal entry to record interest revenue at the end of 19A and 19B.

E10–15   **(Compute Deposit Required and Account for a Single-Sum Savings Account)**

On January 1, 19A, Parent decided to deposit an amount in a savings account that will provide $40,000 four years later to send Offspring to Super University. The savings account will earn 9%, which will be added to the fund each year-end.

Required (show computations and round to the nearest dollar):

a. How much must Parent deposit on January 1, 19A?
b. Give the journal entry that Parent should make on January 1, 19A.
c. What is the time value of the money for the four years?
d. Give the journal entry Parent should make on (1) December 31, 19A, and (2) December 31, 19B.

E10–16   **(Accounting for a Savings Account with Equal Periodic Payments)**

On each December 31, you plan to deposit $1,000 in a savings account. The account will earn 8% annual interest, which will be added to the fund balance at year-end. The first deposit will be made December 31, 19A (end of period).

Required (show computations and round to the nearest dollar):

a. Give the required journal entry on December 31, 19A.
b. What will be the balance in the savings account at the end of the 10th year (i.e., 10 deposits)?
c. What is the time value of money in dollars for the 10 deposits?
d. How much interest revenue did the fund earn in 19B? 19C?
e. Give all required journal entries at the end of 19B and 19C.

E10–17 **(Accounting for a Savings Fund with Periodic Rents)**
You have planned to take a trip around the world upon graduation, four years from now (now it is January 1, 19A). Your grandfather wants to deposit sufficient funds for this trip in a savings account for you. On the basis of a budget, you estimate the trip now would cost $11,000. To be generous, your grandfather decided to deposit $2,800 in the fund at the end of each of the next four years, starting on December 31, 19A. The savings account will earn 7% annual interest, which will be added to the savings account at each year-end.

Required (show computations and round to the nearest dollar):

a. Give the required journal entry on December 31, 19A, to record the first deposit.
b. How much money will you have for the trip at the end of Year 4 (i.e., after four deposits)?
c. What is the time value of the money for the four years?
d. How much interest revenue did the fund earn in 19A, 19B, and 19C?
e. Give the journal entries at the end of 19B and 19C. Yes, you left on January 1, 19E.

E10–18 **(Valuation of an Asset Based on Present Value)**
You have the chance to purchase the royalty interest in an oil well. Your best estimate is that the net royalty income will average $35,000 per year for five years. There will be no residual value at that time. Assume the cash inflow is at each year-end and that, considering the uncertainty in your estimates, you expect to earn 20% per year on the investment.

Required (show computations and round to the nearest dollar):

a. What should you be willing to pay for this investment on January 1, 19A?
b. Give the required journal entry (cash paid in full for the royalty interest) on January 1, 19A.
c. Give the required journal entries on December 31, 19A, assuming the net cash received was 20% above your estimate. Assume the cost of the royalty interest is depleted on a straight-line basis.

E10–19 **(Accounting for Interest-Bearing and Noninterest-Bearing Notes Compared)**
Assume you needed to borrow $3,600 cash for one year. The City Bank charges 12% interest per annum on such loans. Answer the following questions (show computations):

Required:

a. What would be the face amount of the note assuming the bank agreed to accept an interest-bearing note?

b. What would be the face amount of the note assuming the bank insisted on a noninterest-bearing note?

c. Give the journal entries to record the note in *(a)* and *(b).* Set the entries in parallel columns.

d. Give the journal entries at date of maturity in *(a)* and *(b).*

PROBLEMS

PART A

P10–1 **(Record and Report Five Current Liabilities)**

Allen Company completed the transactions listed below during 19B. The annual accounting period ends December 31, 19B.

Jan.   8 Purchased merchandise for resale at an invoice cost of $12,000; terms 2/10, n/60. Record at net (see Chapter 6); assume a periodic inventory system.

      17 Paid invoice of January 8.

Apr. 1 Borrowed $60,000 from the National Bank for general use; executed a 12-month, 10%, interest-bearing note payable.

June 3 Purchased merchandise for resale at an invoice cost of $20,000; terms 1/20, n/30; record at net.

July 5 Paid invoice of June 3.

Aug. 1 Rented two rooms in the building owned by Allen and collected six months' rent in advance amounting to $4,800. Record the collection in a way that will not require an adjusting entry at year-end.

Dec. 20 Received a $500 deposit from a customer as a guarantee to return a large trailer "borrowed" for 30 days.

      31 Wages earned but not paid on December 31 of $8,000 (disregard payroll taxes).

Required:

a. Prepare journal entries for each of the above transactions.

b. Prepare all adjusting entries required on December 31, 19B.

c. Show how all of the liabilities arising from the above transactions would be reported on the balance sheet at December 31, 19B.

P10–2 **(Accounting for an Interest-Bearing Note, with Adjusting Entries)**

On April 1, 19A, Ravina Company bought equipment for $150,000. A cash down payment of $50,000 was made. A $100,000 interest-bearing note (including a mortgage on the equipment) was given for the balance. The note specified 12% annual interest. Two payments on principal of $50,000 each, plus interest on the unpaid balance on March 31, 19B, and March 31, 19C, are required—these will be unequal cash payments. The accounting period ends December 31.

Required:

a. Give all of the related journal entries for the terms of this note. Do not use reversing entries.

b. Show how the liabilities should be reported on Ravina's 19A and 19B balance sheets.

P10–3 **(Accounting for Interest-Bearing and Noninterest-Bearing Notes, Including Adjusting Entries)**

During 19A, Billings Company completed two transactions that involved notes payable. The accounting period ends December 31. The company does not use reversing entries.

May 1, 19A—Borrowed $36,000 cash and signed a one-year, interest-bearing note. The interest rate specified on the note was 10%. The principal and interest are payable on the maturity date, April 30, 19B.

September 1, 19A—Borrowed $30,000 cash and signed a six-month, noninterest-bearing note for $31,500. The note did not give a stated rate of interest. The face amount is payable at maturity date, February 28, 19B.

Required:

a. Give all of the entries related to the $36,000 note from May 1, 19A, through April 30, 19B.

b. Give all of the entries related to the $31,500 note from September 1, 19A, through maturity date, February 28, 19B.

c. Show how the liabilities related to the two notes should be reported on the 19A balance sheet.

P10–4 **(Purchase of a Noncash Asset with a Noninterest-Bearing Note; Including Adjusting Entries)**

On August 1, 19A, Brewer Company purchased a machine that cost $23,000. The company paid cash $5,000 and signed a six-month, noninterest-bearing note with a face amount of $19,080. The note did not specify a stated rate of interest. The accounting period ends December 31.

Required:

a. Compute the implicit rate of interest.

b. Give all entries related to the note from August 1, 19A, through the maturity date, February 1, 19B. Do not use reversing entries.

c. Show how the note should be reported on the 19A balance sheet.

P10–5 **(Record and Report Five Liabilities Including an Interest-Bearing Note and a Noninterest-Bearing Note)**

Saxon Company completed the transactions listed below during 19A. The annual accounting period ends December 31.

May 1 Purchased an operational asset (fixtures) for $40,000; paid $10,000 cash and signed a 12-month, 10%, interest-bearing note payable for the balance.

June 5 Purchased an operational asset (machine) at an invoice cost of $12,000; terms 3/10, n/60.

14 Paid invoice of June 5.

Sept. 1 Collected rent revenue on office space rented to another company; the rent of $6,000 was for the next six months. Record the collection in a way to avoid an adjusting entry at the end of 19A.

Nov. 1 Borrowed $30,000 cash and signed a noninterest-bearing note for $31,800. The note matures on April 30, 19B.

Dec. 31 Received a tax bill for property tax for 19A in the amount of $1,800; the taxes are payable no later than March 1, 19B.

Required:

a. Give the 19A journal entries for each of the above transactions.
b. Prepare any required adjusting entries on December 31, 19A.
c. Show how all liabilities arising from the above transactions would be reported on the 19A balance sheet.

P10–6   **(Deferred Income Tax; Two Differences; Entries; Restate Comparative Income Statement to Include Income Tax)**

Radney Company is preparing comparative statements at December 31, 19B. The records show the following summarized income statement data, exclusive of income tax expense:

	19A	19B
Revenues	$180,000	$190,000
Expenses	(110,000)	(129,000)
Extraordinary item	(10,000)	4,000
Income before income tax	$ 60,000	$ 65,000

Included in the 19B revenues of $190,000 is a revenue item of $20,000 that was included on the income tax return for 19A. Also, included in the 19B expenses of $129,000 was an expense item of $6,000 that was deducted on the income tax return for 19A. Assume an average 20% income tax rate. There were no deferred income taxes on the extraordinary items.

Required:

a. What kind of "tax difference" is represented by the two items? Explain.
b. For each year, compute (1) income tax expense, (2) income tax liability, and (3) deferred income tax.
c. Give the journal entry for each year to record income tax, including any deferred income taxes.
d. Restate the above comparative income statement, including the appropriate presentation of income tax for each year. (Hint: Allocate income tax expense between operations and extraordinary items.)

P10–7   **(Income Tax Timing Difference and Permanent Difference; Comprehensive Problem)**

At December 31, 19A, the records of Laymon Corporation provided the following pretax information:

1. Revenues $150,000
2. Expenses (including $13,000 depreciation expense) 113,000
3. Depreciation expense was computed as follows for income statement purposes:
   Operational asset cost (acquired January 1, 19A) 52,000
   Four-year useful life (no residual value).
   Depreciation expense per year (straight-line, $52,000 ÷ 4 years) 13,000
4. Extraordinary loss 10,000
5. The revenues given in 1 include $5,000 interest on tax-free municipal bonds.
6. Assume an average income tax rate of 20% on both ordinary income and extraordinary gain.
7. Sum-of-the-years'-digits depreciation on the operational asset is used on the income tax return (i.e., $52,000 × 4/10 = $20,800) and straight-line on the income statement (see above).

Required:

a. Compute income tax expense.

b. Compute income tax payable on the tax return.

c. Give the journal entry to record income tax including any deferred income tax.

d. Prepare an income statement.

e. What kind of "tax differences" were involved? Explain the basis for your treatment of them.

P10–8 **(Based on Supplement 10A; Accounting for Payroll Costs)**

Tappen Company completed the salary and wage payroll for March 19A. Details provided by the payroll were:

Salaries and wages earned	$200,000*
Employee income taxes withheld	42,000
Union dues withheld	2,000
Insurance premiums withheld	900

FICA tax rate, 7.15%.
FUTA tax rate, 0.7%.
State unemployment tax rate, 2.7% (based on the same amount of wages as FUTA taxes).

* Subject in full to payroll taxes.

Required:

a. Give the journal entry to record the payroll for March, including employee deductions.

b. Give the journal entry to record the employer's payroll taxes.

c. Give a combined journal entry to show remittance of amounts owed to governmental agencies and other organizations.

d. What was the total labor cost for Tappen Company? Explain. What percent of the payroll was take-home pay?

P10–9 **(Based on Supplement 10B: Application of a Voucher System to Control Cash Expenditures)**

Holt Company uses a voucher system to control cash expenditures. The following transactions have been selected from December 19B for case purposes. The accounting year ends December 31.

Design a voucher register and a check register similar to those shown in Supplement 10B. The transactions that follow will be entered in these two special journals.

Dec. 2 Purchased merchandise from AB Wholesalers for resale, $2,000; terms 2/10, n/30; record purchases at net and assume a periodic inventory system (see Chapter 6); Invoice No. 14; start with Voucher No. 11.

7 Approved contract with Ace Plumbing Company for repair of plumbing, $450; account, Building Repairs, No. 77.

11 Paid Voucher No. 11; start with Check No. 51.

22 Purchased store supplies for future use from Crown Company; Invoice No. 21 for $90; account, Store Supplies Inventory, No. 16.

23 Advertising for pre-Christmas sale, $630; bill received from Daily Press and payment processed immediately; account, Advertising Expense, No. 54.

31 Monthly payroll voucher, total $2,500; $1,500 was selling expense (Sales Salaries, No. 52), and $1,000 was administrative expense (Administrative Salaries,

No. 62). The voucher was supported by the payroll record; therefore, one voucher was prepared for the entire payroll. The voucher was approved for immediate payment. Six checks with consecutive numbers were issued.

Required:

a. Enter the above transactions in the voucher register and the check register.
b. Total the special journals and check the equality of the debits and credits. Set up T-accounts and post both registers. Complete all posting notations. The following accounts may be needed:

Account titles	Account No.
Cash	01
Store supplies inventory	16
Vouchers payable	30
Purchases	40
Selling expense control	50
Subsidiary ledger:	
Sales salaries	52
Advertising expense	54
Administrative expense control	60
Subsidiary ledger:	
Administrative salaries	62
Building repairs	77

c. Reconcile the Vouchers Payable account balance with the Unpaid Vouchers File at the end of December.

PART B

P10–10   (Application of Four PV and FV Concepts)

On January 1, 19A, Vail Company completed the following transactions (use a 10% annual interest rate for all transactions):

1. Deposited $40,000 in a debt retirement fund. Interest will be computed at six-month intervals and added to the fund at those times (i.e., semiannual compounding). (Hint: Think carefully about *n* and *i*.)
2. Established a plant addition fund of $200,000 to be available at the end of Year 5. A single sum will be deposited on January 1, 19A, that will grow to the $200,000.
3. Established a pension retirement fund of $500,000 to be available by the end of Year 6 by making six equal annual deposits each at year-end, starting on December 31, 19A.
4. Purchased a $100,000 machine on January 1, 19A, and paid cash, $20,000. A three-year note payable is signed for the balance. The note will be paid in three equal year-end payments starting on December 31, 19A.

Required (show computations and round to the nearest dollar):

a. In transaction 1 above, what will be the balance in the fund at the end of Year 4? What is the total amount of interest revenue that will be earned?
b. In transaction 2 above, what single sum amount must the company deposit on January 1, 19A? What is the total amount of interest revenue that will be earned?
c. In transaction 3 above, what is the required amount of each of the six equal annual deposits? What is the total amount of interest revenue that will be earned?

d. In transaction 4 above, what is the amount of each of the equal annual payments that must be paid on the note? What is the total amount of interest expense that will be incurred?

P10–11   (Accounting for a Fund; Fund Accumulation Schedule and Entries)

On January 1, 19A, Fast Company decided to accumulate a fund to build an addition to its plant. Fast will deposit $200,000 in the fund at each year-end, starting on December 31, 19A. The fund will earn 8% interest which will be added to the fund at each year-end. The accounting period ends December 31.

Required:

a. What will be the balance in the fund immediately after the December 31, 19C, deposit?
b. Complete the following fund accumulation schedule:

Date	Cash Payment	Interest Revenue	Fund Increase	Fund Balance
12/31/19A				
12/31/19B				
12/31/19C				
Total				

c. Give Fast's journal entries on December 31, 19A, 19B, and 19C.
d. The plant addition was completed on January 1, 19D. The total cost was $670,000. Give the entry assuming this amount is paid in full to the contractor.

P10–12   (Accounting for a Plant Fund; a Single Amount)

River Company will build another plant during 19C estimated to cost $900,000. At the present time, January 1, 19A, the company has excess cash, some of which will be set aside in a savings account to defray $700,000 of the plant cost. The savings account will earn 10% annual interest which will be added to the savings account each year-end.

Required (show computations and round to the nearest dollar):

a. What single amount must be deposited in the savings account on January 1, 19A, to create the desired amount by the end of 19C?
b. What will be the time value of the money by the end of 19C?
c. How much interest revenue will be earned each year (19A through 19C)?
d. Give the following journal entries:
   (1) Establishment of the fund.
   (2) Interest earned at each year-end.
   (3) Use of the fund and other cash needed to pay for the plant (completed December 31, 19C, at a cost of $940,000).

P10–13   (Accounting for a Debt Retirement Fund; a Single Amount)

On January 1, 19A, Reston Company set aside a fund to provide cash to pay off the principal amount of a $90,000 long-term debt that will be due at the end of five years. The single deposit will be made with an independent trustee. The fund will earn 7% annual interest which will be added to the fund balance at each year-end.

Required (show computations and round to the nearest dollar):

a. How much must be deposited as a single sum on January 1, 19A, to pay off the debt?

b. What is the time value of the money in dollars for the five years?

c. How much interest revenue will the fund earn in 19A? 19B?

d. Give the journal entries for Reston Company to record:

   (1) The deposit on January 1, 19A.

   (2) The interest revenue for 19A and 19B (separately).

   (3) Payment of the maturing liability at the end of the fifth year.

e. Show how the effects of the fund will be reported on the 19B income statement and balance sheet.

P10–14   **(Accounting for a Debt Fund; Equal Periodic Rents)**

On December 31, 19A, Cuellar Company set aside, in a fund, cash to pay the principal amount of a $120,000 debt due on December 31, 19D. Cuellar Company will make four equal annual deposits on each December 31, 19A, 19B, 19C, and 19D. The fund will earn 8% annual interest, which will be added to the balance of the fund at each year-end. The fund trustee will pay the loan principal (to the creditor) upon receipt of the last fund deposit. Cuellar's accounting period ends December 31.

Required (show computations and round to the nearest dollar):

a. How much must be deposited each December 31? (Hint: Use Table 10–3.)

b. What will be the time value of the money in dollars for the fund?

c. How much interest revenue will the fund earn in 19A, 19B, 19C, and 19D?

d. Give Cuellar's journal entries on the following dates:

   (1) For the first deposit on December 31, 19A.

   (2) For all amounts at the ends of 19B and 19C.

   (3) For payment of the debt on December 31, 19D.

e. Show how the effects of the fund will be reported on the December 31, 19B, income statement and balance sheet.

P10–15   **(Debt Paid in Equal Installments; Debt Payment Schedule and Entries)**

On January 1, 19A, Big Company sold a new machine to Small Company for $40,000. A cash down payment of $10,000 was made by Small Company. A $30,000, 12% note was signed by Small Company for the balance due. The note is to be paid off in three equal installments due on December 31, 19A, 19B, and 19C. Each payment is to include principal plus interest on the unpaid balance. The purchase was recorded by Small as follows:

January 1, 19A:

Machine 40,000		
Cash	10,000	
Note payable	30,000	

Required (show computations and round to the nearest dollar):

a. What is the amount of the equal annual payment that must be made by Small Company? (Hint: Use Table 10–4.)

b. What was the time value of the money, in dollars, on the note?

c. Complete the following debt payment schedule:

Date	Cash Payment	Interest Expense	Principal Decrease	Unpaid Principal
1/1/19A				
12/31/19A				
12/31/19B				
12/31/19C				
Total				

d. Give the journal entries for each of the three payments.

e. Explain why interest expense decreased in amount each year.

P10–16 **(Payment for Auto in Equal Periodic Installments; Prepare Debt Payment Schedule; Entries)**

On January 1, 19A, you bought a new Super-Whiz automobile for $15,000. You paid a $5,000 cash down payment and signed a $10,000 note, payable in four equal installments on each December 31, the first payment to be made on December 31, 19A. The interest rate is 14% per year on the unpaid balance. Each payment will include payment on principal plus the interest.

Required:

a. Compute the amount of the equal payments that you must make. (Hint: Use Table 10–4.)

b. What is the time value of the money in dollars for the installment debt?

c. Complete a schedule using the format below.

DEBT PAYMENT SCHEDULE

Date	Cash Payment	Interest Expense	Reduction of Principal	Unpaid Principal
1/1/A				
12/31/A				
12/31/B				
12/31/C				
12/31/D				
Total				

d. Explain why the amount of interest expense decreases each year.

e. Give the journal entries on December 31, 19A, and 19B.

P10–17 **(Accounting for a Noninterest-Bearing Note; Time to Maturity, Two Years)**
On January 1, 19A, Design Furniture Company borrowed $40,000 cash from Mellon Financial Corporation. Design signed a two-year noninterest-bearing note. The note plus all interest are payable on the maturity date December 31, 19B. The market rate of interest for this risk level was 12%. The accounting period ends December 31.

Required (show computations and round all amounts to the nearest dollar):

a. Compute the face amount of the note.
b. Give Design's journal entries at the following dates:
   (1) January 1, 19A, date of loan.
   (2) December 31, 19A, end of accounting period.
   (3) December 31, 19B, end of accounting period.
   (4) December 31, 19B, maturity date.
c. Show how Design should report this note on its December 31, 19A, balance sheet.

CASES

C10–1 **(Accounting for Warranty Expense and Warranty Liability; a Challenging Case)**
Hi-Fi Retailers sells television sets, stereos, and other related items. This case relates to stereos. During 19A, Hi-Fi sold stereos for $180,000 cash; the related cost of goods sold was $70,000. Each stereo is guaranteed for one year for defective parts. In case of a defective part, the part is replaced and the labor cost of replacing it involves no cost to the customer. Experience by the manufacturer shows that the average cost to make good the warranty is approximately 5% of cost of goods sold. The company uses a perpetual inventory system and the accounting period ends December 31.

Actual expenditures for warranties (i.e., replacement parts and labor) during 19A was $2,700. During 19A, this amount was debited to an account called Warranty Expense and credited to Cash. Stereo sales were much higher during December than in any other prior month.

Required:

a. Give the two summary journal entries for the company to record the sales of stereos during 19A.
b. Explain why the company debited the actual 19A warranty expenditures to warranty expense.
c. Explain the nature of any liability that the company should record at the end of 19A related to the warranties.
d. Compute the estimated amount of any warranty liability that exists at December 31, 19A.
e. Give any entry needed based on your answer to Requirement (d).
f. Show how warranty expense and any warranty liability should be reported in the 19A income statement and balance sheet.

C10–2 **(Hidden Interest in a Real Estate Deal; PV)**
Slick Doe, a home builder, distributed an advertisement that offered "a $120,000 house with a zero interest rate mortgage for sale." If the purchaser made monthly payments of

$2,000 for five years ($120,000 ÷ 60 months), there would be no additional charge for interest. When the offer was made, mortgage interest rates were 12%. Present value for $n = 60$, and $i = 1\%$ is 44.9550.

Required:

a. Did Slick Doe actually provide a mortgage at zero interest?
b. Estimate the true price of the home that was advertised. Assume that the $2,000 monthly payment was based on an implicit interest rate of 12%.

C10–3 **(Based on Supplement 10C; Alternative Choices Involving Leases; Challenging)**

Several years ago, Rapid Service Company borrowed $10 million from First American Bank. At the time the loan was approved, Rapid Service agreed not to borrow any additional money from any other sources until at least half of the First American loan was repaid. As the result of continued growth, Rapid Service must acquire a large computer during the current year. Unfortunately, Rapid Service does not have sufficient cash to purchase the computer or to repay the loan to First American. You have been engaged as a consultant to Rapid Service. The president of Rapid Service, Allison Payne, described the problem during your first meeting:

> The computer can be purchased from Super Computer Company for $500,000, but we don't have the cash and the bank won't let us borrow any more money. However, the computer company has agreed to lease the computer to us on a 10-year lease, which is the expected useful life of the computer (no residual value). Annual lease payments of $81,372 would be paid based on an interest rate of 10%. I think that this lease deal will solve our problem because we will not violate our agreement with First American as long as we don't report any additional debt on the balance sheet. We must work this out without recording any debt. What do you think?

To help the president understand the required accounting treatment, the president should consider three alternatives as follows:

Alternative No. 1—Rapid Service can purchase the computer but would have to borrow $500,000 with a note payable to the computer company at 10% interest for 10 years. Annual year-end payments for principal and interest amount to $81,372.

Alternative No. 2—Rapid Service could rent the computer on a monthly lease basis. The terms of the lease cause it to be considered an operating lease. Annual rent payments would be $125,000 at each year-end for 10 years.

Alternative No. 3—Rapid Service could acquire the computer on a long-term lease basis. At the expiration date of the lease, the computer would be retained by Rapid for no additional cost. The terms of the lease cause it to be accounted for as a capital lease. The lease payments would be $81,372 for 10 years.

Required:

a. Assume that the computer was acquired on January 1, 19D, which is the beginning of the accounting period. Prepare journal entries to record the acquistion of the computer by Rapid Service under each of the three alternatives.
b. Assume Rapid Service makes cash payments under each alternative on December 31 of each year. Prepare the required journal entries on December 31, 19D (include

adjusting entries, if required). Rapid Service uses straight-line depreciation for all assets.

c. Would the capital lease alternative, described by the president, permit Rapid Service to acquire the computer, and conform to GAAP? Would a capital lease violate the agreement with the bank?

d. What are the primary problems of Alternatives 1 and 2?

C10–4   **(Analysis of Liabilities Reported on an Actual Set of Financial Statements)**
Refer to the financial statements of Chesebrough-Pond's given in Special Supplement B immediately preceding the Index. Answer the following questions for the 1985 annual accounting period.

1. What were the (a) total current liabilities, (b) long-term debt, and (c) any other noncurrent liabilities reported on the balance sheet?
2. How much cash was paid on (a) long-term debt and (b) other noncurrent liabilities?
3. Refer to the notes to the financial statements and complete the following:

   Total long-term debts listed . . . . $ _____
   Less: Current portion . . . . $ _____
   Total long-term debt . . . . $ _____

4. Explain the reason for subtracting the "current portion" in Question 3 above.
5. Did the company disclose any contingent liabilities? Explain.

This chapter discusses a particular liability called bonds payable. Notice below how one well-known company reports its industrial development bonds and its unamortized discount.

D u P o n t   A n n u a l   R e p o r t   1 9 8 5

Consolidated Balance Sheet (Dollars in millions)

		December 31	
See Note		**1985**	1984
Total Current Liabilities		**$ 5,311**	$ 5,117
15 Long-Term Borrowings		**3,191**	3,421
16 Capital Lease Obligations		**93**	104
17 Other Liabilities		**1,475**	1,458
6 Deferred Income Taxes		**2,343**	1,627

Notes to Financial Statements

15 — Long-Term Borrowings

	December 31			December 31	
	1985	1984		1985	1984
U.S. dollar:					
Industrial development bonds					
due 1986-2022	$ 228	$ 259	9.13% debentures due 1999 .	132	139
14.50% notes due 1988	—	375	7.50% debentures due 1999 .	68	72
14.13% notes due 1989	200	200	8.88% debentures due 2001 .	200	200
13.25% notes due 1989	180	17	6.00% debentures due 2001		
Zero coupon notes due 1990			($660 face value, 13.95%		
($300 face value, 13.99% yield			yield to maturity)	327	322
to maturity)	172	150	8.25% notes due 2002	80	80
12.88% notes due 1992	150	150	8.45% debentures due 2004 .	198	198
11.25% notes due 1995	150	150	8.50% debentures due 2006 .	182	182
13.75% retractable notes due			9.38% debentures due 2009 .	200	200
1997	189	189	13.25% debentures due 2011 .	300	300
8.70% notes due 1998	200	217	Other loans (various currencies)		
8.00% notes due 1998	60	63	due 1986-2013	238	241
			Unamortized discount	(263)	(283)
				$3,191	$3,421

MEASURING AND REPORTING BONDS PAYABLE

PURPOSE:

Chapter 10 discussed current liabilities and the concepts of future and present value. This chapter discusses long-term liabilities, with emphasis on bonds payable. Long-term liabilities are an important source of funds that are primarily used to pay for noncurrent assets. Bonds are long-term debt instruments. When bonds are issued (i.e., sold), they represent an investment for the buyer and a liability for the issuer. Accounting for bonds involves some complexities. The purpose of this chapter is to discuss measuring, recording, and reporting the financial effects of bonds payable.

LEARNING OBJECTIVES—TO BE ABLE TO:

1. Define and classify bonds payable.
2. Record and report bonds payable, with discount and premium amortization.
3. Record and report bond sinking funds.
4. Account for debt retirement funds.
5. Expand your accounting vocabulary by learning about the "Important Terms Defined in This Chapter" (page 586).
6. Apply the knowledge gained from this chapter by completing the homework assigned by your instructor.

ORGANIZATION:

Part A—Fundamentals of Measuring, Recording, and Reporting Bonds Payable

1. Characteristics of bonds payable.
2. Interest rates on bonds.
3. Accounting for bonds sold at par, discount, and premium.
4. Advantages and disadvantages of issuing bonds.
5. Financial leverage.

Part B—Additional Problems in Accounting for Bonds Payable

1. Accounting for bonds sold between intere dates.
2. Accounting for bonds with different interest and accounting period dates.
3. Bonds sinking funds.
4. Effective-interest amortization of bond discount and premium.

PART A—FUNDAMENTALS OF MEASURING, RECORDING, AND REPORTING BONDS PAYABLE

CHARACTERISTICS OF BONDS PAYABLE

Funds needed for long-term purposes, such as the acquisition of high-cost machinery or the construction of a new plant, often are obtained by issuing long-term debt instruments. These instruments usually are long-term notes payable (discussed in Chapter 10) and bonds payable. Bonds payable may be **secured** by a mortgage on specified assets, or the bonds may be **unsecured.** Bonds usually are issued in denominations of $1,000 or $10,000, and sometimes in denominations of $100,000. They usually are negotiable (i.e., transferable by endorsement). The bonds of most large companies are bought and sold daily by investors on the major stock exchanges.[1] A typical bond certificate is shown in Exhibit 11–1.

The **principal** of a bond is the amount (a) payable at the maturity date and (b) on which the cash periodic interest payments are computed. The principal is specified on the bond certificate (see Exhibit 11–1), and it does not change. It is also called the par value, face amount, and maturity value. A bond will always specify a **stated rate of interest,** which also is specified on the bond certificate. The stated rate of interest does not change. A bond will specify that **periodic cash interest payments** must be paid—usually annually or semiannually. Each periodic interest payment is computed as **principal times the stated interest rate.** The selling price of a bond does not affect the periodic **cash** payment for interest. For example, a $1,000, 8%, bond would always pay cash interest of (a) annual basis, $80; or (b) semiannual basis, $40.

A bond may sell at its par value, at a discount (below par), or at a premium (above par). The selling price of a bond is **determined by the difference between its stated interest rate and its market rate of interest.** The market rate of interest is the interest rate that investors (i.e., bond buyers) require to adequately compensate them for the risks related to the bonds. If the stated and market rates are the same, a bond will sell at par; if the market rate is higher than the stated rate, a bond will sell at a discount; and if the market rate is lower than the stated rate, the bond will sell at a premium. These relationships will always prevail because (a) the periodic cash interest payment is fixed, (b) the market rate of interest is set by the investors, and (c) the price paid for the bond must earn the market rate of interest for the investors (this is discussed further in the next section).

---

[1] Bonds also are issued by governmental units, such as federal and state governments, cities, counties, school districts, water districts, and by nonprofit institutions. The discussions in this chapter apply to both types, although we will focus mainly on those issued by corporations.

EXHIBIT 11–1

Typical bond certificate

A company that wants to sell a bond issue must prepare a **bond indenture** (or bond contract) that states the legal provisions of the bonds. These provisions include the maturity date, rate of interest to be paid, date of each interest payment, and any conversion privileges (explained later). When a bond is issued, the investor receives a **bond certificate** (i.e., a bond) like the one shown in Exhibit 11–1. All of the bond certificates for a single bond issue are identical. The face of each certificate shows same maturity date, interest rate, interest dates, and other provisions. Usually when a company issues bonds, an **underwriter** is engaged to sell the bonds to the public. A third party, called the **trustee,** usually is appointed to represent the bondholders. The duties of an independent trustee are to ascertain whether the issuing company fulfills all of the provisions of the bond indenture.

Special Characteristics of Bonds

Each bond issue has characteristics that are specified in the bond indenture. The issuing company often will add special characteristics to a bond issue to make the bond more attractive to investors. Bonds may be classified in different ways, depending on their characteristics. Typical bond characteristics and their related classifications are shown in Exhibit 11–2.

MEASURING BONDS PAYABLE AND INTEREST EXPENSE

The accounting approach used to account for bonds payable is based primarily on the **cost** and **matching principles.** When a bond is issued (i.e., sold), the proceeds include the net cash received, plus the market value of any noncash resources received. In conformity with the **cost principle,** bonds payable are recorded at their **issue price,** which is their **current cash equivalent amount.**

Interest Rates on Bonds

A bond specifies its **stated** interest rate, which is multiplied by the bond principal, or par, amount to determine the **cash** interest paid each interest period. This cash payment is unaffected whether the bond sold at par, a premium, or a discount.

In contrast, the **market** rate of interest is determined by competitive forces in the financial markets. It is the agreed rate that borrowers (bond issuers) are willing to pay and lenders (investors) are willing to accept on their money, taking into consideration the perceived level of risk involved. Market rates tend to fluctuate daily, but the stated rate of interest is fixed by contract for the life of the bond. As a result, the market price of a bond is affected by changes in the market rate of interest. The market rate of interest also is called the effective, yield, or coupon rate.

The **cash flows** related to a bond for the bond issuer can be summarized as follows:

1. Cash **received** at issuance date = Market price of the bond (plus any accrued interest since the last interest date, discussed in Part B).
2. Cash **paid** at each interest date = Par value of the bond × Stated rate of interest.
3. Cash **paid** at maturity date = Par value.

When a bond is **issued at par,** the issuer receives **cash** equal to both the par value and market value of the bond. Also, in this case both the stated and market rates of interest are the **same.** When a bond is **issued at a discount,** the issuer receives **less cash** than the par value of the bond. In this case, because

EXHIBIT 11–2

Bond characteristics and classifications of bonds

Bond classification	*Bond characteristic*
1. **On the basis of collateral (assets):**	
a. Unsecured bonds (often called debentures).	*a.* Bonds that do **not** include a mortgage or pledge of specific assets as a guarantee of repayment at maturity.
b. Secured bonds (often designated on the basis of the type of asset pledged, such as a real estate mortgage).	*b.* Bonds that include the pledge of specific assets as a guarantee of repayment at maturity.
2. **On the basis of repayment of principal:**	
a. Ordinary or single-payment bonds.	*a.* The principal is payable in full at a single specified maturity date in the future.
b. Serial bonds.	*b.* The principal is payable in installments on a series of specified maturity dates in the future.
3. **On the basis of early retirement:**	
a. Callable bonds.	*a.* Bonds that may be called for early retirement at the option of the **issuer.**
b. Redeemable bonds.	*b.* Bonds that may be turned in for early retirement at the option of the **bondholder.**
c. Convertible bonds.	*c.* Bonds that may be converted to other securities of the issuer (usually common stock) at the option of the **bondholder.**
4. **On the basis of the payment of interest:**	
a. Registered bonds.	*a.* Payment of interest is made by check and mailed **direct** to the bondholder whose name must be on file (i.e., in the bond register).
b. Coupon bonds.	*b.* Bonds with a printed coupon attached for each interest payment. The bondholder "clips" the coupon on the interest date and deposits it in a bank like a check, or mails it to the issuing company. Then the company mails the interest check direct to the person and address shown on the completed coupon. The interest rate on coupon bonds often is called the coupon rate.

the cash interest payments are unaffected by either the market interest rate or the selling price, the market rate of interest will be **higher** than the stated rate of interest. When a bond is **issued at a premium,** the issuer receives **more cash** than the par value. Because, in this case, the cash interest is unaffected by either the market rate of interest or the selling price, market rate of interest will be **less** than the stated rate of interest.

Each interest period bond interest expense is measured, recorded, and reported in conformity with the **matching principle.** At the end of each period, the amount of interest unpaid must be accrued and reported as expense so that it will be matched with the revenues in the period in which it was incurred. The measurement and reporting of interest on bonds is similar to interest on notes receivable and notes payable. However, when bonds are issued at a premium or discount, an additional measurement problem occurs because (a) interest expense is based on the market rate of interest and (b) interest paid, or payable, is based on the stated rate of interest.

ACCOUNTING FOR BONDS ILLUSTRATED

Accounting and reporting for bonds payable are illustrated in Exhibit 11–3, for three different cases: (1) bonds issued at par, (2) bonds issued at a discount, and (3) bonds issued at a premium. In each of these cases the bonds are sold on the authorization date, January 1, 19A.

Bonds Sold at Par

Bonds sell at their par value when buyers (investors) are willing to invest in them at the stated interest rate on the bond. For example, on January 1, 19A, Mason Corporation issued $400,000 of the bonds payable and received $400,000 in cash. The bonds were dated to start interest on January 1, 19A. The entry by Mason Corporation to record the issuance of these bonds is given in Exhibit 11–3, Case A.

Subsequent to the sale of the bonds, interest at 5% (i.e., 10% per year) on the par value of the bonds must be paid each June 30 and December 31 until maturity. The entries to record the interest payments during 19A are given in Exhibit 11–3, Case A.

At the end of the accounting period, December 31, 19A, the financial statements must report bond interest expense and a long-term liability, as shown in Exhibit 11–3, Case A.

In this case, Mason Corporation received $1,000 cash for each $1,000 bond sold and will pay back $1,000, principal + ($50 × 20 semiannual interest payments) = $2,000. The $1,000 difference is the amount of interest expense for the 10 years; therefore, the interest cost was $100 per year and the market or effective rate of interest was $100 ÷ $1,000 = 10% per year. The stated rate called for on the bond also was 10%.

The $1,000 cash that Mason Corporation received when each bond was sold is the present value of the future cash flows associated with the bond (refer to Chapter 10, Part B) computed as follows:

	Present value
a. Principal: $1,000 × $P_{n=20;\ i=5\%}$ (Table 10–2; 0.3769)	$ 377
b. Interest: $50 × $P_{n=20;\ i=5\%}$ (Table 10–4; 12.4622)	623
Issue (sale) price of one Mason bond	$1,000

When the effective rate of interest is equal to the stated rate of interest, the present value of the future cash flows associated with a bond **always** will equal the bond's par amount.

Bonds Sold at a Discount

Bonds sell at a discount when the buyers (investors) are willing to invest in them only at a market rate of interest that is **higher** than the stated interest rate on the bonds. Case B assumes that capital market established a 12% market rate of interest for the 10-year Mason bonds (Exhibit 11–3). The bonds have a stated rate of 10%, payable semiannually. Therefore, the bonds sold at a **discount.** At a 12% market rate, how much cash would a $1,000 bond of Mason Company generate if sold on January 1, 19A? To compute the cash issue (sale) price of one bond requires computation of its present value, at the **market rate,** of the two future cash flows specified on the bond: (a) the principal ($n = 20, i = 6\%$) and (b) the cash interest paid each semiannual interest period ($n = 20, i = 6\%$). Thus, the cash issue (sale) price of one Mason bond is computed as follows (refer to Chapter 10, Part B):

	Present value
a. Principal: $1,000 × $P_{n=20;\ i=6\%}$ (Table 10–2; 0.3118)	$312
b. Interest: $50 × $P_{n=20;\ i=6\%}$ (Table 10–4; 11.4699)	573
Issue (sale) price of one Mason bond	$885*

* Thus, the issue price was 88.5. Discount: $1,000 − $885 = $115.

The cash issue price of the 400 bonds issued by Mason would be $354,000 (i.e., 400 bonds × $885).

When a bond is sold at a discount (i.e., $115 discount per bond in the above example), the Bonds Payable account is credited for the par or maturity amount and the **discount is recorded as a debit to Discount on Bonds Payable.** The issuance of 400 of the bonds of Mason Company at a cash sale price of $885 per bond (i.e., a 12% market rate) is recorded as shown in Exhibit 11–3, Case B.

The journal entry to record the issuance of the bonds (Exhibit 11–3) shows the discount in a separate contra liability account (Discount on Bonds Payable) as a **debit.** The discount must be given special treatment on the income statement to measure interest expense. Also, the balance sheet reports the bonds payable at their **carrying value** (maturity amount less any **unamortized** discount).

EXHIBIT 11–3

Accounting for bonds payable illustrated

Situation:

Mason Corporation approved a bond issue on January 1, 19A: Bonds payable authorized, 500 bonds, $1,000 par per bond, 10% interest (payable semiannually each June 30 and December 31), maturity in 10 years on December 31, 19J. Mason's accounting period ends December 31.

Case A—Bonds issued at par:

On January 1, 19A, Mason issued 400 bonds at par (i.e., an effective rate of 10%) for $400,000 cash.

Entries during 19A:

January 1, 19A—To record issuance of the bonds at par:
Cash (400 bonds × $1,000) 400,000
   Bonds payable (400 bonds) 400,000

Interest payments during 19A:

	June 30, 19A	December 31, 19A
Bond interest expense	20,000	20,000
Cash ($400,000 × 5%)	20,000	20,000

Financial statement for 19A:

Income statement:
Bond interest expense .... $ 40,000

Balance sheet:
Long-term liabilities:
   Bonds payable, 10% (due December 31, 19J) 400,000

Case B—Bonds issued at a discount:

On January 1, 19A, Mason issued 400 ($400,000 par) of the bonds at an effective interest rate of 12% (i.e., at price of 88.5) for $354,000 cash.

Entries during 19A:

January 1, 19A—To record issuance of the bonds at a discount:
Cash (400 bonds × $885) 354,000
Discount on bonds payable [400 bonds × ($1,000 − $885)] 46,000*
   Bonds payable (400 bonds × $1,000) 400,000*

  * Note: In effect, the bonds are recorded at their **issue price** because the liability is reported on the balance sheet net of these two balances.

Interest payments during 19A:

	June 30, 19A	December 31, 19A
Bond interest expense (cash interest plus amortized discount)	22,300	22,300
Discount on bonds payable, straight-line amortization ($46,000 ÷ 20 periods)	2,300	2,300
Cash ($400,000 × 5%)	20,000	20,000

Financial statements for 19A:

Income statement:
Bond interest expense ($22,300 × 2) .... $ 44,600

Balance sheet:
Long-term liabilities:
   Bonds payable, 10%, due December 31, 19J $400,000
   Less unamortized discount .... 41,400*   358,600†

_____ **EXHIBIT 11–3** *(concluded)* _____

Accounting for bonds payable illustrated

Case B—Bonds issued at a discount (continued)
  Or, alternatively:

  Bonds payable, 10%, due December 31, 19J
    (maturity amount, $400,000, less unamortized discount) . . . .   358,600†

  * $46,000 − $2,300 − $2,300 = $41,400.
  † This amount is called the carrying value or net liability.

Case C—Bonds issued at a premium:
  On January 1, 19A, Mason issued 400 ($400,000 par) of the bonds at an effective interest rate of 8½% (i.e.,
    at a price of 110) for $440,000 cash.

  Entries during 19A:

  January 1, 19A—To record issuance of the bonds at a premium:
    Cash (400 bonds × $1,100) 440,000
        Premium on bonds payable [400 bonds × ($1,100 − $1,000)]   40,000
        Bonds payable (400 bonds × $1,000)   400,000

  Interest payments during 19A:

	June 30, 19A	*December 31, 19A*
Bond interest expense (cash interest less amortized premium)	18,000	18,000
Premium on bonds payable, straight-line amortization		
($40,000 ÷ 20 periods)	2,000	2,000
Cash ($400,000 × 5%)	20,000	20,000

  Financial statements for 19A:

  Income statement:
    Bond interest expense ($18,000 × 2) . . . . $ 36,000

  Balance sheet:
    Long-term liabilities:
      Bonds payable, 10% (due December 31, 19J) $400,000
      Add unamortized premium . . . .   36,000*   436,000†

  Or, alternatively:
    Bonds payable, 10%, due December 31, 19J (maturity amount,
      $400,000, plus unamortized premium) . . . .   436,000†

    * $40,000 − $2,000 − $2,000 = $36,000.
    † This amount is called the carrying value or net liability.

Payment of principal (face) amount at maturity date (all three situations):

  December 31, 19J:

    Bonds payable 400,000
      Cash   400,000

Measuring and recording interest on bonds issued at a discount

In Exhibit 11–3, Case B, the issue price of each bond was $885 (discount $115). During the 10-year term of the bonds, Mason must make 20 semiannual cash interest payments of $50 each (i.e., $50 × 20 = $1,000 total interest) and at maturity pay back the $1,000 cash principal. Therefore, in addition to the cash interest of $1,000, $115 more cash per bond is paid back than was borrowed (i.e., $1,000 − $885). This $115 discount on each bond causes the yield or effective rate to be 12% (instead of the 10% stated on the bonds). The discount is an adjustment of the amount of interest expense that will be **reported** each accounting period on the income statement. Bond discount represents an **increase in bond interest expense.** To give accounting effect to bond discount in periods subsequent to issuance, the $46,000 debit to Discount on Bonds Payable (Exhibit 11–3, Case B) must be apportioned to each semiannual interest period as an increase in bond interest expense from the date of issuance to maturity date. There are two methods for doing this: (1) **straight-line amortization** and (2) **effective-interest amortization.** Straight-line amortization is easy to compute. The effective-interest method is discussed in Part B of this Chapter.

Straight-line amortization.   To amortize the $46,000 bond discount over the period from date of issuance to maturity date on a straight-line basis, an equal dollar amount is allocated to each interest period. The Mason bonds have 20 six-month interest periods. Therefore, the computation would be $46,000 ÷ 20 periods = $2,300 amortization on each semiannual interest date. The interest payment on the bonds during 19A would be recorded as shown in Exhibit 11–3, Case B.

In conformity with *APB Opinion 21*, "Interest on Receivables and Payables," bonds payable should be measured and reported on the balance sheet at their **net liability amount,** that is, the maturity amount less any unamortized bond discount or plus any unamortized bond premium. Therefore, at the end of the accounting period, December 31, 19A, the financial statements would report interest expense and bonds payable as shown in Exhibit 11–3, Case B.

Each succeeding year the unamortized discount will **decrease** by $4,600, therefore, the net liability will **increase** each year by $4,600. At the maturity date of the bonds, the unamortized discount (i.e., the balance in the Discount on Bonds Payable account) will be **zero.** At that time the maturity or face amount of the bonds and the current net liability amount will be the same (i.e., $400,000).

When straight-line amortization of bond discount is used, **interest expense** is computed as the **sum** of the cash, or accrued, interest amount and the periodic amount of discount amortized (see Exhibit 11–3).

Bonds Sold at a Premium

Bond sell at a premium when the buyers (investors) are willing to invest in bonds at a market or yield rate of interest that is **lower** than the stated interest rate on the bonds. For example, the capital market established an 8½% market rate of interest for the 10-year Mason bonds (Exhibit 11–3, Case C, stated rate, 10%, payable on semiannual basis), which means the bonds sold at a **premium.** The cash issue (sale) price of one Mason bond is computed as follows (refer to Chapter 10, Part B):

Present value

a. Principal: $1,000 × $P_{n=20;\ i=4¼\%}$ (Table 10–2; 0.4350) .... $ 435
b. Interest: $50 × $P_{n=20;\ i=4¼\%}$ (Table 10–4; 13.2944) 665
  Issue (sale) price of one Mason bond $1,100

The cash issue price (110) of the 400 bonds issued by Mason would be $440,000 (i.e., 400 bonds × $1,100).

When a bond is sold at a premium ($100 premium per bond in the above case), the Bonds Payable account is credited for the par amount, and the **premium is recorded as a credit to Premium on Bonds Payable.** The issuance of 400 of the bonds of Mason Company at a cash sale price of $1,100 each (i.e., at an 8½% market rate) is recorded as shown in Exhibit 11–3, Case C.

Measuring and recording interest expense on bonds issued at a premium

The premium of $40,000 recorded by Mason must be apportioned to each of the 20 interest periods. Either the effective-interest method or the straight-line method may be used. Using the straight-line method, the amortization of premium each semiannual interest period would be $40,000 ÷ 20 periods = $2,000. Therefore, the payments of interest on the bonds during 19A would be recorded as shown in Exhibit 11–3, Case C.[2]

In the journal entry to record the sale and issuance of the bonds by Mason, the premium was recorded in a separate account, **Premium on Bonds Payable, as a credit.** The premium **decreases** interest expense. Therefore, in each period a portion of it is amortized to interest expense. Notice in Exhibit 11–3, Case C, that Bond Interest Expense was reduced by $2,000 each semiannual period. At the end of 19A, the financial statements of Mason Company would report interest expense and bonds payable as shown in Exhibit 11–3, Case C.

---

[2] The amount of interest expense recorded each semiannual period may be confirmed as follows:

Cash paid out by the borrower:
  Par amount of bonds at maturity $400,000
  Interest payments ($20,000 × 20 periods) 400,000
    Total cash payments 800,000
Cash received by the borrower 440,000
    Total interest expense over 10 years $360,000
Interest expense per semiannual period ($360,000 ÷ 20 periods)* .... $ 18,000

  * Alternatively, $20,000 cash interest − $2,000 premium amortization = $18,000.

When straight-line amortization of bond premium is used, **interest expense** is computed as the cash, or accrued, interest amount **minus** the periodic amount of premium amortized (see Exhibit 11–3).

At maturity date, after the last interest payment, the bond premium of $40,000 will be fully amortized, and the maturity or face amount of the bonds and the current net liability of the bonds will be the same (i.e., $400,000). At maturity, December 31, 19J, the bonds will be paid off in full, resulting in the same entry whether the bond was originally sold at par, a discount, or a premium.

The effect of amortization of bond discount and bond premium on a $1,000 bond is shown graphically in Exhibit 11–4.

The above discussion focused on the fundamental issues in measuring and reporting bonds payable. This discussion provided the background essential to understand the economic impact of bonds payable on the issuing company and its reporting on the periodic financial statements. The next part of the chapter discusses some complexities often encountered in accounting for bonds payable.

EXHIBIT 11–4

Amortization of bond discount and premium compared

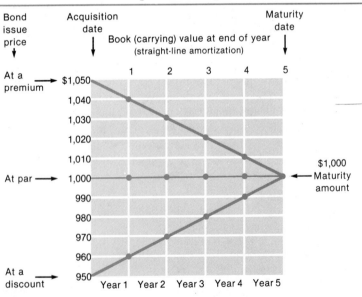

ADVANTAGES OF ISSUING BONDS

A corporation often uses long-term debt to get additional cash rather than by selling its capital stock. The primary advantages of using bonds rather than capital stock are:

1. Ownership and control of the company are not diluted—in contrast to stockholders, bondholders do not participate in the management (by voting) and accumulated earnings of the company.
2. Cash payments to the bondholders are limited to the specified interest payments and the principal of the debt.
3. The net interest cost of borrowed funds often is less because **interest expense** reduces taxable income. Dividends paid to stockholders are not tax deductible.
4. **Positive financial leverage** often occurs. This occurs when the **net interest rate** on debt is less than the interest rate earned by the company on its total assets. For example, if a company borrows funds for an after-tax interest rate of 5.4% and earns 15% on its total assets, the difference, 9.6%, is called positive financial leverage because the company earns more on total invested funds than it pays out to borrow funds. Therefore, the stockholders had a significant benefit because of the relatively low cost of the borrowed cash. **Financial leverage is measured as the difference between the return on stockholders' equity and the return on total assets.**

Financial Leverage Illustrated

Exhibit 11–5 shows two comparative cases for Spicewood Corporation to illustrate the cause and economic effects of financial leverage. Case A assumes that the company has total assets of $500,000, which were provided in full by stockholders (i.e., it has no debt). In contrast, Case B assumes that of the total amount of assets, $300,000 was provided by stockholders and the remaining $200,000 was provided by creditors (i.e., debt). For illustrative purposes, the other variables are held constant in order to demonstrate the cause and economic effects of using debt to help finance a business.

In Exhibit 11–5, Case A, return on stockholders' equity is 15%, and the return on total assets also is 15%. When there is **no debt,** as in Case A, these two rates will **always** be the same.

Now examine Case B, where $200,000 of debt is introduced. The return on stockholders' equity is 21%, and it is 15% on total assets. When debt is introduced, these two rates usually are different—only because of the debt.

This difference of 6% (i.e., 21%–15%) is a measure of **financial leverage** because it measures the effect on owners' equity. Financial leverage may be positive (i.e., favorable to stockholders) or negative. In this case the financial leverage is **positive** because the rate of return on stockholders' equity (21%) is **higher** than the return on total assets (15%).

EXHIBIT 11–5

Effects of financial leverage

SPICEWOOD CORPORATION		
Case A: No debt	**Case B: Debt, $200,000, 9%**	

Balance sheet:

	Case A	Case B	
Total assets	$500,000	....	$500,000
Total debt (9% interest)	–0–	....	200,000
Stockholders' equity			
(10,000 shares)	$500,000	(6,000 shares)	$300,000

Income statement:

	Case A	Case B	
Revenues	$300,000	....	$300,000
Operating expense	(175,000)	....	(175,000)
Income tax			
($125,000 × 40%)	(50,000)	....	(50,000)
Interest expense		($200,000 × 9% = $18,000) –	
(net of income tax)	–0–	($18,000 × 40% = $7,200)	(10,800)
Net income	$ 75,000		$ 64,200

Analysis:

	Case A	Case B	
a. Return on stockholders'			
equity ($75,000 ÷ $500,000)	15%	($64,200 ÷ $300,000)	21%
b. Return on total assets		($64,200 + $10,800 = $75,000)	
($75,000 ÷ $500,000)	15%	÷ $500,000*	15%
c. Financial leverage			
[a] − [b]†	–0–	(21% − 15%)	6%
d. EPS ($75,000 ÷ 10,000			
shares)	$7.50	($64,200 ÷ 6,000 shares)	$10.70

* Interest on debt, net of income tax, is added back to derive total return to all fund providers (also see Chapter 16).
† Also see discussion of financial leverage in Chapter 16.

Notice in Exhibit 11–5, Case B, that to compute return on total assets, net income is increased by interest expense (net of income tax). This increase in net income is necessary because the denominator (total assets) includes resources provided by both owners and creditors. Therefore, the numerator must include the total return (i.e., net income plus the net-of-tax return provided to creditors). The computation in Exhibit 11–5, Case B, is:

$$\frac{\$64{,}200 + (\$18{,}000 \times 60\% = \$10{,}800) = \$75{,}000}{\$500{,}000} = \underline{\underline{15\%}}$$

DISADVANTAGES OF ISSUING BONDS

The primary disadvantages of using bonds are that (a) the required interest payments must be made each interest period, and (b) the large principal amount must be paid at maturity date. Sound financing of a business requires a realistic **balance** between the amounts of debt (including bonds payable) and owners' equity (i.e., common and preferred stock and retained earnings). In Case A, there was no debt, which is the most conservative position. In Case B, the $200,000 of debt was 40% of total assets employed (not an unusual case). However, if Spicewood Corporation had $400,000 debt, the 80% debt to total assets would be considered too high in most cases. It would be considered too high because interest payments to bondholders are **fixed charges.** Interest payments legally must be paid each period, whether the corporation earns income or incurs a loss. In contrast, dividends usually are paid to stockholders only if earnings are satisfactory. Each year, some companies go bankrupt because of their inability to make their required interest payments to creditors.

PART B—ADDITIONAL PROBLEMS IN ACCOUNTING FOR BONDS PAYABLE

This part of the chapter discusses four problems commonly encountered in accounting for bonds payable. These problems are (1) accounting for bonds sold between interest dates, (2) adjusting entries for accrued bond interest, (3) bond sinking funds, and (4) effective-interest amortization.

ACCOUNTING FOR BONDS SOLD BETWEEN INTEREST DATES

Although bonds may be sold on an interest date, market factors often cause them to be sold **between interest dates.** The exact amount of interest stated on the bond certificate for each interest date will be paid, regardless of whether a bond is sold on an interest date or between interest dates. Therefore, when bonds are sold between two interest dates, the investor (i.e., the buyer) must pay the interest that has **accrued since the last interest date** in addition to the market price of the bond. The amount of the next interest payment will be for a **full interest period;** therefore, the accrued interest is returned to the buyer. The net effect is that the investor will realize interest revenue only for the number of months the bonds were held from the date of sale. Similarly, the issuing corporation will incur interest expense for the same period. This case presents two complexities in accounting for bonds: (1) the amount of accrued interest charged to the buyer must be included in the journal entry of the issuer to record the sale of bonds; and (2) any premium or discount must be amortized by the issuer over the remaining period that the bonds will be outstanding; that is, the period from date of sale to date of maturity of the bonds.

In this section, we will illustrate the four problems in accounting for bonds with data for Mendez Corporation, given at the top of Exhibit 11–6. Mendez Corporation issued bonds on August 1, 19A, which was two months after the date of the bonds (June 1, 19A). The time scale given in Exhibit 11–6 will be helpful in analyzing the effect of different dates on the accounting for the bond issue.

On August 1, 19A, date of the issuance of the 100 bonds, Mendez Corporation would receive cash for the sale price of the bonds, plus two months' accrued interest (June 1, 19A, to July 31, 19A), computed as follows (refer to the bond time scale, Exhibit 11–6):

Market price (for 100 bonds)	$96,460
Add accrued interest for 2 months (June and July):	
$100,000 × 12% × 2/12	2,000
Total cash received	$98,460

The bond investors must pay two months of accrued interest to Mendez because the bond indenture (contract) requires that Mendez pay a full six months of interest on the next interest date (i.e., November 30). On the first interest date, the bonds will have been outstanding for only four months (August 1 through November 30). Therefore, on November 30, 19A, the investors have earned four months' interest revenue, and the issuer (Mendez) has incurred four months' interest expense. Payment by the investor to the issuer of two months accrued interest when the bonds are purchased is an offset that causes interest to be adjusted to a four-month basis for both the investor and the issuer.

The journal entry for the issuer, Mendez Corporation, to record the issuance of the 100 bonds payable is shown in Exhibit 11–6. In that entry, Bond Interest Expense was credited for $2,000 accrued interest collected because that amount will be refunded to the investor when the next interest payment is made. That interest payment will be recorded as a credit to Cash and a debit to Bond Interest Expense (Exhibit 11–6).

The $3,540 recorded in the Discount on Bonds Payable account is amortized over the **period outstanding** of 118 months. Therefore, straight-line amortization would be $3,540 ÷ 118 months = $30 per month. The entry to record the first interest payment would include **amortization of discount** only for the four months that the bonds have been outstanding. The first interest payment would be recorded as shown in Exhibit 11–6.

After journal entries are made to record the collection of accrued interest (August 1, 19A) and the payment of interest (November 30, 19A), the Bond Interest Expense account will have a debit balance of $4,120. This amount is equivalent to four months' interest (i.e., $100,000 × 12% × 4/12 = $4,000) plus four months' amortization of discount (i.e., $30 × 4 = $120). The Bond Interest Expense account would appear as follows:

Bond Interest Expense

11/30/19A	6,120	8/1/19A	2,000

(Balance, 11/30/19A, $4,120)

ADJUSTING ENTRY FOR ACCRUED BOND INTEREST

In Chapter 10, we discussed the **adjusting entry** that must be made for any interest expense accrued on a note payable since the last interest payment date. The same adjustment procedure must be applied to bonds payable. However, in the case of bonds, the adjusting entry must include **both the accrued interest and amortization of any bond discount or premium.** For example, Mendez Corporation (Exhibit 11–6) recorded an interest payment on November 30, 19A. Therefore, on December 31, 19A, there is accrued interest for one month. Bond discount also must be amortized for one more month. The adjusting entry at December 31, 19A, is shown in Exhibit 11–6.

After the adjusting entry is posted on December 31, 19A, the Bond Interest Expense account will have a debit balance of $5,150. This amount represents interest expense for the five months that the bonds have been outstanding during 19A (August 1 to December 31). The Bond Interest Expense account for 19A is shown at the bottom of Exhibit 11–6. The ending balance of $5,150 can be verified as follows:

Interest: $100,000 × 12% × 5/12	$5,000
Add discount amortized: $30 × 5	150
Total interest expense for 19A	$5,150

Bond Interest Expense is closed to Income Summary at the end of the accounting period and is reported on the 19A income statement. The Bond Discount account for 19A is reported on the balance sheet as follows:

Long-term liabilities:

Bonds payable	$100,000
Less: Discount on Bonds payable . . .	3,390
Carrying value	$ 96,610

BOND SINKING FUNDS

On the maturity date of bonds payable, the issuing company must have available a large amount of cash to pay off the bondholders. A demand for a large amount of cash might place the issuing company in a financial strain. To avoid this situation, some companies create a separate **cash fund** by making

EXHIBIT 11–6

Accounting for bonds sold between interest dates

Situation:

Mendez Corporation approved the following bond issue on June 1, 19A:

Bonds payable authorized, 200 bonds, $1,000 par per bond, 12% interest (payable each May 31 and November 30), maturity in 10 years on May 31, 19J.

Mendez's accounting period ends December 31.

Bonds issued: 100 bonds (par $100,000) issued on August 1, 19A, for $96,460.

Analysis of the situation (graphic time scale):

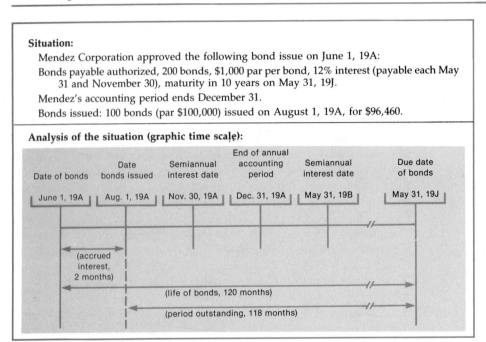

equal annual **contributions** over a period of time in advance of the bond maturity date. This separate cash fund is called a **bond sinking fund.** A bond sinking fund is an asset that is invested pending the due date of the bonds. It is reported on the balance sheet under the caption "Investments and funds."

A bond sinking fund also reduces the risk of nonpayment for the bond-holders. It assures them that funds will be available for retirement of the bonds at their maturity date. Each cash contribution to the fund is deposited with an **independent trustee** (a designated third party such as bank or another financial institution). The trustee invests the funds and adds the fund earnings to the fund balance each year. Interest earned on a sinking fund is recorded as an increase in the fund balance (a debit) and as interest revenue (a credit). Thus, a bond sinking fund has the characteristics of a savings account as shown in Chapter 10, Part B. At the maturity date of the bonds, the balance of the fund is used to pay the bondholders. Any excess cash is returned to the issuing corporation, or in the case of a deficit, it is made up by the issuer.

___ **EXHIBIT 11–6** *(concluded)* ___

Accounting for bonds sold between interest dates

Current 19A entries for bonds sold between interest dates:

August 1, 19A—Issuance of the bonds (par $100,000) for $96,460 plus two months accrued interest prior to issuance date, $2,000.

Cash ($96,460 + $2,000)	98,460	
Discount on bonds payable ($100,000 − $96,460)	3,540	
Bonds payable (100 bonds × $1,000 par)		100,000
*Bonds interest expense ($100,000 × 12% × 2/12)		2,000

    * This could be Bond Interest Payable.

November 30, 19A—First interest payment (issue date to maturity date, 118 months):

Bond interest expense (cash paid + amortized discount)	6,120	
Discount on bonds payable (straight-line;		
$3,540 × 4/118 mos.)		120
Cash ($100,000 × 6%)		6,000

Adjusting entry (end of the accounting period):

December 31, 19A—For 1 month interest since last interest date:

Bond interest expense ($1,000 + $30 amortization)	1,030	
Discount on bonds payable (straight-line;		
$3,540 × 1/118 mos.)		30
Bond interest payable ($100,000 × 12% × 1/12)		1,000

T-accounts for 19A:

Bond Interest Expense				Discount on Bonds Payable			
11/30/19A	6,120	8/1/19A	2,000	8/1/19A	3,540	11/30/19A	120
12/31/19A	1,030					12/31/19A	30

(Balance 12/31/19A, $5,150; close to In-come Summary and report on income statement.)

(Balance 12/31/19A, $3,390; report on bal-ance sheet as a deduction (contra) to Bonds payable.)

Exhibit 11–7 illustrates a bond sinking fund for Mendez Corporation. The fund will be built up over the last five years that the bonds are outstanding by making five equal annual deposits each May 31, starting in 19F. The sinking fund contributions will be deposited with City Bank, as trustee, which will pay 8% annual interest on the fund balance each May 31. The amount of each deposit required can be calculated using the time value of money concepts discussed and illustrated in Chapter 10, Part B. If the fund earned no interest, each deposit would have to be $20,000 (i.e., $100,000 ÷ 5 contributions = $20,000). Instead of $20,000, the annual deposit required is **less** than $20,000

EXHIBIT 11-7

Accounting for a bond sinking fund

Situation:

Mendez Corporation plans to accumulate a bond sinking fund sufficient to retire the $100,000 bond issue outstanding on maturity date, May 31, 19J (see Exhibit 11–6). Five equal annual deposits are to be made on each May 31, starting in 19F. Expected earning rate on the fund is 8%.

Computation of perodic deposits ($n = 5$, years F through J; $i = 8\%$):

Computation (application of future value of annuity of $1):

Future value = Periodic rent $\times$ $F_{n=5;\ i=8\%}$

Substituting:

$100,000 = \quad ? \quad \times 5.8666$ (Table 10–3)

Periodic rent = $100,000 \div 5.8666

= $\underline{\$\ 17,046}$

Entries—for first year of the fund and the second deposit:

May 31,19F—To record the first deposit by Mendez:

Bond sinking fund	17,046	
Cash (computed above)		17,046

May 31, 19G—To record interest revenue for 1 year added to the fund:

Bond sinking fund (notice, not the cash account)	1,364	
Interest revenue ($17,046 $\times$ 8%)		1,364

May 31, 19G—To record the second deposit by Mendez:

Bond sinking fund	17,046	
Cash (computed above)		17,046

Entry at maturity date, (May 31, 19J) to retire the bonds:

Bonds payable	100,000	
Bond sinking fund		100,000

Sinking fund accumulation schedule (Deposits, $17,046; $n = 5$; $i = 8\%$):

Date	Cash Deposit (Credit Cash)	Interest Revenue (Credit)	Fund Increase (Debit Fund)	Accumulated Fund Balance
5/31/19F	17,046[a]		17,046	17,046
5/31/19G	17,046	17,046 $\times$ 8% = 1,364[b]	18,410[c]	35,456[d]
5/31/19H	17,046	35,456 $\times$ 8% = 2,836	19,882	55,338
5/31/19I	17,046	55,338 $\times$ 8% = 4,427	21,473	76,811
5/31/19J	17,046	76,811 $\times$ 8% = 6,143*	23,189	100,000
Totals	85,230	14,770	100,000	

* Rounded $2 to accommodate prior rounding errors.

[a] Computed above.

[b] Interest earned on beginning balance in the fund each period at 8 percent.

[c] Periodic deposit ($17,046) plus interest earned ($1,364) = $18,410 (etc.)

[d] Prior balance ($17,046) plus increase in fund ($18,410) = $35,456 (etc.).

Note: This is an ordinary annuity, i.e., end-of-period contributions.

because the interest earned each year will be added to the fund balance. The $17,046 required annual deposit was computed as shown in Exhibit 11–7.[3]

The journal entries for May 31, 19F, and 19G, for the sinking fund are shown in Exhibit 11–7. Notice that the fund is increased by both the annual deposits and the accumulation of interest. Identical journal entries with different interest amounts would be made for each of the five years of the accumulation period. The interest amounts increase each year because of the increasing balance in the fund. At the maturity date of the bonds, payment will be made to the bond-holders using the cash accumulated in the sinking fund. The journal entry to retire the bonds payable is shown in Exhibit 11–7.

Often it is useful to prepare a fund accumulation schedule as shown in Exhibit 11–7. Notice that the schedule provides data for (1) the entry on each interest date and (2) the buildup of the fund to maturity date.

EFFECTIVE-INTEREST AMORTIZATION
OF BOND DISCOUNT AND PREMIUM

Amortization of bond discount and premium, using the straight-line method, was discussed in Part A (page 568). Another method is called **effective-interest amortization.** This method uses the **present value** (Chapter 10, Part B) to compute the periodic amortization amounts. The concept underlying the effective-interest method is that **interest expense each period is the unpaid balance of the liability multiplied by the effective interest rate (not the stated rate) for the bonds.**

APB Opinion 21, "Interest on Receivables and Payables," **requires effective-interest amortization of bond discounts or premiums. However, the straight-line approach is permitted when the difference in periodic amortization results between the two methods is not material in amount.** Conceptually, the effective-interest method is similar to the debt repayment which was discussed in Chapter 10. Each equal payment made on the debt has two parts: (1) a payment of principal and (2) a payment of interest.

Exhibit 11–8 shows an application of the effective-interest method. The sale price of the West Corporation bonds is the present value of the future cash flows associated with the bonds. The difference between the total par value of the bonds ($10,000) and the present value of the bonds ($8,558) is the discount ($1,442) which must be amortized over the life of the bonds. First, the journal entry to record the issuance of the bonds is shown in Exhibit 11–8.

When the effective-interest amortization method is used, the amount of interest expense and the amount of discount or premium that is amortized **change** each interest period. The amount of cash interest paid does not change

---

[3] A company also may restrict, or appropriate, an equivalent amount of retained earnings as a dividend restriction. Restrictions of retained earnings by a corporation are discussed in Chapter 12.

EXHIBIT 11–8

Effective-interest amortization on bond discount

Situation: West company sold ten, $1,000 bonds as follows:

Bonds payable authorized (10 bonds at $1,000 par each) $10,000
Date printed on each bond . . . .   January 1, 19A
Maturity date (five-year term from January 1, 19A) . . . . December 31, 19E
Interest, **cash payable per annum** each December 31, 8% $800
Issued (sold) all of the bonds . . . .   January 1, 19A
Market interest rate 12%
Sale price (at a discount) $8,558*
End of the accounting period for West . . . .   December 31

   * Issue price computed as follows:
      $10,000 × $p_{n=5;\ i=12\%}$ (Table 10–2; 0.5674) = $5,674
      $800 × $P_{n=5;\ i=12\%}$ (Table 10–4; 3.6048)   = 2,884
                                                          $8,558

Entry to record issuance (sale) of the bonds at a discount:

January 1, 19A:

   Cash (computed above) 8,558
   Discount on bonds payable ($10,000 − $8,558) 1,442
       Bonds payable (10 bonds × $1,000 par)   10,000

Bond payment schedule, effective-interest amortization:

(a) Date	(b) Cash Interest Paid on Each Interest Date ($10,000 × 8%)	(c) Interest Expense (based on beginning unpaid liability at market rate of 12%)	(d) Effective- Interest Amortization (increase of liability)*	(e) Net Liability (unpaid balance)
1/1/19A				8,558
12/31/19A	800	8,558 × 12% = 1,027	227	8,785
12/31/19B	800	8,785 × 12% = 1,054	254	9,039
12/31/19C	800	9,039 × 12% = 1,085	285	9,324
12/31/19D	800	9,324 × 12% = 1,119	319	9,643
12/31/19E	800	9,643 × 12% = 1,157	357	10,000
Subtotal	4,000	5,442	1,442	
12/31/19E	10,000†		10,000	–0–

   * Adjusts the net liability to the maturity amount.
   † Payment of principal.

_____   **EXHIBIT 11–8** *(concluded)* _____

Effective-interest amortization on bond discount

Periodic entries to record interest paid and discount amortization, December 31:	19A	19B	19C	19D	19E
Bond interest expense	1,027	1,054	1,085	1,119	1,157
Discount on bonds payable	227	254	285	319	357
Cash	800	800	800	800	800

Financial statements:	19A	19B	19C	19D	19E
Income statement:					
Bond interest expense	$1,027	$1,054	$1,085	$1,119	$1,157
Balance sheet:					
Bonds payable (maturity amount, $10,000) minus unamortized discount	8,785	9,039	9,324	9,643	–0–

because it is based on the stated rate of interest that is stated on the bond. The amounts for each journal entry to record the payment of interest must be recomputed for each interest period. An organized approach to this computation is based on the preparation of a **debt payment schedule.** Notice that for each period, the first computation is interest expense (Exhibit 11–8, Col. c). It is computed by using the **effective** interest rate. The schedule provides the amortization and interest expense amounts that must be recorded each interest period, as shown in Exhibit 11–8. The journal entries to record periodic interest are based on the amounts in the debt payment schedule. The journal entries for West Corporation are illustrated in Exhibit 11–8.

The effective-interest amortization method is preferred conceptually because it multiplies the **unpaid liability balance** by the effective interest rate to compute periodic interest expense. The amortization amount then is computed as the difference between interest expense and the cash interest paid. For example, West Corporation borrowed $8,558 on January 1, 19A, at a market interest rate of 12%. The interest expense for the first year should be $1,027 (i.e., 12% × $8,558 = $1,027) which is the amount recorded in the journal entry for 19A, in Exhibit 11–8. In contrast, if the straight-line method had been used, the amortization of the bond discount would have been $288 (i.e., $1,442 ÷ 5 = $288), and interest expense would have been $1,088 (i.e., $288 + $800 = $1,088).

To summarize, effective-interest amortization conceptually is superior to straight-line amortization. For each period, consistent with the issue price of the bonds, it measures (1) the true amount of interest expense each period on the income statement and (2) the true current net carrying amount of the bonds outstanding (net liability) on the balance sheet each period. In contrast, straight-line amortization gives approximations of these amounts and can be used only when the difference between the two methods is deemed not material (refer to threshold for recognition, materiality). In such cases, straight-line amortization often is used because it is less complex.

DEMONSTRATION CASE

(Try to resolve the requirements before proceeding to the suggested solution that follows.)

To raise funds to build a new plant, the management of Reed Company issued bonds. A bond indenture was approved by the board of directors. Some provisions in the bond indenture and specified on the bond certificates were:

Par value of the bonds ($1,000 bonds) $600,000
Date of bond issue—February 1, 19A, due in 10 years on January 31, 19K.
Interest—10% per annum, payable 5% on each July 31 and January 31.

All of the bonds were sold on June 1, 19A, at 102½, plus accrued interest. The annual accounting period for Reed Company ends on December 31.

Required:

a. How much cash was received by Reed Company from the sale of the bonds payable on June 1, 19A? Show computations.
b. What was the amount of premium on the bonds payable? Over how many months should it be amortized?
c. Compute the amount of amortization of premium per month and for each six-month interest period; use straight-line amortization. Round to the nearest dollar.
d. Give the journal entry on June 1, 19A, to record the sale and issuance of the bonds payable.
e. Give the journal entry for payment of interest and amortization of premium for the first interest payment on July 31, 19A.
f. Give the adjusting entry required on December 31, 19A, at the end of the accounting period.
g. Give the optional reversing entry that could be made on January 1, 19B.
h. Give the journal entry to record the second interest payment and the amortization of premium on January 31, 19B.
i. Show how bond interest expense and bonds payable is reported on the financial statements at December 31, 19A.

Suggested Solution

Requirement a:

Sale price of the bonds: ($600,000 × 102.5%)	$615,000
Add accrued interest for four months (February 1 to May 31)	
($600,000 × 10% × 4/12)	20,000
Total cash received for the bonds	$635,000

Requirement b:

Premium on the bonds payable ($600,000 × 2.5%)	$ 15,000
Months amortized: From date of sale, June 1, 19A, to maturity date,	
January 31, 19K (120 months − 4 months)	116 months

Requirement c:

Premium amortization: $15,000 ÷ 116 months = $129 per month, or $774 each six-month interest period (straight-line).

Requirement d:

June 1, 19A (issuance date):

Cash (per Requirement [a] above)	635,000	
Premium on bonds payable (per Requirement [b] above)		15,000
Interest expense (per Requirement [a] above)		20,000
Bonds payable		600,000
To record sale of bonds payable at 102½ plus accrued interest for four months, February 1 to May 31, 19A.		

Requirement e:

July 31, 19A (first interest payment date):

Bond interest expense ($30,000 − $258)	29,742	
Premium on bonds payable ($129 × 2 months)	258	
Cash ($600,000 × 5%)		30,000
To record payment of semiannual interest and to amortize premium for two months, June 1 to July 31, 19A.		

Requirement f:

December 31, 19A (end of the accounting period):

Bond interest expense	24,355	
Premium on bonds payable ($129 × 5 months)	645	
Bond interest payable ($600,000 × 10% × 5/12)		25,000
Adjusting entry for five months' interest accrued plus amortization of premium, August 1 to December 31, 19A.		

Requirement g:

January 1, 19B (reversing entry):

Bond interest payable	25,000	
Premium on bonds payable		645
Bonds interest expense		24,355
Reversing entry; optional.		

Requirement h:

January 31, 19B (second interest date and assuming reversing entry [g] was made):[4]

Bond interest expense	29,226	
Premium on bonds payable (per Requirement [c])	774	
Cash ($600,000 × 10% × 6/12)		30,000
To record payment of semiannual interest and to amortize premium for six months.		

---

[4] If no reversing entry was made on January 1, 19B, this entry would be:

Bond interest payable	25,000	
Premium on bonds payable	129	
Bond interest expense	4,871	
Cash		30,000

Requirement i:

Interest expense reported on the 19A income statement should be for the period outstanding during the year (i.e., for seven months, June 1 through December 31). Interest expense, per the above entries, is $29,742 + $24,355 − $20,000 = $34,097; or alternatively, ($600,000 × 10% × 7/12 = $35,000) − ($129 × 7 months = $903) = $34,097.

Income statement for 19A:

Interest expense	$ 34,097

Balance sheet, December 31, 19A:

Long-term liabilities:

Bonds payable, 10% (due January 31, 19K)	$600,000	
Add unamortized premium*	14,097	614,097

* $15,000 − ($258 + $645) = $14,097.

SUMMARY OF CHAPTER

This chapter discussed bonds payable, which represent a primary way to obtain funds to acquire long-term assets and to expand a business. An important advantage of bonds payable is that the **cost** of borrowing the funds—interest expense—is deductible for income tax purposes which reduces the interest cost to the business.

Bonds may be sold at their par (or face) amount, at a premium, or at a discount, depending upon the stated interest rate on the bonds compared with the market (or yield) rate of interest that the bond buyers demand and the issuer will accept. In each case, bonds are measured, recorded, and reported at their current cash equivalent amount. The price of a bond varies based on the relationship between the market and stated rates of interest. If the market rate is higher than the stated rate on the bond, the bonds will sell at a discount. Conversely, if the market rate is lower than the stated rate on the bond, the bonds will sell at a premium.

Discounts and premiums on bonds payable are adjustments of the cash interest payments made by the issuing company during the term of the bonds. Therefore, discount or premium on bonds payable is amortized to interest expense over the period outstanding from issue date to maturity date.

To assure that funds are available to retire bonds payable at maturity, a company may set aside cash in advance by means of periodic contributions to a bond sinking fund. Such a fund is like a savings account. The bond sinking fund usually is administered by an independent trustee. Interest earned on the fund balance is added to the fund each period. At the maturity date of the bonds, the fund is used to pay the bondholders. The fund is reported on the balance sheet under the caption "Investments and funds." Interest earned on the fund is reported on the income statement as "Interest revenue."

IMPORTANT TERMS DEFINED IN THIS CHAPTER

Terms (alphabetically)	Key words in definitions of important terms used in chapter	Page reference
Bond certificate	The bond document; an example is given in Exhibit 11–1.	561
Bond discount	A bond that is sold for less than par is sold at a discount; the difference between selling price and par.	565
Bond premium	A bond that is sold for more than par is sold at a premium; the difference between selling price and par.	568
Bond principal	The amount payable at the maturity of the bond; face amount.	560
Bond sinking fund	A cash fund accumulated for payment of a bond upon maturity.	575
Callable bond	A bond that may be called for early retirement at the option of the issuer.	563
Convertible bond	A bond that may be converted to other securities of the issuer (usually common stock).	563
Coupon rate of interest	The stated rate of interest on coupon bonds.	562
Debenture	An unsecured bond; no assets are specifically pledged to guarantee repayment.	563
Effective-interest rate	Another name for the market rate of interest on a bond when issued; also called the yield rate.	562
Effective-interest amortization	Theoretically preferred method to amortize a bond discount or premium; interest expense is based on the effective interest rate.	579
Face amount	Another name for principal or the principal amount of a bond.	560
Financial leverage	Use of borrowed funds to increase the rate of return on owners' equity; occurs when the interest rate on debt is lower than the earnings rate on total assets.	571
Indenture	A bond contract that specifies the legal provisions of a bond issue.	563
Market interest rate	Current rate of interest on a debt when incurred; also called yield or effective rate.	562
Net interest cost	Interest cost, less any income tax savings associated with interest expense.	571
Par value	Another name for bond principal or the maturity amount of a bond.	560
Redeemable bond	Bond that may be turned in for early retirement at the option of the bondholder.	563
Stated rate	The rate of cash interest per period specified in the bond contract.	560
Straight-line amortization	Simplified method to amortize a bond discount or premium.	568
Trustee	An independent party appointed to represent the bondholders.	576
Yield interest rate	Another name for the market rate of interest on a bond.	562

QUESTIONS

PART A

1. What are the primary characteristics of a bond? For what purposes are bonds usually issued?

2. What is the difference between a bond indenture and a bond certificate?

3. Distinguish between secured and unsecured bonds.

4. Distinguish among callable, redeemable, and convertible bonds.

5. Distinguish between registered and coupon bonds.

6. From the perspective of the issuer, what are some advantages of issuing bonds, as compared with issuing capital stock?

7. As the tax rate increases, the net cost of borrowing money decreases. Explain.

8. Explain financial leverage. Can financial leverage be negative?

9. At the date of issuance, bonds are recorded at their current cash equivalent amount. Explain.

10. What is the nature of the discount and premium on bonds payable? Explain.

11. What is the difference between the stated interest rate and the effective interest rate on a bond?

12. Distinguish between the stated and effective rates of interest on a bond (a) sold at par, (b) sold at a discount, and (c) sold at a premium.

13. Why are bond discounts and premiums amortized over the outstanding life of the related bonds payable rather than the period from the date of the bonds to their maturity date?

14. What is the carrying value of a bond payable?

PART B

15. Why is the lender (i.e., the purchaser of a bond) charged for the accrued interest from the last interest date to the date of purchase of the bonds?

16. If a 10-year bond dated January 1, 19A, is sold on April 1, 19B, how many months is used as the period outstanding for amortizing any bond premium or discount?

17. What is a bond sinking fund? How should a bond sinking fund be reported in the financial statements?

18. Explain the basic difference between straight-line amortization and effective-interest amortization of bond discount or premium. Explain when each method should, or may, be used.

EXERCISES

PART A

E11–1   (Pair Definitions with Terms)

Match the brief definitions given below with the terms by entering the code letters in the blank spaces provided.

Term	*Brief definition (or statement)*
<u> D </u> (1) Secured bonds (example)	A. Amount payable at due date (other than interest).
_____ (2) Principal of a bond	B. An individual or company that is engaged by bond issuers to sell bonds.
_____ (3) Stated interest rate on a bond	C. Arises when a bond is sold for less than its par amount.
_____ (4) Trustee (related to a bond issue)	D. Bond supported by a mortgage on specified assets.
_____ (5) Par value of a bond	E. Same as the face or maturity amount of a bond.
_____ (6) Bond premium	F. The amount of cash interest that must be paid regardless of its issue price.
_____ (7) Carrying value of a bond	G. An independent party appointed to represent bondholders.
_____ (8) Bond indenture	H. Same as the market or yield rate of interest on a bond.
_____ (9) Underwriter	I. Arises when a bond is sold for more than its par amount.
_____ (10) Bond discount	J. A contract that specifies the legal provisions of a bond issue.
_____ (11) Financial leverage	K. Present value of the future cash flows related to a bond.
_____ (12) Primary disadvantage of bonds payable	L. A bond sold at its par value.
_____ (13) Present and par value of a bond are the same	M. Issue price of a bond less any amortized premium or plus any amortized discount.
_____ (14) Effective interest rate	N. Net interest rate on debt is different from interest rate earned on total assets.
_____ (15) Bond issue or selling price	O. Cash payments of interest and principle required, regardless of income or loss.

E11–2   (Pair Bond Characteristics with Bond Classifications)

Match the following bond characteristics with the bond classifications by entering the answer codes in the spaces provided.

Bond classification	*Bond characteristics*
<u> E </u> (1) Serial bonds (example)	A. Bonds with parts attached that are turned in to receive interest.
_____ (2) Unsecured bonds	B. Bonds that are retired early upon request of the issuer.
_____ (3) Convertible bonds	C. The principal amount is payable at a single maturity date.
_____ (4) Ordinary bonds	D. Bonds that may be turned in for early retirement at the option of the bondholders.
_____ (5) Coupon bonds	E. Principal amount is payable in installments.
_____ (6) Redeemable bonds	F. Do not include a mortgage on specific assets.
_____ (7) Registered bonds	G. Bonds that include pledged assets to assure payment at maturity.
_____ (8) Callable bonds	H. Bonds that may be exchanged for other securities at the option of the bondholder.
_____ (9) Secured bonds	I. Interest payments are made by check directly to the bondholders on each interest date.

E11–3   **(Compute Issue Prices of Bonds for Three Cases; Record Bond Issuances)**

Felix Corporation is planning to issue $300,000, five-year, 10% bonds. Interest is payable semiannually each June 30 and December 31. All of the bonds will be sold on January 1, 19A. The bonds mature on December 31, 19E.

Required (round to the nearest 10 dollars):

a. Compute the issue (sale) price on January 1, 19A, for each of the following three independent cases (show computations):

   Case A—The market (yield) rate is 10%.
   Case B—The market (yield) rate is 8%.
   Case C—The market (yield) rate is 12%.

b. Give the journal entry to record the issuance for each case.

E11–4   **(Record Bond Issue and First Interest Payment, with Discount; Verify Issue Price)**

On January 1, 19A, Century corporation sold a $300,000, 7% bond issue for $279,872 (8% market rate). The bonds were dated January 1, 19A, and pay interest each December 31. The bonds mature 10 years from January 1, 19A.

Required:

a. Give the journal entry to record the issuance of the bonds.
b. Give the journal entry to record the interest payment on December 31, 19A. Assume straight-line amortization.
c. Show how the bond interest expense and the bonds payable should be reported on the December 31, 19A, annual financial statements.
d. Verify the sale price of $279,872 (show computations).

E11–5   **(Record Bond Issue and First Interest Payment, with Premium; Show Reporting and Verify the Issue Price)**

Star Corporation sold a $150,000, 10% bond issue on January 1, 19A, for $159,626 (at a market rate of 9%). The bonds were dated January 1, 19A, and interest is paid each December 31. The bonds mature 10 years from January 1, 19A.

Required (round to the nearest dollar):

a. Give the journal entry to record the issuance of the bonds.
b. Give the journal entry for the interest payment on December 31, 19A. Assume straight-line amortization.
c. Show how the bond interest expense and the bonds payable should be reported on the December 31, 19A, annual financial statements.
d. Verify the issue (sale) price (show computations).

E11–6   **(Analysis to Determine Bond Issue Price and Stated Interest Rate; Entries for Issuance and Interest)**

FAB Corporation had $200,000, 10-year, coupon bonds outstanding on December 31, 19A (end of the accounting period). Interest is payable each December 31. The bonds were issued (sold) on January 1, 19A. The 19A annual financial statements showed the following:

> **Income statement:**
> Bond interest expense (straight-line amortization) .... $ 18,600
>
> **Balance sheet:**
> Bonds payable (net liability) 194,600

Required (show computations):

a. What was the issue price of the bonds? Give the issuance entry.

b. What was the coupon rate on the bonds? Give the entry to record 19A interest.

E11–7   (Cash Borrowed; Analyze Financing Cost (Net of Tax) and Determine Financial Leverage)
On January 1, 19A, Snappy Corporation borrowed $120,000 on a three-year note payable. The interest rate is 10% per annum, payable each year-end. The company computed its return on total assets [i.e., Net income ÷ (Liabilities + Owners' equity)] to be 20%. The average income tax rate for the company is 40%.

Required:

a. What amount of interest would be paid for 19A?

b. Considering the effect of income tax, what would be the net interest cost and the net interest rate (net of income tax)?

c. Would financial leverage be present in this situation? Explain.

d. List two primary advantages to Snappy Corporation in favor of the note payable versus selling more of its unissued capital stock to obtain needed funds.

PART B

E11–8   (Accrued Interest on Bond Issue Date; Record Issuance; Reporting at Year-End)
Nevada Corporation authorized the issuance of $300,000, 9%, 10-year bonds. The bonds are dated January 1, 19A. The interest is payable each June 30 and December 31.
On September 1, 19A, the company issued (sold) $200,000 of the bonds at 96 plus any accrued interest. The accounting period ends December 31.

Required:

a. How much cash did Nevada Corporation receive on September 1, 19A? Show computations.

b. Give the journal entry to record the issuance.

c. How much interest expense should be reported on the 19A income statement? Use straight-line amortization.

d. Show how the bonds should be reported on the 19A balance sheet.

E11–9   (Accrued Interest on Bond Issue Date; Straight-Line Amortization; Reporting)
White Corporation issued the following bonds:

> Bonds payable authorized $60,000
> Date on each bond .... Jan. 1, 19A
> Maturity date (10 years) .... Dec. 31, 19J
> Interest, 10% per year, payable each December 31.

White sold all of the bonds on March 1, 19A, and received $62,180 cash which included the accrued interest.

Required:

a. What was the amount of accrued interest and the discount or premium on issuance date?

b. Over what period of time should the discount or premium be amortized?

c. What would be the amortization amount per month assuming straight-line amortization?

d. Give the journal entry to record the issuance.

e. Give the journal entry on first interest payment date.

f. What amount should be reported as interest expense for 19A?

g. What amount of net liability should be shown on the balance sheet at December 31, 19A?

E11–10 **(Accrued Interest on Issuance Date; Recording and Reporting Issuance and Interest)**
Dopuch Corporation issued $10,000, 9% bonds dated April 1, 19A. Interest is paid each March 31. The bonds mature in three years on March 31, 19D. The bonds were sold on June 1, 19A, for $9,660 plus any accrued interest. The accounting period ends each December 31.

Required:

a. Give the journal entry to record the bond issuance on June 1, 19A.

b. Give the adjusting entry required on December 31, 19A. Use straight-line amortization.

c. What amount of interest expense should be reported on the income statement for 19A?

d. Show how the bonds should be reported on the balance sheet at December 31, 19A?

e. Give the journal entry to record the first interest payment on March 31, 19B.

E11–11 **(Accounting and Reporting for a Bond Sinking Fund; Compute the Annual Contribution Needed)**
Tower Corporation has a $100,000 bond issue outstanding that is due four years hence. It wants to set up a bond sinking fund for this amount by making five equal annual contributions. The first contribution will be made immediately (December 31, 19X1) and the last one on the due date (i.e., an ordinary annuity). The corporation will deposit the annual contributions with a trustee who will increase the fund at the end of each year at 8% on the fund balance that existed at the beginning of the year.

Required:

a. Compute the required annual contribution (rent) to the fund.

b. Give the journal entry for the first and second contributions, including interest.

c. Show how the effects of the fund would be reported on the financial statements at the end of the second year.

d. Give the entry to pay the bondholders at maturity date assuming the bond sinking has the exact amount needed.

E11–12 **(Accounting and Reporting for a Bond Sinking Fund; Fund Accumulation Schedule; Entries)**
Small Company has a $90,000 debt that will be due at the end of three years. The management will deposit three equal year-end amounts of $27,723 in a debt retirement

fund (i.e., an ordinary annuity). The fund balance will earn 8% interest which will be added to the fund at each year-end.

Required:

a. Prepare a fund accumulation schedule similar to Exhibit 11–7. Round to the nearest dollar and show computations.
b. Give the journal entry(s) at the end of the second year to record the increase in the fund.
c. Show how the $27,723 was computed.
d. Did the earnings on the fund increase the balance of the company's cash account? Explain.

E11–13   (Analyze a Bond Amortization Schedule; Reporting Bonds Payable)
Jolly Corporation issued a $1,000 bond on January 1, 19A. The bond specified an interest rate of 8% payable at the end of each year. The bond matures at the end of 19C. It was sold at a market rate of 9% per year. The following schedule was completed:

	Cash	Interest	Amortization	Balance
Jan. 1, 19A (issuance)				$ 975
End of Year A	$80	$88	$8	983
End of Year B	80	88	8	991
End of Year C	80	89	9	1,000

Required:

a. What was the issue price of the bond?
b. Did the bond sell at a discount or a premium? How much was the premium or discount?
c. What amount of cash was paid each year for bond interest?
d. What amount of interest expense should be shown each year on the income statement?
e. What amount(s) should be shown on the balance sheet for bonds payable at each year-end (for Year C, show the balance just before retirement of the bond)?
f. What method of amortization was used?
g. Show how the following amounts were computed for Year B: (1) $80, (2) $88, (3) $8, and (4) $991.
h. Is the method of amortization that was used preferable? Explain why.

E11–14   (Prepare a Debt Payment Schedule with Effective-Interest Amortization; Entries)
Butle Company issued a $10,000, 11%, three-year bond on January 1, 19A. The bond interest is paid each December 31. The bond was sold to yield 10% (issue price, $10,249).

Required:

a. Complete a bond payment schedule. Use the effective-interest method.
b. Give the interest and amortization entry at the end of 19A, 19B, and 19C.
c. Show how the $10,249 issue price was computed.

PROBLEMS

PART A

P11-1   **(Bonds Issued at Par, Discount, and Premium Compared; Entries and Reporting)**
To get cash to purchase operational assets, Solect Corporation, whose annual accounting period ends on December 31, issued the following bonds:

Date of bonds: January 1, 19A.
Maturity amount and date: $100,000 due in 10 years (December 31, 19J).
Interest: 11% per annum payable each December 31.
Date sold: January 1, 19A.

Required:

a. Give the journal entry to record the issuance and the first two interest payments under each of three different independent cases (assume straight-line amortization):

Case A: The bonds sold at par.
Case B: The bonds sold at 96.
Case C: The bonds sold at 104.

b. Provide the following amounts to be reported on the 19A financial statements:

	Case A	Case B	Case C
1. Interest expense	$_____	$_____	$_____
2. Bonds payable	_____	_____	_____
3. Unamortized premium or discount	_____	_____	_____
4. Net liability	_____	_____	_____
5. Stated rate of interest	_____	_____	_____
6. Cash interest paid	_____	_____	_____

c. Explain why items 1 and 6 are different in Requirement *(b)*.

P11-2   **(Compute Issue Price of Bonds; Record Issuance and Interest Payments; Reporting)**
Ward Company issued bonds with the following provisions:

Maturity value: $300,000.
Interest: 11% per annum payable semiannually each June 30 and December 31.
Terms: Bonds dated January 1, 19A, due five years from that date.

The annual accounting period for Ward ends December 31. The bonds were sold on January 1, 19A, at a 10% market rate.

Required:

a. Compute the issue (sale) price of the bonds (show computations).
b. Give the journal entry to record issuance of the bonds.
c. Give the journal entries at the following dates (use straight-line amortization): June 30, 19A; December 31, 19A; and June 30, 19B.
d. How much interest expense would be reported on the income statement for 19A? Show how the liability related to the bonds should be reported on the December 31, 19A, balance sheet.

P11-3 **(A Comprehensive Analysis of the Issuance of Bonds at Par, Discount, and Premium; No Entries)**

On January 1, 19A, Beckwith Corporation sold and issued $100,000, 8%, five-year bonds. The bond interest is payable annually each December 31. Assume the bonds were sold under three separate and independent cases: Case A, at par; Case B, at 95; and Case C, at 105.

Required:

a. Complete a schedule similar to the following for each separate case assuming straight-line amortization of discount and premium. Disregard income tax. Give all dollar amounts in thousands.

	At Start of 19A	At End of 19A	At End of 19B	At End of 19C	At End of 19D	At End of 19E Prior to Payment of Principal	At End of 19E Payment of Principal
Case A—Sold at par (100): Pretax cash inflow	$	$	$	$	$	$	$
Pretax cash outflow							
Interest expense on income statement							
Net liability on balance sheet							
Case B—Sold at a discount (95): Pretax cash inflow							
Pretax cash outflow							
Interest expense on income statement							
Net liability on balance sheet							
Case C—Sold at a premium (105): Pretax cash inflow							
Pretax cash outflow							
Interest expense on income statement							
Net liability on balance sheet							

b. For each separate case, calculate each of the following:
   (1) Total pretax cash outflow.
   (2) Total pretax cash inflow.
   (3) Difference—net pretax cash outflow.
   (4) Total pretax interest expense.
c. (1) Explain why the net pretax cash outflows differ among the three cases.
   (2) For each case, explain why the net pretax cash outflow is the same amount as total interest expense.

P11–4   **(Analysis of Differences Among Bonds Issued at Par, Discount, and Premium; Issuance and Interest Entries)**

Southwick Corporation sold a $200,000, 8% bond issue on January 1, 19A. The bonds pay interest each December 31, and will mature 10 years from January 1, 19A. For comparative study and analysis, assume three separate cases. Use straight-line amortization, and disregard income tax unless specifically required.

Case A—The bonds sold at par.
Case B—The bonds sold at 97.
Case C—The bonds sold at 103.

Required:

a. Complete the following schedule to analyze the differences among the three cases.

	Case A (par)	Case B (at 97)	Case C (at 103)
1. Cash inflow at issue (sale) date			
2. Total cash outflow through maturity date			
3. Difference—total interest expense			
Income statement for 19A:			
4. Bond interest expense, pretax			
Balance sheet at December 31, 19A:			
Long-term liabilities:			
5. Bonds payable, 8%			
6. Unamortized discount			
7. Unamortized premium			
8. Net liability			
9. Stated interest rate			
10. Total interest expense, net of income tax (40% tax rate)			

b. Give the journal entries for each case on January 1, 19A, and December 31, 19A (excluding closing entries).
c. For each case, explain why the amounts in items 3, 4, and 10 of Requirement *(a)* are the same, or different.

P11–5   **(Computation and Explanation of Financial Leverage)**

The 19A financial statements of Little Corporation provided the following data:

Balance sheet:
Total assets $100,000
Total liabilities 60,000
Total stockholders' equity 40,000

Income statement:

Total revenues	$150,000
Total expenses (including pretax interest)	135,000
Pretax income	15,000
Income tax ($15,000 × 20%)	3,000
Net income	$ 12,000

Required (round to nearest percent):

a. Compute the following:
   (1) Return on stockholders' equity.
   (2) Return on total assets.
   (3) Financial leverage.
b. Is the financial leverage positive or negative? Explain.

P11–6   **(Compute, Interpret, and Compare Financial Leverage for Two Companies in the Same Industry)**

The information given below is from the 19B annual financial statements of two competing companies in the same industry. Each company had 50,000 shares of common stock outstanding.

	Thousands of dollars	
	Company A	Company B
Balance sheet:		
Total assets	$900	$900
Total liabilities (10% interest)	400	600
Income statement:		
Total revenues	480	421
Total expenses (including income tax)	300	400
Income tax rate	40%	20%

Required:

a. Complete a tabulation similar to the following (show computations):

Item	Company A	Company B
Earnings per share		
Return on stockholders' equity		
Return on total assets		
Financial leverage		

b. Interpret and compare the financial leverage figures for the two companies.

PART B

P11–7   **(Recording and Reporting Bonds Issued between Interest Dates)**

On January 1, 19A, Instate Corporation authorized $500,000, five-year, 10%, bonds payable. The bonds are dated January 1, 19A, and pay semiannual interest each June 30 and December 31. The accounting period ends December 31.

On March 31, 19A, $300,000 of the bonds were sold at 103.

Required (round to the nearest dollar):

a. Give the journal entry to record the issuance of the bonds on March 31, 19A.

b. Give all of the interest entries (excluding closing entries) required during 19A. Use straight-line amortization.

c. Give the amounts that should be reported on the 19A financial statements for:
   (1) Interest expense.
   (2) Bonds payable.
   (3) Unamortized discount or premium.
   (4) Net liability.

d. What would be the 19A aftertax net interest cost (dollars) assuming a 30% income tax rate?

P11–8 **(Bonds Sold at Par, Discount, and Premium between Interest Dates; Compare Cash Flows and Reporting)**

Cody Corporation authorized a $300,000, 10-year bond issue dated July 1, 19A. The bonds pay 8% interest each June 30. The accounting period ends December 31. Assume the bonds were sold on August 1, 19A, under three different cases as follows:

Case A—Sold at par.

Case B—Sold at 98.

Case C—Sold at 102.

Required:

Complete a schedule for Cody Corporation similar to the following assuming straight-line amortization. Show computations.

	Case A par	Case B 98	Case C 102
1. Cash received at issuance (sale) date	$_____	$_____	$_____
2. Cash received for accrued interest at issuance date	_____	_____	_____
3. Amount of premium or discount at issuance date	_____	_____	_____
4. Stated rate of interest (annual)	_____%	_____%	_____%
5. Net cash interest paid during 19A	$_____	$_____	$_____
6. Interest expense reported for 19A	_____	_____	_____
7. Bonds payable reported at end of 19A	_____	_____	_____
8. Unamortized premium or discount reported at end of 19A	_____	_____	_____
9. Net liability (carrying value) reported at end of 19A	_____	_____	_____
10. Interest payable reported at end of 19A	_____	_____	_____

P11–9 **(Recording and Reporting Bonds Issued between Interest Dates and the Interest Period Not at the End of the Accounting Year)**

Fisher Corporation issued bonds with the following provisions and dates:

Maturity amount: $100,000
Interest: 8%, payable each December 31
Dates: Bonds dated January 1, 19A
      Bonds sold, $60,000 at 104 on May 1, 19A
      End of accounting period, June 30
      Maturity date, December 31, 19E (5 years)

Required (round to the nearest dollar):

a. Give the journal entry to record the issuance of the bonds.
b. Give all 19A entries related to the interest on the bonds. Use straight-line amortization and exclude closing entries.
c. Complete the following for the year ending June 30, 19A:

Income statement:
  Interest expense
Balance sheet:
  Current liabilities:
  Long-term liabilities:

P11–10   (Recording and Reporting Bonds Issued between Interest Dates and Interest Period Not at the End of the Accounting Period)

In order to expand to a new region, Utah Manufacturing Company decided to build a new plant and warehouse. Approximately 60% of the resources required would be obtained through a $600,000 bond issue. The company developed and approved a bond indenture with the following provisions:

Date of bonds .... March 1, 19A, due in 10 years
Amount authorized .... $600,000 (par amount)
Interest .... 10% per annum, payable 5% each Feb. 28 and Aug. 31

The annual accounting period ends on December 31. The bonds were issued (sold) on May 1, 19A, at 102.36.

Required:

a. How much cash was received by Utah on May 1, 19A?
b. What was the amount of the premium? Over how many months will it be amortized?
c. Give journal entries, if any, at each of the following dates: May 1, 19A; August 31, 19A; December 31, 19A; and February 28, 19B. Do not use a reversing entry on January 1, 19B.
d. As to the financial statements for December 31, 19A:
   (1) How much interest expense should be reported on the income statement?
   (2) Show how the liabilities related to the bonds should be reported on the balance sheet.

P11–11   (Accounting for a Bond Sinking Fund; Compute Deposits; Entries)

On December 31, 19F, Steady Company had outstanding bonds of $120,000, par (8% annual interest payable each December 31). The bonds will mature at the end of 19J. Anticipating the maturity date, the maturity amount, and some possible miscellaneous related costs, Steady Company decided to accumulate a bond sinking fund of $122,102 so that cash will be available to pay the bonds on maturity date. Steady will make five equal annual deposits on December 31, 19F, G, H, I, and J. The trustee will handle the fund and will increase its balance by 10% at each year-end starting in 19G.

Required:

a. Compute the amount of each of the five equal deposits that Steady Company must make to accumulate $122,102.

b. Give the journal entry to record the first deposit by Steady Company (December 31, 19F).

c. Prepare a fund accumulation schedule for the five annual deposits.

d. Give the journal entry that Steady Company should make on December 31, 19G.

e. Assume it is December 31, 19J.

   (1) Give the journal entry that Steady Company should make to record the payment of the bond principal.

   (2) What balance remains in the bond sinking fund? What disposition should Steady Company make of this amount?

P11–12   **(Accounting for Bonds and Related Bond Sinking Funds; Compute Fund Deposits)**

On January 1, 1972, Boston Corporation issued $500,000, 6% bonds due at the end of 20 years (December 31, 1991). The bonds specified semiannual interest payments on each June 30 and December 31. The bonds originally sold at par. Also, the bond indenture called for the establishment of a bond sinking fund to be accumulated over the last five years by making five equal annual deposits on each December 31, starting in 1987. Interest on the fund balance at 8% will be added to the fund at year-end.

Required:

a. Give the journal entry for issuance of the bonds on January 1, 1972.

b. Give the journal entry for the semiannual interest payment on the bonds on June 30, 1987.

c. Give the journal entry on December 31, 1987, for the first $85,228 contribution of cash to the sinking fund. Show how this amount was computed.

d. Give the sinking fund entry that will be made at the end of 1988.

e. Prepare a fund accumulation schedule.

f. Give the journal entry to record retirement of the bonds at maturity assuming the total bond sinking fund accumulation is $500,000.

P11–13   **(Effective-Interest Amortization of Bond Premium; Analysis of a Prepared Amortization Schedule)**

Foster Corporation issued bonds and received cash in full for the issue price. The bonds were dated and issued on January 1, 19A. The stated interest rate was payable at the end of each year. The bonds mature at the end of four years. The following schedule has been completed:

Date	Cash	Interest	Amortization	Balance
Jan. 1, 19A				$5,173
End of Year 19A	$350	$310	$40	5,133
End of Year 19B	350	308	42	5,091
End of Year 19C	350	305	45	5,046
End of Year 19D	350	304	46	5,000

Required:

a. What was the maturity amount of the bonds?

b. How much cash was received at date of issuance (sale) of the bonds?

c. Was there a premium or a discount? If so, which and how much?

d. How much cash will be disbursed for interest each period and in total for the full life of the bond issue?

e. What method of amortization is being used? Explain.

f. What is the stated rate of interest?

g. What is the effective rate of interest?

h. Show how the following amounts for 19C were computed: (1) $350, (2) $305, (3) $45, and (4) $5,046.

i. What amount of interest expense should be reported on the income statement each year?

j. Show how the bonds should be reported on the balance sheet at the end of each year (show the last year immediately before retirement of the bonds).

k. Why is the method of amortization being used preferable to other methods? When must it be used?

CASES

C11–1   **(Demonstration of Financial Leverage; Computation and Interpretation)**

The financial statements of New Corporation for 19A showed the following:

Income Statement

Revenues	$200,000
Expenses	(139,000)
Interest expense	(1,000)
Pretax income	60,000
Income tax (40%)	(24,000)
Net income	$ 36,000

Balance Sheet

Assets	$150,000
Liabilities (average interest rate, 10%)	$ 10,000
Common stock, par $10	100,000
Retained earnings	40,000
	$150,000

Notice in the above data that the company had a debt of only $10,000 compared with common stock outstanding of $100,000. A consultant recommended the following: debt, $60,000 (at 10%) instead of $10,000 and common stock outstanding of $50,000 (5,000 shares) instead of $100,000 (10,000 shares). That is, the company should have more debt and less owner contributions to finance the business.

Required (round to nearest percent):

a. You have been asked to develop a comparison between the (1) actual results and (2) results had the consultant's recommendation been followed. To do this you decided to develop the following schedule:

Item	Actual results for 19A	Results with an increase in debt of $50,000
a. Total debt	_____	_____
b. Total assets	_____	_____
c. Total stockholders' equity	_____	_____
d. Interest expense (total at 10%)	_____	_____
e. Net income	_____	_____
f. Return on total assets	_____	_____
g. Earnings available to stockholders:		
(1) Amount	_____	_____
(2) Per share	_____	_____
(3) Return on stockholders' equity	_____	_____
h. Financial leverage	_____	_____

b. Based upon the completed schedule in (a), provide a comparative analysis and interpretation of the actual results and the recommendation.

C11–2   (Theoretical—Straight-Line versus Effective-Interest Methods of Amortizing Bond Discount and Premium)

Tumbleweed Corporation manufactures electronic equipment. The board of directors of the company authorized a bond issue on January 1, 19A, with the following terms:

Maturity (par) value: $500,000.
Interest: 9% per annum payable each December 31.
Maturity date: December 31, 19E.

The bonds were sold at an effective interest rate of 13%.

Required:

a. Compute the bond issue price. Explain why both the stated and effective interest rates are used in this computation.
b. Give the entry to record this bond issue.
c. Assume Tumbleweed used the straight-line approach to amortize the discount on the bond issue. Compute the following amounts for each year (19A–19E):
   (1) Cash payment for bond interest.
   (2) Amortization of bond discount or premium.
   (3) Bond interest expense.
   (4) Interest rate indicated (Item 3 ÷ $500,000).
   (5) The straight-line rate is theoretically deficient when interest expense, (4) above, is related to the net liability (i.e., carrying value of the debt). Explain.
d. Assume instead that Tumbleweed used the effective-interest method to amortize the discount. Prepare an effective-interest bond amortization schedule similar to Exhibit 11–8 in the text.
   The effective-interest method provides a constant interest rate when interest expense is related to the net liability. Explain by referring to the bond amortization schedule.
e. Which method should be used by Tumbleweed to amortize the bond discount?

C11-3   (Analysis of Zero-Coupon Bonds)

Early in 1981, J. C. Penney Company issued "zero coupon" bonds with a face (maturity value) of $400 million due in 1989 (8 years after issuance). When the bonds were sold to the public, similar bonds paid a 15 effective interest. An article in *Forbes* magazine (May 25, 1981) discussed the J. C. Penney bonds and stated: "It's easy to see why corporations like to sell bonds that don't pay interest. But why would anybody want to buy that kind of paper (bond)?"

Required:

a. Explain why an investor would buy a J. C. Penney bond with a zero interest rate. If investors could earn 15% on similar investments, how much should they be willing to pay for a J. C. Penney bond with a par value of $1,000 (due eight years after issuance)?

b. Assume that J. C. Penney sold the $400 million bond issue on May 1, 1981, the first day of the term (life) of the bond issue. Give the journal entry to record the sale of the bonds for cash.

c. Assume that the accounting period for J. C. Penney ends on December 31 each year. Give the journal entry required on December 31, 1981, to record accrued interest expense. If none is required, explain.

d. Give the entry on maturity date to pay the bondholders. How much cash interest was paid on the bonds? Explain.

C11-4   (Analysis of the Reporting of Bonds Payable on an Actual Set of Financial Statements)

Refer to the financial statements of Chesebrough-Pond's given in Special Supplement B immediately preceding the Index. Answer the following questions for the 1985 annual accounting period.

1. Did the company report any bonds payable on the balance sheet? Explain.
2. How much cash was provided (or used) from bonds payable? Explain what this means.
3. Refer to the notes to the financial statements and identify all bonds payable included in long-term debts.
4. Are any of the bonds (or indentures) supported by a bond sinking fund?

Owners are particularly interested in the accounting for a company's stock. Dividend policy and the value of the shares of stock will affect the investors' cash flows.

The Penn Central Corporation

Dividend Policy and Stock Market Prices

The Penn Central Corporation Common Stock is listed and traded principally on the New York Stock Exchange. On February 5, 1986 there were approximately 28,400 holders of record of Common Stock.

The Penn Central Corporation has not paid dividends on its Common Stock since its reorganization on October 24, 1978. The Company's Board of Directors periodically considers the payment of dividends on the Common Stock. At the present time, there are no plans to pay a cash dividend.

The following table sets forth the high and low sales prices of the Company's Common Stock for the last two years, as reported on the New York Stock Exchange Composite Tape.

Year-End Book Value and
Market Price Per Share (In dollars)

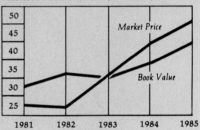

| | 1985 | | 1984 | |
	High	Low	High	Low
First Quarter	$55¼	$46⅛	$44⅛	$36⅝
Second Quarter	58⅝	51	46½	40¾
Third Quarter	55¼	47⅜	50¼	45⅜
Fourth Quarter	53⅞	45	48⅛	43¾

MEASURING AND REPORTING OWNERS' EQUITY

PURPOSE:

A business receives funds from a variety of sources. In the two previous chapters, we discussed accounting for funds provided by creditors (i.e., liabilities). In this chapter, we will examine measuring and reporting funds provided by the owners of a business. Accounting for owners' equity is affected by the types of business organization. Owners' equity appears somewhat differently on the balance sheets of sole proprietorships, partnerships, and corporations. However, given the same set of transactions, the total amount of owners' equity on a given date will be the same (except for income tax effects) for every type of business organization. The focus of this chapter will be primarily on the corporate form because it is the most prominent type of business entity.

LEARNING OBJECTIVES—TO BE ABLE TO:

1. Describe the basic nature of a corporation.
2. Compare and contrast the various types of capital stock.
3. Record transactions involving treasury stock.
4. Account for dividends on common and preferred stock.
5. Record stock dividends and stock splits.
6. Measure and report retained earnings.
7. Expand your accounting vocabulary by learning about the "Important Terms Defined in this Chapter" (page 644).
8. Apply the knowledge gained from this chapter by completing the homework assigned by your instructor.

ORGANIZATION:

Part A—Stockholders' Equity

1. Nature and structure of a corporation.
2. Accounting for various types of capital stock.
3. Treasury stock.

Part B—Accounting for Dividends, Retained Earnings, and Unincorporated Businesses

1. Dividends defined.
2. Dividends on preferred stock.
3. Stock dividends and stock splits.
4. Reporting retained earnings.
5. Unincorporated businesses.

PART A—STOCKHOLDERS' EQUITY

NATURE OF A CORPORATION

A corporation is a separate legal entity that is created by law. It has many of the same rights and duties as individuals. A corporation may be owned by a number of persons and perhaps other business entities. Ownership in the corporation is evidenced by shares of capital stock that typically are traded on established stock exchanges (such as the New York Stock Exchange). The life of a corporation is indefinite and is not affected by changes in the group of individuals, or other entities, that own it.

In terms of volume of business, the corporation is the dominant type of business organization in the United States. This popularity can be attributed to three important advantages that a corporation has over the sole proprietorship and the partnership. First, the corporate form facilitates the bringing together of large amounts of funds through the sale of ownership interests (capital stock) to the public. Second, it facilitates the transfer of separate ownership interests because the shares can be transferred easily to others. Third, it provides the stockholder with limited liability.[1]

The corporation is the only business form that is recognized in law as a separate legal entity. As a distinct entity, the corporation enjoys a continuous existence separate and apart from its owners. It may own assets, incur liabilities, expand and contract in size, sue others, be sued, and enter into contracts independently of the stockholder owners.

STRUCTURE OF A CORPORATION

Ownership of a corporation is evidenced by shares of **capital stock** that are freely transferable without affecting the corporation. The owners of a corporation are known as **stockholders** or **shareholders.**

Each state has different laws that govern the organization and operation of corporations within their boundaries. To create a corporation, an **application for a charter** must be submitted to the appropriate state official. The application must specify the name of the corporation, the purpose (type of business), kinds and amounts of capital stock **authorized,** and a minimum amount of capital (resources) that must be invested by the owners at the date of organization.

---

[1] In case of insolvency of a corporation, the creditors have recourse for their claims only to the assets of the corporation. Thus, the stockholders stand to lose, as a maximum, only their equity in the corporation. In contrast, in the case of a partnership or sole proprietorship, creditors have recourse to the personal assets of the owners if the assets of the business are insufficient to meet the outstanding debts of the business.

EXHIBIT 12–1

Common stock certificate

Most states require a minimum of three stockholders when the corporation is formed. Upon approval of the application, the state issues a **charter** (sometimes called the **articles of incorporation**). The governing body of a corporation is the **board of directors,** which is elected by the stockholders.

When a person acquires shares of capital stock, a **stock certificate** is issued as evidence of an ownership interest in the corporation. The certificate states the name of the stockholder, date of purchase, type of stock, number of shares represented, and the characteristics of the stock. Exhibit 12–1 shows a stock certificate for 50 shares of common stock of Dow Jones & Company. The back of the certificate has instructions and a form to be completed when the shares are sold or transferred to another party.

EXHIBIT 12–2

EXHIBIT 12–2

Typical organizational structure of a corporation

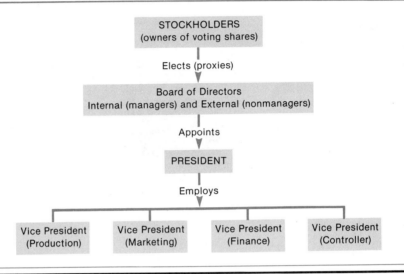

Stockholders have the following basic rights:

1. Vote in the stockholders' meeting (or by proxy) on major issues concerning management of the corporation.[2]
2. Participate proportionately with other stockholders in the distribution of profits of the corporation.
3. Share proportionately with other stockholders in the distribution of corporate assets upon liquidation.
4. Purchase shares of any new issues of common stock on a pro rata basis in order to maintain their percentage of ownership.

Stockholders exercise their control of a corporation by voting in the annual meeting of the stockholders. The usual organizational structure of a corporation is shown in Exhibit 12–2.

AUTHORIZED, ISSUED, AND OUTSTANDING CAPITAL STOCK

The corporate charter states the maximum number of shares of capital stock the corporation can issue. This maximum is called the **authorized** number of **shares.** The number of shares issued and the number of shares outstanding are

---

[2] A voting proxy is a written authority given by a stockholder that gives another party the right to vote the stockholder's shares in the annual meeting of the stockholders. Typically, proxies are solicited by, and given to, the president of the corporation.

determined by the stock transactions of the corporation. Shares of stock that never have been sold to the public are called unissued shares. In some situations, shares of stock may be sold on credit. These shares are called subscribed stock, which will not be issued until cash is collected from the investor. Exhibit 12–3 defines and illustrates the five terms usually used in respect to corporate shares.

Typically, the corporate charter authorizes a larger number of shares than the corporation expects to issue after its organization. This strategy provides future flexibility for the issuance of additional shares without amending the charter.

EXHIBIT 12–3

Authorized, issued, and outstanding shares

Definition	Illustration
Authorized number of shares: The **maximum** number of shares that can be issued as specified in the **charter** of the corporation.	Charter of Tye Corporation specifies "authorized capital stock, **100,000 shares**, par value $1 per share."
Issued number of shares: The total cumulative number of shares that has been issued to date by the corporation.	To date, Tye Corporation sold and issued **30,000** shares of its capital stock.
Unissued number of shares: The number of authorized shares that have never been issued to date.	Authorized shares . . . . 100,000 Issued shares . . . . 30,000 Unissued shares **70,000**
Subscribed number of shares: Shares of authorized stock sold on credit and not yet issued.	Tye Corporation sold 1,000 shares on credit; the shares will be issued when the sale price is collected in full. Subscribed shares = **1,000.**
Outstanding number of shares: The number of shares currently owned by stockholders; that is, the total (maximum) number of shares authorized minus the total number of unissued shares.	Tye Corporation: Authorized shares . . . . 100,000 Unissued shares . . . . 70,000 Outstanding shares **30,000***

* Observe that outstanding shares and issued shares are the same (i.e., 30,000 shares) in this situation. **Treasury stock** (i.e., shares that have been issued then subsequently repurchased by the issuing corporation) will be presented later. When treasury stock is held, the number of shares issued and the number outstanding will differ by the number of shares of treasury stock held (treasury stock is included in "issued" but not in "outstanding").

TYPES OF CAPITAL STOCK

All corporations must issue **common stock** which may be viewed as the "normal" stock of a corporation because it has voting rights. A corporation may issue preferred stock that grants **preferences** that the common stock does not have. These preferences usually specify, as a minimum, that the preferred stockholders must receive their dividends **before** any dividends can be declared or paid to the common stockholders. Because of the important differences between common and preferred stock, they are identified separately in accounting and reporting (and on the stock exchanges).

Common Stock

When only one class of stock is issued, it must be common. It has voting rights and often is called the **residual equity** because it ranks **after** the preferred stock for dividends and assets distributed upon liquidation of the corporation. Common stock does not have a fixed dividend rate (as does most preferred stock). As a result, common stock may pay higher dividends and have significant increases in market value. Common stock may be either par value or nopar value stock.

Par value and nopar value stock

Many years ago, all capital stock had to specify a par value. Par value is a **nominal** value per share established for the stock in the charter of the corporation and is printed on the face of each stock certificate. Stock that is sold by the corporation to investors above par value is said to sell at a **premium;** whereas, stock sold below par is said to sell at a **discount.** In recent years, the laws of all states have been changed to forbid the initial sale of stock by the corporation to investors below par value.[3] Originally, the concept of par value was established as protection for creditors by specifying a permanent amount of capital that could not be withdrawn by the owners as long as the corporation existed. Par value has no relationship to market value. The original idea that it represented protection for creditors was ill conceived. Today, par value, when specified, only identifies the stated or **legal capital** of the corporation (otherwise, it has no particular significance).

The par value concept was ineffective in protecting either creditors or stockholders. For that reason, many states enacted legislation permitting **nopar value** stock. Nopar value common stock does not have an amount per share specified in the charter. It may be issued at any price without a **discount or premium.**

---

[3] Our discussions concerning the sale of capital stock refer to the **initial** sale of the stock by the corporation rather than to later sales between investors as is the common situation in the day-to-day transactions of the stock markets. Because the sale of stock by a corporation at a discount no longer is legal, no further discussion of it is included. The sale of stock among **individuals** is not recorded in the accounts of the corporation.

Nopar value stock avoids giving the impression of a market value. When nopar stock is used by a corporation, the legal, or stated, capital is as defined by the state law.

When par value stock is used, the par value typically is set at a very low amount (such as $1 per share) and the issuing (selling) price is set much higher (such as $10 per share). This arrangement reduces the possibility of a discount.

The term **legal capital** is defined by the law of the state of incorporation. While it varies among states, legal capital usually is viewed as the par value of the stock outstanding (in the case of par value stock), or as either the stated value set by the company or the amount for which the stock was sold originally (in the case of nopar value stock). We shall see later that legal capital usually cannot be used as the basis for dividends. The stock certificate shown in Exhibit 12–1 represents par value common stock (par $1).

Preferred Stock

When stock other than common stock is issued, the additional classes are called **preferred stock.** Preferred stock has some characteristics that make it different from the common stock. The usual characteristics of preferred stock are:

1. Dividend preferences.
2. Conversion privileges.
3. Asset preferences.
4. Nonvoting specifications.

Preferred stock has both favorable and unfavorable characteristics.[4] For example, the nonvoting characteristic is an unfavorable characteristic. Preferred stock may be nopar value, although typically it has a par value. Most preferred stock has a fixed dividend rate. For example, a corporation charter may specify "Authorized capital stock: nonvoting, 6% **preferred stock,** 10,000 shares, par value $10 per share" in addition to the common stock. In this situation, the annual preferred dividend would be 6% of par, or $0.60 per share. In contrast, if the preferred stock is nopar value, the preferred dividend would be specified as $0.60 per share.

A corporation may choose to issue more than one class of stock to (1) obtain favorable control arrangements from its own point of view, (2) issue stock without voting privileges, and (3) appeal to a wide range of investors by offering preferred stock with special provisions.

The dividend preferences of preferred stock take precedence over the common stock, up to a specified limit. Dividend preferences will be discussed in Part B of the chapter. The other features of preferred stock are explained below.

---

[4] A majority of corporations issue only common stock. Often large corporations have both common and preferred in their financial structures. Some large companies also issue more than one class of preferred stock in addition to the common stock.

Convertible preferred stock

Convertible preferred stock provides preferred stockholders the option to exchange their preferred shares for shares of **common** stock of the corporation. The terms of the conversion will specify dates and a conversion ratio. A charter could read: "Each share of preferred stock, at the option of the stockholder, can be converted to two shares of common stock anytime after January 1, 19A."

Asset preferences of preferred stock

Two **asset preferences** usually are specified on preferred stock. One preference is provided with preferred stock that is **callable.** At the option of the issuing corporation, holders of callable preferred stock can be required to return the shares to the corporation for a specified amount of cash. The call price usually is higher than the par value. Upon call of the preferred stock, the preferred stockholders receive cash equal to, but no more than, the asset preference of their stock before any distributions could be made to the common stockholders. For example, a corporate charter could specify that preferred stock with a $10 par value was callable at $15. At this preference rate, a holder of the preferred stock would receive $15 per share upon "call" by the corporation.

The other asset preference on the preferred stock occurs when the corporation **dissolves** (e.g., in the case of termination of operations). Preferred stock usually has a specified preference amount per share that must be paid upon dissolution to the preferred stockholders before any assets can be distributed to the common stockholders. Usually, the preference amount also is the maximum that would be paid to the preferred stockholders.

Nonvoting specifications on preferred stock

Nonvoting preferred stock is customary, even though the nonvoting feature is undesirable to the investors. This feature denies the preferred stockholder the right to vote at stockholder meetings. It is one method for obtaining capital without diluting the control of the common stockholders.

In summary, preferred stock benefits the investor because of dividend, conversion, and asset preferences (to the extent that they are specified). However, preferred stock has the disadvantages of the nonvoting feature and upper dividend limits. In contrast, common stock is not constrained on dividend limits, asset limits on dissolution, and voting rights. If the corporation is profitable, common stock is more attractive to investors than preferred stock. Preferred stock is less risky than common stock because of the dividend, conversion, and asset preferences.

ACCOUNTING FOR, AND REPORTING OF, CAPITAL STOCK

Accounting for stockholders' equity is based upon a **concept of sources.** Under this concept, owners' equity from different sources is recorded in different accounts and reported separately in the stockholders' equity section of the balance sheet. The three basic sources of stockholders' equity are:

1. **Contributed capital (often called paid-in capital)**—the amount invested by stockholders through the purchase of shares of stock from the corporation. Contributed capital has two distinct components: *(a)* stated capital—par or stated value derived from the sale of capital stock; and *(b)* additional contributed capital—amounts derived from the sale of stock in excess of par or stated value. This often is called **additional paid-in capital.**
2. **Retained earnings**—the **cumulative** amount of net income earned since the organization of the corporation less the cumulative amount of dividends paid by the corporation since organization.
3. **Unrealized capital** (discussed in Chapter 13).

Sale and Issuance of Par Value Capital Stock

When par value stock is sold for cash, three accounts are affected: (1) cash is debited for the sale price, (2) the par value amount is credited to an appropriately designated contributed capital account for each type of stock, and (3) any difference between the sale price and the par value of the stock is credited to a separate additional contributed capital account entitled "Contributed Capital in Excess of Par." The par value is recorded in a separate account because it represents legal capital.

The sale of par value common and preferred stock is shown in Exhibit 12–4. Notice in the first journal entry that the preferred and common stock accounts were credited for the **par value** of the shares sold. The differences between the sale prices and the par values were credited to two capital in excess of par accounts. Tye Corporation recognized **two** different sources of stockholders' equity—preferred and common stock—and each source was subdivided between the par value and the excess received over par.[5]

Capital Stock Sold and Issued for Noncash Assets and/or Services

Often **noncash** considerations, such as buildings, land, machinery, and services (e.g., attorney fees), are received in payment for capital stock issued. In these cases, the assets received (or expenses incurred in the case of services) should be recorded by the issuing corporation at the **market value** of the stock issued at the date of the transaction in accordance with the **cost principle.** If the market value of the stock issued cannot be determined, then the market value of the consideration received should be used. Assume Tye Corporation issued 100 shares of preferred stock for legal services when the stock was selling at $12 per share. The second journal entry given in Exhibit 12–4 records this transaction. Notice that the value of the legal services received is assumed to be the same as the value of the stock that was issued.

---

[5] Contributed capital in excess of par sometimes is called premium on capital stock or paid-in capital in excess of par.

___ EXHIBIT 12–4 _____

Sale and issuance of par value capital stock

Situation of Tye Corporation:

Authorized:
  Preferred stock, 6% par $10; 10,000 shares.
  Common stock, par $1, 100,000 shares.

Sale and issuance for cash:

Preferred stock, 1,000 shares @ $12.
Common stock, 30,000 shares @ $5.

Cash (1,000 × $12) + (30,000 × $5)	162,000	
Preferred stock (1,000 × par $10)		10,000
Common stock (30,000 × par $1)		30,000
Contributed capital in excess of par, preferred		
[(1,000 × ($12 − $10)]		2,000
Contributed capital in excess of par, common		
[30,000 × ($5 − $1)]		120,000

Sale and issuance for services:

Issued 100 shares of preferred stock for legal services when the stock was selling at $12.

Legal expense	1,200	
Preferred stock (100 × par $10)		1,000
Contributed capital in excess of par, preferred		
[100 × ($12 − $10)]		200

Reporting on the financial statements:

Balance sheet—stockholders' equity:

Contributed capital:

Preferred stock, 6%, par $10; authorized 10,000 shares, issued and outstanding, 1,100 shares	$ 11,000	
Common stock, par $1; authorized 100,000 shares, issued and outstanding, 30,000 shares	30,000	
Contributed capital in excess of par:		
Preferred stock	2,200	
Common stock	120,000	
Total contributed capital		$163,200
Retained earnings (illustrated later)		

Income statement:

Legal expense		1,200

Reporting Stockholders' Equity

The **full disclosure principle** requires that the major classifications of stock-holders' equity be reported separately. Also, the subdivisions of each of these major classifications must be reported. Exhibit 12–4 shows the typical reporting of **contributed capital** and its subdivisions. Notice the separation of each type of stock and of par values and amounts in excess of par. Also, notice that the number of **shares** of each kind of stock authorized, issued, and outstanding are reported.

Sales and Issuance of Nopar Capital Stock

The laws of all states specify how legal capital must be determined if a par value is not stated in the corporate charter. There are two typical specifications, depending on the particular state that issued the charter, that affect the way the sale and issuance of nopar stock is recorded:

1. In its bylaws, the corporation must specify a **stated** value per share as legal capital. This stated value is a substitute for par value.
2. The corporation must record the **total** proceeds received from each sale and issuance of nopar stock as legal capital.

Recall that **legal** capital is credited to the capital stock account (e.g., common or preferred stock). Any excess of sale price over legal capital is credited to a separate account (e.g., Contributed Capital in Excess of Stated Value, Nopar Common, or Preferred, Stock).

Exhibit 12–5 illustrates the sale and issuance of nopar capital stock.

EXHIBIT 12–5

Sale and issuance of nopar capital stock

Situation of Sun Corporation:

Authorized capital stock—common stock, **nopar,** 200,000 shares.
Issued and sold—60,000 shares @ $6 per share (cash).

Sale and issuance:

Case A—The state law requires that the corporation set a **stated** value per share to represent legal capital for nopar stock. The company's charter specified a stated value of $0.50 per share.

Cash (60,000 × $6)	360,000	
Common stock, nopar (with stated value of $0.50)		
(60,000 × $0.50)		30,000
Contributed capital in excess of stated value		
60,000 × ($6.00 − $0.50)		330,000

Case B—The state law requires that the total proceeds be recorded as legal capital.

Cash	360,000	
Common stock, nopar		360,000

TREASURY STOCK

Treasury stock is a corporation's own capital stock that was issued to stockholders, **reacquired** subsequently by the corporation, and is still held by the corporation. Treasury stock often is bought for sound business reasons, such as to obtain shares needed for employee bonus plans, to increase the earnings per share amount, or to have shares on hand for use in the acquisition of other companies. Treasury stock, while held by the issuing corporation, has no voting, dividend, or other stockholder rights.[6]

When a corporation buys its own capital stock, the assets (usually cash) of the corporation and the stockholders' equity are reduced by equal amounts. When treasury stock is sold, the opposite effects occur. Purchases of treasury stock are recorded by debiting its cost to a stockholders' equity account called Treasury Stock (by type of stock) and crediting Cash. Because the Treasury Stock account has a debit balance, it often is called a **negative** (or contra) stockholders' equity account. When treasury stock is sold, the Treasury Stock account is credited at cost, and Cash is debited. Usually the purchase and sale prices of treasury stock are different, necessitating recording the difference in an appropriately designated **contributed capital** account.[7]

Accounting for treasury stock is shown in Exhibit 12–6. In the journal entry for January 2, 19B, the **Treasury Stock** account is debited for the **cost** of the treasury stock purchased ($3,600). The journal entry on February 15, 19B, credits the Treasury Stock for the **cost** of the 100 shares of treasury stock sold. A corporation is not permitted by GAAP to increase its income or retained earnings by investing in its own stock. In Exhibit 12–6, upon sale of the treasury stock, **contributed capital** was increased by $100, which was the difference between the cost and the sales price of the treasury shares sold [i.e., 100 shares × ($13 − $12)]. This difference was **not** recorded as a gain as would be done for the sale of an asset (such as investments in marketable securities). The basic accounting concept underlying this treatment is that "gains or losses" on transactions involving a corporation's own stock are balance sheet (**stockholders' equity**) items and not income statement items. Therefore, the balance sheet of May Corporation, shown at the bottom of Exhibit 12–6, reports "Contributed capital, treasury stock transactions" of $100.

The Treasury Stock account never has a credit balance, even though owners' equity accounts normally carry a credit balance. The balance in the Treasury

---

[6] The laws of most states impose certain restrictions on the amount of treasury stock a corporation can hold at any one time because the purchase of treasury stock is an avenue for taking resources out of the corporation by the owners (stockholders), which may jeopardize the rights of creditors. The law in some states limits the cost of treasury stock that can be purchased to the balance reflected in the Retained Earnings account.

[7] Two alternative approaches are used to account for treasury stock—the cost method and the par value method. We will limit our discussions to the cost method because it is less complex and used more widely. The par value method is discussed in most accounting texts at the intermediate level.

EXHIBIT 12–6

Accounting for, and reporting of, treasury stock

Situation of May Corporation on January 1, 19B:

MAY CORPORATION
Summarized Balance Sheet
January 1, 19B

Assets		Stockholders' Equity	
Cash	$ 30,000	Contributed capital:	
Other assets	70,000	Common stock, par $10, autho-	
		rized 10,000 shares, issued	
		8,000 shares	$ 80,000
		Retained earnings	20,000
Total assets	$100,000	Total stockholders' equity	$100,000

Purchase of treasury stock:

On January 2, 19B, May Corporation purchased 300 of its own outstanding shares of common stock at $12 per share.

Treasury stock, common (300 shares @ $12 per share	3,600	
Cash		3,600

(Note: This transaction reduces both assets and stockholders' equity by $3,600.)

Sale of treasury stock:

On February 15, 19B, May sold one third of the treasury stock at $13 per share.

Cash (100 shares @ $13)	1,300	
Treasury stock, common (100 shares @ cost, $12)		1,200
Contributed capital, treasury stock transactions		100

(Note: This transaction increases both assets and stockholders' equity by $1,300.)

Reporting treasury stock:

MAY CORPORATION*
Summarized Balance Sheet
February 15, 19B

Assets		Stockholders' Equity	
Cash	$27,700	Contributed capital:	
Other assets	70,000	Common stock, par $10,	
		authorized 10,000 shares, is-	
		sued 8,000, of which 200	
		shares are held as treasury	
		stock	$ 80,000
		Contributed capital, treasury	
		stock transactions	100
		Total contributed capital	80,100
		Retained earnings	20,000
		Total	100,100
		Less cost of treasury stock	
		held	2,400
Total assets	$97,700	Total stockholders' equity	$ 97,700

* Reflects the additional effects of the two transactions given above.

Stock account reflects a **contraction** of stockholders' equity. Therefore, it is a **negative** equity account. The debit balance in the Treasury Stock account represents the acquisition **cost** of the treasury stock still held at the date of the balance sheet. Observe this deduction on the balance sheet for May Corporation at the bottom of Exhibit 12–6.[8] That balance sheet reports the number of shares as:

Classification	Shares
Authorized	10,000
Unissued	(2,000)
*Issued	8,000
Treasury shares	(200)
*Outstanding	7,800

* Different by the number of treasury shares held.

Neither the purchase or sale of treasury stock affects the number of shares of stock that are issued or unissued. Treasury stock does affect the number of shares of **outstanding** stock. The only difference between treasury stock and unissued stock is that treasury stock has been sold at least once.

To illustrate the **resale** of treasury stock at a price **less than cost,** assume that an additional 50 shares of the treasury stock were resold by May Corporation on April 1, 19B, at $11 per share; that is, $1 per share below cost. The resulting journal entry would be:

April 1, 19B:

Cash	550	
Contributed capital, treasury stock transactions	50	
Treasury stock, common (50 shares)		600
Sold 50 shares of treasury stock at $11 per share; cost, $12 per share.		

Notice that the difference between sale price and cost was debited to the same contributed capital account to which the difference in the preceding journal entry (Exhibit 12–6) was credited. Retained Earnings would be debited for some or all of the amount of the difference only if there were an insufficient credit balance in the account Contributed Capital, Treasury Stock Transactions.

---

[8] Some persons argue that the debit balance in the Treasury Stock account should be reported on the balance sheet as an asset rather than as a reduction in stockholders' equity. This position is supported by the argument that the treasury stock could be sold for cash just as readily as the shares of other corporations. The argument is fallacious; all **unissued** stock of the corporation presumably also could be sold for cash, yet unissued shares never are considered to be an asset.

PART B—ACCOUNTING FOR DIVIDENDS AND RETAINED EARNINGS AND UNINCORPORATED BUSINESSES

DIVIDENDS DEFINED

Usually a dividend is a distribution of cash to stockholders by a corporation. Dividends can be paid in assets other than cash or in capital stock of the corporation. Dividends must be approved by the board of directors of the corporation (i.e., a dividend declaration) **before** they can be paid. Without a qualifier, the term **dividend** means a **cash** dividend, which is the most common type. A dividend distribution of the corporation's own stock is called a **stock dividend.** Dividends usually are stated in terms of dollars per share, or as a percent of par value.

The declaration and payment of a **cash dividend** reduces the assets (cash) and the stockholders' equity (retained earnings) by the total amount of the dividend. Exhibit 12–7 illustrates the declaration and payment of a cash dividend. Observe that assets and stockholders' equity **both** were reduced by the amount of the cash dividend ($12,400).

DIVIDENDS FROM THE PERSPECTIVES OF THE INVESTOR AND THE ISSUER

An **investor** acquires shares of stock of a corporation with the expectation of earning a future economic return on the investment, usually in future cash inflows. The investor's future cash inflows from the stock investment come from two sources: (1) periodic cash inflows in the form of dividends on the shares and (2) a cash inflow at the time the stock is sold. The investor anticipates that the sum of the present values of these two cash inflows will be greater than the original investment in the shares. The investor views cash dividends as revenue, that is, the return **on** the investment. The other cash inflow includes a return **of** the investment (from sale of the shares) and will usually result in a **realized gain or loss,** depending on whether the investor sells the shares above or below their acquisition price. The amounts and frequency of dividends paid by a corporation have an effect on the market price of the stock.

The primary financial objective of a corporation is to earn income on the resources provided by stockholders and creditors. The ability to attract and retain resources from present and potential investors depends in good measure upon the income record of the company. The earnings of a corporation may be retained in the business for corporate expansion or paid to the stockholders as dividends. One of the significant decisions faced by the board of directors of a corporation is how much of the earnings should be retained and how much should be distributed to the stockholders as dividends each year.

EXHIBIT 12-7

Declaration and payment of a cash dividend

Situation prior to cash dividend (Box Corporation):

Cash	$ 20,000	
Remaining assets	135,000	
Liabilities	(35,000)	$120,000

Stockholders' equity:

Preferred stock, 6%, par $20, shares outstanding, 2,000	$ 40,000	
Common stock, par $10, shares outstanding, 5,000	50,000	
Retained earnings	30,000	$120,000

Dividend declaration:

"On December 1, 19E, the Board of Directors of Box Corporation hereby declares an annual cash dividend of $2 per share on the common stock and 6% per share on the preferred stock to the stockholders on date of record, December 10, 19E, payable on December 30, 19E."

Journal entries:*

December 1, 19E:

Retained earnings (or Dividends declared which is closed to Retained earnings)	12,400	
Dividends payable (a current liability)		12,400

Declaration of a cash dividend:
Preferred stock (2,000 shares × par $20 × rate 6%) = $ 2,400.
Common stock (5,000 shares × $2)   = 10,000.

December 30, 19E:

Dividends payable	12,400	
Cash		12,400
Payment of dividend liability.		

Effects of the cash dividend on the balance sheet:

Cash	$ 7,600	
Remaining assets	135,000	
Liabilities	(35,000)	$107,600

Stockholders' equity:

Preferred stock	$ 40,000	
Common stock	50,000	
Retained earnings	17,600	$107,600

* These two entries could be combined into one journal entry on the date of payment, as a debit to Retained Earnings and a credit to Cash of $12,400 because they were in the same accounting year.

Exhibit 12–7 demonstrated that a cash dividend reduces both assets (cash) and stockholders' equity (retained earnings). There are two fundamental requirements for the payment of a cash dividend:

1. **Sufficient retained earnings**—The corporation must have accumulated a sufficient amount of retained earnings to cover the amount of the dividend. State incorporation laws usually place restrictions on cash dividends. For example, the state laws often limit cash dividends to the balance in retained earnings. To meet growth objectives, most corporations do not disburse more than 40–60% of the average net income amount as dividends.
2. **Sufficient cash**—The corporation must have access to sufficient cash to pay the dividend and to meet the continuing operating needs of the business. The mere fact that there is a large **credit** in the Retained Earnings account does not mean that the board of directors can declare and pay a cash dividend. The cash generated in the past by earnings represented in the Retained Earnings account may have been expended to acquire inventory, buy operational assets, and/or pay liabilities. Consequently, there is no necessary relationship between the balance of retained earnings and the balance of cash on any particular date (simply, retained earnings is not cash).

Exhibit 12–7 indicated a cash balance of $20,000 and a balance in retained earnings of $30,000. In this example, it appears that cash may be the constraining factor on dividends. Some companies overcome this cash constraint (at least temporarily) by borrowing cash to pay cash dividends. The balance in retained earnings is a more inflexible constraint because retained earnings cannot be borrowed.

DIVIDENDS ON PREFERRED STOCK

Recall that preferred stock gives certain rights that have precedence over the rights of common stock. The primary distinguishing characteristics of preferred stock are dividend preferences. The **dividend preferences** may be classified as follows:[9]

1. Current dividend preference.
2. Cumulative dividend preference.
3. Participating dividend preference.

Preferred stock may have one or a combination of these three dividend preferences. The charter and the stock certificates of the corporation must state the distinctive features of the preferred stock.

---

[9] A dividend preference does not mean that dividends will be paid automatically. Dividends are paid only when **formally declared** by the corporation's board of directors. Thus, the declaration of a dividend is discretionary. A typical dividend problem involves the allocation of a total amount of dividends declared between the preferred stock and common stock as illustrated in the next section.

Current Dividend Preference on Preferred Stock

Preferred stock always carries a **current dividend preference.** It requires that if any dividends are declared, the current preferred dividend must be declared and paid before any dividends can be declared and paid on the common stock. When the current dividend preference is met (and no other preference is operative), dividends then can be paid to the common stockholders. The current dividend preference on par value preferred stock is a specified percent of the par value of the preferred stock.

Declared dividends must be **allocated** between the preferred and common stock. First, the preferences of the preferred stock must be met, then the remainder of the total dividend can be allocated to the common stock. Exhibit 12–8, Case A, illustrates the allocation of the **current dividend** preference under four different assumptions concerning the **total** amount of dividends to be paid.

Cumulative Dividend Preference on Preferred Stock

Cumulative preferred stock has a preference that states if all or a part of the specified current dividend (e.g., 6% in Exhibit 12–8) is not paid in full, the unpaid amount becomes **dividends in arrears.** Thus, when the preferred stock is cumulative, the amount of any preferred dividends in arrears must be paid before any common dividends can be paid. In any one year, preferred stock cannot receive total dividends in excess of the current year dividend preference plus all dividends in arrears. Of course, if the preferred stock is **noncumulative,** dividends never can be in arrears. Therefore any dividends passed (i.e., not declared) are lost permanently by the preferred stockholders. Because preferred stockholders are not willing to accept this unfavorable feature, preferred stock usually is cumulative.

The allocation of dividends between **cumulative** preferred stock and common stock is illustrated in Exhibit 12–8, Case B, under four different assumptions concerning the **total** amount of dividends to be paid. Observe that the dividends in arrears are paid first, next the current dividend preference is paid, and, finally, the remainder is paid to the common stockholders.

Some preferred stock may provide dividends that are greater than the required minimum amount. Participating preferred stock is discussed in Supplement 12A.

STOCK DIVIDENDS

The board of directors may vote to declare and issue a stock dividend instead of a cash dividend. A **stock dividend is a distribution of additional shares of a corporation's own capital stock on a pro rata basis to its stockholders at no cost.** Stock dividends usually consist of common stock issued to the holders of

EXHIBIT 12–8

Dividends on preferred stock

Case A—Current dividend preference only:

Preferred stock outstanding, 6%, par $20; 2,000 shares = $40,000 par.
Common stock outstanding, par $10; 5,000 shares = 50,000 par.

Allocation of dividends between preferred and common stock assuming **current dividend** preference only:

		Amount of dividend paid to stockholders of	
Assumptions	Total dividends paid	6% preferred stock (2,000 shares @ $20 par = $40,000)*	Common stock (5,000 shares @ $10 par = $50,000)
No. 1	$ 1,000	$1,000	–0–
No. 2	2,000	2,000	–0–
No. 3	3,000	2,400	$ 600
No. 4	18,000	2,400	15,600

* Preferred dividend preference, $40,000 × 6% = $2,400; or 2,000 shares × $1.20.

Case B—Cumulative dividend preference:

Preferred and common stock outstanding—same as above. Dividends in **arrears** for the two preceding years.

Allocation of dividends between preferred and common stock assuming **cumulative** preferred stock:

		Amount of dividend paid to stockholders of	
Assumptions (dividends in arrears, 2 years)	Total dividends paid	6% preferred stock (2,000 shares @ $20 par = $40,000)*	Common stock (5,000 shares @ $10 par = $50,000)
No. 1	$ 2,400	$2,400	–0–
No. 2	7,200	7,200	–0–
No. 3	8,000	7,200	$ 800
No. 4	30,000	7,200	22,800

* Current dividend preference, $40,000 × 6% = $2,400; dividends in arrears preference, $2,400 × 2 years = $4,800; and current dividend preference plus dividends in arrears = $7,200.

common stock. **Pro rata basis** means that each stockholder receives additional shares equal to the percentage of shares already held. A stockholder with 10% of the outstanding shares would receive 10% of any additional shares issued as a stock dividend. Therefore, a stock dividend does not change the proportionate ownership of any stockholder. It does not involve the distribution of any assets (e.g., cash) of the corporation to the stockholder, and it does not affect the **total** stockholders' equity of the issuing corporation. Assume King Corporation has outstanding 100,000 shares of common stock, par $5, originally sold at $8 per share. The board of directors voted to declare and issue a 10% common stock dividend (i.e., 10,000 shares) when the market value of the common stock was $11 per share. The entry by King Corporation to record the declaration and issuance of this stock dividend would be:[10]

```
Retained earnings (10,000 shares × $11) ..........................  110,000
     Common stock, par $5 (10,000 shares × $5) ...................           50,000
     Contributed capital in excess of par, common stock
        10,000 shares × ($11 − $5) ...............................           60,000
     Common stock dividend of 10% distributed when the market
     value per share was $11.
```

Observe in the above entry that **retained earnings** was **decreased** by $110,000 and that **contributed capital** (i.e., common stock and contributed capital in excess of par) was increased by $110,000; assets and liabilities were unaffected. Therefore, the stock dividend did **not** change total stockholders' equity—it only changed some of the balances of the accounts that comprise stockholders' equity. This process of transferring an amount from retained earnings to contributed (i.e., permanent) capital often is called **capitalizing earnings** because it reduces the amount of retained earnings available for future dividends.

After a stock dividend, each **stockholder** has the same **proportionate** ownership of the corporation as before, and no additional assets are received by the stockholders (only more shares to represent the same total value previously held). Because more shares now represent the same "value," the **market** price per share of the stock should drop proportionately.

Observe in the previous journal entry, the amount that was transferred from Retained Earnings to Contributed Capital was the **current market value** of the shares issued as a stock dividend. Market value amount is considered appropriate when the stock dividend is "small"; that is, when it is less than 25% of the previously outstanding shares. In those cases where a stock dividend is "large" (i.e., more than 25%), the amount transferred should be the total par value of the shares issued.

---

[10] Some accountants prefer to debit an account called Stock Dividends Distributed, which is closed to Retained Earnings at the end of the period. The effect is the same.

Reasons for Stock Dividends

Stock dividends often serve useful purposes for both the corporation and the individual stockholder. The two primary purposes of a stock dividend are:

1. **To maintain dividend consistency**—Many corporations prefer to declare dividends each year. In the case of a cash shortage, the dividend record may be maintained by issuing a stock dividend. Stock dividends tend to satisfy the demands of stockholders for continuing dividends and yet avoid the demand on cash. Also, a stock dividend is not considered as revenue to the stockholder for income tax purposes. Stockholders view stock dividends as quite different from cash dividends.

2. **To capitalize retained earnings**—A stock dividend is used to transfer retained earnings to permanent capital and thus remove such earnings from cash dividend availability. When a corporation consistently retains a large percent of its earnings for growth, the related funds often are invested permanently in long-term assets such as plant and other property. Therefore, it is realistic to transfer those accumulated earnings to permanent capital. A stock dividend is a convenient approach to capitalize retained earnings.

STOCK SPLITS

Stock splits are **not** dividends. They are (a) similar to a stock dividend, (b) often confused with a stock dividend, and (c) quite different from a stock dividend as to their impact upon the stockholders' equity accounts. In a stock split, the **total** number of authorized shares is increased by a specified amount, such as a two-for-one split. In this instance, each share held is called in, and two new shares are issued in its place. Typically, a stock split is accomplished by **reducing the par or stated value** per share of all authorized shares so that the **total** par value (in dollars) of all authorized shares is unchanged. For example, assume 1,000 shares of $20 par value stock were outstanding before a two-for-one split. This stock split would involve reducing the par value of each new share to $10 and the issuance of 2,000 shares of $10 par value stock. In contrast to a stock dividend, a stock split does **not** result in a transfer of retained earnings to contributed capital. No transfer is needed because the reduction in the par value per share compensates for the increase in the number of shares. The primary reason for a stock split is to **reduce the market price per share,** which tends to increase the market activity of the stock. Sometimes a corporation wants to **reduce** the number of shares outstanding. One way to do this is to implement a **reverse** stock split. A stock dividend requires a journal entry while a **stock split does not require a journal entry.**

In both a stock dividend and a stock split the stockholder receives more shares of stock but does not disburse any additional assets to acquire the additional shares.

The **comparative effects** of a stock dividend versus a stock split may be summarized as follows:

	Stockholders' equity		
	Before a stock dividend or split	After a 100% stock dividend	After a two-for-one stock split
Contributed capital:			
Number of shares outstanding	30,000	60,000	60,000
Par value per share	$ 10	$ 10	$ 5
Total par value outstanding	300,000	600,000	300,000
Retained earnings	650,000	350,000	650,000
Total stockholders' equity	950,000	950,000	950,000

DIVIDEND DATES

The preceding discussions assumed that a dividend was paid immediately after its declaration by the board of directors. Typically, there is a time lag between declaration and payment. A typical dividend declaration is as follows:

On November 20, 19B, the Board of Directors of XY Corporation hereby declares a $0.50 per share cash dividend on the 200,000 shares of nopar common stock outstanding. The dividend will be paid to stockholders of record at December 15, 19B, on January 15, 19C.

This declaration specifies **three important dates:**

1. **Declaration date—November 20, 19B:** This is the date on which the board of directors officially approved the dividend. As soon as a public announcement of the declaration is made, it is irrevocable. Therefore, a **dividend liability** immediately is created when a dividend is declared. On the date of declaration, XY Corporation would record the following journal entry:

November 20, 19B:

Retained earnings (or Dividends declared) 100,000
    Dividends payable 100,000
  Cash dividend declared: 200,000 shares × $0.50 = $100,000.

The December 31, 19B, balance sheet would report **Dividends Payable as a current liability.**

2. **Date of record—December 15, 19B:** This date follows the declaration date, usually by about one month, as specified in the declaration. It is the date on

which the corporation prepares the list of current stockholders based on the **stockholder records.** The dividend is payable only to those names listed on the record date. Thus, share transfers between investors reported to the corporation before this date result in the dividend being paid to the new owner. Changes reported **after** this date result in the dividend being paid to the old owner; the new owner will receive all subsequent dividends. No journal entry would be made on this date.

3. **Date of payment—January 15, 19C:** This is the date on which the **cash** is disbursed to pay the dividend liability. It follows the date of record as specified in the dividend announcement. The entry to record the cash disbursement by XY Corporation would be as follows:

January 15, 19C:		
Dividends payable	100,000	
Cash		100,000
To pay the liability for a cash dividend declared and recorded on November 20, 19B.		

For instructional purposes this time lag may be ignored because it does not pose any substantive issues. Also, when all of the three dates fall in the same accounting period, a single entry on the date of payment may be made in practice for purely practical reasons.

STOCKHOLDER RECORDS

A corporation must keep a record of each stockholder. The record includes at least the name and address of each stockholder, number of shares owned, certificate numbers, and dates acquired. This record is known as the **stockholders'** subsidiary ledger. The Capital Stock account is the **control account** in the general ledger for this subsidiary ledger. Sales of shares by a stockholder to others must be reported to the corporation so that new stock certificates can be issued and the stockholders' subsidiary ledger can be changed. Dividends are sent only to the names and addresses shown in the stockholders' subsidiary ledger on the date of record. Large corporations with thousands of stockholders usually pay an independent **stock transfer agent** to handle the transfer of shares, to issue new stock certificates, and to maintain the equivalent of a stockholders' subsidiary ledger.

An important record that must be kept by all corporations is called the **minute book.** This is an official record of the actions taken at all meetings of the board of directors and of the stockholders. The independent auditor is required to inspect the minute book as a part of the audit program. Often, it is used as evidence in lawsuits and in income tax litigation.

REPORTING RETAINED EARNINGS

The preceding chapters emphasized that the income statement reports two income amounts: (1) income before extraordinary items and (2) net income (i.e., after extraordinary items). *APB Opinion 30* (dated June 1973) defines **extraordinary items** as those transactions and events that meet both of two criteria: (1) **unusual in nature for the business** and (2) **infrequent in occurrence.** Extraordinary items are set out separately on the income statement so that statement users can focus on the usual and frequent results. Income **before** extraordinary items is more reflective of future earnings and cash inflow than is net income (i.e., after extraordinary items).

In several prior chapters we discussed the statement of retained earnings. Although not a required statement, it usually is presented to conform with the **full disclosure principle.** Because retained earnings is one of two basic components of stockholders' equity, users of financial statements need sufficient disclosures to understand the causes of changes in the amount of retained earnings. A typical statement of retained earnings is shown in Exhibit 12–9.

The statement of retained earnings shown in Exhibit 12–9 reports two items that have not been discussed: (1) prior period adjustments and (2) restrictions on retained earnings.

Prior Period Adjustments

Prior period adjustments were defined in *FASB Statement 16*, as follows:

Items of profit and loss related to the following shall be accounted for and reported as prior period adjustments and excluded from the determination of net income for the current period:
a) Correction of an error in the financial statements of a prior period and
b) Adjustments that result from realization of income tax benefits of preacquisition operating loss carryforwards of purchased subsidiaries.[11]

Prior period adjustments must be reported on the statement of retained earnings as an **adjustment of the beginning balance of retained earnings.** These adjustments are not reported on the income statement. Prior period adjustments are closed at the end of the period **directly** to the Retained Earnings account. Examples of prior period adjustments include corrections of **accounting errors** made in a prior period such as in depreciation, revenues, operational assets,

---

[11] *FASB Statement 16*, "Prior Period Adjustments" (Stamford, Conn., 1977), par. 11.

EXHIBIT 12–9

Statement of retained earnings

FERRARI CORPORATION
Statement of Retained Earnings
For the Year Ended December 31, 19C

Retained earnings balance, January 1, 19C		$226,000
Prior period adjustment:		
Deduct adjustment for correction of prior		
accounting error (net of income tax)		10,000
Balance as restated		216,000
Net income for 19C		34,000
Total		250,000
Deduct dividends declared in 19C:		
On preferred stock	$ 6,000	
On common stock	12,000	18,000
Retained earnings balance, December 31, 19C (see Note 5)		$232,000

Note 5. Restrictions on retained earnings; total, $137,400:
  a. Treasury stock—The corporation has treasury stock that cost $37,400. The state law requires that retained earnings equal to the cost of all treasury stock held be restricted from dividend availability.
  b. Bonds payable—The indenture requires that retained earnings be restricted in accordance with an agreed schedule. The schedule amounts for 19B and 19C total $100,000.

liabilities, and expenses. Exhibit 12–9 shows reporting of a prior period adjustment.[12] Observe that prior period adjustments are defined and reported differently than extraordinary items.

Restrictions on Retained Earnings

Often corporations have restrictions on retained earnings. Such a **restriction temporarily removes the restricted amount of retained earnings from availability for dividends.** When the restriction is removed, the amount that was restricted is available for dividends and other "uses" of retained earnings. Restrictions on retained earnings may be voluntary or involuntary. The two restrictions reported on Exhibit 12–9 are involuntary; one was imposed by **law** (i.e., the treasury stock restriction) and the other was imposed by **contract.** On occasion, the management or the board of directors may voluntarily establish a restriction on retained earnings for expansion of the business. The amount of

---

[12] Discussion of the second category of prior period adjustments, which relates to certain income tax benefits due to loss carryforwards, is deferred to more advanced accounting courses.

retained earnings restricted for this purpose often is called "Retained earnings appropriated for earnings invested in plant and equipment." This restriction can be removed by the management or board of directors at any time.

The **full disclosure principle** requires that restrictions on retained earnings be reported on the financial statements or in a separate note to the financial statements. The approach most widely used is by note, as illustrated in Exhibit 12–9.

A practice used widely in past years, but now used less often, was to set up a special retained earnings account for each appropriation. Such accounts, somewhat illogically, often were called reserves. A journal entry to establish a "reserve" for the restriction of retained earnings by Ferrari Corporation (Exhibit 12–9) would be:

Retained earnings 137,400		
Reserve for cost of treasury stock*		37,400
Reserve for bonds payable		100,000

* A much more descriptive title would be preferable, such as "Retained earnings appropriated equal to the cost of treasury stock held."

In preparing the statement of retained earnings, Ferrari Corporation could list the two "reserve" accounts on the statement of retained earnings, and Note 5 would be unnecessary. When the restrictions are removed, the above entry is reversed.

An appropriation (or restriction) of retained earnings is **not cash.** Observe in the above entries that cash was not affected; the **only** effect was to remove a specific amount of retained earnings from dividend availability. In order to set aside cash for a special purpose, cash is credited and a **fund** account (e.g., building construction fund) is debited. Such fund accounts are assets similar to a savings account. Thus, there is no necessary relationship between appropriations of retained earnings and cash.

ACCOUNTING AND REPORTING FOR UNINCORPORATED BUSINESSES

There are three forms of business organizations: **corporations** (i.e., shares of stock owned by a number of individuals), **sole proprietorships** (i.e., one owner), and **partnerships** (i.e., two or more owners). The fundamentals of accounting and reporting for unincorporated businesses are the same as for a corporation except for **owners' equity.** Typical account structures for the three forms of business organizations are outlined in Exhibit 12–10.

Accounting for sole proprietorships and partnerships is discussed in Supplement 12B.

EXHIBIT 12–10

Comparative account structures among types of business entities

TYPICAL ACCOUNT STRUCTURE		
Corporation (stockholders' equity)	**Sole Proprietorship** (proprietor's equity)	**Partnership** (partners' equity)
Capital stock Contributed capital in excess of par	Doe, capital	Able, capital Baker, capital
Retained earnings	Not used	Not used
Dividends paid	Doe, drawings	Able, drawings Baker, drawings
Income summary (closed to Retained Earnings)	Income summary (closed to Doe, Capital)	Income summary (closed to Able, Capital and Baker, Capital)
Revenues, expenses, gains, and losses	Same	Same
Assets and liabilities	Same	Same

DEMONSTRATION CASE

(Try to resolve the requirements before proceeding to the suggested solution that follows.)

This case focuses on the organization and operations for the first year of Shelly Corporation, which was organized on January 1, 19A. The laws of the state specify that the legal capital for nopar stock is the full sale amount. The corporation was organized by 10 local entrepreneurs for the purpose of operating a business to sell various operating supplies to hotels. The charter **authorized** the following capital stock:

Common stock, nopar value, 20,000 shares.

Preferred stock, 5%, $100 par value, 5,000 shares (cumulative, nonparticipating, non-convertible, and nonvoting; liquidation value, $110).

The following summarized transactions, selected from 19A, were completed on the dates indicated:

1. Jan.　Sold a total of 7,500 shares of nopar common stock to the 10 entrepreneurs for cash at $52 per share. Credit the Nopar Common Stock account for the total sales amount.

2. Feb.   Sold 1,890 shares of preferred stock at $102 per share; cash collected in full.

3. Mar.   Purchased land for a store site and made full payment by issuing 100 shares of preferred stock. Early construction of the store is planned. Debit Land (store site). The preferred stock is selling at $102 per share.

4. Apr.   Paid $1,980 cash for organization costs. Debit an intangible asset account entitled "Organization Cost."

5. May   Issued 10 shares of preferred stock to A. B. Cain in full payment of legal services rendered in connection with organization of the corporation. Assume the preferred stock is selling regularly at $102 per share. Debit Organization Cost.

6. June   Sold 500 shares of nopar common stock for cash to C. B. Abel at $54 per share.

7. July   Purchased 100 shares of preferred stock that had been sold and issued earlier. The stockholder was moving to another state and "needed the money." Shelly Corporation paid the stockholder $104 per share.

8. Aug.   Sold 20 shares of the preferred treasury stock at $105 per share.

9. Dec. 31   Purchased equipment for $600,000; paid cash. No depreciation expense should be recorded in 19A.

10. Dec. 31   Borrowed $2,000 cash from the City Bank on a one-year, interest-bearing note. Interest is payable at a 12% rate at maturity.

11. Dec. 31   Gross revenues for the year amounted to $129,300; expenses, including corporation income tax but excluding amortization of organization costs, amounted to $98,000. Assume that these summarized revenue and expense transactions were paid in cash. Because the equipment and the bank loan transactions were on December 31, no related adjusting entries at the end of 19A are needed.

12. Dec. 31   Shelly Corporation decided that a "reasonable" amortization period for organization costs, starting as of January 1, 19A, would be 10 years. This intangible asset must be amortized to expense. Give the required adjusting entry for 19A.

Required:

a. Give appropriate journal entries, with a brief explanation for each of the above transactions.

b. Give appropriate closing entries at December 31, 19A.

c. Prepare a balance sheet for Shelly Corporation at December 31, 19A. Emphasize full disclosure of stockholders' equity.

Suggested Solution

Requirement a—Journal entries:

1. January 19A:

```
Cash ................................................. 390,000
    Nopar common stock (7,500 shares) .....................        390,000
    Sale of nopar common stock ($52 × 7,500 shares = $390,000).
```

2. February 19A:

```
Cash ................................................. 192,780
    Preferred stock, 5%, par $100 (1,890 shares) ..............        189,000
    Contributed capital in excess of par, preferred stock
        [1,890 shares × ($102 − $100)] .......................          3,780
    Sale of preferred stock ($102 × 1,890 shares = $192,780).
```

3. March 19A:

```
Land (store site) ......................................... 10,200
    Preferred stock, 5%, par $100 (100 shares) ................         10,000
    Contributed capital in excess of par, preferred stock ........            200
    Purchased land for future store site; paid in full by issuance of
    100 shares of preferred stock. The market value is, $102 × 100
    shares = $10,200.
```

4. April 19A:

```
Organization cost ......................................... 1,980
    Cash ................................................          1,980
    Paid organization cost.
```

5. May 19A:

> Organization cost 1,020
>   Preferred stock, 5%, par $100 (10 shares) 1,000
>   Contributed capital in excess of par, preferred stock 20
> Organization cost (legal services) paid by issuance of 10 shares
> of preferred stock. The implied market value is, $102 × 10
> shares = $1,020.

6. June 19A:

> Cash 27,000
>   Nopar common stock (500 shares) 27,000
> Sold 500 shares of the nopar common stock ($54 × 500 shares
> = $27,000).

7. July 19A:

> Treasury stock, preferred (100 shares at $104) 10,400
>   Cash 10,400
> Purchased 100 shares of preferred treasury stock ($104 × 100
> shares = $10,400).

8. August 19A:

> Cash (20 shares at $105) 2,100
>   Treasury stock, preferred (20 shares at $104) 2,080
>   Contributed capital from treasury stock transactions 20
> Sold 20 shares of the preferred treasury stock at $105.

9. December 31, 19A:

Equipment	600,000	
Cash		600,000
Purchased equipment.		

10. December 31, 19A:

Cash	20,000	
Note payable		20,000
Borrowed on one-year, 12%, interest-bearing note.		

11. December 31, 19A:

Cash	129,300	
Revenues		129,300
Expenses	98,000	
Cash		98,000
To record summarized revenues and expenses.		

12. December 31, 19A:

Expenses	300	
Organization cost		300
Adjusting entry to amortize organization cost for one year		
($1,980 + $1,020) ÷ 10 years = $300.		

Requirement b—Closing entries:

13. December 31, 19A:

Revenues	129,300	
Income summary		129,300
Income summary	98,300	
Expenses ($98,000 + $300)		98,300
Income summary	31,000	
Retained earnings		31,000
($129,300 − $98,300 = $31,000).		

Requirement c:

SHELLY CORPORATION
Balance Sheet
At December 31, 19A

Assets

Current assets:
Cash .... $ 50,800

Tangible assets:
Land .... $ 10,200
Equipment (no depreciation assumed in the problem) 600,000   610,200

Intangible assets:
Organization cost (cost, $3,000 less amortization, $300) 2,700
Total assets $663,700

Liabilities

Current liabilities:
Note payable, 12% .... $ 20,000

Stockholders' Equity

Contributed capital:
Preferred stock, 5%, par value $100, authorized 5,000 shares,
  issued 2,000 shares of which 80 shares are held as
  treasury stock $200,000
Common stock, nopar value, authorized 20,000 shares,
  issued and outstanding 8,000 shares 417,000
Contributed capital in excess of par, preferred stock 4,000
Contributed capital from treasury stock transactions 20

Total contributed capital 621,020
Retained earnings 31,000

Total 652,020
Less cost of preferred treasury stock held (80 shares) 8,320

Total stockholders' equity 643,700
Total liabilities and stockholders' equity $663,700

SUMMARY OF CHAPTER

This chapter discussed accounting for owners' equity for corporations. Sole proprietorships and partnerships are discussed in Supplement 12B. Except for owners' equity, accounting basically is unaffected by the type of business organization. Accounting for owners' equity is based upon the concept of **source:** each specific source of owners' equity should be accounted for separately. The two basic sources of owners' equity for a corporation are contributed capital and retained earnings. Separate accounts are kept for each type of capital stock.

The earnings of a corporation that are not retained in the business for growth and expansion are distributed to the stockholders by means of dividends. Dividends are paid only when formally declared by the board of directors of the corporation. A cash dividend results in a decrease in assets (cash) and a commensurate decrease in stockholders' equity (retained earnings). In contrast, a stock dividend does not change assets, liabilities, or total stockholders' equity. A stock dividend results in a transfer of retained earnings to the permanent or contributed capital of the corporation by the amount of the stock dividend. Therefore, a stock dividend affects only certain account balances within stockholders' equity. A stock split affects only the par value of the stock and the number of shares outstanding; the individual equity account balances are not changed. Frequently a corporation purchases its own stock in the marketplace. Stock previously issued by the corporation and subsequently reacquired is known as **treasury stock** as long as it is held by the issuing corporation. The purchase of treasury stock is viewed as a contraction of corporate capital, and the subsequent resale of the treasury stock is viewed as an expansion of corporate capital.

SUPPLEMENT 12A—PARTICIPATING DIVIDEND PREFERENCE ON PREFERRED STOCK

Preferred stock may be nonparticipating, fully participating, or partially participating. Participation relates to the dividends that can be paid on preferred stock **after** dividends in arrears and **after** the current dividend preference.

Most preferred stock is **nonparticipating,** as shown in Exhibit 12–8. Preferred stock that is **participating** may be either noncumulative or cumulative.

Fully participating and **noncumulative** preferred stock receives a first priority for the current dividend preference; then a matching proportionate amount is allocated to the common stock; any remaining balance of the total dividend is allocated on a proportionate basis to the preferred and common stock as shown in Exhibit 12–11, Case A.

Fully participating and **cumulative** preferred stock receives a first priority on both dividends in **arrears** and the current dividend preference. After those

EXHIBIT 12–11

Dividends on participating preferred stock

Situation (Box Corporation; refer to Exhibit 12–7):

Preferred stock, 6%, par $20; shares outstanding, 2,000 = $40,000.
Common stock, par $10, shares outstanding, 5,000 = $50,000.
Dividends in arrears for the two previous years.

Allocation of dividends between preferred and common stock assuming fully participating:

		Amount of dividends paid		
	Assumptions (dividends in arrears, two years)	6% preferred stock (total par, $40,000)	Common stock (total par, $50,000)	Total dividends paid
Case A—Preferred stock is fully participating and noncumulative (two years in arrears). Total dividends paid, $7,200:				
Current dividend ($40,000 × 6%)		$ 2,400		$ 2,400
Equivalent amount to common ($50,000 × 6%)			$3,000	3,000
Subtotal				5,400
Full participation—balance allocated in ratio of par values:				
($40,000/$90,000) × ($7,200 − $5,400)		800		800
($50,000/$90,000) × ($7,200 − $5,400)			1,000	1,000
Totals		$ 3,200	$4,000	$ 7,200
Case B—Preferred stock is fully participating and cumulative (two years in arrears). Total dividends paid, $16,500:				
Arrears ($2,400 × 2 years)		$ 4,800		$ 4,800
Current preference ($40,000 × 6%)		2,400		2,400
Equivalent amount to common ($50,000 × 6%)			$3,000	3,000
Subtotal				10,200
Full participation—balance allocated in ratio of par:				
($40,000/$90,000) × ($16,500 − $10,200)		2,800		2,800
($50,000/$90,000) × ($16,500 − $10,200)			3,500	3,500
Totals		$10,000	$6,500	$16,500

preferences are satisfied, a proportionate amount is allocated to the common stock; any remaining balance of total dividends to be paid is allocated on a proportionate basis to the preferred and common stock as shown in Exhibit 12–11, Case B.

Partially participating preferred stock essentially is the same as fully participating. However, the participating preference in excess of the current dividend rate is limited to a stated percent of par. For example, the corporate charter may read, "and partially participating only up to an additional two percent."

Fully participating and partially participating preferred stock preferences are rare.[13]

SUPPLEMENT 12B—ACCOUNTING FOR OWNERS' EQUITY FOR SOLE PROPRIETORSHIPS AND PARTNERSHIPS

A sole proprietorship is an unincorporated business owned by one person. The only owner's equity accounts needed are (1) a capital account for the proprietor (for example, J. Doe, Capital), and (2) a drawing (or withdrawal) account for the proprietor (for example, J. Doe, Drawings). The **capital account** of a sole proprietorship is used for two purposes: to record investments by the owner and to accumulate the periodic income or loss. Thus, the **Income Summary** account is closed to the capital account at the end of each accounting period. The **drawing account** is used to record withdrawals of cash or other assets by the owner from the business. The drawing account is closed to the capital account at the end of each accounting period. The capital account reflects the cumulative total of all investments by the owner, plus all earnings of the entity, less all withdrawals of resources from the entity by the owner. In most respects, the accounting for a sole proprietorship is the same as for a corporation.

Exhibit 12–12 presents the recording of selected transactions and the owner's equity section of the balance sheet of Doe Retail Store to illustrate the accounting for and reporting of **owner's equity** for a sole proprietorship.[14]

There are two more differences between accounting for corporations and sole proprietorships. A sole proprietorship does not pay income taxes. Therefore, the financial statements of a sole proprietorship will not reflect income tax expense or income taxes payable. The net income of a sole proprietorship is taxed when it is included on the **personal** income tax return of the owner. Also, because an employer/employee contractual relationship cannot exist with only one party involved, a "salary" to the owner is not recognized as an expense of a sole proprietorship. The salary of the owner is accounted for as a distribution of profits (i.e., a withdrawal).

Owners' Equity for a Partnership

The Uniform Partnership Act, which has been adopted by most states, defines a partnership as "an association of two or more persons to carry on as co-owners of a business for profit." The partnership form of business is used by

---

[13] Textbooks for more advanced courses in accounting contain additional discussion and illustrations of the participating features and the payment of a dividend in assets other than cash, such as property and stock of other corporations being held as an investment.

[14] Alternatively, the balance sheet may reflect only "J. Doe, capital, December 31,19A, $156,000," with a supplemental or supporting **statement of owner's equity** that would be the same as shown in the exhibit.

EXHIBIT 12–12

Accounting and reporting of owner's equity for a sole proprietorship

Selected entries during 19A:

January 1, 19A:

J. Doe started a retail store by investing $150,000 of personal savings. The journal entry for the business would be as follows:

Cash 150,000
    J. Doe, capital   150,000
Investment by owner.

During 19A:

Each month during the year, Doe withdrew $1,000 cash from the business for personal living costs. Accordingly, each month the following journal entry was made.

J. Doe, drawings 1,000
    Cash   1,000
Withdrawal of cash by owner for personal use.

Note: At December 31, 19A, after the last withdrawal, the drawings account will reflect a debit balance of $12,000.

December 31, 19A:

Usual journal entries for the year, including adjusting and closing entries for the revenue and expense accounts, resulted in an $18,000 **credit balance** in the Income Summary account (i.e., $18,000 net income). The next closing entry will be:

Income summary 18,000
    J. Doe, capital   18,000
Closing entry to transfer net income for the year to the owner's equity account.

December 31, 19A:

The journal entry required on this date to close the drawings account would be:

J. Doe, capital 12,000
    J. Doe, drawings   12,000
Closing entry to transfer drawings for the year to the capital account.

Balance sheet December 31, 19A (partial):

Owner's Equity

J. Doe, capital, January 1, 19A	$150,000	
Add: Net income for 19A	18,000	
Total	168,000	
Less: Withdrawals for 19A	12,000	
J. Doe, capital December 31, 19A		$156,000

small businesses and professionals, such as accountants, doctors, and lawyers. A partnership is formed by two or more persons reaching mutual agreement about the terms of the partnership. The law does not require an application for a charter as in the case of a corporation. The agreement between the partners constitutes a **partnership contract** that should be in writing. The partnership agreement should specify such matters as division of periodic income, management responsibilities, transfer or sale of partnership interests, disposition of assets upon liquidation, and procedures to be followed in case of the death of a partner. If the partnership agreement does not specify on these matters, the laws of the resident state will be binding. The primary advantages of a partnership are (1) ease of formation, (2) complete control by the partners, and (3) no income taxes on the business itself. The primary disadvantage is the unlimited liability of each partner for the liabilities of the partnership.

As with a sole proprietorship, accounting for a partnership follows the same underlying fundamentals of accounting as any other form of business organization, **except for those entries that directly affect owners' equity.** Accounting for partners' equity follows the same pattern as illustrated earlier for a sole proprietorship, except that separate partner capital and drawings accounts must be established for **each** partner. Investments by each partner are credited to the partner's capital account. Withdrawals from the partnership by each partner are debited to the respective drawings account. The net income for a partnership is divided between the partners in the **profit ratio** specified in the partnership agreement. The Income Summary account is closed to the respective partner capital accounts. The respective drawings accounts also are closed to the partner capital accounts. Therefore, after the closing process, the capital account of each partner reflects the cumulative total of all investments of the individual partner, plus the partner's share of all partnership earnings, less all withdrawals by the partner.

Exhibit 12–13 presents selected 19A journal entries and partial financial statements of AB Partnership to illustrate the accounting for and reporting of the distribution of income and partners' equity.

The financial statements of a partnership follow the same format as a corporation, except (1) the income statement includes an additional section entitled "Distribution of net income," (2) the partners' equity section of the balance sheet is detailed for each partner in conformity with the full disclosure principle, as illustrated in Exhibit 12–13, (3) there is no income tax expense or income taxes payable because partnerships do not pay income tax (each partner must report his or her share of the partnership profits on the individual tax return), and (4) salaries paid to partners are not recorded as expense but are treated as a distribution of earnings (i.e., withdrawals).

EXHIBIT 12–13

Accounting for and reporting of partners' equity

Selected entries during 19A:

January 1, 19A:

AB Partnership was organized by A. Able and B. Baker on this date. Able contributed $60,000 and Baker $40,000 cash in the partnership and agreed to divide net income (and net loss) 60% and 40%, respectively. The journal entry for the business to record the investment would be:

Cash 100,000		
A. Able, capital	60,000	
B. Baker, capital	40,000	

Investment to initiate a partnership.

During 19A:

It was agreed that in lieu of salaries, Able would withdraw $1,000 and Baker $650 per month in cash. Accordingly, **each month** the following journal entry for the withdrawals was made:

A. Able, drawings 1,000	
B. Baker, drawings 650	
Cash	1,650

Withdrawal of cash by partners for personal use.

December 31, 19A:

Assume the normal closing entries for the revenue and expense accounts resulted in a $30,000 **credit balance** in the Income Summary account (i.e., $30,000 net income). The next closing entry would be:

Income summary 30,000	
A. Able, capital	18,000
B. Baker, capital	12,000

Closing entry to transfer net income to the respective capital accounts. Net income divided as follows:

A. Able $30,000 × 60% = $18,000
B. Baker $30,000 × 40% =   12,000
Total $30,000

December 31, 19A:

The journal entry required to close the drawings account would be:

A. Able, capital 12,000	
B. Baker, capital 7,800	
A. Able, drawings	12,000
B. Baker, drawings	7,800

Closing entry to transfer drawings for the year to the respective capital accounts.

__EXHIBIT 12–13 *(concluded)*__

Accounting for and reporting of partners' equity

After the closing entries the partners' accounts would reflect the following balances:

Income summary	–0–
A. Able, drawings	–0–
B. Baker, drawings	–0–
A. Able, capital	$66,000
B. Baker, capital	44,200

Reporting partners' distribution of net income and partners' equity:

Income statement for the year ended December 31, 19A:

Net income	$ 30,000

Distribution of net income:

A. Able (60%)	$18,000
B. Baker (40%)	12,000
	$30,000

Balance sheet December 31, 19A:

Partners' Equity

A. Able, capital	$66,000
B. Baker, capital	44,200
Total partners' equity	$110,200

A separate statement of partners' capital similar to the following customarily is prepared to supplement the balance sheet:

AB PARTNERSHIP
Statement of Partners' Capital
For the Year Ended December 31, 19A

	A. Able	B. Baker	Total
Investment, January 1, 19A	$60,000	$40,000	$100,000
Add: Additional investments during the year	–0–	–0–	–0–
Net income for the year	18,000	12,000	30,000
Totals	78,000	52,000	130,000
Less: Drawings during the year	12,000	7,800	19,800
Partners' equity, December 31, 19A	$66,000	$44,200	$110,200

IMPORTANT TERMS DEFINED IN THIS CHAPTER

Terms (alphabetically)	Key words in definitions of important terms used in chapter	Page reference
Authorized shares	Maximum number of shares of the corporation that can be issued as specified in the charter.	608
Charter of a corporation	The legal articles of incorporation by the state that create a corporation; specifies purpose and capital.	606
Common stock	The basic, normal, voting stock issued by a corporation; not preferred stock; residual equity.	610
Convertible preferred stock	Preferred stock that is convertible, at the option of the holder, to common stock.	612
Cumulative dividend preference	Preferred stock preference that dividends not declared for a particular year cumulate as a subsequent preference.	622
Current dividend preference	The basic dividend preference on preferred stock for a particular year.	622
Dividend dates: Declaration	Date dividend declared; entry for cash dividend; dividends payable.	626
Record	Date on which the stockholders are individually identified to receive a declared dividend.	626
Payment	Date on which a cash dividend is paid to the stockholders of record; cash is disbursed.	627
Dividends in arrears	Dividends on cumulative preferred stock that have not been declared in prior years.	622
Issued shares	Total shares of stock that have been issued; shares outstanding plus treasury shares held.	609
Legal or stated capital	Defined by state law; usually par value; provides a "cushion" for creditors; cannot be used for dividends.	611
Minute book	An official record of the actions of the board of directors of a corporation.	627
No par value stock	Shares of capital stock that have no par value specified in the corporate charter.	610
Outstanding shares	Shares of stock, in total, that are owned by stockholders on any particular date.	609
Par value	Nominal value per share of capital stock; specified in the charter; basis for legal capital.	610
Partnership	An unincorporated business owned by two or more persons.	630
Preferred stock	Shares of stock that have specified rights over the common stock.	611
Prior period adjustments	Amounts debited or credited directly to retained earnings resulting from correction of accounting errors.	628
Restrictions on retained earnings	Temporary removal of some or all of the balance of retained earnings from dividend availability.	629
Sole proprietorship	An unincorporated business owned by only one person (one owner).	630
Stock certificate	Evidence of the number of shares of stock held by an investor; ownership interest.	607
Stock dividends	Distribution of additional shares of stock to current stockholders on a proportional basis at no cost; decreases retained earnings.	622

Terms *(alphabetically)*	Key words in definitions of important terms used in chapter	Page reference
Stock splits	The total number of authorized shares is increased by a specified ratio; issued at no cost; does not change proportional ownership of each stockholder; does not decrease retained earnings.	625
Stock transfer agent	An individual or organization appointed by a corporation to transfer shares and maintain stockholders' records.	627
Stockholders' subsidiary ledger	A record, usually maintained by a stock transfer agent, of the names, addresses, and shares owned, of all the stockholders.	627
Treasury stock	A corporation's own stock that has been issued, then reacquired and still held by that corporation.	616
Unissued shares	Shares of a corporation's stock that have never been issued.	609

QUESTIONS

PART A

1. Define a corporation and identify its primary advantages.

2. What is the charter of a corporation?

3. Explain each of the following terms: (a) authorized capital stock, (b) issued capital stock, (c) unissued capital stock, and (d) outstanding capital stock.

4. Distinguish between common stock and preferred stock.

5. Explain the distinction between par value stock and nopar value capital stock.

6. What are the usual characteristics of preferred stock?

7. What are the two basic sources of stockholders' equity? Explain each.

8. Owners' equity is accounted for by source. What is meant by source?

9. Define treasury stock. Why do corporations acquire treasury stock?

10. How is treasury stock reported on the balance sheet? How is the "gain or loss" on treasury stock which has been sold reported on the financial statements?

PART B

11. What are the two basic requirements to support a cash dividend? What are the effects of a cash dividend on assets and stockholders' equity?

12. Distinguish between cumulative and noncumulative preferred stock.

13. Define a stock dividend. How does it differ from a cash dividend?

14. What are the primary purposes in issuing a stock dividend?

15. Identify and explain the three important dates in respect to dividends.

16. Define retained earnings. What are the primary components of retained earnings at the end of each period?

17. Define prior period adjustments. How are they reported?

18. What is meant by restrictions on retained earnings?

EXERCISES

E12–1   **(Pair Definition with Terms)**

Match the following brief definitions with the terms by entering the appropriate letter in each space provided.

Terms	*Description*
_____ (1) Unissued shares	A. Specified by the corporate charter, the maximum number of shares of capital stock the corporation can issue.
_____ (2) Stock dividends	
_____ (3) Dividends in arrears	
_____ (4) Authorized shares	B. The class of stock that is issued when only one kind is issued.
_____ (5) Nopar value stock	
_____ (6) Common stock	C. Provides the option of being exchanged for common stock.
_____ (7) Declaration date	
_____ (8) Stock splits	D. Requires that if dividends are not paid in full, the unpaid amount of dividends accumulates.
_____ (9) Cumulative dividend preference	E. The date on which the board of directors officially approves a dividend.
_____ (10) Record date	F. The date on which the corporation prepares a list of those owning outstanding shares.
_____ (11) Issued shares	
_____ (12) Par value	G. The date cash dividends are disbursed.
_____ (13) Legal or stated capital	H. The accumulated unpaid preferred stock dividends.
_____ (14) Payment date	I. Includes treasury stock.
_____ (15) Treasury stock	J. Par value.
_____ (16) Convertible preferred stock	K. Stock that cannot be sold at a premium or discount.
_____ (17) Preferred stock	L. Nominal value per share established for the stock in the charter of the corporation.
_____ (18) Prior period adjustment	M. Stock whose characteristics usually include: dividend preferences, conversion priviledges, asset preferences, and nonvoting specification.

N. Correction of an error in the financial statements of a prior period that must be reported on the statement of retained earnings.

O. A board of directors may declare and issue this instead of a cash dividend; it decreases retained earnings.

P. Similar to a stock dividend but does not decrease retained earnings.

Q. Capital stock reacquired which reduces cash and stockholders' equity by equal amounts.

R. Authorized shares minus issued shares.

E12–2   **(Preparing the Stockholders' Equity Section of the Balance Sheet)**

Janex Corporation was organized in 19A to operate an engineering service business. The charter authorized the following capital stock: common stock, par value $10 per share, 10,000 shares. During the first year, the following selected transactions were completed:

1. Sold and issued 5,000 shares of common stock for cash at $25 per share.
2. Issued 500 shares of common stock for a piece of land that will be used for a facilities site; construction began immediately. Assume the stock was selling at $27 per share at the date of issuance. Debit land.
3. Sold and issued 1,000 shares of common stock for cash at $27 cash per share.
4. At year-end, the Income Summary account reflected a $7,000 loss. Because a loss was incurred, no income tax expense was recorded.

Required:

a. Give the journal entry required for each of the transactions listed above.
b. Prepare the stockholders' equity section as it should be reported on the year-end balance sheet.

E12–3 **(Analysis of Transactions Affecting Stockholders' Equity)**

Reed Corporation was organized in January 19A by 12 stockholders to operate an air conditioning sales and service business. The charter issued by the state authorized the following capital stock:

Common stock, $1 par value, 100,000 shares.

Preferred stock, $10 par value, 8%, nonparticipating, noncumulative, 30,000 shares.

During January and February 19A, the following stock transactions were completed:

1. Collected $30,000 cash from each of the 12 organizers and issued 1,000 shares of common stock to each of them.
2. Sold 8,000 shares of preferred stock at $30 per share; collected the cash and immediately issued the stock.

Required:

a. Give the journal entries to record the above stock transactions.
b. Net income for 19A was $35,000, cash dividends declared and paid at year-end were $15,000. Prepare the stockholders' equity section of the balance sheet at December 31, 19A.

E12–4 **(Issuing Common and Preferred Stock)**

Sound Systems, Incorporated, was issued a charter on January 15, 19A, that authorized the following capital stock:

Common stock, nopar, 80,000 shares.

Preferred stock, 6%, par value $10 per share, 10,000 shares.

The board of directors established a stated value on the nopar common stock of $1 per share.

During 19A, the following selected transactions were completed in the order given:

1. Sold and issued 30,000 shares of the nopar common stock at $30 cash per share.
2. Sold and issued 4,000 shares of preferred stock at $21 cash per share.
3. At the end of 19A, the Income Summary account had a credit balance of $15,000.

Required:

a. Give the journal entry indicated for each of the above transactions.
b. Prepare the stockholders' equity section of the balance sheet at December 31, 19A.

E12–5   **(Stockholders' Equity Transactions, Including Noncash Consideration)**

Datalife Corporation obtained a charter at the start of 19A that authorized 40,000 shares of nopar common stock and 5,000 shares of preferred stock, par value $10. The corporation was organized by five individuals who "reserved" 51% of the common stock shares for themselves. The remaining shares were to be sold to other individuals at $50 per share on a cash basis. During 19A, the following selected transactions occurred:

1. Collected $20 per share cash from four of the organizers and received two adjoining lots of land from the fifth organizer. Issued 3,000 shares of common stock to each of the five organizers and received title to the land.
2. Sold and issued 5,000 shares of common stock to an "outsider" at $50 cash per share.
3. Sold and issued 4,000 shares of preferred stock at $15 cash per share.
4. At the end of 19A, the Income Summary account, after income taxes, reflected a credit balance of $30,000.

Required:

a. Give the journal entries indicated for each of the transactions listed above.
b. Prepare the stockholders' equity section of the balance sheet at December 31, 19A.
c. Explain the basis that you used to determine the cost of the land.

E12–6   **(Finding Missing Amounts from the Stockholders' Equity Section)**

The stockholders' equity section on the December 31, 19D, balance sheet of Houston Corporation was:

Stockholders' Equity

Contributed capital:
Preferred stock, par value $30, authorized 8,000 shares;___?___ issued, of which 500 shares are held as treasury stock	$165,000
Common stock, nopar, authorized 10,000 shares; issued and outstanding 7,000 shares	630,000
Contributed capital in excess of par, preferred	7,150
Contributed capital, treasury stock transactions	2,000
Retained earnings	40,000
Cost of treasury stock, preferred	16,000

Required:

Complete the following statements and show your computations.

a. The number of shares of preferred stock issued was _____.
b. The number of shares of preferred stock outstanding was _____.
c. The average sale price of the preferred stock when issued was $_____ per share.
d. Have the treasury stock transactions (1) increased corporate resources _____; or (2) decreased resources _____? By how much? _____.
e. How much did the treasury stock transactions increase (decrease) stockholders' equity?
f. How much did the treasury stock held cost per share? $_____
g. Total stockholders' equity is $_____.
h. What was the average issue price of the common stock? $_____.
i. Assuming one fourth of the treasury stock is sold at $30 per share, the remaining balance in the Treasury Stock account would be $_____.

E12–7   (Accounting for Treasury Stock Transactions)

The balance sheet (summarized) of Pope Corporation reflected the information shown below at December 31, 19B:

POPE CORPORATION
Balance Sheet
At December 31, 19B

Assets		Liabilities	
Cash	$100,000	Current liabilities	$ 60,000
All other assets	412,000	Long-term liabilities	80,000
			140,000
		Stockholders' Equity	
		Contributed capital:	
		Common stock, par $20, authorized 20,000 shares; outstanding 12,000 shares	240,000
		Contributed capital in excess of par	72,000
		Retained earnings	60,000
	$512,000		$512,000

During the next year, 19C, the following selected transactions affecting stockholders' equity occurred:

Feb. 1   Purchased in the open market, 500 shares of Pope's own common stock at $40 cash per share.

July 15   Sold 100 of the shares purchased on February 1, 19C, at $41 cash per share.

Sept. 1   Sold 20 more of the shares purchased on February 1, 19C, at $38 cash per share.

Dec. 15   Sold an additional 80 of the treasury shares at $35 per share.

31   The credit balance in the Income Summary account was $31,140.

Required:

a. Give the indicated journal entries for each of the five transactions.

b. Prepare the stockholders' equity section of the balance sheet at December 31, 19C.

PART B

E12–8   (Comparing Various Types of Preferred Stock)

The records of Quality Plumbing Supply Company reflected the following balances in the stockholders' equity accounts at December 31, 19H:

Common stock, par $5 per share, 30,000 shares outstanding.

Preferred stock, 6%, par $10 per share, 3,000 shares outstanding.

Retained earnings, $150,000.

On September 1, 19H, the board of directors was considering the distribution of a $42,000 cash dividend. No dividends were paid during 19F and 19G. You have been asked to determine the total and per share amounts that would be paid to the common stockholders and to the preferred stockholders under three independent assumptions (show computations):

a. The preferred stock is noncumulative and nonparticipating.

b. The preferred stock is cumulative and nonparticipating.

c. The preferred stock is cumulative and fully participating (solve this assumption only if Supplement 12A is assigned for study).

d. Give the journal entry to record dividends separately for preferred and common stock under each assumption.

e. Explain why the dividends per share of common stock was less for each assumption than for the preceding assumption.

f. What factor would cause a more favorable per share result to the common stockholders?

E12–9   (Recording Dividends)

Rye Corporation has the following capital stock outstanding at the end of 19B:

Preferred stock, 8%, par $20, outstanding shares, 6,000.

Common stock, par $5, outstanding shares, 20,000.

On October 1, 19B, the board of directors declared dividends as follows:

Preferred stock, the full cash preference amount; payable December 20, 19B.

Common stock, a 10% common stock dividend (i.e., one additional share for each 10 held), issuable December 20, 19B.

On December 20, 19B, the market prices were: preferred stock, $50, and common stock, $20.

Required:

a. Give any required journal entry(s) to record the declaration and subsequent payment of the dividend on the preferred stock.

b. Give any required journal entry(s) to record the declaration and issuance of the stock dividend on the common stock.

c. Explain the comparative overall effect of each of the dividends on the assets, liabilities, and stockholders' equity of Rye Corporation.

E12–10   (Analysis of Stock Dividends)

On December 31, 19E, the stockholders' equity section of the balance sheet of Hyde Park Corporation reflected the following:

Common stock, par $10, shares authorized 50,000; shares outstanding 20,000	$200,000
Contributed capital in excess of par	15,000
Retained earnings	103,000

On February 1, 19F, the board of directors declared a 15% stock dividend to be issued April 30, 19F. The market value of the stock on February 1, 19F, was $16 per share. The market value will be capitalized.

Required:

a. Give any required journal entry(s) to record the declaration and issuance of the stock dividend.

b. For comparative purposes, prepare the stockholders' equity section of the balance sheet (1) immediately before the stock dividend and (2) immediately after the stock dividend. (Hint: Use two amount columns for this requirement.)

c. Explain the effects of this stock dividend on the assets, liabilities, and stockholders' equity.

E12–11   (Preparation of a Statement of Retained Earnings)

The following account balances were selected from the records of Comed Corporation at December 31, 19E, after all adjusting entries were completed:

Common stock, par $5, authorized 200,000 shares; issued 120,000 shares, of which 500 shares are held as treasury stock	$600,000
Contributed capital in excess of par	280,000
Bond sinking fund	70,000
Dividends declared and paid in 19E	24,000
Retained earnings, January 1, 19E	90,000
Correction of prior period accounting error (a debit, net of income tax)	10,000
Treasury stock at cost (500 shares)	3,000
Income summary for 19E (credit balance)	45,000
Restriction on retained earnings equal to the cost of treasury stock held is required by law in this state.	

Required:

Based upon the above data, prepare *(a)* the statement of retained earnings for 19E and *(b)* the stockholders' equity section of the balance sheet at December 31, 19E. (Hint: Total stockholders' equity is $978,000.)

E12–12   (Preparing the Statement of Retained Earnings)

The data given below were selected from the records of Stonewall Corporation at December 31, 19B.

Common stock, par $2, authorized 300,000 shares, issued 110,000 shares of which 1,000 are held as treasury stock (purchased at $8 per share)	$220,000
Preferred stock, 6%, par $10, authorized 20,000 shares, issued and outstanding 15,000 shares	150,000
Contributed capital in excess of par:	
Common stock	230,000
Preferred stock	120,000
Dividends declared and paid during 19B	24,000
Net income for 19B	64,000
Retained earnings balance, January 1, 19B	130,000
Prior period adjustment (gain, net of income tax)	10,000
Extraordinary loss (unusual and infrequent, net of income tax)	22,000

Required:

a. Prepare a statement of retained earnings for the year ended December 31, 19B.

b. Prepare the stockholders' equity section of the balance sheet dated December 31, 19B. (Hint: Total stockholders' equity is $892,000.)

E12–13   (Comparison of Stock Dividends and Splits)

On July 1, 19B, Brodnik Corporation had the following capital structure:

Common stock, par $2, authorized shares	100,000
Common stock, par $2, unissued shares	80,000
Contributed capital in excess of par, $60,000.	
Retained earnings, $120,000.	
Treasury stock, none.	

Required:

a. The number of issued shares is _____.
b. The number of outstanding shares is _____.
c. Total stockholders' equity is _____.
d. Assume the board of directors declared and issued a 20% stock dividend (i.e., one new share for each five shares already owned) when the stock was selling at $11 per share. Give any required journal entry(s). If none is required, explain why.
e. Disregard the stock dividend in (*d*) above. Assume that the board of directors voted a six-to-five stock split (i.e., a 20% increase in the number of shares). The market price prior to the split was $11 per share. Give any required journal entry(s). If none is required, explain why.
f. Complete the following comparative tabulation followed by comments on the comparative effects:

Items	Before Dividend and Split	After Stock Dividend	After Stock Split
Common stock account	$	$	$
Par per share	$2	$	$
Shares outstanding	#	#	#
Contributed capital in excess of par	$ 60,000	$	$
Retained earnings	$120,000	$	$
Total stockholders' equity	$	$	$

PROBLEMS

PART A

P12–1   **(Preparation of the Stockholders' Equity Section of the Balance Sheet)**
Alliance Corporation received its charter during January 19A. The charter authorized the following capital stock:

Preferred stock, 6%, par $10, authorized 10,000 shares.
Common stock, par $2, authorized 100,000 shares.

During 19A, the following transactions occurred in the order given:

1. Issued a total of 60,000 shares of the common stock to the six organizers at $5 per share. Alliance collected cash in full from five of the organizers, and legal services were received from the other organizer in full payment for the shares. The stock was issued immediately.
2. Sold 3,000 shares of the preferred stock at $22 per share. Collected the cash and issued the stock immediately.
3. Sold 2,000 shares of the common stock at $7 per share and 1,000 shares of the preferred stock at $30. Collected the cash and issued the stock immediately.
4. Total revenues for 19A, $206,000, and total expenses (including income tax), $140,000.

Required:

a. Give all of the journal entries required for the above items including closing entries.

b. Prepare the stockholders' equity section of the balance sheet at December 31, 19A.

c. What was the average issue price of the common stock?

d. Explain the basis you used to value the legal services in the first journal entry.

P12–2   (Analysis of Transactions Affecting Stockholders' Equity)

Xenia Corporation began operations in Janary 19A. The charter authorized the following capital stock:

Preferred stock, 6%, $10 par, authorized 20,000
Common stock, nopar, authorized 100,000 shares.

The corporation, in conformance with state laws, established a stated value per share of $4 for the nopar common stock.

During 19A, the following transactions occurred in the order given:

1. Issued 20,000 shares of the nopar common stock to each of the three organizers. Collected $8 cash per share from two of the organizers and received a plot of land, with a small building thereon, in full payment for the shares of the third organizer and issued the stock immediately. Assume that 20% of the noncash payment received applies to the building.

2. Sold 4,000 shares of the preferred stock at $15 per share. Collected the cash and issued the stock immediately.

3. Sold 200 shares of the preferred stock at $16 and 1,000 shares of the nopar common stock at $10 per share. Collected the cash and issued the stock immediately.

4. Operating results at the end of 19A, were as follows:

Revenue accounts $160,000
Expense accounts, including income taxes 115,000

Required:

a. Give the journal entries indicated (including closing entries) for each of the above transactions.

b. Prepare the stockholders' equity section of the balance sheet at December 31, 19A.

c. Explain what you used to determine the cost of the land and the building in the first journal entry.

P12–3   (Comparison of Par and Nopar Stock)

Myles Company was issued a charter in January 19A, which authorized 75,000 shares of common stock. During 19A, the following selected transactions occurred in the order given:

1. Sold 10,000 shares of the stock for cash at $70 per share. Collected the cash and issued the stock immediately.

2. Acquired land to be used as a future plant site; made payment in full by issuing 500 shares of stock. Assume a market value per share of $70.

3. At the end of 19A, the Income Summary account reflected a credit balance of $40,000.

Three independent cases are assumed as follows for comparative study purposes:

Case A—Assume the common stock was $30 par value per share. The state law specifies that par value is legal capital.

Case B—Assume the common stock was nopar and that the total sale price is credited to the Common Stock, Nopar account because the state law specifies this amount as legal capital.

Case C—Assume the common stock is nopar with a stated value, specified by the board of directors, of $10 per share.

Required:

For each independent case:

a. Give the journal entries for each of the three transactions.
b. Prepare the stockholders' equity section of the balance sheet at December 31, 19A.
c. Should total stockholders' equity be the same amount among the three independent cases? Explain.
d. Should the noncash asset (land) be recorded at the same cost under each of the three independent cases? Explain.

P12–4   (Analysis of Stockholders' Equity Transactions)

Mika Company obtained a charter from the state in January 19A, which authorized 100,000 shares of common stock, $1 par value. The stockholders comprised 20 local citizens. During the first year, the following selected transactions occurred in the order given:

1. Sold 80,000 shares of the common stock to the 20 stockholders at $5 per share. Collected the $400,000 cash and issued the stock.
2. During the year, one of the 20 stockholders needed cash and wanted to sell the stock back to Mika. Accordingly, the corporation purchased the investor's 5,000 shares at $7 cash per share.
3. Two months later, 1,000 of the shares of treasury stock (purchased in 2) were resold to another individual at $7.25 cash per share.
4. An additional 2,000 shares of the treasury stock were sold at $6.90 cash per share.
5. On December 31, 19A, the end of the first year of business, the Income Summary account reflected a credit balance of $28,550.

Required:

a. Give the indicated journal entry for each of the above items.
b. Prepare the stockholders' equity section of the balance sheet at December 31, 19A.
c. What dollar effect did the treasury stock transactions have on the assets, liabilities, and stockholders' equity of Mika Corporation? Explain.

P12–5   (Analysis of Stockholder Transactions Including Noncash Consideration)

Centex Manufacturing Company was granted a charter that authorized the following capital stock:

Common stock, nopar, 50,000 shares. Assume the nopar stock is not assigned a stated value per share.

Preferred stock, 6%, par $10, 10,000 shares.

During the first year, 19A, the following selected transactions occurred in the order given:

1. Sold 20,000 shares of the nopar common stock at $30 cash per share and 3,000 shares of the preferred stock at $22 cash per share. Collected cash and issued the stock immediately. For the nopar stock, credit the full selling price to the common stock account.
2. Issued 1,000 shares of preferred stock as full payment for a plot of land to be used as a future plant site. Assume the stock was selling at $22.
3. Purchased 1,000 shares of the nopar common stock sold earlier; paid cash, $26 per share.
4. Sold all of the treasury stock (common) purchased in 3 above. The sale price was $29 per share.
5. Purchased 200 shares of the company's own preferred stock at $24 cash per share.
6. At December 31, 19A, the Income Summary account reflected a credit balance of $21,200.

Required:

a. Give the journal entries indicated for each of the above transactions.
b. Prepare the stockholders' equity section of the balance sheet at December 31, 19A, end of the annual accounting period.

PART B

P12–6   **(Comparison of Stock and Cash Dividends)**

Providence Equipment Company had the following stock outstanding and retained earnings at December 31, 19E:

Common stock, $10 par, outstanding 20,000 shares $200,000
Preferred stock, 6%, $20 par, outstanding 5,000 shares 100,000
Retained earnings 240,000

The board of directors is considering the distribution of a cash dividend to the two groups of stockholders. No dividends were declared during 19C or 19D. Three independent cases are assumed:

Case A—The preferred stock is noncumulative and nonparticipating; the total amount of dividends is $36,000.

Case B—The preferred stock is cumulative and nonparticipating; the total amount of dividends is $18,000.

Case C—Same as Case B, except the amount is $58,000.

Required:

a. Compute the amount of dividends, in total and per share, that would be payable to each class of stockholders for each case. Show computations.
b. Give the journal entry to record the cash dividends declared and paid in 19E for Case C only. Assume that the declaration and payment occurred simultaneously on December 31, 19E.
c. Give the required journal entry assuming, instead of a cash dividend, the declaration and issuance of a 10% common stock dividend on the outstanding common stock. Assume the market value per share of common stock was $20.

d. Complete the following comparative schedule including explanation of the comparative differences.

Item	Amount of Dollar Increase (Decrease)	
	Cash Dividend—Case C	Stock Dividend
Assets	$	$
Liabilities	$	$
Stockholders' equity	$	$

P12–7 **(Recording Dividends)**

Value Manufacturing Company has outstanding 50,000 shares of $5 par value common stock and 15,000 shares of $10 par value preferred stock (8%). On December 1, 19B, the board of directors voted a 8% cash dividend on the preferred stock and a 20% common stock dividend on the common stock (i.e., for each five shares of common stock held, one additional share of common stock is to be issued as a stock dividend). At the date of declaration, the common stock was selling at $30 and the preferred at $25 per share. The dividends are to be paid, or issued, on February 15, 19C. The annual accounting period ends December 31.

Required:

a. Give any journal entry(s) required to record the declaration and payment of the cash dividend.
b. Give any journal entry(s) required to record the declaration and issuance of the stock dividend.
c. Explain the comparative effects of the two dividends on the assets, liabilities, and stockholders' equity (1) through December 31, 19B, (2) on February 15, 19C, and (3) the overall effects from December 1, 19B, through February 15, 19C. A schedule similar to the following might be helpful:

Item	Comparative Effects Explained	
	Cash Dividend on Preferred	Stock Dividend on Common
1. Through December 31, 19B: Assets		
etc.		

P12–8 **(Analysis of Stockholders' Equity Transactions Including Treasury Stock)**

The accounts of Federated Corporation reflected the following balances on January 1, 19C:

Preferred stock, 5%, $50 par value, cumulative, authorized
    10,000 shares, issued and outstanding 2,000 shares $100,000
Common stock, $10 par value, authorized 100,000 shares,
    outstanding 20,000 shares   200,000
Contributed capital in excess of par, preferred   5,000
Contributed capital in excess of par, common   10,000
Retained earnings   200,000
        Total stockholders' equity $515,000

The transactions during 19C relating to the stockholders' equity are listed below in order:

1. Purchased 200 shares of preferred treasury stock at $150 per share.
2. The board of directors declared and paid a cash dividend to the preferred stockholders only. No dividends were declared during 19A or 19B. The dividend was sufficient to pay the arrears plus the dividend for the current year.
3. The board of directors declared a 1-for-10 (i.e., 10%) common stock dividend on the outstanding common stock. Market value of $20 per share is to be capitalized.
4. Net income for the year was $80,000.

Required:

a. Give the journal entry for each of the above transactions, including the closing entries. Show computations.
b. Prepare a statement of retained earnings for 19C and the stockholders' equity section of the balance sheet at December 31, 19C. (Hint: Total stockholders' equity is $551,500.)
c. Explain the comparative effects on assets and stockholders' equity of the (1) cash dividend and (2) the stock dividend.

P12–9   (Preparing the Stockholders' Equity Section of the Balance Sheet)
EMBA Company is completing its year-end accounting, including the preparation of the annual financial statements, at December 31, 19E. The stockholders' equity accounts reflected the following balances at the end of the year, 19E:

Common stock, par $10, shares outstanding 50,000 .... $500,000
Contributed capital in excess of par   50,000
Retained earnings, January 1, 19E (credit)   300,000
Cash dividends declared and paid during 19E (debit)   30,000
Income summary account for 19E (credit balance; after tax)   60,000

The following selected transactions occurred near the end of 19E; they are not included in the above amounts:

1. During 19D, EMBA Company was sued for $85,000, and it was clear that the suit would be lost. Therefore, in 19D, EMBA should have debited a loss and credited a liability for this amount. This journal entry was not made, and the accounting error was found in 19E. (Hint: Credit Liability for Damages.) Disregard any income tax effects.
2. The board of directors voted a voluntary restriction on retained earnings of $100,000. It is to be designated as "Earnings appropriated for plant expansion" effective for the 19E financial statements.

Required:

a. Give the appropriate journal entries for the events listed immediately above. If no entry is given, explain.

b. Prepare a statement of retained earnings for 19E and the stockholders' equity section of the balance sheet at December 31, 19E. (Hint: The ending balance of stockholders' equity is $795,000.)

P12–10   **(Preparation of the Statement of Retained Earnings)**

Fred Company has completed all of the annual information processing at December 31, 19D, except for preparation of the financial statements. The following account balances were reflected at that date:

FRED COMPANY
Adjusted Trial Balance
December 31, 19D

	Debit	Credit
Cash	$ 57,000	
Accounts receivable (net)	58,000	
Merchandise inventory, December 31, 19D	120,000	
Long-term investment in Company Y	20,000	
Bond sinking fund	40,000	
Land	20,000	
Buildings and equipment (net)	738,000	
Other assets	29,200	
Accounts payable		$ 86,000
Income tax payable		18,000
Bonds payable, 7%, payable December 31		100,000
Preferred stock, par $10, authorized 50,000 shares		100,000
Common stock, par $5, authorized 200,000 shares		660,000
Contributed capital in excess of par, preferred		6,100
Contributed capital in excess of par, common		19,900
Treasury stock, preferred, 10 shares at cost	1,100	
Retained earnings, January 1, 19D		163,300
19D net income		40,000
19D cash dividends on preferred	26,000	
19D common stock dividends distributed (10,000 shares)	70,000	
19D, discovered an accounting error made in 19A in recording a purchase of land (the correction required a net credit to land of $14,000)	14,000	
	$1,193,300	$1,193,300

Note: Retained earnings is restricted in an amount equal to the bond sinking fund per the provisions of the bond indenture.

Required:

Prepare a statement of retained earnings for 19D and a classified balance sheet at December 31, 19D. (Hint: Total stockholders' equity is $878,200.)

P12–11   (Evaluation of an Inaccurately Prepared Statement)

The bookkeeper for Careless Company prepared the following balance sheet:

CARELESS COMPANY
Balance Sheet
For the Year 19W

Assets

Current assets	$ 45,000
Fixed assets (net of depreciation reserves, $70,000)	125,000
Other assets	50,000
Total debits	$220,000

Liabilities

Current liabilities	$ 32,000
Other debts	25,000

Capital

Stock, par $10, authorized 10,000 shares	60,000
Stock premium	30,000
Earned surplus	58,000
Treasury stock (500 shares)	(10,000)
Reserve for treasury stock (required by law)	10,000
Correction of prior year error (a credit, net)	7,000
Cash dividends paid during 19W	(12,000)
Net profit for 19W	20,000
Total credits	$220,000

Required:

a. List all of the deficiencies you can identify in the above statement. Assume the amounts given are correct.

b. Prepare a statement of retained earnings for 19W.

c. Recast the above balance sheet in good form; focus especially on stockholders' equity.

P12–12   (Based on Supplement 12B—Comparison of Stockholders' Equity Sections for Alternative Forms of Organization)

Assume for each of the three independent cases below that the annual accounting period ends on December 31, 19W, and that the Income Summary account at that date reflected a debit balance of $30,000 (i.e., a loss).

Case A—Assume that the company is a **sole proprietorship** owned by Proprietor A. Prior to the closing entries, the capital account reflected a credit balance of $70,000 and the drawings account a balance of $6,000.

Case B—Assume that the company is a **partnership** owned by Partner A and Partner B. Prior to the closing entries, the owners' equity accounts reflected the following balances: A, Capital, $50,000; B, Capital, $45,000; A, Drawings, $7,000; and B, Drawings, $6,000. Profits and losses are divided equally.

Case C—Assume that the company is a **corporation.** Prior to the closing entries, the stockholders' equity accounts showed the following: Capital Stock, par $20, authorized 20,000 shares, outstanding 4,000 shares; Contributed Capital in Excess of Par, $2,000; and Retained Earnings, $40,000.

Required:

a. Give all of the closing entries indicated at December 31, 19W, for each of the separate cases.

b. Show how the owners' equity section of the balance sheet would appear at December 31, 19W, for each case.

CASES

C12–1   (Finding Missing Amounts)

At December 31, 19E, the records of Lone Star Corporation provided the following selected and incomplete data:

Common stock, par $10 (no changes during 19E):
  Shares authorized, 500,000.
  Shares issued _?_ issue price $12 per share; cash collected in full, $1,800,000.
  Shares held as treasury stock, 2,000 shares—cost $15 per share.
Net income for 19E, $176,000.
Dividends declared and paid during 19E, $74,000.
Bond sinking fund balance, $20,000.
Prior perod adjustment—correction of 19B accounting error, $18,000 (a credit, net of income tax).
Retained earnings balance, January 1, 19E, $180,000.
State law places a restriction on retained earnings equal to the cost of treasury stock held.
  The treasury stock was acquired after the stock dividend was issued.
Extraordinary gain (net of income tax), $22,000.

Required:

a. Complete the following tabulation:
  Shares authorized _____.
  Shares issued _____.
  Shares outstanding _____.

b. The balance in the Contributed Capital in Excess of Par account appears to be $_____.

c. EPS on net income is $_____.

d. Dividend paid per share of common stock is $_____.

e. The bond sinking fund should be reported on the balance sheet under the classification _____.

f. Net income before extraordinary items was $_____.

g. The prior period adjustment should be reported on the _____ as an addition _____ or a deduction _____.

h. Treasury stock should be reported on the balance sheet under the major caption _____ in the amount of $_____.

i. The amount of retained earnings available for dividends on January 1, 19E, was $_____.

j. Assume the board of directors voted a 100% stock split (the number of shares will double). After the stock split, the par value per share will be $_____ and the number of outstanding shares will be _____.

k. Assuming the stock split given in (*j*) above, give any journal entry that should be made. If none explain why.

l. Disregard the stock split (assumed in *[j]* and *[k]* above). Assume instead that a 5% stock dividend was declared and issued when the market price of the common stock was $15. Give any journal entry that should be made.

C12–2   (Analysis of Stockholders' Equity Using an Actual Financial Statement)
Refer to the financial statements of Chesebrough-Pond's given in Special Supplement B immediately preceding the Index.

Required:

a. How many shares of treasury stock were purchased during 1984? What was the average cost per share of treasury stock purchased during 1984? Did the company purchase any treasury stock during 1985?

b. How many shares of common stock were issued at the end of 1985? How many shares were authorized? How many shares were outstanding?

c. Has the company issued any preferred stock?

d. How many stockholders own stock in the company?

e. Assume the company declared and paid a $1 per share dividend on December 31, 1985. Prepare the journal entry to record the dividend.

Accounting for long term investments in securities is more complex than accounting for short term investments in securities. Usually a note is included in the financial statement to provide additional information concerning the investment.

Note 4. Investments and Advances

As of December 31, Millions of Dollars	1985	1984
Nonsubsidiary companies and unconsolidated finance subsidiaries accounted for on the equity method:		
Caltex group of companies	$1,163	$1,256
Other companies	750	609
	1,913	1,865
Nonsubsidiary companies—at cost	76	73
	1,989	1,938
Miscellaneous investments (at cost), long-term receivables, etc., less reserve	711	852
Total	$2,700	$2,790

For additional information regarding the Caltex group of companies, reference is made to Note 18.

Texaco's equity in the net income of nonsubsidiary companies and of unconsolidated finance subsidiaries accounted for on the equity method aggregated $485 million in 1985, $642 million in 1984, and $677 million in 1983. Dividends received from all companies accounted for by this method amounted to $480 million in 1985, $503 million in 1984, and $406 million in 1983. Undistributed earnings of these companies included in Texaco's retained earnings amounted to $1,389 million at December 31, 1985, and $1,395 million at December 31, 1984.

MEASURING AND REPORTING LONG-TERM INVESTMENTS

PURPOSE:

One corporation may invest in the capital stock of another corporation for a variety of reasons. Often the investment is for a short term, designed to earn a return on idle funds. Accounting for short-term investments was discussed in Chapter 8. Some investments in the stock of other corporations are for the long term. These investments may be designed to provide the investing corporation with significant influence or control over the other corporation. Long-term investments that do not provide the investor with control are discussed in this chapter. Long-term investments that provide control are discussed in Chapter 14. This chapter also discusses investments in the bonds of another corporation. These investments always are designed to provide a return on idle funds because bond investments never provide the investor with the ability to influence the other corporation (i.e., bonds do not have voting rights).

LEARNING OBJECTIVES—TO BE ABLE TO:

1. Explain and use the cost and equity methods.
2. Account for bonds purchased at par; at a discount; at a premium.
3. Record bonds purchased between interest dates.
4. Use the straight-line and effective-interest amortization methods.
5. Expand your accounting vocabulary by learning about the "Important Terms Defined in This Chapter" (page 686).
6. Apply the knowledge gained from this chapter by completing the homework assigned by your instructor.

ORGANIZATION:

Part A—Long-Term Investments in Equity Securities (Stocks)

1. Cost method—no significant influence.
2. Equity method—significant influence but no control.

Part B—Long-Term Investments in Debt Securities (Bonds)

1. Bonds purchased at par.
2. Bonds purchased at a discount.
3. Bonds purchased at a premium.
4. Bonds purchased between interest dates.
5. Effective-interest amortization on bonds.

PART A—LONG-TERM INVESTMENTS IN EQUITY SECURITIES (STOCKS)

A company may invest in the equity securities (either common or preferred stock) of one or more other corporations for various reasons. Some of the reasons are to earn a return on excess cash; exercise influence or control over the other company; attain growth through sales of new products and new services; and gain access to new markets and new sources of supply. An entity may acquire capital stock of a corporation by purchasing outstanding shares from other stockholders for cash (or other assets); or if the investor is a corporation, by exchanging some of its own capital stock for outstanding capital stock of the other corporation.

When one company purchases **outstanding** shares of stock of another company, the transaction is between the acquiring company and the **stockholders** of the other company (not the other company itself). This kind of transaction affects the acquiring entity only. The accounting of the other company is not affected.

The investor may acquire **some or all** of the outstanding stock of the other company (often called the **investee**). If the purpose of the investment is to gain influence or control, the investor will acquire **common** stock because it has voting rights. The number of shares of outstanding stock of a corporation acquired by another entity usually depends upon the objectives of the investor. For measuring and reporting purposes, **three different levels of ownership** are recognized. The three levels are related to the percentage of the outstanding shares of **voting** capital stock owned by the investor.

MEASURING LONG-TERM INVESTMENTS IN VOTING COMMON STOCK

Accounting for long-term investments in voting stock involves measuring the amount of the investment (reported on the balance sheet) and the periodic investment revenue (reported on the income statement). In conformity with the cost principle, at the dates of acquisition of the shares, long-term investments in the voting stock of another company are measured and recorded as the total consideration given to acquire them. This total includes the market price, plus all commissions and other purchasing costs. Subsequent to acquisition, accounting for long-term investments depends upon the relationship between the investor and the investee company. The relevant characteristic of the relationship is the extent to which the investing company can exercise **significant influence or control over the operating and financial policies** of the other company. Significant influence and control are related to the number of voting shares owned of the investee company in proportion to the total number of such shares outstanding.

EXHIBIT 13–1

Measuring and reporting long-term investments in voting stock of another company

Status of ownership	Method	Measurement at date of acquisition	Measurement after date of acquisition	
			Investment	*Revenue*
1. **Investor can exercise no significant influence or control.** Presumed if investor owns less than 20% of the outstanding voting stock of the investee company.	Cost method	Investor records the investment at cost. Cost is the total outlay made to acquire the shares.	Investor reports the investment on the balance sheet at LCM.	Investor recognizes revenue each period when dividends are declared by the investee company. A realized gain or loss is recognized when the investment is sold.
2. **Investor can exercise significant influence, but not control,** over the operating and financing policies of the investee company. Presumed if the investor owns at least 20% but not more than 50% of the outstanding voting stock of the investee company.	Equity method	Same as above.	Investor measures and reports the investment at cost **plus** the investor's share of the earnings (or less the losses) and **minus** the dividends received from (i.e., declared by) the other company. (Dividends received are not considered revenue. To recognize dividends as revenue, rather than as a reduction in the investment, would involve double counting.)	Investor recognizes as revenue each period the investor's proportionate share of the earnings (or losses) reported each period by the investee company.
3. **Investor can exercise control** over the operating and financing policies of the investee company. Control is presumed if the investor owns more than 50% of the outstanding voting stock of the investee company.	Consolidated financial statement method	Same as above.	Consolidated financial statements required each period. Discussed in Chapter 14.	

APB Opinion 18 defines the term "significant influence" and "control" as follows:

1. **Significant influence**—the ability of the investing company to have an important impact on the operating and financing policies of another company in which it owns shares of the voting stock. Significant influence may be indicated by *(a)* membership on the board of directors of the other company, *(b)* participation in the policy-making processes, *(c)* material transactions between the two companies, *(d)* interchange of management personnel, or *(e)* technological dependency. In the absence of a clear-cut distinction based upon these factors, **significant influence is presumed** if the investing company owns at least 20% but not more than 50% of the outstanding voting shares of the other company.

2. **Control**—the ability of the investing company to determine the operating and financing policies of another company in which it owns shares of the voting stock. For all practical purposes, **control is presumed** when the investing company owns more than 50% of the outstanding voting stock of the other company.

The three levels of ownership that relate to the measuring and reporting of long-term investments in voting capital stock are:

Level of ownership	*Measuring and reporting approach*
1. Neither significant influence nor control	Cost method
2. Significant influence but not control	Equity method
3. Control	Consolidated statement method

Each of these approaches is outlined in Exhibit 13–1. The first two are discussed in this chapter; the third is discussed in Chapter 14.

COST METHOD

The **cost method** of accounting must be used when the number of shares of **voting** capital stock of a corporation does not give the investing corporation the ability to exercise significant influence or control. Under the cost method, the investment is recorded at the acquisition date in conformity with the cost principle, as shown in Exhibit 13–2. Subsequent to acquisition, the investment amount is reported at the **lower of cost or market** (LCM). Cash dividends declared by the investee corporation are reported by the investor as "Revenue from investments" in the period declared.

FASB Statement 12 requires that long-term **equity** investments accounted for under the cost method be valued at LCM after acquisition. At the end of each accounting period, the total cost and the total market value must be computed for the **entire portfolio** of long-term equity investments. Market value is measured as the number of shares owned multiplied by the actual market price per share at the balance sheet date. If total market value is less than total cost, the difference must be recorded as an unrealized loss. This situation is illustrated in Exhibit 13–2 on December 31, 19A. The recording of this unrealized loss does not affect the income statement. If, at the end of a subsequent period, market exceeds the LCM valuation reported the prior period, the portfolio is written up to the new market **not to exceed** the original acquisition cost of the securities portfolio.

When long-term securities are sold, the difference between the sale price and acquisition cost is recorded and reported as a **realized** gain or loss.

In Exhibit 13–2, notice that on December 31, 19A, LCM is applied to the total cost and market amounts for the portfolio (instead of being applied to each individual security amount). The total portfolio was written down to LCM, from cost ($32,000) to market ($31,000), and an unrealized loss of $1,000 was recorded.

On June 15, 19B, 300 shares of Cox stock were sold. The journal entry to record the sale removes the shares from the investment account at the original cost and does not affect the allowance account. The difference between the original cost of the stock ($12,000) and the sale price ($12,300) is recorded as a **realized** gain of $300. The allowance account was not affected in this entry because the account is adjusted **only** at the end of each accounting period to reflect the LCM valuation of the ending portfolio (as illustrated in the journal entry on December 31, 19B).

Exhibit 13–2 gives the reporting effects of the cost method on the income statement and the balance sheet. The unrealized loss account is a **contra equity account,** reported on the balance sheet. The income statement is affected only by dividend revenue and realized gains (losses) on the sale of investments.

The journal entries given in Exhibit 13–2 reflect application of the cost principle at the date of acquisition and application of LCM subsequent to that time. The investment is carried continuously at LCM, and dividend revenue is recognized from the investment **only** in periods in which dividends are declared.

The fact that Able Corporation purchased stock in Baker Corporation and Cox Corporation had no effect on the accounting and reporting by either Baker or Cox Corporations.

All **nonvoting** stock owned as a long-term investment, regardless of the level of ownership, is accounted for under the cost method.

EQUITY METHOD

The equity method must be used when significant influence (but not control) exists. The equity method recognizes a proportionate share of the reported income of the investee company as revenue for the investor. Dividends from the investee company are not recognized as income for the investor.

The concept underlying the equity method is that the investor has earned income from the investment equivalent to its ownership share. This income is recorded as a debit to the investment account and a credit to investment revenue. Dividends from the investee company are treated as a return of a part

EXHIBIT 13–2

Cost method of measuring and reporting long-term investments in equity securities

Situation:

Able Corporation purchased the following long-term investments on February 1, 19A:

Baker Corporation common stock (nopar), 1,000 shares at $12 per share (represents 10% of the outstanding shares).

Cox Corporation, 5% preferred stock (par $20), nonvoting, 500 shares at $40 per share (represents 10% of the outstanding shares).

February 1, 19A, to record the acquisition:

Long-term investments 32,000
    Cash   32,000

Computations:
    Baker common stock, 1,000 shares × $12 = $12,000
    Cox preferred stock, 500 shares × $40   = 20,000
        Total acquisition cost $32,000

November 30, 19A, cash dividends declared (payable in January 19B) as follows: Baker common stock, $1 per share; Cox preferred stock, 5% of par.

Dividends receivable 1,500
    Revenue from investments   1,500

Computations:
    Baker common stock, 1,000 shares × $1   = $1,000
    Cox preferred stock, 500 shares × $20 × 5% =   500
        Total dividends $1,500

December 31, 19A, end of the accounting period, quoted market prices: Baker common stock, $13; Cox preferred stock, $36.

Unrealized loss on long-term investments 1,000
    Allowance to reduce long-term investments to market   1,000

Computations:

	Shares	Market Dec. 31, 19A	Acquisition cost	Market Dec. 31, 19A
Baker common stock	1,000	$13	$12,000	$13,000
Cox preferred stock....................	500	36	20,000	18,000
			$32,000	$31,000

LCM: $32,000 − $31,000 = $1,000 (balance required in the allowance account).

January 15, 19B, received cash for the dividends of Baker and Cox Corporations (declared on November 30, 19A).

Cash 1,500
    Dividends receivable   1,500

June 15, 19B, sold 300 shares of the Cox preferred stock at $41.

Cash (300 shares × $41) 12,300
    Long-term investments (300 × $40)   12,000
    Gain on sale of investment   300

EXHIBIT 13–2 *(concluded)*

Cost method of measuring and reporting long-term investments in equity securities

November 30, 19B, cash dividends declared (payable December 30, 19B) as follows: Baker common stock, $0.90 per share; Cox preferred stock, 5% of par.

Dividends receivable	1,100	
Revenue from investments		1,100

Computations:
Baker common stock, 1,000 shares × $0.90 = $ 900
Cox preferred stock, 200 shares × $20 × 5% =   200
Total dividends $1,100

December 30, 19B, received cash for the dividends of Baker and Cox Corporations (declared on November 30, 19B).

Cash	1,100	
Dividends receivable		1,100

December 31, 19B, end of the accounting period, quoted market prices: Baker common stock, $11; Cox preferred stock, $43.

Allowance to reduce long-term investments to market	600	
Unrealized loss on long-term investments		600

Computations:

	Shares	Market Dec. 31, 19B	Acquisition cost	Market Dec. 31, 19B
Baker common stock	1,000	$11	$12,000	$11,000
Cox preferred stock	200	43	8,000	8,600
			$20,000	$19,600

LCM: $20,000 − $19,600 = $400 (balance required in the allowance account). Reduction in the allowance account: $1,000 − $400 = $600.

December 31, 19A, and 19B, reporting on the **income statement** and **balance sheet** (partial):

	19A	19B
Income statement:		
Revenue from investments	$ 1,500	$ 1,100
Gain on sale of investment		300
Balance sheet:		
Current assets:		
Dividends receivable	1,500	
Investments and funds:		
Investments in equity securities	$32,000	$20,000
Less: Allowance to reduce long-term investments to market	1,000 31,000	400 19,600
Stockholders' equity:		
Unrealized loss on long-term investments	(1,000)	(400)

EXHIBIT 13–3

Equity method of measuring and reporting long-term investments in equity securities

---

Situation:
> Crown Corporation (the investor company) purchased 3,000 shares of the outstanding common stock of Davis Corporation (the investee company) on January 15, 19E, at a cash cost of $120 per share. At date of purchase, Davis Corporation had outstanding 10,000 shares of common stock (par $100 per share).

Analysis:
> The equity method must be used by Crown Corporation because it now owns between 20% and 50% of the outstanding voting stock of the investee company.

January 15, 19E, to record the acquisition:

Investment in common stock, Davis Corporation (3,000 shares) .. 360,000
    Cash   360,000
> Purchased 3,000 shares (30%) of the common stock of Davis Corporation at $120 per share.

December 31, 19E, end of the accounting period, Davis Corporation reported net income of $50,000. On this date, Crown Corporation recognized its proportionate share as follows:

Investment in common stock, Davis Corporation   15,000
    Revenue from investments   15,000
> To record the proportionate share of 19E income reported by Davis Corporation ($50,000 × 30% = $15,000). The credit often is called Equity in Earnings of Partially Owned Company.

December 31, 19E, Davis Corporation declared and paid immediately a $10,000 cash dividend, of which 30% (i.e., $3,000) was received by the investor, Crown Corporation. Crown Corporation recorded its share of the dividend as follows:

Cash   3,000
    Investment in common stock, Davis Corporation   3,000
> To record the receipt of a cash dividend from Davis Corporation ($10,000 × 30% = $3,000).

---

of the investment. Under the equity method, dividends are recorded as a debit to cash and a credit to the investment account.[1] If dividends were recorded as revenue, there would be a double counting of the proportionate share of income and the distribution of that income.

Application of the equity method is shown in Exhibit 13–3.[2] The illustration is

---

[1] When a cash dividend is declared in one year and paid in the following year, the dividend is recognized by the investor when declared by debiting Dividends Receivable (a current asset) instead of Cash. Subsequently, when the cash is received, the Cash account is debited and Dividends Receivable is credited. In contrast, dividends declared and paid in the same year may be recorded by the investor on payment date as a debit to Cash and credit to the investment account.

[2] This example assumes that the investment was purchased at "book value." The accounting procedures for other situations are more complex. They involve asset write-ups and write-downs

EXHIBIT 13–3 *(concluded)*

Equity method of measuring and reporting long-term investments in equity securities

December 31, 19E, the investment and revenue accounts of Crown Corporation for the year 19E would be as follows (based upon the above entries):

Investment in Common Stock, Davis Corporation

1/15/E	Purchased 3,000 shares	360,000	12/31/E	Proportionate share of dividends of Davis Corporation	3,000
12/31/E	Proportionate share of 19E income of Davis Corporation	15,000			

(debit balance, $372,000)

Revenue from Investments

12/31/E	Revenue from Davis Corporation	15,000

December 31, 19E, reporting by Crown Corporation (investor) on the **income statement** and **balance sheet** (partial):

Income Statement
For the Year Ended December 31, 19E

Revenue from investments .... $ 15,000

Balance Sheet
At December 31, 19E

Investments and funds:
  Investment in common stock, Davis Corporation,
    equity basis (cost, $360,000; market, $369,000)* $372,000

* Market is measured as the number of shares owned multiplied by the actual market price per share on the balance sheet date.

based on the assumption that Crown Corporation (the investor company) purchased 3,000 shares (or 30%) of the outstanding common stock of Davis Corporation (the investee company) at a cash price of $120 per share. The equity method must be used because Crown Corporation purchased 30% of the outstanding voting stock of Davis Corporation. The first journal entry in Exhibit 13–3 shows how the investment would be recorded by Crown Corporation.

When the investee corporation reports income (or loss), the investor company

and, perhaps, the recognition of "goodwill." This chapter presents the fundamentals without unnecessary complexity. More advanced accounting courses devote considerable attention to these complexities.

records its percentage share (i.e., equity) of the investment revenue. The second entry by Crown Corporation (the investor company) given in Exhibit 13–3 recognizes its proportionate share of the net income of Davis Corporation.

In Exhibit 13–3, the proportionate share of the net income of Davis Corporation was recorded by Crown Corporation as revenue and as an **increase** in the investment account. When a dividend is received, it is necessary to avoid double-counting the income from the investee company; therefore, the dividend from the investee company is recorded as a debit to Cash and as a **credit to the investment account.** This entry reflects the fact that a dividend represents the conversion of a part of the investment account balance to cash.

The investment and revenue accounts of the investor company, Crown Corporation, are shown in Exhibit 13–3. The financial statements for Crown also are shown in Exhibit 13–3.

LCM is not used with the equity method because under the equity method, investments are accounted for at equity, not cost.

Financial statements must disclose the method used to account for long-term investments. Also, regardless of whether the cost or the equity method is used, the original cost, current market value, and carrying value of the investment should be disclosed.

The cost and equity methods represent a compromise on the part of the accounting profession. Many accountants believe that all marketable securities should be reported at their **current market values** at each balance sheet date. Under this approach, which is not currently acceptable, both dividends received and changes in the market value of the stock since the last period would be reported as revenue (or loss) on the income statement. Accountants who support this approach believe that it meets most closely the objective of reporting the **economic consequences** of holding an investment in marketable securities. The **cost method** measures only the dividends received by the investor as revenue, but dividends may have no relationship to the earnings of the investee company for the period. The cost method does not reflect the earnings pattern of the investee company. The **equity method** overcomes this deficiency; however, it does not reflect the economic impact of market changes in the investment shares held. The effect of such market changes is significant to the investor. The accounting profession has accepted the three different measurement approaches for long-term investments in shares that are outlined in Exhibit 13–1.

PART B—LONG-TERM INVESTMENTS IN DEBT SECURITIES (BONDS)

In Chapter 11 we discussed bonds as long-term liabilities of the issuing corporation. This part of the chapter discusses bonds of another company held as a **long-term investment.** Bonds offer significantly different investment risks and returns than capital stock. Bonds have a stated rate of interest (which determines the amount of cash that will be received on each interest date) and a specified maturity value (which will be received in cash at maturity date). Stockholders receive cash dividends only when they are declared by the board of directors. Dividends tend to vary with the profitability of the corporation. Bondholders have no voting rights.

Similar to capital stock, bonds are bought and sold in the regular security markets. The market price of bonds fluctuates **inversely** with changes in the **market rate** of interest because the **stated rate** of interest remains constant over the life of the bonds (see Chapter 11). If the market rate of interest increases, bond prices fall.

MEASURING AND REPORTING BOND INVESTMENTS

Investors may buy bonds at their date of issuance or at subsequent dates during the life of the bonds. Regardless of the timing of the bonds' acquisition, at the end of each accounting period the investor must measure the (1) cost, adjusted for the cumulative amount of discount or premium that has been amortized; and (2) interest revenue earned.

At the date of acquisition, a bond investment is recorded in conformity with the **cost principle.** The purchase cost, including all incidental acquisition costs (such as transfer fees and broker commissions), is debited to an investment account such as "Long-Term Investment, Bonds of Beta Corporation." The amount recorded is the **current cash equivalent amount.** This amount may be the same as the maturity amount (if acquired at par), less than the maturity amount (if acquired at a discount), or more than the maturity amount (if acquired at a premium).[3] Usually the premium or discount on a bond investment is not recorded in a separate account as is done for bonds payable (Chapter 11). The investment account shows the current book or carrying amount. However, the bond investment account can be debited at par, and a separate discount or premium account can be used with the same results.

If a bond investment was acquired at par, the book value remains constant over the life of the investment because there is no premium or discount to be amortized. In this situation, revenue earned from the investment each period is measured as the amount of cash interest collected (or accrued).

When a bond investment is purchased at a discount or premium, measurement of the book value of the investment after date of acquisition necessitates adjustment of the investment account balance from acquisition cost to maturity amount each period over the life of the investment. This adjustment is the periodic amortization of the discount or premium. The periodic amortization is made as a debit to the investment account if there is a discount, or credit if there is a premium.

When a bond investment is acquired at a discount or premium, the revenue

---

[3] Fees, commissions, and other incidental costs decrease the discount, or increase the premium; therefore, they are amortized over the remaining period to maturity. Alternatively, such costs sometimes are recorded separately and amortized on the same basis as the discount or premium.

from interest each period is measured as the cash interest collected (or accrued) plus or minus the periodic amortization of discount or premium. As was illustrated in Chapter 11 for bonds payable, bond discount or premium may be amortized by using either the straight-line or effective-interest method. The former is simpler, whereas the latter is conceptually preferable. In the following paragraphs, we will assume straight-line amortization; effective-interest amortization is explained at the end of this part.

In contrast to long-term investments, discount or premium is not amortized on bonds held as a **short-term** investment because the bonds will not be held to maturity.

After the date of acquisition, interest revenue must be accrued (by means of an adjusting entry) for periods between the last date on which interest revenue was collected and the end of the accounting period. The procedure for accruing interest expense and interest revenue was discussed in several prior chapters.

ACCOUNTING FOR BONDS ILLUSTRATED

On July 1, 19E, Roth Company purchased $10,000, 8%, 10-year bonds in the open market. The bonds were issued originally on July 1, 19A, and mature on June 30, 19J. The 8% interest is paid each June 30.[4] Roth Company's annual accounting period ends December 31. The sequence of journal entries made by Roth Company during 19E are illustrated under three different purchase cost assumptions as follows:

Assumptions	Exhibits
1. Bond investment purchased at par (100)	13–4
2. Bond investment purchased at a discount (98)	13–5
3. Bond investment purchased at a premium (102)	13–6

BONDS PURCHASED AT PAR

When bond investors accept a rate of interest on a bond investment that is the **same** as the stated rate of interest on the bonds, the bonds will sell at par (i.e., at 100). Bonds that sell at par will not cause a premium or discount. Exhibit 13–4 illustrates the recording and reporting of an **investment** in bonds purchased at par.

BONDS PURCHASED AT A DISCOUNT

When bond investors demand a rate of interest that is higher than the **stated rate,** bonds will sell at a **discount.** When a bond is purchased at a discount, the investor receives the periodic interest payments stated in the bond contract plus

---

[4] Bonds usually pay interest semiannually. Annual interest is used in this illustration to reduce the number of repetitive entries. The concepts are applied the same way in either case.

EXHIBIT 13–4

Bonds purchased at par

Situation:

On July 1, 19E, Roth Company purchased $10,000, 8%, 10-year bonds of Ellsworth Company for cash, $10,000 (i.e., at par). The bonds were issued originally on July 1, 19A, and mature June 30, 19J. Interest is paid each June 30. Roth's accounting period ends December 31.

July 1, 19E, to record purchase of bond investment at par (100):

Long-term investment, bonds of Ellsworth Company	10,000	
Cash		10,000

Purchased at par, $10,000 maturity value, 8% bonds of Ellsworth Company. (Note: Because the bonds were purchased on an interest date, there was no accrued interest.)

December 31, 19E, adjusting entry at end of the accounting period (and each year through maturity date):

Bond interest receivable	400	
Revenue from investments*		400

Adjusting entry to accrue six months interest revenue on Ellsworth Company bonds ($10,000 × 8% × 6/12 = $400).

   * Alternate titles are Interest Revenue and, sometimes, Interest Income.

June 30, 19F, to record annual interest (and each year until maturity):[a]

Cash ($10,000 × 8%)	800	
Bond interest receivable (from December 31 entry)		400
Revenue from investments		400

Receipt of annual interest payment on the Ellsworth Company bonds.

June 30, 19J, maturity date of the bonds; to record cash received for face (maturity) amount of the bond investment:[b]

Cash	10,000	
Long-term investment, bonds of Ellsworth Company		10,000

Retirement of bonds at maturity date (assumes last interest receipt already recorded).

December 31, 19E, Roth Company's **income statement** and **balance sheet** (partial):

Income statement for the year ended December 31, 19E:

   Revenue from investments .... $ 400

Balance sheet at December 31, 19E:

   Current assets:
      Bond interest receivable .... $ 400

   Investments and funds:
      Investment in bonds, at cost (market, $10,125) 10,000

Notes: *a.* This entry presumes that there was no reversal on January 1, 19F, of the prior adjusting entry. A reversing entry is optional because it serves only to facilitate the subsequent entry (see Chapter 5).

      b. Because the bond investment was purchased at par, there was no premium or discount to be amortized.

_____ **EXHIBIT 13–5** _____

Bonds purchased at a discount

> **Situation:**
> Exactly the situation given in Exhibit 13–4, except that on July 1, 19E, Roth Company purchased $10,000 of bonds of Baker Company for $9,800 (i.e., at 98), rather than at par.
>
> July 1, 19E, to record purchase of bond investment at a discount (98):
>
> Long-term investment, bonds of Baker Company (at cost) 9,800
> Cash 9,800
> Purchased $10,000 maturity value, 8% bonds of the Baker Company at 98.
>
> Note: This entry records the investment at its cost; that is, net of any discount or premium. Some accountants prefer to record it at **gross** as follows with the same end result:
>
> Long-term investment 10,000
> Discount on long-term investment 200
> Cash 9,800
>
> ---
>
> December 31, 19E, end of accounting year; to record adjusting entry for interest revenue and amortization of discount on bond investment (and each year until maturity):
>
> Bond interest receivable ($10,000 × 8% × 6/12) 400
> Long-term investment, bonds of Baker Company
> (amortization: $40 × 6/12) 20
> Revenue from investments 420
> Adjusting entry to (1) accrue interest revenue for six months and (2) amortize discount on the bond investment for six months (July 1 to December 31); $200 ÷ 5 years = $40 amortization per year.
>
> ---
>
> June 30, 19F, to record cash interest received and to amortize discount on bond investment (and each year until maturity):
>
> Cash ($10,000 × 8%) 800
> Long-term investment, bonds of Baker Company
> (amortization: $40 × 6/12) 20
> Bond interest receivable (from December 31 entry) 400
> Revenue from investments 420
> Receipt of annual interest on Baker Company bonds and amortization of discount for six months (January 1 to June 30).

the maturity value, which is a greater amount than the initial cash invested. A discount increases the interest revenue earned on a bond investment. Assume that on July 1, 19E, Roth Company purchased a $10,000, 8% bond issued by Baker Company for $9,800 cash. The bond will mature in five years (in 19J). Interest of $10,000 × 8% = $800 will be collected annually.

Although $800 cash is collected each year, the annual revenue **earned** from the investment is $840. The additional $40 is due to amortization of the discount. Analysis of the interest revenue, using straight-line amortization, is as follows:

_____ **EXHIBIT 13–5** *(concluded)* _____

Bonds purchased at a discount

June 30, 19J, maturity date; to record cash maturity amount received:

Cash 10,000
     Long-term investment, bonds of Baker Company   10,000
     Retirement of bonds at maturity (assumes last interest receipt already recorded).

December 31, 19E, long-term investment account for 19E–19J:

Long-Term Investment, Bonds of Baker Company

July 1, 19E At acquisition	9,800	June 30, 19J Retirement	10,000
Yearly amortizations by:			
Dec. 31, 19E	20		
31, 19F	40		
31, 19G	40		
31, 19H	40		
31, 19I	40		
June 30, 19J	20		
	10,000		10,000

December 31, 19E, **income statement** and **balance sheet** for year 19E (partial)

Income statement for the year ended December 31, 19E:

  Revenue from investments .... $ 420

Balance Sheet at December 31, 19E:

  Current assets:
    Bond interest receivable .... $ 400

  Investments and funds:
    Investment in bonds, at amortized cost (market, $10,125)   9,820

Cash inflows from the investment:
  Annual interest collected, July 1, 19E, through
  June 30, 19J ($10,000 × 8% × 5 years) .... $ 4,000
  Collection of bond at maturity date, June 30, 19J 10,000 $14,000

Cash outflow for the investment:
  July 1, 19E—purchase of bond   9,800

  Difference—net increase in cash (the
    total interest earned) .... $ 4,200

Revenue from investment per year: $4,200 ÷ 5 years =
$840 (assuming straight-line amortization).

Exhibit 13–5 illustrates the recording and reporting of a bond investment purchased at a discount.

When a bond is purchased, it is recorded at cost. Therefore, when a bond is purchased at a discount, the investment account balance at the purchase date will be less than par or maturity value. Through **amortization** of the discount, the balance of the investment account is **increased** each period so that the book value will be the same as the par amount on the maturity date. Amortization of the discount each period increases the amount of interest revenue earned. The amount of discount amortized each period is debited to the investment account and credited to Interest Revenue.

In Exhibit 13–5, each year Roth Company must amortize a part of the discount ($10,000 − $9,800 = $200), so that the total discount is amortized over the remaining life of the bond investment. Using straight-line amortization, the amount of discount amortized each full year will be $200 ÷ 5 years = $40 per year.

The balance of the long-term investment account will increase from cost at date of purchase to par value at maturity date because of the amortization of the bond discount. This effect is recorded in Roth's investment ledger account shown in Exhibit 13–5.[5] Also shown in Exhibit 13–5 is 19E financial statement information for Roth Company.

BONDS PURCHASED AT A PREMIUM

When bond investors are willing to invest at a rate of interest that is **less** than the **stated rate** of interest on bonds, the bonds will sell at a **premium.** When bonds are purchased at a premium, the investment account is debited for an amount greater than the par or maturity value of the bonds. Therefore, the premium must be **amortized** over the **remaining life** of the bonds as a **decrease** in the balance of the investment account so that the investment account balance will be the par value on maturity date. The amortization is similar to the procedure illustrated for a discount, except that each period the investment account is credited and the premium amortization **decreases** interest revenue.

Assume Roth Company purchased Garden Company bonds on July 1, 19E, for $10,200 cash. The bonds have an 8% interest rate and mature in five years from that date, on June 30, 19J. Using straight-line amortization, the cash outflow and inflows for this investment may be analyzed to illustrate the effect of the premium on interest revenue as follows:

---

[5] Observe that the amortization of discount or premium on bond investments conceptually is the same as the amortization discussed and illustrated in Chapter 11 in the issuer's accounts. Here, we are looking at the other side of the transaction. A minor procedural difference may be noted. In Chapter 11, premium or discount was recorded in a separate account; in this chapter, the **net amount** (i.e., the cost) was recorded in the investment account. Either procedure can be used in either situation with the same results. Common practice follows the procedures illustrated in the respective chapters.

EXHIBIT 13-6

Bonds purchased at a premium

Situation:

Exactly the same situation given in Exhibit 13-4, except that on July 1, 19E, Roth Company purchased $10,000 of bonds of Garden Company for $10,200 (i.e., at 102), rather than at par.

July 1, 19E, to record purchase of bond investment at a premium (102):

Long-term investment, bonds of Garden Company (at cost)	10,200	
Cash		10,200

Purchased $10,000 maturity value, 8% bonds of Garden Company at 102.

December 31, 19E, end of accounting year; to record adjusting entry for interest revenue and amortization of premium on bond investment (and each year until maturity):

Bond interest receivable ($10,000 × 8% × 6/12)	400	
Long-term investment, bonds of Garden Company (amortization: $40 × 6/12)		20
Revenue from investments		380

Adjusting entry to (1) accrue interest revenue for six months and (2) amortize premium on the investment for six months (July 1 to December 31); $200 ÷ 5 years = $40 amortization per year.

June 30, 19F, to record cash interest received and to amortize premium on bond investment (and each year until maturity):

Cash ($10,000 × 8%)	800	
Bond interest receivable (per December 31 entry)		400
Long-term investment, bonds of Garden Company (amortization: $40 × 6/12)		20
Revenue from investments		380

Receipt of annual interest revenue on Garden Company bonds and amortization of premium for six months (January 1 to June 30).

June 30, 19J, maturity date; to record cash maturity amount received:

Cash	10,000	
Long-term investment, bonds of Garden Company		10,000

Retirement of bonds at maturity (assuming the last interest receipt has been recorded).

December 31, 19E, **income statement** and **balance sheet** for year 19E (partial):

Income statement for year ended December 31, 19E:

Revenue from investments .... $ 380

Balance sheet at December 31, 19E:

Current assets:
Bond interest receivable .... $ 400

Investments and funds:
Investment in bonds, at amortized cost (market, $10,225) 10,180

Cash inflows from the investment:
Annual interest collected, July 1, 19E, through
June 30, 19J ($10,000 × 8% × 5 years) .... $ 4,000
June 30, 19E, collection of bond at maturity 10,000 $14,000

Cash outflow for the investment:
July 1, 19J—purchase of bond   10,200

Difference—net increase in cash (the total
interest revenue earned) .... $ 3,800

Revenue from investment, per year: $3,800 ÷ 5 years = $760

Exhibit 13–6 presents the journal entries and financial statements for the investor, Roth Company.

BONDS PURCHASED BETWEEN INTEREST DATES

Investors usually purchase bonds between the interest dates specified on the bonds. In these situations, the investor must pay the amount of **interest accrued** since the last interest date in addition to the purchase price of the bond. The bond market operates in this manner because the seller of the bond is entitled to interest from the last interest date to the date of the sale transaction; but on the next interest payment date, the new owner will receive interest for the full period between interest dates, regardless of the purchase date. Assume Hays Company purchased a $1,000 bond, 12% interest, payable 6% each March 31 and September 30. The bond was purchased on June 1, 19F, at 100 plus any accrued interest. The purchase of this bond investment is recorded by Hays Company as follows:

June 1, 19F:

Long-term investment, 12% bond 1,000
Revenue from investments ($1,000 × 12% × 2/12)*   20
Cash [$1,000 + ($1,000 × 12% × 2/12)]   1,020

Purchase of a $1,000, 12% bond as a long-term investment at 100 plus accrued interest for two months, March 31, 19F (last interest date) to June 1, 19F (date of purchase).

* Alternatively, an account, Bond Interest Receivable, could have been debited on June 1 for $20 and then credited for that amount on September 30. The net effect would have been the same. When the end of the accounting period falls between the purchase date and the next interest date, such a procedure may be less complex.

Hayes Company debited the long-term investment account for the cost of the investment, which **excludes** the accrued interest. The $20 accrued interest was paid in cash by Hayes Company. However, it will be returned to Hayes Company at the next interest date, September 30, 19F. At that time, Hayes Company will receive the full amount of cash interest for six months, although it has owned the bond for only four months (i.e., June 1 to September 30, 19F).

The journal entry to record the first interest collection after the purchase is:

September 30, 19F:

Cash 60

    Revenue from investments 60

Collected interest for six months on bond investment
    ($1,000 × 6% = $60).

After these two entries are posted, the Revenue from Investments account on the books of Hays Company will reflect $40 interest earned for the four months since purchase as follows:

Revenue from Investments

6/1/19F	20	9/30/19F	60

(balance, $1,000 × 12% × 4/12 = $40 credit)

SALE OF A BOND INVESTMENT

A long-term investment in bonds is accounted for with the expectation that the bonds will be held to maturity. This expectation is the basis for amortizing any premium or discount over the period from the date of purchase to the maturity date. However, the bonds may be sold prior to their maturity date. When an investor sells bonds prior to maturity, the difference between the sale price and the book value of the bonds is recorded as a "Gain (or Loss) on the Sale of Investments."

Assume Carson Corporation has two $1,000 12% bonds of Drake Company that are being held as a long-term investment. Each bond was purchased at 104. The long-term investment account was debited for $2,080. Because of amortization of bond premium to January 1, 19F, the investment account balance is $2,040. On that date one of the bonds was sold at 100. The entry by Carson Company to record the sale is:

Cash 1,000

Loss on sale of investments 20

    Long-term investment, Drake Company bonds 1,020

Sale of long-term investment.

EFFECTIVE-INTEREST AMORTIZATION ON BOND INVESTMENTS

Effective-interest amortization of the discount or premium on a bond investment is similar to the procedures discussed for bonds payable in Chapter 11. This method of amortization is conceptually preferable because (1) interest revenue is measured correctly each period for income statement purposes, and (2) the book value of the investment is measured correctly for balance sheet purposes at the end of each accounting period. Assume that on January 1, 19A, Farmer Company purchased a five-year, $10,000, 8% bond of Research Corporation as a long-term investment. The purchase price, based on a 12% effective-interest rate, was 85.58. Therefore, the cash paid was $8,558 (a $1,442 discount). The bonds have a stated rate of interest of 8% per year, payable each December 31. The acquisition was recorded by Farmer Company as follows:[6]

Long-term investment, Research Corporation bonds		
(maturity amount $10,000)	8,558	
Cash		8,558
Purchase of long-term investment.		

Farmer Company used the effective-interest amortization method to amortize the bond discount. The journal entries for a bond investment are the same regardless of the amortization method used, except for some of the **amounts** in the periodic interest entries.

Computation of effective-interest amortization is shown in Exhibit 13–7. Notice that the effective rate of interest of 12%, rather than the stated rate of 8%, is used to compute the interest revenue amounts.

The first column in Exhibit 13–7 shows the cash inflow each period for interest (based on the stated rate). The second column shows the interest revenue that should be reported on the income statement each period (based on the effective rate). The third column shows the amount of the discount that is amortized (which is the difference between the interest revenue earned and the amount of cash received). The last column shows the book value of the investment (i.e., the unamortized principal) that should be reported on the balance sheet at the end of each period. The entry for interest revenue each period can be taken directly from the schedule (Exhibit 13–7):

---

[6] Given the effective rate of 12%, the price of the bonds can be determined from a bond table or computed as follows:

$$\$10,000 \times P_{n=5,\ i=12\%} = \$10,000 \times .5674 \text{ (Table 10--2)} \quad \$5,674$$
$$\$800 \times P_{n=5,\ i=12\%} = \$800 \times 3.6048 \text{ (Table 10--4)} \quad \underline{2,884}$$
$$\text{Bond price (}PV\text{ of future cash flows)} \quad \underline{\underline{\$8,558}}$$

_____ EXHIBIT 13–7 _____

Schedule of effective-interest amortization

Date	Cash Interest Received Each Interest Date	Interest Revenue (based on beginning balance of investment)	Amortization (increase investment)*	Net Investment
1/1/19A (acquisition)				8,558
12/31/19A	800	8,558 × 12% = 1,027	227	8,785
12/31/19B	800	8,785 × 12% = 1,054	254	9,039
12/31/19C	800	9,039 × 12% = 1,085	285	9,324
12/31/19D	800	9,324 × 12% = 1,119	319	9,643
12/31/19E	800	9,643 × 12% = 1,157	357	10,000
Totals	4,000	5,442	1,442	

Note: This example is identical to the illustration of the issuer's situation shown in Exhibit 11–8. Computation of the sale price of the bonds at an effective rate of 12% is shown in footnote 6.
* Adjusts the net investment balance to the maturity amount.

	Year 1	Year 2	Etc.
Cash	800	800	
Long-term investment	227	254	
Revenue from investments	1,027	1,054	

Conceptually, the effective-interest method derives the true interest revenue earned during each period and the correct book value of the investment at the end of each period. The straight-line approach gives only approximations of these amounts. When there is a material difference between the two methods, *APB Opinion 21* requires use of the effective-interest method. Straight-line amortization often is used because it is simple to apply, and the different amounts of premium or discount amortized each period are not material.

DEMONSTRATION CASE

(Try to resolve the requirements before proceeding to the suggested solution that follows.)

Howell Equipment Corporation sells and services a major line of farm equipment. Both sales and service operations have been profitable. At the beginning of 19S, the company had excess cash. At that time, the management decided to invest in some securities of two of the manufacturers that supply most of the equipment purchased by Howell for resale. The annual accounting period ends on December 31.

This case focuses on the two long-term investments purchased in 19S. One investment was in equity securities, and the other in debt securities. The transactions were:

19S

a. Jan.   1   Purchased 2,000 shares of common stock of Dear Company at $40 per share. This was 1% of the shares outstanding.

b. Aug. 1   Purchased $100,000, 9% bonds payable of the Massey Company at 102, plus any accrued interest. The bonds pay semiannual interest each May 31 and November 30. The bonds mature on May 31, 19X (i.e., five years from June 1, 19S). Brokerage fees were $900.

c. Nov. 30   Received semiannual interest on Massey Company bonds. Use straight-line amortization.

d. Dec. 28   Received $4,000 cash dividend on the Dear Company stock.

e. Dec. 31   Adjusting entry for accrued interest on the Massey Company bonds.

f. Dec. 31   The current market price of the Dear stock is $39 and $103 for the Massey bonds.

g. Dec. 31   Closed Revenue from Investments to Income Summary.

Required:

a. Give the journal entry for each of the above transactions.

b. Show how the two investments, the accrued interest receivable and the related revenue, should be reported on the balance sheet and income statement at December 31, 19S.

Suggested Solution

Requirement a:

a. January 1, 19S:

Long-term investment, stock of Dear Company (2,000 shares)	80,000	
Cash		80,000
Purchased 2,000 shares Dear Company common stock at $40 per share.		

b. August 1, 19S:

Long-term investment, bonds of Massey Company 102,900
Revenue from investments ($100,000 × 9% × 2/12)   1,500
    Cash   104,400
Purchased $100,000 bonds of the Massey Company.

Computations:
  Cost ($100,000 × 1.02) + $900 = $102,900
  Accrued interest for 2 months
  $100,000 × 9% × 2/12   =   1,500
     Total cash paid $104,400

c. November 30, 19S:

Cash 4,500
    Long-term investment, bonds of Massey Company   200
    Revenue from investments   4,300

Computations:
  Semiannual interest: $100,000 × 4½% = $4,500
  Amortization of premium:
    $2,900 ÷ 58 months = $50*
    per month; $50 × 4 months   =   200
     Revenue from investments $4,300
  * August 1, 19S, to May 31, 19X = 58 months remaining life.

d. December 28, 19S:

Cash 4,000
    Revenue from investments   4,000
Received dividend on Dear Company stock.

e. December 31, 19S:

```
Interest receivable .........................................   750
    Long-term investment, bonds of Massey Company .........        50
    Revenue from investments ...............................       700
Adjusting entry for accrued interest and premium amortization
for one month on Massey Company bonds.

  Computations:
    Accrued interest receivable:
      $100,000 × 9% × 1/12            = $750
    Amortization of premium:
      $50 × 1 month                  =   50
    Revenue from investments .......   $700
```

f. December 31, 19S:

```
Unrealized loss on long-term equity investment ................  2,000
    Allowance to reduce long-term investment to LCM .........         2,000
To record LCM on Dear stock:
  2,000 shares × ($40 − $39) = $2,000.
```

g. December 31, 19S:

```
Revenue from investments ...................................  7,500
    Income summary .......................................        7,500
Closing entry: ($4,300 − $1,500 + $4,000 + $700 = $7,500).
```

Requirement b:

HOWELL EQUIPMENT CORPORATION
Balance Sheet (partial)
At December 31, 19S

Current assets:
Interest receivable . . . . $ 750

Investments and funds:
Stock of Dear Company, at LCM, 2,000 shares
  (cost, $80,000) . . . . $ 78,000*
Bonds of Massey Company, at amortized cost
  ($100,000 maturity value; market, $103,000) . . . . 102,650†   180,650

Stockholders' equity:
Unrealized loss on long-term equity investments . . . .   (2,000)

 * Cost of equity securities . . . . $ 80,000
   Less: Allowance to reduce long-term
     equity investment to LCM   2,000
   Equity investment at LCM . . . . $ 78,000

 † Cost of debt securities $102,900
   Less: Amortization of premium
     ($200 + $50)   250
   Debt investment at amortized cost $102,650

HOWELL Equipment Corporation
Income Statement (partial)
For the Year Ending December 31, 19S

Revenue from investments . . . . $ 7,500

SUMMARY OF CHAPTER

This chapter discussed the measuring and reporting of two types of long-term investments: capital stock (equity securities) and bonds (debt securities) of another company. An investor may acquire a part or all of the outstanding capital stock of a corporation by **purchase** of its shares or if the investor is a corporation, by **exchange** of its own stock for shares in the other company. The measuring and reporting of long-term investments in the capital stock of another company are determined by the percent of shares owned in relation to the total number of shares outstanding.

If the ownership level of **voting** shares is less than 20%, or if the ownership is of nonvoting stock, the **cost method** must be used. Under this method, the investment amount reported by the investor is based on the lower of cost or market, and investment revenue is recognized on the basis of dividends declared by the investee corporation.

If the ownership is at least 20% but not more than 50%, the **equity method** must be used. Under this method, the investment is recorded at cost by the investor at date of acquisition. Each period thereafter, the investment amount is increased (or decreased) by the proportionate interest in the income (or loss) reported by the investee corporation and decreased by the proportionate share of the dividends declared by the investee corporation. The LCM basis is not used with the equity method. Each period, the investor recognizes as revenue its proportionate share of the income (or loss) reported by the investee company.

If there is a controlling interest—that is, more than 50% ownership of the outstanding voting stock is held by the investor—the financial statements of the affiliated companies (investor and investee) are **consolidated.** This subject is discussed in Chapter 14.

An investor may purchase the bonds (i.e., debt securities) of another entity as a long-term investment. In contrast to capital stock, bonds are a liability of the issuing company; therefore, bonds (1) have a specified maturity date and maturity amount, (2) require the payment of a stated rate of interest at regular specified interest dates, and (3) do not confer voting rights. At the date of purchase, a long-term investment in bonds is recorded at cost, which may be at par, at a discount, or at a premium. When purchased at a premium or a discount, amortization of the premium or discount over the **remaining life** of the bonds is required. The periodic amortization adjusts (1) the balance of the investment amount so that the book value will be the same as the par value on the maturity date and (2) the interest revenue which is reported on the income statement.

IMPORTANT TERMS DEFINED IN THIS CHAPTER

Terms (alphabetically)	Key words in definitions of important terms used in chapter	Page reference
Control	The ability of an investor to determine the operating and financing policies of another company (the investee).	666
Cost method	Method used by investor if less than 20% of the voting stock of the investee company is owned by the investor.	666
Discount	A bond that is purchased for less than par value is purchased at a discount; the difference between cost and par of a bond.	674
Effective interest	The real or true rate of interest; also called the market rate of interest.	682
Equity method	Method used by investor if 20% to 50% of the voting stock of the investee company is owned by the investor.	667
Premium	A bond that is purchased for more than par value is purchased at a premium; the difference between cost and par of a bond.	678
Significant influence	The ability of an investor to have an important impact on the operating and financing policies of another company (the investee).	666
Stated interest rate	The annual rate of cash interest specified in the bond contract.	674

QUESTIONS

PART A

1. Explain the difference between a short-term investment and a long-term investment.

2. Match the following:

   Measurement method:
   _____ Cost method.
   _____ Equity method.
   _____ Consolidation.

   Level of ownership of the voting capital stock:
   a. More than 50% ownership.
   b. Less than 20% ownership.
   c. At least 20% but not more than 50%.

3. Explain the application of the cost principle to the purchase of capital stock in another company.

4. Under the cost method, when and how is revenue measured by the investor company?

5. Under the equity method, why is revenue measured on a proportionate basis by the investor company when income is reported by the other company, rather than when dividends are declared?

6. Under the equity method, dividends received from the investee company are not recorded as revenue. To record dividends as revenue would involve double counting. Explain.

7. Match the following items that relate to the long-term investment amount reported on the balance sheet of the investor company:

   Measurement method:
   _____ Cost method.
   _____ Equity method.

   Explanation of balance in the investment account:
   a. LCM.
   b. Original cost plus proportionate part of the income of the investee, less proportionate part of the dividends declared by investee.

PART B

8. Explain the difference between an equity security and a debt security.

9. Explain why interest revenue must be accrued on a long-term investment in bonds but not on a long-term investment in capital stock.

10. Under what conditions will a bond sell at (*a*) par, (*b*) a discount, and (*c*) a premium?

11. Distinguish between a long-term investment in bonds and a long-term investment in the capital stock of another company.

12. Why is it necessary to amortize premium or discount that arises from the purchase of a long-term bond investment above or below par? Over what period should the premium or discount be amortized?

13. When a bond investment is purchased between interest dates, the purchaser must pay accrued interest plus the purchase price of the bond. Explain why the accrued interest must be paid.

EXERCISES

PART A

E13–1   (Pair Definitions with Terms)
Match the following brief definitions with the terms by entering the appropriate letter in each space provided.

Terms	Brief description
_____ (1) Significant influence	A. Assumed when the investing company owns more than 50% of the outstanding voting stock of another company.
_____ (2) Discount	
_____ (3) Control	B. Accounting treatment prescribed when an investing company does not have significant influence or control over the other company.
_____ (4) Effective interest	
_____ (5) Equity method	
_____ (6) Stated interest rate	C. Occurs when the stated interest rate is less than the market rate.
_____ (7) Premium	D. Market rate of interest.
_____ (8) Cost method	E. Accounting treatment prescribed when an investing company has significant influence, but not control over the other company.
	F. Occurs when the stated interest rate is more than the market rate.
	G. Presumed if the investing company owns 20% to 50% of the outstanding voting shares of the other company.
	H. When this rate matches a bond investor's required rate of return, the bond will sell at par value.

E13–2   (Compare Primary Characteristics of Cost and Equity Methods)
Company P purchased a certain number of the outstanding voting shares of Company S at $15 per share as a long-term investment. Company S had outstanding 10,000 shares of $10 par value stock. On a separate sheet complete the following matrix relating to the measurement and reporting by Company P after acquisition of the shares of Company S stock.

Questions	Method of Measurement	
	Cost Method	Equity Method
a. What is the applicable level of ownership by Company P of Company S to apply the method?	Percent	Percent
For (b), (e), (f), and (g) that follow, assume: Number of shares acquired of Company S stock Net income reported by Company S in the first year Dividends declared by Company S in the first year Market price at end of first year, Company S stock, $13.50	1,000 $40,000 $15,000	3,000 $40,000 $15,000
b. At acquisition, the investment account on the books of Company P should be debited at what amount?	$	$
c. On what basis should Company P recognize revenue earned on the stock of Company S? Explanation required.		
d. After acquisition date, on what basis should Company P change the balance of investment account in respect to the stock of Company S owned (other than for disposal of the investment)? Explanation required.		
e. What would be the balance in the investment account on the books of Company P at the end of the first year?	$	$
f. What amount of revenue from the investment in Company S should Company P report at the end of the first year?	$	$
g. What amount of unrealized loss should Company P report at the end of the first year?	$	$

E13–3   **(Identification and Use of Proper Method to Account for a Long-Term Investment in Equity Securities)**

During 19B, Eli Company acquired some of the 60,000 outstanding shares of the common stock, par $10, of Cox Corporation as a long-term investment. The accounting period for both companies ends December 31. The following transactions occurred:

19B
July   2   Purchased 9,000 shares of Cox common stock at $20 per share.
Dec. 31   Received the 19B annual financial statement of Cox Corporation that reported net income of $40,000.
       31   Cox Corporation declared and paid a cash dividend of $0.50 per share.
       31   Market price of Cox stock was $19 per share.

Required:

a. What accounting method should Eli Company use? Why?

b. Give the required journal entries for Eli Company for each transaction. If no entry is required, explain why.

c. Show how the long-term investment and the related revenue should be reported on the 19B financial statements of Eli Company.

E13–4   **(Recording and Reporting a Long-Term Investment in an Equity Security)**

Black Company acquired some of the 40,000 shares of outstanding common stock (nopar) of Noe Corporation during 19E as a long-term investment. The annual accounting period for both companies ends December 31. The following transactions occurred during 19E:

19E

Jan.   10   Purchased 16,000 shares of Noe common stock at $30 per share.

Dec.   31   Received the 19E financial statement of Noe Corporation which reported net income of $80,000.

      31   Noe Corporation declared and paid a cash dividend of $1.25 per share.

      31   Market price of Noe stock was $25 per share.

Required:

a. What method of accounting should Black Company use? Why?

b. Give the journal entries by Black Company for each of the above transactions. If no entry is required, explain why.

c. Show how the long-term investment and the related revenue should be reported on the 19E financial statements of Black Company.

E13–5   **(Identify and Use the Proper Method to Account for a Long-Term Investment in an Equity Security)**

D··ring 19H, Steven Company purchased some of the 100,000 shares of common stock, par $5, of Salt Marine, Inc., as a long-term investment. The annual accounting period for each company ends December 31. The following transactions occurred during 19H.

19H

Jan.   7   Purchased 15,000 shares of Salt Marine common stock at $15 per share.

Dec.   31   Received the 19H financial statement of Salt Marine, which reported net income of $70,000.

      31   Salt Marine declared and paid a cash dividend of $2 per share.

      31   Market price of Salt Marine stock was $18 per share.

Required:

a. What method of accounting should Steven Company use? Why?

b. Give the journal entries for Steven Company for each of the above transactions. If no entry is required, explain why.

c. Show how the long-term investment and the related revenue should be reported on the 19H financial statements of Steven Company.

E13–6   **(Identify and Use the Proper Method to Account for a Long-Term Investment in an Equity Security)**

Use the same situation for Steven Company and the data given in Exercise 13–5, **except** for the January 7, 19H, transaction. Assume it was as follows:

19H
Jan. 7 Purchased 30,000 shares of Salt Marine stock at $15 per share.

(The data for December 31 are unchanged.)

Required:

a. What method of accounting should Steven Company use? Why?
b. Give the journal entries for Steven Company for each transaction (refer also to transactions given in Exercise 13–5). If no entry is required, explain why.
c. Show how the long-term investment and the related revenue should be reported on the 19H financial statements of Steven Company.

PART B

E13–7   **(Accounting for a Debt Security from Purchase Date to Maturity Date)**

On July 1, 19A, AB Company purchased at par a $10,000, 9%, 20-year bond of CD Corporation as a long-term investment. The annual bond interest is payable each year on June 30. The accounting period for AB Company ends December 31. At the date of purchase, the bond had five years remaining before maturity.

Required:

Give the journal entries on the books of AB Company for the following transactions:

a. July 1, 19A, acquisition date.
b. December 31, 19A.
c. June 30, 19B.
d. Maturity date of the bond, June 30, 19F.

E13–8   **(Accounting for a Debt Security from Purchase Date to Maturity Date)**

On April 1, 19A, Rover Company purchased at par ten $1,000, 9%, 10-year bonds of HI Corporation as a long-term investment. The bond interest is payable semiannually each March 31 and September 30. The accounting period for Rover Company ends on December 31. At the date of purchase, the bonds had six years remaining to maturity.

Required:

Give the journal entry for each of the following dates in the accounts of Rover Company in respect to the long-term investment: April 1, 19A; September 30, 19A; December 31, 19A; March 31, 19B; and the maturity date.

E13–9   **(Recording an Investment in Bonds)**

On February 1, 19A, Jones Company purchased at par a $15,000, 10%, 30-year bond of Lam Corporation as a long-term investment. The bond interest is payable semiannually each January 31 and July 31. The accounting period for Jones Company ends December 31. At the date of purchase, the bonds had four years remaining to maturity.

Required:

Give all journal entries required in the accounts of Jones Company for the period February 1, 19A, through January 31, 19B, and on the maturity date.

E13–10   (Compare Bonds Sold at Par; at a Discount; at a Premium)

On July 1, 19B, Tiana Company purchased three different bonds as long-term investments. Data about the three bonds and the purchase prices are:

Bond designation	Par of bond	Annual interest	Payable semiannually	Remaining years to maturity	Market purchase price*
A	$1,000	10%	Dec. 31 and	7	$1,000
B	1,000	9	June 30	10	960
C	1,000	12	each year	5	1,050

* These amounts do not include any accrued interest.

Required:

a. Give the journal entries to record separately the purchase of each bond.
b. Give the journal entries to record separately collection of interest on the first interest date after purchase. Use straight-line amortization of any discount or premium.
c. Give the journal entries to record separately the maturity of each bond.

E13–11   (Entries and Reporting for a Debt Security Using Straight-Line Amortization)

On May 1, 19B, American Company purchased $9,000 maturity value bonds of Opel Corporation at 96.25 (plus any accrued interest) as a long-term investment. The bond interest rate is 10% per annum payable 5% each April 30 and October 31. The bonds mature in four years from May 1, 19B.

Required:

a. Give the journal entries for American Company on May 1, 19B; October 31, 19B; and December 31, 19B (adjusting entry for accrued interest). Use straight-line amortization and round all amounts to the nearest dollar.
b. Show how this long-term investment and the related revenue should be shown on the December 31, 19B, annual financial statements of American Company. (Hint: Include the investment, interest receivable, and revenue.)

E13–12   (Entries and Reporting for a Debt Security Using Straight-Line Amortization)

On May 1, 19B, State Company purchased $10,000 of the 8% bonds of Cook Corporation, at 112 (plus any accrued interest) as a long-term investment. The bonds pay interest each April 30 and October 31. The bonds mature in five years on April 30, 19G.

Required:

a. Give the journal entries for State Company on May 1, 19B; October 31, 19B; and December 31, 19B (adjusting entry for accrued interest). Use straight-line amortization and round to the nearest dollar.
b. Show how this long-term investment should be shown on the December 31, 19B, annual financial statements of State Company.

E13–13 **(Entries and Reporting for a Debt Security Purchased between Interest Dates; Straight-Line Amortization)**

On March 1, 19B, Erbs Corporation purchased $6,000 of the 12% bonds of TU Corporation as a long-term investment. The bonds pay interest each June 30 and December 31. The bonds mature in 10 years on December 31, 19K. The purchase price was $6,236, plus any accrued interest.

Required:

a. Give the journal entry by Erbs Corporation to record the purchase on March 1, 19B.
b. Give the journal entry to record the interest received on June 30 and December 31, 19B. Use straight-line amortization.
c. What was the amount of interest revenue in 19B? At what amount should the bond investment be reported on the balance sheet at December 31, 19B?

E13–14 **(Analysis of an Effective-Interest Amortization Schedule)**

On January 1, 19A, Cotton Company purchased, as a long-term investment, a $3,000 bond of Devons Company for $2,922 (plus any accrued interest). The bond had a stated interest rate of 7%, payable each January 1. The bond matures in three years on December 31, 19C. Cotton Company uses effective-interest amortization. The amortization table given below was developed.

Date	Cash inflow	Interest revenue	Investment change	Investment balance
January 1, 19A				$2,922
End year 19A	$210	$234	$24	2,946
End year 19B	210	236	26	2,972
End year 19C	210	238	28	3,000

Required:

a. How much was the discount or premium?
b. What was the total cash outflow and the total cash inflow over the life of this investment? What does the difference represent? Explain.
c. How much interest revenue should be recognized on the income statement each year and in total?
d. What amounts should be reported on the balance sheet each year? For the last year give the amounts just prior to collection of the maturity amount.
e. What was the effective rate of interest per year? Show computations.
f. Show how the four different amounts that are listed on the line 19B were computed.
g. Show how the price of the bond of $2,922 was computed.

E13–15 **(Prepare an Effective-Interest Amortization Schedule; Entries and Reporting)**

On January 1, 19A, Indian Company purchased, as a long-term investment, a $10,000 par value, 12% bond issued by Jackson Corporation. The bond pays interest each year on December 31 and has five years remaining life to maturity from January 1, 19A. The accounting period for Indian Corporation ends December 31.

The bond was purchased to yield a 10% effective rate of interest; therefore, the price of the bond was computed as follows:

$$\$10,000 \times P_{n=5;\ i=10\%} (0.6209) = \$\ 6,209$$
$$\$1,200 \times \mathbf{P}_{n=5;\ i=10\%} (3.7908) = \underline{\ 4,549}$$
$$\text{Sales price} \dots \dots \dots \dots \underline{\$10,758}$$

Required:

a. Give the journal entry for Indian Company to record the purchase of the bond on January 1, 19A.

b. Prepare a schedule of effective-interest amortization.

c. Give the journal entries for the collection of interest on the bond investment during 19A and 19B.

d. Complete the following schedule (show computations):

	December 31	
	19A	19B
Income statement:		
Revenue from bond investment . . . . $ _____	$ _____	
Balance sheet:		
Bond-interest receivable	_____	_____
Long-term investment, bond of		
Jackson Corporation	_____	_____

PROBLEMS

PART A

P13–1   **(Identify, Record, and Report Using the Proper Method to Account for an Equity Investment)**

During January 19A, Quick Company purchased 10,000 shares of the 100,000 out-standing common shares (nopar value) of Eleven Corporation at $40 per share. This block of stock was purchased as a long-term investment. Assume the accounting period for each company ends December 31.

Subsequent to acquisition, the following data were available:

	19A	19B
Income reported by Eleven Corporation		
at December 31	$60,000	$70,000
Cash dividends declared and paid by		
Eleven Corporation during the year	25,000	30,000
Market price per share of Eleven common stock		
on December 31	37	39

Required:

a. What accounting method should be used by Quick Company? Why?

b. Give the journal entries for Quick Company for each year (use parallel columns) for the following (if none, explain why):

(1) Acquisition of Eleven Corporation stock.

(2) Net income reported by Eleven Corporation.

(3) Dividends received from Eleven Corporation.

(4) Market value effects at year-end.

c. Show how the following amounts should be reported on the financial statements for Quick Company for each year:

(1) Long-term investment.

(2) Stockholders' equity—unrealized loss.

(3) Revenues.

P13–2 **(Identify, Record, and Report Using the Proper Method to Account for Two Different Equity Investments)**

During January 19A, John Corporation purchased the shares listed below as a long-term investment:

| | | Number of shares | | |
Corporation	Stock	Out-standing	Purchase	Cost per share
M	Common (nopar)	80,000	12,000	$10
N	Preferred, nonvoting (par $10)	10,000	4,000	15

The accounting period of each company ends on December 31. Subsequent to acquisition, the following data were available:

	19A	19B
Net income reported at December 31:		
Corporation M	$20,000	$25,000
Corporation N	30,000	38,000
Dividends declared and paid per share during the year:		
Corporation M common stock	$ 1.00	$ 1.10
Corporation N preferred stock	0.20	0.30
Market value per share at December 31:		
Corporation M common stock	8.00	8.00
Corporation N preferred stock	15.00	16.00

Required:

a. What accounting method should be used by John for the M common stock? N preferred stock? Why?

b. Give the journal entries for John Corporation for each year in parallel columns (if none, explain why) for each of the following:
   (1) Purchase of the investments.
   (2) Income reported by Corporations M and N.
   (3) Dividends received from Corporations M and N.
   (4) Market value effects at year-end.

c. For each year, show how the following amounts should be reported on the financial statements for 19A:
   (1) Long-term investment.
   (2) Stockholders' equity—unrealized loss.
   (3) Revenues.

P13–3 **(Compare Methods to Account for Various Levels of Ownership of Voting Stock)**

Company S had outstanding 20,000 shares of common stock, par value $15 per share. On January 1, 19B, Company P purchased some of these shares at $20 per share. At the end of 19B, Company S reported the following: income, $40,000; and cash dividends declared and paid during the year, $15,000. The market value of Company S stock at the end of 19B was $17 per share.

Required:

a. For each case given below (in the tabulation), identify the method of accounting that should be used by Company P. Explain why.

b. Give the journal entries for Company P at the dates indicated below for each of the two independent cases. If no entry is required, explain why. Use the following format:

Tabulation of items	Case A—2,000 shares purchased	Case B—8,000 shares purchased
1. Entry to record the acquisition at January 1, 19B.	————	————
2. Entry to recognize the income reported by Company S for 19B.	————	————
3. Entry to recognize the dividends declared and paid by Company S for 19B.	————	————
4. Entry to recognize market value effect at end of 19B.	————	————

c. Complete the following schedule to show the separate amounts that should be reported on the 19B financial statements of Company P.

	Dollar amounts	
	Case A	Case B
Balance sheet:		
Investments and funds	————	————
Stockholders' equity	————	————
Income statement:		
Revenue from investments	————	————

d. Explain why assets, stockholders' equity, and revenues are different between the two cases.

P13–4 **(Compare the Cost and Equity Methods)**

Orban Company purchased, as a long-term investment, some of the 100,000 shares of the outstanding common stock of Towns Corporation. The annual accounting period for each company ends December 31. The following transactions occurred during 19E.

19E
Jan. 10 Purchased shares of common stock of Towns at $10 per share as follows:

Case A—10,000 shares.

Case B—30,000 shares.

Dec. 31 Received the 19E financial statements of Towns Corporation; the reported net income was $80,000.
  31 Received a cash dividend of $0.30 per share from Towns Corporation.
  31 Market price of Towns stock, $8 per share.

Required:

a. For each case, identify the accounting method that should be used by Orban. Explain why.

b. Give the journal entries for Orban Company for each case for the above transactions. If no entry is required, explain why. (Hint: Use parallel columns for Case A and Case B.)

c. Give the amounts for each case that should be reported on the 19E financial statements of Orban Corportion. Use the following format:

	Case A	Case B
Balance sheet (partial):		
Investments and funds:		
Investment in common stock, Towns Corporation	_____	_____
Stockholders' equity:		
Unrealized loss	_____	_____
Income statement (partial):		
Revenue from investments	_____	_____

P13–5   **(Compare the Cost and Equity Methods)**

Sub Corporation had outstanding 200,000 shares of nopar common stock. On January 10, 19B, Par Company purchased a block of these shares in the open market at $20 per share. At the end of 19B, Sub Corporation reported net income of $210,000 and cash dividends of $0.50 per share. At December 31, 19B, the Sub stock was selling at $18 per share. This problem involves two separate cases:

Case A—Par Company purchased 30,000 shares of Sub common stock.

Case B—Par Company purchased 60,000 shares of Sub common stock.

Required:

a. For each case, identify the accounting method that should be used by Par Company? Explain why.

b. For each case, in parallel columns, give the journal entries for Par Company for each of the following (if no entry is required, explain why):
   (1) Acquisition.
   (2) Revenue recognition.
   (3) Dividends received.
   (4) Market value effects.

c. For each case show how the following should be reported on the 19B financial statements of Par Company:
   (1) Long-term investments.
   (2) Market effects.
   (3) Revenues.

d. Explain why the amounts reported (in Requirement [c]) are different between the two cases.

PART B

P13–6   **(Compare Accounting for Equity Securities with Accounting for Debt Securities)**

On January 1, 19B, Ace Company purchased $60,000, 11% bonds of Bye Company as a long-term investment, at 100 (plus any accrued interest). Interest is payable annually on December 31. The bonds have six years to maturity from December 31, 19A. The annual accounting period for Ace Company ends December 31. In addition, on January 2, 19B, Ace Company purchased in the market 5% of the 10,000 shares of outstanding common stock of Bye Company at $30 per share.

Required:

a. Give the journal entry for Ace Company to record the purchase of the bonds on January 1, 19B.

b. Give the journal entry to record the purchase of the common stock on January 2, 19B.

c. Give the journal entry assuming a cash dividend of $3 per share was declared and received on the Bye stock on December 28, 19B.

d. Give the journal entry for the receipt of the interest on the Bye bonds on December 31, 19B.

e. Show how the long-term investments and the related revenues should be reported on the 19B annual financial statements of Ace Company. Market price of Bye stock was $31 at the end of 19B.

P13–7   **(Reporting Bond Investments Using Straight-Line Amortization of the Discount)**
On May 1, 19B, Moon Company purchased $30,000, 8% bonds of Taylor Company as a long-term investment. The interest is payable each April 30 and October 31. The bonds have four years to maturity from May 1, 19B. The bonds were purchased at 95 (plus any accrued interest). In addition, brokerage fees of $540 were paid by Moon Company.

Required:

a. Give the 19B journal entries for Moon Company on the following dates:

May   1 Purchase.
Oct. 31 First interest date. Use straight-line amortization.
Dec. 31 Adjusting entry for accrued interest at the end of the annual accounting period.

b. Show how the investment, interest receivable, and related revenue should be reported on the 19B annual financial statements of Moon Company.

c. Give the journal entry at the maturity date of the bonds.

P13–8   **(Reporting for a Debt Security Using Straight-Line Amortization of a Bond Premium)**
On June 1, 19B, Fred Company purchased $30,000, 12% bonds of Gray Company, as a long-term investment. The interest is payable each April 30 and October 31. The bonds have five years to maturity from the issue date, May 1, 19B. The bonds were purchased at 105 (plus any accrued interest). In addition, Fred Company paid brokerage fees of $270. The annual accounting period for Fred Company ends December 31.

Required:

a. Give the journal entries for Fred Company on the following dates:

June   1 Purchase plus any accrued interest.
Oct. 31 First interest date. Use straight-line amortization.
Dec. 31 Adjusting entry for accrued interest.

b. Show how the investment, interest receivable, and related revenue should be reported on the 19B annual financial statements of Fred Company.

c. Give the journal entry at the maturity date of the bonds, April 30, 19G.

P13–9   **(Compare Entries and Reporting for Bonds Purchased at Par; at a Discount; at a Premium)**
During 19A, Akers Company purchased the following bonds of Jackson Corporation as a long-term investment:

	Series A	Series B	Series C	Series D
Maturity amount	$10,000	$10,000	$10,000	$10,000
Date purchased	7/1/19A	7/1/19A	7/1/19A	9/1/19A
Interest per annum	8%	7%	9%	9%
Interest dates, annual	June 30	June 30	June 30	June 30
Maturity date	6/30/19F	6/30/19F	6/30/19F	6/30/19F
Purchase price*	100	95	106	100

  * Plus any accrued interest.

Required:

a. Give the journal entries to record separately the purchase of the long-term investments.

b. Give the adjusting entries of Akers Company for December 31, 19A, assuming this is the end of the accounting period. Give a separate journal entry for each series. Use straight-line amortization.

c. Give the journal entry of Akers Company for each separate series that should be made on June 30, 19B, for collection of the first interest payment.

d. Complete the following schedule to show the amounts that should be reported on the 19A financial statements (show each series separately):

> **Income statement (19A):**
> Revenue from investments .... $ _____
> **Balance sheet (at December 31, 19A):**
> Long-term investment, bonds of Jackson Corporation ..... $ _____

P13–10 **(Analyze Effective-Interest Amortization; Prepare Schedule and Entries)**

On January 1, 19A, Austin Corporation purchased $50,000, 9% bonds of Boston Company to yield an effective rate of 10%. The bonds pay the interest on June 30 and December 31 and will mature on December 31, 19C.

This long-term investment was recorded by Austin Corporation as follows:

January 1, 19A:

Long-term investment, Boston Company bonds 48,730
    Cash   48,730

    Computations:
    Principal—$50,000 × $P_{n=6;\ i=5\%}$ (0.7462)   = $37,310
    Interest—$2,250 × $P_{n=6;\ i=5\%}$ (5.0757)   =   11,420
        Bond price $48,730

Required:

a. What were the stated and effective rates of interest?

b. What was the amount of the discount or premium? What would be the amount of discount or premium amortization each interest period assuming straight-line amortization?

c. Prepare a schedule of effective-interest amortization similar to Exhibit 13–7.

d. Give the journal entries to record interest (including amortization) on June 30 and December 31, 19A, assuming (1) straight-line and (2) effective-interest amortization.

e. Explain when it is appropriate to use each method of amortization.

CASES

C13–1   (Analyze the Financial Effects of the Cost and Equity Methods)

On January 1, 19B, Emerson Company purchased 40% of the outstanding common stock of Reed Corporation at a total cost of $780,000. On December 31, 19B, the investment in Reed Corporation was reported by Emerson as $950,000, but Emerson did not purchase any additional Reed stock. Emerson Company received $100,000 in cash dividends from Reed. The dividends were declared and paid during 19B. Emerson used the equity method to account for its investment in Reed. The market price of Reed stock increased during 19B.

Required:

a. Explain why the investment account balance increased from $780,000 to $950,000 during 19B.

b. What amount of revenue from the Reed investment was reported by Emerson during 19B?

c. If Emerson used the cost method, what amount of revenue from the Reed investment should have been reported in 19B?

d. If Emerson used the cost method, what amount should be reported as the investment in Reed Corporation on the December 31, 19B, Emerson Company balance sheet?

C13–2   (Analyzing and Understanding Effective-Interest Amortization)

On January 1, 19A, Evans Corporation purchased, as a long-term investment, a bond of Fable Corporation. The following schedule was prepared based on the investment (table captions have been omitted intentionally):

January 1, 19A				$10,339
End year 19A	$800	$724	$76	10,263
End year 19B	800	718	82	10,181
End year 19C	800	713	87	10,094
End year 19D	800	706	94	10,000

Required:

Respond to the following questions in respect to the investment by Evans Corporation:

a. What was the maturity amount of the bond?

b. What was the acquisition price of the investment?

c. Give the journal entry that Evans Corporation should make at acquisition date.

d. Was the bond acquired at a premium or discount? How much?

e. What was the stated rate of interest per year? Show computations.

f. What method of amortization apparently will be used? Explain.

g. What was the effective rate of interest?

h. What were the total cash inflow and total cash outflow on the investment? What does the difference represent? Explain.

i. How much interest revenue should be reported each period on the income statement? How does this amount relate to the difference in (*h*)?

j. What amount will be reported on the balance sheet at the end of each year? (Show the amount for year 19D just prior to collection of the maturity amount.)

k. How were the amounts in each of the four columns of the above schedule computed? Use year 19B to demonstrate the computations.

l. Why is the method of amortization being used conceptually preferable?

C13-3   **(Analysis of the Cost and Equity Methods Using an Actual Financial Statement)**
Refer to the financial statements of Chesebrough-Pond's given in Special Supplement B immediately preceding the Index.

Required:

a. Does the company consolidate all of its wholly owned subsidiaries? If not, why and what method is used?

b. How much of the company's 1985 income is associated with investments accounted for under the equity method?

c. If the company used the cost method instead of the equity method for certain of its investments, would you expect the company's income to increase or decrease? Why?

d. The company does not consolidate the "associated companies" shown in footnote 11. Explain why.

e. Assume Pond's Limited, a 40% owned associated company, increased its dividend payment from $1 million to $1.5 million. What impact would the increase have on Chesebrough-Pond's income?

Most large corporations prepare consolidated financial statements. They include a note that describes the consolidation process.

Ex-Cell-O Corporation

(1) Significant accounting policies

Notes to consolidated financial statements
Principles of consolidation

The consolidated financial statements include the accounts of the company and its subsidiaries, except for Ex-Cell-O Credit Corporation (See Note 6), which is included on an equity basis. All significant intercompany balances and transactions have been eliminated in consolidation. Investments in affiliated companies are recorded principally on the equity method.

Goodwill

The excess of cost of investment over the fair value of net assets acquired is being amortized primarily by the straight-line method over 40 years.

CONSOLIDATED STATEMENTS— MEASURING AND REPORTING

PURPOSE:

The previous chapter discussed accounting for long-term investments when one company owns less than 50% of the voting stock of another corporation. This chapter discusses those situations in which one corporation has a controlling influence over another corporation as the result of owning more than 50% of the outstanding voting stock of the other corporation. Often, when a corporation has a controlling influence in another corporation, the financial statements for each corporation are combined into a single set of financial statements by an accounting process called consolidation. Because most large companies prepare consolidated financial statements, an understanding of the consolidation process is important for both accounting majors and anyone who uses financial statements.

LEARNING OBJECTIVES—TO BE ABLE TO:

1. Identify necessary criteria for consolidated statements.
2. Specify appropriate use of the pooling and purchase methods.
3. Apply the pooling and purchase methods.
4. Compare the pooling and purchase methods.
5. Expand your accounting vocabulary by learning about the "Important Terms Defined in This Chapter" (page 735).
6. Apply the knowledge gained from this chapter by completing the homework assigned by your instructor.

ORGANIZATION:

Part A—Acquiring a Controlling Interest

1. Criteria for consolidated statements.
2. Pooling of interests.
3. Purchase method.

Part B—Reporting Consolidated Operations after Acquisition

1. Impact of pooling and purchase methods after acquisition.
2. Comparison of pooling and purchase methods.

PART A—ACQUIRING A CONTROLLING INTEREST

CRITERIA FOR CONSOLIDATED FINANCIAL STATEMENTS

A **parent** and **subsidiary** relationship exists when a company owns more than 50% of the outstanding voting stock of another corporation. The investing corporation is known as the parent company, and the other corporation is called a subsidiary. Both corporations are **separate legal entities.** Each company has its own accounting system, and each prepares its own financial statements. However, because of their special relationship, they are viewed as a **single economic entity** for financial reporting. Because the parent and subsidiary are viewed as a single economic entity, the parent company (but not the subsidiary) is required to prepare **consolidated financial statements.** The individual financial statements of the parent and each of its subsidiaries are combined by the parent company into one overall or consolidated set of financial statements. The consolidated financial statements report on the single economic entity. Each of the three required statements—balance sheet, income statement, and statement of changes in financial position—is consolidated by the parent company.

There are a number of operating, economic, and legal advantages to the parent-subsidiary relationship. Therefore, most large corporations, and many medium-sized corporations, have a controlling interest in one or more other corporations. For example, Sears, Roebuck and Company has acquired a controlling interest in many of the companies that manufacture the products that are sold by Sears. As a result, Sears is assured of getting the quality and quantity of product that it wants at the price that it wants to pay.

Consolidated financial statements are prepared when two basic elements exist. These two basic elements are control and economic compatibility.

Control is presumed to exist when one investor owns more than 50% of the outstanding voting stock of an entity. Nonvoting stock is not included in the determination of control because it does not provide the investor with any ability to influence the policies of the subsidiary. Effective control may not exist even though an investor owns more than 50% of the voting stock. This situation may exist when the subsidiary is located in a foreign country where **governmental restrictions** prevent the parent company from exercising meaningful control. In circumstances where control is lacking, consolidated statements are not appropriate.

Economic compatibility means that the operations of the affiliated companies are related so that one complements the other. The operations of an automobile manufacturer (such as General Motors) are economically compatible with the operations of a company that manufactures spark plugs. On the other hand, a manufacturing company and a bank lack economic compatibility and should not be consolidated.

Consolidated statements are not prepared when an investor lacks either *(a)* meaningful control or *(b)* economic compatibility with the other company. In such situations, the investment is reported as a long-term asset on the balance sheet of the parent as "Investment in unconsolidated subsidiary." The investment is accounted for under the **equity method** as discussed in Chapter 13 and is not consolidated.

Consolidated statements affect only the **reporting** by the parent company of the financial results of the parent and its subsidiaries. The accounting for each subsidiary company is not affected. The fact that a parent company owns a controlling interest has no effect on the accounting of a subsidiary. At the end of the accounting period, the subsidiary prepares its own financial statements. Also, the parent company accounts for its own operations in the normal manner and prepares its own financial statements at the end of each period.

When consolidation is appropriate, the financial statements of the parent and the subsidiaries are prepared in the normal manner and then are combined by the parent company on an **item-by-item basis.** Thus, the consolidated statement concept does not affect the recording of transactions by the parent and subsidiaries. It affects only the **reporting phase** of the combined entity represented by the parent company and its subsidiaries.

METHODS OF ACQUIRING A CONTROLLING INTEREST

One corporation may acquire a controlling interest in another corporation either *(a)* by creating a new corporation and **retaining** more than 50% of the voting stock of the new entity or *(b)* by **acquiring** more than 50% of the outstanding voting stock of an existing corporation. Both ways of acquiring a controlling interest are used widely. A parent company may acquire the voting capital stock of an existing corporation in either of two ways:

1. **Exchanging shares of parent company voting stock for more than 50% of the outstanding voting capital stock of the subsidiary (owned by the stockholders of the subsidiary)**—If certain additional criteria are met, this type of acquisition is called a **pooling of interests.** In this situation, the stockholders of the subsidiary give up their subsidiary shares and become stockholders of only the parent company.
2. **Purchasing by the parent, using cash, other assets, or debt, of more than 50% of the outstanding voting shares from the stockholders of the subsidiary**—This type of acquisition is known as a **combination by purchase.** In this situation, the stockholders of the subsidiary sell more than 50% of their voting shares and are not stockholders of either the parent or the subsidiary.[1]

The pooling and purchase methods have different impacts on the consolidated financial statements. In the next few paragraphs, we will discuss the

---

[1] There is a distinction between a pure combination by pooling of interest and a pure purchase. However, a controlling interest may be acquired in part by a stock exchange and in part by a cash purchase. In these "nonpure" situations, a rigid list of criteria must be met to qualify as a pooling of interest (see footnote 2); otherwise, the combination must be accounted for as a combination by purchase.

EXHIBIT 14–1

Illustrative data for consolidation

COMPANY P AND COMPANY S
Separate Balance Sheets
January 1, 19A, Immediately before Acquisition

	Company P		Company S	
Assets				
Cash		$205,000		$ 35,000
Accounts receivable (net)*		15,000		30,000
Receivable from Company S		10,000		
Inventories		170,000		70,000
Plant and equipment (net)*		100,000		45,000
Total assets		$500,000		$180,000
Liabilities and Stockholders' Equity				
Liabilities:				
Accounts payable		$ 60,000		$ 20,000
Payable to Company P				10,000
Stockholders' equity:				
Common stock, Company P (par $6)	$300,000			
Common stock, Company S (par $10)			$100,000	
Retained earnings	140,000	440,000	50,000	150,000
Total liabilities and stockholders' equity		$500,000		$180,000

* Accounts receivable, less the allowance for doubtful accounts; and plant and equipment, less accumulated depreciation. The net amounts are used to simplify the example. The end results will be the same as they would have been had the separate control accounts been used.

consolidation process and the effects of the alternative methods of acquiring a controlling interest. Throughout the chapter we will use a continuing example to illustrate the consolidation process. We will use data for Company P (the parent) and Company S (the acquired subsidiary) shown in Exhibit 14–1.

POOLING OF INTERESTS METHOD

When one corporation acquires more than 50% of the voting stock of another corporation by **exchanging** stock, the stockholders of the two corporations have pooled their ownership interests. This transaction is not viewed as a purchase/ sale transaction, and as a result, the cost principle is **not** applied to pooling of interests acquisitions.[2] After a pooling of interests, the consolidated statements

---

[2] AICPA, *APB Opinion No. 16*, "Business Combinations" (New York, August 1970), states precise conditions under which a business combination **must** be measured and reported as a pooling of interests. The *Opinion* states: "The combination of existing voting common stock interests by the

EXHIBIT 14–2

Balance sheets immediately after acquisition (pooling of interests method)

COMPANY P AND COMPANY S
Separate Balance Sheets (pooling of interests method)
January 1, 19A, Immediately after Acquisition

	Company P	Company S
Assets		
Cash	$205,000	$ 35,000
Accounts receivable (net)	15,000	30,000
Receivable from Company S	10,000	
Inventories	170,000	70,000
Investment in Company S (100%)	150,000*	
Plant and equipment (net)	100,000	45,000
Total assets	$650,000	$180,000
Liabilities and Stockholders' Equity		
Accounts payable	$ 60,000	$ 20,000
Payable to Company P		10,000
Common stock, Company P	360,000*	
Common stock, Company S		100,000
Contributed capital from pooling of interests	90,000*	
Retained earnings, Company P	140,000	
Retained earnings, Company S		50,000
Total liabilities and stockholders' equity	$650,000	$180,000

* Amounts changed from preacquisition balance sheets given in Exhibit 14–1.

reflect the book values of each company, as shown on their respective financial statements and not the market value of the assets of the subsidiary on the date of the exchange of stock.

To illustrate the consolidation process, we will combine the two separate balance sheets shown in Exhibit 14–2 into a single **consolidated balance sheet.** Basically, consolidation involves combining the balances in each account on the financial statements of the parent and subsidiary companies. The result is the consolidated financial statements that would appear if there were a **single entity.** When the parent company consolidates the balance sheets shown in Exhibit 14–2, the consolidated balance sheet will report a cash balance of $240,000 (i.e., $205,000 + $35,000). During consolidation, some accounts are

exchange of stock is the essence of a business combination accounted for by the pooling of interests method." The *Opinion* specifies a number of additional conditions that if present **require** use of the pooling of interests method. Because of these conditions, many stock exchanges (particularly if cash also is involved) do not qualify for the pooling of interests method. All combinations not meeting the specified conditions for pooling of interests must be accounted for by the purchase method. The usual, although not exclusive, mode of combination in these latter situations is by disbursement of cash or by incurrence of debt for the stock.

eliminated (or adjusted) to avoid including amounts that would not be reported if only a single entity existed. For example, the balance sheet of Company P shows a receivable from Company S of $10,000, and the balance sheet of Company S shows a payable to Company P of $10,000. During consolidation, these accounts must be eliminated (which means that they will not be reported on the consolidated balance sheet). The consolidated balance sheet is prepared as if a single entity existed, and it would not be proper to report an amount that the entity owed to itself.

Two items must be eliminated when the balance sheets shown in Exhibit 14–2 are consolidated under the pooling of interests method:

a. The debit balance of $150,000 in Company P's investment account will be replaced on the consolidated balance sheet with the assets (less the liabilities) of Company S. To prevent double counting, the investment account must be eliminated. The credit balance of $100,000 in the Company S common stock account is owned by Company P. It is an intercompany item that must be eliminated. Finally, the difference between the balances in the investment account and the common stock account of Company S ($150,000 − $100,000 = $50,000) must be eliminated from Contributed Capital from Pooling of Interests (on Company P's books). This elimination is necessary because it is an intercompany amount. These three eliminations are made by Company P to avoid double counting. They can be summarized as follows:[3]

	Eliminations	
	Consolidated assets	Consolidated stockholders' equity
Investment account—decrease	−$150,000	
Common stock, Company S—decrease		−$100,000
Contributed capital from pooling of interests—decrease (for the difference)		− 50,000

b. Company P shows a receivable of $10,000 from Company S, and the accounts of Company S show this as a payable to Company P. This amount is called an **intercompany debt.** When the two balance sheets are combined into a single consolidated balance sheet, intercompany debt must be eliminated because there is no external debt or receivable for the combined entity. Thus, the following elimination must be made when the two balance sheets are combined:

	Eliminations	
	Consolidated assets	Consolidated liabilities
Receivable from Company S—decrease	−$10,000	
Payable to Company P—decrease		−$10,000

---

[3] This tabulation also can be viewed in the debit/credit format as follows:

Common stock, Company S	100,000	
Contributed capital from pooling of interests	50,000	
Investment in Company S		150,000

The balance sheets of Company P and Company S are shown separately in Exhibit 14–3. In the last column, these balance sheets are combined on a line-by-line basis, after deducting the "Eliminations," to develop the "Consolidated balance sheet." In an external consolidated financial statement, only the last column—the "Consolidated balance sheet" (and not the "Separate balance sheets")—would be reported by the parent company.

Review the "Consolidated balance sheet" by the pooling of interests method shown in the last column of Exhibit 14–3. Notice the following measurement procedures: (1) the amounts on each line for the consolidated assets, liabilities, and stockholders' equity are the **combined book values** of the parent and the subsidiary as were shown on the separate balance sheets; (2) the intercompany amounts for investment, subsidiary common stock, a part of contributed capital

---

EXHIBIT 14–3

Preparation of consolidated balance sheet (pooling of interests method)

COMPANY P and Its Subsidiary, COMPANY S (100% owned)
Consolidated Balance Sheet (pooling of interests method)
At January 2, 19A, Immediately after Acquisition

	Separate balance sheets			Consolidated balance sheet
	Company P*	Company S*	Eliminations*	
Assets				
Cash	$205,000	$ 35,000		$240,000
Accounts receivable (net)	15,000	30,000		45,000
Receivable from Company S	10,000		(b) − 10,000	–0–
Inventories	170,000	70,000		240,000
Investment in Company S	150,000		(a) − 150,000	–0–
Plant and equipment (net)	100,000	45,000		145,000
Total assets	$650,000	$180,000		$670,000
Liabilities				
Accounts payable	$ 60,000	$ 20,000		$ 80,000
Payable to Company P		10,000	(b) − 10,000	–0–
Stockholders' Equity				
Common stock, Company P	360,000			360,000
Common stock, Company S		100,000	(a) − 100,000	–0–
Contributed capital from pooling	90,000		(a) − 50,000	40,000
Retained earnings, Company P	140,000			} 190,000
Retained earnings, Company S		50,000		
Total liabilities and stockholders' equity	$650,000	$180,000		$670,000

* Included for instructional purposes only. A worksheet usually is used to derive the consolidated amounts. See Supplements 14A and 14B.

from pooling, and the intercompany debt are eliminated; and (3) the **consoli-dated** retained earnings amount is the sum of the two separate retained earnings amounts ($140,000 + $50,000 = $190,000).[4]

The $100,000 balance shown in the capital stock account of Company S is eliminated because it is an intercompany item (all of the capital stock is owned by Company P). Retained earnings of Company S is not eliminated because it is not an intercompany item. The old stockholders of Company P plus the former Company S stockholders (who are now stockholders of Company P) have dividend claims on the **total** of retained earnings for the combined unit.

PURCHASE METHOD

The preceding discussion considered the pooling of interests method (an exchange of stock). In contrast, when a corporation pays cash to acquire the stock of another corporation, a **purchase** transaction takes place.[5] The purchase of assets must be recorded in conformity with the **cost principle.** Thus, on the acquisition date, the investment account for the parent company must be mea-sured at cost, which is the **market value of the acquired shares at date of purchase** (i.e., the cash or cash equivalent paid).

To illustrate a combination by **purchase,** we will use the balance sheets of Companies P and S as given in Exhibit 14–1. Assume that on January 2, 19A, Company P **purchased** from stockholders 100% of the outstanding voting stock of Company S for $165,000 and paid cash. On this date, Company P would make the following journal entry in its accounts:

January 2, 19A:		
Investment in stock of Company S (10,000 shares, 100%)	165,000	
Cash		165,000
Acquisition by purchase.		

Note that Company P paid $165,000 cash for 100% of the owners' equity of Company S, although the **total book value** of the stockholders' equity of Company S that was purchased was only $150,000. Thus, Company P paid $15,000 more than "book value." In consolidating the two balance sheets, this $15,000 difference must be taken into account as explained below.

This purchase by Company P will have no effect on the accounting and

---

[4] The pooling of interests method also requires that all comparative statements presented for prior years must be restated as if consolidated statements had been prepared.

[5] Refer to footnote 2. In some instances, exchanges of shares do not qualify for the pooling method. In these instances, the purchase method must be used.

reporting by the subsidiary Company S because the stock was sold (and cash was received) by the stockholders of Company S (and not by Company S itself).

After the above journal entry is posted to the accounts of Company P, the two separate balance sheets would be changed as shown in the first two columns of Exhibit 14–4. Compare these two columns with Exhibit 14–1, and you will see that for (a) Company P cash decreased by $165,000 and the investment increased by the same amount and (b) Company S accounts are unchanged.

Observe the consolidated balance sheet under the **purchase method** shown in Exhibit 14–4. The two separate balance sheets for Companies P and S were combined immediately after acquisition to develop the consolidated balance sheet. The consolidation process for a purchase is similar to consolidation for a pooling of interests (as illustrated in Exhibit 14–3). There are two intercompany

---

EXHIBIT 14–4

Preparation of a consolidated balance sheet (purchase method)

COMPANY P and Its Subsidiary, COMPANY S (100% owned)
Consolidated Balance Sheet (purchase method)
At January 2, 19A, Immediately after Acquisition

	Separate balance sheets			Consolidated balance sheet
	Company P*	Company S*	Eliminations*	
Assets				
Cash	$ 40,000	$ 35,000		$ 75,000
Accounts receivable (net)	15,000	30,000		45,000
Receivable from Company S	10,000		(b) − 10,000	–0–
Inventories	170,000	70,000		240,000
Investment in Company S	165,000		(a) − 165,000	–0–
Plant and equipment (net)	100,000	45,000	(a) + 5,000	150,000
Goodwill†			(a) + 10,000	10,000
Total assets	$500,000	$180,000		$520,000
Liabilities				
Accounts payable	$ 60,000	$ 20,000		$ 80,000
Payable to Company P		10,000	(b) − 10,000	–0–
Stockholders' Equity				
Common stock, Company P	300,000			300,000
Common stock, Company S		100,000	(a) − 100,000	–0–
Retained earnings, Company P	140,000			140,000
Retained earnings, Company S		50,000	(a) − 50,000	–0–
Total liabilities and stockholders' equity	$500,000	$180,000		$520,000

* Included for instructional purposes only. A worksheet usually is used to derive the consolidated amounts. See Supplements 14A and 14B.

† A title preferred by most accountants is "Excess of purchase price over the current value of the net assets of the subsidiary" rather than "Goodwill." However, the length of this term causes the shorter term to be used extensively.

items that require eliminations like those shown for the pooling of interests method. Notice, however, one item differs significantly. The two eliminations are:

a. The P Company investment account balance of $165,000 represents **market value** at the date of acquisition. It must be eliminated against the stock-holders' equity of the subsidiary, which is at **book value.** Company P paid $15,000 more than book value (i.e., $165,000 − $150,000) to acquire Company S for two reasons: (1) The plant and equipment owned by Company S had a market value of $50,000 at acquisition (compared with the book value of $45,000 reported by Company S), and (2) Company S had developed a good reputation with its customers which increased the overall value of Company S. The difference between the cost and the book value of the investment may be analyzed as follows:

Purchase price for 100% interest in Company S		$165,000
Net assets purchased, value at market:		
Book value, $180,000 + market value increment		
of plant and equipment, $5,000 = ...	$185,000	
Less liabilities assumed	30,000	
Total market value purchased		155,000
Goodwill purchased		$ 10,000

Company P paid $165,000 cash for Company S, which had net assets (total assets minus liablities) with a **market** value of $155,000. Therefore, the good-will of Company S cost $10,000. **Goodwill** is the amount that an investor paid for the good reputation, customer appeal, and general acceptance of the business that an acquired company had developed over the years. All suc-cessful companies have some amount of goodwill. Its "value" is never known except when a business is purchased, as it was in this case. To eliminate the Company P investment account and the owner's equity accounts of Com-pany S, the following five steps must be completed:

1. Increase the plant and equipment of Company S from the book value of $45,000 to market value of $50,000; the increase is $5,000.
2. Recognize the $10,000 goodwill purchased as an asset.
3. Eliminate the investment account balance of $165,000.
4. Eliminate the Company S common stock balance of $100,000.
5. Eliminate the Company S retained earnings balance of $50,000.

These five steps are implemented as follows:[6]

---

[6] This tabulation also can be viewed in the debit-credit format as follows (see supplements):

Plant and equipment	5,000	
Goodwill	10,000	
Common stock, Company S	100,000	
Retained earnings, Company S	50,000	
Investment, Company S		165,000

	Eliminations	
	Consolidated assets	Consolidated stockholders' equity
Plant and equipment—increase	+$ 5,000	
Goodwill—increase	+ 10,000	
Investment—decrease	− 165,000	
Common stock Company S—decrease		−$100,000
		− 50,000

b. The intercompany debt must be eliminated:

	Eliminations	
	Consolidated assets	Consolidated liabilities
Receivable from Company S—decrease	−$10,000	
Payable to Company P—decrease		−$10,000

When the purchase method is used, the balance of Retained Earnings of the subsidiary at acquisition is eliminated. In contrast, under the pooling of interest method, retained earnings is not eliminated. This elimination is made with the purchase method because the retained earnings of the subsidiary were in effect paid to the former stockholders of Company S when they were bought out for cash.

The accounts of Company S are not affected by a purchase because the transaction was between the parent company and the former stockholders of the subsidiary.

The two "Separate balance sheets" are shown in Exhibit 14–4. After eliminations, they are combined on a line-by-line basis to develop the "Consolidated balance sheet" of Company P shown in the last column. In an external consolidated financial statement of Company P, only the "Consolidated balance sheet" shown in the last column (and not the "Separate balance sheets") would be reported.

To reemphasize, when the purchased method is used, the **market values** at date of acquisition of the subsidiary's assets are added on an item-by-item basis to the **book values** of the parent.

COMPARISON OF THE EFFECTS ON THE BALANCE SHEET OF POOLING VERSUS PURCHASE METHODS

To examine the differences in balance sheet amounts that arise when the pooling of interests method is used versus the purchase method, we can compare several of the consolidated amounts shown in Exhibits 14–3 and 14–4 as follows:

	Acquisition method		
	Pooling method	Purchase method	Difference
1. Cash	$240,000	$ 75,000	$(165,000)
2. Plant and equipment (net)	145,000	150,000	5,000 *
3. Goodwill		10,000	10,000 *
4. Common stock Company P	360,000	300,000	(60,000)
5. Contributed capital from pooling	40,000		(40,000)
6. Retained earnings Company P	190,000	140,000	(50,000)*

* These three amounts reflect the basic differences between the two methods (see footnote 7).

The $165,000 difference in cash was the purchase price of the subsidiary (under the pooling method, only stock was exchanged). The $100,000 difference in the amount of common stock is due to the effect of issuing stock under pooling of interests rather than paying cash when the purchase method is chosen.[7] The plant and equipment amount is higher when the purchase method is used because the purchase method requires application of the cost principle. Under the cost principle, the **market value** at date of acquisition rather than book value must be recognized for the assets of the subsidiary. Usually, goodwill arises in purchase but not pooling of interests. These higher amounts for assets under the purchase method mean higher expenses will be reported on the income statements in the future periods. In this case, depreciation expense and amortization expense for goodwill will be higher. Finally, under the pooling of interests method, the reported retained earnings amount is higher because the amount of retained earnings of the subsidiary must be added to that of the parent as shown in Exhibit 14–3.

When the pooling of interests and purchase methods are compared, three items usually stand out on the consolidated balance sheet:

1. Operational assets almost always are valued higher under the purchase method because they are recorded at market rather than at the subsidiary's book values.
2. Goodwill often is recorded under the purchase method but never is recorded under the pooling of interests method.
3. Retained earnings is lower under the purchase method because only the parent company's retained earnings is reflected, while under the pooling of interests method consolidated retained earnings always is the sum of the parent and subsidiary retained earnings.

Part B will discuss other significant effects that are reflected on the consolidated income statement of the parent company.

---

[7] In the example of the purchase method, the subsidiary stock was purchased by Company P for cash without borrowing or selling unissued stock. Had Company P borrowed the $165,000, the cash position would have been unaffected; however, there would have been an increase in debt by the same amount. Alternatively, Company P could have sold the 10,000 shares of its common stock for $165,000 cash and then purchased the 10,000 shares of Company S stock with that cash. In this scenario, the cash position and the contributed capital accounts would have been the same under both methods.

PART B—REPORTING CONSOLIDATED OPERATIONS AFTER ACQUISITION

The preceding discussions focused on the effects of the consolidation process on the consolidated balance sheet immediately after acquisition. Consolidation has important effects on the income statement and for accounting periods subsequent to the year of acquisition. Exhibit 14–5 presents the consolidated

EXHIBIT 14–5

Consolidated financial statements under the pooling and purchase methods one year after acquisition

COMPANY P and Its Subsidiary, COMPANY S (100% Owned)
Consolidated Financial Statements
Pooling and Purchase Methods Compared
At December 31, 19A, One Year after Acquisition

	Consolidated statements	
	Pooling method	*Purchase method*
Income statement (for the year ended December 31, 19A):		
Sales revenue	$ 510,000	$ 510,000
Expenses:		
Cost of goods sold	(279,000)	(279,000)
Expenses (not detailed)	(156,500)	(156,500)
Depreciation expense	(14,500)	(15,000)
Amortization expense (goodwill)		(500)
Income tax expense	(26,000)	(26,000)
Net income (carried to retained earnings)	$ 34,000	$ 33,000
Balance sheet (at December 31, 19A):		
Assets		
Cash	$ 271,500	$ 106,500
Accounts receivable (net)	46,000	46,000
Inventories	250,000	250,000
Plant and equipment (net)	130,500	135,000
Goodwill		9,500
Total assets	$ 698,000	$ 547,000
Liabilities		
Accounts payable	$ 74,000	$ 74,000
Stockholders' Equity		
Common stock	400,000*	300,000
Retained earnings	190,000	140,000
Add: Net income (from above)	34,000	33,000
Total liabilities and stockholders' equity	$ 698,000	$ 547,000

* Includes contributed capital from pooling of interests, $40,000.

income statement and balance sheet for Company P and its subsidiary, Company S, after one year of operations. Observe that the amount of net income that is reported will differ depending on whether the pooling of interests or purchase method is used. The underlying data and consolidation procedures used to derive these two financial statements are shown in Supplement 14A, Exhibit 14–10, and Exhibit 14–11. Compare the financial statements shown in Exhibits 14–10 and 14–11 to get an overview of the effect of consolidation on the income statement.

The primary objective of Part B is to discuss the impact of the pooling of interests and purchase methods on reporting consolidated results after acquisition.

THE IMPACT OF THE POOLING AND PURCHASE METHODS ONE YEAR AFTER ACQUISITION

Recall that at the date of acquisition, the plant and equipment shown on the balance sheet of Company S had a market value of $5,000 in excess of book value. These assets are being depreciated by Company S over a remaining life of 10 years. Also, the acquisition of Company S resulted in the recognition of $10,000 goodwill when the purchase method was used. This goodwill will be amortized over the next 20 years.[8]

A comparison of the impact of the pooling method and the purchase method on the consolidated statements of Company P after one year of operations is shown in Exhibit 14–6.

The comparison in Exhibit 14–6 shows that 11 amounts were different because of the alternative consolidation methods. Net income was $1,000 less under the purchase method because **additional** depreciation expense and amortization expense (goodwill) must be recognized in consolidation when the assets of the subsidiary are recorded at their market values on the date of acquisition. The causes of the $1,000 difference are:

	Items	Difference
a. Depreciation expense on pooling of interests method (on parent and subsidiary assets at book value)	$14,500	
Add depreciation on the increased asset amount of the subsidiary (to market value from book value, $5,000 ÷ 10 years)	500	$ 500
Depreciation expense on purchase method (on parent assets at book value and subsidiary assets at market value)	$15,000	
b. Amortization expense on the intangible asset, goodwill, of $10,000, which is to be amortized over the next 20 years ($10,000 ÷ 20 years)		500
(There is no goodwill recognized under pooling of interests.)		
Total of the differences		$1,000

---

[8] *APB Opinion No. 17*, "Accounting for Intangible Assets" (New York, August 1970), states: "The cost of each type of intangible asset [including goodwill] should be amortized on the basis of the estimated life of that specific asset. . . ." The *Opinion* limits the amortization to a maximum of 40 years.

EXHIBIT 14–6

Comparison of pooling of interests and purchase methods one year after acquisition

| | Acquisition approach | | |
	Pooling method	Purchase method	Difference
Income statement:			
1. Depreciation expense	$ 14,500	$ 15,000	$ 500*
2. Amortization expense (goodwill)		500	500*
3. Net income	34,000	33,000	$ 1,000*
Balance sheet:			
4. Cash	271,500	106,500	$165,000
5. Plant and equipment (net)	130,500	135,000	(4,500)
6. Goodwill		9,500	(9,500)
7. Total	698,000	547,000	$151,000
8. Common stock	360,000	300,000	$ 60,000
9. Contributed capital from pooling of interests	40,000		40,000
10. Retained earnings	224,000	173,000	51,000
11. Total	698,000	547,000	$151,000

* Basic differences on the income statement.

When the purchase method is used, net income will be less because of the additional expenses that must be recognized in each year subsequent to acquisition. Businesses usually do not like this unfavorable impact of the purchase method.

The $151,000 difference in the balance sheet totals shown in Exhibit 14–6 is caused by the (1) different way in which the stock was acquired (shares exchanged versus cash payment) and (2) accounting measurements implicit in each of the two methods. These differences may be explained as follows:

Cash—The $165,000 difference reflects the cash price paid for the stock of the subsidiary purchased under the purchase method instead of the exchange of shares under pooling of interests (see footnote 7).

Plant and equipment (net)—This difference reflects the effects of including the plant and equipment of the subsidiary at book value under the pooling of interests method compared with including them at **acquisition** market value under the purchase method. The $4,500 difference in plant and equipment may be explained as follows:

<pre>
Difference between market value and book value of
   subsidiary assets at date of acquisition $5,000
Deduct depreciation on the difference for one year
   ($5,000 ÷ 10 years)   500
      Difference: Operational assets (higher under purchase method) $4,500
</pre>

Goodwill—Goodwill often is recognized under the purchase method (and amortized over 40 years or less); it is not recognized under pooling of interests.

Common stock—The common stock of Company P is greater by $60,000 under a pooling of interests because of the issuance of shares in exchange for the shares of Company S. Note that this amount is the same as it was at acquisition.

Contributed capital from pooling of interests—This amount arises only under pooling of interests as a result of the exchange of shares. In consolidation, a part or all of it is eliminated.

Retained earnings—Retained earnings is $51,000 more under the pooling of interests method than under the purchase method. This difference is due to two factors:

<pre>
Amount of retained earnings eliminated:
   Under pooling of interests method .... $ –0–
   Under purchase method 50,000 $50,000
Amount of consolidated net income:
   Under pooling of interests method   34,000
   Under purchase method   33,000   1,000
      Difference: Retained earnings (higher under
         pooling of interests method) $51,000
</pre>

The pooling of interests method usually is preferred by the management of acquiring companies because it (1) requires little or no disbursement of cash, other assets, or the creation of debt; (2) results in a higher net income reported on the consolidated income statement than does the purchase method; (3) reports higher retained earnings; and (4) is susceptible to manipulation, which was evidenced by numerous abuses prior to the issuance of *APB Opinion 16* (August 1970). However, in the opinion of many persons, the opportunities for manipulation of net income are significant deficiencies of the pooling of interests method. Three fairly common manipulative practices of the past were:

1. **Instant earnings**—Assume Company P acquired Company S through a pooling of interests. At the acquisition date, Company S owned a factory that had a book value of $100,000 and a market value of $600,000. Following the pooling of interests method, the $100,000 book value of the factory was reported on the consolidated balance sheet as an asset. During the next year the factory was sold for the $600,000 market value. The result was a reported gain on the sale of operational assets of $500,000 (disregarding income taxes), even though a factory that cost $600,000 was sold for $600,000. This transaction was called, in a derogatory way, "instant earnings." The reported gain

would significantly increase **net income** and EPS and often caused the price of the shares of Company P to rise. At the higher stock prices, shares were sold to the public and/or used for another round of mergers following the same pattern. Many persons believe that there was no economic gain because the cost of the plant to the acquiring company was the market value of the shares given in exchange (and that it should have been recorded at this amount). If the asset were recorded at acquisition cost, no gain would be reported when the plant was sold for $600,000.

2. **Escalating EPS**—This term refers to what was a common practice of seeking out smaller successful companies to acquire through a pooling of interests, so that their earnings could be **added** to those of the parent. Thus, by the simple expedient of year-end pooling acquisitions, the acquiring company could escalate net income and EPS reported on the consolidated income statement. This action became a favorite way to "doctor" net income and EPS at year-end.

3. **Tricky mixes**—This situation represented the ultimate in misleading and illogical accounting. It was referred to as "part-purchase, part-pooling of interests accounting." In acquiring another company by pooling, a corporation often found a number of stockholders of the other company who would not accept shares in exchange; they wanted cash immediately. It might work out that two thirds of the shares of the subsidiary would be acquired by exchange of shares, and the remaining third would be purchased for cash. In order to derive some of the "reporting benefits" of pooling of interests accounting, two thirds of the acquisition would be accounted for as a pooling and one third as a purchase—thus part-purchase, part-pooling accounting. This mixture of accounting approaches not only was theoretically untenable but also was misleading. It was stopped by *APB Opinion 16*.

The "merger movement" in the 1960s came under considerable criticism because pooling of interests accounting often was used in situations that were, in substance, purchases. In response to extensive criticism, the APB issued *Opinion 16*, "Business Combinations," and *Opinion 17*, "Intangible Assets," which stopped the abuses cited above. *Opinion 16* states 12 criteria that if met require use of the pooling method. If any one of the criteria is not met, the purchase method must be used. A number of the members of the APB strongly believed, both for conceptual and practical reasons, that pooling of interests accounting should be disallowed completely. The conceptual argument against the pooling of interests method is that it ignores the market values on which the parties traded shares and substitutes, in violation of the cost principle, the book values carried in the accounts of the subsidiary. The practical argument against the pooling of interests method is that it leads to abuses such as those cited above.

The primary arguments in favor of the pooling of interests method of reporting are (1) it avoids the problems of measuring the market value of the different assets of the subsidiary at acquisition date; (2) it avoids the necessity of recognizing goodwill, then having to amortize it as an expense in future periods; and (3) the exchange of shares is not a purchase/sale transaction but, rather, is a joining of common interests and risks. Many accountants predict that the FASB eventually will eliminate the pooling of interests method.

DEMONSTRATION CASE

On January 1, 19A, Connaught Company purchased 100% of the outstanding voting shares of London Company in the open market for $85,000 cash. On the date of acquisition, the market value of the operational assets of London Company was $79,000.

Required:

a. Was this a combination by pooling of interests or by purchase? Explain.
b. Give the journal entry that should be made by Connaught Company at date of acquisition. If none is required, explain why.
c. Give the journal entry that should be made by London Company at date of acquisition. If none is required, explain why.
d. Analyze the acquisition to determine the amount of goodwill purchased.
e. Should the assets of London Company be included on the consolidated balance sheet at book value or market value? Explain.

Suggested Solution

a. The purchase method should be used because the stock of the subsidiary was acquired for cash.
b. January 1, 19A:

Investment in subsidiary	85,000	
Cash		85,000

c. London Company would not record a journal entry related to the purchase of stock by Connaught Company. The transaction was between Connaught and the stockholders of London Company. The transaction did not directly involve the London Company.

d. Purchase price for London Company $85,000
Market value of net assets purchased 79,000
Goodwill .... $ 6,000

e. Under the purchase method, the assets of London Company should be included on the consolidated balance sheet at their market values as of the date of acquisition. The cost principle applies because a purchase/sale transaction is assumed when the combination is accounted for as a purchase. When the pooling of interests method is used, the assets of the subsidiary are reported on the consolidated balance sheet at their book value.

SUMMARY OF CHAPTER

Consolidated financial statements are required in most situations when one corporation owns more than 50% of the outstanding voting stock of another corporation. The concept of consolidation is based upon the view that a parent company and its subsidiaries constitute one economic entity. Therefore, the separate income statements, balance sheets, and statements of changes in financial position should be combined each period on an item-by-item basis as a single set of consolidated financial statements.

Ownership of a controlling interest of another corporation may be accounted for as either a pooling of interests or combination by purchase. The measurement of amounts reported on the consolidated financial statements is influenced by these two different accounting methods.

The pooling of interests method usually is used when the parent company exchanges shares of its own voting stock for a controlling interest in the voting shares of the subsidiary. In this situation, there is no purchase/sale (exchange) transaction. Rather, there was a joining of interests by exchanging stock and the cost principle is not applied. Therefore, in preparing consolidated statements under the pooling of interests method, the book values of each related company are added together. Acquisition market values are disregarded.

Under the purchase method, the parent company usually pays cash and/or incurs debt to acquire the voting shares of the subsidiary. In these circumstances, a purchase/sale transaction has been completed, and the acquisition is accounted for in conformity with the cost principle. Therefore, the assets of the subsidiary must be measured at their acquisition market values when combined with the statements of the parent company.

The differences between the pooling of interests and purchase methods are summarized in Exhibit 14–7. The acquisition of a controlling interest **does not** affect the accounting and reporting of the subsidiary companies (the subsidiary companies do not prepare consolidated statements).

SUPPLEMENT 14A—CONSOLIDATION PROCEDURES—100% OWNERSHIP

This supplement discusses in more depth the measurement procedures used in preparing consolidated financial statements. To accomplish this objective, we use a **consolidation worksheet** because it brings the underlying concepts and measurement procedures into sharp focus. The worksheet should be viewed as a learning device and not something only to be mastered mechanically. The worksheet and the entries made on it are **supplemental** to the ledger accounts of the parent company. **The worksheet entries are not recorded in the ledger**

EXHIBIT 14–7

Differences between the pooling of interests and purchase methods summarized

Item	Pooling of Interests	Purchase
1. Measuring and recording at date of acquisition by the parent company.	Acquisition is accomplished by exchanging shares of stock. A purchase/sale transaction is not assumed; therefore, the cost principle is **not** applied. The investment account is debited for the **book value** of the subsidiary stock acquired.	Acquisition usually is accomplished by purchasing the shares with cash and/or debt. A purchase/sale transaction is assumed; therefore, the cost principle is applied. On acquisition date the investment account is debited for the **market value** of the resources acquired.
2. Goodwill.	Goodwill is not recognized by the parent company.	Goodwill is recognized by the parent company to the extent that the purchase price exceeds the sum of acquisition market values of the assets (less the liabilities) of the subsidiary.
3. Method of aggregating or combining by the parent company to derive the consolidated balance sheet.	Assets and liabilities (less any eliminations) of the subsidiary are added, at **book value,** to the book values of the parent.	Assets and liabilities (less any eliminations) of the subsidiary are added, at their acquisition **market values,** to the book values of the assets and liabilities of the parent.
4. Method of aggregating or combining by the parent company to derive the consolidated income statement.	Revenues and expenses as reported by each company, less any eliminations, are aggregated.	Revenues as reported, less any eliminations, are aggregated. Expenses, plus additional depreciation and amortization of goodwill, less any eliminations, are aggregated.
5. Eliminations.	Eliminate all intercompany debts, revenues, and expenses. Eliminate investment account on parent's books and owners' equity of the subsidiary, excluding retained earnings.	Eliminate all intercompany debts, revenues, and expenses. Eliminate the investment account on parent's books and common stock and retained earnings of the subsidiary.
6. Usual comparative effects on the consolidated financial statements.	Expenses—lower Net income—higher EPS—higher Assets—higher cash Noncash assets—lower Liabilities—same Capital stock—higher Retained earnings—higher	Expenses—higher Net income—lower EPS—lower Assets—lower cash Noncash assets—higher Liabilities—same Capital stock—lower Retained earnings—lower

accounts under any circumstances because the worksheet is an analytical device only. The example for Company P and its subsidiary, Company S, given in Exhibit 14–1, will be continued for all of the illustrations in this supplement.

Developing Consolidated Statements for Periods Subsequent to Acquisition

At the end of each accounting period after acquisition, a consolidated balance sheet, income statement, and statement of changes in financial position must be prepared by the parent company. A single worksheet can be used to prepare both a consolidated balance sheet and a consolidated income statement for accounting periods subsequent to acquisition.

Recall that on January 2, 19A, Company P acquired 100% of the outstanding stock of Company S. Assume that it is now December 31, 19A. After operating for a year, each company prepared its separate income statement and balance sheet as shown in Exhibit 14–8. Two sets of financial statements are shown for Company P; the first is based on the assumption that Company S was acquired through an exchange of stock (pooling of interests), and the second is based on the assumption that Company S stock was acquired with cash (purchase).

At the end of 19A, the following additional data were available to Company P:

a. The Investment in Company S balance of $165,000 was the same as at date of acquisition; the balance of Retained Earnings of Company S at acquisition was $50,000.

b. At date of acquisition, January 2, 19A, the plant and equipment of Company S had an acquisition market value of $5,000 above book value and goodwill purchased amounted to $10,000.

c. Intercompany debt owed by Company S to Company P was $6,000 at the end of 19A.

d. The plant and equipment owned by Company S had a 10-year remaining life from January 1, 19A, for depreciation purposes. The company uses straight-line depreciation.

e. Goodwill is to be amortized from January 1, 19A, over 20 years on a straight-line basis.

f. During December 19A, Company S declared and paid a $10,000 cash dividend to Company P. Each company made the following journal entry in its accounts:

Company P		Company S	
Cash 10,000		Dividends declared	
Revenue from		and paid 10,000	
investments	10,000	Cash	10,000

EXHIBIT 14–8

Illustrative data for consolidated financial statements subsequent to acquisition (100% ownership)

COMPANY P AND COMPANY S
Separate Financial Statements for 19A (unclassified)

At December 31, 19A

	Company P		
	Exchange of stock	*Purchase with cash*	*Company S*
Income statement (for 19A):			
Sales revenue	$ 400,000	$ 400,000	$ 110,000
Revenue from investments			
(dividend from Company S)	10,000	10,000	
Cost of goods sold	(220,000)	(220,000)	(59,000)
Expenses (not detailed)	(130,000)	(130,000)	(26,500)
Depreciation expense	(10,000)	(10,000)	(4,500)
Income tax expense	(20,000)	(20,000)	(6,000)
Net income	$ 30,000	$ 30,000	$ 14,000
Balance sheet (at December 31, 19A):			
Cash	$ 226,000	$ 61,000	$ 45,500
Accounts receivable (net)	18,000	18,000	28,000
Receivable from Company S	6,000	6,000	
Inventories	185,000	185,000	65,000
Investment in Company S			
(by purchase, at cost)	150,000*	165,000*	
Plant and equipment (net)	90,000	90,000	40,500
	$ 675,000	$ 525,000	$ 179,000
Accounts payable	$ 55,000	$ 55,000	$ 19,000
Payable to Company P			6,000
Common stock, par $10	360,000	300,000	100,000
Contributed capital in excess of par	90,000		
Beginning retained earnings*	140,000	140,000	50,000
Dividends declared and paid during 19A			(10,000)
Net income for 19A (per above)	30,000	30,000	14,000
	$ 675,000	$ 525,000	$ 179,000

* Balance at date of acquisition.

A consolidated income statement and balance sheet must be prepared at the end of 19A. These statements were shown in Exhibit 14–5, assuming (1) pooling of interests method and (2) purchase method. A separate consolidation worksheet for each method will be discussed.

Pooling of interests method—income statement and balance sheet

This worksheet (Exhibit 14–9) has side captions for each income statement and balance sheet account, and column headings for the parent company, the subsidiary company, eliminations, and the **Consolidated Balances.** The amounts entered in the first two columns are taken directly from the separate 19A financial statements prepared by the parent and the subsidiary (as given in Exhibit 14–8).

The worksheet is designed so that the eliminations are entered in debit and credit format. This format provides an excellent check on the accuracy of the work. Remember that the elimination entries are **worksheet entries only;** they are never entered into the accounts of either the parent or the subsidiary. Consolidated statements represent a **reporting approach** that does not affect the ledger accounts of either the parent or the subsidiaries.

To complete the worksheet, the elimination entries must be entered. Then, each line is accumulated horizontally to derive the consolidated amount in the last column.

Under the pooling of interests method, there are three elimination entries that must be made on the worksheet:

a. Eliminate the investment in Company S with offsets to the accounts for (1) Common Stock, Company S, and (2) Contributed Capital from Pooling. These eliminations can be accomplished using the following intercompany elimination entry on the worksheet (which is shown in a journal entry format):

Common stock, Company S	100,000	
Contributed capital from pooling of interests	50,000	
Investment in Company S		150,000

b. Eliminate the intercompany debt of $6,000 owed by Company S to Company P. These two eliminations can be accomplished by means of the following intercompany elimination entry on the worksheet:

Payable to Company P	6,000	
Receivable from Company S		6,000

EXHIBIT 14–9

Consolidation worksheet (pooling of interests methods; 100% ownership)

COMPANY P and Its Subsidiary, COMPANY S
Consolidation Worksheet (pooling of interests) for the Balance Sheet
and Income Statement December 31, 19A (100% ownership)

| Items | Statements | | Intercompany Eliminations | | Consolidated Balances |
	Company P	Company S	Debit	Credit	
Income statement:					
Sales revenue	400,000	110,000			510,000
Revenue from investments	10,000		(c) 10,000		
Cost of goods sold	(220,000)	(59,000)			(279,000)
Expenses (not detailed)	(130,000)	(26,500)			(156,500)
Depreciation expense	(10,000)	(4,500)			(14,500)
Income tax expense	(20,000)	(6,000)			(26,000)
Net income (carried down)	30,000	14,000			34,000
Balance sheet:					
Cash	226,000	45,500			271,500
Accounts receivable (net)	18,000	28,000			46,000
Receivable from Company S	6,000			(b) 6,000	
Inventories	185,000	65,000			250,000
Investment in Company S	150,000*			(a) 150,000	
Plant and equipment (net)	90,000	40,500			130,500
	675,000	179,000			698,000
Accounts payable	55,000	19,000			74,000
Payable to Company P		6,000	(b) 6,000		
Common stock, Company P	360,000*				360,000
Common stock, Company S		100,000	(a) 100,000		
Contributed capital from pooling	90,000*		(a) 50,000		40,000
Beginning retained earnings, Company P	140,000				140,000
Beginning retained earnings, Company S		50,000			50,000
Dividends declared and paid during 19A		(10,000)		(c) 10,000	
Net income, 19A (from above; not added across)	30,000†	14,000†			34,000†
	675,000	179,000	166,000	166,000	698,000

Explanation of eliminations:
  (a) To eliminate Investment in Company S against Common Stock of Company S and Contributed Capital from Pooling of Interests.
  (b) To eliminate the intercompany debt.
  (c) To eliminate the intercompany revenue and dividends (paid by the subsidiary to the parent).
  * These amounts are based upon the pooling of interests method. The parent would have made the following journal entry at acquisition date:

Investment in Company S 150,000
    Common stock, Company P   60,000
    Contributed capital from pooling of interests   90,000
  † Carried down from above.

c. During the year, Company S declared and paid dividends amounting to $10,000. Because Company P owned 100% of the outstanding stock, all of the dividends were paid to Company P. This intercompany item must be eliminated. The Revenue from Investments account of Company P is debited on the worksheet, and the Dividends Declared and Paid account of the subsidiary is credited for $10,000. Observe that separate lines are set up on the worksheet for dividends and net income. This is done for convenience and clarity. The worksheet entry for these two eliminations is:

Revenue from investments	10,000	
Dividends declared and paid (Retained earnings, Company S)		10,000

Purchase Method—Income Statement and Balance Sheet

Under the purchase method, a few more eliminations are needed because of the use of acquisition market values for the subsidiary. The intercompany eliminations on the worksheet (Exhibit 14–10) under the purchase method are:

a. Eliminate the investment account against the subsidiary owners' equity accounts. This elimination entry will be the same each year because it is based upon the values recognized at the date of acquisition. The $15,000 difference between the purchase price and the book value must be allocated to the subsidiary company's assets (including goodwill). The **worksheet** entry is as follows (illustrated in a journal entry format):

Common stock, Company S	100,000	
Retained earnings, Company S	50,000	
Plant and equipment	5,000	
Goodwill	10,000	
Investment in Company S		165,000

b. Eliminate the intercompany debt of $6,000 with the following entry on the worksheet:

Payable to Company P	6,000	
Receivable from Company S		6,000

EXHIBIT 14–10

Consolidation worksheet (purchase method; 100% ownership)

COMPANY P and Its Subsidiary, COMPANY S
Consolidation Worksheet (by purchase) for the Balance Sheet
and Income Statement
December 31, 19A (100% ownership)

Items	Statements		Intercompany Eliminations		Consolidated Balances
	Company P	Company S	Debit	Credit	
Income statement:					
Sales revenue	400,000	110,000			510,000
Revenue from investments	10,000		(e) 10,000		
Cost of goods sold	(220,000)	(59,000)			(279,000)
Expenses (not detailed)	(130,000)	(26,500)			(156,500)
Depreciation expense	(10,000)	(4,500)	(c) 500		(15,000)
Amortization expense (goodwill)			(d) 500		(500)
Income tax expense	(20,000)	(6,000)			(26,000)
Net income (carried down)	30,000	14,000			33,000
Balance sheet:					
Cash	61,000	45,500			106,500
Accounts receivable (net)	18,000	28,000			46,000
Receivable from Company S	6,000			(b) 6,000	
Inventories	185,000	65,000			250,000
Investment in Company S (at cost)	165,000			(a) 165,000	
Plant and equipment (net)	90,000	40,500	(a) 5,000	(c) 500	135,000
Goodwill			(a) 10,000	(d) 500	9,500
	525,000	179,000			547,000
Accounts payable	55,000	19,000			74,000
Payable to Company P		6,000	(b) 6,000		
Common stock, Company P	300,000				300,000
Common stock, Company S		100,000	(a) 100,000		
Beginning retained earnings, Company P	140,000				140,000
Beginning retained earnings, Company S		50,000	(a) 50,000		
Dividends declared and paid during 19A		(10,000)		(e) 10,000	
Net income, 19A (from above; not added across)	30,000*	14,000*			33,000*
	525,000	179,000	182,000	182,000	547,000

* Carried down from above.
Explanation of eliminations:
(a) To eliminate the investment account against the subsidiary stockholders' equity and to allocate the difference between purchase price and book value purchased to the appropriate accounts.
(b) To eliminate the intercompany debt.
(c) To record additional depreciation for one year on the asset increase resulting from the acquisition.
(d) To record amortization for one year on the goodwill recognized.
(e) To eliminate intercompany revenue and dividends (paid by the subsidiary to the parent).

c. Because the plant and equipment amount for Company S was increased by $5,000 to reflect acquisition market value, additional depreciation must be recorded on the $5,000 increment. The depreciation reflected on the statements of Company S is based on original acquisition cost and does not include this $5,000 increase to market value. Therefore, the worksheet entry must be:

```
Depreciation expense (Company S) ..........................   500
    Plant and equipment (Company S)
        (or accumulated depreciation) .........................        500
    $5,000 ÷ 10 years = $500.
```

d. Goodwill must be amortized over a realistic period not longer than 40 years *(APB Opinion 17)*. Company P decided to use a 20-year life. $10,000 goodwill was recognized in entry *(a)* above. This amount must be amortized. Therefore, the worksheet entry to accomplish this effect is:

```
Amortization expense (goodwill) ..........................   500
    Goodwill ............................................        500
    $10,000 ÷ 20 years = $500.
```

e. During the year, Company S declared and paid dividends amounting to $10,000. Because Company P owned 100% of the outstanding stock, all of the dividends were paid to Company P. This intercompany item must be eliminated. The Revenue from Investments account of Company P must be debited on the worksheet, and the Dividends Declared and Paid account of the subsidiary credited for $10,000. Observe that separate lines are set up on the worksheet for dividends and net income. This procedure is for convenience and clarity. The worksheet entry for these eliminations is:

```
Revenue from investments ..................................   10,000
    Dividends declared and paid (retained earnings,
        Company S) .........................................        10,000
```

After all of the intercompany eliminations have been entered on the work-sheet, the consolidated financial statement amounts are determined by ac-cumulating each line horizontally to derive the balances in the last column. The balances in the last column of the worksheet are classified in the normal manner in preparing the consolidated income statement and balance sheet.

SUPPLEMENT 14B—CONSOLIDATION PROCEDURES— LESS THAN 100% OWNERSHIP

When the parent company owns a controlling interest that is less than 100%, most of the consolidation procedures are the same as the procedures for 100% ownership. Certain eliminations differ because they are based upon the **propor-tionate** ownership level. When the parent company does not own 100% of the subsidiary, there will be a group of stockholders of the subsidiary company called the **minority stockholders.** Their interest in the subsidiary is not affected by the parent's interest. The minority stockholders' interest must be accorded appropriate measurement and reporting on the consolidated financial state-ments. **Minority interest** includes the minority stockholders' proportionate share of both the earnings and the stockholders' equity of the subsidiary.

To illustrate consolidated statements with a minority interest, we will adapt the data for Company P and Company S given in Exhibit 14–1. Assume that on January 2, 19A, Company P purchased 80% of the 10,000 shares of outstanding capital stock of Company S for $132,000 cash.[9] At acquisition date, Company P recorded the purchase of the 8,000 shares of capital stock as follows:

Investment, stock of Company S (80% ownership)	132,000	
Cash		132,000
Acquisition of 8,000 shares (80%) of the capital stock of Company S at $16.50 per share.		

On the acquisition date, the owners' equity for Company S showed the following amounts: capital stock, $100,000; and retained earnings, $50,000 (total owners' equity was $150,000). Company P paid $132,000 cash for 80% of the owners' equity of Company S. The book value of the investment was $120,000 ($150,000 × 80%). Thus, Company P paid $12,000 more than the book value of Company S. The market value of the subsidiary company's plant and equipment was $5,000 more than its book value. Therefore, of the $12,000 cost in excess of book value that P Company paid, $4,000 (i.e., $5,000 × 80%) was for the greater

---

[9] Ownership interests of less than 100% usually are on the purchase basis. *APB Opinion 16* does not permit use of the pooling of interest basis when the ownership interest held by the parent company is less than 90%.

EXHIBIT 14-11

Illustrative data for consolidation (less than 100% ownership)

COMPANY P AND COMPANY S
Separate Financial Statements for 19A

	Company P	Company S
Income statement (for 19A):		
Sales revenue	$ 400,000	$ 110,000
Revenue from investments (dividends from Company S)	8,000	
Cost of goods sold	(220,000)	(59,000)
Expenses (not detailed)	(130,000)	(26,500)
Depreciation expense	(10,000)	(4,500)
Income tax expense	(20,000)	(6,000)
Net income	$ 28,000	$ 14,000
Balance sheet (at December 31, 19A):		
Cash	$ 92,000	$ 45,500
Accounts receivable (net)	18,000	28,000
Receivable from Company S	6,000	
Inventories	185,000	65,000
Investment in Company S (80%, at cost)	132,000	
Plant and equipment	90,000	40,500
	$ 523,000	$ 179,000
Accounts payable	$ 55,000	$ 19,000
Payable to Company P		6,000
Common stock, par $10	300,000	100,000
Beginning retained earnings	140,000	50,000
Dividends declared and paid during 19A		(10,000)
Net income for 19A (from above)	28,000	14,000
	$ 523,000	$ 179,000

market value of the plant and equipment. The remaining amount, $8,000, was for **goodwill**. The analysis of the purchase transaction, at date of acquisition, follows:[10]

Purchase price for 80% interest in Company S	$132,000
Net assets purchased, valued at market:	
Book value, $120,000 + market value increment of plant and equipment, $5,000 × 80% =	124,000
Goodwill purchased	$ 8,000

On December 31, 19A, both companies had completed one year's operations as affiliated companies. Each company has prepared the separate 19A financial statements shown in Exhibit 14–11.

---

[10] Some accountants believe that the plant and equipment difference should be 100% (i.e., $5,000) rather than 80 percent (i.e., $4,000). This difference in opinion has not been resolved; however, it appears that most companies currently use the lower amount.

Additional data developed by Company P for the consolidation worksheet:

a. Investment account balance of $132,000 to be eliminated against 80% of stockholders' equity of subsidiary.
b. Plant and equipment of Company S to be increased by $4,000 to market value (i.e., the increment acquired by Company P). Goodwill will be recognized, $8,000 (see analysis of purchase transaction above).
c. Company S owed Company P $6,000 on December 31, 19A.
d. The plant and equipment is being depreciated on a straight-line basis over a remaining life of 10 years by Company S (no residual value).
e. Goodwill will be amortized over 20 years.
f. Company S declared and paid $10,000 cash dividends on December 15, 19A.

The consolidation worksheet under the purchase method is shown in Exhibit 14–12. It is the same as the worksheet shown in Exhibit 14–10 for 100% ownership, except for elimination entries (a), (c), (d), and (e). These intercompany eliminations differ only in **their amounts. They have been reduced to the 80% ownership level.**

EXHIBIT 14–12

Consolidation worksheet (purchase method; less than 100% ownership)

COMPANY P and Its Subsidiary, COMPANY S
Consolidation Worksheet (by purchase) for the Balance Sheet and Income Statement
December 31, 19A (80% ownership)

Items	Statements		Intercompany Eliminations		Consolidated Balances
	Company P	Company S	Debit	Credit	
Income statement:					
Sales revenue	400,000	110,000			510,000
Revenue from investments	8,000		(e) 8,000		
Cost of goods sold	(220,000)	(59,000)			(279,000)
Expenses (not detailed)	(130,000)	(26,500)			(156,500)
Depreciation expense	(10,000)	(4,500)	(c) 400		(14,900)
Amortization expense					
(goodwill)			(d) 400		(400)
Income tax expense	(20,000)	(6,000)			(26,000)
Net income	28,000	14,000			33,200
Carried down:					
Minority interest					
($14,000 × 20%)					2,800 M*
Parent interest income					30,400

EXHIBIT 14–12 *(concluded)*

Consolidation worksheet (purchase method; less than 100% ownership)

COMPANY P and Its Subsidiary, COMPANY S
Consolidation Worksheet (by purchase) for the Balance Sheet and Income Statement
December 31, 19A (80% ownership)

Items	Statements		Intercompany Eliminations		Consolidated Balances
	Company P	Company S	Debit	Credit	
Balance sheet:					
Cash	92,000	45,500			137,500
Accounts receivable (net)	18,000	28,000			46,000
Receivable from Company S	6,000			(b) 6,000	
Inventories	185,000	65,000			250,000
Investment in Company S					
(at cost)	132,000			(a) 132,000	
Plant and equipment (net)	90,000	40,500	(a) 4,000	(c) 400	134,100
Goodwill			(a) 8,000	(d) 400	7,600
	523,000	179,000			575,200
Accounts payable	55,000	19,000			74,000
Payable to Company P		6,000	(b) 6,000		
Common stock, Company P	300,000				300,000
Common stock, Company S		100,000	(a) 80,000		20,000 M
Beginning retained earnings,					
Company P	140,000				140,000
Beginning retained earnings,					
Company S		50,000	(a) 40,000		10,000 M
Dividends declared and paid					
during 19A		(10,000)		(e) 8,000	(2,000)M
Net income, 19A (from above;					
not added across)	28,000	14,000			30,400
	523,000	179,000	146,800	146,800	575,200

M—Minority interest.

* The minority interest in the earnings of the subsidiary is unaffected by the consolidation procedures of the parent company. Thus, the minority interest in the earnings is $14,000 × 20% = $2,800. This amount is subtracted from consolidated income to derive the amount of consolidated income identifiable with the controlling interest. The two separate amounts then are carried down to the balance sheet section.

Explanation of eliminations:

(a) To eliminate the investment account against 80% of the owners' equity of the subsidiary and to allocate the difference between purchase price and book value to the appropriate accounts.

(b) To eliminate the intercompany debt.

(c) To record depreciation for one year on the asset increase resulting from the acquisition.

(d) To amortize goodwill recognized (one year).

(e) To eliminate intercompany revenue arising from dividends declared and paid by the subsidiary.

EXHIBIT 14–13 _____

Consolidated financial statements (with minority interest)

COMPANY P and Its Subsidiary, COMPANY S
Consolidated Income Statement (purchase method)
For the Year Ended December 31, 19A

Sales revenue		$510,000
Cost of goods sold		279,000
Gross margin		231,000
Less:		
Expenses (not detailed)	$156,500	
Depreciation expense	14,900	
Amortization expense (goodwill)	400	
Income tax expense	26,000	197,800
Consolidated net income		33,200
Less: Minority interest in net income		2,800
Controlling interest in net income		$ 30,400

EPS of common stock ($33,200 ÷ 30,000 shares) = $1.107
(some accountants prefer to use $30,400 as the numerator).

COMPANY P and Its Subsidiary, COMPANY S
Consolidated Balance Sheet (purchase method)
At December 31, 19A

Assets

Current assets:		
Cash	$137,500	
Accounts receivable (net)	46,000	
Inventories	250,000	$433,500
Tangible operational assets:		
Plant and equipment (net)		134,100
Intangible operational assets:		
Goodwill (or excess of cost over market value of assets		
of subsidiary)		7,600
Total assets		$575,200

Liabilities

Current liabilities:		
Accounts payable		$ 74,000

Stockholders' Equity

Contributed capital:		
Common stock, par $10, 30,000 shares outstanding	$300,000	
Retained earnings	170,400	
Total	470,400	
Minority interest	30,800*	
Total stockholders' equity		501,200
Total liabilities and stockholders' equity		$575,200

   * $20,000 + $10,000 + $2,800 − $2,000 = $30,800.

On the worksheet, the minority interest (20%) is designated with an "M." In the income statement portion of the worksheet, 20% of the **subsidiary** net income (i.e., $2,800) is coded "M," and the remainder ($30,400) is identified with the parent. Notice that the minority stockholders do not share in the income of the parent company. On the worksheet, the income amounts are carried down to the retained earnings section of the balance sheet. The 20% of subsidiary stockholders' equity owned by the minority stockholders was not eliminated as an intercompany item. Therefore, it is carried across as minority interest and coded "M." Aside from these adaptations, the Consolidated Balances column is completed as previously explained.

The consolidated income statement and balance sheet, based on the data in the Consolidated Balances column of the worksheet, are shown in Exhibit 14–13. The **minority interest** share of net income is identified separately on the income statement. Also, the minority interest share of stockholders' equity is identified separately on the balance sheet. Alternatively, the minority interest share of stockholders' equity often is shown as a special caption between liabilities and stockholders' equity rather than as illustrated in Exhibit 14–13.

IMPORTANT TERMS DEFINED IN THIS CHAPTER

Terms (alphabetically)	Key words in definitions of important terms used in chapter	Page reference
Consolidation	The accounting process of combining financial statements from related companies into a single set of financial statements.	706
Control	Presumed to exist when more than 50% of the voting stock of an entity is owned by one investor.	706
Economic compatibility	The operations of affiliated companies complement each other.	706
Goodwill	The amount that was paid for the good reputation and customer appeal of an acquired company.	714
Minority interest	The proportionate share of both the earnings and the contributed capital of the subsidiary that is now "owned" by the parent.	732
Parent company	The company that has a significant investment in a subsidiary company.	706
Pooling of interests	An acquisition that is completed by exchanging parent company stock for subsidiary voting capital stock.	708
Purchase	An acquisition which is completed by purchasing subsidiary company voting capital stock for cash.	612
Subsidiary	The company that is owned by a parent company as evidenced by more than 50% of the voting capital stock.	706

QUESTIONS

PART A

1. What is a parent-subsidiary relationship?

2. Explain the basic concept underlying consolidated statements.

3. What two basic elements must be present before consolidated statements are appropriate?

4. The concept of consolidated statements relates only to reporting as opposed to preparing and posting journal entries in the ledger accounts. Explain.

5. What is pooling of interests?

6. What is a combination by purchase?

7. The investing corporation debits a long-term investment account when it acquires a controlling influence in another corporation. In the case of a pooling of interests, describe how to determine the amount that is debited to the investment account.

8. What are intercompany eliminations?

9. Explain why the investment account must be eliminated against stockholders' equity when consolidated statements are prepared.

10. Explain why the "book values" of the parent and subsidiary are aggregated on consolidated statements when there is a pooling of interests, but acquisition market values of the subsidiary assets are used when the combination is by purchase.

11. Why is goodwill not recognized in a pooling of interests? Why is it recognized in a combination by purchase?

PART B

12. Explain why additional depreciation expense usually must be recognized on consolidation when the combination was by purchase.
13. What is goodwill?
14. Explain why pooling of interests was more popular in the merger movement than combination by purchase.
15. Explain the basis for each of the following statements:
    a. Pooling of interests, given the same situation, reports a higher net income than combination by purchase.
    b. The cash position, other things being equal, usually is better when the combination is by pooling of interests than when the combination is by purchase.
    c. Pooling of interests, other things being equal, reports a higher amount of retained earnings than does combination by purchase.

EXERCISES

PART A

E14–1   (Pair Definition with Terms)
    Match the following brief definitions with the terms by entering the appropriate letter in each space provided.

Term	*Brief definition*
_____ (1) Subsidiary	A. Required because a parent and subsidiary are considered
_____ (2) Economic compatibility	one economic entity.
	B. Ownership of voting stock provides more than signifi-
_____ (3) Purchase	cant influence.

Term	Brief definition
_____ (4) Minority interest	C. A requirement for consolidating financial statements when one company owns more than 50% of another company.
_____ (5) Control	
_____ (6) Consolidation	
_____ (7) Pooling of interests	D. An amount whose "value" is never known except when a business is purchased.
_____ (8) Goodwill	
_____ (9) Parent company	E. Only comes into existence when there is less than 100% ownership by the parent company.
	F. The company that owns more than 50% of the outstanding voting stock of another corporation.
	G. This transaction often is not viewed as a purchase/sale transaction; therefore, the cost principle is not applied.
	H. In this transaction, the purchase of a controlling interest in another company is recorded under the cost principle.
	I. The company that is owned by another company.

E14–2 (Preparation of a Consolidated Balance Sheet)

On January 2, 19A, Company P acquired all of the outstanding voting stock of Company S by exchanging, on a share-for-share basis, its own unissued stock for the stock of Company S. Immediately after the acquisition of Company S, the separate balance sheets showed the following:

	Balances, January 2, 19A, immediately after acquisition	
	Company P	*Company S*
Cash	$ 38,000	$12,000
Receivable from Company S	7,000	
Inventory	35,000	18,000
Investment in Company S (100%)	60,000	
Operational assets (net of accumulated depreciation)	80,000	50,000
Total	$220,000	$80,000
Liabilities	$ 25,000	$13,000
Payable to Company P		7,000
Common stock (Company P, par $5) (Company S, par $5)	140,000	40,000
Contributed capital from pooling of interests	20,000	
Retained earnings	35,000	20,000
Total	$220,000	$80,000

Required:

a. Is this a pooling of interests or a combination by purchase? Explain why.

b. Give the journal entry that was made by Company P to record the acquisition.

c. Prepare a consolidated balance sheet immediately after the acquisition.

d. Were the assets of the subsidiary added to those of the parent, in the consolidated balance sheet, at book value or at market value? Explain why.

e. What were the balances in the accounts of Company P immediately prior to the acquisition for (1) investment and (2) common stock? Were any other account balances for either Company P or Company S changed by the acquisition? Explain.

E14–3 (Comparison of the Pooling and Purchase Methods)

On January 1, 19A, Company P acquired 100% of the outstanding common stock of Company S. At date of acquisition, the balance sheet of Company S reflected the following book values (summarized):

Total assets (market value, $220,000)* $180,000
Total liabilities   30,000

Stockholders' equity:
　　Common stock, par $10   100,000
　　Retained earnings   50,000

　　　* One half subject to depreciation; 10-year remaining life
and no residual value.

Two separate and independent cases are given below that indicate how Company P acquired 100% of the outstanding stock of Company S:

　Case A—Exchanged two shares of its own common stock (par $1) for each share of Company S stock.

　Case B—Paid $20 per share for the stock of Company S.

Required:

　For each case, answer the following:

　a. Was this a combination by pooling of interests or by purchase? Explain.
　b. Give the journal entry that Company P should make to record the acquisition. If none, explain why.
　c. Give the journal entry in the accounts of Company S to record the acquisition. If none, explain why.
　d. Analyze the transaction to determine the amount of goodwill purchased. If no goodwill was purchased, explain why.
　e. In preparing a consolidated balance sheet, should the subsidiary assets be included at book value or market value? Explain.

E14–4   (Identification of the Appropriate Consolidation Method)

　On January 1, 19A, Company P purchased 100% of the outstanding voting shares of Company S in the open market for $70,000 cash. On that date (prior to the acquisition) the separate balance sheets (summarized) of the two companies reported the following book values:

	Prior to acquisition	
	Company P	*Company S*
Cash	$ 80,000	$18,000
Receivable from Company P		2,000
Operational assets (net)	80,000	60,000
Total	$160,000	$80,000
Liabilities	$ 28,000	$20,000
Payable to Company S	2,000	
Common stock:		
Company P, nopar	100,000	
Company S, par $10		50,000
Retained earnings	30,000	10,000
Total	$160,000	$80,000

　It was determined on date of acquisition that the market value of the operational assets of Company S was $66,000.

Required:

a. Was this a combination by pooling of interests or by purchase? Explain why.

b. Give the journal entry that should be made by Company P at date of acquisition. If none is required, explain why.

c. Give the journal entry that should be made by Company S at date of acquisition. If none is required, explain why.

d. Analyze the acquisition to determine the amount of goodwill purchased.

e. Should the assets of Company S be included on the consolidated balance sheet at book value or market value? Explain.

f. Prepare a consolidated balance sheet immediately after acquisition.

E14–5 (Preparation of a Consolidated Balance Sheet after Acquisition)

On January 4, 19A, Company P acquired all of the outstanding stock of Company S for $10 cash per share. At the date of acquisition, the balance sheet of Company S reflected the following:

Common stock, par $5 ..... $50,000
Retained earnings 30,000

Immediately after the acquisition, the balance sheets reflected the following:

	Balances, Jan. 4, 19A, immediately after acquisition	
	Company P	*Company S*
Cash	$ 13,000	$17,000
Receivable from Company P		3,000
Investment in Company S (100%), at cost	100,000	
Operational assets (net)	122,000	70,000*
Total	$235,000	$90,000
Liabilities	$ 22,000	$10,000
Payable to Company S	3,000	
Common stock, par $5	150,000	50,000
Retained earnings	60,000	30,000
Total	$235,000	$90,000

* Determined by Company P to have a market value of $78,000 at date of acquisition.

Required:

a. Was this a combination by pooling of interests or by purchase? Explain why.

b. Give the journal entry that should be made by Company P to record the acquisition.

c. Analyze the acquisition to determine the amount of goodwill purchased.

d. Should the assets of Company S be included on the consolidated balance sheet at book value or market value? Explain.

e. Prepare a consolidated balance sheet immediately after acquisition.

PART B

E14–6 (Completion of a Consolidation Worksheet)

On January 1, 19A, Company P acquired all of the outstanding voting stock of Company S by exchanging one share of its own stock for each share of Company S stock. At the date of the exchange, the balance sheet of Company S showed the following:

Common stock, par $10 ..... $40,000
Retained earnings 10,000

One year after acquisition the two companies prepared their separate financial statements as shown on the following worksheet:

	COMPANY P and Its Subsidiary, COMPANY S (100% owned) Consolidated Balance Sheet and Income Statement December 31, 19A			
Items	Separate Statements		Eliminations	Consolidated Statements
	Company P	Company S		
Income statement (for 19A):				
Sales revenue	96,000	42,000		
Revenue from investments	4,000			
Cost of goods sold	(60,000)	(25,000)		
Expenses (not detailed)	(17,000)	(10,000)		
Net income	23,000	7,000		
Balance sheet (at December 31, 19A):				
Cash	21,000	19,000		
Receivable from Company P		2,000		
Investment in Company S (100%)	50,000			
Operational assets (net)	59,000	47,000		
Total	130,000	68,000		
Liabilities	17,000	15,000		
Payable to Company S	2,000			
Common stock, Company P (par $10)	50,000			
Contributed capital from pooling of interests	10,000			
Common stock, Company S (par $10)		40,000		
Beginning retained earnings, Company P	28,000			
Beginning retained earnings, Company S		10,000		
Dividend declared and paid, 19A; Company S		(4,000)		
Net income, 19A (from above)	23,000	7,000		
Total	130,000	68,000		

Required:

a. Give the journal entry that was made by Company P to record the pooling of interests on January 1, 19A.
b. Complete the Eliminations column in the above worksheet, then combine two sets of statements in the last column to develop the consolidated income statement and balance sheet. (Hint: Eliminate Revenue from Investments against Dividends Declared and Paid because this represents an intercompany transaction. The consolidated net income is $26,000.)

E14–7   (Analysis of a Consolidation Worksheet)

On January 1, 19A, Company P purchased all of the outstanding voting stock of Company S at $2.50 per share. At that date the balance sheet of Company S reflected the following:

Common stock, par $1 ..... $20,000
Retained earnings 10,000

One year after acquisition each company prepared its own separate financial statements and Company P set up the following consolidation worksheet (partially completed):

Items	Separate Statements		Intercompany Eliminations		Consolidated Balances
	Company P	Company S	Debit	Credit	
Income statement (for 19A):					
Sales revenue	99,000	59,000			
Revenues from investments	6,000		*(e)* 6,000		
Expenses (not detailed)	(71,000)	(40,400)			
Depreciation expense	(9,000)	(3,600)	*(c)* 1,200		
Amortization expense (goodwill)			*(d)* 400		
Net income	25,000	15,000			
Balance sheet (at December 31, 19A):					
Cash	16,000	6,000			
Receivable from Co. P		4,000		*(b)* 4,000	
Investment in Co. S	50,000			*(a)* 50,000	
Operational assets (net)	90,000	40,000*	*(a)* 12,000	*(c)* 1,200	140,800
Goodwill (amortize over 20 years)			*(a)* 8,000	*(d)* 400	
Totals	156,000	50,000			170,400
Liabilities	15,000	11,000			
Payable to Co. S	4,000		*(b)* 4,000		
Common stock, Co. P	80,000				
Common stock, Co. S		20,000	*(a)* 20,000		
Beginning retained earnings, Co. P	32,000				
Beginning retained earnings, Co. S		10,000	*(a)* 10,000		
Dividends declared and paid, Co. S, 19A.		(6,000)		*(e)* 6,000	
Net income, 19A (per above)	25,000†	15,000†			32,400†
Totals	156,000	50,000	81,600	81,600	

* Market value of the operational assets at acquisition was $12,000 above book value and their remaining useful life was 10 years.
† Carried down.

Required:

a. Give the journal entry made by Company P on January 1, 19A, to record the purchase of Company S stock.

b. Show how the $8,000 of goodwill was computed.

c. Complete the last column of the worksheet (note that under "Eliminations" debit/credit instead of +/− were used).

d. Give a brief explanation of eliminations *(c)*, *(d)*, and *(e)*.

PROBLEMS

PART A

P14–1   **(Analysis of Acquisition and Preparation of a Consolidated Balance Sheet)**
During January 19A, Company P acquired all of the outstanding voting shares of Company S by exchanging one share of its own unissued voting common stock for two shares of Company S stock. Immediately prior to the acquisition, the separate balance sheets of the two companies reflected the following:

	Balances immediately prior to acquisition	
	Company P	*Company S*
Cash	$200,000	$ 32,000
Receivable from Company P		3,000
Inventory	75,000	5,000
Operational assets (net of accumulated depreciation)	75,000	80,000
Total	$350,000	$120,000
Liabilities	$ 57,000	$ 30,000
Payable to Company S	3,000	
Common stock, Company P (par $4)	180,000	
Common stock, Company S (par $5)		50,000
Contributed capital from pooling		
Retained earnings	110,000	40,000
Total	$350,000	$120,000

Additional data:

At the date of acquisition, the market price of Company S stock was $16 per share; there was no established market for Company P stock.

The operational assets of Company S were appraised independently at the date of acquisition at $130,000.

Required:

a. Is this a purchase or a pooling of interests? Explain why.

b. What account balances on each of the above balance sheets would be changed by the exchange of shares? List each account and amount.

c. Give the journal entry that should be made by each company to record the exchange; if no entry is required, explain why.

d. How much goodwill should be recognized? Why?

e. Prepare a consolidated balance sheet immediately after the acquisition.

f. Did you use any market values in solving the above requirements? Explain why.

P14–2   **(Analysis of Acquisition and Preparation of a Consolidated Balance Sheet)**
Assume the same facts given in P14–1 except that instead of an exchange of shares of stock, Company P purchased from the stockholders 100% of the outstanding voting shares of Company S at a cash price of $160,000.

Required:

a. Is this a purchase or a pooling of interests? Explain why.

b. What account balances on each of the balance sheets would be changed by the purchase of the shares? List each account and amount.

c. Give the journal entry that should be made by each company to record the exchange; if no entry is required, explain why.

d. How much goodwill should be recognized? Why?

e. Prepare a consolidated balance sheet immediately after acquisition.

f. Did you use any market values in solving the above requirements? Explain why.

P14–3   **(Analysis of Entry to Record Acquisition and Preparation of a Consolidated Balance Sheet)**
On January 1, 19A, the separate balance sheets of two corporations showed the following:

	Balances, Jan. 1, 19A	
	Company P	*Company S*
Cash	$ 21,000	$ 9,000
Receivable from Company P		4,000
Operational assets (net)	99,000	32,000
Total	$120,000	$45,000
Accounts payable	$ 16,000	$10,000
Payable to Company S	4,000	
Common stock, par $20	60,000	20,000
Retained earnings	40,000	15,000
Total	$120,000	$45,000

On January 3, 19A, Company P acquired all of the outstanding voting shares of Company S by exchanging one share of its own stock for two shares of Company S stock.

Required:

a. Was this a combination by pooling of interests or by purchase? Explain why.

b. Company P made the following journal entry on its books, at the date of acquisition, to record the investment:

January 3, 19A:

Investment in Co. S	35,000	
Common stock		10,000
Contributed capital from pooling of interests		25,000

Explain the basis for each of the three amounts in this entry.

c. Should any goodwill be recognized on the consolidated balance sheet? Explain why.

d. Prepare a consolidated balance sheet immediately after the acquisition.

P14–4   **(Analysis of Consolidation Method and Preparation of a Consolidated Balance Sheet)**
On January 2, 19A, Company P acquired all of the oustanding stock of Company S by exchanging its own stock for the stock of Company S. One share of Company P stock was exchanged for two shares of Company S stock. Immediately after the acquisition was recorded by Company P, the balance sheets showed the following:

	Balances, Jan. 2, 19A, immediately	
	Company P	Company S
Cash	$ 38,000	$26,000
Receivable from Company S	6,000	
Inventory	30,000	10,000
Investment in Company S (100%)	70,000	
Operational assets (net)	90,000	50,000
Other assets	6,000	4,000
Total	$240,000	$90,000
Liabilities	$ 16,000	$14,000
Payable to Company P		6,000
Common stock, par $5	125,000	50,000
Contributed capital from pooling of interests	45,000	
Retained earnings	54,000	20,000
Total	$240,000	$90,000

Required:

a. Was this a combination by pooling of interests or by purchase? Explain why.

b. Give the journal entry that was made by Company P to record the acquisition on January 2, 19A. Explain the basis for each amount included in the entry.

c. Should the assets of Company S be included on the consolidated balance sheet at book value or market value? Explain.

d. Will any goodwill be recognized on the consolidated balance sheet? Explain why.

e. Prepare a consolidated balance sheet immediately after acquisition.

P14–5   **(Analysis of Goodwill and Preparation of a Consolidated Balance Sheet)**
On January 5, 19A, Company P purchased all of the outstanding stock of Company S for $100,000 cash. Immediately after the acquisition the separate balance sheets of the two companies showed the following:

	Jan. 5, 19A, immediately after acquisition	
	Company P	Company S
Cash	$ 22,000	$ 9,000
Accounts receivable (net)	14,000	6,000
Receivable from Company S	4,000	
Inventory	50,000	25,000
Investment in Company S (at cost)	100,000	
Operational assets (net)	153,000	67,000
Other assets	7,000	3,000
Total	$350,000	$110,000

	Jan. 5, 19A, immediately after acquisition	
	Company P	Company S
Accounts payable	$ 20,000	$ 16,000
Payable to Company P		4,000
Bonds payable	90,000	
Common stock, par $5	180,000	60,000
Contributed capital in excess of par	8,000	
Retained earnings	52,000	30,000
Total	$350,000	$110,000

The operational assets of Company S were estimated to have a market value at date of acquisition of $71,000.

Required:

a. Was this a combination by pooling of interests or by purchase? Explain why.
b. Give the journal entry that Company P should make at the date of acquisition.
c. Analyze the acquisition to determine the amount of goodwill purchased.
d. Should the assets of Company S be included on the consolidated balance sheet at book value or market value? Explain.
e. Prepare a consolidated balance sheet immediately after acquisition.

P14–6 **(Analysis of an Acquisition and Completion of a Worksheet to Prepare a Consolidated Balance Sheet)**

On January 4, 19A, Company P purchased 100% of the outstanding common stock of Company S for $240,000 cash. Immediately after the acquisition, the separate balance sheets for the two companies were prepared as shown in the worksheet below.

COMPANY P and Its Subsidiary, COMPANY S
Consolidated Balance Sheet
January 4, 19A, Immediately after Acquisition

	Separate balance sheets		Eliminations	Consolidated balance sheet
	Company P	Company S		
Assets				
Cash	$ 80,000	$ 40,000	_____	_____
Accounts receivable (net)	26,000	19,000	_____	_____
Receivable from Company P		8,000	_____	_____
Inventories	170,000	80,000	_____	_____
Long-term investment, bonds, Z Company	15,000		_____	_____
Long-term investment, Company S	240,000		_____	_____
Land	12,000	3,000	_____	_____
Plant and equipment (net)	157,000	130,000	_____	_____
Goodwill			_____	_____
Total assets	$700,000	$280,000	_____	_____

| | Separate balance sheets | | | |
	Company P	Company S	Eliminations	Consolidated balance sheet
Liabilities				
Accounts payable	$ 22,000	$ 40,000	_____	_____
Payable to Company S	8,000		_____	_____
Bonds payable, 5%	100,000	30,000	_____	_____
Stockholders' Equity				
Common stock, Company P	500,000		_____	_____
Common stock, Company S (par $10)		150,000	_____	_____
Retained earnings, Company P	70,000		_____	_____
Retained earnings, Company S		60,000	_____	_____
Total liabilities and stockholders' equity	$700,000	$280,000	_____	_____

It was determined at the date of acquisition that on the basis of a comparison of market value and book value, the assets as shown on the books of Company S should be adjusted as follows: *(a)* inventories should be reduced by $3,000, *(b)* plant and equipment should be increased to $148,000, and *(c)* land should be increased by $2,000.

Required:

a. Was this a combination by pooling of interests or by purchase? Explain why.
b. Give the journal entry that was made on the books of Company P to record the acquisition.
c. Analyze the acquisition transaction to determine the amount of goodwill purchased. Use data from the worksheet if needed.
d. At what amount will the assets of Company S be included on the consolidated balance sheet? Explain.
e. Complete the "Eliminations" column in the worksheet and then extend the amounts for the consolidated balance sheet.

PART B

P14–7   (Analysis of Consolidation Elimination Entries and Completion of a Worksheet)
On January 1, 19A, Company P acquired 100% of the outstanding stock of Company S for $106,000 cash. At the date of acquisition the balance sheet of Company S showed the following:

> Total assets (including operational assets*) 115,000
> Total liabilities 25,000
> Common stock, par $10 60,000
> Retained earnings 30,000
>
>   * Book value, $42,000; market value, $48,000 (20-year remaining life).

One year after acquisition the two companies prepared their December 31, 19A, financial statements. Company P developed the following consolidation worksheet (partially completed):

COMPANY P AND ITS SUBSIDIARY, COMPANY S
Consolidation Worksheet
Income Statement and Balance Sheet, December 31, 19A (100% ownership)

Items	Separate Statements		Eliminations		Consolidated Balances
	Company P	Company S	Debit	Credit	
Income statement:					
Sales revenue	80,000	47,000			
Revenue from investments	4,000		(e) 4,000		
Cost of goods sold	(45,000)	(25,000)			
Expenses (not detailed)	(15,000)	(10,000)			
Depreciation expense	(4,000)	(2,000)	(c) 300		
Amortization of goodwill			(d) 500		
Net income	20,000	10,000			
Balance sheet:					
Cash	15,000	10,000			
Accounts receivable (net)	19,000	9,000			
Receivable from Co. P		1,000		(b) 1,000	
Inventories	70,000	50,000			
Investment in Co. S (100%)	106,000			(a) 106,000	
Plant and equipment (net)	80,000	40,000	(a) 6,000	(c) 300	
Goodwill			(a) 10,000	(d) 500	
	290,000	110,000			
Accounts payable	26,000	14,000			
Payable to Co. S	1,000		(b) 1,000		
Common stock, Co. P	200,000				
Common stock, Co. S		60,000	(a) 60,000		
Beginning retained earnings, Co. P	50,000				
Beginning retained earnings, Co. S		30,000	(a) 30,000		
Dividends declared and paid during 19A, Co. P	(7,000)				
Dividends declared and paid during 19A, Co. S		(4,000)		(e) 4,000	
Net income (from above)	20,000	10,000			
	290,000	110,000	111,800	111,800	308,200

Required:

a. Was this a purchase or pooling? Explain.

b. Give the journal entry made by each company to record the acquisition.

c. Complete the last column of the worksheet to develop the consolidated income statement and balance sheet.

d. How much goodwill was recognized? How was it computed?

e. Briefly explain each of the eliminations shown on the worksheet. Note that debit and credit rather than plus and minus were used in the Eliminations column.

P14–8   **(Comparison and Analysis of the Pooling of Interests and the Purchase Methods)**
This problem presents the income statement and the balance sheet on a consolidated basis for Company P and its subsidiary, Company S, one year after acquisition, under two different assumptions: Case A—pooling of interests, and Case B—purchase. The two different assumptions are used so that we can compare and analyze the differences between the pooling and purchase methods.

On January 2, 19A, Company P acquired all of the outstanding common stock of Company S. At that date the stockholders' equity of Company S showed the following: common stock, par $10, $50,000; and retained earnings, $20,000. The journal entry made by Company P to record the acquisition under each case was as follows:

Case A—Pooling of Interests method:

Investment in Company S (5,000 shares, 100%)	70,000	
Common stock, par $8		40,000
Contributed capital from pooling		30,000

Case B—Purchase method:

Investment in Company S (5,000 shares, 100%)	80,000	
Cash		80,000

On January 2, 19A, the acquisition by purchase (Case B) was analyzed to determine the goodwill as follows:

Purchase price paid for 100% interest in Company S	$80,000
Net assets purchased, value at market:	
Book value of net assets ($50,000 + $20,000 =	
$70,000 + increase of $2,000 in operational	
assets to market value)	72,000
Goodwill purchased	$ 8,000

For consolidated statement purposes the operational assets are being depreciated over 10 years remaining life, and the goodwill will be amortized over 20 years.

One year after acquisition, the two companies prepared separate income statements and balance sheets (December 31, 19A). These separate statements have been consolidated under each case as shown below.

Required:

a. Prepare a schedule of amounts that shows what items are different between each statement for Case A, compared with Case B.
b. Explain the reasons why net income is different under pooling of interests versus purchase. Use amounts from the two statements in your explanation and tell why they are different.
c. Explain why the cash balance is different between the two cases.
d. What was the balance in the account "Investment in Company S" in each case prior to its elimination? Explain.
e. Explain why the operational asset (net) amounts are different between the two cases.
f. Why is there a difference in goodwill between the two cases? Provide computations.
g. How much was eliminated for intercompany debt? Why was it eliminated?
h. What amount of "Common stock, Company S," was eliminated? Why was it eliminated?
i. Why was only $20,000 of the $30,000 of contributed capital from pooling of interests eliminated?

j. Explain why the account "Contributed capital in excess of par, $10,000," was not eliminated.

k. Explain why "Beginning retained earnings, Company S, $20,000," is shown under Case A (pooling) but not under Case B (purchase).

COMPANY P and Its Subsidiary, COMPANY S (100% owned)
Consolidated Income Statement and Balance Sheet
December 31, 19A

	Consolidated statements December 31, 19A	
	Pooling method (Case A)	Purchase method (Case B)
Income statement (for the year ended December 31, 19A):		
Sales revenue	$ 236,000	$ 236,000
Revenue from investments ($4,000, eliminated)		
Cost of goods sold	(112,000)	(112,000)
Expenses (not detailed to simplify)	(75,500)	(75,500)
Depreciation expense	(12,500)	(12,700)
Amortization expense (goodwill)		(400)
Net income	$ 36,000	$ 35,400
Balance sheet (at December 31, 19A):		
Assets		
Cash	$ 128,000	$ 48,000
Accounts receivable (net)	53,000	53,000
Receivable from Company S ($5,000, eliminated)		
Inventory	37,000	37,000
Investment in Company S (eliminated)		
Operational assets (net)	125,000	126,800
Goodwill		7,600
Total	$ 343,000	$ 272,400
Liabilities		
Current liabilities	$ 30,000	$ 30,000
Payable to Company P (eliminated)		
Bonds payable	50,000	50,000
Stockholders' Equity		
Common stock, Company P	140,000	100,000
Common stock, Company S (eliminated)		
Contributed capital in excess of par	10,000	10,000
Contributed capital from pooling of interests ($20,000, eliminated)	10,000	
Beginning retained earnings, Company P	47,000	47,000
Beginning retained earnings, Company S	20,000	
Dividends declared and paid in 19A (eliminated)		
Net income, 19A (from income statement above)	36,000	35,400
Total	$ 343,000	$ 272,400

P14–9 **(Preparation of a Consolidated Balance Sheet and Income Statement Using a Worksheet—Based on Supplement 14A)**

On January 1, 19A, Company P purchased 100% of the outstanding capital stock of Company S for $98,000 cash. At that date the stockholders' equity section of the balance sheet of Company S showed the following:

Capital stock, $10 par, 5,000 shares outstanding $50,000
Retained earnings 30,000
                                                  $80,000

At the date of acquisition, it was determined that the market values of certain assets of Company S, in comparison with the book values of those assets as shown on the balance sheet of Company S, should be shown by *(a)* decreasing inventories by $2,000 and *(b)* increasing equipment by $8,000.

It is now one year after acquisition, December 31, 19A, and each company has prepared the following separate financial statements (summarized):

	Company P	Company S
Balance sheet (at December 31, 19A):		
Cash	$ 52,000	$ 30,000
Accounts receivable (net)	31,000	10,000
Receivable from Company P		3,000
Inventories	60,000	70,000
Investment in Company S (at cost)	98,000	
Equipment	80,000	20,000
Other assets	9,000	17,000
	$ 330,000	$ 150,000
Accounts payable	$ 42,000	$ 30,000
Payable to Company S	3,000	
Bonds payable, 10%	70,000	30,000
Capital stock, $10 par	140,000	50,000
Beginning retained earnings	50,000	30,000
Dividends declared and paid during 19A	(10,000)	(5,000)
Net income, 19A (from income statement)	35,000	15,000
	$ 330,000	$ 150,000
Income statement (for 19A):		
Sales revenue	$ 360,000	$ 140,000
Revenue from investments	5,000	
Cost of goods sold	(220,000)	(80,000)
Expenses (not detailed)	(106,000)	(44,000)
Depreciation expense	(4,000)	(1,000)
Net income	$ 35,000	$ 15,000

Additional data during 19A:

1. Near the end of 19A, Company S declared and paid a cash dividend of $5,000.
2. The equipment is being depreciated on the basis of a 20-year remaining life (no residual value).
3. Goodwill is to be amortized over a 40-year period.

Required:

a. Give the journal entry that Company P should make to record the acquisition of the capital stock of Company S on January 1, 19A.
b. Analyze the acquisition of the stock to determine the purchased goodwill.
c. Prepare a consolidation worksheet (purchase method) for the year 19A as a basis for the 19A income statement and balance sheet. (Hint: Consolidated net income is $44,300.)
d. Prepare a consolidated income statement and balance sheet based on the data provided by the consolidation worksheet.

P14–10 **(Preparation of a Consolidated Balance Sheet and Income Statement with Minority Interest—Based on Supplement 14B)**

On January 1, 19A, Company P purchased 90% of the outstanding voting stock of Company S for $100,000 cash. At the date of acquisition, the stockholders' equity accounts of Company S reflected the following: Capital Stock (par $10), $60,000; Contributed Capital in Excess of Par, $10,000; and Retained Earnings, $20,000. At that date it was determined that the book value of the operational assets was $10,000 less than their market value.

It is now December 31, 19A, and each company has prepared the following separate financial statements (summarized):

	Company P	Company S
Balance sheet (at December 31, 19A):		
Cash	$ 23,000	$ 11,000
Accounts receivable (net)	57,000	13,000
Receivable from Company P		7,000
Inventories	110,000	24,000
Investment in Company S (at cost; 90% owned)	100,000	
Operational assets (net)	120,000	50,000
Other assets	6,000	5,000
	$ 416,000	$ 110,000
Accounts payable	$ 30,000	$ 8,000
Payable to Company S	7,000	
Bonds payable, 9%	80,000	10,000
Capital stock, $10 par	200,000	60,000
Contributed capital in excess of par	4,000	10,000
Beginning retained earnings	80,000	20,000
Dividends declared and paid, 19A	(15,000)	(8,000)
Net income (from income statement)	30,000	10,000
	$ 416,000	$ 110,000
Income statement (for 19A):		
Sales revenue	$ 195,000	$ 75,000
Revenue from investments	7,200	
Cost of goods sold	(115,000)	(43,000)
Expenses (not detailed)	(52,200)	(19,500)
Depreciation expense	(5,000)	(2,500)
	$ 30,000	$ 10,000

Required:

a. Give the journal entry that Company P should make to record the acquisition of the stock of Company S.

b. Analyze the stock purchase to determine the amount of goodwill purchased.

c. Prepare a consolidation worksheet (purchase method) for a balance sheet and income statement for 19A. Assume the operational assets of Company S have a 10-year remaining life and that any goodwill will be amortized over 20 years. (Hint: Consolidated net income is $31,400.)

d. Prepare an income statement and balance sheet for 19A based upon the data provided by the consolidation worksheet.

e. What is the minority interest claim to earnings and stockholders' equity at December 31, 19A?

CASES

C14–1   (Analysis of Consolidation Policy)

Sears, Roebuck and Company and J.C. Penney are large retailers that have 100% owned finance subsidiaries. Sears includes its finance subsidiary in its consolidated financial statements, but J.C. Penney does not. J.C. Penney uses the equity method to account for its finance subsidiary.

Required:

a. How do you think the management of Sears and J.C. Penney justify their consolidation policy for their finance subsidiaries?
b. Describe the impact of the different consolidation policies on the balance sheets of Sears and J.C. Penney.
c. Which consolidation policy do you prefer? Why?

C14–2   (Comparison of the Pooling of Interests and the Purchase Methods)

Some analysts believe that management would prefer to account for an acquisition under the pooling of interests method instead of the purchase method. Accounting rules do not permit management to select the method, but these analysts believe that management will structure the transaction so that it will be accounted for as a pooling. One of the alleged benefits of the pooling of interests method for management is that return on investment (net income/total assets) is usually higher under pooling. Why would you expect return on investment to be higher under pooling?

C14–3   (Analysis of Consolidation Using an Actual Financial Statement)

Refer to the financial statements of Chesebrough-Pond's given in Special Supplement B immediately preceding the Index.

Required:

a. What amount of 1985 sales revenue reported by the company is the result of transactions between companies in the Consumer Products Group and companies in the Chemical Products Group?
b. By what amount would liabilities increase if all of the "associated companies and unconsolidated subsidiaries" were consolidated in 1985?
c. Was the acquisition of Stauffer Chemical Company accounted for as a purchase or a pooling? Why?
d. Was any goodwill recorded as the result of the Stauffer Chemical Company acquisition? If so, what amount?
e. Explain the nature of minority interest reported on the balance sheet. How is it related to the investment in associated companies?

This chapter discusses the statement of changes in financial position (sources and uses of cash). The company identified below (a) reports cash sources and cash uses on a 3-year comparative basis (format shown below for 1985) and (b) presents a graphic display of cumulative cash sources and uses for the last 5 years (pie charts shown below).

The Penn Central Corporation and Consolidated Subsidiaries

(a) Format:

Statement of Changes in Financial Position

(Dollars in Millions)	For the Years Ended December 31,	1985	1984	1983
Source (Use) of Cash				
Net income				
etc.				

(b) Graphic display:

Five year principal sources of cash
Cumulative sources: $4.4 billion

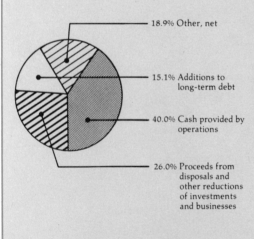

- 18.9% Other, net
- 15.1% Additions to long-term debt
- 40.0% Cash provided by operations
- 26.0% Proceeds from disposals and other reductions of investments and businesses

Five year principal uses of cash
Cumulative uses: $4.4 billion

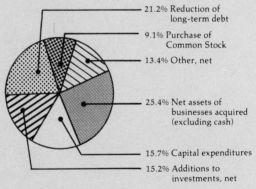

- 21.2% Reduction of long-term debt
- 9.1% Purchase of Common Stock
- 13.4% Other, net
- 25.4% Net assets of businesses acquired (excluding cash)
- 15.7% Capital expenditures
- 15.2% Additions to investments, net

STATEMENT OF CHANGES IN FINANCIAL POSITION

PURPOSE:

Three basic statements are required for external reporting purposes—income statement, balance sheet, and statement of changes in financial position (abbreviated SCFP). This chapter will discuss the concepts of the SCFP, stress its usefulness to decision makers, and show how it is prepared. The chapter discusses two alternative concepts of the SCFP—the cash basis and the working capital basis.

ORGANIZATION:

1. Concepts of the statement of changes in financial position (SCFP).
2. How the SCFP helps decision makers.
3. Format of the SCFP.
4. Preparing the SCFP, cash basis.
5. Preparing the SCFP, working capital basis.
6. Working capital versus cash basis for the SCFP.

LEARNING OBJECTIVES—TO BE ABLE TO:

1. Identify and explain the concepts of the SCFP.
2. Prepare a SCFP, cash basis.
   a. Using the direct analysis for simple situations.
   b. Using the worksheet analysis for complex situations.
3. Prepare a SCFP, working capital basis.
4. Explain how the SCFP, cash basis, helps decision makers.
5. Expand your accounting vocabulary by learning the "Important Terms Defined in This Chapter" (page 788).
6. Apply the knowledge gained from this chapter by completing the homework assigned by your instructor.

PART A—STATEMENT OF CHANGES IN FINANCIAL POSITION, CASH BASIS

CONCEPTS OF THE STATEMENT OF CHANGES IN FINANCIAL POSITION

The income statement and balance sheet are based on **accrual accounting.** That is, revenues, expenses, gains, losses, assets, liabilities, and owners' equity amounts are recognized when the transaction occurs regardless of when the related cash is received or paid. A statement of changes in financial position is often called a **funds** statement because it can be prepared on either a:[1]

1. Cash basis, to report cash inflows (i.e., cash receipts) and outflows (i.e., cash payments), or
2. Working capital basis, to report inflows and outflows of working capital.[2]

The working capital basis was used more frequently in the past. However, there has been a major shift to the cash basis. A recent survey of the financial reports of 600 major companies showed the following:[3]

	1984		1983		1982		1981	
SCFP basis	No.	%	No.	%	No.	%	No.	%
Cash	356	59	314	52	254	42	134	22
Working capital	244	41	286	48	346	58	466	78
Total	600	100	600	100	600	100	600	100

Most companies prepare monthly cash basis SCFP reports for internal use by the management to assess, plan, and control cash. Since cash flow information is important to both external and internal decision makers and is being used increasingly, the SCFP, cash basis, is discussed in Part A. Part B discusses the working capital basis.

The SCFP, cash basis, recognizes only those transactions that involve either a cash inflow (i.e., a cash receipt) or a cash outflow (i.e., a cash payment).[4] For example, a sale of goods or services **on credit** in 19A and collected in 19B would be recognized on the 19A income statement as revenue. The sale would not be recognized on the 19A SCFP, cash basis, because it was not a cash inflow. Instead, the cash collection transaction would be reported on the 19B SCFP as a source of cash (i.e., a cash inflow). A cash dividend is recorded on the accrual basis when declared, but it is reported on the SCFP, cash basis, only when the cash is paid (i.e., a cash outflow).

---

[1] AICPA, *APB Opinion 19*, "Reporting Changes in Financial Position" (New York, March 1971).

[2] Working capital is defined as current assets minus current liabilities. The general term **funds** is used for SCFP purposes and refers to **either** cash or working capital.

[3] AICPA, *Accounting Trends & Techniques*, 39th ed. (New York, 1985), p. 358.

[4] An exception, called direct exchanges, is discussed later.

Transactions involving a cash inflow are called **investing activities.** Transactions involving a cash outflow are called **financing activities.**

The SCFP is a **change statement** because it reports the **causes** of the change (increase or decrease) in cash from the beginning to the end of the accounting period. For example, Hypothetical Company started Year 19X with a cash balance of $20,000; the 19X ending cash balance was $35,000. The 19X SCFP, cash basis, showed: **Sources** (inflows) of cash (detailed), $100,000; **Uses** (outflows) of cash (detailed), $85,000; and **Increase in cash** of $15,000 during 19X.

HOW THE SCFP, CASH BASIS, HELPS DECISION MAKERS

Statement users need to know the accrual basis results reported on the income statement and balance sheet. They also need financial information about the **timing, amounts, and causes of the cash inflows and cash outflows** of the entity during the accounting period. Knowledge about the **liquidity** (i.e., cash availability) of an entity is important to statement users because the success of an entity is measured by the cumulative amount of net cash inflow that it gives. Investors and creditors are concerned about the net cash inflow of an entity because it is the source of their cash returns (e.g., dividends or interest, and cash received upon disposition of their shares or maturity of debt). Also, the existence of an entity depends upon cash flows; sufficient cash must be received and be available monthly (even daily) to pay for such items as salaries, rent, interest and principal on debt, assets purchased, and cash dividends. The first sign of an impending economic problem usually is a shortage of cash. Therefore, financial statement users need current and direct data about the timing, sources, and uses of cash by the entity during the period covered by the financial statements. The **statement of changes in financial position, cash basis,** provides cash flow (i.e., liquidity) information for the statement users.[5] The SCFP supplements, but does not replace, the income statement and balance sheet because the SCFP gives information that is not given by the other two statements.[6]

Complementing the income statement and balance sheet, the SCFP, cash basis, provides information that is useful to users of the financial statements in answering questions such as:

1. How much cash was provided by the **normal operations** of the entity?
2. What were the primary sources of cash from such activities as borrowing, issuance of capital stock, and sale of operational assets?

---

[5] FASB, *Statement of Financial Accounting Concepts No. 1,* "Objectives of Financial Reporting by Business Enterprises" (Stamford, Conn., November 1978), states: "Since investors' and creditors' cash flows are related to enterprise cash flows, financial reporting should provide information to help investors, creditors, and others assess the amounts, timing, and uncertainty of prospective net cash inflows to the related enterprise."

[6] *APB Opinion 19* states: "The funds statement cannot supplant either the income statement or the balance sheet but is intended to provide information that the other statements either do not provide or provide only indirectly about the flow of funds and changes in financial position during the period."

3. How much cash was derived from **nonrecurring** transactions?
4. How much cash was used to pay long-term debts?
5. How much cash was used to acquire operational assets?
6. Why were large borrowings necessary? What users were made of the cash borrowed?
7. What are the causes of any liquidity problems of the entity?
8. Is a future cash flow problem reasonably possible or imminent?
9. What was the financial effect of noncash exchanges (such as the settlement of a debt by issuing company shares)?
10. Does the company have idle cash? How does the company "use" its idle cash?
11. What is the ability of the company to consistently produce cash in the long term?

The SCFP, cash basis, has an important purpose because it can assist the users of financial statements in answering the above questions.

FORMAT OF THE SCFP, CASH BASIS

The SCFP, cash basis, is easy to understand and interpret because it shows only three primary captions—sources, uses, and net increase (decrease) in cash during the accounting period. There are three major sources of cash and three major uses. A cash basis SCFP also is easy to understand because everyone knows what cash means.[7] Exhibit 15–1 shows the format of an SCFP, cash basis. This format was designed for instructional purposes. In particular, notice the numbered **subcaptions.**

Sources of Cash

Sources of cash come from completed cash transactions. These transactions involve an immediate **debit** to the Cash account. The three major sources of cash are from normal operations, sale of noncash assets, and financing. A fourth category, other or miscellaneous sources, usually is needed for practical reasons. Exhibit 15–1 shows examples of each of these sources. All of the sources, except **cash from normal operations,** are usually easy to identify. Cash from normal operations requires that all of the **revenues and expenses** reported on the income statement (i.e., accrual basis) be converted to a strictly cash basis. This conversion to the cash basis is discussed later in this chapter in the section "Preparing the SCFP, Cash Basis" (see page 763).

---

[7] For SCFP purposes, companies often combine cash and short-term investments in marketable securities in the designation cash. This procedure is reasonable because such securities can be immediately converted to cash when needed.

_____ **EXHIBIT 15–1** _____

SCFP, cash basis (instructional format)

HYPOTHETICAL COMPANY
Statement of Changes in Financial Position, Cash Basis
For the Year Ended December 31, 19X
(in thousands)

Sources (inflows) of cash:
1. Cash from normal operations:
   Cash collected for goods and services sold less
   cash paid for expenses $60
2. Sale of noncash assets:
   Investment in bonds $15
   Equipment 5   20
3. Financing:
   Note payable (cash borrowed) 10
   Sale and issuance of company stock 6   16
4. Other sources:
   Insurance indemnity received for fire loss   4

   Total cash sources during 19X $100

Uses (outflows) of cash:
1. Payments to creditors:
   Mortgage payable 30
   Note payable, short term 4   34
2. Purchase of noncash assets:
   Equipment 12
   Investment in land 5   17
3. Payments to owners:
   Dividends 10
   Treasury stock 8   18
4. Other uses:
   Payment for extraordinary loss (damages)   16

   Total cash uses during 19X   85
Net increase (decrease) in cash during 19X .... $ 15*

   * Agrees with the change in the cash account.

Uses of Cash

Uses of cash come from completed cash transactions. These transactions involve an immediate credit to the Cash account. The three major uses of cash are payments to creditors, purchase of noncash assets, and payments to owners. A fourth category, other or miscellaneous uses, usually is needed for practical reasons. All of these uses are usually easy to identify. Notice that cash paid for **expenses** is not shown under uses. Instead, as explained later, it is included in computing and reporting cash from normal operations as shown in Exhibit 15–1.

Net Increase (Decrease) in Cash during the Accounting Period

This amount sometimes is referred to as the "bottom line" on the SCFP. It must agree with the change in the Cash account during the period. Thus, it is a "check figure" that is available before the development of the SCFP. For example, Hypothetical Company's 19X Cash account showed the following (in thousands):

Beginning balance (January 1, 19X) $20
Ending balance (December 31, 19X) 35
Net increase (decrease) in cash during 19X $15

Financial statement users do not have access to a company's Cash account. However, they can verify the net change in cash during the accounting period that should be reported on the SCFP by looking at the cash line reported on the **comparative** balance sheet. The 19X comparative balance sheet for Hypothetical Company would show cash balances of December 31, 19W, $20; and December 31, 19X, $35.

ALL-RESOURCES CONCEPT OF THE SCFP

Often a company buys an asset without the immediate payment of any cash. Examples are (a) the purchase of a machine with payment by trading in another asset and (b) the payment of a debt by issuing capital stock. Because there is no cash payment in these examples at transaction date, should such transactions be reported on the SCFP?

Noncash transactions are called **direct exchanges** for SCFP purposes. They must be reported on the SCFP because of the **all-resources** concept. On transaction date, a direct exchange does not cause a cash flow; however, a direct exchange must be reported on the SCFP "as if" there were a simultaneous **source** of funds and **use** of funds. Consider the following two cases:

Case A:

AB Company acquired a $6,000 machine by issuing 100 shares of its own common stock, par $50 per share. The stock was selling regularly at $60 per share. Therefore, the company recorded this transaction in the accounts as follows:

Machine (100 shares × $60) 6,000
    Common stock, par $50 (100 shares × $50)   5,000
    Contributed capital in excess of par (100 shares × $10)   1,000

In conformity with the all-resources concept, this direct exchange is reported on the SCFP, cash basis, as follows:

Sources of cash:
Issuance of common stock (Note A) $6,000

Uses of cash:
Purchase of machine (Note A) 6,000

Note A: This was a direct exchange. A machine was acquired at a cost of $6,000; payment was made by issuing 100 shares of common stock par $50 per share that had a total market value of $6,000.

Case B:

BC Company owed a $30,000 note payable. The note was paid off in full by issuing 500 of its own common shares, par $50, with a $60 market value per share. The company recorded this transaction as follows:

Note payable 30,000		
Common stock, par $50 (500 shares × $50)		25,000
Contributed capital in excess of par (500 shares × $10)		5,000

This direct exchange is reported on the SCFP as follows:

Sources of cash:
Issuance of common stock (Note A) $30,000

Uses of cash:
Payment of note payable (Note A) 30,000

Note A: This transaction was a direct exchange. Debt was paid by issuing 100 shares of common stock, par $50 per share; total market value $30,000.

PREPARING THE SCFP, CASH BASIS[8]

Preparing the SCFP, cash basis, can be done by using one of three kinds of analyses:

1. **Direct analysis** is a "pick and choose" analysis. It is useful for instructional purposes and in simple cases. A direct analysis is illustrated below for Hypothetical Company.
2. **Worksheet analysis** uses a Debits-Credits type of worksheet similar to the worksheet used to prepare the income statement and balance sheet (see Chapter 5). This kind of analysis also is discussed below.
3. **T-account analysis** is a Debits-Credits analysis using T-accounts. It is used primarily for instructional purposes and simple cases. Except for the format, this analysis is the same as the worksheet analysis. It is illustrated in Supplement 15A.

---

[8] This section can have a low priority or may be omitted if there is a time constraint. It does not have a significant impact on subsequent chapters.

Direct Analysis to Prepare the SCFP, Cash Basis

This analysis involves examination of the income statement, the balance sheet, and related records to identify each source and each use of cash during the reporting period. However, it is not used for complex cases because it is (a) time consuming and (b) subject to omissions and errors. This analysis is illustrated below for Hypothetical Company.

Exhibit 15–1 shows that the Company reported **cash from normal operations, $60.** This amount of cash is from the cash revenues, less the cash expenses, implicit in the 19X income statement. In short, it is the amount of "cash" income that would be reported on a strictly **cash basis** income statement for 19X. Notice that the **cash received** during 19X from the sales of goods and services and the **cash paid** during 19X for expenses are not separately reported on the 19X SCFP (Exhibit 15–1). Instead, the SCFP combines the cash inflow from revenues with the cash outflow for expenses. The combined amount is reported on the SCFP as cash from normal operations.

Normal operations are defined as the usual and continuing operating activities of the business. For Hypothetical Company, normal operations include all items reported on the income statement except unusual items, nonrecurring items, and extraordinary gains and losses.

The conversion of net income (accrual basis) to a cash basis requires an analysis of the current asset and liability accounts **directly related to normal operations.** Hypothetical's 19X net income of $75 (accrual basis) was converted to a cash basis amount as follows:

```
Hypothetical Company, 19X (thousands):
  Cash from normal operations:
    Net income (from 19X income statement) ................... $ 75
    Additions (deductions) to convert to cash basis:
      Depreciation expense (from income statement) ...........    6
      Increase in accounts receivable (from balance sheet) .......  (18)
      Decrease in inventory (from balance sheet) ..............   12
      Decrease in accounts payable (from balance sheet) ........  (15)
        Cash inflow from operations .........................        $60
```

This computation is reported in its entirety on the SCFP, cash basis (for another example, see Exhibit 15–6). Let's look at the above conversion analysis and identify all "noncash effects" in the income statement.

Depreciation expense.   The income statement is studied to identify all **noncash expenses** reported. These are expenses reported on the current income statement that did not require cash payments during the current accounting period. Depreciation expense of $6,000, reported by Hypothetical Company, is a noncash expense for 19X because no cash was paid during 19X for the assets depreciated. The cash was paid when these assets were acquired. Depreciation expense is **added** back to net income because it is a noncash expense that was deducted from revenue to derive net income (thus, the addition removes its effect).

Next, the beginning and ending balance sheets are compared to identify changes in the current assets and current liabilities directly related to normal operations. Hypothetical's 19X comparative balance sheet reported three such items.

Accounts receivable increased, $18.   This increase means that $18 of sales revenue was not collected during 19X. This cash collection will be made in later accounting periods. This amount is a **noncash revenue** because it did not cause cash to increase during the current accounting period. Therefore, $18 must be deducted from accrual income to convert it to a cash basis for this item. If accounts receivable had decreased, the amount would have been added.

Inventory decreased, $12.   This inventory decrease means that goods were taken from inventory during 19X without paying cash for them (the cash was paid in a prior period). Therefore, this noncash expense must be added to net income to convert it to the cash basis for this time. If inventory had increased, the change would be deducted because cash was paid for inventory items that were not included in computing net income.

Accounts payable decreased, $15.   This decrease means that during 19X more cash was paid for expenses than the amount of expenses reported on the 19X income statement (i.e., unpaid expenses from the prior year were paid during the current year). Therefore, this $15 change must be deducted from net income to convert it to a cash basis for this item. If accounts payable increased, the change would be added because some expenses reported on the current income statement have not been paid.[9]

The **other sources** of cash usually can be identified by a direct analysis of the Cash account and the cash receipt records. Also, the **cash uses** can be identified by a direct analysis of the Cash account and the cash payment records.

---

[9] The adjustments to convert accrual income to cash flow from operations are varied. Although careful analysis is needed, the following table may be useful for checking purposes:

Item	Plus and minus adjustments to convert income to net cash flow from operations	
	When item increases	When item decreases
Accounts receivable (trade)	−	+
Accounts payable (trade)	+	−
Accrued liability and unearned revenue	+	−
Prepaid asset and accrued revenue	−	+
Inventory	−	+
Depreciation, depletion, and amortization	+	
Amortization of discount on bonds payable	+	
Amortization of premium on bonds payable	−	
Amortization of discount on bond investment	−	
Amortization of premium on bond investment	+	

Relationships among the Income Statement, Balance Sheet, and the SCFP

The income statement, balance sheet, and SCFP are interrelated. The **income statement** reports net income on the **accrual** basis. This amount is converted to the **cash basis** which is reported on the SCFP (e.g., $60,000 for Hypothetical Company, Exhibit 15–1). The income statement and the SCFP are called **change statements** because they "explain" why the **ending balance sheet** amounts for the accounting period are different from the **beginning balance sheet** amounts of that same period. As change statements, both the income statement and the SCFP are dated "For the Year Ended December 31, 19X." In contrast, the balance sheet is dated "At December 31, 19X," because it is a **position** statement rather than a change statement.

The **income statement** "explains" the **changes** between the beginning and ending balance sheet amounts **caused by accrual basis** revenues, expenses, and extraordinary gains and losses. There are numerous **changes** in the beginning and ending balance sheet amounts (e.g., buying an operational asset) that are **not** reported on the accrual basis income statement.

In contrast, the **SCFP, cash basis,** gives the **cash effects of all changes** between the beginning and ending balance sheets. Exhibit 15–1 shows how the cash change effects are reported on the SCFP.

Exhibit 15–2 focuses on the relationships between the balance sheet and the SCFP, cash basis. It shows the interrelationships between the beginning balance sheet, the SCFP, cash basis, and the ending balance sheet. Notice that the SCFP ties the two consecutive balance sheets together. This relationship is for cash changes only, even though both balance sheets are on the accrual basis. Notice that the SCFP "explains" the changes in each balance sheet item in terms of the actual cash inflows and cash outflows and the **causes** of each of those changes.

WORKSHEET ANALYSIS TO PREPARE SCFP, CASH BASIS

The worksheet analysis is an organized and efficient way to prepare a SCFP in most cases. Its built-in system of checks and balances is very helpful. The worksheet analysis requires data from the comparative balance sheet. The worksheet provides for:

a. Analysis of the change in each **noncash** balance sheet account (the top portion), and
b. Classification of all of the **sources and uses** of cash during the period (the bottom portion).

To facilitate the analysis, the worksheet has four money amount columns: Column 1, Beginning Balance Sheet; Columns 2 and 3, Analysis of Interim Entries; and Column 4, Ending Balance Sheet.

EXHIBIT 15-2

Relationship between the SCFP, Cash Basis and the balance sheet (SCFP data is from Exhibit 15-1)

Balance Sheet
At December 31, 19W

Cash	$ 20
Noncash assets	130
Total	$150
Liabilities	$ 30
Owners' equity:	
Common stock	100
Treasury stock	—
Retained earnings	20
Total	$150

Statement of Changes in Financial Position
For the Year Ended December 31, 19X

* Sources of Cash (cash debits)

Causes	Amount
Disposals (sold)	$ 20
Borrowing	10
Issuance of stock (sold)	6
Normal operations	60
Insurance indemnity	4
Total	$100

† Uses of Cash (cash credits)

Causes	Amount
To increase cash	$ 15
Purchases	17
Payments	34
Purchase of stock	8
Dividends	10
Extraordinary loss	16
Total	$100

Balance Sheet
At December 31, 19X

Cash		$ 35
= Noncash assets		127
Total		$162
= Liabilities		$ 6
Owners' equity:		
= Common stock		106
= Treasury stock		(8)
= Retained earnings		58
Total		$162

A change statement that explains the causes of the changes in the balance sheet accounts—assets, liabilities, and owners' equity. (Assumptions: Funds measured as cash and no direct exchanges.)

* Financing activities.
† Investing activities.

The worksheet analysis involves four simple steps: (1) collect data, (2) set up the worksheet, (3) complete the worksheet, and (4) prepare the formal SCFP.

Exhibit 15–3 gives the 19B comparative balance sheets and income statement for Fina Company. These data will be used for illustrative purposes.

Step 1—**Collect data.** Obtain the current income statement and comparative balance sheets (Exhibit 15–3).

Step 2—**Set up the worksheet.** Label the five column headings as shown in Exhibit 5–4. List the debit accounts and amounts in the first, second, and last columns, followed by the credits as shown in Exhibit 15–4, **Part A.** Next, in **Part B** list the side captions for the SCFP, cash basis. These side captions, with enough space between each one, are **sources** of cash (from normal operations and from other sources) and **uses** of cash. The caption "From normal operations" provides for the **conversion** of net income (accrual basis) to the cash basis.

Step 3—**Complete the worksheet.** The heading "Analysis of Interim Entries" provides for the analysis of all changes in the **noncash** accounts during the current accounting period. **Analytical entries are entered under this heading to identify and classify each source and each use of cash.** For accuracy, each entry maintains the Debit = Credits feature. **Instead of entering cash debits and credits in the Cash account (line 1 on the worksheet), they are entered under Part B, "Sources of Cash" (debits) and "Uses of Cash" (credits).** (See Exhibit 15–2.) The analytical entries for this case are explained in Exhibit 15–5.

The worksheet is complete when the change **on each line** (in Part A of the worksheet) between the beginning and ending balances is fully accounted for. At this time the change in the Cash account during the period (as shown on the first line) can be entered on the first line under "Analysis of Interim Entries" and at the bottom of the worksheet. The debit and credit columns in the bottom portion of the worksheet may be summed to test for equality. This step is a partial check on the accuracy of the results. Finally, the total debit and total credit in the "Analysis of Interim Entries" columns should be tested for equality.

Exhibit 15–4 shows the completed worksheet for Fina Company (data given in Exhibit 15–3). Notice the following: Part A—analysis of the balance sheet accounts, Part B—SCFP outlined, and the balancing features—Debits = Credits in each pair of money columns.

Step 4—**Prepare the formal SCFP.** All of the information needed to prepare the formal SCFP is shown in Part B of the worksheet. The SCFP, cash basis, for Fina Company (Exhibit 15–6) was prepared directly from Exhibit 15–4. Some variations in terminology and classifications may be seen in actual practice.

EXHIBIT 15-3

Comparative balance sheets and income statements (for SCFP)

FINA COMPANY
Balance Sheets
At December 31, 19B, and 19A

	December 31, 19B		December 31, 19A[a]	
Assets				
Current assets:				
Cash	$ 41,300		$31,000	
Accounts receivable (net)[b]	25,000		20,000	
Inventory (periodic)	20,000	$ 86,300	24,000	$ 75,000
Long-term investments:				
Common stock of X Corporation		1,000		6,000
Operational assets:[b]				
Equipment (net)[c]	59,000			
Patent (cost, $3,400 − amortization, $200)	3,200	62,200		60,000
Total assets		$149,500		$141,000
Liabilities				
Current liabilities:				
Accounts payable	$ 22,000		$20,000	
Income tax payable	500		1,000	
Short-term note payable (nontrade)	10,000	$ 32,500	14,000	$ 35,000
Long-term liabilities:				
Long-term note payable	10,000			
Bonds payable	32,000	42,000		40,000
Stockholders' Equity				
Stockholders' equity:				
Common stock, par $10	60,000		50,000	
Contributed capital in excess of par	6,000		5,000	
Treasury stock (at cost)	(3,000)			
Retained earnings[d]	12,000	75,000	11,000	66,000
Total liabilities and stockholders' equity		$149,500		$141,000

[a] The ending balance sheet for the prior period is the beginning balance sheet for the current period.

[b] In analyzing and reporting changes in financial position, accounts receivable and operational assets usually are shown net of the contra accounts for convenience.

[c] A machine that cost $5,000 was acquired on January 1, 19B. Payment in full was made by exchanging $5,000 of the investment in the common stock of X Corporation (the carrying value of these shares was the same as their current market value).

[d] Dividends declared and paid during 19B amounted to $7,000.

FINA COMPANY
Income Statement
For the Year Ended December 31, 19B

Sales revenue		$100,000
Cost of goods sold		60,000
Gross margin		40,000
Less expenses:		
Expenses (not detailed)	$23,800	
Depreciation expense	6,000	
Amortization expense (patent)	200	
Income tax expense	2,000	32,000
Net income		$ 8,000

EXHIBIT 15–4

Worksheet to prepare SCFP, Cash Basis (Fina Company for the year ended December 31, 19B)

Part A—Analysis of Balance Sheet Accounts:

Col. 1	Col. 2	Col. 3	Col. 4	Col. 5
		Analysis of Interim Entries*		Ending Balances Dec. 31, 19B
Items	Balances Dec. 31. 19A	Debit	Credit	
Debits				
Cash account	31,000	(√) 10,300		41,300
Noncash accounts:				
Accounts receivable (net)	20,000	(d) 5,000		25,000
Inventory	24,000		(e) 4,000	20,000
LT investment, X Corp. stock†	6,000		(f-1) 5,000	1,000
Equipment (net)	60,000	(f-2) 5,000	(b) 6,000	59,000
Patent (net)		(g) 3,400	(c) 200	3,200
Total	141,000			149,500
Credits				
Accounts payable	20,000		(h) 2,000	22,000
Income tax payable	1,000	(i) 500		500
Short-term note payable (non-trade)	14,000	(j) 4,000		10,000
Long-term note payable			(k) 10,000	10,000
Bonds payable	40,000	(l) 8,000		32,000
Common stock, par $10	50,000		(m) 10,000	60,000
Contributed capital in excess of par	5,000		(m) 1,000	6,000
Treasury stock		(n) 3,000		(3,000)
Retained earnings	11,000	(o) 7,000	(a) 8,000	12,000
Total	141,000	46,200	46,200	149,500

Analysis of Disposal of an Asset

The Fina Company case did not show how the disposal of a **noncash** asset would be analyzed for the SCFP. The disposal of a noncash asset usually causes a gain or loss on disposal which is reported on the income statement. This gain or loss must be removed from income as one of the conversion adjustments because it is not the total amount of cash inflow from the disposal. The total cash flow from a disposal must be reported on the SCFP, "From other sources." Assume that Fina Company sold equipment that had a book value of $2,000 for $3,000 cash. The $1,000 gain would be deducted from net income. The $3,000 cash inflow would be reported under "From other sources." If the $1,000 gain is

_____ EXHIBIT 15–4 *(concluded)* _____

Worksheet to prepare SCFP, Cash Basis (Fina Company for the year ended December 31, 19B)

Part B—SCFP Outlined:

Items	Income and Additions	Income Deductions	
Sources of cash:			
From normal operations:			
Net income	*(a)* 8,000		⎫
Depreciation expense	*(b)* 6,000		Cash from
Amortization of patent	*(c)* 200		normal
Accounts receivable increase		*(d)* 5,000	operations,
Inventory decrease	*(e)* 4,000‡		$14,700
Accounts payable increase	*(h)* 2,000‡		
Income tax payable decrease		*(i)* 500	⎭
	Sources	**Uses**	
From other sources:			
Exchange of investment for equipment	*(f-1)* 5,000		
LT note payable	*(k)* 10,000		
Sold and issued common stock	*(m)* 11,000		
Uses of cash:			
Exchange of investment for equipment		*(f-2)* 5,000	
Purchase of patent		*(g)* 3,400	
Payment on ST note		*(j)* 4,000	
Payment on bonds payable		*(l)* 8,000	
Purchase of treasury stock		*(n)* 3,000	
Declared and paid cash dividend		*(o)* 7,000	
Net increase in cash (per line 1, Part A)		(√) 10,300	
	46,200	46,200	

* These entries are keyed for ready reference to the text discussion; see Exhibit 15–5.
† Equipment was acquired in exchange for common stock of X Corporation, which was being held as a long-term investment.
‡ These two items may be combined as a conversion of cost of goods sold on the accrual basis to a cash basis as follows:

CGS—accrual basis (Exhibit 15–3)	$ 60,000
Inventory change—decrease (Exhibit 15–3)	(4,000)
Purchases—accrual basis	56,000
Accounts payable change—increase (Exhibit 15–3)	(2,000)
CGS—Cash basis	$ 54,000
Adjustment (add) for conversion of CGS to cash basis ($60,000 − $54,000) = ...	$ 6,000

The worksheet analytical entry would be:

Cost of goods sold adjustment	6,000	
Inventory		4,000
Accounts payable		2,000

EXHIBIT 15–5

Analytical worksheet entries (see Exhibit 5–4)

Code	Data source	Analytical entry with explanation
(a)	Income statement (Exhibit 15–3)	Sources of cash (income) . . . . 8,000 Retained earnings 8,000
		This analytical entry in (1) Part A of the worksheet partially accounts for the $1,000 net credit increase in retained earnings and (2) Part B shows income as a source of cash. Because net income of $8,000 is an **accrual basis** amount, additions and subtractions must be made in subsequent analytical entries to convert it to a **cash basis** (see entries [b], [c], [d], [e], [h], and [i]).
(b)	Income statement (Exhibit 15–3)	Sources of cash (income addition) . . . . 6,000 Equipment (or accumulated depreciation) 6,000
		This analytical entry in (1) Part A accounts for the $6,000 credit increase in the equipment account and (2) Part B adds the $6,000 to income because depreciation is a **noncash** expense that was deducted to derive accrual income.
(c)	Income statement (Exhibit 15–3)	Sources of cash (income addition) . . . . 200 Patent (or Accumulated amortization) 200
		This analytical entry has the same effects as entry (b) except that it relates to an intangible asset account.
(d)	Balance sheet (Exhibit 15–3)	Accounts receivable (trade) . . . . 5,000 Sources of cash (income deduction) 5,000
		This analytical entry in (1) Part A accounts for the $5,000 net debit increase in accounts receivable and (2) Part B deducts the $5,000 from accrual income because credit sales were more than cash sales by this amount; it is noncash sales for the period.
(e)	Balance sheet (Exhibit 15–3)	Sources of cash (income addition) . . . . 4,000 Merchandise inventory 4,000
		This analytical entry in (1) Part A, accounts for the net credit decrease in inventory and (2) Part B adds the $4,000 to income because that amount of goods was withdrawn from inventory in excess of purchases. Thus, it is a noncash expense (cost of goods sold) for this period which was deducted to derive accrual net income.

EXHIBIT 15–5 *(continued)*

Analytical worksheet entries (see Exhibit 5–4)

(f)	Balance sheet (Exhibit 15–3 and related data about the direct exchange)	*(f-1)* Sources of cash (direct exchange) 5,000
		        LT investment, stock of X Corp. 5,000
		(f-2) Machine 5,000
		        Uses of cash (direct exchange) 5,000
		
		This was a **direct exchange;** therefore two entries were required. Analytical entry (f-1) reflects the **financing activity;** the debit recognizes the implied ''as if'' source of cash and the credit accounts for the net credit decrease in the investment account. Analytical entry (f-2) reflects the **investing activity;** the credit recognizes the implied use of cash and the debit accounts for the increase in the asset account. This $5,000 debit increase and the $6,000 credit decrease for depreciation expense (entry [b]) account fully for the $1,000 net credit decrease in the equipment account.

(g)	Balance sheet (Exhibit 15–3 and related data)	Patent .... 3,400 Uses of cash (purchase of patent) .... 3,400 This analytical entry in (1) Part A accounts for a $3,400 debit increase in the patent account (which was its cost) and (2) Part B recognizes a use of cash. This $3,400 debit increase and the $200 credit decrease for amortization (entry [c]) account fully for the net credit increase of $3,200 in the patent account.
(h)	Balance sheet (Exhibit 15–3)	Sources of cash (income addition) .... 2,000 Accounts payable .... 2,000 This analytical entry in (1) Part A accounts for the $2,000 credit increase in accounts payable and (2) Part B adds the $2,000 to income because the accrual expenses deducted to derive income amounted to $2,000 more than the cash currently paid; thus, this amount is recognized as a noncash expense for the period.
(i)	Balance sheet (Exhibit 15–3)	Income tax payable .... 500 Sources of cash (income deduction) .... 500 This analytical entry in (1) Part A accounts for the net debit increase in income tax payable and (2) Part B deducts $500 from income because income tax expense deducted to derive accrual income was $500 less than the cash currently paid for income taxes; thus, this amount was an additional **cash** expense for the current period.
(j)	Balance sheet (Exhibit 15–3)	ST note payable (nontrade) .... 4,000 Uses of cash (payment of debt) .... 4,000 This analytical entry in (1) Part A accounts for the net debit decrease in note payable and (2) Part B shows a use of cash to pay debt.

EXHIBIT 15–5 *(concluded)*

Analytical worksheet entries (see Exhibit 5–4)

(k)	Balance sheet (Exhibit 15–3)	Sources of cash (LT note) .... 10,000 LT note payable 10,000	

This analytical entry in (1) Part A accounts for the $10,000 net credit increase in LT note payable and (2) Part B shows a source of cash.

(l)	Balance sheet (Exhibit 15–3)	Bonds payable .... 8,000 Uses of cash (payment on bonds) 8,000	

This analytical entry in (1) Part A accounts for the $8,000 net debit decrease in bonds payable and (2) Part B shows a use of cash to pay debt.

(m)	Balance sheet (Exhibit 15–3)	Sources of cash (issued capital stock) 11,000
		    Common stock, par $10 10,000
		    Contributed capital in excess of par 1,000	

This analytical entry in (1) Part A accounts for the credit increases in the two capital stock accounts and (2) Part B shows a cash source.

(n)	Balance sheet (Exhibit 15–3)	Treasury stock 3,000
		    Uses of cash (purchase of treasury
		      stock) 3,000	

This analytical entry in (1) Part A accounts for the debit increase in the treasury stock account and (2) Part B shows a use of cash.

(o)	Statement of retained earnings	Retained earnings .... 7,000 Uses of cash 7,000	

This analytical entry for cash dividends declared and paid during 19B in (1) Part A accounts for a $7,000 debit decrease in retained earnings and (2) Part B shows a use of cash. When this $7,000 debit decrease is combined with the $8,000 credit increase (entry [a]) the net credit increase in the retained earnings account is fully accounted for. Note: A cash dividend declared in 19A and paid in 19B would not decrease **cash** until 19B. However, the declaration would decrease **working capital** in 19A (because of the credit to dividends payable) but would have no effect on working capital in 19B.

not subtracted from net income, the gain would be "double counted" as a source of cash from (1) normal operations and (2) from other sources. The **analytical entry** on the worksheet would be:

Sources of cash, from other sources 3,000
    Equipment (net)   2,000
    Sources of cash (income deduction to remove its
      effect from income)   1,000

EXHIBIT 15-6

Statement of changes in financial position, cash basis

FINA COMPANY
Statement of Changes in Financial Position, Cash Basis
For the Year Ended December 31, 19B[a]

Sources of cash:[b]
From normal operations:

Income	$ 8,000	
Add (deduct) adjustments to convert to cash basis:		
Accounts receivable increase	(5,000)	
Depreciation expense	6,000	
Amortization expense (patent)	200	
Merchandise inventory decrease	4,000	
Accounts payable increase	2,000	
Income tax payable decrease	(500)	
Net cash from normal operations		$14,700[c]

From other sources:

Borrowing on long-term note	10,000	
Sale of unissued common stock	11,000	
Disposal of long-term investment (Note A)	5,000	
Total cash from other sources		26,000
Total cash generated (inflow) during the period		40,700

Uses of cash:[b]

Cash dividend on common stock declared and paid during 19B	7,000	
Payment on bonds payable	8,000	
Payment on notes payable, short term (nontrade)	4,000	
Purchase of patent	3,400	
Purchase of treasury stock	3,000	
Acquisition of equipment (Note A)	5,000	
Total cash used (outflow) during the period		30,400
Net increase of cash during the period		$10,300

Note A: Equipment was acquired in exchange for common stock of X Corporation, which was being held as a long-term investment.

[a] Source of data. Exhibit 15-4.

[b] Sometimes referred to as "Cash generated" and "Cash applied," respectively.

[c] Some persons prefer to set the computations above this line in a way to separate revenues from expenses, which has two distinct advantages: (1) separate computing and reporting of the cash inflows from revenues and the cash outflows for expenses and (2) no implication that depreciation and amortization expenses are sources of cash. To illustrate:

Revenues		$ 100,000
Add (deduct) adjustments to convert to cash basis:		
Accounts receivable increase		(5,000)
Cash generated from revenues		$95,000
Expenses ($60,000 + $32,000)		92,000
Add (deduct) adjustments to convert to cash basis:		
Depreciation expense		(6,000)
Amortization expense		(200)
Merchandise inventory decrease		(4,000)
Accounts payable increase		(2,000)
Income tax payable decrease		500
Cash disbursed for expenses		80,300
Net cash inflow from operations		$14,700

PART B—STATEMENT OF CHANGES IN FINANCIAL POSITION, WORKING CAPITAL BASIS

CONCEPT OF WORKING CAPITAL[10]

The only difference between the SCFP prepared on a working capital basis and one prepared on a cash basis is how the "funds" are **measured.** This part of the chapter discusses the sources and uses of funds in terms of **working capital** instead of cash. Compared with cash, working capital is a broader and significantly different concept of funds because it involves an arithmetical difference—**total current assets minus total current liabilities.** Thus, working capital is an abstraction because it does not represent a single asset, or group of similar assets; rather it includes total current assets and an offset—total current liabilities. It cannot be counted, handled, or used to settle receivables and payables. Because of its abstract nature, working capital often is not fully understood by statement users. Although working capital is used widely as the SCFP measurement basis, a growing use of the cash basis is evident.

To understand and interpret the SCFP prepared on the working capital basis, you should clearly understand the concept of working capital as a measurement of **funds.** As a basis for discussion, notice in Exhibit 15–3, for Fina Company, that the comparative balance sheets reported working capital that may be tabulated as follows:

	December 31		Working capital increase (decrease)
	19B	19A	19A to 19B
Current assets:			
Cash	$41,300	$31,000	$ 10,300
Accounts receivable	25,000	20,000	5,000
Inventory	20,000	24,000	(4,000)
Total current assets	86,300	75,000	
Current liabilities:			
Accounts payable	22,000	20,000	(2,000)
Income tax payable	500	1,000	500
Short-term note payable (nontrade)	10,000	14,000	4,000
Total current liabilities	32,500	35,000	
Working capital (at year-end)	$53,800	$40,000	$ 13,800

Examination of the working capital tabulation above shows two fundamental relationships that relate directly to the SCFP, working capital basis:

1. Increases in current assets and/or decreases in current liabilities **increase**

---

[10] Before this book went to press, the FASB distributed an exposure draft that would require the SCFP to be a cash basis statement. If this draft is approved, the SCFP, working capital basis would not be required for external reporting purposes.

working capital, and decreases in current assets and/or increases in current liabilities **decrease working capital.**

2. A transaction that affects only working capital accounts during a given period does **not** change the amount of working capital for that period because only the components of working capital are changed. The **total amount** of working capital during a given period is changed only by transactions that affect one or more **noncurrent** (i.e., nonworking capital) accounts; that is noncurrent assets, noncurrent liabilities, and owners' equity accounts. Therefore, an analysis of the **noncurrent** balance sheet accounts is used to develop a SCFP on the working capital basis.

Sources of Working Capital

Transactions that **increase** working capital are called **sources of working capital.** These transactions involve a debit to either a current asset or current liability account and a credit to one or more **nonworking capital accounts.** The four primary sources of working capital are:

1. **From normal operations**—Net income (accrual basis) must be converted to working capital basis. As goods and services are sold during the period, there is an inflow of cash and/or accounts receivable (both working capital items). Also, during the period, as expenses are incurred, usually there is a decrease in working capital because of cash payments and/or the incurrence of current liabilities (both working capital items). Therefore, a reported income usually results in an increase (source) of working capital. In the case of a loss, working capital usually will decrease. The conversion to working capital is done like the conversion for cash. The main difference is that the conversion adjustments that must be made affect **only nonworking capital accounts.** Because they do not include changes in only current assets and current liabilities, they usually are limited to depreciation amortization, depletion, and gains and losses. For example, conversion of net income to the working capital basis is as follows:

Income	$ 8,000
Add (deduct) to convert to working capital basis:	
Depreciation expense	6,000
Amortization expense	200
Net working capital from normal operations	$14,200

    * See Exhibits 15–7 and 15–8.

2. **Sale of capital stock for cash or short-term receivables**—A sale of capital stock is a source of working capital because cash or a short-term receivable is received for the sale price of the stock.
3. **Sale of noncurrent assets**—When a long-term investment, an operational asset, or an "other noncurrent asset" is sold, working capital is increased by the total amount of the cash and/or short-term receivable that results from its disposition (the increase is not the amount of the disposal gain or loss).

4. **Long-term borrowing**—When a loan is obtained on a long-term basis, working capital (cash) is increased by the proceeds of the loan. In contrast, when a **short-term** loan is obtained, working capital is **not** increased because a working capital account (Cash) is increased and another working capital account (a current liability) is increased by the same amount. Because the two changes offset each other, working capital (current assets minus current liabilities) does not change. To illustrate, if Fina Company borrowed $5,000 cash on a 90-day loan near the end of 19B, the working capital effect would be as follows:

	Before short-term loan	Effect of short-term loan	After short-term loan
Current assets	$ 86,300	+$ 5,000	$ 91,300
Current liabilities	(32,500)	+ (5,000)	(37,500)
Working capital	$ 53,800	–0–*	$ 53,800

* Effect on working capital = (+$5,000) − (+$5,000) = 0.

Uses of Working Capital

Transactions that **decrease** working capital are called **uses of working capital.** These transactions involve a credit to a working capital account and a debit to a **nonworking capital account.** The three main uses of working capital are:

1. **Purchase operational assets and other noncurrent assets for cash or short-term debt**—These transactions usually require a payment of cash and, sometimes, the creation of a short-term debt. To the extent that cash is paid or short-term debt is incurred, working capital is reduced.
2. **Declare cash dividends**—This transaction causes the recognition of a current liability; therefore, working capital is reduced (used) by that amount. However, the subsequent cash payment of the dividend already declared does not reduce working capital.[11]
3. **Pay a long-term liability**—Payments on long-term notes and bonds and other long-term obligations involve an outflow of cash; therefore, they represent uses of working capital. In contrast, the payment of a **current liability does not change working capital** for the same reason explained above in respect to borrowing (source) on a short-term debt basis; that is, the two working capital effects offset one another.

---

[11] When a dividend is declared, working capital is reduced by the amount of the dividend even though payment in cash is in a later period. In this case, the dividend payable is recorded as a current liability on declaration date. The cash payment in the later period does not affect working capital at that time because equal debits and credits to working capital accounts will be made. This distinction is important only when declaration and payment dates fall in different accounting periods. The declaration and payment of a cash dividend in the same year reduces both cash and working capital for that year.

To summarize, (1) working capital is not increased or decreased by any transaction that involves **only** debits and credits to working capital accounts, and (2) working capital is increased or decreased by each transaction that involves debits and/or credits to working capital accounts and **also debits and/or credits to nonworking capital accounts.**

FORMAT FOR THE SCFP, WORKING CAPITAL BASIS

Exhibit 15–8 shows the SCFP, working capital basis, for Fina Company. The standard format for the SCFP, working capital basis, has two distinct parts (in contrast to the SCFP, cash basis, which needs only the first part):

Part A—Sources and uses of working capital

Part B—Changes in working capital during the period

Part A reports the financing activities (sources of working capital) and the investing activities (uses of working capital) during the period. Part A is the basic report. Part B lists each current asset and current liability, the resulting increases and decreases, and the net change in working capital during the period.[12] The format in Part A of the statement follows the cash basis format, except that it relates only to the sources and uses of **working capital.**

WORKSHEET TO PREPARE THE SCFP, WORKING CAPITAL BASIS

Exhibit 15–7 shows a worksheet to prepare the SCFP. Compare this exhibit with Exhibit 15–4 (cash basis worksheet). Notice that the working capital worksheet is different only in the following ways:

1. All of the working accounts are grouped on the first line called "Working capital."
2. Only the nonworking capital accounts are listed in Part A of the worksheet.
3. Part B captions follow the reporting format of the SCFP, working capital basis.
4. The entries in the columns "Analysis of Interim Entries" are limited to the nonworking capital accounts. On the cash basis worksheet the entries are related to all accounts except cash.
5. The "check" figure is the change in working capital from the beginning to the end of the accounting period.

---

[12] Part B is copied from the related comparative balance sheets. Therefore, some accountants consider Part B to be redundant; however, it is required by *APB Opinion 19*. The two parts of the SCFP, working capital basis, are not called "Part A and Part B" in actual practice; this designation is used here only for instructional convenience.

EXHIBIT 15-7

Worksheet to prepare SCFP, Working Capital Basis (Fina Company)

Part A—Analysis of the Noncurrent Balance Sheet Accounts:

Items	Balances Dec. 31, 19A	Analysis of Interim Entries†		Ending Balances Dec. 31, 19B
		Debit	Credit	
Debits				
Working capital	40,000	(√) 13,800		53,800
Noncurrent accounts:				
LT investment, X Corp. stock	6,000		(f-1) 5,000	1,000
Equipment (net)	60,000	(f-2) 5,000	(b) 6,000	59,000
Patent (net)		(g) 3,400	(c) 200	3,200
Total	106,000			117,000
Credits				
LT note payable (nontrade)			(k) 10,000	10,000
Bonds payable	40,000	(l) 8,000		32,000
Common stock, par $10	50,000		(m) 10,000	60,000
Contributed capital in excess of par	5,000		(m) 1,000	6,000
Treasury stock		(n) 3,000		(3,000)
Retained earnings	11,000	(o) 7,000	(a) 8,000	12,000
Total	106,000	40,200	40,200	117,000

Steps to Prepare the SCFP, Working Capital Basis

The consecutive steps to prepare a SCFP, working capital basis, are:

Step 1—Collect data. Obtain the current income statement and comparative balance sheets (see Exhibit 15–3).

Step 2—Set up the worksheet. See Exhibit 15–7. In Part A of the worksheet, list each noncurrent (i.e., nonworking capital) account and its balances as reported on the comparative balance sheets. Use the first line for the working capital amounts (these are "balancing" amounts). Notice in Exhibit 15–7 how the accounts, beginning balances and ending balances, are entered on the worksheet.

Step 3—Complete the worksheet. The analytical entries are entered only on the worksheet. They follow the pattern of regular journal entries and must account for all of the net increases and decreases in the noncurrent accounts in Part A of the worksheet. The offsetting debits and credits that show

_____ **EXHIBIT 15–7** *(concluded)* _____

Worksheet to prepare SCFP, Working Capital Basis (Fina Company)

Part B—SCFP Outlined:

Items	Income and Additions	Income Deductions	
Sources of working capital:			Net working capital inflow from normal operations, $14,200; see Exhibit 15–8.
From normal operations:			
Net income	*(a)* 8,000		
Depreciation expense	*(b)* 6,000		
Amortization expense	*(c)* 200		
	Sources	**Uses**	
From other sources:			
Exchange of investment for equipment*	*(f-1)* 5,000		
LT note payable	*(k)* 10,000		
Sold and issued common stock	*(m)* 11,000		
Uses of working capital:			
Exchange for investment for equipment*		*(f-2)* 5,000	
Purchased patent		*(g)* 3,400	
Payment on bonds payable		*(l)* 8,000	
Purchased treasury stock		*(n)* 3,000	
Declared and paid a cash dividend		*(o)* 7,000	
Increase in working capital (line 1)		(√) 13,800	
	40,200	40,200	

   * Equipment acquired in exchange for common stock of X Corporation, which was being held as a long-term investment.

   † These entries are keyed for ready references to the text discussions (see Exhibit 15–5). The analytical entries for working capital do not include all of the analytical entries that were required for the cash basis; therefore, some of the code letters are not shown here.

increases and decreases of working capital are recorded in Part B of the worksheet (Debits = Sources and Credits = Uses). The analytical entry codes used in Exhibit 15–4 (cash basis) also were used in Exhibit 15–7 (working capital basis) to make study and comparison easier. You should reread the explanations in Exhibit 15–5 for entries *(a)*, *(b)*, *(c)*, *(f)*, *(g)*, *(k)*, *(l)*, *(m)*, *(n)*, and *(o)* (i.e., the working capital analytical entries).

Step 4—Prepare the formal SCFP. Part B of the worksheet completed in Step 3 provides all of the data needed to complete the "Sources and uses" part of the formal SCFP. The second part of the SCFP is copied directly from the comparative balance sheets. Exhibit 15–8 shows the formal SCFP, working capital basis.

EXHIBIT 15–8

Statement of changes in financial position, working capital basis

FINA COMPANY
Statement of Changes in Financial Position, Working Capital Basis
For the Year Ended December 31, 19B

Part A—Sources and uses of working capital during the period:

Sources of working capital:

From normal operations:

Income	$ 8,000	
Add (deduct) to convert to working capital basis:		
Depreciation expense	6,000	
Amortization expense (patent)	200	
Total working capital generated from normal operations		$14,200
From other sources:		
Borrowed on long-term note	10,000	
Sale of unissued common stock	11,000	
Disposal of long-term investment (Note A)	5,000	
Total working capital generated from other sources		26,000
Total working capital generated during the period		40,200

Uses of working capital:

Cash dividend on common stock declared and paid during 19B	7,000	
Payment on bonds payable	8,000	
Purchase of patent	3,400	
Purchase of treasury stock	3,000	
Acquisition of equipment (Note A)	5,000	
Total working capital used during the period		26,400
Net increase in working capital during the period		$13,800*

Part B—Changes in working capital during the period:

	Balances, December 31		Working capital increase (decrease)
Working capital accounts	*19B*	*19A*	
Current assets:			
Cash	$41,300	$31,000	$ 10,300
Accounts receivable (net)	25,000	20,000	5,000
Merchandise inventory	20,000	24,000	(4,000)
Total current assets	86,300	75,000	
Current liabilities:			
Accounts payable	22,000	20,000	(2,000)
Income tax payable	500	1,000	500
Note payable, short term (nontrade)	10,000	14,000	4,000
Total current liabilities	32,500	35,000	
Working capital	$53,800	$40,000	$ 13,800*

Note A: Equipment was acquired in exchange for common stock of X Corporation, which was being held as a long-term investment.
Part A—source of data, Exhibit 15–7.
Part B—source of data, Exhibit 15–3.
* These two amounts must agree.

WORKING CAPITAL VERSUS CASH BASIS FOR THE SCFP

The SCFP, working capital basis, has the following advantages over the SCFP, cash basis: *(a)* it is broader in scope because working capital includes all current assets and current liabilities; *(b)* it is easier to prepare; and *(c)* it has been used extensively in the past (see page 758). In contrast, the advantages of the SCFP, cash basis, are: *(a)* cash is the primary resource of interest to decision makers because they need to project future cash flows; *(b)* cash is understood by most persons whereas working capital (being an abstract amount) often is not understood by decision makers; and *(c)* recently there has been a significant increase in the use of the cash basis (see page 758).

FASB Concepts Statement No. 5, "Recognition and Measurement in Financial Statements of Business Enterprises" (December 1984) gives the needs for a cash flow statement, but it does not mention the working capital basis. It is likely that the FASB soon will require only the cash basis SCFP. The *FASB Status Reports,* dated July 10, 1985, and September 17, 1986, read:

> The Board added to its agenda during the second quarter a project to develop standards for cash flow statements. The cash flow project is of limited scope and will aim to (a) establish the objectives of a cash flow statement; (b) define the "elements," the few major components, of a cash flow statement; and (c) require a cash flow statement as part of a full set of financial statements. The standards would amend or replace APB Opinion No. 19, "Reporting Changes in Financial Position."

If adopted as a final statement, the provisions of the exposure draft would be effective for financial statements for fiscal periods ending after June 30, 1987.

If this position is adopted by the FASB, the SCFP, working capital basis, will probably no longer be given in external financial statements (see footnote 10).

DEMONSTRATION CASE

The 1982 statement of changes in consolidated financial position of Dennison Manufacturing Company and Subsidiaries was taken from the annual report:

	(Thousands of Dollars)		
Years Ended December 31	**1982**	1981	1980
Cash Provided by Operations:			
Net earnings	**$20,637**	$ 30,074	$ 23,255
Non-cash items included in net earnings:			
Depreciation	**18,353**	15,432	13,826
Deferred income taxes	**521**	655	985
Other	**298**	591	476
	39,809	46,752	38,542
Increase (decrease) in cash caused by certain working capital items:			
Trade accounts receivable	**2,474**	(16,812)	(5,404)
Inventories	**(1,582)**	(15,933)	(1,300)
Prepaid expenses and other current assets	**306**	(13)	2,031
Accounts payable	**(52)**	8,183	3,839
Other current liabilities	**5,980**	3,297	2,266
Effect of exchange rate changes	**(181)**	(477)	
Net Cash Flow from Operations	**46,754**	24,997	39,974
Financing Activities:			
Issuance of long-term debt	**2,500**	27,000	
Payment of long-term debt	**(1,104)**	(3,785)	(2,222)
Increase in current notes payable to banks	**2,622**	1,799	6,313
Payments from Employee Stock Ownership Trust	**703**	1,267	1,289
Common Stock issued in connection with acquisition of a business		2,278	
Proceeds from the exercise of stock options	**24**	487	217
Other—net	**592**	(427)	591
	5,337	28,619	6,188
Net Cash Provided from All Sources	**52,091**	53,616	46,162
Cash Used for:			
Purchase of property, plant, and equipment, net	**23,206**	29,001	24,885
Net non-current assets of businesses acquired	**5,724**	6,690	
Acquisition of minority interests		2,840	
Cash dividends to shareholders	**14,048**	12,551	11,004
	42,978	51,082	35,889
Net Increase in Cash and Marketable Securities	**9,113**	2,534	10,273
Cash and marketable Securities at Beginning of Year	**15,505**	12,971	2,698
Cash and Marketable Securities at End of Year	**$24,618**	$15,505	$12,971

Required:

a. What period does this statement cover? How does Dennison define "funds"?
b. Explain why (1) depreciation and (2) deferred income taxes are added to net earnings to determine cash inflow from operations.
c. Explain why (1) accounts receivable was added to and (2) inventories was deducted from net earnings to calculate cash inflow based on operations.

d. What was the amount of net cash flow from the income statement?

e. Explain why (1) the issuance of long-term debt was added and (2) the payment of long-term debt was deducted to determine net cash provided from all sources.

f. Assume the 1982 income statement and balance sheet are available. Explain how you could verify the overall accuracy of the SCFP.

Suggested Solution

a. Period covered by the SCFP, **Year ended December 31** for each year (1980, 1981, and 1982). The SCFP uses the term **cash;** however, the last three lines show that the cash definition includes **cash and short-term marketable securities.**

b. On the SCFP, net earnings, **accrual** basis (i.e., $20,637), must be converted to the cash basis by making certain adjustments. **Depreciation** is added to change net earnings to the cash basis because (1) it is a noncash expense and (2) was deducted to compute net earnings. **Deferred income taxes** is a liability; the related part of income tax expense is added to change net earnings to the cash basis because (1) it is a noncash expense and (2) was deducted to compute net earnings.

c. During 1982, **accounts receivable decreased** by $2,474, which increased cash inflow (compared to accrual revenue); therefore, that amount was added to net earnings to convert it to the cash basis. **Inventories increased** during 1982 by $1,582, which caused cash of this amount to be paid (when purchased or when the related accounts payable is paid); therefore, this amount must be deducted from net earnings to change it to the cash basis.

d. Net cash inflow from operations (i.e., the income statement) was $46,754.

e. Long-term debt of $2,500 was added because it is a source of cash borrowing. In contrast, long-term debt of $1,104 was deducted because this was the total payment on debts.

f. The accuracy of the SCFP can be proven by referring to the beginning and ending balances of the two "cash equivalent" accounts:

	Beginning balance	Ending balance	Net increase
Cash	$ *	$ *	$ *
Short-term marketable securities	$ *	$ *	$ *
Total	$15,505	$24,618	$9,113†

* Not given in case data.
† Check figure for the SCFP.

SUMMARY OF CHAPTER

The SCFP is a required statement. Its purpose is to provide financial statement users with information about the sources and uses of cash (or working capital) during the accounting period. This information is needed to help them project the future cash flows of the entity. To accomplish this purpose, the SCFP

EXHIBIT 15–9

SCFP, cash basis; T-account analysis

FINA COMPANY
T-Account Approach to Develop Sources and Use of Cash
Noncash Balance Sheet Accounts

Accounts Receivable (net)			Inventory			LT Investment— Stock X Corporation		
NC	5,000			NC	4,000		NC	5,000
(d)	5,000			(e)	4,000		(f-1)	5,000

Equipment (net)			Patent (net)			Accounts Payable		
	NC	1,000	NC	3,200			NC	2,000
(f-2)Pur. 5,000	(b)	6,000	(g) Pur. 3,400	(c) Amort. 200			(h)	2,000

Income Tax Payable			ST Note Payable (nontrade)			LT Note Payable		
NC	500		NC	4,000			NC	10,000
(i)	500		(j)	4,000			(k)	10,000

Bonds Payable			Common Stock, Par $10			Contributed Capital in Excess of Par		
NC	8,000			NC	10,000		NC	1,000
(l)	8,000			(m)	10,000		(m)	1,000

Treasury Stock (cost)			Retained earnings		
NC	3,000			NC	1,000
(n)	3,000		(o) Div. 7,000	(a) NI	8,000

NC = Net change from 19A to 19B.

EXHIBIT 15–9 *(concluded)*

SCFP, cash basis; T-account analysis

From Normal Operations			
Sources		**Uses**	
Income Plus Additions		*Income Reductions*	
(a) Net income	8,000	(d) Accounts receivable increase	5,000
(b) Depreciation expense	6,000	(i) Income tax payable decrease	500
(c) Amortization of patent	200		
(e) Inventory decrease	4,000		
(h) Accounts payable increase	2,000		

From Other			
Sources		**Uses**	
(f-1) Exchange of investment for equipment	5,000	(f-2) Exchange of investment for equipment	5,000
(k) LT note payable	10,000	(g) Purchased patent	3,400
(m) Sold and issued common stock	11,000	(j) ST note payable (nontrade)	4,000
		(l) Payment on bonds payable	8,000
		(n) Purchased treasury stock	3,000
		(o) Paid cash dividend	7,000
		Check: Change in Cash account ($41,300 − $31,000)	10,300
Totals	46,200		46,200

reports on the **liquidity** (i.e., cash availability) of the company. It reports the **causes** of the inflows and outflows of resources. The SCFP may be prepared using **either** (1) cash or (2) working capital as the measure of funds. When prepared on a cash basis, the sources and uses of funds are measured in terms of a specific asset, cash. When prepared on a working capital basis, the sources and uses of funds are measured in abstract terms because working capital is the difference between the total current assets and total current liabilities. Working capital cannot be counted, handled, and used like cash.

The main source of funds during the period is **normal operations** (i.e., from the revenues, less the expenses reported on the income statement). This source is determined by changing net income (accrual basis) to a cash basis amount. Other common sources of funds are borrowing, sale of operational assets, and the sale and issuance of capital stock. Common uses of funds are payments on debt, purchases of operational assets, long-term investments, and payments of cash dividends.

SUPPLEMENT 15A—T-ACCOUNT ANALYSIS
TO DEVELOP THE SCFP, CASH BASIS

The SCFP can be prepared by using (1) a direct analysis, (2) worksheet analysis, or (3) a T-account analysis. The T-account analysis is used for instructional purposes, while the worksheet analysis is used in practice and in cases that are complex and have extensive data. The direct and worksheet analyses were illustrated in the chapter.

This supplement presents a T-account analysis using the cash basis. The Fina Company case given in the chapter also is used in this supplement. The T-account analysis presented in this supplement parallels the worksheet analysis in all ways except format. Each account is analyzed in a Debits = Credits manner, and the **analytical entries are identical** to those used in the worksheet analysis. The worksheet has the advantage that the bottom portion may suffice for the formal SCFP in many problem and examination situations (see Exhibit 15–4).

The T-account analysis to develop the SCFP, cash basis, begins by setting up **separate T-accounts for each noncash** account reported on the comparative balance sheets and then entering in each account the net change (NC) in the account balance from the beginning and ending balance sheets (this is equivalent to Part A of the worksheet). Also, two T-accounts are set up to account for sources and uses of cash. These T-accounts are labeled "From normal operations" and "From other." In these two accounts, Debits = Sources and Credits = Uses (this is equivalent to Part B of the worksheet). Next, the **analytical entries** are entered in the T-accounts. These entries are **identical** to those that would be entered on the worksheet analysis (Exhibit 15–4). The T-account analysis is shown in Exhibit 15–9.

IMPORTANT TERMS DEFINED IN THIS CHAPTER

Terms (alphabetically)	Key words in definitions of important terms used in chapter	Page reference
All-resources concept	SCFP must report all sources and uses of funds; this includes direct nonfund exchanges (direct swaps).	762
Analytical entries, SCFP	Entries used on a SCFP worksheet to reconcile the nonfund accounts and to develop the SCFP.	768 & 774
Change statements	Statements that explain why balance sheet accounts change during a period; income statement and SCFP.	766
Direct exchanges, SCFP	Transactions that involve the exchange of only nonfund assets, liabilities, or capital stock; direct swaps.	762
Funds (resources)	For the SCFP it means either cash or working capital.	758
Investing activities	Transactions and activities that cause a decrease in funds during the period (uses of funds).	759
Liquidity	Cash availability; nearness of noncash assets to cash.	759
Noncash expenses	Expenses reported on the income statement that did not require cash payments during the period; depreciation.	764

Terms (alphabetically)	Key words in definitions of important terms used in chapter	Page reference
Noncash revenues	Revenues of a period reported on the income statement that did not cause funds to increase during that period.	765
SCFP, cash basis	SCFP that reports sources and uses of funds in terms of cash or cash equivalents.	758
SCFP, working capital basis	SCFP that reports sources and uses of funds in terms of working capital.	776
Sources of cash	Activities and transactions that cause a cash inflow into a company; from operations, borrowing, etc.	760
Sources of working capital	Transactions that cause working capital to increase; debits to working capital accounts.	777
T-account approach, SCFP	Used to develop the SCFP; an organized approach used for instructional purposes; uses T-accounts.	786
Uses of cash	Transactions that decrease cash; purchase of noncash assets; payment of debts, dividends, etc.	761
Uses of working capital	Transactions that decrease working capital; credits to working capital accounts.	778
Working capital	Current assets minus current liabilities; one way to measure funds on the SCFP.	776
Worksheet analysis, SCFP	Used to develop the SCFP; an organized and systematic approach; analyzes the nonfund accounts; used for either cash or working capital.	766 & 780

QUESTIONS

PART A

1. What are the financial statements that are required in the external financial report? What does each statement report?

2. What are the main sources and uses of funds in a business?

3. What is the basic difference between a SCFP prepared on a (a) cash basis and (b) working capital basis?

4. Company X acquired a tract of land in exchange for a $10,000 bond payable. How does this transaction relate to the SCFP all-resources concept?

5. What is a direct exchange? How does a direct exchange affect the SCFP?

6. Why is the SCFP called a change statement?

7. Define the following terms. Give two examples of each.
   a. Nonfund asset accounts.
   b. Nonfund liability accounts.

8. Why is income (i.e., from normal operations) often the primary source of funds in a business in the long term?

9. In developing "sources of funds, from operations (cash or working capital)," on the SCFP, explain why depreciation, amortization of intangible assets, and depletion are added back to net income.

10. Why is the SCFP, cash basis, relevant to external statement users?

11. Explain why the SCFP, cash basis, requires the conversion of net income to another amount.

12. You are completing a SCFP, cash basis, and have the data listed below. Complete the blanks to the right.

Income (accrual basis) $10,000
Increase in accounts receivable .... $1,400   _____
Depreciation expense 1,500   _____
Amortization of patent 200   _____
Decrease in merchandise inventory 2,200   _____
Decrease in accounts payable 1,000   _____
Net cash inflow from normal
   operations for the period .... $_____

13. You are preparing a SCFP, cash basis, and have the data listed below. Complete the blanks to the right.

Income (accrual basis) $20,000
Decrease in accounts receivable .... $2,000   _____
Decrease in accounts payable 3,000   _____
Depreciation expense 8,000   _____
Gain on sale of operational asset (cash
   sale price, $3,000; book value,
   $2,000) 1,000   _____
Net cash inflow from normal operations ...... $_____

14. Total sales revenue for 19B was $300,000, of which one third was on credit. The balances in accounts receivable at year's end were 19B, $15,000; and 19A, $23,000. The cash inflow from sales revenue during 19B was $_____.

15. Total expenses for 19B was $200,000, of which $10,000 was depreciation expense and $30,000 was on credit (accounts payable). The balances in accounts payable at year's end were 19A, $16,000; and 19B, $12,000. The cash outflow for expenses during 19B was $_____.

16. Company X is preparing the SCFP, cash basis, for 19B. During the year, the company acquired a tract of land and paid in full by issuing 1,000 shares of its own capital stock, par $10 per share (market value $15 per share). Show how this transaction should be reported on the SCFP. Explain. Would this transaction be reported in the same manner on the SCFP, working capital basis? Why?

PART B

17. Complete the following tabulation:

	Working capital	
Transactions	Source	Use
a. Collected an account receivable, $150	$_____	$_____
b. Sold land for $4,000, one half collected in cash and the balance on one-year note; gain; $500	_____	_____
c. Paid a bond payable, $1,000	_____	_____
d. Sold and issued common stock, $2,500 cash	_____	_____
e. Paid short-term note payable, $1,300	_____	_____

18. Complete the following tabulation:

Income, $32,000 (accrual basis) .... $ _____
Depreciation expense, $5,000 .... _____
Inventory increase, $10,000 (paid cash) .... _____
Working capital from normal operations .... _____

19. Company T reported working capital at year-end of 19A, $90,000; and 19B, $75,000. During 19B, the company (a) paid a $5,000 short-term note and (b) paid a $15,000 long-term note. Disregarding interest, how much did each of these transactions change working capital during 19B? Explain.

20. Company S bought a machine that cost $30,000; payment was made as follows: cash, $10,000; short-term payable, $4,000; and long-term note payable, $16,000. How much did working capital change? Explain.

21. What are the two basic parts of a SCFP, working capital basis? Why is the second part considered redundant by some people?

22. As a statement user interested in the statement of changes in financial position, would you prefer the (a) cash basis or (b) working capital basis? Explain.

EXERCISES

PART A

E15–1   (Pairing Definitions with Terminology)

Match the definitions or statements with the terms by entering the appropriate letters to the left.

Term	*Definition or statement*
__G__ (1) Working capital (example)	A. SCFP must report direct exchanges both as a source and use of cash.
____ (2) Financing activities	B. Revenues reported on the income statement that did not cause fund (cash) increases.
____ (3) Noncash expenses	
____ (4) Noncash revenues	C. Worksheet entries made to determine sources and uses of funds.
____ (5) Direct exchange	
____ (6) Liquidity	D. Statement of changes in financial position.
____ (7) All-resources concept	E. Cash availability; nearness to cash.
____ (8) SCFP, cash basis	F. Depreciation, depletion, and amortization.
____ (9) Analytical entries	G. Current assets minus current liabilities.
____ (10) Investing activities	H. Transactions that cause funds (cash or working capital) to increase.
____ (11) Funds	
____ (12) Increase (decrease) in funds during the period	I. A general term used to mean either cash or working capital.
	J. Transactions that cause a decrease in funds (cash or working capital).
____ (13) Cash from normal operations	K. Transactions that do not increase or decrease funds but must be reported on the SCFP as both a source and use of funds.
____ (14) SCFP	L. Total fund inflows minus total fund outflows.
	M. SCFP basis that is more useful in projecting future cash flows.
	N. Net income is converted to this item (cash basis).

E15–2   Below are a number of transactions of Rye Company during 19B. For each transaction, enter a letter to the right to indicate its SCFP effect on funds measured on the cash basis. Use S for source, U for use, and N for neither of these. Assume cash if not stated otherwise.

	Effect on funds measured on cash basis
Transactions	
a. Income (accrual basis)	_____
b. Write off of a bad debt (allowance method)	_____
c. Purchased an operational asset	_____
d. Depletion expense (on gravel pit)	_____
e. Declared a cash dividend (cash to be paid in the next year)	_____
f. Depreciation expense	_____
g. Collection on a long-term note	_____
h. Issued a stock dividend	_____
i. Sold a long-term investment	_____
j. Borrowed cash on a long-term note	_____
k. Sold an operational asset at a loss	_____
l. Amortization of discount on bonds payable	_____
m. Purchased treasury stock	_____
n. Payment on bonds payable	_____
o. A stock split	_____
p. Extraordinary gain	_____
q. Amortization of premium on bond investment	_____
r. Purchased a long-term investment	_____
s. Exchange of unissued stock for operational asset	_____
t. Exchange of land for equipment	_____
u. Sale of treasury stock	_____
v. Payment of debt by issuance of company shares	_____
w. Net loss	_____
x. Amortization of patent	_____
y. Bad debt expense recorded	_____
z. Declared and paid a property dividend	_____
zz. Paid the dividend declared in *(e)* above	_____

E15–3   (Compute Cash from Normal Operations; Use Direct Analysis)

The 19D income statement of Coffey Company is summarized below. Additional 19D data from the 19C and 19D balance sheets are as follows:

a. Decrease in accounts receivable (for services sold) during 19D, $14,000.

b. Bought a small service machine, $6,000 (cash).

c. Increase in salaries payable during 19D, $8,000.

d. Decrease in service revenue collected in advance during 19D, $5,000.

e. Decrease in income tax payable during 19D, $7,000.

Income Statement 19D

Items	Accrual Basis	Net Cash Inflow (Outflow) from Operations	
		Explanation	Amount
Service revenues	$ 60,000		
Expenses:			
Salaries	51,000		
Depreciation	11,000		
Depletion	200		
Utilities (cash)	4,000		
Remaining expenses (cash)	3,800		
Income tax	–0–		
Total expenses	70,000		
Net income (loss)	$(10,000)		

Required:

a. Complete the above income statement schedule to determine the "net cash inflow (outflow) from normal operations."

b. Because there is a net loss for 19D would you expect the net cash flow from normal operations to be negative (i.e., an outflow)? Explain.

c. Give proof of your answer to Requirement (a) by starting with the $10,000 loss and ending with your answer to Requirement (a).

E15–4   (Prepare SCFP, Cash Basis; Use Direct Analysis)

Davis Company has finished its income statement and comparative balance sheet at December 31, 19B. The following data are from those statements:

Net income	$32,000
Depreciation expense	5,000
Purchase of operational assets for cash	26,000
Sale of long-term investment (sold at book value for cash, $6,000)	6,000
Inventory increase during the period	3,000
Declared and paid cash dividends during 19B	9,000
Borrowed on short-term note	20,000
Accounts payable decrease	1,000
Payment of long-term note	30,000
Acquired land for future use; issued capital stock in payment (market value)	25,000

Required:

Prepare the SCFP, cash basis, properly classified. Use the direct analysis.

E15–5   (Prepare SCFP, Cash Basis; Use Direct Analysis)

Fisher Corporation has finished its 19A income statement and balance sheet. The SCFP, cash basis, must be prepared. The following 19A data have been extracted from the income statement, balance sheet, and other company records:

a. Depreciation expense, $9,000.

b. Bought treasury stock, $4,000 (cash).

c. Sold a long-term investment at book value, $6,000 (cash).

d. Declared and paid a $7,000 cash dividend during 19A.

e. Salaries recorded but unpaid on December 31, 19A, $1,000.

f. Income, accrual basis, $30,000 (from the 19A income statement).

g. Borrowed $10,000 on a one-year interest-bearing note (15% interest).

h. Service revenue recorded but uncollected on December 31, 19A, $3,000.

i. Sold 200 shares of its own common stock, par $1, for $5 per share (cash).

j. Paid a $16,000 note payable plus $800 interest.

k. Bought operational assets, $30,000 (cash).

Required:

a. Prepare the 19A SCFP, cash basis, for Fisher Corporation (use direct analysis).

b. Reconcile income (accrual basis) with the net increase (decrease) in cash during 19A. Use designations and amounts.

E15–6   **(Prepare a SCFP, Cash Basis Using Direct Analysis)**

The accounting department of Snow Company assembled the following unclassified SCFP data at December 31, 19B, end of the accounting period.

| | Cash* | |
Transactions	Sources	Uses
Net income (Revenues, $210,000 − Expenses, $170,000)	$40,000	
Depreciation expense	8,000	
Purchase of operational assets for cash		$45,000
Wages payable increase	6,000	
Inventory decrease	4,000	
Accounts payable decrease		9,000
Declared and paid a cash dividend on common stock during 19B		25,000
Amortization of patent	1,000	
Payment on short-term note payable (nontrade)		40,000
Sale of common stock for cash	20,000	
Sale of operational assets for cash (sold at book value, $9,000)	9,000	
Accounts receivable increase		7,000
Long-term borrowing during the period	50,000	
Purchase of long-term investment, stock of X Co. (paid cash)		20,000

* Including income additions and deductions.

Required:

a. Use the above data to prepare a SCFP, cash basis, properly classified. Use a direct analysis.

b. Answer the following questions:

(1) What adjustment item(s) are related to revenues, and what effect did the item(s) have on cash flow?

(2) What two adjustment items affected cost of goods sold (cash basis)? What cash flow effects did they have?

(3) What was the amount of the increase or decrease in cash as reported on the balance sheet?

(4) What was the effect of the increase in wages payable on cash flow for 19B?

(5) Would the declaration and issuance of a stock dividend be reported on the SCFP, cash basis? Explain.

E15–7 **(Reporting Direct Exchanges on the SCFP, Cash Basis)**

The SCFP must be based on the all-resources concept. During 19B, West Corporation finished the two transactions below.

1. West acquired a large machine that had a list price of $25,000. Since West was short of cash, it paid for the machine in full by giving a $10,000, 15%, interest-bearing note due at the end of two years, and 200 shares of its capital stock, par $50 (market value $60) per share.

2. West acquired a small machine (list price $9,995). Full payment was made by transferring a tract of land that had a market value of $9,500 (this was also its book value).

Required:

For each machine show what should be reported on the SCFP, cash basis, under (a) sources of cash and (b) uses of cash. Explain the basis for your responses.

E15–8 **(Compute Net Cash Flow from Normal Operations; Includes the Sale of a Noncash Asset at a Gain)**

Blue Company prepared the tabulation below at December 31, 19E. Give the correct amount for each blank. Use parentheses for deductions, and enter a zero if no conversion is needed.

Sources of cash	*SCFP, cash basis*
From normal operations:	
Net income (accrual basis)	$200,000
Add (deduct) to convert to cash basis:	
Depreciation expense, $25,000	_____
Increase in trade accounts receivable, $9,000	_____
Decrease in inventory, $12,000	_____
Amortization of patent, $2,000	_____
Decrease in rent revenue receivable, $1,000	_____
Increase in prepaid insurance, $3,000	_____
Decrease in trade accounts payable, $8,000	_____
Decrease in income tax payable, $4,000	_____
Gain on sale of operational asset $3,000	
(sold for cash, $9,000)	_____
Net cash inflow from normal operations .... $	_____

E15–9 **(Critique and Recast a Defective SCFP)**

The following actual statement was taken from the annual financial statements of Lazy Corporation:

LAZY CORPORATION
Funds Statement
Year, December 31, 19B

Funds generated:

Sales and service revenue	$85,000	
Depreciation	6,000	
Accounts receivable decrease	700	
Merchandise inventory decrease	3,000	
Borrowing (short-term note)	20,000	
Sale of unissued stock	15,000	
Total cash		$129,700

Funds applied:

Cost of sales	48,000	
Expenses (including depreciation and income tax)	20,000	
Accounts payable decrease	1,000	
Income tax payable decrease	300	
Payment on long-term mortgage	25,000	
Acquisition of operational asset	9,000	
Dividends (cash) declared and paid during 19B	7,000	
Total		110,300
Increase in funds		$ 19,400

Required:

a. Is this a cash basis or a working capital basis statement? Give the basis for your answer.

b. Did Lazy give enough attention to the communication of financial information to stockholders?

c. What was the amount of net income (or loss) reported for 19B?

d. Recast the above statement in good form (and preferred terminology).

e. Did operations generate more or less cash than net income? What caused the difference?

PART B

E15-10   (Comparison of Cash versus Working Capital from Normal Operations; Use a Direct Analysis)

Below is a tabulation that gives information about both cash and working capital for Ross Company.

Transactions	(a) Cash basis	(b) Working capital basis
Net income reported (accrual basis)	$17,000	$17,000
Depreciation expense, $2,700		
Increase in wages payable, $500		
Decrease in trade accounts receivable, $6,800		
Increase in merchandise inventory, $9,300		
Amortization of patents, $300		
Increase in bonds payable, $10,000		
Decrease in trade accounts payable, $7,400		
Sale of unissued common stock, $5,000		
Total cash generated from operations	$	
Total working capital generated from operations		$20,000

Required:

a. Give the correct amounts for each of the blanks in the above tabulation; if none, enter a zero.

b. Compare the total of cash with the total of working capital. Why are they different?

c. Which result do you think would be of most use to statement users? Why?

E15–11 **(Prepare SCFP, Working Capital Basis; Use a Direct Analysis)**

Busby Company finished the income statement and the comparative balance sheet at year-end, December 31, 19B. A statement of changes in financial position must be developed. The following data are available:

	Balances at Dec. 31	
	19A	*19B*
From balance sheet:		
Current assets:		
Cash	$ 8,000	$15,000
Accounts receivable (net)	17,000	12,000
Inventory	15,000	18,000
Current liabilities:		
Accounts payable	10,000	12,000
Notes payable, short term	18,000	13,000
From income statement:		
Net income		$20,000
Depreciation expense		6,000
From other records:		
Purchase of long-term investment		15,000
Payment of long-term note		5,000
Sale of unissued capital stock		10,000
Declaration and payment of cash dividend during 19B		8,000
Purchased land for future plant site, issued		
capital stock as payment in full		25,000

Required:

Prepare a SCFP, working capital basis. Use a direct analysis.

E15–12 **(Prepare a SCFP, Working Capital Basis; Use a Direct Analysis)**

Cullen Company has never prepared a SCFP. At the end of 19B, the company bookkeeper assembled the data given below (which is correct) to develop this statement:

	Balances at Dec. 31	
	19A	*19B*
From the balance sheet:		
Current assets:		
Cash	$ 15,000	$ 20,000
Accounts receivable (net)	24,000	17,000
Merchandise inventory	30,000	27,000
Current liabilities:		
Accounts payable	(19,000)	(15,000)
Notes payable, short term	(10,000)	(12,000)
Working capital	$ 40,000	$ 37,000

	Balances at Dec. 31
	19B
From the income statement and other sources:	
Net income	$ 21,000
Depreciation expense	4,500
Amortization of patent	500
Purchase of operational assets	(6,000)
Sale of operational assets (at book value) for cash	2,000
Payment of long-term note payable	(40,000)
Issuance of bonds payable for cash	30,000
Sale and issuance of common stock for cash	10,000
Declaration and payment of a cash dividend on common stock during 19B	(25,000)
Difference	$ (3,000)

Required:

Prepare a SCFP, working capital basis, for 19B. Use a direct analysis.

E15–13   (Prepare a Worksheet Analysis to Develop a SCFP, Working Capital Basis)

Lakeland Company is developing its annual financial statements at December 31, 19B. The income statement and balance sheet are finished, and the SCFP, working capital basis, is being developed. The income statement and comparative balance sheets are summarized below:

	19A	19B
Balance sheet at December 31:		
Cash	$12,800	$10,800
Accounts receivable (net)	9,000	10,500
Merchandise inventory	6,600	5,000
Operational assets (net)	40,000	43,000
Patent	3,000	2,700
	$71,400	$72,000
Accounts payable	$11,000	$ 9,000
Income tax payable	400	500
Notes payable, long term	10,000	5,000
Common stock (nopar)	42,000	45,000
Retained earnings	8,000	12,500
	$71,400	$72,000
Income statement for 19B:		
Sales revenue		$60,000
Cost of goods sold		35,000
Gross margin		25,000
Expenses (including depreciation, $4,000, and patent amortization, $300)		18,000
Net income		$ 7,000

Additional data for 19B:
Purchased operational assets for cash, $7,000.
Paid $5,000 on long-term note payable.
Sold and issued common stock for $3,000 cash.
Declared and paid a $2,500 cash dividend on capital stock during 19B.

Required:

a. Based upon the above data, prepare a worksheet analysis using the SCFP, working capital basis.

b. Prepare the formal SCFP, working capital basis.

PROBLEMS

PART A

P15–1 **(Distinguish between SCFP, Cash Basis and Working Capital Basis)**

Below is a list of 19B transactions that involve sources and uses of funds. Some of the transactions relate only to sources and uses of cash; others relate to sources and uses of working capital. Analyze each transaction and enter its 19B dollar effect in the spaces to the right. Assume cash transactions unless stated otherwise.

	Cash		Working capital	
Transactions during 19B	*Sources*	*Uses*	*Sources*	*Uses*
a. Sold a short-term investment for cash, $500.	$_____	$_____	$_____	$_____
b. Sold an operational asset and received a short-term note, $600.	_____	_____	_____	_____
c. Prepaid a one-year insurance premium, $200.	_____	_____	_____	_____
d. Purchased a small machine (an operational asset) and gave a short-term note, $150.	_____	_____	_____	_____
e. Sold a patent for $700 cash (book value, $500; gain, $200).	_____	_____	_____	_____
f. Purchased land, $9,900 cash.	_____	_____	_____	_____
g. Sold a long-term investment, $9,000; collected cash, $1,000, short-term note, $3,000, and long-term note, $5,000.	_____	_____	_____	_____
h. Purchased an operational asset, $9,000; paid cash, $4,000, short-term note, $3,000, and long-term note, $2,000.	_____	_____	_____	_____
i. Declared and paid a preferred stock cash dividend, $3,000 during 19B.	_____	_____	_____	_____
j. Declared a common stock cash dividend, $4,000 during 19B which is payable during 19C.	_____	_____	_____	_____

P15–2   **(Compute Cash from Normal Operations Using a Direct Analysis)**
The income statement of Josey Corporation is given below.

JOSEY CORPORATION
Income Statement for the Year Ended December 31, 19C
Accrual Basis

		Cash flow
Sales revenue (one third on credit; accounts receivable year's end—19A, $11,000; 19B, $15,000)	$300,000	$ _____
Cost of goods sold (one fourth on credit; accounts payable year's end—19A, $9,000; 19B, $8,000 (net); inventory at year's end—19A, $50,000; 19B, $45,000)	180,000	_____
Gross margin on sales	120,000	

Expenses:

Salaries and wages (including accrued wages payable at year's end—19A, $500; 19B, $300)	$44,000		
Depreciation expense	8,000		
Rent expense (no accruals)	6,000		_____
Bad debt expense	300		_____
Remaining expenses (no accruals)	11,700		_____
Income tax expense (income tax payable at year's end—19A, $2,000; 19B, $3,000)	10,000		_____
Total expenses		80,000	
Net income		$ 40,000	_____
Cash inflow from normal operations			$ _____

Proof of results:

Net income (accrual basis)	$40,000
Add (deduct) to convert to cash basis:	
_____	_____
_____	_____
_____	_____
_____	_____
_____	_____
_____	_____
_____	_____
_____	_____
Cash inflow from normal operations	$ _____

Note: This problem shows two different approaches to derive cash inflow from operations; the proof-of-results approach above is the one usually used because it is more direct.

Required:

a. Enter the correct cash amounts needed for cash from normal operations in the blanks provided. Use parentheses to show cash deductions, and enter a zero for no change (use direct analysis).

b. Prove your answer to Requirement (a) by starting with net income (accrual basis).

P15-3   **(Critique and Restate a Defective SCFP; Direct Analysis)**

The following statement has just been prepared by Cheep Corporation:

CHEEP CORPORATION
Funds Flow Statement
Year, December 31, 19E

Funds earned:

Sales and other incomes	$ 95,000
Accounts receivable decrease	3,200
Expenses (including depreciation and income tax)	(70,000)
Depreciation	3,000
Inventory increase	(4,000)
Accounts payable increase	1,000
Prepaid insurance increase	(100)
Income tax payable decrease	(200)
Common stock	6,000
Total funds earned	$ 33,900

Funds spent:

Equipment	(8,000)
Bonds payable	(30,000)
Dividends declared and paid	(2,900)
Total funds spent	$ 40,900

Required:

a. Is the above statement based on a working capital or on a cash basis? How did you determine the basis on which the statement was prepared?

b. List the format and terminology deficiencies on the statement.

c. Recast the above statement using preferred format and terminology.

P15-4   **(Analyze and Recast a Deficient SCFP; Includes a Direct Exchange; Direct Analysis)**

The following statement was prepared by Old Corporation:

OLD CORPORATION
Funds Statement
December 31, 19X

Where got:

Revenues		$ 180,000
Accounts receivable decrease		15,000
Expenses (including depreciation and income tax)		(160,000)
Depreciation		14,000
Inventory increase		(6,000)
Accounts payable increase		7,000
Income tax payable decrease		(3,000)
Total		$ 47,000
Sale of permanent assets (at book value)		17,000
Issuance of common stock for land		25,000
Borrowing—short-term note		40,000
Total cash received		$129,000

Where gone:

Dividends	20,000	
Payment on long-term mortgage	80,000	
Machinery	15,000	
Land (5,000 shares of stock)	25,000	
Funds (decrease)	(11,000)	
Total		$129,000

Required:

a. Is this a cash basis or a working capital basis statement? Explain the basis for your answer.

b. What was the amount of net income reported for 19X?

c. Did cash increase or decrease? Explain. How can this amount be verified independent of the SCFP?

d. Did the company give enough attention to communication of financial information to the stockholders? Explain the basis for your response.

e. Recast the above statement using preferred format and terminology.

f. What was the amount of the difference between net income and cash generated from normal operations? Why were they different?

g. Do you suspect any potential problems for this company? Explain the basis for your response.

P15–5   **(Complete a Worksheet Analysis to Prepare a SCFP, Cash Basis)**
Mason Company is developing the annual financial statements at December 31, 19B. The statements are complete except for the SCFP, cash basis. The completed comparative balance sheets and income statement are summarized below:

	19A	19B
Balance sheet at December 31:		
Cash	$ 20,000	$ 31,500
Accounts receivable (net)	26,000	25,000
Merchandise inventory	40,000	38,000
Operational assets (net)	64,000	67,000
	$150,000	$ 161,500
Accounts payable	$ 24,000	$ 27,000
Wages payable	500	400
Notes payable, long term	35,000	30,000
Common stock, nopar	70,000	80,000
Retained earnings	20,500	24,100
	$150,000	$ 161,500
Income statement for 19B:		
Sales		$ 90,000
Cost of goods sold		(52,000)
Expenses (including depreciation expense, $4,000)		(32,000)
Net income		$ 6,000

Required:

a. Set up a worksheet analysis to develop the SCFP, cash basis. Analytical entries should be made for the following:

   a. Net income—from income statement.

   b. Depreciation expense—from income statement.

   c. Bought operational assets for cash, $7,000.

   d. Paid $5,000 on the long-term note payable.

   e. Sold unissued common stock for $10,000 cash.

   f. Declared and paid a $2,400 cash dividend.

   g. Accounts receivable decrease—from balance sheets.

   h. Merchandise inventory decrease—from balance sheets.

i. Accounts payable increase—from balance sheets.

j. Wages payable decrease—from balance sheets.

b. Based upon the analysis completed in Requirement *(a)*, prepare the formal SCFP, cash basis.

P15–6 **(Complete a Worksheet Analysis to Prepare a SCFP, Cash Basis; Includes a Direct Exchange)**

Hamilton Company is developing the 19B annual report. A SCFP, cash basis, is being developed. The following worksheet has been set up to develop the statement:

Hamilton Company
Worksheet Analysis to Develop Statement of Changes in Financial Position, Cash Basis
For the Year Ended December 31, 19B

Items	Ending Balance, Dec. 31, 19A	Analysis of Interim Entries		Ending Balances, Dec. 31, 19B
		Debit	Credit	
Debits				
Cash account	24,000			32,200
Noncash accounts:				
Accounts receivable (net)	26,000			30,000
Inventory	30,000			28,000
Prepaid insurance	1,200			800
Investments, long term	10,800			8,000
Operational assets (net)	30,000			39,000
Patent (net)	3,000			2,700
	125,000			140,700
Credits				
Accounts payable	21,000			18,000
Wages payable	3,000			2,000
Income tax payable	1,000			1,200
Note payable, long term	25,000			20,000
Common stock, par $10	60,000			70,000
Contributed capital in excess of par	1,000			3,000
Retained earnings	14,000			26,500
	125,000			140,700
Sources of cash:				
Uses of cash:				
Change in cash				

Additional data for 19B:

a. Revenues, $120,000; expenses, $100,000; and net income, $20,000.

b. Depreciation expense, $3,000.

c. Amortization of patent, $300.

d. Sale of long-term investment, $2,800 cash, which was equal to its book value.

e. Purchased operational assets and issued 1,000 shares of its common stock as full payment (market value, $12 per share).

f. Declared and paid cash dividend, $7,500.

g. Increase in accounts receivable balance during the period.

h. Decrease in inventory during the period.

i. Decrease in prepaid insurance balance during the period.

j. Decrease in accounts payable balance during the period.

k. Decrease in wages payable balance during the period.

l. Increase in income tax payable balance during the period.

Required:

Complete the above worksheet on a cash basis. Also, show on the worksheet "Net cash inflow from normal operations."

P15–7   **(Complete a Worksheet Analysis to Prepare a SCFP, Cash Basis; Includes a Direct Exchange and Gain on Disposal)**

Texmo Company is preparing its 19B financial statements, which include the following information:

	Comparative	
	19A	*19B*
Balance sheet:		
Cash	$ 40,000	$ 52,000
Inventory	30,000	37,000
Accounts receivable (net)	20,000	17,000
Long-term investment, stock Co. A	10,000	3,000
Machinery and equipment (net)	80,000	75,000
	$180,000	$ 184,000
Accounts payable	$ 15,000	$ 11,000
Income tax payable	4,000	6,000
Note payable, long term	20,000	10,000
Bonds payable	30,000	10,000
Common stock, par $10	100,000	110,000
Contributed capital in excess of par	8,000	11,000
Retained earnings	3,000	26,000
	$180,000	$ 184,000
Income statement:		
Revenue		$ 140,000
Cost of goods sold		(65,000)
Depreciation expense		(8,000)
Patent expense (cash for royalty paid)		(600)
Remaining operating expenses		(28,400)
Income tax expense		(9,000)
Gain on disposal of machine (net of tax)		1,000
Net income		$ 30,000

Additional data for 19B:

1. Machinery that had a book value of $10,000 was sold for $11,000 cash.

2. Long-term investment (shares of Company A stock) was sold for $7,000 cash, which had a carrying value of $7,000.

3. Equipment was acquired, and payment in full was made by issuing 1,000 shares of capital stock that had a market value of $13 per share.

4. Payments on debt: long-term note, $10,000; bonds payable, $20,000.
5. Declared and paid a cash dividend, $7,000.

Required:

a. Prepare either a worksheet analysis or a T-account analysis to develop a SCFP, cash basis.
b. Prepare the formal SCFP, cash basis.

PART B

P15–8   **(Emphasizes Working Capital Effects—Schedule 1; and Differences between SCFP, Cash versus Working Capital—Schedule 2)**

Schedule 1—effect on working capital of increases and decreases of the components of working capital. Provide the missing amounts.

Current (Working Capital) Accounts	December 31		Working Capital
	19B	19A	Increase (Decrease)
1. Cash	$?	$30,000	$(29,000)
2. Short-term investment in securities	5,000	20,000	?
3. Accounts receivable (net)	70,000	?	30,000
4. Inventory	95,000	70,000	?
5. Prepaid expense (e.g., insurance)	?	2,000	1,000
6. Accounts payable	74,000	?	(4,000)
7. Income tax payable	4,000	6,000	?
8. Revenue collected in advance (unearned)	?	1,000	(1,000)
9. Product warranty liability (estimated)	3,000	4,000	?
10. Working capital	?	?	10,000

Schedule 2—differences between the SCFP, cash basis, versus the SCFP, working capital basis. Give the correct dollar amounts in the blank spaces to the right on the following schedule of SCFP sources and uses. Assume cash transactions unless otherwise stated.

Transaction	Cash Basis		Working Capital Basis	
	Sources	Uses	Sources	Uses
1. Sold and issued capital stock, $5,000 cash.	$	$	$	$
2. Declared and paid a cash dividend, $3,000.				
3. Sold a short-term investment, $2,000 cash.				
4. Borrowed on a long-term note, $8,000.				
5. Sold an operational asset, $7,500 cash.				
6. Purchased an operational asset; gave a one-year interest-bearing note, $6,000.				
7. Declared a cash dividend (payable next year), $1,500.				
8. Paid a short-term note, $2,500.				
9. Collected a short-term note, $1,800.				
10. Collected a long-term note, $7,000.				
11. An operational asset was sold at a gain on disposal of $500; it originally cost $10,000 and was 75% depreciated (straight line). Cash was collected for the sale price.				
12. Sales revenue during 19B amounted to $100,000; the balances in Accounts Receivable at year's end were 19A, $20,000; and 19B, $14,000.				
13. Sold and issued 1,000 shares of common stock, par $10; credited Contributed Capital in Excess of Par in the amount of $5,500. Cash was collected for half of the issue price and the balance is due at the end of one year.				

P15–9   **(Analysis, Interpretation, and Recasting of a Deficient SCFP, Working Capital Basis)**
The following "Funds Statement" was taken from the annual financial statements of Fisher Corporation:

FISHER CORPORATION
Funds Statement
December 31, 19B

Funds generated:

Net profit (plus $10,000 depreciation)	$18,000
Common stock	9,000
Long-term debt	10,000
Total	$37,000

Funds applied:

Equipment	$15,000
Dividend	8,000
Debt	12,000
Change	2,000
Total	$37,000

Working capital:

	19B	Change
Cash	$ 3,200	$ 6,500
Receivables	7,500	5,000*
Inventory	30,000	13,500*
Payables (trade)	(4,800)	2,500*
Notes	(12,000)	7,500*
Total	$ 23,900	$ 2,000*

* Increase.

Required:

a. What was the 19B income?

b. Is this a working capital or cash basis statement? Explain the basis for your response.

c. Did working capital increase or did it decrease? By how much?

d. Did "operations" generate more or less working capital than income? Explain why.

e. Why is the amount of the change in working capital different than income.

f. Assess the soundness of the cash dividend.

g. Can you spot any potential problems for Fisher Corporation? Explain.

h. Did Fisher Corporation give enough attention to communication of financial information to stockholders? Explain the basis for your response.

i. Was the dividend paid or only declared? Explain.

j. Compare and explain the amounts of change in working capital versus cash.

k. Was the equipment purchased on credit? Explain.

l. Recast the above statement in good form consistent with your comments in Requirement *(h).*

P15–10   **(Interpret and Recast a Deficient SCFP, Working Capital Basis; Includes a Direct Exchange)**

The following actual SCFP was extracted from the published annual financial statements of Laird Corporation:

LAIRD CORPORATION
Statement of Working Capital
December 31, 19B

Working capital provided:

Net income	$14,000	
Add: Depreciation	15,000	
Patent amortization	1,000	
Total	30,000	
Bonds	50,000	
Common stock (for equipment)	15,000	
Total working capital provided		$95,000

Working capital applied:

Mortgage	60,000	
Equipment	15,000	
Dividends	10,000	
Total working capital applied		85,000
Working capital increase		$10,000

Working capital changes:

	19B	Change
Cash	$ 7,400	$(12,400)
Accounts receivable	9,000	6,000
Inventory	24,900	19,900
Accounts payable	(7,000)	(4,000)
Other short-term debt	(1,400)	500
Total	$ 32,900	$ 10,000

Required:

a. Compare and explain the significance of the change in cash with the change in working capital.

b. Why is the amount of the change in working capital different from the amount of net income?

c. What were the largest source and use of working capital?

d. Is the working capital position sound? Explain.

e. Compare the cash position with the working capital position.

f. List all of the communication weaknesses in the above format.

g. Recast the above statement to correct it for the weaknesses you listed in Requirement (f).

P15-11 **(Prepare a Worksheet Analysis to Develop a SCFP, Working Capital Basis; Includes a Direct Exchange)**

All-Steel Company is preparing the annual financial statements, including a SCFP, working capital basis, at December 31, 19B. The 19B comparative balance sheet and the income statement and some additional data are summarized below:

	19B	19A
Balance sheet at December 31:		
Cash	$ 21,500	$ 15,000
Accounts receivable (net)	23,000	20,000
Merchandise inventory	27,000	22,000
Prepaid insurance	300	600
Investments, long term (S Corp. stock)	12,000	
Operational assets (net)	220,000	134,000
Patent (net)	16,000	
	$319,800	$191,600
Accounts payable	$ 18,000	$ 12,000
Note payable, short term (nontrade)	10,000	18,000
Wages payable	800	1,000
Income tax payable	1,000	600
Note payable, long term	10,000	30,000
Bonds payable	100,000	
Common stock, par $10	140,000	100,000
Contributed capital in excess of par	6,000	5,000
Retained earnings	34,000	25,000
	$319,800	$191,600
Income statement for 19B:		
Sales revenue		$200,000
Cost of goods sold		126,000
Gross margin on sales		74,000
Expenses (not detailed)	$39,000	
Depreciation expense	14,000	
Amortization of patent	1,000	
Income tax expense	7,000	61,000
Net income		$ 13,000

Additional data for 19B:

1. Bought patent on January 1, 19B, for $17,000 cash.
2. Bought stock of S Corporation as a long-term investment for $12,000 cash.
3. Paid $20,000 on the long-term note payable.
4. Sold and issued 4,000 shares of common stock for $41,000 cash.
5. Declared and paid a $4,000 cash dividend.
6. Acquired a building (an operational asset) and paid in full for it by issuing $100,000 bonds payable at par to the former owner—date of transaction was December 30, 19B.

Required:

a. Based upon the above data, prepare a worksheet analysis to develop the SCFP, working capital basis.

b. Based upon the completed worksheet, prepare a formal SCFP, working capital basis.

P15–12 **(Prepare a Worksheet Analysis to Develop a SCFP, Working Capital Basis; Includes a Loss on Sale of a Noncash Asset and a Direct Exchange)**

Riverside Company is preparing its 19B financial statements. The following information is given by the completed 19B comparative balance sheet and income statement:

	19A	19B
Balance sheet:		
Cash	$ 10,000	$ 2,000
Accounts receivable (net)	16,600	21,000
Inventory	17,000	25,000
Prepaid expenses	1,400	400
Operational assets (net)	59,000	68,000
Plant site		20,000
Long-term investment	16,000	7,000
	$120,000	$ 143,400
Accounts payable	$ 8,000	$ 12,000
Wages payable	1,000	1,500
ST note payable (interest, December 31)	6,000	3,000
LT note payable (interest, December 31)	10,000	4,000
Bonds payable (interest, December 31)	30,000	50,000
Common stock, par $10	60,000	60,500
Contributed capital in excess of par	3,000	3,400
Retained earnings	2,000	9,000
	$120,000	$ 143,400
Income statement:		
Revenues		$ 135,000
Depreciation expense		(15,000)
Remaining expenses		(95,000)
Loss on sale of long-term investment		(3,000)
Net income		$ 22,000

Additional data:

1. Purchased operational asset for cash, $24,000.
2. Sold long-term investment for $6,000 cash; carrying value, $9,000.
3. Sold 50 shares of common stock at $18 cash per share.
4. Declared and paid a cash dividend of $15,000.
5. Payment on short-term note, $3,000.
6. Payment on long-term note, $6,000.
7. Acquired plant site and issued bonds, $20,000, for full purchase price (the bonds were selling at par).

Required:

a. Prepare a worksheet analysis to develop a SCFP, working capital basis.
b. Prepare the formal SCFP, working capital basis.

CASES

C15–1 **(Analysis of the SCFP Effect of Different Amounts of Depreciation and the Disposal of an Operational Asset)**

Problem A—Ransom Company (a sole proprietorship) reported net income of $100,000. To compute cash from normal operations, the corporation added the recorded depreciation expense ($20,000, on the straight-line basis) to net income getting a cash basis amount of $120,000 because "depreciation is one of the largest sources of cash in our company." The company could have used accelerated depreciation instead of straight-line depreciation and reported $30,000 depreciation expense. Would this change increase the cash inflow (there would be no income tax considerations)? Explain and illustrate your response.

Problem B—Ransom Company sold an old machine (an operational asset) for $28,000 cash. At date of sale the accounting records showed the following:

Machine No. 12 (cost) $30,000
Accumulated depreciation (Machine No. 12) 10,000

At year-end the income statement (summarized) reported the following:

Revenues (all cash) .... $ 900,000
Expenses (all cash except depreciation expense
  of $60,000) .... (796,000)
Gain on sale of operational asset 8,000
Net income .... $ 112,000

Explain and illustrate how the disposal (sale) of the machine and depreciation expense should be shown on the SCFP, cash basis.

C15–2   **(Explanation and Interpretation of a SCFP, Cash Basis)**

The following statement has been prepared by Young Corporation:

YOUNG CORPORATION
Statement of Changes in Financial Position, Cash Basis
For the Year Ended December 31, 19B

Sources of cash:
From normal operations:
  Net loss .... $(10,000)
  Add (deduct) adjustments to convert to cash basis:
    Accounts receivable decrease 2,000
    Depreciation expense 3,000
    Amortization expense 300
    Inventory increase .... (1,500)
    Accounts payable decrease .... (1,000)
    Prepaid insurance decrease 200
      Cash generated from (used in) operations ... $ (7,000)
From other sources:
  Sale of capital stock 10,000
  Long-term note payable 30,000
  Land (exchanged for machinery) 7,000
  Cash from other sources 47,000
    Total cash generated during the period 40,000

Uses of cash:
Machinery (acquired in exchange for land) 7,000
Payment on mortgage 6,000
Cash dividends declared and paid 12,000
  Total cash expended during the period 25,000
Net increase in cash during the period .... $ 15,000

Required:

a. Why was the net loss $3,000 more than the cash "used" in operations?

b. How did the company show a net increase in cash of $25,000 more than the net loss?

c. Explain the land transaction. Why is it reported under two different captions on the above SCFP?

d. Why is the decrease in accounts receivable "added" as an adjustment to the net loss?

e. Why are both the inventory increase and the accounts payable decrease "deducted" as an adjustment to the net loss?

f. How can the amount "Net increase in cash during the period, $15,000" be proven independent of the SCFP computations?

C15–3   (Interpretation of a SCFP, Working Capital Basis)

The following statement has just been prepared by Slow Company:

SLOW COMPANY
Statement of Changes in Financial Position, Working Capital Basis
For the Year Ended December 31, 19B

Sources of working capital:

From operations:

Net income		$ 2,000
Add expenses not requiring working capital:		
Depreciation expense	4,000	
Patent amortization expense	1,000	
Total working capital generated by operations		$ 7,000
From other sources:		
Sale of unissued common stock	10,000	
Long-term loan	33,000	
Sale of land (at cost)	5,000	
Total working capital from other sources		48,000
Total working capital generated during the period		55,000

Uses of working capital:

Acquisition of machinery	22,000	
Payment of mortgage	20,000	
Cash dividend declared and paid	12,000	
Total working capital applied during the period		54,000
Net increase in working capital during the period		**$ 1,000**

Changes in working capital accounts:

	Balances at December 31		Working capital increase (decrease)
	19B	*19A*	
Current assets:			
Cash	$ 1,000	$ 9,000	$ (8,000)
Accounts receivable	31,000	24,000	7,000
Inventory	38,000	21,000	17,000
Total current assets	70,000	54,000	
Current liabilities:			
Accounts payable	18,000	15,000	(3,000)
Short-term notes payable	22,000	10,000	(12,000)
Total current liabilities	40,000	25,000	
Working capital	$30,000	$29,000	$ 1,000

Required:

a. Was there an increase or decrease in working capital? How much? What were the primary source and the major use of working capital?

    b. How was working capital of $55,000 generated when income was only $2,000?

    c. Explain the fact that while working capital increased $1,000, cash decreased $8,000.

    d. How much cash was generated, and how much was used? How much cash was generated by normal operations?

    e. What current asset increased the most? What current liability increased the most? How were these two changes related to cash?

    f. Assess the soundness of the cash dividend.

    g. Can you identify a potential problem about liabilities? Explain.

    h. Evaluate the cash and working capital positions at the end of 19B.

C15–4   **(Analysis of the SCFP Reported in an Actual Set of Financial Statements)**

Refer to the financial statements of Chesebrough-Pond's given in Special Supplement B immediately preceding the Index. Answer the following questions for the 1985 annual accounting period.

    1. What title and date caption did the company use on the SCFP?

    2. What definition of "cash" did the company use on the SCFP? Explain.

    3. What is the title and amount reported on the last line of the SCFP. Give your interpretation of this line. Verify whether or not this amount is correct.

    4. Use subtotals to show how the $30,602 decrease was computed on the SCFP. Any comments?

Many financial analysts use ratios to help evaluate companies. Some financial statements include the calculation of selected ratios.

 # DAYTON HUDSON CORPORATION

Return on Investment
Achieving our performance objectives depends largely upon our ability to produce a superior return on investment (ROI). We believe that ROI is the most important single measure of financial performance. ROI is the primary financial tool we use to manage our business.
    We define ROI as our after-tax return before borrowing costs on unleveraged investment.

$$\text{ROI} = \frac{\text{Sales}}{\text{Investment}} \times \frac{\text{Earnings}}{\text{Sales}}$$

	ROI =	Investment Turnover ×	Return on Sales
1984	12.1% =	2.85 ×	4.23%
1983	13.0% =	2.88 ×	4.52%

The following table shows the calculation for ROI for 1983 and 1984.

(Millions of Dollars)	1984	1983
Net earnings	$ 259.3	$ 245.5
Interest expense—after tax(a)	49.7	41.6
Interest equivalent in leases—after tax(b)	22.6	20.6
Earnings before financing costs	$ 331.6	$ 307.7
Working capital(c)	$ 877.2	$ 728.2
Net property & equipment	1,370.6	1,199.2
Capital leases	115.8	97.9
Other non-current assets	14.7	12.4
Present value of operating leases	373.0	323.5
Total investment at beginning of year	$2,751.3	$2,361.2
Return on investment	12.1%	13.0%

USING AND INTERPRETING FINANCIAL STATEMENTS

PURPOSE:

Throughout the preceding chapters, we emphasized the conceptual basis of accounting. An understanding of the rationale underlying accounting is important for both preparers and users of financial statements. In this chapter we introduce the use and analysis of financial statements. Many widely used analytical techniques are discussed and illustrated. As you study this chapter, you will see that an understanding of accounting rules and concepts is essential for effective analysis of financial statements.

ORGANIZATION:

1. Financial reports in the decision-making process.
2. Ratio and percentage analysis.
3. Widely used ratios.
4. Interpreting ratios.
5. Impact of accounting alternatives on ratio analysis.

LEARNING OBJECTIVES—TO BE ABLE TO:

1. Identify the major users of financial statements and explain how they use statements.
2. Explain the objectives of ratio analysis.
3. Identify and compute 13 widely used accounting ratios.
4. Interpret accounting ratios.
5. Describe how accounting alternatives affect ratio analysis.
6. Expand your accounting vocabulary by learning about the "Important Terms Defined in This Chapter" (page 838).
7. Apply the knowledge learned from this chapter by completing the homework assigned by your instructor.

FINANCIAL REPORTS IN THE DECISION-MAKING PROCESS

The objective of financial statements is to provide information that helps users make better economic decisions. There are two broad groups of decision makers who use financial statements. One group is the management of the business who rely on accounting data to make important management decisions. The second group is "external" decision makers. This group consists primarily of investors (both present and potential owners), investment analysts, creditors, government, labor organizations, and the public. Financial accounting and the external financial reports serve a diverse group of decision makers with different information needs.

Users of financial statements are interested in three types of information:

1. **Information about past performance**—Information concerning such items as income, sales volume, extraordinary items, cash flows, and return earned on the investment helps assess the success of the business and the effectiveness of the management. Such information also helps the decision maker compare one entity with others.
2. **Information about the present condition of a business**—This type of information helps answer such questions as: What types of assets are owned? How much debt does the business owe, and when is it due? What is the cash position? How much of the earnings have been retained in the business? What are the EPS, return-on-investment, and debt/equity ratios? What is the inventory position? Answers to these and similar economic questions help the decision maker assess the successes and failures of the past; but, more importantly, they provide useful information in assessing the cash flow and profit potentials of the business.
3. **Information about the future performance of the business**—Decision makers select from among several alternative courses of action. Each course of action will cause different results. All decisions are future oriented because they do not (and cannot) affect the past. However, in predicting the probable future impact of a decision, reliable measurements of what has happened in the recent past are valuable. For example, the recent sales and earnings trends of a business are good indicators of what might be expected in the future. The primary objective of measuring past performance and the present condition of a business is to aid in predicting the future cash flows of the business.

Some decisions are made intuitively and without much supporting data. In such cases there is no systematic attempt to collect relevant data. Therefore, it is practically impossible to array, measure, and evaluate each alternative. Intuitive decision making is used for several reasons. The time and cost of collecting data may prevent a careful analysis. Sometimes the decision maker is unsophisticated and may not understand more systematic approaches to decision making. Unsophisticated decision makers tend to oversimplify the decision-making process, disregard basic information, and often overlook the financial effects of a decision.

In contrast, sophisticated decision makers prepare a systematic analysis of each alternative. Information regarding each alternative is collected and evaluated. For most business decisions, the financial statements provide critical financial data for effective decision makers.

Financial statement users should understand what was measured and how it was measured. Even if you do not plan to major in accounting, you will use extensively the information that you have studied in this book to evaluate the data presented in the financial reports of a business. One of the objectives of the preceding chapters was to help you understand and evaluate financial statements as a decision maker.

Financial statements are general-purpose statements that are designed primarily to meet the special needs of external decision makers. Because of the varied needs of these users, supplementary financial data may be needed for many decisions.

INVESTORS

The investor group includes current owners, potential owners, and investment analysts (because they advise investors). Investors include individuals, mutual funds, other businesses, and institutions, such as your college or university.

Most investors do not seek a controlling interest when they buy stock. Instead, they invest with the expectation of earning a return on their investment. The return on a stock investment has two components: (1) dividend revenue during the investment period and (2) increases in the market value of the shares owned. When considering an investment of this type, the investor has the problem of predicting the future **income** and **growth** of the business. Investors are interested in enterprise income because it is the "source" of future dividends. They are interested in enterprise growth because it tends to cause the market value of the shares to increase. In making these predictions, the investor should consider three factors:

1. **Economy-wide factors**—Often the overall health of the economy will have a direct impact on the performance of an individual business. Investors should consider such data as the gross national product, productivity, unemployment rate, general inflation rate, and changes in interest rates.
2. **Industry factors**—Certain events have a major impact on each company within an industry but have only a minor impact on other companies. For example, changes in the cost of oil products have a significant effect on the airline industry but only a minor effect on the electronics industry.
3. **Individual company factors**—These factors may be either quantifiable or nonquantifiable. Nonquantifiable factors include the introduction of a new product, a lawsuit, and changes in key personnel. Information concerning nonquantifiable factors often is presented in notes to the financial statements. Data pertaining to quantifiable factors are presented in the basic

__EXHIBIT 16–1__

Illustration of comparative financial statements

PACKARD COMPANY
Comparative Income Statements (simplified for illustration)
For the Years Ended December 31, 19B, and 19A

	Year ended Dec. 31		Increase (decrease) 19B over 19A	
	19B	19A*	Amount	Percent
Sales revenue	$120,000	$100,000	$20,000	20.0
Cost of goods sold	72,600	60,000	12,600	21.0
Gross margin on sales	47,400	40,000	7,400	18.5
Operating expenses:				
Distribution expenses	22,630	15,000	7,630	50.9
Administrative expenses	11,870	13,300	(1,430)	(10.8)
Interest expense	1,500	1,700	(200)	(11.8)
Total expenses	36,000	30,000	6,000	20.0
Pretax income	11,400	10,000	1,400	14.0
Income taxes	2,600	2,000	600	30.0
Net income	$ 8,800	$ 8,000	$ 800	10.0

* Base year for computing percents.

financial statements. The income statement provides significant information for the investor, such as revenue from products and services, extraordinary items, income tax impacts, net income, and earnings per share. Other relationships, such as gross margin, profit margin, and expense relationships, can be computed. Also, the balance sheet, the statement of changes in financial position, and the notes to the financial statements provide measurements of past profit performance, cash flow, and current financial position. These data constitute an important base from which predictions of future income and growth can be made. These data are particularly useful when compared with recent past periods as shown in Exhibit 16–1.

CREDITORS

Suppliers, financial institutions, and individuals provide long-term and short-term credit to businesses. Creditors lend money with the expectation that they will earn a return on their money and that funds will be repaid in accordance with the loan agreement. Creditors are concerned about the following:

EXHIBIT 16–1 *(concluded)*

Illustration of comparative financial statements

PACKARD COMPANY
Comparative Balance Sheets (simplified for illustration)
At December 31, 19B, and 19A

	At December 31		Increase (decrease) 19B over 19A	
	19B	19A*	Amount	Percent
Assets				
Current assets:				
Cash	$ 13,000	$ 9,000	$ 4,000	44.4
Accounts receivable (net)	8,400	7,000	1,400	20.0
Merchandise inventory	54,000	60,000	(6,000)	(10.0)
Prepaid expenses	2,000	4,000	(2,000)	(50.0)
Total current assets	77,400	80,000	(2,600)	3.3
Investments:				
Real estate	8,000	8,000		
Operational assets:				
Equipment and furniture	82,500	75,000	7,500	10.0
Less accumulated depreciation	(23,250)	(15,000)	8,250	55.0
Total operational assets	59,250	60,000	(750)	(1.3)
Other assets	1,900	2,000	(100)	(5.0)
Total assets	$146,550	$150,000	$(3,450)	(2.3)
Liabilities				
Current liabilities:				
Accounts payable	$ 13,200	$ 12,000	$ 1,200	10.0
Notes payable, short term	15,000	20,000	(5,000)	(25.0)
Accrued wages payable	7,200	8,000	(800)	(10.0)
Total current liabilities	35,400	40,000	(4,600)	(11.5)
Long-term liabilities:				
Notes payable, long term	7,150	10,000	(2,850)	(28.5)
Total liabilities	42,550	50,000	(7,450)	(14.9)
Stockholders' Equity				
Common stock, par $10	85,000	85,000		
Retained earnings	19,000	15,000	4,000	26.7
Total stockholders' equity	104,000	100,000	4,000	4.0
Total liabilities and stockholders' equity	$146,550	$150,000	$(3,450)	(2.3)

* Base year for computing percents.

1. Profit potential of the business because a profitable entity is more likely to meet its credit obligations.
2. Ability of the business to generate cash from recurring operations because it will be in a more favorable position to pay its debts.
3. Financial position of the business because the assets are security for the debts and the debts indicate the future demand for cash at debt maturity dates.

Creditors use the financial reports for information concerning the business. To enhance the credibility of these reports, creditors often require that the reports be audited by an independent CPA.

ANALYSIS OF FINANCIAL STATEMENTS

Financial statements include a large volume of quantitative data supplemented by disclosure notes. The notes are an integral part of the financial statements and help users interpret the statements. Notes elaborate on accounting policies, major financial effects and events, and certain nonquantifiable events that may contribute to the success or failure of the firm. The notes often include supplemental schedules, such as listings of assets by geographic region or lines of business. The statements also include a letter from the chief executive officer that contains a management discussion and analysis of the operations of the company.

Four techniques are used to help decision makers understand and interpret the external financial statements: (1) comparative financial statements, (2) long-term summaries, (3) graphic presentations, and (4) ratio analyses.

COMPARATIVE FINANCIAL STATEMENTS

Accounting rules require the presentation of **comparative financial statements** covering, as a minimum, the current year and the immediately prior year.

Most financial statements present, side by side, the results for the current and the preceding years (similar to the statements shown in Exhibit 16–1). Analysis of comparative statements is made easier if two additional columns are added for (1) the **amount** of change for each item and (2) the **percent** of change. These data are shown in Exhibit 16–1. Often the percent of change from the prior period is more helpful for interpretative purposes than the absolute dollar amount of change. Notice on each line that the percents are determined by dividing the amount of the change by the amount for the preceding year. For example, in Exhibit 16–1, the percentage on the Cash line was computed as $4,000 \div \$9,000 = 44.4\%$. The amount from the earlier year is used as the base amount.

LONG-TERM SUMMARIES

In the interest of full disclosure, annual reports often give 5-, 10-, and even 20-year summaries of certain basic data, such as sales revenue, net income, total assets, total liabilities, total owners' equity, and selected ratios. Data for a series of years are important in interpreting the financial statements for the current period. Misinterpretation is likely when the statement user limits consideration to only the last one or two periods. The vagaries of business transactions, economic events, and accounting techniques are such that the financial reports for a single time period usually do not provide a sound basis for assessing the long-term potential of a business. Sophisticated financial analysts use data for a number of periods so that trends may be identified.

Care should be used in interpreting long-term summaries. Data for a period in the distant past may not be comparable because of changes in the company, industry, and environment. For example, Exxon is a very different company now than it was when a gallon of gasoline sold for 25 cents.

In interpreting comparative data, the items showing significant increases and decreases should receive special attention. Analysts should identify significant **turning points,** either upward or downward, in trends for important items such as net income and cash flow. The turning points often provide indication of significant future trends. Analysts should determine the **underlying causes** for significant favorable or unfavorable changes.

RATIO AND PERCENTAGE ANALYSIS

Some amounts on financial statements, such as net income, are significant in and of themselves. Other data are more significant when expressed as a relationship to other amounts. Significant relationships can be examined through the use of an analytical tool called **ratio** or **percentage analysis.** A ratio or percent expresses the proportionate relationship between two different amounts. A ratio or percent is computed by dividing one quantity by another quantity. For example, the fact that a company earned net income of $500,000 assumes greater significance when net income is compared with the stockholders' investment in the company. Assuming that stockholders' equity is $5,000,000, the relationship of earnings to stockholder investment is $500,000 ÷ $5,000,000 = 0.1, or 10%. This ratio indicates a different level of performance than would be the case if stockholders' equity was $50,000,000. Ratio analysis helps decision makers to identify significant relationships and to compare companies more realistically than if only single amounts were analyzed.

There are two kinds of ratio analysis: (1) relationships **within one period** and (2) relationships **between periods.** Also, ratios may be computed with amounts within one statement, such as the income statement, or between different statements, such as the income statement and the balance sheet. In Exhibit 16–1, the percents of change represent a percentage analysis between periods within each statement.

Financial statement analysis is a judgmental process. No single ratio or percentage can be identified as appropriate to all situations. Each analytical situation may require the calculation of several ratios. However, there are several ratios or percentages that usually are used because they are appropriate to many situations.

COMPONENT PERCENTAGES

Component percentages are used to express each item on a particular statement as a percentage of a single **base amount** (i.e., the denominator of the ratio). Exhibit 16–2 shows a component analysis for the 19A and 19B income statements and balance sheets for Packard Company. To compute component percentages for the income statement, the base amount is **net sales revenue.** Therefore, each expense is expressed as a percent of net sales revenue. On the balance sheet, the

_____ EXHIBIT 16–2 _____

Illustration of component percentages

PACKARD COMPANY
Income Statements (simplified for illustration)
For the Years Ended December 31, 19B, and 19A

	For the year ended			
	Dec. 31, 19B		Dec. 31, 19A	
	Amount	Percent	Amount	Percent
Sales revenue (net)*	$120,000	100.0	$100,000	100.0
Cost of goods sold	72,600	60.5	60,000	60.0
Gross margin on sales	47,400	39.5	40,000	40.0
Operating expenses:				
Distribution expenses	22,630	18.9	15,000	15.0
Administrative expenses	11,870	9.9	13,300	13.3
Interest expense	1,500	1.2	1,700	1.7
Total expenses	36,000	30.0	30,000	30.0
Pretax income	11,400	9.5	10,000	10.0
Income taxes	2,600	2.2	2,000	2.0
Net income	$ 8,800	7.3	$ 8,000	8.0

* Base amount.

EXHIBIT 16–2 *(concluded)*

Illustration of component percentages

PACKARD COMPANY
Balance Sheets (simplified for illustration)
At December 31, 19B, and 19A

	Dec. 31, 19B		*Dec. 31, 19A*	
	Amount	*Percent*	*Amount*	*Percent*
Assets				
Current assets:				
Cash	$ 13,000	8.9	$ 9,000	6.0
Accounts receivable (net)	8,400	5.7	7,000	4.6
Merchandise inventory	54,000	36.8	60,000	40.0
Prepaid expenses	2,000	1.4	4,000	2.7
Total current assets	77,400	52.8	80,000	53.3
Investments:				
Real estate	8,000	5.5	8,000	5.3
Operational assets:				
Equipment and furniture	82,500	56.3	75,000	50.0
Less accumulated depreciation	(23,250)	(15.9)	(15,000)	(10.0)
Total operational assets	59,250	40.4	60,000	40.0
Other assets	1,900	1.3	2,000	1.4
Total assets*	$146,550	100.0	$150,000	100.0
Liabilities				
Current liabilities:				
Accounts payable	$ 13,200	9.0	$ 12,000	8.0
Notes payable, short term	15,000	10.2	20,000	13.3
Accrued wages payable	7,200	4.9	8,000	5.3
Total current liabilities	35,400	24.1	40,000	26.6
Long-term liabilities:				
Notes payable, long term	7,150	4.9	10,000	6.7
Total liabilities	42,550	29.0	50,000	33.3
Stockholders' Equity				
Common stock, par $10	85,000	58.0	85,000	56.7
Retained earnings	19,000	13.0	15,000	10.0
Total stockholders' equity	104,000	71.0	100,000	66.7
Total liabilities and stockholders' equity*	$146,550	100.0	$150,000	100.0

* Base amount.

base amount is **total assets.** The percents are derived by dividing each balance sheet account by total assets.

Component percentages are useful because they reveal important proportional relationships. For example, on the income statement in Exhibit 16–2, observe that distribution expenses were 18.9% of sales revenue in 19B, compared with 15% in 19A. On the balance sheet, notice that merchandise inventory was 36.8% of total assets for 19B, compared with 40% for 19A. These changes in important relationships often suggest the need for further inquiry because they may suggest opportunities for corrective action and increased profitability.

SOME WIDELY USED RATIOS

Numerous ratios and percentages can be computed from a single set of financial statements, but only a selected number may be useful in a given situation. A common approach is to compute certain widely used ratios and then decide which additional ratios are relevant to the particular decision.

Balance sheet amounts relate to one instant in time, and income statement amounts relate to a period of time. Therefore, care should be exercised when calculating ratios that use amounts from both statements. When an income statement amount is compared with a balance sheet amount, a balance sheet **average amount** often is used to reflect changes in the balance sheet amounts. The selected balance sheet amount usually is computed as the average of the amounts shown on the beginning and ending balance sheets. When additional information is available, such as monthly or quarterly data, an average of the additional data often is more representative.

Commonly used financial ratios can be grouped into the five categories shown in Exhibit 16–3.

TESTS OF PROFITABILITY

Profitability is a primary measure of the overall success of a company. Indeed, it is a necessary condition for survival. Investors and creditors would prefer a **single measure** of profitability that would be meaningful in all situations. Unfortunately, no single measure can be devised to meet this comprehensive need. Tests of profitability focus on measuring the adequacy of income by comparing it with one or more primary activities or factors that are measured in the financial statements. Five different tests of profitability are explained below.

1. Return on owners' investment (ROI_o)

This ratio is a fundamental test of profitability. It relates income to the investment that was made by the owners to earn the income. This ratio can be used to measure the profitability of any investment, whether for a company, a

EXHIBIT 16–3

Widely used accounting ratios

Ratio	Basic computation
Tests of profitability:	
1. * Return on owners' investment (ROI_o).	$\dfrac{\text{Income}}{\text{Average owners' equity}}$
2. Return on total investment (ROI_t).	$\dfrac{\text{Income + Interest expense (net of tax)}}{\text{Average total assets}}$
3. Financial leverage ($ROI_o - ROI_t$).	$\dfrac{\text{Return on}}{\text{owners' investment}} - \dfrac{\text{Return on}}{\text{total investment}}$
4. Earnings per share.	$\dfrac{\text{Income}}{\text{Average number of shares of common stock outstanding}}$
5. Profit margin.	$\dfrac{\text{Income (before extraordinary items)}}{\text{Net sales revenue}}$
Tests of liquidity:	
6. Working capital ratio.	$\dfrac{\text{Current assets}}{\text{Current liabilities}}$
7. Quick ratio.	$\dfrac{\text{Quick assets}}{\text{Current liabilities}}$
8. Receivable turnover.	$\dfrac{\text{Net credit sales}}{\text{Average net trade receivables}}$
9. Inventory turnover.	$\dfrac{\text{Cost of goods sold}}{\text{Average inventory}}$
Test of solvency and equity position:	
10. Debt/equity ratio.	$\dfrac{\text{Total liabilities}}{\text{Owners' equity}}$
Market tests:	
11. Price/earnings ratio.	$\dfrac{\text{Current market price per share}}{\text{Earnings per share}}$
12. Dividend yield ratio.	$\dfrac{\text{Dividends per share}}{\text{Market price per share}}$
Miscellaneous ratio:	
13. Book value per share.	$\dfrac{\text{Common stock equity}}{\text{Number of shares of common stock outstanding}}$

 * The numbers to the left are used in the following discussions to facilitate reference.

project, or an individual. The return on owners' investment ratio is computed as follows:

$$\text{Return on owners' investment} = \frac{\text{Income*}}{\text{Average owners' equity†}}$$

$$\text{Packard Company, 19B} = \frac{\$8,800*}{\$102,000†} = 8.6\%$$

Based on Exhibit 16–2.
* Income **before** extraordinary items should be used.
† Average owners' equity is preferable when available, that is ($100,000 + $104,000) ÷ 2 = $102,000.

Packard Company earned 8.6%, after income taxes, on the investment provided by the **owners.** Return on owners' investment is a particularly useful measure of profitability from the **viewpoint of the owners.** It relates two fundamental factors—the amount of the owners' investment and the return earned for the owners on that investment.

2. Return on total investment (ROI$_t$)

Another view of the return on investment concept relates income to **total assets** (i.e., total investment) used to earn income. Under this broader concept, return on total investment is computed as follows:

$$\text{Return on total investment} = \frac{\text{Income* + Interest expense (net of tax)}}{\text{Average total assets†}}$$

$$\text{Packard Company 19B} = \frac{\$8,800* + (\$1,500 \times 77\%)}{\$148,275†} = 6.7\%$$

Based on Exhibit 16–2.
* Income before extraordinary items should be used. This illustration assumes an average income tax rate of 23%.
† Average total assets should be used; that is ($150,000 + $146,550) ÷ 2 = $148,275.

Packard Company earned 6.7% on the **total resources it used** during the year. Under this concept, **investment** is the amount of resources provided by both owners and creditors. Return is measured as the return to both owners and creditors. To compute return on **total** investment, interest expense (net of income tax) is added back to income because interest is the return on the creditors' investment. It must be added back because it was previously deducted to derive net income. The denominator represents **total** investment, therefore, the numerator (income) must include the total return that was available to the suppliers of funds. The interest is measured net of income tax because it represents the net cost to the corporation for the funds provided by creditors.

Return on total investment reflects the combined effect of both the operating and the financing activities of a company as shown in Exhibit 16–4 (remember that total assets always equals total liabilities plus total owners' equity).

Most analysts compute the two return-on-investment ratios shown above.

EXHIBIT 16–4

Components of return on total investment

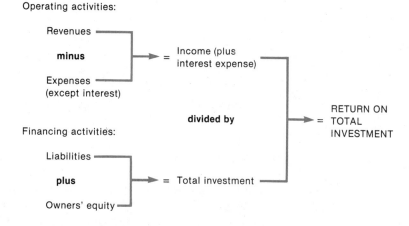

Return on total investment is the preferable measure of **management performance** in using all of the resources available to the company. The return on owners' equity is relevant to the owners because it measures the return that has "accrued" to them.

3. Financial leverage

Financial leverage is the advantage, or disadvantage, which occurs as the result of earning a return on owners' investment that is different from the return earned on total investment (i.e., $ROI_o - ROI_t$). Most companies have positive leverage. Positive leverage occurs when the rate of return on a company's investments is higher than the average aftertax interest rate on borrowed funds. Basically, the company borrows at one rate, and invests at a higher rate of return.

Financial leverage can be measured by comparing the two return-on-investment ratios as follows:

$$\text{Financial leverage} = \frac{\text{Return on}}{\text{owners' investment}} - \frac{\text{Return on}}{\text{total investment}}$$

Packard Company, 19B = 8.6% − 6.7% = 1.9% (positive leverage)

When a company can borrow funds at an aftertax interest rate and invest those funds to earn a higher aftertax rate of return, the difference "accrues" to the benefit of the owners. This is the primary reason that most companies obtain a significant amount of resources from creditors rather than obtaining resources only from the sale of their capital stock.

4. Earnings per share (EPS)

This ratio evaluates profitability strictly from the common stockholders' point of view. Instead of being based on the dollar amount of the investment, it is based on the number of shares of common stock outstanding. EPS is computed as follows:

$$\text{Earnings per share} = \frac{\text{Income}}{\text{Average number of shares of common stock outstanding}}$$

$$\text{Packard Company, 19B} = \frac{\$8,800}{8,500} = \$1.04 \text{ per share}$$

EPS usually is computed on three amounts if extraordinary items are reported on the income statement: (1) income before extraordinary items (required), (2) extraordinary items (optional), and (3) net income (required). Of the three EPS amounts, the first one is considered the most relevant because extraordinary items are unusual and do not reoccur.

5. Profit margin

This percent is based on two income statement amounts. It is computed as follows:

$$\text{Profit margin} = \frac{\text{Income (before extraordinary items)}}{\text{Net sales}}$$

$$\text{Packard Company, 19B} = \frac{\$8,800}{\$120,000} = 7.3\%$$

This profitability test is the percent of each sales dollar, on the average, that is profit. For Packard Company, each dollar of sales generated 7.3 cents of profit. Care must be used in analyzing the profit margin because it does not consider the amount of resources employed (i.e., total investment) to earn income. For example, the income statements of Company A and Company B may show the following:

	Company A	Company B
a. Sales revenue	$100,000	$150,000
b. Income	$ 5,000	$ 7,500
c. Profit margin (b) ÷ (a)	5%	5%
d. Total investment	$ 50,000	$125,000
e. Return on total investment* (b) ÷ (d)	10%	6%

    * Assuming no interest expense.

In this example, both companies reported the same profit margin (5%). Company A, however, appears to be performing much better because it is earning a 10% return on the total investment versus the 6% earned by Company B. The profit margin percents do not reflect the effect of the $50,000 total investment in Company A compared to the $125,000 total investment in Company B. The effect of the different amounts of investment in each company is reflected in the return on investment (ROI) percents. Thus, the profit margin omits one of the two important factors that should be used in evaluating return on the investment.

Comparing profit margins for companies in different industries is difficult. For example, profit margins in the food industry are very low while profit margins in the jewelry business are large. Both types of businesses can be quite profitable because they differ in terms of investment. Grocery stores have small margins but require a relatively small investment. Jewelry stores earn more profit from each sales dollar but require a large investment.

TESTS OF LIQUIDITY

Liquidity refers to a company's ability to meet its currently maturing debts. Tests of liquidity focus on the relationship between current assets and current liabilities. The ability of a company to pay its current liabilities is an important factor in evaluating short-term financial strength. For example, a company that does not have cash available to pay for purchases on a timely basis will lose its cash discounts and run the risk of discontinued credit by vendors. Two ratios are used to measure liquidity: the working capital (or current) ratio and the quick ratio. Recall that working capital is the difference between total current assets and total current liabilities.

6. Working capital ratio

This ratio measures the relationship between total current assets and total current liabilities at a specific date. It is computed as follows:

$$\text{Working capital ratio} = \frac{\text{Current assets}}{\text{Current liabilities}}$$

$$\text{Packard Company, 19B} = \frac{\$77,400}{\$35,400} = 2.2 \text{ times or 2.2 to 1}$$

At year-end, current assets for Packard Company were 2.2 times current liabilities or, alternatively, for each $1 of current liabilities there were $2.20 of current assets. The working capital ratio measures the cushion of working capital maintained in order to allow for the inevitable unevenness in the flow of "funds" through the working capital accounts.[1]

---

[1] Occasionally, "working capital" is used to mean total current assets. This usage is confusing and unnecessary because "total current assets" is more descriptive. Sometimes the term **net working capital** is used to describe the difference between current assets and current liabilities. Throughout this book, we have followed the more general use of working capital to mean the difference between current assets and current liabilities.

7. Quick ratio (or acid test ratio)

This ratio is similar to the working capital ratio except that it is a more stringent test of short-term liquidity. It is computed as follows:

$$\text{Quick ratio} = \frac{\text{Quick assets}}{\text{Current liabilities}}$$

$$\text{Packard Company, 19B} = \frac{\$21,400}{\$35,400} = 0.60 \text{ times or } 0.60 \text{ to } 1$$

Quick assets are readily convertible into cash at approximately their book values. Quick assets include cash, short-term investments, and accounts receivable (net of the allowance for doubtful accounts). Inventories usually are omitted from quick assets because of the uncertainty of when cash will be received from the sale of inventory in the future. In unusual circumstances, if the inventory will turn to cash very quickly, it should be included. In contrast, prepaid expenses do not "convert" to cash and are excluded from quick assets. Thus, the quick or acid-test ratio is a more severe test of liquidity than is the working capital ratio.

8. Receivable turnover

Short-term liquidity often is measured in terms of **turnover** of certain current assets. Two additional ratios that measure nearness to cash are receivable turnover and inventory turnover.

Receivable turnover is computed as follows:

$$\text{Receivable turnover} = \frac{\text{Net credit sales*}}{\text{Average net trade receivables}}$$

Packard Company, 19B
(net credit sales assumed
to be $77,000 for 19B)

$$= \frac{\$77,000}{(\$7,000 + \$8,400) \div 2} = 10 \text{ times}$$

* When the amount of credit sales is not known, total sales may be used as a rough approximation.

This ratio is called a turnover ratio because it reflects how many times the trade receivables were recorded, collected, then recorded again during the period (i.e., "turnover"). Receivable turnover expresses the relationship of the average balance in Accounts Receivable to the transactions (i.e., credit sales) that created those receivables. This ratio measures the effectiveness of the credit-granting and collection activities of the company. A high receivable turnover ratio suggests effective collection activities. Granting credit to poor credit risks and ineffective collection efforts will cause this ratio to be low. A very low ratio is obviously a problem, but a very high ratio can also be a problem. A very high ratio may indicate an overly stringent credit policy that would cause lost sales and profits.

The receivable turnover ratio often is converted to a time basis known as the average age of receivables. The computation is as follows:

$$\text{Average age of trade receivables} = \frac{\text{Days in year}}{\text{Receivable turnover}}$$

$$\text{Packard Company, 19B} = \frac{365}{10} = 36.5 \text{ average days to collect}$$

The effectiveness of credit and collection activities sometimes is judged by the "rule of thumb" that the **average days to collect** should not exceed 1½ times the credit terms. For example, if the credit terms are 2/10, n/30, the average days to collect should not exceed 45 days (i.e., not more than 15 days past due). Like all rules of thumb, this one has many exceptions. However, an increase or decrease in the average days to collect would suggest changes in the credit policies and/or changes in collection efficiency.

9. Inventory turnover

Inventory turnover measures the liquidity (i.e., nearnesss to cash) of the inventory. It reflects the relationship of the inventory to the volume of goods sold during the period. The computation is as follows:

$$\text{Inventory turnover} = \frac{\text{Cost of goods sold}}{\text{Average inventory}}$$

$$\text{Packard Company, 19B} = \frac{\$72,600}{(\$60,000 + \$54,000) \div 2} = 1.3 \text{ times}$$

The inventory "turned over" 1.3 times during the year because cost of goods sold was 1.3 times the average inventory level. Because profit normally is realized each time the inventory is sold (i.e., turned over), an increase in the ratio is usually favorable. However, if the ratio is too high, sales may be lost because of items that are out of stock. The turnover ratio often is converted to a time-basis expression called the **average days' supply in inventory**. The computation is:

$$\text{Average days' supply in inventory} = \frac{\text{Days in year}}{\text{Inventory turnover}}$$

$$\text{Packard Company, 19B} = \frac{365}{1.3}$$

$$= \frac{281 \text{ average day's supply in}}{\text{inventory}}$$

Turnover ratios are used extensively because they are easy to understand. Normal (or average) inventory turnover ratios vary significantly by industry classification. Companies in the food industry (grocery stores and restaurants) have high inventory turnover ratios while companies that sell expensive merchandise (automobile dealers and high-fashion clothes) have much lower ratios.

TESTS OF SOLVENCY AND EQUITY POSITION

Solvency refers to the ability of a company to meet its **long-term obligations** on a continuing basis. Certain critical relationships can be identified by analyzing how a company has financed its assets and activities. The relative amount of resources provided by creditors and owners is known as a company's **equity position.** The debt/equity ratio is used to reflect the equity position of a company.

10. Debt/equity ratio

This ratio expresses the direct proportion between debt and owners' equity.[2] It is computed as follows:

$$\text{Debt/equity ratio} = \frac{\textbf{Total liabilities (i.e., creditors' equity)}}{\textbf{Owners' equity}}$$

$$\textbf{Packard Company, 19B} = \frac{\$42{,}550}{\$104{,}000} = \textbf{0.41 (or 41\%)}$$

This ratio means that for each $1 of owners' equity, there was $0.41 of liabilities.

Debt is risky for a company because it imposes important contractual obligations. There are *(a)* specific maturity dates for the principal amounts and *(b)* specific interest payments that must be made. Debt obligations are enforceable by law and do not depend upon the earnings of the company. In contrast, dividends for stockholders are always at the discretion of the company and are not legally enforceable until declared by the board of directors. Owner's equity is "permanent" capital that does not have a maturity date. Thus, equity capital usually is seen as much less risky than debt for a company.

---

[2] The relationship between debt and owners' equity alternatively may be calculated with the following two ratios:

$$\text{Owners' equity to total equities} = \frac{\text{Owners' equity}}{\text{Total equities}}$$

$$\text{Packard Company, 19B} = \frac{\$104{,}000}{\$146{,}550} = 71\%$$

$$\text{Creditors' equity to total equities} = \frac{\text{Creditors' equity}}{\text{Total equities}}$$

$$\text{Packard Company, 19B} = \frac{\$42{,}500}{\$146{,}550} = 29\%$$

Despite the risk associated with debt, most companies get significant amounts of resources from creditors because of the advantages of financial leverage. Typically, the return on company investments is higher than the aftertax interest rate paid to creditors. By accepting the risk associated with debt, management may earn a higher return for the owners because of positive financial leverage. For example, assume a company is earning 15% return on total investment, while its average interest rate on debt is 7% (net of income tax). The difference between the earnings rate on total resources (15%) and the interest paid to the creditors (7%) "accrues" to the benefit of the stockholders.[3] The stockholders benefit by the 15% earned on the resources provided by them, plus the difference between the 15% return and the 7% interest rate paid on the resources provided by the creditors. A company with a high proportion of debt is **highly levered.** The debt/equity ratio shows the balance that the management has attained between the resources provided by creditors and the resources provided by owners.

MARKET TESTS

Several ratios have been developed to measure the "market worth" of a share of stock. These market tests relate the current market price of a share of stock to an indicator of the return that might accrue to the investor. The tests focus on the **current market price** of the stock because that is the amount the buyer would invest. Two market test ratios used by analysts and investors are the price/earnings ratio and the dividend yield ratio.

11. Price/earnings (P/E) ratio

This ratio measures the relationship between the current market price of the stock and its earnings per share. Assuming a current market price of $15.60 per share for Packard Company common stock in 19B and earnings per share of $1.04, the P/E ratio is computed as follows:

$$\text{Price/earnings ratio} = \frac{\text{Current market price per share}}{\text{Earnings per share}}$$

$$\text{Packard Company, 19B} = \frac{\$15.60}{\$1.04} = 15 \text{ (or 15 to 1)}$$

Packard stock was selling at 15 times the EPS. The P/E ratio often is referred to as the **multiple.** The P/E ratio is used as an indicator of the future performance of

---

[3] Interest expense on debt is a deductible expense on the income tax return; in contrast, dividend payments to stockholders are not deductible. Thus, in addition to the lower stated rate for debt, funds obtained by means of debt tend to be less costly because of the income tax saving. The real cost of debt in the above example depends upon the income tax rate.

the stock. Analysts use the P/E ratio to predict how the stock price may react to a change in the level of the company's earnings.

Sometimes the components of the P/E ratio are inverted, giving the **capitalization rate.** This is the rate at which the stock market apparently is capitalizing the current earnings. Computation of the capitalization rate on current earnings per share for Packard Company would be $1.04 ÷ $15.60 = 6.67%.

12. Dividend yield ratio

This ratio measures the relationship between the dividends per share paid and the current market price of the stock. Assuming dividends paid by Packard Company of $0.75 per share for 19B and a current market price per share of $15.60, the ratio is computed as follows:

$$\text{Dividend yield ratio} = \frac{\textbf{Dividend per share}}{\textbf{Market price per share}}$$

$$\text{Packard Company, 19B} = \frac{\$0.75}{\$15.60} = 4.81\%$$

This ratio measures the current dividend yield to the investor, based upon the dividends declared per share against the current market price per share. Like the P/E ratio, it is a volatile measure because the price of stock may change materially over short periods of time, and each change in market price or dividend payment changes the ratio.

MISCELLANEOUS RATIO

13. Book value per share

The book value per share of stock measures the owners' equity in terms of each share of common stock outstanding. In the case of a simple capital structure, with **only** common stock outstanding, the computation of book value per share is not difficult. To illustrate, assume Day Corporation had total owners' equity of $250,000 and 10,000 outstanding shares of common stock, par $10. The computation of book value per share would be as follows:

$$\frac{\textbf{Book value per}}{\textbf{common share}} = \frac{\textbf{Total owners' equity}}{\textbf{(applicable to common shares)}} \Big/ \textbf{Common shares outstanding}$$

$$\text{Packard Company, 19B} = \frac{\$250,000}{10,000 \text{ shares}} = \$25$$

Computation of book value per share is more difficult if both common and preferred shares are outstanding. In this situation, total owners' equity must be allocated between common and preferred stock. This allocation is accomplished by assigning an amount to preferred stock, based on its preferences, and, then, assigning the remaining amount of owners' equity to common stock. Assume Bye Corporation had total owners' equity of $273,000; 1,000 shares outstanding of its 5% preferred stock, par $20, cumulative (no dividends in arrears for past years), and liquidation value of $22 per share; and 10,000 outstanding shares of common stock, par $10.

Allocation:

Total owners' equity		$273,000
Less equity allocated to preferred stock:		
Liquidation value (1,000 shares × $22)	$22,000	
Cumulative dividend preference for the current year		
(1,000 shares × $20 × 5%)	1,000	
Amount allocated to preferred stock		23,000
Remainder allocated to common stock		$250,000

Book value per share:
Preferred, $23,000 ÷ 1,000 shares = $23
Common, $250,000 ÷ 10,000 shares = $25

Book value per share has limited significance because it has no necessary relationship to market value. Because it is a low conservative amount (historical cost basis), some analysts consider a market value below book value to imply underpriced shares.

INTERPRETING RATIOS

The computation of any particular ratio is not standardized. Neither the accounting profession nor security analysts have prescribed the manner in which a ratio must be computed (except for earnings per share). Thus, users of financial statements should compute the various ratios in accordance with their decision objectives. Before using ratios computed by others, the user should determine the computational approach that was used. This section discusses commonly used approaches.

To interpret a ratio, it should be compared with some **standard** that represents an optimal or desirable value. For example, the return-on-investment ratio may be compared with alternative investment opportunities. Some ratios, by their characteristics, are unfavorable if they are **either** too high or too low. For example, analysis may indicate that a working capital ratio of approximately 2:1 may be considered optimal for a company. In this situation, a ratio of 1:1 may indicate a danger of being unable to meet maturing debts. A ratio of 3:1 may indicate that excess funds are being left idle rather than being employed profitably. Furthermore, an optimal ratio for one company often is not the optimal ratio for another company. Comparisons of ratios for different companies are appropriate only if the companies are indeed comparable. Differences in industry, nature of operations, size, and accounting policies make many comparisons of questionable value.

Most ratios represent **averages.** Therefore, they may obscure underlying factors that are of interest to the analyst. To illustrate, a working capital ratio of 2:1 may be considered optimal. But even an optimal working capital ratio may obscure a short-term liquidity problem if the company has a very large amount of inventory and a minimal amount of cash with which to pay debts as they mature. Careful analysis can uncover this liquidity problem. In other cases, careful analysis cannot uncover obscured problems. For example, consolidated statements include financial information about the parent and its subsidiaries. The parent company may have a high working capital ratio and the subsidiary a very low ratio. When the statements are consolidated, the working capital ratio (in effect, an average of the parent and the subsidiary) may be within an acceptable range. Obscured is the fact that the subsidiary may have a very serious liquidity problem.

Despite limitations, ratio analysis is a useful analytical tool. Financial ratios are effective in predicting bankruptcy. Exhibit 16–5 gives the working capital ratio and the debt/equity ratio for Braniff International Corporation. Notice the deterioration of these ratios each year. In 1981, the independent auditor issued a qualified audit opinion and noted, "there are conditions which indicate that the company may be unable to continue as a going concern." In the spring of 1982, Braniff filed for bankruptcy. Analysts who studied the financial ratios each year probably were not surprised by the bankruptcy of Braniff. After selling many of its assets and undergoing a complete financial restructuring, Braniff was able to resume limited flight operations.

Financial analysts often use four types of "standards" against which ratios and percents are compared:

1. **Comparison of the ratios for the current year with the historical ratios for the same company**—Particular attention is given to the **trend** of each ratio over time.
2. **Comparison of the ratios for the current year with ratios of other companies for the same year**—These comparisons include the use of ratios and percents from other similar companies and from industry averages. Industry averages

---

EXHIBIT 16–5

Selected financial ratios for Braniff International

	1977	1978	1979	1980	1981
Working capital ratio	1.20	0.91	0.74	0.60	0.49
Debt/equity ratio	2.03	2.45	4.88	15.67	N/A*

* In 1981, Braniff reported negative owners' equity as the result of a large net loss that produced a negative balance in retained earnings. Creditors' equity exceeded **total** equities.

are published by many companies, trade associations, and governmental agencies. For example, a variety of ratios can be found in the publications of Dun & Bradstreet, Inc., Moody's *Manual of Investments,* and Standard & Poor's *Corporation Records.*

3. **Experience of the analyst who has a subjective feel for the "right" relationships in a given situation**—These subjective judgments of an experienced and competent observer tend to be more reliable than purely mechanical comparisons.

4. **Comparison of the ratios for the current year with planned goals and objectives expressed as ratios**—Many companies prepare comprehensive profit plans (i.e., budgets) on a continuing basis that incorporate realistic plans for the future. These plans usually incorporate planned goals for significant ratios, such as profit margin, return on investment, and EPS. Internal plans seldom are available to external parties because managers are reluctant to share their business plans with competitors. Some companies have begun to experiment with methods to make this information available to users. Days Inn Corporation recently included proforma (estimated) financial statements for the future as part of their annual report.

IMPACT OF ACCOUNTING ON ANALYSIS

Financial statements provide information for the average investor. Users who understand basic accounting are able to more effectively analyze the information contained in financial statements. While studying this book, you have developed an understanding of the accounting vocabulary. A knowledge of this vocabulary is necessary to understand financial statements.

Also, familiarity with the underlying accounting concepts is essential for proper analysis of statements. Some unsophisticated users do not understand the cost principle and believe that assets are reported on the balance sheet at their fair market value. We have stressed accounting concepts throughout the book because it is impossible to interpret accounting numbers without an understanding of the concepts that were used to develop the numbers.

When comparing companies, it is rare to find that they use exactly the same accounting policies. If the comparisons are to be useful, the analyst must understand the impact of various accounting alternatives. One company may use very conservative accounting alternatives such as accelerated depreciation and LIFO while another may use "income maximizing" alternatives, such as straight-line depreciation and FIFO. Users who do not understand the effects of accounting methods may misinterpret financial results. Perhaps the most important first step in analyzing financial statements is a review of the accounting policies that the company has selected. This information must be disclosed in a note to the statements. An example of this disclosure is shown in the annual report in Special Supplement B.

SUMMARY OF CHAPTER

Interpretation of amounts reported on financial statements may be enhanced by expressing certain relationships as ratios or percents. Although many ratios can be calculated, only a few will be useful for a given decision. Having selected the relevant ratios, the analyst has the problem of evaluating the results. This evaluation involves the task of selecting one or more realistic standards with which to compare the results. Four types of standards are used: (1) historical standards, (2) external standards, (3) experience, and (4) planned standards. The interpretation of ratios may suggest strengths and weaknesses in the operations and/or the financial position of the company that should be accorded in-depth investigation and evaluation.

IMPORTANT TERMS DEFINED IN THIS CHAPTER

Terms (alphabetically)	Key words in definitions of important terms used in chapter	Page references
Common ratios	Selected ratios that are used widely. Exhibit 16–3 presents a list of 13 commonly used accounting ratios.	825
Comparative statements	Financial statements for several years, amounts are presented side by side for comparative purposes.	820
Component percentages	A percentage that expresses each item on a particular financial statement as a percent of a single base amount.	822
Long-term summaries	Summaries of basic accounting data for many years (typically 10 years).	821
Market tests	Ratios that tend to measure the "market worth" of a share of stock.	833
Ratio analysis	An analytical tool designed to identify significant relationships; measures proportional relationship between two financial statement amounts.	821
Tests of liquidity	Ratios that measure a company's ability to meet its currently maturing obligations.	829
Tests of solvency	Ratios that measure a company's ability to meet its long-term obligations.	832

QUESTIONS

1. What are three fundamental uses of external financial statements by decision makers?

2. What are some of the primary items on financial statements about which creditors usually are concerned?

3. Explain why the notes to the financial statements are important to decision makers.

4. What is the primary purpose of comparative financial statements?

5. Why are statement users interested in financial summaries covering several years? What is the primary limitation of long-term summaries?

6. What is ratio analysis? Why is ratio analysis useful?

7. What are component percentages? Why are component percentages useful?

8. Explain the two concepts of return on investment.

9. What is financial leverage? How is financial leverage measured?

10. Is profit margin a useful measure of profitability? Explain.

11. Compare and contrast the working capital ratio and the quick ratio.

12. What does the debt/equity ratio reflect?

13. What are "market tests?"

14. What are the primary problems when using ratios?

EXERCISES

E16–1   (Pair Definition with Terms)

Match the following brief definitions with the terms by entering the appropriate letter in each space provided.

Term	*Brief definitions*
_____ (1) Long-term summaries	A. Ratios and percentages calculated from financial statements to give greater insight into the profitability, liquidity, solvency, and market status of a company.
_____ (2) Market tests	
_____ (3) Common ratios	
_____ (4) Tests of solvency	B. These could be used to compare and contrast a company's financial position from year to year.
_____ (5) Comparative statements	C. If you were to compute these percentages for an income statement, the denominator would be net sales revenue.
_____ (6) Tests of liquidity	D. These documents are useful in tracking a company's progress over a long period of time.
_____ (7) Component percentages	E. Examples of these are the price/earnings ratio and the dividend yield ratio.
_____ (8) Ratio analysis	F. Used to analyze relationships both within one period and between periods.
	G. These tests focus on the relationship between current assets and current liabilities.
	H. An example of this kind of test is the debt/equity ratio.

E16–2 **(Analysis of Comparative Financial Statements Using Percentages)**

The comparative financial statements prepared at December 31, 19B, for Doan Company showed the following summarized data:

	19B	19A
Income statement:		
Sales revenue	$150,000*	$140,000*
Cost of goods sold	90,000	85,000
Gross margin	60,000	55,000
Operating expenses and interest expense	43,000	40,500
Pretax income	17,000	14,500
Income tax	5,000	4,500
Net income	$ 12,000	$ 10,000
Balance sheet:		
Cash	$ 7,000	$ 11,000
Accounts receivable (net)	12,000	14,000
Inventory	30,000	28,000
Operational assets (net)	50,000	43,000
	$ 99,000	$ 96,000
Current liabilities (no interest)	$ 14,000	$ 17,000
Long-term liabilities (10% interest)	35,000	35,000
Common stock (par $10)	40,000	40,000
Retained earnings†	10,000	4,000
	$ 99,000	$ 96,000

* One third were credit sales.
† During 19B, cash dividends amounting to $6,000 were declared and paid.

Required:

a. Complete the following columns for each item in the above comparative financial statements:

	Increase (decrease)	
	19B over 19A	
	Amount	*Percent*

b. Answer the following questions:
   (1) Compute the percentage increases in sales revenue, net income, cash, inventory, liabilities, and owners' equity.
   (2) By what amount did working capital change?
   (3) What was the percentage change in the average income tax rate?
   (4) What was the amount of cash inflow from revenues for 19B?
   (5) By what percent did the average markup realized on goods sold change?
   (6) How much did the book value per share change?

E16–3   **(Analysis of a Financial Statement Using Component Percentages and Selected Ratios)** Use the data given in Exercise 16–2 for Doan Company.

Required:

a. Present component percentages for 19B only.

b. Answer the following questions for 19B:
   (1) What was the average percentage markup on sales?
   (2) What was the average income tax rate?
   (3) Compute the profit margin. Was it a good or poor indicator of performance? Explain.
   (4) What percent of total resources was invested in operational assets?
   (5) Compute the debt/equity ratio. Does it look good or bad? Explain.
   (6) What was the return on owners' investment?
   (7) What was the return on total investment?
   (8) Compute the financial leverage percent. Was it positive or negative? Explain.
   (9) What was the book value per share of common stock?

E16–4   **(Analysis of a Financial Statement Using Each Ratio Discussed in the Chapter)** Use the data given in Exercise 16–2 for Doan Company. Use a separate sheet and complete the following tabulation for 19B only (assume a common stock price of $33 per share); compute the ratios that usually are included under each category:

Name and Computation of the Ratio (show computations)	Brief Explanation of the Ratio

A. **Tests of profitability:**
   1. Return on owners' investment
   2. Etc.	

B. **Tests of liquidity:**
   1. Working capital ratio
   2. Etc.	

C. **Tests of solvency and equity position:**
   1. Debt/equity ratio
   2. Etc.	

D. **Market tests:**
   1. Price/earnings ratio
   2. Etc.	

E. **Miscellaneous ratio:** 1. Book value per share	

E16–5 **(Match Each Ratio with its Computational Definition)**

Match the following by entering the appropriate letters in the blanks.

Ratio or percent

_____ (1) Profit margin
_____ (2) Inventory turnover
 ratio
_____ (3) Average collection
 period
_____ (4) Creditors' equity to
 total equities
_____ (5) Dividend yield ratio
_____ (6) Return on owners'
 investment
_____ (7) Working capital ratio
_____ (8) Debt/equity ratio
_____ (9) Price/earnings ratio
_____ (10) Financial leverage
_____ (11) Receivable turnover
 ratio
_____ (12) Average days' supply of inventory
_____ (13) Owners' equity to
 total equities
_____ (14) Earnings per share
_____ (15) Return on total investment
_____ (16) Quick ratio
_____ (17) Book value per share

Computation

A. Income (before extraordinary items) ÷ Net sales.
B. Days in year ÷ Receivable turnover.
C. Income ÷ Average owners' equity.
D. Income ÷ Average number of shares of common stock
 outstanding.
E. Return on owners' investment − Return on total invest-
 ment.
F. Quick assets ÷ Current liabilities.
G. Current assets ÷ Current liabilities.
H. Cost of goods sold ÷ Average inventory.
 I. Net credit sales ÷ Average net trade receivables.
J. Creditors' equity (debt) ÷ Total equities.
K. Days in year ÷ Inventory turnover.
L. Total liabilities ÷ Owners' equity.
M. Dividends per share ÷ Market price per share.
N. Owners' equity ÷ Total equities.
O. Current market price per share ÷ Earnings per share.
P. Owners' equity ÷ Shares outstanding.
Q. Income + Interest expense (net of tax) ÷ Total assets.

E16–6 **(Analysis of the Impact of Selected Transactions on the Working Capital Ratio, Accounts Receivable and Inventory Turnover, and Financial Leverage)**

Case A—Current assets totaled $60,000, and the working capital ratio was 1.5. As-sume the following transactions were completed: (1) purchased merchandise for $3,000 of which one third was on short-term credit; and (2) purchased a delivery truck for $8,000, paid $2,000 cash, and signed a two-year interest-bearing note for the balance. Compute the cumulative working capital ratio after each transaction.

Case B—Sales for the year were $600,000 of which one half was on credit. The average gross margin rate was 40% on sales. Account balances were:

	Beginning	Ending
Accounts receivable (net)	$30,000	$20,000
Inventory	20,000	16,000

Compute the turnover for the accounts receivable and inventory, the average age of receivables, and the average days' supply of inventory.

Case C—The financial statements reported the following at year-end:

Total asssets	$100,000
Total debt (10% interest)	60,000
Net income (average tax rate 30%)	12,000

Compute the financial leverage. Was it positive or negative?

E16-7 **(Analysis of a Financial Statement Using Ratios and Percentage Changes)**
Ryan Retail Company has just prepared the comparative annual financial statements for 19B given below:

RYAN RETAIL COMPANY
Income Statement
For the Year Ended December 31, 19B and 19A

		For the year ended	
		19B	19A
Sales revenue (one half on credit)		$100,000	$ 95,000
Cost of goods sold		48,000	46,000
Gross margin		52,000	49,000
Expenses (including $3,000 interest expense each year)		34,000	33,000
Pretax income		18,000	16,000
Income tax on operations (22%)		3,960	3,520
Income before extraordinary items		14,040	12,480
Extraordinary loss	$3,000		
Less income tax saved	660	2,340	
Extraordinary gain			$1,000
Applicable income tax			220	780
Net income		$ 11,700	$ 13,260

RYAN RETAIL COMPANY
Balance Sheet
At December 31, 19B and 19A

	19B	19A
Assets		
Cash	$ 47,200	$ 20,000
Accounts receivable (net) (terms 1/10, n/30)	35,000	30,000
Inventory	30,000	40,000
Operational assets (net)	90,000	100,000
Total assets	$202,200	$190,000
Liabilities		
Accounts payable	$ 60,000	$ 50,000
Income tax payable	1,500	1,000
Note payable, long term	25,000	25,000
Stockholders' Equity		
Capital stock, par $10	80,000	80,000
Retained earnings	35,700	34,000
Total liabilities and stockholders' equity	$202,200	$190,000

Required (round percents and ratios to two decimal places):

a. For 19B, compute the tests of (1) profitability, (2) liquidity, (3) solvency, and (4) market. Assume the quoted price of the stock was $26.50 for 19B. Dividends declared and paid during 19B were $10,000.

b. Respond to the following for 19B:
   (1) Compute the percentage changes in sales, income before extraordinary items, net income, cash, inventory, and debt.
   (2) What appears to be the pretax interest rate on the note payable?
c. Identify at least two problems facing the company that are suggested by your responses to (a) and (b).

PROBLEMS

P16–1   **(Analysis of a Financial Statement Using All of the Ratios Discussed in the Chapter; Emphasis on Assessing Liquidity)**

Peterson Corporation has just completed its comparative statements for the year ended December 31, 19B. At this point, certain analytical and interpretative procedures are to be undertaken. The completed statements (summarized) are as follows:

	19B	19A
Income statement:		
Sales revenue	$400,000*	$390,000*
Cost of goods sold	220,000	218,000
Gross margin	180,000	172,000
Operating expenses (including interest on bonds)	147,000	148,000
Pretax income	33,000	24,000
Income tax	9,000	7,000
Net income	$ 24,000	$ 17,000
Balance sheet:		
Cash	$ 5,400	$ 2,700
Accounts receivable (net)	44,000	30,000
Merchandise inventory	30,000	24,000
Prepaid expenses	600	500
Operational assets (net)	120,000	130,000
	$200,000	$187,200
Accounts payable	$ 19,000	$ 20,000
Income tax payable	1,000	1,200
Bonds payable (10% interest rate)	50,000	50,000
Common stock, par $10	100,000†	100,000
Retained earnings	30,000‡	16,000
	$200,000	$187,200

* Forty percent were credit sales.
† The market price of the stock at the end of 19B was $30 per share.
‡ During 19B, the company declared and paid a cash dividend of $10,000.

Required:

a. Complete a table similar to the following (show computations; round percents and ratios to two places):

Name and Computation of the 19B Ratio	Brief Explanation of the Ratio

Tests of profitability:
  1. Return on owners'
     investment.
  2. Etc.
 	
Tests of liquidity:
  1. Working capital ratio.
  2. Etc.
 	
Tests of solvency and equity position:
  1. Debt/equity ratio.
  2. Etc.
 	
Market tests:
  1. Price/earnings ratio.
  2. Etc.	

b. Answer the following questions for 19B:
  (1) Evaluate the financial leverage. Explain its meaning using the computed amount(s).
  (2) Evaluate the profit margin amount and explain how a stockholder might use it.
  (3) Explain to a stockholder why the working capital ratio and the quick ratio are different. Do you observe any liquidity problems? Explain.
  (4) Assuming credit terms are 1/10, n/30, do you perceive an unfavorable situation for the company related to credit sales? Explain.

P16–2   (Use Ratios to Analyze Several Years of Financial Data; Identify Favorable and Unfavorable Factors; Give Recommendations to Improve Operations)

The following information was contained in the annual financial statements of Taterwood Company, which started business January 1, 19A (assume account balances only in Cash and Capital Stock on this date; all amounts are in thousands of dollars).

	19A	19B	19C	19D
Accounts receivable (net) (terms n/30)	$ 8	$10	$ 16	$ 22
Merchandise inventory	10	12	20	25
Net sales (¾ on credit)	40	60	100	120
Cost of goods sold	26	36	64	80
Net income (loss)	(10)	6	14	10

Required (show computations and round to two decimal places):

a. Complete the tabulation given below.
b. Evaluate the results of the three related ratios 1, 2, and 3, to identify the favorable or unfavorable factors. Give your recommendations to improve Taterwood's operations.
c. Evaluate the results of the last four ratios (4, 5, 6, and 7) and identify any favorable or unfavorable factors. Give your recommendations to improve Taterwood's operations.

Items	19A	19B	19C	19D
1. Profit margin—percent.				
2. Gross margin—ratio.				
3. Expenses as a percent of sales, excluding cost of goods sold.				
4. Inventory turnover.				
5. Days' supply in inventory.				
6. Receivable turnover.				
7. Average days to collect.				

P16–3   **(Compare Alternative Investment Opportunities Using All of the Ratios Discussed in the Chapter; Prepare Investment Recommendation)**

The 19B financial statements for Able and Baker companies are summarized below:

	Able Company	Baker Company
Balance sheet:		
Cash	$ 25,000	$ 11,000
Accounts receivable, net	30,000	17,000
Inventory	80,000	20,000
Operational assets, net	125,000	300,000
Other assets	40,000	252,000
Total assets	$ 300,000	$ 600,000
Current liabilities	$ 90,000	$ 40,000
Long-term debt (10%)	50,000	60,000
Capital stock, par $20	120,000	400,000
Contributed capital in excess of par	10,000	60,000
Retained earnings	30,000	40,000
Total liabilities and stockholders' equity	$ 300,000	$ 600,000
Income statement:		
Sales revenue (on credit) (⅓) (⅕)	$ 600,000	$ 900,000
Cost of goods sold	(350,000)	(450,000)
Expenses (including interest and income tax)	(205,000)	(360,000)
Net income	$ 45,000	$ 90,000
Selected data from the 19A statements:		
Accounts receivable, net	$ 25,000	$ 19,000
Inventory	70,000	24,000
Long-term debt	50,000	60,000
Other data:		
Per share price at end of 19B (offering price)	$ 50	$ 40
Average income tax rate	30%	30%
Dividends declared and paid in 19B	$ 25,800	$ 150,400

Able and Baker companies are in the same line of business and are direct competitors in a large metropolitan area. They have been in business approximately 10 years, and each has had steady growth. The two managements have different viewpoints in many respects; however, Baker is the more conservative, and as the president said, "We avoid what we consider to be undue risks." Neither company is publicly held. Able Company has an annual audit by a CPA but Baker Company does not.

Required:

a. Complete a schedule that reflects a ratio analysis of each company. Compute the 13 ratios discussed in the chapter.

b. A client of yours has the opportunity to buy 10% of the shares in one or the other company at the per share prices given above. Your client has decided to invest in one of the companies. Based on the data given, prepare a comparative evaluation of the ratio analyses (and any other available information) and give your recommended choice with the supporting explanation.

P16–4 **(Comparison of Loan Requests from Two Companies Using All of the Ratios Discussed in the Chapter)**

The 19B financial statements for Doe and Roe companies are summarized below:

	Doe Company		Roe Company
Balance sheet:			
Cash	$ 20,000		$ 40,000
Accounts receivable, net	60,000		10,000
Inventory	120,000		30,000
Operational assets, net	500,000		150,000
Other assets	155,000		54,000
Total	$ 855,000		$ 284,000
Current liabilities	$ 100,000		$ 20,000
Long-term debt (10%)	200,000		50,000
Capital stock, par $10	500,000		200,000
Contributed capital in excess of par	25,000		2,000
Retained earnings	30,000		12,000
Total	$ 855,000		$ 284,000
Income statement:			
Sales revenue (on credit) (½)	$ 900,000	(⅓)	$ 300,000
Cost of goods sold	(522,000)		(180,000)
Expenses (including interest and income tax)	(288,000)		(84,000)
Net income	$ 90,000		$ 36,000
Selected data from the 19A statements:			
Accounts receivable, net	$ 50,000		$ 14,000
Long-term debt (10% interest)	200,000		50,000
Inventory	100,000		45,000
Other data:			
Per share price at end of 19B	$ 12.75		$ 10.50
Average income tax rate	30%		20%
Dividends declared and paid in 19B	$ 40,000		$ 13,125

These two companies are in the same line of business and in the same state but in different cities. Each company has been in operation for about 10 years. Doe Company is audited by one of the "Big-8" accounting firms, and Roe Company is audited by a local accounting firm. Both companies received an unqualified opinion (i.e., the independent auditors found nothing wrong) on the financial statements. Doe Company wants to borrow $75,000 cash, and Roe Company needs $30,000. The loans will be for a two-year period and are needed for "working capital purposes."

Required:

a. Complete a schedule that reflects a ratio analysis of each company. Compute the ratios discussed in the chapter.

b. Assume you work in the loan department of a local bank. You have been asked to analyze the situation and recommend which loan is preferable. Based on the data given, your analysis prepared in *(a)*, and any other information, give your choice and the supporting explanation.

P16–5   **(Assess the Solvency of an Actual Company Using Selected Ratios)**

The following information was contained in the actual financial statements of a large manufacturing company that currently is listed on The New York Stock Exchange:

Balance Sheet	December 31 (millions of dollars)	
	19B	19A
Assets		
Current Asssets		
Cash	$ 188.2	$ 123.2
Time deposits	120.8	248.8
Marketable securities	165.3	150.8
Accounts receivable (less allowance for doubtful accounts: 19B—$34.9 million; 19A—$16.7 million)	610.3	848.0
Inventories—at the lower of cost (substantially FIFO) or market	1,873.8	1,980.8
Prepaid insurance, taxes, and other expenses	162.3	210.2
Total Current Assets	3,120.7	3,561.8
Total Investments and Other Assets	1,183.5	1,396.5
Property, Plant, and Equipment		
Land, buildings, machinery, and equipment	3,733.1	3,391.3
Less accumulated depreciation	2,097.1	1,963.9
	1,636.0	1,427.4
Special tools	712.9	595.5
Net Property, Plant, and Equipment	2,348.9	2,022.9
Total Assets	$ 6,653.1	$ 6,981.2
Liabilities and Stockholders' Investment		
Current Liabilities		
Accounts payable	$ 1,530.4	$ 1,725.0
Accrued expenses	807.9	698.0
Short-term debt	600.9	49.2
Payment due within one year on long-term debt	275.6	12.4
Taxes on income	16.8	1.2
Total Current Liabilities	3,231.6	2,485.8
Total Long-term Debt and Other Liabilities	1,559.1	1,564.1
Minority interest in consolidated subsidiaries	38.3	4.8
Preferred stock—nopar value	218.7	217.0
Common stock—par value $6.25 per share	416.9	397.7
Additional paid-in capital	692.2	683.1
Net earnings retained	496.3	1,628.7
Total Liabilities and Stockholders' Investment	$ 6,653.1	$ 6,981.2

Income Statement

	Year Ended December 31 (millions of dollars)	
	19B	19A
Net sales	$12,004.3	$13,669.8
Cost of goods sold	11,631.5	12,640.1
Depreciation of plant and equipment	180.6	154.0
Amortization of special tools	220.0	198.2
Selling and administrative expenses	598.5	572.1
Pension plans	260.6	262.3
Interest expense	215.4	128.9
	13,106.6	13,955.6
Loss Before Taxes on Income	(1,102.3)	(285.8)
Taxes on income (credit)	(5.0)	(81.2)
Net Loss	$(1,097.3)	$ (204.6)

Required:

a. Calculate the following ratios:

   (1) Return on owners' investment.

   (2) Return on total investment.

     (For purposes of this case, assume that the interest expense reported on the income statement is net of income taxes.)

   (3) Financial leverage.

   (4) Earnings per share.

   (5) Working capital ratio.

   (6) Quick ratio.

   (7) Inventory turnover.

   (8) Debt/equity ratio.

b. Based on your analysis of the ratios that you calculated in Requirement (a), do you think that this company will be able to continue in existence? Explain. Would you be willing to invest in this company? Explain.

P16–6   (Analysis of the Impact of Alternative Inventory Methods on Selected Ratios)

Aggressive Company uses the FIFO method to cost inventory, and Conservative Company uses the LIFO method. The two companies are exactly alike except for the difference in inventory costing methods. Costs of inventory items for both companies have been rising steadily in recent years, and each company has increased its inventory each year. Each company has paid its tax liability in full for the current year (and all previous years), and each company uses the same accounting methods for both financial reporting and income tax reporting. Identify which company will report the higher amount for each of the following ratios. If it is not possible, explain why.

a. Working capital ratio.

b. Quick ratio.

c. Debt/equity ratio.

d. Return on owners' investment.

e. Earnings per share.

CASES

C16–1   **(Analysis of the Impact of Alternative Depreciation Methods on Ratio Analysis)**
Fast Company uses the sum-of-years'-digits method to depreciate its property, plant, and equipment, and Slow Company uses the straight-line method. Both companies use 175% declining balance depreciation for income tax purposes. The two companies are exactly alike except for the difference in depreciation methods.

Required:

a. Identify the financial ratios discussed in Chapter 16 that are **likely** to be affected by the difference in depreciation methods.
b. Which company will report the higher amount for each ratio that you have identified? If you cannot be certain, explain why.

C16–2   **(Analysis of the Impact of Business Transactions on Ratio Analysis)**
Nearly Broke Company requested a sizable loan from Second City National Bank in order to acquire a large tract of land for future expansion. Nearly Broke reported current assets of $1,750,000 ($475,000 in cash) and current liabilities of $975,000. Second City denied the loan request for a number of reasons including the fact that the working capital ratio was below two to one. When Nearly Broke was informed of the loan denial, the comptroller of the company immediately paid $470,000 that was owed to several trade creditors. The comptroller then asked Second City to reconsider the loan application. Based on these abbreviated facts, would you recommend that Second City approve the loan request? Why?

C16–3   **(Compute Accounting Ratios Based on the Actual Financial Statement)**
Refer to the financial statements of Chesebrough-Pond's given in Special Supplement B immediately preceding the Index.

Required:

Compute each of the 13 accounting ratios (for 1985) discussed in the chapter. If you are unable to compute a particular ratio, explain why. Assume the tax rate is 46%.

This chapter discusses accounting for the impact of changing prices (i.e., inflation and market value changes). Most large corporations report this information in a note to their financial statements.

BRUSHWELLMAN

Supplemental Statement of Income
Adjusted for Changing Prices

Year ended December 31, 1985
(Dollars in thousands)

	As Reported	Adjusted for Changes in Specific Prices
Net sales	$242,902	$242,902
Cost of sales	146,996	146,994
Other costs and expenses	32,036	32,036
Depreciation and amortization	15,710	17,806
Income taxes	20,248	20,248
Net Income From Continuing Operations	$ 27,912	$ 25,818

Other Information:
  Gain from decline in purchasing power of net monetary
    amounts owed during the year: .... $ 560

  Increases in cost of inventories and property, plant
    and equipment held during the year

        Due to increase in general price level.................. $ 8,559
        Due to increase in specific prices* (current costs)   439

        Excess of increase in general price level over
          increase in specific prices .... $ 8,120

*At December 31, 1985 the estimated current cost of inventories was $80,166 and of property, plant and equipment, net of allowances for depreciation and amortization, was $147,127.

FINANCIAL REPORTING AND CHANGING PRICES

PURPOSE:

Accounting is based on the cost principle. Our discussions in the previous chapters have been based on that principle. Some accountants question the relevancy of historical costs during a period of rapidly changing prices (e.g., inflation). This chapter discusses two alternatives to historical cost. This discussion of alternatives to historical cost is not merely theoretical because the FASB issued a *Statement* that encourages most large corporations to report supplemental information about the impact of changing prices on their financial statements. This chapter provides a complete understanding of these important disclosures.

ORGANIZATION:

Part A—Reporting the Effects of General Price Level Changes

1. Using price level index numbers.
2. Concepts underlying constant dollar (CD) restatement.
3. CD restatement procedures.
4. Overview of CD effects.

LEARNING OBJECTIVES—TO BE ABLE TO:

1. Identify the causes of changing prices.
2. Use price level index numbers.
3. Restate historical costs to constant dollars.
4. Identify monetary and nonmonetary items.
5. Compute the purchasing power gain (loss) on net monetary items.
6. Define three concepts of current value.
7. Prepare current cost financial statements.
8. Compute the real holding gain (loss) on nonmonetary items.
9. Expand your accounting vocabulary by learning about the "Important Terms Defined in This Chapter" (page 875).
10. Apply the knowledge learned from this chapter by completing the homework assigned by your instructor.

Part B—Reporting Current Cost Changes

1. Definitions of current value.
2. Concepts underlying current cost/constant dollar (CC/CD) reporting.
3. CC/CD reporting procedures.
4. Overview of CC/CD effects.
5. Reporting the effects of changing prices.

PART A—REPORTING THE EFFECTS OF GENERAL PRICE LEVEL (GPL) CHANGES

The current rate of inflation in our economy is relatively low. However, the United States has recently experienced periods of rapid inflation. It now costs more than three dollars to purchase the goods and services that one dollar would have purchased less than 20 years ago. In periods of inflation, traditional historical cost financial statements aggregate amounts that include dollars of different purchasing power. This aggregation of "apples and oranges" has caused the accounting profession to consider alternatives to historical cost measurements. Beginning in 1979, the FASB required most large companies to disclose inflation adjusted accounting information as a supplement to the historical cost statements. Accountants, economists, and persons in business and government do not agree about what should be done to make financial statements more useful under conditions of significant price changes.

Many people incorrectly believe that "inflation" and "changing prices" are synonymous terms. They are not. Inflation is the general rise of prices in the economy as the result of an excessive supply of money. Inflation is measured as the change in the general purchasing power of the dollar. Prices of specific goods and services may change more or less rapidly than the general inflation rate. Some prices may actually decrease during a period of inflation. During the double-digit inflation year of 1979, computer prices fell significantly. Changing prices may be caused by either general inflation or changes in the supply and demand for a specific item. Controversy exists today concerning whether accounting data should be adjusted to reflect the impact of general inflation or the changes in costs of the actual goods and services that a business acquires. We will consider both accounting alternatives in this chapter. First, we discuss accounting for the impact of general inflation. Reporting the effects of general price level (GPL) changes on financial statements requires that the traditional historical cost (HC) financial statements be **restated** from the HC basis to the latest GPL adjusted dollars, usually called **constant dollars.** This restatement requires use of general price level (GPL) index numbers.[1] The resulting financial statements are called historical cost/constant dollar (HC/CD) financial statements.

USING PRICE LEVEL INDEX NUMBERS

The federal government publishes price level index numbers that may be used to restate HC financial statement amounts for price changes. A **price level index** is a statistical value that expresses relative price levels for each of a series

---

[1] In this chapter the descriptive term **restated** is used because the HC basis amounts are restated to current GPL or constant dollars. Alternatively, the term **adjusted** sometimes is used. It is less descriptive and suggests the notion of "adjusting" entries, which is based on a different concept.

of periods. To construct a price level index, the price of a specific item, or a group of items, in one period is expressed as a relationship to a price at another period. A base year is selected and assigned the base index value of 100. Subsequent changes in prices are expressed in relation to this base. Two kinds of indexes are used widely:

1. **General price level (GPL) index**—A GPL price index measures the rate of inflation. These indexes are computed on the basis of an **average** "market basket" of commodities and services.[2] The index is computed by collecting the prices of each of the many items that make up the average market basket. Each period the average price of the basket is computed and then related to the base year index of 100. A GPL index is used to measure the effects of general price level (GPL) changes and to restate the HC financial statements to the latest constant dollar (CD) basis. Assume a tract of land was purchased in 1967 at a cost of $10,000 when the GPL index was 100. At the end of the current year, the land is still owned, and the GPL index is 280. The $10,000 cost of the land is reported on a HC/CD balance sheet at $10,000 × 280/100 = $28,000. The GPL increase was $18,000 (i.e., $28,000 − $10,000).

2. **Specific price level index**—A specific price level index is computed in the same way as a GPL index except that it measures the price change of a **single** item (or small group of homogeneous items). It is not a measure of general inflation. Specific price index values are used to estimate the current replacement cost of **specific** commodities or services. Assume that in the example given above, the land (HC, $10,000) had a specific price index of 120 when acquired in 1967 and has a specific price index of 240 at the end of the current year. The current replacement cost of the land can be estimated as $10,000 × 240/120 = $20,000. This computuation shows that the specific value of the land increased by $10,000, which was less than the GPL increase of $18,000. Use of specific index numbers is illustrated in Part B of this chapter.

The pervasiveness of **general inflation** in recent years is reflected in the index values from the Consumer Price Index for all Urban Consumers (CPI-U) given in Exhibit 17–1.

The use of a GPL index may be illustrated by considering the effect of general inflation on the cost of attending college. Assume that the cost of attending "Big State University" changes with the general inflation rate and that in 1967 the average cost of tuition for two semesters was $4,000 per student. Using the CPI-U index amounts given in Exhibit 17–1, we can estimate the cost of tuition for several years:

---

[2] The two GPL series usually are the Gross National Product Deflator (which is published quarterly) and the Consumer Price Index for all Urban Consumers (CPI-U) which is published monthly. Both indexes are published by the U.S. Department of Labor. The CPI-U index is the more widely used index in accounting.

EXHIBIT 17–1

Selected consumer price index values

	CPI-U index*	
Year	Average for the year	At year-end
1967 (base year)	100.0	101.6
1970	116.3	119.1
1971	121.3	123.1
1972	125.3	127.3
1973	133.1	138.5
1974	147.7	155.4
1975	161.2	166.3
1976	170.5	174.3
1977	181.5	186.1
1978	195.4	202.9
1979	217.4	229.9
1980	246.8	258.4
1981	272.4	281.5
1982	289.1	292.4
1983	298.4	303.5
1984	311.1	315.5
1985	322.2	327.4

* Source: Economic Indicators Joint Economic Committee, U.S. Government Printing Office (monthly).

Year	CPI-U index (average)	Restatement computation	Average cost per student
1967	100.0		$4,000
1970	116.3	$4,000 × 116.3/100.0 =	4,652
1975	161.2	$4,000 × 161.2/100.0 =	6,448
1979	217.4	$4,000 × 217.4/100.0 =	8,696
1985	322.2	$4,000 × 322.2/100.0 =	12,888

UNIT-OF-MEASURE ASSUMPTION

The **unit-of-measure assumption** (Exhibit 4–5) states that with many diverse items and transactions to be accounted for, it is necessary that a single unit of measure be adopted. In our country, accounting uses the dollar as the common denominator in the measurement process. Implicit in this use is the assumption that the dollar has a constant value, which is an important measurement characteristic (a "meterstick" is always one meter long!). However, during a period of inflation the constant value assumption is not valid. The monetary unit literally becomes a "rubber" measuring unit (it stretches) during a period of inflation.

The dollar is used in accounting because it is the accepted measure of value in our society. The dollar commands a certain amount of goods and services in the marketplace at a given time. Unfortunately, the dollar (or any other currency) does not maintain a stable value in terms of the goods and services it can command.

Over time, a dollar will command fewer goods and services in the case of inflation or, alternatively, more goods and services in the case of deflation. In other words, the purchasing power of the dollar changes over time. As a result of using the cost principle, transactions are recorded in historical cost (HC) basis dollars. Some of those dollar amounts (such as the cost of a factory) remain in the accounts and are reported in the financial statements over many years. Thus, the accounting system accumulates and reports dollars that have different purchasing power. Under historical cost (HC) accounting, dollars with different real values are **aggregated** on the balance sheet and **matched** on the income statement. During periods of significant inflation, financial statement amounts may reflect considerable distortion from current dollars because of the effects of purchasing power changes.

Consider a company that bought a building for $200,000 when the GPL index was 100. Assuming straight-line depreciation, no residual value, and a 40-year life, the annual depreciation is $5,000 per year. The current year is Year 30 (since acquisition), and the current GPL index is 300. At the end of Year 30, the financial statements would show the following amounts, based on historical cost (HC):

Balance sheet:
  Operational assets:
    Building (at cost) $200,000
    Accumulated depreciation ($5,000 × 30 years) 150,000
      Carrying value $50,000

Income statement:
  Depreciation expense   5,000

All of the amounts shown above represent dollars "valued" 30 years earlier, with a purchasing power equivalent of 100 (the GPL index). These amounts are aggregated with other dollar amounts that have different purchasing power equivalents. On the income statement, depreciation expense, expressed in dollars with one purchasing power (index 100), is matched with revenue, which is in current dollars with another purchasing power (index 300). The current GPL index of 300 means that each current dollar will command (buy) only one third (i.e., 100/300) as many goods and services as when the index was 100. The historical cost amounts can be restated to constant dollars by multiplying the HC amount by a CD index ratio in the following manner:

$$\begin{array}{l} \text{Historical} \\ \text{cost (HC)} \\ \text{amount} \end{array} \times \frac{\text{Current period GPL index}}{\text{Transaction date GPL index}} = \begin{array}{l} \text{CD} \\ \text{restated} \\ \text{amount} \end{array}$$

The calculations and the resulting CD restated amounts for the data given above would be as follows:

Item	HC basis	CD restatement computation	CD restated amount
Balance sheet amounts:			
Operational assets:			
Building	$200,000	× 300/100 =	$600,000
Accumulated depreciation	150,000	× 300/100 =	450,000
Carrying value	$ 50,000	× 300/100 =	$150,000
Income statement amount:			
Depreciation expense	$ 5,000	× 300/100 =	$ 15,000

CONCEPTS UNDERLYING CD RESTATEMENT OF FINANCIAL STATEMENTS

Constant dollar (CD) restatement of financial statements is a **supplementary reporting approach.** The traditional HC financial statements are prepared each period in conformity with GAAP. The HC statements continue as the basic periodic reports of the entity. HC/CD information is prepared by restating historical cost information in current end-of-period dollars (i.e., in constant dollars). Thus, the HC/CD financial statements continue to be cost basis statements except that all dollar amounts are in **constant dollars,** that is, dollars of constant purchasing power. CD restated information often is called HC/CD information to emphasize that it is cost data restated for the effects of changes in the purchasing power of the dollar. The CD restatement computations involve three steps:

Step 1:   Classify all accounts on the financial statements as either monetary or nonmonetary (defined later in the chapter). **Monetary** items are **not** restated on the HC/CD financial statements while the **nonmonetary** items **are** restated. Exhibit 17–2 gives the classification of several accounts.

Step 2:   Restate each **nonmonetary** item by multiplying its HC amount by the appropriate restatement ratio (i.e., the current period GPL index divided by the GPL index that existed at the date on which the transaction was recorded).

Step 3:   Calculate the purchasing power gain or loss on monetary items. This gain or loss is measured as the difference between the HC amount and the CD restated amount for each monetary item. Each of these steps is discussed in the remainder of this part of the chapter.

EXHIBIT 17–2

Classification of monetary and nonmonetary items

	Monetary	Nonmonetary
Assets		
Cash	X	
Marketable securities:		
Most common stock		X
Most bonds	X	
Accounts and notes receivable	X	
Allowance for doubtful accounts	X	
Inventories		X
Prepaid expense:		
Claims to future services		X
Prepayments that are deposits or advance payments	X	
Long-term receivables	X	
Property, plant, and equipment		X
Accumulated depreciation		X
Patents and trademarks		X
Goodwill		X
Liabilities		
Accounts and notes payable	X	
Accrued expenses	X	
Cash dividends payable	X	
Bonds payable and other long-term debt	X	
Premium or discount on bonds payable	X	
Deferred income taxes	X	
Owners' Equity		
Preferred stock (nonmonetary if not carried at a fixed redemption price)	X	
Common stock		X
Retained earnings		
This amount usually is restated as a plug or balancing amount		X

Source: Adapted from *FASB Statement 33*, "Financial Reporting and Changing Prices," (Stamford, Conn., September, 1979).

CD RESTATEMENT—ILLUSTRATIVE CASE

A simplified situation is used as the basis for discussing the computations used to develop HC/CD financial statements.

ACE Corporation was organized December 31, 19A, when the GPL index was 120. The accounting period ends December 31. Preparation of HC/CD financial statements of ACE Corporation is discussed in the following paragraphs. Exhibit 17–3 gives background data for ACE Corporation.

EXHIBIT 17–3

Historical cost and GPL data of ACE Corporation

Summary of transactions:

Year 19A:
a. December 31, 19A: Sold and issued capital stock (nopar) for $80,000 cash (GPL index, 120).
b. December 31, 19A: Borrowed $40,000 cash from a local bank; signed a $40,000 interest-bearing note due December 31, 19C (GPL index, 120).
c. December 31, 19A: Purchased equipment for use in the business at a cash cost of $60,000 (GPL index, 120).

Year 19B:
d. March 19B: Purchased land for use in the business at a cash cost of $6,350 (GPL index, 127).
e. During 19B: Purchased merchandise (evenly throughout the year) at a cash cost of $121,500 (average GPL index for 19B, 135). Assume a perpetual inventory system (average costing), cost of goods sold, $108,000, and an ending inventory of $13,500 (i.e., total, $121,500).
f. During 19B: Sales revenue, $162,000, sold evenly throughout the year (average GPL index for 19B, 135). Assume total cash collections on sales of $129,600 and accounts receivable at year-end of $32,400 (i.e., total, $162,000).
g. During 19B: Expenses paid in cash $27,000, which included interest expense and income tax expense but excluded depreciation expense (average GPL index for 19B, 135).
h. July 1, 19B: Declared and paid a cash dividend, $2,700 (GPL average index, 135).
i. December 31, 19B: Depreciation expense on equipment (estimated five-year life and no residual value), $60,000 ÷ 5 years = $12,000.

Balance sheet, at December 31, 19B (HC basis amounts):

Assets		Liabilities	
Cash	$32,050	Note payable, long term	$ 40,000
Accounts receivable (net)	32,400		
Inventory	13,500	**Stockholders' Equity**	
Equipment	60,000	Capital stock (nopar)	80,000
Accumulated depreciation	(12,000)	Retained earnings	12,300
Land	6,350		
Total	$132,300	Total	$132,300

Income statement, for the year ended December 31, 19B (HC basis amounts):

Sales revenue	$162,000
Cost of goods sold	(108,000)
Depreciation expense	(12,000)
Remaining expenses	(27,000)
Net income	$ 15,000

Statement of retained earnings, at December 31, 19B (HC basis amounts):

Beginning balance, January 1, 19B	$ –0–
Add: Net income of 19B	15,000
Deduct: Dividends of 19B	(2,700)
Ending balance, December 31, 19B	$12,300

GPL index data:

December 31, 19A	120
January 1, 19B	120
Average during 19B	135
December 31, 19B	150

Step 1—Identify Monetary and Nonmonetary Items

Preparation of HC/CD financial statements requires that a careful distinction be made between **monetary items** and **nonmonetary items.** These items cause different economic effects on their holder (owner) when the real value of the dollar changes as the result of inflation or deflation.

A **monetary item,** by its nature or as the result of a contract, is stated in a **fixed** number of dollars. This fixed number of dollars does not change in response to changes in price levels. Monetary items include cash, payables, and receivables but do not include revenues or expenses. Because inflation does not affect the amount of cash held or the number of dollars to be paid or received for monetary items, these items are **not restated** on HC/CD financial statements.

While monetary items are not restated on HC/CD financial statements, the **purchasing power** of monetary items is affected by inflation. Consider what would happen if you left $100 in your wallet during a year in which the inflation rate was 20%. At the end of the year, you could buy less goods and services with the $100 than you could have bought at the beginning of the year. Your loss of purchasing power on this **monetary asset** was $20 [i.e., $100 − ($100 × 120/100)]. This $20 loss is called a purchasing power loss on monetary items.

In contrast, if you held **monetary liabilities** during a period of inflation, you would experience a purchasing power gain on monetary items because the liabilities will be paid in dollars that have less purchasing power than the dollars that were borrowed. A dollar owed through a period of inflation is still a dollar owed, although it will command fewer goods at the end of the period.

In summary, monetary assets and monetary liabilities are not restated on the HC/CD financial statements. However, their existence can cause the holder (or debtor) to incur a real gain or loss during a period of inflation. A purchasing power **gain** on net monetary items is reported on HC/CD financial statements if the purchasing power gain on monetary liabilities is more than the purchasing power loss on monetary assets. Alternatively, a purchasing power **loss** is reported if the purchasing power loss on monetary assets is more than the purchasing power gain on monetary liabilities.

Notice in Exhibit 17–4 that the three monetary items (cash, accounts receivable, and note payable) are not restated in the HC/CD financial statements. However, a purchasing power loss on monetary items of $5,050 is reported on the HC/CD income statement (this loss is computed in Exhibit 17–5).

Nonmonetary items are all items on the financial statement that are not classified as monetary assets and liabilities. Examples of nonmonetary items are shown in Exhibit 17–2.[3] Nonmonetary items have dollar amounts that are **not** fixed in the future by their nature or by contract. The value of a nonmonetary

---

[3] Preferred stock usually is classified as a monetary item because it usually has a fixed redeemable value. In contrast, receivables and liabilities that can be settled with goods and services (rather than cash) are classified as nonmonetary items.

___EXHIBIT 17–4___

CD restatement of financial statements, ACE Corporation, year-end 19B

Items	HC Basis	CD Restatement Computations	HC/CD Basis
Balance sheet, at December 31, 19B:			
Assets			
Cash	$ 32,050	Monetary, not restated	$ 32,050
Accounts receivable (net)	32,400	Monetary, not restated	32,400
Inventory	13,500	Nonmonetary, $13,500 × 150/135	15,000
Equipment	60,000	Nonmonetary, $60,000 × 150/120	75,000
Accumulated depreciation (credit)	(12,000)	Nonmonetary, $12,000 × 150/120	(15,000)
Land	6,350	Nonmonetary, $6,350 × 150/127	7,500
Total	$ 132,300		$ 146,950
Liabilities			
Note payable, long term	$ 40,000	Monetary, not restated	$ 40,000
Stockholders' Equity			
Capital stock, nopar	80,000	Nonmonetary, $80,000 × 150/120	100,000
Retained earnings	12,300	Nonmonetary, plug, $146,950 − $40,000 − $100,000	6,950
Total	$ 132,300		$ 146,950
Income statement, for the year ended December 31, 19B:			
Sales revenue	$ 162,000	Nonmonetary, $162,000 × 150/135	$ 180,000
Deduct:			
Cost of goods sold	(108,000)	Nonmonetary, $108,000 × 150/135	(120,000)
Depreciation expense	(12,000)	Nonmonetary, $12,000 × 150/120	(15,000)
Remaining expenses	(27,000)	Nonmonetary, $27,000 × 150/135	(30,000)
Income from normal operations	$ 15,000		$ 15,000
Purchasing power gain (loss on monetary items		Computed, per Exhibit 17–5	(5,050)
Income, CD restated		Carry to statement of retained earnings	$ 9,950
Statement of retained earnings, at December 31, 19B			
Beginning balance, January 1, 19B	$ –0–	Nonmonetary	$ –0–
Add: Income of 19B	15,000	Nonmonetary, from restated income statement	9,950
Deduct: Dividends of 19B (debit)	(2,700)	Nonmonetary, $2,700 × 150/135	(3,000)
Ending balance, December 31, 19B	$ 12,300	Proof: check per balance sheet plug amount	$ 6,950

EXHIBIT 17–5

Computation of the purchasing power gain (loss) on net monetary items—ACE Corporation, year-end 19B

Items	HC Basis	CD Restatement Computations	CD Restated Basis	Purchasing Power Gain (Loss) on Net Monetary Items
Cash:[a]				
Beginning balance	$ 60,000	$ 60,000 × 150/120	$ 75,000	
Debits:				
Sales and accounts receivable	129,600	129,600 × 150/135	144,000	
Credits:				
Purchase of land	(6,350)	6,350 × 150/127	(7,500)	
Merchandise, expenses, and dividends ($121,500 + $27,000 + $2,700)	(151,200)	151,200 × 150/135	(168,000)	
Ending balance	$ 32,050		$ 43,500	$(11,450)
Accounts receivable:[b]				
Ending balance	$ 32,400	32,400 × 150/135	$ 36,000	(3,600)
Note payable:[c]				
Beginning balance	$ 40,000	40,000 × 150/120	$ 50,000	10,000
Purchasing power net gain (loss) on net monetary items (to income statement)				$ (5,050)

Explanation:

[a] Restatement of an account that has several changes during the period at **different** GPL ratios requires restatement of each increase and decrease separately. Thus, the beginning balance and each change (grouped by GPL index numbers) are restated.

[b] Accounts receivable can be restated in this case on the basis of the ending balance because (1) there was no beginning balance and (2) the increases and decreases during the year were at the average GPL index (135).

[c] Note payable can be restated in this case on the basis of the beginning balance because there were no increases or decreases in the account during the year (the beginning balance was recorded on December 31, 19A, when the GPL index was 120).

item tends to move up and down with inflation and deflation. A tract of land purchased for $6,350 when the GPL index was 127 would **tend** to increase in market value to $7,500 as a result of an increase of the GPL price index to 150 (i.e., $6,350 × 150/127 = $7,500). This price change on the land would not provide the owner with a real gain because if the land was sold for $7,500, the

$7,500 would purchase (at the date of sale of the land) the same quantity of real goods and services that the $6,350 would have bought when the owner originally purchased the land. A real value change would occur only if the price of the land changed more or less rapidly than the general inflation rate.

Step 2—CD Restatement of HC Financial Statements

CD restatement of each HC financial statement for ACE Corporation is shown in Exhibit 17–4.

Restatement of the balance sheet

The ACE Corporation balance sheet shows three monetary items: cash, accounts receivable, and the note payable. These three **monetary items** were not restated because each has a fixed monetary amount that is not affected by inflation or deflation. The three HC amounts for monetary items were extended across on the balance sheet to the CD restatement column. In contrast, the four nonmonetary asset amounts on the balance sheet were CD restated because their market prices are free to change as a result of changes in the general price level.

Notice in Exhibit 17–4 that 10 **nonmonetary items** are restated on the HC/CD balance sheet and income statement. Also, notice that there is not any real gain or loss on the **nonmonetary** items reported on the HC/CD financial statements (see Part B of this chapter).

Exhibit 17–4 gives the CD restatement computation for each nonmonetary item. For example, the Land account was restated as follows:

$$\begin{array}{c} \text{Historical cost} \\ \text{(HC) basis} \\ \text{amount} \end{array} \times \frac{\text{Current period GPL index}}{\text{Transaction date GPL index}} = \begin{array}{c} \text{CD} \\ \text{restated} \\ \text{amount} \end{array}$$

$$\text{Land, \$6,350} \times \frac{150}{127} = \$7,500$$

Restatement of the income statement

All items on the income statement are **nonmonetary**; therefore, each item is restated. The numerator of the CD restatement ratio is the ending GPL index. The denominator usually is the average GPL index for the current period because it is assumed that price changes and business transactions occurred evenly throughout the period. Notice that depreciation expense always is restated by using the same GPL index amounts that were used to restate the related asset (150/120 in the illustration). Notice the "Purchasing power gain (loss) on monetary items." This **gain or loss** must be computed separately on the monetary assets and monetary liabilities as shown in Step 3 (Exhibit 17–5).

Step 3—Computation of the Purchasing Power Gain or Loss on Net Monetary Items

Computation of the purchasing power gain or loss requires restatement of each monetary asset and each monetary liability. Often this is the most tedious phase of CD restatement. Monetary items that have identical numerator indexes and identical denominator indexes can be grouped for computation purposes with the same results.

Computation of the purchasing power gain (loss) on the monetary items for ACE Corporation is shown in Exhibit 17–5. Notice in this exhibit that the HC amount of each monetary item (first money column) is CD restated by using the appropriate numerator and denominator indexes. The net gain or loss on each monetary item is the difference between its **ending** actual HC basis amount and its **ending** CD restated amount (i.e., for cash, $32,050 − $43,500 = $11,450 loss).

The beginning balance of each monetary item as well as each transaction that affects the account must be restated with the appropriate GPL indexes. **Monetary** items are restated **only** for purposes of calculating the purchasing power gain or loss on net monetary items. They are **not** restated on the balance sheet.

The total purchasing power gain (loss) on monetary items is the sum of the purchasing power **losses on monetary assets** and the purchasing power **gains on monetary liabilities.** In the illustration, the $5,050 is a loss during a period of inflation because the monetary assets exceeded the monetary liabilities. This purchasing power gain (loss) is reported on the HC/CD income statement (as shown in Exhibit 17–4) because it represents an economic gain or loss.

In summary, HC/CD financial statements are prepared by restating the **nonmonetary** HC items on the balance sheet, income statement, and statement of retained earnings. The monetary items are included in the HC/CD financial statements at their HC basis amounts. However, the **monetary** assets and liabilities are restated separately to compute the purchasing power gain or loss on monetary items, which is reported on the income statement. The CD restated net income is carried to the HC/CD statement of retained earnings, and the CD restated ending balance of retained earnings is reported on the HC/CD balance sheet.[4]

---

[4] In view of CD restatement on the balance sheet of only the nonmonetary items (not the monetary items), the question always arises as to why a HC/CD balance sheet "balances." Technically, the reason is that the monetary assets and monetary liabilities are not restated on the balance sheet, but total owners' equity is restated. Therefore, owners' equity includes a restatement for both nonmonetary items and monetary items. Inclusion of the purchasing power gain (loss) on monetary items on the income statement (and hence in retained earnings on the balance sheet) provides the mathematically necessary amount to bring the equation $A - L = OE$ into balance on the HC/CD balance sheet.

OVERVIEW OF CD EFFECTS

A comparison of the HC and HC/CD balance sheets presented in Exhibit 17–4 shows that the CD restatement increased total assets from $132,300 to $146,950 (an 11.1% increase). In contrast, the income statement reflected a decrease in reported income of $15,000 to $9,950 which was a 34% decrease. When there is inflation and the relationship between monetary assets and monetary liabilities remains essentially constant, **CD restated income** usually will be lower than the HC amount, primarily because of higher restated assets and correspondingly higher restated depreciation expense.

HC financial statements rest on the unit-of-measure assumption (Exhibit 4–5), which states that each transaction should be measured in those dollars that "existed" at the date of each transaction. During periods of inflation or deflation, HC financial statements contain dollars that have different amounts of purchasing power. In contrast, the concept of HC/CD financial statements retains the HC amounts except that they are restated in constant dollars. Therefore, all nonmonetary HC dollar amounts (but not the monetary amounts) reflected in the HC statements are restated to constant dollars. The HC/CD income statement reports a special type of gain or loss: purchasing power gain or loss on monetary items.

Advocates of CD restatement contend that two sets of financial statements should be presented: (1) one set prepared on the traditional HC basis, and (2) another set prepared on the CD restated basis. The primary **arguments for** presenting HC/CD financial statements are (1) during periods of significant inflation, HC basis statements contain serious measurement distortions; (2) the CD restated amounts, including the purchasing power gain or loss on monetary items, are relevant to the users of financial statements; and (3) the HC approach essentially is retained with all amounts stated in terms of dollars of the same purchasing power. In contrast, the primary **arguments against** HC/CD statements are (1) two sets of financial statements (restated and not restated) may confuse statement users, (2) it is difficult to justify a particular GPL price index to use for restatement purposes, (3) statement users do not find the restated amounts to be particularly useful, and (4) GPL effects and real value changes on **nonmonetary** items are not reported separately (discussed in Part B).

FASB *Statement of Financial Accounting Standards 33*, "Financial Reporting and Changing Prices," which applies only to very large companies, states that:

> for fisal years ended on or after December 25, 1979, enterprises are required to report:
>
> *a.* Income from continuing operations adjusted for the effects of general inflation.
>
> *b.* The purchasing power gain or loss on monetary items.[5]

---

[5] In September, 1986, the FASB completed a review of *Statement 33* and concluded that further supplementary disclosure of inflation-adjusted data should be encouraged but not required.

These minimum requirements usually are met by including the two required amounts in the notes to the financial statements. *FASB Statement 33* does not require a complete set of HC/CD financial statements, although complete and comprehensive CD reporting (as illustrated on Exhibit 17–4) is to be encouraged.

PART B—REPORTING CURRENT COST CHANGES

The primary argument for reporting current cost information in the financial statements is that users are more interested in the current "worth" of assets rather than in the HC amounts reported under GAAP. Basically, current cost is the price a company would have to pay today to replace an asset. The acceptance of current cost accounting has been slow because of the difficulty associated with measuring current cost. *FASB Statement 33* requires certain large corporations to report current cost information adjusted for general inflation. This combination approach is called current cost/constant dollar (CC/CD) accounting. In the following discussions, the **combination reporting approach** is used because it provides considerable information on both current cost changes and GPL effects.

DEFINITION OF CURRENT VALUE IN FINANCIAL REPORTING

The term **current value** is a general term that refers to three different concepts of value:

1. **Present value** is measured as the present value of the expected net future cash inflow attributable to an asset. The expected net future cash inflows are discounted to the present at an appropriate interest rate. Although this approach is conceptually superior to HC or CD, it is not used in financial statements because of uncertainty in (*a*) projecting the future cash inflows by period and (*b*) selecting an appropriate interest rate.
2. **Net realizable value** is measured as the expected price at which an asset could be sold in its present condition, less all disposal costs. This concept of asset value was discussed in Chapter 7 in respect to inventories. This method of asset valuation is used in cases in which current value cannot be determined reasonably by other approaches.[6]
3. **Current cost (CC)** is measured as the cost of replacing the asset in its present operating condition with either an identical asset or one with the same "service potential." Estimating the current cost of some assets is hard because there may not be a current market for certain unique assets (such as a nuclear power plant). For other assets, estimating current cost may be simple because

---

[6] *FASB Statement 33* specifies that current cost cannot exceed net realizable value for financial statement reporting purposes.

there are established markets. Typically for inventory items, standard price lists or active markets can be used to estimate current cost.

CONCEPTS UNDERLYING CC/CD FINANCIAL REPORTING

CC/CD financial reporting does **not** require the recording of current costs in the accounts. The following discussions treat CC/CD as a supplementary reporting approach without entering the current costs in the accounts.

When CC/CD financial statements are prepared, the HC amounts are converted to CC/CD amounts. CC/CD reports price changes in the **nonmonetary** asset and income statement amounts. For **monetary items,** the HC amounts and CC/CD amounts usually are the same. Preparation of CC/CD financial statements has the following steps:

Step 1: At the end of each accounting period a **current cost value** is obtained for each nonmonetary item by using current price lists, prices for comparable used assets, specific price indexes, and professional appraisals.

Step 2: On the CC/CD balance sheet, the **monetary** items are not changed from the historical cost amounts. The **nonmonetary** amounts are changed from historical cost to current cost and are reported on the CC/CD balance sheet in constant dollars.

Step 3: On the CC/CD income statement, revenues are reported at historical cost restated for the GPL change that occurred during the year. Expenses are reported at current cost restated for GPL changes.

Step 4: A new item, "CC/CD real holding gain (loss) on **nonmonetary** items," is computed and reported on the CC/CD income statement. This holding gain (loss) is computed as the difference between the constant dollar restated historical cost and the current cost of all nonmonetary items. A holding gain (loss) is reported whenever the actual cost of nonmonetary items changes more (less) rapidly than the inflation rate. These gains and losses are aggregated and reported on the CC/CD income statement as a single amount.[7]

Some current cost amounts are not measured in end-of-period dollars. These amounts can be restated to end-of-period constant dollars. This combination approach has the advantage of reporting both CC and GPL effects. This approach is discussed in the next section.[8]

CC/CD FINANCIAL REPORTING—ILLUSTRATIVE CASE

The data for ACE Corporation (used in Part A) will be continued in this part of the chapter. The HC financial statements are shown in Exhibit 17–3.

---

[7] This amount can be separated into two amounts: (1) unrealized, which relates to assets still owned, and (2) realized, which relates to assets sold during the period.

[8] Another variation of CC reporting does not include the CD feature.

Step 1—Determine Current Cost Data

The first step in developing CC/CD financial statements is to determine current cost data for each **nonmonetary** item. Current cost amounts for ACE Corporation are given in Exhibit 17–6.

EXHIBIT 17–6

Current cost/constant dollar data for ACE Corporation

Item	Current Cost Determination*	CC Valuation Amount (in Constant Dollars at Dec. 31, 19B)
Ending inventory, December 31, 19B	The specific price index at year's end of the inventory, based on CC, was 120% of HC. $13,500 × 1.20 =	16,200
Equipment	The specific price index at year's end of the equipment, based on estimated current cost in present condition, was 130% of HC. $60,000 × 1.30 =	78,000
Accumulated depreciation, equipment	The equipment has a five-year useful life, no residual value, and is being depreciated on a straight-line basis. At the end of 19B, CC accumulated depreciation is one fifth of the CC amount for equipment: $78,000 × ⅕ =	15,600
Depreciation expense	The CC amount for this expense is determined by applying the depreciation rate (one fifth) to the **average** CC amount for equipment during the year 19B and restating the result to end-of-period constant dollars: $\left(\dfrac{\$60{,}000\ +\ \$78{,}000}{2}\right) \times \dfrac{1}{5} \times \dfrac{150}{135} =$	15,330
Land	Professionally appraised at year's end	6,985
Cost of goods sold	The average specific price index, based on the current cost when the goods were sold, was 108% of HC. $108,000 × 1.08 × 150/135	129,600
Remaining expenses	HC average and CC average were the same for the year. $27,000 × 150/135 =	30,000

* For GPL data, refer to Exhibits 17–3 and 17–4.

Step 2—Determine Balance Sheet Changes

Exhibit 17–7 shows the *(a)* HC financial statements and *(b)* CC/CD financial statements. The basis used to determine each current cost amount also is shown in Exhibit 17–7. Notice: (1) the difference in the current cost accounting treatment of monetary and nonmonetary items, (2) the variety of approaches used to determine the current cost amounts, and (3) the restatement of all items in year-end constant dollars.

In Exhibit 17–7, the monetary assets and liabilities were reported at historical cost because monetary items do not respond to changes in price levels. The nonmonetary assets were stated in current cost amounts determined at year's end. As a result, it was not necessary to CD restate the current cost amounts.

Step 3—Determine Income Statement Changes

It is not necessary to determine the current cost of sales revenue because it reflects "current value" on the date of the sale. However, sales revenue must be CD restated to reflect GPL changes during the year. CC/CD cost of goods sold is determined by using the average specific price index (108) when the goods were sold. This current cost amount is also CD restated to reflect GPL changes during the year. Notice that the same CD index ratio (150/135) is used to restate sales revenue and cost of goods sold. CC/CD depreciation expense was determined by multiplying the current cost of the equipment by the depreciation rate and then restating the result in year-end constant dollars.

Step 4—Determine Real Holding Gain (Loss) on Nonmonetary Items

There are two types of holding gains (losses) reported on the CC/CD income statement. One is based on the **monetary items,** and the other is based on **nonmonetary items.**

1. Purchasing power gain (loss) on monetary items, $5,050—This real gain or loss occurs when monetary items are held during a period of inflation or deflation. It is the same calculation that was discussed in Part A (Exhibit 17–5).
2. CC real holding gain (loss) on nonmonetary items, $13,015—This real gain or loss occurs when nonmonetary assets that are still owned at the end of the period and expenses of the period change in dollar value more or less rapidly than the inflation rate. Computation of this amount is illustrated in Exhibit 17–8.

Computation of CC **real holding** gains and losses on **nonmonetary** items (Exhibit 17–8) reflects the following conceptual differences between **GPL fictional changes** and **CC real value changes:**

EXHIBIT 17–7

Current cost (in constant dollars) financial statements, ACE Corporation, end of Year 19B

Items	HC Basis	CC/CD Basis of Determination	CC/CD Amount
Balance sheet, at December 31, 19B:			
Assets			
Cash	$ 32,050	Monetary—HC and CC are the same	$ 32,050
Accounts receivable (net)	32,400	Monetary—HC is net realizable value	32,400
Inventory	13,500	× specific price index (at year's end), 1.20	16,200
Equipment	60,000	× specific price index (at year's end), 1.30	78,000
Accumulated depreciation (credit)	(12,000)	× specific price index (at year's end), 1.30	(15,600)
Land	5,350	Per professional appraisal (in constant dollars)	6,985
Total	$ 132,300		$ 150,035
Liabilities			
Note payable, long term	$ 40,000	Monetary—HC and CC are the same	$ 40,000
Stockholders' Equity			
Capital stock (nopar)	80,000	× GPL index, 150/120 (to restate in constant dollars)	100,000
Retained earnings	12,300	To balance (plug) $150,035 − $40,000 − $100,000	10,035
Total	$ 132,300		$ 150,035
Income statement, for the year ended December 31, 19B:			
Sales revenue (credit)	$ 162,000	× GPL index, 150/135 (to restate in constant dollars)	$ 180,000
Deduct:			
Cost of goods sold (debit)	(108,000)	× specific price index, 1.08 × 150/135 (to restate in constant dollars)	(129,600)
Depreciation expense (debit)	(12,000)	Calculated by applying depreciation rate to average CC of equipment $\dfrac{\$60,000 + \$78,000}{2} \times \dfrac{1}{5} \times \dfrac{150}{135}$	(15,330)*
Remaining expenses (debit)	(27,000)	× GPL index, 150/135 (to restate in constant dollars)	(30,000)
Income from operations	$ 15,000		5,070
Purchasing power gain (loss) on net monetary items (Exhibit 17–5)			(5,050)
CC real holding gain (loss) on non-monetary items (Exhibit 17–8)			13,015
CC/CD income			$ 13,035
Statement of retained earnings, at December 31, 19B:			
Beginning balance	$ –0–		$ –0–
Add: Income of 19B	15,000	Per income statement	13,035
Deduct: Dividends of 19B	(2,700)	× GPL index, 150/135 (to restate in constant dollars)	(3,000)
Ending balance, December 31, 19B	$ 12,300	Carried to balance sheet	$ 10,035

* This solution follows *FASB 33*. Note that accumulated depreciation and depreciation expense for this first year are different by $270. We believe a conceptually preferable approach would reflect the same amount for the increase in accumulated depreciation and depreciation expense. This approach would increase the CC real holding gain on nonmonetary items by $270.

EXHIBIT 17-8

Computation of CC real holding gains (losses) on nonmonetary items, ACE Corporation

	HC Basis A	CD Restated Basis (See Exhibit 17-2) B		CC/CD Basis C		Total Change HC to CC C–A	GPL Fiction Change Gain (Loss) B–A	CC Real Holding Gain (Loss) C–B
Nonmonetary assets:								
Inventory	$ 13,500	A × 150/135	$ 15,000	A × 1.20	$ 16,200	$ 2,700	$ 1,500	$ 1,200
Equipment	60,000	A × 150/120	75,000	A × 1.30	78,000	18,000	15,000	3,000
Accumulated depreciation (credit)	(12,000)	A × 150/120	(15,000)	A × 1.30	(15,600)	(3,600)	(3,000)	(600)
Land	6,350	A × 150/127	7,500	Appraisal	6,985	635	1,150	(515)
Operations:								
Sales revenue (credit)	(162,000)	A × 150/135	(180,000)	A × 150/135*	(180,000)	(18,000)	(18,000)	–0–
Deduct:								
Cost of goods sold	108,000	A × 150/135	120,000	A × 1.08 × 150/135†	129,600	21,600	12,000	9,600
Depreciation expense	12,000	A × 150/120	15,000	From Exhibit 17-7	15,330	3,330	12,000	330
Remaining expenses	27,000	A × 150/135	30,000	A × 150/135*	30,000	3,000	3,000	–0–
Totals	$ 52,850		$ 67,500		$ 80,515	$ 27,665	$ 14,650	$ 13,015

* No CC change specified in the problem; to convert to constant dollars.

† Observe that the related assets (e.g., inventory and equipment) are "CC valued" at the **year's end specific index**, while the expenses (i.e., cost of goods sold, depreciation expense, etc.) are "CC valued" at the **average specific index** when incurred and then are CD restated to year-end.

1. **GPL fictional changes on nonmonetary items** are differences between historical costs and CD restated amounts. These differences are **not real value changes** because they represent only the number of dollars required to exactly keep even with general inflation.
2. **CC real holding gains (losses) on nonmonetary items** are differences between current costs and CD restated amounts. These differences represent **real value changes** because they measure the extent to which current costs changed more or less than the general inflation rate.

To illustrate, the 19B ending inventory in Exhibit 17–6 was reported as follows: HC, $13,500; and CC, $16,200. The total price difference between these two amounts, $2,700, represents the effects of two different kinds of price changes:

1. GPL fictional change:
      CD, restated, $15,000 − HC, $13,500 = $1,500 GPL fictional gain
2. CC real holding gain:
      CC, $16,200 − CD restated, $15,000   =   1,200 CC real holding gain
            Total price change $2,700

The above analysis may be shown graphically as follows:

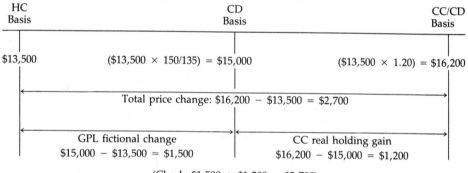

(Check: $1,500 + $1,200 = $2,700)

While the computation of the CC real holding gain or loss on **nonmonetary** items (Exhibit 17–8) looks complicated, it is based on the concept shown in the previous graph. Notice the application of this concept in Exhibit 17–8. Nonmonetary items are listed at their historical costs in Column A; HC/CD amounts are computed in Column B; and CC/CD amounts are computed in Column C. The remaining columns reflect the differences caused by the price changes of each item—total change, GPL fictional, and CC real holding gains and losses. The **CC real holding gain (loss) on nonmonetary items** (the last column) is the difference between the CC/CD amounts and the HC/CD amounts. The CC real holding gain (loss) on nonmonetary items is reported on the CC/CD income statement (Exhibit 17–7). The GPL fictional gain (loss) (the fifth column) is not reported separately on the CC/CD financial statements because the GPL effects are included in the various nonmonetary CC amounts.

OVERVIEW OF CC/CD EFFECTS

HC financial statements are distorted during periods of significant inflation because of the decline in the purchasing power of the dollar. Inflation results in aggregating dollars with different values (in terms of purchasing power) in the financial statements. This "adding of apples and oranges" is not very meaningful for measuring financial results. On the other hand, historical cost reporting is **objective** because the recorded amounts are established by actual transactions between parties who bargain in their own economic interest.

HC/CD financial statements report the effects of inflation by restating historical costs in terms of the current purchasing power of the dollar. Also, CD restatement measures the real purchasing power gain or loss on net monetary items held during a period of inflation. CD restatement does not report changes in the actual costs of goods and services purchased by a company. Some financial statement users believe that information concerning changes in actual costs is more relevant than information concerning the effect of general inflation.

CC/CD financial statements report the effects of both general inflation and changes in the specific prices paid by a company for the goods and services that it acquires. CC/CD financial statements report all amounts at their current cost and express current costs in terms of constant dollars.[9] The conceptual objective of CC/CD reporting is to tell decision makers the current "worth" of each item reported. This objective is important because decision makers must evaluate the current situation and make predictions about the future. Current values are relevant for most decisions. For example, a person who is thinking about buying a 20-year-old office building would be concerned primarily about (1) its value today and (2) its potential to generate net cash inflows during the expected holding period. The historical cost of the building would not be relevant to the purchase decision.

CC/CD is a conceptually sound reporting approach, but it has a significant implementation problem. It is often difficult to attain objectivity and accuracy in determining current costs. In some situations, it is easy to determine current costs, but it is difficult in others. Some accountants believe that the relevancy of current cost information justifies reporting data that are based on subjective determinations.

REPORTING THE EFFECTS OF CHANGING PRICES

FASB Statement 33, "Financial Reporting and Changing Prices," requires, at a minimum, the supplementary reporting of certain HC/CD and CC/CD information. Many accountants and statement users questioned the relevancy of the required HC/CD disclosures. In 1984, the FASB responded to the criticism and

---

[9] *FASB Statement 33* specifies that the GPL (constant dollars) may be expressed as (1) at year-end or (2) the average for the year.

issued *FASB Statement 82* which eliminated the HC/CD disclosure requirements for companies that present CC/CD information.

FASB Statement 33 (as amended) requires the following disclosures:[10]

1. CC/CD basis:
   a. Information about income from continuing operations for the current reporting year on a CC/CD basis.
   b. The CC amounts of inventory and property, plant, and equipment at the end of the current reporting year.
   c. Increases or decreases for the current reporting year in the CC amounts of inventory and property, plant, and equipment, before and after adjusting for the effects of inflation.
   d. The principal types of information used to calculate the CC of inventory and property, plant, and equipment.
   e. Differences between the depreciation methods, estimates of useful lives, and values of assets used to calculate CC/CD depreciation and the methods and estimates used to calculate HC depreciation.

2. Summary of the most recent five years:
   a. Net sales and other operating revenues.
   b. Income from continuing operations on a CC/CD basis.
   c. Purchasing power gain or loss on net monetary items.
   d. Increases or decreases in the CC amounts of inventory and property, plant, and equipment, net of inflation.
   e. Net assets at year-end on a CC/CD basis.
   f. Income per common share from continuing operations on a CC/CD basis.

The information required by the *Statement* usually is presented in the notes to the statements instead of in comprehensive CC/CD financial statements, as illustrated in this chapter. By studying comprehensive HC/CD and CC/CD statements, you have a better understanding of the uses and limitations of the information required by *FASB Statement 33* (as amended) and the concepts underlying the preparation of accounting data adjusted for changing prices.

IMPORTANT TERMS DEFINED IN THIS CHAPTER

Terms (alphabetically)	Key words in definitions of important terms used in chapter	Page reference
CD restatement	Restatement of financial statements to reflect general price level changes.	858
Constant dollars	Dollars with constant (or equal) purchasing power.	858
CPI-U	Consumer Price Index for All Urban Consumers; a measure of general inflation.	855

---

[10] In September, 1986, the FASB proposed a new statement that would make the disclosure of inflation adjusted data voluntary rather than required for fiscal years ending after March 15, 1987.

Terms (alphabetically)	Key words in definitions of important terms used in chapter	Page reference
Current cost	The cost of replacing an asset in its present operating condition.	867
GPL index	Any price index which measures general inflation.	855
Monetary items	Cash or the obligation to pay or receive a fixed number of dollars (Exhibit 17–2).	861
Nonmonetary items	All items which are not properly classified as monetary items (Exhibit 17–2).	861
Purchasing power gain (or loss)	The gain (or loss) in purchasing power that results from holding monetary items during a period of inflation (or deflation).	865
Specific price index	Similar to a general price level index except that it is related to a single item (or a small group of homogeneous items).	855

QUESTIONS

PART A

1. Explain the difference between general price level changes and specific price level changes.

2. What is a price level index? Explain the difference between a general price level index and a specific price level index.

3. What happens to the "value" of a dollar during a period of inflation or deflation?

4. A tract of land was acquired for $15,000 when the GPL index was 150. Five years later the GPL index was 270. At what price would the land have to sell for the owner to keep up exactly with inflation? Explain.

5. Define monetary items and nonmonetary items. Give some examples of each. Explain why a careful distinction between monetary and nonmonetary items is essential when HC/CD financial statements are prepared.

6. At the beginning of the current period, the Land account had a balance of $18,000 (GPL index at acquisition date, 100). The Note Payable account had no beginning balance but had an ending balance of $30,000 (GPL index at transaction date, 150). The GPL index at the end of the current period was 200. Compute the purchasing power gain (loss) on monetary items. Explain the nature of this gain or loss.

7. Items on the balance sheet may be either monetary or nonmonetary, while all items on the income statement are nonmonetary. Is this statement true or is it false? Explain why.

PART B

8. Briefly define each of the following concepts of "current value": (a) present value, (b) net realizable value, and (c) current cost (CC).

9. Are current costs usually entered into the journal and ledger when CC/CD statements are prepared? Explain.

10. Explain the nature and composition of the item "CC real holding gain (loss) on nonmonetary items." Contrast it with the "purchasing power gain (loss) on monetary items."

11. Contrast "GPL fictional changes" with "CC real value changes."

12. A tract of land was bought for $10,000 when the GPL was 100. At the end of Year 5, the GPL was 240 and the appraised value of the land was $27,000. Prepare a diagram that shows the price change effects.

EXERCISES

PART A

E17–1   (Pair Definitions with Terms)

Match the following brief definitions with the terms by entering the appropriate letter in each space provided.

Term	*Brief definitions*
_____ (1) Nonmonetary items	A. When this supplementary reporting approach is used, the historical cost basis financial statements are restated in current end-of-period dollars.
_____ (2) Constant dollars	
_____ (3) Specific price index	
_____ (4) CD restatement	B. Monetary units restated so as to represent the same general purchasing power.
_____ (5) Monetary items	
_____ (6) Current cost	C. A price index used to measure general inflation; Consumer Price Index − Urban Consumers.
_____ (7) CPI-U	
_____ (8) GPL index	D. Costs at present-day price levels.
_____ (9) Purchasing power gain (or loss)	E. Any index intended to measure general inflation or deflation.
	F. Includes cash, payables, and receivables, but not revenues or expenses.
	G. Includes property, plant, and equipment, and goodwill.
	H. Computation of this requires restatement of each monetary asset and each monetary liability.
	I. Used to estimate the current replacement cost of specific commodities or services.

E17–2   (Use a Price Index to Analyze Price Changes)

During 1967, a Quality Stereo set sold for $250. Assume that each year this particular set increased in price exactly the same as the changes in the GPL index. However, in 1987 it sold for $695.

Required:

a. What was the selling price in 1970, 1975, and 1978? Use the average CPI-U index values given in the chapter and round to the nearest dollar. Show computations.

b. Analyze the change in price during 1987. Assume that the CPI-U for 1987 was 310.

E17–3   (CD Restatement of an Operational Asset and the Related Depreciation Expense)

In 1967, Tower Company purchased a plant site for $23,100. Immediately thereafter, construction of a plant building was started. The building was completed in January 1968 at a cost of $336,000. The building is being depreciated on a straight-line basis assuming an estimated useful life of 30 years and no residual value.

Assume the GPL index in 1967 was 110, in 1968 it was 112, and at the end of 1987 it was 310.

Required:

a. Complete a schedule similar to the following:

	Amount to be reported assuming	
	HC basis	CD restated
Balance sheet at December 31, 1987:		
Operational assets:		
Land		
Building		
Less accumulated depreciation (20 years)		
Income statement for 1987:		
Depreciation expense		

Show your computations.

b. Would the CD restatement affect income tax expense for the company? Explain. Do you think it should? Explain.

E17–4   **(CD Restatement of Selected Balance Sheet Accounts and Calculation of the Purchasing Power Gain [Loss] on Monetary Items)**

The HC balance sheet for Fargo Company was prepared on December 31, 19F. Supplemental HC/CD statements are to be developed. The following four items were selected from the balance sheet:

Items	HC basis (when acquired)	GPL index (when acquired or incurred)
Receivables	$69,000	115
Investment, common stock	42,000	105
Land, plant site	20,000	100
Payables	99,000	110

The GPL at the end of 19F was 120.

Required:

a. Indicate which items are monetary and which are nonmonetary.

b. Set up a schedule to derive the amount "CD restated basis" that should be shown on the supplementary HC/CD balance sheet for each item. Show computations.

c. Compute the purchasing power gain (loss) on monetary items that should be reported on the HC/CD income statement. Show computations.

d. Explain why certain items were omitted from your computation in *(c).*

E17–5   **(Prepare a HC/CD Balance Sheet and Determine HC/CD Net Income)**

The items listed below were taken from the December 31, 19A, HC balance sheet of Environmental Systems Company. This date is the end of the first year of operations. The GPL index at January 1, 19A, was 200, and at December 31, 19A, it was 220.

	Debits	Credits	GPL index transaction date
Cash	$ 26,000		210†
Accounts receivable (net)	45,000		210†
Investments, common stock	12,000		215
Land	15,000		205
Equipment	100,000		200
Accumulated depreciation		$ 8,000	
Accounts payable		23,000	210†
Notes payable		43,000	200
Capital stock (nopar)		110,000	200
Retained earnings*			
	$198,000	$198,000	

* Cash dividends declared and paid on December 31, 19A, amounted to $4,000.

† Average.

Required:

a. Prepare a HC/CD balance sheet. Use a format similar to Exhibit 17–4 and round all amounts to the nearest dollar.

b. What was the amount of HC/CD income for 19A? Explain.

c. Compute the amount of HC/CD income from normal operations assuming the purchasing power gain on monetary items is $2,014. Show how this gain was computed.

E17–6   (Prepare a HC/CD Income Statement)

At the end of 19A (the first year of operations), Weber Company prepared the summarized HC income statement shown below. At January 1, 19A, the GPL index was 220; and at December 31, 19A, it was 260.

WEBER COMPANY
Income Statement
For the Year Ended December 31, 19A

	Amount	GPL index at average transaction date
Sales revenue	$ 330,000	234
Cost of goods sold	(165,000)	234
Depreciation expense*	(11,000)	
Remaining expenses	(94,000)	230
Pretax income	60,000	
Income tax expense	(18,000)	260
Net income	$ 42,000	

* The related asset was acquired when the GPL index was 220.

Required:

a. Prepare a HC/CD income statement. Use a format similar to Exhibit 17–4. The monetary items and their GPL indexes at transaction dates were: receivables, $32,000 (index 234), and liabilities, $16,000 (index 220). Round all amounts to the nearest dollar.

b. Prepare a HC/CD statement of retained earnings assuming cash dividends of $6,000 were declared but not paid on December 31, 19A.

E17-7   **(Compute Purchasing Power Gains [Losses] in Situations that Involve Numerous Transactions)**

At December 31, 19D, the GPL index was 132. The following summary data were taken from the ledger:

Transactions	GPL at transaction date	Cash	Payable
Beginning balance	120	$ 30,000	$18,000
Purchased land	125		+12,000
Sales revenue	130	+150,000	
Borrowing on note	120	+60,000	+60,000
Payment	122	−15,000	−15,000
Payment	132	−42,000	−42,000
Expenses paid	130	−90,000	
Dividends paid	132	−10,000	
Equipment purchased	120	−80,000	
Payment	125		−13,000
Ending balance		+ 3,000	$20,000

Note: GPL index numbers: January 1, 19D, 120; December 31, 19D, 132.

Required:

Compute the purchasing power gain or loss on monetary items for each account (cash and payable) separately. Round all amounts to the nearest dollar.

PART B

E17-8   **(Compute Purchasing Power Gain [Loss] on Monetary Items and Holding Gain [Loss] on a Nonmonetary Asset)**

On January 1, 19A, Lone Star Gas Company acquired a tract of land that cost $120,000 when the GPL was 120. Payment was made in cash, $50,000, plus a $70,000 three-year, interest-bearing note. One year later the note was still outstanding, and the GPL index was 150. The specific index, related to the land, was 100 at the beginning of 19A and was 145 at the end of 19A. The land and the note will be included on December 31, 19A, CC/CD financial statements.

Required (show computations and round to the nearest dollar):

a. The CC/CD value for the land that should be reported on the 19A CC/CD balance sheet is $_____.

b. The purchasing power gain (loss) on the monetary liability which should be reported on the 19A CC/CD income statement is $_____.

c. The CC real holding gain (loss) on the nonmonetary asset that should be reported on the 19A CC/CD income statement is $_____.

d. The amount of the GPL fictional change on the land was $_____.

e. Diagram the above responses in respect to the land (not the note payable).

E17-9   **(Analysis of GPL Fictional Price Changes)**

On January 1, 19A, Reston Company purchased a machine (an operational asset) that cost $15,000. Cash paid was $10,000 and a $5,000, three-year, interest-bearing note was given to the seller. On January 1, 19A, the GPL index was 100. At the end of 19A, the Accumulated Depreciation account reflected $3,000 (i.e., straight-line depreciation; estimated life five years and no residual value). During 19A, the average GPL index was 115 and at the end of 19A the GPL index was 120. The specific price index for the machine was 110 at the beginning of 19A and 143 at the end of 19A. The machine, accumulated depreciation, and note payable will be reported on the 19A CC/CD financial statements.

Required (show computations and round to the nearest dollar):

a. Complete the following tabulation of the amounts that should be reported on the 19A financial statements:

Item	HC basis	CC/CD basis
Balance sheet:		
Machine		
Accumulated depreciation		
Note payable		
Income statement:		
Depreciation expense		

b. The purchasing power gain (loss) on monetary items that should be reported on the CC/CD income statement is $_____.

c. The CC real holding gain (loss) on nonmonetary items that should be reported on the income statement is $_____.

d. The amounts of the GPL fictional changes were:
   (1) Machinery, net, $_____.
   (2) Depreciation expense, $_____.

E17–10   (Analysis of GPL Fictional Price Changes)

First Austin Company purchased merchandise for resale during 19A (the first year of operations) that cost $76,000. Payment was in cash except for an $11,400 ending balance in Accounts Payable. The purchases, and payments on accounts payable, occurred evenly throughout the year. The average GPL index for 19A was 190 and at the end of 19A it was 200.

The ending inventory was $15,200; therefore, cost of goods sold was $60,800. Current cost of the ending inventory was $17,000 and $68,000 for cost of goods sold (the CC cost of goods sold is based on the average cost during the year). Accounts payable, inventory, and cost of goods sold will be reported on the 19A CC/CD financial statements.

Required (show computations and round to the nearest dollar):

a. Complete the following tabulation of amounts that should be reported at the end of 19A:

Item	HC basis	CC/CD basis
Balance sheet:		
Inventory		
Accounts payable		
Income statement:		
Cost of goods sold		

b. The purchasing power gain (loss) on monetary items that should be reported on the CC/CD income statement is $_____.

c. The CC real holding gain (loss) on the nonmonetary items that should be reported on the CC/CD income statement is $_____.

d. The amounts of the GPL fictional changes were:
   (1) Inventory, $_____.
   (2) Cost of goods sold, $_____.

PROBLEMS

PART A

P17–1   **(CD Restate Selected Balance Sheet Accounts and Compute Purchasing Power Gain [Loss] on Monetary Items)**

Hill Company has prepared the annual HC basis financial statements at December 31, 19F. The company must prepare supplemental HC/CD statements. The following seven items were selected from the balance sheet:

Items	HC basis (when acquired)	GPL index (when acquired or incurred)
1. Cash:		
Beginning balance	$ 20,000	141.5
Debits	38,800	146*
Credits	(44,600)	147*
2. Merchandise inventory (average cost)	58,000	145
3. Accounts receivable, net	28,800	144*
4. Land (no changes during 19F)	12,000	100
5. Building, net (no changes during 19F)	157,500	105
6. Accounts payable	42,000	140*
7. Bonds payable (no changes during 19F)	90,000	110

At the end of 19F the price-level index was 150.
* Average GPL index for these items.

Required:

a. Group the above items into two categories: monetary and nonmonetary.
b. Set up a schedule and compute the amount "CD restated basis" that should be shown on the HC/CD balance sheet for each of the items. Show calculations.
c. Set up a schedule and compute the purchasing power gain or loss on monetary items that will be shown on the HC/CD income statement. Show calculations and round to the nearest $100.
d. Explain why some of the seven items were omitted from your computations in (c).

P17–2   **(Prepare HC/CD Balance Sheet and Income Statement)**

At the end of the first year of operations, DE Company prepared the following balance sheet and income statement (HC basis):

DE COMPANY
Balance Sheet
At December 31, 19A

Assets

Cash	$ 3,330
Accounts receivable (net)	5,650
Inventory	46,000
Operational assets (net)	55,000
Total	$ 109,980

Liabilities

Accounts payable	$ 3,480
Bonds payable	23,000

Stockholders' Equity

Capital stock (nopar)	66,000
Retained earnings	17,500
Total	$ 109,980

Income Statement
For the Year Ended December 31, 19A

Revenues	$ 69,000
Expenses (not detailed)	(46,000)
Depreciation expense	(5,500)
Net income	$ 17,500

Items	GPL (when acquired or incurred)
GPL at start of year—110	
GPL at end of year—120	
Cash (no beginning balance)	111*
Accounts receivable	113*
Inventory	115
Operational assets	110
Accounts payable	116
Bonds payable	115
Revenues	115*
Expenses	115*
Depreciation expense	110
Capital stock (nopar)	110

* Average GPL index for all items in the account.

Required:

a. Restate the income statement and balance sheet; use the following headings: (1) HC Basis, (2) Restatement Computations, and (3) HC/CD Basis. Round amounts to the nearest $10.

b. Explain why net income is different between the two statements; identify amounts.

c. Why were the nonmonetary items, but not the monetary items, restated on the balance sheet?

d. Does the HC/CD income statement better match expenses with revenues? Explain.

P17–3 (Prepare HC/CD Balance Sheet and Income Statement)

After operating for one year, DO Company completed the following income statement and balance sheet:

DO COMPANY
Balance Sheet
At December 31, 19A

Assets

Cash	$42,300*
Accounts receivable (net)	29,580
Long-term investment, common stock	7,400
Land	11,200
Plant	154,000
Accumulated depreciation	(14,000)
Total	$230,480

Liabilities

Accounts payable	$ 5,880
Bonds payable	28,000

Stockholders' Equity

Capital stock (nopar)	182,000
Retained earnings	14,600
Total	$230,480

Income Statement
For the Year Ended December 31, 19A

Revenues	$ 87,000
Expenses (not detailed)	(58,400)
Depreciation expense†	(14,000)
Net income	$ 14,600

* Beginning balance, $58,800 (GPL index, 140); debits $49,600 (GPL index, 148); credits, $66,100 (GPL index, 145.3).

† Depreciation is recorded on a straight-line basis; estimated life of the plant is 11 years and no residual value.

Items	GPL (when acquired or incurred)
GPL index at start of year—140	
GPL index at end of year—150	
GPL index average for 19A—145	
Cash	* above
Accounts receivable	141†
Long-term investment purchased, common stock	148
Land purchased	140
Plant acquired	140
Accounts payable	147†
Bonds payable	140
Capital stock (nopar)	140
Revenues	145†
Expenses	146†
Depreciation expense	140

† Average GPL for these amounts.

Required:

a. Restate the income statement and balance sheet with the following headings: (1) HC Basis, (2) Restatement Computations, and (3) HC/CD Basis. Round amounts to the nearest $10.
b. Explain why net income is different between the two statements; identify amounts.
c. Why were the nonmonetary items, but not the monetary items, restated on the balance sheet?
d. Does the HC/CD income statement better match expenses with revenues? Explain.

P17–4   **(Prepare HC/CD Balance Sheet and Compute Purchasing Power Gain [Loss] on Monetary Items)**

The transactions summarized below were completed by Sullins Company during its first year of operations. The accounting period ends December 31. The GPL index on January 1, 19A, was 100, on December 31, 19A, it was 144, and the average for the year was 120.

January 1, 19A: Issued 10,000 shares of capital stock (nopar) for $60,000 cash and borrowed $36,000 cash on a two-year, interest-bearing note (GPL index, 100).

February 1, 19A: Purchased equipment for use in the business, $75,000 cash (GPL index, 105).

During 19A: Purchased merchandise on credit (evenly throughout the year), $180,000 (GPL average index, 120).

During 19A: Sales revenues (evenly throughout the year), $300,000, all cash (GPL average index, 120).

During 19A: Paid expenses (evenly throughout the year), $80,000 (GPL average index, 120); includes all expenses except depreciation expense.

During 19A: Paid accounts payable, $161,200 (GPL average index on payments, 124).

December 1, 19A: Declared and paid a cash dividend of $6,900 (GPL index, 138).

December 31, 19A: Depreciation on equipment based on estimated life of 10 years and a $5,000 residual value.

December 31, 19A: Cost of goods sold, $170,000 (GPL average index for cost of goods sold and ending inventory, 120).

The above entries resulted in the following preclosing HC account balances at December 31, 19A (the 19A adjusting entries already have been completed).

Debits

Cash	$ 72,900
Inventory	10,000
Equipment	75,000
Cost of goods sold	170,000
Expenses	80,000
Depreciation expense	7,000
Retained earnings (dividend declared and paid)	6,900
Total	$421,800

Credits

Accumulated depreciation	$ 7,000
Accounts payable	18,800
Note payable	36,000
Capital stock (nopar)	60,000
Revenues	300,000
Total	$421,800

Required:

    a. Set up a format similar to Exhibit 17–4 to derive HC/CD financial statements. Enter the HC basis amounts for each statement.

    b. Restate each item on each statement on a CD basis. Prepare a separate schedule similar to Exhibit 17–5 to compute the purchasing power gain or loss on monetary items. Round all amounts to the nearest dollar. (Hint: There was a $32,083 monetary loss on cash.)

P17–5   **(Prepare HC/CD Balance Sheet and Compute Purchasing Power Gain [Loss] on Monetary Items)**

    Small Company was organized on January 1, 19A, at which time the GPL index was 150. The accounting period ends December 31. The transactions completed during 19A were:

    a. January 1, 19A: Sold and issued 10,000 shares of capital stock (par $10) for $150,000 cash (GPL index, 150).

    b. January 1, 19A: Purchased merchandise on credit for resale, $60,000 (GPL index, 150).

    c. February 1, 19A: Purchased equipment for use in the business; paid cash, $31,000, and gave a $46,500, interest-bearing note due December 31, 19C (GPL index, 155).

    d. During 19A: Sales revenue, $180,000 (sold evenly throughout the year); one third was on credit (GPL average index, 165).

    e. During February–December 19A: Purchased merchandise on credit (evenly throughout the year) for resale, $44,000 (GPL index, 165).

    f. During 19A: Collected accounts receivable, $50,000 (average GPL index for collections, 170).

    g. During 19A: Paid accounts payable, $84,000 (average GPL index for payments, 160).

    h. During 19A: Paid expenses in cash (evenly throughout the year), $61,000 (average GPL index, 165), which included interest, income tax, and all other expenses except depreciation expense.

    i. July 1, 19A: Invested $96,000 cash for common stock of X Corporation (GPL index, 160).

    j. December 31, 19A: Declared and paid a dividend of $10,000 (GPL index, 180).

    k. December 31, 19A: Depreciation expense on equipment, $14,000.

    l. December 31, 19A: Cost of goods sold, $84,000 (average GPL index for cost of goods sold and ending inventory, 156).

    The above transactions resulted in the following preclosing HC account balances (adjusting entries already have been made):

Debits

Cash	$ 38,000
Accounts receivable (net)	10,000
Inventory	20,000
Investment, common stock	96,000
Equipment	77,500
Cost of goods sold	84,000
Expenses	61,000
Depreciation expense	14,000
Retained earnings (dividend)	10,000
	$410,500

Credits

Accumulated depreciation	$ 14,000
Accounts payable	20,000
Note payable	46,500
Capital stock (par $10)	100,000
Contributed capital in excess of par	50,000
Revenues	180,000
	$410,500

Required:

a. Set up a format similar to Exhibit 17–4 to derive HC/CD financial statements. Enter the historical cost basis amounts for each statement. The GPL index at December 31, 19A, was 180.

b. Restate each item on each statement on a CD basis. Prepare a separate schedule similar to Exhibit 17–5 to compute the purchasing power gain or loss on monetary items. (Hint: There was a $10,805 monetary loss on cash). Round all amounts to the nearest dollar.

PART B

P17–6 (Prepare CC/CD Balance Sheet and Income Statement)

This problem is based on the data given in P17–3 (DO Company). The balance sheet and income statement (HC basis) and the GPL index numbers are not changed. Current cost (CC) information is as follows:

Item	Current cost (CC) data, December 31, 19A
Long-term investment, common stock	Based on stock market quotation .... $ 8,500
Land	Per professional appraisal 14,000
Plant (net)	Specific index, 1.10 of carrying value.
Expenses (not detailed)	HC average and CC average the same.
(GPL index data given in Problem 17–3)	

Required (show computations and round all amounts to the nearest $10):

a. Set up a schedule similar to Exhibit 17–7 to develop a CC/CD balance sheet and income statement at December 31, 19A. Enter the HC data and complete the CC/CD amounts through "Income from operations." The purchasing power loss on monetary items was $2,500.

b. Compute the CC real holding gains (losses) on nonmonetary items.

c. Use the amounts computed in (b) to complete the CC/CD income statement. (Hint: The CC/CD balance sheet totals are $248,380.)

P17–7 (Prepare CC/CD Balance Sheet and Income Statement)

Thu Company began operations on January 1, 19A, at which time the GPL index was 130. The 19A balance sheet and income statement, along with relevant GPL index numbers and CC information, are given below. The 19A average GPL index was 143, and it was 156 at December 31, 19A.

	HC basis	GPL index at transaction date	CC valuations (which are different from HC) at December 31, 19A
Balance sheet:			
Assets:			
Cash	$ 14,300	143	
Accounts receivable	28,600	143	
Inventory (average)	57,200	143	Specific index, 165/143 of HC
Equipment	78,000	130	Specific index, 1.282 of HC
Accumulated depreciation	(7,800)	130	Specific index, 1.282 of HC
Other assets	19,500	130	Specific index, 160/130 of HC
Total	$ 189,800		
Liabilities:			
Accounts payable	$ 14,300	143	
Note payable	39,000	130	
Stockholders' equity:			
Capital stock	130,000	136.84	
Retained earnings	6,500		
Total	$ 189,800		
Income statement:			
Revenue	$ 114,400	143	
Cost of goods sold	(71,500)	143	Average specific price index, 1.0577 of HC
Depreciation expense*	(7,800)	143	Based on average CC of equipment during 19A
Remaining expenses	(28,600)	143	HC and CC averages are the same
Net income	$ 6,500		

* Straight-line depreciation, 10-year estimated life and no residual value (Cost, $78,000 ÷ 10 years = $7,800).

Required:

Based on the above data, the company wants to construct a CC/CD balance sheet and income statement at December 31, 19A. Show all computations and round to the nearest $10.

a. Set up a schedule similar to Exhibit 17–7 to develop CC/CD statements. Enter the HC data given above and complete the CC/CD amounts through "Income from operations."

b. The purchasing power gain on monetary items was $5,200. Show how this was computed (refer to Exhibit 17–5).

c. Compute the CC real holding gain (loss) on nonmonetary items (refer to Exhibit 17–8).

d. Use the amounts computed in (b) and (c) to complete the CC/CD income statement. (Hint: The CC/CD balance sheet totals are $222,900.)

CASES

C17–1   (Compute and Analyze Purchasing Power Gain on Debt)

Frank Smith, president of Delta Corporation, has asked that you help him understand inflation accounting. During a meeting, Mr. Smith made the following comments:

I have been told that it is possible to make money by borrowing money during a period of inflation. I plan to recommend that Delta borrow $10 million, at 10% interest, on January 1, 19D, and deposit the money in Delta's checking account (which does not pay interest). One year later, we will repay the money. The average inflation rate during 19D is expected to be 5%, consequently Delta should have a purchasing power gain on the debt. Delta will be able to use the cash from the purchasing power gain to pay a dividend to the stockholders of the company. The only thing I don't understand is why bankers are willing to lend money during a period of inflation. If we can make money by borrowing, don't the bankers lose money by lending money?

Required:

a. Determine the amount of the purchasing power gain that Mr. Smith **expects** Delta to earn by borrowing $10 million. Will Delta actually earn the purchasing power gain that Mr. Smith expects? Explain why. Would your answer be different if the $10 million were invested in a tract of land during the year? Why?
b. Evaluate Mr. Smith's plan to use cash from a purchasing power gain on monetary items to pay a cash dividend to the stockholders.
c. Prepare a response to Mr. Smith's question concerning why bankers are willing to lend money during a period of inflation.

C17–2 **(Analysis of HC/CD and CC/CD Data Using an Actual Financial Statement)**
Refer to the financial statements of Chesebrough-Pond's given in Special Supplement B immediately preceding the Index.

Required:

a. What was the current cost of inventories at December 31, 1985? What was the current cost of net property, plant, and equipment?
b. Is the company in a net monetary asset or a net monetary liability position? Explain.
c. Did the company have a real holding gain or loss on inventories and property, plant, and equipment?
d. The sales revenue as reported in the 1985 HC financial statements was $2,699.5 million. The HC/CD sales revenue reported in the "five-year comparison of selected financial data adjusted for changing prices" is $2,699.5 million. Why are the HC and HC/CD sales revenue the same?
e. Has the amount of sales revenue increased every year for the past five years?

SPECIAL SUPPLEMENT A— OVERVIEW OF INCOME TAXES

PURPOSE:

Income taxes are complex and pervasive; they affect most persons and businesses. Each individual and manager should consider the income tax implications when making economic decisions. A general knowledge of income taxes enables the decision maker to (a) recognize the importance of various income tax implications, (b) know when to seek professional help, and (c) carry on tax planning to minimize income taxes.

Federal, state, and local governments not only assess income taxes but also property taxes (i.e., on real property), sales taxes (i.e., on the sale of goods and services), and excise taxes (i.e., on gasoline). Because income taxes are levied by the federal government and most states, the total amount exceeds any other tax, and as a result, it exerts a pervasive effect on many business decisions. Basically there are three major groups of taxpayers: individuals, corporations, and fiduciaries (that is, trusts and estates).

The purpose of this supplement is to present an overview of **federal income taxes** applicable to **individuals** and **corporations**. This overview is designed to (a) enhance your general knowledge of the primary federal income tax provisions, (b) give you a basic undertanding of income tax returns, and (c) provide an overview of the relationship between **accounting income** (reported on the income statement) and **taxable income** (reported on the income tax return).[1] The discussion in this supplement is based upon current income tax information. By the time you read this supplement, certain tax provisions may be out of date. However, the discussion still will be relevant because it deals with key concepts and terminology rather than with the numerous exceptions and detailed rules. We reemphasize that our objective is to give a broad overview of income tax provisions rather than a highly technical view. The examples given are intended to

---

[1] It appears that the first U.S. federal income tax was proposed in 1815. Later during the Civil War, a federal income tax law was enacted, and income taxes were collected; however, this law was repealed shortly thereafter. During 1894, another income tax law was passed, which was soon held to be unconstitutional. At the outset of World War I, the 16th Amendment to the Constitution was passed that made income taxes constitutionally allowable. Our present federal income tax law dates from measures passed by the U.S. Congress in 1913.

illustrate key concepts and terminology. Congress may change the tax rates or specific tax law which may make certain illustrations out of date, but our educational objective will remain intact. For example, a change in the individual income tax rates will not affect the method used to calculate the tax obligation.

To accomplish this purpose, the supplement is subdivided as follows:

ORGANIZATION:

Part A—Income taxes paid by individuals

1. Income tax filing requirements
2. Computation of taxable income
3. Computation of income tax liability

Part B—Income taxes paid by corporations

1. Special income tax provisions for corporations
2. Computation of corporate income tax
3. Modified cash basis and accrual basis
4. Tax planning

LEARNING OBJECTIVES—TO BE ABLE TO:

1. Learn about the federal income tax provisions and the general reporting requirements
2. Understand the primary distinctions between income tax requirements for individuals and corporations.
3. Define taxable income for individuals and corporations.
4. Understand the nature and importance of income tax planning.
5. Expand your knowledge by learning some of the primary terms used in income tax reporting.
6. Apply the knowledge learned from this supplement by completing the homework assigned by your instructor.

PART A—INCOME TAXES PAID BY INDIVIDUALS

Current income tax law (as set forth in the Internal Revenue Code) states the legal provisions for all taxpayers, including individuals and corporations. Due to the complexity of the tax law, the Treasury Department issues **regulations** that state the government's position on that law and provide guidelines for implementing it. Much of the Code and the regulations apply to both individual and corporate taxpayers; however, there are certain provisions that apply only to individuals and not to corporations, and vice versa. For example, different tax rates apply to each. This part of the supplement will give an overview of the income tax provisions that specifically apply to **individuals,** including a sample tax return.

INCOME TAX FILING REQUIREMENTS

An individual must file an annual tax return on a *(a)* calendar-year basis (ending December 31), or *(b)* fiscal-year basis (ending on the last day of a month other than December). The tax return must be filed on or before the 15th day of the fourth month following the taxable year-end (i.e., April 15 for the calendar-year basis). Most individual taxpayers file the standard form entitled "Form 1040, U.S. Individual Income Tax Return" (Exhibit A–3). This form is submitted to the appropriate regional service center of the Internal Revenue Service, Department of the Treasury.

In 1986, a return must be filed if the **gross income** of a taxpayer under age 65 is equal to or more than (a) $3,560 if single or head of household; (b) $4,750 if a surviving spouse; (c) $3,560 if married, filing jointly; or (d) $400 of self-employed income.[2] If a taxpayer is 65 years of age or older, or if blind, these amounts increase by $1,080 for each such incidence.[3]

The income tax is computed by multiplying an amount called taxable income by the appropriate income tax rate for the individual taxpayer. A discussion of the determination of **taxable income** follows.

GROSS INCOME

Computation of **taxable income** starts with determination of gross income. For an individual taxpayer, **gross income** is broadly defined as income from any source. Gross income for the individual taxpayer may be measured on the (a) cash basis or (b) accrual basis.[4] Exhibit A–1 lists different income items that may be included in **gross income.** Of these, the most typical items are wages and salaries, rental income, investment income, and business income.

Most individual taxpayers receive a W-2 or a Form 1099 from each source of income. These forms are required by tax law and provide some of the income data needed to complete the individual tax return. Exhibit A–2 shows examples of these two forms for the Doe family. Notice that these standard forms report the amounts of (a) total earnings and (b) income taxes withheld (i.e., prepayments of income tax) for the tax year. Also, the individual taxpayer usually should refer to tax law and regulations to determine whether a particular receipt or payment will affect the amount of taxable income.

Some amounts are excluded in full, or in part, from gross income for tax purposes. Typical examples are interest on state and municipal bonds used for governmental operations (called tax-exempt bonds), most life insurance proceeds, gifts, inheritances, most workers' compensation, some social security

---

[2] For tax years beginning in 1987 and after, these amounts will change.

[3] The Tax Reform Act of 1986 adjusts the standard deduction upward by $600 for each condition (i.e., age, blindness) for married taxpayers and by $750 for each condition for unmarried taxpayers for 1987 and later years.

[4] Other options, which are modifications of these two bases, are available. Discussion of these options is beyond the scope of this supplement. Most individual taxpayers elect the cash basis because (a) it does not require the taxpayer to maintain a formal set of books and (b) it provides the taxpayer opportunities to time cash receipts and payments to effect tax savings.

EXHIBIT A–1

Overview of Form 1040, Individual Income Tax Return

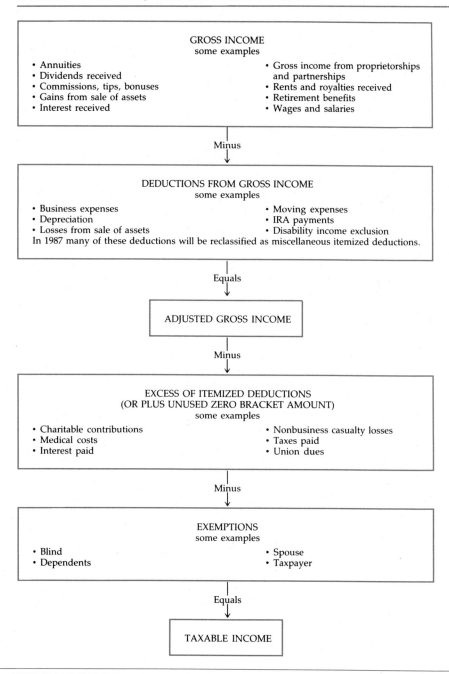

EXHIBIT A-2

Forms used to report income earned and taxes withheld (W-2 and 1099)

1 Control number 22222 OMB No. 1545-0008		
2 Employer's name, address, and ZIP code University of Texas at Austin Austin, Texas 78712	3 Employer's identification number 74-2333444	4 Employer's state I.D. number
	5 Statutory employee ☐ Deceased ☐ Legal rep. ☐ 942 emp. ☐ Subtotal ☐ Void ☐	
	6 Allocated tips	7 Advance EIC payment
8 Employee's social security number 123-45-6789	9 Federal income tax withheld 6,800.00	10 Wages, tips, other compensation 50,000.00	11 Social security tax withheld 3003.00

12 Employee's name, address, and ZIP code John J. Doe 1770 Mountain Drive Austin, Texas 78703	13 Social security wages 42,000.00	14 Social security tips
	16	16a Fringe benefits incl. in Box 10
	17 State income tax	18 State wages, tips, etc.	19 Name of state
	20 Local income tax	21 Local wages, tips, etc.	22 Name of locality

Form **W-2 Wage and Tax Statement**   **1986**

Copy 1 For State, City, or Local Tax Department
Employee's and employer's copy compared ☐

PAYER'S name, street address, city, state, and ZIP code TYE Savings and Loan Assoc. P.O. Box 9877 Austin, Texas 78701		OMB No.1545-0112 **1986** **Interest Income** Statement for Recipients of
PAYER'S Federal identification number 74-1667889	RECIPIENT'S identification number 123-45-6789	1 Earnings from savings and loan associations, credit unions, bank deposits, bearer certificates of deposit, etc. $1,250.00	**Copy C For Payer**
RECIPIENT'S name (first, middle, last) John J. Doe		2 Amount of forfeiture 3 U.S. Savings Bonds, etc.	For Paperwork Reduction Act Notice and
Street address 1770 Mountain Drive		4 Federal income tax withheld	instructions for completing this form, see
City, state, and ZIP code Austin, Texas 78703		5 Foreign tax paid (if eligible for foreign tax credit) 6 Foreign country or U.S. possession	Instructions for Forms 1099, 1098, 5498,
Account number (optional)			1096, and W-2G.

☆ U.S. GOVERNMENT PRINTING OFFICE: 1985-463-163   Form **1099-INT**   Department of the Treasury - Internal Revenue Service

benefits, disability pensions to veterans, GI benefits, compensation for damages, and $100 of dividend income per taxpayer.[5]

An individual taxpayer may own a small business (a proprietorship) or an interest in a partnership. In either case, these two types of business entities do not pay income taxes. Rather, each owner's share of the net income or loss from the business is included on the owner's individual tax return (see Exhibit A-3, lines 12 and 18). If the individual taxpayer derives business income from a sole proprietorship, "Schedule C, Profit (Loss) from Business or Profession" must be attached to the income tax return. A typical Schedule C is shown in Exhibit A-4.

DEDUCTIONS FROM GROSS INCOME

The overview given in Exhibit A-1 lists different **deductions** from gross income. Generally, these deductions are of two kinds: (1) expenses incurred in the production of income (e.g., depreciation on rental property) and expenses in operating a business, or (2) personal deductions (e.g., alimony paid). The operating expenses of a sole proprietorship are reported as a direct reduction of the income from the business on Schedule C, Profit or Loss from Business or Profession (see Exhibit A-4). The **personal deductions** are reported directly on Form 1040, lines 24–30 (see Exhibit A-3).[6]

In 1982, tax legislation created a new deduction for married couples filing a joint return in cases when each spouse earned income (Form 1040, line 30).[7] The amount of the deduction is 10 percent times the amount of qualified earned income (limited to $30,000) of the spouse with the lower amount of earned income. Therefore, for years 1983 and later, the maximum deduction allowable is $3,000 (or 10 percent times $30,000 of earned income).

ADJUSTED GROSS INCOME

Gross income **less** the deductions from gross income gives an amount that is called **adjusted gross income** (AGI). This amount is significant because the actual amount of certain **itemized deductions** is based on it. For example, the 1986 deduction for medical expenses is limited to 5 percent of adjusted gross income (7.5 percent in 1987). A more detailed discussion of itemized deductions follows.

---

[5] The dividend exclusion is repealed by the Tax Reform Act of 1986 for tax years beginning after December 31, 1986.

[6] Note that these personal deductions are not the same as "itemized deductions" which are discussed in a later section of this supplement.

[7] The tax Reform Act of 1986 repeals this deduction for tax years begining after 1986.

Form 1040 Department of the Treasury—Internal Revenue Service
U.S. Individual Income Tax Return 1986

For the year January 1-December 31, 1986, or other tax year beginning _____ , 1986, ending _____ , 19 ____ | OMB No. 1545-0074

Use IRS label. Otherwise, please print or type.		
Your first name and initial (if joint return, also give spouse's name and initial) **John J. and Jane A.**	Last name **Doe**	Your social security number **123 45 6789**
Present home address (number and street or rural route). (If you have a P.O. Box, see page 4 of Instructions.) **1770 Mountain Drive**		Spouse's social security number **789 56 1234**
City, town or post office, state, and ZIP code **Austin, Texas 78703**	If this address is different from the one shown on your 1985 return, check here ▶	

Presidential Election Campaign ▶
Do you want $1 to go to this fund? .... Yes ☐ No **X**
If joint return, does your spouse want $1 to go to this fund?. Yes ☐ No **X**

Note: Checking "Yes" will not change your tax or reduce your refund.

For Privacy Act and Paperwork Reduction Act Notice, see Instructions.

Filing Status

Check only one box.

1 ☐ Single
2 **X** Married filing joint return (even if only one had income)
3 ☐ Married filing separate return. Enter spouse's social security no. above and full name here. _____
4 ☐ Head of household (with qualifying person). (See page 5 of Instructions.) If the qualifying person is your unmarried child but not your dependent, enter child's name here. _____
5 ☐ Qualifying widow(er) with dependent child (year spouse died ▶ 19 ____). (See page 6 of Instructions.)

Exemptions

Always check the box labeled Yourself. Check other boxes if they apply.

					Enter number of boxes checked on 6a and b ▶	2
6a	**X** Yourself	☐ 65 or over	☐ Blind			
b	**X** Spouse	☐ 65 or over	☐ Blind			

c First names of your dependent children who lived with you **John Jr. (son), Joyce (daughter)**

Enter number of children listed on 6c ▶ **2**

d First names of your dependent children who did not live with you (see page 6). _____
(If pre-1985 agreement, check here ▶ ☐ .)

Enter number of children listed on 6d ▶

e Other dependents:		(3) Number of months lived in your home	(4) Did dependent have income of $1,080 or more?	(5) Did you provide more than one-half of dependent's support?	
(1) Name	(2) Relationship				Enter number of other dependents ▶

Add numbers entered in boxes above ▶ **4**

f Total number of exemptions claimed (also complete line 36). ....

Income

Please attach Copy B of your Forms W-2, W-2G, and W-2P here.

If you do not have a W-2, see page 4 of Instructions.

7	Wages, salaries, tips, etc. (attach Form(s) W-2)	7	50,000	00
8	Interest income (also attach Schedule B if over $400)	8	2,650	00
9a	Dividends (also attach Schedule B if over $400) 1,200 00, 9b Exclusion 200 00			
c	Subtract line 9b from line 9a and enter the result	9c	1,000	00
10	Taxable refunds of state and local income taxes, if any, from the worksheet on page 9 of Instructions.	10		
11	Alimony received	11		
12	Business income or (loss) (attach Schedule C)	12	4,900	00
13	Capital gain or (loss) (attach Schedule D)	13		
14	40% of capital gain distributions not reported on line 13 (see page 9 of Instructions)	14		
15	Other gains or (losses) (attach Form 4797)	15		
16	Fully taxable pensions, IRA distributions, and annuities not reported on line 17 (see page 9).	16		
17a	Other pensions and annuities, including rollovers. Total received 17a _____			
b	Taxable amount, if any, from the worksheet on page 10 of Instructions	17b		
18	Rents, royalties, partnerships, estates, trusts, etc. (attach Schedule E)	18		
19	Farm income or (loss) (attach Schedule F)	19		
20a	Unemployment compensation (insurance). Total received . . 20a _____			
b	Taxable amount, if any, from the worksheet on page 10 of Instructions	20b		
21a	Social security benefits (see page 10). . . . 21a _____			
b	Taxable amount, if any, from worksheet on page 11. { Tax-exempt interest _____ }	21b		
22	Other income (list type and amount—see page 11 of Instructions) _____	22		
23	Add the amounts shown in the far right column for lines 7 through 22. This is your total income . ▶	23	58,550	00

Adjustments to Income

(See Instructions on page 11.)

24	Moving expenses (attach Form 3903 or 3903F)	24		
25	Employee business expenses (attach Form 2106).	25		
26	IRA deduction, from the worksheet on page 12	26		
27	Keogh retirement plan and self-employed SEP deduction . .	27		
28	Penalty on early withdrawal of savings	28		
29	Alimony paid (recipient's last name _____ and social security no. _____)	29		
30	Deduction for a married couple when both work (attach Schedule W)	30		
31	Add lines 24 through 30. These are your total adjustments . . . . ▶	31		

Adjusted Gross Income

32 Subtract line 31 from line 23. This is your adjusted gross income. If this line is less than $11,000 and a child lived with you, see "Earned Income Credit" (line 58) on page 16 of Instructions. If you want IRS to figure your tax, see page 13 of Instructions . . . . ▶ | 32 | 58,550 | 00

Form 1040 (1986)   John J. and Jane A. Doe   S.S.No. 123-45-6789   Page 2

Tax Compu-tation (See Instructions on page 13.)	33	Amount from line 32 (adjusted gross income).	**33** 58,550 00
	34a	If you itemize, attach Schedule A (Form 1040) and enter the amount from Schedule A, line 26 . .	**34a** 7,282 00
		Caution: If you have unearned income and can be claimed as a dependent on your parents' return, see page 13 of Instructions and check here ▶ ☐ . Also see page 13 if you are married filing a separate return and your spouse itemizes deductions, or you are a dual-status alien.	
	b	If you do not itemize but you made charitable contributions, enter your cash contributions here. (If you gave $3,000 or more to any one organization, see page 14.) **34b**	
	c	Enter your noncash contributions *(you must attach Form 8283 if over $500)* **34c**	
	d	Add lines 34b and 34c. Enter the total	**34d**
	35	Subtract line 34a or line 34d, whichever applies, from line 33	**35** 51,268 00
	36	Multiply $1,080 by the total number of exemptions claimed on line 6f (see page 14) . . .	**36** 4,320 00
	37	**Taxable income.** Subtract line 36 from line 35. Enter the result (but not less than zero)	**37** 46,948 00
	38	Enter tax here. Check if from ☐ Tax Table, ☒ Tax Rate Schedule X, Y, or Z, or ☐ Schedule G	**38** 9,728 00
	39	Additional taxes (see page 14 of Instructions). Enter here and check if from ☐ Form 4970, ☐ Form 4972, or ☐ Form 5544	**39**
	40	Add lines 38 and 39. Enter the total . . . . ▶	**40** 9,728 00
Credits (See Instructions on page 14.)	41	Credit for child and dependent care expenses *(attach Form 2441)* **41**	
	42	Credit for the elderly or for the permanently and totally disabled *(attach Schedule R)* **42**	
	43	Partial credit for political contributions for which you have receipts **43**	
	44	Add lines 41 through 43. Enter the total	**44** 9,728 00
	45	Subtract line 44 from line 40. Enter the result (but not less than zero)	**45**
	46	Foreign tax credit *(attach Form 1116)* **46**	
	47	General business credit. Check if from ☐ Form 3800, ☐ Form 3468, ☐ Form 5884, ☐ Form 6478, or ☐ Form 6765 **47**	
	48	Add lines 46 and 47. Enter the total	**48**
	49	Subtract line 48 from line 45. Enter the result (but not less than zero) . . . . ▶	**49** 9,728 00
Other Taxes (Including Advance EIC Payments)	50	Self-employment tax *(attach Schedule SE)*.	**50**
	51	Alternative minimum tax *(attach Form 6251)*.	**51**
	52	Tax from recapture of investment credit *(attach Form 4255)*	**52**
	53	Social security tax on tip income not reported to employer *(attach Form 4137)*	**53**
	54	Tax on an IRA *(attach Form 5329)* . . . . ▶	**54**
	55	Add lines 49 through 54. This is your **total tax** . . . . ▶	**55** 9,728 00
Payments Attach Forms W-2, W-2G, and W-2P to front.	56	Federal income tax withheld **56** 6,800 00	
	57	1986 estimated tax payments and amount applied from 1985 return **57** 4,000 00	
	58	Earned income credit (see page 16) **58**	
	59	Amount paid with Form 4868 . . . . **59**	
	60	Excess social security tax and RRTA tax withheld (two or more employers) **60**	
	61	Credit for Federal tax on gasoline and special fuels *(attach Form 4136)* **61**	
	62	Regulated investment company credit *(attach Form 2439)* . . . **62**	
	63	Add lines 56 through 62. These are your **total payments** . . . . ▶	**63** 10,800 00
Refund or Amount You Owe	64	If line 63 is larger than line 55, enter amount **OVERPAID** . . . . ▶	**64** 1,072 00
	65	Amount of line 64 to be **REFUNDED TO YOU** . . . . ▶	**65** 1,072 00
	66	Amount of line 64 to be applied to your 1987 estimated tax . . . . ▶ **66**	
	67	If line 55 is larger than line 63, enter **AMOUNT YOU OWE.** Attach check or money order for full amount payable to "Internal Revenue Service." Write your social security number, daytime phone number, and "1986 Form 1040" on it . . . . ▶	**67**
		Check ▶ ☐ if Form 2210 (2210F) is attached. See page 17. **Penalty: $**	

Please Sign Here

Under penalties of perjury, I declare that I have examined this return and accompanying schedules and statements, and to the best of my knowledge and belief, they are true, correct, and complete. Declaration of preparer (other than taxpayer) is based on all information of which preparer has any knowledge.

Your signature ▶	Date	Your occupation
Spouse's signature (if joint return, BOTH must sign) ▶	Date	Spouse's occupation

Paid Preparer's Use Only

Preparer's signature ▶	Date	Check if self-employed ☒	Preparer's social security no. 477 : 82 : 5555
Firm's name (or yours, if self-employed) and address ▶ Jones & Jones, CPA 1400 First Street Austin, Texas		E.I. No. 74 : 2225555	ZIP code 78701

SCHEDULE C (Form 1040) Department of the Treasury Internal Revenue Service	**Profit or (Loss) From Business or Profession** (Sole Proprietorship) Partnerships, Joint Ventures, etc., Must File Form 1065. ▶ Attach to Form 1040, Form 1041, or Form 1041S. ▶ See Instructions for Schedule C (Form 1040).	OMB No. 1545-0074 19**86** Attachment Sequence No. 09

Name of proprietor	Social security number
John J. Doe	123 45 6789

A Principal business or profession, including product or service (see Instructions)
Retail Sales - Antiques

B Principal business code   (from page 2) ▶

C Business name and address ▶ Doe's Antiques; 10800 Industrial Blvd.; Austin, Texas 78746

D Employer ID number

E Method(s) used to value closing inventory:
- (1) ☒ Cost   (2) ☐ Lower of cost or market   (3) ☐ Other (attach explanation)

F Accounting method: (1) ☒ Cash   (2) ☐ Accrual   (3) ☐ Other (specify) ▶ ....

	Yes	No
G Was there any change in determining quantities, costs, or valuations between opening and closing inventory? . . . . If "Yes," attach explanation.		X
H Did you deduct expenses for an office in your home?		X

I If this schedule includes a loss, credit, deduction, income, or other tax benefit relating to a tax shelter required to be registered, check here. ▶ ☐
If you check this box, you **MUST** attach Form 8271.

Part I Income

1a Gross receipts or sales	1a	13,100 00
b Less: Returns and allowances	1b	1,100 00
c Subtract line 1b from line 1a and enter the balance here	1c	12,000 00
2 Cost of goods sold and/or operations (from Part III, line 8)	2	3,000 00
3 Subtract line 2 from line 1c and enter the **gross profit** here	3	9,000 00
4a Windfall profit tax credit or refund received in 1986 (see Instructions) . . .	4a	
b Other income	4b	
5 Add lines 3, 4a, and 4b. This is the **gross income.** . . . . ▶	5	9,000 00

Part II Deductions

6 Advertising	100 00	**20** Office expense		40 00
7 Bad debts from sales or services (Cash		**21** Pension and profit-sharing plans . .		
method taxpayers, see Instructions.)		**22** Rent on business property		600 00
8 Bank service charges	20 00	**23** Repairs		400 00
9 Car and truck expenses		**24** Supplies (not included in Part III below)		350 00
10 Commissions		**25** Taxes (Do not include windfall profit		
11 Depletion		tax here. See line 29.)		160 00
12 Depreciation and section 179 deduction from Form 4562 (not included in Part III below)		**26** Travel and entertainment		
		27 Utilities and telephone		450 00
13 Dues and publications	30 00	**28a** Wages . . .	1,500 00	
14 Employee benefit programs		**b** Jobs credit . .		
15 Freight (not included in Part III below) .		**c** Subtract line 28b from 28a . . .		1,500 00
16 Insurance	150 00	**29** Windfall profit tax withheld in 1986		
17 Interest:		**30** Other expenses (specify):		
a Mortgage (paid to financial institutions)		**a**		
b Other		**b**		
18 Laundry and cleaning		**c**		
19 Legal and professional services . . .	300 00	**d**		

31 Add amounts in columns for lines 6 through 30d. These are the **total deductions** . . . . ▶	31	4,100 00
32 Net profit or (loss). Subtract line 31 from line 5 and enter the result. If a profit, enter on Form 1040, line 12, and on Schedule SE, line 2 (or line 5 of Form 1041 or 1041S). If a loss, you **MUST** go on to line 33 . .	32	4,900 00

33 If you have a loss, you **MUST** answer this question: "Do you have amounts for which you are not at risk in this business (see Instructions)?" . . ☐ Yes ☒ No
If "Yes," you **MUST** attach Form 6198. If "No," enter the loss on Form 1040, line 12, and on Schedule SE, line 2 (or line 5 of Form 1041 or Form 1041S).

Part III Cost of Goods Sold and/or Operations (See Schedule C Instructions for Part III)

1 Inventory at beginning of year (If different from last year's closing inventory, attach explanation.)	1	7,200 00
2 Purchases less cost of items withdrawn for personal use	2	50,000 00
3 Cost of labor (Do not include salary paid to yourself.)	3	
4 Materials and supplies	4	
5 Other costs	5	
6 Add lines 1 through 5	6	57,200 00
7 Less: Inventory at end of year	7	54,200 00
8 Cost of goods sold and/or operations. Subtract line 7 from line 6. Enter here and in Part I, line 2, above. .	8	3,000 00

For Paperwork Reduction Act Notice, see Form 1040 Instructions.

Schedule C (Form 1040) 1986

Itemized Deductions

Broadly defined, itemized deductions are certain personal expenditures paid by the taxpayer that are specifically deductible under tax law. Exhibit A–1 lists some itemized deductions. These deductions reduce adjusted gross income (see Exhibit A–3, Form 1040, line 32). The individual taxpayer may (1) itemize the personal deductions by using "Schedule A—Itemized Deductions" (presented in Exhibit A–5) or (2) use a standard amount (included in the tax tables) called the zero bracket amount.[8] The taxpayer may also deduct one half of contributions to qualified charitable organizations in 1986 if the zero bracket amount option is used. For 1986, the zero bracket amount (ZBA) is $2,480 for single individuals, $3,670 for married individuals filing jointly, and $1,835 for married individuals filing separately. These zero bracket amounts have been built into the tax rate schedules (see Exhibit A–6).[9] Therefore, if the total **itemized** deductions are equal to, or less than the ZBA, no amount for itemized deductions is entered on the tax return (Form 1040, line 34a). To illustrate, John and Jane Doe reported total itemized deductions of $10,952 for 1986 (see Exhibit A–5, line 24). However, on Form 1040, line 34a (see Exhibit A–3), $7,282 was reported (i.e., $10,952 − $3,670, the zero bracket amount).

1986 will be the last year individuals who do not itemize their deductions on Schedule A will be able to deduct one half of their contributions to qualified charitable organizations. The deduction is claimed by completing lines 34b through 34d of Form 1040. In some cases, this deduction may be more advantageous than deducting the amount of excess itemized deductions.

Exemptions

In addition to itemized deductions, personal and dependency exemptions from adjusted gross income are allowed. Exemptions of $1,080 each are allowed for the taxpayer, the taxpayer's spouse, the taxpayer and/or spouse who is blind, the taxpayer and/or spouse 65 years of age or older, and dependents. In general, a dependent (a) is a close relative of the taxpayer, (b) has gross income of less than $1,080 for the tax year, and (c) has over half of the dependent's support furnished by the taxpayer. The exemptions are entered directly on the income tax return. Form 1040, lines 6a through 6f (see Exhibit A–3). The total deduction then is taken on Form 1040, line 36 (see Exhibit A–3).

TAXABLE INCOME

Now that all of the components used to compute **taxable income** have been discussed, we can focus on the overall computation of taxable income outlined in Exhibit A–1:

---

[8] For tax years beginning after 1986, the charitable contribution deduction for non-itemizers is repealed.

[9] Beginning in 1987, the ZBA is replaced by the "standard deduction," which is not built into the tax tables.

SCHEDULES A&B
(Form 1040)

Department of the Treasury
Internal Revenue Service

Schedule A—Itemized Deductions

(Schedule B is on back)

▶ Attach to Form 1040. ▶ See Instructions for Schedules A and B (Form 1040).

OMB No. 1545-0074

19 86

Attachment
Sequence No. 07

Name(s) as shown on Form 1040   Your social security number

John J. and Jane A. Doe   123 45 6789

Medical and Dental Expenses (Do not include expenses reimbursed or paid by others.) (See Instructions on page 19.)	1 Prescription medicines and drugs; and insulin	1	600 00	
	2 a Doctors, dentists, nurses, hospitals, insurance premiums you paid for medical and dental care, etc.	2a	2,850 00	
	b Transportation and lodging	2b	50 00	
	c Other (list—include hearing aids, dentures, eyeglasses, etc.) ▶	2c		
	3 Add lines 1 through 2c, and enter the total here	3	3,500 00	
	4 Multiply the amount on Form 1040, line 33, by 5% (.05)	4	2,928 00	
	5 Subtract line 4 from line 3. If zero or less, enter -0-. **Total** medical and dental ▶	5		572 00
Taxes You Paid (See Instructions on page 20.)	6 State and local income taxes	6		
	7 Real estate taxes	7	1,200 00	
	8 a General sales tax (see sales tax tables in instruction booklet)	8a	360 00	
	b General sales tax on motor vehicles	8b		
	9 Other taxes (list—include personal property taxes) ▶	9		
	10 Add the amounts on lines 6 through 9. Enter the total here. **Total taxes** ▶	10		1,560 00
Interest You Paid (See Instructions on page 20.)	11 a Home mortgage interest paid to financial institutions (report deductible points on line 13)	11a	5,500 00	
	b Home mortgage interest you paid to individuals (show that person's name and address) ▶	11b		
	12 Total credit card and charge account interest you paid	12	80 00	
	13 Other interest you paid (list payee's name and amount) ▶	13	240 00	
	14 Add the amounts on lines 11a through 13. Enter the total here. **Total interest** ▶	14		5,820 00
Contributions You Made (See Instructions on page 21.)	15 a Cash contributions. (If you gave $3,000 or more to any one organization, report those contributions on line 15b.)	15a	2,500 00	
	b Cash contributions totaling $3,000 or more to any one organization. (Show to whom you gave and how much you gave.) ▶	15b		
	16 Other than cash. (You must attach Form 8283 if over $500.)	16		
	17 Carryover from prior year	17		
	18 Add the amounts on lines 15a through 17. Enter the total here. **Total contributions** ▶	18		2,500 00
Casualty and Theft Losses	19 Total casualty or theft loss(es). (You must attach Form 4684 or similar statement.) (See page 21 of Instructions.) ▶	19		150 00
Miscellaneous Deductions (See Instructions on page 22.)	20 Union and professional dues	20	100 00	
	21 Tax return preparation fee	21	250 00	
	22 Other (list type and amount) ▶	22		
	23 Add the amounts on lines 20 through 22. Enter the total here. **Total miscellaneous** ▶	23		350 00
Summary of Itemized Deductions (See Instructions on page 22.)	24 Add the amounts on lines 5, 10, 14, 18, 19, and 23. Enter your answer here.	24		10,952 00
	25 If you checked Form 1040 { Filing Status box 2 or 5, enter $3,670 / Filing Status box 1 or 4, enter $2,480 / Filing Status box 3, enter $1,835 }	25		3,670 00
	26 Subtract line 25 from line 24. Enter your answer here and on Form 1040, line 34a. (If line 25 is more than line 24, see the Instructions for line 26 on page 22.) ▶	26		7,282 00

For Paperwork Reduction Act Notice, see Form 1040 Instructions.   Schedule A (Form 1040) 1986

EXHIBIT A-6

Income tax rate schedules for individuals

1986 SCHEDULE X SINGLE INDIVIDUALS				
Taxable Income Over	But Not Over	Pay	% on + Excess	of the amount over—
$ 0—$ 2,480		$ 0.00	0	. . . . .
2,480—	3,670	0.00	11	$ 2,480
3,670—	4,750	130.90	12	3,670
4,750—	7,010	260.50	14	4,750
7,010—	9,170	576.90	15	7,010
9,170—	11,650	900.90	16	9,170
11,650—	13,920	1,297.70	18	11,650
13,920—	16,190	1,706.30	20	13,920
16,190—	19,640	2,160.30	23	16,190
19,640—	25,360	2,953.80	26	19,640
25,360—	31,080	4,441.00	30	25,360
31,080—	36,800	6,157.00	34	31,080
36,800—	44,780	8,101.80	38	36,800
44,780—	59,670	11,134.20	42	44,780
59,670—	88,270	17,388.00	48	59,670
88,270—	. . . . .	31,116.00	50	88,270

1986 SCHEDULE Y—MARRIED INDIVIDUALS SEPARATE RETURNS—MARRIED PERSONS				
Taxable Income Over	But Not Over	Pay	% on + Excess	of the amount over—
$ 0—$ 1,835		$ 0.00	0	. . . . .
1,835—	2,970	0.00	11	$ 1,835
2,970—	4,100	124.85	12	2,970
4,100—	6,420	260.45	14	4,100
6,420—	8,635	585.25	16	6,420
8,635—	10,900	939.65	18	8,635
10,900—	13,275	1,347.35	22	10,900
13,275—	16,135	1,869.85	25	13,275
16,135—	18,990	2,584.85	28	16,135
18,990—	24,710	3,384.25	33	18,990
24,710—	32,375	5,271.85	38	24,710
32,375—	46,185	8,184.55	42	32,375
46,185—	59,025	13,984.75	45	46,185
59,025—	87,625	19,762.75	49	59,025
87,625—	. . . . .	33,776.75	50	87,625

1986 SCHEDULE Y—MARRIED INDIVIDUALS JOINT RETURNS AND SURVIVING SPOUSES				
Taxable Income Over	But Not Over	Pay	% on + Excess	of the amount over—
$ 0—$ 3,670		$ 0.00	0	. . . . .
3,670—	5,940	0.00	11	$ 3,670
5,940—	8,200	249.70	12	5,940
8,200—	12,840	520.90	14	8,200
12,840—	17,270	1,170.50	16	12,840
17,270—	21,800	1,879.30	18	17,270
21,800—	26,550	2,694.70	22	21,800
26,550—	32,270	3,739.70	25	26,550
32,270—	37,980	5,169.70	28	32,270
37,980—	49,420	6,768.50	33	37,980
49,420—	64,750	10,543.70	38	49,420
64,750—	92,370	16,369.10	42	64,750
92,370—	118,050	27,969.50	45	92,370
118,050—	175,250	39,525.50	49	118,050
175,250—	. . . . .	67,553.50	50	175,250

1986 SCHEDULE Z HEADS OF HOUSEHOLDS				
Taxable Income Over	But Not Over	Pay	% on + Excess	of the amount over—
$ 0—$ 2,480		$ 0.00	0	. . . . .
2,480—	4,750	0.00	11	$ 2,480
4,750—	7,010	249.70	12	4,750
7,010—	9,390	520.90	14	7,010
9,390—	12,730	854.10	17	9,390
12,730—	16,190	1,421.90	18	12,730
16,190—	19,640	2,044.70	20	16,190
19,640—	25,360	2,734.70	24	19,640
25,360—	31,080	4,107.50	28	25,360
31,080—	36,800	5,709.10	32	31,080
36,800—	48,240	7,539.50	35	36,800
48,240—	65,390	11,543.50	42	48,240
65,390—	88,270	18,746.50	45	65,390
88,270—	116,870	29,042.50	48	88,270
116,870—	. . . . .	42,770.50	50	116,870

$$\begin{matrix} \text{Gross} \\ \text{income} \end{matrix} - \text{Deductions} - \begin{matrix} \text{Excess itemized} \\ \text{deductions} \\ \text{(or non-itemized} \\ \text{charitable contribution)} \end{matrix} - \text{Exemptions} = \begin{matrix} \text{Taxable} \\ \text{income} \end{matrix}$$

The individual taxpayer uses taxable income, to compute his or her income tax liability for the year.

COMPUTATION OF INCOME TAX LIABILITY

The amount of income tax payable is computed by multiplying taxable income by the appropriate income tax rates. The income tax rates often are changed by legislation. Current rates are different for individual taxpayers than they are for corporate taxpayers. Exhibit A–6 gives the four 1986 Income Tax Rate Schedules for individual taxpayers. Note the different tax rates for each group of taxpayers.

To calculate the income tax liability, taxpayers must use the rate schedule that corresponds to their tax filing status. To illustrate, taxpayer Smith is a single individual with taxable income of $14,000. The 1986 rate schedule for this taxpayer (Exhibit A–6) shows $13,920 with a corresponding tax liability of $1,706.30 plus 20 percent of the $80 excess of $14,000 over $13,920 (an additional $16), giving a total tax liability of $1,722 (i.e., $1,706.30 + $16). Although the **marginal tax rate** (i.e., the tax rate on the next dollar of taxable income) is 20 percent, the **average** tax rate is only 12.3 percent (i.e., $1,722.30 ÷ $14,000). Additional examples are:

Individual	Taxable income	Computation of total income tax	Computed average tax rate
Smith	$ 14,000	$ 1,706.30 + ($ 80 × 20%) = $ 1,722.30	12.3
Jones	30,000	$ 4,441.00 + ($ 4,640 × 30%) = $ 5,833.00	19.4
Brown	70,000	$17,388.00 + ($10,330 × 48%) = $22,346.40	31.9
Wilson	150,000	$31,116.00 + ($61,730 × 50%) = $61,981.00	41.3

COMPLETION OF THE INDIVIDUAL INCOME TAX RETURN ILLUSTRATED

The preceding discussions included an income tax return for John and Jane Doe. At this point, you should review the following steps used to complete Form 1040. U.S. Individual Income Tax Return (Exhibit A–3):

Step	Activity	Source of information
1	Enter name, address, and other required taxpayer information—top portion of Form 1040	Taxpayer
2	Enter filing status of taxpayer, lines 1–5	Taxpayer
3	Enter exemptions, lines 6a through 6f	Taxpayer
4	Enter amount of exemptions, line 36 (exemptions multiplied by $1,080)	Line 6f and tax code

Step	Activity	Source of information
5	Enter gross income, lines 7–23	
	Line 7, wages and salaries	W-2
	Line 8, interest income	1099
	Line 9, dividend income	1099
	Line 12, business income (loss)	Schedule C
	Line 23, total	Summation
6	Adjustments to income, lines 24–30	Taxpayer records
7	Compute adjusted gross income, line 32	Line 23 minus line 31
8	Compute income tax, lines 33 through 40	
	Line 33, adjusted gross income	Line 32
	Line 34a, itemized deductions	Schedule A
	Lines 34b–34e, nonitemizer charitable contribution deduction	Taxpayer records
	Line 37, taxable income	Line 35 minus line 36
	Line 40	Summation
9	Total personal credits, lines 41–45	Taxpayer records
	Total business and other credits, lines 47–49	Taxpayer records
10	Other taxes, lines 51–55	Taxpayer records
11	Compute total tax, add lines 50 through 55	Summation
12	Compute tax payments (already made), lines 56–62	
	Line 56, income taxes withheld	W-2 and 1099
	Line 57, estimated income tax paid	Taxpayer records
	Line 63	Summation
	Compute refund due or amount owed	Line 55 compared with line 63

CAPITAL GAINS AND LOSSES (FOR INDIVIDUAL TAXPAYERS)

For income tax purposes a capital gain or loss results from the sale or exchange of a capital asset. A **capital asset** includes any item of property owned **except** merchandise inventories, depreciable property, and three other types of special assets (e.g., copyrights). For example, the personal residence, furnishings, and autos of an individual taxpayer would be capital assets.

A capital gain or loss may be either long term or short term. A **long-term** capital gain or loss generally results from the sale or exchange of a capital asset after being held for more than six months; a **short-term** capital gain or loss results if the asset as been held for six months or less. This distinction between long-term and short-term capital gains and losses is important for income tax purposes.[10]

For income tax purposes, a capital gain or loss is measured as the difference between the "amount realized" and its "adjusted basis" at the date of disposal. A **net short-term capital gain** results when the short-term capital gains **exceed** the short-term capital losses for the tax year. Short-term capital gains are taxed at

---

[10] The Tax Reform Act of 1986, however, repeals the 60 percent exclusion granted to individuals for their long-term capital gains prior to December 31, 1986. As a result, this distinction becomes significantly less important. However, the definition of capital asset is retained in the Internal Revenue Code to make it easier to reinstate a capital gains rate differential if tax rates increase in the future.

ordinary tax rates; whereas long-term capital gains had been accorded favorable tax treatment prior to the end of 1986 (i.e., only 40 percent of long-term capital gains were taxed). Long-term capital gains subsequent to December 31, 1986, will be taxed at ordinary tax rates. A **net short-term capital loss** results when the short-term capital losses exceed short-term capital gains for the tax year.[11]

Because taxpayers have been creative and aggressive in the past in having (1) long-term capital gains rather than short-term capital gains and (2) long-term losses to offset short-term gains during the tax year, complex tax regulations in the area of capital gains and losses have been developed by the Treasury Department to constrain these taxpayer strategies. Detailed discussion of the complexities of capital gains and losses is beyond the scope of this overview of income taxes.

TAX PLANNING FOR THE INDIVIDUAL TAXPAYER

Individual taxpayers should plan to minimize their income tax liabilities, within the provisions of the tax law. There are two ways to accomplish this objective: (1) timing and/or structural strategies and (2) tax return strategies. Some suggested strategies that should be discussed with a competent tax adviser are:[12]

Timing and/or structural strategies	Tax return preparation strategies
1. Investments in equity securities versus debt securities.	1. Whether to itemize deductions or to use the zero bracket amount.
2. Investments in tax-exempt municipal bonds.	2. Use of credit cards; an expenditure when charged for a "cash basis" return.
3. Individual retirement accounts (IRAs).	3. Choice of depreciation method used for income producing property.
4. Long-term versus short-term capital gains and losses.	4. Control of cash payments near year-end.
5. Income tax shelters (risk).	5. Deductions for sales taxes, property taxes, and licenses.
6. Ownership and operation of incorporated businesses.	6. Interest expense (prepaid interest).
7. Investment tax credits (recapture provisions).	7. Casualty and theft losses, and related insurance recovery.
8. Sale of personal residence.	8. Child care, job-seeking costs, medical costs, education costs.
9. Energy savings credits and pollution controls.	9. Short-term and long-term capital gains and losses (carryforwards).
10. Gifts, contributions, trusts, estate planning.	10. Avoidance of interest and penalties for incorrect and late tax return and tax payments (estimated).

Note: The Tax Reform Act of 1986 changes the applicability of several of these strategies (e.g., IRAs, capital gains, tax shelters, investment tax credits, certain energy credits, itemized deductions for consumer interest and sales tax, etc.). For example, most investment tax credits were repealed for tax years beginning on or after January 1, 1987.

---

[11] Casualty and theft losses (i.e., involuntary losses) usually are not capital losses; they are deducted as itemized deductions. The deduction for a personal casualty loss is subject to a $100 floor for each loss. A taxpayers' aggregate personal casualty and theft loss, less the $100 floor for each separate loss, is deductible only to the extent that the total losses exceed 10 percent of adjusted gross income.

[12] Tax planning should not be confused with tax evasion. Tax evasion involves illegal activities to reduce the tax liability, such as not reporting cash receipts from a source other than recorded income (e.g., tips). Severe penalties are prescribed for tax evasion activities.

PART B—INCOME TAXES PAID BY CORPORATIONS

A business may be organized as a sole proprietorship, partnership, or corporation. Sole (or single) proprietorships and partnerships are not required to pay income taxes.[13] In Part A we explained that the earnings (or losses) of sole proprietorships and partnerships must be included on the individual income tax return(s) of the owner(s). In contrast, a **corporation,** as a separate taxable entity, is required to file an annual income tax return and to pay any income taxes based upon its taxable income. The **stockholders** of a corporation pay income taxes on the corporation's earnings only when, and to the extent that, they receive dividends (out of corporate "earnings and profits").[14]

INCOME TAX RATES FOR CORPORATIONS

Corporate income tax rates for 1986 are as shown below along with an illustration of their application.[15]

Corporate income tax		Illustration assuming
Rate	Bracket	taxable income of $150,000
15%	on first $25,000	15% × $25,000 = $ 3,750
18%	on next 25,000	18% × $25,000 = 4,500
30%	on next 25,000	30% × $25,000 = 7,500
40%	on next 25,000	40% × $25,000 = 10,000
46%	on remaining income over $100,000	46% × $50,000 = 23,000
		Total income tax $48,750

Both individual and corporate income taxpayers may have to estimate their income tax liability. Corporations may be required to make quarterly installment payments based on these estimates during the year. Individual taxpayers usually have taxes withheld from wages by their employers; however, when they have taxable income that is not subject to withholding, they also may be required to make quarterly estimated tax payments.

SPECIAL INCOME TAX PROVISIONS FOR CORPORATIONS

Taxable income for a corporation is determined in much the same manner as it is for individual taxpayers. However, there are some differences in the income tax provisions for corporations including the following:

---

[13] Federal income tax law views sole proprietorships and partnerships as conduits for earnings to flow through to the owners. Partnerships must file an information return showing the determination of net income and the share of that income allocated to each partner. Distribution of assets to partners are not considered as partnership expenses for income tax purposes.

[14] Some people criticize this tax structure on the basis that the earnings of a corporation are subject to double taxation—once when earned and again when those earnings are distributed to stockholders as cash dividends.

[15] When fully phased-in, the Tax Reform Act of 1986 provides only two corporate tax rates: 15 percent and 34 percent.

1. The required tax forms—Form 1120, U.S. Corporation Income Tax Return, is significantly different from Form 1040, U.S. Individual Income Tax Return (compare Exhibits A–3 and A–8).
2. Currently, a corporation may elect to use either the cash or accrual basis for measuring **taxable income;** however, when the production, purchase, or sale of goods is a significant activity of the corporation, the accrual basis must be used.[16]
3. There is no category "itemized deductions" or a "zero bracket amount" for corporations; also, corporations cannot have personal deductions.
4. A corporation may exclude from taxable income 85 percent of any **dividend** revenue received from taxable domestic corporations (it is 100 percent under specified conditions).[17]
5. A corporation may deduct **organization** expenditures and amortize them over a five-year period or longer.
6. Corporations can deduct charitable contributions up to 10 percent of income before the contribution deduction. Any contribution in excess of this limit may be carried forward to five successive years provided that the 10 percent limit is not exceeded in any of those years.
7. Corporations may deduct, as expense, salaries paid to stockholders (i.e., owners) to the extent that the amount paid is reasonably related to the services performed.
8. A corporation must present beginning and ending balance sheets with the annual tax return.
9. The annual tax return of a corporation must include a reconciliation of the ending balance of retained earnings with the income data presented on the tax return.
10. A corporation has the option of using a 28 percent tax rate on its capital gains.[18]

COMPUTATION OF CORPORATE INCOME TAX

Taxable income of a corporation is computed as GROSS INCOME minus ORDINARY DEDUCTIONS minus SPECIAL DEDUCTIONS. Exhibit A–7 gives an overview of the corporate tax return and lists the specific items that are included in gross income, ordinary deductions, and special deductions. This overview of "Form 1120, U.S. Corporation Income Tax Return" is presented to help you understand the basic components of the corporate income tax return.

---

[16] The Tax Reform Act of 1986 generally limits the use of the cash method to corporations with three-year average annual gross receipts of less than $5 million. Other corporations will be required to use the accrual method of reporting taxable income.

[17] The dividend received deduction is changed to 80 percent for dividends subsequent to December 31, 1986.

[18] The Tax Reform Act of 1986 also repeals the preferential capital gains rate for corporations.

EXHIBIT A–7

Overview of Form 1120, Corporation Income Tax Return

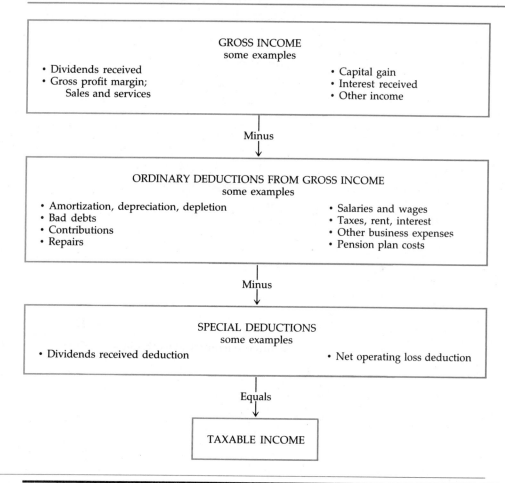

Exhibit A–8 shows a copy of the 1985 **corporation** income tax return; the basic tax return (Form 1120) has the following nine attached schedules to support it:

Schedule designation	Schedule title
A	Cost of goods sold
C	Dividends and special deductions
E	Compensation of officers
F	Bad debts, reserve method
J	Tax computation
—	Additional information
L	Balance sheets

U.S. Corporation Income Tax Return

Form 1120

Department of the Treasury
Internal Revenue Service

U.S. Corporation Income Tax Return

For calendar 1985 or tax year beginning _____, 1985, ending _____, 19 ____

▶ **For Paperwork Reduction Act Notice, see page 1 of the instructions.**

OMB No. 1545-0123

1985

Check if a—

A Consolidated return ☐
B Personal Holding Co. ☐
C Business Code No. (See the list in the Instructions)

Use IRS label. Otherwise please print or type.

Name

Number and street

City or town, state, and ZIP code

D Employer identification number

E Date incorporated

F Total assets (see Specific Instructions)
Dollars | Cents

G Check box if there has been a change in address from the previous year . . . . ▶ ☐ $

Income

1 a Gross receipts or sales _____ b Less returns and allowances _____ Balance ▶	1c
2 Cost of goods sold and/or operations (Schedule A)	2
3 Gross profit (line 1c less line 2)	3
4 Dividends (Schedule C)	4
5 Interest	5
6 Gross rents	6
7 Gross royalties	7
8 Capital gain net income (attach separate Schedule D)	8
9 Net gain or (loss) from Form 4797, line 17, Part II (attach Form 4797)	9
10 Other income (see instructions—attach schedule)	10
11 TOTAL income—Add lines 3 through 10 and enter here . . . . . ▶	11

Deductions

12 Compensation of officers (Schedule E)	12
13 a Salaries and wages _____ b Less jobs credit _____ Balance ▶	13c
14 Repairs	14
15 Bad debts (Schedule F if reserve method is used)	15
16 Rents	16
17 Taxes	17
18 Interest	18
19 Contributions (**see instructions for 10% limitation**)	19
20 Depreciation (attach Form 4562) 20	21b
21 Less depreciation claimed in Schedule A and elsewhere on return . 21a	
22 Depletion	22
23 Advertising	23
24 Pension, profit-sharing, etc. plans	24
25 Employee benefit programs	25
26 Other deductions (attach schedule)	26
27 TOTAL deductions—Add lines 12 through 26 and enter here . . . . . . ▶	27
28 Taxable income before net operating loss deduction and special deductions (line 11 less line 27) .	28
29 **Less: a** Net operating loss deduction (see instructions) 29a	29c
b Special deductions (Schedule C) 29b	
30 Taxable income (line 28 less line 29c)	30
31 TOTAL TAX (Schedule J)	31

Tax and Payments

32 Payments:

a 1984 overpayment allowed as a credit . . .		
b 1985 estimated tax payments		
c Less 1985 refund applied for on Form 4466 . . ( )		
d Tax deposited with Form 7004		
e Credit from regulated investment companies (attach Form 2439) . .		
f Credit for Federal tax on gasoline and special fuels (attach Form 4136)	32	

33 Enter any **PENALTY** for underpayment of estimated tax—check ▶☐ if Form 2220 is attached	33
34 **TAX DUE**—If the total of lines 31 and 33 is larger than line 32, enter AMOUNT OWED	34
35 **OVERPAYMENT**—If line 32 is larger than the total of lines 31 and 33, enter AMOUNT OVERPAID	35
36 Enter amount of line 35 you want: **Credited to 1986 estimated tax** ▶ _____ Refunded ▶	36

Please Sign Here

Under penalties of perjury, I declare that I have examined this return, including accompanying schedules and statements, and to the best of my knowledge and belief, it is true, correct, and complete. Declaration of preparer (other than taxpayer) is based on all information of which preparer has any knowledge.

▶ _____   _____   ▶ _____
Signature of officer   Date   Title

Paid Preparer's Use Only

Preparer's signature ▶	Date	Check if self-employed ▶ ☐
		Preparer's social security number
Firm's name (or yours, if self-employed) and address ▶		E.I. No. ▶
		ZIP code ▶

Schedule designation	Schedule title
M-1	Reconciliation of income per books with income per tax return
M-2	Analysis of unappropriated retained earnings per books

(Other special schedules are available and used as needed.)

The corporate income tax form is presented in Exhibit A–8 for the sole purpose of giving you an idea of the nature and complexity of a corporation tax return. You may wish to compare it with the individual tax return (given in Exhibit A–3).

ACCOUNTING INCOME VERSUS TAXABLE INCOME

Accounting income is reported on the income statement; it measures the income or loss of a business on the accrual basis in conformity with generally accepted accounting principles (GAAP). In contrast, **taxable income** is reported on the income tax return; it is determined according to current tax law and regulations. The U.S. Congress identifies the objectives and specifies in general terms the manner of computing taxable income. These objectives usually are different than the objectives of financial reporting (per GAAP). The objectives of the income tax system include (a) providing revenue to meet the expenditures of the federal government and (b) implementing certain public policy decisions (such as defense, social programs, education, and foreign aid). Therefore, it is no surprise that in a given year accounting income and taxable income of a particular corporation may differ significantly. To illustrate, consider six of the major areas of difference: (1) cash versus accrual basis of accounting, (2) the modified accrual basis used for tax versus the strict accrual basis used for accounting purposes, (3) special tax provisions for recognizing certain revenues and expenses, (4) capital gains and losses, (5) tax-exempt income, and (6) use of different accounting methods for some items, such as depreciation. To illustrate, we discuss three major areas: (1) revenue and expense recognition, (2) modifications of the "cash" and "accrual" bases, and (3) use of different accounting methods.

REVENUE AND EXPENSE RECOGNITION FOR INCOME TAX PURPOSES

Many, but not all, of the income tax provisions are designed to prevent both individual and corporate taxpayers from manipulating the timing and structuring of transactions to shift income (or loss) among periods simply to take advantage of more favorable tax policy and tax rates. There is a never-ending "battle" between the taxing authorities and the taxpayers (who become very creative). As a consequence, tax provisions dealing with revenue and expense recognition often cause major differences between accounting income and taxable income. Some of the more common examples are:

1. Interest revenue on state and municipal bonds is generally excluded from taxable income, although it is included in accounting income.
2. Amortization of purchased goodwill is not deducted in computing taxable income, although it is deducted in computing accounting income.
3. Statutory depletion, rather than depletion based on cost, sometimes may be used to compute taxable income, but cannot be used to compute accounting income.
4. Rent revenue collected in advance is included in taxable income when collected, but it is included in accounting income on the accrual basis.

MODIFIED CASH BASIS AND MODIFIED ACCRUAL BASIS USED FOR MEASURING TAXABLE INCOME

As discussed throughout this book, accounting income must be measured using a pure accrual basis. Under this basis, **recognition** occurs when revenues are realized (i.e., when the earnings process is essentially completed) and when expenses are incurred, regardless of the timing of the related cash flows. GAAP prohibits use of cash basis accounting because it does not appropriately measure income.

In contrast, for income tax purposes either a (1) modified accrual basis or (2) a modified cash basis may be used. The **modified accrual basis** excludes certain revenues (such as interest on tax-exempt bonds, capital gains and losses). In respect to expenses, the timing of recognition may be different (e.g., depreciation expense), and some expenses are not deductible for income tax purposes (e.g., amortization of goodwill). The **modified cash basis** used to measure taxable income is not strictly cash receipts minus cash payments. Cash receipts are measured as taxable revenue when the cash has been **constructively received** (constructive receipt means although not yet in possession, but so much within the control of the taxpayer that possession is reasonably assured). In respect to expenses, cash payments cannot include cash paid to purchase **depreciable property** that has an estimated useful life of more than one year. Under the cash basis for computing taxable income, such a purchase is an acquisition of an asset which must be depreciated for tax purposes. Thus, the cash basis treats such property as if the accrual basis is being used.

USE OF DIFFERENT ACCOUNTING METHODS

Tax law and the regulations permit use of accounting methods for computing taxable income that differ from those permitted for determining accounting income. For example, a company may use the straight-line method of depreciation for computing accounting income, but use an accelerated depreciation method to compute taxable income. Four other common examples relate to depletion, profit on long-term construction contracts, capital gains and losses, and gross margin or profit on installment sales.[19]

TAX PLANNING BY BUSINESS MANAGERS

Because income tax rates are high and the related income tax law and regulations are complex, tax planning is an important consideration in most business decisions made by the management of any business. The basic objective of tax planning is to minimize income taxes within the framework of the tax law and regulations prescribed by the Treasury Department. Tax planning focuses on anticipated tax consequences of future transactions. To provide an overview of tax planning we will discuss three of the major areas that affect most business entities: (1) selecting the type of business organization, (2) financing the business, and (3) structuring transactions before they occur.

Selecting the Type of Business Organization

Sole proprietorships, partnerships, and corporations have different income tax implications for owners and managers. When starting a new business, selecting the type of business organization poses several substantive issues, one of which is the long-term income tax implications. The tax obligation related to the operations of a sole proprietorship depends upon the marginal income tax rate of the individual owner, and for a partnership it depends upon the marginal tax rates of each partner. Marginal tax rates are applied to the annual earnings of the business whether they are withdrawn by the owners or not. In contrast, the tax obligation on corporate earnings depends upon (a) the tax rates of the corporation (when the earnings are realized) and (b) the marginal tax rates of the stockholders when the corporation pays dividends out of those earnings. The relevant income tax provisions for these issues are beyond the scope of this overview. However, they have significant impact at date of organization, over the life of the business, and eventually upon dissolution of the business.

Financing a Business

A business obtains funds (e.g., cash) from three primary sources: (1) investments by owners, (2) borrowing, and (3) earnings of the business. Often when additional funds are needed (e.g., for operations and expansion), the management of the company must decide between equity and debt (or some combination) as the source(s) of funds. Such decisions have important income tax implications, particularly for a corporation, because interest on debt is a fully deductible expense in computing taxable income; in comparison dividends paid

---

[19] The installment method of income recognition permits taxpayers to defer income recognition until cash is collected, and therefore the taxpayer has the funds to pay the tax.

to stockholders (of common and preferred stock) are not deductible. To illustrate, assume Tye Corporation needs $500,000 cash to acquire a new productive facility. The management is considering two alternatives as follows:

Alternative A—Borrow the needed funds at 12 percent interest; the marginal income tax rate for the company is 46 percent.

Alternative B—Issue for cash, 50,000 shares of the company's cumulative 8 percent, preferred stock, at $10 par value per share.

The two financing alternatives can be analyzed as follows:

Alternative A, borrowing:

$$\$500,000 \times 12\% \times (1.00 - .46) = \$32,400 \text{ aftertax cost per year}$$
$$\text{Net interest rate: } \$32,400 \div \$500,000 = \underline{6.48\%}$$

Alternative B, issue capital stock:

$$\$500,000 \times 8\% = \$40,000 \text{ aftertax cost per year}$$
$$\text{Net interest rate: } \$40,000 \div \$500,000 = \underline{8.0\%}$$

Note: The lower tax rates resulting from the Tax Reform Act of 1986 would have some bearing on Alternative A.

The borrowing alternative was less costly because the interest expense is deducted in full from taxable income at the 46 percent marginal tax rate. However, a number of other factors should be considered in making this decision. The company is legally required to make the fixed interest payments of $60,000 per year and to repay the $500,000 principal amount on maturity date, regardless of whether the company earned income or incurred a loss. In contrast, by choosing to issue capital stock, these fixed payments may be avoided. Dividends can be paid only if there are accumulated earnings (i.e., a positive balance in retained earnings) and there is no payment on a maturity date for the shares issued.

Structuring and Timing Transactions to Minimize Income Taxes

Business transactions often can be structured and/or timed in ways to maximize their favorable, or minimize their unfavorable, income tax consequences. Structuring and timing must be accomplished before the transaction has been completed. Some typical transactions that can be structured or timed for this purpose are:

1. Leasing versus purchase of operating assets.
2. Installment sale of real estate.
3. Valuation of several "used" assets bought at a lump-sum price (i.e., land and the building thereon).
4. Valuation of assets and liabilities of a purchased business.
5. Allocation of the lump-sum purchase price of depreciable versus nondepreciable assets.

6. Recognition of investment tax credit (deferral versus flow through).
7. Accelerated depreciation (change in mid-life).
8. Energy credits and pollution control costs.
9. Tax-free exchanges of certain types of assets.
10. Capital gains and losses (short term versus long term).
11. The wide range of approved "tax shelters."
12. Purchase of merchandise for inventory (related to the inventory flow method, such as LIFO).

Note: Some of these items are affected by the Tax Reform Act of 1986 (e.g., the investment tax credit has been repealed). A detailed discussion is beyond the scope of this chapter.

DEMONSTRATION CASE

(To illustrate, for instructional purposes only, computation of income tax without using the required standardized forms.)

The accounting records of Dow Corporation (no subsidiaries) provided the following 19D data:

Sales revenue	$700,000	Cash dividends received	$ 8,000
Interest revenue	3,000	Compensation of officers	125,000
Bad debt expense	1,800	Advertising expense	7,000
Taxes (excluding income tax)	5,000	Interest expense	15,000
Depreciation expense	20,000	Repair expense	1,200
Charitable contributions		Salaries and wages	121,000
(net allowable)	4,000	Special deductions	9,000
19D estimated income tax		Employee benefit programs	40,000
payments (total paid)	30,000		
Cost of goods sold	242,000		

Required:

Prepare a schedule to compute the 19D income tax for Dow Corporation. To compute total tax, assume there are no additional complications such as investment tax credit, jobs credit, personal holding company, minimum tax, etc. Set up the major captions listed in Exhibit A–8. Use terminology and identifying lines from Form 1120. Assume that 1986 income tax rates apply.

Suggested Solution

Line	Item	Amount
	Gross income:	
1	Sales revenue	$ 700,000
2	Cost of goods sold	(242,000)
3	Gross profit	458,000
4	Dividends	8,000
5	Interest	3,000
11	Total income	$ 469,000

Line	Item	Amount	
		Amount	
	Ordinary deductions:		
12	Compensation of officers	125,000	
13	Salaries and wages	121,000	
14	Repairs	1,200	
15	Bad debts	1,800	
17	Taxes	5,000	
18	Interest	15,000	
19	Contributions	4,000	
20	Depreciation	20,000	
23	Advertising	7,000	
25	Employee benefit programs	40,000	
27	Total deductions		340,000
28	Taxable income before special deductions		129,000
	Special deductions:		
29b	Special deduction		(9,000)
30	Taxable income		$ 120,000
	Tax:		
31	Total tax*	34,950	
32	Credits:		
	(b) 19D estimated tax payments	(30,000)	
34	Tax due		$ 4,950

* Computation:
(15% × $25,000) + (18% × $25,000) + (30% × $25,000) + (40% × $25,000) + (46% × $20,000)
= $34,950.

QUESTIONS

PART A

1. (a) What is the form number and title of the individual income tax return? (b) When and where must the return be filed? (c) What are the minimum gross income amounts for 1986 that make the filing of an individual income tax return required?

2. Why do most individual taxpayers elect the cash basis to measure taxable income?

3. Give the formula for determining taxable income for an individual taxpayer.

4. The files of Dr. Joe Rock, an optometrist, showed that $60,000 cash was collected from patients during 19X. At the beginning of 19X, total receivables from patients amounted to $12,000, and at the end of 19X the amount was $8,500. What amount of gross income should be included in the computation of taxable income assuming the (a) cash basis $_____ and (b) the accrual basis $_____?

5. John P. Jones is regularly employed by CT Company as personnel director. His monthly salary during 19G (before any deductions) was $36,000. During 19G, Jones collected $7,500 cash from another source for independently contracted consulting services. List the two forms that Jones should receive relating to his earnings and indicate basically what each form should report.

6. Explain the income tax treatment of interest received on state and municipal bonds.

7. What is a capital asset for tax purposes? What are the two kinds of gains or losses that usually arise when capital ╕   ˙s are sold?

PART B

8. Indicate whether each of the following types of business organization is required to file a separate income tax return: *(a)* sole proprietorship, *(b)* partnership, and *(c)* corporation. Explain the basis for each answer.

9. Complete the following tabulation based on the 1986 corporate tax rates:

Case	Taxable income	Amount of income tax
A	$ 25,000	_____
B	56,000	_____
C	110,000	_____

10. Give the formula for determining taxable income for a corporation.

11. Form 1120, U.S. Corporation Income Tax Return, is a one-page standardized form; however, attached to it are nine subschedules. What is the primary purpose of these nine subschedules?

12. List and briefly explain three areas in which there are differences between corporate accounting income and taxable income.

13. If a corporate taxpayer uses the cash basis to measure taxable income, it must generally depreciate (not expense as one amount) property having a useful life of more than one year (as is done in accrual accounting). Is this statement true or false? Explain.

14. Explain why a corporation often prefers to obtain needed cash (e.g., for expansion) by selling bonds rather than by issuing shares of its own capital stock.

EXERCISES

PART A

EA–1.   (Emphasizes Effect on Income Tax of Client Filing Status and Level of Earnings) Assume you are a CPA in public practice and have agreed to speak on the subject of income taxes. You have decided to use transparencies with data on some of your typical clients. Two of the transparencies will be organized as shown below.

Required:

Complete the following transparencies:

a. Clients A, B, C, and D each have taxable income of $40,000. Use 1986 tax rates.

Client Filing Status	Taxable Income	Income Tax		Average Tax Rate
		Computation	Amount	
A. Single	$40,000			
B. Head of household	40,000			
C. Married, separate	40,000			
D. Married joint	40,000			

What primary point on this transparency would you emphasize?

b. Clients E, F, and G, each married, will file jointly with the indicated income.

Client	Taxable Income	Income Tax		Average Tax Rate
		Computation	Amount	
E	$ 12,000			
F	50,000			
G	130,000			

What point on this transparency would you emphasize?

EA–2.   (Emphasizes the Effect on Taxable Income of the Marital Status of the Taxpayer) On Form 1040, U.S. Individual Income Tax Return, Line 6f is entitled "Total number of exemptions claimed." Assume you are preparing income tax returns for eight different clients.

Required:

a. Based on the data given below, determine the number of exemptions to which each taxpayer is entitled and complete the last column of the following schedule:

Client	Filing Status	Age	Number of Dependents	Blind	Form 1040, Line 6f Exemptions Claimed
A	Single	22	0	No	
B	Married, separately	33*	2	No	
C	Married, jointly	41*	9	No	
D	Head of household	65	1	No	
E	Single	66	0	Yes	
F	Married, separately	67*	1	No	
G	Married, jointly	75*	0	Yes	
H	Head of household	65	2	No	

* Age of spouse:
Client B, 28; Client C, 37; Client F, 43; and Client G, 72 and blind.

b. Assume that the amount for each one of the above taxpayers on Form 1040, line 35, is $30,000. Compute taxable income (line 37).

EA–3. (Emphasizes the Difference Between Itemized Deductions and the Zero Bracket Amount) Assume you are a CPA in public practice and that the amounts given below are the total itemized deductions for six of your clients.

Client and Filing Status	Total Itemized Deductions	Zero Bracket Amount	Amount that Should Be Entered on Form 1040, Line 34a
A. Single	$5,000		
B. Single	2,000		
C. Single	3,300		
D. Married, jointly	2,000		
E. Married, jointly	7,000		
F. Married, jointly	3,670		

Required:

a. Complete the above schedule, assuming the year is 1986.
b. Explain the basis for each amount that you entered in the last column.

EA–4.   (Compute Income Tax Amount for a Couple with Four Children) Two of your clients, Samuel and Sue Smith, have engaged you to prepare their 19C, U.S. individual income tax return. They have four children and will file a joint return (cash basis). Sam and Sue are 36 and 34, respectively. They have provided you with the following information.

Salary (W-2) $75,000
Income taxes withheld (W-2) 14,000
Business income, consulting (net of applicable expenses) 5,000
Interest revenue (including $2,000 on tax-exempt bonds) 10,000
Rental revenue (per Schedule E) 6,000
Casualty loss theft, from residence (net of $100 deduction) ... 1,800
Interest paid (on residence) 23,000
Medical deductions .... None
Property taxes paid (on residence) 2,100
Sales taxes paid (including $200 on vehicles) 2,000
Payments to Keogh (HR10) retirement plan 7,000
Estimated payments on 19C income tax 3,000

Required:

Set up an abbreviated schedule in a manner similar to the demonstration case (instead of using Form 1040) and compute the amount of the required income tax payment (or refund) on April 15, 19D. Use the major captions shown in Exhibit A–1 and show all computations. Use terminology and identifying lines from Form 1040. Use 1986 rates.

PART B

EA–5.   (Compute Income Tax for a Corporation Starting with Taxable Income) Doss Corporation is preparing its 19G federal income tax return. Taxable income has been computed at $115,000 (accrual basis). An overpayment of income tax for 19F of $9,000 was carried over and will be applied to the 19G income tax liability. Also, the company remitted 19G total estimated income tax payments of $18,000.

Required:

Refer to Exhibit A–8 and complete lines 30–34 of the 1985 corporate tax return. Show computations.

EA–6.   (Comparison of Items on the Tax Return of an Individual Versus a Corporation) Below is a list of 20 items, each of which may or may not be related to taxable income (either as an increase or decrease). For each item, enter a check mark under either "Yes" or "No" to indicate whether that item should be included in measuring taxable income. Assume the individual taxpayer does not own a sole proprietorship or an interest in a partnership, or rental properties.

Item	Included in Computation of Taxable Income			
	Individual*		Corporation	
	Yes	No	Yes	No
1. Interest revenue on tax-exempt municipal bonds				
2. Cost of traveling from home to place of employment (by owner[s])				
3. Fee paid to CPA for preparing tax return				
4. Interest paid on debt on residence of owner(s)				
5. Storm damage to personal auto				
6. Contributions to charity				
7. IRS penalty for late tax return				
8. Income taxes withheld (reported on W-2)				
9. State income taxes				
10. Medical expenses				
11. Insurance on residence of owner(s)				
12. Depreciation expense				
13. Amortization of organization expenditures				
14. Exemptions (personal)				
15. Depletion expense (oil and gas)				
16. Union dues paid				
17. Presidential election campaign (deduction)				
18. Bad debts				
19. Casualty insurance on residence of owner(s)				
20. Zero bracket amount				

* With no separate sole proprietorship or partnership interest.

EA-7.   (Compute Income Tax for a Corporation) Reneau Corporation's 19W income statement reported pretax items as follows:

Sales revenue	$1,033,000
Interest revenue (including $4,000 on interest-free municipal bonds)	9,000
Salaries and wages paid	102,000
Repairs	7,000
Bad debts (Schedule F)	2,000
Cost of goods sold (Schedule A)	460,000
Gross rent received	7,200
Compensation of officers (Schedule E)	130,000
Gross royalties received	4,800
Rents paid	8,000
19W estimated income tax payments	60,000
Special deduction (Schedule C)	15,000
Depreciation (Form 4562)	18,000
Advertising	20,000
Interest paid and accrued	30,000
Contributions	4,000
Overpayment of 19V income tax (applicable to 19W)	6,000
Taxes paid (on property)	24,000

Required:

Prepare a schedule to compute the income tax due when the tax return is filed. Assume there are no complications other than those presented above. Set up the major captions given in Exhibit A–7. Use terminology and identifying lines from the 1985 Form 1120. Use 1986 tax rates.

PROBLEMS

PART A

PA-1.   (Compute Income Tax for a Single Individual) The following information has been provided to you by your client, Gene Horton:

Salary	$55,000
Charitable contributions, cash (allowable)	5,000
Interest on home mortgage	2,300
Interest on VISA charge card*	78
Interest on school loan*	149
Federal income taxes withheld (Form W-2)	20,000
Property taxes	780
Sales tax*	164
Rental income	1,800
Professional dues (AICPA)*	50
Interest income	200
Penalty on early withdrawal of savings	54
Contribution to IRA*	1,000

* Provisions in the Tax Reform Act of 1986 affect deductibility of these items after 1986.

Gene is a single, 44-year-old, cash basis, calendar-year taxpayer. Assume that 1986 rates apply.

Required:

Using the demonstration case in the chapter as a model, set up an abbreviated schedule to compute the amount of income tax due or the refund for this year. Show computations, and use terminology from Form 1040.

PA–2. (Analysis of Income Tax Effects to Determine Whether a Couple Should File Separate or Joint Tax Returns) Two of your clients, Raymond and Sherry Stewart, engaged you to prepare their 19C individual income tax return. They want to file the return in a manner that will minimize their tax liability. Raymond and Sherry have asked you to evaluate whether it would be more beneficial for them to file a joint return or to file separately (using the tax tables for married filing separately). Assume that 1986 income tax rates apply.

Salary from Raymond's W-2	$27,000
Salary from Sherry's W-2	25,000
Sherry's consulting revenue (net of applicable expenses)	18,250

There are no other sources of income and their total deductions do not exceed the zero bracket amount.

Required:

a. What would you recommend with respect to their tax return(s)? Show calculations to support your recommendations.

b. What would you recommend assuming Raymond did not earn a salary in 19C?

PART B

PA–3. (Analysis of Income Tax Effects to Determine Whether a New Business Should be Organized as a Proprietorship or a Corporation) John Springer, a single individual, age 31, wants to incorporate his small business. As a primary job, John works as an engineer for TPX Corporation and receives a yearly salary of $41,000 ($10,000 was withheld from his paycheck for 19C). Two years ago John started a small business which has been operated as a sole proprietorship. Gross revenues from the business average about $12,000 per year, with the following expenses:

Advertising	$500
Supplies	700
Interest	800
Depreciation	450
Travel	910
Telephone	360
Legal and professional fees	240

John expects his income from TPX to remain approximately the same for the next several years, but foresees considerable growth potential in his own consulting business. Assume 1986 rates apply in all situations, and that self-employment tax on the consulting revenues does not apply.

Required:

a. Compute John's total income tax expense based on the assumption that his consulting business is continued as a sole proprietorship. Alternatively, what would the income tax be if he incorporates his consulting business and withdraws all of its earnings as dividends?

b. Would your answer to requirement *a* be different if the **taxable income** (Schedule C) from John's consulting business was $100,000? Support your response with calculations.

PA–4.   (Analysis of Income Tax Effects of Financing with Capital Stock Versus Bonds) XYZ Corporation is considering financing alternatives to expand its current facilities at a cost of $300,000. The president of XYZ suggests issuing 30,000 shares of its 10 percent preferred stock, cumulative, par $10 to finance the expansion. The controller recommends that XYZ sell 300 bonds with a stated rate of 10 percent paid annually (yield rate, 10 percent) to get the funds. Each bond has a par value of $1,000 and matures in 10 years. Assume 1986 tax rates apply.

Required:

a. Assume taxable income, before interest expense, of $150,000. What effect does each alternative have on income taxes?
b. Evaluate the two alternatives in terms of cash flows now and in future years.
c. What alternative would you recommend? Explain the basis for your recommendation.

SPECIAL SUPPLEMENT B— 1985 FINANCIAL STATEMENTS OF CHESEBROUGH-POND'S, INC.

Management's Discussion and Analysis

1985 Net Sales by Operating Division

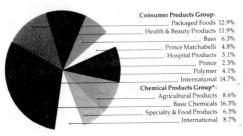

Consumer Products Group:
Packaged Foods 12.9%
Health & Beauty Products 11.9%
Bass 6.3%
Prince Matchabelli 4.8%
Hospital Products 3.1%
Prince 2.3%
Polymer 4.1%
International 14.7%

Chemical Products Group*:
Agricultural Products 8.6%
Basic Chemicals 16.3%
Specialty & Food Products 6.3%
International 8.7%

*The results of the Chemical Products Group are included in the consolidated results only from the acquisition date of March 1985.

Results of Operations

Net Sales

Consolidated net sales from continuing operations increased 77.3 per cent in 1985 compared with a 9.9 per cent increase in 1984. The 1985 sales increase includes Stauffer Chemical Company, acquired March 15, 1985. (See Note 2 to the Consolidated Financial Statements). Excluding the effects of the Stauffer and Polymer acquisitions, net sales from continuing operations increased 2.9 per cent over 1984.

The Packaged Foods Division's sales increased 0.7 per cent in 1985 and 3.9 per cent in 1984. The sales increase in 1985 was primarily due to increased sales of *Ragú* Traditional sauces and the new Traditional II flavors (Extra Cheese and Extra Garlic) introduced during the third quarter of 1985, offset by lower sales of other *Ragú* spaghetti sauces. The sales increase in 1984 was due to full-year sales of *Ragú* Chunky Gardenstyle spaghetti sauce, somewhat offset by lower sales of other *Ragú* spaghetti sauces and *Ragú Pizza Quick* products.

The Health & Beauty Products Division's sales increased 9.4 per cent in 1985 and 2.1 per cent in 1984. The sales increase in 1985 reflects higher sales of existing brands such as *Pond's* creams, *Vaseline Intensive Care* lotions, *Cutex* nail polish remover and *Vaseline* petroleum jelly. In addition, *Cutex* Eyes, *Rave* Hair Masque conditioner, *Vaseline Lip Therapy* and *Cutex Nailcolor Pen*, contributed to the increase. The sales increase in 1984 reflects higher sales of *Q-tips* products and the introductions of *Cutex* lipsticks, *Rave* Hair Masque conditioner and *Vaseline Lip Therapy*.

The Bass Division's sales decreased 1.0 per cent in 1985 and increased 19.7 per cent in 1984. The sales decrease in 1985 was due to overall lower sales at the wholesale level for *Bass* women's footwear. On the retail level, however, sales were up substantially in 1985 as the full-line, full-price Bass retail stores, including The Shoe Box chain of retail stores in Texas, continued to show strong growth. The sales increase in 1984 reflected a significant increase in the division's retail operations.

The Prince Matchabelli Division's sales increased 0.5 per cent in 1985 and 9.7 per cent in 1984. The increase in 1985 was due primarily to sales of the new *Vervé* Body Scenting Mist and the *Aziza Polishing Pen* automatic nail color. Offsetting these increases were significant declines in the *Cachet Noir* and *Béret* women's fragrance lines, reflecting overall softness in the fragrance category and inventory reductions by key retailers. The sales increase in 1984 includes sales of the *Aziza Polishing Pen* automatic nail color, introduced during the third quarter of 1984, and reflects increased sales for the *Aviance Night Musk* and *Wind Song* women's fragrance lines.

The Polymer Corporation was purchased by the company during the third quarter of 1984. (See Note 2 to the Consolidated Financial Statements). Sales for 1985 compared to full-year sales for 1984 decreased 0.3 per cent due to reduced pricing as a result of an overall weakness in the industrial market. Full-year 1984 sales increased 18.4 per cent due to increased sales of plastic shapes and parts, and coating powders.

The Hospital Products Division's sales increased 13.1 per cent in 1985 and 6.3 per cent in 1984. The sales increase in 1985 reflects increases in most major product lines including the *Kangaroo* line of enteral feeding systems which was enhanced during the year by the acquisition of a line of nutritional feeding products. The sales increase in 1984 was due primarily to increased sales for the *Kangaroo* line of enteral feeding systems which was expanded during 1984.

The Prince Division's sales decreased 5.4 per cent in 1985 and increased 2.1 per cent in 1984. The sales decrease in 1985 was due to lower sales of *Prince* tennis racquets as a result of the continued decline in the domestic tennis racquet category. The sales increase in 1984 reflected sales of two new tennis racquet models, the *Prince* Precision Graphite and the *Prince* Magnesium Pro, and sales increases for tennis accessories. These increases were partially offset by selling-price adjustments made to broaden the appeal of *Prince* racquets.

The Consumer Products Group's International Division sales increased 1.7 per cent in 1985 and 5.4 per cent in 1984. Declines in most foreign currencies relative to the U.S. dollar reduced the dollar value of the division's 1985 sales by about $192 million, and price increases had the effect of increasing sales by about $177 million. In 1984, declines in most foreign currencies reduced the dollar value of sales by about $152 million, and price increases had the effect of increasing sales by about $154 million. Unit sales were particularly strong in

France, West Germany, Italy, England and in certain African markets in 1985 and Argentina, France, Japan, the United Kingdom, Venezuela and West Germany in 1984.

The Chemical Products Group (Stauffer Chemical Company), a worldwide manufacturer and marketer of a wide range of agricultural and food products, as well as chemical products and services, was purchased by the company during the first quarter of 1985. Sales for the Chemical Products Group have been included in the consolidated financial statements since the acquisition date.

The Agricultural Products Division's full-year sales increased 9.3 per cent in 1985 benefitting from volume increases for hybrid seeds and strong sales for intermediates.

The Basic Chemicals Division's full-year sales decreased 5.9 per cent in 1985 due to decreased sales for the phosphorus and chlor-alkali businesses, reflecting the general sluggishness in the economy during the year.

The Specialty & Food Products Division's full-year sales increased 3.4 per cent in 1985 due to strong sales contributions from specialty chemical products and food ingredient products.

The Chemical Products Group's International Division full-year sales increased 3.2 per cent despite lower than expected agricultural chemical sales in Europe, South Africa and China.

The consolidated sales increase of 77.3 per cent in 1985 consisted of volume growth of 2.6 per cent, price increases of 12.9 per cent and sales from acquired companies of 74.4 per cent. The consolidated sales increase of 9.9 per cent in 1984 consisted of volume growth of 4.5 per cent, price increases of 12.2 per cent and sales from acquired companies of 4.2 per cent. In addition, changes in relative rates of foreign exchange reduced sales by 12.6 per cent in 1985 and by 11.0 per cent in 1984.

Cost of Products Sold

Cost of products sold as a per cent of sales was 58.5 per cent, 45.6 per cent and 43.1 per cent in 1985, 1984 and 1983, respectively. The Consumer Products Group cost of sales ratio increased to 47.1 per cent in 1985 from 45.6 per cent in 1984 due partially to selling-price adjustments and higher cost of sales ratios in the Bass, Prince Matchabelli, Polymer and International divisions. In addition, 1985 includes the Chemical Products Group, whose cost of sales ratio was relatively higher than the Consumer Products Group. The increase in 1984 was due to higher cost of sales ratios in

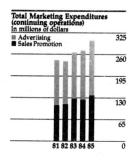

Total Marketing Expenditures
(continuing operations)
In millions of dollars

■ Advertising
■ Sales Promotion

325

260

195

130

65

81 82 83 84 85   0

most divisions due to increased sales of higher-cost products and selling-price adjustments. In addition, 1984 includes the Polymer Division, whose cost of products sold ratio was relatively higher than most other divisions.

Selling, Advertising and Administrative Expenses
Selling, advertising and administrative expenses absorbed 33.4 per cent of each sales dollar in 1985, compared with 42.4 per cent in 1984 and 43.9 per cent in 1983. The Consumer Products Group selling, advertising and administrative expenses increased to 43.2 per cent in 1985 from 42.4 per cent in 1984 due to higher marketing expenditures in all divisions except the Packaged Foods and Prince divisions. In addition, 1985 includes the Chemical Products Group, whose selling, advertising and administrative expenses as a per cent of sales were relatively lower than the Consumer Products Group. The decrease as a per cent of sales in 1984 was due to a reduction in marketing expenditures in all divisions except the Hospital Products and International divisions.

Interest Expense/Income
The increase in interest expense in 1985 was due primarily to the financing for the acquisition of Stauffer and a higher average level of borrowings to finance working capital needs. The increase in 1984 was due primarily to a higher average level of borrowings to finance working capital needs, the acquisition of The Polymer Corporation and the purchase of 1.8 million of the company's shares at the August 6, 1984 closing market price of 38 ⅛ in a privately negotiated transaction.

Interest income increased in 1985, due primarily to the interest income associated with the termination of the overfunded Stauffer pension plans and interest income relative to Stauffer's foreign operations. Interest income increased in 1984, due principally to an increase in investments held by the company's Puerto Rico operations.

Provision for Income Taxes
The provision for income taxes as a per cent of income from consolidated operations before provision for income taxes, was 16.5 per cent in 1985, 39.0 per cent in 1984 and 41.1 per cent in 1983. The decrease in 1985 was due to the reduced domestic income primarily resulting from interest expense associated with the Stauffer acquisition and a lower effective tax rate relative to Stauffer's foreign operations. The decrease in 1984 was due to a decrease in the overall foreign tax rate, an increase in the relationship of tax-exempt earnings from Puerto Rico operations to total consolidated pre-tax income and an increase in investment tax credits. A reconciliation of the 1985, 1984 and 1983 effective tax rates to the Federal statutory rate is presented in Note 17 to the Consolidated Financial Statements.

Minority Interest
Minority interest increased in 1985 as a result of the acquisition of Stauffer Chemical Company subsidiaries which are not 100 per cent owned.

Equity in Earnings of Associated Companies
Equity in earnings of associated companies increased in 1985 due to the acquisition of Stauffer Chemical Company. The decrease in 1984 was due to a decline in the income from the company's equity interest in its India operation. (See Note 11 to the Consolidated Financial Statements).

Financial Condition
Following the $1.3 billion acquisition of Stauffer in March, the company's financial position has steadily improved and remains sound. The acquisition, which was initially financed by a bank revolving credit agreement, increased the company's total debt to total capital employed ratio to 78 per cent, but as a result of an aggressive debt reduction program, including the sale of the Health-tex Division, termination of the overfunded Stauffer pension plans, repatriation of a significant portion of Stauffer's overseas funds and several sale-leaseback transactions, the company has successfully reduced the total debt to total capital employed ratio to 60.2 per cent as of December 31, 1985. The company's stated goal is to further reduce this ratio to below the 50 per cent range. In a step towards this goal, the company sold in late February 1986, through an underwritten public offering, 6,900,000 newly issued shares of common stock. (See Note 10 to the Consolidated Financial Statements). The cash proceeds from the sale of common

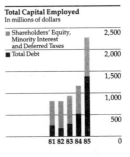

Total Capital Employed
In millions of dollars

- ▨ Shareholders' Equity, Minority Interest and Deferred Taxes
- ■ Total Debt

81 82 83 84 85

stock will be utilized to repay commercial paper and bank borrowings currently classified as long-term debt. The ratio was 44.0 per cent at December 31, 1984 and 29.0 per cent at December 31, 1983 with the principal reasons for the increase in 1984 being higher borrowing levels to support increased working capital needs, the acquisition of The Polymer Corporation and the purchase of 1.8 million of the company's common shares. Total debt includes notes payable, current portion of long-term debt and long-term debt; total capital employed includes total debt, deferred income taxes, minority interest and total shareholders' equity.

To further improve its capital structure, the company issued approximately $420 million of fixed-rate, long-term debt in the domestic and international capital markets during 1985 with the majority of the proceeds used to repay the bank revolving credit borrowings incurred in connection with the acquisition of Stauffer. The company's long-term debt is rated Baa/BBB by Moody's and Standard & Poor's, respectively.

Cash provided from continuing operations earnings increased 83.5 per cent to $255.6 million in 1985 after increasing 2.6 per cent to $139.3 million in 1984. The significant increase in 1985 is due primarily to the increased depreciation charges and other non-cash expenses relating to Stauffer. Dividends paid during 1985 were $70.1 million, up 4.3 per cent from $67.2 million in 1984, which was up 2.1 per cent from $65.8 million in 1983. The payout as a per cent of net income was 85.3 per cent in 1985, 56.2 per cent in 1984 and 51.5 per cent in 1983. The dramatic increase in the payout ratio in 1985 is due to the decline in earnings. After considering working capital requirements (primarily inventories and accounts receivable), dividends, and investment and financing activities, cash and short-term investments decreased $30.6 million in 1985 following a $12.6 million increase in 1984.

Capital expenditures were $161.1 million in 1985, up from $59.3 million in 1984 and $42.2 million in 1983. Of these amounts, about 79 per cent was for domestic operations in 1985, compared with about 75 per cent in 1984. The remainder was spent primarily in Spain, Italy and the United Kingdom of the Consumer Products Group International Division in 1985 and in Canada, Italy, Mexico, South Africa, Spain and the United Kingdom in 1984. Domestically, major expenditures were made for new machinery and equipment, primarily in the Health & Beauty, Packaged Foods

and Basic Chemicals divisions in 1985 and the Health & Beauty Products, Health-tex and Packaged Foods divisions in 1984. Major expenditures for new and improved manufacturing, warehouse and office facilities were made primarily in the Packaged Foods and Bass divisions in 1985 and the Bass, Health-tex and Packaged Foods divisions in 1984. Capital expenditures for 1986 are projected to be about $160 million, primarily in the International, Packaged Foods, Polymer and Bass divisions of the Consumer Products Group and the Basic Chemicals, Agricultural Products and International divisions of the Chemical Products Group.

The current ratio decreased to 1.8 at December 31, 1985, compared with 2.0 at December 31, 1984 and 2.5 at December 31, 1983. The decrease in the ratio in 1985 was primarily the result of a higher level of current liabilities as a result of the Stauffer acquisition. The decrease in the ratio in 1984 was primarily the result of a higher level of short-term borrowings due to increased inventory levels, particularly in the Bass and Health-tex divisions.

To meet its short-term domestic financing needs throughout the year, the company issues commercial paper and borrows from commercial banks. Also, at December 31, 1985 the company had available a $600 million bank revolving credit facility. (See Note 8 to the Consolidated Financial Statements). Overseas, the company's external financing needs are met primarily by bank loans.

Inflation Information

The company's income from continuing operations after adjusting for the effects of inflation is less than income from continuing operations in the primary financial statements. For more complete information on the impact of inflation on the company, see Note 20 to the Consolidated Financial Statements.

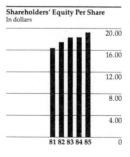

Shareholders' Equity Per Share
In dollars

	20.00
	16.00
	12.00
	8.00
	4.00
81 82 83 84 85	0

Ten-Year Financial Summary

(dollars in thousands except per share data)	1985(a)	1984
For the Year (b):		
Net sales	$2,699,498	$1,522,148
Cost of products sold	1,579,690	693,670
Selling, advertising and administrative expenses	902,708	645,757
Income from operations	217,100	182,721
Interest expense	179,056	55,070
Income from consolidated operations before provision for income taxes	77,445	146,485
Provision for income taxes	12,776	57,083
Income from continuing operations	67,960	92,347
Income from discontinued operations	14,214	27,182
Net income	82,174	119,529
Dividends paid	70,116	67,211
Capital expenditures (c)	161,124	59,262
Depreciation	118,547	24,748
At Year-End (c):		
Current assets	$1,343,709	$1,006,445
Current liabilities	764,113	506,927
Other assets	640,115	111,543
Working capital	579,596	499,518
Net property, plant and equipment	1,024,226	329,322
Total assets	3,008,050	1,447,310
Short-term debt including current portion of long-term debt	194,687	269,468
Long-term debt	1,174,349	243,929
Minority interest	87,293	1,164
Shareholders' equity	678,273	625,617
Total capital employed	2,275,626	1,166,867
Number of shareholders	17,234	15,712
Number of employees	25,719	25,471
Common Stock Data (b):		
Per Share:		
Earnings from continuing operations	$1.94	$2.63
Earnings from discontinued operations	.41	.77
Earnings	2.35	3.40
Dividends	2.00	1.92
Shareholders' equity	19.20	18.30
Stock price range	48½-31	39⅞-32⅛
Weighted average shares outstanding	34,997,000	35,132,000
Shares outstanding at year-end	35,320,000	34,183,000
Key Ratios:		
Current ratio (c)	1.8	2.0
Return on net sales from continuing operations (b)	2.5%	6.1%
Return on average capital employed (c)	10.4%	14.3%
Return on average shareholders' equity (c)	12.6%	18.7%
Total debt to total capital employed (c)	60.2%	44.0%

(a) 1985 amounts reflect the acquisition of Stauffer Chemical Company on March 15, 1985 and the September 30, 1985 disposition of the Health-tex Division. (b) Income statement data for 1984–1976 has been restated to reflect the 1985 disposition of the Health-tex Division. (c) Prior year balances have not been restated to reflect the disposition of the Health-tex Division.

Net Sales
In millions of dollars

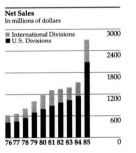

■ International Divisions
■ U.S. Divisions

Chesebrough-Pond's Inc. and Subsidiaries

1983	1982	1981	1980	1979	1978	1977	1976
$1,385,128	$1,342,421	$1,308,128	$1,189,563	$1,008,489	$816,639	$669,064	$626,562
596,810	578,054	559,517	520,224	441,647	344,551	282,276	278,766
607,525	584,261	572,475	507,111	431,502	352,625	291,794	259,928
180,793	180,106	176,136	162,228	135,340	119,463	94,994	87,868
31,142	31,332	29,726	22,322	14,953	11,866	9,497	9,033
161,140	165,991	155,602	144,448	121,754	105,115	84,702	80,102
66,212	66,219	64,110	62,963	54,528	50,361	40,592	39,533
98,812	99,772	91,492	81,485	67,226	54,754	44,110	40,569
29,066	25,493	25,929	18,253	13,870	13,601	14,803	12,753
127,878	125,265	117,421	99,738	81,096	68,355	58,913	53,322
65,841	58,983	49,659	41,416	34,869	30,390	27,072	24,423
42,203	41,973	57,450	45,139	38,563	34,976	17,977	14,911
21,570	19,985	18,265	15,136	12,357	10,071	8,812	7,961
$850,611	$727,470	$738,096	$642,634	$531,737	$477,063	$387,814	$347,595
340,288	226,215	299,840	277,711	240,619	183,486	137,080	116,745
79,455	75,223	90,692	83,727	82,075	77,497	60,630	45,942
510,323	501,255	438,256	364,923	291,118	293,577	250,734	230,850
241,844	240,727	239,185	204,887	179,350	155,275	128,696	123,525
1,171,910	1,043,420	1,067,973	931,248	793,162	709,835	577,140	517,062
141,260	33,471	82,560	68,566	60,670	48,262	30,649	26,888
131,784	143,321	165,170	130,674	97,829	120,955	75,492	72,172
—	—	(8)	42	140	111	1,170	1,026
649,945	625,082	565,436	491,681	427,945	382,343	343,529	311,109
939,959	819,266	826,661	701,635	595,867	560,792	459,409	417,037
16,070	16,270	15,737	14,735	13,906	14,134	14,359	14,156
22,056	21,059	21,555	20,759	19,478	18,616	16,728	15,997
$2.76	$2.84	$2.65	$2.38	$1.97	$1.61	$1.30	$1.19
.82	.72	.75	.53	.40	.40	.44	.38
3.58	3.56	3.40	2.91	2.37	2.01	1.74	1.57
1.84	1.72	1.52	1.28	1.08	.94	.84	.76
18.27	17.41	16.32	14.31	12.53	11.26	10.13	9.11
46¾-36¼	47¼-30½	39⅞-27	31⅞-19⅛	25⅝-20⅞	27⅛-20¼	26⅞-20⅛	32½-22½
35,768,000	35,196,000	34,513,000	34,243,000	34,183,000	33,972,000	33,883,000	34,063,000
35,584,000	35,913,000	34,648,000	34,368,000	34,154,000	33,945,000	33,905,000	34,153,000
2.5	3.2	2.5	2.3	2.2	2.6	2.8	3.0
7.1%	7.4%	7.0%	6.8%	6.7%	6.7%	6.6%	6.5%
16.5%	17.4%	17.5%	17.3%	15.6%	14.7%	14.6%	14.4%
20.1%	21.0%	22.2%	21.7%	20.0%	18.8%	18.0%	18.1%
29.0%	21.6%	30.0%	28.4%	26.6%	30.2%	23.1%	23.8%

Income from Continuing Operations
In millions of dollars

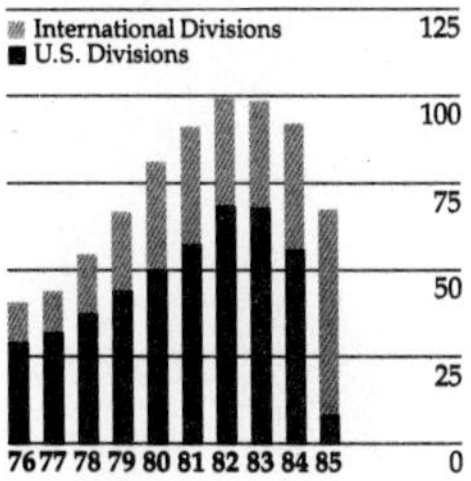
International Divisions
U.S. Divisions
125
100
75
50
25
0
76 77 78 79 80 81 82 83 84 85

Distribution of Income from Continuing Operations
In millions of dollars

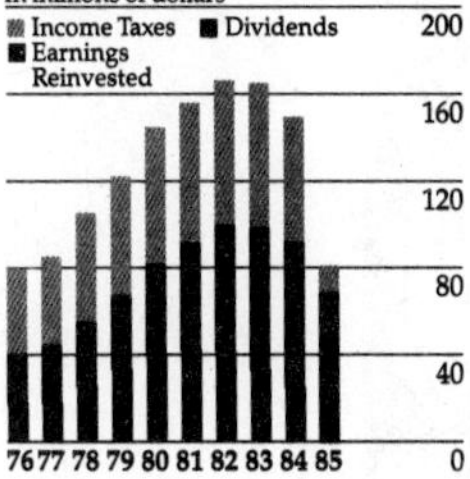
Income Taxes
Dividends
Earnings Reinvested
200
160
120
80
40
0
76 77 78 79 80 81 82 83 84 85

Distribution of Earnings Per Share from Continuing Operations
In dollars

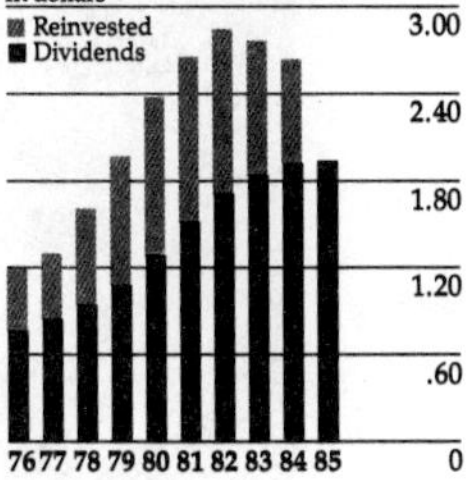
Reinvested
Dividends
3.00
2.40
1.80
1.20
.60
0
76 77 78 79 80 81 82 83 84 85

Consolidated Statement of Income

	Year Ended December 31,		
(dollars in thousands except per share data)	1985	1984	1983
Net Sales	$2,699,498	$1,522,148	$1,385,128
Cost of products sold	1,579,690	693,670	596,810
Selling, advertising and administrative expenses	902,708	645,757	607,525
Operating costs and expenses	2,482,398	1,339,427	1,204,335
Income from Operations	217,100	182,721	180,793
Other income (expense):			
Interest expense	(179,056)	(55,070)	(31,142)
Interest income	34,368	15,068	10,356
Gain on foreign exchange	12,256	3,639	1,044
Miscellaneous—net	(7,223)	127	89
Total other income (expense)	(139,655)	(36,236)	(19,653)
Income from consolidated operations before provision for income taxes	77,445	146,485	161,140
Provision for income taxes	12,776	57,083	66,212
Minority interest	(4,319)	47	—
Equity in earnings of associated companies	7,610	2,898	3,884
Income from Continuing Operations	67,960	92,347	98,812
Discontinued operations	14,214	27,182	29,066
Net Income	$ 82,174	$ 119,529	$ 127,878
Weighted average shares outstanding	34,997,000	35,132,000	35,768,000
Earnings per Share:			
Continuing operations	$1.94	$2.63	$2.76
Discontinued operations	.41	.77	.82
Earnings per share	$2.35	$3.40	$3.58

See accompanying notes.

Consolidated Balance Sheet

Chesebrough-Pond's Inc. and Subsidiaries

(in thousands)	December 31, 1985	1984	1983
Assets			
Current Assets:			
Cash and short-term investments	$ 69,964	$ 100,566	$ 88,014
Accounts receivable	506,519	365,054	335,516
Inventories	657,498	502,894	396,515
Prepaid expenses	59,503	37,931	30,566
Net assets of businesses held for sale	50,225	—	—
Total current assets	1,343,709	1,006,445	850,611
Property, Plant and Equipment:			
At cost	1,252,068	508,748	399,209
Less accumulated depreciation	227,842	179,426	157,365
Net property, plant and equipment	1,024,226	329,322	241,844
Investments and Other Assets	184,169	53,092	40,558
Goodwill and Trademarks	455,946	58,451	38,897
	$3,008,050	$1,447,310	$1,171,910
Liabilities and Shareholders' Equity			
Current Liabilities:			
Notes payable	$ 109,615	$ 265,952	$ 130,408
Accounts payable	207,681	80,111	59,273
Accrued liabilities	297,661	128,538	109,004
Income taxes payable	64,084	28,810	30,751
Current portion of long-term debt	85,072	3,516	10,852
Total current liabilities	764,113	506,927	340,288
Long-Term Debt	1,174,349	243,929	131,784
Deferred Income Taxes	141,024	26,689	16,970
Other Non-Current Liabilities	162,998	42,984	32,923
Minority Interest	87,293	1,164	—
Shareholders' Equity:			
Common stock (shares issued: 36,180,438—1985; 36,180,436—1984; 36,111,956—1983)	36,180	36,180	36,112
Additional paid-in capital	92,678	96,331	95,079
Retained earnings	671,210	659,152	606,834
Foreign currency translation adjustment	(88,973)	(89,892)	(67,408)
	711,095	701,771	670,617
Less treasury stock, at cost	32,822	76,154	20,672
Total shareholders' equity	678,273	625,617	649,945
	$3,008,050	$1,447,310	$1,171,910

See accompanying notes.

Consolidated Statement of Changes in Financial Position

Chesebrough-Pond's Inc. and Subsidiaries

(in thousands)	Year Ended December 31,		
	1985	1984	1983
Cash Provided (Used) by Operations:			
Continuing operations:			
Income	$ 67,960	$ 92,347	$ 98,812
Non-cash expenses:			
Depreciation	118,547	24,748	21,570
Stock Award Plan compensation	11,375	10,581	10,493
Deferred income taxes	41,883	10,038	863
Amortization of goodwill and trademarks	9,661	1,088	842
Other	6,170	457	3,157
Cash provided by continuing operations earnings	255,596	139,259	135,737
Changes in Working Capital Items—Operations:			
Accounts receivable...	62,030	(3,710)	(58,110)
Inventories	21,923	(69,892)	(36,723)
Prepaid expenses	(13,740)	(3,787)	(8,081)
Accounts payable/accrued liabilities/income taxes payable	40,991	10,699	323
Foreign currency translation adjustment—working capital.................	(8,638)	(15,522)	(14,101)
	102,566	(82,212)	(116,692)
Cash Provided (Used) by Continuing Operations	358,162	57,047	19,045
Discontinued operations:			
Income (including gain on disposal)	14,214	27,182	29,066
Non-cash expenses:			
Depreciation	4,010	5,382	4,863
Gain on disposal of Health-tex Division	(9,877)	—	—
Deferred income taxes and other	12,764	3,753	2,787
Cash provided by discontinued operations..........................	21,111	36,317	36,716
Cash Provided (Used) by Operations	379,273	93,364	55,761
Cash Provided (Used) by Investment Activities:			
Purchase price of acquisitions	(1,253,858)	(105,311)	(8,072)
Stauffer cash and short-term investments at acquisition....................	192,427	—	—
Disposal of Health-tex Division	215,100	—	—
Pension termination	150,689	—	—
Sale of receivables	100,000	—	—
Additions to property, plant and equipment............................	(161,124)	(59,262)	(42,203)
Purchase of treasury stock..	—	(68,635)	(32,770)
Non-current liabilities..	(18,348)	(7,294)	(17,455)
Investments and other assets—net	(75,576)	(9,565)	(2,475)
Net book value of disposed assets	10,282	1,546	2,527
	(840,408)	(248,521)	(100,448)
Net Change in Cash from Operations and Investment Activities	(461,135)	(155,157)	(44,687)
Dividends..	(70,116)	(67,211)	(65,841)
Cash Provided (Used) by Financing Activities:			
Notes payable	(445,474)	125,693	97,896
Issuance of common stock under Stock Award Plan	10,939	10,693	11,115
Sale of common stock to employee stock plan	19,101	—	—
Long-term debt, including current portion.............................	734,911	94,811	(967)
Proceeds from sale/leasebacks	179,237	—	11,698
Other—net	1,935	3,723	4,572
	500,649	234,920	124,314
Increase (Decrease) in Cash and Short-term Investments	$ (30,602)	$ 12,552	$ 13,786

See accompanying notes.

34

Consolidated Statement of Shareholders' Equity

Chesebrough-Pond's Inc. and Subsidiaries

(in thousands except share data)	Common Shares $1 Par Value	Additional Paid-in Capital	Retained Earnings	Foreign Currency Translation Adjustment	Treasury Stock Shares	Cost
Balance at January 1, 1983	36,054,823	$95,670	$544,797	$47,122	141,510	$ 4,318
Debenture conversions	57,133	1,462	—	—	—	—
Stock Award Plan	—	(5,110)	—	—	(408,313)	(16,225)
Net income	—	—	127,878	—	—	—
Dividends paid ($1.84 per share)	—	—	(65,841)	—	—	—
Executive Incentive Profit-Sharing Plan	—	—	—	—	(5,065)	(182)
Treasury stock purchases	—	—	—	—	800,002	32,770
Foreign currency translation adjustment	—	—	—	20,286	—	—
Other	—	3,057	—	—	(227)	(9)
Balance at December 31, 1983	36,111,956	95,079	606,834	67,408	527,907	20,672
Debenture conversions	68,480	1,765	—	—	—	—
Stock Award Plan	—	(1,662)	—	—	(315,580)	(12,355)
Net income	—	—	119,529	—	—	—
Dividends paid ($1.92 per share)	—	—	(67,211)	—	—	—
Executive Incentive Profit-Sharing Plan	—	—	—	—	(4,259)	(165)
Treasury stock purchases	—	—	—	—	1,806,200	68,635
Foreign currency translation adjustment	—	—	—	22,484	—	—
Dividend Reinvestment Plan	—	(89)	—	—	(16,306)	(622)
Other	—	1,238	—	—	(265)	(11)
Balance at December 31, 1984	36,180,436	96,331	659,152	89,892	1,997,697	76,154
Stock Award Plan	—	(50)	—	—	(288,257)	(10,989)
Stock ownership plan	—	(3,208)	—	—	(585,207)	(22,309)
Net income	—	—	82,174	—	—	—
Dividends paid ($2.00 per share)	—	—	(70,116)	—	—	—
Executive Incentive Profit-Sharing Plan	—	—	—	—	(7,344)	(280)
Foreign currency translation adjustment	—	—	—	(919)	—	—
Dividend Reinvestment Plan	—	(1,213)	—	—	(236,906)	(9,029)
Other	2	818	—	—	(19,049)	(725)
Balance at December 31, 1985	36,180,438	$92,678	$671,210	$88,973	860,934	$32,822

See accompanying notes.

Notes to Consolidated Financial Statements

1. Summary of Significant Accounting Policies

Principles of Consolidation
The consolidated financial statements include the accounts of all majority-owned subsidiaries with the exception of two wholly-owned insurance subsidiaries, which are accounted for on the equity method due to dissimilar business activities. Investments in associated companies are stated at cost plus equity in undistributed earnings. Intercompany accounts and transactions have been eliminated in consolidation.

Foreign Currency Translation
All assets and liabilities in the balance sheets of foreign subsidiaries whose functional currency is other than the U.S. dollar are translated at year-end exchange rates. Translation gains and losses are not included in determining net income but are accumulated in a separate component of shareholders' equity. For subsidiaries considered to be operating in highly inflationary countries and for certain other subsidiaries, the U.S. dollar is the functional currency, and translation gains and losses are included in determining net income. Foreign currency transaction gains and losses generally are included in determining net income.

Inventories
Inventories are valued at the lower of cost or market. Market is estimated net realizable value. Cost for the Consumer Products Group is generally determined using the FIFO (first-in, first-out) method. Cost for the Chemical Products Group for domestic and certain foreign inventories is generally determined using the LIFO (last-in, first-out) method. Cost for other inventories is generally determined using the average cost method.

Property, Plant and Equipment
Property, plant and equipment is stated at cost. Depreciation, which includes amortization of assets recorded under capital leases, is provided on a straight-line basis for financial accounting purposes, while accelerated methods are used for income tax purposes.

Income Taxes
Deferred income taxes result from timing differences between the amounts reported for financial accounting and income tax purposes. These differences relate primarily to depreciation, sales returns, installment sales, incentive compensation and certain sales promotion expenses. Investment tax credits are applied as a reduction of the provision for income taxes in the year the related property is placed in service.

Goodwill and Trademarks
Goodwill, or excess of the purchase price over the fair value of the net assets of acquired companies, and trademarks are being amortized on a straight-line basis over periods not exceeding 40 years.

Advertising and Sales Promotion Costs
Advertising costs are expensed as incurred, and sales promotion costs are expensed during the period of the promotional program.

Retirement Plans
The company has various retirement plans covering the majority of its employees worldwide. The company's financial accounting policy is to expense current service costs and to amortize prior service costs over periods from 10 to 30 years.

Earnings Per Share
The computation of earnings per share is based on the weighted average number of shares outstanding (34,997,000, 35,132,000 and 35,768,000 in 1985, 1984 and 1983, respectively).

Reclassification
Certain prior year amounts have been reclassified to conform to the 1985 presentation, principally related to minority interest and equity in earnings of associated companies. No reclassification has been made of the December 31 balance sheets relative to the disposition of the Health-tex Division.

2. Acquisitions

Effective March 15, 1985, the company acquired Stauffer Chemical Company ("Stauffer") through a cash tender offer for all shares of Stauffer common stock for approximately $1.3 billion, including expenses of acquisition. The business combination was accounted for as a "purchase" and accordingly, Stauffer's results of operations are reflected from March 15, 1985. Consolidated results include approximately $1.1 billion in sales and a $7.8 million loss, net of acquisition related interest expense from these operations. The accounts of Stauffer, after adjustments to reflect the fair value assigned to Stauffer's assets and liabilities, have been included in the company's Consolidated Balance Sheet at December 31, 1985. The excess of the purchase price over the fair value of the net assets of Stauffer at date of acquisition approximated $387 million and is being amortized on a straight-line basis over forty years.

The table below summarizes on an unaudited, pro forma basis the combined results of operations of the company and Stauffer for the twelve month periods ended December 31, 1985 and 1984 as if the companies had been combined for those periods. The adjustments made in preparing this pro forma information consist primarily of interest expense on debt incurred, depreciation expense on revalued property, plant and equipment, amortization of acquisition goodwill, elimination of Stauffer's 1984 extraordinary gain, other miscellaneous expense adjustments, and, where applicable, related income tax effects. These pro forma results are presented for comparative purposes only, and are not necessarily indicative of future results of operations or of what results would have been for the combined companies.

Pro Forma Results (unaudited) (in thousands except per share data)	December 31, 1985	1984
Net sales	$3,011,335	$2,915,654
Income from continuing operations	$50,962	$16,491
Earnings per share from continuing operations	$1.46	$.47

During 1984 the company acquired The Polymer Corporation, a worldwide manufacturer of engineered plastics, for $95.6 million, including expenses of acquisition. In addition, four smaller companies were acquired during the year for a total purchase price of $9.7 million. Results of operations of these purchases, which were not material to the company's consolidated results, have been included since their acquisition dates. The excess of the purchase price over the fair value of the net assets for these acquisitions of $34.7 million is being amortized on a straight-line basis over forty years.

3. Dispositions

Effective September 30, 1985 the company completed the sale of its Health-tex Division to a group of investors, headed by former division management. The company sold to the investor group the assets of the Health-tex Division other than cash and marketable securities relating to Health-tex's Puerto Rico operations and a New Jersey property with an aggregate value of approximately $37,400,000 which were retained by the company, and the investors assumed principally all liabilities of the Health-tex Division. The investors purchased the Health-tex Division for an aggregate purchase price of $233,056,000, consisting of $215,100,000 in cash and $17,956,000 principal amount of a junior subordinated 10 per cent promissory note due March 31, 1997.

Discontinued operations of the Health-tex Division for the nine months ended September 30, 1985 and the twelve months ended December 31, 1984 and 1983 have been included under the caption "Discontinued operations" in the Consolidated Statement of Income and are summarized as follows:

(in thousands)	1985	1984	1983
Net sales	$241,962	$335,182	$300,289
Income from operations (net of applicable income tax expense (benefit) of $(3,368), $17,764 and $21,324 in 1985, 1984 and 1983, respectively)	4,337	27,182	29,066
Gain on disposal (net of income tax expense of $9,819)	9,877	—	—
Discontinued operations	$ 14,214	$ 27,182	$ 29,066

During the third quarter of 1985, the Health-tex Division adopted the last-in, first-out (LIFO) method of inventory valuation for financial reporting purposes retroactively to January 1, 1985. The effect of the change on discontinued operations was immaterial.

Included in the "Net assets of businesses held for sale" in the Consolidated Balance Sheet are the net assets of Applied Solar Energy Corporation, Psychiatric Diagnostic

Laboratories of America, Inc. and Stauffer Oil and Gas, Inc., all acquired in the Stauffer acquisition.

4. Accounts Receivable

Accounts receivable at December 31 were:

(in thousands)	1985	1984	1983
Trade:			
Consumer Products			
Group	$304,911	$345,735	$311,097
Chemical Products			
Group	136,615	—	—
	441,526	345,735	311,097
Allowance for doubtful			
accounts	12,509	9,168	6,391
	429,017	336,567	304,706
Other	77,502	28,487	30,810
Total	$506,519	$365,054	$335,516

In 1985, other receivables includes $26,188,000 relating to income taxes refundable. Also in 1985, the company sold $100,000,000 of Chemical Products Group trade receivables without right of recourse to the company.

In 1984 and 1983, Consumer Products Group trade receivables include $35,317,000 and $29,080,000 respectively, relating to discontinued operations.

5. Inventories

Inventories at December 31 were:

(in thousands)	1985	1984	1983
Consumer Products Group:			
Raw materials and work-			
in-process	$132,344	$198,235	$178,221
Finished goods	220,729	304,659	218,294
Total Consumer			
Products Group	353,073	502,894	396,515
Chemical Products Group:			
Raw materials and			
supplies	97,718	—	—
Finished goods and work-			
in-process	206,707	—	—
Total Chemical			
Products Group	304,425	—	—
Total	$657,498	$502,894	$396,515

Inventories stated using LIFO amounted to approximately 66 per cent of the inventory of the Chemical Products Group at December 31, 1985.

Included in the 1984 and 1983 inventory amounts are $154,715,000 and $119,385,000 respectively, relating to discontinued operations.

6. Property, Plant and Equipment

Property, plant and equipment at December 31 was:

(in thousands)	1985	1984	1983
Land	$ 105,916	$ 12,013	$ 9,844
Buildings and building			
improvements	183,204	142,008	114,598
Machinery and equipment	876,210	317,619	247,170
Leasehold improvements	19,537	21,584	16,726
Construction-in-progress	67,201	15,524	10,871
	1,252,068	508,748	399,209
Less accumulated			
depreciation	227,842	179,426	157,365
Net property, plant and			
equipment	$1,024,226	$329,322	$241,844

Included above is net property, plant and equipment relative to capital leases of $15,807,000, $29,358,000 and $19,944,000 for 1985, 1984 and 1983, respectively.

Unexpended appropriations for property, plant and equipment approximated $49,000,000 at December 31, 1985. Portions of these appropriations are covered by firm commitments. In 1985 the company capitalized $6,196,000 of interest costs into the value of property, plant and equipment. Comparable amounts for 1984 and 1983 were not material.

7. Notes Payable

Notes payable at December 31 were:

(in thousands)	1985	1984	1983
Banks and other	$109,615	$112,379	$ 20,711
Commercial paper	—	153,573	109,697
Total	$109,615	$265,952	$130,408

The company has various established lines of credit on a worldwide basis. Domestic lines of credit require a fee equal to ¼ per cent of the total lines of credit. Certain international lines of credit require compensating balances which in the aggregate are not significant. At December 31, 1985 worldwide unused lines of credit were $152,626,000.

8. Long-Term Debt

Long-term debt at December 31 was:

(in thousands)	1985	1984	1983
Commercial paper	**$ 342,163**	$ 40,000	$ 40,000
Bank loans	**100,000**	99,375	—
10⅞% debentures due 1995	**99,851**	—	—
10½% notes due 1991	**99,639**	—	—
12% notes due 1993	**99,450**	—	—
8.85% debentures due 2001	**75,986**	—	—
8⅛% notes due 1986	**74,961**	—	—
5½% notes due 1995	**69,562**	—	—
10⅝% notes due July 1990	**69,122**	69,104	69,087
9¾% notes due 2000	**49,880**	—	—
8⅛% debentures due 1996	**29,830**	—	—
Other	**148,977**	38,966	33,549
	1,259,421	247,445	142,636
Less current portion	**85,072**	3,516	10,852
Total	**$1,174,349**	$243,929	$131,784

The $442,163,000 of commercial paper and bank loans is supported by a $600 million revolving credit agreement with various banks which requires a commitment fee of ¼ per cent per annum on the average daily unused amount. This agreement expires on February 17, 1989, at which time any outstanding borrowings can be converted into a four-year term loan. This agreement supports the classification of $442,163,000 of commercial paper and bank loans outstanding as long-term debt. This debt has a weighted average interest rate of 8⅝ per cent. (See Note 10 to Consolidated Financial Statements).

The 8.85 per cent debentures due 2001 and the 8⅛ per cent debentures due 1996 are supported by annual sinking fund requirements which have been met through 1991 and 1987, respectively.

Other long-term debt includes capital leases, term loans and industrial revenue bonds of $83,777,000 payable 1987 to 2012 at fixed rates from 5.3% to 11¾% and variable rates of 55% to 70% of prime.

The company continues to guarantee industrial development revenue bonds issued by the Health-tex Division amounting to approximately $18,000,000 at December 31, 1985.

The amounts of long-term debt due during the years 1987 through 1990 are: 1987—$10,172,000; 1988—$13,365,000; 1989—$12,445,000; 1990—$81,621,000.

9. Capital Stock

At December 31, 1985, 1,000,000 shares of $1.00 par value preferred stock were authorized and unissued, and 50,000,000 shares of $1.00 par value common stock were authorized.

10. Subsequent Event

In late February 1986, the company sold through an underwritten public offering 6,900,000 newly issued shares of common stock for a price, prior to underwriters' commissions, of $40.50 per share. The cash proceeds from the sale will be used to repay commercial paper and bank borrowings currently classified as long-term debt.

The unaudited pro forma effect of issuing 6,900,000 shares of common stock as of January 1, 1985 would be to increase net income by $12,200,000 and decrease earnings per share by $.10.

11. Associated Companies and Unconsolidated Subsidiaries

Operations of associated companies and two wholly-owned insurance subsidiaries, which are accounted for under the equity method, are summarized as follows:

(in thousands)	1985	1984	1983
Net sales	**$203,552**	$52,961	$44,364
Net income	**$19,197**	$5,958	$3,197
Assets	**$203,348**	$47,538	$33,789
Liabilities	**$86,824**	$30,653	$22,837
Total equity	**$116,524**	$16,885	$10,952
Chesebrough share:			
Net income	**$7,610**	$2,898	$3,884
Dividends	**$7,703**	$2,284	$259
Undistributed income	**$13,738**	$7,818	$5,639
Equity, including advances	**$64,391**	$15,084	$11,491

The company had outstanding indebtedness of $25,500,000 to certain of its associated companies at December 31, 1985.

The company's investment in associated companies and un-consolidated subsidiaries at December 31, 1985 consisted of:

Consumer Products Group: Merritt Insurance Company Limited (100% owned), Benedict Insurance Co. Ltd. (100% owned), Pond's (India) Limited (40% owned), Pond's Taiwan Ltd. (30% owned), Nippon Polypenco Limited (45% owned), Polydrop S.A. (50% owned), Polypenco (Proprietary) Limited (50% owned), and Chesebrough-Nutricia Inc. (50% owned).

Chemical Products Group: Stauffer-Wacker Silicones Corpora-tion (50% owned), Texas Alkyls, Inc. (50% owned), Texas Alkyls Belgium, S.A. (50% owned), Kali-Chemie Stauffer G.m.b.H. (50% owned), Toyo-Stauffer Chemical Co., Ltd. (50% owned), Pacific Chemicals Industries Pty., Ltd. (49% owned) and Cornwall Chemicals, Limited (50% owned).

12. Stock Award and Stock Ownership Plans

The Stock Award Plan provides that no more than 500,000 shares of the company's common stock can be allocated in any one year and no more than four per cent thereof can be allocated to any one officer or key employee in any year. Shares are delivered over three years and participants may defer the receipt of the shares until separation from the com-pany, in which case shares in lieu of dividends are credited to the account of the participant.

The activity of the plan was:

	Shares		
	1985	1984	1983
Outstanding, January 1.....	**827,942**	800,389	947,568
Allocated	**475,662**	389,508	300,483
Delivered	**(288,252)**	(315,580)	(401,451)
Cancelled	**(145,092)**	(52,518)	(51,073)
Shares in lieu of dividends...........	**5,066**	6,143	4,862
Outstanding, December 31 ..	**875,326**	827,942	800,389
Shares reserved............	**1,716,543**		

For financial accounting purposes, compensation expense is recognized over the period of delivery of the shares and the amount charged to income from continuing operations was $11,375,000, $10,581,000 and $10,493,000 in 1985, 1984 and 1983, respectively. The measurement dates and the timing of expense for financial accounting and income tax purposes

differ, and deferred income taxes have been provided for the related future tax benefits. Tax effects arising from the change in market values at the different measurement dates are applied to additional paid-in capital.

With the acquisition of the Stauffer Chemical Company, the company acquired for cash all of the common shares of Stauffer Chemical held by an employee stock ownership plan (ESOP). Subsequent to the acquisition, the ESOP was amended to allow for the purchase of the company's stock. In accordance with this change, 585,207 shares were pur-chased from the company for $19,100,000.

13. Incentive Plans

The company has an Executive Incentive Profit-Sharing Plan in which the total allotment to any participating officer or key employee for any calendar year may not exceed 50 per cent of the participant's annual base salary. In addition, the company (including Stauffer for 1985) has various discre-tionary cash award incentive plans. In 1985, 1984 and 1983, $9,866,000, $6,625,000 and $6,498,000, respectively, were charged to continuing operations for the above men-tioned plans.

14. Rent Expense and Lease Commitments

The company has operating leases, primarily for distribu-tion warehouses, general office facilities, research and development facilities, transportation equipment, data processing and other equipment. Net rent expense charged to income from continuing operations relative to these leases was $61,366,000, $37,147,000 and $30,231,000 in 1985, 1984 and 1983, respectively. In addition, the company has capital leases for certain manufacturing, warehouse and general office facilities.

At December 31, 1985 future minimum lease payments for capital leases and the minimum rental payments under non-

40

cancellable operating leases with a term in excess of one year were:

(in thousands)	Capital Leases	Operating Leases
1986	$ 4,700	$ 64,200
1987	5,900	59,700
1988	5,800	54,900
1989	4,200	47,800
1990	5,600	42,800
1991 and beyond	41,600	635,700
Total minimum lease payments	67,800	$905,100
Less amount representing interest	28,100	
Total obligations under capital leases	39,700	
Less obligations due within one year	1,500	
Long-term obligations under capital leases	$38,200	

15. Retirement Plans and Postretirement Benefits

Retirement expense charged to income from continuing operations for 1985, 1984 and 1983 was $17,336,000, $8,414,000 and $6,774,000, respectively.

For 1985 the company expects to fund the minimum contribution required by the Employee Retirement Income Security Act of 1974 (ERISA), which approximates current service cost. For 1984 the company funded the minimum contribution and for 1983 did not fund the domestic retirement plan due to prior years' prepayments.

In connection with the acquisition of Stauffer (see Note 2 to the Consolidated Financial Statements), the company terminated Stauffer's overfunded pension plans and provided earned benefits for covered employees through the purchase of annuity contracts. Future benefits, including the effects of salary increases for earned benefits, will be provided through the company's plans. The overfunded status of the Stauffer plans at date of acquisition, including the impact of estimated future salary increases for benefits earned through the acquisition date, was reflected in the fair value of the acquired net assets. Subsequent to acquisition and prior to final liquidation, Stauffer's plans' assets appreciated in value resulting in additional overfunding of approximately $16,000,000. Such gain has been deferred at December 31, 1985 and will be recognized on an after-tax basis in accordance with recently promulgated standards on pension accounting.

The assumed rate of return used in calculating the actuarial present value of accumulated plan benefits for the company was 8½ per cent for 1985, 1984 and 1983. The 1984 actuarial present value of accumulated plan benefits and net assets available for benefits reflect the inclusion of the pension plan for The Polymer Corporation. The 1984 assumed rate of return for this pension plan was 6.5 per cent. At January 1, 1985, 1984 and 1983, the actuarial present value of accumulated plan benefits and the net assets for all domestic pension plans of the company were:

(in thousands)	1985	1984	1983
Actuarial present value of accumulated plan benefits:			
Vested	$ 77,521	$ 71,011	$50,281
Nonvested	10,612	10,138	7,821
	$ 88,133	$ 81,149	$58,102
Net assets available for benefits	$119,896	$112,991	$86,915

The company's foreign pension plans are not required to comply with ERISA. Therefore, the actuarial present value of accumulated plan benefits and the net assets available for benefits have not been determined. However, the company believes there is no material unfunded liability related to its foreign pension plans.

The company and its subsidiaries provide certain health care and life insurance benefits for retired employees. Most of the company's employees may become eligible for these benefits if they reach normal retirement age while still employed by the company. The company recognizes the cost of providing these benefits on a "pay-as-you-go" basis through payments to an insurance company. The cost of providing these benefits for retirees was $1,502,000 and $620,000, for 1985 and 1984, respectively.

16. Research and Development

In 1985, 1984 and 1983, $66,742,000, $19,637,000 and $16,897,000, respectively, were charged to continuing operations for company-sponsored research to develop and improve products.

17. Provision for Income Taxes

Income from consolidated operations before provision for income taxes consisted of:

(in thousands)	1985	1984	1983
United States	$(11,656)	$ 81,910	$113,999
Foreign	89,101	64,575	47,141
Total	$ 77,445	$146,485	$161,140

The provision for income taxes applicable to continuing operations consisted of:

(in thousands)	1985	1984	1983
Current:			
Federal	$(52,036)	$26,830	$43,930
Foreign	27,743	17,259	16,425
State and local	(4,814)	2,956	4,994
	(29,107)	47,045	65,349
Deferred:			
Federal	38,025	6,011	178
Foreign	1,271	2,948	1,361
State and local	2,587	1,079	(676)
	41,883	10,038	863
Total	$ 12,776	$57,083	$66,212

Included in the 1985, 1984 and 1983 deferred income tax amounts are $35,252,000, $3,870,000 and $2,514,000, respectively, resulting from accelerated depreciation.

The effective tax rate from continuing operations differs from the Federal statutory rate as a result of the following factors:

	1985	1984	1983
Federal statutory rate	46.0%	46.0%	46.0%
State and local income taxes, net of Federal income tax benefit	(1.6)	1.5	1.5
Net difference in effective tax rate of foreign operations	(19.9)	(3.5)	(2.2)
Puerto Rico operations	(0.7)	(3.8)	(3.3)
Investment tax credits	(10.7)	(1.4)	(1.1)
Goodwill amortization	4.7	0.2	0.1
Other	(1.3)	—	0.1
Effective tax rate	16.5%	39.0%	41.1%

In connection with the acquisition of Stauffer, the company plans to remit the accumulated earnings of Stauffer's foreign subsidiaries at acquisition date. The estimated additional U.S. tax to be incurred on such remittance was included in the determination of the fair value of acquired net assets.

No provision has been made for Federal income taxes on unremitted foreign earnings that are intended to remain permanently invested or that will be remitted in future tax free liquidations. Should such earnings be distributed, the related U.S. income taxes would be partially offset by available tax credits. Such unremitted earnings aggregated $220,579,000 at December 31, 1985.

The company has three operating subsidiaries in Puerto Rico which are exempt from Federal income taxes. In addition, two of these subsidiaries are 100 per cent exempt and the other is 90 per cent exempt from Puerto Rico income tax under tax exempt grants expiring in 1990, 1991 and 1994.

18. Segments of Business

The company operates in twelve industry segments.

Consumer Products Group:
The Packaged Foods segment manufactures, markets and distributes, through food brokers, specialty foods, including spaghetti and other sauces, pasta meals, meat tenderizers and seasonings.

The Health & Beauty Products segment manufactures, markets and distributes, through various retail stores, cosmetic, toiletry and medicinal products, including skin creams and lotions, cotton swabs, lipsticks, nail and hair care products and petroleum jellies, among others.

The Bass segment manufactures, markets and distributes casual and fashion footwear through retail stores, including some company operated stores.

The Prince Matchabelli segment manufactures, markets and distributes, through retail stores, fragrances and

42

cosmetics, including perfumes, colognes, makeup products and other skin care preparations.

The Polymer segment manufactures, markets and distributes, principally through authorized distributors and direct to other manufacturers, engineered industrial plastic shapes and parts, coating powders and hoses.

The Hospital Products segment manufactures, markets and distributes supplies to hospitals, including enteral feeding systems, respiratory therapy aids, sterile gauze dressings, cotton swabs, bandages, thermometers, arterial blood-gas syringes and urological devices.

The Prince segment manufactures, markets and distributes tennis racquets, apparel, shoes and equipment, principally through retail stores or professional and specialty tennis shops.

The International segment manufactures, markets and distributes, primarily through retail stores abroad, toiletries, cosmetics, specialty foods and fragrances.

Chemical Products Group:

The Agricultural Products segment manufactures, markets and distributes, primarily to farm distributors and dealers and direct to manufacturers, insecticides, proprietary pesticides, agricultural, pharmaceutical and industrial intermediates and hybrid seeds.

The Basic Chemicals segment manufactures, markets and distributes, primarily to industrial customers, chlor-alkali products, sulfuric products, phosphorus products, rubber industry products and natural soda ash.

The Specialty & Food Products segment manufactures, markets and distributes, primarily to other manufacturers and the food processing industry, flame retardants, hydraulic fluids, catalysts, food grade phosphates, sodium bicarbonate, formulated food systems and fabricated products.

The International segment has both agricultural and chemical operations, which manufacture, market and distribute, primarily to growers and industrial customers abroad, substantially the same products as those sold in domestic markets.

Significant intersegment sales which are transferred between domestic segments, at cost, and transferred to the International segment at market for 1985 are approximately: Agricultural Products $19,900,000, Basic Chemicals $69,800,000, Specialty & Food Products $6,800,000.

The company's industry segments are substantially consistent with its operating divisional structure. However, as required by Statement of Financial Accounting Standards No. 14, certain corporate expenses and assets have been allocated to industry segments, and export sales and related profits, as well as assets, have been identified with the appropriate industry segments. Divisional information presented in the Shareholder Letter, Management's Discussion and Analysis and elsewhere in this report is before the corporate allocations and reflects certain export operations within the International divisions, which are responsible for the selling, marketing and distribution of these exported products.

(in thousands)	1985	1984	1983
Net Sales			
Consumer Products Group:			
Packaged Foods	$ 349,878	$ 347,511	$ 334,065
Health & Beauty Products ..	332,273	304,277	300,527
Bass	170,462	172,127	143,799
Prince Matchabelli	138,411	139,773	127,325
Polymer	109,208	52,541	—
Hospital Products	84,407	74,608	70,188
Prince	61,945	65,495	64,176
International	374,184	365,816	345,048
Total Consumer Products Group	1,620,768	1,522,148	1,385,128
Chemical Products Group:			
Agricultural Products......	243,162	—	—
Basic Chemicals...........	450,152	—	—
Specialty & Food Products ..	176,283	—	—
International	209,133	—	—
Total Chemical Products Group	1,078,730	—	—
Consolidated Total	$2,699,498	$1,522,148	$1,385,128

The net sales of the Consumer Products Group International segment were primarily comprised of health & beauty products. The net sales of the Chemical Products Group International segment were as follows: agricultural products approximately 48 per cent and chemical products approximately 52 per cent.

(in thousands)	1985	1984	1983
Income from Consolidated Operations before Provision for Income Taxes			
Consumer Products Group:			
Packaged Foods	**$ 66,175**	$ 59,187	$ 61,423
Health & Beauty Products ..	**62,850**	59,178	53,178
Bass	**(21,456)**	(1,258)	5,275
Prince Matchabelli	**5,585**	13,288	14,378
Polymer	**2,312**	4,653	—
Hospital Products	**10,058**	7,843	9,183
Prince	**4,090**	4,913	8,429
International	**36,932**	45,611	39,214
Total Consumer Products Group	**166,546**	193,415	191,080
Chemical Products Group:			
Agricultural Products......	**5,747**	—	—
Basic Chemicals...........	**32,168**	—	—
Specialty & Food Products ..	**12,623**	—	—
International	**9,555**	—	—
Total Chemical Products Group	**60,093**	—	—
Discontinued operations*....	**(9,539)**	(10,694)	(10,287)
Total income from operations	**217,100**	182,721	180,793
Total other income (expense)	**(139,655)**	(36,236)	(19,653)
Income from consolidated operations before provision for income taxes	**$ 77,445**	$146,485	$161,140

* Reflects corporate expenses allocated to discontinued operations.

(in thousands)	1985	1984	1983
Identifiable Assets			
Consumer Products Group:			
Packaged Foods	**$ 161,602**	$ 149,417	$ 145,980
Health & Beauty Products ..	**144,304**	149,473	154,420
Bass	**198,405**	192,231	149,421
Prince Matchabelli	**102,059**	114,803	108,053
Polymer	**131,814**	121,257	—
Hospital Products	**63,165**	57,199	55,610
Prince	**44,340**	51,984	34,906
International	**326,074**	273,092	273,171
Total Consumer Products Group.................	**1,171,763**	1,109,456	921,561
Chemical Products Group:			
Agricultural Products......	**407,928**	—	—
Basic Chemicals...........	**777,029**	—	—
Specialty & Food Products ..	**163,825**	—	—
International	**421,985**	—	—
Total Chemical Products Group.................	**1,770,767**	—	—
Total identifiable assets from continuing operations ...	**2,942,530**	1,109,456	921,561
Corporate assets (principally domestic cash, security investments and deferred income taxes)	**65,520**	73,968	49,902
Continuing operations.......	**3,008,050**	1,183,424	971,463
Discontinued operations.....	**—**	263,886	200,447
Total assets..............	**$3,008,050**	$1,447,310	$1,171,910

(in thousands)	1985	1984	1983
Capital Expenditures			
Consumer Products Group:			
Packaged Foods	$ 18,614	$10,350	$ 7,621
Health & Beauty Products ..	6,189	6,511	5,224
Bass	5,182	6,093	6,395
Prince Matchabelli	3,035	2,493	1,704
Polymer	7,737	2,899	—
Hospital Products	4,074	4,309	3,751
Prince	1,108	1,380	1,256
International	21,086	14,807	8,994
Total Consumer Products Group	67,025	48,842	34,945
Chemical Products Group:			
Agricultural Products	14,044	—	—
Basic Chemicals	53,412	—	—
Specialty & Food Products ..	4,691	—	—
International	13,734	—	—
Total Chemical Products Group	85,881	—	—
Continuing operations	152,906	48,842	34,945
Discontinued operations	8,218	10,420	7,258
Total capital expenditures	$161,124	$59,262	$42,203
Depreciation			
Consumer Products Group:			
Packaged Foods	$ 5,725	$ 4,898	$ 4,360
Health & Beauty Products .	4,947	4,511	4,657
Bass	4,073	3,118	2,634
Prince Matchabelli	1,903	1,641	1,633
Polymer	5,368	2,603	—
Hospital Products	2,665	2,024	2,644
Prince	672	697	557
International	4,769	4,610	4,340
Discontinued operations*..	—	646	745
Total Consumer Products Group	30,122	24,748	21,570
Chemical Products Group:			
Agricultural Products	15,665	—	—
Basic Chemicals	58,007	—	—
Specialty & Food Products..	5,254	—	—
International	9,499	—	—
Total Chemical Products Group	88,425	—	—
Total depreciation	$118,547	$24,748	$21,570

* Reflects corporate expenses allocated to discontinued operations

Geographic segment information was:

(in thousands)	1985	1984	1983
Net Sales			
United States	$2,084,982	$1,144,339	$1,037,535
Europe..................	277,374	148,122	131,506
Other	337,142	229,687	216,087
Total net sales	$2,699,498	$1,522,148	$1,385,128

Export sales included in the United States amount are $80,867,000, $24,268,000 and $27,582,000 for 1985, 1984 and 1983, respectively.

	1985	1984	1983
Income from Operations			
United States	$167,016	$135,980	$141,203
Europe..................	25,025	16,195	10,448
Other	25,059	30,546	29,142
Total income from operations	$217,100	$182,721	$180,793
Identifiable Assets			
United States	$2,164,925	$ 820,574	$ 647,411
Europe..................	395,614	156,273	145,052
Other	381,991	132,609	129,098
Total identifiable assets ..	$2,942,530	$1,109,456	$ 921,561
Corporate assets (principally domestic cash, security investments and deferred income taxes)	65,520	73,968	49,902
Continuing operations	3,008,050	1,183,424	971,463
Discontinued operations ..	—	263,886	200,447
Total assets	$3,008,050	$1,447,310	$1,171,910

The consolidated balance sheet at December 31, 1985, 1984 and 1983 includes net assets of $528,734,000, $213,086,000 and $207,458,000, respectively, for subsidiaries and branches in foreign countries.

19. Quarterly Data (unaudited)

The quarterly results were:

(in thousands except per share data)	1st Quarter	2nd Quarter	3rd Quarter	4th Quarter
1985:				
Net sales	$438,037	$825,929	$746,019	$689,513
Gross profit	215,410	328,982	310,749	264,667
Income from continuing operations	14,844	23,876	21,674	7,566
Discontinued operations	5,079	350	8,785	—
Net income	19,923	24,226	30,459	7,566
Earnings per share:				
Continuing operations	.43	.68	.61	.21
Discontinued operations	.15	.01	.25	—
Earnings per share	.58	.69	.86	.21
Dividends per share	.50	.50	.50	.50
Stock price range:				
High	38¼	36¾	34⅞	48½
Low	31½	31¾	31	31⅞
1984:				
Net sales	$333,322	$363,331	$410,431	$415,064
Gross profit	185,991	199,612	221,136	221,739
Income from continuing operations	10,112	18,484	31,975	31,776
Discontinued operations	8,502	4,828	8,995	4,857
Net income	18,614	23,312	40,970	36,633
Earnings per share:				
Continuing operations	.28	.52	.92	.93
Discontinued operations	.24	.13	.26	.14
Earnings per share	.52	.65	1.18	1.07
Dividends per share	.48	.48	.48	.48
Stock price range:				
High	39⅞	38¾	38¾	37⅝
Low	33⅜	32⅜	34⅛	32⅛

(in thousands except per share data)	1st Quarter	2nd Quarter	3rd Quarter	4th Quarter
1983:				
Net sales	$317,251	$332,039	$372,583	$363,255
Gross profit	184,172	190,105	209,668	204,373
Income from continuing operations	21,234	20,312	35,861	21,405
Discontinued operations	7,617	4,150	8,864	8,435
Net income	28,851	24,462	44,725	29,840
Earnings per share:				
Continuing operations	.60	.56	1.00	.60
Discontinued operations	.21	.12	.25	.24
Earnings per share	.81	.68	1.25	.84
Dividends per share	.46	.46	.46	.46
Stock price range:				
High	46¾	43⅛	40¾	42⅝
Low	37	37⅜	37	36¼

20. Inflation Accounting (unaudited)

Introduction

The primary financial statements, which are prepared under generally accepted accounting principles, are based on transactions recorded at the actual value of dollars received or expended (i.e., nominal dollars) without regard to the effects of inflation on business enterprises. The Financial Accounting Standards Board requires the experimental disclosure of certain supplementary information to reflect

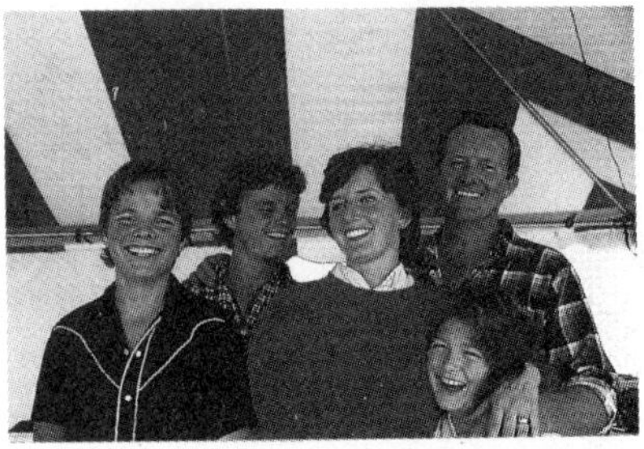

the effects of changes in the specific prices of certain assets (i.e., current cost accounting). This information is presented in the accompanying tables. In preparing this information, historical amounts were translated into U.S. dollars and then restated to reflect changes in specific prices during the periods being measured.

The reader should keep in mind that the current cost method involves the extensive use of assumptions, estimates and subjective judgments. Therefore, the resulting measurements should be viewed in that context and not as precise indicators of the effects of inflation on the company.

Current Cost Information
Current cost income from continuing operations represents income as reported in the Consolidated Statement of Income adjusted to restate cost of products sold and depreciation expense for the effects of changes in the specific prices of the related assets.

The current cost of inventories for the Consumer Products Group was calculated on the basis of historical standard product costs which were adjusted to reflect estimated current costs of materials, labor and overhead, including current cost depreciation expense. Cost of products sold on a current cost basis was estimated by adjusting historical cost of products sold to recognize cost increases during the approximate time lag between acquiring or producing the inventories and the time of sale.

The current cost of property, plant and equipment for the Consumer Products Group was determined in various ways. Land values were based on estimates of current market prices. Values for buildings and building improvements were based on indices developed from published current construction cost data as well as management's estimates based on recent construction cost experience. Values for machinery and equipment and leasehold improvements were based on indices developed by obtaining price data from equipment suppliers. Depreciation expense on a current cost basis was calculated based on these new asset values.

Current cost of inventories and property, plant and equipment for the Chemical Products Group were based on a study undertaken to determine the fair value of Stauffer's assets as a result of accounting for the acquisition.

Current cost depreciation assumptions (i.e., methods, estimates of useful lives, etc.) are the same as in the primary financial statements.

The amount of net assets under the current cost method is higher than the amount of net assets in the primary financial statements (i.e., shareholders' equity) due primarily to the inflationary impact on the values of property, plant and equipment. At December 31, 1985, the current cost of inventories was $659.3 million and the current cost of net property, plant and equipment was $1,134.7 million.

Monetary items are assets or liabilities which will be converted into a fixed number of dollars regardless of changes in prices. Examples of monetary assets are cash and accounts receivable; examples of monetary liabilities are accounts and notes payable, income taxes payable and long-term debt. A gain in purchasing power is achieved when a net monetary liability position exists in a period of inflation, since the liquidation of those liabilities in the future will require fewer units of general purchasing power. This purchasing power gain can be viewed as a reduction of interest expense since interest rates are generally increased during periods of inflation.

Other Data
In the accompanying five-year comparison of selected financial data, all dollar amounts have been restated into average 1985 dollars using the Consumer Price Index for All Urban Consumers (CPI-U).

47

Consolidated Statement of Income Adjusted for Changing Prices

(in millions except per share data)	As Reported 1985	Current Cost 1985
Net sales	$2,699.5	$2,699.5
Cost of products sold*	1,475.9	1,479.6
Selling, advertising and administrative expenses*	887.9	887.9
Depreciation expense	118.5	125.6
Other expense—net	139.7	139.7
Provision for income taxes	12.8	12.8
Total costs and expenses	2,634.8	2,645.6
Minority interest	(4.3)	(4.3)
Equity in earnings of associated companies	7.6	7.6
Income from continuing operations	$ 68.0	$ 57.2
Earnings per share from continuing operations	$1.94	$ 1.64
Increase in current costs		$ 7.9
Increase in general price level of inventories and property, plant and equipment		32.3
Excess of increase in current costs over increase in general price level		$(24.4)

* Excludes depreciation expense.

Key Ratios:

Dividend payout ratio (continuing operations)	103.2%	122.5%
Effective income tax rate (continuing operations)	16.5%	19.1%

Five-Year Comparison of Selected Financial Data Adjusted for Changing Prices**

(dollars in millions except per share data)	1985	1984	1983	1982	1981
Net sales	$2,699.5	$1,576.5	$1,495.6	$1,496.1	$1,547.3
Current cost information:					
Income from continuing operations	$57.2	$72.5	$88.9	$97.0	$77.5
Earnings per share from continuing operations	$1.64	$1.97	$2.67	$2.56	$2.35
Net assets at year-end	$778.8	$773.9	$837.5	$842.7	$813.0
Excess of increase in current costs over increase in general price level of inventories and property, plant and equipment	$(24.4)	$25.8	$19.6	$17.8	$(24.2)
Foreign currency translation adjustment	$(3.3)	$28.9	$25.2	$92.1	—
Other information:					
Purchasing power gain on net monetary items	$57.4	$4.8	$1.2	$4.0	$7.7
Dividends per share	$2.00	$1.99	$1.99	$1.92	$1.80
Market price per share at year-end	$41.95	$34.34	$39.41	$49.59	$38.63
Average CPI-U	322.2	311.1	298.4	289.1	272.4

** Expressed in average 1985 dollars.

48

Report of Certified Public Accountants

 A MEMBER OF ARTHUR YOUNG INTERNATIONAL

Arthur Young

277 Park Avenue
New York, New York 10172

To the Shareholders of Chesebrough-Pond's Inc.:

We have examined the accompanying consolidated balance sheet of Chesebrough-Pond's Inc. and subsidiaries at December 31, 1985, 1984 and 1983, and the related consolidated statements of income, shareholders' equity and changes in financial position for the years then ended. Our examinations were made in accordance with generally accepted auditing standards and, accordingly, included such tests of the accounting records and such other auditing procedures as we considered necessary in the circumstances.

In our opinion, the statements mentioned above present fairly the consolidated financial position of Chesebrough-Pond's Inc. and subsidiaries at December 31, 1985, 1984 and 1983, and the consolidated results of operations and changes in financial position for the years then ended, in conformity with generally accepted accounting principles applied on a consistent basis during the period.

Arthur Young + Company

February 27, 1986

Management's Responsibility for Financial Reporting

To the Shareholders of Chesebrough-Pond's Inc.:

Management is responsible for the company's financial statements and other financial information in this report. The financial statements have been prepared in conformity with generally accepted accounting principles consistently applied and include amounts that are based on our best estimates and judgements. The independent public accountants provide an objective review as to the fairness of the reported operating results and financial condition.

The company believes its accounting and internal control systems provide reasonable assurance that assets are safeguarded and that transactions are properly executed and recorded in all material respects. These systems are supported by written policies, internal audits and training of qualified personnel.

The Audit Committee of the Board of Directors, composed entirely of outside directors, approves the scope of the audit program, reviews audit findings and evaluates the adequacy of the company's internal control and financial reporting. The internal auditors and independent public accountants meet periodically with the Audit Committee, without management present, to discuss matters relating to their audits.

Ralph E. Ward
Chairman and
Chief Executive Officer

Donald G. Wiesen
Vice Chairman and
Chief Financial Officer

49

INDEX

This book has been set Linotron 202 in 10 and 9 point Palatino, leaded 2 points. Chapter numbers are 14 and 36 point Palatino Bold. Chapter Titles are 30 point Palatino Bold. The size of the type area is 34 by 48½ picas.